Professional Responsibility

TEXT

Professional Responsibility

ETHICS BY THE PERVASIVE METHOD

Second Edition

Deborah L. Rhode

McFarland Professor of Law
Stanford University

Director
Keck Center on Legal Ethics
and the Legal Profession

Formerly published by
Little, Brown and Company

A Division of Aspen Publishers, Inc.
A Wolters Kluwer Company

Permissions
Aspen Law & Business
A Division of Aspen Publishers, Inc.
1185 Avenue of the Americas
New York, NY 10036

Printed in the United States of America

2 3 4 5 6 7 8 9 0

Library of Congress Cataloging-in-Publication Data

Rhode, Deborah L.
    Professional responsibility : ethics by the pervasive method /
Deborah L. Rhode. -- 2nd ed.
        p.   cm.
    Includes index.
    ISBN 1-56706-542-2
    1. Legal ethics--United States. I. Title.
KF306.R47   1998
174'.3'0973--dc21
                                                        97-51275
                                                        CIP

About Aspen Law & Business, Law School Division

In 1996, Aspen Law & Business welcomed the Law School Division of Little, Brown and Company into its growing business—already established as a leading provider of practical information to legal practitioners.

Acquiring much more than an outstanding collection of educational publications by the country's foremost authors, Aspen Law & Business inherited the long-standing Little, Brown tradition of excellence—born over 150 years ago. As one of America's oldest and most venerable publishing houses, Little, Brown and Company commenced in a world of change and challenge, innovation and growth. Sharing that same spirit, Aspen Law & Business has dedicated itself to continuing and strengthening the integrity begun so many years ago.

ASPEN LAW & BUSINESS
A Division of Aspen Publishers, Inc.
A Wolters Kluwer Company

Summary of Contents

PART I

Professional Responsibility and Regulation: Core Concepts

1

PART II

Legal Ethics in Legal Context   427

Table of Contents

PART I

PROFESSIONAL RESPONSIBILITY AND REGULATION: CORE CONCEPTS

Chapter VIII.   NEGOTIATION AND MEDIATION   337

Chapter IX. THE LAWYER-CLIENT RELATIONSHIP   377

PART II

LEGAL ETHICS IN LEGAL CONTEXT   427

Chapter X.   CIVIL PROCEDURE   429

Chapter XI.   CONSTITUTIONAL LAW   459

Chapter XII. CONTRACTS   511

Chapter XIII.   CORPORATE LAW   543

Chapter XIV. CRIMINAL LAW AND PROCEDURE   595

Chapter XVIII.   TAX   755

Chapter XIX. TORTS 789

Preface

This book seeks to revive an abandoned ideal. For most of its history, American legal education aspired to teach professional responsibility through the "pervasive method." This book aims to make that aspiration possible not just in theory but in practice.

Until the mid-1970s, the traditional view was that professional responsibility issues would arise naturally and pervasively throughout the curriculum. The reality was rather different, and the inadequacy of this approach led almost all schools to require a separate course in legal ethics or the legal profession. Yet paradoxically, these requirements also removed pressure to treat professional responsibility issues throughout the law school experience. By limiting discussion of legal ethics to a single course, many institutions have risked marginalizing, and ultimately subverting, their intended goal.

This book has broad aspirations. It provides coverage of all the core professional responsibility issues that can constitute a basic course in the subject, as well as materials for integrating such issues into the broader curriculum. The aim is to address professional responsibility in all substantive courses because it arises in all substantive fields, and because it involves values that are central to lawyers' personal and professional lives.

As its title implies, Part I of this book explores the central concepts in professional responsibility. It includes an overview of all the basic topics: traditions of moral reasoning, regulation of the profession, the advocate's role, the adversary system, confidentiality, conflicts of interest, negotiation and mediation, and the lawyer-client relationship. Coverage includes relevant provisions of the Model Rules of Professional Conduct and the Code of Professional Responsibility, as well as excerpts or summaries of leading cases, commentary, bar ethics rulings, and related regulatory material. This first half of the book is suitable for standard courses on legal ethics and the legal profession, or for orientation programs and other innovative approaches to these issues.

Part II of the book provides similar material for integrating professional responsibility materials into the core first-year and advanced courses: civil procedure, constitutional law, contracts, corporate law, criminal law and procedure, evidence and trial advocacy, family law, property, tax, and torts. An extensive cross-reference system avoids repetition and permits discussion of particular topics in either concise or comprehensive form. For example, Chapter VI in Part I includes basic rules, policy considerations, and hypothetical problems on confidentiality. Part II provides further discussion of that topic as it arises in particular contexts, such as criminal procedure, corporate counseling, family law, evidence, and so forth. A class using Part I for a standard professional responsibility course could include additional materials from Part II to supplement particular topics. A class using a chapter from Part II in connection with a substantive course could include as much of the basic background materials from Part I as time permitted.

The material in both sections of the book aims to avoid recurring complaints about legal ethics — that they are too theoretical or not theoretical enough; too removed from the day-to-day realities of practice and too uninformed by the broader historical, philosophical, psychological, and economic perspectives. To avoid these inadequacies, this volume centers discussion around concrete problems, drawn from fact patterns in reported cases, commentary, and related sources. The book also includes substantial interdisciplinary materials that situate these problems in a wider context. The objective is both to broaden and deepen understanding of the ethical issues that arise in legal practice and the regulatory strategies necessary to address them.

In order to provide a wide range of coverage in a single volume, this book relies on summaries and carefully edited excerpts. That editing strategy rests on the assumption that this book often will be used in conjunction with other materials. Where it is the sole text, and further cases are desirable, they can be added without the copyright problems that arise in reproducing other supplementary materials.

In some respects, this book aspires to its own obsolescence. Ideally, sufficient material on professional responsibility would appear in standard casebooks; no supplementary volume would be necessary. However, we remain some distance from that goal. In a recent survey of some 130 leading texts, the median amount of coverage was less than 2 percent of total pages. Much of that coverage consisted of simple reprinting bar rules.[1] This volume, the first publication of its kind, aims to encourage better integration of

---

1. Deborah L. Rhode, Ethics by the Pervasive Method, 42 J. Legal Educ. 31, 41 (1992).

professional responsibility issue throughout the curriculum by both individual faculty and casebook editors. Law schools have long proclaimed their commitment to fostering high ethical standards within the bar. The material that follows is offered in that spirit.

Deborah L. Rhode

February 1998

Acknowledgments

It is so customary for authors to embellish in acknowledgments that any accurate statement here risks seeming overdrawn, banal, or both. However, since this is a book on ethics, my hope is that readers will accept on faith that this project owes more debts than I can ever adequately acknowledge. The greatest of these are to my husband Ralph Cavanagh, and my assistant, Mary Tye. Among their most characteristic contributions were to absolve me of any necessity for recognition.

This research was supported by the Walter and Elise Haas Fund, the Evelyn and Walter Hass, Jr. Fund and the Stanford Legal Fund, made possible by a bequest from Ira S. Lillick, and gifts from other friends of the Stanford Law School. Its intellectual debts are far greater and more widely shared. The text builds on a rich array of other work that is acknowledged explicitly in the materials below. In addition, a number of colleagues offered invaluable comments on the second edition: Barbara Babcock, Joseph Bankman, Rory Little, William Simon, and Bernard Wolfman. Stanford students Dawn Dekle and Sarah Killingsworth provided research assistance of exceptional quality. The librarians at Stanford were unparalleled in their skills and dedication. To Dave Bridgman, Andy Eisenberg, Paul Lomio, and Erika Wayne I am especially grateful.

This book is dedicated to Paul Brest, Dean of Stanford Law School, whose vision, commitment, and support made this project possible.

I am grateful to the following sources for permission to reprint excerpts of their work:

Alschuler, Albert W., Personal Failure, Institutional Failure, and the Sixth Amendment, 14 N.Y.U. Rev. L. & Soc. Change 149 (1986). Reprinted by permission.

American Academy of Matrimonial Lawyers, Standards 2.11, 2.26, 2.27, and 3.6. Copyright ©1992. Reprinted by permission of the American Academy of Matrimonial Lawyers and the American Bar Association. A copy of this publication is available from Order Fulfillment, American Bar Association, 570 North Lake Shore Drive, Chicago, IL 60611.

American Bar Association, Divorce and Family Mediation: Standards of Practice of the ABA Task Force on Mediation, Section of Family Law. Copyright © 1986. Reprinted by permission of the American Bar Association. A copy of this publication is available from Order Fulfillment, American Bar Association, 750 North Lake Shore Drive, Chicago, IL 60611.

American Bar Association, Formal Ethics Opinion 85-352. Copyright © 1985. A copy of this publication is available from Order Fulfillment, American Bar Association, 750 North Lake Shore Drive, Chicago, IL 60611.

American Bar Association, Model Code of Professional Responsibility, selected Disciplinary Rules and Ethical Considerations. Copyright © 1983. Reprinted by permission of the American Bar Association. A copy of this publication is available from Order Fulfillment, American Bar Association, 750 North Lake Shore Drive, Chicago, IL 60611.

American Bar Association, Model Rules of Professional Conduct, selected Rules. Copyright © 1993. Reprinted by permission of the American Bar Association. A copy of this publication is available from Order Fulfillment, American Bar Association, 750 North Lake Shore Drive, Chicago, IL 60611.

American Bar Association, Residential Real Estate Transactions: The Lawyer's Proposed Role 2-5, 8-9 (1978). Copyright © 1978. Reprinted by permission.

American Bar Association, Standards Relating to the Administration of Criminal Justice, The Prosecution Function (1978). Reprinted by permission.

Ames, Matthew C., Formal Opinion 352: Professional Integrity and the Tax Audit Lottery, 1 Geo. J. Legal Ethics 411 (1987). Reprinted by permission.

Amsterdam, Anthony, Correspondence, October 1990. Reprinted by permission.

Angelos, Claudia, Correspondence, October 1990. Reprinted by permission.

Aronson, Robert H., What About Children? Are Family Lawyers the Same (Ethically) as Criminal Lawyers? A Morality Play, 1 J. Institute for Study of Legal Ethics 141 (1996). Reprinted by permission.

Association of the Bar of the City of New York, Committee on Professional Ethics, Inf. Ref. 82-79 (1982). Copyright © 1982. Reprinted by permission of The Association of the Bar of the City of New York and the American Bar Association. A copy of this publication is available from Order Fulfillment, American Bar Association, 750 North Lake Shore Drive, Chicago, IL 60611.

Bell, Derrick A., Jr., Serving Two Masters: Integration Ideals and Client Interests in School Desegregation Litigation, 85 Yale L. J. 470 (1976). Reprinted by permission of The Yale Law Journal and Fred B. Rothman & Company.

Bellows, Randy, Notes of a Public Defender, in Social Responsibility of Lawyers: Case Studies 69 (Publishers Foundation Press, 1988). Reprinted by permission.

Bok, Sissela, Blowing the Whistle, in Public Duties: The Moral Obligations of Government Officials 204 (Joel L. Fleishman, Lance Liebman & Mark H. Moore, eds.). Reprinted by permission of the publisher. Cambridge, Mass.: Harvard University Press. Copyright © 1981 by The President and Fellows of Harvard College.

Bok, Sissela, Lying — Moral Choice in Public and Private Life (Pantheon, 1978). Reprinted by permission.

Brill, Steven, Roy Cohn Rides Again. Steven Brill is the editor-in-chief of The American Lawyer. This article is reprinted with permission from the March 1980 issue of The American Lawyer, page 5. Copyright © 1980, The American Lawyer.

Burns, Sarah E., Correspondence, October 1990. Reprinted by permission.

Coffee, John C., Jr., Beyond the Shut-Eyed Sentry: Toward a Theoretical View of Corporate Misconduct and an Effective Legal Response, 63 Va. L. Rev. 1099 (1977). Copyright © 1977. Reprinted by permission of the Virginia Law Review Association and Fred B. Rothman & Company.

Corneel, Frederic G., Guidelines to Tax Practice Second, 43 Tax Lawyer 297 (1990). Copyright © 1990. Reprinted by permission of the American Bar Association.

Cramton, Roger C., Problem and Summary of *Washington State Physicians Ins. Exchange & Assn. v. Fisons Corp.* (1994). Reprinted by permission.

Davis, Peggy, Correspondence, October 1990. Reprinted by permission.

Days, Drew S., III, *Brown* Blues: Rethinking the Integrative Ideal, 34 Wm. & Mary L. Rev. 53 (1992). Copyright © 1992, William and Mary Law Review. Reprinted by permission.

Dorsen, Norman, Correspondence, October 1990. Reprinted by permission.

Ellman, Ira M., Paul M. Kurtz, and Katharine T. Bartlett, Family Law: Cases, Texts, Problems. Copyright © 1991. Reprinted by permission of the Michie Company.

Fisher, Roger, A Code of Negotiation Practices for Lawyers, 2 Negotiation J. 105 (1985). Reprinted by permission of Plenum Publishing Corporation.

Frankel, Marvin E., The Search for Truth: An Umpireal View, 123 U. Pa. L. Rev. 1031 (1975). Reprinted by permission of the author, University of Pennsylvania Law Review, and Fred B. Rothman & Company.

Freedman, Monroe H., Muzzling Trial Publicity: New Rule Needed, Apr. 5, 1993, at page 24. Reprinted by permission.

Freedman, Monroe H., Professional Responsibility of the Criminal Defense Lawyer: The Three Hardest Questions, 64 Mich. L. Rev. 1469 (1966).

Fried, Charles, The Lawyer as Friend: The Moral Foundations of the Lawyer-Client Relation, 85 Yale L. J. 1060 (1976). Copyright © Charles Fried, 1976, 1992. Reprinted by permission of The Yale Law Journal Company and Fred B. Rothman & Company.

Fuller, Lon L. and John D. Randall, Professional Responsibility: Report of the Joint Conference of the American Bar Association and American Association of Law Schools, 44 A.B.A.J. 1159 (1958). Reprinted by permission.

Gillers, Stephen, Regulation of Lawyers: Problems of Law and Ethics (3d ed. 1992). Reprinted by permission.

Gillers, Stephen, Correspondence, October 1990. Reprinted by permission.

Gordon, Robert W., The Independence of Lawyer, 68 B.U. L. Rev. 1 (1988). Reprinted by permission.

Gordon, Robert W., Unfreezing Legal Reality: Critical Approaches to the Law, 15 Fla. St. U.L. Rev. 195 (1987). Reprinted by permission.

Goulden, Joseph C., The Superlawyers: The Small and Powerful World of the Great Washington Law Firms (Weybright and Talley 1972). Copyright © 1970 by Joseph C. Goulden. Reprinted by permission of Brandt & Brandt Literary Agents, Inc.

Hazard, Geoffrey C., Ethics in the Practice of Law (1978). Copyright © 1978, Yale University Press. Reprinted by permission.

Hazard, Geoffrey, C., Jr., Panel Discussion on Professional Responsibility and the Model Rules of Professional Conduct, 35 U. Miami L. Rev. 639 (1981). Copyright © 1981 by University of Miami Law Review. Reprinted by permission.

Irons, Peter, Justice at War (New York: Oxford University Press 1983). Reprinted by permission.

Jackall, Robert, Moral Mazes: The World of Corporate Managers (Oxford University Press 1988). Reprinted by permission.

Kassin, Saul M., An Empirical Study of Rule 11 Sanctions (Federal Judicial Center 1985). Reprinted by permission.

Kennedy, Duncan, Rebels from Principle: Changing the Corporate Law Firm from Within, Harvard Law School Bulletin, vol. 33, no. 2, pp. 36-38 (1982). Reprinted by permission.

Kester, John G., Correspondence, Harvard Law School Bulletin, vol. 33, no. 2, pg. 32 (Spring 1982). Reprinted by permission.

Lavelle, Mariane, Placing a Price on Human Life: A Legal Puzzle, National Law Journal Oct. 10, 1988, at page 1. Reprinted by permission.

Law, Sylvia, Correspondence, October 1990. Reprinted by permission.

Luban, David, The Adversary System Excuse, in The Good Lawyer 93 (D. Luban, ed.). Copyright © 1984, Rowman and Littlefield Publishers. Reprinted by permission.

Luban, David, Lawyers and Justice: An Ethical Study (1988). Copyright © 1988 by Princeton University Press. Reprinted by permission of Princeton University Press.

Luban, David, Partisanship, Betrayal and Autonomy in the Client-Lawyer Relationship: A Reply to Stephen Ellman, 90 Colum. L. Rev. 1004 (1990). Reprinted by permission of Columbia Law Review.

Macey, Jonathan R., and Geoffrey Miller, The Plaintiff's Attorney's Role in Class Action and Derivative Litigation: Economic Analysis and Recommendation for Reform, 58 U. Chi. L. Rev. 1 (1991). Reprinted by permission.

MacIntyre, Alisdair, Utilitarianism and Cost-Benefit Analysis: An Essay on the Relevance of Moral Philosophy to Bureaucratic Theory, in Values in the Electric Power Industry (Kenneth M. Sayre ed., 1977). Reprinted by permission.

Mann, Kenneth, Defending White-Collar Crime (Yale University Press, 1985). Reprinted by permission.

Melilli, Kenneth J., Prosecutorial Discretion in an Adversary System, 1992 B.Y.U.L. Rev. 669. Copyright © 1992, Brigham Young University Law Review. Reprinted by permission.

Menkel-Meadow, Carrie, Toward Another View of Legal Negotiation: The Structure of Problem-Solving, 31 UCLA L. Rev. 754 (1984). Copyright © 1984, The Regents of the University of California. All rights reserved. Reprinted by permission of UCLA Law Review and Fred B. Rothman & Company.

Miller, Geoffrey P., Government Lawyers' Ethics in a System of Checks and Balances, 54 U. Chi. L. Rev. (1987). Reprinted by permission.

Mitchell, John, The Ethics of the Criminal Defense Attorney — New Answers to Old Questions, 32 Stan. L. Rev. 293 (1980). Copyright © 1980 by the Board of Trustees of the Leland Stanford Junior University. Reprinted by permission.

Morawetz, Nancy, Correspondence, October 1990. Reprinted by permission.

Neely, Richard, The Primary Caretaker Parent Rule: Child Custody and the Dynamics of Greed, 3 Yale L. & Poly. Rev. 168 (1984). Reprinted by permission.

Neuborne, Burt, Correspondence, October 1990. Reprinted by permission.

Paul, Randolph, The Responsibility of the Tax Adviser, 63 Harv. L. Rev. 377 (1950). Copyright © 1950 by the Harvard Law Review Association. Reprinted by permission.

Post, Robert C., On the Popular Image of the Lawyer: Reflections in a Dark Glass, 75 Cal. L. Rev. 379 (1987). Reprinted by permission.

Uviller, Richard H., The Virtuous Prosecutor in Quest of an Ethical Standard: Guidance from the ABA, U. Mich. L. Rev. 1145 (1978). Copyright © 1978 by the Michigan Law Review Association. Reprinted by permission.

Van Voris, Bob, Marden Problem Pulled, Reinstated, The Commentator, Oct. 18, 1990. Reprinted by permission.

Wasserstrom, Richard, Lawyers as Professionals: Some Moral Issues, 5 Human Rights 1 (1975). Reprinted by permission.

White, Lucie E., To Learn and Teach: Lessons from Driefontein on Lawyering and Power, 1988 Wis. L. Rev. 699. Reprinted by permission.

Williams, Harold, Professionalism and the Corporate Bar, 36 Business Law 159 (1980). Copyright © 1980. Reprinted by permission of the American Bar Association.

PART I

Professional Responsibility and Regulation: Core Concepts

Chapter I

Introduction

Each lawyer's vision of society and his or her dedication to the dignity of individuals will affect the quality of life in our country in ways that mere technical skill in drafting a document, constructing a statute, writing a brief, or authoring a law review article can never approach. If . . . lawyers are to play . . . important social and moral roles . . . , we must begin by recognizing that our nation's basic human problems never have arisen because the legal profession misunderstood Blackstone or the Bluebook, the Uniform Commercial Code or the Federal Rules of Evidence. Poverty, hatred, malnutrition, inadequate health care and housing, corruption in government, and the failures of our public school system continue to haunt us today because those in power often have lacked personal morality or failed to make real the values that they have professed to hold in the abstract. To paraphrase Justice Holmes, the life of the law must not be mere logic; it must also be values. . . . Each lawyer must consciously and constantly assess his or her values and goals in forging rules of law for the future.

A. Leon Higginbotham, Jr.[1]

What is the "ethics" in legal ethics? That in itself is a matter of ethical debate. In a narrow sense, the term refers to the law of lawyering — the formal rules governing attorneys' conduct. In a broader sense, legal ethics involves application of ethical theory and implicates deeper questions about the moral dimensions of our professional lives. These different meanings have inspired different conceptions of legal ethics courses. At the theoretical level, these courses reflect a variety of objectives: reinforcing moral values, teaching ethical analysis, building awareness of applicable rules, preventing future misconduct, and encouraging regulatory reform. At the practical level, professional responsibility instruction reflects differing views of educational method. How should we teach? Should instruction occur primarily in specialized courses or in coverage that is pervasive throughout the curriculum? How much do our choices matter? Is legal ethics "like politeness on subways . . . or fidelity in marriage" — a matter of core values that cannot be acquired through professional education?[2]

For most of American history, these issues were not central to legal education. The traditional view was that instruction in professional responsibility was someone else's responsibility. Although ethical issues arise in all substantive areas, such issues have received little coverage in standard courses or casebooks. Legal ethics classes have often been regarded as intellectual interlopers, taught to "vacant seats and vacant minds."[3] Until quite recently, materials for these classes were frequently criticized as too theoretical and not theoretical enough: too removed from the actual context of practice, and too uninformed by historical, philosophical, and social science materials.[4]

This book responds to these traditional limitations in professional responsibility instruction. It aims to straddle the theory-practice divide by situating concrete problems in a broader, interdisciplinary context. The hypothetical circumstances that these problems describe are not hypothetical only. They draw on reported cases and other published accounts. They involve real people and real consequences. Any adequate analysis of these problems requires attention to the contexts in which they arise and the values that they implicate. To that end, the chapters that follow include background on moral reasoning, social psychology, economic pressures, historical developments, practice norms, legal rules, and regulatory structures. The objective is not only to build awareness of professional responsibility issues but also to enhance capacities for individual and institutional responses.

This book also addresses debates over pervasive versus specialized coverage by providing materials for both approaches. Underlying this strategy is the premise that law schools should address professional responsibility issues throughout the curriculum as well as in courses specifically focused on the legal profession. Legal ethics deserves discussion in all substantive areas because it arises in all substantive areas. To confine its analysis to a single course under-cuts its significance and its central message — that moral responsibility is a crucial concern in all legal practice. Curricular priorities are apparent not only in what is said but also in what is unsaid, and pervasive silence makes a statement that no single course can counteract.

Yet a course or orientation program that centers on professional responsibility also permits a depth and range of coverage that is difficult to achieve by intermittent coverage throughout the curriculum. Many ethical issues cut across substantive areas, and some sustained treatment avoids the risk of repetitive or unsystematic discussion. Other issues, such as those involving bar regulatory structures, may fall through the cracks if not made the focus of one specialized course. Accordingly, this volume can serve as a text for a basic legal ethics class as well as for pervasive coverage.

The materials that follow explore legal ethics on two levels: individual choice and collective responsibility. These dimensions are related because many individual dilemmas are partly due to problems in the structure of legal practice and bar regulatory processes. Many of these dilemmas are not readily resolved. Any adequate response requires attention to complex relationships among personal morality, professional roles, collegial pressures, economic incentives, doctrinal gaps, and enforcement limitations. No classroom setting can fully duplicate these multiple forces. Yet by the same token, the relative freedom from self–interest in law school contexts may permit a more reflective assessment of competing values than is possible in daily practice.

Despite this obvious advantage, some skepticism about professional responsibility instruction remains common. One concern is that ethics courses will not significantly affect ethical values. A related concern is that ethical values will not override the practical pressures influencing professional conduct. Both of these views deserve closer scrutiny.

Legal Education and Ethical Values. The first concern takes several forms. Some individuals assume that professional responsibility is largely a matter of moral integrity, which reflects early socialization.[5] Adherents of this view question (most often rhetorically) whether it is possible to alter in a few classroom hours the values that individuals have acquired over long periods from family, friends, schools, churches, and popular culture. A second concern builds on still more skeptical premises. It assumes that ethical questions worth discussing have no "right" answers and that faculty should not turn their podiums into pulpits. Alternatively, other critics assume that when professors studiously avoid imposing their views, ethics courses can readily lapse into a form of "values clarification" that erodes values. If everyone's view is as good as everyone else's, what is the point of classroom debate?

Such critiques, however, undervalue the possibility of a middle ground. As Chapter II's overview of moral reasoning suggests, we can encourage toleration without endorsing skepticism. Although on many issues there are no objectively valid answers, not all answers are equally valid; some are more logical, consistent, coherent, respectful of evidence, and so forth. Nor do all issues of professional responsibility present insoluble value-laden dilemmas. Many regulatory issues call for the same skills of legal and policy analysis that are standard fare in law school classrooms. The most effective way to secure substantial changes in professional ethics is often through reforming regulatory standards and economic incentives, and legal education can contribute to that effort.

So too, a substantial body of evidence suggests that ethical values are by no means as fixed as critics contend. Recent psychological research indicates that significant changes occur during early adulthood in people's basic strategies for dealing with moral issues.[6] Through well-designed curricula, individuals can enhance skills in moral analysis and build awareness of the situational factors that skew judgment. More than a hundred studies evaluating ethics courses find that appropriately designed classes can significantly improve capacities for moral reasoning and that adults in their twenties and thirties gain more than younger students.[7]

Ethical Reasoning and Ethical Conduct. Increasing capacity for ethical analysis can also affect ethical conduct, although its impact is constrained by other forces. Such constraints are clearly apparent in both historical and psychological studies. They demonstrate that moral conduct is partly situational. Individuals differ in their responses to temptation, but contextual pressures also shape moral conduct independent of any generalized "integrity."[8] One sobering survey found no significant differences in the moral beliefs characteristic of Chicago ministers and inmates of the state penitentiary.[9] Differences showed up not in ethical values but in the pressures and incentives that confronted these individuals in daily life. So too, in psychologist Stanley Milgram's well-known experiment, two-thirds of the subjects complied with directions to administer apparently dangerous electric shocks to co-participants despite their cries of pain.[10]

Moreover, self-interest often skews interpretation of moral action. Individuals selectively perceive information that is consistent with their desires, discount contrary evidence, and adopt euphemistic labels to justify preferred conduct.[11] Diffusion of responsibility and distance from victims also affect moral perceptions and priorities.

These patterns suggest reasons to avoid overstating the potential contributions of ethics instruction but not reasons to avoid including it in law school curricula. Despite the importance of situational pressures, most psychological research finds a modest relationship between moral judgment and moral behavior.[12] How individuals evaluate the consequences of their actions affects their conduct, and education can influence those evaluative processes. It can also make individuals aware of ways that economic and peer pressures, structures of authority, and diffusion of responsibility skew judgment. For example, in Milgram's obedience studies, participants were far less likely to impose shocks if others refused to do so. Such findings highlight the importance for lawyers of finding sympathetic colleagues and ensuring support for whistleblowers when ethical problems arise in later professional life.

Such problems do arise. A well-constructed ethics curriculum addresses issues of far greater personal relevance than much of what is tested in law courses or bar exams. Many practitioners will never encounter a shifting (or springing) executory interest; all will confront questions of honesty, loyalty, confidentiality, and conflicts of interest. Practitioners who have taken legal ethics courses have credited them with later helping to resolve ethical issues.[13] And surveyed lawyers have generally favored maintaining or expanding ethics coverage.[14] There is, in short, more evidence on the effectiveness of professional responsibility education than that of other law school classes.

For law schools to refuse, explicitly or implicitly, to address ethical issues that arise throughout the curriculum encourages future practitioners to do the same. One primary cause of unethical conduct, particularly in organizational settings, is the assumption that moral responsibility lies elsewhere. Legal education cannot afford to mirror this approach in classroom priorities. Although no law school course can fully mirror the pressures of practice, it can provide a setting to explore their causes. Particularly in areas where the interests of the profession and the public do not coincide, future lawyers can benefit from analyzing the gap before they have a vested interest in ignoring it.

In essence, we should neither overstate nor undervalue the significance of legal ethics education. No law school course can of itself instill integrity or ensure effective regulation. But a collective effort to make ethical issues more central throughout the educational experience can serve more modest objectives. If ethics by the pervasive method is our aspiration, ethics as a central priority could be the result.

Endnotes

1. A. Leon Higginbotham, Jr., The Life of the Law: Values, Commitment, and Craftsmanship, 100 Harv. L. Rev. 795, 815 (1987).

2. Eric Schnapper, The Myth of Legal Ethics, 64 A.B.A.J. 202, 205 (1978). For a more extended review of the issues in this Introduction, see Deborah L. Rhode, Into the Valley of Ethics: Professional Responsibility and Educational Reform, 58 Law & Contemp. Probs. 139 (1995); Ethics by the Pervasive Method, 42 J. Legal Educ. 31 (1992).

3. Dale C. Moss, Out of Balance: Why Can't Law Schools Teach Ethics?, 20 Student Law. 18, 19 (Oct. 1991).

4. Frances K. Zemans & Victor G. Rosenblum, The Making of a Public Profession 165-196 (1981); Ronald M. Pipkin, Law School Instruction in Professional Responsibility: A Curricular Paradox, 1979 Am. B. Found. Res. J. 247 (1979).

5. Orville G. Brim, Jr., Socialization Through the Life Cycle, in Socialization After Childhood: Two Essays 1 (Orville G. Brim, Jr. & Stanton Wheeler eds., 1966); Lawrence Kohlberg, Moral Stages and Moralization: The Cognitive-Developmental Approach, in Moral Development and Behavior: Theory, Research, and Social Issues 31 (Thomas Lickona ed., 1976); see Rhode, Ethics, supra note 2, at 44.

6. James R. Rest, Can Ethics Be Taught in Professional Schools? The Psychological Research, in Ethics: Easier Said Than Done 22, 23-24 (Winter 1988) [hereinafter Can Ethics Be Taught?]; James R. Rest, Muriel Bebeau & Joseph Volker, An Overview of the Psychology of Morality, in Moral Development: Advances in Research and Theory 3, 14 (James R. Rest et al. eds., 1986).

7. Rest, Can Ethics Be Taught?, supra note 6. See also James S. Leming, Curricular Effectiveness in Moral-Values Education: A Review of Research, 10 J. Moral Educ. 147 (1981).

8. See research surveyed in Rhode, Ethics, supra note 2, at 45; Walter Mischel, Personality and Assessment 26 (1968); David L. Rosenhan, Bert S. Moore & Bill Underwood, The Social Psychology of Moral Behavior, in Moral Development and Behavior, supra note 5, at 241.

9. Peter Caws, On the Teaching of Ethics in a Pluralistic Society, 8 Hastings Center Report 32 (Oct. 1978).

10. Stanley Milgram, Obedience to Authority: An Experimental View 35 (1974).

11. See Albert Bandura, Social Cognitive Theory of Moral Thought and Action, in 1 Handbook of Moral Behavior and Development 45 (William M. Kurtines & Jacob L. Gewirtz eds., 1991); Leon Festinger, A Theory of Cognitive Dissonance (1957); and sources cited in Rhode, Ethics, supra note 2, at 45.

12. Walter Mischel & Harriet N. Mischel, A Cognitive Social-Learning Approach to Morality and Self-Regulation, in Moral Development and Behavior, supra note 5, at 84, 101-107; Bandura, supra note 11, at 53; Rest, Can Ethics Be Taught?, supra note 6; Rest, Development in Judging Moral Issues 180-195 (1979); Augusto Blasi, Bridging Moral Cognition and Moral Action: A Critical Review of the Literature, 88 Psychol. Bull. 1 (1980).

13. Zemans & Rosenblum, supra note 4, at 176-177.

14. Id. at 180.

Chapter II

Traditions of Moral Reasoning

Moral talk is often rather repugnant. Leveling
moral accusations . . . passing moral
judgment . . . justifying oneself, and above all
moralizing—who can enjoy such talk? And who
can like or trust those addicted to it?

Kurt Baier[1]

"Legal ethics" is a term often misused and abused. Popular
resentment of lawyers traditionally has found expression in cynicism
about their moral standards. Legal ethics has been dismissed as
either a contradiction in terms or a poor relation to philosophical
theory. As one cliche puts it, legal ethics is to ethics as military
music is to music.

Unsurprisingly, this book takes a different view and this chapter presents a less jaundiced account of the relationship between
moral reasoning and legal ethics. It begins by clarifying terms and
then surveys the central traditions of moral philosophy.

A.   THE NATURE OF ETHICS

Most scholars trace *ethics* to the Greek words *ethikos*, which means pertaining to custom, and *ethos*, which refers to character. *Morality* comes from the Latin *mores*, which refers to character or custom and habit. In contemporary societies, both terms have become somewhat detached from their original meaning. Philosophers generally consider ethics to be the study of morality and morality to involve universal principles of right and wrong.[2] In popular usage, the terms are largely interchangeable, and this volume will treat them as synonymous.

Ethics as a field of study has three primary branches: *metaethics, normative ethics*, and *applied* or *practical ethics*. *Metaethics* involves the semantic or logical analysis of moral concepts. It focuses on the meaning of expressions such as "right," "good," or "obligation," and on ways of validating moral claims. *Normative ethics* concerns the justifications for moral values. It seeks coherent theories of virtue, moral obligation, and the nature of good and evil. *Applied ethics* relates general normative theories to concrete practical problems. It explores the moral dilemmas that arise in particular contexts. Legal ethics is a form of applied ethics.[3]

These fields of inquiry all seek to promote human welfare and to identify principles that advance the common good.[4] Such principles are distinctive in two crucial respects: they are both universal and generalizable. Christianity's Golden Rule and Immanuel Kant's Categorical Imperative are well-known illustrations. In one formulation, Kant's imperative demands: "[a]ct only according to that maxim . . . [which] should become a universal law."[5] The "moral point of view" in most Western philosophy assumes a universal standpoint; its judgments are those that an impartial spectator would accept and generalize.[6]

This assumption is not without critics. Recent work in communitarian, feminist, and religious ethics reflects long-standing challenges. Such work questions the premise that an adequate understanding of moral life can emerge from abstract, universal principles formulated by disinterested, disembodied subjects.[7] According to many critics, moral identity depends on roles, relationships, communities, traditions, and religious commitments. To focus solely on principles is to ignore much that structures human values.

One common response to such critiques is that generalizable principles can acknowledge the value of special relationships and commitments. In formulating such principles, a disinterested observer can take account of particular loyalties. However, the point of hypothesizing such a neutral third party is to place some check on biases that we would not want others to indulge. In an interdependent world, the only way to ensure respect for our own commitments is to provide a similar respect for the commitments of others.

B. MORAL JUSTIFICATION AND MORAL REASONING

In order to evaluate various moral frameworks, it is necessary to have some sense of how ethical judgments can be justified. One position is that they cannot be, and such skepticism underpins many claims that lawyers should defend, not judge, their clients.

This book, like other recent work in legal ethics, rejects such amoral conceptions of the attorney's role. Subsequent chapters on advocacy and the adversary system argue that lawyers, no less than other individuals, must remain accountable for the moral consequences of their professional acts. Although there may be no single, objectively "right" answer to the ethical dilemmas of legal practice, some answers are more justifiable than others. And there are better and worse ways of analyzing the questions.

This chapter seeks to assist such analysis by reviewing arguments about the possibility of moral justification. The aim is not to endorse a particular position or to attempt a complete summary. Rather, the point is to clarify central ethical debates and to challenge some common forms of moral skepticism.

1. Arguments from Knowledge and Culture: Relativism and Realism

Traditions ranging from classical Greek skepticism to modern pragmatism and postmodernism maintain that we cannot understand the world apart from our own cultural concepts and categories. One group of theories is, to varying degree, "antirealist" about knowledge and denies that there is a "real world" that we can know in any objective "true" sense. A related group of theories is, to varying extent, relativist about morality: these theories deny the existence of any universal ethical principles. Relativism holds that values are always culturally grounded, and that there is no objective basis for justifying one set of ethical beliefs over another.

Although these theoretical traditions are related, not all individuals who are relativist about values reject realism about the world. And not all those who reject truth claims about the world are equally skeptical about values. For example, some people believe that disagreements about morality are qualitatively different from disagreements about the natural order. Over time, as more information becomes more widely available, consensus about factual claims becomes more likely. According to some theorists, no such convergence necessarily occurs on moral claims. Nor is there any way of testing them that is comparable to the logical methods of mathematics or to the empirical methods of science. From this perspective, ethical judgments appear subjective to a degree that scientific judgments do not.

By contrast, other commentators argue that we often have far more grounds for confidence in our moral than in our factual assessments. Even expert physicists may be more certain that genocide is wrong than that contemporary theories about subatomic particles are right.

Antirealist and relativist claims both have generated extensive challenges. Most fall into two general categories, which a recent survey labels arguments by "death and furniture."

> When relativists talk about the social construction of reality, truth, cognition, scientific knowledge, technical capacity, social structure and so on, their realist opponents sooner or later start hitting the furniture, invoking the Holocaust, talking about rocks, guns, killings, human misery, tables and chairs. The force of these objections is to introduce a bottom line, a bedrock of reality. . . . There are two related kinds of moves: Furniture (tables, rocks, stones, etc. — the reality that *cannot* be denied) and Death (misery, genocide, poverty, power — the reality that *should not* be denied).[8]

To most individuals, the realist position has considerable intuitive appeal. It seems plausible to assume that some objective world exists independent of our perceptions. Something makes a table solid that hurts when we hit it. Antirealists, however, respond that this "something" still has to be represented and interpreted through cultural concepts. Indeed, physicists looking at a chair might insist that "at a certain level of analysis, there is nothing at all solid down there, down at . . . the contested [level] of subatomic space. Its solidity then, is ineluctably a perceptual category."[9] Drawing on postmodern and pragmatist strains from a variety of disciplines, antirealists maintain that all knowledge is socially constructed. What pass for "objective" conclusions rest on the culturally contingent methodology used to determine them: the answers we get depend on how we frame the questions and what we count as proof. Many "scientific truths" of prior generations have turned out to lack empirical foundations.

Relativists make similar arguments about "moral truths." As they note, ethical convictions vary widely across cultures. To take only the most obvious examples, practices that contemporary Americans would find abhorrent — torture, infanticide, slavery — have been widely accepted in other societies.

However, the fact that cultures and communities disagree about moral values does not of itself prove that moral justification is impossible. Here again, challenges to relativism are intuitively appealing. Given the legacy of Nazi Germany, few individuals are prepared to follow cultural relativism to its seemingly logical conclusion and concede that genocide violates no universal principle.[10] Building on such reactions, theorists who reject relativism generally argue that reflective decision-making will eventually yield consensus on basic moral premises. Given full information and an opportunity for dispassionate and disinterested judgment, individuals will agree about certain essential values — honesty, benevolence, and so forth. To be sure, disagreements may remain about the application of those values in particular cases. Nonetheless, many theorists maintain that we have no categorical reason to be more skeptical of our considered ethical convictions than our considered factual conclusions.

For those concerned with practical resolution of ethical dilemmas, three central points about these debates over realism and relativism bear emphasis. The first involves the importance of reflective reasoning. Whether or not one believes that objectively or universally valid answers are possible on factual or moral questions, some answers are clearly more valid than others. Even the most committed relativists, who maintain that ethical judgments are inevitably shaped by social practices, will agree that some judgments are more consistent, coherent, self-critical, and respectful of available evidence.

A second crucial point concerns the relation between facts and values. Much of the variation in beliefs on moral questions involves less subjectivity than we often assume. Such variation frequently reflects not a difference in ethical principles but a difference in factual assumptions, traditions, and circumstances.[11] Virtually all societies condemn unjustified killing but disagree as to what constitutes a justification. Thus, views on infanticide may depend in part on nonmoral variables such as poverty, access to birth control and medical services, dependence on healthy children for labor and support in later life, and social customs that devalue daughters. Similarly, many ethical disputes in legal practice turn largely on factual rather than moral disputes. As Chapter VI reflects, arguments about lawyers' duties of confidentiality depend largely on empirical assertions about whether limited disclosure obligations will significantly impair client trust or avert substantial public harms.

A final point involves the relation between commitment and tolerance. Even those who believe most passionately in the truth of their moral position need not seek to impose it on others. Individuals can, for example, believe that abortion is wrong without insisting that the state should criminalize others who act on contrary views. So too, on many issues of legal ethics, lawyers with high moral principles may differ on what those principles require in hard cases. Particularly where competing values and factual uncertainties are involved, the most professionally responsible approach may require respect for differing personal judgments.

2.   Arguments from Language: Moral Meaning

An alternative way of thinking about moral justification is to refine how we think about moral language. One common position is that of "intuitionism." It holds that terms expressing moral values, such as "good," "right," or "ought," refer to "non-natural" as opposed to factual properties. From this perspective, the truth or falsity of ethical judgments is self-evident; it depends on intuition rather than empirical observation or logical deduction. According to intuitionists, we can believe that people should be just, kind, and honest without assessing the consequences of such actions or formulating universal principles.[12]

This theory is, however, difficult to square with the historical and anthropological evidence noted earlier. Different cultures and different groups within the same culture have had very different intuitions on certain moral issues. Once we move beyond the most basic propositions, such as honesty is generally good and torture is generally wrong, our intuitions are less reliable guides. That is particularly true when values conflict, as happens often in legal ethics. How lawyers should balance competing concerns such as protecting client confidences versus preventing injury to third parties is not intuitively self-evident without regard to consequences.

Other theories of moral meaning are often grouped under the awkward label of "noncognitivism." Such approaches share one central feature: they hold that value judgments are matters of attitude rather than cognition or knowledge. According to these theories, moral claims are not factual statements susceptible to verification. Unlike intuitionism, such frameworks assume that ethical beliefs cannot be true or false. The most extreme theoretical position is held by emotivists, who believe that moral assertions are simply expressions of emotion, not statements capable of rational evaluation or justification.[13]

This perspective is not widely shared, in part because it fails to capture what most of us experience when making moral statements or engaging in moral argument; we believe that there are non-arbitrary foundations for ethical reasoning. What is the basis for our emotion if not some belief in the validity of our convictions? If noncognitivists were correct, and every statement that "x is wrong" meant only "I think x is wrong," then moral disagreement would be impossible. Speakers would simply be describing their own attitudes and no one could dispute their assessments. Our persistence in fighting, sometimes even dying, for moral principles exposes the problems with noncognitivism in its most extreme form.

Other noncognitivist positions, however, have attracted broader support. Existentialists, for example, ground morality in personal choice, while many theologians place emphasis on divine command. Despite other differences, these frameworks share a central philosophical premise: values cannot be rationally justified. More moderate views of the possibilities of moral justification also have emerged from both religious and secular theorists. Some contemporary theologians maintain that ethical principles arise from a fusion of reason and faith, while some analytic philosophers argue that such principles are forms of recommendation, evaluation, or prescription.[14] What allies these otherwise diverse theories is a belief that moral convictions are in some sense rational, if not verifiable. To say that something is good or right implies that we are prepared to generalize or universalize our judgments and that our reasons are not purely subjective.

3. Arguments from Rational Choice: "Practical Theory"

Other theorists take a somewhat more practical view of moral justification. These theories are often allied with moderate noncognitivist positions and share a common premise. They claim that moral standards cannot be shown to be true but can be subject to rational evaluation. Practical theories propose criteria for evaluating moral standards and justify those criteria in terms of rational choice or practical reason. For example, some commentators argue that valid moral standards are those that rational persons would choose under ideal conditions involving freedom from coercion or self-interest. Contemporary practical theories generally draw on hypothesized social contracts or rational choice models. John Rawls offers a variation of this approach in defending principles that he believes individuals would accept in "the original position," that is, behind a "veil of ignorance," without knowledge of their own life circumstances.[15]

The way to resolve moral questions, these theorists often argue, is to find a "reflective equilibrium." According to Rawls, ethical decision-making involves a search for principles that will accommodate our "considered" moral beliefs or intuitions. Such beliefs are those formed under "favorable circumstances," which require an absence of undue pressure, emotional disturbance, or self-interest. Yet even these considered views may often involve inconsistencies and distortions. The process of ethical judgment thus requires testing such views against traditional moral principles such as utilitarianism. These principles may cause us to revise our beliefs, and these revised beliefs may prompt changes in our principles. Through this process we will eventually reach a reflective equilibrium in which our moral values cohere.[16]

4.   Arguments from Pluralism

A final group of theorists argues that values and principles are too diverse to be reconciled into any single harmonious moral scheme. Unlike relativists, who also stress the diversity of moral beliefs, these theorists do not view values as subjective. Rather, their position is that not all values are compatible; resolution of concrete dilemmas requires recognition of pluralism. According to some philosophers, such as Michael Walzer and Virginia Held, individuals inhabit multiple domains in which different moral principles assume different priorities.[17] Such frameworks have particular relevance for legal ethics, since they recognize different norms for different social roles.

However one assesses these debates about moral justification, a final point deserves emphasis. Even if one remains uncertain about the validity of a particular approach or judgment, it does not follow that indifference is the appropriate response. Just as we must often act on factual beliefs despite the risk of error, we will often need to take a moral stand despite the absence of certainty. In many professional contexts, we have no choice but to choose. We do, however, have choices about how to go about making an ethical judgment. Whatever their other differences, ethical theorists generally agree about the importance of the moral reasoning process.

Consider the preceding frameworks in light of your own understanding of moral judgment. How would you describe the meaning of value statements and the approach you would use to justify them?

C.   NORMATIVE THEORY

Normative ethical theory has two primary branches. One approach judges the morality of acts or dispositions in terms of their results. A second approach judges acts in terms of their conformity to basic rights and duties. Each of these frameworks has many variations; the most important are reviewed below.

1.   The Pursuit of Justifiable Ends: Utilitarian and Virtue-Based Frameworks

Theories that evaluate the moral worth of actions by the goodness of their ultimate results are termed "teleological," from the Greek word *telos*, or end. The most common of these frameworks involve consequential or utilitarian reasoning. Under these frameworks, the rightness of an action depends on the extent to which it produces good consequences. Two more long-standing approaches assess acts in light of whether they will advance the agent's own well-being (i.e., egoism) or the agent's character (i.e., virtue and self-realization).

a. Egoism

Versions of ethical egoism were popular among some classical Greek philosophers and have been revived in qualified form by some contemporary rational choice theorists.[18] Egoistic frameworks, however, do not enjoy broad support. In many contexts such frameworks appear self-defeating; it will not be to an individual's advantage to have everyone pursue his or her own self-interest. Nor does egoism adequately account for relationships that engage altruistic emotions such as sympathy, empathy, and care. Self-seeking behavior also gives rise to what philosophers have labeled the hedonistic paradox: those who single-mindedly pursue pleasure seldom if ever achieve it. To obtain satisfaction, we need to desire something else such as meaningful work or personal relationships and then find ways to satisfy that desire.[19]

b. Virtue and Self-Realization

Virtue-based theories of morality also grow out of Greek classical traditions and also are attracting renewed interest among contemporary theorists. According to Aristotle, virtues are dispositions to act and judge in accordance with "right reason," and the exercise of virtues is the end of life. These dispositions, such as courage, justice, and temperance, are acquired through habit and training as well as practical intelligence, which unifies intellectual and moral insight. The influential contemporary philosopher, Alisdair MacIntyre, similarly argues that we derive moral traditions from lives where virtues flourish. Unlike other moral theories, which focus either on abstract rules and principles or on the consequences of individual action, virtue ethics focuses on the character of moral agents.[20] Under this approach, sometimes labeled self-realization ethics, right actions both reflect and contribute to human excellence.

Anthony Kronman, in The Lost Lawyer, draws heavily on Aristotelian traditions in arguing for a richer sense of professionalism in the American bar.[21] According to Kronman, effective lawyering requires practical reasoning, which depends on well-developed capacities for empathy and contextual judgment. Building on similar arguments, many communitarian and feminist theorists argue that the morality of actions and dispositions cannot be analyzed in the abstract. Ethical decision-making must be evaluated in context, with attention to individuals' roles, relationships, and communities. Morality, in this view, is not reducible to universal rules, nor are virtues reducible to those traits emphasized by traditional philosophy. Rather, virtues such as care and concern for others, which traditionally have been associated with women and essential for community survival, deserve equal emphasis.[22]

c. Utilitarianism

The most familiar consequentialist theory is utilitarianism. In its classic form, developed by Jeremy Bentham, John Stuart Mill, and Henry Sidgwick, utilitarianism holds that the morally right action is the one that produces the greatest balance of happiness over unhappiness for the greatest number of people. Under this theory, each person's welfare is equally important: "As between his [or her] own happiness, and that of others, utilitarians require [each individual] to be as sincerely impartial as a disinterested and benevolent spectator."[23]

Not all consequentialist theories take this form. Some theorists, variously labeled "ideal utilitarians" or "nonutilitarian consequentialists," define the good to be maximized as encompassing not simply individuals' subjective happiness but also objective conditions such as freedom, knowledge, beauty, fairness of resource distribution, and capacity for individual self-realization.[24] By broadening the definition of welfare, these approaches respond to many of the objections directed against classical utilitarianism noted below, for example, objections based on the failure to consider distributive issues or to safeguard individual rights. But this broader framework also creates other difficulties. It is by no means clear what to do when objectives such as freedom and fairness conflict. Discussion here will focus primarily on classical utilitarianism, since it has had the widest influence. Its significance has been particularly apparent in economic theory, which often views satisfaction of personal preferences as society's fundamental objective.

One other distinction with particular relevance for legal ethics involves the difference between "act utilitarianism" and "rule utilitarianism." The first approach analyzes the morality of each act directly to determine whether it produces the greatest good for the greatest number. The second approach establishes general rules that produce the greatest good for the greatest number and then assesses each act according to whether it conforms to the morally justified rule. The difference between these frameworks is apparent in considering a central question in legal ethics. Should lawyers disclose client confidences in order to prevent harm to innocent third parties? An act utilitarian would require an assessment of the benefits and harms of disclosure in the particular case. To be sure, the lawyer should consider the likely consequences of his decision in affecting future decisions: would clients be less likely to have trusting and candid relationships with their lawyer if they knew that disclosure of secrets was possible? If so, would the cost of somewhat diminishing client trust outweigh the concrete benefits of protecting nonclients under the circumstances at issue? By contrast, a rule utilitarian would attempt to formulate general principles governing confidentiality that would take account of the costs and benefits of disclosure across all cases. For reasons set forth in Chapter VI, a typical rule utilitarian might conclude that the best general standard for the legal profession is that attorneys should maintain client confidences except under limited circumstances (such as to prevent a future crime or an act likely to cause grave bodily danger). Under this approach, the question to consider in any given case would be how to comply with the relevant rule.

Many philosophers, however, believe that the rule/act distinction collapses in practice. In cases where an act utilitarian has valid reasons to violate a general rule such as maintaining secrets, the rule utilitarian would want to modify the rule to include exceptions for that case.[25] Other philosophers respond that the point of having a rule is to absolve individuals from having to make a case-by-case assessment of whether compliance is justified. Given the difficulties in identifying, measuring, and comparing all relevant factors in an unbiased fashion, reliance on general rules has obvious advantages. Consider these arguments in light of your own experience. Which approach, a rule or an act-based approach, seems most helpful?

That question may, in turn, suggest certain broader issues about the usefulness of any utilitarian approach in addressing ethical dilemmas in legal practice. Critics of utilitarianism object that it is both too demanding and not demanding enough. It asks too much both in requiring individuals to set aside their own special relationships and projects in favor of the common good, and in insisting that all consequences of a given action be measured and compared. Conversely, it asks too little by failing to ensure minimum rights, by ignoring distributional issues, and by declining to recognize that not all interests stand on equal footing.

The first objection is that utilitarianism's mandates of strict impartiality run counter to our deepest moral interests. Few of us believe that we should subordinate all personal, professional, and family commitments in favor of the general welfare. Fewer still live in accordance with that principle. As Bernard Williams notes, "there can come a point at which it is quite unreasonable for a man to give up, in the name of the impartial good ordering of the world . . . something which is a condition of his having any interest in being around in the world at all."[26]

Philosopher Gilbert Harnan brings the point home:

> Consider your own present situation. You are reading a . . . book about ethics. There are many courses of action open to you that would have much greater social utility. If, for example, you were immediately to stop reading and do whatever you could to send food to places like Africa or India, where it is scarce, you could probably save hun-

dreds, even thousands of lives. . . . According to utilitarianism, therefore, you are not now doing what you ought morally to be doing and
this will continue to be true throughout your life.[27]

To make every action as morally good as possible would edge out
many interests that we consider part of a well-lived life — such as the
pursuit of excellence or the nurturance of friendships.[28]

Defenders of utilitarianism usually respond that the theory is
capable of recognizing the need for special projects and relationships.
From their perspective, the way to maximize happiness or general
welfare is for individuals to forge commitments that sustain and give
meaning to life. Yet this response also underscores the second sense
in which critics find utilitarianism problematic: its indeterminacy.
How can we be sure what will in fact produce the greatest good for
the greatest number? To identify, weigh, and compare all the consequences of a given action against the alternatives is extremely difficult. How do we measure the value of undertaking at least some
famine relief efforts as against the value of pursuing more
self-interested projects? Recent economic work highlights the problems in making interpersonal comparisons of utility and in attempting trade-offs between incommensurable values.[29] There is, for
example, no uncontested way of assessing the benefits of encouraging client trust when measured against the benefits of averting
client fraud, or of using a given percentage of law firm profits for pro
bono efforts when measured against improving the work conditions
for support staff or providing more adequate parental leaves for
lawyers.

The difficulties become still greater if we consider the remote
and indirect consequences that philosophers label "ripple effects."[30]
Thus, Sissela Bok argues below that the costs and benefits of any lie
must take into account not just the likely impact on those most immediately involved, but also the far more elusive and intangible
corrosive effects, such as reducing levels of trust in the community
generally or lowering resistance to lying. Complicating the evaluative process still further are the personal biases and information
constraints that individuals generally bring to the decision-making
process.

To this argument, defenders of utilitarianism have only partial
answers. One response is to acknowledge the need for rules that will
avoid the constant indeterminacies and biases of judging particular
acts. Yet that response only pushes the ambiguities back one step to
the point at which rules are formulated. An alternative approach is
to concede the problem but to argue that no other normative theory
escapes it. Certainly the leading contenders, the rights-based theories discussed below, present analogous difficulties.

While one group of critics has presented utilitarianism as too
demanding, a second group paints it as too permissive. For some
philosophers, a fundamental flaw lies in the theory's failure to pro-

tect individual rights irrespective of majority interests. Several well-known hypothetical situations illustrate this concern. For example, critics argue that, in a context of racial violence, utilitarians should have no moral objection to convicting an innocent man if it would appease a mob and avert many further deaths. Nor should utilitarians object to enslaving the few if it would help the many, or removing the organs of one healthy individual if their distribution could save the lives of several. By contrast, most defenders of utilitarianism deny that such actions would in fact serve the greatest good of the greatest number; they argue that respect for basic human rights can be justified on utilitarian grounds such as maximizing happiness and the common welfare.

Other similar objections generate similar responses. Critics claim that utilitarianism is insensitive to distributional issues and to qualitative differences between the preferences that it seeks to maximize. On this view, a utilitarian would have no moral basis for preferring a society in which a minority enjoyed great happiness and a majority enjoyed relatively little happiness to another society in which greater equality prevailed, provided that the overall level of happiness was comparable. Nor would a classical utilitarian have any moral grounds for distinguishing between preferences founded on irrationality, ignorance, bigotry, or addictions and those grounded in love of nature, beauty, art, and so forth. To a large extent, our desires are socially constructed and constrained; we want what appears possible and appropriate to want. And if maximizing happiness is the ultimate goal, we have no basis for challenging the structures that lead to certain preferences.[31]

In response to such concerns, defenders of utilitarianism take two approaches. On the distributional issue, some commentators invoke the principle of declining marginal returns. Greater equality, they argue, should yield greater aggregate happiness if other factors are held constant; giving additional income to the poor typically will produce more satisfaction than giving it to the wealthy, whose basic needs already are satisfied. An alternative response, common among ideal utilitarians, is to define the good according to objective standards that give moral priority to certain preferences and values, including distributional fairness.[32] The problem, of course, is that justifying those priorities requires some nonutilitarian principle, which raises all the metaethical problems noted in the preceding section.

2. Respect for Obligations: Rights-Based Frameworks

A second major tradition of normative theory is deontological, from the Greek word *deon*, meaning duty. Under this approach, actions are morally right when they conform to a universal, generalizable principle of obligation, irrespective of their consequences. Immanuel Kant, the leading deontological theorist among Western philosophers, believed that any ethically justifiable conduct must satisfy one ultimate moral principle, or categorical imperative. As noted earlier, the primary formulation of this principle requires us to act according to maxims that we would accept as universal laws. At other points in his work, Kant offered a second formulation of the categorical imperative: "act so that you treat humanity whether in your own person or in that of another, always as an end and never as a means only." Scholars have long debated whether or why Kant believed these rules were equivalent. For purposes of this discussion, however, that question is less important than more general issues concerning the strengths and limitations of deontological approaches in applied ethics.

At the core of such approaches is respect for individual dignity, freedom, and self-determination. Kant believed that each human being has intrinsic worth because of the capacity for rationality. He further assumed that rational agents who engaged in a disinterested, reflective moral reasoning process would support a principle requiring universal, generalizable rules. That principle underpins not only the categorical imperative but also religious injunctions to love one's neighbor as oneself and popularized versions of the Golden Rule.[33]

In applying these frameworks, philosophers have attempted to identify obligations that would satisfy moral principles of universality, generalizability, and respect for individuals. Such obligations typically include duties of fidelity (keeping promises and avoiding deception); benevolence (helping others and avoiding harm); and justice (treating individuals in similar circumstances similarly and respecting just distributional principles). Because these obligations imply corresponding rights, deontological approaches are often labeled "rights-based approaches," and that usage will be followed throughout this book.

According to leading theorists such as John Rawls, these fundamental rights and obligations are those that free and rational agents would accept if they were totally disinterested. In essence, Rawls attempts to identify principles that individuals would want for a society in which they did not know their own place: Moral responsibilities are those that would command consensus from individuals in an "original position," behind a "veil of ignorance" where they would be unaware of their abilities, social position, and other personal characteristics that might influence their status.

Critics argue that the strength of deontological approaches is also the source of their limitations. A rule that we are prepared to universalize will often need to be framed at such a level of abstraction that it cannot resolve particular cases. Nor is it self-evident what individuals would want in an original position. The more content we give to their ethical choices, the more controversial those presumed choices become; the less content we supply, the less useful they prove in guiding decisions. Formulas such as the categorical imperative have no specific content and cannot resolve ethical questions that implicate competing values. A requirement that rules be generalizable is of limited help in legal ethics when the issue is which rule we should generalize.[34]

As noted earlier, much communitarian, feminist, and critical social theory also calls into question the assumption that we can develop adequate moral standards by hypothesizing abstract agents behind a veil of ignorance. According to critics, such an approach denies decision-makers access to the experiences and commitments that construct our moral sensibilities. From this perspective, a focus on universal rules undervalues the significance of concrete relationships in ethical decision-making. Our attachments to family, friends, colleagues, community, and religious institutions shape our identity in ways that abstract rights-based frameworks fail to acknowledge.[35]

Finally, critics question frameworks that give priority to preserving rights irrespective of their consequences in all cases. For example, as discussion in Part D below suggests, many individuals reject the notion that we should always tell the truth, whatever the human and societal costs.

In response to such criticisms, contemporary theorists often emphasize that deontological approaches need not be entirely insensitive to consequences when formulating rights and responsibilities. In practice, deontological and utilitarian approaches often converge. Just as utilitarians can value rights when determining what will promote good consequences, nonutilitarians can consider consequences when determining what rights should be protected. We can, in short, arrive at similar ethical results through different ethical frameworks.[36]

In some contexts, however, it will matter whether we place priority on the intrinsic quality of an act or its extrinsic results. Which of the preceding ethical approaches best captures your view? Under what professional circumstances would you be most likely to use utilitarian, rights-based, or character-based approaches? When might you expect different outcomes? Why?

3.   Pro Bono Service: Utilitarian and Rights-Based Approaches Compared

To explore how different ethical traditions might approach issues of lawyers' conduct, it is helpful to work through a controversial question. One example is whether lawyers have an ethical obligation to provide pro bono services. An early draft of the Model Rules of Professional Conduct would have required 40 hours of such assistance from each attorney each year. Rule 6.1 of the current Model Rules provides that "a lawyer should aspire to render at least

50 hours of pro bono public legal services per year" to persons of limited means or to organizations assisting such persons.

A rights-based argument favoring pro bono service might begin from the premise that access to legal services is a basic entitlement. As the Supreme Court has recognized in other contexts, the right to sue and defend "is the right conservative of all other rights" and would often be of little value if it did not encompass legal assistance.[37] Access to such assistance is necessary to ensure governmental legitimacy, protect fundamental interests, safeguard procedural due process, and promote participatory values.[38]

Recent surveys suggest that a wide gap remains between America's aspirations to equal justice under law and current distributional patterns. Studies of low-income groups find that over three-quarters of legal needs remain unmet. Studies cutting across income groups estimate that individuals do not obtain lawyers' help for between 30 to 40 percent of their personal legal needs.[39] Mandatory pro bono service by the private bar could help fill the gap. Under current voluntary programs, relatively few lawyers perform significant pro bono work for low-income clients. The average for the profession as a whole is estimated at less than a half an hour per week.[40] Advocates of mandatory pro bono argue that the profession's monopoly over the provision of legal services should carry with it a corresponding obligation to make such services more available.

Utilitarians might appeal to similar values in defending pro bono requirements. Their defense, however, would turn not on rights to legal assistance but on the positive consequences of expanding its availability. Such consequences might include promoting more just outcomes in legal disputes; enabling more individuals to enforce their entitlements to crucial benefits; enhancing the legitimacy of the justice system; increasing public regard for lawyers; and expanding attorneys' opportunities for satisfying work and their awareness of how the law functions, or fails to function, for low income groups.

Opposition to pro bono obligations has also invoked both rights-based and utilitarian arguments. One line of criticism has emphasized the infringement of lawyers' own rights.[41] Other licensed professionals are not expected to provide free goods and services. Why then should lawyers bear special burdens? From this perspective, conscripting attorneys undermines their fundamental rights of due process and just compensation. If society wishes to expand legal access, society as a whole should pay the cost.

Utilitarians stress different objections. From their vantage, pro bono obligations are not an efficient way of realizing the benefits of broadened access to services. Lawyers who lack expertise and motivation to serve under-represented groups will not provide cost-effective representation. Requiring attorneys to provide a miminal level of services of largely unverifiable quality cannot begin to meet this nation's massive problem of unmet legal need. Worse still, such token responses to distributional inequalities may deflect attention from the fundamental problems that remain and from more productive ways of addressing them. Preferable strategies might include simplification of legal procedures, expanded subsidies for poverty law programs, and elimination of the professional monopoly over routine legal services.

How would you respond to these arguments? Would you support the pro bono requirements for law students that about fifteen schools have adopted? Which theoretical framework — the utilitarian or rights-based approach — seems most helpful?

Under what other circumstances in legal practice would you be most likely to use utilitarian, rights-based, or character-based approaches? Why?

See Chapter XI, Constitutional Law
   • Mandatory Pro Bono Representation
      (pages 504-506)

See also Chapter VI, Confidentiality and Client Counseling
   • Consumer Safety and Corporate Counseling
      (pages 263–278)

D.   MORAL REASONING IN PROFESSIONAL CONTEXT: DECEPTION AS A CASE STUDY

1.   Introduction

To make the preceding analysis more concrete, the remainder of this chapter applies different ethical frameworks to one representative set of professional dilemmas, those involving deception. Under conventional definitions, deception involves any effort to create a belief different from one's own understanding of the truth. Such efforts fall along a spectrum and encompass knowingly false statements (i.e., lies) as well as other representations or omissions that are designed to mislead. Opportunities for deceptive conduct arise in all areas of legal practice and figure prominently in several chapters of this volume. To ground discussion here, it may be useful to consider some of the problems involving candor in negotiations (Chapter VIII) and in litigation (Chapter V). Those problems raise certain recurrent questions. What circumstances might justify deceptive behavior? When is letting someone believe a lie the moral equivalent of actually telling one? What are lawyers' responsibilities when clients are engaged in deceptive conduct?

SISSELA BOK, LYING: MORAL CHOICE IN PUBLIC AND PRIVATE LIFE

24-28 (1978)

THE PERSPECTIVE OF THE LIAR

Those who adopt the perspective of would-be-liars, on the other hand, have different concerns. For them, the choice is often a difficult one. They may believe, with Machiavelli, that "great things" have been done by those who have "little regard for good faith." They may trust that they can make wise use of the power that lies bring. And they may have confidence in their own ability to distinguish the times when good reasons support their decision to lie.

Liars share with those they deceive the desire not to *be* deceived. As a result, their choice to lie is one which they would like to reserve for themselves while insisting that others be honest. They would prefer, in other words, a "free-rider" status, giving them the benefits of lying without the risks of being lied to. Some think of this free-rider status as for them alone. Others extend it to their friends, social group, or profession. This category of persons can be narrow or broad; but it does require as a necessary backdrop the ordinary assumptions about the honesty of most persons. The free rider trades upon being an exception, and could not exist in a world where everybody chose to exercise the same prerogatives.

At times, liars operate as if they believed that such a free-rider status is theirs and that it excuses them. At other times, on the contrary, it is the very fact that others *do* lie that excuses their deceptive stance in their own eyes. It is crucial to see the distinction between the freeloading liar and the liar whose deception is a strategy for survival in a corrupt society.

All want to avoid being deceived by *others* as much as possible. But many would like to be able to weigh the advantages and disadvantages in a more nuanced way whenever they are themselves in the position of choosing whether or not to deceive. They may invoke special reasons to lie such as the need to protect confidentiality or to spare someone's feelings. They are then much more willing, in particular, to exonerate a well-intentioned lie on their own part; dupes tend to be less sanguine about the good intentions of those who deceive them.

But in this benevolent self-evaluation by the liar of the lies he might tell, certain kinds of disadvantage and harm are almost always overlooked. Liars usually weigh only the immediate harm to others from the lie against the benefits they want to achieve. The flaw in such an outlook is that it ignores or underestimates two additional kinds of harm: the harm that lying does to the liars themselves, and the harm done to the general level of trust and social cooperation. Both are cumulative; both are hard to reverse.

How is the liar affected by his own lies? The very fact that he *knows* he has lied, first of all, affects him. He may regard the lie as an inroad on his integrity; he certainly looks at those he has lied to with a new caution. And if they find out that he has lied, he knows that his credibility and the respect for his word have been damaged. When Adlai Stevenson had to go before the United Nations in 1961 to tell falsehoods about the United States' role in the Bay of Pigs invasion, he changed the course of his life. He may not have known beforehand that the message he was asked to convey was untrue; but merely to carry the burden of being the means of such deceit must have been difficult. To lose the confidence of his peers in such a public way was harder still.

Granted that a public lie on an important matter, once revealed, hurts the speaker, must we therefore conclude that *every* lie has this effect? What of those who tell a few white lies once in a while? Does lying hurt them in the same way? It is hard to defend such a notion. No one trivial lie undermines the liar's integrity. But the problem for liars is that they tend to see *most* of their lies in this benevolent light and thus vastly underestimate the risks they run. While no one lie always carries harm for the liar, then, there is *risk* of such harm in most.

These risks are increased by the fact that so few lies are solitary ones. It is easy, a wit observed, to tell a lie, but hard to tell only one. The first lie "must be thatched with another or it will rain through." More and more lies may come to be needed; the liar always has more mending to do. And the strains on him become greater each time; many have noted that it takes an excellent memory to keep one's untruths in good repair and disentangled. The sheer energy the liar has to devote to shoring them up is energy the honest man can dispose of freely.

After the first lies, moreover, others can come more easily. Psychological barriers wear down; lies seem more necessary, less reprehensible; the ability to make moral distinctions can coarsen; the liar's perception of his chances of being caught may warp. These changes can affect his behavior in subtle ways; even if he is not found out he will then be less trusted than those of unquestioned honesty. And it is inevitable that more frequent lies *do* increase the chance that some will be discovered. At that time, even if the liar has no personal sense of loss of integrity from his deceitful practices, he will surely regret the damage to his credibility which their discovery brings about. Paradoxically, once his word is no longer trusted, he will be left with greatly *decreased* power, even though a lie often does bring at least a short-term gain in power over those deceived.

Even if the liar cares little about the risks to others from his deception, therefore, all these risks to himself argue in favor of at least weighing any decision to lie quite seriously. Yet such risks rarely enter his calculations. Bias skews all judgment, but never more so than in the search for good reasons to deceive. Not only does it combine with ignorance and uncertainty so that liars are apt to overestimate their own good will, high motives, and chances to escape detection; it leads also to overconfidence in their own imperviousness to the personal entanglements, worries, and loss of integrity which might so easily beset them.

The liar's self-bestowed free-rider status, then, can be as corrupting as all other unchecked exercises of power. There are, in fact, very few "free rides" to be had through lying. I hope to examine . . . those exceptional circumstances where harm to self and others from lying is less likely, and procedures which can isolate and contain them. But the chance of harm to liars can rarely be ruled out altogether.

Bias causes liars often to ignore the second type of harm as well. For even if they make the effort to estimate the consequences to *individuals*, themselves and others, of their lies, they often fail to consider the many ways in which deception can spread and give rise to practices very damaging to human communities. These practices clearly do not affect only isolated individuals. The veneer of social trust is often thin. As lies spread, by imitation, or in retaliation, or to forestall suspected deception, trust is damaged. Yet trust is a social good to be protected just as much as the air we breathe or the water we drink. When it is damaged, the community as a whole suffers; and when it is destroyed, societies falter and collapse.

---

2. Rights-Based Approaches

Kant believed that lying was always morally unjustified whatever its consequences. In his view, deception, even from benevolent motives, ran counter to both formulations of the categorical imperative. Dishonesty failed to respect the integrity of either the deceiver or the deceived and treated the duped individual as a means to other goals. Lying also violated the injunction to act only in accordance with universal, generalizable principles, because if everyone lied whenever they felt the ends justified it, such deception would ultimately prove self-defeating. People could no longer afford to trust each other and neither liars nor truthtellers could count on being believed.[42]

This categorical prohibition against lying has attracted widespread criticism. One well-known hypothetical involves a ship captain who is stopped by Nazis and asked if he has knowledge of any Jews aboard his boat. To answer truthfully would expose his hidden Jewish passengers to virtually certain death. According to many rights-based theorists (as well as utilitarians), a lie in this case is morally justified. The rule against dishonesty that these theorists are willing to universalize includes an exception to save innocent lives or to withhold truth from someone who has no moral right to demand it.[43]

Deception in legal practice rarely involves preservation of life. The question then becomes what other circumstances might justify deceit. Rights-based theorists generally support prohibitions on dishonesty with narrow exceptions because this approach minimizes the indeterminacies and biases that Sissela Bok describes. Bok herself recommends a "test of publicity," which asks what lies reasonable persons would find legitimate and be willing to justify publicly. She assumes that such persons would look for nondeceptive alternatives and would assess the moral justifications for and against deception from the perspective of individuals potentially affected by deception. Her rule would consider whether persons had implicitly consented to dishonesty (as in playing poker or bargaining in a bazaar). Where such consent is absent, her standard would weigh not only the interests of the parties in maintaining their credibility and reputation, but also the value to society of encouraging trust and a sense of individual integrity.[44]

3.   Utilitarian Approaches

Unlike Kant, utilitarians do not consider deception to be intrinsically evil; its morality depends on its consequences. Nonetheless, many rule utilitarians end up with an approach quite similar to Bok's and for the same reasons. They want a rule that maximizes good results across the broad category of cases, and that allows dishonesty only in limited circumstances, such as those Bok identifies. Most act utilitarians also consider the same factors as Bok's framework but would weigh them in each case.

The main difference between these two utilitarian approaches lies in the confidence they place in general standards to capture appropriate exceptions. Those who prefer rule-based approaches worry that individuals will not be able to make disinterested judgments or to assess all relevant costs in particular cases. Those who prefer act-utilitarian approaches worry that any rules general enough to be universalizable will not be specific enough to resolve particular dilemmas.

4.   Alternative Approaches

An alternative set of frameworks denies that abstract rules or principles can take into account all of the contextual factors that should influence judgment. Preserving relationships is one such factor. Communitarian and feminist theorists, for example, would take a far more tolerant view than many rights-based theorists of "white lies" that serve to protect family, friends, or community bonds. Thanking a host for a "lovely" evening or a colleague for "helpful" criticism are examples of social conventions that often may be preferable to total candor. Virtue-based approaches place less emphasis on detailed prohibitions and more emphasis on personal integity, enforced by informal sanctions.

Critics of such approaches have raised a number of concerns related to legal ethics. Research on moral behavior leaves doubt that honesty reflects a fixed and consistent personality trait that does not vary under situational influences.[45] So too, communitarian and feminist approaches that stress relational values may prove of limited help when the issue is which relationship to value. If, as examples in Chapter XVI (Family Law) suggest, maintaining a client's confidence will jeopardize the needs of unrepresented children, which interests should take priority?

Consider these different ethical frameworks in assessing problems of candor in negotiation (Chapter VIII), trial testimony (Chapter V), and discovery (Chapter V). In determining whether deception is justifiable, when should lawyers defer to a client's ethical decisions and when should they insist on making their own judgments? To what extent would your view depend on the underlying merits of a client's action?

For example, how would you analyze the case of the woman on welfare that William Simon discusses in Chapter IV (Advocacy)? See page 151. Assume that the only persuasive interpretation of the rules would deprive the client of sufficient resources to bring her family up to subsistence levels. Which of the ethical traditions discussed above would you find most helpful in analyzing the lawyer's responsibility in such contexts?

See Chapter V, The Adversary System

See Chapter VIII, Negotiation and Mediation
  • Candor in Representations of Fact and Value
    (pages 342–347)

Endnotes

1. Kurt Baier, The Moral Point of View 3 (1969).

2. G.W.F. Hegel, Phenomenology of Spirit 266-294 (A.V. Miller trans., 1977); John Hartland-Swann, An Analysis of Morals (1960).

3. Joan C. Callahan, Basics and Background in Ethical Issues in Professional Life 7-9 (Joan C. Callahan ed., 1988); Victor Grassian, Moral Reasoning: Ethical Theory and Some Contemporary Moral Problems 4 (1981); William Frankena, Ethics 4-5 (1963).

4. See, e.g., J.L. Mackie, Ethics: Inventing Right and Wrong (1977); Geoffrey James Warnock, The Object of Morality 26 (1971).

5. Immanuel Kant, Foundations of the Metaphysic of Morals (L. Beck trans., 2d ed. 1990) (1959).

6. See Baier, supra note 1.

7. Alisdair MacIntyre, After Virtue: A Study in Moral Theory (1981); Virginia Held, Feminism and Moral Theory, in Women and Moral Theory 111 (Eva Fedar Kittey & Diana T. Meyers eds., 1987); Stanley Hauerwas & David B. Burrell, From System to Story: An Alternative Pattern for Rationality in Ethics, in Truthfulness and Tragedy: Further Investigations in Christian Ethics (Stanley Hauerwas ed., 1977).

8. Derek Edwards, Malcolm Ashmore & Jonathan Potter, Death and Furniture: The Rhetoric, Politics, and Theology of Bottom Line Arguments Against Relativism, 8 History of the Human Sciences 25, 26 (1995).

9. Id. at 29.

10. Morris Ginsburg, On the Diversity of Morals, in 1 Essays on Sociology and Social Philosophy 97-129 (1956); Michael Moore, Moral Reality, 1982 Wis. L. Rev. 1061, 1088-1096 (1982).

11. Grassian, supra note 3, at 28-29.

12. Henry Sidgwick, The Methods of Ethics (Book III) (5th ed. 1893); see William K. Frankena, Ethics 102-103 (2d ed. 1973).

13. See, e.g., Alfred Jules Ayer, Language, Truth and Logic (1936). This work draws on logical positivist theories of language that statements are "true" only if they can be deduced by logic or verified by experience.

14. Compare Christian Ethics (Waldo Beach & H. Richard Niebuhr eds., 1955); Edward LeRoy Long Jr., A Survey of Recent Christian Ethics

(1982); James F. Bresnahan, Ethical Theory and Possible Contributions of Religious Ethics to Dialogue About Professional Ethics of Attorneys, 37 The Jurist 56 (1977), with analytic approaches described in Frankena, supra note 12, at 106; and David O. Brink, Moral Realism and The Foundation of Ethics 30 (1989).

15. John Rawls, A Theory of Justice (1971). However, since Rawls also appeals to moral considerations and viewed his project as normative rather than metaethical, he is not a "pure" practical theorist in the sense that philosophers often use the term. See David Copp, Metaethics, in 2 Encyclopedia of Ethics 793 (Lawrence C. Becker & Charlotte B. Becker eds., 1992).

16. Rawls, supra note 15, at 47-51.

17. Michael Walzer, Spheres of Justice: A Defense of Pluralism and Equality (1983); Virginia Held, Rights and Goods: Justifying Social Action (1984).

18. Rational choice theory offers an economic analysis of decision-making that builds on consequentialist philosophy. Its essential premise is that individuals act rationally to maximize their interests, and its focus is on the implications of this premise in various strategic and collective contexts. See Dennis Mueller, Public Choice II (1979); David Gauthier, Morals by Agreement (1986).

19. Frankena, supra note 12, at 19-23; Peter Singer, Practical Ethics 201 (1979); Joel Feinberg, Psychological Egoism, in Reason & Responsibility 529, 533 (Joel Feinberg ed., 1978).

20. Aristotle, Nichomachean Ethics (W.D. Ross trans., 1915); Alisdair MacIntyre, After Virtue (1981) and Three Rival Versions of Moral Enquiry: Encyclopaedia, Genealogy, and Tradition (1990); The Virtues: Contemporary Essays on Moral Character (Robert B. Kruschwitz & Robert C. Edwards eds., 1987).

21. Anthony Kronman, The Lost Lawyer (1993).

22. See Feminist Ethics (Claudia Card ed., 1991); Alison M. Jaggar, Feminist Ethics, in 1 Encyclopedia of Ethics 361 (Lawrence C. Becker & Charlotte B. Becker eds., 1992).

23. John Stuart Mill, Utilitarianism (Oscar Piest ed., Liberal Arts Press 1957). See Jeremy Bentham, An Introduction to the Principles of Morals and Legislation, in A Fragment on Government and An Introduction to the Principles of Morals and Legislation (Wilfrid Harrison ed., 1948); Henry Sidgwick, The Methods of Ethics (5th ed. 1893).

24. See Brink, supra note 14.

25. Bernard Williams, Morality: An Introduction to Ethics 102 (1922); David Lyons, Forms and Limits of Utilitarianism 119-160 (1965).

26. Brink, supra note 14, at 280 (quoting Bernard Williams); see also Shelly Kagan, The Limits of Morality 263 (1989); Samuel Scheffler, The Rejection of Consequentialism: A Philosophical Investigation of the Considerations Underlying Rival Moral Conceptions (1982).

27. Gilbert Harman, The Nature of Morality: An Introduction to Ethics 157 (1977).

28.   Susan Wolf, Moral Saints, 79 J. Philosophy 419 (1982).

29. Amartya K. Sen, Collective Choice and Social Welfare 118-148 (1970).

30. J.J.C. Smart & Bernard Williams, Utilitarianism: For and Against 33 (1973).

31. See Roberto Mangabeira Unger, Critical Legal Studies, 96 Harv. L. Rev. 561, 657-658 (1983); Amartya Sen & Bernard Williams, Introduction, in Utilitarianism and Beyond 15 (Amartya Sen & Bernard Williams eds., 1982).

32. See text at note 28 and J.L. Mackie, Ethics 147 (1977); Brink, supra note 14, at 226-236.

33. Formulations of the Golden Rule appear in a wide variety of religious and cultural traditions. See H. Rost, The Golden Rule: A Universal Ethic (1986).

34. See Roberto Mangabeira Unger, Knowledge and Politics 54 (1975) (noting that "do unto others" is unhelpful when we are unsure what it is that we want them to do unto us); Alisdair MacIntyre, A Short History of Ethics 197-198 (1966).

35. See, e.g., sources cited in note 7 and Jennifer Nedelsky, Reconceiving Autonomy: Sources, Thoughts and Possibilities, 1 Yale J. Law & Feminism 7 (1989); Susan Okin, Justice, Gender and the Family 89-109 (1989).

36. Judith Lichtenberg, The Right, the All Right, and the Good, 92 Yale L.J. 54, 56 (1983) (book review of Samuel Scheffler, The Rejection of Consequentialism (1982)).

37. Chambers v. Baltimore & Ohio R.R., 207 U.S. 142, 148 (1907).

38. See David Luban, Lawyers and Justice: An Ethical Study 263-264 (1988); Frank Michelman, The Supreme Court and Litigation Access Fees: The Right to Protect One's Rights, Part I, 1973 Duke L.J. 1153, 1172.

39. See studies cited in Roy W. Resse & Carolyn A. Eldred, Institute for Survey Research, Temple University for Consortium on Legal Services and the Public, American Bar Association, Legal Needs Among Low-Income and Moderate-Income Households: Summary of Findings from the Comprehensive Legal Needs Study 7-30 (1994); Deborah L. Rhode & David Luban, Legal Ethics (2d ed. 1995).

40. See surveys summarized in Deborah L. Rhode, Lawyers, Wm. & Mary L. Rev. (forthcoming 1997).

41. See Deborah L. Rhode, Ethical Perspectives on Legal Practice, 37 Stan. L. Rev. 589, 610 (1985) (quoting commentators who objected to the Model Rules' proposed requirement on grounds that it constituted "involuntary servitude" and an "improper intrusion into the lawyer's right of free determination"). For an overview of cases raising involuntary servitude objections to court appointments of uncompensated counsel, see Deborah L. Rhode & David Luban, Legal Ethics 805 (2d ed. 1995).

42. Immanuel Kant, Duties Towards Others: Truthfulness, in Lectures on Ethics 224-235 (Hollis Infield ed., Harper and Row 1963) (1930), and On the Supposed Right to Lie from Benevolent Motives, in Critique of Practical Reason and Other Writings in Moral Philosophy (Lewis White Beck ed., 1949).

43. See generally Charles Fried, Right and Wrong 60-72 (1978).

44. See Sissela Bok, Lying: Moral Choice in Public and Professional Life 100-104 (1978), and the materials on candor in negotiations in Chapter VIII.

45. See Deborah L. Rhode, Moral Character as a Professional Credential, 94 Yale L.J. 491, 556-560 (1985); Hugh Hartshorn & Mark Arthur May, Studies in Nature of Character; Studies in Deceit, Book 1 at 377-412, Book 2 at 41-43 (1928); and discussion in Chapter III (Regulation of the Profession, Part C), infra.

Chapter III

Regulation of the Profession

A. THE NATURE OF A PROFESSION

American lawyers have long prided themselves on being part of a profession. That status is critical to attorneys' personal identity, social position, and regulatory independence. Since the notion of professionalism carries so much significance for lawyers both individually and collectively, it is worth focusing on what exactly the concept means.

Historically, the term "profession" is both elastic and elusive; its definition has varied considerably over time and cultures. Who can claim that status has been a matter of political as well as theoretical dispute? Occupations that we now consider "professional" have been in existence for well over 2,000 years, although the term itself and the distinctive features of these vocational groups did not begin to emerge until the sixteenth century. "Profession" comes from the Latin, *professionem*, meaning to make a public declaration. The term evolved to describe occupations that required new entrants to take an oath professing their dedication to the ideals and practices of a learned calling.[1]

Current usage has become considerably more varied. Many individuals use "professional" simply to convey competence or to distinguish between amateurs and paid practitioners. However, the occupations that historically have been considered professions have emphasized a more restrictive definition. According to a recent American Bar Association report, professionals are those who "pursue a learned art . . . in the spirit of public service."[2] These two central characteristics, specialized knowledge and social responsibility, have been thought to account for other distinguishing features of professions, such as ethical codes, regulatory autonomy, prescribed forms of training, and a monopoly over certain work.

This understanding of professionalism has attracted increasing challenge from all points on the ideological spectrum. Commentators from both the left and right argue that professionals' claims to specialized competence are no different in kind from the claims of other groups that lack professional status, such as plumbers or paralegals. Critics also question the extent to which public service orientations are more prevalent among those with recognized professional status, such as attorneys, architects, or academics, than among those traditionally viewed as nonprofessionals, such as midwives or elementary school teachers.

Neoclassical economists have been particularly critical of the way professional claims serve to rationalize anticompetitive protections, such as overly restrictive regulations concerning admission, advertising, and nonlawyer practice.[3] Theorists on the left similarly argue that professionals do not simply fill a recognized social need; rather, they actively work to create a market for their claimed expertise and then rely on such expertise to legitimize professional power, social status, and economic prerogatives.[4] From this perspective, lawyers are largely responsible for, and beneficiaries of, unnecessarily complex, jargon-laden, and expensive legal procedures.

Yet even those most critical of professional privileges often acknowledge that the interests at issue are more complicated than any reductive economic account might suggest. Many professionals pursue ideals as well as profits, and regulatory policies have provoked frequent conflicts among practitioners.[5] Within the American bar, there are strong "economic differences between those who wis[h openly] to compete and those who [do] not and ideological disagreements between those seeking to elevate the status of the profession by giving it a noncommercial tone and others relatively unconcerned about status."[6] Similar tensions arise between those committed to increasing access to legal services and those wary about creating greater demands for pro bono services and cheaper non-lawyer alternatives.

These internal divisions have become increasingly apparent over the last quarter century. Changes in the market for legal services have intensified competition, diminished collegiality, and discouraged nonprofit-oriented activities.[7] In 1986, an American Bar

Association Commission on Professionalism expressed widespread concerns:

> [A central question facing today's bar is]: Has our profession abandoned principle for profit, professionalism for commercialism?
>
> The answer cannot be a simple yes or no. The legal profession is more diverse and provides more legal services to more people today than ever before. These are not inconsiderable achievements. Further, most lawyers, the Commission believes, are conscientious, fair, and able. They serve their clients well and are a credit to the profession. Yet the practices of some lawyers cry out for correction. . . .
>
> The public views lawyers, at best, as being of uneven character and quality. In a survey conducted by this Commission . . . only 6% of corporate users of legal service rated "all or most" lawyers as deserving to be called "professionals." Only 7% saw professionalism increasing among lawyers; 68% said it had decreased over time. Similarly, 55% of the state and federal judges questioned in a separate poll said lawyer professionalism was declining.
>
> The primary question for this Commission thus becomes what, if anything, can be done to improve both the appearance and the reality of lawyer professionalism.[8]

In response, the Commission proposed various strategies, including more legal ethics education, more efforts to promote civility in litigation, improvements in bar disciplinary procedures, and greater pro bono service. Following release of the ABA report, many state and local bar associations convened their own committees on professionalism, which generally expressed views similar to those of the national commission.

Underlying these reports is a widespread disaffection about the increasing pressures of contemporary practice — its higher billable hour requirements, lower partner-associate ratios, more aggressive pursuit of clients, less stable law firm relationships, and increasingly combative tactics. Accompanying these concerns is a widespread nostalgia for a hypothesized happier era, such as de Tocqueville described in a celebrated passage in Democracy in America:

> The people in democratic states do not mistrust the members of the legal profession, because it is known that they are interested to serve the popular cause. . . .
>
> In America there are no nobles or literary men, and the people are apt to mistrust the wealthy; lawyers consequently form the highest political class and the most cultivated portion of society. . . . If I were asked where I place the American aristocracy, I should reply without hesitation that it is not among the rich, who are united by no common tie, but that it occupies the judicial bench and the bar.[9]

Whether any "golden era" of professionalism has ever in fact existed is open to dispute. Historians generally paint a less glowing picture than de Tocqueville did. As they note, lawyers have long been targets of public abuse as well as respect, and bar leaders have lamented the decline of law into a business throughout the last two centuries.[10]

But whether or not the contemporary situation is worse, the critical issue is how to remedy it. And that task presents substantial challenges. As Robert Nelson and David Trubeck argue:

> To be sure, many within the legal profession might . . . prefe[r] stable markets and stable relationships guided by "professional" rather than commercial values. But this option . . . has never really been available in recent history. The bar is too fragmented to agree on what relationships and values should be fostered. It has been too tolerant of entrepreneurship and too leery of effective professional association or governmental control to develop truly powerful regulatory mechanisms . . . or do anything significant about the trends [bar leaders have decried]. The result [has been] a vague and general invocation of "shared" values that really aren't shared and a symbolic and nostalgic crusade in the name of an ideology almost no one really believes in fully and which has little to do with the everyday working visions of American lawyers.[11]

Do you agree? If so, what follows from this diagnosis? How are "professions" different from other occupational groups? What would it mean for lawyers truly to put "professionalism" first, as the ABA Commission recommends? Consider that issue in light of the materials on professional codes, discipline, and regulation of competition that follow.

B. PROFESSIONAL REGULATION

1. Introduction

In the United States, law is a self-regulating profession. American lawyers are subject to a complex set of formal and informal norms that are largely under the control of the profession. This chapter summarizes the most important oversight structures.[12]

a. Courts

Courts traditionally have asserted "inherent power" to regulate the practice of law, an authority rooted in constitutional provisions governing the separation of government power. Some exercises of the inherent power doctrine are simply instances of common law adjudication in the context of specific cases. For example, courts have applied contract, fiduciary, and related principles to govern lawyers in areas such as malpractice, fee disputes, and conflicts of interest.

In addition, the judiciary has claimed authority to adopt procedural rules and ethical codes outside the context of specific cases or controversies. Virtually all state supreme courts have asserted control over bar admission, discipline, and unauthorized practice of law. Federal judges enjoy analogous inherent authority as well as statutory power to regulate admission, discipline, and trial conduct for those who practice before them. For substantive standards, federal courts generally rely on the ethical codes and common law of the jurisdictions in which they sit. To varying degrees, judges in both state and federal systems have enforced legislative regulation that they view as consistent with their own oversight objectives.

b. Bar Associations

In exercising their inherent powers, courts frequently have deferred or delegated authority to bar associations. About two-thirds of the states have "integrated" bars, which require lawyers to belong to state bar associations as a condition of practice. In some states, bar organizations largely control admission and disciplinary structures, although the judiciary exercises nominal supervision. Other states have separate organizations or committees that assert regulatory power subject to judicial review. In either case, although non-lawyers often have representation in the process, the profession exercises control. The organized bar generally has defined the relevant standards through committee recommendations and legislative lobbying.

In addition to state bar associations, many lawyers belong to national, local, or other bar organizations, such as those structured around fields of practice, political and legal causes, or race, gender, and ethnicity. The largest of these organizations, representing just over one-third of the nation's attorneys, is the American Bar Association.

c. Ethical Codes

One of the most significant activities of bar associations has been formulating ethical codes. The ABA is responsible for the two major codes currently in use. The Model Rules of Professional Conduct were approved by the ABA in 1983 and adopted in whole or in part by about two-thirds of the states, usually through their supreme courts on advice from state bar committees. Other states, with the exception of California, have versions of an earlier Model Code of Professional Responsibility, approved by the ABA in 1970. California has a unique system that grants its Board of Bar Governors statutory power to promulgate rules directly, subject to approval by the California Supreme Court. These rules draw on the ABA Code but are in some respects different.

In most jurisdictions, bar ethical codes have the force of law as a result of state supreme court decrees. In a minority of jurisdictions, courts have ratified bar codes only as guidelines. In either case, codified provisions are relevant primarily in setting standards for lawyer discipline. However, many courts have also looked to bar requirements in establishing civil liability, despite drafters' disclaimers of any such intent.[13] During the late 1980s and early 1990s, a number of state and local bars also adopted codes of civility. For the most part, these establish voluntary standards, but a few codes have been approved or adopted by a court.

d.   Other Sources of Authority

Other primary sources of regulation include bar ethics committees, administrative agencies, and specialized bar associations or their subdivisions. Rulings by state, local, and national bar committees have played a significant, although declining, role in defining lawyers' ethical responsibilities. Traditionally, these opinions have responded to direct inquiries by attorneys and have claimed to set standards for bar disciplinary proceedings. However, as courts have grown increasingly active in disciplinary and malpractice proceedings, and as voluntary bar organizations have grown increasingly concerned about avoiding antitrust violations, ethics committee opinions have become less influential.[14]

The role of administrative agencies has grown correspondingly greater. Federal and some state courts have allowed legislatures and administrative agencies to define standards for parties appearing before them. Some agencies, such as the United States Patent Office, admit non-lawyers as well as lawyers who satisfy special eligibility requirements. Certain agencies such as the Securities and Exchange Commission also have power to discipline practitioners who have engaged in unethical or illegal acts. Bar associations and other professional organizations also have promulgated standards for lawyers practicing in specified areas. For example, the ABA's Standards Relating to the Administration of Criminal Justice have often been an important source of guidance for practitioners, courts, ethics codes, and bar committees. The American Law Institute's forthcoming Restatement of the Law Governing Lawyers is likely to have a similar impact.

A final, and in some respects the most significant, source of regulatory authority is workplace norms. Some institutions have specific procedures, committees, policy manuals, or codes concerning ethical issues. For example, large firms often have elaborate structures for dealing with potential conflicts of interest; many district attorneys' offices specify procedures governing plea-bargaining and press statements; some corporations have codified provisions governing whistle-blowing; and so forth. Of equal or greater importance are the informal norms that attorneys observe among colleagues in their offices. In one of the few studies on point, lawyers ranked such collegial practices as the second most significant factor, after general upbringing, in helping to resolve questions of professional responsibility.[15]

2. Historical Background: Bar Associations, Ethical Codes, and Regulatory Policies

The first formulations of professional ethics date back 2,500 years to principles established by medical practitioners. Some Roman legal advisors and advocates also developed ethical standards, as did certain law guilds in medieval Europe. By the mid-eighteenth century, British practitioners were subject to comprehensive regulations, but it was not until this century that lawyers in the United States formalized similar codes. During the American bar's early years, its ethical norms developed largely through professional traditions and informal community oversight. Judicial sanctions were relatively rare and usually occurred only in response to violations of criminal or civil law.[16]

During the mid-nineteenth century, David Hoffman, a Maryland law professor, and George Sharswood, a Pennsylvania judge, each published a treatise that influenced subsequent codes. Both Hoffman's Fifty Resolutions in Regard to Professional Deportment (1836) and Sharswood's Essay on Professional Ethics (1854) focused heavily on etiquette as well as on ethics, and their standards discouraged any dishonorable or self-promoting conduct that might reflect adversely on attorneys' public standing.

Such concerns also underpinned the development of the first formal bar associations. By the late eighteenth century, many lawyers belonged to local professional associations that generally served social and disciplinary functions as well as provided library facilities. After the Revolutionary War, as the cultural mood became more populist and bar regulation became more lax, these organizations largely disappeared or became purely social. In the late nineteenth century, lawyers again began forming professional associations, primarily to combat corruption in municipal governments, to restrict activities of non-lawyer competitors, to upgrade professional standards, and to sponsor collegial activities. By 1925, bar organizations existed in virtually all states and territories.

The most prominent professional organization has been the American Bar Association. Formed at a resort in Saratoga in 1878, it began as an elite group with selective membership policies and a mix of both social and law reform purposes. Initially, its major activities included promotion of uniform state laws and the Canons of Ethics for lawyers. The 1906 ABA Committee Report recommending adoption of the Canons is suggestive of the drafters' objectives:

... [W]ith the ranks of our profession ever extending, its fields of activities ever widening, the lawyer's opportunities for good and evil are correspondingly enlarged. . . . We cannot be blind to the fact that, however high may be the motives of some, the trend of many is away from the ideals of the past and the tendency more and more to reduce our high calling to the level of a trade, to a mere means of livelihood or of personal aggrandizement. With the influx of increasing numbers, who seek admission to the profession mainly for its emoluments, have come new and changed conditions. Once possible ostracism by professional brethren was sufficient to keep from serious error the practitioner with no fixed ideals of ethical conduct; but now the shyster, the barratrously inclined, the ambulance chaser . . . pursue their nefarious methods with no check . . . so long as they stop short of actual fraud and violate no criminal law.[17]

Following this report, the ABA approved 32 Canons with little controversy or debate. They were modeled on an earlier Alabama Code, which in turn had borrowed heavily from Sharswood and Hoffman. Most states eventually adopted the Canons through judicial or legislative enactment; others treated them as authoritative guidelines in judicial and bar disciplinary actions. Substantial problems in enforcement persisted, however, in part because of the standards' brevity, generality, and attempts to combine moral exhortation with disciplinary mandates. The situation worsened as the number of Canons multiplied. By the late 1960s there were 47 Canons and some 1,400 formal and informal ABA committee opinions interpreting them, many of questionable clarity and consistency. The forms of conduct most clearly prohibited were thefts of clients' funds and competition with fellow attorneys. Direct professional rivalry was strictly condemned and broadly construed. Studies of state bar ethics committees during the early twentieth century indicate that they spent more effort refining and enforcing restrictions on advertising and solicitation than on any other subject; even overly ostentatious letterheads or Christmas cards revealing a professional affiliation could constitute grounds for sanctions.[18]

Part of bar leaders' animosity toward competition reflected class, racial, religious, and ethnic biases. Established lawyers could afford to demand that "business seek the young attorney" rather than the converse.[19] But lawyers from less privileged backgrounds and those who served less privileged clients could not always afford that luxury. Discrimination was common throughout the nineteenth and early twentieth centuries not only by bar associations but also by employers, clients, law schools, and moral character committees. Racial and ethnic minorities, immigrants, and Jews were common targets and many faced considerable difficulties in establishing a practice. Clients from similar backgrounds had related difficulties finding or paying for legal assistance.[20] Women also were subject to pervasive discrimination both as lawyers and clients. Until the early twentieth century, most states denied female applicants admission to the bar and even after formal barriers were removed, widespread gender bias persisted.[21]

Bar associations' responses on issues of both access to legal services and discrimination within the profession were mixed. In the 1920s, the ABA began providing modest financial support to the nation's tiny number of understaffed legal aid offices.[22] However, at the same time, many bar leaders opposed government funding out of concerns about "socialized" lawyering. These leaders also opposed advertising and solicitation methods designed to increase access to legal services among lower income clients. The situation changed dramatically during the War on Poverty and social activism of the 1960s. Poverty and public interest law attracted both a large influx of government and private subsidies and increased levels of bar support. In the face of subsequent federal cutbacks, the organized bar became one of the staunchest and most powerful allies of legal aid programs. Its efforts helped preserve a federal Legal Services Corporation, which now has an annual budget of some $250 million for civil legal assistance.

On issues of discrimination, the record reflects similarly uneven but steady progress. In 1919, the ABA's inadvertent admission of three African-American attorneys prompted substantial controversy. Efforts to prevent reversal of the admissions were successful, but subsequent applicants had to identify themselves by race. The ABA's membership remained almost all white for most of the next half century.[23] The Association's opposition to the appointment of Louis Brandeis, a Jew and a progressive, to the United States Supreme Court in 1916 revealed similar prejudices. Discrimination by local bars was even more persistent and prompted many African Americans, women, and other ethnic minorities to form their own associations. Politically "radical" lawyers and causes faced comparable biases, and during the McCarthy era the ABA supported loyalty oaths as a condition of admission.[24]

Again, the activism of the 1960s both reflected and reinforced substantial changes. Bar associations altered their own policies and many contributed to civil rights and public interest movements. During the next quarter century, as the profession grew in size and diversity, the influence and agendas of bar organizations also expanded. By the end of the 1990s about 385,000 of the nation's 900,000 lawyers belonged to the ABA and many more were members of state and local associations. These organizations pursued a wide range of public policy initiatives as well as professional education, regulation, and collegial activities. See Chapter XI (Constitutional Law).

Bar leadership also devoted increasing attention to issues of discrimination. As section 5 indicates below, an ABA Task Force on Minorities in the Profession and an ABA Commission on the Status of Women in the Legal Profession have both played important roles in documenting the persistence of bias and in recommending strategies for change.

3.   The Structure of Regulation

In 1970, the ABA responded to long-standing problems in bar regulatory structures by adopting the Model Code of Professional Responsibility. It has two main parts, which a Preliminary Statement describes as follows:

> The Ethical Considerations [ECs] are aspirational in character and represent the objectives toward which every member of the profession should strive. . . . The Disciplinary Rules [DRs], unlike the Ethical Considerations, are mandatory in character. The Disciplinary Rules state the minimum level of conduct below which no lawyer can fall without being subject to disciplinary action.

The inspiration for this approach came from Lon Fuller, whose book, The Morality of Law (1964), argued for a distinction between moralities of duty and moralities of aspiration. Other commentators similarly supported a structure that included ethical considerations in addition to disciplinary rules because such considerations could "deal with questions less easily codified."[25] As these commentators emphasized, many ethical issues confronting lawyers called "not for simple 'dos' and 'don'ts', but for an enlarged and more sensitive consciousness of the variety of values at stake."[26]

Although the ABA adopted the Code with little debate or dissension, its content and structure soon began to provoke increasing criticism. According to some observers, the disparity between what the Ethical Considerations exhorted and what the Disciplinary Rules required was fostering cynicism and creating confusion in enforcement efforts. Other critics identified further problems with the Code, including its ambiguities, its failure to distinguish among various functions that lawyers performed (such as advocate, counselor, intermediary), and its lack of attention to certain crucial issues (such as conflicts of interests involving former clients or lawyers in organizational settings). Problems also had arisen in the interpretation of Ethical Considerations. Not all of these Considerations appeared only "aspirational in character"; some provided important clarification of the Rules and used mandatory rather than permissive phrasing (see, e.g., EC 5-15). In addition, a series of Supreme Court decisions in the 1970s on advertising, solicitation, fees, and group legal services forced reconsideration of Code provisions concerning professional competition. Within a decade after the Code's adoption, a special ABA Commission was already recommending an alternative set of standards, the Model Rules of Professional Conduct.

Unlike their predecessors, these Rules inspired considerable dispute within the profession. After heated debates over a series of preliminary drafts, the ABA in 1983 approved a final version. Controversy then shifted to the states. Fifteen years later, 41 states had adopted the Model Rules in large part, although with changes in certain substantive provisions. Other jurisdictions retained the Code, sometimes with revisions based on Model Rules standards. California kept its own state code, but with certain amendments. Federal courts generally have adopted the provisions in force in the jurisdictions in which they sit, although many cite both the Code and Model Rules as guidance.

The format of the Model Rules marks a significant departure from earlier codes. It provides black-letter standards with interpretative comments and little of the moral exhortation characteristic of the Rules' predecessors. A note on the Rules' scope states that "the Comments are intended as guides to interpretation, but the text of each Rule is authoritative." In short, the trend in professional standards over the last century has been toward substituting legal requirements for ethical aspirations. The assumption of current bar leaders is that codes should "walk like law and squawk like law"; rather than attempting to describe "the good lawyer" they should focus on describing "the bad lawyer."[27] This trend raises two issues: what should be the primary functions of professional standards, and should the profession have exclusive power to determine their content?

Codified standards serve several objectives. Most obviously, they clarify the minimum obligations that lawyers owe to clients, to the legal system, and to society generally. As the profession grows larger and more diverse, this function becomes more critical: the less cohesive the community, the less it can assume consensus about appropriate norms and the less able it becomes to rely on informal regulation based on reputation and collegial sanctions. Under such circumstances, clear minimal standards are increasingly necessary to prevent a "race to the bottom." Without such rules, ethical attorneys could often be undercut by colleagues with fewer compunctions. As economists note, a principal objective of professional codes is to prevent individuals from becoming "free riders" on the profession's general reputation for integrity without observing ethical standards themselves.[28]

To the extent that such codes are actively enforced, either in disciplinary or civil liability proceedings, they serve important deterrent and socializing functions. Even where enforcement is sporadic, codes can perform a useful task in sensitizing individuals to the full implications of their acts:

> [A] collective affirmation of professional values may have some effect simply by supplying, or removing, one source of rationalization for dubious conduct. . . . [S]tandards pitched at a more demanding level can reinforce the lawyer who would prefer the ethical course but is reluctant to appear sanctimonious.[29]

How well the bar's regulatory frameworks serve these functions has been a matter of considerable dispute. Although the Model Rules avoid some of the Code's greatest deficiencies, the reliance on bright-line rules creates its own set of problems. In order for codified provisions to gain acceptance within an increasingly diverse profession practicing in increasingly varied contexts, ethical standards frequently require formulation at a highly abstract level. Neither the Model Rules nor their predecessors have been able to escape heavy reliance on "weasel words" such as "reasonable," "imprudent," "[un]justifiable," and so forth. Moreover, the same pressures to gain consensus often result in codification of the lowest common denominator of conduct that a diverse bar is willing to brand as deviant. Such pressures also encourage standards that give priority to the profession's interests over those of clients or the public generally. To label these standards "ethical" is misleading, and the danger is that they will pass for ethics. New practitioners are socialized to the minimal requirements that a highly self-interested constituency will acknowledge as a potential basis for disciplinary proceedings or civil liability.

As this latter point suggests, there are inherent limitations in any regulatory code that is formulated exclusively by those subject to regulation. Traditionally, those limitations have been thought less problematic than the risks of sharing control over the drafting process. As the Preamble to the Model Rules notes, self-regulation

> helps maintain the legal profession's independence from government domination. An independent legal profession is an important force in preserving government under law, for abuse of legal authority is more readily challenged by a profession whose members are not dependent on government for the right to practice.

However, as subsequent discussion suggests, majoritarian governmental control and total professional autonomy are not the only alternatives. And the public pays a substantial price for ceding exclusive power over regulatory standards to the profession's own membership. Most issues that ethical codes address are not too esoteric for non-lawyers to understand. Unlike regulatory commissions in some countries, which have had a majority or substantial minority of non-lawyers, the 12-member committee that drafted the Code had no lay representatives, and the 13-member Model Rules Commission had only one.[30] Yet, as critics note,

> [t]his imbalance between professional and public representation in the drafting phase is exacerbated by a ratification process in which only the views of professionals are systematically solicited, and in which they alone cast the decisive vote.
>
> Such a process is hardly conducive to an unbiased accommodation of the diverging interests at stake. Without impugning the good faith of those involved in the enterprise, it is legitimate to inquire whether the bar as a whole can rise above parochial concerns on issues that place its income or status at risk. Pure altruism may be

possible, but the architects of our regulatory processes generally have proceeded on a contrary assumption. . . .

Neither the Code nor the Model Rules indicate why the bar should proceed as if it were exempt from the natural human tendency to prefer private over public ends. Confronted with conflict between their self-interest and their perception of societal interests, many individuals will attempt to discount or reconstrue the less immediate concern so as to reduce internal tension. Simply through normal processes of cognitive dissonance-reduction and acculturation, . . . professionals may lose sensitivity to interests at odds with their own. Nothing in the bar's extended history of self-governance suggests it to be an exception. . . .

In a celebrated history of the profession prepared under ABA auspices, Roscoe Pound reassured his sponsor that it was not, after all, "the same sort of thing as a retail grocers' association." If he was right, it was almost certainly for the wrong reasons. Lawyers no less than grocers are animated by parochial concerns. What distinguishes professionals is their relative success in packaging occupational interests as societal imperatives. In that regard, codes of ethics have proved highly useful. Seldom, of course, are such documents baldly self-serving; it is not to a profession's long-term advantage that it appear insensitive to the common good. But neither are any profession's own encyclicals likely to incorporate public policies that might significantly compromise members' status, monopoly, working relationships, or autonomy.

In part, the problem is one of tunnel vision. Without doubt, most lawyers, including those [involved in bar regulation], are committed to improving the legal system in which they work. What *is* open to doubt is whether a body of rules drafted, approved, and administered solely by attorneys is the most effective way of realizing that commitment. No matter how well-intentioned and well-informed, lawyers regulating lawyers cannot escape the economic, psychological, and political constraints of their position.[31]

Do you agree? According to the trial lawyer who headed the Roscoe Pound American Trial Lawyers' Foundation study of bar regulatory codes, "[p]utting lawyers in charge of their own ethics is like putting Dracula in charge of the blood bank."[32] How would bar leaders respond? How would you respond?

In analyzing ethical standards in the chapters that follow, consider whether a drafting commission more broadly representative of the general public would have adopted the same provisions. It is critical to approach those provisions not as fixed mandates but as starting points for discussion about what appropriate policy should and could be. As Charles Frankel noted after the ABA's adoption of the Code of Professional Responsibility:

> [In] the legal profession, as in most other domains of life, the elevation of standards comes in the main from neither exhortation nor codification. It comes from renewed attention to first principles, from a freshened awareness of the changed problems people confront, and from a sustained debate about the best ways to deal with them.[33]

This debate is the subject of the material that follows.

4.   Bar Associations and Public Policy

See Chapter XI, Constitutional Law
  • Role of Bar Associations
      (pages 466–468)

5.   Bias in the Profession: Issues of Race, Ethnicity, Gender, and Sexual Orientation

a.   Introduction

During the 1980s and early 1990s, most states established commissions or task forces to consider bias in the courts and many created separate task forces to address racial and ethnic bias. In addition, the American Bar Association as well as state or local bar organizations established commissions on the status of women and on minorities in the legal profession. A smaller number of organizations formed task forces on sexual orientation. These commissions generally had two primary objectives: obtaining and distributing information about the extent of bias and formulating recommendations to address it. By the mid-1990s, most state and national commissions had released at least preliminary reports. These varied considerably in scope but certain common themes emerged.

(1)   Racial and Ethnic Bias

(a)   Demeaning and Stereotypical Treatment

Despite recent progress, racial bias remains a significant problem. Reports of degrading and stereotypical treatment are still common. The New York Judicial Commission on Minorities found that 14 percent of all surveyed litigators indicated that judges, attorneys, or courtroom personnel publicly repeat ethnic jokes, use racial epithets, or make demeaning remarks about a minority group often or very often. Another 23 percent said that such remarks occur sometimes.[34] Comments range from the obviously invidious (including use of terms such as "nigger" and "tarbaby") to the ostensibly benign (compliments for being "a credit to your race").[35] Attorneys of color frequently have been mistaken for the defendant or for clerical or janitorial staff. In one recent report by the ABA's Multicultural Women Attorneys Network, a black woman partner from a major Chicago firm noted that she had been taken for a court reporter at every deposition she had ever attended.[36]

(b) Professional Opportunities

Beginning in the 1960s, minority representation in the legal profession began to increase substantially, but progress remained limited. By the mid-1990s, when African Americans, Latinos, Native Americans, and Asian Americans accounted for almost a quarter of the American population, they constituted only about 12 percent of the nation's law students, less than 8 percent of its lawyers, 6 percent of its law professors, and 3 percent of the partners at the nation's largest law firms.[37]

Part of the problem stems from often unconscious biases that diminish minorities' opportunities to enter law school and that constrain their advancement once they graduate. Some of the problems are comparable to those confronting women of all races: the devaluation of competence; the special scrutiny that accompanies token status; the exclusion from informal networks of advice and assistance; and the absence of mentors and role models.[38] In addition, barriers of race and ethnicity intersect with barriers of class.

Minorities' underrepresentation in the law school applicant pool is partly attributable to inadequate financial resources and educational preparation. These factors, together with pressures resulting from isolation and biased treatment, contribute to a racially disproportionate attrition rate during law school.[39] Overreliance on grades as a hiring credential particularly penalizes African-American and Hispanic job applicants. Once hired, nonwhite attorneys often experience a biased or unsupportive working environment, which leads to further attrition. Senior attorneys then become reluctant to invest time in mentoring young minority lawyers, and the cycle becomes self-perpetuating. Many organizations remain committed to diversity in principle but have not made it a priority in practice.[40]

(2) Gender Bias

(a) Demeaning, Stereotypical, and Harassing Treatment

Virtually every gender-bias commission report has found substantial evidence of disrespectful, stereotypical, and patronizing conduct, as well as substantial disparities in men's and women's perceptions of such behavior. In nearly every study, between two-thirds and three-fourths of the women surveyed indicate that they have experienced some form of bias, while only one-fourth to one-third of the men report observing such conduct.[41] Female attorneys have had to cope with labels such as "honey," "babe," "little lady," and "lawyerette," or questions such as "Ladies and Gentlemen, can you believe this pretty little thing is an Assistant Attorney General?" or "Do you really understand all the economics involved in this [antitrust] case?" or "Are you satisfied with the representation you had at trial, even though [your lawyer] was a woman?"[42]

Such gender bias is often viewed as harmless, and women who object are frequently dismissed as humorless or oversensitive. Yet such ridicule both compounds women's injury and discourages protests that might prevent it. Even well-intentioned gallantry or seemingly trivial asides can undercut women's credibility and professional status.[43]

(b)   Professional Opportunities

Research on women in the profession reveals that they are significantly underrepresented in positions of greatest power, status, and economic reward, such as law firm partners, tenured law school faculty, federal judges, and bar association leaders. Female lawyers also have lower rates of pay and promotion and higher rates of dissatisfaction with practice than male lawyers with similar backgrounds.[44]

What accounts for these disparities is a matter of dispute. Many observers believe that factors other than discrimination explain most differences. One common view is that current gender inequalities reflect women's prior underrepresentation in the profession, and that over time any sex-biased disparity will naturally erode. This claim is reinforced by some economic theories, which assume that well functioning markets will eliminate discriminatory patterns. According to these theories, employers who do not indulge arbitrary preferences will have a competitive advantage. As Richard Epstein puts it, "constraints of reputation and survival are powerful checks against any firmwide effort to engage in sex discrimination."[45]

In practice, however, researchers have found that occupational stratification and reward structures can be highly resistant to change, and that professional employment markets are not always perfectly competitive. Within the bar, status and income disparities between women and men cannot be explained by length of time in practice or other objectively quantifiable factors. In law, as in other elite professions, female members advance less far and less quickly than male colleagues with comparable qualifications.[46]

In accounting for these disparities, some researchers place primary importance on men's and women's different choices. According to human capital theories, women seek to reconcile competing job and family demands by making a lower investment in their professions. Economist Victor Fuchs argues that the "conflicts between career and family are stronger for women than for men. . . . [A]n average woman feels a stronger desire for children than do men and a greater concern for their welfare after they are born."[47] Richard Epstein similarly maintains that the "extensive differences in occupational patterns for men and women . . . [are attributable] not to discrimination by employers but to the different preference structures of men and women."[48]

Feminists respond to these claims on several levels. As a threshold matter, they generally agree that women experience greater difficulties than men in reconciling work and family obligations. However, most feminists do not view this gender difference solely as a function of natural preferences. Rather, these commentators emphasize sex-based socialization patterns and employment cultures that encourage women to form lower aspirations for vocational achievement and to assume a greater share of family responsibilities.[49] Moreover, in feminists' view, women's career sacrifices are attributable to the choices not simply of individual women but also of employers, male partners, and societal decision-makers. Inadequate support for child care, flexible or part-time schedules, or equal division of household obligations contributes greatly to female attorneys' problems in accommodating work and family commitments.

Finally, feminists emphasize the significances of gender stereotypes and unconscious biases in accounting for gender inequalities. The mismatch between characteristics traditionally associated with women and those typically associated with professional success also leaves female lawyers in a long-standing double bind. They remain vulnerable to criticism for being "too feminine" or "not feminine enough." What is assertive in a man is abrasive in a woman. A wide array of experiential and clinical evidence indicates that profiles of successful professionals conflict with profiles of normal or ideal women.[50] The aggressiveness, competitiveness, and emotional detachment traditionally presumed necessary for advancement in the most prestigious and well-paid occupations are incompatible with traits commonly viewed as attractive in women: cooperativeness, deference, sensitivity, and self-sacrifice. From most feminists' perspective, what needs to change are workplaces, not women.

So too, women in male-dominated occupations face continuing problems of "fitting in" and forming the client and collegial relationships necessary for advancement:

> Female professionals often lack access to the informal networks of advice, collaboration, and contacts on which successful careers depend. Women of color face unconscious discrimination on two fronts and their small numbers amplify problems such as high visibility, few mentors and role models, and additional counseling and committee responsibilities. . . .
>
> Given these biases, women, particularly minorities, must work harder than men to succeed. Those who do not advance under such circumstances, or who become frustrated and opt for different employment, confirm the adverse stereotypes that worked against their advancement in the first instance. The perception remains that women cannot succeed by conventional standards, or are less committed to doing so than men. In either event, female professionals do not warrant the same investment in training, assistance, and other op-

portunities as their male counterparts. Women employees disproportionately drift off the occupational fast track, leaving the most powerful sectors of the professions insulated from alternative values. Again, the result is a subtle but self-perpetuating cycle in which individual choices are constrained by gender biases.[51]

(3)   Sexual Orientation Bias

"Don't have any. Don't want any." That was one employer's response to a Los Angeles bar survey about gay and lesbian attorneys.[52] As that and other recent bar association studies demonstrate, such views remain all too common within the legal community. In both the Los Angeles and New York surveys, about 40 percent of lawyers reported witnessing or experiencing sexual orientation bias in professional settings, even though both cities have ordinances prohibiting it.[53] A majority of the gay and lesbian attorneys in the Los Angeles survey also felt that their sexual orientation had adversely affected their careers.[54] Those perceptions are consistent with other bar research finding lower earnings and promotion rates among gay and lesbian attorneys.[55]

Rarely does discrimination based on sexual orientation result in complaints, and seldom do complaints result in effective responses. Only 7 percent of some 1100 Legal Aid attorneys in the New York survey were aware of a complaint involving sexual orientation bias although six times that number were aware of bias-related incidents. A related New York bar survey of some 220 gay and lesbian attorneys found that disciplinary action occurred in less than 4 percent of reported incidents of discrimination.[56]

Inadequate remedies both mask and perpetuate the problem. Most victims of discrimination see little point in raising concerns that might harm their own reputations more than those of their offenders. Risks of blacklisting make litigation involving employment discrimination particularly unlikely. As a Los Angeles bar report notes, gay and lesbian practitioners generally would "rather have a career than a lawsuit."[57]

PROBLEM 3A

For this problem, the class should break into teams of four or five students. Some teams should constitute committees charged with policies governing diversity-related issues. Topics to consider include hiring, promotion, harassment, mentoring, part-time work, childcare, and domestic partners. Different teams can represent different practice settings (large firm, small firm, government agency, in-house corporate counsel, etc.).

Other teams should act as subcommittees of the Board of Governors of the American Bar Association or a local bar organization that is considering whether to adopt an ethical rule banning discrimination by lawyers. These subcommittees should formulate policy recommendations concerning the scope and advisability of such a rule. What forms of bias in what contexts should be subject to bar oversight?

PROBLEM 3B

Parts 1 and 4 of the following problem draw on more extended monologues that appear in Stephen Gillers, Regulation of Lawyers: Problems of Law and Ethics (3d ed. 1992).[58]

1. You are the managing partner in a Midwest law firm. A fifth-year associate in the litigation department comes to you with a major grievance. The senior partner in charge of a matter on which she has worked for the last two years has told her that she will not be part of the team that actually tries the case. The proceedings start next month in a small Southern city. According to the partner, the area is a "haven for rednecks" and the lead litigators believe that a Jewish woman trial attorney will not go over well with a local jury. The partner promises that her career will not suffer and that she will be reassigned to another case offering equivalent trial experience.

She is furious. "All the partner spoke about was the firm's responsibility to the client. What about its responsibilities to me and to other lawyers not to discriminate on the basis of sex or religion?" In her view, if customer prejudice is not a justification for discrimination under civil rights law, juror prejudice should not be justification for litigation assignments by "officers of the court."

The senior partner disagrees. Juror bias "is a fact of life and there are plenty of cases that a WASP Yankee like me would never take to trial." He notes that an adverse judgment in this litigation could cost the client between $20 to $30 million, and the resulting publicity would hardly be helpful to the firm's reputation. The associate should recognize her own interest in seeing the litigation department do well in this case. The only way her career could suffer is if she "makes a stink" about the reassignment.

How do you respond? Would it matter if the client's general counsel had explicitly requested that the associate not be part of the trial team?

2. Your law firm specializes in representing women in divorce cases. A father whom you refused to represent in a custody dispute filed a complaint with the Massachusetts Commission Against Discrimination, which is described in Problem 4B, Chapter IV (Advocacy), at page 154. After the Commission has ruled in the client's favor and imposed a $5,000 fine, do you appeal the ruling? How would you decide the case as a member of the state bar task force on bias in the profession?

3. Suppose that you were supervising the prosecution of O.J. Simpson. Would it be appropriate to consider race in assigning the trial responsibilities of your team? Would similar considerations be appropriate if you were supervising the defense in a case alleging race discrimination? Are there circumstances in which you would refuse to

accept an assignment because of race, ethnicity, gender, religion, or sexual orientation?

4. As managing partner in the Midwest firm described above, you face problems with another female associate. She is also unhappy but for different reasons. The difficulties involve her refusal to join a litigation team on a three-month trial in another city that takes ten hours to reach. She has an eighteen-month-old infant and this is the third case involving travel that she has declined since returning from parental leave. She is working full-time, largely because the firm's policy is not to consider any part-time lawyer for promotion to partnership. Although she has cut back on her time in the office, she is still meeting the firm's annual billable hours quota. Given the sacrifices that she is making to pull her load, she feels that the least the firm can do is excuse her from out-of-state travel. However, since she refused the two preceding cases, she has been receiving fewer interesting or challenging matters, and she no longer has supervisory responsibilities. She worries that rejecting this case will compound the problem and further jeopardize her partnership prospects.

When you raise the issue with her supervisor, he is quite defensive. In his view, the litigation department has leaned over backward to ac-commodate the associate's needs, but 40 percent of the firm's trial work involves out-of-state matters and almost no one likes to travel. "It simply isn't fair to other associates to keep granting her requests for special treatment and making them pay the price. Other lawyers have families, and she can't be a full-time litigator if she isn't prepared to take some inconvenient assignments." Nearly everyone in the department agrees that her attitude and schedule cannot help but affect her chances for partner. "Clients expect lawyers to be on call, and parents who need to be home by 6:00 aren't in a position to respond." They also are not likely to be doing their "fair share" of after-hours activities that generate new business. Although the associate is a "perfectly competent lawyer," she is not exceptional, and the senior litigator cannot help feeling that she would be better off in another specialty with more predictable hours or in another firm with less demanding work.

How do you respond? Assume that you are helping to revise the firm's part-time policy. What provisions would you make for compensa-tion, travel, and eligibility for partnership? Should flexible or reduced schedules be equally available to lawyers and non-lawyer staff? Should the policy be limited to family or medical needs, or should it be available for other reasons, such as a desire to write or do extensive pro bono work?

b. Regulatory Codes

Strategies for combating bias take several forms. One response is to amend state codes of judicial conduct along the lines proposed by the American Bar Association. In 1990, the ABA adopted new sections in Canon 3 providing that:

A judge shall perform judicial duties without bias or prejudice. A judge shall not, in the performance of judicial duties, by words or conduct manifest bias or prejudice, including but not limited to bias or prejudice based upon race, sex, religion, national origin, disability, age, sexual orientation or socioeconomic status, and shall not permit staff, court officials and others (including lawyers) subject to the judge's direction and control to do so. . . . This Section 3B(6) does not preclude legitimate advocacy when race, sex, religion, national origin, disability, age, sexual orientation or socioeconomic status, or other similar factors, are issues in the proceeding.[59]

Some commentators have advocated similar prohibitions for lawyers' codes of professional conduct, and a few jurisdictions have considered or adopted such provisions. For example, California's Rule 2-400 prohibits lawyers from engaging in unlawful discrimination in employment or in accepting and terminating representation of a client. Rule 8.4(g) of the New Jersey Rules of Professional Conduct provides:

> It is professional misconduct for a lawyer to: engage in a professional capacity, in conduct involving discrimination (except employment discrimination unless resulting in a final agency or judicial determination) because of race, color, religion, age, sex, sexual orientation, national origin, marital status, socioeconomic status, or handicaps where the conduct is intended or likely to cause harm.

Other rules and proposed rules vary widely. Some reach broadly to prohibit discrimination based on sexual orientation or socioeconomic status and some cover private conduct, such as belonging to single-sex organizations. Exceptions for constitutionally protected speech appear in some but not all policies. In 1995, the American Bar Association adopted a statement condemning bias by lawyers in their professional activities except for "legitimate advocacy." However, the ABA has declined to include such a prohibition in its Model Rules of Professional Conduct.[60]

How effective do you believe such codified provisions would be? Would they raise significant constitutional problems? Should lawyers be free to join clubs that discriminate or to advocate some forms of discrimination?[61] Is it necessary or appropriate to implement *ethical* provisions banning discrimination that is already "unlawful"? Should law firms ever consider race, religion, gender, ethnicity, or sexual orientation in work assignments or affirmative action policies? What, if any, forms of bias should be subject to formal sanctions by a court or by a state bar disciplinary committee?

c. Bar Initiatives

(1) Minorities

Groups such as the American Bar Association's Task Force on Minorities in the Legal Profession have issued a broad range of recommendations. Employers should intensify their efforts in hiring, retaining, and promoting minority lawyers. Recruitment procedures and evaluation criteria should be reassessed if they have a disproportionate racial impact. Recruiters should target more minority student associations, conferences, and law schools that have substantial minority enrollments. Hiring standards should avoid excessive reliance on first-year grades, LSAT scores, and law review experience, which disproportionately exclude students of color and do not measure the full range of skills that are necessary for successful practice. Promotion criteria such as collegiality and ability to attract client business need to take into account the special obstacles facing minority lawyers. Employers should also be encouraged to create a favorable working environment for underrepresented groups. Key priorities should include diversity education, mentoring programs, and equal opportunities for desirable assignments and client contact.

Minority task forces also have recommended efforts to expand access to the profession by assisting disadvantaged students. Such steps include greater financial support, recruitment efforts, educational preparation programs, and bar review assistance.

Many state and local bar organizations, as well as public and private employers, have made efforts along these lines. A wide variety of diversity education programs and client networking groups are available. For example, under the California Minority Counsel Program, every participating corporation agrees to hire and promote more lawyers of color, to use more minority-owned firms for outside legal work, and to encourage other firms that it employs to assign lawyers of color to its work. Participating non-minority law firms must accept the affirmative action goals approved by the bar and make other equal opportunity efforts.

(2) Gender and Sexual Orientation

Comparable initiatives have been identified by gender bias task forces and bar commissions. Strategies to assist women include model parental leave and part-time policies that do not penalize lawyers with substantial family commitments; hiring and promotion goals in contexts where female practitioners are underrepresented; improved sexual harassment policies and enforcement structures; mentoring and support programs; and gender bias education for the bench and bar.

On issues of sexual orientation, bar reports agree that the first priority is for associations, law firms, and other organizations employing lawyers to enact and enforce clear prohibitions on sexual orientation bias. That will, in turn, require adequate formal policies, publicized complaint procedures, and significant sanctions. Medical, family, and related benefit policies should cover same-sex relationships and domestic partners should be welcome at employer-sponsored events.

d.   Future Directions for Anti-Bias Strategies

Recent government and bar reports suggest certain key strategies in effective antibias programs:

- Demonstrate a substantial, visible commitment to diversity by the organization's management.
- Hold managers and supervisors accountable for progress.
- Use affirmative action strategies to ensure equal opportunity.
- Establish formal mentoring programs and channels for expressing diversity-related concerns.
- Provide training to sensitize employees about gender, racial, ethnic, and cultural bias.
- Adopt policies that accommodate the balance between work and family.[62]

What other strategies would you add to this agenda? What are the major barriers to its implementation, and how can they be addressed?

In commenting on the contributions of recent antibias initiatives, Judith Resnick notes that significant progress has occurred. "Legislation has been passed, policies have been developed, educational programs have been implemented, and concerns of underrepresented groups have been placed on reform agendas." But Resnick concludes:

> What has not happened is the howl of pain that such findings of [discrimination] might have prompted nor the transformations that appear to have been demanded. Words like "there is evidence that bias does occur with disturbing frequency at every level of the legal profession and court system" are uttered, repeated, printed, pronounced, but without much interim effect. Rather, the reports and their conclusions are absorbed, calmed, and transformed into another form of polite conversation about the administration of justice, albeit one that affects somewhat the administration.[63]

Do you agree with that assessment? If so, what follows from it?

C. ADMISSION TO THE BAR

1. Introduction

For most of this nation's history, bar admission standards were strikingly permissive. Until the late nineteenth century, the chief method of legal education was apprenticeship. Students read law in a licensed attorney's office and did much of the tedious copying of legal documents that was necessary before typewriters and duplicating machines. Training was often inadequate, but most bar applicants had no realistic alternative. Except for a few fairly short-lived efforts by independent "proprietary" law schools, American legal education remained rudimentary until the turn of this century.[64]

Requirements for admission to the bar varied but were rarely rigorous. At their lowest point, during the populism of the Jacksonian era, applicants simply had to satisfy good moral character requirements and pass an informal oral exam. The experience of one candidate is illuminating. His examination took place with Abraham Lincoln, who was taking a bath in his hotel room. Lincoln made a few "meager inquiries" concerning extremely basic issues such as the definition of a contract, and certified the applicant as competent to practice.[65]

The same forces contributing to the rise of bar associations brought increased efforts to upgrade admission standards, and these associations actively assisted the campaign. Between 1880 and 1920, states established centralized boards of bar examiners and adopted additional entry requirements such as written exams and investigation by bar character committees. The exams were not overly demanding; some surveys suggested that about 90 percent of those who took the test eventually passed.[66] For certain groups, the moral character investigation proved more of a barrier. Racial, ethnic, and religious minorities, as well as political nonconformists, were frequently deterred or harassed and sometimes excluded.[67] Although such overt biases are no longer common, other problems involving bar screening procedures remain, as the following materials suggest.

2. Competence

As noted earlier, qualifications for practicing lawyers are established or approved by state supreme courts. In most jurisdictions, the bar's primary methods of screening for competence are the bar exam and a three-year law school graduation requirement. Critics claim that both methods are over- and underinclusive. They exclude individuals with experience and practice skills who would be perfectly competent to practice in specialized areas, while providing no assurance that those who pass are, or will remain, competent in their chosen fields. Related criticisms of bar exams involve the disproportionate exclusion of minority candidates; the time, effort, and expense spent on rote memorization of information unrelated to practice needs; the arbitrary selection of passing scores; the inhibition of law school curricular approaches that do not directly aid exam preparation; the barriers to practitioners' mobility across state lines; and the failure to test many capabilities essential to effective lawyering such as research, negotiation, and counseling skills.[68]

Such criticisms have often emerged in the context of equal protection challenges. Many state bar exams have racially discriminatory impacts, and petitioners have argued that these tests fail to meet the requirement of job relatedness set forth in Washington v. Davis, 426 U.S. 229 (1976). In response, bar examiners usually have claimed that they design questions to test practice skills and that applicants' exam scores correlate with grades in law school. Courts uniformly have found such evidence sufficient to uphold exams, despite the absence of any showing that either these tests or law school grades predict successful performance as attorneys, or that passing scores are linked with minimal competence.[69] Would you reach the same result?

Defenders of bar examinations frequently make two further claims. First, they defend standardized tests as a useful incentive for students to synthesize their knowledge and to recognize legal issues in areas outside their own expected specialty. To the extent that current bar exams do not provide a useful learning experience, defenders wish to improve, not eliminate, testing procedures. Second, these commentators generally fear that the likely alternative to bar exams would be worse. If, for example, a license to practice was granted to all graduates of accredited law schools, states might seek to interfere with curricular offerings or graduation and admission requirements.

Such concerns, together with practicing lawyers' sense of hard-won entitlement and desire to avoid an oversupply of competitors, have worked against significant change. A few states have made modest reforms by expanding the skills tested. Several jurisdictions have waived exam requirements for graduates of in-state law schools. On the whole, however, the bar shows little enthusiasm for modifying the existing admission system. Between 80 to 90 percent of surveyed lawyers believe that bar exams should continue. Although about two-thirds of attorneys think that the current system measures minimum knowledge, they also agree that the exams do not adequately assess the ability to practice law, and slightly over half prefer a national exam with character evaluations by individual states.[70]

What is your view? Would it be preferable to replace or supplement the exam with an apprenticeship system or some intensive course in skills training? Should accreditation standards for law schools permit a wider range of degree options so that graduates of one- or two-year specialty programs could practice in limited fields?

 3.   Character

PROBLEM 3C

You are a member of your state bar moral character committee. Would you vote to deny or delay admission of any of the following applicants? What factors would be relevant to your decision? Would it affect your judgment to know that about half of surveyed law students admit to some form of cheating in law school and about 15 to 20 percent default on student loans?[71]

1. A candidate who was suspended for plagiarism during his second year of law school.[72]
2. A candidate who discharged his student loans in bankruptcy after a temporary loss of employment, without experiencing "exceptional financial or health problems [or] major misfortunes" and without making significant efforts to repay.[73]
3. Candidates who completed prison terms for first-degree murder, child molestation, income tax evasion, sale of marijuana, or harassment and destruction of property in connection with antiabortion activities.[74]

Every American jurisdiction requires applicants to the bar to establish their good moral character. To meet that burden, prospective lawyers supply extensive personal information to boards of examiners or character committees, whose decisions are subject to judicial oversight. The scope and formality of the process vary considerably by state, although all denials of admission must meet minimum due process standards of notice and an opportunity to be heard. Willner v. Committee on Character and Fitness, 373 U.S. 96 (1963).

Courts and commentators have traditionally identified two major objectives for the moral character requirement. The first is safeguarding clients and the administration of justice from lawyers likely to engage in misconduct. A second less frequently articulated rationale for character screening rests on the bar's own interest in maintaining its public image and sense of professional community with shared norms and values. Whether current procedures adequately serve these objectives has, however, been open to challenge.

As the United States Supreme Court has acknowledged, the moral character requirement is "unusually ambiguous" and "any definition will necessarily reflect the attitudes, experiences, and prejudices of the definer." Konigsberg v. State Bar, 353 U.S. 252, 263 (1957). In general, the Court has required that any criteria for disqualification have a "rational connection with the applicant's fitness or capacity to practice law." Schware v. Board of Bar Examiners, 353 U.S. 232, 239 (1957). More specifically, the focus is on whether a "reasonable [person] could fairly find that there were substantial doubts about the [applicant's] honesty, fairness, and respect for the rights of others and for the laws of the state and nation." Konigsberg, 353 U.S. at 264. According to recent case law and the Code of Recommended Standards for Bar Examiners, relevant factors include the recurrence, seriousness, and circumstances of the conduct; evidence of rehabilitation; and candor in the application process.

The problem is that reasonable people can and do disagree about what sort of conduct raises substantial doubts and what, if any, evidence of rehabilitation will allay concern. A comprehensive survey of contemporary bar committee and judicial decision-making reveals highly idiosyncratic and inconsistent judgments, both within and across jurisdictions:

> The conventional view has been that certain illegal acts, regardless of the likelihood of their repetition in a lawyer-client relationship, evidence attitudes toward law that cannot be countenanced among its practitioners; to hold otherwise would demean the profession's reputation and reduce the character requirement to a meaningless pretense. The difficulty, of course, is that this logic licenses inquiry into any illegal activity, no matter how remote or minor, and could justify excluding individuals convicted of any offense that affronted the sensibilities of a particular court or character committee. In fact, bar inquiry frequently extends to juvenile offenses, . . . parking violations, and [civil disobedience]. Conduct warranting exclusion has been thought to include traffic convictions and cohabitation. . . . Violation of a fishing license statute ten years earlier was sufficient to cause one local Michigan committee to decline certification. But, in the same state, at about the same time, other examiners sitting on the central board admitted individuals convicted of child molesting and conspiring to bomb a public building. . . . Decisions concerning drug and alcohol offenses have proved particularly inconsistent. Convictions for marijuana are taken seriously in some jurisdictions and overlooked in others.
>
> Attitudes toward sexual conduct such as cohabitation or homosexuality [as well as financial mismanagement] reflect similar diversity. Some bar examiners do not regard that activity as "within their purview," unless it becomes a "public nuisance" or results in criminal charges. . . . [In other jurisdictions] cohabitation and homosexuality [have triggered] extensive inquiry and delay, and some slight possibility of denial. . . . Most jurisdictions make no inquiries concerning debts past due (73%), while others demand detailed information ranging from parking fines to child support obligations. . . . Discharges [in bankruptcy] to avoid payment of student loans have resulted in denial in some jurisdictions. Yet about a third of all state bar applications made no inquiries in this area, and some [surveyed] examiners, particularly those who handle bankruptcies in private practice, felt that individuals had a right to such remedies.
>
> [A fundamental difficulty with such screening processes is that] a vast array of social science research has failed to find evidence of consistent character traits. . . . [E]ven the slightest change in situational variables dramatically alter[s] tendencies toward deceit; one [cannot] predict cheaters in one class on the basis of cheating in another. . . . [Most] findings suggest that the person with a "truly generalized conscience . . . is a statistical rarity." Although individuals clearly differ in their responses to temptation, contextual pressures have a substantial effect on moral conduct. . . . Although empirical evidence on lawyers' ethics is fragmentary, it also suggests that . . . an

attorney's willingness to violate legal or professional rules depends heavily on the exposures to temptation, client pressures, and collegial attitudes in his practice setting. . . .[75]

The point is not that moral acts are unrelated or entirely unpredictable. Rather, the problem is that it is necessary to know a great deal about how individuals perceive particular situations and why they respond in particular ways in order to gauge how they will react in situations that are somewhat different.[76]

So too, a comparison of bar admission and disciplinary processes raises further doubts about the justifications for current character screening procedures. Although practicing attorneys have a greater stake in retaining their professional licenses than bar applicants, practitioners' conduct is also more probative of risks to the public.

[From a public policy perspective, the rationale for disciplinary oversight is stronger for abuses committed within a lawyer-client relationship than for offenses occurring prior to the point of licensure.] Yet the bar's administration of admission and disciplinary processes has yielded precisely [the reverse] double standard; both substantive and procedural requirements are more . . . [forgiving for] practitioners than applicants. . . . Except in the most egregious cases, the bar has always been disinclined to cast out a colleague. . . .

The disparity between entry and exclusion standards raises a number of awkward questions about the current scope of certification procedures. If certain nonprofessional conduct is sufficiently probative to withhold a license, why is it not also grounds for license revocation? As long as bar members are unwilling to monitor their colleagues' parking violations, psychiatric treatment, and alimony payments, what justifies their reliance on such evidence in screening applicants? Insofar as the profession is truly committed to public rather than self-protection, the incongruity between disciplinary and certification procedures is untenable.[77]

A final criticism of moral character inquiries involves their costs. The current certification process subjects applicants to burdensome and sometimes unduly intrusive inquiries in order to identify the small number of individuals raising serious concerns. Only a tiny number of candidates are actually denied admission on character grounds (an estimated 2 percent of all applicants). However, some substantial number may be deterred from applying or may avoid conduct that could delay or prevent their admission, such as engaging in civil disobedience, filing lawsuits, seeking psychiatric assistance, or acknowledging their homosexuality. Such a character screening system raises obvious due process and first amendment concerns. The indeterminate and idiosyncratic nature of bar decision-making provides inadequate notice of the professional consequences of prior activities and chills protected conduct.[78] In critics' views, the system as currently implemented trivializes and subverts the moral ideals it intends to affirm.

How would you respond to such criticisms? Consider the rationale for virtue-based ethical frameworks in Chapter II. Is the bar's moral character system an appropriate application of these frameworks? Could it do better? Should some of the resources now spent on predicting misconduct at the application stage be diverted to responding to misconduct through the disciplinary process?

Would you advocate efforts to restrict or replace the current system with a more rule-bound structure? For example, state boards could specify the kind of conduct that would presumptively or categorically prevent admission, such as conviction of a felony or a misdemeanor involving dishonesty within a specific period prior to application. Alternatively, bar examiners could identify certain conduct that would not be grounds for exclusion, such as outpatient mental health treatment, homosexual activity with consenting adults, or involvement in a political protest. If such changes are desirable, how might they be achieved?

D.   COMPETENCE AND DISCIPLINE

1.   Discipline

a.   *Introduction*

American courts' power to discipline attorneys has its roots in English practices dating from the thirteenth century. "Disbarment" described proceedings in which attorneys guilty of misconduct were literally cast over the bar, a wooden barrier separating judges from others in the courtroom.

In this country, eighteenth and nineteenth century courts seldom exercised their disciplinary power. Community disapproval was the primary sanction for professional misconduct, and the inadequacy of this approach was a major impetus for the formation of bar associations. By the early twentieth century, all states and several hundred localities had voluntary organizations of lawyers with grievance committees to handle reports of attorney misconduct. Such committees were demonstrably inadequate for the task because they lacked power to compel attendance of witnesses or to impose discipline. With the rise of integrated (i.e., compulsory) bar associations in the early twentieth century came an expansion in regulatory power. Under legislative or judicial mandates, both voluntary and integrated associations gradually acquired authority to investigate misconduct and to impose sanctions, subject to court oversight.

Since current disciplinary proceedings are "quasi-criminal" in nature, courts have extended basic due process safeguards, such as (1) the opportunity to confront evidence and cross-examine witnesses, Willner v. Committee on Character and Fitness, 373 U.S. 96

(1963); (2) the right to present witnesses and argument, In re Ginger, 372 F.2d 620 (6th Cir. 1967) (per curiam); and (3) the privilege against self-incrimination, Spevack v. Klein, 385 U.S. 511 (1967); In re Ruffalo, 390 U.S. 544 (1968). In addition to these constitutional mandates, most states have afforded procedural protections to their members, including requirements that formal charges be established by clear and convincing evidence.

The purpose of disciplinary proceedings is to protect the public and the administration of justice from attorneys who violate professional standards. Civil malpractice litigation has the additional function of providing remedies for individuals injured by such misconduct.

PROBLEM 3D

1. You are representing a local hospital, which is a codefendant in a malpractice suit. The other defendant, a doctor, is represented by a solo practitioner with whom you have worked before. In both of your prior experiences with that attorney, she was totally incompetent. In this case, the attorney, who is charging by the hour, has insisted on attending depositions for which she is demonstrably unprepared, and has scheduled several unnecessary meetings. Throughout those depositions, she repeatedly referred to Hispanic witnesses by their first names while calling white males by their surnames. When you objected, she initially corrected the practice but told you to "lighten up" and later lapsed back into the pattern. The lawyer also has misrepresented to the presiding judge the reasons for seeking a continuance and has asserted what you consider to be several unfounded claims of the attorney-client privilege.

What, if any, actions should you take? Would your actions differ if the lawyer were representing your adversary or if you suspected that some of her problems were due to substance abuse? Is your knowledge of the attorney's practice in the preceding cases confidential? If so, how do you reconcile the duty of confidentiality with the duty to report lawyer misconduct?

2. If you were aware of such conduct as a judge, how would you respond? What factors would influence your decision?

3. If a complaint involving these facts came before you as a member of a bar disciplinary board, what would you recommend? Suppose a complaint also was filed against the hospital's lawyer for failing to report collegial misconduct. Would you impose sanctions?

IN RE HIMMEL

533 N.E.2d 790 (Ill. 1989)

[The case arose after Tammy Forsberg retained attorney John R. Casey to represent her in a personal injury action. Having settled the claim for $35,000, Casey (who was entitled to a one-third contingency fee) declined to provide Forsberg with her two-thirds share of the recovery. After several unsuccessful efforts to collect, Forsberg hired James Himmel to represent her. Casey subsequently agreed to pay $75,000 in settlement of the claim, and Forsberg agreed not to initiate criminal, civil, or disciplinary charges. When Casey failed to honor that agreement, Himmel sued and won a judgment of $100,000. However, he received no fee since despite the judgment, Forsberg ultimately collected only $15,400 and Himmel's retainer agreement gave him one-third of the recovery in excess of the amount owed on the original claim.

Prior to retaining Himmel, Forsberg had contacted the Illinois Attorney Registration and Disciplinary Committee (ARDC). When investigation revealed other complaints against Casey, ARDC initiated an action and subsequently disbarred Casey by consent. The ARDC then pursued charges against Himmel for failing to report Casey's misconduct. On appeal, the Illinois Supreme Court sustained those charges.]

STAMOS, J.: We begin our analysis by examining whether a client's complaint of attorney misconduct to the Commission can be a defense to an attorney's failure to report the same misconduct. Respondent offers no authority for such a defense and our research has disclosed none. Common sense would dictate that if a lawyer has a duty under the Code, the actions of a client would not relieve the attorney of his own duty. Accordingly, while the parties dispute whether or not respondent's client informed the Commission, that question is irrelevant to our inquiry in this case. We have held that the canons of ethics in the Code constitute a safe guide for professional conduct, and attorneys may be disciplined for not observing them. . . .

As to respondent's argument that he did not report Casey's misconduct because his client directed him not to do so, we again note respondent's failure to suggest any legal support for such a defense. A lawyer, as an officer of the court, is duty-bound to uphold the rules in the Code. . . .

Respondent contends that the information was privileged information received from his client, Forsberg, and therefore he was under no obligation to disclose the matter to the Commission. Respondent argues that his failure to report Casey's misconduct was motivated by his respect for his client's wishes, not by his desire for financial gain. To support this assertion, respondent notes that his fee agreement with Forsberg was contingent upon her first receiving all the money Casey originally owed her. Further, respondent states that he has received no fee for his representation of Forsberg.

Our analysis of this issue begins with a reading of the applicable disciplinary rules. Rule 1-103(a) of the Code states:

(a) A lawyer possessing unprivileged knowledge of a violation of Rule 1-102(a)(3) or (4) shall report such knowledge to a tribunal or other authority empowered to investigate or act upon such violation.

107 Ill. 2d R. 1-103(a).

Rule 1-102 of the Code states:

(a) A lawyer shall not
    (1) violate a disciplinary rule;
    (2) circumvent a disciplinary rule through actions of another;
    (3) engage in illegal conduct involving moral turpitude;
    (4) engage in conduct involving dishonesty, fraud, deceit, or misrepresentation; or
    (5) engage in conduct that is prejudicial to the administration of justice.

107 Ill. 2d R. 1-102.

These rules essentially track the language of the American Bar Association Model Code of Professional Responsibility, upon which the Illinois Code was modeled. Therefore, we find instructive the opinion of the American Bar Association's Committee on Ethics and Professional Responsibility that discusses the Model Code's Disciplinary Rule 1-103 (Model Code of Professional Responsibility DR 1-103 (1979)). Informal Opinion 1210 states that under DR 1-103(a) it is the duty of a lawyer to report to the proper tribunal or authority any unprivileged knowledge of a lawyer's perpetration of any misconduct listed in Disciplinary Rule 1-102. (ABA Committee on Ethics & Professional Responsibility, Informal Op. 1210 (1972) (hereinafter Informal Op. 1210).) The opinion states that "the Code of Professional Responsibility through its Disciplinary Rules necessarily deals directly with reporting of lawyer misconduct or misconduct of others directly observed in the legal practice or the administration of justice." Informal Op. 1210, at 447. . . .

We agree with the Administrator's argument that the communication regarding Casey's conduct does not [fall under the attorney-client privilege]. The record does not suggest that this information was communicated by Forsberg to the respondent in confidence. We have held that information voluntarily disclosed by a client to an attorney, in the presence of third parties who are not agents of the client or attorney, is not privileged information. . . . In this case, Forsberg discussed the matter with respondent at various times while her mother and her fiance were present. . . . The record [also] shows that respondent, with Forsberg's consent, discussed Casey's conversion of her funds with the insurance company involved, the insurance company's lawyer, and with Casey himself. Thus, under [prior precedent] the information was not privileged.

Though respondent repeatedly asserts that his failure to report was motivated not by financial gain but by the request of his client, we do not deem such an argument relevant in this case. This court has stated that discipline may be appropriate even if no dishonest motive of the misconduct exists. . . . In addition, we have held that client approval of an attorney's action does not immunize an attorney from disciplinary action. . . .

The third issue concerns the appropriate quantum of discipline to be imposed in this case. . . . [Respondent's] failure to report resulted in interference with the Commission's investigation of Casey, and thus with the administration of justice. Perhaps some members of the public would have been spared from Casey's misconduct had respondent reported the information as soon as he knew of Casey's conversions of client funds. We are particularly disturbed by the fact that respondent chose to draft a settlement agreement with Casey rather than report his misconduct. As the Administrator has stated, by this conduct, both respondent and his client ran afoul of the Criminal Code's prohibition against compounding a crime, which states in section 32-1:

> (a) A person compounds a crime when he receives or offers to another any consideration for a promise not to prosecute or aid in the prosecution of an offender.
> (b) Sentence. Compounding a crime is a petty offense. . . .

Both respondent and his client stood to gain financially by agreeing not to prosecute or report Casey for conversion. According to the settlement agreement, respondent would have received $17,000 or more as his fee. If Casey had satisfied the judgment entered against him for failure to honor the settlement agreement, respondent would have collected approximately $25,588.

We have held that fairness dictates consideration of mitigating factors in disciplinary cases. . . . Therefore, we do consider the fact that Forsberg recovered $10,400 through respondent's services, that respondent has practiced law for 11 years with no record of complaints, and that he requested no fee for minimum collection of Forsberg's funds. However, these considerations do not outweigh the serious nature of respondent's failure to report Casey, the resulting interference with the Commission's investigation of Casey, and respondent's ill-advised choice to settle with Casey rather than report his misconduct.

Accordingly, it is ordered that respondent be suspended from the practice of law for one year.

---

b. *Barriers to Reporting*

Critics of bar disciplinary processes identify weaknesses along several dimensions that Problem 3D suggested.

Current regulatory structures rest on inconsistent premises. Standards governing admission and [non-lawyer] competition assume that a free market in legal services is inappropriate; clients are not in a position to make informed judgments about the quality and appropriate cost of services received. Yet bar disciplinary systems have generally worked on the opposite assumption: they rely almost exclusively on client grievances (together with felony convictions) as sources of information about attorney misconduct.

As the ABA Commission on Professionalism notes, lawyers and judges have traditionally been reluctant to file disciplinary charges. That reluctance arises from a variety of social, psychological, and economic factors. Part of the problem is the level of abstraction at which rules of professional conduct are formulated. What constitutes an incompetent performance or unreasonable fee is often difficult to assess except at the extremes. A sense of professional humility or concern about personal hypocrisy may also be at work. Many lawyers do not feel sufficiently blameless to cast the first stone unless they are sure of a fellow practitioner's serious misconduct, and the incentives to gather the relevant information are quite limited. So too, like other professionals, attorneys are often reluctant to expose colleagues' "dirty linen" to public scrutiny.

The general cultural ethos against informing pushes in similar directions. As Gerald Lynch notes, "the very term informer evokes a sense of betrayal." Bonds of friendship and collegiality create loyalties that individuals are often unwilling to jeopardize in the service of some more abstract social objective. To many lawyers, the issue of informing evokes sentiments similar to those that prompted E.M. Forster's celebrated aphorism: "If I had to choose between betraying my country and betraying my friend, I hope I should have the guts to betray my country."

. . . Current disciplinary structures reflect classic free rider/common action problems. Prosecution of disciplinary charges benefits society and the profession as a whole, but often not complainants or their clients. In explaining why he had not filed a grievance against a fellow practitioner who had allegedly committed a serious breach of ethics, one prominent New York attorney explained that he represented "Ford Motor Company, not the next guy. . . . I have a very narrow balance sheet." To many lawyers [as Geoffrey Hazard points out], reporting misconduct seems little more than "buying trouble. In a small community you start a feud. In a big community, you probably won't have to deal with the guy again anyway."

Even lawyers and judges willing to take a broader view of their balance sheets are often unwilling to file charges with disciplinary agencies that have proved ineffective in responding. The assumption that "nothing will happen anyway" has been a major rationale and rationalization for non-reporting. So too, the sense of diffused responsibility that deters good samaritanism in other contexts may play a role in professional oversight. Attorneys may justify inaction on the premise that if the pattern of misconduct was really serious, others would see it and respond to it.[79]

These patterns are compounded by clients' frequent lack of information about misconduct or bar disciplinary processes and their lack of incentives to file complaints.[80] Since clients actually benefit from some forms of attorney misconduct (e.g., discovery abuse), and rarely gain adequate restitution through the disciplinary system, they often see no reason to pursue bar grievance procedures.

Although these barriers are not easily overcome, many commentators believe that the profession should take more active steps to encourage reporting by clients, judges, and lawyers. One obvious strategy, as in In re Himmel, supra, is to impose sanctions for failing to report collegial misconduct. Although the ABA Commission of Evaluation of Disciplinary Enforcement recommended such sanctions, the *Himmel* court's step in that direction provoked substantial controversy. Part of the controversy may have been inevitable since the decision was the first reported instance in which an attorney was disciplined solely for failure to report another attorney's misconduct.[81] Some commentators noted with approval that lawyers' reports of misconduct increased after the court's judgment in *Himmel*.[82] Others felt that the decision would compromise client confidentiality, encourage frivolous retaliatory complaints, and unfairly penalize an attorney for conduct that was pervasive within the bar.

What is your view? Under what, if any, circumstances would you impose sanctions on lawyers for failing to report collegial misconduct? How certain about such misconduct should the reporting lawyer be in order to incur disclosure obligations? Compare DR 1-103, which requires reporting by lawyers who have "unprivileged knowledge of a violation of the [Disciplinary Rules]," with Model Rule 8.3, which requires reporting of violations that raise a "substantial question as to [another] lawyer's honesty, trustworthiness or fitness" unless the knowledge of the violation was received through a privileged communication. "Substantial," according to the Model Rule Comment, refers to the "seriousness of the possible offense and not the quantum of evidence of which the lawyer is aware."

To improve reporting channels, commentators have proposed various initiatives. One strategy for increasing lawyers' willingness to report professional misconduct is to provide greater safeguards against retaliation. The New York Court of Appeals set an important example along those lines in Wieder v. Skala, 80 N.Y.2d 628 (1992), excerpted in Part E of Chapter XII (Contracts).

To encourage greater client protection, experts have recommended measures such as greater public outreach; consumer access to disciplinary data banks concerning bar discipline; increased recognition of complainant rights, such as notice and opportunities to be heard in discipline and reinstatement hearings; and more frequent remedies that provide client restitution, such as fines, mandatory fee arbitration, and expanded bar security funds. Expansion of proactive efforts could also be helpful, such as substance abuse education and assistance, random audits of client trust fund accounts, and quality control measures comparable to those involved in peer review. In addition, as ABA Commissions have frequently noted, clients, attorneys, and judges would also be more likely to report misconduct if they had more reason to anticipate effective responses.

c. Responses to Misconduct

One of the strongest criticisms of current disciplinary systems is the inadequacy of remedies for clients. Most consumer grievances do not fall within disciplinary agency jurisdiction; complaints involving neglect, negligence, or fee disputes are generally excluded on the ground that other remedies are available through arbitration processes and civil suits claiming malpractice or breach of contract. However, as subsequent discussion suggests, litigation is too expensive for most grievances, and arbitration systems have been hampered by the lack of lawyer support. Few jurisdictions make arbitration mandatory and the clients most in need of assistance seldom find their attorneys willing to cooperate.

Moreover, around 90 percent of complaints are dismissed without investigation because they lack probable cause or fall outside agency jurisdiction. Less than 2 percent result in public discipline.[83] Many of these complaints are dismissed because they are inherently implausible or reflect dissatisfaction with outcomes rather than deficiencies in attorney performance. However, the low level of sanctions also reflects a lack of investigatory and prosecutorial resources. State disciplinary agencies are generally underfunded and understaffed and often rely on overmatched volunteer counsel. So too, most jurisdictions have no time limits for resolving cases and decline to proceed during the pendency of civil actions; these delays can prevent successful prosecution and expose more clients to misconduct.[84]

A final criticism of bar disciplinary processes involves their secrecy and lack of public accountability. Except in Oregon, states generally do not disclose the existence of complaints at least until an agency's finding of probable cause to believe that misconduct has occurred. Thus, in some jurisdictions, lawyers with as many as 20 complaints under investigation can receive a clean bill of health if a potential client seeks information about their records.[85] According to many critics, the bar's long-standing failure to address problems in the disciplinary process argues for placing supervisory power in a more publicly accountable structure, such as a commission with broad-based membership ultimately subject to supreme court control. For example, a bill proposed in California would have created a Commission on Attorney Discipline and Competency, appointed by several constituencies: the bar, the California Judicial Council, the Governor, and the Speaker of the California Assembly.[86]

In 1992, in response to some of these criticisms, the American Bar Association House of Delegates approved certain recommendations of its Commission on Evaluation of Disciplinary Enforcement.

The most important proposals included creating a consumers' bill of rights (including notice and opportunities to appear and seek review of dismissed complaints); having a prosecuting attorney appointed by the court and not the bar; and establishing a system with multiple remedial structures, such as mandatory fee arbitration systems, voluntary malpractice arbitration processes, and special substance abuse programs. However, the House of Delegates also rejected proposals that complaints be made public from the time of filing and that control over the disciplinary process be shared with legislatures.[87] The latter vote was based in part on the Commission's failure to find persuasive evidence that legislative regulation of other professions has resulted in better protection of the public.[88] Legislatively created agencies often suffer from the same problems of understaffing, underfunding, and delays as bar regulatory bodies. In addition, as David Wilkins points out, politically accountable agencies also confront the same barriers to reporting and some of the same risks of capture as current disciplinary authorities.[89]

However, other commentators note that the ABA's Commission, like the Association itself, is composed solely of lawyers, and that other oversight our processes generally are built on the assumption that regulatory decisions should not be made solely by the groups to be regulated. What is your view? What strategies for reforming the disciplinary process strike you as most promising?

See Chapter XII, Contracts
  • Part E. Employment at Will and Whistle-Blowing Responsibilities
    (pages 536–540)

2. Sanctions

Jurisdictions vary somewhat in their disciplinary sanctions. Disbarment is the most uniform but also the most infrequent response; it refers to a permanent or indefinite withdrawal of the license to practice law, although many states allow an attorney to apply for reinstatement after some prescribed number of years. Suspension refers to a temporary prohibition on practice either for a specified period (usually ranging from several months to several years) or until compliance with certain specified conditions and an order of the court. Less stringent sanctions include public and private censures, reprimands, admonitions, warnings, and cautions. Some jurisdictions permit lawyers under investigation to resign, although that act is generally treated as an admission of guilt; attorneys who later seek reinstatement following resignation must make the same showing of rehabilitation as disbarred attorneys who seek readmission.

PROBLEM 3E

Consider the following conduct. If you were chair of your state bar's disciplinary committee, what sanctions would you impose?

Kevin A. Holloway

Holloway "deceived clients, failed to promptly deliver unearned fees and other funds rightfully belonging to a client, neglected his clients' cases and abused his clients' trust."[90]

Robert E. Moore

Moore "knew [that] marijuana was growing on his premises and he failed to destroy the plants."[91]

Richard W. Kleindienst

During Senate confirmation hearings on his nomination as Attorney General of the United States, Kleindienst

> expressly asserted that no effort had been made by anyone at the White House directed at influencing the Department of Justice in its conduct of antitrust litigation challenging mergers by International Telephone & Telegraph, Inc. with the Canteen Corporation, the Hartford Corporation, and the Grinnell Corporation. To the contrary, a tape-recorded telephone conversation between [Kleindienst] and then-President Nixon reveals that [Kleindienst] was ordered to "stay . . . out of [the case]. . . . Don't file the brief [in the Supreme Court]. . . . [D]rop the . . . thing!"[92]

In a plea agreement with the Watergate special prosecutor, Kleindienst pleaded guilty to a misdemeanor and received a suspended sentence of a fine and one month's imprisonment. Prior to that incident, Kleindienst had a distinguished record of public service.

Mahlon Perkins, Jr. and Joseph Fortenberry

Perkins, a partner at a large Wall Street firm, falsely stated at a deposition that he had inadvertently destroyed certain documents. He subsequently disclosed the perjury, was convicted of a misdemeanor, and served a one-month prison sentence. Fortenberry, an associate present at the deposition, allegedly reminded the partner that the documents were not destroyed. However, he remained silent after the partner did not correct the misstatement.[93] See the discussion in Part E, Supervisory and Subordinate Lawyers, pages 82-89.

Laura Beth Lamb

Lamb faced disciplinary charges for taking the California bar exam for her husband. At the time of the exam, she was seven months pregnant and suffering complications from chronic diabetes. Her husband, who had previously failed exams in both Texas and California, had bouts of rage and depression during which he threatened to kill Lamb and her unborn child if she did not take the test in his place. She agreed, disguised herself as her husband, and scored ninth out of some 7,000 applicants. After an anonymous tip revealed the matter to the state bar, she pleaded guilty to felony impersonation and deception. She received a $2,500 fine, probation, and a sentence of 200 hours of community service. When she was fired from her job at the SEC, she took a position as a legal secretary. She also divorced her husband and received psychological treatment. In a letter to the court passing on the disciplinary motion, Lamb's therapist concluded that she "was unlikely to do anything remotely like this again. [Her] prognosis for the future is good provided that she remains in therapy long enough to develop the psychic structures that have not yet matured. . . . This will require a long-term commitment."[94]

The following sanctions were imposed in each case.

Holloway. The Indiana Supreme Court imposed a 45-day suspension because Holloway's "numerous acts of professional misconduct have served to tarnish the integrity of the legal profession [and] exemplify [his] repeated inability to grasp the importance of adhering to professional ethics."[95]

Moore. The Indiana Supreme Court ordered disbarment. Moore "acted in contravention of the laws of . . . Indiana at the time he was serving a public trust to enforce such laws. . . . A lawyer who betrays his public trust and ignores his responsibility for the impartial administration of justice, not only suggests to the public an absence of integrity, but also demonstrates an unfitness to continue in practice."[96]

Kleindienst. The Arizona Supreme Court, a District of Columbia bar disciplinary hearing committee, and the District of Columbia Court of Appeals all concluded that Kleindienst had violated bar Disciplinary Rule 1-102(A), prohibiting "dishonesty, fraud, deceit, or misrepresentation." After the Arizona Supreme Court imposed censure, the D.C. bar disciplinary committee recommended a one-year suspension. Its decision rested primarily on the need to avoid "erosion of public confidence in the [profession]," and de-emphasized other factors such as public protection and deterrence by example. The D.C. Court of Appeals rejected the committee's recommendation as overly punitive, and instead imposed a 30-day suspension. In reaching that decision, the court focused on Kleindienst's distinguished career and the stress created by a "highly charged political atmosphere."[97]

Several years later, Kleindienst was disciplined for lying under oath to an Arizona bar disciplinary committee investigating charges of misconduct in his dealings with insurance officials.[98]

Perkins and Fortenberry. See the discussion in Part E, Supervisory and Subordinate Lawyers, pages 82–89.

Laura Beth Lamb. By a 6-1 vote, the California Supreme Court revoked Lamb's license. In its view:

> [Lamb's] deceitful acts were of exceptional gravity. Her conduct threatened innumerable clients with significant injury through unknowing exposure to an unqualified practitioner. It undermined the integrity of the State Bar's admission system, on which public confidences in the competence of attorneys is founded. . . . Though replete with testimonials to her talent and general character, the record contains . . . no "clear and convincing" indication of [her] *sustained and complete* rehabilitation from chronic personal problems which led to her catastrophic misjudgment. . . . The legal, ethical, and moral pressures of daily practice come in many forms. Besides raw avarice and self-aggrandizement, they may include the sincere but misguided desire to please a persuasive or overbearing client. . . . Despite our sympathetic feelings, . . . we believe that reinstatement proceedings are the means by which petitioner should demonstrate her clear rehabilitation after "the passage of considerable time."

In re Lamb, 776 P.2d at 768-770 (Cal. 1989).

Justice Kaufman, dissenting, responded:

> . . . Contrary to the majority's premise, there is no danger to the public or anyone else from petitioner's one-time, aberrational conduct stemming from circumstances that no longer exist and as to which there is not the slightest possibility of recurrence. . . . [Disbarment] serves only to punish an apparently talented lawyer whose misconduct resulted from the most desperate, life-threatening circumstances. Indeed, such drastic discipline serves the public interest *less* well than would a long period of probation on appropriate conditions . . . including proof of fitness before returning to the practice of law.

Id. at page 771.

What sanctions would you have imposed in these cases? How should the bar treat "one-time aberrational" acts? Would you respond differently to a lawyer convicted of a single act of domestic violence?[99]

At an abstract level, there is general agreement about the factors relevant in imposing disciplinary sanctions. However, more concrete questions provoke considerable disagreement.

a. Stringency of Sanctions

One perennial dispute has involved the stringency of sanctions. While courts and disciplinary agencies generally have been reluctant to withdraw an individual's means of earning a living, commentators have repeatedly criticized the leniency of discipline, particularly in cases like *Holloway* involving repeated instances of neglect, misrepresentation, or incompetence.

b. Mitigation

A related controversy has centered on the role of mitigating factors. Some courts and bar disciplinary officials have been sympathetic toward offenses that apparently stemmed from psychological problems, such as exceptional stress or family and marital difficulties; other court decision-makers have been reluctant to view such difficulties as adequate mitigation. The significance of lawyers' feelings of remorse and willingness to provide client compensation has provoked related disputes. According to Americans for Legal Reform, it is a disciplinary agency's job to make sure that the risk to clients is "eliminated or minimized, not excused. The kind of leniency [granted to lawyers] is not accorded elsewhere; one can hardly imagine a bank forgiving a teller's theft of thousands of dollars and keeping them on the job based on excuses such as alcoholism, mental disability, or willingness to pay it back."[100] Is this an appropriate analogy?

Similar controversies involve questions about whether the attorney has "suffered enough." To some judges and bar officials disbarment seems gratuitous for a prominent lawyer who, like Kleindienst or Perkins, has undergone the humiliation of public disciplinary proceedings, particularly those accompanied by criminal charges or involuntary resignation from employment. Yet, as in the sentencing of white-collar criminals, the class bias underlying such views remains problematic. It is equally arguable that attorneys who have attained positions of wealth and status should meet higher, not lower, standards of conduct, especially since these practitioners generally have little financial excuse and their cases are likely to attract more attention than the usual proceedings. How would you respond to those concerns in Problem 3E?

c.   Fines

Unlike the disciplinary systems in other countries, American procedures generally do not permit a monetary fine, although they do sometimes make restitution of client losses a condition of the lawyer's continued practice. The stated rationale is that fines constitute punishment, and that the purpose of disciplinary procedures is protection. A related concern is that monetary sanctions would make disciplinary procedures resemble those of the criminal justice system and would accordingly require comparable due process safeguards (e.g., proof beyond a reasonable doubt). By contrast, some commentators argue that fines may offer more effective deterrence than warnings or reprimands. A lawyer, it is assumed, is even more likely than the average person to engage in cost-benefit calculations and to have information about the risks of misconduct. In addition, courts may be less reluctant to level fines than to impose sanctions amounting to the loss of an individual's livelihood.

What is your view? If fines are appropriate in cases involving white-collar crime and Rule 11 misconduct, should they also be available for ethical violations?

d.   Organizational Liability

A related issue is whether disciplinary sanctions, including fines, should be directed at organizations as well as individuals. In jurisdictions like New York that permit institutional liability, the aim is to encourage better internal methods of preventing or responding to misconduct. Organizational sanctions also avoid the need to scapegoat individuals in circumstances of diffused or shared responsibility.[101]

Under what, if any, circumstances do you think disciplinary agencies should enforce concepts of enterprise liability? Consider Model Rule 5.1(a), which requires "reasonable efforts to ensure that the firm has in effect measures giving reasonable assurance that all lawyers in the firm conform to the rules of professional conduct." What circumstances should prompt organizational sanctions for violation of this Rule? For example, should discovery abuse, overbilling, sexual harassment, racial bias in recruitment, or sexual relations with clients be grounds for institutional accountability?

e.   The Scope of Disciplinary Authority

Problems involving the scope of disciplinary regulation are well illustrated by controversies involving attorney-client sexual relationships. Such relationships are hardly a new development. What is new, however, is the dispute about appropriate regulatory responses.

According to a national survey in the early 1990s, about a third of responding lawyers knew of one or more instances in which other lawyers had been sexually involved with clients.[102] Six percent acknowledged having such relationships themselves, a figure that may be somewhat understated but is not inconsistent with surveys involving other professionals, such as mental health practitioners.[103] In those surveys, patients overwhelmingly report adverse effects from sexual involvement with their therapists, a finding that has led most mental health associations to impose a flat ban.[104]

In arguing for a similar rule for lawyers, commentators point to a variety of harms that can arise from intimate relationships. For example, sexual involvement may discourage divorce clients from reconciliation or provoke punitive responses toward the client by judges or ex-spouses.[105] Intimate relationships are also likely to compromise independent judgment by both clients and lawyers. Attorneys who want to prolong or terminate sexual involvement might skew their legal advice accordingly. Not all clients who are involved in such relationships may feel able to challenge the quality of assistance provided, the strategies proposed, or the fees requested. Nor will some clients feel free to refuse or end a sexual involvement if they fear that their legal representation might suffer and that hiring another lawyer would impose undue delay or expense. These clients also may be unwilling to later seek malpractice remedies given the financial expense, public humiliation, problems of proof, and absence of clear rules governing attorney conduct.

In recognition of these problems, about two-thirds of surveyed attorneys have indicated that ethical codes should address lawyer-client sexual involvement, and about half have supported prohibitions on all such relationships. Most bar leaders, however, have been reluctant to regulate on this issue. Many feel that existing rules on conflicts of interest and breach of fiduciary obligations are adequate, that not all areas of legal practice present significant potential for abuse, and that categorical restrictions would interfere with lawyers' privacy and associational rights. As one practitioner put it, "consenting and competent adults should be able to sort out their sexual activities without any advice from the state bar."[106]

Proponents of more specific regulations agree that lawyers *should* be able to do so, but point to a growing number of cases in which the reality appears otherwise. Bar committees and courts increasingly have been called on to sort out the propriety of attorneys' conduct after the fact, and the results have been inconsistent. In some instances, decision-makers have found no duty to refrain from sexual relationships or have imposed only nominal sanctions. In other cases, such relationships have resulted in significant penalties.[107] The ABA's Standing Committee on Ethics and Professional Responsibility warns that if sexual relationships become issues in disciplinary proceedings, lawyers should "bear a heavy burden to

demonstrate that their representation was not adversely affected."
Formal Opinion No. 92-364.

Would you support more explicit regulations? Should the bar
prohibit all lawyer-client sexual relationships as many commentators and some ethics committees have proposed? Or would you favor
a ban in specific practice contexts such as matrimonial law, or under
certain circumstances presenting clear risks of abuse.[108]   See California Rule of Professional Conduct 3-120, which prohibits attorneys
from demanding or requiring sexual relationships with clients, from
employing coercion or undue influence in entering into sexual relationships, and from continuing representation if a relationship
causes incompetent performance. How would you counsel the lawyer
in Problem 16H at page 726? See the discussion of attorney-client
relationships in matrimonial cases in Chapter XVI (Family Law), at
pages 726–727.

f. Misconduct Outside Lawyer-Client Relationships

Cases involving discipline for conduct occurring outside a lawyer's professional relationships raise a final and somewhat different
set of concerns. As discussion in Part C on admissions notes, the bar
has been much more active in policing moral character among applicants than among admitted attorneys. From a public policy standpoint, this double standard is problematic. Of course, practicing
lawyers have a greater vested interest in their professional licenses
than do applicants to the bar. However, acts committed after admission are also more probative of future threats to the public than acts
committed before becoming an officer of the court.[109]

Disciplinary cases have differed widely in their treatment of
conduct outside a lawyer-client relationship.[110] Some states mandate
automatic disbarment for attorneys convicted of any felony. Other
jurisdictions specify certain offenses or acts involving "moral turpitude," a standard open to widely varying interpretations.

[Some] leading definitions border on tautology. Thus, the California
Supreme Court has declared: "To hold that an act of a practitioner
constitutes moral turpitude is to characterize him as unsuitable to
practice law." . . . [Certain offenses such as those involving marijuana,
political protest, tax evasion, and sexual misconduct have proved particularly divisive.] State courts are currently split as to whether willful evasion of taxes or failure to file a return constitutes moral
turpitude. Even within the same jurisdiction, local disciplinary committees have different views of comparable cases. . . .
    [A]lthough a Florida lawyer lost his license following a convic-
tion for indecent exposure in a public lavatory, an Indiana practitioner received only a year suspension for making sexual advances to
one client and offering to exchange his legal services for nude photographs of another client and her daughter; only the latter attorney's

activities were deemed "personal and unrelated" to professional practice.[111]

How would you respond to such conduct? Should the primary issue be public protection, public confidence, or public image? Would automatic disbarment for any felony be preferable to ad hoc decision-making? Alternatively, should disciplinary committees consider only misconduct that is committed in a lawyer-client relationship and leave other considerations to the criminal justice system? Is there a more desirable intermediate position?

g. Substance Abuse

Drug and alcohol problems present related controversies and figure in an increasing percentage of disciplinary cases; estimates in different jurisdictions range between 20 and 75 percent. How to respond to such problems raises more fundamental questions about both the nature of the disciplinary process and the nature of substance abuse. Should discipline be seen purely as a protective system, concerned with an attorney's fitness to practice? Alternatively, should it reflect considerations of public image and deterrence? Under either framework, what implication does addiction carry? Standard 9.3 of the ABA Standards for Imposing Lawyer Sanctions allows "physical" or "mental" disabilities or chemical dependence as mitigating factors but notes in the commentary that courts are divided on this issue.

Courts are also divided on the applicability of the Americans with Disabilities Act, which prohibits discrimination based on disabled status. What is your view? Consider, for example, a District of Columbia disciplinary committee's recommendation of leniency for a lawyer recovering from cocaine addiction who was under adequate supervision to prevent abuse. In challenging that decision, bar counsel argued that "people go to jail for conduct that [the attorney] offers as a mitigating factor. An informed public would find it intolerable that such a lawyer be granted special grace."[112] How should the bar balance public image versus public protection?

On one point, however, there is little disagreement. Confidential assistance for impaired attorneys not yet charged with disciplinary violations can be of enormous assistance to those attorneys and to their clients, colleagues, and families. Diversion to special treatment and monitoring programs for impaired lawyers guilty of minor misconduct has proved of similar value. Recovery rates among professionals who obtain adequate treatment are encouragingly high, and increasing support for assistance programs should become a greater priority throughout the bar.[113]

E. SUPERVISORY AND SUBORDINATE LAWYERS

PROBLEM 3F

Suppose the facts had been as follows in the Berkey-Kodak case described below.

1. You are an associate with Donovan Leisure.

(a) For the past two years you have worked primarily for one senior partner on a large antitrust suit brought by Berkey Photo against your client, Eastman Kodak. One of the major issues in the suit concerns whether Kodak's acquisitions of early competitors or its superior product innovations were the primary cause of its dominant market position. In connection with that issue, Kodak has retained a highly regarded Yale economics professor to study the photography industry in the hope that he will develop an expert opinion that Kodak's innovations, rather than acquisitions, enabled it to attain dominance. Ultimately, the professor does develop such a theory. However, in one early letter to the senior partner, the expert indicates he is unable to explain how Kodak's early acquisitions could be irrelevant to its present market position.

This letter and certain documents used by the economist have not been produced in response to Berkey's discovery demand for all such documents and for "interim reports" prepared by the economist. At the expert's deposition, the partner makes an assertion, which he later repeats in an affidavit under oath, that he inadvertently destroyed the documents, believing them to be duplicates of material still available. The partner also privately maintains that he does not consider the economist's correspondence to be a "report" within the meaning of the discovery demand.

You find that interpretation contrived and try unsuccessfully to convince the partner that the expert's preliminary expression of doubt is precisely the sort of interim statement that Berkey is seeking for cross-examination purposes. At the very least, you believe the trial court should be asked to rule on the question. You also know that the documents have not been destroyed, although they reveal nothing of critical substantive value to Berkey. You greatly respect the senior partner and are at a loss to explain his behavior. What is your response?

(b) Assume that you describe the situation to another litigation partner whose opinion you value. He questions whether you can be absolutely certain that your supervising partner has knowingly suppressed evidence and lied under oath. In the litigator's view, a public charge might ruin the supervising attorney's life and taint the firm's reputation, as well as jeopardize the client's case and subject the firm to a million-dollar malpractice suit if the trial is affected. Without proof, the litigation partner is unwilling to take further steps himself. What do you do?

(c) Assume that before you take any action, Berkey makes a settlement offer that Kodak is willing to accept. Does that affect your plans?

2. You are the chair of the New York Bar Disciplinary Committee. Suppose that there was no settlement offer in the Berkey-Kodak case. Assume also that the existence of the letter came to light during trial, and that the partner disclosed the perjury to one of his colleagues, who brought it to the court's attention. The presiding judge refers the case to your committee. What, if any, disciplinary action do you recommend against the firm and the attorneys involved? Consider DR 1-102 and Model Rules 5.2 and 8.3.

3. You are a member of Donovan Leisure's executive committee. You have worked with the attorneys whose conduct is now open to question and, prior to this incident, you liked and respected all of those involved. What action do you believe the firm should take with respect to the supervising partner, the litigating partner, and the associate? Consider Model Rule 5.1.[114]

Although most ethical standards and moral theories are framed with reference to individual decision-makers, most legal practice occurs in organizational contexts. These contexts often pose special challenges because information and responsibility are divided. Consider whether bar ethical rules deal adequately with such situations. The Code does not explicitly address issues of supervisory relationships. Model Rule 5.1 holds supervising lawyers responsible for a subordinate's disciplinary violation when they order or ratify the conduct, or when they knowingly fail to take reasonable remedial action. Rule 5.1 also makes partners responsible for ensuring that firm policies give "reasonable assurance" that all lawyers conform to rules of professional conduct. Supervisors also must make reasonable efforts to ensure conformity by lawyers under their supervision. Under Rule 5.2, subordinate lawyers do not violate professional standards if they act in accordance with a supervisory lawyer's "reasonable resolution" of an arguable question of professional duty.

Similarly, an opinion by the Association of the Bar of the City of New York, Commission on Professional and Judicial Ethics, Inq. Ref. 82-79 (1982), concluded that an associate who questions the propriety of a partner's conduct should raise the matter within the firm, either with the partner or with other partners, committees, or department heads, before reporting to a court or disciplinary committee.

Compare this approach to the military's principles, set forth in the Nuremberg Charter and the Army's Law of Land Warfare. These principles hold government officials and commanding officers responsible for war crimes committed by subordinates. Subordinates are also accountable for their own actions, although their status may mitigate punishment. Should lawyers be held to similar standards?

Problem 3F is modeled on a case that has been the subject of several journalistic accounts. Although they vary in some respects, the basic facts appear consistent with part 1(a) of the problem. The associate, Joseph Fortenberry, had been present at the deposition at which the senior partner, Mahlon Perkins, first misrepresented that documents had been inadvertently destroyed. According to Perkins' later testimony, Fortenberry had whispered something in Perkins' ear reminding him that they still had a suitcase containing the documents. Fortenberry denied this.[115] It is, however, extremely likely that Fortenberry knew of the perjury and never again raised the matter with Perkins, discussed it with other lawyers, or disclosed it to the presiding judge, Marvin Frankel.[116] Nor does it appear that Fortenberry or other lawyers working on the case challenged the decision not to disclose the expert's early letter.

Both matters eventually came to light. The existence of the expert's correspondence emerged after cross-examination when Berkey's counsel asked him whether there were any documents "on this matter" prepared prior to a given date. When the expert responded by seeking a definition of "on this matter," counsel for Berkey pursued the issue and District Judge Frankel required disclosure of the letter.[117] After this ruling, Perkins voluntarily disclosed his perjury, first to the Donovan partner in charge of the case and then to the court.

Everyone did not live happily ever after. In his summation to the jury, Berkey's counsel made the most of the opposition's "sordid spectacle of dissembling, evasiveness, deception, and concealment."[118] Judge Frankel also made clear his own dissatisfaction with Donovan Leisure's performance. He began by noting that Perkins had executed his false affidavit in response to a partner's request for something stronger that would "satisfy" the court as to why documents couldn't be produced. Frankel then questioned whether it was sufficient "for Mr. Perkins' partners to demand more positiveness or whether it wasn't incumbent on everyone concerned to press Mr. Perkins more vigorously than he appears to have been pressed for the truthful account we received so many months later." As for the failure to disclose the expert's early letter, Frankel questioned why lead counsel "did not see fit to let me look at that document," and condemned the firm's single-minded interest "in winning, winning, winning."[119]

A week after the jury awarded Berkey a total of $113 million in damages, Kodak announced that Sullivan and Cromwell was taking over the litigation. On appeal, the Second Circuit reversed the lower court judgment and remanded the case for further proceedings. Kodak eventually settled the matter for $6.75 million. Donovan Leisure reportedly paid $675,606 to Kodak to settle claims concerning its handling of the case.[120] Kodak had previously been Donovan Leisure's largest client, accounting for $3 to $5 million of the firm's estimated $22 to $24 million in annual gross billings.[121]

How the incident affected Fortenberry's career is a matter of some dispute. Stephen Brill in Esquire magazine claimed that

Fortenberry (Harvard B.A. and Yale J.D.) was "brilliant," "engaging," and "enjoyable" to work with, and had an excellent chance of making partner prior to the incident with Perkins.[122] By contrast, James Stewart's account suggests that Fortenberry was something of an "oddball" and had been passed over for partnership before the incident; the firm reportedly concealed its adverse decision to enhance his chances of obtaining other employment.[123] There is no dispute that after the Berkey-Kodak events, Fortenberry failed to receive any job offers from private firms. He was not, however, charged with any disciplinary violations. Should he have been? Should the firm have been subject to any sanctions for failure to establish adequate internal reporting channels for misconduct?

Ironically enough, Mahlon Perkins may have emerged with the least long-term damage. He resigned from Donovan Leisure, pleaded guilty to a reduced misdemeanor charge of contempt of court, and spent 27 days in jail where he served as assistant to the chaplain.[124] At Perkins' sentencing hearing for criminal contempt, his lawyer made the following statement:

> Those in our profession who know about this, if they are honest about it, would admit that there, possibly but for the grace of God, go I, because of the pressures which come upon men and women who practice law in big cases.[125]

Similar considerations may have moved the New York Court of Appeals, which passed on disciplinary charges against Perkins. Because prosecutors allowed Perkins to plead guilty to a misdemeanor, he was not subject to New York's requirement of automatic disbarment for convicted felons. In explaining its decision to impose only severe censure rather than more stringent sanctions, the court observed:

> Having served a term of imprisonment, suffered resignation from partnership in a major law firm, tarnishing his previously impeccable reputation with consequent humiliation and disgrace, we believe that the conduct is not likely to recur, and accordingly, we consider severe censure to be [adequate].[126]

The court also noted that the misconduct had come to light through Perkins' own disclosures and that he had a distinguished record of community and war service.

Would you have reached a similar decision? Just before the appellate court decision, a report by a special committee of the city bar of New York had criticized the laxity of discipline for Wall Street lawyers.[127] Should the court have taken that criticism into account in sanctioning Perkins? What about concerns of general deterrence? Would other disciplinary options have been appropriate, such as community service?

Following his resignation, Perkins retired on his Donovan Leisure pension and initially devoted much of his time to charitable
work for the Greenwich, Connecticut, Philharmonic Orchestra. He
was reportedly much happier in that pursuit than in practicing
law.[128] Several years later, he returned to legal practice. Working pro
bono for the New York Center for Constitutional Rights, he developed a reputation for "productivity, effectiveness, dedication, and
modesty" in civil liberties cases. By his own account, his ordeal in
the Kodak litigation was a blessing in disguise because it forced him
into a career he found more satisfying but might never have had the
courage to choose. It "wasn't a very good way to have gotten out," he
noted, "but at this point, I'm very happy not to be there and very
happy to be here."[129] Does knowing how the story ends affect your
view of any of the events along the way, including the appropriateness of the disciplinary sanctions against Perkins?

Consider the following exchange between Duncan Kennedy and
John Kester. Whose position do you find more persuasive?

DUNCAN KENNEDY, REBELS FROM PRINCIPLE: CHANGING THE CORPORATE LAW FIRM FROM WITHIN

Harv. L. Sch. Bull. 36 (Fall 1981)

... My grandfather, who graduated from Harvard Law School about
75 years ago, was a corporate lawyer in upstate New York. By the
twenties he was a senior partner in his firm, and one of their clients
was a chemical company engaged in making, among other things,
poison gas for the War Department. The factory was a pretty Victo-
rian building by a river, but the neighbors complained about the
smells, and they claimed they couldn't grow anything in their gar-
dens anymore. They threatened law suits. One way the client dealt
with the threats was by putting magnificent geraniums in window
boxes across the front of the building, with the windows open and
the fumes coming out. It was a visual argument that the complaints
were crazy. But in order for it to work, every Monday morning about
3 AM the client sent a grounds crew to replace all the flowers before
they died. It went on week after week through the growing season.

My grandfather didn't, that I know, take any action. He should
have tried to do something about it. That doesn't mean that there
was, in fact, anything he could have done that would have worked.
But he might have taken a riskless step out of a sense of moral
outrage, or a very slightly risky step, or he might have done something that would have risked losing the client. If you were a young
associate in his firm, and knew what was going on, you should have
confronted him, maybe, and tried to get him to do something. He
died when I was small, and I have no real sense of how he would

have reacted and that's important to what I'm saying. I'm not advocating suicidal moralism on the part of associates with left liberal or radical personal political opinions. But I think we should ask of our students that in practice they try to figure out whether there are intelligent, more or less controlled risks they can take to put their careers behind their opinions.

According to my students, they "impliedly agreed" not to do any such thing, and if they tried, they'd be fired, or never make partner. But that is a self-serving lie. They *want* to think that so they'll have an excuse for total passivity once they've made their pact with the Devil. There are many variations on law firm hierarchy. There are firms in which senior partners test associates to see if they are such sell-outs that they'll do anything, no matter how ethically questionable, and firms in which someone will put a black mark in a mental book if you show the slightest hesitation about putting your arm to the elbow in muck. There are firms where you can get out of doing bad things with the equivalent of "please, not tonight, dear, I have a headache," and firms where you can engage your coworkers in a serious dialogue about the ethics of particular cases.

Most of the lawyers I know have no idea which of these descriptions fits their firm, because they've never made the slightest effort to politicize their work situations. Sometimes they *think* they know, but you just *don't* know until you've tried, and as soon as you do try, you change everything one way or another, and most of what you thought you knew becomes irrelevant. Let me say again that I'm not advocating self-immolation, more like sly, collective tactics within the institution where you work, to confront, outflank, sabotage or manipulate the bad guys and build the possibility of something better.

. . . Rebelliousness is like a muscle. You can strengthen it or you can let it atrophy. It is only if you engage in perennial collective resistance while you are young that you'll be strong enough to do anything when control is finally handed to you by the simple facts of aging and death. If you fight now, if you come to stand for something now, you'll be able to make things different when you own the place. If you've done nothing during the long interval but cave in, and cave in, and cave in, you won't even know it when you own the place, or if you know it you won't care. . . .

Let me close with two tactical maxims. The first is that what is at issue is politics, not grandstanding or heroism. If you think before you act, if you are subtle, collusive, skillful and tricky, if you use confrontation when confrontation will work, you should be able to do left office politics without being fired, and make partner. All you need is the persistent will to do it, a willingness to experiment, modest expectations of success, and some psychological armor against the feeling that nothing you do can make any difference to the course of world history. So what if it doesn't make any difference to the course of world history.

The second maxim is "find another person." The left slogan of community applies very powerfully to resistance within elite bureaucratic organizations. If you are alone, you will fail. If you can't find someone else, you shouldn't even try it. But there is *always* someone else, if you look hard enough and are willing to help the most likely prospects move little by little from mere disaffection to active resistance.

JOHN G. KESTER, CORRESPONDENCE

Harv. L. Sch. Bull. 32 (Spring 1982)

Putting to one side his slogans and fantasies about recreating society, there are three things to say about Professor Duncan Kennedy's homily in the Fall Bulletin.

The first, and least important, is that he is frighteningly naive. . . .

A second comment is that some of the issues he touches on do matter. The bar ought more often to admit that there is more to professional morality than staying a millimeter this side of the Canons of Ethics: there is the question of what one does with one's life. A lawyer whose scruples haven't atrophied from too many trips to the bank has to consider what he owes the public for the talents and opportunities he was given. And although everyone is entitled to counsel if the system is to work, it's true also that not all clients are equally attractive (though few are easily labeled all good or all bad, and nearly all look better after you meet the people on the other side).

It is more, though, a question of the totality of one's effort than of political judgments about individual cases. One should not barter one's soul to practice law, and one does not have to. It is inconceivable to me that any attorney in my firm would be forced to work on a case if he found it morally offensive. But you can't expect to be a habitual conscientious objector and still plan to be a general. No law graduates were ever conscripted to join my firm (or to go to law school, for that matter). If they do so, it's because they seek challenging work, development of skills, able co-workers, an opportunity to help people, and wealth for themselves. If you are far to the left and only support causes you like, then you ought not be offering yourself for general hire as a lawyer. The problem is not with the clients or the cases, it's with you, you are in the wrong line of work.

Which brings up the third, and most troubling, aspect of Professor Kennedy's advice: that he is implicitly contemptuous of those he is advising, and offers them only the unhappiness of acting out his own daydreams.

Why does Professor Kennedy not do his young readers the respect of assuming they are people of honor? Why does he not address the ethical problems of accepting a law firm's bread while at the same time being "subtle, collusive, skillful and tricky" in order to "sabotage and manipulate"? Are not young lawyers who do that going to wind up either self-deluded or guilt-ridden?

To the dilemma of career choice Professor Kennedy holds out the answer every child wants to hear: that you can have it both ways. You can drive a BMW, live in a stylish apartment, work for greedy clients, and still stay pure at heart and be on the winning side, come the revolution. All you need do is occasionally snarl at your bosses and organize the oppressed classes around the Lexis computer and the coffee machine until the dictatorship of the proletariat arrives. . . .

In the end, his moralism has no root in practice and his practical suggestions lack morality. Kennedy's political agenda may be fun for the classroom, but one hates to think of others being moved to act out his obsessions at the expense of their own lives. It isn't just that Professor Kennedy is a bewildered shepherd; it's that he's positively dangerous to his sheep.

> John G. Kester '63
> Washington, D.C.

See Chapter IX, The Lawyer-Client Relationship
  • Part B. The Counseling Role
    (pages 390–398)

F. MALPRACTICE

PROBLEM 3G

You are an associate in a large firm specializing in insurance defense for medical malpractice cases. An old friend of your family asks for an interview. She believes that she may have a claim against a local hospital and one of its surgeons. You arrange an interview with your firm's leading trial attorney. After discussing the matter for about 45 minutes, he tells her that the claim is not one that the firm is "interested in handling." He subsequently tells you that it was pointless to arrange a consultation with someone interested in suing a hospital that has been a frequent client. When you run into the woman later at a social event, she indicates that she hasn't pursued the legal issue because your colleague obviously thought it lacked merit. Since you don't know exactly what your partner said, you are noncommittal.

After the statute of limitations on the claim has run, the woman discovers that it had been quite likely to succeed. She sues your firm. The partner claims that he informed her about the statute and the need to consult another lawyer if she wanted to pursue the matter. He also argues that there was no attorney-client relationship. By contrast, the woman denies that he mentioned the limitations problem, and emphasizes that he never informed her about the conflict of interest or recommended another attorney. Nor did you when she mentioned her reasons for dropping the matter. Your firm is self-insured for malpractice claims. How should it respond? What, if anything, should you or the partner have done differently?[130]

1. Introduction

Three decades ago, malpractice claims against attorneys were so rare that insurance coverage was almost unavailable on the domestic market. By the mid-1990s, that situation had dramatically changed. Recent estimates suggest that about two-thirds of lawyers have some form of insurance and 10 to 20 percent are facing malpractice exposure.[131] The increase in such claims reflects the same factors that have fueled tort actions against other professionals: a rising sense of consumer activism and expectations; an increasing willingness among some practitioners to testify against colleagues; a search for "deep pockets" to sue following financial scandals; an expansion of third party obligations; and a growing number of lawyers specializing in plaintiff personal injury work. Some commentators also believe that increasing competition within the profession has increased incompetent practice by encouraging lawyers to cut corners and to handle matters beyond their expertise.

Despite the escalation of malpractice claims, the barriers to recovery remain substantial. Although data on plaintiffs' success rates are incomplete and sometimes inconsistent, it generally appears that most claims result in little or no recovery. Successful actions typically involve obvious errors such as missing deadlines, neglecting to file documents, or failing to contact clients and follow their instructions.[132] In cases presenting less objective evidence of error, clients often have difficulty determining and proving whether the lawyer's performance fell below average standards within the relevant community. Yet despite these difficulties, the threat of malpractice litigation has had a profound effect on practice. Insurance companies and lawyers, through their insurance premiums, spend an estimated four billion dollars annually in resolving malpractice claims.[133]

Current debates over the appropriate scope of malpractice liability center on four main issues: how to set performance standards; what proof of causation should be necessary; who should be entitled to sue; and what damages should be recoverable.

2. Performance Standards

Courts and commentators have divided over whether community standards set the appropriate benchmark for professional practice, and, if so, how the legal community should be defined; should it be the locality, the state, or the legal profession more generally? According to the Vermont Supreme Court, the "minimum knowledge required should not vary with geography. . . . The fact that a lower degree of care or less able practice may be prevalent in a particular local community should not dictate the standard of care." Russo v. Griffin, 510 A.2d 436, 438 (Vt. 1986) (holding that the state was the relevant community). Other commentators have raised more fundamental objections to making liability depend on prevailing practices in the community. In their view, such an approach adopts a "perpetrator" rather than "victim" perspective; it grants the profession the power to dictate its own standard of conduct. Moreover, in most areas of practice, no reliable data are available on how lawyers generally handle legal tasks. To these critics, a preferable approach is for judges and juries to determine what constitutes reasonable performance under the totality of the circumstances, including clients' legitimate expectations. A related dispute involves the significance of professional rules. Some courts hold that, as a matter of law, these rules establish the appropriate standard of conduct. By contrast, most other courts view the profession's codes as establishing relevant but not determinative standards.

What is your view? Consider these issues in light of Aloy v. Mash, 696 P.2d 656 (Cal. 1985), where the court permitted a malpractice claim to go to trial where an attorney had done inadequate research in an unsettled area of marital pension rights, even though his advice turned out to be consistent with a later United States Supreme Court holding. Since it was unlikely that this holding would be retroactively applied, a majority of justices saw no reason to bar the plaintiff's claim. Three justices dissented on the theory that an attorney should not be held liable for counsel that later turned out to be correct.

From a societal standpoint, which decisions make most sense? The majority in *Aloy* focused on the standard of care owed to the client, while the dissent concentrated on whether the client got the result that was ultimately held to be correct. What should be the primary objective of malpractice litigation: client compensation or establishment of an appropriate standard of attorney care?

3. Causation

In order to recover for malpractice, plaintiffs generally must establish that the lawyer's inadequate performance was a "but for" cause of quantifiable damage. For claims involving litigation (which comprise about half of all malpractice complaints), that burden requires a trial within a trial; plaintiffs must establish that, but for the lawyer's negligence, they would have prevailed in the original proceeding. That standard has also been severely criticized. Should malpractice clients be required to show only that the attorney's negligence resulted in the loss of a substantial possibility of recovery, as some commentators argue and some European law provides?

4. Third Party Obligations

A related controversy involves lawyers' liability to nonclients for violations of professional rules. Although traditional privity standards prevented such suits, courts gradually began recognizing exceptions. Some jurisdictions now hold that lawyers who undertake responsibilities that foreseeably affect a third party owe a duty of care to that individual. Such holdings rely on fiduciary/agency principles, third party beneficiary theories, or a balancing test that considers the predictability and certainty of harm, the defendant's moral culpability, and so forth.[134] Underlying this line of cases is a desire to place responsibility for maintaining insurance on the individual best able to prevent losses.

By contrast, other courts have concluded that making lawyers liable to third parties would introduce "undesirable self-protective" interests into the fiduciary relationship, erode loyalty to client interests, and unduly burden the profession.[135] That issue assumed increasing importance during the late 1980s and early 1990s in the aftermath of the collapses of speculative financial ventures. In your view, should investors who lost money from junk-bond deals or savings-and-loan failures have any right to sue lawyers who gave negligent advice to management or who failed to blow the whistle on obvious frauds? Should legislatures impose on attorneys greater statutory responsibilities to government regulators or third party victims? See Chapter XIII (Corporate Law).

5. Damages

Finally, should punitive damages be available for gross negligence, or should compensation be available for non-economic losses? See Patrick v. Williams, 402 S.E.2d 452 (N.C. 1991) (holding punitive damages available where the attorney failed to inform clients about an offer of settlement and to file timely appeal); Tara Motors v. Superior Court, 276 Cal. Rptr. 603 (1990) (permitting damages for emotional distress where lawyer failed to follow proper procedures in terminating client's daughter as general manager of a family auto dealership). Alternatively, should greater recoveries be available from bar-sponsored client security funds? Existing funds attempt to provide compensation for intentional wrongdoing where recovery against the attorney is impossible. Yet these funds generally require proof of fraud or dishonesty and place a cap on payment; most are too limited to cover more than a small fraction of client grievances.

6.   Prevention

Both lawyers and clients stand to gain from a greater focus on preventive techniques. For example, a time-management system can be effective in helping lawyers meet appropriate deadlines, especially if it allocates responsibility for ensuring compliance with someone other than the lawyer who is to perform the services. Adequate systems for monitoring conflicts of interest and client funds should be high priorities. Effective communication with clients is equally critical; disputes can often be prevented by providing detailed written retainer agreements, ongoing reports (such as copies of filings), and realistic assessments of outcome, delays, and costs.

Contrary to popular assumptions, it is not young, inexperienced attorneys who experience most malpractice claims, but lawyers with over ten years in practice.[136] The same financial and psychological factors that help lead to disciplinary charges also contribute to malpractice: unrealistic caseloads, acceptance of cases outside the attorney's expertise, drug and alcohol abuse, and personal stresses such as divorce and burnout. The best protection for both lawyers and their clients is professional help when such problems arise, together with comprehensive malpractice coverage.

G.   COMPETITION

1.   Introduction

The final section of this chapter explores representative policies governing competition among lawyers. Like the earlier discussion of bar regulatory structures, the following analysis focuses on three related questions. What are the appropriate objectives of professional rules? How well do existing standards serve those objectives? Who should decide those questions?

The rationale for regulating professional competition rests on what economists describe as imperfections in the market for legal services: information barriers, adverse selection, free riders, and externalities.

a.   Information Barriers

An initial difficulty stems from many consumers' inability to make accurate assessments about cost-effective legal services either before or after purchase. Most individual (as opposed to organizational) clients are one-shot purchasers; many will not consult an attorney more than once and, of those who do, a majority will select a different lawyer for subsequent work.[137] This lack of experience, coupled with the expense and difficulties of comparative shopping for professional assistance, makes it hard for such clients to identify services that will best suit their needs. In the absence of some external regulation, these clients may suffer from incompetent, overpriced, or unethical representation.

b. Adverse Selection

A related problem involves the adverse effects of information barriers on the quality of legal assistance. If clients cannot accurately discriminate among the services available, and no regulatory body enforces performance standards, lawyers will lack adequate incentives to invest time, education, and resources in providing quality representation.

c. Free Riders

An additional difficulty involves "free riders," that is, attorneys who gain benefits without contributing to collective goods. For example, the bar as a whole has an interest in securing the public's trust and in having lawyers conduct themselves in ways likely to maintain that trust. However, absent effective regulatory structures, individual attorneys will have inadequate economic incentives to avoid cheating; they can benefit as free riders from the bar's general reputation without adhering to the standards that sustain it.

d. Externalities

A final category of problems involves the external costs to society and third parties from conduct that may be advantageous to particular clients and their lawyers. For example, the public generally has an interest in seeing just and expeditious resolution of disputes in circumstances where individual clients would be willing to pay lawyers to frustrate truth-finding processes.[138]

Although commentators on the legal profession generally agree that these problems call for regulatory intervention, there is considerable dispute about the forms it should take.

2.   Advertising

PROBLEM 3H

You are the chair of a committee appointed by your state supreme court to recommend modifications in the rules governing attorney advertising. The lawyers who form a majority of members on your committee favor a restrictive approach. They would follow the lead of states that prohibit testimonial endorsements, lyrics, jingles, dramatizations, animations, and self-laudatory or undignified claims.[139] The non-lawyer members of your committee support the proposal of a Federal Trade Commission study, which would ban only false or deceptive communications.[140] How would you vote? Would it bother you to submit recommendations that lawyer members supported and non-lawyer members opposed? If so, how would you proceed? Would any compromise proposal be preferable?

Committee members have collected the following examples from various jurisdictions that suggest areas where guidance would be useful. Under the standard that you favor, how would you rule on the following advertisements?

1. A television advertisement features a man truthfully stating that after his third arrest for drunk driving, "They wanted to put me in jail for a year and take away my driver's license for ten years. That's when I called the lawyers at the Ticket Center. They got my case thrown out of court. No jail. No suspension. Nothing."[141]

2. A suggestive picture of an attractive blonde attorney wearing a miniskirt and spiked heels, lying prone across her desk, with a caption stating: "Does this firm have a reputation? You bet it does."[142]

3. An advertisement asserts that attorneys certified by the state bar as specialists provide "the best" legal representation, where the certification program requires only that specialists spend at least 60 percent of their time in their field during the five years preceding application and that they attend continuing legal education courses in the field.[143]

4. A full-page advertisement features a taxi-fare meter, a headline that reads "How to Hire a Lawyer Without Getting Taken for a Ride," and a text that states, "Few things are as frustrating as retaining an attorney. Because the minute you walk into their office the meter starts to run. For reasonable fees for routine services, call [X]."[144]

5. A television ad presents a lawyer wearing striped pajamas. He plays a convict whose final words to the chaplain from the electric chair are that he wishes he'd called the Hur legal clinic.[145]

6. An ad offers the following limerick:

A careless roadrunner named Fred
Slipped under a light that was red.
He thought he'd go free with a "No Contest" plea
But now he's a jailbird instead.[146]

7. An advertisement claims that the lawyer can obtain "fast fair cash compensation" for accident victims, and a television dramatization features a happy woman leaving a lawyer's office with an eight-foot check, while the lawyer promises: "I can't guarantee that I will get you a check that big, but I will evaluate your case free of charge."[147]

a. Introduction

Although many attorneys view advertising by their fellow professionals as a recent and lamentable development, it is in fact restrictions on advertising that are recent. Lawyers in ancient Greece and Rome were not shy about promoting their services. Neither were distinguished eighteenth- and nineteenth-century American attorneys, including Abraham Lincoln, who employed circulars or newspaper listings.[148] However, as earlier discussion indicated, after the turn of this century, bar leaders became increasingly concerned with promotional practices, and both the Canons of Ethics and the initial version of the Code of Professional Responsibility banned most advertisements.

During the 1960s and early 1970s, a growing constituency both inside and outside the profession challenged traditional constraints on competition. The increasing size and heterogeneity of the bar, the rise of an organized consumer movement, and a widening concern about access to legal services all set the stage for legal challenges that eventually reached the Supreme Court.

The first of these suits, Bates v. State Bar of Arizona, 433 U.S. 350 (1977), involved a relatively colorless advertisement for a legal clinic offering "legal services at very reasonable fees." The ad also listed charges for certain routine services such as uncontested divorces, adoptions, and simple personal bankruptcies. The Supreme Court held that lawyer advertising could not be subjected to blanket suppression, and that the advertisement at issue fell within first amendment protections. In a subsequent decision, In re RMJ, 455 U.S. 191, 203 (1982), the Court again struck down content restrictions on nonmisleading commercial speech and summarized its approach as follows:

> Truthful advertising related to lawful activities is entitled to the protections of the First Amendment. But when the particular content or method of the advertising suggests that it is inherently misleading or when experience has proved that in fact such advertising is subject to abuse, the States may impose appropriate restrictions. Misleading advertising may be prohibited entirely. But the States may not place an absolute prohibition on certain types of potentially misleading information, e.g., a listing of areas of practice, if the information also may be presented in a way that is not deceptive. . . . Although the potential for deception and confusion is particularly strong in the context of advertising professional services, restrictions upon such ad-

vertising may be no broader than reasonably necessary to prevent the deception.

Even when a communication is not misleading, the State retains some authority to regulate. But the State must assert a substantial interest and the interference with speech must be in proportion to the interest served. . . . Restrictions must be narrowly drawn and the State lawfully may regulate only to the extent regulation furthers the State's substantial interest.[149]

Subsequent cases held that bar ethics rules could not prohibit nondeceptive graphic illustrations or descriptions of ongoing litigation, Zauderer v. Office of Disciplinary Counsel, 471 U.S. 626 (1985);[150] mailings targeted to a specific recipient, Shapero v. Kentucky Bar Assn., 486 U.S. 466 (1988);[151] or accurate identification of an attorney as a certified trial specialist, Peel v. Attorney Registration and Disciplinary Commn., 496 U.S. 91 (1990).[152] The Bar could, however, prohibit targeted mail solicitations to accident victims and their families for 30 days following the accident. Florida Bar v. Went For It, 115 S. Ct. 2371 (1995).

The invalidation of advertising restrictions has provoked strong dissents within the Court and widespread opposition within the bar. Surveys following the *Bates* opinion generally have found that most lawyers oppose mass media advertising. A significant number of practitioners also agree with former Chief Justice Burger that such self-promotion is one of the most "unethical things a lawyer can do."[153] By contrast, most consumers believe that advertising is informative and is professionally acceptable, and a substantial minority within the bar believes that it is personally profitable and socially desirable.[154]

That controversy is reflected in continuing challenges to bar ethical rules and committee opinions governing advertising. DR 2-101 identifies in detail the information that lawyers can permissibly advertise and prohibits use of any public communication that is "undignified" or that includes a "false, fraudulent, misleading, deceptive, self-laudatory or unfair statement or claim." Model Rule 7.1 provides:

RULE 7.1 COMMUNICATIONS CONCERNING A LAWYER'S SERVICES

A lawyer shall not make a false or misleading communication about the lawyer or the lawyer's services. A communication is false or misleading if it:

(a) contains a material misrepresentation of fact or law, or omits a fact necessary to make the statement considered as a whole not materially misleading;

(b) is likely to create an unjustified expectation about results the lawyer can achieve, or states or implies that the lawyer can achieve results by means that violate the rules of professional conduct or other law; or

(c) compares the lawyer's services with other lawyers' services, unless the comparison can be factually substantiated.

Many states have modified or interpreted these rules to require additional disclaimers or to prohibit dramatizations, testimonials, and so forth. Consider what restrictions make sense in light of the following traditional justifications for restricting attorneys' commercial speech.

b. Deception

As the majority in *Bates* noted, opponents of advertising often claim that it "inevitably will be misleading . . . because such services are so individualized with regard to content and quality as to prevent informed comparison on the basis of advertisement, [and] . . . because advertising by attorneys will highlight irrelevant factors and fail to show the relevant factor or skill." 433 U.S. at 372. Although acknowledging the force of this objection, the *Bates* majority felt that the preferred remedy was "more disclosure rather than less." Id. at 375. It seemed "peculiar to deny the consumer, on the ground that the information is incomplete, at least some of the relevant information needed to reach an informed decision." Id. at 374.

c. Coercion and Invasion of Privacy

A further concern, particularly with respect to targeted mailings, is that unsophisticated consumers might find it difficult to ignore legal advice that seems directed at them personally. Zauderer v. Office of Disciplinary Counsel, 471 U.S. 626 (1985); Shapero v. Kentucky State Bar Assn., 486 U.S. 466 (1988) (O'Connor, J., dissenting). On this point, a majority of the Court has disagreed and has trusted in the ability of most individuals to disregard unwanted offers when not under pressure of direct in-person solicitation. However, the law has also recognized a valid interest in protecting the privacy of victims and their families in the aftermath of an accident. Florida Bar v. Went For It, 115 S. Ct. 2371 (1995).

d. Cost and Quality

Opponents of advertising claim that its likely result will be to raise the price and lower the quality of services. Attorneys assertedly will pass on their additional costs of marketing in the form of higher fees, and practitioners who advertise prices also will be inclined to provide a "standard package [of services] regardless of whether it fits the client's needs." Bates v. State Bar of Arizona, 433 U.S. at 378. The Court in *Bates* rejected these arguments as empirically "dubious" and constitutionally "[ir]relevant." Id. at 377. As the majority pointed out, price competition generally results in lower fees, and the bar's own support for prepaid group legal services programs with fixed rates undercut its opposition to standardized services. Id. at 378.

Many experts similarly believe that greater competition, by decreasing charges, will increase demand, expand volume, and encourage economies of scale through specialization and efficient use of paralegals and technology.[155] The limited research available generally suggests that advertising has a favorable effect on price and an uncertain effect on quality.[156] In any event, experts generally agree with the *Bates* majority that restraints on advertising are an "ineffective way of deterring shoddy work." 433 U.S. at 378.

e. *Professionalism and Administration of Justice*

Critics of advertising claim that it stirs up unnecessary litigation, undermines lawyer professionalism, and damages the bar's public image. Bates v. State Bar of Arizona, 433 U.S. at 368. In rejecting such claims, the *Bates* majority responded:

> At its core, the [professionalism] argument presumes that attorneys must conceal from themselves and from their clients the real-life fact that lawyers earn their livelihood at the bar. We suspect that few attorneys engage in such self-deception. . . . Bankers and engineers advertise, and yet these professions are not regarded as undignified. . . . Since the belief that lawyers are somehow "above" trade has become an anachronism, the historical foundation for the advertising restraint has crumbled. . . . Although advertising might increase the use of judicial machinery, we cannot accept the notion that it is always better for a person to suffer a wrong silently than to redress it by legal action.

433 U.S. at 368-376.

In Zauderer v. Office of Disciplinary Counsel, 471 U.S. at 648, the majority opinion similarly stated: "[W]e are unsure that the State's desire that attorneys maintain their dignity in their communications with the public is an interest substantial enough to justify the abridgment of their First Amendment rights. . . . [T]he mere possibility that some of the population might find advertising embarrassing or offensive cannot justify suppressing it." By contrast, in Florida Bar v. Went For It, the Court held that the bar had a "substantial interest both in protecting injured Floridians from invasive conduct by lawyers and in preventing the erosion of confidence in the profession that such repeated invasions have engendered." 115 S. Ct. at 2381.

What is your position? Are you troubled by attorneys who, in Chief Justice Burger's phrase, "sell law like laxatives"? Surveys that attempt to gauge advertising's effect on professional image have reached mixed results. Some studies suggest that consumers who are aware of lawyers' ads rate the bar lower on characteristics such as trustworthiness, professionalism, honesty, and integrity. Even individuals who generally believe that lawyer advertising is beneficial give the lawyers who place such advertisements lower ratings in trustworthiness, ethical conduct, and legal ability.[157] However, other research, including a national study by the ABA, finds that advertising is not a major factor in shaping public impressions of the bar and that "dignified" advertisements reflect favorably on the profession and on attorneys who advertise.[158]

Given this evidence, how much restriction of nondeceptive commercial speech is appropriate? Who should decide that question? Should authority to regulate attorney advertising rest with the organized bar or with a consumer protection organization subject to judicial review? Does it affect your view to know that in surveyed states like California, over 90 percent of all complaints to the bar about advertising come from other lawyers, and that only about 1 to 2 percent of consumer complaints about lawyers' conduct involve advertising?[159] Consider Linda Morton's proposal that consumer protection commissions should have jurisdiction over lawyer advertisements and should make findings about what messages are false and misleading. Under Morton's system, once a consumer brings a complaint, the attorney's conduct would be judged by juries, not by a judge or practicing bar. All malpractice verdicts would be published and records kept for easy access by consumers.[160]

Do you agree? If rules on marketing require some trade-offs among competing values, such as broadening access, encouraging more cost-effective services, and preserving a professional image, which values should take precedence? How should that decision be made?

3. Solicitation

PROBLEM 3I

1. You are a member of the Alabama Supreme Court, which is considering bar disciplinary findings of improper solicitation. The case arose after the death of a young child, who was left unattended for over six hours in a day-care van. According to Alabama attorney Robert Norris, an anonymous caller contacted his firm, claimed to be a friend of the family, and asked his office to help. The caller reportedly added that the parents were too poor even to buy flowers for the funeral. Norris had a member of his staff deliver a wreath to the funeral home with a firm brochure and a letter to the family stating:

Please accept our deepest sympathy in the loss of Randy. We know that you are presently being faced with many difficult decisions and will soon be faced with others. If we may be of assistance to you in any regard, do not hesitate to contact us at [the firm's phone number].

Someone contacted the bar instead. The mother denounced the lawyer and his associates as "vultures," and the bar's disciplinary board imposed a two-year suspension. In challenging that decision, the lawyer argued that Alabama's prohibitions against solicitation referred only to contact made "in person or by telephone."[161] The board rejected that argument on the ground that the rule was "clear as to its purpose and spirit" and the types of conduct it listed were simply examples. How would you vote? Would it matter if the law firm had just sent the wreath without the cover letter?

2. You are the president of the North Carolina bar, which is similarly enmeshed in disputes over solicitation. At issue is the conduct of a Washington, D.C., attorney who sent a mailing to potential North Carolina clients after a major plant fire. Although the local bar set up an information booth to advise victims and their relatives following the disaster, some individuals also responded to the D.C. lawyer's mailings. When a local prosecutor brought misdemeanor solicitation charges, the lawyer denounced the prosecution as an effort to protect local attorneys' "home turf." He characterized state bar officials as "sanctimonious yahoos" who "worry about their image and their pocketbooks rather than their clients."[162]

How would you respond? Suppose that following the disaster many potential claimants received a letter and follow-up call from the plant's insurance company seeking to negotiate an "immediate, full, and fair" resolution of any potential claims. Would you support a rule like Florida's, which prohibits plaintiffs' personal injury lawyers from contacting accident victims or their families for 30 days after the accident? Would it matter whether similar prohibitions were applicable to defense lawyers or insurance agents? Florida Bar v. Went For It, 115 S. Ct. 2371 (1995).

3. You are an attorney with a small civil rights firm that handles plaintiffs' Title VII suits. Your litigation is now supported primarily by contingent fee recoveries and fee awards under federal statutes, although you also sometimes receive project grants from foundations.

Over the last two years, several individuals have discussed potential claims of race discrimination by Allard, Inc., a large manufacturing conglomerate, but none have decided to file suit. Last month, while attending a reception for a local artist, you met one of Allard's few upper-level Hispanic executives. When you mention your area of work, he describes some of his own experiences of racial bias at Allard. You suggest that if he is interested in pursuing the matter, he should contact your firm.

He does so. Although he is interested in filing suit, he is unwilling to underwrite the costs of the litigation. You explain that although he must agree to be nominally liable for litigation expenses, your firm would never seek to recover costs from him. He wants you to put that representation into your retainer agreement.

You seek advice from a fellow attorney. She believes that the solicitation-maintenance issue could become sticky and advises you to refer the client to another lawyer. While you are quite reluctant to pass up this opportunity for a suit likely to generate substantial publicity and fees, you agree to think the matter over. On reflection, what do you do?

If you decide to accept the case, may you call or write the other Allard employees who previously approached you and ask whether they would be interested in joining a class action? Alternatively, may you or your client hold a general meeting for Allard employees to inform them of the litigation and suggest that anyone interested in filing suit contact your firm?[163]

Prohibitions on personal solicitation of clients originated in medieval England. These prohibitions were linked with three practices that the profession sought to discourage: maintenance (assisting others to prosecute or defend a suit without just cause); champerty (assisting a suit in return for a share of the recovery); and barratry (stirring up quarrels and litigation).[164] In this country, experience with solicitation has been mixed. Some of the nation's most significant public interest litigation has resulted from lawyers' personal contact with potential clients.[165] The practice has also had a seamier side, known colloquially as ambulance-chasing.

Although there is much to dislike in the coercive and intrusive practices linked with solicitation, there is also much to deplore in the biases that informed traditional prohibitions. As historian Jerold Auerbach notes, bans on advertising and solicitation

> rewarded the lawyer whose law-firm partners and social contacts made [such practices] unnecessary at the same time that it attributed inferior character and unethical behavior to attorneys who could not afford to sit passively in their offices awaiting clients; it thus penalized both them and their potential clients, who might not know whether they had a valid legal claim or where, if they did, to obtain legal assistance. . . . The Canons [of Ethics] especially impeded those lawyers who worked in a highly competitive urban market with a transient clientele. . . . [M]ethods of solicitation were condemned, but nothing was said about company claim agents who visited hospitalized workers to urge a quick and inexpensive settlement. [Plaintiffs'attorneys'] fees were isolated for judicial scrutiny, but larger corporate retainers were ignored by professional associations. . . . Not only were [plaintiffs' lawyers] criticized for professional malfeasance; their speech was mocked (many were recent immigrants) and their perseverance was denigrated as aggressiveness (many were Jewish). Commercialization, speculation, solicitation, and excessive litigation were decried, but there was no mention of the contribution of contingent fees to the enforcement of legitimate claims otherwise denied by the victim's poverty. . . . Rules of ethical deviance were . . . applied by particular lawyers to enhance their own status and prestige.[166]

Are any similar biases present in the current Code and Model Rules? DR 2-104(A) provides:

A lawyer who has given in-person unsolicited advice to a layperson that he should obtain counsel or take legal action shall not accept employment resulting from that advice, except that:

(1) A lawyer may accept employment by a close friend, relative, former client (if the advice is germane to the former employment), or one whom the lawyer reasonably believes to be a client.

(2) A lawyer may accept employment that results from his participation in activities designed to educate laypersons to recognize legal problems, to make intelligent selection of counsel, or to utilize available legal services if such activities are conducted or sponsored by a qualified legal assistance organization.

(3) A lawyer who is recommended, furnished or paid by a qualified legal assistance organization enumerated in DR 2-103(D)(1) through (4) may represent a member or beneficiary thereof, to the extent and under the conditions prescribed therein.

(4) Without affecting his right to accept employment, a lawyer may speak publicly or write for publication on legal topics so long as he does not emphasize his own professional experience or reputation and does not undertake to give individual advice.

(5) If success in asserting rights or defenses of his client in litigation in the nature of a class action is dependent upon the joinder of others, a lawyer may accept, but shall not seek, employment from those contacted for the purpose of obtaining their joinder.

Model Rule 7.3 provides:

(a) A lawyer shall not by in-person or live telephone contact solicit professional employment from a prospective client with whom the lawyer has no family or prior professional relationship when a significant motive for the lawyer's doing so is the lawyer's pecuniary gain.

(b) A lawyer shall not solicit professional employment from a prospective client by written or recorded communication or by in-person or telephone contact even when not otherwise prohibited by paragraph (a), if:

(1) the prospective client has made known to the lawyer a desire not to be solicited by the lawyer; or

(2) the solicitation involves coercion, duress or harassment.

(c) Every written or recorded communication from a lawyer soliciting professional employment from a prospective client known to be in need of legal services in a particular matter, and with whom the lawyer has no family or prior professional relationship, shall include the words "Advertising Material" on the outside envelope and at the beginning and ending of any recorded communication.

OHRALIK v. OHIO STATE BAR ASSOCIATION

436 U.S. 447 (1978)

Mr. Justice POWELL delivered the opinion of the Court. . . .

[In 1974, the appellant, an Ohio attorney, learned about an automobile accident involving Carol McClintock, an 18-year-old woman with whom he had a casual acquaintance. Through a phone call to her parents he learned that she was in the hospital. When he suggested that he might visit her there, Mrs. McClintock agreed, but requested that he stop by their home first.]

I

. . . During appellant's visit with the McClintocks, they explained that their daughter had been driving the family automobile on a local road when she was hit by an uninsured motorist. Both Carol and her passenger, Wanda Lou Holbert, were injured and hospitalized. In response to the McClintocks' expression of apprehension that they might be sued by Holbert, appellant explained that Ohio's guest statute would preclude such a suit. When appellant suggested to the McClintocks that they hire a lawyer, Mrs. McClintock retorted that such a decision would be up to Carol, who was 18 years old and would be the beneficiary of a successful claim.

Appellant proceeded to the hospital, where he found Carol lying in traction in her room. After a brief conversation about her condition, appellant told Carol he would represent her and asked her to sign an agreement. Carol said she would have to discuss the matter with her parents. She did not sign the agreement, but asked appellant to have her parents come to see her. Appellant also attempted to see Wanda Lou Holbert, but learned that she had just been released from the hospital. He then departed for another visit with the McClintocks.

On his way appellant detoured to the scene of the accident, where he took a set of photographs. He also picked up a tape recorder, which he concealed under his raincoat before arriving at the McClintocks' residence. Once there, he re-examined their automobile insurance policy, discussed with them the law applicable to passengers, and explained the consequences of the fact that the driver who struck Carol's car was an uninsured motorist. Appellant discovered that the McClintocks' insurance policy would provide benefits of up to $12,500 each for Carol and Wanda Lou under an uninsured-motorist clause. . . . Two days later appellant returned to Carol's hospital room to have her sign a contract, which provided that he would receive one-third of her recovery.

In the meantime, appellant obtained Wanda Lou's name and address from the McClintocks after telling them he wanted to ask her some questions about the accident. He then visited Wanda Lou at her home, without having been invited. He again concealed his tape recorder and recorded most of the conversation with Wanda Lou. After a brief, unproductive inquiry about the facts of the accident, appellant told Wanda Lou that he was representing Carol and that he had a "little tip" for Wanda Lou: the McClintocks' insurance policy contained an uninsured-motorist clause which might provide her with a recovery of up to $12,500. The young woman, who was 18 years of age and not a high school graduate at the time, replied to appellant's query about whether she was going to file a claim by stating that she really did not understand what was going on. Appellant offered to represent her, also, for a contingent fee of one-third of any recovery, and Wanda Lou stated "O.K."

Wanda's mother attempted to repudiate her daughter's oral assent the following day, when appellant called on the telephone to speak to Wanda. Mrs. Holbert informed appellant that she and her daughter did not want to sue anyone or to have appellant represent them, and that if they decided to sue they would consult their own lawyer. Appellant insisted that Wanda had entered into a binding agreement. A month later Wanda confirmed in writing that she wanted neither to sue nor to be represented by appellant. She requested that appellant notify the insurance company that he was not her lawyer, as the company would not release a check to her until he did so. Carol also eventually discharged appellant. Although another lawyer represented her in concluding a settlement with the insurance company, she paid appellant one-third of her recovery in settlement of his lawsuit against her for breach of contract. . . .

After a hearing, the Board found that appellant had violated Disciplinary Rules (DR) 2-103(A) and 2-104(A) of the Ohio Code of Professional Responsibility. . . . The Supreme Court of Ohio adopted the findings of the Board, reiterated that appellant's conduct was not constitutionally protected, and increased the sanction of a public reprimand recommended by the Board to indefinite suspension. . . .

II

. . . In-person solicitation by a lawyer of remunerative employment is a business transaction in which speech is an essential but subordinate component. While this does not remove the speech from the protection of the First Amendment, as was held in *Bates* and [Virginia Pharmacy v. Virginia Citizens' Consumer Council, 425 U.S. 748 (1976)], it lowers the level of appropriate judicial scrutiny. . . . Unlike a public advertisement, which simply provides information and leaves the recipient free to act upon it or not, in-person solicitation may exert pressure and often demands an immediate response, without providing an opportunity for comparison or reflection. The aim and effect of in-person solicitation may be to provide a one-sided presentation and to encourage speedy and perhaps uninformed decisionmaking: there is no opportunity for intervention or counter-education by agencies of the Bar, supervisory authorities, or persons close to the solicited individual. . . . In-person solicitation is as likely as not to discourage persons needing counsel from engaging in a critical comparison of the "availability, nature, and prices" of legal services, cf. *Bates*, 433 U.S., at 364, it actually may disserve the individual and societal interest, identified in *Bates*, in facilitating "informed and reliable decisionmaking." Ibid.

It also is argued that in-person solicitation may provide the solicited individual with information about his or her legal rights and remedies. In this case, appellant gave Wanda Lou a "tip" about the prospect of recovery based on the uninsured-motorist clause in the McClintocks' insurance policy, and he explained that clause and Ohio's guest statute to Carol McClintock's parents. But neither of the Disciplinary Rules here at issue prohibited appellant from communicating information to these young women about their legal rights and the prospects of obtaining a monetary recovery, or from recommending that they obtain counsel. DR 2-104(A) merely prohibited him from using the information as bait with which to obtain an agreement to represent them for a fee. The Rule does not prohibit a lawyer from giving unsolicited legal advice; it proscribes the acceptance of employment resulting from such advice. . . .[16]

A lawyer's procurement of remunerative employment is a subject only marginally affected with First Amendment concerns. It falls within the State's proper sphere of economic and professional regulation. See [NAACP v. Button]. While entitled to some constitutional protection, appellant's conduct is subject to regulation in furtherance of important state interests.

. . . The substantive evils of solicitation have been stated over the years in sweeping terms: stirring up litigation, assertion of fraudulent claims, debasing the legal profession, and potential harm to the solicited client in the form of overreaching, overcharging, underrepresentation, and misrepresentation. The American Bar Association, as amicus curiae, defends the rule against solicitation primarily on three broad grounds: It is said that the prohibitions embodied in DR 2-103(A) and 2-104(A) serve to reduce the likelihood of overreaching and the exertion of undue influence on lay persons, to protect the privacy of individuals, and to avoid situations where the lawyer's exercise of judgment on behalf of the client will be clouded by his own pecuniary self-interest.

We need not discuss or evaluate each of these interests in detail as appellant has conceded that the State has a legitimate and indeed "compelling" interest in preventing those aspects of solicitation that

---

16. . . . In recognizing the importance of the State's interest in regulating solicitation of paying clients by lawyers, we are not unmindful of the problem of the related practice, described in [Railroad Trainmen v. Virginia Bar, 377 U.S. 1 (1964)], of the solicitation of releases of liability by claims agents or adjusters of prospective defendants or their insurers. Such solicitations frequently occur prior to the employment of counsel by the injured person and during circumstances posing many of the dangers of overreaching we address in this case. Where lay agents or adjusters are involved, these practices for the most part fall outside the scope of regulation by the organized Bar, but releases of settlements so obtained are viewed critically by the courts.

involve fraud, undue influence, intimidation, overreaching, and other forms of "vexatious conduct." Brief for Appellant 25. . . .

III

Appellant's concession that strong state interests justify regulation to prevent the evils he enumerates would end this case but for his insistence that none of these evils was found to be present in his acts of solicitation. . . .

Appellant's argument misconceives the nature of the State's interest. The Rules prohibiting solicitation are prophylactic measures whose objective is the prevention of harm before it occurs. The Rules were applied in this case to discipline a lawyer for soliciting employment for pecuniary gain under circumstances likely to result in the adverse consequences the State seeks to avert. In such a situation, which is inherently conducive to overreaching and other forms of misconduct, the State has a strong interest in adopting and enforcing rules of conduct designed to protect the public from harmful solicitation by lawyers whom it has licensed.

The State's perception of the potential for harm in circumstances such as those presented in this case is well founded. The detrimental aspects of face-to-face selling even of ordinary consumer products have been recognized and addressed by the Federal Trade Commission, and it hardly need be said that the potential for overreaching is significantly greater when a lawyer, a professional trained in the art of persuasion, personally solicits an unsophisticated, injured, or distressed lay person. Such an individual may place his trust in a lawyer, regardless of the latter's qualifications or the individual's actual need for legal representation, simply in response to persuasion under circumstances conducive to uninformed acquiescence. Although it is argued that personal solicitation is valuable because it may apprise a victim of misfortune of his legal rights, the very plight of that person not only makes him more vulnerable to influence but also may make advice all the more intrusive. Thus, under these adverse conditions the overtures of an uninvited lawyer may distress the solicited individual simply because of their obtrusiveness and the invasion of the individual's privacy, even when no other harm materializes. Under such circumstances, it is not unreasonable for the State to presume that in-person solicitation by lawyers more often than not will be injurious to the person solicited.

The efficacy of the State's effort to prevent such harm to prospective clients would be substantially diminished if, having proved a solicitation in circumstances like those of this case, the State were required in addition to prove actual injury. Unlike the advertising in *Bates*, in-person solicitation is not visible or otherwise open to public scrutiny. . . . It therefore is not unreasonable, or violative of the

Constitution, for a State to respond with what in effect is a prophylactic rule. . . .

Mr. Justice MARSHALL, concurring in part and concurring in the judgments. . . .

What is objectionable about Ohralik's behavior here is not so much that he solicited business for himself, but rather the circumstances in which he performed that solicitation and the means by which he accomplished it. Appropriately, the Court's actual holding in *Ohralik* is a limited one: that the solicitation of business, under circumstances, such as those found in this record, presenting substantial dangers of harm to society or the client independent of the solicitation itself, may constitutionally be prohibited by the State. In this much of the Court's opinion in *Ohralik*, I join fully. . . .

Notwithstanding the injurious aspects of Ohralik's conduct, even his case illustrates the potentially useful, information-providing aspects of attorney solicitation. Motivated by the desire for pecuniary gain, but informed with the special training and knowledge of an attorney, Ohralik advised both his clients (apparently correctly) that, although they had been injured by an uninsured motorist, they could nonetheless recover on the McClintocks' insurance policy. The provision of such information about legal rights and remedies is an important function, even where the rights and remedies are of a private and commercial nature involving no constitutional or political overtones.

In view of the similar functions performed by advertising and solicitation by attorneys, I find somewhat disturbing the Court's suggestion in *Ohralik* that in-person solicitation of business, though entitled to some degree of constitutional protection as "commercial speech," is entitled to less protection under the First Amendment than is "the kind of advertising approved in *Bates*." The First Amendment informational interests served by solicitation, whether or not it occurs in a purely commercial context, are substantial, and they are entitled to as much protection as the interests we found to be protected in *Bates*.

. . . Not only do prohibitions on solicitation interfere with the free flow of information protected by the First Amendment, but by origin and in practice they operate in a discriminatory manner. As we have noted, these constraints developed as rules of "etiquette" and came to rest on the notion that a lawyer's reputation in his community would spread by word of mouth and bring business to the worthy lawyer. Bates v. State Bar of Arizona, supra, 433 U.S. at 371-372, 374-375 n.30. The social model on which this conception depends is that of the small, cohesive, and homogeneous community; the anachronistic nature of this model has long been recognized. If ever this conception were more generally true, it is now valid only with respect to those persons who move in the relatively elite social and educational circles in which knowledge about legal problems, legal remedies, and lawyers is widely shared.

The impact of the nonsolicitation rules, moreover, is discriminatory with respect to the suppliers as well as the consumers of legal services. Just as the persons who suffer most from lack of knowledge about lawyers' availability belong to the less privileged classes of society, so the disciplinary rules against solicitation fall most heavily on those attorneys engaged in a single-practitioner or small-partnership form of practice, attorneys who typically earn less than their fellow practitioners in larger, corporate-oriented firms. Indeed, some scholars have suggested that the rules against solicitation were developed by the professional bar to keep recently immigrated lawyers, who gravitated toward the smaller, personal injury practice, from effective entry into the profession. See J. Auerbach, Unequal Justice 42-62, 126-129 (1976). In light of this history, I am less inclined than the majority appears to be to weigh favorably in the balance of the State's interests here the longevity of the ban on attorney solicitation.

. . . By discussing the origin and impact of the nonsolicitation rules, I do not mean to belittle those obviously substantial interests that the State has in regulating attorneys to protect the public from fraud, deceit, misrepresentation, overreaching, undue influence, and invasions of privacy. But where honest, unpressured "commercial" solicitation is involved, a situation not presented in either of these cases, I believe it is open to doubt whether the State's interests are sufficiently compelling to warrant the restriction on the free flow of information which results from a sweeping nonsolicitation rule and against which the First Amendment ordinarily protects. While the State's interest in regulating in-person solicitation may . . . be somewhat greater than its interest in regulating printed advertisements, these concededly legitimate interests might well be served by more specific and less restrictive rules than a total ban on pecuniary solicitation. For example, the Justice Department has suggested that the disciplinary rules be reworded "so as to *permit* all solicitation and advertising except the kinds that are false, misleading, undignified or champertous."

IN RE PRIMUS, 436 U.S. 412 (1978). This was a companion case to *Ohralik*. It involved a South Carolina attorney who provided pro bono services for the American Civil Liberties Union and paid assistance to the South Carolina Council on Human Relations. During the early 1970s, Gary Allen, a representative of an organization serving poverty populations, requested that the Council provide information to pregnant welfare recipients who were being sterilized or threatened with sterilization as a condition of receiving Medicaid funds. At a meeting with some of these women in Allen's office, Primus provided advice about their legal rights and suggested the possibility of a lawsuit.

A month later, Primus learned from the ACLU that it was willing to provide representation to mothers who had been sterilized, and learned from Allen that one woman, Mary Williams, was interested in taking legal action. Primus then wrote Williams as follows:

> You will probably remember me from talking with you at Mr. Allen's office in July about the sterilization performed on you. The American Civil Liberties Union would like to file a lawsuit on your behalf for money against the doctor who performed the operation. We will be coming to Aiken [South Carolina] in the near future and would like to explain what is involved so you can understand what is going on. . . . About the lawsuit, if you are interested, let me know, and I'll let you know when we will come down to talk to you about it. We will be coming to talk to Mrs. Waters at the same time; she has already asked the American Civil Liberties Union to file a suit on her behalf.

436 U.S. at 417 n.6.

Shortly after receiving this letter, Williams visited the doctor who had performed the sterilization to discuss her third child, who was then ill. At the doctor's office, she encountered his attorney and, at the latter's request, signed a release of liability for the sterilization. She also provided them a copy of Primus' letter and called Primus from the doctor's office to communicate the decision not to file suit. There was no further contact between Williams and Primus.

The South Carolina Board of Commissions on Grievances and Discipline subsequently found that Primus had solicited a client on behalf of the ACLU in violation of DR 2-103(D)(5)(a) and (c) and DR 2-104(A)(5) of the Code and recommended a private reprimand. The Supreme Court of South Carolina accepted those findings and increased the sanction to a public reprimand.

The Supreme Court reversed. Speaking through Justice Powell, the majority emphasized that "[t]his was not in-person solicitation for pecuniary gain. [Primus] was communicating an offer of free assistance by . . . the ACLU . . . to advance civil liberties' objectives." 436 U.S. at 422.

Although the ACLU had a policy of seeking court-awarded counsel fees, the majority did not find that fact controlling because "fees are awarded in the discretion of the court, awards are not drawn from the plaintiff's recovery and are usually premised on a successful outcome; and the amounts awarded often may not correspond to fees generally obtainable in private litigation." Id. at 430. Under policies in force at the time of Primus' letter, any fee award would have gone to the ACLU, not to her. In a footnote, the Court noted that the ACLU's policy had later changed to permit sharing of fees between the organization and cooperating attorneys. The majority "express[ed] no opinion whether [its] analysis in this case would be different had the later policy been in effect during the period in question." Id. at 430 n.24.

In the majority's view, the record did not support the bar's claim of "undue influence, overreaching, misrepresentation, or invasion of privacy":

> Appellant's letter of August 30, 1973, followed up the earlier meeting, one concededly protected by the First and Fourteenth Amendments, by notifying Williams that the ACLU would be interested in supporting possible litigation. The letter imparted additional information material to making an informed decision about whether to authorize litigation, and permitted Williams an opportunity, which she exercised, for arriving at a deliberate decision. The letter was not facially misleading, indeed, it offered "to explain what is involved so you can understand what is going on." The transmittal of this letter, as contrasted with in-person solicitation, involved no appreciable invasion of privacy; nor did it afford any significant opportunity for overreaching or coercion. Moreover, the fact that there was a written communication lessens substantially the difficulty of policing solicitation practices that do offend valid rules of professional conduct. . . .
>
> The State is free to fashion reasonable restrictions with respect to the time, place, and manner of solicitation by members of its Bar. The State's special interest in regulating members of a profession it licenses, and who serve as officers of its courts, amply justifies the application of narrowly drawn rules to proscribe solicitation that in fact is misleading, overbearing, or involves other features of deception or improper influence. As we decide today in *Ohralik*, a State also may forbid in-person solicitation for pecuniary gain under circumstances likely to result in these evils. And a State may insist that lawyers not solicit on behalf of lay organizations that exert control over the actual conduct of any ensuing litigation.

436 U.S. at 435-439.

Justice Rehnquist dissented. In his view, the majority's focus on motive invited manipulation by clever practitioners. The next lawyer in Ohralik's shoes would be sure to assume the "prescribed mantle of 'political association' to assure that insurance companies do not take unfair advantage of policyholders." 436 U.S. at 442. Justice Rehnquist was also unable to

> share the Court's confidence that the danger of [such consequences] is minimized simply because a lawyer proceeds from political conviction rather than for pecuniary gain. A State may reasonably fear that a lawyer's desire to resolve "substantial civil liberties questions" may occasionally take precedence over his duty to advance the interests of his client. It is even more reasonable to fear that a lawyer in such circumstances will be inclined to pursue both culpable and blameless defendants to the last ditch in order to achieve his ideological goals. Although individual litigants, including the ACLU, may be free to use the courts for such purpose, South Carolina is likewise free to restrict the activities of the members of its Bar who attempt to persuade them to do so.

Id. at 445-446.

_____

Which of the perspectives in these cases, Justice Powell's, Justice Rehnquist's, or Justice Marshall's, is closest to your own? Consider the harms that the *Ohralik* decision attributed to solicitation, such as over-reaching, undue influence, conflicts of interest, and invasion of privacy. To what extent can these occur irrespective of who initiates contact? What evidence supports the Court's assumption that these harms are particularly likely to accompany fee-generating cases that result from personal solicitation? Note the frequency of terms such as "may" and "likely" in the majority decision in *Ohralik*. In contexts involving first amendment interests, should the state be required to establish a firmer causal relationship between prohibited expression and the harms that assertedly follow from it?

Under the Court's analysis in these companion cases, how critical should attorneys' motives be in determining whether their conduct is constitutionally protected? If Primus had been entitled to share court-awarded fees, should she have been subject to disciplinary action? Consider the following claim:

> [M]any civil rights attorneys during the last century have found personal persuasion to be the most effective means of rousing relevant constituencies. To cite only the most notable example, the named plaintiff in Brown v. Board of Education was initially "anything but eager" to incur the risks of legal proceedings [and was recruited through in-person conversation]. . . . Without personal contact, many victims of constitutional violations will remain unaware of potential remedies or means to pursue them.
>
> Lawyers willing to skirt the official rules on decorum have made for a more humane social order in both public and private law contexts. By helping to redistribute the costs of accidents, the personal injury bar has increased incentives for reducing accidents while ameliorating the conditions of victims and their dependents. Similarly, by raising the costs and consciousness of various constitutional and statutory violations, entrepreneurial public interest attorneys have helped produce some of the most progressive social changes in this nation's history. . . .
>
> Prevailing constitutional doctrine and codified standards, by focusing on attorneys' motives rather than conduct, have misconstrued the problem and misconceived the solution. The kind of pure [charitable] intent ostensibly present in *Primus* has become increasingly unusual given recent legislation expanding the potential for fee recoveries in public interest litigation. Since unalloyed altruism is rare, to prohibit personal contact except in the highly atypical circumstances where lawyers have no conceivable financial interest in the outcome is both over- and under-inclusive. Such an approach bans conduct that need not result in overreaching or underrepresentation, and it ignores the ways in which nonmonetary concerns can compromise counsels' fiduciary obligations. Attorneys' personal interests and ideologies are often implicated in pro bono contexts. . . . A constituency more concerned with the fact than the image of impropriety should seek a different regulatory framework. . . .[167]

One possible alternative would be the Federal Trade Commission's proposed rule banning in-person solicitation that

1. involves harassment, coercion, or undue influence;
2. involves communication with persons who have expressed a desire not to be contacted; or
3. occurs when a potential client is unable to exercise reasonable, considered judgment.[168]

Would such a prohibition, coupled with strict enforcement rules on fraud, unreasonable fees, and incompetent representation, be adequate to address the abuses historically linked to solicitation? To what extent should solicitation rules respond to the profession's interest in preventing an image of lawyers as greedy, ghoulish souls who hope to turn scenes of human distress into lucrative retainers? Alternatively, to what extent should those rules respond to victims' need for assistance, which is met principally by lawyers with an economic stake in the representation? Could those victims' needs be adequately met through more active bar association efforts, such as mass disaster referral plans, together with greater restriction of insurance company contacts?

Endnotes

1. See Stephen F. Barker, What Is a Profession?, 1 Professional Ethics 73 (1992).

2. American Bar Association Commission on Professionalism, In the Spirit of Public Service: A Blueprint for the Rekindling of Lawyer Professionalism (1986) (quoting Roscoe Pound, The Lawyer from Antiquity to Modern Times 5 (1953)).

3. Milton Friedman, Capitalism and Freedom 136-160 (1962); Sylvia Ostry, Competition Policy and the Self-Regulating Professions, in The Professions and Public Policy 17, 19-22 (Philip Slayton & Michael Trebilcock eds., 1978).

4. Magali Sarfatti Larson, The Rise of Professionalism: A Sociological Analysis (1977); Richard L. Abel, The Rise of Professionalism, 6 Brit. J. Law & Socy. 82 (1979).

5. Robert W. Gordon & William H. Simon, The Redemption of Professionalism, in Lawyers' Ideals/Lawyers' Practices: Transformation in the American Legal Profession 230 (Robert L. Nelson, David M. Trubeck & Rayman L. Solomon eds., 1992).

6. Richard L. Abel, United States: The Contradictions of Professionalism, in 1 Lawyers in Society: The Common Law World 186, 187 (Richard L. Abel & Philip S.C. Lewis eds., 1988).

7. See Anthony Kronman, The Lost Lawyer (1993); Deborah L. Rhode, The Professionalism Problem, Wm. & Mary L. Rev. (forthcoming 1997).

8. ABA Commission on Professionalism, supra note 2, at 1-3. For more recent accounts finding that only 40 percent of surveyed Americans have favorable views of lawyers, see Rhode, supra note 7; Gary A. Hengstler, Vox Populi, The Public Perception of Lawyers: ABA Poll, A.B.A.J., Sept. 1993, at 62.

9. Alexis de Tocqueville, 1 Democracy in America 275-278 (Henry Reeve trans., Phillips Bradley ed., Francis Bowen rev. ed., 1989) (lst ed. 1835).

10. For popular mistrust, see Lawrence M. Friedman, A History of American Law (1985). For continuities in what Robert Gordon labels

"declension rhetoric" (i.e., law's decline into a business), see Robert Gordon, "The Ideal and the Actual in the Law": Fantasies and Practices of New York City Lawyers, 1870-1970, in The New High Priests: Lawyers in Post-Civil War America 51 (Gerard W. Gawalt ed., 1984).

11. Robert L. Nelson & David M. Trubeck, New Problems and New Paradigms in the Studies of the Legal Profession, in Lawyers' Ideals, supra note 5, at 1.

12. For a more extensive review, see Charles W. Wolfram, Modern Legal Ethics 20-78 (1986), and sources cited.

13. The Preliminary Statement to the Code of Professional Responsibility makes clear that it does not undertake to define standards for civil liability of lawyers. The introductory provision governing the "scope" of the Model Rules of Professional Conduct similarly asserts that they are not designed to be a basis for civil liability.

14. Wolfram, supra note 12, at 65-67. In the aftermath of the settlement of a government antitrust suit against the ABA, its ethics committee issued an opinion declaring that its rulings were not binding on lawyers. ABA Comm. on Ethics and Professional Responsibility, Informal Op. 1420 (1978).

15. Fran Zemans & Victor Rosenblum, The Making of a Public Profession (1984).

16. Professionalization 129 (Howard M. Vollmer & Donald L. Mills eds., 1966); C.F. Tausch, Professional Ethics, 12 Encyclopedia Soc. Sci. (1934); Deborah L. Rhode, Moral Character as a Professional Credential, 94 Yale L.J. 491 (1985).

17. American Bar Association, Report of the Committee on [the] Code of Professional Ethics, 1906 American Bar Association Report 600, 600-604.

18. See sources cited in Deborah L. Rhode & David Luban, Legal Ethics 623 (2d ed. 1995).

19. George Sharswood, Essay on Professional Ethics (1854), quoted in Jerold S. Auerbach, Unequal Justice: Lawyers and Social Change in Modern America 41 (1976).

20. In 1919, Reginald Heber Smith's Justice and the Poor revealed a total of only 40 legal aid organizations throughout the country, with a combined budget of over $200,000. Earl Johnson, Jr., Justice and Reform: The Formative Years of the OEO Legal Services Program 5-7 (1974). For an overview of discrimination against lawyers from less privileged backgrounds, see Auerbach, supra note 19; Rhode & Luban, supra note 18, at 69-70.

21. See Deborah L. Rhode, Justice and Gender (1989); Karen Morello, The Invisible Bar: The Woman Lawyer in America, 1638 to the Present (1986).

22. See note 20.

23. Auerbach, supra note 19; Geraldine Segal, Blacks in the Law (1983).

24. Auerbach, supra note 19.

25. Charles Frankel, Review, 43 U. Chi. L. Rev. 874, 880 (1976) (examining the Code of Professional Responsibility).

26. Id.

27. David Luban & Michael Milleman, Good Judgment: Ethics Teaching in Dark Times, 9 Geo. J. Legal Ethics 31, 46 (1995); Robert F. Cochran, Lawyers and Virtues: A Review Essay, 71 Notre Dame L. Rev. 707, 722 (1996).

28. Roland N. McKean, Some Economic Aspects of Ethical-Behavioural Codes, 27 Political Studies 251, 253 (June 1979) (discussing ethical behavior as a public good); see also S. David Young, The Rule of Experts: Occupational Licensing in America 16 (1987).

29. Deborah L. Rhode, Ethical Perspectives on Legal Practice, 37 Stan. L. Rev. 589, 648 (1985).

30. See the discussion of the British Royal Commission on Legal Services, which had a majority of non-lawyers, and the proposed Independent Legal Profession Council for New South Wales in Rhode & Luban, supra note 18, at 126-127.

31. Deborah L. Rhode, Why the ABA Bothers: A Functional Perspective on Professional Codes, 59 Tex. L. Rev. 689, 720 (1981).

32. Quoted in Milton R. Wessel, Science and Conscience 67 (1980).

33. Frankel, supra note 25, at 886.

34. Arthur S. Hayes & Amy Stevens, Racism Is Said to Pervade New York Courts, Wall St. J., June 5, 1991, at B6.

35. Race Bias Commission Hears from Worcester, Mass. Lawyers Wkly., Oct. 14, 1991, at 3; Salvatore Arena, Racial Slam for Court, N.Y. Daily News, June 5, 1991; Jeannie Wong, Panel Hears How Minorities See Court System, Sacramento Bee, Apr. 11, 1992, at B1, B2.

36. ABA Multicultural Women Attorneys Network, The Burdens of Both, The Privileges of Neither 1 (1994).

37. Ann Davis, Big Jump in Minority Associates, But, Natl. L.J., Apr. 29, 1996, at A1.

38. Id.; American Bar Association Task Force on Minorities and the Legal Profession, Report with Recommendations (1986); Steven Keeva, Unequal Partners: It's Tough at the Top for Minority Lawyers, A.B.A.J., Feb. 1993, at 50.

39. ABA Task Force, supra note 38.

40. David B. Wilkins & G. Mitu Gulati, Why Are There So Few Black Lawyers in Corporate Law Firms, 84 U. Cal. L. Rev. 493 (1996); Committee on Minority Employment, Bar Association of San Francisco, Goals 95 Report: Goals and Timetables for Minority Hiring and Advancement (1996).

41. Ann J. Gelles, Great Expectations: Women in the Legal Profession: A Commentary on State Studies, 66 Ind. L.J. 941, 971 (1991). See also Ellen S. Podger, Lawyer Professionalism in a Gendered Society, 47 S.C. L. Rev. 323, 343 (1996); Judith Resnick, Asking About Gender in the Courts, 21 Signs 952 (1996).

42. Report of the Maine Commission on Gender, Justice, and the Courts, 49 Me. L. Rev. 135, 169-70 (1997); Lynn Hecht Schafran, Eve, Mary, and Superwoman: How Stereotypes About Women Influence Judges, 24 Judges J. 12, 15 (1985); American Bar Association Commission on Women in the Profession, Report to the House of Delegates 10 (1988); Report of the Florida Supreme Court, Gender Bias Study Commission 199 (1990).

43. See ABA Commission, supra note 42, at 10.

44. American Bar Association Commission on Women in the Profession, Unfinished Business: Overcoming the Sisyphis Factor (1995); Podger, supra note 41, at 343-441; Deborah L. Rhode, Gender and Professional Roles, 63 Fordham L. Rev. 39 (1994); Cynthia Fuchs Epstein et al., Glass Ceilings and Open Doors: Women's Advancement in the Legal Profession, 64 Fordham L. Rev. 291 (1995); Deborah L. Rhode, Myths of Meritocracy, 65 Fordham L. Rev. 585 (1996); Chris Klein, Women's Progress Slow at Top Firms, Natl. L.J., May 6, 1996, at A1.

45. Richard A. Epstein, Forbidden Grounds: The Case Against Employment Discrimination Laws 77 n.16 (1992).

46. See sources cited in note 44.

47. Victor R. Fuchs, Women's Quest for Economic Equality 3-4 (1988); Gary Becker, Human Capital 178-180 (2d ed. 1975).

48. Epstein, supra note 45, at 391.

49. See, e.g., sources cited in Deborah L. Rhode, Justice and Gender 165-167 (1989), and Speaking of Sex 6-8, 148-53 (1997).

50. See sources cited in Deborah L. Rhode, Gender and Professional Roles, 63 Fordham L. Rev. 39, 67 (1994), and ABA Commission on the Status of Women in the Profession, Fair Measure: Toward Effective Performance Evaluation (1997).

51. Deborah L. Rhode, Perspectives on Professional Women, 40 Stan. L. Rev. 1163, 1192 (1988).

52. Los Angeles County Bar Association Report on Sexual Orientation Bias, 4 S. Cal. Rev. L. & Women's Studies 295, 305 (1995).

53. Id. at 197; Report of the Council on Lesbian and Gay Men in the Legal Profession, Association of the Bar of the City of New York, 48 The Record 843, 860 (1993).

54. Los Angeles County Bar Report, supra note 52, at 341.

55. California Bar Association, Report and Recommendations Regarding Sexual Orientation Discrimination in the California Legal Profession (1996).

56. Report of the Council, supra note 53, at 854; Association of the Bar of the City of New York, Committee on Lesbians and Gay Men in the Legal Profession, Report of Findings from the Survey on Barriers and Opportunities Related to Sexual Orientation, 51 The Record 130 (1996).

57. Los Angeles County Bar Report, supra note 52, at 355.

58. Professor Gillers and New York University School of Law have produced two videotapes containing a total of 15 dramatic scenes, including the two represented in Problem 3B. Information about the videotapes can be obtained from Professor Gillers.

59. American Bar Association, Model Code of Judicial Conduct, Canon 3B(5), (6) (1990).

60. See Andrew E. Taslitz & Sharon Styles Anderson, Regulating Race, Gender, and Ethnic Bias in the Legal Profession: A Modest Proposal, The Professional Lawyer, May 1996, at 10.

61. See Brenda Jones Quick, Ethical Rules Prohibiting Discrimination by Lawyers: The Legal Profession's Response to Discrimination on the Rise, 7 Notre Dame J.L. Ethics & Pub. Poly. 5, 49, 55 (1993) (raising constitutional questions, including vagueness and overbreadth, about the proposed codes).

62. A Solid Investment: Making Full Use of the Nation's Human Capital, Recommendations of the Federal Glass Ceiling Commission (Nov. 1995); Committee on Minority Employment, supra note 40, at 27-37.

63. Judith Resnick, Ambivalence: The Resiliency of United States Legal Culture, 45 Stan. L. Rev. 1525, 1533-1534 (1993) (quoting Michigan Race/Ethnicity report).

64. James Willard Hurst, The Growth of American Law 256-284, 292-293 (1950); Robert Stevens, Law School: Legal Education in America from the 1850s to the 1980s (1983).

65. Len Yang Smith, Abraham Lincoln as a Bar Examiner, 51 Bar Examiner 35, 37 (Aug. 1982).

66. Hurst, supra note 64.

67. Rhode, Moral Character as a Professional Credential, supra note 16, at 500-502 (1985), and sources cited within.

68. American Bar Association Task Force on Law Schools and the Profession, Narrowing the Gap: Legal Education and Professional Development — An Educational Continuum (1992).

69. For representative cases, see Richardson v. McFadden, 540 F.2d 744 (4th Cir. 1976), on rehearing, 563 F.2d 1130 (4th Cir. 1977), cert. denied, 435 U.S. 968 (1978); Parrish v. Board of Commissioners of Alabama State Bar, 533 F.2d 942 (5th Cir. 1976). For bar examiners' claims that racial differences in exam performance reflect differences in law school admission standards, see Deirdre Shesgreen, Law Schools Get Their Report Cards, Legal Times, May 12, 1997, at A23. For a critical review, see David M. White, The Definition of Legal Competence: Will the Circle Be Unbroken?, 18 Santa Clara L. Rev. 641 (1978).

70. Paul Reidinger, Law Poll: Bar Exam Blues, 73 A.B.A.J. 34 (July 1987); Law Poll, 68 A.B.A.J. 544 (May 1982).

71. Soozhana Chai, How Many of Your Classmates Cheat? Natl. Justice (Nov.-Dec. 1996); Ann Davis, Graduate Debt Burden Grows, Natl. L.J., May 22, 1995, at A1, A25.

72. In re Zbiegien, 433 N.W.2d 871 (Minn. 1988) (admitting applicant who plagiarized paper due to stress and wife's illness).

73. Application of William W. Gahan, 279 N.W.2d 826 (Minn. 1979) (denying applicant whose discharge of loans suggested flagrant disregard for responsibility to other students and inability to manage finances). Compare In re Application for Certification for C.R.W., 481 S.E.2d 511 (Ga. 1997) (denying applicant who failed to make good faith effort to pay student loans); Florida Board of Bar Examiners re S.M.D., 609 So. 2d 1309 (Fla. Sup. Ct. 1992) (admitting applicant who declared bankruptcy during law school because she was unsuccessful in job search).

74. Cases discussed in Jane Gross, A Killer in Law School: Admirable or Abominable, N.Y. Times, Sept. 13, 1993, at A14, and Rhode, Moral Character, supra note 16, at 538.

75. Rhode, id. at 537-559. See also M.A. Cunningham, The Professional Image Standard: An Untold Standard of Admission to the Bar, 66 Tul. L. Rev. 1015, 1037-1039 (1992) (discussing gender, race, and class biases). See Donald H. Stone, The Bar Admission Process, Gatekeeper or Big Brother: An Empirical Study, 15 N. Ill. U.L. Rev. 331 (1995).

76. Walter Mischel & Yuichi Shoda, A Cognitive Affective Theory of Personality: Reconceptualizing Situations, Dispositions, Dynamics, and Invariance in Personality Structure, 10 Psychological Rev. 246 (1995); see sources cited in Rhode & Luban, supra note 18, at 859 n.2; and Abdon M. Pollasch, Screening Process May Become Screaming Process for Bar Applicants, Chicago Law., Sept. 1997, at 4.

77. Rhode, supra note 16, at 547-549.

78. See Law Students Civil Rights Research Council v. Wadmond, 401 U.S. 154 (1971) (rejecting due process and first amendment challenges to New York character review system but acknowledging that a "wise policy," if not constitutional mandates, might dictate reliance on disciplinary rather than screening mechanisms); Stone, Bar Admission Process, supra note 75.

79. Deborah L. Rhode, Professionalism in Perspective (1991) (in Deborah L. Rhode & David Luban, Legal Ethics 946-947 (1992)). For a comprehensive overview of problems in any system for regulating lawyers,

see David B. Wilkins, Who Should Regulate Lawyers?, 105 Harv. L. Rev. 799 (1992).

80. See, e.g., the ABA Commission on Evaluation of Disciplinary Enforcement, Report to the American Bar Association House of Delegates 23-26 (1991); Richard Abel, American Lawyers 144 (1989) (reporting that only 13 percent of surveyed clients were aware of bar disciplinary processes); Robert Fellmeth, The Discipline System of the California State Bar: An Initial Report, 7 Cal. Regulatory L. Reporter 1, 5-6 (Summer 1987) (noting bar's failure even to list phone numbers for client complaints).

81. Anthony Blackwell, Wieder's Paradox: Reporting Legal Misconduct in Law Firms, 1992-1993 Annual Survey Am. L. 9, 10 n.7; Laura Gatland, The *Himmel* Effect, A.B.A.J., Apr. 1997, at 24.

82. See Ronald D. Rotunda, The Lawyer's Duty to Report Another Lawyer's Unethical Violations in the Wake of *Himmel*, 1988 U. Ill. L. Rev. 977 (1989).

83. American Bar Association Center for Professional Responsibility and the Standing Committee on Professional Discipline, Survey on Lawyer Discipline Systems 9 (1990); HALT (Americans for Legal Reform), Attorney Discipline: National Survey and Report 1 (1990); Don J. DeBenedictis, ABA Adopts Most Discipline Proposals, 78 A.B.A.J. 28 (Apr. 1992). See sources cited in Rhode & Luban, supra note 18, at 859 n. 2.

84. ABA Commission on Evaluation of Disciplinary Enforcement, supra note 80, at 35-41; American Bar Association Commission on Professionalism, In the Spirit of Public Service: A Blue Print for the Rekindling of Lawyer Professionalism 45 (1986).

85. Fellmeth, supra note 80, at 7; HALT, supra note 83.

86. Although the bill did not pass, it helped stimulate other substantial reforms; see Rhode & Luban, supra note 79, at 953-954. For later similar legislation, see Reynolds Holding, Legislators Consider Bill to Eliminate State Bar, San Francisco Chron., July 27, 1992, at A1. For an analysis of the competing interests at issue, see Wilkins, supra note 79, at 845-847.

87. DeBenedictis, supra note 83.

88. ABA Commission on Evaluation of Disciplinary Enforcement, supra note 80, at 4.

89. Wilkins, supra note 79, at 844-847.

90. In re Holloway, 452 N.E.2d 934, 935 (Ind. 1983) (per curiam).

91. In re Moore, 453 N.E.2d 971, 974 (Ind. 1983) (per curiam).

92. District of Columbia Bar v. Kleindienst, 345 A.2d 146, 147 (D.C. 1975) (per curiam).

93. James B. Stewart Jr., The Partners (1983). See the discussion in Part E at pages 82–89 and in Chapter V (The Adversary System) at pages 195–208.

94. In re Laura Beth Lamb, 776 P.2d 765, 767 (Cal. 1989).

95. In re Holloway, 452 N.E.2d 934, 935 (Ind. 1983) (per curiam).

96. In re Moore, 453 N.E.2d 971, 974-975 (Ind. 1983) (per curiam).

97. District of Columbia Bar v. Kleindienst, 345 A.2d 146 (D.C. 1975) (per curiam).

98. In re Kleindienst, 644 P.2d 249 (Ariz. 1982).

99. See Darryl Van Lleech, Lawyers Who Abuse Could Be Disbarred, Natl. L.J., Aug. 19, 1996, at A6.

100. HALT (Americans for Legal Reform), Attorney Discipline 16 (1988).

101. Theodore Schneyer, Professional Discipline for Law Firms, 77 Cornell L. Rev. 1 (1991); Christopher D. Stone, The Place of Enterprise Liability in the Control of Corporate Conduct, 90 Yale L.J. 1, 27 (1980).

102. J.L. Bernard et al., Dangerous Liaisons, 78 A.B.A.J. 82 (Nov. 1992).

103. Id.; Jacqueline Bouhoutsos et al., Sexual Intimacy Between Psychotherapists and Patients, 14 Prof. Psychology: Research & Practice 185 (1983).

104. Bouhoutsos et al., supra note 103 (90 percent of patients reported adverse effects); see Note, Attorney-Client Sex, 92 Colum. L. Rev. 887, 920 n.175 (1992). For discussion of rules by the American Psychiatric Association and the American Psychological Association, see Sex and the Divorce Lawyer, 1 Geo. J. Legal Ethics 585, 615 (1988).

105. Drucker's Case, 577 A.2d 1198, 1199 (N.H. 1990) (finding that sexual relationship with lawyer caused client to take action in marriage that she otherwise might have avoided); Doe v. Roe, 756 F. Supp. 353, 355 (N.D. Ill. 1991) (husband breaches promise to pay wife's attorney's fees after learning of sexual relationship); In re Lehr, 583 P.2d 1157, 1158 (Or. App. 1978) (custody granted to father in part because of mother's cohabitation with lawyer).

106. Joanne Pitulla, Unfair Advantage, 78 A.B.A.J. 76 (Nov. 1992) (quoting Joseph Hurley); Bernard et al., supra note 102. See Yaet Levy, Attorneys, Clients and Sex: Conflicting Interests in the California Rule, 5 Geo. J. Legal Ethics 649 (1992).

107. See, e.g., In re Disciplinary Proceedings Against Gibson, 369 N.W.2d 695 (Wis. 1985) (bar sought disbarment for unwanted sexual advances and referee recommended 90-day suspension); Suppressed v. Suppressed, 565 N.E.2d 101 (Ill. App. 1990) (sexual relationships did not violate fiduciary obligations even though the client's consent was not knowledgeable or voluntary); United States v. Babbitt, 26 M.J. 157, 159 (C.M.A. 1986) (rejecting defendant's claim that she was denied effective assistance of counsel because she was involved in a sexual relationship with her defense attorney; a review of the record indicated that the attorney was "if anything spurred on" by the relationship); Drucker's Case, 577 A.2d 1198 (N.H. 1990) (imposing two-year suspension on lawyer who had sex with divorce client while knowing she was under psychiatric care and who subsequently terminated their affair); Doe v. Roe, 756 F. Supp. 353 (N.D. Ill. 1991), aff'd, 958 F.2d 763 (7th Cir. 1992) (dismissing RICO complaint against same lawyer involved in Suppressed v. Suppressed who threatened client with reprisals from "very 'Italian' friends" if she did not pay her bill and suggested that she work off the charges through sexual relations; under the court's analysis, since the client complied and paid her bills with sex, she suffered no federally cognizable economic loss).

108. Nancy Goldberg Wilks, Sex in the ABA: Impotent Standing Committee or the Proverbial Fox? 6 Md. J. Cont. Legal Issues 205 (1995).

109. See Rhode, supra note 16, at 546-549.

110. Id.; Cynthia Kelly, Lawyer Sanctions: Looking Back Through the Looking Glass, 1 Geo. J. Legal Ethics 469, 471 (1988).

111. Rhode, supra note 16, at 552-554.

112. Panel Allows ADA Defense for Addicted Lawyers, The Recorder, Jan. 14, 1997, at 3.

113. Michael A. Bloom & Carol Lynn Wallinger, Lawyers and Alcoholism: Is It Time for a New Approach?, 61 Temp. L.Q. 1409 (1988).

114. This problem is modeled on a similar hypothetical in Rhode & Luban, Legal Ethics, supra note 79, at 395-396.

115. James B. Stewart, Jr., Kodak and Donovan Leisure: The Untold Story, The American Lawyer, Jan. 1983, at 24, 62, excerpted from James B. Stewart, Jr., The Partners (1983).

116. Trial Transcript, Jan. 14, 1978, at 16739.

117. Walter Kiechel III, The Strange Case of Kodak's Lawyers, Fortune, May 8, 1978, at 188, 193-194.

118. Stewart, supra note 115, at 29.

119. Trial Transcript, Jan. 21, 1978, at 16742.

120. Stephen Wermiel, Lawyers' Public Image Is Dreadful, Spurring Concern by Attorneys, Wall St. J., Oct. 11, 1983, at 1.

121. Kiechel, supra note 117, at 194.

122. Steven Brill, When a Lawyer Lies, Esquire, Dec. 19, 1978, at 23.

123. Stewart, supra note 115, at 62.

124. Id.

125. Tom Goldstein, Ex-Partner in a Major Law Firm Is Spared Disbarment, N.Y. Times, July 23, 1979, at B3.

126. Id.

127. Id.

128. Stewart, supra note 115, at 62.

129. David Margolick, A Lawyer, After the Fall, San Francisco Chron., Jan. 28, 1990, at A8.

130. For a related case finding liability, see Togstad v. Vesley, Otto, Miller & Keeh, 291 N.W.2d 686 (Minn. 1980).

131. See sources cited in Rhode & Luban, supra note 79, at 886; Manuel R. Ramos, Legal Malpractice: No Lawyer or Client Is Safe, 47 Fla. L. Rev. 1, 5 (1995).

132. Standing Committee on Lawyer's Professional Liability, Characteristics of Legal Malpractice: Report of the National Malpractice Data Center 2-3 (1989); John Gibeaut, Good News, Bad News in Malpractice, A.B.A.J., Mar. 1997, at 101 (noting that vast majority of claims result in no payment and successful ones typically pay out under $10,000).

133. Ramos, supra note 131, at 5.

134. Flaherty v. Weinberg, 492 A.2d 618 (Md. 1985); Steve Gillers, Ethics That Bite: Lawyer's Liability to Third Parties, Litig., Winter 1987, at 8; John Leubsdorf, Legal Malpractice and Professional Responsibility, 48 Rutgers L. Rev. 101 (1995); Forest Bowman, Lawyer Liability to Non-Clients, 97 Dick. L. Rev. 267 (1993).

135. See Goodman v. Kennedy, 556 P.2d 737 (Cal. 1976), and cases cited in Rhode & Luban, supra note 18, at 960.

136. See sources cited in Rhode & Luban, supra note 18, at 893-894; Characteristics of Legal Malpractice, supra note 132.

137. Barbara A. Curran, The Legal Needs of the Public: The Final Report of a National Survey 190 (1977).

138. See generally Roland N. McKean, Some Economic Aspects of Ethical-Behavioural Codes, 27 Pol. Stud. 251 (1979); John Leubsdorf, Three Models of Professional Reform, 67 Cornell L. Rev. 1021 (1982); Regulating the Professions: A Public-Policy Symposium (Roger D. Blair & Stephen Rubin eds., 1980).

139. See, e.g., Florida Bar Petition to Amend the Rules Regulating the Florida Bar, Advertising Issues, 571 So. 2d 451 (Florida); Iowa Code of Professional Responsibility DR 2-101(B)(5) (1990). During the early 1990s,

about 20 states were considering restrictive advertising regulations. Jim Rossi & Mollie Weighner, An Empirical Examination of the Iowa Bar's Approach to Regulating Lawyer Advertising, 77 Iowa L. Rev. 179, 181 n.4 (1991).

140. Federal Trade Commission, Improving Consumer Access to Legal Services: The Case for Removing Restrictions on Truthful Advertising (1984).

141. Milo Geyelin, Debate Intensifies over State Regulations That Restrict TV Advertising by Lawyers, Wall St. J., Aug. 31, 1992, at B1.

142. Evelyn Nieves, Using a Feminine Edge to Open a Man's World, N.Y. Times, Nov. 28, 1995, at 13.

143. David Margolick, At the Bar, N.Y. Times, Jan. 10, 1992, at B9. See Rhode & Luban, supra note 18, at 663.

144. See Matter of Marcus, 320 N.W.2d 806, 809 (Wis. 1985).

145. Gail Diane Cox, Battle on Legal Ads Comes Down to Class, Natl. L.J., Aug. 10, 1992, at 1.

146. Lori B. Andrews, The Selling of a Precedent, 10 Student Law. 12, 49 (1982).

147. Capoccia v. Committee on Professional Standards, 1990 W.L. 21189 (N.D.N.Y. 1990); Nina Bernstein, Battles over Lawyer Advertising Divide the Bar, N.Y. Times, July 19, 1997, at A9.

148. William Forsyth, The History of Lawyers (1873); Lori Andrews, Birth of a Salesman: Lawyer Advertising and Solicitation 1 (1980); Richard Abel, American Lawyers (1989).

149. The case involved a successful challenge to Missouri regulations that narrowly limited advertising to certain specified categories of information and designated areas of practice.

150. At issue was an advertisement featuring a drawing of the Dalkon Shield, accompanied by the question, "DID YOU USE THIS IUD?" The ad stated that the device was alleged to cause certain serious complications, that the lawyers' firm was representing women with claims against the manufacturer, and that "the cases are handled on a contingent fee basis of the amount recovered. If there is no recovery, no legal fees are paid by our clients." The Court held that the state bar could impose discipline for only the last sentence of the advertisement, which did not distinguish between fees and costs and which therefore might mislead lay persons to believe they had no liability in a losing cause. 471 U.S. at 652-653. The Court also found reasonable the Ohio Supreme Court's suggestion that attorneys advertising their availability on a contingency fee basis must also disclose their rates. Id. at 653 n.15.

151. The mailing at issue was directed to individuals subject to mortgage foreclosure proceedings.

152. The attorney's letterhead stated that he was a "certified civil trial specialist by the National Board of Trial Advocacy [NBTA]." The lower court made no finding of actual deception, and because the NBTA standards were verifiable and rigorous, the Supreme Court did not find the advertisement inherently misleading despite the absence of an official state certification program.

153. Archer W. Honeycutt & Elizabeth A. Wibker, Consumers' Perceptions of Selected Issues Relating to Advertising by Lawyers, 7 J. of Prof. Services Marketing 119, 120 (1991). See Bernstein, supra note 147, at A9; William E. Hornsley Jr. & Kurt Schimmel, Regulating Lawyer Advertising: Public Images and Irresistible Aristotelian Impulses, 9 Geo. J.

Legal Ethics 325, 336-337 (1996) (87 percent of surveyed lawyers believe advertising negatively influences profession's image).

154. American Bar Association, Lawyer Advertising at the Crossroads (1994); Honeycutt & Wibker, supra note 153; Geyelin, supra note 141, at B1, B4; Diane B. MacDonald & Mary Anne Raymond, Attorney Advertising: Do Attorneys Know Their Clients? 7 J. of Prof. Services Marketing 99 (1991); Hornsley & Schimmel, supra note 153; Bernstein, supra note 147, at A9 (discussing findings that lower income consumers were most likely to believe lawyers who advertised were better).

155. Geoffrey Hazard, Jr., Russell Pearce & Jeffrey Stempel, Why Lawyers Should Be Allowed to Advertise: A Market Analysis of Legal Services, 58 N.Y.U.L. Rev. 1084 (1983).

156. For a comprehensive review of existing research, see Stewart Macaulay, Lawyer Advertising: Yes But (working paper 7-3) (Institute for Legal Studies, Madison, Wisconsin, 1985), excerpted in Rhode & Luban, Legal Ethics, supra note 79, at 673; Rossi & Weighner, supra note 139, at 224-231.

157. W. Ward Reynoldsen, The Case Against Lawyer Advertising, A.B.A.J., Jan. 1989, at 60; Rossi & Weighner, supra note 139, at 223, 253-255.

158. Honeycutt & Wibker, supra note 153, at 124; ABA Commission on Advertising, Report on the Survey on the Image of Lawyers in Advertising (Jan. 1990); Lloyd B. Snyder, Rhetoric, Evidence and Bar Agency Restrictions on Speech by Lawyers, 28 Creighton L. Rev. 3, 386 (1995).

159. Brae Conlen, Injured? Call Now, Cal. Law., Jan. 1995, at 30; Poll Shows Public Has Diminishing Respect for Attorneys, Natl. L.J., Aug. 9, 1993, at 1; Wiese Research Associates, Attorney Advertising Perceptions Study 10-11 (1994).

160. Linda Morton, Finding a Suitable Lawyer: Consumers Can't Always Get What They Want and What the Legal Profession Should Do About It, 25 U.C. Davis L. Rev. 283, 303 (1992).

161. Mark Hansen, Solicitation or Sympathy?, A.B.A.J., Sept. 1991, at 34. See also Norris v. Alabama State Bar, 582 So. 2d 1034 (Ala. 1991); Christine Biederman, Families of Crash Victims Say Lawyers Ignore Solicitation Ban, N.Y. Times, June 4, 1996, at 149 (describing flowers sent by lawyers following Valuejet aircrash).

162. Henry J. Reske, Lawyer Charged with Soliciting, A.B.A.J., Dec. 1991, at 26.

163. Part 3 of this problem draws on a related hypothetical case in Rhode & Luban, Legal Ethics, supra note 18, at 651-652.

164. See Wolfram, supra note 12, at 489-490.

165. See id. at 786 (discussing, for example, Abraham Lincoln, the Aaron Burr litigation, and the Dred Scott case); and text at note 167 infra (discussing Brown v. Board of Education).

166. Jerold S. Auerbach, Unequal Justice: Lawyers and Social Change in Modern America 43-50 (1976).

167. Deborah L. Rhode, Solicitation, 36 J. Legal Educ. 317, 325-329 (1986).

168. Federal Trade Commission, supra note 140.

Chapter IV

Advocacy

A. THE MORALITY OF ROLES

Randall Jarrell once described a college president as "so well adjusted to his environment that sometimes you could not tell which was the environment and which was President Robbins."[1] That characterization reflects an integration of identity and role that is central to debates about professional ethics.

The concept of role has both factual and moral dimensions. Social scientists use the term to describe a status carrying a distinct set of cultural expectations and obligations. According to sociologist Erving Goffman, there is no self outside of roles; in all our daily interactions we are playing some part, as parent, student, friend, employee, customer.[2] Generalizing from such patterns, some philosophers have maintained that ethical behavior requires adherence to the particular norms that are appropriate to particular roles. These defenders of "role-differentiality morality" often conclude that individuals occupying a given status cannot "do right" without "doing wrong," at least as measured by ordinary ethical principles. Thus, for example, a political or military leader confronting terrorism might justifiably employ deceptive tactics that would be ethically indefensible in other contexts.[3] The following essay by Richard Wasserstrom critically evaluates this concept of role-differentiated morality for lawyers.

RICHARD WASSERSTROM, LAWYERS AS PROFESSIONALS: SOME MORAL ISSUES

5 Human Rights 1-14 (1975)

... [The first] issue I propose to examine concerns the ways the professional-client relationship affects the professional's stance toward the world at large. The primary question that is presented is whether there is adequate justification for the kind of moral universe that comes to be inhabited by the lawyer as he or she goes through professional life. For at best the lawyer's world is a simplified moral world; often it is an amoral one; and more than occasionally, perhaps, an overtly immoral one. . . .

As I have already noted, one central feature of the professions in general and of law in particular is that there is a special, complicated relationship between the professional, and the client or patient. For each of the parties in this relationship, but especially for the professional, the behavior that is involved is to a very significant degree, what I call, role-differentiated behavior. And this is significant because it is the nature of role–differentiated behavior that it often makes it both appropriate and desirable for the person in a particular role to put to one side considerations of various sorts, and especially various moral considerations, that would otherwise be relevant if not decisive. . . .

[For example, to be a parent is,] in probably every human culture, to be involved in role-differentiated behavior. In our own culture, and once again in most, if not all, human cultures, as a parent one is entitled, if not obligated, to prefer the interests of one's own children over those of children generally. That is to say, it is regarded as appropriate for a parent to allocate excessive goods to his or her own children, even though other children may have substantially more pressing and genuine needs for these same items. . . .

It is, of course, conceivable that plausible and even thoroughly convincing arguments exist for the desirability of the role-differentiated behavior and its attendant neglect of what would otherwise be morally relevant considerations. Nonetheless, it is, I believe, also the case that the burden of proof, so to speak, is always upon the proponent of the desirability of this kind of role-differentiated behavior. . . .

Consider, more specifically, the role-differentiated behavior of the lawyer. Conventional wisdom has it that where the attorney-client relationship exists, the point of view of the attorney is properly different, and appreciably so, from that which would be appropriate in the absence of the attorney-client relationship. For where the attorney-client relationship exists, it is often appropriate and many times even obligatory for the attorney to do things that, all other things being equal, an ordinary person need not, and should not do. What is characteristic of this role of a lawyer is the lawyer's required indifference to a wide variety of ends and consequences that in other contexts would be of undeniable moral significance. Once a lawyer represents a client, the lawyer has a duty to make his or her expertise fully available in the realization of the end sought by the client, irrespective, for the most part, of the moral worth to which the end will be put or the character of the client who seeks to utilize it. Provided that the end sought is not illegal, the lawyer is, in essence, an amoral technician whose peculiar skills and knowledge in respect to the law are available to those with whom the relationship of client is established. The question, as I have indicated, is whether this particular and pervasive feature of professionalism is itself justifiable. At a minimum, I do not think any of the typical, simple answers will suffice. . . .

[T]he role-differentiated character of the lawyer's way of being tends to render irrelevant what would otherwise be morally relevant considerations. Suppose that a client desires to make a will disinheriting her children because they opposed the war in Vietnam. Should the lawyer refuse to draft the will because the lawyer thinks this is a bad reason to disinherit one's children? Suppose a client can avoid the payment of taxes through a loophole only available to a few wealthy taxpayers. Should the lawyer refuse to tell the client of a loophole because the lawyer thinks it an unfair advantage for the rich? Suppose a client wants to start a corporation that will manufacture, distribute and promote a harmful but not illegal substance, e.g., cigarettes. Should the lawyer refuse to prepare the articles of incorporation for the corporation? In each case, the accepted view within the profession is that these matters are just of no concern to the lawyer qua lawyer. The lawyer need not of course agree to represent the client (and that is equally true for the unpopular client accused of a heinous crime), but there is nothing wrong with representing a client whose aims and purposes are quite immoral. And having agreed to do so, the lawyer is required to provide the best possible assistance, without regard to his or her disapproval of the objective that is sought. . . .

More specifically, if it is correct that this is the perspective of lawyers in particular and professionals in general, is it right that this should be their perspective? Is it right that the lawyer should be able so easily to put to one side otherwise difficult problems with the answer: but these are not and cannot be my concern as a lawyer? What do we gain and what do we lose from having a social universe in which there are professionals such as lawyers, who, as such, inhabit a universe of the sort I have been trying to describe?

One difficulty in even thinking about all of this is that lawyers may not be very objective or detached in their attempts to work the problem through. For one feature of this simplified, intellectual world is that it is often a very comfortable one to inhabit.

To be sure, on occasion, a lawyer may find it uncomfortable to represent an extremely unpopular client. On occasion, too, a lawyer may feel ill at ease invoking a rule of law or practice which he or she thinks to be an unfair or undesirable one. Nonetheless, for most lawyers, most of the time, pursuing the interests of one's clients is an attractive and satisfying way to live in part just because the moral world of the lawyer is a simpler, less complicated, and less ambiguous world than the moral world of ordinary life. There is, I think, something quite seductive about being able to turn aside so many ostensibly difficult moral dilemmas and decisions with the reply: but that is not my concern; my job as a lawyer is not to judge the rights and wrongs of the client or the cause; it is to defend as best I can my client's interests. . . .

But there is, of course, also an argument which seeks to demonstrate that it is good and not merely comfortable for lawyers to behave this way.

It is good, so the argument goes, that the lawyer's behavior and concomitant point of view are role-differentiated because the lawyer qua lawyer participates in a complex institution which functions well only if the individuals adhere to their institutional roles.

For example, when there is a conflict between individuals, or between the state and an individual, there is a well-established institutional mechanism by which to get that dispute resolved. That mechanism is the trial in which each side is represented by a lawyer whose job it is both to present his or her client's case in the most attractive, forceful light and to seek to expose the weaknesses and defects in the case of the opponent.

When an individual is charged with having committed a crime, the trial is the mechanism by which we determine in our society whether or not the person is in fact guilty. Just imagine what would happen if lawyers were to refuse, for instance, to represent persons whom they thought to be guilty. In a case where the guilt of a person seemed clear, it might turn out that some individuals would be deprived completely of the opportunity to have the system determine whether or not they are in fact guilty. The private judgment of individual lawyers would in effect be substituted for the public, institutional judgment of the judge and jury. The amorality of lawyers helps to guarantee that every criminal defendant will have his or her day in court.

In addition, of course, appearances can be deceiving. Persons who appear before trial to be clearly guilty do sometimes turn out to be innocent. Even persons who confess their guilt to their attorney occasionally turn out to have lied or to have been mistaken. . . .

Nor is the amorality of the institutional role of the lawyer restricted to the defense of those accused of crimes. As was indicated earlier, when the lawyer functions in his most usual role, he or she functions as a counselor, as a professional whose task it is to help people realize those objectives and ends that the law permits them to obtain and which cannot be obtained without the attorney's special competence in the law. The attorney may think it wrong to disinherit one's children because of their views about the Vietnam war, but here the attorney's complaint is really with the laws of inheritance and not with his or her client. The attorney may think the tax provision an unfair, unjustifiable loophole, but once more the complaint is really with the Internal Revenue Code and not with the client who seeks to take advantage of it. And these matters, too, lie beyond the ambit of the lawyer's moral point of view as institutional counselor and facilitator. If lawyers were to substitute their own private views of what ought to be legally permissible and impermissible for those of the legislature, this would constitute a surreptitious and undesirable shift from a democracy to an oligarchy of lawyers. For given the fact that lawyers are needed to effectuate the wishes of clients, the lawyer ought to make his or her skills available to those who seek them without regard for the particular objectives of the client.

Now, all of this certainly makes some sense. These arguments are neither specious nor without force. . . . As I indicated earlier, I do believe that the amoral behavior of the *criminal* defense lawyer is justifiable. But I think that jurisdiction depends at least as much upon the special needs of an accused as upon any more general defense of a lawyer's role-differentiated behavior. As a matter of fact I think it likely that many persons such as myself have been misled by the special features of the criminal case. Because a deprivation of liberty is so serious, because the prosecutorial resources of the state are so vast, and because, perhaps, of a serious skepticism about the rightness of punishment even where wrongdoing has occurred, it is easy to accept the view that it makes sense to charge the defense counsel with the job of making the best possible case for the accused, without regard, so to speak, for the merits. This coupled with the fact that it is an adversarial proceeding succeeds, I think, in justifying the amorality of the criminal defense counsel. But this does not, however, justify a comparable perspective on the part of lawyers generally. Once we leave the peculiar situation of the criminal defense lawyer, I think it quite likely that the role-differentiated amorality of the lawyer is almost certainly excessive and at times inappropriate. That is to say, this special case to one side, I am inclined to think that we might all be better served if lawyers were to see themselves less as subject to role-differentiated behavior and more as subject to the demands of the moral point of view. In this sense it may be that we need a good deal less rather than more professionalism in our society generally and among lawyers in particular.

Moreover, even if I am wrong about all this, four things do seem to me to be true and important.

First, all of the arguments that support the role-differentiated amorality of the lawyer on institutional grounds can succeed only if the enormous degree of trust and confidence in the institutions themselves is itself justified. If the institutions work well and fairly, there may be good sense to deferring important moral concerns and criticisms to another time and place, to the level of institutional criticism and assessment. But the less certain we are entitled to be of either the rightness or the self-corrective nature of the larger institutions of which the professional is a part, the less apparent it is that we should encourage the professional to avoid direct engagement with the moral issues as they arise. And we are, today, I believe, certainly entitled to be quite skeptical both of the fairness and of the capacity for self-correction of our larger institutional mechanisms, including the legal system. To the degree to which the institutional rules and practices are unjust, unwise or undesirable, to that same degree is the case for the role-differentiated behavior of the lawyer weakened if not destroyed.

Second, it is clear that there are definite character traits that the professional such as the lawyer must take on if the system is to work. What is less clear is that they are admirable ones. Even if the role-differentiated amorality of the professional lawyer is justified by the virtues of the adversary system, this also means that the lawyer qua lawyer will be encouraged to be competitive rather than cooperative; aggressive rather than accommodating; ruthless rather than compassionate; and pragmatic rather than principled. . . . It is surely neither accidental nor unimportant that these are the same character traits that are emphasized and valued by the capitalist ethic, and on precisely analogous grounds. Because the ideals of professionalism and capitalism are the dominant ones without our culture, it is harder than most of us suspect even to take seriously the suggestion that radically different styles of living, kinds of occupational outlooks, and types of social institutions might be possible, let alone preferable.

Third, there is a special feature of the role-differentiated behavior of the lawyer that distinguishes it from the comparable behavior of other professionals. What I have in mind can be brought out through the following question: Why is it that it seems far less plausible to talk critically about the amorality of the doctor, for instance, who treats all patients irrespective of their moral character than it does to talk critically about the comparable amorality of the lawyer? . . .

The answer, I think, is twofold. To begin with (and this I think is the less interesting point) it is, so to speak, intrinsically good to try to cure disease, but in no comparable way is it intrinsically good to try to win every lawsuit or help every client realize his or her objective. In addition (and this I take to be the truly interesting point), the lawyer's behavior is different in kind from the doctor's. The lawyer, and especially the lawyer as advocate, directly says and affirms things. The lawyer makes the case for the client. He or she tries to explain, persuade and convince others that the client's cause should prevail. The lawyer lives with and within a dilemma that is not shared by other professionals. If the lawyer actually believes everything that he or she asserts on behalf of the client, then it appears to be proper to regard the lawyer as in fact embracing and endorsing the points of view that he or she articulates. If the lawyer does not in fact believe what is urged by way of argument, if the lawyer is only playing a role, then it appears to be proper to tax the lawyer with hypocrisy and insincerity. To be sure, actors in a play take on roles and say things that the characters, not the actors, believe. But we know it is a play and that they are actors. The law courts are not, however, theaters, and the lawyers both talk about justice and they genuinely seek to persuade. The fact that the lawyer's words, thoughts, and convictions are, apparently, for sale and at the service of the client helps us, I think, to understand the peculiar hostility which is more than occasionally uniquely directed by lay persons toward lawyers. The verbal, role-differentiated behavior of the lawyer qua advocate puts the lawyer's integrity into question in a way that distinguishes the lawyer from the other professionals.

Fourth, and related closely to the three points just discussed, even if on balance the role-differentiated character of the lawyer's way of thinking and acting is ultimately deemed to be justifiable within the system on systemic instrumental grounds, it still remains the case that we do pay a social price for that way of thought and action. For to become and to be a professional, such as a lawyer, is to incorporate within oneself ways of behaving and ways of thinking that shape the whole person. . . . In important respects, one's professional role becomes and is one's dominant role, so that for many persons at least they become their professional being. This is at a minimum a heavy price to pay for the professions as we know them in our culture, and especially so for lawyers. Whether it is an inevitable price is, I think, an open question, largely because the problem has not begun to be fully perceived as such by the professionals in general, the legal profession in particular, or by the educational institutions that train professionals.

Critiques of role morality generally take two forms. One school of thought, following lines set out in Wasserstrom, stresses the corrosive aspects of role identification. In critics' view, the submersion of self into role is particularly damaging for lawyers, whose work often rewards deception, combativeness, and insensitivity to nonclient interests. Identification with role enables individuals to detach themselves from professional actions, but this strategy comes at a cost. Philosopher Gerald Postema describes the price:

> [This detachment] in turn encourages an uncritical, uncommitted state of mind, or worse a deep moral skepticism. . . . In a large portion of his daily experience, in which [a lawyer] is acting regularly

in the moral arena, he is alienated from his own moral feelings and attitudes and indeed from his moral personality as a whole. . . . The social costs of cutting off professional deliberation and action from their sources in ordinary moral experience are even more troubling. First, cut off from sound moral judgment, the lawyer's ability to do his job well, to determine the applicable law and effectively advise his clients, is likely to be seriously affected. . . . But the lawyer who must detach professional judgment from his own moral judgment is deprived of the resources from which arguments regarding his client's legal rights and duties can be fashioned. In effect, the ideal of neutrality and detachment wars against its companion ideal of zealous pursuit of client interests. . . .

[M]ost importantly, when professional action is estranged from ordinary moral experience, the lawyer's sensitivity to the moral costs in both ordinary and extraordinary situations tends to atrophy. The ideal of neutrality permits, indeed requires, that the lawyer regard his professional activities and their consequences from the point of view of the uninvolved spectator. . . . As Bernard Williams argued, "only those who are [by practice] reluctant or disinclined to do the morally disagreeable when it is really necessary have much chance of not doing it when it is not necessary. . . . [A] habit of reluctance is an essential obstacle against the happy acceptance of the intolerance."[4]

From this perspective, role obligations should be abandoned when the moral costs of adhering to role are too great for lawyers, society, or third parties. In essence, this critique of role morality is analogous to the critique of rule utilitarianism discussed in Chapter II (Traditions of Moral Reasoning). Rule utilitarianism assumes that the greatest good for the greatest number comes from adhering to general rules even if it results in occasional injustice, just as role morality assumes that conformity with roles is generally appropriate even when it produces unjust outcomes in particular cases. Yet, as critics note, "whatever the general validity of having a certain rule [or role], if one has actually reached the point of seeing that the utility of breaking it on a certain occasion is greater than that of following it . . . then surely it would be pure irrationality not to break it."[5]

A second line of criticism emphasizes not the costs of role morality, but the possibility of distinguishing it from "ordinary" moral decision-making. As contemporary philosophers have often noted, "no one is ever an abstract moral agent."[6] Both "ordinary" morality and role-differentiated approaches assume that "persons in different circumstances and with different abilities have different obligations."[7]

Contemporary work on legal ethics has been increasingly influenced by these critiques of role morality. Some commentators advocate abandoning the concept altogether. In their view, lawyers should assess the morality of their professional conduct in the same way that they evaluate other ethical issues. Since role considerations are an inherent part of ordinary ethical analysis, there is no need or justification for retreat into a fixed set of conventions. In essence, individuals can neither deny the force of roles nor escape moral accountability for their consequences; to attempt either would be a form of what Jean-Paul Sartre called "bad faith."[8] Under an "ordinary morality" approach, a lawyer might conclude that requirements of an attorney-client relationship such as loyalty and confidentiality are presumptively justifiable, but that they should be qualified in particular cases where other morally compelling interests are implicated. For example, David Luban argues that an appeal to role is a "shorthand method of appealing to the moral reasons incorporated in that role. And these may be, must be, balanced against the moral reasons for breaking the role expressed in common morality."[9]

Consider these approaches in light of the ethical problems that arise for lawyers as advocates in civil cases. How convincing are the traditional justifications for the adversary system and the role obligations that have been associated with it? To what extent should individuals depart from conventional roles to accommodate competing moral interests?

B. THE TRADITIONAL RATIONALE AND CONTEMPORARY CHALLENGES

1. Introduction

In a celebrated 1820 divorce trial of England's Queen Caroline on charges of adultery, her defense counsel Lord Brougham offered a classic definition of the advocate's role:

> An advocate, in the discharge of his duty, knows but one person in all the world, and that person is his client. To save that client by all means and expedients, and at all hazards and costs to other persons, and, amongst them, to himself, is his first and only duty; and in performing this duty he must not regard the alarm, the torments, the destruction which he may bring upon others.[10]

Brougham's definition encompasses two central principles, often referred to as the "standard conception of the advocate's role." These principles have been described by William Simon as the principles of neutrality and partisanship. The first principle, that of neutrality,

> prescribes that the lawyer remain detached from his client's ends. The lawyer is expected to represent people who seek his help regardless of his opinion of the justice of their ends. In some cases, he may have a duty to do so; in others, he may have the personal privilege to refuse. But whenever he takes a case, he is not considered responsible for his client's purposes. . . .
>
> The second principle of conduct is partisanship. This principle prescribes that the lawyer work aggressively to advance his client's

ends. The lawyer will employ means on behalf of his client which he would not consider proper in a non-professional context even to advance his own ends. These means may involve deception, obfuscation, or delay . . . [although they are qualified by certain minimum responsibilities of lawyers] as officers of the Court.[11]

Yet American legal traditions have always included other conceptions of the advocate's role. Professional ideals have cast lawyers not simply as neutral partisans but also as public servants and moral activists, with civic as well as client obligations. And the pressures of professional practice have often led attorneys to qualify their partisanship in order to preserve their reputations and relationships with other participants in the legal process and other sources of legal business.[12]

Alternative models of advocacy have deep historical roots. Many leaders of the eighteenth- and nineteenth-century bar viewed the attorney's role as mediating between the needs of the legal order and the desires of clients. This understanding of the lawyer as civic statesman helped inspire de Tocqueville's vision of the legal profession as America's natural aristocracy, capable of checking popular passions and self-interest.[13] Similarly, many progressive era leaders echoed Louis Brandeis' assumption that attorneys should take advantage of the "opportunity in law" to promote justice through reform activity and client counseling.[14]

These competing visions of the advocacy role have long coexisted in standards governing lawyers' ethics. In the first American treatise on the subject, Maryland law professor David Hoffman argued for principles of direct moral accountability rather than neutral partisanship. "My client's conscience, and my own, are distinct entities," wrote Hoffman. "It would be dishonorable folly in me to endeavor to incorporate [any unmeritorious claim] into the jurisprudence of the country."[15]

Judge George Sharswood, the other major nineteenth-century theorist on the subject, attempted to accommodate principles of both neutral partisanship and accountability. Under his analysis, the advocate was

> not morally responsible for the act of the party in maintaining an unjust cause, nor for the error of the court . . . in deciding it in his favor. . . . The lawyer, who refuses his professional assistance because in his judgment the case is unjust and indefensible, usurps the functions of both judge and jury.[16]

Yet, somewhat inconsistently, Sharswood also argued that counsel "have an undoubted right, and are in duty bound" to refuse assistance to a plaintiff "aiming to perpetrate a wrong through the means of some advantage the law may have afforded him." And, when defending an "unrighteous" action, the advocate "may and even ought to refuse to act under instructions from his client to defeat what he believes to be an honest and just claim, by insisting upon the slips of the opposite party, by sharp practice, or special pleading. . . ."[17]

Over the last century, the principles of neutral partisanship have grown more dominant. A variety of forces have contributed to this trend, including the increased commercialism, competitiveness, and complexity of legal practice. American lawyers increasingly have found themselves in a society without a shared vision of civic virtue. According to many legal historians, "the most available redefinition of the lawyer's role, in the context of a democratic market society, was that the lawyer would do the greatest good by submitting to the will of his clients" and that attorneys' expertise should be understood as "technical" rather than "moral."[18] For most of the bar, obligations of public service became increasingly removed from daily practice, to be accommodated in separate career paths or in separate pro bono work.

Contemporary ethical codes embody neutral partisanship principles. Both the Code of Professional Conduct and the Model Rules of Professional Responsibility require zealous representation of a client's interests. See EC 7-1 and Comment, Model Rule 1.3. According to DR 7-101(A) of the Code, "[a] lawyer shall not intentionally . . . [f]ail to seek the lawful objectives of his client through reasonably available means or prejudice or damage his client during the course of the professional relationship." Model Rule 1.2 provides that a lawyer "shall abide by a client's decisions concerning the objectives of representation" and that legal assistance "does not constitute an endorsement of the client's political, economic, social or moral views or activities."

Bar rules do include some important qualifications. Neither the Code nor the Model Rules require that lawyers accept a client or cause that they find unjust, and neither authorize offensive although legal tactics. Both permit lawyers to seek the client's consent to limit the objectives of representation or to forgo actions that lawyers consider "repugnant or imprudent." Model Rule 1.2. See also DR 7-101 and Model Rule 1.3.[19] Under the Code, lawyers may withdraw from representation with client consent, or, if a matter is not pending before a tribunal, whenever a client insists on conduct contrary to their advice. DR 2-110(C). Under the Model Rules, withdrawal is permissible with consent if it can be accomplished without prejudice or if the client insists on pursuing a matter that the lawyer considers repugnant or imprudent. However, both the Code and the Model Rules also emphasize that lawyers should not decline representation because a cause is unpopular. And if lawyers do not withdraw from representation, then the client's decisions on substantive matters must prevail, and lawyers must keep confidences and pursue interests that may seriously injure innocent third parties.[20]

The following materials explore the most frequent justifications for the conventional neutral partisan role. The first justification rests on instrumental, utilitarian premises; it assumes that an adversarial clash between two advocates is the best available way to discover truth. A second rationale invokes non-instrumental, rights-based values; it assumes that partisan advocacy provides the most effective protection for individual autonomy. In many respects, these justifications parallel and overlap the arguments for an adversary system, explored more fully in Chapter V (The Adversary System). However, it bears emphasis that the vast majority of lawyers' work occurs outside the full protections of the adversary system. Over 90 percent of all civil and criminal cases are settled without trial, and most legal counseling, drafting, and negotiation proceed without the oversight of an impartial tribunal. Thus, the standard conception of the advocacy role cannot entirely depend on the arguments supporting an adversarial adjudicative process.

Nor can conventional justifications for neutral partisanship rest on the lawyer's function in criminal defense. As Wasserstram's analysis and Chapter XIV (Criminal Law and Procedure) suggest, criminal proceedings are distinctive in several respects: in their reliance on state power, their potential for governmental oppression, and their impact on individual life, liberty, and reputation. For the same reasons that our constitutional traditions impose special protections for criminal cases — practices such as proof beyond a doubt and the privilege against self-incrimination — most commentators suggest that the justifications for neutral partisanship are strongest in that context.[21] To be sure, in some civil matters, the potential for abusive power or the constraints on fundamental rights may raise concerns analogous to those at issue in criminal proceedings. While zealous advocacy has been of enormous social value in those contexts, such cases do not constitute the mainstay of legal work. And since relatively few lawyers handle criminal defense matters, the professional norms appropriate for those cases should not serve as the paradigm for all legal practice.

Accordingly, the following materials focus on advocacy in the civil context. In assessing the persuasiveness of traditional justifications for neutral partisanship, it may be helpful to consider some paradigm cases. Problems 4A to 4C summarize some widely discussed instances of morally questionable means or ends. How would you resolve them? Do current ethical rules provide appropriate guidance?

PROBLEM 4A

You are an attorney for a large Kansas City law firm that represents several major tobacco companies. Over the last three decades, the firm has represented these clients on a variety of matters, including lobbying efforts on regulatory issues, international marketing arrangements, and defense of product liability claims. This work provides about 20 percent of the firm's revenues.

A growing number of firm lawyers would like to phase out such representation entirely. Others would like to limit involvement to defense of past conduct and eliminate lobbying and marketing activities. However, attorneys who work on tobacco matters defend their role on several grounds. They claim that other products also create health problems, that every client is entitled to counsel, that smokers are aware of risks, and that tobacco companies are looking for constructive solutions to liability and regulatory issues.[22] Some lawyers, echoing a comment by Abe Fortas concerning his representation of Philip Morris, maintain that "[y]ou don't walk away from a client who is in trouble."[23] In addition, since your firm could not readily replace the volume of work supplied by tobacco clients, withdrawal from representation would result in considerable economic losses and termination of employment for some attorneys and support staff.

What position do you take? Which of the following arguments concerning the advocate's role do you find most persuasive in reaching your decision?

2. Truth

One defense of neutral partisanship principles, explored more fully in Chapter V (The Adversary System), involves their value in discovering truth and ensuring substantively correct results. Most versions of this argument presuppose an objective view of truth and assume that competitive partisan efforts are the best way to get at it. Robert Kutak, chair of the commission that drafted the Model Rules of Professional Conduct, traced this assumption to America's most fundamental social, economic, and political institutions. Our adversarial preferences reflect "the same deep-seated values we place on competition" in other contexts. We believe in "an individualistic system of judicial process for an individualistic society."[24]

As the Preamble to the Model Rules maintains, "when an opposing party is well represented, a lawyer can be a zealous advocate on behalf of a client and at the same time assume that 'justice is being done.'" If the opposing party lacks such assistance, the conventional "solution to this problem is not to impose on counsel the burden of representing interests other than those of his client, but rather to take appropriate steps to insure that all interests are effectively represented."[25]

To critics of neutral partisanship, this defense is inadequate on several grounds. The most obvious difficulty arises from the qualification acknowledged in the Model Rules' Preamble. The assumption about effective representation of all interests proceeds in

a social and economic vacuum. The conventional paradigm presupposes combatants with roughly equal incentives, resources, and capabilities. How frequently those suppositions hold is open to question in a social order that tolerates vast disparities in wealth, renders most litigation enormously expensive, and allocates civil legal assistance almost entirely through market mechanisms. Under these circumstances, one would expect that the "haves" generally come out ahead.[26]

Critics of neutral partisanship also challenge its objectivist view of truth and its formalist conception of justice. Truth is constructed, not simply discovered in legal processes. The assumption that "justice is being done" through adversarial processes confuses procedural and substantive justice. Wealth, power, and prejudice can often skew decision-making. Even if partisanship results in a rational application of law to fact, the result may be unfair because the law is itself flawed. No legal system will perfectly reflect societal values. Policy-makers may not have access to all relevant information, single-interest groups may exercise undue influence, and formal rules may be inevitably under- or overinclusive because the costs of fine-tuning are too great.

Partly in response to such criticisms, some defenders of partisan principles start from a more realistic factual premise, although they arrive at a similar conclusion. These commentators take a skeptical view of knowledge and assume that advocates have no special expertise that entitles their version of truth or justice to prevail. Whether client conduct is in fact unconscionable, fraudulent, or unduly hazardous will often be open to dispute. As Samuel Johnson put it to Boswell:

> Sir, you do not know . . . [a cause] to be good or bad till the Judge determines it. . . . An argument which does not convince yourself, may convince the Judge to whom you urge it: [A]nd if it does convince him, why then Sir, you are wrong, and he is right.[27]

To critics, it seems equally plausible that Johnson was wrong. Given all the limitations of adversarial processes noted previously and explored below, attorneys with access to confidential information and unrehearsed witnesses are often in a better position than a court to assess their clients' position. And since the vast majority of cases never reach a neutral decision-maker, lawyers' assessments, however flawed, will necessarily assume controlling significance.

As critics of neutral partisanship also note, advocates play an indispensable role in helping individuals define their interests and evaluate their options. Clients often have multiple, competing, or ambiguous goals, and one of lawyers' greatest contributions has always been assisting individuals to act in accordance with their best, not worst, instincts.[28] Thus, competent professional practice often requires evaluations of the sort skeptics renounce. Clients pay large sums for attorneys' judgments on issues such as what a statute means by "equitable" or what most courts would find to be unconscionable. Lawyers can rely on the same reasoning processes in other contexts where the morality of client conduct is at issue.

3. Rights and Relationships

A second defense of neutral partisanship invokes non-instrumental values, such as respect for individual dignity, autonomy, and relationships involving loyalty and trust. Stephen Pepper sets forth that argument:

> Our first premise is that law is intended to be a public good which increases autonomy. The second premise is that increasing individual autonomy is morally good. The third step is that in a highly legalized society such as ours, autonomy is often dependent upon access to the law. Put simply, first-class citizenship is dependent on access to the law. And while access to law . . . is formally available to all, in reality it is available only through a lawyer. . . .
>
> For the lawyer to have moral responsibility for each act he or she facilitates, for the lawyer to have a moral obligation to refuse to facilitate that which the lawyer believes to be immoral, is to substitute lawyers' beliefs for individual autonomy and diversity. Such a screening submits each to the prior restraint of the judge/facilitator and to rule by an oligarchy of lawyers. . . . If [a client's] conduct is sufficiently "bad," it would seem that it ought to be made explicitly unlawful. If it is not that bad, why subject the citizenry to the happenstance of the moral judgment of the particular lawyer to whom each has access? If making the conduct unlawful is too onerous because the law would be too vague, or it is too difficult to identify the conduct in advance, or there is not sufficient social or political concern, do we intend to delegate to the individual lawyer the authority for case-by-case legislation and policing?[29]

★ good argument

Under this standard defense of neutral partisanship, respect for clients' autonomy implies respect for clients' rights to pursue legal actions. That respect is necessary even when such actions do not conform to lawyers' own ethical principles, or when the client is not someone whom the lawyer finds morally sympathetic. Any alternative principle would be "equivalent to saying that saints must have a monopoly of lawsuits" and that lawyers should have a monopoly of deciding who qualifies for sainthood.[30] Since lawyers have no special expertise on ethical matters, their role, as Clarence Darrow once summarized it, is "not to judge a man . . . [but to] defend him."[31]

Advocates' neutral partisan role thus encourages crucial assistance to unsympathetic clients and essential protection to an attorney who defends them. The promise of nonjudgmental advocacy may encourage legal consultation by those most in need of ethical counseling. And while lawyers may not impose their personal morality, their advice may include moral as well as legal considerations. To defenders of neutral partisanship, any risk that counsel will help some clients pursue unethical objectives is offset by the prospect that other clients will be deterred. By absolving lawyers from account-ability for their clients' acts, the traditional advocacy role also encourages representation of those most vulnerable to public preju-dice and state oppression. Our history provides ample illustration of the social and economic sanctions directed at attorneys with un-popular clients. Consider how much worse it would have been for counsel in early southern civil rights litigation or in McCarthy era persecutions without the claim that attorneys' representation is not an endorsement of client conduct.[32]

A second, somewhat related, claim is that lawyers' own auton-omy and individuality entitle them to give special weight to the interests of clients with whom they have personal relationships. In a well-known article on the "Lawyer as Friend," Charles Fried devel-ops this metaphor as a justification for the lawyer's neutral partisan role.

CHARLES FRIED, THE LAWYER AS FRIEND: THE MORAL FOUNDATIONS OF THE LAWYER-CLIENT RELATION

85 Yale L.J. 1060-1062, 1070-1088 (1976)

. . . [It] is not only consonant with, but also required by, an ethics for human beings that one be entitled first of all to reserve an area of concern for oneself and then to move out freely from that area if one wishes to lavish that concern on others to whom one stands in concrete, personal relations. Similarly, a person is entitled to enjoy this extra measure of care from those who choose to bestow it upon him without having to justify this grace as either just or efficient. We may choose the individuals to whom we will stand in this special relation, or they may be thrust upon us, as in family ties. . . . In explicating the lawyer's relation to his client, my analogy shall be to friendship, where the freedom to choose and to be chosen expresses our freedom to hold something of ourselves in reserve, in reserve even from the universalizing claims of morality. These personal ties and the claims they engender may be all-consuming, as with a close friend or family member, or they may be limited, special-purpose claims, as in the case of the client or patient. The special-purpose claim is one in which the beneficiary, the client, is entitled to all the special consideration *within* the limits of the relationship which we accord to a friend or a loved one. . . .

SPECIAL-PURPOSE FRIENDS

How does a professional fit into the concept of personal relations at all? He is, I have suggested, a limited-purpose friend. A lawyer is a friend in regard to the legal system. He is someone who enters into a personal relation with you, not an abstract relation as under the concept of justice. That means that like a friend he acts in your interests, not his own; or rather he adopts your interests as his own. I would call that the classic definition of friendship. . . .

The lawyer-client relation is a personal relation, and legal counsel is a personal service. This explains directly why, *once the relation has been contracted*, considerations of efficiency or fair distribution cannot be allowed to weaken it. The relation itself is not a creature of social expediency (though social circumstances provide the occasion for it); it is the creature of moral right, and therefore expediency may not compromise the nature of the relation. This is true in medicine because the human need creates a relation of dependence which it would be a betrayal to compromise. In the lawyer-client relation, the argument is more complex but supports the same conclusion. The relation must exist in order to realize the client's rights against society, to preserve that measure of autonomy which social regulation must allow the individual. But to allow social considerations, even social regulations, to limit and compromise what by hypothesis is an entailment of the original grant of right to the individual is to take away with the left hand what was given with the right. Once the relation has been taken up, it is the client's needs which hold the reins, legally and morally.

So much for the integrity of the relation once it has taken hold. But what of the initial choice of client? Must we not give some thought to efficiency and relative need at least at the outset, and does this not run counter to the picture of purely discretionary choice implicit in the notion of friendship? The question is difficult, but before considering its difficulties we should note that the preceding argumentation has surely limited its impact. We can now affirm that whatever the answer to this question, the individual lawyer does a morally worthy thing whomever he serves and, moreover, is bound to follow through once he has begun to serve. In this he is like the doctor. . . .

Must the lawyer expend his efforts where they will do the most good, rather than where they will draw the largest fee, provide the most excitement, prove most flattering to his vanity, whatever? Why must he? If the answer is that he must because it will produce the most good, then we are saying to the lawyer that he is merely a scarce resource. But a person is not a resource. He is not bound to lead his life as if he were managing a business on behalf of an impersonal body of stockholders called human society. It is this monstrous conception against which I argued earlier. Justice is not all; we are entitled to reserve a portion of our concern and bestow it where we will. We may bestow it entirely at our discretion as in the case of friendship, or we may bestow it at what I would call "constrained discretion" in the choice and exercise of a profession. That every exercise of the profession is morally worthwhile is already a great deal to the lawyer's credit. Just as the principle of liberty leaves one morally free to choose a profession according to inclination, so within the profession it leaves one free to organize his life according to inclination. The lawyer's liberty, moral liberty, to take up what kind of practice he chooses and to take up or decline what clients he will is an aspect of the moral liberty of self to enter into personal relations freely.

I would not carry this idea through to the bitter end. It has always been accepted, for instance, that a court may appoint an available lawyer to represent a criminal defendant who cannot otherwise find counsel. Indeed, I would be happy to acknowledge the existence of some moral duty to represent any client whose needs fit one's particular capacities and who cannot otherwise find counsel. [However] . . . this kind of representation should always be compensated, [since] the duty to the client who cannot afford representation is initially a duty of society, not of the individual lawyer. . . .

Immoral Means

. . . I come to what seems to me one of the most difficult dilemmas of the lawyer's role. It is illustrated by the lawyer who is asked to press the unfair claim, to humiliate a witness, to participate in a distasteful or dishonorable scheme. I am assuming that in none of these situations does the lawyer do anything which is illegal or which violates the ethical canons of his profession; the dilemma arises if he acts in a way which seems to him personally dishonorable, but there are no sanctions, legal or professional, which he need fear. . . . But here we have a specific victim as well as a specific beneficiary. The relation to the person whom we deceive or abuse is just as concrete and human, just as personal, as to the friend whom we help. . . .

It is not wrong but somewhat lame to argue that the lawyer like the client has autonomy. From this argument it follows that the lawyer who is asked to do something personally distasteful or immoral (though perfectly legal) should be free either to decline to enter into the relationship of "legal friendship" or to terminate it. And if the client can find a lawyer to do the morally nasty but legally permissible thing for him, then all is well, the complexities of the law have not succeeded in thwarting an exercise of autonomy which the law was not entitled to thwart. So long as the first lawyer is reasonably convinced that another lawyer can be found, I cannot see why he is less free to decline the morally repugnant case than he is the boring or poorly paid case. True, but lame, for one wants to know not whether one *may* refuse to do the dirty deed, but whether one is morally *bound* to refuse, bound to refuse even if he is the last lawyer in town and no one else will bail him out of his moral conundrum.

If personal integrity lies at the foundation of the lawyer's right to treat his client as a friend, then surely consideration for personal integrity, his own and others', must limit what he can do in friendship. Consideration for personal integrity forbids me to lie, cheat, or humiliate, whether in my own interests or those of a friend, so surely they prohibit such conduct on behalf of a client, one's legal friend. This is the general truth, but it must be made more particular if it is to do service here. For there is an opposing consideration. Remember, the lawyer's special kind of friendship is occasioned by the right of the client to exercise his full measure of autonomy within the law. This suggests that one must not transfer uncritically the whole range of personal moral scruples into the arena of legal friendship. After all, not only would I not lie or steal for myself or my friends, I probably also would not pursue socially noxious schemes, foreclose on widows or orphans, or assist in the avoidance of just punishment. So we must be careful lest the whole argument unravel on us at this point.

Balance and structure are restored if we distinguish between kinds of moral scruples. Think of the soldier. If he is a citizen of a just state, where foreign policy decisions are made in a democratic way, he may well believe that it is not up to him to question whether the war he fights is a just war. But he is personally bound not to fire dum-dum bullets, not to inflict intentional injury on civilians, and not to abuse prisoners. These are personal wrongs, wrongs done by his person to the person of the victim. So also, the lawyer must distinguish between wrongs that a reasonably just legal system permits to be worked by its rules and wrongs which the lawyer personally commits. . . .

Consider the difference between humiliating a witness or lying to the judge on one hand, and on the other hand, asserting the statute of limitations or the lack of a written memorandum to defeat what you know to be a just claim against your client. In the latter case, if an injustice is worked, it is worked because the legal system not only permits it, but also defines the terms and modes of operation. Legal institutions have created the occasion for your act. What you do is not personal; it is a formal, legally-defined act. But the moral quality of lying or abuse obtains both without and within the context of the law. Therefore, my general notion is that a lawyer is morally entitled to act in this formal, representative way even if the result is an injustice, because the legal system which authorizes both the injustice (e.g., the result following the plea of the statute of limitations) and the formal gesture for working it insulates him from personal moral responsibility. I would distinguish between the lawyer's own wrong and the wrong of the system used to advantage by the client. . . .

Critics of neutral partisanship challenge these arguments on several grounds. Some take issue with the friendship analogy. For example, William Simon argues:

[T]he classical notion of friendship includes a number of other qualities foreign to the relation Fried describes. These missing qualities
include affection, admiration, intimacy and vulnerability. On the
other hand, if Fried's definition is amplified to reflect the qualification . . . that the lawyer adopts the client's interests *for money*, it becomes apparent that Fried has described the classical notion, not of
friendship, but of prostitution.[33]

According to Simon, the "dominant conception of the lawyer's professional responsibility," which underpins Fried's defense of neutral
partisanship, erodes the connections "between the practical tasks of
lawyering and the value of justice that ultimately undergird the
lawyer's role."[34] Other commentators, more sympathetic to the
friendship analogy, deny that it supports neutral partisanship.
Philosopher Susan Wolf argues that "if one adopts some interests as
one's own, it would seem one becomes to that extent personally
accountable for them."[35] If there are individuals we would not choose
as a friend, and acts we would not commit in a friend's behalf, the
same should be true for lawyers and clients. How would defenders of
neutral partisanship respond? How would you?

Other commentators raise more general objections to rights-
based justifications for neutral partisanship. The first has to do with
the importance of autonomy. In one of the most extensive and sophisticated treatments of this issue, David Luban argues that the
standard defense of neutral partisanship blurs the distinction between the "desirability of people acting autonomously and the desirability of their autonomous act." It may be "desirable . . . for me to
make my own decisions about whether to lie to you; it is . . . undesirable for me to lie to you." Autonomy, Luban argues, has no
intrinsic value; rather, its importance derives from the values it
fosters, such as authenticity, creativity, and responsibility. If a
particular client objective does not, in fact, promote those values, or
does so only at much greater cost to third parties, then a lawyer's
assistance is not morally justifiable.[36]

Other commentators, while acknowledging autonomy to be a
significant value in itself, deny that it should be the preeminent
consideration where broader societal interests are at issue. Why, for
example, should we give ethical priority to a client's autonomous
desire to maximize profits through environmentally risky, but
imperfectly regulated, methods? A related claim is that many ethical
dilemmas for lawyers arise in contexts that involve the autonomy of
third parties as well as clients. Why clients' interests should remain
paramount requires some further justification, particularly where
the client is an organization rather than an individual. As critics of
Fried's article suggest, it is far easier to defend neutral partisanship
principles when the lawyer appears as a "protector of the persecuted
rather than friend of the finance company."[37] Yet, it is scarcely

self-evident that concerns of human dignity and autonomy are best served by lawyers' undivided commitment to organizational objectives, whatever the consequences to individual third parties such as victims of unjust or hazardous activities.

A further difficulty with rights-based justifications of neutral partisanship is that they collapse legal and moral entitlements. Such justifications assume that clients have a right to do what the law fails to prohibit. Yet some conduct that would generally be condemned may remain legal because adequate prohibitions appear too difficult or expensive to enforce, or because decision-making bodies are too uninformed, overextended, or co-opted by special interests to make socially optimal choices.[38]

Critics of neutral partisanship also believe that lawyers can recognize instances in which legal and moral rights diverge. Although attorneys may have no special expertise on moral issues, they may also have a somewhat more disinterested perspective than clients on the ethical dimensions of certain conduct. Moreover, to accept moral responsibility is not necessarily to impose it. Unless the lawyer is the last in town, his or her refusal to aid particular actions will not necessarily preempt a client's autonomous choice. It may simply prompt reevaluation or exact the psychological and financial costs of finding alternative counsel.

So too, as critics note, the neutral partisan's agnosticism is highly selective. When regulation involving their own conduct is at issue, attorneys generally have no difficulty in determining where the "public interest" lies. Indeed, the organized bar has often sought exclusive authority to resolve value-laden questions, such as whether a client's desire for confidentiality should trump other societal interests, or whether lawyers should be accountable for assisting conduct that injures third parties.

From critics' vantage, the question then is not by what right do lawyers impose their moral views, but by what right should they evade the responsibility of all individuals for the moral consequences of their decisions? As the discussion of skepticism and relativism in Chapter II makes clear, a belief that ethical judgments are subjective or open to dispute does not establish that suspending judgment is the appropriate response. Even assuming that there are no objectively valid moral decisions, it does not follow that all views are equally valid. Some positions are more coherent, free of bias or self-interest, supported by reliable evidence, and so forth. Lawyers often can and should act on the basis of their own principled convictions even when they recognize that others could in good faith hold different views.

How would you evaluate these arguments for and against neutral partisanship? Do you find Fried's friendship analogy convincing?

See Chapter XI, Constitutional Law
   • The Advocate's Role in the Pursuit of Principles:
      Unpopular Positions and Constitutional Values
         (pages 459–466)

See also Chapter XII, Contracts
   • The Morality of Roles: Formal Justice and Substantive
      Justice
         (page 516)

See also Chapter XIII, Corporate Law
   • Lawyer's Obligations in Banking Contexts
      (Problem 13G, pages 582–587)

C. ALTERNATIVE VISIONS

1. Introduction

Most alternative models of the advocate's role reject neutrality and partisanship as preeminent norms. These frameworks generally begin from the premise that lawyers should accept moral accountability for the consequences of their professional acts and that obligations to clients may need to be qualified by other values.

In other respects, such proposals vary considerably. Some, like Rhode's and Postema's frameworks, remain at a fairly general level and suggest that attorneys, like any individuals making moral judgments, should seek consistent, disinterested, and generalizable foundations for conduct.[39] Roger Cramton, following Lon Fuller, argues that lawyers' primary obligation is not to clients, but to the integrity of the "procedures and institutions of the law."[40]

Other commentators have been more specific. Murray Schwartz argues that in civil matters where a neutral arbiter is absent, advocates should refrain from unconscionable means and ends.[41] Similarly, David Luban proposes that lawyers should be allowed to forgo immoral tactics or the pursuit of unjust ends without withdrawing from a case. His model of advocacy would include four restrictions:

   (1) on modes of practice that inflict morally unjustifiable damage
        on other people, especially innocent people;
   (2) on deceit, i.e., actions that obscure truths or that lure people
        into doing business under misapprehensions, even if these
        are legally permissible;
   (3) on manipulations of morally defensible law to achieve out-
        comes that negate its [purpose] or violate its spirit, and, . . .
   (4) on the pursuit of substantively unjust results.[42]

William Simon argues for a contextual approach in which lawyers exercise ethical discretion to promote justice.[43] One distinctive aspect of Simon's decision-making structure is that it is grounded in the values of the system itself. Consider the arguments for such an alternative, as set forth in the excerpt below. Do you find this model more justifiable than the standard conception of neutral partisanship?

WILLIAM H. SIMON, ETHICAL DISCRETION IN LAWYERING

101 Harv. L. Rev. 1083, 1083-1084, 1090-1109 (1988)

Lawyers should have ethical discretion to refuse to assist in the pursuit of legally permissible courses of action and in the assertion of potentially enforceable legal claims. This discretion involves not a personal privilege of arbitrary decision, but a professional duty of reflective judgment. One dimension of this judgment is an assessment of the relative merits of the client's goals and claims and those of other people who might benefit from the lawyer's services. Another is an attempt to reconcile the conflicting considerations that bear on the internal merits of the client's goals and claims. In both dimensions, the basic consideration should be whether assisting the client would further justice. . . .

THE DISCRETIONARY APPROACH

The basic maxim of the approach I propose is this: The lawyer should take those actions that, considering the relevant circumstances of the particular case, seem most likely to promote justice. This "seek justice" maxim suggests a kind of noncategorical judgment that might be called pragmatist, ad hoc, or dialectical, but that I will call discretionary. "Discretionary" is not an entirely satisfactory term; I do not mean to invoke its connotations of arbitrariness or nonaccountability, but rather its connotations of flexibility and complexity. . . .

In the context of professional responsibility, lawyers tend to be skeptical that judgments applying abstract ideals to particular cases could be anything but arbitrary. Yet lawyers also tend to regard discretionary judgment as plausible in the context of the judicial role. The kind of complex, flexible judgment proposed here has been extensively defended against more categorical styles in some of the best-known literature of judicial decisionmaking. Although this portrayal has been challenged, it has gained wide acceptance, even among lawyers hostile to this style of decision in legal ethics.

Another pertinent context in which lawyers have been relatively willing to accept the possibility of meaningful discretionary judgment is that of the public prosecutor. Indeed, my formulation of the basic maxim of the discretionary approach has been partly inspired by the maxim the Code prescribes for the prosecutor: "The responsibility of a public prosecutor differs from that of the usual advocate; his duty is to seek justice, not merely to convict."

To propose a style of ethical judgment for private lawyers analogous to that familiarly associated with judges or prosecutors is not to say that lawyers should act as if they were judges or prosecutors. The analogy is to the style of judgment, not necessarily to the particular decisions that judges and prosecutors make. The discretionary approach incorporates much of the traditional lawyer role, including the notion that lawyers can serve justice through zealous pursuit of clients' goals. Although it assumes a public dimension to the lawyer's role as well, that dimension is grounded in the lawyer's age-old claim to be an "officer of the court" and in notions about the most effective integration of the lawyering role with other roles in the legal system.

There are two dimensions to the judgment that the discretionary approach requires of the lawyer. The first is an assessment of the relative merits of the client's goals and claims and the goals and claims of others whom the lawyer might serve. The second is an effort to confront and resolve the competing factors that bear on the internal merits of the client's goals and claims.

Relative Merit

Neither of the dominant approaches adequately confronts a central fact about the legal system: Most people are unable to enforce most of their rights most of the time. An important reason is that enforcement requires resources, and the most important resource is professional assistance. The problem is not simply the bar's failure to live up to its professed commitment to provide assistance to those who cannot afford it. At any plausible level of expanded pro bono activity, the problem would remain, because hardly anyone in the society would want to devote the resources needed to bring us even close to a state in which rights could be generally enforced. Thus, legal services are necessarily a scarce resource. . . .

In deciding whether to commit herself to a client's claims and goals, a lawyer should assess their merits in relation to the merits of the claims and goals of others whom she might serve. The criteria the lawyer should employ in making this assessment are suggested by the bases of legal concern about the distribution of services: the extent to which the claims and goals are grounded in the law, the importance of the interests involved, and the extent to which the representation would contribute to the equalization of access to the legal system.

Of course, merit cannot be the only consideration to determine how the lawyer allocates her efforts. The lawyer's financial interests are also necessarily important. But the financial considerations that tacitly determine the distribution of legal services under the dominant approaches are substantially arbitrary in relation to the most basic goals of the legal system, those concerning legal merit. Lawyers can mitigate the tendency of the market to produce an inappropriate distribution of legal services by integrating considerations of relative merit into their decisions about whom to represent and how to do so. In making such judgments, lawyers will have to balance their legitimate financial concerns with their commitment to a just distribution of legal services. A lawyer who cannot refuse to assist a particular client without impairing her ability to earn a reasonable income may have to compromise her judgments of relative merit more than one who can say no without great financial sacrifice. It may or may not be desirable for the bar to prescribe collectively how individual lawyers should strike this balance. The minimum that the discretionary approach requires is that the lawyer try in good faith to take account of relative merit in her decisions.

The type of considerations urged here simply extends to conventional practice the kind of judgments many lawyers now make in pro bono practice. Lawyers who do pro bono work usually choose cases in accordance with some estimate of the relative merits of the claims competing for their services. The judgments made in pro bono practice illustrate the possibility of judgments of relative merit, and they show that financial considerations do not invariably swamp ethical ones in practice. However, the limitation of this type of ethical discretion to the pro bono sphere is arbitrary. A client's ability to pay is not an irrelevant consideration, but there is no reason why it should preclude all assessment of relative merit.

In 1985, Covington & Burling, the Washington D.C. law firm, decided to stop representing the government-owned South African Airways. . . . Let us assume, as seems quite likely, that South African Airways [was] implicated in the South African system of racial subordination in a variety of ways: through its employment and customer practices in South Africa, through its contribution to an international network of businesses that enriches South Africa and strengthens the current regime, and through its participation in the United States in public relations efforts that promote or apologize for South Africa's racial policies. Let us further assume that although the representation in question [did] not directly involve defending South African racism, it [made] no contribution to alleviating it either.

Given these assumptions, the airline's request for representation even in conventional business matters should have had a low priority.

Internal Merit

The second aspect of the lawyer's assessment of merit involves an attempt to reconcile the conflicting legal values implicated directly in the client's claim or goal. These conflicts usually arise in the form of the overlapping tensions between substance and procedure, purpose and form, and broad and narrow framing. . . .

Substance Versus Procedure . . .

The basic response of the discretionary approach to the substance-procedure tension is this: the more reliable the relevant procedures and institutions, the less direct responsibility the lawyer need assume for the substantive justice of the resolution; the less reliable the procedures and institutions, the more direct responsibility she need assume for substantive justice. . . .

Consider a case in which the breakdown arises from incapacity on the part of official institutions. Suppose an experienced tax practitioner has conceived a new tax avoidance device. She herself is convinced that it is improper, but there is a nonfrivolous argument for its legality. The lawyer might believe that the Internal Revenue Service and the courts are best situated to resolve such questions. She might reason that the agency and the courts have greater expertise than she, that they are better able to resolve issues in a way that can be uniformly applied to similar cases, and that they are subject to various democratic controls. However, such arguments are plausible only to the extent that the agency and the courts *will in fact make an informed decision on the matter*. The arguments do not warrant the lawyer using the device in a case where the agency and the courts will never effectively review it. This might happen because the agency lacks sufficient enforcement resources to identify the issue or to take the matter to court. In such a situation, the lawyer should respond to the procedural failure. She can do so by trying to remedy it, for example, by bringing the issue to the attention of the IRS. If that course is not possible (for example, because the client will not permit it), or if it will not be sufficient to remedy the procedural deficiencies (for example, because the agency is so strapped that it cannot even respond to such signals), then the lawyer has to assume more direct responsibility for the substantive resolution. If she thinks that the device should be held invalid, she should refuse to assist with it. In these circumstances, she is the best situated decisionmaker to pass on the matter.

Purpose Versus Form

Part of the substance versus procedure tension could be considered a special variation of the purpose versus form tension. When the lawyer impeaches a witness she knows to be truthful, when she objects to hearsay she knows to be accurate, when she puts the opposing party to proof on a matter the client has no legitimate interest in disputing, she takes advantage of procedural rules designed to promote accurate, efficient decisionmaking in a way that frustrates this purpose. When judges apply rules, we expect them to take account of the purposes underlying the rules. But the judge often lacks sufficient knowledge to determine whether the relevant purposes would be served by applying the rules. The lawyer, however, often does have sufficient knowledge to do so. . . .

The discretionary approach responds to the purpose versus form tension in terms of the following maxim: the clearer and less problematic the relevant purposes, the more the lawyer should consider herself bound by them; the less clear and more problematic the relevant purposes, the more justified the lawyer is in treating the relevant norms formally. Treating them formally means understanding them to permit any client goal not plainly precluded by their language. "Problematic" purposes are purposes that pose an especially grave threat to fundamental legal values . . . [such as] civil burdens on constitutional rights. Other kinds of purposes that have been considered problematic include those of transferring wealth to or conferring economic power on powerful interest groups. . . .

. . . [C]onsider a case in which the relevant purpose is [not entirely clear or unproblematic]. The client is a public assistance recipient under the Aid to Families with Dependent Children program. She and her child live, rent-free, in a home owned by her cousin. Under the applicable regulations, the receipt of lodging "at no cost" is considered "income in kind" that requires a reduction of about $150 in the welfare grant. The lawyer has to decide whether to recommend that the client make a nominal payment of, say, five dollars to the cousin so that she would no longer be receiving lodging "at no cost," and thus avoid the $150 reduction in her grant.

Again, assume that some institutional failure requires that the lawyer take some responsibility for the substantive merits. Upon examination, she is unable to come up with a sense of legislative purpose as clear and coherent as the one involved in the tax case. On the other hand, the benefit reduction seems designed to reflect the lesser needs of people who live rent free, and the fact that the provision could be effectively nullified by the type of financial planning in question suggests that such planning was not contemplated. On the other hand, nothing in the language of the regulation suggests an intention to preclude such planning, although it would have been simple enough to do so by providing for a benefit reduction in cases of low rent payments. . . . In this situation, the lawyer has no clear sense of which course of action would be most consistent with legislative purpose. It is thus proper for her to treat the regulation formally. . . .

Broad Versus Narrow Framing

This tension arises as ethical issues are defined. If we define an issue narrowly in terms of a small number of characteristics of the parties and their dispute, it will often look different than if we define it to encompass the parties' identities, relationship, and social circumstances. On the one hand, legal ideals encourage narrow definition of legal disputes in order to limit the scope of state intrusion into the lives of private citizens and to conserve scarce legal resources. On the other hand, making rights enforcement effective and meaningful often seems to require broadening the definition of disputes. . . .

The discretionary approach gives individual lawyers substantial responsibility for determining whether broad or narrow framing is appropriate in the particular case. It suggests that the lawyer should frame ethical issues in accordance with three general standards of relevance. First, a consideration is relevant if it is implicated by the most plausible interpretation of the applicable law. Issues tend to be defined more narrowly under legal norms that regulate narrowly. For example, traffic laws suggest narrower framing than family laws. Second, a consideration is relevant if it is likely to have a substantial practical influence on the resolution. Issues tend to be defined more narrowly to the extent that the parties are situated so that substantively irrelevant factors are not likely to influence the resolution. Equality of resources and of access to information are among the more important factors weighing toward narrow definition under this second standard. Third, knowledge and institutional competence will affect the appropriate framing. More broadly framed issues tend to require more knowledge and more difficult judgments. When the lawyer lacks needed knowledge or competence, narrow framing becomes more appropriate.

These alternative models of advocacy have been criticized as too demanding or not demanding enough, and as promising a too significant or too insignificant departure from existing standards. Defenders of current partisanship norms question whether clients would continue to place the same reliance on lawyers who had divided allegiance. Critics of those existing norms also wonder whether significant change would come from attempting to alter the ideology of advocacy as long as social and economic pressures reinforce client loyalty. As is clear from the materials on moral psychology in Chapter I, situational influences play a major role in shaping ethical attitudes and conduct. Demands that lawyers assume moral accountability for their actions may not significantly alter conduct where lawyers feel pressure to identify with client objectives.[44]

Questions have also been raised about proposals like Simon's, which rely on current legal standards as the benchmark for ethical decision-making. How satisfactory will such proposals be where the standards themselves are unjust or inadequate? Consider, for example, the welfare case that Simon discusses. Suppose that legislative history indicated that rental payments below market value would not be sufficient to avoid a reduction in benefits. However, the statutory language did not so provide. Nor did the lawyer believe that the client's grant before any reduction was anywhere near adequate to provide for her family's basic needs, including the special demands of a disabled child. Does Simon's approach suggest a satisfactory resolution?

At a later point in his article, Simon suggests that some lawyers might argue that

> a norm of minimal subsistence income is so fundamental that it amounts to a precondition of legal legitimacy. Such a lawyer might reason that a core value of legality is the autonomy of the individual and that a person who lacked minimal material subsistence would be so dependent and debilitated that she would be incapable of exercising the autonomy that legality aspires to safeguard. In this way, the lawyer might conclude that this value is fundamental and hence that norms that violate it are not entitled to respect. [Under such circumstances] . . . the lawyer needs to consider whether the lawyering role allows her nullifying powers of the sort commonly imputed to the roles of prosecutor, jury, and judge, and, less commonly, private citizen [through civil disobedience].[45]

Does this suggest that an advocate could exercise ethical discretion to help a client violate any welfare provision, subject only to concerns about getting caught? Are there differences in kind or only in degree between actions such as filing papers that knowingly misrepresent a client's assets or interpreting welfare regulations contrary to their purpose? Is there also a distinction between powers of nullification when exercised privately by an attorney or publicly by a judge, juror, prosecutor, or political activist whose conduct is subject to review? If so, what follows from such distinctions? Under what, if any circumstances, would you exercise "nullifying powers"? Consider one of Simon's other examples — lawyers in the era preceding no-fault divorce who assisted couples in fabricating evidence that would satisfy one of the limited grounds for divorce (such as adultery or physical cruelty).[46] Would you defend or engage in such conduct?

As a general matter, do you find any of these alternatives of advocacy more helpful than neutral partisanship principles in resolving the ethical issues raised by Problems 4A, 4B, and 4C? In Rameau's Nephew, the famous eighteenth-century French philosopher Denis Diderot claimed that "the job is worth what the man is worth and in the end vice versa. . . . So we make the job worth as much as we can." If that is our objective, how should we define our professional role?

2.   Moral Principles and Unpopular Positions

PROBLEM 4B

1. Your law firm specializes in representing women in divorce cases. A man whom you refused to represent on divorce related issues filed a complaint with the Massachusetts Commission Against Discrimination. He argues that the firm has violated the state's public accommodation law, which prohibits discrimination based on various factors, including sex, by "any place which is open to and accepts or solicits patronage of the general public."

The Commission has ruled in the man's favor and imposed a $5,000 fine. How do you proceed? Do the merits of the case matter? Is it relevant that the complainant was the primary caretaker of the couple's children? If you were a member of the state bar commission on bias in the profession, what position would you take on such issues? Would you view decisions based on race the same as those based on sex?[47]

2. You are an attorney with the Illinois office of the American Civil Liberties Union. Your office has been asked to represent the American Nazi party in its efforts to parade through a predominantly Jewish suburb of Chicago. Many ACLU members adamantly oppose accepting the case. As they note, such an exercise of first amendment principles would cause enormous pain to the Holocaust survivors and families of victims living in the area. Given the scarcity of organizational resources, why should the ACLU "defend the free speech rights of would-be tyrants [who would] . . . crush free speech rights the moment they get power"?[48] Since large numbers of ACLU members are prepared to resign if the office takes the case, such a decision would further restrict resources. How would you vote on whether to accept representation of the Nazis?[49]

3. You are the chair of the board of the Port Arthur, Texas branch of the NAACP. Anthony Griffin is an African-American lawyer who serves as your organization's general counsel. Griffin is also a cooperating attorney for the American Civil Liberties Union, and in that capacity he has agreed to represent Michael Lowe, the Grand Dragon of the Texas Ku Klux Klan. Lowe is challenging efforts by the Texas Commission on Human Rights to compel disclosure of Klan membership lists.[50]

The controversy arose after the Klan began a systematic campaign to harass and intimidate blacks who were moved into all-white housing projects in the predominantly white city of Vidor, Texas. This desegregation effort followed a federal court's finding of blatant discrimination by Texas public housing officials. In defending his representation, Griffin pointed to an important line of first amendment cases where blacks successfully resisted hostile government efforts to obtain membership lists. See NAACP v. Alabama, 357 U.S. 449 (1958). According to Griffin, "If you create a rule of law to have Klan lists obtained, you create a law that also comes back and gets you."[51] Forced disclosure of members' identities often subjects them to harassment and deters others from joining.

To many NAACP members, however, there is a principled argument for distinguishing the Klan and the civil rights organizations involved in NAACP v. Alabama and its progeny: the Klan has a demonstrated history of violence and intimidation and the others do not.[52] These members also believe that Klan representation by a black lawyer is likely to enhance its credibility and legitimacy, and increase the risks to potential victims. Because the NAACP eventually might want to become involved in the Vidor dispute, either by representing residents in civil suits against the Klan or by supporting an exception to NAACP v. Alabama, Griffin faces a potential conflict of interest.

Your board is now about to vote on whether to fire Griffin as general counsel. What is your position? Should Griffin have taken the ACLU case? Would it have made a difference if he was not African American or not counsel for the NAACP?

4. Your firm is considering whether to take two other cases. One pro bono matter involves a law student's challenge to a state university hate-speech regulation. The student ran through a dormitory, shouting "Faggot, hope you die of AIDS" in the direction of a gay resident advisor's suite. The university has instituted disciplinary charges under a provision banning "harassment by personal vilification." That provision prohibits expression that (a) is intended to stigmatize on the basis of sex, race, color, handicap, religion, sexual orientation, or national and ethnic origin; (b) is addressed directly to the individual student(s) whom it insults or stigmatizes; and (c) makes use of insulting or "fighting" words or nonverbal symbols.[53]

Lawyers in your office are divided over whether to accept the case. It poses two issues: first, whether the campus code is constitutionally valid, and, second, whether the code governs this conduct, given that it refers to students and the resident advisor was not a student at the time. Some of your gay colleagues believe that the code is sufficiently narrow to satisfy first amendment standards. These staff members also feel that the organization should not expend scarce resources to defend homophobic conduct, particularly since the case could be decided on a narrow jurisdictional issue with little precedential significance. Other colleagues disagree. They maintain that such codes chill protected expression and that the firm should defend a student who cannot afford paid counsel and cannot find other pro bono representation. Which way do you vote? How should your office make decisions about what cases lawyers may pursue pro bono on firm time with firm resources?

In the second case, two partners in your firm want to represent ten paying clients who belong to Operation Rescue. These individuals face criminal trespass charges arising from protest activities at a local abortion clinic. They claim that their restriction of access to the clinic was a justifiable act of civil disobedience, and that the trespass statute is overbroad. Pro-choice lawyers and legal support staff in your office are planning to picket the office if the firm takes the case. The partners respond that they should have freedom to decide what work to accept, and that other firm attorneys have represented Planned Parenthood pro bono.[54]

If you were managing partner, how would you resolve these cases?

These cases involve variations on two of the most fundamental questions of legal ethics: when should advocates use morally legitimate means for morally questionable ends, and how should those ends be evaluated when competing moral values are at issue?

Lawyers who represent unpopular parties have long paid a substantial price, including loss of other clients, community ostracism, death threats, disbarment proceedings, and contempt prosecutions. For example, defense attorneys for British soldiers during pre-Revolutionary uprisings, counsel for alleged communists during the McCarthy era, civil rights activists in the 1950s and 1960s, and counsel for Oklahoma bombing suspects in the mid-1990s all suffered such harassment. As a consequence, effective legal assistance has often been unavailable to individuals subject to public prejudice.[55]

Partly in response to this history, both the Code and Model Rules emphasize that representation of an unpopular client does not imply endorsement of that client's action but rather is consistent with the highest standards of the profession.[56] Indeed, the Commentary to Model Rule 6.2 emphasizes that every lawyer has a responsibility to provide pro bono service, which requires accepting a "fair share of unpopular matters or indigent or unpopular clients." Yet at the same time, both codes acknowledge attorneys' right to decline or withdraw from representation that they consider morally repugnant.[57]

In attempting to reconcile these provisions, many commentators argue that lawyers have an obligation to accept unpopular matters only under certain situations. Charles Wolfram posits a "duty to rescue" only if the lawyer is the last in town who is willing and able to take the case and if the client asserts a legal right to a fundamental human need.[58] William Simon proposes a somewhat more elaborate test; lawyers should consider whether taking a case will promote norms of fair access and fair procedure or will improve the substantive law. Under this approach, questions of access turn on whether the lawyer feels some obligation to compensate for a scarcity of legal services that is partly created by the bar's own collective actions (such as restrictions on admission and lay competition). If a case fails to advance these procedural or substantive objectives, lawyers should not care if legal representation is unavailable.[59]

Other commentators draw a distinction between defending crucial moral principles even when that action assists morally objectionable clients, and providing general assistance to such clients even when no important principles are at stake. Thus, David

Luban argues that an ACLU lawyer who fights for the Nazis' right to march stands on ethically different footing than a lawyer who is on retainer to the Nazis, who is uncommitted to the first amendment, and who would argue against it if that would help her clients.[60] Luban defends the ACLU attorney on principles analogous to what philosophers refer to as the doctrine of "double effect." This doctrine holds that "it is permissible to perform an act likely to have evil indirect [and unintended] consequences (like helping Nazis) only if its direct [and intended] effect, in this case the vindication of the First Amendment, is morally acceptable and the . . . actor aims only at the acceptable effect."[61] So too, in the case described in Problem 4B(3), the lawyer for the Ku Klux Klan made clear that he would represent the Grand Dragon only on issues regarding membership lists, not on criminal charges involving harassment of black residents.[62]

Do you find these distinctions persuasive? Do any of these frameworks help in resolving Problem 4B(4), the case concerning campus homophobia? How should an attorney balance the value of protecting unpopular expressions against the costs of allowing hate speech that may silence subordinate groups?

How should an organization decide how to allocate scarce public interest resources? For example, some ACLU members objected to the representation of Nazis in the Skokie case on the ground that the organization was entitled to "a better class of victims."[63] Would making such distinctions about the value of clients' speech be consistent with ACLU principles? What procedures for accepting cases pro bono would you support for public interest organizations or private law firms?

3. The Morality of Means and the Morality of Ends

PROBLEM 4C

1. Your firm represents Metro, a transportation company, in a negligence suit filed by some 400 personal injury victims. Although the lead attorney working on the case believes that the victims have substantively valid claims, he also believes that the client may be able to escape liability by arguing that the court in which the cases are filed lacks jurisdiction. The charter establishing Metro did not name that court as the correct forum, since it did not exist at the time the charter was signed, and other evidence suggests that a different court may be appropriate. If that argument is accepted, the cases will be barred by the statute of limitations.[64]

Extensive prior dealings with Metro convince you that its management and board of directors will wish to assert the technical defense and escape liability, despite the adverse publicity and personal hardships that will result. The lead attorney asks you if he is ethically obligated to draw the client's attention to the jurisdictional claim, which is otherwise likely to remain unnoticed.

2. "A lawyer employed by the United States Department of Justice is assigned to handle a case filed in a federal district court against the Social Security Administration (SSA). Plaintiff is a widow who claims that the SSA has unlawfully denied her Social Security benefits. In her complaint, she asserts that the benefits are her only source of income and that without them she will be destitute. Upon reviewing the case, the government lawyer determines that the agency violated its own regulations in handling the claim and that, under its regulations, the plaintiff would have been entitled to Social Security benefits. The government lawyer also determines, however, that the statute of limitations has run and that the claim is time barred. [Should] the government lawyer . . . assert the statute of limitations defense?"[65]

3. You represent a local church that subsidizes a home for a small number of elderly indigent men. The home's funding comes from a bequest, which has trust income sufficient to support the men and to provide a comfortable living for the church warden who runs the home. An attorney from another city has filed a contingent-fee suit on behalf of the men, claiming that all of the income from the bequest should go for their support. The suit is filed against the warden and the home, but fails to name the church, which is in fact the appropriate party. That failure is, in your opinion, sufficient to bar the claim under applicable law because the statute of limitations has now run. The church has not been prejudiced by the failure, since its leadership has had notice of the claim. Nonetheless, those leaders would like to invoke the defense because that would be the least risky and most inexpensive way to win the lawsuit.

The warden, however, would greatly prefer a defense on the merits so that he could receive a public declaration of entitlement to the income.[66] You believe that the chance of obtaining such a declaration is excellent if the case proceeds to trial, but victory isn't certain and litigation costs could be substantial. You also believe that you might be able to pressure the church leaders into a defense on the merits by threatening to withdraw. What do you do?

Lawyers' reliance on technically valid claims raises long-standing disputes about the use of morally defensible rules for morally indefensible goals. During the nineteenth century, the two leading American commentators divided on that question. For example, in the context of statutes of limitations, David Hoffman argued that lawyers should never plead the statute if their clients admitted liability; no one should make attorneys "a partner in [such] knavery."[67]

George Sharswood was more equivocal. He maintained that clients who knew that they owed the amount claimed and that the delay in repayment had been attributable to their opponents' "indulgence or confidence" should not plead the statute of limitations. However, an attorney should not insist on such conduct; "the lawyer, who refuses his professional assistance because in his judgment the case is unjust and indefensible, usurps the functions of both judge and jury."[68] Who was right about the lawyer's responsibilities?

Contemporary ethical codes, consistent with neutral partisanship principles, suggest that a decision whether to invoke a lawful claim, issue, or defense rests with the client. As noted earlier, however, lawyers may ask their clients to forgo such an action, may counsel their clients concerning its moral significance, and may withdraw under certain circumstances. And if attorneys anticipate the relevance of a technical defense, they can, of course, decline the case or limit their scope of representation.[69]

Critics of neutral partisanship often argue that lawyers should not exploit procedural or technical provisions to defeat valid claims. Kenney Hegland, for example, argues that in civil matters, it should be "unprofessional conduct for a lawyer to assert any legal doctrine or rule on behalf of a client unless the lawyer has a good faith belief that the assertion of the doctrine or rule in the particular case will further a policy behind the doctrine or rule."[70] Under Hegland's framework, lawyers should not, for example, assert the statute of limitations unless doing so would serve statutory purposes. The objective of the statute of limitations is to prevent stale claims and to allow individuals to get on with their lives; it protects those who would otherwise be unable to defend themselves because memories fade, witnesses vanish, and documents are lost or destroyed. Given these purposes, does it follow, under Hegland's analysis, that the lawyers in Problem 4C should not have asserted technical defenses?

Hegland defends his view on reasoning similar to Simon's. From their perspective, clients have neither a legal nor a moral right to lawyers' "quibbles, nitpicks, and afterthoughts." These are largely "the product of the legal imagination. If the profession can create them, it can prohibit them."[71] In response to concerns about abandoning bright-line rules, Hegland writes:

> The efficiency argument is that we should apply rules without reference to underlying policies because it is simply too costly to figure out when to make exceptions. . . . "Even though our goal is to protect defendants from stale claims, it is too costly to determine staleness as a matter of fact; we must simply assume, pursuant to our rule, that claims are stale after four years." I have always had problems with this cavalier approach to the pressing problems of citizens. "Yes, you should probably win this case but, quite frankly, it would take us too much time to figure out why, so best of luck in life."[72]

In assessing lawyers' reliance on "quibbles," should it matter whether they believe that their clients' substantive position is legally or morally defensible? In another case around the same time as the

Metro claims described in Problem 4C(1), attorneys for Haitian refugees attempted to get their clients released from an Immigration and Naturalization Service detention center by invoking "every possible legal issue to trap the government in its own bureaucratic tangle," including arguments that the center was unlawful because it lacked an environmental impact statement.[73] David Luban notes that attorneys for both Metro and the refugees used the law in ways that had little to do with the purposes it was meant to fulfill. Yet for him, the cases stand on different footing because of the substantive objectives involved.[74]

Do you agree? If so, does it follow that in Problem 4C(3) lawyers who agreed with their client's position could appropriately capitalize on their opponents' mistake? In what sort of professional culture would you prefer to practice, one in which lawyers take advantage of any slip-up by their adversaries, or one in which technical errors are overlooked in the absence of real prejudice? In theory, clients whose suits are barred because of mistakes by their attorney have a remedy through malpractice litigation. In practice, such suits are rarely worthwhile except in the unusual case where clients can clearly establish that, but for the lawyer's negligence, they would have obtained a substantial recovery. See Chapter III (Regulation of the Profession). Given the inevitable overinclusiveness of many technical defenses and the unavoidability of adversaries' mistakes, how should lawyers' ethical codes respond?

Should lawyers for the government have any special obligation to "do justice," rather than simply minimize financial liability? In commenting on that issue, Judge Jack Weinstein describes a condemnation case in which he once served as county attorney. The opposing parties, an elderly husband and wife, were not represented by counsel and were not aware of how much their property had increased in value. Weinstein convinced them to demand a higher price than they had initially sought. In his view, such conduct was consistent with government counsel's obligation to "seek justice." EC 7-14.[75] Do you agree?

So too, when Barbara Babcock served as Assistant Attorney General for the Justice Department's Civil Division during the Carter administration, she implemented a policy preventing government lawyers from collecting costs from losing parties in discrimination cases despite a statutory entitlement to such costs unless the claims involved bad faith, harassment, or abusive conduct.[76] Her successor abandoned the policy. What would you have done? Would you have permitted government lawyers to file time-barred claims in contexts where their adversaries were unlikely to recognize that they had a defense? See ABA Formal Opinion 94-387 (Sept. 26, 1994).

Are administrative agency officials entitled to the same zealous representation as private clients, or does a lawyer representing "the public" have an independent obligation to evaluate the public interest?[77] Which way does that interest cut when taxpayers end up paying the price?

Under what circumstances should lawyers be prepared to decline a case or withdraw from representation rather than defeat what they perceive to be a valid claim? Consider Abraham Lincoln's advice to a potential client:

> Yes . . . we can doubtless gain your case for you; . . . we can distress a widowed mother and her six fatherless children and thereby get you six hundred dollars to which you seem to have a legal claim, but which rightfully belongs, it appears to me, as much to the woman and her children as it does to you. You must remember that some things that are legally right are not morally right. We shall not take your case but will give you a little advice for which we will charge you nothing. You seem to be a sprightly, energetic man; we would advise you to try your hand at making six hundred dollars in some other way.[78]

Would Lincoln give the same advice to any of the lawyers in Problem 4C?

4. Epilogue

Much of the ethical tension that arises in advocacy contexts has deeper cultural roots. Robert Post, in analyzing popular opinion polls, literary images, and media portrayals of lawyers, points to a recurring paradox: lawyers are both honored and condemned for their partisanship.

ROBERT C. POST, ON THE POPULAR IMAGE OF THE LAWYER: REFLECTIONS IN A DARK GLASS

75 Cal. L. Rev. 379, 386, 389 (1987)

[L]awyers are especially disliked because they manipulate the legal system in the interests of their particular clients, without regard to the common, universal values of right and wrong. But recall also that lawyers are praised because their first priority is to the private perspective of their clients. Lawyers, in other words, bestride the following cultural contradiction: we both want and in some respects have a universal, common culture, and we simultaneously want that culture to be malleable and responsive to the particular and often incompatible interests of individual groups and citizens. We expect lawyers to fulfill both desires, and so they are a constant irritating reminder that we are neither a peaceable kingdom of harmony and order, nor a land of undiluted individual autonomy, but somewhere disorientingly in between. Lawyers, in the very exercise of their profession, are the necessary bearers of that bleak winter's tale, and we hate them for it.

We hate them, that is, because they are our own dark reflection. We use lawyers both to express our longing for a common good, and to express our distaste for collective discipline. . . .

Analyzed in this way, the special hatred which popular culture holds for the lawyer can be an illuminating resource for understanding cultural contradictions of the deepest and most profound kind. The lawyer is the public and unavoidable embodiment of the tension we all experience between the desire for an embracing and common community and the urge toward individual independence and self-assertion. . . . In popular imagery the lawyer is held to strict account for the discrepancy between our aspirations and our realities. But this discrepancy is not the lawyer's alone, and once we understand this we may also come to see that in popular culture the lawyer is so much our enemy, because his failings are so much our own.

Endnotes

1. Randall Jarrell, Pictures from an Institution 11 (1954).

2. Erving Goffman, Encounters 105-110, 132, 152 (1961). For a crucial early formulation, see Ralph Linton, The Study of Man (1936).

3. See Michael Walzer, Political Action: The Problem of Dirty Hands, 2 Phil. & Pub. Aff. 160 (1973); Stuart Hampshire, Public and Private Morality, in Public and Private Morality 23 (Stuart Hampshire ed., 1978). See generally F.H. Bradley, Ethical Studies 160 (1927).

4. Gerald J. Postema, Moral Responsibility in Professional Ethics, 55 N.Y.U. L. Rev. 63 (1980). See also Wayne Brazil, The Attorney as Victim: Toward More Candor About the Psychological Price Tag of Litigation Practice, 3 J. Legal Prof. 10 (1978).

5. Bernard Williams, Morality: An Introduction to Ethics 102 (1972).

6. Alasdair MacIntyre, What Has Ethics to Learn from Medical Ethics, 2 Phil. Exchange 37, 46 (1978); Jack L. Sammons, Jr., Professing: Some Thoughts on Professionalism and Classroom Teaching, 3 Geo. J. Legal Ethics 609, 616 n.15 (1990).

7. Virginia Held, The Division of Moral Labor and the Role of the Lawyer, in The Good Lawyer: Lawyers' Roles and Lawyers' Ethics 60, 67 (David Luban ed., 1984).

8. Jean-Paul Sartre, Being and Nothingness 86-116 (Hazel E. Barnes trans., 1966).

9. David Luban, Lawyers and Justice: An Ethical Study 125 (1988). See Deborah L. Rhode, Ethical Perspectives on Legal Practice, 37 Stan. L. Rev. 589 (1985); Richard Wasserstrom, Roles and Morality, in The Good Lawyer, supra note 7, at 25; and discussion in Part C infra.

10. For competing views on the historical context and contemporary significance of Lord Brougham's statement, see Deborah L. Rhode, An Adversarial Exchange on Adversarial Ethics: Text, Subtext, and Context, 41 J. Legal Educ. 29 (1991).

11. William H. Simon, The Ideology of Advocacy: Procedural Justice and Professional Ethics, 1978 Wis. L. Rev. 30, 36 (1978).

12. Theodore Schneyer, Moral Philosophy's Standard Misconception of Legal Ethics, 1984 Wis. L. Rev. 1529; and Schneyer, Some Sympathy for the Hired Gun, 41 J. Legal Educ. 11 (1991).

13. Alexis de Tocqueville, Democracy in America, vol. I (H. Reeve trans. & P. Bradley ed., 1973) (1st ed. 1835). See Robert W. Gordon, The Ideal and the Actual in the Law: Fantasies and Practices of New York City Lawyers 1870-1910, in The New High Priests: Lawyers in Post Civil War America (Gerard W. Gawalt ed., 1984).

14. Louis D. Brandeis, The Opportunity in the Law, in Business: A Profession 329 (1933). See Gordon, supra note 13.

15. David Hoffman, Resolutions in Regard to Professional Deportment, in A Course of Legal Study 755 (2d ed. 1836).

16. George Sharswood, An Essay on Professional Ethics 84-85 (3d ed. 1869).

17. Id. at 97-98, 99-100.

18. Michael Schudson, Public, Private, and Professional Lives: The Correspondence of David Field and Samuel Bowles, 21 Am. J. Legal Hist. 191, 192-193 (1977) (quoting Mark de Wolfe Howe). See also Gordon, supra note 13.

19. Disciplinary Rule 7-101 provides that a lawyer does not violate his obligations by avoiding offensive tactics, and the Commentary to Model Rule 1.3 similarly notes that a "lawyer is not bound to press for every advantage that might be realized for a client. A lawyer has professional discretion in determining the means by which a matter should be pursued."

20. See EC 2-27, EC 7-9, and Commentary to Model Rule 1.2.

21. See Luban, supra note 9; Richard Wasserstrom, Lawyers as Professionals: Some Moral Issues, 5 Human Rights 1 (1975); Rhode, supra note 9, at 606-607; Chapter XIV (Criminal Law).

22. David Margolick, "Tobacco" Its Middle Name, Law Firm Thrives for Now, N.Y. Times, Nov. 20, 1992, at A1, B9 (referring to such arguments by lawyers at Shook, Hardy & Bacon).

23. Joseph C. Goulden, The Superlawyers: The Small and Powerful World of the Great Washington Law Firms 132 (1972).

24. Robert J. Kutak, The Adversary System and the Practice of Law, in The Good Lawyer, supra note 7, at 172, 174.

25. Abe Krash, Professional Responsibility to Clients and the Public Interest: Is There a Conflict?, 55 Chi. B. Rec. 31, 37 (1974).

26. Rhode, supra note 9, at 597.

27. Boswell's Life of Johnson 47 (George Hill ed., 1964).

28. See, e.g., Model Rule 2.1 (in rendering advice, a lawyer may refer not only to law but to other considerations such as moral, economic, social, and political factors that may be relevant to the client's situation); EC 7-8 (in assisting the client to reach a proper decision, it is often desirable for a lawyer to point out those facts that may lead to a decision that is morally just as well as legally permissible); William H. Simon, Visions of Practice in Legal Thought, 36 Stan. L. Rev. 469 (1984).

29. Stephen L. Pepper, The Lawyer's Amoral Ethical Role: A Defense, a Problem, and Some Possibilities, 1986 Am. B. Found. Res. J. 613, 617-618. See also Alan Donagan, Justifying Legal Practice in the Adversary System, in The Good Lawyer, supra note 7, at 123.

30. This phrase comes from Samuel Bowles' defense of a prominent New York lawyer's willingness to defend two notorious robber barons. Michael Schudson, Public, Private, and Professional Lives: The Corre-

spondence of David Field and Samuel Bowles, 21 Am. J. Legal Hist. 191 (1977).

31. Clarence Darrow, quoted in John Basten, Control and the Lawyer-Client Relationship, 6 J. Legal Prof. 7, 15 (1981). See also Baron Bramwell, quoted in John V. Barry, The Ethics of Advocacy, reprinted in Julian Disney et al., Lawyers 690 (1977) ("A client is entitled to say to his counsel, I want your advocacy and not your judgment").

32. Kenney Hegland, Quibbles, 67 Tex. L. Rev. 1491, 1497 (1989). For accounts of the pressures against lawyers' acceptance of such cases, see Jerold S. Auerbach, Unequal Justice: Lawyers and Social Change in Modern America 254 (1976); Daniel H. Pollitt, Counsel for the Unpopular Cause: The Hazard of Being Undone, 43 N.C.L. Rev. 9 (1964).

33. Simon, supra note 11, at 108.

34. Simon, The Practice of Justice (1998).

35. Susan Wolf, Ethics, Legal Ethics, and the Ethics of Law, in The Good Lawyer, supra note 7, at 38, 59 n.4.

36. David Luban, The Lysistratian Prerogative: A Response to Stephen Pepper, 1986 Am. B. Found. Res. J. 637, 639 (1987); David Luban, Partisanship, Betrayal, and Autonomy in the Lawyer-Client Relationship: A Reply to Stephen Ellman, 90 Colum. L. Rev. 1004 (1990).

37. Rhode, supra note 9, at 607-608.

38. Duncan Kennedy, Legal Formality, 2 J. Legal Stud. 351, 394 (1973).

39. Postema, supra note 4, at 82-83; Rhode, supra note 9; Deborah L. Rhode, Lawyers, Wm. & Mary L. Rev. (forthcoming 1997).

40. Roger C. Cramton, On Giving Meaning to Professionalism (1997); Professional Responsibility: Report of the Joint Conference, 44 A.B.A.J. 1159 (1958).

41. Murray L. Schwartz, The Professionalism and Accountability of Lawyers, 66 Cal. L. Rev. 669 (1978); and Schwartz, The Zeal of the Civil Advocate, in The Good Lawyer, supra note 7, at 150.

42. Luban, supra note 9, at 157.

43. Simon, supra note 34, at 2.

44. See Schneyer, Moral Philosophy's Standard Misconception, supra note 12, at 1543 (arguing that the financial, psychological, and organizational pressures of law practice explain exclusively client-regarding behavior better than rules of legal ethics). For discussion of these pressures, see Deborah L. Rhode, Institutionalizing Ethics, 44 Case W. Res. L. Rev. 665 (1994).

45. William H. Simon, Ethical Discretion in Lawyering, 101 Harv. L. Rev. 1083, 1116 (1988).

46. Simon, supra note 34.

47. Stropnicky v. Nathanson, discussed in Deborah L. Rhode, Can A Lawyer Insist On Clients of One Gender, Natl. L.J., Dec. 1, 1997, at A21.

48. The High Cost of Free Speech, Time, June 26, 1978, at 63 (paraphrasing William Kuntsler). See generally Anthony Lukas, The A.C.L.U. Against Itself, N.Y. Times Mag., July 9, 1978, at 9.

49. In the case on which this problem is based, NSPA v. Skokie, 432 U.S. 43 (1976), 30 percent of Illinois ACLU members resigned in protest over the organization's stand, forcing a 40 percent budget cut; 15 percent of the organization's national membership resigned. See sources cited in note 48.

50. For an extended analysis of this case, see David B. Wilkins, Race, Ethics, and the First Amendment: Should a Black Lawyer Represent the Ku Klux Klan?, 63 George Wash. L. Rev. 1030 (1995).

51. Sue Anne Presley, Klan Leader and NAACP Counsel Make an Odd Couple of Civil Rights, Wash. Post, Sept. 29, 1993, at A3 (quoting Griffin).

52. See 357 U.S. at 465.

53. This hypothetical is based on a 1992 incident at Stanford University. The quoted language is drawn from the university's "Fundamental Standard" governing student expression.

54. Wendy Olson, WSL, NLG Take Action on Abortion Issues, 19 Stan. L.J. 1, 15 (Feb. 1989).

55. Pollitt, supra note 32; cases cited in Rhode, supra note 10, at 29; Aryeh Neier, Defending My Enemy (1979).

56. EC 2-29; Model Rules 1.2, 6.2.

57. DR 2-110; EC 7-8; EC 2-30; Model Rule 6.2.

58. Charles W. Wolfram, A Lawyer's Duty to Represent Clients Repugnant and Otherwise, in The Good Lawyer, supra note 7, at 214.

59. Simon does suggest that if the lawyer is the *only* one in town, that might impose a duty to take extra care in scrutinizing the merits. Simon, supra note 45.

60. Luban, supra note 9, at 161.

61. Id. at 162. That doctrine underpins the principle of "just wars," which excuses soldiers whose actions in a just war inevitably, but inadvertently, kill some innocent civilians.

62. Wilkins, supra note 50, at 1044.

63. Lukas, supra note 48, at 29.

64. These facts are drawn from a Washington, D.C., case discussed in Al Kamen, Metro Lawyers Using Loophole in Injury Cases, Wash. Post, Dec. 8, 1981, at A1.

65. This case is from Catherine J. Lanctot, The Duty of Zealous Advocacy and the Ethics of the Federal Government Lawyer: The Three Hardest Questions, 64 S. Cal. L. Rev. 951, 951-952 (1991).

66. The case is based on one in Anthony Trollope, The Warden (1855).

67. Hoffman, supra note 15, at 752, 754.

68. Sharswood, supra note 16, at 84-85. However, Sharswood was not entirely consistent on such issues. He also maintained that it would be "an immoral act [for a lawyer] to afford . . . assistance . . . when his conscience told him that the client was aiming to perpetrate a wrong through the means of some advantage the law may have afforded him." Id. at 98.

69. See DR 7-101(A); DR 2-110; Model Rule 1.2, discussed in the text accompanying note 19, supra.

70. Hegland, Quibbles, supra note 32, at 1494.

71. Id. at 1500. See also Simon, Practice of Justice, supra note 34.

72. Hegland, supra note 32, at 1502, 1506-1507.

73. Luban, supra note 9, at 17.

74. Id.

75. Jack B. Weinstein & Gay A. Crosthwait, Some Reflections on Conflicts Between Government Attorneys and Clients, 1 Touro L. Rev. 1, 6 (1985).

76. See Barbara A. Babcock, The Role of the Government Lawyer, 13 Stan. Law. 3 (1978).

77. For contrasting views, see Part C of Chapter XI (Constitutional Law) and Eric Schnapper, Legal Ethics and the Government Lawyer, 32

The Record 649 (1977); Lanctot, supra note 65; Barbara A. Babcock, Defending the Government: Justice and the Civil Division, 23 Clev. Marshall L. Rev. 181 (1990).

78. William H. Herndon & Jesse William Weik, 2 Herndon's Lincoln 346 (1890).

Chapter V

The Adversary System

A. THE TRADITIONAL RATIONALE AND CONTEMPORARY CHALLENGES

1. Introduction

An adversary legal system has several defining characteristics. It relies on party presentations in a competitively structured trial setting before a neutral, largely passive, judge.[1] Such features distinguish adversarial procedures from the "inquisitorial" systems that most countries employ. These inquisitorial systems, which are described more fully in Part B below, rely primarily on judges rather than on litigants and their lawyers to develop a record.

The Anglo-American adversary process has its roots in various rituals of dispute resolution, including trial by combat and trial by ordeals such as drowning or burning. Depending on the ritual, the accused party's survival served as proof of guilt or innocence.[2] The Normans introduced jury systems, which initially offered few procedural protections and depended on panels of male landowners who knew enough about the dispute to render a decision. By the seventeenth century, when British colonists brought their legal practices to the New World, more formal procedural safeguards had developed. Initially, however, some colonists viewed such formality as too expensive and cumbersome for American needs. A general distrust of lawyers, who were accused of stirring up disputes, also inspired efforts to develop simple dispute resolution procedures.

Yet as American society became more complex and its commercial activity more extensive, the need for legal safeguards and specialists became more obvious. So too, many members of the emerging middle and upper classes in America wished both to restrain the power of the state and to prevent the development of an aristocracy. An adversarial system appeared consistent with these objectives. It limited the role of the judge and gave a large measure of control to litigants and their chosen attorneys. As long as those attorneys were members of an independent professional class, they could provide an important check on central government authority. As Chapter IV (Advocacy) noted, a competitive dispute resolution process also suited the values reflected and reinforced by capitalist market structures.

This complex set of historical, political, and socioeconomic forces played an influential role in the development of American legal procedures. The framers of the Bill of Rights included provisions that fortified an adversarial system, such as rights to counsel, due process, and trial by jury. Those provisions were, in turn, interpreted by a legal profession interested in maintaining its own independence and influence. Over the next two centuries, the American bar developed a deep commitment to an adversarial process and to the values underlying it, which are reviewed in the readings below.[3]

Traditional justifications for the adversary system parallel and overlap the traditional justifications for the advocate's neutral partisanship role. One rationale stresses the adversary system's ability to discover truth; an alternative rights-based rationale stresses the system's capacity to promote values of individual dignity, autonomy, and expression. In the following excerpts, the Joint Conference Report defends the truth-related justification and David Luban challenges its premises.

2.   The Search for Truth

LON L. FULLER & JOHN D. RANDALL, PROFESSIONAL RESPONSIBILITY: REPORT OF THE JOINT CONFERENCE OF THE AMERICAN BAR ASSOCIATION (ABA) AND THE ASSOCIATION OF AMERICAN LAW SCHOOLS (AALS)

44 A.B.A.J. 1159, 1160-1161 (1958)

. . . The lawyer appearing as an advocate before a tribunal presents, as persuasively as he can, the facts and the law of the case as seen from the standpoint of his client's interest. . . .

In a very real sense it may be said that the integrity of the adjudicative process itself depends upon the participation of the advocate. This becomes apparent when we contemplate the nature of the task assumed by any arbiter who attempts to decide a dispute without the aid of partisan advocacy.

Such an arbiter must undertake, not only the role of judge, but that of representative for both of the litigants. Each of these roles must be played to the full without being muted by qualifications derived from the others. When he is developing for each side the most effective statement of its case, the arbiter must put aside his neutrality and permit himself to be moved by a sympathetic identification sufficiently intense to draw from his mind all that it is capable of giving, in analysis, patience and creative power. When he resumes his neutral position, he must be able to view with distrust the fruits of this identification and be ready to reject the products of his own best mental efforts. The difficulties of this undertaking are obvious. . . .

What generally occurs in practice is that at some early point a familiar pattern will seem to emerge from the evidence, an accustomed label is waiting for the case and, without awaiting further proofs, this label is promptly assigned to it. It is a mistake to suppose that this premature cataloguing must necessarily result from impatience, prejudice or mental sloth. Often it proceeds from a very understandable desire to bring the hearing into some order and coherence, for without some tentative theory of the case there is no standard of relevance by which testimony may be measured. But what starts as a preliminary diagnosis designed to direct the inquiry tends quickly and imperceptibly, to become a fixed conclusion, as all that confirms the diagnosis makes a strong imprint on the mind, while all that runs counter to it is received with diverted attention.

An adversary presentation seems the only effective means for combatting this natural human tendency to judge too swiftly in terms of the familiar that which is not yet fully known. The arguments of counsel hold the case, as it were, in suspension between two opposing interpretations of it. . . .

These, then, are the reasons for believing that partisan advocacy plays a vital and essential role in one of the most fundamental procedures of a democratic society. But if we were to put all of these detailed considerations to one side, we should still be confronted by the fact that, in whatever form adjudication may appear, the experienced judge or arbitrator desires and actively seeks to obtain an adversary presentation of the issues. Only when he has had the benefit of intelligent and vigorous advocacy on both sides can he feel fully confident of his decision.

Viewed in this light, the role of the lawyer as a partisan advocate appears not as a regrettable necessity, but as an indispensable part of a larger ordering of affairs. The institution of advocacy is not a concession to the frailties of human nature but an expression of human insight in the design of a social framework within which man's capacity for impartial judgment can attain its fullest realization.

When advocacy is thus viewed, it becomes clear by what principle limits must be set to partisanship. The advocate plays his role well when zeal for his client's cause promotes a wise and informed decision of the case. He plays his role badly, and trespasses against the obligations of professional responsibility, when his desire to win leads him to muddy the headwaters of decision, when, instead of lending a needed perspective to the controversy, he distorts and obscures its true nature.

DAVID LUBAN, THE ADVERSARY SYSTEM EXCUSE

The Good Lawyer: Lawyers' Roles and Lawyers' Ethics 83, 93-97 (David Luban ed., 1983)

CONSEQUENTIALIST JUSTIFICATIONS OF THE ADVERSARY SYSTEM

Truth

The question whether the adversary system is, all in all, the best way of uncovering the facts of a case at bar sounds like an empirical question. I happen to think that it is, an empirical question, moreover, that has scarcely been investigated, and that is most likely impossible to answer. This last is because one does not, after a trial is over, find the parties coming forth to make a clean breast of it and enlighten the world as to what *really* happened. A trial is not a quiz show with the right answer waiting in a sealed envelope. We can't learn directly whether the facts are really as the trier determined them because we don't ever find out the facts. . . .

Given all this, it is unsurprising to discover that the arguments purporting to show the advantages of the adversary system as a fact-finder have mostly been nonempirical, a mix of a priori theories of inquiry and armchair psychology.

Here is one, based on the idea, very similar to Sir Karl Popper's theory of scientific rationality, that the way to get at the truth is a wholehearted dialectic of assertion and refutation. If each side attempts to prove its case, with the other trying as energetically as possible to assault the steps of the proof, it is more likely that all of the aspects of the situation will be presented to the fact-finder than if it attempts to investigate for itself with the help of the lawyers.

This theory is open to a number of objections. First of all, the analogy to Popperian scientific methodology is not a good one. Perhaps science proceeds by advancing conjectures and then trying to refute them, but it does not proceed by advancing conjectures that the scientist knows to be false and then using procedural rules to exclude probative evidence.

The two adversary attorneys, moreover, are each under an obligation to present the facts in the manner most consistent with their client's position, to prevent the introduction of unfavorable evidence, to undermine the credibility of opposing witnesses, to set unfavorable facts in a context in which their importance is minimized, to attempt to provoke inferences in their client's favor. The assumption is that two such accounts will cancel out, leaving the truth of the matter. But there is no earthly reason to think this is so; they may simply pile up the confusion. . . .

The other side, of course, can cross-examine . . . a witness to get the truth out. Irving Younger, perhaps the most popular lecturer on trial tactics in the country, tells how. Among his famous "Ten Commandments of Cross-Examination" are these:

- Never ask anything but a leading question.
- Never ask a question to which you don't already know the answer.
- Never permit the witness to explain his or her answers.
- Don't bring out your conclusions in the cross-examination. Save them for closing arguments when the witness is in no position to refute them.

Of course, the opposition may be prepared for this; they may have seen Younger's three-hour, $425 videotape on how to examine expert witnesses. They may know, therefore, that the cross-examiner is saving his or her conclusions for the closing argument. Not to worry: Younger knows how to stop an attorney from distorting the truth in closing arguments. "If the opposing lawyer is holding the jury spellbound . . . the spell must be broken at all cost [sic]. [Younger] suggests the attorney leap to his or her feet and make furious and spurious objections. They will be overruled, but they might at least break the opposing counsel's concentration."

My guess is that this is not quite what Sir Karl Popper had in mind when he wrote, "The Western rationalist tradition . . . is the tradition of critical discussion, of examining and testing propositions or theories by attempting to refute them." . . .

No trial lawyer seriously believes that the best way to get at the truth is through the clash of opposing points of view. If a lawyer did believe this, the logical way to prepare a case for trial would be to hire two investigators, one taking one side of every issue and one taking the other. After all, the lawyer needs the facts, and if those are best discovered through an adversary process, the lawyer would be irresponsible not to set one up. That no lawyer would dream of such a crazy procedure should tip us off that the Joint Conference Report premise is flawed.

The Joint Conference Report employs two subsidiary psychological arguments as well. The first is that the adversary system will "hold the case . . . in suspension between two opposing interpretations of it," so the finder of fact will not jump to hasty conclusions. The second is that if the judge and not the lawyer had to "absorb" the disappointments of his or her theory of the case being refuted, he or she would be "under a strong temptation to keep the hearing moving within the boundaries originally set for it"; then it would not be a fair trial so much as a "public confirmation for what the tribunal considers it has already established in private."

Let me reiterate that these arguments, however plausible they sound on paper, are untested speculations from the armchair. But let us suppose for the sake of argument that they are right. They still do not show why we must have an adversary system. Consider three other possible systems: (1) a three-judge panel, two of whom investigate and present the case from the points of view of the respective litigants, making the strongest arguments they can but also pointing out weaknesses in their side's case and strengths in the other; (2) a system like our own, except that the advocates are under an affirmative duty to point out facts or arguments in the other side's favor if the adversary is unaware of them (or, perhaps, a system in which the court awards attorney's fees on the basis of how helpful they are in the overall search for truth); (3) the French system in which one judge investigates the case beforehand and presents a dossier to [a different] trial judge.

Now, I don't recommend any of these as a practical alternative to the existing adversary system; they have their drawbacks. But notice that (1) and (2) do just as good a job as the adversary system at holding the case in suspension, while all three do just as good a job at shifting the onus of being wrong away from the tribunal. All three, moreover, sever the search for truth from the attorney's need to win, which under the adversary system ties the attorney to the client's victory by bonds of self-interest. All three, therefore, are likely to avoid the most extravagant tactics currently employed by lawyers. The Joint Conference Report does not even consider this as a possibility.

Indeed, it seems to take as a premise the idea that truth is served by self-interested rather than disinterested investigation. "The lawyer appearing as an advocate before a tribunal presents, as persuasively as he can, the facts and the law of the case *as seen from the standpoint of his client's interest*" [emphasis added]. The emphasized phrase is accurate, but it gives the game away. For there is all the difference in the world between "the facts seen from X's standpoint" and "the facts seen from the standpoint of X's interest." Of course it is important to hear the former — the more perspectives we have, the better informed our judgment. But to hear the latter is not helpful at all. It is in the murderer's *interest* not to have been at the scene of the crime; consequently, the "facts of the case as seen from the standpoint of [the] client's interest" are that the client was elsewhere that weekend. From the standpoint of my *interest*, the world is my cupcake with a cherry on top; from the standpoint of yours, its streets are paved with gold. Combining the two does not change folly to truth.

All this does not mean that the adversary system may not in fact get at the truth in many hard cases. (Trial lawyers' war stories are mixed.) I suppose that it is as good as its rivals. But, to repeat the point I began with, nobody knows how good that is. . . .

The argument that the adversary system is the best available means of discovering truth rests on several premises:

1. There is some stable, knowable reality that an effective legal process can uncover.
2. The prospect of victory will motivate adversaries to put maximum effort into developing their case, while in inquisitorial systems, adjudicators may simply seek the simplest way to get through their caseloads and their day.
3. Proof requires hypotheses and if adjudicators develop the proof, their preliminary hypotheses will too easily bias their final decision.[4]
4. The advantages of competitive, party-controlled processes outweigh their costs.

Each of these premises has attracted considerable criticism. First, as Chapter II noted, many commentators challenge the assumption that there are fixed, objective truths waiting to be discovered through competitive presentations. Rather, as postmodern and pragmatist frameworks suggest, facts are constructed, not just revealed, and decision-makers' own interests and identities affect their interpretations. Critics of adversarial assumptions worry that our reliance on two oppositional stories and our faith in neutral adjudicators may mask the multiplicity of perspectives and biases of decision-makers involved.[5]

Moreover, the lawyer's role is, in some important respects, at odds with adversarial premises. As Plato pointed out centuries ago, the advocate is not a seeker of truth but a producer of belief.[6] Marvin Frankel, a former federal court judge and member of the Model Rules Commission, makes the same point; he argues that current procedural and ethical norms in practice rank truth too low:

> Despite untested statements of self-congratulation, we know that others searching after facts, in history, geography, medicine, whatever, do not emulate our adversary system. We know that most countries of the world seek justice by different routes. What is much more to the point, we know that many of the rules and devices of adversary litigation as we conduct it are not geared for, but are often aptly suited to defeat, the development of the truth. . . . Employed by interested parties, the process often achieves truth only as a convenience, a byproduct, or an accidental approximation. The business of the advocate,

simply stated, is to win. . . . His is not the search for truth as such. To put that thought more exactly, the truth and victory are mutually incompatible for some considerable percentage of the attorneys trying cases at any given time.[7]

As discussion in Part C reflects, the absence of disclosure obligations and common techniques of witness preparation and cross-examination often serve to multiply expenses and to obfuscate rather than reveal relevant information. Participants may then be trapped in an adversarial arms race. Both sides might gain from a more cooperative structure, but neither can afford individually to abandon partisan practices.[8]

In an adversarial model, the merits will win out only if the contest is a balanced one, that is, if each side has roughly equal access to relevant legal information, resources, and advocacy skills. How often that balance occurs in practice is open to doubt. Consider first the problems that arise from disparities in legal representation. According to courthouse graffiti, trial by jury is "twelve people deciding who has the best lawyer."[9] Douglas Rosenthal's study of personal injury litigation offers a case in point. As one of an insurance company's defense lawyers explains:

> Frankly, we are in business to wear out plaintiffs. . . . We're not a charity out to protect the plaintiff's welfare. Take the case I was trying today. The other lawyer [for the plaintiff] earns twice what I do and drives around in a Cadillac. But he doesn't know what he's doing. His client's got a good claim for a fractured skull. *I want this bastard to win* . . . and he'll blow it. Today I laid the foundation for contributory negligence, which is very doubtful, and the other lawyer made no attempt to knock it down. The plaintiff is a sweet, gentle guy, a Puerto Rican. I met him in the john at recess and I told him that there was nothing personal in my working against him, that I was just doing my job. I think he understood this. . . .
>
> It's not my fault, I want him to win. It's his lawyer's fault and his own fault for not getting a better lawyer like me. If the client gets nothing, it won't be my doing; it will be the jury's responsibility and that stupid contributory negligence rule.[10]

Inequalities in advocacy are usually symptomatic of broader inequalities. Disparities in parties' financial resources, access to information, and inclination to litigate will inevitably skew results. Marc Galanter's classic account of "Why the Haves Come Out Ahead" charts the systematic disparities between "repeat players" [RP] who frequently engage in similar litigation and their "one shot" [OS] adversaries.[11] Although acknowledging that these characterizations are somewhat oversimplified, Galanter finds them useful to illustrate the advantages available to frequent litigators such as prosecutors, creditors, or insurance companies:

(1) RPs, having done it before, have advance intelligence; they are able to structure the next transaction and build a record.

It is the RP who writes the form contract, requires the security deposit, and the like.

(2) RPs develop expertise and have ready access to specialists. They enjoy economies of scale and have low start-up costs for any case.

(3) RPs have opportunities to develop . . . [helpful] relations with institutional [players such as court clerks, police].

(4) The RP's . . . interest in his "bargaining reputation" serves as a resource to establish "commitment" to his bargaining positions. With no bargaining reputation to maintain, the OS has more difficulty in convincingly committing himself in bargaining.

(5) RPs can play the odds and adopt strategies calculated to maximize gain over a long series of cases, even where this involves the risk of maximum loss in some cases.

(6) RPs can play for rules as well as immediate gains. First, it pays an RP to expend resources in influencing the making of the relevant rules by such methods as lobbying. (And his accumulated expertise enables him to do this persuasively.)

(7) RPs can also play for rules in litigation itself, whereas an OS is unlikely to. . . . Since they expect to litigate again, RPs can select to adjudicate (or appeal) those cases which they regard as most likely to produce favorable rules. On the other hand, OSs should be willing to trade off the possibility of making "good law" for tangible gain. . . .

(8) RPs, by virtue of experience and expertise, are more likely to be able to discern which rules are likely to [make a tangible difference] and which are likely to remain merely symbolic commitments.[12]

Do these inequalities undercut the instrumental, truth-related rationale for the adversary system? If so, should we make greater efforts to reduce the disparities among litigants or reduce the effects that such disparities have on legal outcomes? Consider that issue in light of the dilemmas raised in Problems 5A to 5E and the alternatives proposed in Part B.

3.   The Protection of Rights and the Value of Participation

A second rationale for adversarial processes involves their capacity to protect individual rights and the underlying values of autonomy and dignity that such rights preserve. Allowing parties to shape their "day in court" fosters a sense of self-expression and self-respect; it gives individuals a sense of "having their will 'counted' in societal decisions."[13] Whether litigants feel that their views have been considered is central to whether they perceive the process as fair.[14]

The adversary system's effectiveness in serving these goals is open to question. By and large, losing litigants "do not feel they have been near the heartbeat of justice," and most surveys suggest that the greater experience individuals have with the legal process, the less their confidence in its fairness.[15] As discussion in Part H reflects, participants frequently report greater satisfaction with alternative dispute resolution procedures than with the existing adversary system.

To many critics, that system too often subverts the very values of dignity and autonomy that the process is designed to serve. The rights-based rationale for adversary procedures, like the rights-based rationale for neutral partisanship, fails to explain why the rights of a particular client should trump those of all other parties whose interests are inadequately represented. The weakness of such justifications is most obvious when organizational clients are unevenly matched with unsophisticated one-shot players in circumstances like the one Douglas Rosenthal described. How is individual dignity served by letting an insurance company deny a badly injured victim's valid claim because of opposing counsel's ineptitude? How are individual autonomy and self-expression fostered by the bar's rejection of a proposed ethical rule prohibiting lawyers who appear against unrepresented parties from "unfairly exploiting . . . [their] ignorance or procur[ing] unconscionable results"?[16]

Critics of the proposed rule concerning unrepresented parties claimed that unfairness and unconscionability were overly vague standards and would impair clients' rights to loyal advocacy. According to some commentators, opposing parties "too cheap to hire a lawyer" should not be "coddled by special treatment."[17] Proponents of the rule responded that non-lawyers are frequently subject to broad standards such as unconscionability, good faith, or fair dealing. Why should lawyers need greater regulatory precision? In a system where not everyone can afford partisan advocacy or function effectively without it, clients should have no right to unconstrained representation.

Given all these limitations in conventional rationales for adversarial processes, some commentators argue that the current system is justifiable only on weak pragmatic grounds: it is not demonstrably worse than other systems, the costs of radical restructuring would be substantial, and the devil you know is better than the devil you don't.[18] However, these commentators join other critics in suggesting that lawyers should respond both individually and collectively to problems in existing structures. Attorneys should support changes in legal norms, ethical rules, and the distribution of services, as well as exercise discretion to prevent injustice in particular cases.

How would you assess these justifications and critiques of adversarial processes? Consider the reform proposals set forth in Part B. How well would they address the general weaknesses in adversarial procedures noted above and the specific dilemmas arising in Problems 5A to 5E below?

PROBLEM 5A

Consider the statement of Lord Brougham, when representing Queen Caroline in her 1820 adultery trial before the House of Lords, quoted in Chapter IV, page 133: Do you agree that "to protect [a] client at all . . . costs . . . is the highest and most unquestioned of [a lawyer's] duties"?

Would you accept the implications of that view in the case Douglas Rosenthal describes on page 176.[19]

B. PROCEDURAL STRUCTURES AND ETHICAL CONSTRAINTS

1. Introduction

The problems in adversarial processes described above have prompted various responses. One approach is to reduce disparities in legal representation through the kind of distributional and regulatory strategies that are described in Chapter II (Traditions of Moral Reasoning), Part C, at pages 18–27; Chapter III (Regulation of the Profession), Part D, at pages 65–81; and Chapter XIV (Criminal Law and Procedure), Part E, at pages 610–621. A second strategy is to alter substantive and procedural rules in ways that minimize incentives for abuse. If noncompliance with legal standards is widespread, the best solution at times may be to modify these doctrines rather than to enlist lawyers as enforcement agents. As the subsequent analysis of witness preparation dilemmas suggests, one way of minimizing perjury is to eliminate dysfunctional barriers to legal relief; an apt illustration is the elimination of fault-based divorce requirements that encouraged fabricated evidence. An alternative response to biased testimony or abusive discovery involves procedural controls like those in place in the European civil law systems described in section 3 below. Finally, in the absence of procedural or substantive reforms, strengthening ethical requirements for lawyers may be the only realistic alternative.

2. Ethical Rules

Current ethical codes impose certain important obligations on lawyers as officers of the court, which are discussed more fully in the sections that follow. Many of these obligations incorporate provisions of the substantive law applicable to all citizens, such as prohibitions on knowing use of perjured or false testimony and knowing misstatements of law or fact.[20] In addition, a lawyer may not assist conduct known to be illegal or fraudulent and may not participate in

the creation of evidence that they know is false.[21] Attorneys who
have knowledge of a fraud perpetrated on a tribunal must take some
remedial measures.[22] Both the Code and Model Rules prohibit actions that are undertaken merely to harass or that would not be
warranted under existing law unless they can be supported by a
good faith argument for modification.[23] And both codes impose
obligations to disclose to a tribunal controlling legal authority known
to be directly adverse to the client's position and not revealed by
opposing counsel.[24]

However, many commentators have argued that these rules are
inadequate, and the drafters of the Model Rules of Professional
Conduct initially proposed a number of provisions that would have
increased lawyer's obligations to the fact-finding process. Those
provisions, explored in the sections that follow, would have prohibited lawyers from

- engag[ing] in any procedure or tactic having no substantial
  purpose other than delay or to increase the burdens on an adversary initiating actions unless a lawyer acting in good faith
  would conclude there is a reasonable basis for doing so;
- offering evidence, without suitable exploration, that the lawyer knows is substantially misleading;
- failing to disclose adverse facts to a tribunal when disclosure
  would probably have a substantial effect on the determination
  of a material issue.[25]

These initial proposals also gave lawyers discretion to disclose
favorable evidence to an opposing party and obligated them to
correct manifest misapprehensions of fact resulting from their own
or their client's previous representations in negotiation.[26]

Marvin Frankel, a member of the drafting commission, had
proposed comparable provisions in an earlier influential article on
lawyers' obligations to truth, excerpted below. Would you support his
or the drafters' proposals? Would they be likely to improve current
adversarial procedures, or are more comprehensive institutional
changes necessary, along the lines suggested by the civil law inquisitorial systems described in section 3, infra? If none of these proposals
seem desirable, what correctives for current adversarial problems
would you support?

MARVIN FRANKEL, THE SEARCH
FOR TRUTH: AN UMPIREAL VIEW

123 U. Pa. L. Rev. 1031, 1056-1059 (1975)

If the lawyer is to be more truth-seeker than combatant, troublesome
questions of economics and professional organization may demand
early confrontation. How and why should the client pay for loyalties
divided between himself and the truth? Will we not stultify the

energies and resources of the advocate by demanding that he judge the honesty of his cause along the way? Can we preserve the heroic lawyer shielding his client against all the world, and not least against the State, while demanding that he honor a paramount commitment to the elusive and ambiguous truth? It is strongly arguable, in short, that a simplistic preference for the truth may not comport with more fundamental ideals, including notably the ideal that generally values individual freedom and dignity above order and efficiency in government. Having stated such issues too broadly, I leave them in the hope that their refinement and study may seem worthy endeavors for the future. . . .

[However, truth is surely one of the adversary system's paramount objectives, and bar ethics rules should be better suited to promote that aim.] The rules of professional responsibility should compel disclosures of material facts and forbid material omissions rather than merely proscribe positive frauds. . . . In an effort to be still more specific, I submit a draft of a new disciplinary rule. . . . The draft says:

> (1) In his representation of a client, unless prevented from doing so by a privilege reasonably believed to apply, a lawyer shall:
> (a) Report to the court and opposing counsel the existence of relevant evidence or witnesses where the lawyer does not intend to offer such evidence or witnesses.
> (b) Prevent, or when prevention has proved unsuccessful, report to the court and opposing counsel the making of any untrue statement by client or witness or any omission to state a material fact necessary in order to make statements made, in the light of the circumstances under which they were made, not misleading.
> (c) Question witnesses with a purpose and design to elicit the whole truth, including particularly supplementary and qualifying matters that render evidence already given more accurate, intelligible, or fair than it otherwise would be.
> (2) In the construction and application of the rules in subdivision (1), a lawyer will be held to possess knowledge he actually has or, in the exercise of reasonable diligence, should have.

Key words in the draft, namely, in (1)(b), have been plagiarized, of course, from the Securities and Exchange Commission's rule 10b-5. That should serve not only for respectability; it should also answer, at least to some extent, the complaint that the draft would impose impossibly stringent standards. The morals we have evolved for business clients cannot be deemed unattainable by the legal profession.

Harder questions suggest themselves. The draft provision for wholesale disclosure of evidence in litigation may be visionary or outrageous, or both. It certainly stretches out of existing shape our conception of the advocate retained to be partisan. As against the yielding up of everything, we are accustomed to strenuous debates about giving a supposedly laggard or less energetic party a share in his adversary's litigation property safeguarded as "work product." A

lawyer must now surmount partisan loyalty and disclose "information clearly establishing" frauds by his client or others. But that is a
far remove from any duty to turn over all the fruits of factual investigation, as the draft proffered here would direct. It has lately come
to be required that some approach to helpful disclosures be made by
prosecutors in criminal cases; "the suppression by the prosecution of
evidence favorable to an accused upon request violates due process
where the evidence is material either to guilt or to punishment,
irrespective of the good faith or bad faith of the prosecution. . . . "
But even that restricted rule is for the *public* lawyer. Can we, should
we, adopt a far broader rule as a command to the bar generally?

   That question touches once again the most sensitive nerve of all.
A bar too tightly regulated, too conformist, too "governmental," is not
acceptable to any of us. We speak often of lawyers as "officers of the
court" and as "public" people. Yet our basic conception of the office is
of one essentially private, private in political, economic, and ideological terms, congruent with a system of private ownership, enterprise, and competition, however modified the system has come to be.
It is not necessary to recount here the contributions of a legal profession thus conceived to the creation and maintenance of a relatively
free society. It *is* necessary to acknowledge those contributions and
to consider squarely whether, or how much, they are endangered by
proposed reforms.

   If we must choose between truth and liberty, the decision is not
in doubt. If the choice seemed to me that clear and that stark, this
essay would never have reached even the tentative form of its present submission. But I think the picture is quite unclear. I lean to the
view that we can hope to preserve the benefits of a free, skeptical,
contentious bar while paying a lesser price in trickery and obfuscation.

---

3.   Cross-Cultural Comparisons

   Some nations have procedural norms that could inspire reforms
in American legal processes. Comparative legal scholars generally
identify three major systems of justice. Common law English-
speaking nations have adversarial structures comparable to the
United States system. Civil law countries in Western Europe and
Latin America employ an inquisitorial process, and totalitarian
governments have generally adopted variations on that process. A
smaller number of nations, primarily in Africa and the Mideast,
have systems based on religious traditions. The following discussion
focuses on the civil law inquisitorial model because it is the source of
most American reform proposals.[27]

   To many individuals, the term "inquisitorial procedure" evokes
visions of state torture reminiscent of the Spanish Inquisition. That

image is highly misleading. In fact, the primary distinction between adversarial and inquisitorial systems lies in the distribution of authority between lawyers and judges. In an adversary system attorneys for the parties develop the case and the judge is a largely passive umpire. In an inquisitorial system, the judge, or panel of judges, plays a far more central role in structuring the litigation.

For example, German civil cases begin with a complaint, which alleges the basis for a claim and proposes means of proof. The complaint includes or identifies relevant documents and lists potential witnesses. The defendant's answer follows the same pattern. Typically, however, neither counsel will have undertaken any significant investigation for evidence beyond what their clients have provided. A presiding judge will review these materials, order relevant documents, and conduct a series of hearings with counsel and sometimes with parties and witnesses. If no settlement occurs, the court establishes a sequence for taking proof and decides which witnesses should be called, which documents are necessary, and which experts, if any, to appoint. The court also takes responsibility for examining witnesses and summarizing their testimony for the record, although lawyers may occasionally ask supplemental questions or suggest changes in wording.

Unlike the American system, with its sharp division between trial and pretrial proceedings, the inquisitorial format involves a series of proceedings that seeks to minimize overpreparation, inefficiency, and surprise. If, for example, a key issue involves the validity of an affirmative defense, the court can take evidence on that point first and, if it finds for the defendant, avoid the need for proof on other aspects of the case. If a new question unexpectedly surfaces, the judge can delay the proceedings to allow investigation. Civil cases are resolved without juries and generally by a panel of judges; appellate review involves a de novo consideration of the record, supplemented if necessary by additional evidence.

The lawyers in such proceedings play a circumscribed role, and their partisanship is subject to certain important restrictions. Attorneys may comment on the court's decisions through oral or written submissions and may suggest additional lines of inquiry. However, they may not influence witnesses and are discouraged even from contacting them. Lawyers may not contradict an opponent's statement if they believe it to be true, and have some obligation to verify a client's representation before attesting to its validity. Fees are set by statute, based largely on the type of case and amount in controversy, irrespective of the hours involved. Contingent fees are not permissible.

Despite such constraints on partisanship, German lawyers generally believe that their primary loyalty is to the client rather than to the state. German and American attorneys often report similar economic pressures and distortions of the decision-making process. However, the structure of German proceedings and billing practices works against certain abuses that plague American adversarial processes. Lawyers who cannot charge by the hour, who have no chance for pretrial depositions, and who need not worry about surprise have fewer incentives for unnecessary preparation and meter-running. Prohibitions on influencing witnesses and hiring experts minimize some of the obfuscating tactics described in Part E below. Inquisitorial proceedings that resemble "routine business meetings" rather than sporting contests or theatrical performances make disparities in lawyers' quality and gamesmanship less relevant.[28]

There are, of course, countervailing disadvantages to a system that relies so heavily on judicial control. One continuing concern, developed more fully by the Joint Conference Report, is that the judge who "opens his mouth closes his mind," and de novo appellate review is an expensive and only partial corrective.[29] Americans traditionally have been reluctant to vest so much power in decision-makers who are largely insulated from direct popular accountability. Some wariness may also stem from this nation's frequent practice of appointing or electing judges based on political connections rather than merit, experience, or training.

Of course, distinctions between adversarial and inquisitorial models should not be overstated. Many European systems are moving toward increased procedural protections and greater reliance on counsel.[30] So too, American judges, particularly in discovery matters and complex cases, are assuming more activist roles. Moreover, the vast majority of America's cases settle without the full adversarial protections that distinguish its legal process.

Nonetheless, there are some general differences in procedural systems that both reflect and reinforce differences in national temperament. What is effective in one cultural context may prove unworkable or unacceptable in another. As comparativists note, inquisitorial systems typically place less importance on protection of individual freedom and more on efficiency, uniformity, and equality of treatment. Our priorities are often reversed. Yet, even granting these cultural variations, many American experts believe that some aspects of the civil law system are worth emulating. As John Merryman notes:

> For those who are concerned about the relative justice of the two systems, a statement made by an eminent scholar after long and careful study is instructive: he said that if he were innocent, he would prefer to be tried by a civil law court, but that if he were guilty, he would prefer to be tried by a common law court. This is, in effect, a judgment that criminal proceedings in the civil law world are more likely to distinguish accurately between the guilty and the innocent.[31]

Consider this claim in light of the problems in adversarial practices described in general terms above and set forth in more detail below.

C. THE TACTICAL USE OF PROCEDURE

On such an afternoon [when the dense fog is densest, and the muddy streets are muddiest], some score of members of the High Court of Chancery bar ought to be — as here they are — mistily engaged in one of the ten thousand stages of an endless cause, tripping one another up on slippery precedents, groping knee-deep in technicalities, running their goat-hair and horsehair warded heads against walls of words, and making a pretence of equity with serious faces, as players might. On such an afternoon, the various solicitors in the cause, some two or three of whom have inherited it from their fathers, who made a fortune by it, ought to be — as are they not — ranged in a line, in a long matted well (but you might look in vain for Truth at the bottom of it), between the registrar's red table and the silk gowns, with bills, cross-bills, answers, rejoinders, injunctions, affidavits, issues, references to masters, masters' reports, mountains of costly nonsense, piled before them. . . .

Jarndyce and Jarndyce drones on. This scarecrow of a suit has, in course of time, become so complicated that no man alive knows what it means. The parties to it understand it least; but it has been observed that no two Chancery lawyers can talk about it for five minutes without coming to a total disagreement as to all the premises. Innumerable children have been born into the cause; innumerable young people have married into it; innumerable old people have died out of it. Scores of persons have deliriously found themselves made parties in Jarndyce and Jarndyce, without knowing how or why; whole families have inherited legendary hatreds with the suit. . . . [T]here are not three Jarndyces left upon the earth perhaps, since old Tom Jarndyce in despair blew his brains out at a coffee-house in Chancery Lane; but Jarndyce and Jarndyce still drags its dreary length before the Court, perennially hopeless. . . .

"Mr. Tangle," says the Lord High Chancellor, latterly something restless under the eloquence of that learned gentleman.

"Mlud," says Mr. Tangle. Mr. Tangle knows more of Jarndyce and Jarndyce than anybody. He is famous for it — supposed never to have read anything else since he left school.

"Have you nearly concluded your argument?"

"Mlud, no — variety of points — feel it my duty to tsubmit—ludship," is the reply that slides out of Mr. Tangle.

"Several members of the bar are still to be heard, I believe?" says the Chancellor, with a slight smile.

Eighteen of Mr. Tangle's learned friends, each armed with a little summary of eighteen hundred sheets, bob up like eighteen hammers in a pianoforte, make eighteen bows, and drop into their eighteen places of obscurity.

Charles Dickens
Bleak House (1853)

1.   The Scope of the Problem

As the excerpt from Bleak House suggests, complaints about the expense and delay of legal proceedings are by no means new or unique to the United States. However, in the last quarter century, the American bar has experienced increased concerns about frivolous claims and abusive tactics. Factors contributing to these concerns include

- the growth in substantive rights that can give rise to legal claims;
- the growth in scale and complexity of some forms of litigation;
- the increased use of billing by the hour for litigation matters;
- the growth in size and competitiveness of the bar; and
- the related decline in informal community sanctions.

Yet while perceptions of a problem have become more widespread, the scope of that problem remains open to some dispute. Whether "frivolous" cases should be a paramount concern is not self-evident because what constitutes frivolity is itself controversial. The United States' current litigation rates are not exceptionally high, either in comparison with prior historical eras or with other western nations not known for undue contentiousness, such as Canada, Australia, England, and Denmark.[32] Many arguments about America's "legal hypochondria" or "hyperlexis" rest on largely anecdotal evidence of trivial cases: football fans suing referees, suitors suing dates, and beauty contestants suing each other.[33] However, such examples do not of themselves establish that America has exceptional problems with frivolous suits or that they occupy an undue amount of judicial time. The issue is always: compared with what?

Historical and cross-cultural research reveals comparable claims such as a 1965 Belgrade court coping with 9,000 slander suits.[34] What constitutes frivolity is often in the eye of the beholder, and the boundary between vindictiveness and vindication is often difficult to draw. Consider, for instance, what a prominent law school dean once labeled as "inappropriate" claims: sex discrimination suits against Little Leagues.[35] Is it self-evident that such claims are a "waste" of judicial resources given the importance this nation attaches to sports, its long-standing inequalities in male and female athletic opportunities, and the gender stereotypes that such inequalities reinforce?

Another equally problematic example involves a multimillion-dollar punitive damages award against McDonald's for serving coffee at scalding temperatures. Commentators offered endless variations on the theme summarized by the national Chamber of Commerce: "Is it fair to get a couple of million dollars from a restaurant just because you spilled hot coffee on yourself?" On closer examination, that question no longer seems rhetorical. The plaintiff, a 79-year-old woman, spent eight days in the hospital after suffering acutely painful third-degree burns from 180° coffee. Only after McDonald's refused to reimburse her medical expenses did she bring suit. At trial, jurors learned of 700 other burn cases involving McDonald's coffee during the preceding decade. Their verdict of $2.3 million represented two days of coffee sales revenues, and the judge reduced the judgment to $640,000. To avoid an appeal, the plaintiff then settled the case for an undisclosed amount, and McDonald's, as well as other fast-food chains, put warnings on cups and signs.[36] Does this case reflect what's wrong or what's right with the current system? By what criteria?

Although the scope of the "litigiousness" problem is subject to dispute, there is widespread agreement that some litigation-related problems exist. Courts, practitioners, and researchers report unacceptable levels of abusive conduct in high-stakes cases. While the vast majority of state and federal proceedings involve relatively little discovery and relatively few reported difficulties, lawyers in large complex cases report chronic abuses. The average litigant is "over-discovered . . . over-charged, over-exposed, and over-wrought."[37] In Wayne Brazil's study of Chicago litigators, 62 percent complained about overdiscovery, and 80 percent complained about incomplete or evasive responses to requests. Lawyers who handled large cases reported that in about half the matters that settled and in about 30 percent of those that tried, they had significant information that had not been discovered by other parties.[38]

Techniques for evading or exhausting an adversary are not in short supply. Examples include:

- Abusive scheduling practices, such as arranging depositions in order to impose maximum inconvenience and expense, and refusing to acquiesce in reasonable requests or extensions of time;
- Objectionable questioning techniques, such as seeking embarrassing but unnecessary information, objecting to reason-

able inquiries, inappropriately coaching witnesses, or instructing them not to answer;

- Overuse of depositions and interrogatories, such as drafting
  inquiries "with 2800 questions including subparts" and (so
  that "no one will mistake the attorney's virility") labeling
  these the "First Set of Interrogatories";[39]
- Evasive strategies, such as promising but failing to answer at
  a later date; asserting the attorney-client privilege without
  an adequate basis; referring to an entire transcript of a related case; reshuffling documents to prevent an opponent
  from locating relevant materials; or placing the "smoking pistol" in an "irrelevant mess in the middle of [a] warehouse and
  invit[ing] the adversary to visit for a spell."[40]

Such practices arise from a complex set of economic, social, and
psychological factors. By prolonging proceedings, some clients can
continue engaging in profitable activity, maintain use of the money
at stake, avoid publicizing unfavorable facts, or obtain time to respond to unwelcome contingencies, such as a corporate takeover bid
or property development project. By turning litigation into an expensive war of attrition, parties may also be able to force a favorable
settlement or discourage other potential adversaries from filing suit.
As the materials in Chapter I indicate, some discovery abuse may
also be the result of prisoner's dilemmas: clients who fear that their
adversaries are playing with "hardball" tactics may decide that the
only prudent strategy is to follow a similar approach. As a consequence, both sides may sometimes end up paying more for discovery
than either would prefer.

Lawyers' own incentives also contribute to discovery problems.
In wars of attrition, arms suppliers are often the largest winners,
and attorneys are the functional equivalent. Counsel seeking to
maximize billable hours have an obvious interest in meter-running,
a practice that litigators frequently report experiencing but never
committing.[41] Many lawyers are understandably risk-averse, and
leaving no stone unturned has obvious advantages "if you can charge
by the stone."[42] Prolonging pretrial maneuvers to force settlements
can also avoid the costs of defeat and the loss of reputation that it
might entail. As pretrial proceedings become more and more likely to
replace trials, litigators become less and less likely to have courtroom experience. They also become less and less willing to assume
the risk of going to trial, which reinforces the incentives for pretrial
maneuvers.[43] Finally, lawyers as well as clients can easily become
used to a combative approach, and retaliation has its own rewards.
Two wrongs don't make a right, but they may be the next best thing
when locking horns with a "paper warrior."[44]

There are, however, significant countervailing concerns. As
many prominent litigators note, abusive tactics carry a cost for
perpetrators as well as their opponents and can often prove counter-

productive. In the short run, evasive, harassing, or overly aggressive behavior can provoke retaliation or sanctions and undercut construc-tive settlement efforts. In the long term, such conduct can compro-mise a lawyer's reputation for integrity and reasonableness. The result is likely to be less credibility and fewer referrals from courts and opponents, as well as more acrimonious working environments.[45]

Relations with clients may also suffer. For some individuals, having lawyers who are known for honesty and fairness is a way of avoiding "prisoners' dilemmas." As discussion in Chapter VIII (Nego-tiation and Mediation) indicates, such dilemmas arise when people find it individually rational to act against their collective best inter-est because they cannot be sure how another party will act. Assume, for example, that two parties are fighting over ownership of a million dollars' worth of property. Each side has material information not known to the other side, some favorable and some unfavorable. Suppose that if both cooperate with discovery requests, each will have minimal disclosure costs and that a neutral decision-maker would split the million dollars between them. If neither cooperates, they will end up with the same decision but each will need to spend substantial resources on discovery. For example, they may need to fight over what information is privileged; sift through irrelevant or nonresponsive materials; and attempt to verify lawyers' representa-tions. If one party cooperates and the other does not, the "sucker" has greater costs, receives less information, and may obtain a less favorable outcome than his adversary. Given this payoff structure, parties who are uncertain about their adversaries' behavior may decide against cooperation and thus prevent the most desirable mutual outcome. By contrast, if both sides hire attorneys known to avoid discovery abuse, the costs of litigation may be lower and the possibility of acceptable settlements may be greater.[46]

How best to curb procedural abuse and prevent prisoners' dilemmas is a matter of long-standing controversy. Although law-yers place primary responsibility with the courts, judges have their own reasons to avoid involvement. Sorting out who is at fault in pretrial disputes is a time-consuming and frequently thankless enterprise. It often requires more knowledge than overburdened judges have time to acquire, particularly on matters that are un-likely to require trial or that do not involve clear villains and vic-tims. Most judges also dislike antagonizing lawyers by imposing sanctions, because that can compromise settlement efforts, risk reversal on appeal, provoke retaliation in elections or bar opinion polls, and make the proceedings less pleasant.[47] If counsel cannot manage to behave civilly toward one another, a traditional judicial response has been to let them pay the price.

Yet the costs of procedural abuse are not borne by the parties alone. Legal costs are passed on to consumers in the form of higher prices and subsidized by taxpayers through public funding for the courts and tax deductions for business expenses. How to modify the incentive structures that contribute to abusive tactics has become a matter of public as well as professional interest.

PROBLEM 5B

You are a former legal aid lawyer who occasionally represents tenants pro bono in disputes with their landlords. In the local housing court in which you practice, about 90 percent of tenants are unrepresented by counsel, and the vast majority of judges (appointed by a conservative governor) are unsympathetic to defenses in routine evictions. Crushing caseloads have exacerbated the problem; over two-thirds of all cases are handled in under fifteen minutes and a third in under six. Landlords have therefore become somewhat lax in complying with procedural formalities, including notice requirements. Your former legal aid office has decided to challenge such practices in an effort to increase tenants' bargaining leverage and opportunities for a hearing. You have agreed to help.

One of your current cases involves a client facing eviction for nonpayment of rent. Unless the court is willing to overlook a well-established line of cases holding that building code violations are not a defense in suits for nonpayment of rent, the tenant has no chance for success. However, by preparing a general denial of the complaint and demanding a jury trial, you can delay the proceeding for 60 days. That would give your client sufficient time to save enough cash for a security deposit on another apartment. You could also demand a hearing on service of process, which would gain the tenant another two weeks.

As is common in the area, the process server slipped the eviction notice under your client's door rather than complying with a statutory requirement that personal service should be attempted first and, if that proves impossible, the notice should be taped to the door and a copy sent by registered mail. Although your client received actual notice of the eviction proceeding, you have reason to believe that other tenants in the area are victims of "sewer service"; courts often enter default judgments before the renter learns of the hearing. Your former legal aid colleagues are convinced that the best way to curb such practices is to force landlords to prove compliance with statutory formalities in every case for which a lawyer is available.

Your state code of civil procedure has a provision identical to Federal Rule 11. You are also subject to the Model Rules of Professional Conduct, including Rules 3.1 and 3.2, which prohibit frivolous claims and require "reasonable efforts to expedite litigation consistent with the interests of the client." Under those provisions, can you file a general denial of the landlord's claim and demand a hearing on service of process? Should you? Would it matter why your client has not paid the rent?

Suppose the trial court finds that building code violations are not a defense to your client's nonpayment of rent. In your judgment, the chances that an appellate court will overrule that determination are minimal, but the appointment of one new judge makes it theoretically possible that the issue might receive reconsideration. Can you file the appeal? If you were counsel for the landlord and the tenant appealed, would you move for sanctions?[48]

For related problems, see Chapter XVII (Property), Problem 17A at page 735, and Chapter X (Civil Procedure), Problem 10A at pages 430–431.

PROBLEM 5C

You are on the court of appeals in a suit brought by former United States Attorney General Ramsey Clark on behalf of Libyan citizens. The plaintiffs sought to recover damages from the United Kingdom and United States governments as well as various named officials for losses resulting from the United States' 1986 air strikes on Libya. The strikes were launched from British airbases for the ostensible purpose of retaliating against Libyan-sponsored attacks, particularly the bombing of a Berlin nightclub. However, West German authorities had concluded prior to the U.S. strikes that Libya was not involved in the bombing, and no evidence challenging that conclusion was ever presented.[49]

The trial court held that British defendants were protected from suit by existing immunity provisions and act of state doctrine, and that the United States defendants were protected by sovereign immunity. In short, the case offered "no hope whatsoever of success and plaintiffs' attorneys surely knew it." Saltany v. Reagan, 702 F. Supp. 319, 320 (D.D.C. 1988). However, because "the injuries for which the suit is brought are not insubstantial," the court viewed the case as "not frivolous so much as it is audacious." Id. In the trial judge's view, courts could "serve in some respects as a forum for making [political] statements, and should continue to do so." Id. Accordingly, he imposed no Rule 11 sanctions.

The defendants have appealed the denial of sanctions. If you agree with the trial court's assessment of the chances of success, what do you decide concerning sanctions?

Enforcing prohibitions against frivolous claims presents inherent difficulties. Positions that appear frivolous today may become law tomorrow, and any sanction sufficient to deter truly meritless actions may deter innovative ones as well. This tension is captured in debates over subjective versus objective standards. If the test is subjective, the difficulties of proving bad faith will make prohibitions on frivolous suits extremely difficult to enforce. Alternatively, if the standard is objective, based on a reasonable person's perspective, then the cost of chilling novel claims can be substantial. That cost will be even greater if the standard is itself unclear about what constitutes reasonableness. Do current ethical and procedural rules provide sufficient guidance on these matters? What percentage of lawyers would have to view a claim as frivolous and how convinced would they need to be before sanctions are appropriate? If a reasonable lawyer would find a claim non-frivolous, does it matter if the client's motive is delay?

In 1895, in Plessy v. Ferguson, 163 U.S. 537, the United States upheld "separate but equal" racial segregation. Would immediately arguing for a contrary conclusion have been frivolous? If so, what changes would need to occur before the argument became permissible? Should it matter whether the Court was virtually certain to reaffirm *Plessy* if the lawyer was equally certain that the case was wrongly decided? Consider Jules Lobel's argument that "[i]t was the political climate in 1890 that made even counsel for Plessy realize the hopelessness of a favorable outcome in the Supreme Court, not the weakness of the claims." In Lobel's view, hopeless claims aren't necessarily frivolous; they may serve important purposes in publicizing issues, encouraging political action, and laying groundwork for legal change.[50] What is your view? How should courts and ethical codes balance the values of legal reform versus stare decisis?

Does the *Plessy* analogy hold for circumstances like Problem 5B? Critics of such practices argue that they constitute an inequitable wealth transfer from the nonlitigious to litigious poor; landlords will pass on the costs of tenants who don't pay their rent to tenants who do. In commenting on a case with some similarities to Problem 5B, a New York attorney writes:

> Such efforts should not be considered "pro bono" because they vindicate no public interest. They do nothing more than shift the cost from one party to another without regard to the equities of the situation. Indeed, such efforts might more accurately be characterized as "anti bono" because they actually work against the public interest. They flood the courts with meritless litigation. They delay the progress of legitimate litigation. And they increase the cost of doing business, both for public agencies and private landlords, which is then passed along to the ultimate consumers, the taxpayers and the tenants who pay their rent.[51]

Do you agree? Does your assessment depend on whether you believe that landlords in fact can transfer such costs in the form of higher rent? Are other "equities" besides the amount of rent due also relevant, such as the difficulties of enforcing warranties of habitability and ensuring fair eviction notice procedures?

On the facts in Problem 5C, the United States Court of Appeals for the District of Columbia held that sanctions were appropriate. Unlike the trial court, the appellate panel did "not conceive it a proper function of a federal court to serve as a forum for 'protests,' to the detriment of parties with serious disputes waiting to be heard." Saltany v. Regan, 886 F.2d 438 (1989).[52] Do you agree?

PROBLEM 5D

1. Consider the issue of discovery abuse in the Berkey-Kodak case, described in Chapter III (Regulation of the Profession) at pages 82–86. If

you had been the associate, what would you have done? Alternatively, suppose you had been the trial judge, and lawyers for Berkey had requested sanctions based on Kodak's failure to disclose a letter from its expert witness. Berkey's discovery request had called for all "interim reports" prepared by that witness, and Kodak lawyers claimed that the letter constituted correspondence rather than a report. Berkey's counsel responded that the letter expressed a position contrary to that taken at trial and that it was obviously the sort of preliminary statement of opinion that the discovery demand meant to include. From their perspective, Kodak's artificially narrow construction of the discovery request constituted bad faith, because its lawyers could have resolved any genuine ambiguity through clarification by the court. What would you decide?

2. You are a mid-level law firm associate in charge of responding to discovery requests in a $50 million dispute. On the day the responses are due, there is a computer crash, and you cannot print out the final text until shortly after midnight. In order for the responses to qualify as timely, someone must certify that they were put into the mail by midnight. Sanctions for a late filing could include a decision by the court to deem the responses admitted at trial. A secretary offers to certify that the documents were mailed before midnight. What do you do? To what extent does your answer depend on:

- Why no margin for error was available;
- Whether the supervising partner assures you not to worry about the certification because "this sort of thing happens all the time";
- How significant the admissions would be if the case went to trial;
- How you assess the conduct of opposing counsel;
- What effect your decision might have on your status in the firm?

What other factors would be relevant?

3. You are the lawyer responsible for discovery in the case described in Problem 10A, Chapter X (Civil Procedure), at page 430. How do you respond?

Consider the material on deception in Chapter II (Traditions of Moral Reasoning) at pages 27–32 and on subordinate attorneys in Chapter III (Regulation of the Profession) at pages 82–89. Do the partners' judgments in Problems 5D(1) and 5D(2) qualify as "reasonable resolutions of an arguably professional duty" under Model Rule 5.3? What could law firms do to assist associates facing these sorts of dilemmas?

Assume that the associate in 5D(1) does nothing and that the associate in 5D(2) authorizes a perjurious certification. If the full facts later come to light, how should the firms respond? Would bar disciplinary sanctions be appropriate?

In her analysis of lying, excerpted in Chapter II (Traditions of Moral Reasoning) at pages 28–30, Sissela Bok observes that all want to avoid being deceived by *others* as much as possible. But many would like to be able to weigh the advantages and disadvantages in a more nuanced way whenever they are themselves in the position of choosing whether or not to deceive. They may invoke special reasons to lie . . . and are then much more willing . . . to exonerate a well-intentioned lie on their own part.

But in this benevolent self-evaluation by the liar of the lies he might tell, certain kinds of disadvantage and harm are almost always overlooked. Liars usually weigh only the immediate harm to others from the lie against the benefits they want to achieve. The flaw in such an outlook is that it ignores or underestimates two additional kinds of harm, the harm that lying does to the liars themselves and the harm done to the general level of trust and social cooperation. Both are cumulative; both are hard to reverse.[53]

As Bok notes, the liar is affected by his own lie in several ways. It is an "inroad on his integrity," and after the first lie, "others can come more easily. Psychological barriers wear down; lies seem more necessary . . . the ability to make moral distinctions can coarsen."[54] And with more lies come more chances that the true facts will come to light, with all the costs that public exposure may entail.

Does this suggest that the considerations noted at the end of Problem 5D(2) were inadequate? How would you weigh the relevant factors?

2.   The Range of Possible Responses

The principal means of enforcing prohibitions against discovery abuse has been Rule 11 and its state court analogues, discussed in Chapter X (Civil Procedure) at pages 430–437. The inadequacies of this approach have led to other proposals, including voluntary bar civility codes.

Such codes reflect widespread concerns. In one of the most comprehensive surveys, involving some 1,300 lawyers and judges, a committee of the Seventh Circuit Federal Judicial Circuit found that 45 percent of judges and 42 percent of lawyers agreed that civility was lacking.[55] Most respondents also targeted discovery as the major source of conflict.

Such perceptions have prompted various initiatives. In 1988, the ABA House of Delegates adopted a recommendation that state and local bar associations "encourage their members to accept . . . a lawyers' creed of professionalism," although nothing in such a creed should supersede existing disciplinary rules or establish liability standards. The Los Angeles County Bar Association's Litigation Guidelines are a representative example. They include requirements that lawyers refrain from

- communicating with their adversaries in anything other than "civil and courteous" fashion;

- using interrogatories, document demands, or depositions as a means to harass or to generate expense;
- engaging in any conduct during a deposition that would not be allowed in the presence of a judicial officer;
- coaching deponents while a question is pending;
- reading interrogatories or document demands in an artificially restrictive manner to avoid disclosure.

Would you support such a code? Would you prefer to practice in a jurisdiction where lawyers complied with its standards? How successful do you think such voluntary standards will be in affecting conduct? Consider critics' claim that an unenforceable code will be ineffective, that an enforceable code with more stringent standards than existing rules will be confusing, and that an enforceable code with comparable standards will be redundant.[56] Do you agree?

Other commonly proposed responses to procedural abuse include law firm policies and training programs; more resources to encourage managerial judging; greater use of special masters; standing referees provided through bar associations; more disciplinary actions against lawyers and law firms; replacement of hourly billing structures with flat-fee rates that would eliminate incentives for overdiscovery; requirements that losers pay winners' legal fees and court costs; and orders that parties who make burdensome discovery requests subsidize their opponents' compliance.[57] In addition, many commentators place primary responsibility on law schools to instill ethical standards.[58] Which of these approaches to procedural abuse would strike you as most promising?

D. DISCLOSURE OF FACTS AND LAW

See Chapter X, Civil Procedure
- Procedural Values and Litigation Strategies: Disclosure of Facts and Law
  (pages 439–446)

E. RELATIONS WITH WITNESSES

1. Witness Preparation

PROBLEM 5E

You are a struggling solo practitioner specializing in plaintiffs' personal injury actions. A young woman seeks your advice about any legal claim she might have arising from a fall outside her apartment six months ago. She recalls walking up Third Avenue, day-dreaming and worrying about where she might find a permanent job, when she stepped off a curb and landed flat on her back. A young man ran across the street to help her. While supporting herself by leaning on barriers at a Commonwealth construction site several feet from the accident, she flagged a taxi. The bystander accompanied her to the emergency room of a nearby hospital. Since the accident, she has been unemployed and in more or less constant pain as a result of a ruptured spinal disc.

Under prevailing law, the woman has no chance for recovery unless she (1) tripped over loose sidewalk or construction debris, neither of which she has mentioned, and (2) was not so inattentive as to be contributorily negligent. Her chances of recovery against the store that is undertaking the construction would likely depend on whether there was sufficient evidence of debris and passenger footprints in the area to suggest that the owners had constructive notice of the danger.

1. Do you inform her of these facts before asking whether she noticed any cement chunks or construction material in the vicinity? If you do, and if she responds that there may well have been some object causing her to trip, what is your response?

2. Assume that you have accepted the case and are preparing your client for deposition. How do you suggest she describe her mental state at the time of the injury?

3. Do you suggest that you or your client contact the bystander? What, if anything, do you tell the prospective witness about prevailing law at the outset of the interview? If it appears that your client has already correctly explained the law to the witness, who thinks perhaps he may have seen a loose piece of sidewalk but can't be certain, what is your response?[59]

PROBLEM 5F

Consider the following lawyers' statements in preparing witnesses for testimony. Are any ethically impermissible or tactically inappropriate?

Instructions on Recollection, Vocabulary, and Demeanor

1. If there is any uncertainty in your mind, say you don't recall. It's almost impossible to prove that "I don't recall" is a false answer.

2. I'm hearing you say that the green car was traveling very fast when it hit the truck. Why don't you say that the green car "smashed" into the truck? Is that word OK by you?

3. If you are unable to say that the contract was "critical," then we might as well go home.

4. It seems to me that this employee was always interfering in other people's projects. Isn't that right?

5. This attorney gets flustered because he has difficulty asking clear questions. Stare at him as if he's speaking a foreign language.

Information on Law and Facts

6. We need to show that if the plaintiff had looked around for alternatives beginning the day we terminated the sales contract, the plaintiff could have found a suitable replacement with little or no effort. If we prove that, we win the case. How can we show that?

7. Before I ask you about your recollection, let me tell you what Mary Smith recalls.[60]

Ethical problems in witness preparation fall across a spectrum. At one end lie overt efforts to create false evidence. Such conduct clearly violates Model Rule 3.3 and DR 7-102, which prohibit an attorney from knowingly using false evidence or perjured testimony. At the other end of the spectrum lie inadvertent effects: a wide array of evidence makes clear that lawyers' discussions with clients can significantly alter recollections and descriptions of events, even when neither intend to lie.[61] A considerable amount of coaching behavior falls in between, and neither ethical rules nor court and bar opinions provide detailed guidance.

Model Rule 1.2 provides that "a lawyer shall not counsel a client to engage or assist a client in conduct that the lawyer knows is criminal or fraudulent . . . but may counsel or assist a client to make a good faith effort to determine the validity, scope, meaning or application of the law." What constitutes "good faith" in Problem 5E? If the client remembers the facts differently after learning the law, does the attorney "know" that she is lying? How certain does a lawyer need to be? Does it matter whether the case is criminal or civil (see Chapter XIV (Criminal Law and Procedure) at pages 595–608), or what the attorney thinks about the legitimacy of the underlying law (see Simon's divorce and welfare examples, pages 151–154)?

Consider one personal injury practitioner's views on witness preparation:

> The classic case for coaching is what we call the "fall-down case." You have the supermarket, with the freshly mopped floor or the aisle covered with produce. Along comes Mrs. Smith, who falls on her ass and breaks her hip. Now in Pennsylvania an airtight defense under contributory negligence can be built with one question: "Did you look before you walked?" If she says no, good-bye, her case is over.
>
> Now this is ridiculous, for the *leitmotif* of a supermarket is to attract the customer's attention with bright displays and piles of fancy foods. . . . Hell, if customers walked around with their heads down, it would be catastrophic to the national economy. But the law says this must be done, otherwise you bust your ass at your own expense. So again you resort to coaching to fit the facts to the cubbyhole. An intelligent client, once he hears your lecture, can come up with any number of answers: "I stepped around a crate on the floor and fell on the first step before I had a chance to see what was before me. . . ." "The shopping cart blocked my view." "I was carrying a shopping bag, and doing my best to see where I was going. . . ."

I'd like a system of justice where you could lay out the facts and
let common sense prevail, and not some doctrines the insurance industry managed to wheedle through the Pennsylvania legislature and
the Pennsylvania Supreme Court. This would mean an effective end
to lawyering, I suppose, but more and more I feel like a coach, not a
trial lawyer.[62]

A long-standing debate has centered on the technique, summarized by Marvin Frankel, of "telling the client 'the law' before eliciting the facts, i.e. telling the client what facts would constitute a
successful claim or defense and only then asking the client what the
facts happen perchance to be."[63] Robert Traver's Anatomy of a Murder (1958) offers a well-known fictional account of the technique.
After receiving instruction about what constituted a defense of
impaired mental capacity, a murder defendant conveniently recalls
facts that fit the defense.

Where is the boundary between "helping [to present] what the
witness knows and . . . helping the witness to know new things?"[64]
Monroe Freedman defends the practice of disclosing the law before
discussing the facts on the ground that "[i]t is not the lawyer's
function to prejudge his client as a perjurer. He cannot presume that
the client will make unlawful use of his advice. . . . [T]here is a
natural predisposition in most people to recollect facts, entirely
honestly, in a way most favorable to their own interest. . . . Before he
begins to remember essential facts, the client is entitled to know
what his own interests are. . . . To decide otherwise would . . .
penalize the less well-educated defendant."[65]

Other commentators make similar factual assumptions but
arrive at a different conclusion. In their view, it is asking too much
of human nature to provide a motive for lying and then to ask for the
truth. While well-informed clients may be better able to deceive
without assistance, it does not follow that a lawyer's role is to give
everyone equal skills in deception. Advising parties about the law
under circumstances that will tempt them to conceal documents or
misrepresent facts can be imprudent as well as unethical. As Chapter VI on Confidentiality and Client Counseling makes clear, attorneys often face enough difficulties obtaining truthful information
without supplying a motive for distortion.[66] If an attorney strongly
suspects a potential witness of lying, others may as well. As one
lawyer explained in Kenneth Mann's study of white-collar criminal
defense work, "I don't want to be associated with a client who is
concealing facts from me; my career is more valuable than any single
client's needs."[67] Attorneys in Mann's study often found non-judg-
mental ways of counseling their clients against perjury or destruction of evidence:

I don't say, "Look, I can't allow you do to do that." That puts me
in a one-up moral position and is most embarrassing for the client. I
usually say something like, "The penalties are very severe,
and . . . [the truth] may turn up later and cause you more trouble, so I

advise you not to do it." That makes it seem more like I'm helping him
protect himself rather than demonstrating some kind of moral superiority.[68]

A related issue involves helping witnesses to accurately or
effectively describe events. Again, pretrial preparation can assist as
well as distort fact-finding processes. It can prompt recollection;
encourage careful choice of language; alert participants to unfavorable facts; eliminate annoying or suspicious mannerisms; prevent
unduly technical or rambling presentations; and aid unsophisticated,
nervous, or reticent individuals in making effective presentations.[69]
Such assistance can often make a substantial difference in the way
fact-finders view a case. For example, in one study, subjects who
watched the same collision gave differing estimates of the speed of
the vehicles depending on how the impact was described; "smashed"
resulted in average responses of 41 miles per hour, "hit" yielded 34
miles per hour, and "contacted" yielded 32 miles per hour.[70]

An interesting exchange on the rationale and risks of witness
preparation occurred on the seventy-fifth anniversary of the notorious Triangle Shirtwaist factory fire. In that disaster, 146 women,
mostly immigrants, burned to death. The incident became a turning
point in the struggle for protective labor legislation and also resulted
in prosecution of the factory owners for violation of safety statutes.
At trial, after poignant testimony from one of the victims, defense
counsel requested her to repeat her narrative. When she provided an
almost verbatim repetition, the lawyer asked about one word she had
used in her first but not second account. After repeating the testimony silently to herself, moving her lips slightly in the process, the
witness confirmed that she had erroneously omitted the word. After
briefly changing the subject, counsel then repeated the strategy with
similar results. The obviously rehearsed nature of the victim's
testimony helped undermine the credibility of the prosecution's case
and secure an acquittal. A New York Law Journal article com-
mending the defense counsel for exposing canned testimony provoked an angry letter to the editor. Its authors noted that many
women who testified in the case needed rehearsing; they spoke little
or no English and were traumatized by the fire and court proceedings.[71]

How would you have handled the Triangle factory case? Were
other options available for the plaintiffs' attorney, such as insisting
on an interpreter? Note that even with interpreters, subtle differences in cultural meanings can open avenues for misleading cross-
examination, particularly among unsophisticated witnesses.[72]

Are different circumstances presented by the "day-dreaming"
client in Problem 5E? How would you distinguish between helping
her recollect and helping her revise reality? According to Opinion 79
of the Committee on Legal Ethics of the District of Columbia (1980),
a lawyer may suggest language as long as the "substance of the
testimony is not, as far as the lawyer knows or ought to know, false

or misleading." What would constitute "misleading" on the facts of Problem 5E?

Would more stringent standards concerning witness preparation be desirable? A preliminary draft of the Model Rules included a provision that would have prohibited lawyers from offering advice that they could "reasonably foresee will aid a client in giving false testimony." Would such a standard, whether formally codified or informally followed, provide useful guidance? Would you prefer the approach of many civil law countries, which forbids lawyers' preparation of witnesses?

See Chapter XV, Evidence and Trial Advocacy
  • Witness Preparation
       (pages 662–669)

2.   Impeachment

> One would naturally imagine . . . that an undis-
> turbed thread of clear evidence would be best
> obtained from a man whose position was made
> easy and whose mind was not harassed; but this
> is not the fact; to turn a witness to good account,
> he must be badgered this way and that till he is
> nearly mad; he must be made a laughing stock
> for the court; his very truths must be turned
> into falsehoods, so that he may be falsely
> shamed; he must be accused of all manner of
> villainy, threatened with all manner of punish-
> ment; he must be made to feel that he has no
> friend near him, that the world is all against
> him; he must be confounded till he forget his
> right hand from his left, till his mind be turned
> into chaos, and his heart into water; and then
> let him give his evidence. What will fall from his
> lips when in this wretched collapse must be of
> special value, for the best talents of practiced fo-
> rensic heroes are daily used to bring it about.
>
> *Anthony Trollope*[73]

PROBLEM 5G

1. You represent a lawyer on criminal charges growing out of his representation of an 89-year-old woman. She lived alone with no family nearby and retained the lawyer to take care of a few monthly expenses such as rent and utility bills. After she gave him her bankbooks to withdraw the necessary funds, he withdrew over $100,000 for the purchase of a Cadillac and investments listed in his own and his wife's names. A neighbor's discovery of these withdrawals led to criminal indictment.

Your client's defense is that the woman lent him some of the money and asked him to invest the remainder. However, he neglected to keep copies of the promissory notes. The widow recalls no such agreement and prosecutors have located no such notes.

The client refused to plea bargain or to make any restitution, and the case proceeded to trial. You cross-examined the woman about details unrelated to the incident in an effort to establish her faulty memory. She became quite confused about the date of her birth and her husband's death, but is clear about the recent events surrounding the lawyer's conduct. After lengthy deliberations, the jury deadlocked 11 to 1 in favor of conviction and the judge declared a mistrial.

While waiting for a new trial you learn that the woman is in ill health and lacks sufficient funds to pay for medical care. Although the bar has filed disciplinary charges against your client, its backlog of cases is so great that the woman will probably not survive long enough to testify. The client is pleased with your representation and again refuses any plea bargains. He asks if there is anything he can do to help delay the proceeding. Your partners ask if there is anything you can do to withdraw from representation. How do you respond? Would your answer be different if the case involved civil fraud charges, not a criminal prosecution?[74]

2. You represent an indigent 13-year-old boy accused of sexually molesting an 8-year-old boy. Your client was himself the victim of sexual abuse by his now incarcerated father. You have good reason to believe that the 8-year-old is telling the truth. While you and the prosecutor both agree that your client belongs in a therapeutic setting, she is insisting on a facility far from the boy's home. Your client is unwilling to accept that placement and insists that he will run away if cut off from his family. If the matter proceeds to trial, are you obligated to impeach the testimony of the 8-year-old?[75]

3. You represent one codefendant in a campus rape case. The incident took place after the complainant, a sophomore, originally from Jamaica, accepted a ride home with your client following rifle club practice. He is a college senior from a middle-class white family and this is the second time he has been accused of sexual assault. According to the complainant, on the evening in question your client said he needed to stop off at his fraternity house and invited the woman in. A number of his friends, all white, were drinking. They pressured the woman into joining them. One guided a cup to her lips. When she indicated that she felt sick, she was taken upstairs. She slid down on a couch and the defendant began undressing her. She protested but was too sick and scared to resist physically. She passed out and, when she awoke, three fraternity brothers were taking turns sodomizing her. They continued despite her screams but eventually allowed her to leave. Your client insists that he believed the woman consented. His fraternity has a history of initiating "little sisters" through drinking and group sex, and he thought this woman was aware of the tradition. He also tells you that Caribbean women are "hot-blooded" and "highly sexed," and he's sure that fact will be relevant to a jury.

Investigators hired by the defendant's family have discovered a disaffected former boyfriend of the victim. He is willing to testify that she was "flirtatious," that she was taking birth control pills, and that she often did what was necessary to "fit in" and "be accepted." According to investigator's reports, the woman is from a conservative Catholic family. You suspect that vigorous pretrial questioning about her provocative dress and her prior sexual relationships might persuade her to drop the case. Under your state's rape shield statute, a victim's prior sexual conduct is not admissible unless "it is material to negating . . . force or coercion." Findings from a recent state task force report on gender bias convince you that some judges would admit this evidence in order to avoid reversal on appeal. You also know that some prosecutors avoid objecting to questions about sexual history because they don't want the complainant to look as if she has something to hide.

Under prevailing case law, the prior allegation of rape against your client is likely to appear too prejudicial and too dissimilar from this incident to be admissible at trial. In that earlier case, the victim decided not to press charges after being harassed by the defendant's friends and humiliated by pretrial proceedings. You are concerned that a similar outcome in this case would discourage other women from coming forward and would add to the well-documented problems of campus sexual assault. You also worry that as defense counsel, that's not what you should be worrying about.

How do you proceed? Would your answer be different if you were a public defender, your client was from a poor black family, and the victim was from a wealthy white family?[76]

Problem 5G raises a number of fundamental questions of legal ethics:

1. What are lawyers' responsibilities when they believe that their client is guilty or wishes to assert a position that is factually untrue?

2. Are clients entitled to a defense that includes impeaching a witness whom the lawyer believes is telling the truth?

3. Do the answers to those questions vary depending on whether that case is civil or criminal? Should lawyers' obligations take into account the costs to potential witnesses? If so, does rape stand on a different footing from other civil or criminal proceedings? Alternatively, does any matter involving particularly vulnerable victims present special considerations?

4. Should the lawyer's gender affect resolution of these issues? Does a defendant gain an extra and unwarranted advantage from representation by a female attorney in a case where the sexual history of a witness is relevant? Might a juror assume that no woman would zealously attack another woman's credibility without a belief that she was testifying untruthfully?

5. Do the bar's ethical rules provide adequate guidance on these questions? Consider the following provisions:

AMERICAN BAR ASSOCIATION, STANDARDS RELATING TO THE ADMINISTRATION OF CRIMINAL JUSTICE, THE DEFENSE FUNCTION (1991)

Standard 4-7.6

(a) The interrogation of all witnesses should be conducted fairly, objectively, and with due regard for the dignity and legitimate privacy of the witness, and without seeking to intimidate or humiliate the witness unnecessarily. Proper cross-examination can be conducted without violating rules of decorum.

(b) Defense counsel's belief or knowledge that the witness is telling the truth does not preclude cross-examination.

(c) Defense counsel should not ask a question which implies the existence of a factual predicate for which a good faith belief is lacking.

AMERICAN BAR ASSOCIATION, MODEL CODE OF PROFESSIONAL RESPONSIBILITY (1981)

Disciplinary Rule 7-106(c)

A lawyer shall not . . .

(2) Ask any question that he has no basis to believe is relevant to the case and that is intended to degrade a witness or another person.

Disciplinary Rule 7-101

(A) A lawyer shall not intentionally:

(1) Fail to seek the lawful objectives of his client through reasonable available means permitted by law and the Disciplinary Rules. . . . A lawyer does not violate this Disciplinary Rule, however, . . . by avoiding offensive tactics, or by treating with courtesy and consideration all persons involved in the legal process.

AMERICAN BAR ASSOCIATION, MODEL RULES OF PROFESSIONAL CONDUCT (1983)

Model Rule 4.4

In representing a client, a lawyer shall not use means that have no substantial purpose other than to embarrass, delay, or burden a third person, or use methods of obtaining evidence that violate the legal rights of such a person.

a. *Truthful Witnesses and Guilty Clients*

The role of lawyers in defending guilty clients or false claims is explored more fully in Parts D and E(1) and in Chapters XIV (Criminal Law and Procedure) and XV (Evidence and Trial Advocacy). In essence, the justification for a vigorous defense in criminal contexts is that the system cannot guarantee due process if attorneys deny adequate representation to any client they assume is guilty. The only way to ensure that the state has met its burden of proof is for lawyers to put questions that might raise a reasonable doubt, irrespective of their personal beliefs in the truth of the witnesses' account. So too, the only way to ensure trust and candor in attorney-client relationships is to avoid penalizing clients for compromising disclosures. According to Monroe Freedman, "when a lawyer fails to crossexamine only because his client, placing confidence in the lawyer, has been candid with him, the basis for such confidence and candor collapses. Our legal system cannot tolerate such a result."[77] Like other procedural protections, such as the prohibition against unreasonable searches and the privilege against self-incrimination, impeachment of a truthful witness may impede accurate decision-making in particular cases but serve other values in the system as a whole.

Not all commentators, however, believe that truth should rank lower than those other values. The initial version of the ABA Standards for Criminal Justice, Defense Standard 7.6(b) (1971), provided that a lawyer "should not misuse the power of cross examination or impeachment by employing it to discredit or undermine a witness if he knows the witness is testifying truthfully." Would you support such a rule? If so, how would you define "knowledge?"

b. Criminal-Civil Distinctions

Whether similar arguments hold for civil cases has been a matter of considerable dispute, as Chapter IV (Advocacy) reflects. Many commentators take the position that criminal defense entails special obligations of zealous advocacy, both because of the potential for abusive state power and because of the special stakes for the defendant whose liberty, reputation, and perhaps even life may be at risk. Other commentators respond that such categorical distinctions are unpersuasive. In their view, the stakes sometimes can be as great for civil awards, and the exercise of private power can have as coercive or adverse an impact as the exercise of public power. That is particularly true when health and safety are at issue. Consider, for example, the humiliating cross-examinations of victims described in Chapter XV (Evidence and Trial Advocacy). Which position on the civil-criminal distinction do you find most persuasive?

Should the public have any role in formulating policies on impeachment of truthful witnesses? In one of the rare studies comparing lawyer and non-lawyer attitudes, participants responded to a hypothetical in which an attorney is "certain" that a witness' testimony is "accurate and truthful." However, through skillful cross-examination attacking first the witness' memory and then his motives, the attorney discredits the testimony. About three-quarters of the lawyers, but just under half the non-lawyers, thought that the attack on memory was appropriate. Two-thirds of the lawyers but only about 40 percent of the non-lawyers supported the attack on motive.[78]

c.   *Special Cases: Rape*

To some commentators, impeachment of truthful witnesses is especially problematic in rape cases. Zealous advocacy in that context may carry special costs because of the particularly grave potential for humiliation; the deterrent that such conduct creates for other victims; and the societal impact of sanctioning "rape myths" suggesting that complainants provoke, desire, or deserve what they get. Lawyers' appeals to such myths are often effective. Jurors are less likely to convict a defendant if evidence suggests that the victim engaged in nonmarital sex, drank, used drugs, dressed "provocatively," or knew the defendant, however brief their acquaintance. The same information affects judicial decision-making, and racial bias amplifies these effects when the complainant is a woman of color.[79] According to some public defenders, "[n]o other criminal complainant comes to court burdened by the presumption of incredibility borne by the rape complainant."[80] In addition, rape victims often suffer from rape trauma syndrome, which may lead them to suppress details of an assault.[81] Zealous cross-examination on such details may unduly discredit a victim's basically accurate account.

Exploitation of rape complainants' special vulnerability can have a corrosive impact on the entire law enforcement system. Rape is the most underreported felony, in part because of a further victimization of victims that rape shield statutes have only partially addressed. To commentators such as David Luban, such considerations suggest limits on lawyers' roles:

> The real value underlying the advocate's role is the protection of individuals against institutions that pose chronic threats to their well-being. The state is the most conspicuous of these, but in point of fact no institution has ever posed a more chronic and pervasive threat to the well-being of individual women than that of patriarchy, the network of cultural expectations and practices that engenders and encourages male sexual violence. . . . Thus, the moral limits to the advocate's role in rape cases must be designed to maximize the protection of jeopardized individuals against both these threatening institutions. Placing the brutal cross-examination of the truthful victim off limits serves precisely that function. . . .
>
> Matters would be different if rape were rare and false accusations of rape occurred regularly. Then the advocate's role would properly focus on the vulnerability of men, not of women. Suffice it to say that the world is not this way. [Susan] Estrich speculates that the law of rape has been shaped by "[t]he male rape fantasy . . . a nightmare" in which the man is accused of rape after having sex with a woman who said no but did not resist. Certainly this improbable "nightmare" lends urgency to the traditional advocate's role in rape cases; but unlike the male rape fantasy, the nightmare of the woman who has been raped on a date and does not report it because she is afraid of what will happen to her reputation during the trial is real. In my view, then, the advocate's role should stop well short of an all-out assault on the prosecutrix. . . . The lawyer can ask the victim whether she con-

sented. The lawyer can also argue reasonable doubt to the jury. What she cannot do is cross-examine her to make her look like a whore.[82]

Do you agree? Does Luban sufficiently consider the costs to male defendants who may misjudge consent? Given the brutal conditions of this nation's prisons and the permanent stigma that may attach to rape convictions, should defendants be entitled to have the jury see the case from their perspective? What about other contexts in which plaintiffs are vulnerable and particularly wary about reporting abuse? For example, the threat of intrusive or demeaning questions also deters elderly complainants and sex harassment plaintiffs.[83] Do rape victims face a unique combination of intrusiveness, stigma, and credibility problems, or are comparable ethical concerns at issue in certain other cases?

How would you weigh the competing considerations in Problem 5G? Consider the following statements by criminal defense attorneys. Do any describe your own position?

TIMOTHY BENEKE, MEN ON RAPE
104-105 (1982)

. . . The bottom line is in getting my client off. If I saw myself appealing to the jury's sexism I would probably wonder about it and, it's true, I don't look at it as harshly as appealing to the jury's racism. The effect of the women's movement on me has been as strong as on anyone else, but I'm no one special; I try to win my cases. If I could get my client off by appealing to the jury's sexism I probably would, because I'd be more concerned with this one guy and his freedom than the ethical issue of sexism. If I didn't appeal to their sexism and I thought I could've to get my client off, and he went to prison, I probably would feel pretty bad about it. In the heat of the battle I probably pull out a lot of stops and I may have appealed to the jury's sexism without even realizing it.

COOKIE RIDOLFI, STATEMENT ON REPRESENTING RAPE DEFENDANTS
(July 26, 1989) (unpublished manuscript, on file with author at Santa Clara Law School)

I have never felt conflicted about what side I stand on in a criminal trial. My political sensibilities keep me firmly planted on the side of the defendant. As a public defender for nearly seven years, I have seen that my clients are victims of poverty, racism, and a criminal justice system that, despite its lofty ideals, presumes guilt, not innocence. My experience has shown me that the system is stacked against an accused and doubly stacked against those who are not white or are poor. . . .

However, my role as a defender in sexual assault cases is not clear or simple. These cases frequently require that I, a feminist who rejects harmful stereotypes of women, exploit those same stereotypes in defense of my client. In the majority of sexual assault cases, the complainant and defendant know one another and fabrication or consent is raised as a defense....As a consequence, in most sex cases, my role is to charge the complainant with having agreed to the sexual encounter, or having asked for it, or of being a woman scorned whose feelings of rejection caused her to cry rape as an act of revenge.

Some defense attorneys believe that effective cross-examination can be done in a way that does not demean the complainant. I disagree. No matter what tone of voice is used or how politely the questions are put, a good cross-examination must still ultimately demonstrate that the complaining witness is a liar.

Moreover, if the defense attorney is respectful of the complainant's feelings, she lends credibility to the prosecution's case. The more successful the defense counsel is at cutting away at the complainant's credibility, the more effective the defense and necessarily, more damaged the complainant is. An attorney who is concerned about a complainant's feelings necessarily compromises her client's right to an advocate with exclusive loyalty.

In the conflict between my commitment to defender work and my increasing distress over what is required of me in a sex case, the fact that my own gender is also an issue at trial weighs heavily. Last year I defended a man charged with assault and rape. He and the complainant were dance partners in a club featuring provocative "live dancing." She testified that the defendant appeared at her door late one night, forced his way inside, then dragged her into the basement where he viciously raped and beat her. The client said that he had been invited into the house for sex which was interrupted when the complainant's husband came home; it was her husband who beat her, not him.

After more than a week of trial where emotions ran high for everyone, the jury acquitted him. Afterwards, I met with jurors. One woman juror told me that she believed in his innocence because she was certain that I could not have fought for him in the way that I did had he committed that crime. . . . I later learned that he was arrested and convicted in two new rape/assault cases similar to the one I had tried. . . . [T]hat trial and that complainant still haunt me. I think of the horror described from the witness stand and I believe now that it is true. I think about the fact that the defendant left the courthouse a free man and returned to a community that pitied him as a victim and despised her as the victimizer. I think about the two women that were beaten and raped by him just a few months later. Finally, I think about my role in that.

Despite this experience and my growing discomfort with my own participation in the defense of rape cases, I remain firm in my belief that every person, no matter what the charge or circumstances of the case, deserves dedicated and competent counsel. I also know that some men are victims of a woman's false charges of rape and agree strongly that this defense must be pursued when a defendant makes this claim. I am not critical of any other woman who chooses to defend a man charged with rape. But for all of the reasons I have given, I would find it difficult to again be in the position where I would have to challenge a woman's claim of rape knowing that what she claims may be true.

3.   The Role of Experts

See Chapter XV, Evidence and Trial Advocacy
  • Relations with Witnesses: Experts
        (pages 671–673)

4.   Misleading the Witness

See Chapter XV, Evidence and Trial Advocacy
  • Impeachment
        (page 669)

F.   TRIAL TACTICS

See Chapter XV, Evidence and Trial Advocacy
  • Adversarial Tactics in Personal Injury and Criminal
      Proceedings
        (pages 655–662)

G.   TRIAL PUBLICITY

See Chapter XI, Constitutional Law
  • Freedom of Expression and Association: The Fair
      Trial/Free Press Balance
        (pages 492–499)

H.   ALTERNATIVE DISPUTE RESOLUTION

> Discourage litigation. Persuade your neighbors
> to compromise whenever you can. . . . As a
> peace-maker the lawyer has a superior opportu-
> nity of being a good man. There will still be
> business enough.
>
> *Abraham Lincoln*[84]

1. The Rationale for Alternative Dispute Resolution

Alternative dispute resolution (ADR) proceedings are not a new phenomenon; what is new is the level of interest in their application. Throughout American history, some groups have sought methods of handling conflict that are less costly and contentious than traditional adversarial structures. A number of early colonies, as well as later religious and utopian communities, attempted to prevent the use of lawyers and to handle disputes through church or secular arbitration and mediation systems. During the nineteenth and twentieth centuries, some commercial and labor disputes were resolved through analogous procedures. In 1913, Cleveland established the first small claims "conciliation" branch of a local court, and other jurisdictions experimented with such systems for certain kinds of cases.[85]

Beginning in the 1960s, interest in alternative dispute procedures markedly increased. Dissatisfaction with traditional adjudication structures takes a variety of forms:

Expense, Delay, and Inaccessibility. In many litigation contexts, the costs of legal proceedings have appeared grossly out of proportion to their benefits. The Rand study of asbestos claims, for example, found that for every dollar received by claimants, legal expenses totaled $2.72. Backlogs for civil cases in some jurisdictions have delayed trial for four to five years. Additional barriers include inconvenient courthouse locations and schedules, as well as lack of support services.

Unjust Results. Parties' unequal ability to bear the cost, uncertainty, and delay of litigation, together with lawyers' unequal skills in exploiting legal advantages, have led to inaccurate or inequitable outcomes.

Insufficient Party Participation. Procedural complexity has restricted individuals' direct participation in dispute resolution and often has alienated them from the results. Giving parties the opportunity to structure the proceedings and to choose a third party decision-maker or mediator can enhance satisfaction.

Inadequacy of Adjudicative Resources and Expertise. Overburdened courts have difficulty handling certain kinds of disputes, particularly those involving complex technical matters. Attempting to educate judges or juries about issues requiring highly specialized knowledge has appeared less efficient than relying on neutral experts.

Inability to Address Underlying Issues. Conventional doctrinal and remedial tools often have diverted attention from problems that give rise to disputes.

Undue Contentiousness and Remedial Inflexibility.   The adversarial nature of proceedings and reliance on win/lose outcomes have exacerbated antagonisms.

Lack of Confidentiality.   Except in extremely limited circumstances, judicial proceedings and court records are open to the public. Private dispute resolution procedures offer opportunities to prevent disclosure of confidential information and adverse publicity.

Lack of Community Involvement.   Seldom have traditional court structures functioned effectively to strengthen communities or to integrate judicial and social services. By contrast, neighborhood justice centers and related programs seek to coordinate governmental efforts and to construct dispute resolution procedures in light of local needs.

Dissatisfaction with conventional adjudication has prompted interest in a variety of alternative dispute resolution processes. The appropriate scope and structure of these processes have sparked heated disputes, summarized in the Rhode and Luban excerpt below. As a general matter, however, several considerations are widely believed to be relevant in matching procedural mechanisms to categories of cases. According to Frank Sander, such considerations fall into three general categories:

1.   NATURE OF CASE
[Dispute resolution mechanisms] should be designed to handle a novel claim challenging the constitutionality of a statute quite differently from a claim applying established principles to a specific set of facts. Only the former merits unique skills and resources of a court. The latter can be more expeditiously and inexpensively dealt with by arbitration.

2.   RELATIONSHIP OF DISPUTANTS
Adjudication typically seeks to make a definitive determination with respect to past events, while mediation attempts to restructure the relationship of disputants. Thus, mediation best resolves cases involving long-term relationships extending into the future. . . .

A significant qualification, however, is presented in the case where the two disputants have substantially disparate bargaining power. In such a case, mediation is either pointless, or worse yet, threatens to take undue and unfair advantage of the weaker party.

3.   SIZE AND COMPLEXITY OF CLAIM
Society has already taken some account of the size and complexity criterion in establishing, on an optional basis, small claims courts for the processing of minor disputes. Some states have even experimented with the use of different tracks for cases of different complexity. Generally, however, transaction costs in processing disputes have largely been ignored. To be sure, certain cases (e.g., a serious crime or a major constitutional challenge) should not be measured by the amount of controversy. Beyond those cases and others raising similar

considerations, however, should not we lawyers be more attuned to the immense public cost every time a lawsuit is processed in court? If a case involves only $1000 and does not raise larger issues of public policy, should society not *require* such a case to be processed in small claims court or its functional equivalent? The counterargument, of course, is that for the low-income consumer a claim of $1000 over his defective refrigerator is as important as a multi-million dollar claim is for General Motors. That argument, however, misses the point. If the larger claim is also a straightforward collection action, it also does not deserve access to the deluxe adjudication model. These factors and others need further exploration.[86]

2. Forms of Alternative Dispute Resolution

Some alternative dispute resolution procedures have developed under federal and state legislative mandates or judicial decrees; others have evolved through private initiatives. A summary of significant national legislation and procedural alternatives appears below.

a. *Federal Mandates*

1. The Federal Court Pilot Project, §901 of the Judicial Improvements and Access to Justice Act, 28 U.S.C. §§651-658, creates an experimental arbitration program in selected federal judicial districts. Under this program, trial courts may require parties to submit to arbitration if the complaint seeks only money damages and the amount in controversy is $100,000 or less, unless the case falls into certain recognized exceptions such as civil rights or federal constitutional claims.

2. The Judicial Improvements Act (Civil Justice Reform Act), Pub. L. No. 101-650, 104 Stat. 5089, requires every federal district court to study its caseload and to develop a plan to "facilitate . . . adjudication of civil cases on the merits, monitor discovery, improve litigation management and ensure just, speedy and inexpensive resolution of civil disputes." Among the strategies courts should consider in formulating their plan is authorizing trial judges to refer appropriate cases to alternative dispute resolution.

3. The Administrative Dispute Resolution Act, Pub. L. No. 101-552, 104 Stat. 2736, requires every federal agency to adopt an alternative dispute resolution policy that encourages use of alternative techniques where all disputants consent.

b. *Procedural Variations*

Alternative dispute resolution procedures vary along a number of dimensions:

1. *The role of third parties.* Who selects the decision-maker or facilitator and by what criteria? Is special expertise required?
2. *The enforceability of the outcome.* Is the outcome binding or is it subject to review?
3. *Consent.* Is the procedure voluntary or mandatory?
4. *Relationship to the government.* Is the procedure connected to a state or federal court system?
5. *Formality.* Is the procedure formally structured by fixed rules or by agreement of the parties, or is it relatively informal and flexible?

c.   *The Range of Alternative Structures*

Arbitration.   In arbitration, parties submit their dispute to a neutral decision-maker, often someone who has particular expertise in the matters at issue. The American Arbitration Association handles close to 10,000 commercial disputes each year, and large numbers of additional labor, tort, and consumer controversies are arbitrated under private contractual arrangements. Some governmental agencies and industry groups such as the Better Business Bureau also have systems for mediating claims.

Over half the states have statutes modeled on the Uniform Arbitration Act, 7 U.L.A. 5 (1985), that govern enforcement of arbitration agreements. Enforcement may also be available under the Federal Arbitration Act, 9 U.S.C. §§1-14 (1992), and the Labor Management Relations Act of 1947, 29 U.S.C. §185 (1988). A number of federal and state courts require submission of certain cases to court-annexed arbitration, although parties generally have a right to trial de novo.

Private Adjudication.   Some statutes and rules of court permit referral of cases to privately selected and compensated adjudicators. Under such referral programs, sometimes labeled "rent-a-judge," the private adjudicator's decision is entered as the judgment of the court. Unlike an arbiter's award, the judgment is normally appealable.

Summary Jury Trial.   Under this procedure, lawyers give a summary of their trial presentation to a jury, usually without witnesses or exhibits. The jury then renders a verdict that is not binding, although the jurors are not informed of this fact before reaching their decision.

Minitrials.   Minitrials, or "structured settlement" negotiations, offer opportunities for lawyers to present an abbreviated version of their case to a decision-making panel. In one common variation, a neutral advisor and decision-making executives of the disputing parties participate on the panel. After the advisor gives an opinion of what would happen if the case were litigated, the principals attempt to negotiate a settlement. In some minitrials, the neutral advisor will render an advisory opinion only if the parties initially fail to reach an agreement.

Mediation. Mediation is an informal process in which a neutral third party helps the parties resolve a dispute or structure a transaction. Ordinarily, this third party facilitates but does not impose a solution, and the parties voluntarily choose the mediator. However, some jurisdictions require mediation for some types of disputes. See Chapter VIII (Negotiation and Mediation) at pages 362–372.

Ombudsperson. Ombudspersons are officials appointed by organizations to prevent, investigate, and informally resolve disputes. In the private sector, ombudspersons function primarily in employer/employee relations. In the public sector, their role is broader. The U.S. Administrative Conference has recommended that all federal agencies with a significant public function consider establishing ombudsperson offices. See 1 C.F.R. §305.90-2.

Neighborhood Justice Centers. Neighborhood justice centers, citizen complaint bureaus, or other community-based centers function as free-standing institutions or court-affiliated agencies. These organizations typically receive referrals from courts, prosecutors, police, or other community agencies, as well as walk-in clients. Professional mediators or community volunteers with mediation training handle a variety of disputes, including landlord-tenant, family, and neighbor relations.

Early Neutral or Expert Evaluation. This technique, which is used both in private dispute resolution and in court-annexed settings, involves reliance on an experienced attorney or technical expert to evaluate a case. After summary presentations by each side, the evaluator assesses disputed issues in an effort to facilitate settlement.

Such processes raise a wide range of ethical issues. For example, on a substantive/jurisprudential level, what determines whether an outcome or process is fair and just? On a jurisdictional level, what professional body should regulate ADR processes? How should conflicts be handled between ethical regulations by different professional bodies in different localities? To what extent should private ADR processes be subject to public accountability? How should more specific issues concerning confidentiality, conflicts of interest, and power imbalances be resolved?[87]

PROBLEM 5H

1. You are chair of your state's Commission on the Administration of Justice. The Commission's charge is to make recommendations to various legislative and judicial bodies concerning alternative dispute resolution procedures. How would you assess the merits of the procedures described above? Would it affect your assessment to learn that a Rand Institute evaluation of federal Justice Reform Act mediation and arbitration programs found that they did not significantly decrease litigation costs or delays?[88] Do such programs further other important values? If most states' experience suggests that voluntary options will not be popular enough to reduce court caseloads appreciably, would you support mandatory programs? Consider, for example, California's mandatory mediation for contested custody issues (see Chapter VIII (Negotiation and Mediation) at pages 360–370) and Hawaii's mandatory arbitration program for all tort cases valued at $150,000 or less.

2. A former client asks your advice on whether to hire a retired judge or a minitrial consultant to resolve a million-dollar contract dispute. Your sister also wants your opinion about whether she should agree to her husband's proposal that they hire a mediator rather than lawyers to handle their divorce. What questions would you ask, and what considerations would be most relevant to your advice?

3. You are president of your local bar association. The association is considering a proposed modification of the state ethics code modeled on a Colorado ethics rule. That rule, in force since 1992, provides that in "a matter involving or expected to involve litigation, a lawyer should advise the client of alternative forms of dispute resolution which might reasonably be pursued to . . . reach the legal objective sought."

Members of your state bar are divided on the proposal. Some object that the provision is toothless; they prefer an earlier formulation of the Colorado rule, which had used the term "shall" rather than "should" and had clearly required disclosure of ADR options. Other lawyers oppose any rule out of concern that even precatory language might interfere with professional judgment and invite unjustified disciplinary or malpractice actions.[89] What position do you take?

3. Alternative Perspectives on Alternative Processes

DEBORAH L. RHODE & DAVID LUBAN, LEGAL ETHICS

783-784 (2d ed.1995)

. . . These varied dispute resolution procedures have sparked an equally varied set of critiques. Paradoxically enough, many of the same criticisms leveled at litigation-based strategies also have been directed at more informal alternatives. Critics have often claimed that alternative dispute resolution procedures do more to defuse than to resolve conflict. By individualizing grievances shared by many people (for example complaints by tenants against a single slumlord), such procedures deflect attention from common problems and the collective efforts necessary to address them. By expanding "access to justice," dispute resolution reforms also may foster the illusion that "justice" has been done. Parties may settle for opportunities to ventilate grievances while leaving intact the power structure that perpetuates them. The net effect, these critics maintain, is to legitimate a fundamentally illegitimate system.

A second cluster of criticisms has an equally paradoxical quality; alternative dispute resolution is criticized for being both too available and not available enough. Some commentators complain that options such as rent-a-judge or minitrials are affordable only by the wealthy. Such a market-based structure institutionalizes "legal apartheid" — convenient, speedy justice for the haves and cumbersome, inefficient processes for the have-nots. By creating a two-track system, alternative dispute procedures also may reduce pressure to reform the judicial system that makes such alternatives necessary.

Conversely, another group of critics charge that informal remedies are too accessible for the non-privileged classes and that such remedies offer a form of second-class justice. In any context where parties' resources are imbalanced, the inaccessibility of neutral adjudicators may lead to skewed settlements. As some commentators have noted, informal, streamlined structures can deprive the poor of crucial strategic tools. A case in point involved a landlord-tenant court in the South Bronx in which legal services lawyers were initially able to gain substantial concessions from slum landlords by invoking burdensome procedural formalities. Landlords eventually responded by lobbying for creation of a streamlined system that greatly reduced these advantages.

Feminist critics have raised related concerns. Mediation between parties with unequal power may reinforce their inequality and encourage negotiation of rights that should be non-negotiable. For example, divorcing wives have often traded necessary child support to avert custody battles and battered wives may agree to avoid "nagging" in exchange for their husbands' promises to refrain from physical assaults. Although some mediators attempt to mitigate certain disparities in parties' bargaining capacities, or refuse to ratify settlements that seem clearly unfair, such non-neutral conduct raises its own set of ethical difficulties. Not only can it compromise mediators' credibility and capacity to achieve solutions, it subjects participants to manipulation by mediators with undisclosed standards and no formal mechanisms of accountability. Risks are particularly great for subordinate groups.

These examples also suggest some of the concerns which Owen Fiss [has summarized]: that informal processes oriented toward private settlements undervalue society's interest in having publicly accountable officials interpret and implement publicly acceptable norms. A process geared toward compromise may also provide inadequate deterrence of unlawful conduct. From this perspective, arbitrators appear "well, arbitrary" in a sense judges do not. . . . As other critics have also noted, it is difficult to generalize about the virtues of alternative dispute resolution techniques given the variation in their structures, outcomes, and factual settings.

It is, however, difficult to generalize about the deficiencies of ADR techniques. For example, William Simon points out that in the Bronx landlord-tenant courts described earlier, legal formalism benefitted the poor only because of particular circumstances; lawyers were available to exploit procedural options, and the burden of initiative in eviction processes rested on the landlord. Had the burdens been differently distributed by allowing landlord self-help, the tenants would have been disadvantaged by formal requirements and their accompanying expense and delay. So too, although procedural formality benefitted the poor tenants facing evictions, it hindered those seeking housing code enforcement.

The point of Simon's analysis is that the evaluation of alternative dispute resolution should not proceed in the abstract; its social, political, and economic implications depend heavily on context. And for reasons noted in prior discussion [see Marc Galanter's analysis of haves and have-nots at pages 176–177], it seems unlikely that the poor generally fare better in formal than informal tribunals.

That point suggests broader lessons about the limits of categorical critiques. Too often, analysis proceeds by comparing alternative dispute processes to an idealized image of adjudication. Yet before denouncing such initiatives as second-class justice, it is important to inquire whether first class is likely to be available and on what terms. Under current adjudicative processes, informal settlement is the norm; less than 10% of cases filed receive the full process that Owen Fiss endorses, and the vast majority of grievances never even reach the filing stage. Even in the small minority of cases that are adjudicated, the due process that is available often looks more impressive in theory than in practice. . . .

[M]any commentators believe that the current system already offers "apartheid justice"; extensive resources are available for commercial litigation that parties can afford to subsidize, while other matters, such as those involving family issues for nonwealthy parties, are resolved with only the most cursory attention. Moreover, what limited empirical evidence is available suggests that most litigants do not place the high value on [formal] process that legal commentators assume and that participants often prefer informal dispute resolution to current alternatives. While parties' satisfaction should not be the sole criteria for evaluation, it is surely relevant.

While we can and should be wary that development of informal dispute resolution processes will remove some pressure to reform the existing system, that is not an inherent or inevitable feature of such innovations. A more hopeful possibility is that such strategies may suggest directions for reforms that will better integrate the strengths and weaknesses of various alternative approaches.

As the authors of a major civil litigation study point out, the distinction between traditional adjudication and alternative dispute resolution is often overdrawn. Much of the literature "naively assumes that what occurs in courts is adjudication, in the classical sense. . . . [But] in the world of ordinary litigation . . . settlement is the rule, not the exception."[90] Moreover, much of what occurs in the world of ADR does not reflect the party control and empowerment that proponents assume. For some categories of cases, informal coercion may be the rule, not the exception.

Such coercion is of particular concern in contexts such as domestic violence or contractual disputes involving repeat players who impose mandatory arbitration clauses on one-shot participants. For example, in a recent study involving these clauses in employment cases, the odds of winning were five to one against an employee.[91] Only repeat players have the resources and incentives to track the predispositions of arbitrators and effectively manipulate procedural norms. Since arbitration doesn't ensure full discovery or appeal of outcomes, the consequences of systemic biases can be substantial.

Other critics of ADR raise further concerns. Some focus on the lack of visibility and public accountability of the process. Other commentators worry about lack of licensing and training requirements for ADR professionals. Most states impose more requirements to become a hair stylist than a mediator.[92] Cost is also a concern, particularly since parties have to subsidize alternative processes, and recent research raises doubts that mediation and arbitration are generally cheaper than adjudication. ADR defenders respond that some of these financial concerns could be met through public subsidies and that the current system is inappropriately skewed in favor of an adversarial system that may not best suit participants' needs.

What is your view? How would you address the problems in alternative dispute resolution procedures? How well do these alternatives respond to problems in adversarial processes?

Endnotes

1. Stephan Landsman, The Adversary System: A Description and Defense 2 (1984).

2. See Marion Neef & Stuart Nagel, The Nature of the American Legal System: A Historical Perspective, in Lawyer's Ethics 73 (Allan Gerson ed., 1980); Theodore F.T. Plucknett, A Concise History of the Common Law 217 (5th ed. 1956).

3. See generally Lawrence M. Friedman, A History of American Law (2d ed. 1985); Kermit Hall, The Magic Mirror (1989).

4. Geoffrey Hazard, Ethics in the Practice of Law 120-135 (1978); Samuel R. Gross, The American Advantage: The Value of Inefficient Litigation, 85 Mich. L. Rev. 734 (1987). One effort to test these premises empirically found that in experimental contexts, adversarial roles had somewhat greater success than neutral inquisitorial roles in counteracting bias and fostering development of a case for parties with initially weak claims. John Thibeaut & Laurens Walker, Procedural Justice: A Psychological Analysis (1975). For a critical review of this study, see Mirjan Damaska, Presentation of Evidence and Fact-Finding Precision, 123 U. Pa. L. Rev. 1083 (1975).

5. Carrie Menkel-Meadow, The Trouble with the Adversary System in a Post-Modern, Multicultural World, 1 J. Inst. for Study of Legal Ethics 801 (1996).

6. Plato, Gorgias (T. Irwin trans., 1979), discussed in Anthony T. Kronman, Forward: Legal Scholarship and Moral Education, 90 Yale L.J. 955, 959 (1981).

7. Marvin E. Frankel, The Search for Truth: An Umpireal View, 123 U. Pa. L. Rev. 1031, 1036-1037 (1975).

8. William Simon, The Practice of Justice (1998).

9. Marvin E. Frankel, Partisan Justice 34 (1980).

10. Douglas E. Rosenthal, Lawyer and Client: Who's in Charge? 82-83 (1974).

11. Marc Galanter, Why the Haves Come Out Ahead: Speculations on the Limits of Legal Change, 9 Law & Socy. Rev. 95 (1974).

12. Id. at 98-103.

13. Frank I. Michelman, The Supreme Court and Litigation Access Fees: The Right to Protect One's Rights, Part I, 1973 Duke L.J. 1153, 1172. See Thibeaut & Walker, supra note 4, at 72-77; Hazard, supra note 4, at 120-135.

14. Tom R. Tyler, Why People Obey the Law (1990).

15. Martin Mayer, The Lawyers 257 (1967); Gary A. Hengstler, Vox Populi, A.B.A.J., Sept. 1993, at 62; William H. Simon, The Ideology of Advocacy: Procedural Justice and Professional Ethics, 1978 Wis. L. Rev. 30, 104-106, 124-130; Jonathan D. Casper, Having Their Day in Court: Defendant Evaluations of the Fairness of Their Treatment, 12 Law & Socy. Rev. 235 (1978).

16. Discussion Draft, Model Rules of Professional Conduct (1980), Rule 3.6.

17. Deborah L. Rhode, Ethical Perspectives on Legal Practice, 37 Stan. L. Rev. 589, 612 (1985) (citing bar commentary).

18. David Luban, Lawyers and Justice: An Ethical Study 92-93 (1988).

19. See the debate published as Deborah L. Rhode, An Adversarial Exchange on Adversarial Ethics: Text, Subtext, and Context, 41 J. Legal Educ. 29 (1991).

20. DR 7-102(A)(4) & (5); Model Rule 3.3(a)(1) & (4).

21. DR 7-102(A)(6); Model Rule 3.3(a)(4); DR 7-102(B)(1) & (2).

22. DR 7-102(B); Model Rule 3.3(4).

23. DR 7-102(A)(1) & (2); Model Rule 3.1.

24. DR 7-106(B)(1); Model Rule 3.3(a)(3).

25. Discussion Draft, Model Rules of Professional Conduct (1980), Rules 3.3(b) and 3.1.

26. Id., Rule 4.2.

27. The material in this section draws on Lawyers in Society (Richard L. Abel & Philip S. Lewis eds., 1988) (3 vols., Vol. 1: The Common Law World; Vol. 2: The Civil Law World; Vol. 3: Comparative Theories); Nigel G. Foster, German Law and Legal System 27 (1993); Edward A. Tomlinson, Nonadversarial Justice: The French Experience, 42 Md. L. Rev. 131, 150-164 (1983); John H. Langbein, The German Advantage in Civil Procedure, 52 U. Chi. L. Rev. 823, 826-831 (1985).

28. Langbein, supra note 27.

29. W. Zeidler, Evaluation of the Adversary System: As Comparison, Some Remarks on the Investigatory System of Procedure, 55 Aust. L.J. 390, 395 (1981) (quoting Chief Baron Palles of Ireland).

30. Abraham Goldstein, Reflections on Two Models: Inquisitorial Themes in American Criminal Procedure, 26 Stan. L. Rev. 1017, 1020 (1974).

31. John H. Merryman, The Civil Law Tradition 132 (2d ed. 1985).

32. Marc Galanter, The Day After the Litigation Explosion, 46 Md. L. Rev. 3 (1986); Marc Galanter, The Life and Times of the Big Six; or, the Federal Courts Since the Good Old Days, 1988 Wis. L. Rev. 921; Lawrence M. Friedman, Litigation and Society, 15 Am. Rev. Soc. 17 (1989).

33. See sources cited in Deborah L. Rhode & David Luban, Legal Ethics 722 (2d ed. 1995).

34. Spite Feuds Fill Yugoslavian Courts, N.Y. Times, Oct. 16, 1966.

35. Thomas Ehrlich, Legal Pollution, N.Y. Times Magazine, Feb. 8, 1976, at 17.

36. Ralph Nader & Wesley J. Smith, No Contest 267-273 (1997); Aric Press, Are Lawyers Burning America? Newsweek, Mar. 20, 1995, at 32.

37. 33 Bus. Law. 817, 834 (1978) (comments of Lester Pollack). For small cases, see David M. Trubek et al., The Costs of Ordinary Litigation, 31 UCLA L. Rev. 72, 90 (1983). For an overview, see Charles W. Sorensen, Jr., Disclosure Under Federal Rule of Civil Procedure 26(a) — "Much Ado About Nothing?" 46 Hastings L. Rev. 679, 705-709 (1995).

38. Wayne D. Brazil, Views from the Front Lines: Observations by Chicago Lawyers About the System of Civil Discovery, 1980 Am. B. Found. Res. J. 219 (1980).

39. Frank F. Flegal, Discovery Abuse: Causes, Effects and Reform, 3 Rev. of Litig. 1, 21-22 (1982).

40. Id. at 23.

41. Brazil, Views from the Front Lines, supra note 38.

42. Rhode, supra note 17, at 635.

43. Weyman I. Lundquist, Trial Lawyer or Litigator, 7 Litig. 3, 4 (1981).

44. Clifford Geertz, Local Knowledge 171 (1983); Nader & Smith, supra note 36, at 35, 103-104.

45. Robert N. Saylor, Rambo Litigator: Why Hardball Tactics Don't Work, A.B.A.J., Mar. 1988, at 79; Bartlett H. McGuire, Rambo Litigation: A Losing Proposition, Am. Law., May 1996, at 39-40.

46. Ronald J. Gilson & Robert H. Mnookin, Disputing Through Agents: Cooperation and Conflict Between Lawyers in Litigation, 94 Colum. L. Rev. 509, 514-27 (1994).

47. Sorenson, supra note 37, at 713; Arthur R. Miller, The Adversary System: Dinosaur or Phoenix, 69 Minn. L. Rev. 1 (1985); Brazil, supra note 38, at 886-888.

48. This problem draws in part on the discussion of South Bronx legal services in Mark H. Lazerson, In the Halls of Justice, the Only Justice Is in the Halls, in The Politics of Informal Justice 119 (Richard L. Abel ed., 1982); Jan Hoffman, Chaos Presides in New York Housing Courts, N.Y. Times, Dec. 28, 1994, at A2; Woodruff Corp. v. Lucien Lacrete, 154 Misc. 2d 301, 585 N.Y.S. 2d 956 (Kings Cty. 1992).

49. Bruce Shapiro, Hard Case, The Nation, Dec. 7, 1992, at 689.

50. Sanford Levinson, Frivolous Cases: Do Lawyers Really Know Anything at All?, 24 Osgoode Hall L.J. 353, 375 (1987); Jules Lobel, Losers, Fools and Prophets: Justice as Struggle, 80 Cornell L. Rev. 1331, 1332, 1346 (1995).

51. Harry Steinberg, Pro Bono? Publico?, N.Y.L.J., Mar. 12, 1992, at 2.

52. Counsel for the plaintiffs ended up paying $36,852.07. Shapiro, supra note 49, at 688.

53. Sissela Bok, Lying: Moral Choice in Public and Private Life 23-24 (1978).

54. Id. at 24-25.

55. Report of the Committee on Civility of the Seventh Federal Judicial Circuit 6 (1991).

56. Geoffrey Hazard, Civility Code May Lead to Less Civility, Natl. L.J., Feb. 26, 1990, at 13.

57. Report of the Committee on Civility, supra note 55, at 40 (training); Judith Resnik, Managerial Judges, 96 Harv. L. Rev. 376 (1982) (managing); Ted Schneyer, Professional Discipline for Law Firms?, 77 Cornell L. Rev. 1 (1991) (discipline); Thomas Ferraro, Administration Seeks to Stem Lawsuits, United Press Internatl., Feb. 4, 1992 (fee-shifting recommendations of the President's Council on Competitiveness).

58. Report of the Committee on Civility, supra note 55, at 40 (a majority of surveyed lawyers and judges selected more law school training as the best way to address civility problems).

59. This hypothetical is modeled on a fact situation that a reporter posing as a client put to randomly selected Manhattan attorneys. See Jane Berentsen, Integrity Test: Five of Thirteen Lawyers Fail, Am. Law., May 1980, at 15-18.

60. These examples are from John Steele, The Ethics of Witness Preparation (unpublished manuscript 1996).

61. For such evidence and discussion of this issue, see Richard C. Wydick, The Ethics of Witness Coaching, 17 Cardozo L. Rev. 1 (1995); Daniel Schacter, Searching for Memory 115 (1996).

62. Joseph C. Goulden, The Million Dollar Lawyers 139-140 (1977).

63. Frankel, supra note 9, at 15.

64. Id.

65. Monroe H. Freedman, Professional Responsibility of the Criminal Defense Lawyer: The Three Hardest Questions, 64 Mich. L. Rev. 1460, 1479, 1481 (1966).

66. Anthony Amsterdam, Lectures on Trial Practice (1981) (unpublished, Stanford Law School).

67. Kenneth Mann, Defending White Collar Crime: A Portrait of Attorneys at Work 122 (1985).

68. Id. at 118.

69. Wydick, supra note 61, at 13-14; John S. Applegate, Witness Preparation, 68 Tex. L. Rev. 277 (1989).

70. Monroe H. Freedman, Counseling the Client: Refreshing Recollection or Prompting Perjury?, 2 Litig. 35, 46 (Spring 1976).

71. Daniel J. Kornstein, A Tragic Fire, A Great Cross-Examination, N.Y.L.J., Mar. 28, 1986, at 2; Ann Ruben & Emily Ruben, Letter to the Editor, N.Y.L.J., Apr. 14, 1986, at 2, in Stephen Gillers & Norman Dorsen, Regulation of Lawyers: Problems of Law and Ethics 492-496 (2d ed. 1989).

72. Maria L. Ontiveros, Rosa Lopez, David Letterman, Christopher Darden, And Me: Issues of Gender, Ethnicity, and Class in Evaluating Witness Credibility, 6 Hastings L.J. 135 (1995).

73. Anthony Trollope, quoted in Jerome Frank, Courts on Trial 83 (1949).

74. E.R. Shipp, Fear and Confusion in Court Plague Elderly Crime Victims, N.Y. Times, Mar. 13, 1983, at A1, discussed in Gillers & Dorsen, Regulation of Lawyers, supra note 71, at 488.

75. David Luban & Michael Millman, Good Judgment: Ethics Teaching in Dark Times, 9 Geo. J. Legal Ethics 31, 69-70 (1995).

76. This problem combines facts from two widely reported cases, one involving St. John's University students and one concerning Glen Ridge, New Jersey students, as well as assaults described in Peggy Sanday, Fraternity Gang Rape (1990). Neither the Glen Ridge nor the St. John's case involved a disaffected boyfriend or prior allegations of rape. Both victims were subject to extensive cross-examination, and sexual history evidence was admitted in the Glen Ridge case. See Bernard Lefkowitz, Our Guys (1997), and Peggy Reeves Sanday, A Woman Scorned (1996).

77. Freedman, supra note 65, at 1474-1475.

78. Wes Hansen, Lawyers, Lawyers, Lawyers, Ethics: Easier Said Than Done 38 (1993).

79. See Deborah L. Rhode, Speaking of Sex 121-127 (1997); Peter M. Hazleton, Rape Shield Laws: Limits on Zealous Advocacy, 19 Am. J. Crim. L. 35 (1991).

80. Abby Smith, When Ideology and Duty Conflict, in Ethical Problems Facing the Criminal Defense Lawyer 26 (Rodney J. Uphoff ed., 1995).

81. See Patricia Frazier & Eugene Borgida, Juror Common Understanding and the Admissibility of Rape Trauma Syndrome Evidence in Court, 12 Law & Hum. Behavior 101 (1988).

82. David Luban, Partisanship, Betrayal and Autonomy in the Lawyer-Client Relationship: A Reply to Stephen Ellmann, 90 Colum. L. Rev. 1004, 1028-1031 (1990).

83. See sources cited in Rhode, supra note 17 at 102, and in the notes for Problem 5E (pages 195–196) and Problem 15D (page 669).

84. Abraham Lincoln, Notes for a Law Lecture, July 1, 1850, in The Life and Writings of Abraham Lincoln 329 (Philip Van Doren Stern ed., 1992), quoted in Gilson & Mnookin, supra note 46.

85. Jerold S. Auerbach, Justice Without Law? 115-137 (1983).

86. Frank E.A. Sander, Alternative Methods of Dispute Resolution: An Overview, 37 Fla. L. Rev. 1, 13-14 (1985).

87. Carrie Menkel-Meadow, Ethics in Alternative Dispute Resolution: New Issues, No Answers from the Adversary Conception of Lawyers' Responsibilities, 38 Tex. L. Rev. 407 (1997).

88. Rand Institute for Civil Justice, Just, Speedy, and Inexpensive? An Evaluation of Judicial Case Management Under the Civil Justice Reform Act (1997).

89. Compare Frank E.A. Sander, Yes: An Aid to Clients, A.B.A.J., Nov. 1990, at 50 with Michael Prigoff, No: An Unreasonable Burden, A.B.A.J., Nov. 1990, at 50.

90. David Trubek et al., The Costs of Ordinary Litigation, 31 UCLA L. Rev. 72, 122 (1983).

91. Richard Reuban, The Lawyer Turns Peacemaker, A.B.A.J., Aug. 1996, at 61.

92. Id. at 60; Nader & Smith, supra note 36, at 299-301.

Chapter VI

Confidentiality and Client Counseling

A. THE ATTORNEY-CLIENT PRIVILEGE AND BAR ETHICAL OBLIGATIONS

One of lawyers' most crucial fiduciary obligations involves confidentiality. In general, attorneys have a duty not to disclose confidential information acquired during the course of representation without the client's consent. This duty is grounded in the law of evidence and in bar ethical rules. As subsequent discussion indicates, the evidentiary lawyer-client privilege protects confidential client communications from disclosure in legal proceedings. The ethical obligation of confidentiality is broader than the privilege in two primary respects. This obligation encompasses information from any source, not only clients, and applies in all contexts, not only in legal proceedings involving lawyers as witnesses.

1. The Evidentiary Privilege

The lawyer-client privilege arose in the seventeenth century as an outgrowth of the general principle that it is dishonorable to reveal another's confidence.[1] During the eighteenth and nineteenth centuries, the rationale gradually shifted to the proper functioning of the legal system as a whole, along the lines discussed in Part B below.

In its traditional form, the attorney-client privilege holds that

> (1) Where legal advice of any kind is sought (2) from a professional legal adviser in his capacity as such, (3) the communications relating to that purpose, (4) made in confidence (5) by the client, (6) are at his instance permanently protected (7) from disclosure by himself or by the legal adviser, (8) except [if] the protection be waived.[2]

Each of these eight subsections has generated an extensive body of case law. Among the most important provisions are those governing waiver. The privilege is inapplicable if communications take place in the presence of a third party, if clients disclose the communications to a third party, or if clients or their agents implicitly or explicitly consent to disclosure. The privilege also does not apply to disclosures by jointly represented clients in any subsequent dispute arising between them. Other significant exceptions to the privilege involve information regarding client identity, future crimes, and continuing frauds, all of which are discussed at length below.

2.   Bar Ethical Obligations

Attorneys' confidentiality obligations are defined by bar ethical codes as well as evidence law. These ethical mandates are more recent in origin than the lawyer-client privilege. No requirement of confidentiality appeared in either of the two main nineteenth-century treatments of professional responsibility — those by David Hoffman and by George Sharswood. The privilege was, however, part of David Dudley Field's 1849 Civil Procedure Code and was later incorporated in bar ethical regulations.

Both the current Code and the Model Rules impose a broader obligation than the attorney-client privilege. As the earlier discussion notes, they enjoin attorneys from revealing confidential information from any source (not just clients) in any setting (not just legal proceedings). Disciplinary Rule 4-101 of the ABA Code protects both "confidences" and "secrets." It defines "confidence" as any information protected by the attorney-client privilege, and "secret" as "other information gained in the professional relationship that the client has requested be held inviolate" or that could be "embarrassing" or "detrimental" if disclosed. Model Rule 1.6(a) states simply that "[a] lawyer shall not reveal information relating to representation of a client."

These ethical mandates also include exceptions. Both the Code and the Model Rules permit lawyers to reveal confidences if the client consents or if necessary to defend themselves from accusations of wrongful conduct or to establish claims and collect fees from a client. Disciplinary Rule 4-101 of the Code allows lawyers to reveal confidences if required by law or court order. Model Rule 1.6(a) exempts from confidentiality "disclosures that are impliedly authorized in order to carry out the representation." Most authorities agree that disclosures required by law are so authorized.

Finally, both the Code and the Model Rules allow the lawyer to disclose information to protect third party interests in certain limited circumstances. Disciplinary Rule 4-101(C)(3) permits but does not require a lawyer to reveal "the intention of his client to commit a crime and the information necessary to prevent the crime." One version of DR 7-102(B), applicable in some states, obligates lawyers to rectify frauds perpetrated during the course of representation. Model Rule 1.6(b)(1) permits but does not require a lawyer to disclose confidential information "to the extent the lawyer reasonably believes necessary to prevent the client from committing a criminal act that the lawyer believes is likely to result in imminent death or substantial bodily harm."

These exceptions, particularly the Model Rule provisions, are strikingly limited. Rule 1.6(b) does not *require* disclosure of confidential information in any circumstances and does not even permit such disclosure to prevent noncriminal but life-threatening acts. Nor does the rule permit disclosures to prevent financial rather than physical injuries. In general, the lawyer's only recourse is to withdraw from representation and to disavow any prior opinion that might assist criminal or fraudulent conduct. Rule 1.6, Comment.

As discussion in Part D indicates, many state ethical codes impose somewhat greater disclosure obligations than the Model Code and Model Rules prescribe. However, all jurisdictions still provide extensive protection for client confidences. Consider the traditional rationale for such protections discussed below. Does it justify current confidentiality rules? If not, what modifications would you propose?

B. JUSTIFICATIONS AND CRITIQUES

In a well-known critique of the attorney-client privilege, Jeremy Bentham questioned why lawyers should not disclose confidences to establish a client's guilt. After all, Bentham argued, the "conviction and punishment of . . . [a guilty defendant] is beneficial to society." If the result of such disclosures was that fewer confidences would be shared, then, asked Bentham, "wherein will consist the mischief? The man by the supposition is guilty; if not, . . . there is nothing to betray." And if confidential communications become less frequent, then "a guilty person will not in general be able to derive quite so much assistance from his law adviser, in the way of concerting a false defence, as he may do at present."[3]

Such critiques of the attorney-client privilege have generated two main responses. These defenses of confidentiality obligations parallel the traditional rationales for the adversary system and the advocate's neutral partisanship role. One line of argument rests on the value of individual legal rights and the importance of confidentiality in ensuring their protection. A second line of argument focuses on the instrumental value of confidentiality in promoting just resolution of legal issues and in promoting compliance with legal obligations.

1.   Rights-Based Justifications of Confidentiality

The basic rights-based argument for confidentiality requirements builds on several assumptions about societal values and client conduct. First, an overarching objective of the legal system is to preserve individual rights. In a complex society, people require lawyers' assistance in order to protect their legal interests. Lawyers cannot provide adequate representation unless clients feel free to provide all relevant information. Many individuals will be unwilling to consult lawyers or to disclose essential facts without assurances that their disclosure will remain confidential. From this perspective, Bentham was wrong in supposing that only the guilty benefit from the lawyer-client privilege. Many innocent individuals may fear the revelation of information that would be legally helpful. As an example, Monroe Freedman cites the case of a battered wife who is afraid to acknowledge shooting her brutal husband because she is unaware that her act would qualify as self-defense.[4]

In addition, confidentiality obligations serve not only to safeguard legal rights in general but also to preserve certain specific entitlements including privacy, effective assistance of counsel, and the protection against self-incrimination. By allowing clients to prevent disclosure of potentially damaging information, confidentiality rules help to ensure a domain of personal autonomy and intimate relationships. Without such rules, persons accused of a crime could not fully exercise both their sixth amendment right to counsel and their fifth amendment privilege against self-incrimination. If counsel could be compelled to reveal client disclosures, defendants' reliance on one constitutional guarantee would effectively compromise the other.

Whether these arguments justify the current broad scope of confidentiality protections is, however, open to dispute. Critics of existing norms raise several objections. First, they note that concerns about criminal defendants' fifth and sixth amendment rights do not justify sweeping protections in civil contexts. Nor do concerns about individual privacy and autonomy explain the extension of such confidentiality protections to corporations. More fundamentally, it is not self-evident why the rights of clients should always take priority over the rights of others, particularly where health and safety interests are implicated. According to commentators such as William Simon, the priorities underlying the traditional confidentiality rationale are "perverse" because they categorically favor clients who withhold information out of irresponsible or guilty motives at the expense of innocent third parties.[5] Similarly, critics also challenge the implicit hierarchy in current bar codes, which require disclosure to prevent fraud on a tribunal but not to save a life, and which permit disclosure to enable lawyers to collect their fees but not to prevent fraud against thousands of innocent investors.

Many commentators also challenge the effectiveness of broad confidentiality protections in preserving legal rights. Research summarized in Chapter XIV (Criminal Law and Procedure) makes clear that defendants aware of the privilege are often reluctant to confide in lawyers whom they cannot discharge or who might have competing loyalties.[6] Moreover, current confidentiality mandates are riddled with exceptions and indeterminacies that few clients now comprehend. Existing research leaves doubt whether adding further qualifications would significantly alter client behavior.

For example, in one Yale Law Journal study, most people were either unaware of the attorney-client privilege or believed that it extended to other professional relationships as well.[7] So too, Fred Zacharias' research in Tompkins County, New York found that surveyed lawyers almost never inform their clients about the duty of confidentiality; that many clients substantially misunderstand the scope of confidentiality; that only 30 percent of former clients report giving information to their lawyers that they would not have given without a guarantee of confidentiality; and that about half of the surveyed individuals predict that they would withhold information without a guarantee of confidentiality.[8]

Moreover, many individuals who would like to withhold compromising information may be unable to do so because they are unaware what material would present problems, because their lawyer has other sources for such information, or because their need for informed legal assistance outweighs other concerns. Historical, cross-cultural, and cross-professional research makes clear that practitioners have long provided counseling on confidential matters without the sweeping freedom from disclosure obligations that the American bar has now obtained.[9]

Given this evidence, it is appropriate to consider whether lawyers' confidentiality rules would look the same if they were drafted by individuals whose self-interest were not so directly involved. In evaluating disclosure obligations for other professionals (such as psychiatrists), legal decision-makers generally have concluded that the benefits of unqualified confidentiality are too conjectural to outweigh concrete risks to third parties.[10] So too, when lawyers' own needs for disclosure are at issue, even the bar's most fervent defenders of an absolute privilege rarely have pursued the logic of their position. Few confidentiality rules have evoked greater consensus within the bar than the provision allowing attorneys to reveal confidential information when necessary to collect fees or to establish their own position in a dispute with the client.[11] Yet it is scarcely obvious why disclosures to protect third party victims will erode client trust, while disclosures to protect lawyers' financial interests will not. As Geoffrey Hazard and Susan Koniak note:

> [O]n general legal principles, such a preference for lawyers as compared with third party victims seems very difficult to justify, to put it mildly. As compared with other victims, the lawyer is likely to be in a superior position to prevent the wrong . . . [and] probably runs a lesser risk of suffering actual injury if the fraud is consummated.[12]

It is, of course, possible to justify the exception for lawyers on other grounds: clients who put their counsel's conduct at issue do not deserve confidentiality protections. But on that logic, one could argue that clients guilty of criminal or fraudulent conduct are equally undeserving. Indeed, that was Bentham's point. Is there a persuasive response?

2.   Instrumental Defenses of Confidentiality

An alternative justification for broad confidentiality protections is that they promote justice. By encouraging individuals to seek legal advice and to disclose all relevant information, the attorney-client privilege and related ethical rules promote compliance with legal norms. Lawyers can counsel individuals about their legal obligations and encourage appropriate resolution of legal disputes. To perform this function, attorneys need a level of trust that is incompatible with whistle-blowing obligations. As John Wigmore noted, "[c]ertainly the position of the legal advisor would be a difficult and disagreeable one . . . [if the advisor is made] at the same time the solicitor and revealer [of confidences]."[13] Lawyers' disclosure of adverse information not only may impair their own relationships with clients, it may also contribute to a climate of suspicion that undermines the bar's socially beneficial counseling functions.

In essence, this argument draws on the rule-utilitarian framework discussed in Chapter II. Proponents of broad confidentiality protections acknowledge that in particular cases the costs of silence may seem greater than the benefits. But, they maintain, if we consider the effects of disclosure across a broad range of circumstances, society is better off with a rule requiring confidentiality than any alternative. It would not, for example, prove feasible for attorneys to evaluate the appropriateness of confidentiality on a case-by-case basis (the act-utilitarian approach) because they would have no ready way of quantifying the cumulative effects of disclosure on other clients' candor.

Critics of this approach argue that it has the same flaws in contexts involving confidentiality as in other circumstances. If disclosure in some cases has greater benefits than silence, why not adopt a rule that will take account of these exceptions? For all the reasons summarized above, it is difficult to maintain that allowing any exceptions to confidentiality obligations would preempt the lawyer's counseling role. Exceptions already exist, most clients are unaware of their scope, and many clients have sufficient independent reasons to confide or not confide in their attorney.

From critics' perspective, current confidentiality norms rest on unverifiable assumptions and impose demonstrable costs. We lack adequate evidence about how effective lawyers now are in promoting client compliance, or how important current confidentiality rules are in enabling lawyers to perform that function. While we also lack systematic data on the price of confidentiality, some case studies are suggestive. Problems 6A, 6C, 6D, 6F, and 6I offer representative illustrations of the substantial costs of lawyers' silence in the face of dangerous or fraudulent conduct. At least some of those adverse consequences affect attorneys as well as third parties. Although Wigmore was undoubtedly accurate about the "difficult and disagreeable" aspects of whistle-blowing, it is often no easier for lawyers to sit silently by and watch client misconduct jeopardize innocent victims' lives, health, and savings.

In addressing the Problems set forth below, consider whether any changes in current standards seem appropriate. Would you support the initial Model Rules proposal, rejected by the ABA but adopted by some states, that would require disclosures necessary to prevent death or substantial bodily harm to a third party? What about the proposal adopted by some states, but also rejected by the ABA, that would permit lawyers to disclose confidences of clients who used lawyers' services in committing criminal or fraudulent acts? Proponents argue that such exceptions serve professional as well as societal objectives by shielding lawyers from becoming accomplices or helpless bystanders in wrongful conduct. Opponents claim that such exceptions would "threaten the very cornerstone of the attorney-client relationship" and expose the bar to malpractice suits by clients for disclosing confidences or suits by third parties for failing to do so.[14] How would you vote on such proposals? Are there other modifications that you would prefer?

C.   THE MORAL LIMITS OF CONFIDENTIALITY

SPAULDING v. ZIMMERMAN, 116 N.W.2D 704 (MINN. 1962).   This case involved a claim by Theodore Spaulding on behalf of his 20-year-old minor son David for injuries arising out of a 1956 automobile accident. David Spaulding was a passenger in a car driven by one defendant, John Zimmerman, which collided with a car driven by the codefendant Florian Ledermann and owned by the codefendant John Ledermann. The case arose on appeal of an order setting aside the parties' settlement, which the plaintiff had initially accepted and later challenged on the ground that it rested on material misinformation.

Following the accident, Spaulding's family physician diagnosed various injuries, including rib fractures and a cerebral concussion with possible brain hemorrhages. The physician then referred Spaulding to an orthopedic specialist, who took chest x-rays and concluded that the heart, aorta, and lung fields were normal. That specialist referred Spaulding to another physician, who also found no problems with the aorta. At defendants' request, Spaulding was then examined by Dr. Hewitt Hannah, a neurologist. The Minnesota Supreme Court describes the subsequent events.

> [Dr. Hannah] reported to [counsel] for defendant John Zimmerman, as follows:
>
>> The one feature of the case which bothers me more than any other part of the case is the fact that this boy of 20 years of age has an aneurysm, which means a dilatation of the aorta and the arch of the aorta. Whether this came out of this accident I cannot say with any degree of certainty and I have discussed it with the Roentgenologist and a couple of Internists. . . . Of course an aneurysm or dilatation of the aorta in a boy of this age is a serious matter as far as his life. This aneurysm may dilate further and it might rupture with further dilatation and this could cause his death.
>>
>> It would be interesting also to know whether the X-ray of his lungs, taken immediately following the accident, shows this dilatation or not. If it was not present immediately following the accident and is now present, then we could be sure that it came out of the accident.
>
> Prior to the negotiations for settlement, the contents of the above report were made known to counsel for defendants Florian and John Ledermann. The case was called for trial . . . [at which time] neither David nor his father . . . was then aware that David was suffering the aorta aneurysm. . . . On the following day an agreement for settlement was reached. . . . [The trial court subsequently vacated the order, stating in part]:
>
>> it is not possible to escape the inference that defendants' representatives knew, or must be here charged with knowing, that plaintiff under all the circumstances would not accept the sum of $6500.00 if he or his representatives knew of the aneurysm and its possible serious consequences. Moreover, there is no showing by defendants that would support an inference that plaintiff and his representatives knew of the existence of the aneurysm but concluded that it was not causally related to the accident. . . .

To hold that the concealment was not of such character as to result in an unconscionable advantage over plaintiff's ignorance or mistake, would be to penalize innocence and incompetence and reward less than full performance of an officer of the Court's duty to make full disclosure to the Court when applying for approval in minor settlement proceedings. . . .

While no canon of ethics or legal obligation may have required [defense counsel] to inform plaintiff or his counsel with respect [to the aneurysm], or to advise the court therein, it did become obvious to them at the time, that the settlement then made did not contemplate or take into consideration the disability described. This fact opened the way for the court to later exercise its discretion in vacating the settlement and under the circumstances described we cannot say that there was any abuse of discretion on the part of the court in so doing. . . .

116 N.W.2d at 707-710.

PROBLEM 6A

You are an associate in the law firm defending Florian Ledermann in Spaulding v. Zimmerman. You have just seen a copy of the medical report describing the plaintiff's life-threatening aneurysm. You are appalled to learn that your supervising partner has no intention of disclosing the report to the plaintiff. According to the partner, he has no legal duty to provide the information under the state's discovery and disciplinary rules, no moral obligation to do so in light of opposing counsel's failure to request the report, and no right to do so, given that the report was prepared for the codefendant Zimmerman, who would be adversely affected by its disclosure.

Do you find that reasoning persuasive? If not, how do you proceed? Consider the material on the responsibilities of subordinate attorneys in Chapter III (Regulation of the Profession) at pages 82-89.

According to the court in *Spaulding*, there was "no doubt of the good faith of both defendants' counsel"; during adversarial settlement negotiations, "no rule required or duty rested upon defendants or their representatives" to disclose Spaulding's aneurysm. 116 N.W.2d at 709. Do you agree? What does "good faith" mean in this context? Would the Code or Model Rules require or permit disclosure? Should they? Would recent changes in discovery rules, if adopted by the state, require the defendant to reveal the report? See Part B of Chapter X (Civil Procedure). In overturning the settlement, the trial court appears to reason that once the parties were in court seeking approval for their agreement, the defendants had disclosure obligations to the judge. Does that reasoning imply that while defendants' counsel had no obligation to save an adversary's life, they did have a duty not to mislead a trial court? Is that reasoning consistent with professional rules? What about moral principles or societal interests?

The trial judge reserves his criticism for Spaulding's lawyer, who failed "to use available rules of discovery" to obtain the medical reports of defendants' physician. Only the fact that Spaulding was a minor prevented the judge from "denying plaintiff's motion to vacate, leaving him to whatever questionable remedy he may have against his doctor and against his lawyer." Id. In your view, who is primarily to blame in this instance? Does it matter for purposes of assessing defense counsel's disclosure obligations? Do you agree that the plaintiff's age is critical in determining those obligations? Would the problem in *Spaulding* have been less likely to arise under a system of court-appointed experts? See the discussion in Chapter XV (Evidence and Trial Advocacy) at pages 671–673.

Do the traditional justifications for confidentiality set forth above justify nondisclosure on the facts of *Spaulding*? Consider Zacharias' research, which surveyed New York lawyers' and clients' responses to various hypothetical situations, including one modeled on *Spaulding*. Of the responding lawyers, about two-thirds would disclose a life-threatening medical condition to their adversary; one-third would not. Of the responding clients, about 90 percent believed that lawyers should disclose such information and 60 percent believed that lawyers could do so under existing ethical rules. Only 10 percent of the clients felt that allowing such disclosure would make them less likely to use an attorney's services.[15] Would such findings affect your judgment if you were a member of an appellate court or bar drafting commission charged with formulating confidentiality rules?

How would you respond to a proposed standard for lawyers like the American Medical Association's Standard for doctors, which permits exceptions to confidentiality obligations based on "overriding social considerations"? Ethical Opinion 5.05 (1994).[16] How would you respond as legal counsel in cases where you might acquire information that suggests conduct posing serious risks to third parties? Suppose, for example, that you had a client who was HIV-positive and was engaging in unprotected sexual activity?[17]

D.   THE SCOPE OF THE PRIVILEGE

1.   Waivers

PROBLEM 6B

You are a litigator who, during pretrial discovery, receives certain material from opposing counsel by mistake. Without reviewing the contents of the material, you can tell from its label and the context of the case that it clearly falls within the attorney-client privilege. How do you proceed? Consider the materials on discovery in Chapter V (The Adversary System) at pages 185-195. What factors would be relevant to your decision?

Under generally accepted principles codified by proposed Federal Rule of Evidence 511, a holder of the attorney-client privilege waives its protection if he or she "voluntarily discloses or consents to disclosure of any significant part of the matter or communication. This rule does not apply if the disclosure is itself a privileged communication." Thus, if a client discloses the contents of her conversation with an attorney to a friend, the privilege is waived, but not if she discloses it to her husband. A client may also waive protection by testifying in court concerning part of a privileged communication. For example, if she states that her attorney advised her that certain conduct would be legal, she is subject to cross-examination about what else the attorney told her.

Since the privilege belongs to the client, no waiver occurs if an attorney discloses protected information without the client's consent. Even after such disclosure, the privilege remains available to prevent admission of the privileged material at trial. Paradoxically, although intentional unauthorized revelations by an attorney will not constitute a waiver, some courts have found that a negligent act will. Where litigators have mistakenly released a privileged document to their opponent, some, but not all, courts have found the privilege inapplicable.[18]

This doctrine has caused understandable alarm among trial attorneys, particularly given the general rule that disclosure of any part of privileged matter constitutes a waiver of other privileged matter on the same subject. Some commentators have accordingly argued that such waiver rules impair the discovery process by encouraging broad claims of privilege in order to prevent inadvertent disclosure of potentially protected material. These commentators often argue that waivers are inappropriate if attorneys who unintentionally release privileged material take prompt steps to recover it prior to reliance by an opponent.[19]

Even without such prompt actions, the American Bar Association Committee on Ethics has advised that lawyers who receive materials that on their face appear to be subject to the attorney-client privilege or "otherwise confidential" should refrain from examining them when it is clear that their disclosure was not intended. Recipients of such materials should notify the sending lawyer and abide by that lawyer's instructions as to the disposition of the materials. Formal Opinion 92-368 (Nov. 10, 1992). In so ruling, the Committee reasoned that waivers were too high a penalty for clients to pay for accidents that were sometimes inevitable. Would you follow that ruling if case law in your jurisdiction imposed no such obligations?

Similar considerations arise with respect to sharing of materials between parties in the same or connected suits. In such circumstances, some commentators recommend focusing on fairness: the issue should be whether the opponent will be "unfairly hampered" without access to the material.[20] Do you agree? If so, would you apply such an analysis if you were litigating a case or only if you were a trial court adjudicating the dispute?

2.   Client Identity and Fee Arrangements

PROBLEM 6C

Mark Baltes was killed in a hit-and-run accident in Palm Beach, Florida. Shortly after the collision, the driver requested the help of Barry Krischer, a local attorney. The driver asked Krischer to negotiate a resolution of the matter without revealing his identity. Krischer then consulted a second lawyer and asked him to negotiate with the prosecutor on the driver's behalf. The prosecutor declined to bargain but did not attempt to compel disclosure of the client's identity.

Two years later, when investigations had proven unsuccessful, Krischer attempted to reopen negotiations without identifying the driver. At that point, Baltes' parents filed a tort action against an unnamed defendant and sought to compel the lawyer to disclose his client's identity. Legal ethics experts lined up on both sides of the issue, and, as one put it, "if there was ever a case to test the sanctity of the attorney-client privilege, this one is it."[21]

If you were the presiding judge, how would you rule? If you were the prosecutor, would you attempt to compel disclosure of the driver's identity?

Under traditional definitions, the attorney-client privilege does not encompass the identity of clients or information concerning payment of their fees. The theory behind this limitation is that the purpose of the privilege is to encourage trust and candor by those who consult attorneys, and clients generally have no choice but to be candid about their identity and to pay fees. Courts and commentators also reason that fee payments are not communications and that society has no interest in encouraging third party subsidies of legal services. Accordingly, these matters do not require protection against disclosure.[22]

This understanding of the privilege has been widely criticized and has generated significant exceptions. Conceptually, these exceptions draw on an influential Ninth Circuit opinion, Baird v. Koerner, 279 F.2d 623 (1960), and its progeny. Baird was a tax lawyer who was consulted by another attorney regarding clients who had underpaid their income tax. These taxpayers wished to be in the most favorable position possible if they were ever to face criminal charges, but they also wanted to avoid triggering an indictment. Accordingly, the attorney gave Baird a cashier's check to pay the amount due anonymously. When the IRS sought to compel disclosure of the taxpayers and their attorney, Baird invoked the privilege and the federal court of appeals upheld his claims. In so ruling, the court identified several rationales. The most influential is the "communications" rationale. The court reasoned that identifying the taxpayers would convey information that would normally be considered a privileged communication, namely, that they owed more taxes than they had paid.

This doctrine has generated a series of inconsistent and increasingly controversial precedents. The cases provoking dispute typically fall into one of five fact patterns. The first is where parties who wish not to link themselves with a wrongful act hire an attorney to make restitution (as in *Baird*), to negotiate a plea bargain for an uncharged crime (as in Problem 6C), to return stolen property, or to perform similar services. A second situation involves an informer who wants to reveal misconduct by another individual while remaining anonymous. A third category of cases concerns prosecutors' efforts to discover details about fee payments by clients whose identity is already known. This information may provide evidence of unreported income or wealth that is likely to have come from criminal activity. A fourth variation arises when persons paying a client's fee or posting bond would like to keep their identity confidential. For example, when low-level members of an organized crime conspiracy are arrested, those higher up may wish to subsidize a defense without revealing their ties to the defendant. Prosecutors seek such information both to link these unidentified benefactors to the conspiracy and to discover payments that exceed reported income or that suggest illegal sources of wealth. A final category of cases involves cash clients. Section 60501 of the Internal Revenue Code requires all persons engaged in a trade or business, including lawyers, to report cash transactions in excess of $10,000 on Form 8300. This requirement was intended not only to encourage disclosure of taxable income but also to trace criminal activity.[23]

Whether the privilege should apply to such cases and on what theory has generated an increasingly confused and confusing series of precedents. Some prominent commentators and bar ethics opinions maintain that allowing ready access to information about client fees and identity creates too great a potential for prosecutorial abuse. The practice of subpoenaing attorneys has grown significantly in recent years and may serve to harass particularly successful defense counsel or to reduce their clients' trust and confidence. Additional problems of conflicts of interest arise where information about tainted fees may expose the lawyers themselves to liability and force their disqualification.[24]

How would you respond to these concerns? Consider the five common fact situations noted above. Under what, if any, circumstances, would you protect client identity and fee information? Could concerns about prosecutorial abuse be met by judicial review of prosecutors' issuance of attorney subpoenas?

3.   The Crime-Fraud Exception

a.   The Attorney-Client Privilege

From the standpoint of legal ethics, the most significant exception to lawyers' confidentiality obligations involves future crimes and frauds. That exception has three primary conditions. First, a client must intend to commit the illegal act; however, it does not matter whether the act actually occurs or whether the lawyer knows of the client's motives. Second, the burden of showing that the privilege is inapplicable lies with the party trying to invoke the crime-fraud exception. Traditionally, this burden required evidence of crime or fraud sufficient to establish a prima facie case or probable cause. More recently, courts have demanded only some foundation in fact, which can be established by the communication itself. Third, the exception applies only to ongoing or future crimes and frauds, not to past illegalities, and the distinction is based on the point at which clients communicate with the attorney, not when they assert the privilege.[25]

McCormick explains the traditional rationale for the exemption:

> Since the policy of the [attorney-client privilege] is that of promoting the administration of justice, it would be a perversion of the privilege to extend it to the client who seeks a chance to help him in carrying out an illegal or fraudulent scheme. Advice given for those purposes would not be professional services, but participation in a conspiracy.[26]

The theory underlying this distinction, like that underpinning the privilege, is that clients are entitled to informed professional assistance in defending their past conduct, but not in planning future illegal activity. This distinction has, however, been criticized on both theoretical and practical grounds. As Geoffrey Hazard notes:

> The distinction between past and future conduct is even more difficult to maintain in practical terms, at least for the modern business lawyer. The rules of confidentiality assume that all real modern instances fall into one of two stock situations. In the first situation, the client walks in, says to the lawyer that he is charged with murder, and then admits he shot the guy. Under the rules, that disclosure is confidential. In the other situation, the client walks in, discloses to the lawyer that he wants to kill the guy, and then goes out and does so. That disclosure is not confidential until the fatal shot is fired, although, as we have seen, the lawyer does not have to disclose it unless asked, which ordinarily he would not be until after the victim is already dead. The realities of modern business, on the other hand, bear

little relation to this tidy dichotomy. They involve clients who "walked in" years ago and have since been continually provided with advice and assistance on all kinds of matters. They involve courses of client activity that originated years ago, continue in the present, and whose consequences will ramify into the more or less indefinite future. They also involve a complex web of legal rules governing the client, many of them carrying both penal sanctions and possibilities of ruinous civil liability and all of them ones which the client has both a duty to obey and incentives to avoid or violate.

To impose on such realities a distinction between past, present, and future is casuistical at best and often simply nonsense. Yet as the confidentiality rule now stands, the distinction is crucial.[27]

Consider Problems 6C to 6I. Is Hazard's analysis persuasive? If so, does it suggest any need for changes in rules concerning the attorney-client privilege?

b.   *Bar Ethics Rules*

These same issues arise in the application of bar ethical rules. Lawyers have always been forbidden to assist future criminal or fraudulent conduct, DR 7-102(A)(7) and Model Rule 1.2, but what they should do on learning of past or continuing illegalities has generated long-standing controversy and confusion. Until the mid-1970s, the ABA Code required lawyers to make disclosures necessary to rectify a fraud perpetrated during the course of representation, DR 7-102(B). The Code also permitted disclosures in order to prevent a crime, DR 4-101. In 1974, the ABA adopted an amendment to DR 7-102(B)(1), which removed any duty to report information concerning frauds if the information was protected as confidential under DR 4-101. See ABA Ethics Committee, Formal Opinion 341. This amendment was a response to the Securities and Exchange Commission's widely publicized efforts to impose liability on lawyers for failure to prevent or report fraudulent client conduct.[28] Most states refused to adopt the amendment. In those that did, lawyers retained discretion to report future crimes under DR 4-101, but were instructed to remain silent regarding past crimes and frauds unless disclosures were "required by law." DR 7-102(A)(3).

The American Bar Association revisited the issue in the early 1980s in debates over the Model Rules. Proponents of broad confidentiality protections defeated various proposals for limited disclosure requirements, largely on the ground that such duties would increase lawyers' exposure to third party liability. Model Rule 1.6 permitted disclosures only to the extent that the lawyer reasonably believed necessary to prevent criminal acts likely to result in death or substantial bodily harm. No disclosures were required and none were even permitted for noncriminal acts or for financial rather than physically threatening misconduct. However, critics of such sweeping confidentiality protections won a concession in the comment to

Rule 1.6, which acknowledges that nothing in the rules "prevents the lawyer from giving notice of the fact of withdrawal [from representing a client], and the lawyer may also withdraw or disaffirm any opinion, document, affirmation or the like." This "noisy withdrawal" provision allows lawyers in at least some situations to accomplish indirectly what they cannot do directly: to warn possible victims of client misconduct.

Such tension between the black-letter rule and the comment has proved to be an unstable compromise. Of the jurisdictions that have ethics codes based to some degree on the Model Rules, only a few have enacted Rule 1.6 without modification. The most common amendments include

- requiring, rather than merely permitting, disclosures to prevent clients from committing a crime;
- including all crimes, not just those likely to result in death or severe bodily harm;
- extending disclosure provisions to encompass frauds as well as crimes; and
- allowing disclosure to rectify the consequences of a criminal or fraudulent act that involved the lawyer's services.

In most states, disclosure beyond what the ABA contemplated has appeared appropriate in light of existing common law, committee rulings, and societal interests.

Proponents of greater disclosure believe that it serves the interests of the bar as well as innocent third parties because it allows lawyers to maintain their good reputations, reduces their chances of being sued as co-conspirators, and enables them to minimize the damages for which they might be held partly accountable. Despite such arguments and the trends in state law, the ABA House of Delegates has rejected proposed changes in the Model Rules.[29]

The ABA Standing Committee on Professional Ethics and Responsibility, however, has made some effort to reconcile the Model Rules formulation and state versions of Rule 1.6. Formal Opinion 92-366 concludes that if a lawyer learns that a client is using legal assistance to defraud third parties:

First, the lawyer must withdraw from any representation that, directly or indirectly, would assist the client's continuing or intended fraud.

Second, the lawyer *may* withdraw from all representation of the client, and *must* withdraw from all representation if the fact of such representation is likely to assist fraud, for example by encouraging third parties' [misplaced confidence in the client].

Third, the lawyer may disavow any of her work product to prevent its use in the client's continuing or intended future fraud even if this indirectly would reveal confidential information.

Fourth, if the fraud is completed, and the lawyer does not know or reasonably believe that the client intends to continue the fraud or commit a future fraud by use of the lawyer's services or work product, the lawyer may withdraw from the representation of the client but may not disavow any work product.

Not all commentators agree with the Committee's opinion and its persuasive authority is not entirely clear. Nor is there agreement on what lawyers should do on facts like those in Problem 6H infra, Problem 13E in Chapter XIII (Corporate Law), and Problems 16D and 16E in Chapter XVI (Family Law). How would you respond in these circumstances? When would you hold lawyers liable — morally and legally — for failing to disclose a crime or fraud?

Of course, disclosure obligations become relevant only when the lawyer knows or has reason to know of client misconduct. What counts as knowledge can often be a matter of some dispute, as subsequent discussion of client perjury indicates. See Part F infra. Moreover, various psychological tendencies can often work against lawyers' recognition or acknowledgement of misconduct. "Cognitive conservatism" encourages individuals not to retain information that is incompatible with established beliefs or earlier decisions, such as decisions that a client deserves zealous representation. Similarly, after coming to such conclusions, individuals tend to reduce "cognitive dissonance" by suppressing or reconstruing facts that cast doubt on their judgment. As Donald Langevoort notes, such psychological tendencies, together with financial self-interest and collegial pressure, may keep lawyers from acknowledging client fraud.[30] It is therefore important that rules of ethics and malpractice liability give lawyers incentives to acquire adequate information and avoid complicity in client misconduct. Do current rules strike the right balance?

4.   The Attorney-Client Privilege in Organizations

See Chapter XIII, Corporate Law
 • Part B. Confidentiality and Disclosure Obligations
   (pages 560–571)

E.   THE DESTRUCTION AND DISCLOSURE OF EVIDENCE

1.   Introduction

PROBLEM 6D

1. Francis Belge and Frank Armani were New York attorneys appointed to defend Robert Garrow on charges of murder. During the course of representation, Garrow acknowledged committing two other

unsolved murders and disclosed the location of the bodies. The lawyers confirmed that location and photographed the bodies. In subsequent plea negotiations with the district attorney, Belge suggested that he could provide information concerning the two unsolved murders in return for a favorable plea disposition.

After several months, and hundreds of thousands of dollars spent on police searches, students stumbled on the bodies of both victims. Law enforcement officials, however, could not connect the crimes with Garrow until his trial on the initial murder charge. Then, in an unsuccessful effort to establish an insanity defense, he confessed to both murders as well as seven rapes. The jury convicted Garrow of first-degree murder and the judge sentenced him to 25 years to life imprisonment, the maximum penalty.

Both lawyers subsequently were called before the grand jury. Belge was indicted for violating two sections of the New York Public Health Law, which require, respectively, that a decent burial be accorded to the dead, and that anyone knowing of the death of a person without medical attendance must report the death to the proper authorities. After state courts dismissed that indictment, the New York Bar Association Committee on Professional Ethics considered the propriety of Belge's conduct.

If you were a member of the committee charged with analyzing Belge's conduct under the Code of Professional Responsibility, how would you vote? Suppose Belge had learned the information from a source other than his client. Would his obligations have been different? Alternatively, assume that Belge knew that another person had been charged with the kidnapping of one of the victims. If Garrow had not wanted his guilt revealed in plea negotiations, what would Belge's responsibilities have been?

What if there had been no plea negotiations and Belge had anonymously informed the authorities of the location of the bodies? Would the appropriateness of his conduct depend on whether investigators were able, or might have been able, to link Garrow to the murders? What should Belge have done if he had strongly suspected that Garrow would attempt other assaults or dispose of the victims' bodies while on bail? If Garrow had also revealed the location of the murder weapon, or had left it in Belge's custody, what would Belge's obligations have been?

2. After his conviction on the initial murder charge, Garrow pled guilty to the other offenses in exchange for concurrent sentences. He then sued Belge and Armani for several million dollars based on allegedly ineffective assistance of counsel, and sued the state for $10 million based on allegedly improper medical treatment of wounds he sustained while being captured by police. In exchange for dropping the claims against the state, he received a transfer to a medium security correctional facility for elderly and handicapped prisoners. The security proved inadequate to his talents and he escaped shortly after his transfer.

The police then asked Armani for any information that might help recapture his former client. According to Armani's subsequent account of the case, he described some of the tactics Garrow had reported using to escape the police: "[Garrow] once told me that he would hole up in the underbrush until the cops gave up the search in that area and pulled out."[31] Based in part on that information, police concentrated search efforts on the underbrush near the prison. As they approached Garrow's cover, he fired on the patrol. They fired back and he was killed instantly.

Did Armani breach the Code of Professional Responsibility in disclosing confidential information about Garrow's past escapes? Would you have acted differently? If Armani had declined to answer any questions about his client's prior strategies in avoiding capture, could he have been required to disclose confidential information? Was he obligated, morally or legally, to volunteer what he knew?

In dismissing the indictment against Belge, the New York trial court concluded that the information was privileged and applauded counsel for acting with "all the zeal at [his] command to protect the constitutional rights of his client." However, the court also acknowledged that its task would have been "much more difficult" had Belge been indicted for obstructing justice rather than for circumventing the "trivia of a pseudo-criminal statute." People v. Belge, 83 Misc. 2d 186, 191 (1975). The appellate court, while affirming dismissal of the indictment, expressly declined to reach the "ethical questions" underlying the case. It did, however, voice "serious concern" about the applicability of the attorney-client privilege in a context where counsel had obligations dictated not only by the bar's code but also by "basic human standards of decency." People v. Belge, 50 A.D.2d 1088 (1975). What do such standards require on the facts of *Belge*? Are they in conflict with the Code of Professional Responsibility?

In a television documentary following the case, the district attorney acknowledged that defense counsel had understandable reasons for not revealing the bodies' location because disclosure might have led to incriminating information. However, he found reprehensible counsel's effort to use information about those crimes to plea bargain for a sentence that would have put the defendant back on the street. Armani later defended his actions on the ground that the "right of confidentiality . . . must exist even for unpopular people and causes, or it exists for no one." If the Constitution "doesn't protect the worst of us . . . it doesn't protect the best of us."[32] "There was," Armani later told the grand jury, "nothing else I could do."[33]

Do you agree? Most members of the attorneys' immediate community did not. Armani, who had taken the case to "forge his reputation as a topflight criminal lawyer," found himself the target of hate mail, death threats, and public vilification.[34] Armani had to lay off his three associate lawyers and support staff; Belge left the country. Yet the attorneys were also convinced that if they had disclosed the location of the victims' bodies, their practices and those of other lawyers would have suffered in other ways. It would have "take[n] years to re-establish [the] principle of lawyer-client confidentiality."[35] Are you persuaded? If so, should Armani also have been concerned about the disclosures he made leading to Garrow's death?

These confidentiality issues have been long-standing subjects of debate. One of the most celebrated early twentieth-century cases involved the disclosure in an autobiography by Atlanta attorney Arthur Powell that a former client had acknowledged committing the murder for which another man had been convicted. In that case, Leo Frank, a Jewish factory owner, was accused of murdering his 14-year-old employee, Mary Phagan. Anti-Semitic prejudice ran high and the jury imposed the death penalty. Powell's client, after a promise of complete confidentiality, revealed his guilt. He would not, however, surrender to authorities or allow Powell to disclose his confession. Powell then contacted the governor and asserted Frank's innocence, but refused to identify the source of his information. After the governor commuted Frank's sentence, a lynch mob gathered under the banner "Knights of Mary Phagan." They hanged Leo Frank and formed the group that subsequently became the Ku Klux Klan.

Powell later defended his actions on the ground that the Constitution guaranteed the right to counsel, and "we lawyers, no matter what we think of it, have no duty but to protect and obey it. Such is our duty; such is our oath." However, Powell also added, "I would be strongly tempted to break my oath before I would let an innocent man hang, but would know that I was violating the law and my oath if I did so."[36]

Discussion of similar issues recurred in 1992 when a New Jersey couple, Arthur and Irene Seale, was indicted for conspiracy, kidnapping, and extortion in connection with the disappearance of Exxon's president, Sidney Reso. Before authorities located Reso's body, dispute centered on whether attorneys for the Seales had any duty to reveal information about the victim's condition and location. As one lawyer put it, "From a purely cold-blooded criminal-defense standpoint, I would think cooperation would be ill-advised. . . . By locating the body, they're adding the additional element of, unfortunately, murder. Whatever they'd be gaining by mitigation, they would be losing in terms of criminal exposure and culpability."[37]

If you had been the defense lawyer in the Reso or the Leo Frank case, would you have felt obligated to take a "cold-blooded" perspective? If the kidnapping victim had been alive, should the lawyers have had ethical duties to disclose his location? During ABA debates over early Model Rule provisions on confidentiality, some commentators cited the Frank case in support of a mandatory disclosure rule to prevent death or bodily injury. In rejecting any such requirement, the majority of the ABA's House of Delegates appeared concerned about the implications of such an obligation not only for clients but also for lawyers facing civil liability. Some commentators have maintained that a discretionary standard is an appropriate way of responding to an issue that fails to generate societal consensus. Are you persuaded by these arguments? Is there a significant absence of consensus concerning disclosure obligations within society or only within the legal profession?[38]

PROBLEM 6E

Consider the following situations:

1. A client leaves in the lawyer's possession the "fruits or instru-mentalities of a crime," such as stolen property or weapons.
2. A third party turns over such evidence to the lawyer or reveals its location.
3. The lawyer receives documents from the client implicating him in criminal activity.
4. A client describes to the lawyer the location of incriminating evidence and asks the lawyer for advice or assistance in main-taining its privacy.
5. After discovering the location of evidence, the lawyer realizes that it will be irretrievably lost or destroyed if she takes no action.
6. A client asks the lawyer whether certain material could establish criminal liability and what the consequences would be if the evi-dence were lost or inadvertently destroyed.
7. The lawyer discovers that incriminating documents have inexpli-cably vanished.
8. A client asks the lawyer to formulate a document retention program that will prevent the accumulation of legally damaging material.

How should the lawyer respond in these contexts? Does it matter whether a legal proceeding is pending or imminent? Should it?

PROBLEM 6F

You are counsel to the President while the Senate is investigating the break-in of the Democratic National Committee headquarters at the Watergate Hotel. You have just listened to President Nixon's tapes, which implicate various members of the Administration in the break-in and its cover-up. These tapes are not under subpoena, and there is no pending grand jury investigation. Assuming that the tapes are private property, the President would like to know if he has any legal obligation to retain them. Under federal obstruction of justice statutes, it is a crime to destroy evidence that is relevant to a pending grand jury or criminal proceeding. Assume that in the District of Columbia it is not otherwise illegal to destroy documents, even if they are relevant to foreseeable proceedings. It is quite apparent to you after listening to the tapes that if they ever became public, a criminal investigation would be virtually certain.

Edward Bennett Williams, a renowned defense lawyer, was reportedly convinced that he could have prevented Richard Nixon's resignation. According to a New York Times account,

> [Williams] who has been heard privately to refer to Mr. Nixon as "old snake
> brains," says confidently: "I could have won it. The first thing, I would have
> told him to burn the tapes. I would have advised him, before they were
> ever called for, before they were ever subject to any subpoena, to make a
> public disposition of these things. It would have had to be premised on the
> fact that there were all kinds of state secrets, private conversations with
> heads of state that would be embarrassing to the United States worldwide
> if exposed. So the tapes would have to be destroyed for national-security
> reasons."
>
> Not all lawyers would admire this kind of advice. Yale Kamisar, a spe-
> cialist in criminal procedure and constitutional law at the University of
> Michigan Law School, replied, when asked for his opinion, that he was
> "taken aback" by [the proposal]. . . . "I think it would have been unethical,
> even though it would be difficult to prove the real reasons for destroying
> the tape. I hate to say this, because I am a great admirer of Edward
> Bennett Williams. First of all, he would have been misrepresenting the real
> reasons for burning the tapes. It would have had nothing to do with
> national security. It would have been to put his client in a better position to
> prevail in a lying contest."[39]

Williams, however, added that he was "happy for the country that
things turned out the way they did."[40] Nixon was less pleased. In retro-
spect, he wished that he had destroyed the tapes. When the subject
arose during a 1984 television interview, Nixon indicated that he had
kept the recordings partly as "insurance" against lies by other
participants in the taped conversations, partly because disclosure of
these recordings occurred while he was hospitalized with pneumonia
and unable to make a "tough decision," and partly because he had bad
advice from "well-intentioned lawyers who had sort of the cockeyed
notion that I would be destroying evidence."[41]

Nixon's counsel, Leonard Garment, recalls the situation somewhat
differently. At the time, he had been concerned that destruction would
spark impeachment proceedings. Fifteen years later, he acknowledged
that Nixon probably could have remained in office by producing the tapes
that were inconclusive, and justifying his destruction of the remainder as
necessary to protect state secrets.[42]

If you had been Nixon's counsel, what advice would you have
provided? Assume that disclosure of the tapes with incriminating material had nothing that could plausibly have presented national security
problems. Would other concerns about the country's welfare have
affected your view?

Do bar ethical standards provide adequate guidance for circumstances like Problem 6E and 6F? Under both the Code and the Model
Rules, lawyers' obligations concerning physical evidence track those
defined by criminal laws and procedural rules. Disciplinary Rule

7-109(A) provides that "[a] lawyer shall not suppress any evidence that he or his client has a legal obligation to reveal or produce." Other provisions direct that a lawyer shall not "[i]ntentionally or habitually violate any established rule of procedure or of evidence" (DR 7-106(C)(7)), engage in "illegal conduct involving moral turpitude" (DR 1-102(A)(3)), or engage "in conduct that is prejudicial to the administration of justice." DR 1-102(A)(5). Model Rule 3.4 provides that a lawyer shall not falsify evidence or "unlawfully obstruct another party's access to evidence or unlawfully alter, destroy, or conceal a document or other material having potential evidentiary value." Nor may a lawyer "counsel or assist another person to do any such act" or engage in conduct "prejudicial to the administration of justice." Rule 8.4(d).

Laws concerning the retention of evidence vary in scope. Some statutes prohibit intentional destruction or concealment if the evidence is relevant to a pending criminal proceeding; other prohibitions also cover material relevant to an ongoing investigation. Model Penal Code §241.7 and its state analogues criminalize destruction or concealment if the actor believes that an official proceeding or investigation is pending or about to be instituted. A few states impose liability for actions intended to prevent production of evidence in a legal proceeding regardless of when the actions take place. Thus, attorneys' ethical responsibilities regarding potential evidence will vary depending upon when destruction or concealment is contemplated, what statutes are controlling, and whether the material is subject to any court order. Interpretation of these responsibilities has produced several clear rules and certain murky norms.

2. Possession of Evidence

Prevailing case law generally holds that attorneys may not actively participate in concealing the fruits or instrumentalities of a crime. Lawyers who come into possession of such material must turn it over to the prosecution. The leading cases are State v. Olwell, 394 P.2d 681 (Wash. 1964); In re Ryder, 263 F. Supp. 360 (E.D. Va.), aff'd, 381 F.2d 713 (4th Cir. 1967); and Morrell v. State, 575 P.2d 1200 (Alaska 1978). In *Olwell*, the court held that an attorney must turn over an incriminating weapon when requested by subpoena and should do so on his own initiative without revealing the source or manner in which it was obtained. *Ryder* reached a similar result, and suspended a lawyer who moved a sawed-off shotgun and apparently stolen money from his client's safety deposit box to his own. In *Morrell*, a friend of the defendant cleaned out his car at his attorney's request. On discovering a kidnap plan, the friend turned it over to the attorney. After consulting the state bar ethics committee, the attorney withdrew from representation and helped arrange the transfer of the evidence to the police. The defendant was convicted and appealed on grounds of ineffective assistance of counsel. In rejecting that claim, the court reasoned that the attorney would have been obligated to see that the evidence reached the prosecutor even if he had received it from the defendant, and that his obligation was even stronger because he had acquired it from a third party. 575 P.2d at 1211.

Although attorneys are required to turn over evidence in their possession, they cannot be compelled to disclose confidences concerning its origin or how they learned of its location. Some judges have required defendants to stipulate where evidence originated. Others have excluded material when the prosecutor had no way except through defense counsel to establish its link with the defendant (such as through fingerprints, bank serial numbers, or the like).[43]

These approaches have attracted significant criticism. Excluding the evidence entirely allows defendants to dispose of incriminating material by leaving it with their lawyers.[44] Yet requiring defendants to stipulate facts linking themselves to such material penalizes confidential disclosures and accomplishes indirectly what the privilege was meant to prevent. Some commentators question why attorneys should be treated differently from other citizens, who don't have an affirmative obligation to produce evidence. Moreover, as a practical matter, the *Olwell* rule is almost never invoked in white-collar cases; attorneys are not penalized for failure to volunteer incriminating records in their possession.[45]

How should lawyers and the legal system handle the problem of confidential disclosures and physical evidence? Does the prevailing notion that lawyers can "look but not touch" make sense? Are cases like *Belge* and *Morrell* logically consistent? Are they ethically defensible?

3.   Document Retention

Businesses are generating an increasing number of documents and government decision-makers are generating an increasing number of regulations concerning document retention. By the early 1980s, the federal government had over 1,300 statutes or regulations requiring retention of certain records for certain periods, and every state and most municipalities had comparable rules.[46] In order to ensure compliance while minimizing costs and risks of legal liability, corporations and their counsel have focused greater attention on information retention policies.

Establishing a general retention program has a variety of advantages. It can minimize the expense of storage and retrieval of documents, as well as reduce the legal risks from records that are erroneous, misleading, or indicative of liability. Yet such programs also have costs, including the administrative expenses of ensuring compliance; the difficulties of establishing facts once certain documents are destroyed; and the adverse inferences observers may draw from incomplete compliance with the program or selective destruction outside its boundaries.[47]

Attorneys often play a pivotal role in weighing these costs and benefits and in counseling clients about document production whether or not they have a formal program. That role often presents difficult ethical dilemmas. As Geoffrey Hazard observes:

> [One] way to cope with the problem is to redefine it. . . . [I]t is unethical to counsel the systematic destruction of evidence that might eventually be embarrassing under the antitrust or tax laws; it is not unethical to provide a projection of the legal aspects of a records retention policy. . . . The cynical ideal would be to formulate a problem in a way that is perfectly ethical from the lawyer's viewpoint and perfectly opportunistic from the client's viewpoint.[48]

The more sophisticated the client, the more attractive this solution.

Is this the "ideal" that current ethical rules legitimate? Consider the conduct of the lawyer described by Goulden in Problem 14B at page 608 and Kenneth Mann in White Collar Crime, below.

On the one hand, clients have strong interests in eliminating documents before they become evidence, and lawyers are under strong pressures to please clients. As litigators often note: "Paper kills and more paper kills more." "Purge Your Files Now or Pay Later."[49] Document control programs speak to this problem by targeting entire categories of material for elimination once they reach a certain age to avoid the suggestion that any selective destruction occurred. Employees also benefit from counseling about the need to "think about how [something] would sound in court." If they "wouldn't care to explain it from the witness stand," they shouldn't write it.[50]

On the other hand, as Geoffrey Hazard notes, "suggesting the destruction of evidentiary documents is as illegal and unethical as counseling perjury. Moreover, in this era in which any piece of paper may have been photocopied, destruction of documents can be much easier to prove than perjury."[51] As senior executives belatedly learned in the celebrated Texaco case involving taped discussions disclosing racial bias, careers may be destroyed by discussing removal of evidentiary documents in meetings that could be recorded or recalled by a non-team player.[52]

Once litigation is pending or imminent, some clients also require counseling about the retention of all the material they wish hadn't been written. If particular employees may have motives to destroy particular documents, counsel should take immediate steps to ensure that those records are secure and that reliable individuals are in charge of storage and file searches. In many cases, pragmatic and ethical considerations point in similar directions. Destruction that can be documented can also be disastrous for clients as well as counsel. Fact-finders are entitled to draw adverse inferences from destruction and significant sanctions can result.[53]

Yet as the preceding discussion suggests, statutory prohibitions leave significant gaps. In some jurisdictions, destruction is legal if a proceeding is foreseeable but not pending. And lawyers who suspect but do not "know" that their client has engaged in illegal destruction may not reveal that fact. For that reason, some commentators have argued that lawyers as well as clients should face tort liability for "spoliation of evidence," the intentional or negligent destruction of material "[known] to be essential to a civil action." See Smith v. Superior Court, 151 Cal. App. 3d 491, 495 (1984).[54] Some courts have also concluded that lawyers should be accountable for failing to make "credible attempt[s] to insure or monitor" the client's compliance with a discovery order or to "intercede to prevent destruction of documents." William T. Thompson Co. v. General Nutrition Corp., 593 F. Supp. 1443, 1455 (C.D. Cal. 1984). Would you support sanctions in such cases? If not, can you suggest other regulatory responses?

KENNETH MANN, DEFENDING WHITE COLLAR CRIME: A PORTRAIT OF ATTORNEYS AT WORK

103-104, 109-110, 112-118, 120-123 (1985)

. . . Defense attorneys know that they walk a narrow line between helping and hurting their case when they facilitate or allow a client to hide facts from the attorney himself. Not having knowledge of an inculpatory fact that the government discovers can completely destroy a defense attorney's argument. . . . But of the attorneys I studied, most either said that they sometimes preferred not to get certain facts from a client or showed by their actions that they felt this way. . . .

LEGAL ADVICE AND LACK OF INQUIRY

. . . Here is an archetype scenario of the attorney in the inquiry avoidance role: a subpoena is issued by a court calling for the client to produce all documents related to a certain transaction. Upon receipt, the client takes the subpoena to an attorney and asks, "How do I proceed?" In the characteristic case of avoidance, the attorney begins by explaining to the client what is called for by the subpoena and what significance certain types of documents would have for the course of the investigation. He will not blandly ask the client what documents currently exist but will explain to the client what the subpoena indicates about the subject and scope of the investigation. Some attorneys go one step further and explain to the client what kinds of documents could be used against the client "*if* they exist." For example, the attorney says, "The government is trying to establish that officers in the corporation had knowledge of the improper evaluation of assets before the public distribution of the prospectus; if there are any documents which show such knowledge, these may be used by the prosecution as evidence for an indictment. Or if there is any document which indicates that an officer requested certain financial analyses that were not made, this may also be problematic." In this fashion, an attorney educates a client as to what constitutes a potentially adverse document. Subsequently, the client takes several weeks to conduct an independent search.

In many instances, such a discussion is the last detailed consideration of the type and possible existence of the requested documents. The client is later asked to report to the attorney whether any such documents were found. And then he is instructed how to make a formal reply on the date of appearance before the prosecutor to answer the subpoena. An attorney who is avoiding inquiry will not ask, "Did such documents ever exist?" or "Was document X or document Y found?" His interaction with the client is likely to be limited to a narrower question: "Do you have anything to present in response to the subpoena?". . .

Another attorney was asked directly about the attorney-client relationship in IRS summons compliance procedures. He stated:

> There are many cases in which one would surmise that documents summoned from the client existed at the time the summons was issued. My function in this procedure is a very limited one. I, of course, do not want the client convicted of an obstruction of justice charge, and I do warn him of the dire consequences of such a happening. But in the end it is the client's choice. I have no doubt that clients destroy documents. Have I ever "known" of such an occurrence? No. But you put two and two together. You couldn't convict anyone on such circumstantial evidence, but you can draw your own conclusion.

Still another attorney summed up the same views when he replied to an associate who seemed to think that a client was not being completely honest: "What you are trying to tell me is that the client is not telling the truth. What I am saying is that the response is credible. We are not law enforcement agents."

These interview comments represent the widespread view that it is not the attorney's task to enforce his client's compliance with the law. His obligation, even if it is an obligation not met all the time by all attorneys, is to refrain from actively facilitating or knowingly taking part in law violations. It is not a defense attorney's obligation to go into the corporate and personal records or send associates to conduct a search. Nor is it his obligation to find out what happened to missing documents. The attorney's limited role in this particular procedure is to serve his client by educating him. . . .

FACILITATION OF CONCEALMENT

. . . A large number of respondents indicated that some clients make open proposals to destroy or manipulate evidence. One attorney stated the following:

When you have a client who's in a very bad bind and he's going to have to essentially convict himself by turning over bank records, or accountant records, or what have you, the client has a very strong impulse to do something about it, to save his own neck. From the client's point of view, there is not much to lose at that stage — he know's he's stuck if he doesn't do something. Occasionally, a client will say something like, "If I get rid of the records now, isn't it true that no one will know the difference?" . . . I don't say, "Look, I can't allow you to do that." That puts me in a one-up moral position and is most embarrassing for the client. I usually say something like, "The penalties are very severe, and it is true that it may turn up later and cause you more trouble, so I advise you not to do it." That makes it seem more like I'm helping him protect himself rather than demonstrating some kind of moral superiority. . . .

It was evident from the behavior and attitudes of many of the attorneys that they believed that even if the most passive attorney were joined with the most actively obstructionist client, there would be no ethical problem unless there were some kind of "direct" involvement of the attorney. What was meant by direct was not specified. . . . As one [attorney] stated,

It's my mission and obligation to defend the client, not to sit in moral, ethical, or legal judgment of him. I cannot join him in transgressing the law, but whatever he does of his own impetus, whatever way he conducts himself in attempting to protect himself, is a decision he has to make independent of what I do. I must inform him of the consequences and significance of his action but not punish him or sanction him or in other ways initiate law enforcement actions against him. My role in the adversary system is to protect him.

This attorney was not concerned about potential backfire if his client were to be prosecuted for obstruction of justice. He explained that in the aggregate there is a high degree of certainty that some clients will help themselves by destroying or altering evidence and others will hurt themselves. From this perspective, the person faced with the tragedy of a criminal prosecution should not be told by an attorney how to handle the evidence that can lead to a conviction. As long as the attorney does not involve himself directly, it is the client's choice. By controlling the conversation, the attorney can protect himself from legal responsibility.

The attorneys who took an active stance by warning their clients about obstructive behavior and by making a diligent effort to discover the presence of all inculpatory evidence appeared to do so out of a long-range concern for the penalty exposure that results when a client conceals evidence or destroys it. One attorney put it this way:

My job is to keep the client out of jail. Some of my clients have ended up in jail not because of the crime for which they were being investigated, but because they lied, or burned documents, or altered them in the course of the investigation. So I tell them right off the bat that if they want to stay out of jail, let me know what's there, and keep hands off.

None of the defense attorneys interviewed said that he attempted to get all the information from the client because he thought that there was an ethical obligation inherent in the public mission of the profession. The attorneys most committed to actively preventing their clients from obstructive behavior appear to be so because they are highly motivated to build and protect a reputation. A client who embarrasses the attorney damages his reputation. He must therefore conscientiously avoid being surprised and avoid making representations that may later be proved wrong. Above all, building a good reputation among the elite of the bar means that he can be trusted, not only by his client, but by his opponent. The test of his reputation is that when he tells an opponent that his client did not see a document, he is believed and relied on. . . . [As one attorney put it], "I do not want to be associated with a client who is concealing facts from me; my career is more valuable than any single client's needs." . . .

The underlying notion of an adversary system helps the attorney to cope with uneasiness he may have about specific actions he takes. The adversary system as a whole is assumed to serve the greater social good, even if some of its details do not appear so. Thus, if a rule mandates or permits a specific behavior, such as an attorney's answering questions posed by the clients as hypotheticals, that behavior is legitimate because it is part of a system that works. It is a deductive logic: if the system works, then the specific rules are right.

F.   CLIENT PERJURY

> *Lawyer*: Do you know what the penalties are for perjury?
> *Client*: Yes, and they're a hell of a lot better than the penalties for murder.

1.   Introduction

No issue in legal ethics has attracted a larger cottage industry of commentary than client perjury. How often the problem arises in practice is highly speculative, but it is often a possibility, and it always poses fundamental questions of professional role. Lawyers' obligations in response to perjury establish the boundaries of their duties of confidentiality. These boundaries help determine what lawyers tell a client about their responsibilities in the first instance, what clients believe they can tell their lawyers, how cases are investigated, and how legal options are evaluated.

Bar ethical rules have taken varying positions on the problem of client perjury. Although both the Code and the Model Rules prohibit knowing use of false testimony (DR 7-102 A(4) and Model Rule 3.3), they differ over how lawyers should respond once they know that perjury has occurred. As Part B indicated (pages 225–229), DR 7-102(B) of the Code requires lawyers to reveal a fraud upon the court except when the information is "protected as a privileged communication." Many states have not, however, adopted the exception. And as noted below, opinions interpreting the Code have taken inconsistent positions about lawyers' responsibilities to disclose perjury.[55]

These inconsistencies came to the fore during debates over the Model Rules. Rule 3.3 resolved the issue by requiring lawyers to take "reasonable remedial measures" when they know a client has committed perjury and to disclose material facts when "necessary" to avoid assisting such misconduct. The comment to the rule makes clear that these requirements apply in criminal as well as civil cases, unless a jurisdiction's constitutional interpretations mandate a different course of action. Consider how well these rules respond to the dilemmas described below.

In several leading works, including the excerpt that follows, Monroe Freedman criticizes these ethical rules' response to lawyers' responsibilities as a "perjury trilemma." This trilemma arises from competing obligations of criminal defense attorneys. To provide effective advocacy, the attorney first has an obligation to learn all the significant facts. At the same time, the attorney also has obligations of confidentiality to the client as well as candor to the court. According to Freedman, attorneys confronting client perjury can fulfill at most two of these three obligations. If they have acquired all relevant information, they will know that the testimony is perjurious, and then must breach either their duties of confidentiality or candor. Those duties can be reconciled only if lawyers remain selectively ignorant, which compromises their ability to provide effective advocacy.

Freedman argues that in cases of conflict, it is the obligation of candor to the court that must give way. In his view, the duties of confidentiality and zealous advocacy are of paramount constitutional and moral significance in criminal cases, for they are essential to the fifth amendment privilege against self-incrimination and the sixth amendment right to representation.[56]

When initially presented, Freedman's argument provoked outrage and even calls for his disbarment. How would you assess its merits? How does it compare with the attorney's strategies that Kenneth Mann describes below? What should lawyers do when they believe a client has lied? How certain should they be before taking remedial measures and what measures are "reasonable"? Does your answer differ for criminal and civil cases?

PROBLEM 6G

1. You represent a defendant on charges of robbery. Your client denies committing the offense but has difficulty remembering where he was on the evening in question. Your investigation fails to confirm either his first recollection, that he was with an former girlfriend, or his second account, that he was at a party with an old high school classmate. The defendant then recalls that he was babysitting for his sister. She is willing to testify on his behalf. If you do not find the alibi credible but your client insists on testifying himself and having his sister take the stand, what do you do?

Assume that you allow the defendant to testify. When cross-examination reveals that he might have committed the robbery after leaving his sister, the defendant indicates that he spent the rest of the evening with his former girlfriend. How do you proceed? If you seek to withdraw, how should the trial court proceed?

2. A matter now pending before your state bar disciplinary committee involves a public defender appointed to represent an indigent defendant. During the course of representation, the client revealed that, contrary to his representations in pretrial proceedings, he in fact had $1,300 in a savings account. Access to those funds placed the defendant outside the statutory definition of indigency. The public defender neither revealed that fact to the court nor moved to withdraw from the case.

In justifying his conduct to the committee, the attorney explained that the client had indicated that these funds were necessary for his father's medical expenses. Apparently, the client had represented that his father had chronic liver disorders and inadequate medical insurance. On investigation, the committee learns that the father has no health problems.

As a member of the committee, what is your recommended disposition? Would it matter whether the attorney learned of the savings from a source other than his client?

3. You are defending your client in a drug sale case. Your investigation, together with facts your client has admitted, leaves no doubt in your mind that he sold the drugs. He will not be testifying. You know that the prosecution plans to put on the buyer as a witness, and that the buyer thinks your client was the person who sold her the drugs, but is not sure.

You are thinking about starting your closing argument as follows:

Your Honor, Mr. Simpson is not guilty of distribution of marijuana. Mr. Simpson was not the man who sold the drugs to Ms. Carter. The police arrested the wrong man.

Can you say that? Would you say that?[57]

MONROE FREEDMAN, PROFESSIONAL RESPONSIBILITY OF THE CRIMINAL DEFENSE LAWYER: THE THREE HARDEST QUESTIONS

64 Mich. L. Rev. 1469, 1470-1472, 1475-1478 (1966)*

The adversary system has further ramifications in a criminal case. The defendant is presumed to be innocent. The burden is on the prosecution to prove beyond a reasonable doubt that the defendant is guilty. The plea of not guilty does not necessarily mean "not guilty in fact," for the defendant may mean "not legally guilty." Even the accused who knows that he committed the crime is entitled to put the government to its proof. Indeed, the accused who knows that he is guilty has an absolute constitutional right to remain silent. The moralist might quite reasonably understand this to mean that, under these circumstances, the defendant and his lawyer are privileged to "lie" to the court in pleading not guilty. . . .

Some derive solace from the sophistry of calling the lie a "legal fiction," but this is hardly an adequate answer to the moralist. Moreover, this answer has no particular appeal for the practicing attorney, who knows that the plea of not guilty commits him to the most effective advocacy of which he is capable. Criminal defense lawyers do not win their cases by arguing reasonable doubt. Effective trial advocacy requires that the attorney's every word, action, and attitude be consistent with the conclusion that his client is innocent. As every trial lawyer knows, the jury is certain that the defense attorney knows whether his client is guilty. The jury is therefore alert to, and will be enormously affected by, any indication by the attorney that he believes the defendant to be guilty. Thus, the plea of not guilty commits the advocate to a trial, including a closing argument, in which he must argue that "not guilty" means "not guilty in fact." . . .

[One of the hardest questions for defense attorneys is whether it is proper to put a witness on the stand when the attorney knows that he will commit perjury.]

Perhaps the most common method for avoiding the ethical problem just posed is for the lawyer to withdraw from the case, at least if there is sufficient time before trial for the client to retain another attorney. The client will then go to the nearest law office, realizing that the obligation of confidentiality is not what it has been represented to be, and withhold incriminating information or the fact of his guilt from his new attorney. On ethical grounds, the practice of withdrawing from a case under such circumstances is

---

*Professor Freedman has updated this article, and has analyzed the issues in light of the Model Code, the Model Rules, and Nix v. Whiteside (pages 295-260 infra) in his book, Understanding Lawyers' Ethics (Matthew Bender 1990).

indefensible, since the identical perjured testimony will ultimately be presented. More important, perhaps, is the practical consideration that the new attorney will be ignorant of the perjury and therefore will be in no position to attempt to discourage the client from presenting it. Only the original attorney, who knows the truth, has that opportunity, but he loses it in the very act of evading the ethical problem.

The problem is all the more difficult when the client is indigent. He cannot retain other counsel, and in many jurisdictions, including the District of Columbia, it is impossible for appointed counsel to withdraw from a case except for extraordinary reasons. Thus, appointed counsel, unless he lies to the judge, can successfully withdraw only by revealing to the judge that the attorney has received knowledge of his client's guilt. Such a revelation in itself would seem to be a sufficiently serious violation of the obligation of confidentiality to merit severe condemnation. In fact, however, the situation is far worse, since it is entirely possible that the same judge who permits the attorney to withdraw will subsequently hear the case and sentence the defendant. When he does so, of course, he will have had personal knowledge of the defendant's guilt before the trial began. Moreover, this will be knowledge of which the newly appointed counsel for the defendant will probably be ignorant.

The difficulty is further aggravated when the client informs the lawyer for the first time during trial that he intends to take the stand and commit perjury. The perjury in question may not necessarily be a protestation of innocence by a guilty man. . . .

If a lawyer has discovered his client's intent to perjure himself, one possible solution to this problem is for the lawyer to approach the bench, explain his ethical difficulty to the judge, and ask to be relieved, thereby causing a mistrial. This request is certain to be denied, if only because it would empower the defendant to cause a series of mistrials in the same fashion. At this point, some feel that the lawyer has avoided the ethical problem and can put the defendant on the stand. However, one objection to this solution, apart from the violation of confidentiality, is that the lawyer's ethical problem has not been solved, but has only been transferred to the judge. Moreover, the client in such a case might well have grounds for appeal on the basis of deprivation of due process and denial of the right to counsel, since he will have been tried before, and sentenced by, a judge who has been informed of the client's guilt by his own attorney.

A solution even less satisfactory than informing the judge of the defendant's guilt would be to let the client take the stand without the attorney's participation and to omit reference to the client's testimony in closing argument. The latter solution, of course, would be as damaging as to fail entirely to argue the case to the jury, and failing to argue the case is "as improper as though the attorney had told the jury that his client had uttered a falsehood in making the statement."

Therefore, the obligation of confidentiality, in the context of our adversary system, apparently allows the attorney no alternative to putting a perjurious witness on the stand without explicit or implicit disclosure of the attorney's knowledge to either the judge or the jury. . . .

Of course, before the client testifies perjuriously, the lawyer has a duty to attempt to dissuade him on grounds of both law and morality. In addition, the client should be impressed with the fact that his untruthful alibi is tactically dangerous. There is always a strong possibility that the prosecutor will expose the perjury on cross-examination. However, for the reasons already given, the final decision must necessarily be the client's. The lawyer's best course thereafter would be to avoid any further professional relationship with a client whom he knew to have perjured himself.

KENNETH MANN, DEFENDING WHITE COLLAR CRIME: A PORTRAIT OF ATTORNEYS AT WORK

103-106, 120 (1985)

Two possible goals related to information control motivate the attorney in his meetings with clients. The first goal is to obtain adequate information about the situation being investigated. . . . The second goal, which can exist only in conjunction with the first, is to keep the client from communicating too much information to the attorney, information that would interfere with his building a strong defense.

There are some attorneys who say that they never facilitate a client's not giving them facts relevant to a criminal investigation. Others go further and say that they always actively probe the client for every piece of information that could relate to an investigation, even if some of it would negatively affect the attorney's defense plans. But many attorneys pursue the two goals simultaneously, encouraging disclosure of certain facts, discouraging disclosure of other facts. They want to extract all the information from the client that will facilitate good defense decisions: details about the potential charge, what the government might use to prove it, and what the "worst case" picture for the client looks like. But they also want clients to conceal from them information that is not essential to these ends and that either limits the attorney's ability to argue certain defenses or puts him in a difficult ethical position.

Some attorneys, for instance, discourage the disclosure of facts that would negate a defense of lack of knowledge. They would not want to find out that a client actually had knowledge of a fact that would prove criminal intent, knowledge of a report or the action of another person, if the government was also not going to find this out. The attorney can then more forcefully argue that the client did not know of the report or action. In other cases, attorneys prefer not to know that the client is continuing to commit the very crime that the government is investigating. In still other cases, clients commit new crimes aimed at obstructing the advancement of an investigation. Knowledge of these acts could raise [problems]. . . .

The "nonprobers," if you will, do not believe that they are in violation of ethical standards. Most of them do not tell a client, "I don't really want to know if you saw the document, let's talk around that." They have more refined ways of accomplishing that goal. The refinement is essential to their own sense of the proper role of the defense attorney in the adversary system and of the ethical and moral standards that govern the legal profession in the context of a criminal investigation. . . .

AVOIDANCE TECHNIQUES

If an attorney believes that it will be useful to a possible defense strategy not to be informed by the client of everything the client knows, he can simply not inquire. A general apprehension about pushing clients to disclose all information about an alleged crime was expressed by one attorney in the following manner.

> I can remember years ago when I represented a fellow in a massive case of political corruption. I was very young, and I asked him, "Would you please tell me everything that happened." And he said, "What, are you out of your mind?" Today my feeling is that I never ask anybody to tell me anything except what they want to tell me. I am not interested in fairy tales, and I am certainly interested in knowing at least what they [the clients] have told the investigators. But I think it is absolutely ridiculous for a lawyer to say I can't help you unless I know everything. If a fellow wants to conceal something, that is because if you probe unnecessarily, he is going to tell you what you don't want to hear and it is going to be devastating. Most clients, I think, have enough brains not to tell everything. It is understandable. And if they engaged in some kind of corruption, they are not going to tell you they are going to engage in another transaction tomorrow. . . .

It would be completely inaccurate to say that the attorneys studied here believe that their work is ethically or morally improper, or that they believe that they are serving incorrect social ends by defending their clients in criminal cases. . . . Deeply imbedded in these attorneys is the idea of an adversary as a person who settles doubt in favor of his client, and therefore he looks for doubt and uses what may appear to be doubtful techniques and doubtful strategies, because it is part of his professional mandate.

---

2. Competing Values and Ethical Mandates

Lawyers' responsibilities concerning client perjury continue to provoke heated debate. A widely read 1992 ethics opinion by the

National Association of Criminal Defense Lawyers came to a conclusion similar to Monroe. Freedman's on similar reasoning.[58] Its assumption, like that underlying the attorney-client privilege in general, is that without protection against disclosure, defendants will decline to be candid with their counsel.

By contrast, other commentators, including philosopher Alan Donegan, have dismissed this assumption as implausible:

> It need not be denied that sometimes even the most adroit lawyer may be unable to persuade a timid and ignorant innocent [person] to give information without promising strict confidentiality with respect to past crimes; but is there the slightest reason to suppose that this will be generally the case? It seems more probable that a lawyer of ordinary competence would be able to discern the nature of the fears that might prompt a client to lie or to conceal the truth, and that it would be enough to explain what the law in fact is. . . . [T]here is no reason to believe that, with reasonably competent lawyers, innocent clients [generally] will be deterred from confiding in them. . . . As for clients who are in fact guilty, while they have a legal right not to incriminate themselves, they have no moral right to enlist informed professional help in concealing their guilt.[59]

Some commentators have suggested ways of resolving the perjury trilemma that do not involve a lawyer's complicity. In an early review of Freedman's book, then professor, now federal judge, John Noonan concluded:

> Dean Freedman rightly points out that the attorney's difficulty is particularly acute when the client is indigent, since he cannot retain other counsel. Moreover, in many jurisdictions appointed counsel or the public defender may only withdraw from a case for extraordinary reasons, which would necessarily require revealing the client's perjurious intent to the very judge before whom he will be tried and sentenced. But Dean Freedman ignores an alternative to the problem: allow the attorney to withdraw without breaching the confidence and if prejudicial inferences are likely to be drawn, assign both a new judge and a new attorney. . . .
>
> Yet the problem remains, says Freedman, since the client, "realizing that the obligation of confidentiality is not what it has been represented to be," will withhold incriminating information or the fact of guilt from the new attorney and perjured testimony will be presented by an unwitting attorney. That may be true, but there is a crucial difference this time around: neither the first nor the second attorney has knowingly acquiesced in perjury, a result of no small importance in preserving the integrity of a truth-seeking system.[60]

Moreover, as other commentators have noted, if the first lawyer declines to assist perjury and the client then finds a second lawyer to do so, the result for the fact-finding process is no worse than the one Freedman's proposed solution reaches.

Some courts and commentators have proposed a different compromise: lawyers should allow a defendant to testify falsely in narrative form, but provide no assistance through direct questioning and make no reference to the false claims in closing argument. Proponents of this approach claim that it offers the best accommodation of the two competing principles; it avoids implicating lawyers in perjury but gives clients whose life and liberty are at risk an opportunity to plead their cases.[61] By contrast, the Comment to Model Rule 3.3 concludes that this strategy "compromises both contending principles: it exempts the lawyer from the duty to disclose false evidence but subjects the client to an implicit disclosure of information imparted to counsel." According to the Comment:

> If withdrawal will not remedy the situation or is impossible, the advocate should make disclosure to the court. It is for the court then to determine what should be done, making a statement about the matter to the trier of fact, ordering a mistrial or perhaps nothing. . . . If there is an issue whether the client has committed perjury, the lawyer cannot represent the client in resolution of the issue and a mistrial may be unavoidable. . . .

The Comment also recognized that some jurisdictions had resolved the issue differently under constitutional principles of due process and effective assistance of counsel. As the Comment acknowledged, these decisions took precedence over bar ethical rules. However, after the ABA's adoption of the Model Rules, the Supreme Court largely removed the constitutional basis for objections to disclosure of client perjury. In Nix v. Whiteside, 475 U.S. 157 (1986), the Court held that a lawyer did not provide ineffective assistance of counsel by discouraging his client from giving what the lawyer believed would be false testimony.

NIX v. WHITESIDE, 475 U.S. 157 (1986).   This case involved a defendant convicted of the second-degree murder of Calvin Love. The killing took place when Whiteside and two companions visited Love's apartment and an argument began over the ownership of a certain amount of marijuana. At one point Love directed his girlfriend to get his "piece." 475 U.S. at 160. According to Whiteside's testimony, Love then started to reach under his pillow and moved toward Whiteside. Whiteside stabbed Love in the chest, inflicting a fatal wound.

After Whiteside was charged with murder, he gave a statement to Gary Robinson, his court-appointed attorney. In that statement, Whiteside indicated that he had stabbed Love as the latter "was pulling a pistol from underneath the pillow on the bed." Id. Upon questioning by Robinson, however, Whiteside indicated that he had not actually seen a gun, but that he was convinced that Love had a gun. A police search uncovered no weapon, and none of Whiteside's companions reported seeing a gun. Robinson advised Whiteside that the existence of a gun was not necessary to establish the claim of self-defense; it was enough if the defendant held a reasonable belief that the victim had a gun nearby.

About a week before trial, Whiteside for the first time told Robinson that he had seen something "metallic" in Love's hand. On closer questioning, Whiteside explained, "If I don't say I saw a gun, I'm dead." 475 U.S. at 161. According to Robinson's testimony, he then told Whiteside that as "officers of the court," Robinson and his co-counsel could not allow a client to testify falsely and that if he did so, they would have to advise the judge and would seek to withdraw as counsel. Robinson also indicated that he might have to impeach any false testimony. Id.

At trial, Whiteside took the stand and stated that he "knew" that Love had a gun, but admitted on cross-examination that he had not actually seen one. Robinson presented evidence that Love had carried a gun on other occasions, that the police search finding no weapon might have been careless, and that the victim's family might have removed the evidence.

The jury returned a verdict of second-degree murder, and the Iowa Supreme Court affirmed. Whiteside then petitioned for a writ of habeas corpus claiming that his lawyer's threat to disclose confidences had denied him effective assistance of counsel.

The United States Supreme Court unanimously disagreed. Chief Justice Burger's majority opinion, in which Justices White, Powell, and Rehnquist joined, concluded that nothing Robinson did deprived Whiteside of effective assistance; "at most, [it] deprived Whiteside of his contemplated perjury." 475 U.S. at 172. In the majority's view, the "responsibility of an ethical lawyer . . . is essentially the same whether the client announces an intention to bribe or threaten witnesses or jurors, or to commit or procure perjury." 475 U.S. at 174. Justice Blackmun's concurrence, in which Justices Brennan, Marshall, and Stevens joined, emphasized that the sole issue before the Court was whether Whiteside's sixth amendment rights had been violated. In their view, they had not. The only effect that Robinson's threat had on the trial was that Whiteside did not testify falsely. And, "[t]o the extent that Whiteside's claim rests on the assertion that he would have been acquitted had he been able to testify falsely, he claims a right that the law simply does not recognize." 475 U.S. at 186. Moreover, if Whiteside had lied on the stand, he would have faced a potential perjury prosecution and could have been subject to impeachment by other witnesses. Accordingly, he could not claim prejudice from his counsel's decision.

Except among criminal defense lawyers, the *Whiteside* decision meets with broad agreement within the bar.[62] However, considerable dispute centers on two questions that the Supreme Court did not resolve. First, what standard of knowledge is required before the lawyer concludes that a defendant's testimony is (or would be) false? Second, what should the lawyer and the court do if the defendant insists on testifying? *Whiteside* held that a lawyer would not violate constitutional standards by disclosing perjury. The Court did not resolve whether a lawyer must make such disclosure.

Knowledge. When do lawyers "know" that their clients will commit perjury within the meaning of bar ethical rules? Some criminal defense lawyers insist that they virtually never have such knowledge. Defendants who plan to lie generally have no reason to announce it to their lawyers, particularly if they are indigent and don't entirely trust their court-appointed attorneys. If lawyers are convinced that a client is lying, they often predict that jurors and judges will share that assessment, and try to persuade their client not to testify. Attorneys facing severe constraints of time and resources also have little incentive to pursue investigations that would establish beyond a reasonable doubt that a client's final story is false. But it is by no means self-evident that absolute certainty should be the standard since this is not our commonsense understanding of what knowledge usually requires.

Courts and commentators have divided on the level of certainty that is appropriate in this context. Under the Model Rules' somewhat circular standard, "knowingly" means "actual knowledge of the facts in question . . . which may be inferred from circumstances." Some jurisdictions, following Commentary to a former Criminal Defense Standard, have interpreted "knowledge" to require a defendant's admission of inculpatory facts to his lawyer that are corroborated by the lawyer's own investigations.[63] Other courts have proceeded with less rigorous requirements, such as a lawyer's good faith belief.[64] Although the trend at the appellate level is to demand a clear expression of perjurious intent, trial judges frequently have failed to make any factual inquiry into the basis of lawyers' conclusions or have implied that a client's inconsistent representations would be sufficient to suggest perjury.[65] How would you define knowledge? Should courts and counsel require proof beyond a reasonable doubt, clear and convincing evidence, a firm factual basis, a good faith belief, or some other degree of knowledge?

Procedural Requirements. A related question involves the procedure that courts should use if a client insists on giving testimony that the lawyer expects will be false, or if a client offers such testimony while on the witness stand. In most settings, the prescribed response to client misconduct is withdrawal. However, courts and commentators have generally found this unsatisfactory in criminal cases, since it would simply transfer the problem to the next attorney and would give a defendant the opportunity to trigger a mistrial by insisting on the right to testify. Particularly in jury trials, courts are reluctant to permit withdrawal unless the attorney-client relationship has deteriorated to such a point that effective representation is impossible.

If a client insists on testifying over counsel's objections, should the trial court conduct an inquiry or make findings on whether the proposed testimony would constitute perjury?[66] If the issues cannot be clearly resolved, should defendants have the option of testifying in narrative form? If a court permits the defendant's testimony and defense counsel fails to rely on it in closing, may the prosecutor comment on this fact and invite the jury to draw the appropriate inferences? See State v. Long, 714 P.2d 465 (Ariz. 1986) (finding a due process violation on such facts).

Would a better accommodation of competing values result from following the European approach of allowing a defendant to testify without being under oath?[67] Consider the alternative that New York judge and former criminal defense attorney Harold Rothwax proposes. Defendants who wish to obtain discovery of the prosecution's case would have to provide a written version of their defense, to be sealed until trial. If the defendants choose to testify, their original version of events would be available to determine whether they changed their story and would be admissible for impeachment purposes. Rothwax argues that such a system would not "violate a defendant's rights. . . . It merely prevents the lie." Do you agree?[68]

G.   DILEMMAS IN COUNSELING

Geoffrey Hazard notes that "[m]any courses of action taken by a client are 'wrong' at least in the exacting sense that they are not what would be done by a supremely moral person unconcerned with costs. If this were the standard by which a lawyer should judge whether to continue his association with a client, there would be few of either clients or lawyers."[69] The following materials explore how lawyers can and should respond when they believe a client's decision is morally "wrong" in at least some sense.

This issue requires analysis along three dimensions. First, how does any decision-maker determine the morality of a business judgment when incommensurable values such as cost and safety are involved? Second, who should make such decisions: how much discretion should rest with corporate officers, directors, government regulators, consumers, or other affected parties? Third, what actions should lawyers take when they disagree either with a substantive decision or with the allocation of decision-making authority?

1. Lawyers' Professional and Social Responsibilities: Consumer Safety and Corporate Counseling

a. Introduction

PROBLEM 6H

1. Assume that members of Ford Motor Company's legal staff have access to the information presented in the excerpt that follows. During the early 1970s, one of the company's design experts approaches in-house counsel and expresses a concern that Ford, in its rush to market a model competitive with small foreign cars, has been unwilling to make certain safety improvements in the fuel tank placement of Pinto automobiles. Based on counsel's preliminary investigation, management undertakes a full review of safety test results and alternative design plans for the Pinto fuel system. After extensive consultation with the engineering and legal staff, Ford's chief executive officer determines that the system, although susceptible to explosion if punctured from the rear, nonetheless meets federal safety standards and that the expenses of improvement would exceed the costs of liability in foreseeable tort litigation. Accordingly, the officer determines to market the model as is and there is no reason to believe that the board of directors would arrive at a different conclusion.

Assume that you are a member of the in-house legal staff. What would you do? If you disagree with the chief executive officer's decision, but are unable to alter his views, what would be your possible courses of action? What factors would be relevant to your judgment?

2. You are head of the litigation department in a firm that General Motors has just hired to defend product liability claims involving its pickup trucks. The claims involve fuel tank explosions resulting from design defects similar to those in Ford Pintos. Two practices of GM's in-house counsel cause you concern. One involves a dispute with a company safety engineer who has testified for GM in several trials. The engineer recently learned facts about safety tests casting doubt on his prior views, and he has resigned after 28 years of service. GM is refusing to honor his pension rights unless he signs a confidential agreement barring any public statements regarding GM product safety.

Your second concern involves a practice that the engineer is prepared to disclose if called as a witness by plaintiffs: namely that GM places sensitive safety reports in individual engineers' files rather than in general product files. Because of this practice, GM lawyers do not find such reports when responding to plaintiffs' search requests for safety-related documents involving certain products.[70]

How should you proceed?

DAVID LUBAN, LAWYERS AND JUSTICE: AN ETHICAL STUDY

206-213 (1988)

The shockers came on three successive days, October 13, 14 and 15, 1979, in three successive front-page Chicago Tribune headlines:

October 13   Ford ignored Pinto fire peril, secret memos show
October 14   How Ford put a price tag on autos' safety
October 15   U.S. official sees cover-up in Ford safety test policy

Of course, everyone knew about the celebrated exploding Pinto long before that time. In February 1978, a California jury had awarded $125 million, later reduced to $6.6 million by a judge, to a teenager who had suffered horrendous burns in a Pinto accident. By the summer of 1978, the macabre gagline "Shut up or I'll back my Pinto into you" was circulating. And the Tribune's research was initiated because a grand jury in Indiana had indicted Ford for reckless homicide in the burning deaths of three teenage women whose 1973 Pinto had exploded after being struck from behind by a van on 10 August 1978.

The secret internal Ford memos revealed in the first two Tribune articles made it all worse. They seemed to show a level of foreknowledge and coldblooded calculatedness on Ford's part that appalled many readers.

The first day's memos showed that Ford engineers knew that Pinto gastanks would be pierced by bolts when struck from behind at speeds as low as 21 m.p.h. This would allow gasoline to leak out, so that any spark, caused, for example, by metal scraping over payment, would explode the fuel supply. Other memos discussed several modifications in the Pinto design that would make it safer. These were rejected on the grounds that they cost too much money (various figures were cited, ranging from $5.08 to $11 per car), and because some would decrease trunk space.

According to the first Tribune article, a Ford memo of 10 November 1970 commented that government-proposed fuel tank safety standards "are too strict and come too soon. Ford executives list lesser standards that the Department of Transportation 'can be expected to buy' as alternatives." A "confidential" memo dated 22 April 1971 recommended that one of the safety devices not be installed until 1976, to save Ford $20.9 million. Another "confidential" memo of October 26, 1971 stated that no additional "fuel system integrity" changes would be made until "required by law." As a result of lobbying by the auto industry, the more stringent legal requirements did not go into effect until 1977; the 1977 Pinto was designed to meet the new requirements. Ford, faced with a government investigation, voluntarily recalled 1.5 million 1971-76 Pintos and Bobcats; as it happened, however, the recall notice was not sent out until twelve days after the Indiana accident.

These memos, in short, indicated that Ford engineers and executives were aware of Pinto's design problem, and that instead of repairing it, they acted deliberately to avoid regulatory and financial consequences to the company. . . . The major document was prepared by Ford as an argument to the federal government against a higher safety standard. According to a Ford spokesman, "who uttered a profanity when a Tribune reporter mentioned the study to him," the government itself had established the dollar value assigned to death and injury by the study. The government, however, claimed that these numbers had been prepared for an entirely different purpose, a federal study of the loss to the national economy brought about by traffic accident injuries.

TABLE 2
Benefits and Costs Relating to
Fuel Leakage Associated with the
Static Rollover Test Portion of FMVSS 208

Cost/benefit analysis

Benefits: *Savings* — 180 burn deaths, 180 serious burn injuries, 2100 burned vehicles.
wrongful death
Unit Cost — $200,000 per death, $67,000 per injury, $700 per vehicle. (*govt #*)
Total Benefit — 180 × ($200,000) + 180 × ($67,000) + 2100 × ($700) = $49.5 million.

Costs: *Sales* — 11 million cars, 1.5 million light trucks.
Unit Cost — $11 per car, $11 per truck.
Total Cost — 11,000,000 × ($11) + 1,500,000 × ($11) = $137 million.

Cheaper to ignore federal safety regulations

Source: Strobel, Lee, "How Ford put a price tag on autos' safety," *Chicago Tribune* 14 October 1979, p.18. [Table taken from Ford's study]

The final day's stories focused on statements by federal officials that Ford's way of handling the crash-test data on Pinto might amount to a cover-up. . . . According to the Tribune, Ford engineers had known since 1968 that fuel tanks in the position of the Pinto's were liable to rupture "at very low speed," and discussions of how to deal with the problem in Pintos had been going on since at least 1970. Yet until the lawsuits began, the public had no inkling of the matter. And the consequences were severe: the company itself could estimate how many people would be immolated in their Pintos. During 1976 and 1977 alone "thirteen Pintos, more than double the number that might be expected in proportion to their numbers, were involved in fiery rear-end crashes resulting in deaths" while the VW Rabbit and Toyota Corolla suffered none. Some might say that it is a mistake to dwell on the particulars: it makes our reactions too emotional. On the contrary, I think that in problems such as this we cannot afford to forget the three teenagers who perished in a one-thousand-degree fire. And, if the Tribune stories are accurate, Ford knew precisely what it was doing. . . .

WHAT'S WRONG WITH TRADING LIVES FOR CASH?

Before turning to our principal question, however, the question of what Ford's attorneys should have done, we must address a prior one: assuming that the facts of the case are as the newspapers stated them, did Ford do anything immoral?

This question sounds absurd. If allowing innocent people to be immolated for no other reason than cold, cold cash isn't immoral, what is? Only one thing, we might answer: doing a study on it first and then covering up the whole horrible process.

Despite this understandable reaction, there is another way to look at the matter. What was it that Ford did? It traded off cost for safety. But that is what car manufacturers must always do. Safety costs money, and people may not be willing to pay the price. Hence, the cheaper, in both senses, car. (Iacocca introduced the Pinto to break into the under-two-thousand-pounds-and-two-thousand-dollars market.) Government regulations set minimum safety standards, but after these are met, the marketplace sets the level of safety. . . . The Pinto's gastank was punctured at twenty-one m.p.h. collisions. For $6.65 extra, it would have withstood thirty m.p.h. But it still would have gone at forty. For more money, it would have stood up to fifty-five (Pinto would then have resembled an armored half-truck). But no car is totally safe, and thus they will all generate their grotesque cost-benefit analyses. Indeed, a standard test of negligent design in tort law is simply that the risk of the design outweighs the benefits; even in strict liability, where the only issue is whether the product is defective and not whether the manufacturer was negligent, one well-known definition of "defective design" is just "design that is not optimally risk-beneficial." Thus, not only does the law contemplate the trade-off of safety against price, compliance with it will require cost-benefit studies such as Ford's.

This brings us to the second part of the response. To a sophisticated reader, Ford's cost-benefit study is nothing to get excited about. First of all, that number of deaths is simply an actuarial statistic and does not by any means show a callous attitude toward human life, any more than does a similar study by your insurance company or by the manufacturer of the safest car money can buy. Every car has a small but calculable probability of burning you to death. Multiply a tiny probability by millions of cars and you will get a body count like Ford's. One hundred and eighty deaths out of 12.5 million vehicles translates into the statistic that the gastank Ford was using increased your chance of death by one in seventy thousand over the safer alternative. That doesn't sound as bad as actually writing down the number of deaths; nevertheless, mathematically the numbers are equivalent. (Many people would bet their lives against eleven dollars at seventy thousand to one odds: you take a worse bet by far every time you ride without a seatbelt.)

Nor is that two hundred thousand dollars per death figure beyond the pale of humanity. Personal injury lawyers use formulas for computing the value of a wrongful death: it's just one of the things that must be done to compensate, as far as possible, for irreversible losses. The fact that we normally do not put a price tag on human life does not mean that its economic meaning is incalculable, and indeed, we "calculate" it every time we choose not to invest in a piece of safety equipment.

So, at any rate, goes the argument. It says that Ford was not doing anything improper or out of the ordinary: it just got caught with a lot of embarrassing memos that made for good copy but really signified nothing.

We should reject this argument for several reasons. The most important and obvious one is that the Pinto did not represent a safety-versus-price trade-off. It represented a blunder. Ford could have built Pintos with safer over-the-axle rather than puncturable behind-the-axle gastank mountings, but it did not, because it had tooled up too quickly. Its cost-benefit analyses did not, as a consequence, address the question of safety-versus-price; rather, they addressed the question of **recall-versus-price**, given the prior mistake.

On either of two standard legal tests of defective design, the Pinto's design was defective. The first, as we have seen, is that a safer design was available for the price. And indeed, Ford's cost-benefit study indicates that the problem could have been fixed for eleven dollars per vehicle, a negligible price difference of about .1 percent. The second test (developed by California courts) is that the product "fails to perform as safely as an ordinary consumer would expect when used in an intended or reasonably foreseeable manner." No ordinary consumer, I suppose, expects a car to explode in a twenty-one m.p.h. fender-bender.

Second, even on economic grounds, Ford's decision was indefensible. The theory that the market should set safety levels presupposes informed consumers who decide how much safety they are willing to pay for. For eleven dollars, at most, Pinto's margin of safety could have been upped from twenty m.p.h. to thirty m.p.h. One supposes that most informed consumers would be willing to pay such a small amount for such a large increase in safety. Ford, however, did not give them the option. When consumers are kept ignorant, the market model makes little sense.

Finally, if the Tribune was right, Ford was within federal guidelines because it had lobbied for more relaxed guidelines. In general, federal safety standards in most arenas do not necessarily mean "safety" in a common sense understanding of the term: they are all the result of political compromises among various powerful special interests; this case is no exception. It is disingenuous to argue, as did Ford executives, that "in every model year the Pinto has been tested and met or surpassed the federal fuel-system integrity standard applicable to it."

The Pinto case evokes two common reactions among lawyers and law students. One is the kind of revulsion about openly "trading lives for cash" that David Luban explores and that jurors obviously expressed in their large verdicts against Ford. A converse reaction is a kind of worldly regret that jurors were so "sentimental" that they punished Ford for doing explicitly what countless public and private sector decision-makers have done implicitly.[71]

By contrast, many commentators propose an alternative, more contextual, framework. This approach begins from the premise that society cannot avoid trade-offs that place some value on human life. Federal executive orders require administrative agencies to weigh costs against benefits before approving regulations, and other governmental bodies operate under similar mandates. For example, every time highway administrators decide not to build an overpass for a railroad crossing, they can estimate the number of deaths that will result. When businesses decide not to incorporate certain safety features in products or workplaces, they can often predict some price in human lives.

Yet to acknowledge that trade-offs are inevitable is not to imply that Ford's approach was adequate. There are, as the following article indicates, a wide range of methods for valuing life. How would you assess Ford's strategy in light of these alternatives? How would you recommend that business and governmental decision-makers deal with the wide variation in standards that currently exists?

MARIANE LAVELLE, PLACING A PRICE ON HUMAN LIFE: A LEGAL PUZZLE
National Law Journal, Oct. 10, 1988, at 1

The problem . . . is that Uncle Sam has decided, on different days and in different ways, that the dollar value of a life is as little as $70,000, as much as $132 million, anywhere in between and impossible to measure.

Separate numbers and philosophies have been adopted by many of the 90-some agencies, charged with assuring Americans have clean air and safe food and products, according to the Administrative Conference report. . . . To Ralph A. Luken, a chief economist with the Environmental Protection Agency, using dollars to represent lives saved by regulation is a straightforward process that helps the agency compare oranges with oranges. "We try to the extent possible to monetize things, because otherwise it's relatively difficult to make comparisons." He says, "How do you compare crop loss to sick days? You need to integrate information."

At the opposite end of the spectrum, Barry Felrice, an administrator at the National Highway Traffic Safety Authority, says his agency eschews quantification of life as a matter of principle. Although the agency estimates how many lives could be saved by air bags, child restraints or the like, NHTSA refuses to translate that benefit into dollars. "Our statute tells us explicitly that safety shall be given an overriding concern." . . .

That doesn't mean regulation at all costs; the proposals are analyzed for their "practicability," says Mr. Felrice. "We interpret that to mean we don't put the car companies out of business." . . .

Different philosophies have bred differing values of life, according to the Gillette-Hopkins report, prepared for the Administrative Conference of the United States, a government think tank that looks for ways to improve efficiency in the federal bureaucracy.

At the extremes, the Consumer Product Safety Commission judged a life to be worth $70,000 in a 1980 proposal for regulation of space heaters, while the Food and Drug Administration's 1979 ban of the pesticide DES in cattle feed judged each life saved to be worth $132 million.

The Nuclear Regulatory Commission, meanwhile, has a unique system that takes into account the number of people affected multiplied by possible amounts of radiation released. By one calculation, the professors found the NRC's so called person-rem standard translates to $7.4 million per life saved.

Juries, on average, award $950,000 as the value of a man in his 30s, according to Jury Verdict Research Co. of Solon, Ohio. The approach used in most courtrooms can be summed up in the phrase, "You are what you earn," a theory articulated as long ago as 1776, by Adam Smith in "Wealth of Nations." . . .

But what is standard operating procedure in the courtroom is considered passe in most of the regulatory world. If human value is equivalent only to potential earnings, then women, children, minorities and the elderly lose their worth. As Jury Verdict Research Co. documents, the average jury settlement for the death of a woman over 65 years old is $85,000.

Most agencies, therefore, have moved to a life valuation method called "willingness-to-pay," which has gained wide acceptance among economists.

How much is a person willing to pay to avoid death? Economists derive this seemingly unknowable number by looking at workers in high-risk jobs such as mining and construction. How much of a pay premium do employers have to offer to lure employees into these dangerous occupations? Using those premium figures and a complex formula, economists have determined value-of-life figures that, for the most part, put jury verdicts to shame.

The value of life appears to be about $1.95 million, give or take $500,000, according to about 25 studies judged credible by economist

Ted R. Miller of the liberal Washington think tank, the Urban Institute. . . . Despite high praise, willingness-to-pay has its drawbacks. For example, it assumes workers fully know and understand the risks involved in jobs, and freely accept the wages fairly offered.

That particular set of assumptions proves the economists are "not in commuting distance with this galaxy," says lawyer David Vladeck of Ralph Nader's Public Citizen Litigation Group. Because the real world rarely achieves the free-market ideal, economists have not quite perfected the willingness-to-pay process.

Although the figures do hover around $2 million, Mr. Miller has seen studies come up with life values ranging from $500,000 to more than $10 million. At the EPA, which has studied the process more than any other federal agency, willingness-to-pay has produced values ranging from $400,000 to $7 million.

With that much play in the figures, politics enters the picture. So many numbers are being juggled that there's a danger of regulators setting figures that purposefully make their proposals look good or bad, [an] Administrative Conference report warns.

The report urges OMB to take a stronger role, updating its own value-of-life methods and acting as a clearinghouse for information on how this tough decision should be made. . . .

Not everyone agrees with this suggestion. Calling OMB "the Darth Vader of the regulatory process," Public Citizen attorney Mr. Vladeck shudders at the prospect of more control in the executive agency's hands. But Mr. Luken, the EPA economist, says, "OMB hasn't enforced [cost-benefit analysis] even to the minimal extent it should have." He says scrutiny from Public Citizen, Congress and others has restrained OMB from checking agency math.

That's all to the good, in Mr. Vladeck's view. "I don't think there's a place for [value-of-life calculations] yet, if ever," he says. "There are too many serious flaws in the methodology to allow it to be a useful tool."

Mr. Gillette admits, "Everyone is a little uneasy about charging government with the responsibility of deciding how much a life's worth." But he argues that more serious thought about the worth of human life in regulation could lead to greater care for safety, not less. The highly publicized case of Jessica McClure, the baby saved after two days trapped in an open well in 1987, serves as an example of how money might have been better spent on prevention.

"We were willing to spend all sorts of money to save her," says Mr. Gillette, "even though no one thought for a minute about whether it was worth spending any money at all to plug up the wells."

Consider the actions in Problems 6H and 6I along the three dimensions noted earlier: how should decision-makers trade off incommensurable values; who should make such decisions; and what should lawyers do if they disagree?

b.   Decision-Making Frameworks

(1)   Utilitarian Approaches

Price/safety trade-offs lend themselves most readily to a utilitarian analysis. An explicit calculation of the costs and benefits of particular improvements appears to be the most straightforward and ethically justifiable way of proceeding. However, for reasons explored more fully in Chapter II (Traditions of Moral Reasoning), utilitarian frameworks have certain limitations in contexts like those of Problem 6H. In an essay on the relevance of moral theory to bureaucratic structure, Alasdair MacIntyre explores several of these limitations.

First, decision-makers must find a way to limit the alternative courses of action under consideration. That requires some "principle of restriction" that cannot itself be utilitarian. For, as MacIntyre notes, if this principle

> were to be justified by the test of beneficial and harmful consequences as against alternative proposed principles of restriction, we should have to find some [further] principle of restriction in order to avoid paralysis by the construction of an indefinitely long list of principles of restriction. And so on.[72]

The decision about which alternatives to consider can often determine the outcomes reached. So, for example, in the Ford Pinto case, it matters which safety improvement the decision-maker subjects to cost-benefit calculation. Should it be the $11 it would cost per car to fix the problem, or the much more modest cost involved in reducing the hazard through partial adjustments or in averting the risk through better design in the first instance?[73] Although private sector decision-makers often claim that it is profitability that restricts their range of alternatives, this response ignores the role that they themselves play in determining what is profitable. Consumer markets are "*made*, not just given," and the product characteristics that car manufacturers advertise affect the characteristics that consumers want.[74]

A second related problem with utilitarian analysis is how to rank incommensurable values, and how to decide whose ranking controls in contexts of disagreement. As then EPA administrator Carol Browner puts it, "How should I value the loss of I.Q. points by children exposed to lead?"[75] This process of making incommensurable values commensurable also requires some nonutilitarian principle of evaluating costs and benefits. Consider MacIntyre's questions:

How are we to weigh the benefits of slightly cheaper power against the loss forever of just one beautiful landscape? How are we to weigh the benefits of increased employment and lessened poverty in Detroit against a marginal increase in deaths from automobile accidents? . . . [I]t is clear not only that there are alternative methods of rank-ordering, but also that different types of people will adopt and argue for different methods. The old do not weigh harms and benefits in the same way as the young; the poor have a different perspective from the rich; the healthy and the sick often weigh pain and suffering differently. "Everybody is to count for one and nobody for more than one," declared Bentham; but others, Sir Karl Popper, for one, have suggested that the relief of pain or suffering always should take precedence over the promotion of pleasure or happiness.[76]

This point has obvious relevance for the Ford Pinto case. As Mariane Lavelle's article notes, decision-makers have adopted widely varying estimates of the value of human life, and many would challenge the figure Ford used as unrealistically low. For example, in reaching the $67,000 cost, analysts made a number of intermediate estimates, such as $10,000 for pain and suffering per victim. Is this a figure that seems plausible, given the range of jury verdicts that the cases actually brought in? Moreover, the $67,000 total does not include certain social costs, such as taxpayer subsidies for the legal expenses involved in resolving tort claims. In commenting on this valuation problem, MacIntyre points out:

> Writers on cost-benefit analysis techniques have devised four alternative methods for computing the cost of a person's life. One is that of discounting to the present the person's expected future earnings; a second is that of computing the losses to others from the person's death so as to calculate their present discounted value; a third is that of examining the value placed on an individual life by presently established social policies and practices, e.g., the benefits in increased motor traffic which society at the present moment is prepared to exchange for a higher fatal accident rate; and a fourth is to ask what value a person placed on his or her own life, by looking at the risks which that person is or was prepared to take and the insurance premiums which he or she was prepared to pay. Clearly, those four criteria will yield very different answers on occasion. . . . [In effect, one approach] considers the individual's own earnings, one the losses to others, one certain socially established norms, and one the individual's own risk-taking. . . . To adopt one of these methods rather than another is precisely to decide who is to decide what counts as a cost and what counts as a benefit.[77]

A similar difficulty involves how to determine what in fact is a consequence of some given action. Utilitarian frameworks generally suggest that all "predictable" effects should be measured, but this raises questions about what are reasonable standards of prediction. For example, in the Pinto case, did Ford consider all foreseeable costs? What about adverse publicity? Related problems also arise in selecting a time frame for measuring consequences; the longer our frame, the greater our difficulties in prediction. As MacIntyre notes:

Our assessment of long-term risks and of long-term probabilities is generally more liable to error than our assessment of short-term risks and probabilities. Moreover, it is not clear how we ought to weigh short-term harms and benefits against long-term contingencies; are our responsibilities the same to future generations as they are to the present one or to our own children? How far ought the present to be sacrificed to the future? Here again we have a range of questions to which non-utilitarian answers have to be given or at least presupposed before any utilitarian test can be applied.[78]

So, for example, if costly safety features make certain cars noncompetitive in their particular market, various adverse results could follow, such as layoffs and plant closings. Such events would, in turn, be likely to increase rates of suicide, alcoholism, and domestic violence among unemployed workers. Thus, the longer the time frame and broader the standard for assessing potential consequences, the more speculative the calculation becomes.

One final difficulty with utilitarianism is its insensitivity to distributional issues. As Chapter II notes, aggregate measures of costs and benefits ignore the relative hardship that certain decisions entail. Thus, Ford's calculation fails to note that those victims least likely to gain adequate compensation for tort claims are concentrated among low-income, nonwhite groups, in part because those groups are least able to shop for attorneys, to hold out for generous settlements, or to command jury sympathy. Of course, those groups are also the least able to afford price increases from heightened safety measures.

Such different distributional results occur in a wide range of regulatory contexts. To take an obvious illustration, trade-offs between environmental quality and economic development have varying implications depending on the individual's geographic location, income, and employment status. Preventing certain farming or logging practices will often be socially justifiable from a long-term cost-benefit standpoint, but the short-run economic consequences for specific employees can be devastating. To make distributional issues relevant, some strategy other than simply measuring aggregate effects is necessary.

(2)   Rights-Based Frameworks

Critics of utilitarianism often suggest that a rights-based approach offers a useful alternative framework in contexts involving competing values. Under this framework, described more fully in Chapter II, the justification for a particular decision would depend on whether it could satisfy a principle that the decision-maker was prepared to see become a universal law. Such a principle might, for example, establish a right not to be subject to unreasonable risks. Or, under the approach of the highway traffic administrators described by Lavelle, the standard might be the maximum level of safety that is economically practical.

Formulating a right in these terms would, of course, require consideration of most of the same factors that would be relevant under utilitarian analysis. To decide what is reasonable or practical, decision-makers would need to limit the range of alternatives under review, assess their costs, and predict their consequences. These evaluations would involve the same indeterminacies noted earlier. However, a rights-based analysis could also yield somewhat different questions and outcomes than a pure utilitarian approach because it can presuppose certain priorities, such as safety, or establish certain minimum standards and external benchmarks.

Thus, in the Pinto case, a rights-based approach would not focus directly on Ford's costs and benefits of remedying the design defect but rather on the degree of risk that an informed buyer should reasonably expect in light of prevailing industry standards. This is in effect the California torts standard that Luban describes. Industry standards would, of course, be affected by the costs and benefits of safety features. However, the final outcome would not be skewed by Ford's initial mistake or its restricted choice of alternatives in comparing price and risk.

To be sure, this approach raises some of the same ambiguities as utilitarian analysis. For example, should we assess consumer expectations in light of an automobile's overall safety record or on the basis of rear-end fire fatalities? Is the latter issue one on which many consumers have expectations? Which framework we select is highly relevant in cases like the Ford Pinto. According to tort expert Gary Schwartz's meticulous research, the Pinto's overall safety record during the relevant period was quite "respectable," in part because only 1 percent of all traffic crashes result in fires and only 4 percent of accident fatalities occur in fire crashes.[79] According to Dennis Gioia, one of Ford's recall coordinators involved in the Pinto case, many subcompact cars "suffered appalling deformities in relatively low-speed collisions, [and] the Pinto was merely the worst of the lot."[80] However, the Pinto did include a significant design defect and did perform worse regarding rear-end fire fatalities than most subcompacts.

Decision-makers in a situation like the Pinto case could thus arrive at much the same outcome through either a utilitarian or rights-based approach. A utilitarian who began with a less limited set of alternatives and costs than Ford's might end up protecting a reasonable expectation of safety. But as Chapter II indicated, the two ethical frameworks can yield different outcomes, particularly where certain fundamental principles are at issue. To take one of Lavelle's examples, consider the baby trapped in an open well. Assume that for about the same cost of rescuing her, we could require mine safety investments that would, on the average, save three lives over the next decade. Or suppose that we could save the life of a child involved in a Pinto crash but only through quite costly intensive care. If we let her die, we could use several of her organs to save the lives of other children. A strict utilitarian might prefer to maximize the lives saved; a rights-based approach, grounded in respect for each individual life, would decline to sacrifice one innocent person for the good of several others.

Which of these ethical frameworks makes most sense on the facts in Problem 6H? How would you judge Ford's decision under each standard? Consider Gary Schwartz's claim that cases like the Pinto reflect a "two cultures problem." On the one hand, we expect both governmental and corporate decision-makers to consider risk-benefit trade-offs when setting safety standards or evaluating design alternatives. Indeed, product liability law requires such an evaluation. On the other hand, when we are dealing not with statistical probabilities but with identifiable victims such as the trapped child or Pinto driver, the prospect of trading cash for lives offends deeply felt moral values.[81]

How the tort system should respond to this ambivalence has been a subject of considerable debate. However one resolves that question in general, and however one assesses Ford's conduct in particular, the point that bears emphasis here is that lawyers counseling corporations need to consider the moral dimensions of risk-benefit analysis. Such dimensions are crucial for attorneys not only in evaluating their own comfort level with a decision, but in predicting their clients' potential legal liabilities and public relations consequences.

c. *Decision-Making Authority*

If reasonable people can disagree about the morality of a particular organizational action, whose decision should control?

(1) Corporate Officers and Directors

Ethical Consideration 5-18 of the Code maintains that a lawyer employed by a corporation "owes his [or her] allegiance to the entity, and not to a stockholder, director, officer or . . . other representative." However, as a practical matter, an entity can only speak through such an agent, and, as Model Rule 1.13 recognizes, that agent is generally management. Under normal circumstances, corporate officers have the expertise and responsibility to make business decisions, including those involving product safety. Under exceptional circumstances of managerial misconduct, such authority rests with the board of directors. According to conventional views of professional responsibility, lawyers ought not to second-guess good-faith decisions of officers and directors. See Rule 1.3 and accompanying Comment, discussed below.

This view has been subject to criticism on several grounds. As one overview concludes:

Corporate structures inevitably tend to fragment moral responsibility. The impersonal character of bureaucracies, their departmentalized concepts of accountability, their claims of personal loyalty, and their devaluation of concerns not readily translated into relatively short-term advantages all conspire to circumscribe ethical vision. Since prestige in the business world turns heavily on abilities to maximize organizational size and growth, less tangible values are often discounted.[82]

If a company's chief executive officer believes, as did Lee Iacocca, that "safety doesn't sell," problems like the Pinto fuel tank placement will too frequently remain unremedied.[83] Nor will sufficient attention focus on externalities, such as environmental risks, unless they become the basis for legal liability or a public relations crisis. Although lawyers may have no special expertise in ethical analysis,

their distance from organizational incentive structures may at least permit a more disinterested perspective than that of corporate officers. By exploring the moral consequences of a client's contemplated actions, counsel may broaden the agenda of decisionmaking. Conversely, by declining that role, lawyers may compound the deflection of responsibility that too often characterizes organizational behavior. Clients can justify asocial action on the ground that counsel have pronounced it not unlawful, while counsel can rationalize their participation by deferring to client autonomy.[84]

(2)   Government Regulation

A common claim by corporate clients and their lawyers is that responsibility for protecting health, safety, or environmental quality rests with government. It is for politically accountable officials, not self-appointed attorney moralists, to make difficult trade-offs between lives and costs. As long as managers comply with existing regulations, their duties are satisfied. In the final analysis, the "social responsibility of business is to make profits."[85]

This view has also attracted frequent criticism. Part of the problem is its failure to acknowledge the limitations of interest-group politics. In contexts like the Ford Pinto case, single-interest industry organizations exercise far more influence over regulatory structures and enforcement than unorganized and uninformed consumers. Inadequate information among regulators may allow distribution of a product without adequate review of risks, as was the case with asbestos and Dalkon shields.[86] In some contexts, corporate or industry organizations are reluctant even to conduct adequate research on safety risks for fear that government agencies will "take the data out of context" and force expensive remedial measures such as recalls, retrofitting, and product or workplace redesign.[87]

From a moral standpoint, this implicit preference for profits over safety is difficult to justify. As Christopher Stone notes, shareholders who are dissatisfied with corporate profits can "sell out." Those who "work in the plants, [unwittingly] buy the products, and consume the effluents, cannot remove themselves from the structure with a phone call."[88] Commentators who stress corporate social responsibility accordingly argue that an organization's compliance with minimum standards should not end analysis. Even assuming that the most appropriate ultimate solution for inadequate regulation is regulatory reform, unless and until appropriate safeguards are in place, neither management nor its lawyers are entitled to defer to governmental standards.

What is your view? If you had been a juror in one of the Pinto cases, how would you have responded to arguments about the company's compliance with applicable regulations? How would you have responded as in-house counsel?

(3) The Market

A related issue of decision-making authority involves the rights of consumers, workers, or other affected parties to make their own trade-offs between dollars and risks. Corporate clients and their counsel often claim that their primary obligation is to make sufficient disclosures for informed choice; it is not their role to impose personal preferences on others about what level of safety to demand.

How plausible is this alternative in circumstances such as the Pinto case? How much information about how many features of how many comparable models would consumers need in order to make a truly rational choice? Studies of informed consent in medical contexts indicate that most individuals do not adequately understand or recall disclosures concerning risky or experimental procedures.[89] When making car purchases, how many prospective buyers are likely to focus on rear-end collision fatalities? Even when the issue was brought to their attention, about half of Pinto purchasers did not respond to Ford's recall notice and obtain free safety improvements.[90] Indeed Gioia, the company's former recall coordinator, now notes with some chagrin that he not only owned a Pinto at the time of the fires, but also that he sold it to his sister.[91] Consumers' reluctance to focus on risks is one reason why many manufacturers don't advertise their products' relative performance. In that sense, Iacocca was right in his assessment that safety doesn't sell.

Was he right, however, in the priorities that the company drew from that fact? Does it follow that consumers are unconcerned with safety simply because they do not make it central in their final decisions? Might they simply assume that government standards establish adequate protection? And if such standards in fact fall short, is there a role for paternalism along the lines suggested in Chapter IX (The Lawyer-Client Relationship) at pages 377–390? Would it also make sense for the government to require some disclosure of safety figures that could be readily compared? Consider

Schwartz's suggestion of stickers indicating a model's overall fatality and severe injury rates.[92]

Would such a disclosure system be adequate? Even if one believes in full consumer sovereignty, might some level of governmental, managerial, and attorney oversight be appropriate to cope with externalities? It is not only purchasers of Pintos who will bear the costs of their price/risk trade-off. Other drivers, passengers, and family members will also be affected.

(4)   Strategies of Dissent

A final issue involves lawyers' obligations if they disagree with a client's substantive decision or allocation of decision-making authority. In the Pinto case, what should attorneys have done if they believed that Ford's management had relied on unrealistic cost estimates and inadequate government regulations? What strategies for challenging a client's decision are consistent with current ethical rules and your own sense of moral obligations?

See Chapter IX, The Lawyer-Client Relationship
   • Part B. The Counseling Role
      (pages 390–398)

See Chapter XV, Evidence and Trial Advocacy
   • Witness Preparation
      (Problem 15C, pages 662–669)

2.   Whistle-Blowing in Organizational Contexts

[Three elements,] each jarring, and triply jarring when conjoined, lend acts of whistleblowing a special urgency and bitterness: dissent, breach of loyalty, and accusation.

Like all dissent, first of all, whistleblowing makes public a disagreement with an authority or a majority view. But . . . whistleblowing has the narrower aim of casting light on negligence or abuse, of alerting the public to a risk and of assigning responsibility for that risk. In the second place, the message of whistleblowers is seen as a breach of loyalty because it comes from within . . . [and creates a] sense of betrayal. . . .

It is the third element of accusation, of calling a "foul" from within, that arouses the strongest reactions on the part of the hierarchy. Explicitly or implicitly, it singles out specific groups or persons as responsible: as those who knew or should have known what was wrong

and what the dangers were, and who had the
capacity to make different choices.

Sissela Bok[93]

In debates over bar confidentiality rules, opponents of broader
disclosure requirements often argue by epithet. In their view,
imposing obligations on lawyers to parties other than clients would
turn counsel into "whistle-blowers," "policemen," and "informers."
This argument generally assumes that such a role is, if not morally
odious, then professionally suicidal and socially counterproductive.
Lawyers individually and collectively cannot expect to retain client
trust if they are willing to betray it.

This claim depends on factual assumptions about client behavior
that earlier discussion called into question. However, contexts
involving organizational clients present further complications.
Under ethical codes and common law, lawyers representing such
clients owe their obligation to the entity, not to any particular
subgroup such as officers, directors, shareholders, or employees. In
some instances, lawyers have knowledge about dangerous misjudg-
ments or misconduct that threatens organizational interests. Under
those circumstances, some form of whistle-blowing may be what
obligations to the entity require. Yet for reasons Bok suggests, this
function is inevitably uncomfortable. Even organizations that
endorse whistle-blowing in theory seldom reward it in practice.

In exploring attorneys' role as whistle-blowers, it is helpful to
focus on several related issues. What are lawyers' duties under
existing rules? What societal and professional interests justify or fail
to justify those rules? Where lawyers have discretion about how to
proceed, what considerations should inform their decisions? In
addressing these issues, it is also useful to distinguish between
external whistle-blowing, which involves disclosure to parties
outside the client organization, and internal whistle-blowing, which
involves reporting to organizational decision-makers outside the
normal channels of review.

a. *Current Rules*

The Code does not speak specifically to lawyers' confidentiality
obligations in organizational settings; its governing norms are set
out in the Disciplinary Rules discussed in Parts A and D above.
Model Rule 1.13 provides more explicit guidance:

RULE 1.13 ORGANIZATION AS CLIENT
    (a) A lawyer employed or retained by an organization represents
the organization acting through its duly authorized constituents.
    (b) If a lawyer for an organization knows that an officer, employee
or other person associated with the organization is engaged in action,

intends to act or refuses to act in a matter related to the representation that is a violation of a legal obligation to the organization, or a violation of law which reasonably might be imputed to the organization, and is likely to result in substantial injury to the organization, the lawyer shall proceed as is reasonably necessary in the best interest of the organization. In determining how to proceed, the lawyer shall give due consideration to the seriousness of the violation and its consequences, the scope and nature of the lawyer's representation, the responsibility in the organization and the apparent motivation of the person involved, the policies of the organization concerning such matters and any other relevant considerations. Any measures taken shall be designed to minimize disruption of the organization and the risk of revealing information relating to the representation to persons outside the organization. Such measures may include among others:

(1) asking reconsideration of the matter;

(2) advising that a separate legal opinion on the matter be sought for presentation to appropriate authority in the organization; and

(3) referring the matter to higher authority in the organization, including, if warranted by the seriousness of the matter, referral to the highest authority that can act in behalf of the organization as determined by applicable law.

(c) If, despite the lawyer's efforts in accordance with paragraph (b), the highest authority that can act on behalf of the organization insists upon action, or a refusal to act, that is clearly a violation of law and is likely to result in substantial injury to the organization, the lawyer may resign in accordance with rule 1.16. . . .

Comment

[4] When constituents of the organization make decisions for it, the decisions ordinarily must be accepted by the lawyer even if their utility or prudence is doubtful. Decisions concerning policy and operations, including ones entailing serious risk, are not as such in the lawyer's province. However, different considerations arise when the lawyer knows that the organization may be substantially injured by action of [a] constituent that is in violation of law. In such a circumstance, it may be reasonably necessary for the lawyer to ask the constituent to reconsider the matter. If that fails, or if the matter is of sufficient seriousness and importance to the organization, it may be reasonably necessary for the lawyer to take steps to have the matter reviewed by a higher authority in the organization. Clear justification should exist for seeking review over the head of the constituent normally responsible for it. The stated policy of the organization may define circumstances and prescribe channels for such review, and a lawyer should encourage the formulation of such a policy. Even in the absence of organization policy, however, the lawyer may have an obligation to refer a matter to higher authority, depending on the seriousness of the matter and whether the constituent in question has apparent motives to act at variance with the organization's interest. Review by the chief executive officer or by the board of directors [or by independent directors] may be required when the matter is of importance commensurate with their authority. At some point it may be useful or essential to obtain an independent legal opinion.

In effect, Rule 1.13 permits internal but not external whistle-blowing. Once an organization's highest authority has reviewed the issue, the only further action that the Model Rules authorize is withdrawal. As noted earlier, Rule 1.16 requires lawyers to withdraw if representation will result in violation of bar ethical rules or other law and permits withdrawal if their services have been used to perpetrate a crime or fraud. Under DR 2-110 of the Code, a lawyer must withdraw to avoid violating a disciplinary rule and may do so to avoid involvement with an illegal course of conduct. Consider whether these rules make adequate provision for whistle-blowing in light of the policy considerations summarized below.

b. Policy Considerations

From a societal standpoint, whistle-blowing by lawyers, like other employees, can promote crucial interests. Most significantly, it can prevent future health, safety, environmental, or financial injuries.[94] Such preventive action may also avert or mitigate harms to the organization such as fines, liability judgments, and impaired reputation and morale. In cases of past misconduct, whistle-blowing may also help mitigate or compensate injuries as well as deter future abuse. From the standpoint of whistle-blowers, acting on principle carries obvious psychological rewards. It may also serve some less commendable objectives such as gaining personal recognition or settling personal grudges, although available research suggests that such motivations are less common than is often supposed.[95] Most whistle-blowers attempt internal review before going public, and the external rewards are rarely sufficient to outweigh the career costs.

Those costs can be substantial. Harassment, isolation, retaliatory dismissals, transfers, and blacklisting are not uncommon.[96] In two major studies involving thousands of federal employees, whistle-blowers suffered retaliation in about 20 percent of all cases.[97] In some smaller-scale studies including private sector employees, the frequency of reprisals was considerably higher.[98] Lawyers who report on a colleague or client may also encounter ostracism; like the employees that Robert Jackall describes (see pages 286–292), they fall "out of the loop" of information exchange and institutional leverage.

The personal price of whistle-blowing, of course, depends heavily on context. Those who go outside the organization typically run greater risks because the major beneficiaries of such action are also outsiders.[99] For the organization itself, the costs of external whistle-blowing in legal liability and adverse publicity often outweigh any gains. The principal exception is where illegal or immoral actions would probably come to light eventually and early disclosure could prevent or significantly reduce their costs. However, in the most common cases of external whistle-blowing, disclosure benefits individual victims or society generally rather than the organization. This asymmetrical reward structure helps account for many well-documented instances of corrupt, illegal, and hazardous conduct in which no whistles are in use.[100]

Fred Zacharias' study of New York lawyers and clients suggests an example. Under one hypothetical in his survey,

> [t]he general counsel to a firm that produces a metal alloy used in the manufacture of airplanes learns of a company study that suggests that in some high altitude flight patterns the alloy might weaken and cause a plane to explode. The alloy does, however, meet the minimum safety standards set by the government. The lawyer urges the Board of Directors to recall the alloy or at a minimum to inform users of its potential danger. The Board decides that the study is too inconclusive to warrant action in light of the dire financial consequences of disclosure to the company.[101]

Over three-quarters of surveyed lawyers indicated that they would not disclose the information, a decision consistent with the New York bar ethical code. Approximately half of the surveyed clients believed (incorrectly) that attorneys had discretion to disclose under current rules, 85 percent believed that attorneys should disclose, and only 15 percent indicated that disclosure would affect their willingness to use an attorney's services.[102] If such findings are indicative of broader patterns, do they suggest a need for different confidentiality norms within the bar?

In analyzing whether whistle-blowing is appropriate, ethics experts generally focus on three basic considerations. Does the practice at issue result in serious harm? Has the individual taken reasonable steps to exhaust internal channels of review? Does the employee have documentation of the objectionable practice and a reasonable basis for believing that public disclosure will bring significant change?[103] In your view, should these be the primary considerations for lawyers? If not, what other factors would be crucial? What changes in bar codes, legal doctrine, and organizational practices might encourage socially desirable whistle-blowing?

c.   Strategies for Change

(1)   Bar Codes

Proponents of greater whistle-blowing by lawyers suggest changes in bar ethical rules along the lines of early Model Rule proposals. One such proposal would have required lawyers to report present or imminent violations of the law to shareholders or to the appropriate government agency. A somewhat later proposal would have allowed lawyers to take "remedial actions," including disclosure of confidential information to persons outside the organization, if (1) its highest authority had acted out of personal or financial interest that conflicted with the organization's interest and (2) such disclosure was "necessary in the best interests of the organization."[104] Several states, including Maryland, Michigan, New Hampshire, and

New Jersey, have adopted this second version. Compare these proposals to the Code of Ethics for Engineers:

> Should the Engineer's professional judgment be overruled under circumstances where the safety, health, and welfare of the public are endangered, the Engineers shall inform their clients or employers of possible consequences and notify other proper authority of the situation, as may be appropriate.[105]

Would any of these formulations of professional responsibility be appropriate for lawyers?

(2)   Legislation

Several legislative strategies are possible. One is to expand compulsory reporting obligations for employees who become aware of unsafe conditions or illegal activity. For example, under Nuclear Regulatory Commission mandates, employees who know of certain nuclear safety risks must inform government officials. In the highly publicized proceeding against the law firm of Kaye, Scholer, discussed in Chapter XIII (Corporate Law) at page 583, the Office of Thrift Supervision argued that, under certain circumstances, lawyers for regulated banking institutions have the same obligation as their clients to disclose material facts and omissions to regulatory agencies.

A second possibility is to provide greater safeguards against reprisal for internal and external whistle-blowers. Over the last half century, Congress has extended protection for federal employees who disclose fraud, corruption, and waste, as well as for other individuals who report violations of certain federal safety and environmental statutes. Over the past decade, about two-thirds of the states have also passed legislation providing some similar safeguards.[106] However, this protective patchwork still excludes most private sector employees. Many state statutes cover only civil servants or reports to government agencies. For that reason, commentators have proposed model legislation that would extend whistle-blower protections more broadly. For example, it could be an unfair labor practice to discharge an employee who reports to management or government agencies any activity reasonably believed to be illegal, against public policy, or inconsistent with employer policy.[107] Would you support such a proposal?

d.   Common Law

In the absence of adequate legislative protections, increased attention has focused on changes in the common law. By the early 1990s, about half of all jurisdictions recognized exceptions to employers' rights to fire at will for at least some cases involving whistle-blowers. Yet although most courts have allowed employees to sue for wrongful discharge if they are fired for refusing to do something illegal, similar protection has not been available where employees lose their jobs after aggressively reporting unethical or unlawful conduct to management.

In the few cases that have arisen involving lawyers, courts have reached varying results. Several well-publicized decisions have not permitted attorneys' claims to proceed to trial. In Herbster v. North American Co. for Life and Health Ins., 501 N.E.2d 343 (Ill. 1986), cert. denied, 484 U.S. 850 (1987), an attorney sought compensatory and punitive damages after he was fired for allegedly disobeying management's request to destroy certain files. The district court granted the insurance company's motion to dismiss on the ground that the communications alleged in the complaint were protected under the attorney-client privilege.[108]

In the aftermath of the *Herbster* case, the Illinois legislature considered legislation that would explicitly allow in-house counsel to sue for retaliatory discharge if they were fired for refusing to obey corporate orders to violate a law or rule of ethics. That legislation would also have permitted lawyers bringing such actions to reveal confidences obtained in the course of employment.[109]

Would you support such a provision? Does it make sense, as in *Herbster*, that an attorney can disclose confidences to collect a fee or to establish a defense in claims initiated by a client, but cannot make similar disclosures to justify whistle-blowing? Could concerns regarding confidentiality be met by judicial orders sealing records?

Other courts have been more receptive to whistle-blowers. These decisions have relied on three major theories. Discharges of whistle-blowers are thought to violate public policy; to breach an implied covenant of good faith and fair dealing; or to violate an implicit term of attorneys' employment contract. For example, in Mourad v. Automobile Club Ins. Assn., 465 N.W.2d 395 (Mich. 1991), the Michigan Court of Appeals upheld a $1.25 million jury award to an in-house lawyer who sued for retaliatory discharge and demotion. His claim was based on pressure from the defendant insurance company to cut corners and costs in defending policyholders. In the appellate court's view, the company should have known in hiring the attorney that he would be bound by the Code of Professional Responsibility and should have "incorporated this fact in creating a just cause employment contract." So too, in Balla v. Gambro, Inc., 560 N.E.2d 1043 (Ill. 1990), the defendant's General Counsel and Manager of Personnel sued for retaliatory discharge, claiming that he was fired after advising that the sale of defective kidney dialyzers would have to be reported to the FDA. The Illinois Court of Appeals remanded for a determination (1) whether the plaintiff's discharge resulted from privileged information; (2) if so, whether the privilege was waived; and (3) whether any countervailing public policies favored disclosure of privileged information. The court distinguished

Herbster on the ground that it did not involve policy concerns relating to the conduct of illegal activities and protection of human life.

In subsequent decisions, the California and Massachusetts Supreme Courts both upheld a corporate counsel's right to sue for wrongful discharge under certain specified circumstances. GTE Products Corp. v. Stewart, 653 N.E.2d 161, 166-167 (Mass. 1995), made remedies available for a retaliatory discharge involving "(1) explicit and unequivocal statutory or ethical norms, (2) policies of importance to the public at large in the circumstances of the particular case, and (3) [a claim that] . . . can be proved without any violation of the attorney's obligation to respect client confidences and secrets." Similarly, General Dynamics Corp. v. Superior Court, 876 P.2d 487 (Cal. 1994), held that lawyers could sue for terminations that implicated a "fundamental and clearly established policy" serving the public at large; that involved disclosure of illegal conduct or refusal to commit a crime; and that could be proven without violating the attorney-client privilege.

Finally, in Wieder v. Skala, 80 N.Y.2d 628 (1992), discussed in Chapter III (Regulation of the Profession) at page 71, and in Chapter XII (Contracts) at page 537, the New York Court of Appeals found an implied-in-law contractual obligation to protect an associate who allegedly was fired after insisting that another law firm associate's misconduct be reported to state disciplinary authorities.

Would any of these approaches adequately address the dilemma in Problem 6I below?

e. *Institutional Strategies*

Changing the ethos against whistle-blowing will require more than changes in formal rules; organizational norms must also change. Commentators have proposed a number of strategies:

- creation of internal hotlines, ethics or audit committees, and inspector general/ombudsperson positions;[110]
- increased resources for enforcement of existing anti-reprisal regulations;
- creation of governmental review agencies; and
- support for whistle-blowers by professional organizations, such as legal funds to pursue wrongful discharge claims or awards for ethical resistance.[111]

In addition, organizations need to make ethics a consideration in job descriptions, training, mentoring, and reward structures.[112]

Which of these strategies strike you as most promising? Would they affect your decisions in Problem 6I?

PROBLEM 6I

1. You are the lawyer for Covenant Corporation in the circumstances that the following excerpt from Moral Mazes, describes. How should you respond? According to Robert Jackall, "[d]rawing lines when information is scarce becomes doubly ambiguous" because it is not entirely clear what can, must, or should be done about it. If you were the general counsel for Covenant, what steps would you take to anticipate these circumstances?

2. Assume that you are the general counsel in Moral Mazes who consults with the accountant Brady. What advice would you have provided?

See Chapter IX, The Lawyer-Client Relationship
   • Part B. The Counseling Role
      (pages 390–398)

ROBERT JACKALL, MORAL MAZES: THE WORLD OF CORPORATE MANAGERS

122-123; 17, 19-21, 106-112 (1988)

... Drawing lines when information is scarce becomes doubly ambiguous, a problem that often emerges in shaping relationships with one's colleagues. For instance, Black, a lawyer at Covenant Corporation, received a call from a chemical plant manager who had just been served with an order from the local fire department to build retaining dikes around several storage tanks for toxic chemicals so that firemen would not be in danger of being drenched with the substance should the tanks burst if there were a fire at the plant. The plant manager indicated that meeting the order would cause him to miss his numbers badly that year and he wondered aloud if the fire chief might, for a consideration, be persuaded to forget the whole thing. Black pointed out that he could not countenance even a discussion of bribery; the plant manager laughed and said that he was only joking and would think things over and get back to Black in a few weeks. Black never heard from the plant manager about this issue again; when they met on different occasions after that, the conversation was always framed around other subjects. Black did inquire discreetly and found out that no dikes had been built; the plant manager had apparently gone shopping for a more flexible legal opinion. Should he, Black wondered, pursue the matter or in the absence of any firm evidence just let things drop, particularly since others, for their own purposes, could misconstrue the fact that he had not acted on his earlier marginal knowledge? Feeling that one is in the dark can be somewhat unnerving.

More unnerving, however, is the feeling that one is being kept in the dark. Reed, another lawyer at Covenant, was working on the legal issues of a chemical dumpsite that Alchemy Inc. [a subsidiary of Covenant] had sold. He suddenly received a call from a former employee who had been having trouble with the company on his pension payments; this man told Reed that unless things were straightened out in a hurry, he planned to talk to federal officials about all the pesticides buried in the site. This was alarming news. Reed had no documentation about pesticides in the site; if Alchemy had buried pesticides there, a whole new set of regulations might apply to the situation and to Covenant as the former owner. Reed went to the chemical company's director of personnel to get the former employee's file but was unable to obtain it. Reed's boss agreed to help, but still the director of personnel refused to release the file. After repeated calls, Reed was told that the file had been lost. Reed went back to his boss and inquired whether it might be prudent for Covenant to repurchase the site to keep it under control. This was deemed a good idea. However, the asking price for the site was now three times what Covenant had sold it for. Everyone, of course, got hesitant; another lawyer became involved and began working closely with Reed's boss on the issue. Gradually Reed found himself excluded from discussions about the problem and unable to obtain information that he felt was important to his work. His anxiety was heightened because he felt he was involved in a matter of some legal gravity. But, like much else in the corporation, this problem disappeared in the night. Eventually, Reed was assigned to other cases and he knew that the doors to the issue were closed, locked, and bolted.

. . . The hierarchical authority structure that is the linchpin of bureaucracy dominates the way managers think about their world and about themselves. Managers do not see or experience authority in any abstract way; instead, authority is embodied in their personal relationships with their immediate bosses and in their perceptions of similar links between other managers up and down the hierarchy. When managers describe their work to an outsider, they almost always first say: "I work for [Bill James]" or "I report to [Harry Mills]" or "I'm in [Joe Bell's] group," and only then proceed to describe their actual work functions. . . .

. . . [The] "management-by-objective" system, as it is usually called, creates a chain of commitments from the CEO down to the lowliest product manager or account executive. In practice, it also shapes a patrimonial authority arrangement that is crucial to defining both the immediate experiences and the long-run career chances of individual managers. In this world, a subordinate owes fealty principally to his immediate boss. This means that a subordinate must not overcommit his boss, lest his boss "get on the hook" for promises that cannot be kept. He must keep his boss from making mistakes, particularly public ones; he must keep his boss informed, lest his boss get "blindsided.". . . A subordinate must also not circumvent his boss nor ever give the appearance of doing so. He must never contradict his boss's judgment in public. To violate the last admonition is thought to constitute a kind of death wish in business. . . .

In return, [a subordinate] can hope for those perquisites that are in his boss's gift — the better, more attractive secretaries, or the nudging of a movable panel to enlarge his office, and perhaps a couch to fill the added space, one of the real distinctions in corporate bureaucracies. He can hope to be elevated when and if the boss is elevated, though other important criteria intervene here. He can also expect protection for mistakes made, up to a point. However, that point is never exactly defined and depends on the complicated politics of each situation. The general rule is that bosses are expected to protect those in their bailiwicks. Not to do so, or to be unable to do so, is taken as a sign of untrustworthiness or weakness. If, however, subordinates make mistakes that are thought to be dumb, or especially if they violate fealty obligations — for example, going around their boss — then abandonment of them to the vagaries of organizational forces is quite acceptable. . . .

It is characteristic of this authority system that details are pushed down and credit is pulled up. Superiors do not like to give detailed instructions to subordinates. The official reason for this is to <u>maximize subordinates' autonomy</u>. The underlying reason is, first, to get rid of tedious details [and also to insulate supervisors from pressures, mistakes, and guilty knowledge]. . . . [B]ecause they are unfamiliar with, indeed deliberately distance themselves from, entangling details, corporate higher echelons tend to expect successful results without messy complications. This is central to top executives' well-known aversion to bad news and to the resulting tendency to kill the messenger who bears the news. . . .

[An example involves Brady, an accountant.] Brady was disturbed to discover, upon first taking office, that there were a number of financial irregularities occurring in his company, including sizable bribery payments to officials of developing countries. Brady immediately had himself and his staff examined by his company's internal auditors, sent them to Mexico and Venezuela to do detailed field investigations of the bribes, and had the auditors send copies of the report to the CEO. In effect, he "blew the whistle on himself" and was later glad he did since the U.S. Attorney's office subsequently came in to investigate the matter; with the aid of the federal investigation, Brady was able to eliminate the irregular payments. . . .

As it happened, however, he soon came across much more serious and potentially damaging information. Key people in the corporation — at this stage Brady was not sure just who was involved — were using about $18 million from the employee pension fund as a profit slush fund. Essentially, there was too much money in the pension fund. Explicit rules govern such a contingency but these were being ignored. The money was not declared as an asset but concealed and moved in and out of the corporation's earnings statements each year so that the corporation always came in exactly on target. In fact, each October key officials could predict earnings per share for the year to the penny even though one-third of all earnings were in foreign currency. This uncanny accuracy assured top executives, of course, of completely reliable bonus payments. These were tied to hitting profit targets and gave top managers in the company up to 100 percent of the annual salary in deferred income in stock on top of whatever benefits they had accrued in the pension plan. Whatever money was not needed to make the incentive program work to its maximum immediate benefit was set aside for a rainy day. . . .

Brady saw the pension fund manipulation as a direct violation of fiduciary trust, as depriving stockholders not only of their rightful knowledge but also of material benefits and as a misuse of other people's money for personal gain. It was, he felt, a practice that could in hard times jeopardize the employees' pension fund. He now had no way of reporting the matter through normal channels. His boss, the corporate vice-president for finance, had been hostile to him ever since Brady came under his control, distrusting Brady, it seems, because of his attempted reporting of the doctored invoices. . . .

[Accordingly, Brady wrote an anonymous memorandum detailing the problem and had a colleague present it to a key member of the board of directors. After that director discussed the matter with the CEO, the colleague was fired. At that point, Brady realized that the CEO was responsible for "fiddling with the numbers." Brady then disclosed what he knew to the highest ranking in-house lawyer.]

The lawyer "did not want to touch the issue with a barge pole." He sent a friend of Brady's, yet another corporate vice-president, to Brady to cool things down. According to Brady, the vice-president argued: "Look, why don't you just forget the whole thing. Everyone does it. That's just part of the game in business today." When Brady persisted, the vice-president asked if Brady could not just go along with things even if he did not agree. Brady said that he could not. Brady mentioned the managerial bonus program and acknowledged that that too could be adversely affected by his action. The vice-president blanched and became quite upset. Right after Brady's boss returned from Europe, Brady was summarily fired and he and his belongings were literally thrown out of the company building.

It is important to note the sharp contrast between Brady's reasons for acting as he did and other corporate managers' analyses of his actions. For Brady, the kinds of issues he confronted at work were distinctly moral issues, seen through the prism of his professional code. He says:

> So what I'm saying is that at bottom, I was in jeopardy of violating my professional code. And I feel that you have to stick up for that. If your profession has standing, it has that standing because *someone stood up for it*. If the SEC [the Securities and Exchange Commission] had come in and did an analysis and then went into the details of the case

and put me up on the stand and asked me, What is your profession? Was this action right or wrong? Why did you do it then? I would really be in trouble . . . with myself most of all. I am frightened of losing respect, my self-respect in particular. And since that was tied with my respect for my profession, the two things were joined together. I had such a fear of losing that precisely because of my high respect for it.

He goes on to comment further about his relation to professional standards and how those standards contrast with the prevailing ethos of corporate life.

I have fears in a situation like that. . . . . It's not exactly a fear of what could happen to me, although that certainly crossed my mind. What it is is a fear of being found out not to stand up to standards that I have claimed as my own. It is a fear of falling down in a place where you have stuck a flag in the ground and said: "This is where I stand." I mean, why is it in life today that we have to deny any morality at all? But this is exactly the situation here. I was just too honest for that company. What is right in the corporation is not what is right in a man's home or in his church. *What is right in the corporation is what the guy above you wants from you.* That's what morality is in the corporation.

The corporate managers to whom I presented this case see Brady's dilemma as devoid of moral or ethical content. In their view, the issues that Brady raises are, first of all, simply practical matters. His basic failing was, first, that he violated the fundamental rules of bureaucratic life [by not dropping a matter his supervisors wanted dropped]. . . .

Second, the managers that I interviewed feel that Brady had plenty of available legitimations to excuse or justify his not acting. Clearly, they feel, a great many other executives knew about the pension fund scam and did nothing; everybody, especially the top bosses, was playing the game. The problem fell into other people's areas, was their responsibility, and therefore their problem. Why, then, worry about it? Besides, Brady had a number of ways out of the situation if he found it intolerable, including resigning. Moreover, whatever action he took would be insignificant anyway so why bother to act at all and jeopardize himself? Even a fool should have known that the CEO was not likely to take whatever blame resulted from the whole affair.

Third, these managers see the violations that disturbed Brady, irregular payments, doctored invoices, shuffling numbers in accounts, as small potatoes indeed, commonplaces of corporate life. One cannot, for example, expect to do business abroad, particularly in the Third World, without recognizing that "one man's bribe is another man's commission." As long as one does not try to extort an unfair market advantage but rather simply facilitates or speeds along already assigned duties, bribes are really the grease that makes the world work. Moreover, as managers see it, playing sleight of hand with the monetary value of inventories, post- or predating memoranda or invoices, tucking or squirreling large sums of money away to pull them out of one's hat at an opportune moment are all part and parcel of managing in a large corporation where interpretations of performance, not necessarily performance itself, decide one's fate. . . .

Even more to the point, Brady called others' organizational morality, their acceptance of the moral ethos of bureaucracy, into question, made them uncomfortable, and eroded the fundamental trust and understanding that make cooperative managerial work possible. One executive elaborates a general sentiment:

> What it comes down to is that his moral code made other people uncomfortable. He threatened their position. He made them uncomfortable with their moral standards and their ethics. If he pursued it, the exposé would threaten their livelihood and their way of life. So they fired him. I personally believe that people in high places in big companies at some stage lose sight of the objectives of their companies and begin to focus on their positions. That's the only way you can really rationalize the pension fund issue. . . .

The finale to the story is worth recounting. After Brady was fired, the CEO retired and elevated to his position a man known throughout the company as "Loyal Sam." The latter had "tracked" the CEO throughout his career. The CEO went back to his old corner office on a middle floor, his home before he ascended to power, and took an emeritus position with the firm, chief of the internal audit department. He now travels around the world, writing scrutinizing reports about the same companies on which he worked his legerdemain when he was CEO. When the managers to whom I present the case hear the outcome, they laugh softly, nod their heads, and give even an outsider like myself one of the sharp, knowing looks that one imagines they usually reserve for trusted others in their world.

Karl Mannheim points out that bureaucracy turns all political issues into matters of administration. One can see a parallel alchemy in managers' responses to Brady's dilemma. Bureaucracy transforms all moral issues into immediately practical concerns. A moral judgment based on a professional ethic makes little sense in a world where the etiquette of authority relationships and the necessity for protecting and covering for one's boss, one's network, and oneself supersede all other considerations and where nonaccountability for action is the norm. As a matter of survival, not to mention advancement, corporate managers have to keep their eye fixed not on abstract principles but on the social framework of their world and its requirements. Thus, they simply do not see most issues that confront them as moral concerns even when problems might be posed in moral terms by others.

SISSELA BOK, BLOWING THE WHISTLE

Public Duties: The Moral Obligations of Government Officials 204, 205, 210-211, 213-214 (J. Fleishman, L. Liebman & M. Moore eds., 1981)

Given the indispensable services performed by so many whistle-blowers, as during the Watergate period and after, strong public support is often merited. But the new climate of acceptance makes it easy to overlook the dangers of whistleblowing: of uses in error or in malice; of work and reputations unjustly lost for those falsely accused; of privacy invaded and trust undermined. There comes a level of internal prying and mutual suspicion at which no institution can function. And it is a fact that the disappointed, the incompetent, the malicious, and the paranoid all too often leap to accusations in public. Worst of all, ideological persecution throughout the world traditionally relies on insiders willing to inform on their colleagues or even on their family members, often through staged public denunciations or press campaigns.

INDIVIDUAL MORAL CHOICE

What questions might those who consider sounding an alarm in public ask themselves? How might they articulate the problem they see and weigh its injustice before deciding whether or not to reveal it? How can they best try to make sure their choice is the right one?

In thinking about these questions it helps to keep in mind the three elements mentioned earlier: dissent, breach of loyalty, and accusation. They impose certain requirements: of accuracy and judgment in dissent; of exploring alternative ways to cope with improprieties that minimize the breach of loyalty; and of fairness in accusation. For each, careful articulation and testing of arguments are needed to limit error and bias.

Dissent by whistleblowers, first of all, is expressly claimed to be intended to benefit the public. It carries with it, as a result, an obligation to consider the nature of this benefit and to consider also the possible harm that may come from speaking out: harm to persons or institutions, and ultimately to the public interest itself. Whistle-blowers must therefore begin by making every effort to consider the effects of speaking out versus those of remaining silent. They must assure themselves of the accuracy of their reports, checking and rechecking the facts before speaking out; specify the degree to which there is genuine impropriety; and consider how imminent is the threat they see, how serious, and how closely linked to those accused of neglect or abuse.

If the facts warrant whistleblowing, how can the second element, breach of loyalty, be minimized? The most important question here is whether the existing avenues for change within the organization have been explored. It is a waste of time for the public as well as harmful to the institution to sound the loudest alarm first. Whistle-blowing has to remain a last alternative because of its destructive side effects: it must be chosen only when other alternatives have been considered and rejected. They may be rejected if they simply do not apply to the problem at hand, or when there is not time to go through routine channels, or when the institution is so corrupt or coercive that steps will be taken to silence the whistleblower should he try the regular channels first.

What weight should an oath or a promise of silence have in the conflict of loyalties? Those sworn to silence are doubtless under a stronger obligation because of the oath taken. They have bound themselves, assumed specific obligations beyond those assumed in merely taking a new position. But even such promises can be overridden when the public interest at issue is strong enough. They can be overridden if they were obtained under duress or through deceit. They can be overridden, too, if they promise something that is in itself wrong or unlawful. The fact that one has promised silence is no excuse for complicity in covering up a crime or a violation of the public's trust.

From the public's point of view, accusations that are openly made by identifiable individuals are more likely to be taken seriously. Since the open accusation is felt to be fairer to the accused, and since it makes the motives of the whistleblower open to inspection, the audience is more confident that the message may have a factual basis. As a result, if whistleblowers still choose to resort to surreptitious messages, they have a strong obligation to let the accused know of the accusation leveled, and to produce independent evidence that can be checked.

During this process of weighing the legitimacy of speaking out, the method used, and the degree of fairness needed, whistleblowers must try to compensate for the strong possibility of bias on their part. They should be scrupulously aware of any motive that might skew their message: a desire for self-defense in a difficult bureaucratic situation, perhaps, or the urge to seek revenge, or [benefits from publicity]. . . . If, for example, a government employee stands to make large profits from a book exposing the iniquities in his agency, there is danger that he will, perhaps even unconsciously, slant his report in order to cause more of a sensation. If he supports his revelation by referring to the Code of Ethics for Government Service urging that loyalty to the highest moral principles and to country be put above loyalty to persons, party, or government department, he cannot ignore another clause in the same Code, specifying that he "ought never to use any information coming to him confidentially in the performance of government duties as a means for making private profits." . . .

To weigh all these factors is not easy. The ideal case of whistle-blowing, where the cause is a just one, where all the less dramatic alternatives have been exhausted, where responsibility is openly accepted, and where the whistleblower is above reproach, is rare. The motives may be partly self-serving, the method questionable, and still we may judge that the act was in the public interest. In cases where the motives for sounding the alarm are highly suspect, for example, but where clear proof of wrongdoing and avoidable risk is adduced, the public may be grateful that the alarm was sounded.

Endnotes

1. Geoffrey Hazard, An Historical Perspective on the Attorney-Client Privilege, 66 Cal. L. Rev. 1061, 1069-1073 (1978); John H. Wigmore, 8 A Treatise on the Anglo-American System of Evidence in Trials at Common Law §2290 (John T. McNaughton ed., rev. ed. 1961).

2. Wigmore, supra note 1, §2292, at 554.

3. Jeremy Bentham, 5 Rationale of Judicial Evidence 302-304 (Hunt & Clarke eds., 1827).

4. Monroe Freedman, Lawyers' Ethics in an Adversary System 4 (1975).

5. William Simon, Ethical Discretion in Lawyering, 101 Harv. L. Rev. 1083, 1142 (1988).

6. See discussion in Part F infra and sources cited in Harry I. Subin, The Lawyer as Superego: Disclosure of Client Confidences to Prevent Harm, 70 Iowa L. Rev. 1091, 1164 (1985).

7. Note, Functional Overlap Between the Lawyer and Other Professionals: Implications for the Privilege Communication Doctrine, 71 Yale L.J. 1226 (1962).

8. Fred C. Zacharias, Rethinking Confidentiality, 74 Iowa L. Rev. 351, 382-383 (1989).

9. Deborah L. Rhode, Ethical Perspectives on Legal Practice, 37 Stan. L. Rev. 589, 614 (1985). See also Canon 41 of the ABA Canons of Ethics.

10. Tarasoff v. Board of Regents of the University of California, 551 P.2d 334 (Cal. 1976) (holding that psychiatrist had duty to warn victim of patient's threat).

11. Rhode, supra note 9, at 615.

12. Geoffrey C. Hazard, Jr. & Susan P. Koniak, The Law and Ethics of Lawyering 279 (1990).

13. Wigmore, supra note 1, §2291, at 553. See also Robert A. Burt, Conflict and Trust Between Attorney and Client, 69 Geo. L.J. 1015 (1981).

14. Henry J. Reske & Don J. DeBenedictis, Ethics Proposals Draw Fire, A.B.A.J., Oct. 1991, at 34 (quoting Terence F. MacCarthy). For opposition to earlier Model Rule proposals, see Rhode, supra note 9, at 612-615.

15. Zacharias, supra note 8, at 392-395.

16. Council on Ethical and Judicial Affairs, Code of Medical Ethics: Current Opinions with Annotations (Chicago, Ill.: American Medical Association, 1994).

17. Laurie S. Kahn, Infecting Attorney-Client Confidentiality: The Ethics of HIV Disclosure, 9 Geo. J. Legal Ethics 547 (1996).

18. See cases cited in James M. Grippando, Attorney-Client Privilege: Implied Waiver Through Inadvertent Disclosure of Documents, 39 U. Miami L. Rev. 511 (1985). For further examples, see Wendy R. Liebowitz, Legal Ethics in an Electronic Age: Where No One Has Gone Before, Natl. L.J., Mar. 24, 1997.

19. See George A. Davidson & William H. Voth, Waiver of the Attorney Client Privilege, 64 Or. L. Rev. 637 (1986). See also Richard L. Marcus, The Perils of Privilege: Waiver and the Litigator, 84 Mich. L. Rev. 1605, 1654-1655 (1986).

20. Marcus, supra note 19, at 1654-1655.

21. Professor Andrew Kaufman, quoted in Lawyer May Be Forced to Identify Client, N.Y. Times, Oct. 13, 1988, at A22. The case was Baltes v. Doe, No. 88-1145-AD Sep. Op. (Fla. Dist. Ct. App., Oct. 13, 1988). See also Jeffrey Schmalz, Lawyer Granted Right to Conceal Client's Identity, N.Y. Times, Oct. 14, 1988, at A1 (reporting debate between Geoffrey C. Hazard, Jr. opposing application of the privilege and Alan Dershowitz supporting it); Steven Goode, Identity, Fees, and the Attorney-Client Privilege, 59 Geo. Wash. L. Rev. 307 (1991); and Dietz v. Doe, 935 P.2d 611 (Wash. 1997).

22. Wigmore, supra note 1, §2313 at 609-610; Vingelli v. United States, 992 F.2d 449 (2d Cir. 1993); Tornay v. United States, 840 F.2d 1424 (9th Cir. 1988); In re Shargel, 742 F.2d 61 (2d Cir. 1984); Restatement of the Law Governing Lawyers §119 cmt. G.

23. For examples of such factual situations, see Confidentiality, 55 ABA/BNA Manual of Professional Conduct 307 (1994); Goode, supra note 21; Developments in the Law, Privileged Communications, 98 Harv. L. Rev. 1501, 1517 n.91 (1985). For detailed discussion of §60501, see Ellen S. Podgor, Form 8300: The Demise of Law as a Profession, 5 Geo. J. Legal Ethics 485, 491 (1991).

24. Fred C. Zacharias, A Critical Look at Rules Governing Grand Jury Subpoenas of Attorneys, 76 U. Minn. L. Rev. 917, 921-923 (1992); William J. Genego, The New Adversary, 54 Brook. L. Rev. 781, 874-875 (1988).

25. See generally Charles Fried, Too High a Price for Truth: The Exception to the Attorney-Client Privilege for Contemplated Crimes and Frauds, 64 N.C.L. Rev. 443 (1986).

26. Charles T. McCormick, Evidence 199, §95 (Edward W. Cleary, 2d ed., 1972).

27. Geoffrey C. Hazard, Jr., Ethics in the Practice of Law 29-30 (1978).

28. The case was SEC v. National Student Marketing, 457 F. Supp. 682 (D.D.C. 1978), discussed in Chapter XIII (Corporate Law) at pages 576–579.

29. Geoffrey Hazard, Jr., Lawyers and Client Fraud: They Still Don't Get It, 6 Geo. J. Legal Ethics 701, 721-722 (1993).

30. See Donald C. Langevoort, Where Were the Lawyers? A Behavioral Inquiry into Lawyers' Responsibility for Clients' Fraud, 46 Vand. L. Rev. 75 (1993); Deborah L. Rhode, Institutionalizing Ethics, 44 Case Western L. Rev. 665 (1994).

31. Tom Alibrani with Frank H. Armani, Privileged Information 199 (1984).

32. Id. at 3; id. at 97 (quoting a law school dean who advised Armani on his confidentiality obligations).

33. Id. at 189.

34. Id. at 116. See Lawyer-Client Privilege Gets Severe Test, 64 A.B.A.J. 664 (1978); Jeffrey F. Chamberlain, Legal Ethics: Confidentiality and the Case of Robert Garrow's Lawyers, 25 Buff. L. Rev. 211, 221 n.64 (1975).

35. Alibrani with Armani, supra note 31, at 98 (quoting a law school dean).

36. Arthur Powell, Privilege of Counsel and Confidential Communications, 6 Ga. B.J. 334, 345 (1964) (discussing I Can Go Home Again (1943)); Leonard Dinnerstein, The Leo Frank Case 125 (1968).

37. David Margolick, Kidnapping? Or Murder, Too?, N.Y. Times, June 26, 1992, at A14 (quoting Jack Arseneault).

38. For research suggesting that there may be more social consensus on certain disclosure obligations than the bar acknowledges, see Zacharias, supra note 8, at 392-395. For example, Zacharias found that 80 percent of surveyed clients believed that lawyers should reveal information that would exonerate a defendant falsely accused of a crime if they could do so without implicating the client even though the client objects. About two-thirds of surveyed lawyers would make such disclosure.

39. Phil Gailey, Behind the Scenes with Ed Williams, N.Y. Times Magazine, Apr. 17, 1983, at 55.

40. Id.

41. John Herbers, Nixon in TV Talk, Shuns Watergate Apology, N.Y. Times, Apr. 6, 1984, at A17.

42. Henry Brandon, What If Nixon . . . , N.Y. Times, Aug. 18, 1988, at A27 (quoting Garment).

43. Confidentiality, 55 ABA/BNA Manual on Professional Conduct 312 (1994); Geoffrey Hazard Jr. & William Hodes, The Law of Lawyering §1.6:401, at 194; §3.4:204, at 631 (1990).

44. Stephen A. Salzburg, Communications Falling Within the Attorney-Client Privilege, 66 Iowa L. Rev. 811, 830 (1981).

45. Kevin R. Reitz, Clients, Lawyers and the Fifth Amendment: The Need for a Projected Privilege, 41 Duke L.J. 572, 597-602, 627 (1991).

46. John M. Fedders & Lauryn H. Guttenplan, Document Retention and Destruction: Practical, Legal, and Ethical Considerations, 56 Notre Dame Law. 5, 8-9 (1980).

47. Id. at 13.

48. Hazard, supra note 27, at 85.

49. Michael Allen, Cleaning House: U.S. Companies Pay Increasing Attention to Destroying Files, Wall St. J., Sept. 2, 1987, at 1 (quoting Judah Best); Ralph Nader & Wesley J. Smith, No Contest 148 (1996) (quoting Philip Lacovara).

50. J. Goulden, The Super-Lawyers 292 (1971).

51. Geoffrey C. Hazard, Jr., Quis custodiet ipsos custodes?, 95 Yale L.J. 1523, 1532, 1534-1535 (1986) (reviewing Kenneth Mann, Defending White Collar Crime (1985)).

52. Kurt Eichenwald, Texaco's Tale of the Tapes, N.Y. Times, Jan. 10, 1996, at E2. For other examples, see Nader & Smith, supra note 49, at 141-157 (1996).

53. For example, courts may award the costs of reconstructing evidence and litigating the motion; make findings of fact or grant claims based on assumptions about what the evidence showed; and impose tort liability

for spoliation of evidence or negligent misrepresentation of fact. See generally Lawrence Solum & Jamie S. Gorelick, Destruction of Evidence (1989); Barry S. Marvin, Do Not Burn, Shred, or Mutilate, Cal. Law., Nov. 1991, at 69-70.

54. Thomas Greene, Wages of Destruction, Cal. Bar J., Sept. 1995, at 15.

55. Hazard & Hodes, supra note 43, §3.3:212 at 597-598 (1991 Supp.). See R.W. Nahstoll, The Lawyer's Allegiance: Priorities Regarding Confidentiality, 41 Wash. & Lee L. Rev. 421 (1984).

56. Monroe Freedman, Lawyers' Ethics in an Adversary System 4, 27 (1975); Freedman's analysis of the perjury trilemma appears in id., Chapter 3.

57. I am indebted for this example to Kim Taylor, Professor, New York University Law School, based on her experience at the Washington, D.C., Public Defender Office.

58. The Ethics Advisory Committee of NACDL, Formal Op. 92-2, reprinted in The Champion 23 (Mar. 1993).

59. Alan Donegan, Justifying Legal Practice in the Adversary System, in The Good Lawyer: Lawyer's Roles and Lawyer's Ethics 123, 145-146 (David Luban ed., 1983).

60. John T. Noonan, Jr., Professional Ethics or Personal Responsibility?, 29 Stan. L. Rev. 363, 364-365 (1977) (reviewing Lawyers' Ethics in an Adversary System).

61. This was the approach proposed in an earlier version of Standard 4-7.7, ABA Proposed Standards for Criminal Justice (2d ed. 1980). It continues to attract some support. See Terence E. MacCarthy & Carol A. Brook, Anticipated Client Perjury: Truth or Dare Comes to Court, in Ethical Problems Facing the Criminal Defense Lawyer 155 (Rodney J. Uphoff ed., 1995).

62. See Formal Op. 92-2, supra note 58.

63. That standard was withdrawn in 1979 on the understanding that it would be supplanted by the Model Rules ABA Standards Relating to the Administration of Criminal Justice 4.94-4.95 (2d ed. 1980) (Editorial Note to deleted Standard 4-7.7).

64. See Monroe H. Freedman, But Only If You Know, in Ethical Problems, supra note 61, at 138-139; Developments, Client Perjury and the Duty of Candor, 6 Geo. J. Legal Ethics 1003, 1008-1009 (1993) (discussing appellate cases); 61 ABA/BNA Lawyers' Manual on Professional Conduct 1407 (1996).

65. See cases summarized in Norman Lefstein, Client Perjury in Criminal Cases: Still in Search of an Answer, 1 Geo. J. Legal Ethics 521, 538-541 (1988); Monroe H. Freedman, Client Confidences and Client Perjury: Some Unanswered Questions, 136 U. Pa. L. Rev. 1939 (1988) (discussing oral argument in Nix regarding the standard of knowledge). See State v. Berrysmith (Wash. App. Div. 1997), 13 ABA/BNA Manual on Professional Conduct 267 (1997) (where client's change in story led to lawyer's reasonable belief that client intended to commit perjury, lawyer entitled to withdraw before trial).

66. See Witherspoon v. United States, 557 A.2d 587 (D.C. App. 1989); United States v. Long, 857 F.2d 436 (8th Cir. 1988).

67. Mary Ann Glendon, Michael Wallace Gordon & Christopher Osakwe, Comparative Legal Traditions 189 (1985).

68. Harold J. Rothwax, Guilty 185 (1995).

69. Hazard, supra note 27, at 136.

70. Part 1 of this problem appears in Deborah Rhode & David Luban, Legal Ethics 358-359 (2d ed. 1995); part 2 of this problem is based on liti-

gation described in Nader & Smith, supra note 49, at 194-200. For similar recent cases, see id. and Tim Golden, Lawsuit Asserts Ford Knowingly Installed Defective Mechanism in Millions of Vehicles, N.Y. Times, Sept. 6, 1997, at A8.

71. Mark Dowie, Pinto Madness, Mother Jones, Sept./Oct. 1977, at 18, 31 (quoting Ford spokesperson who lamented the sentimentality of jurors who "see those charred remains and forget the evidence").

72. Alasdair MacIntyre, Utilitarianism and Cost-Benefit Analysis: An Essay on the Relevance of Moral Philosophy to Bureaucratic Theory, in Values in the Electric Power Industry 221 (Kenneth M. Sayre ed., 1977).

73. For example, installation of a $5 safety device would have resulted in a considerably lower rate of risk. See Dowie, supra note 71, at 28-29.

74. MacIntyre, supra note 72, at 226.

75. Carol Browner, quoted in Nader & Smith, supra note 49, at 361.

76. MacIntyre, supra note 72, at 222, 226.

77. Id. at 227-228.

78. Id. at 223-224.

79. During the period in question, the Pinto accounted for 1.9 percent of the automobile population and 1.9 percent of fatal accidents accompanied by fire, but 4.1 percent of all rear-end fire-related fatalities. Gary T. Schwartz, The Myth of the Ford Pinto Case, 43 Rutgers L. Rev. 966, 1032 (1992).

80. Dennis A. Gioia, Pinto Fires and Personal Ethics: A Script Analysis of Missed Opportunities, 11 J. Bus. Ethics 380, 382 (1992).

81. Schwartz, supra note 79, at 1032.

82. Rhode, supra note 9, at 624.

83. Iacocca, quoted in Dowie, supra note 71.

84. Rhode, supra note 9, at 624.

85. Senior executives quoted in Leonard Silk & David Vogel, Ethics and Profits 139 (1976).

86. See, e.g., Paul Brodeur, Outrageous Misconduct: The Asbestos Industry on Trial (1985); Susan Perry & Jim Dawson, Nightmare: Women and the Dalkon Shield 208 (1985) (discussing Dean et al. v. A.H. Robins Co., Inc., 101 F.R.D. 21 (Minn. 1984)).

87. Eugene Bardach & Robert Kagen, Going by the Book 111 (1982) (quoting Al Schaefer).

88. Christopher Stone, Where the Law Ends 85 (1975) (quoting Ted Jacobs).

89. See, e.g., Jon F. Merz & Baruch Fischoff, Informed Consent Does Not Mean Rational Consent, 11 J. Legal Med. 321, 343-344 (1990); Barrie R. Cassileth et al., Informed Consent, Why Are Its Goals Imperfectly Realized?, 302 New Eng. J. Med. 896 (1980).

90. Schwartz, supra note 79, at 1041-1043.

91. Gioia, supra note 80, at 384.

92. Schwartz, supra note 79, at 1055.

93. Sissela Bok, Secrets 213-227 (1982).

94. Myron P. Glazer & Penina M. Glazer, The Whistleblowers: Exposing Corruption in Government and Industry (1989); Alan F. Westin, Whistle Blowing: Loyalty and Dissent in the Corporation (1981).

95. Terry M. Dworkin & Elletta S. Callahan, Internal Whistleblowing Protecting the Interests of the Employee, the Organization, and Society, 29 Am. Bus. L.J. 267, 301 (1991); Marcia P. Miceli & Janet P. Near, The Relationship Among Beliefs, Organizational Position, and Whistle-Blowing Status: A Discriminant Analysis, 27 Acad. of Mgmt. J. 687 (1984).

96. See Linda K. Trevino & Bart Victor, Peer Reporting of Unethical Behavior: A Social Context Perspective, 35 Acad. of Mgmt. J. 38 (1992); see also K. Soeken & D. Soeken, A Survey of Whistleblowers: Their Stressors and Coping Strategies, in Senate Committee on Governmental Affairs, Hearings on S. 508 before Subcommittee on Federal Services, Post Office, and Civil Service, 100th Cong., 1st Sess., 20 & 31 July 1987, pp.537-548.

97. Office of Merit Systems Review and Studies, Merit Systems Protection Board, Blowing the Whistle in the Federal Government: A Comparative Analysis of 1980 and 1983 Survey Findings 6, 7 (1984); Office of Merit Systems Review and Studies, Merit Systems Protection Board, Whistleblowing and the Federal Employee 3 (1981); Marcia P. Miceli & Janet P. Near, The Incidence of Wrongdoing, Whistle-blowing, and Retaliation: Results of a Naturally Occurring Field Experiment, 2 Employee Responsibilities & Rts. J. 91, 100-102 (1989).

98. Glazer & Glazer, supra note 94, at 210 (citing study in which only about one-third of employees retained their position).

99. Dworkin & Callahan, supra note 95, at 301.

100. See, e.g., Ralph Estes, The Tyranny of the Bottom Line 103-131 (1996); Brodeur, supra note 86; Report of the Trustee Concerning Fraud and Other Misconduct in the Management of the Debtor, discussed in In Re OPM Leasing Services, Debtor, 61 B.R. 596, 597 (Bankr. S.D.N.Y. 1986); Perry & Dawson, supra note 86, at 175, 202-220.

101. Zacharias, supra note 8, at 362-363. The hypothetical comes from John M. Ferren, The Corporate Lawyer's Obligation to the Public Interest, 33 Bus. Law. 1253, 1253-1254 (1978).

102. Zacharias, supra note 8, at 362-363.

103. Gene G. James, In Defense of Whistleblowing, in Ethical Issues in Professional Life 315, 317 (Joan Callahan ed., 1988); Richard T. DeGeorge, Business Ethics 230 (2d ed. 1986).

104. Model Rules of Professional Conduct (Discussion Draft 1980 and Proposed Final Draft 1981), discussed in Steven Gillers, Model Rule 1.13 Gives the Wrong Answer to the Question of Corporate Counsel Disclosure, 1 Geo. J. Legal Ethics 289, 291-292 (1987).

105. 1974 Code of Ethics for Engineers of the Engineer's Council for Professional Development, quoted in John Kultgen, The Ideological Use of Professional Codes, in Ethical Issues in Professional Life, supra note 103, at 411, 415.

106. Dworkin & Callahan, supra note 95, at 269-275; Stephen M. Kohn & Michael D. Kohn, An Overview of Federal and State Whistleblowing Protections, 4 Antioch L.J. 104, 107-111 (1986).

107. Robert D. Boyle, A Review of Whistle Blower Protections and Suggestions for Change, 41 Labor Law J. 821, 825 (1990); Dworkin & Callahan, supra note 95, at 306-307.

108. For a holding similar to *Herbster*, see Willy v. Coastal Corp., 647 F. Supp. 116 (S.D. Tex. 1986) (a lawyer allegedly terminated for insisting that employer comply with environmental and securities laws is not entitled to sue for wrongful discharge).

109. Yosh Golden, In-House Lawyers Seeking Protection from Unfair Firing, Chi. Daily Law. Bull., Apr. 22, 1988, at 1, 14.

110. Consider, for example, Stephen Gillers' proposal that organizations establish Ethical Resolution Committees to which lawyers could appeal for assistance in preventing misconduct or retaliation against whistle-blowers. Gillers, Protecting Lawyers Who Just Say No, 5 Ga. St. U.L. Rev. 1, 25-26 (1988).

111. See Boyle, supra note 107, at 827.

112. Gioia, supra note 80, at 388; Robert W. Gordon, Corporate Law Practice as Public Calling, 49 Md. L. Rev. 255, 282 (1990).

Chapter VII

Conflicts of Interest

A. INTRODUCTION

Conflicts of interest have become increasingly significant in American legal practice, both because of their frequency and the stakes involved. Such conflicts arise in a wide variety of circumstances but generally involve five patterns:

1. Simultaneous representation: representing multiple clients in the same matter;
2. Successive representation: representing a current client against a former client in a related matter;
3. Positional conflicts: representing a client whose legal position could adversely affect another client in a factually unrelated matter;
4. Lawyer-client conflicts: representing clients in a context where their interests may conflict with the attorney's own financial, professional, or other interests (including those of close family members);
5. Vicarious conflicts of interest: representing clients in a matter where another member of the lawyer's firm has one of the preceding conflicts.

In recent years, conflicts problems have grown increasingly common. A rapid growth in the size of private firms and their organizational clients, together with the expansion of branch offices and corporate subsidiaries, has increased the possibility of attenuated or inadvertent conflicts. Similarly, a growing specialization in legal practice within and among firms has generated greater pressure for successive representation. The more technically complex the matter, the greater the value of prior expertise and the greater the likelihood that clients will seek an attorney who has had some previous involvement with their opponent. So too, an unqualified requirement of vicarious disqualification becomes harder to justify as firms become increasingly departmentalized, as lawyers' lateral movement among firms becomes more common, and as dual-career couples constitute a greater share of the profession.

A final factor contributing to the rise in conflicts disputes involves the nature of their remedy. Unlike other ethical rules, where enforcement occurs largely through bar disciplinary actions after the fact, violations of conflicts provisions can result in disqualification of the offending attorneys before or during representation. If a court finds that attorneys have misused confidential information, it may also prohibit them from turning over their work product to successor counsel. Such disqualification remedies are a powerful strategy for increasing an opponent's expense and delay. The strategic value of such remedies, together with their financial implications for the bar, may help explain why conflicts doctrine has been so extensively litigated. Given the costs to lawyers as well as to clients from stringent disqualification rules, alternatives to traditional approaches are beginning to emerge, such as the screening mechanisms discussed in Parts D and E. Consider the need for such alternatives in light of the problems discussed below.

B. SIMULTANEOUS REPRESENTATION OF MULTIPLE INTERESTS

1. Introduction

The term "lawyer for the situation" was coined by Louis Brandeis in the 1916 Senate hearings on his United States Supreme Court confirmation. Brandeis' appointment had aroused considerable opposition largely on the unstated ground that he was liberal, Jewish, and intellectual. The stated objections alleged improprieties in his professional conduct. For example, his opponents charged that he had represented conflicting interests by acting as counsel for a family business in a dispute among family members, by overseeing a business transaction for several parties, and by mediating differences between owners and creditors of a business in order to keep it afloat. Brandeis' opponents questioned whether he could ethically represent such potentially conflicting interests and whether he had adequately conveyed to the parties the nature of the possible conflicts. While acknowledging that his disclosures may not always have been sufficient, Brandeis defended his practice of acting as "lawyer for the situation." Eventually his opponents' charges subsided in the face of concessions by other reputable lawyers that they had engaged in similar conduct.[1]

Brandeis' view of the lawyer's role has inspired continuing debate. Critics have regarded his concept as incoherent; the lawyer, they note, is not retained by a "situation," and practitioners may have different views than the parties as to what a given situation requires.[2] Moreover, the allegations concerning Brandeis' conduct illustrate the risks attorneys assume when representing multiple clients. Their interests are seldom totally congruent, and subsequent disputes can always arise. Thus, as Geoffrey Hazard notes, the issue is not whether parties have divergent concerns, but how far they wish to pursue their separate interests.[3] That, in turn, often depends on legal advice, which threatens to make the conflict inquiry circular. The parties are asking the lawyer, and the lawyer is asking the parties, whether problems are likely to develop.

Yet multiple representation also carries obvious advantages. To avoid needless expense and acrimony, clients may be willing to assume some risk of conflict. For lawyers, such joint representation also has benefits; it may generate additional fees and good relationships.

In general, the price of these benefits is greater vulnerability for both clients and practitioners. If a conflict develops, clients can end up with additional costs and delays by hiring separate counsel and duplicating or contesting prior legal work. When such conflicts occur, attorneys run the risk of becoming scapegoats for problems not of their making. In contexts of multiple representation, lawyers are expected both to *be* fair and to *seem* fair to everyone. They are also expected to predict the likelihood of conflict at the outset. This is an inherently difficult task, since it will depend not only on the objective facts of a transaction but also on the subjective attitudes of parties, both of which can change over time. The lawyer for the situation, as Hazard puts it, is often "advocate, mediator, entrepreneur, and judge, all in one. He could be said to be playing God. Playing God is a tricky business."[4]

The primary ethical rules governing conflicts in simultaneous representation appear in Model Rule 1.7, DR 5-105, and California Rule 3-310(B). All of these provisions require clients' informed consent. In addition, the Code demands that lawyers decline representation if their professional judgment on behalf of another client will be "adversely affected," or if it is not "obvious" that they can "adequately represent the interests of each." The Model Rules prohibit representation that will be adverse to another client or "materially limited" by obligations to another client unless the lawyer reasonably believes that representation will not be "adversely affected." Although California rules do not, by their terms, impose comparable restrictions, California courts have declined to permit joint representation as long as clients provide informed consent, that poses an actual (as opposed to potential) conflict during litigation. A purported consent to such dual representation would, in the California Supreme Court's view, be "neither intelligent nor informed."[5]

In assessing whether clients are in a position to give informed consent, courts and commentators stress several factors:

1. the nature of client interests and services to be provided;
2. the timing, extent, and intelligibility of lawyers' disclosures;
3. clients' capacity to assess the nature of their interests and the consequences of joint representation; and
4. clients' ability to exercise uncoerced choice.

factors lawyers should look at:

So, for example, in matters involving large stakes, adversarial negotiations, unstable conditions, or coercive relationships, joint representation is far less likely to be appropriate than in matters involving smaller stakes, routine services, and cooperative, ongoing relationships. The middle ground between these extremes is where most problems arise.

Clients can also waive future conflicts of interest. However, as the ABA Ethics Committee emphasized in Formal Opinion 93-372 (Apr. 16, 1993), such a waiver must meet all the requirements of a waiver of contemporaneous conflicts. The waiver must also contemplate future conflicts with sufficient clarity so that the client's consent is truly informed. A prospective waiver that did not identify either the potential opposing party or at least the class of potentially conflicting clients would be unlikely to survive scrutiny. Id.

A related standard concerning simultaneous representation appears in Model Rule 2.2. This rule, governing the lawyer's role as an intermediary, is explored at length in Chapter VIII (Negotiation and Mediation) at pages 360–367. According to the Comment to Rule 2.2, its terms are intended to apply when lawyers seek "to establish or adjust a relationship between clients on an amicable and mutually advantageous basis; for example, in helping to organize a business . . . or arranging a property distribution in settlement of an estate or mediating a dispute between clients." As under Model Rule 1.7, the lawyer must obtain informed consent to the common representation. In addition, the lawyer must "reasonably believe that the matter can be resolved on terms compatible with the client's best interests; that each client will be able to make adequately informed decisions in the matter; that there is little risk of material prejudice to the interests of any of the clients if the contemplated resolution is unsuccessful; and that the representation can be undertaken impartially and without improper effect on other responsibilities the lawyer has to any of the clients." If at any point during the representation these conditions are no longer satisfied or if any client so requests, the lawyer must withdraw.

How this rule interacts with ethical rules governing joint representation or mediation is not entirely clear. According to the Comment, Rule 2.2 does "not apply to a lawyer acting as an arbiter or mediator between or among parties who are not clients." Thus, the rule *would not* govern counsel who are simply providing information to facilitate agreement but who do not represent the legal interests of the parties. By contrast, the rule *would* govern mediations where counsel purports to have a lawyer-client relationship with each participant.[6] However, the Comment does not explicitly distinguish between situations governed by Rule 2.2 and those governed by Rule 1.7, and commentators have taken different views. Common approaches for determining whether Rule 2.2 is applicable include focusing on clients' legal needs or objectives: that is, are they seeking a particular type of adjustment of their interests through common legal representation?[7] As a practical matter, it often will make little difference which rule is thought most applicable since their protections are quite similar; norms governing confidentiality and loyalty are comparable.[8]

All the provisions governing conflicts of interest reflect these two general concerns: loyalty and confidentiality. How would you interpret such concerns and codified norms on the facts of Problems 7A to 7E? What factors would be most relevant in determining whether multiple representation would be appropriate?

2.   Criminal Contexts

PROBLEM 7A

You are an attorney specializing in white-collar criminal defense. A large corporation retains your firm in connection with an antitrust investigation by the Department of Justice. At the request of senior management, you conduct an internal inquiry that reveals informal but plainly illegal market control agreements negotiated by a corporate division chief. At least one other subordinate employee had some peripheral role in the negotiations, and a third has knowledge of incriminating evidence. You believe that if all three employees decline to cooperate with government investigators, liability will be impossible to prove. What advice do you give these employees concerning what they disclose to you and whether they should retain separate counsel? Under what circumstances would you be willing to provide joint representation?

KENNETH MANN, DEFENDING WHITE COLLAR CRIME: A PORTRAIT OF ATTORNEYS AT WORK
169-174 (1985)

Where inculpatory information is held by more than one person, it is always to the advantage of the defense attorney for the main target to represent as many of the persons as possible. . . . Once a multiple representation situation is established, the attorney is faced with the problem of deciding how to represent each client without compromising the interest of the others. In one possible situation, each client holds inculpatory evidence against the other, and the government has just enough evidence to consider asking for an indictment against each, but not enough to dismiss the option of granting immunity to one client in order to get determinative evidence against the other. In this evidentiary context, it is difficult for an attorney to act without compromising one of the clients' interests. If he advises neither to make a deal because he believes that he may be able to win the case for both, he is sacrificing a certain success for one of them. And he clearly cannot advise one to make a deal against the other's interest. Some attorneys are able to obtain informed consent in this situation, after explaining the implications of the multiple representation. They then continue to represent all clients in a strategy based on total noncooperation. It is often the case that no client is willing to voluntarily become an informer against other clients. The stonewall defense continues until the government decides to force immunity on one of the clients, at which time the attorney will then have to divide representation. . . .

[In other circumstances, developments in the government's case give one client] an opportunity to make a good deal with the government, to the detriment of the other client or clients. When an attorney is enthusiastically trying to manage a stonewall defense he may fail to give proper attention to this opportunity and compromise the interest of the client who is the potential beneficiary. An attorney representing multiple clients must constantly reevaluate the relative position of his clients, making certain that each client is well informed of his individual opportunities. . . . [As one attorney put it],

> My own belief is that the more information you control as defense lawyer, the more effective you are, meaning that the only weapon you have as a defense lawyer in my view is control of information. You do not have much else. The prosecution has all the cards, they have the grand jury, they have in effect the presumption, they have all the investigative agencies, they have awesome powers. The only thing you have is sometimes you can stonewall an investigation. Now some people claim that that is obstructing justice. I don't, if you do it ethically and you do it out front, it's not. . . .

[Another attorney described his strategy for handling such situations:]

> In one matter I've got now, I'm representing two defendants whose interests may conflict down the line, but in the meantime, I've shown each why it would be better for both of them to stay with me. My evaluation of the situation is that it may be worse for both if one of them talks. In order to protect each from the other's potential sellout, I'm meeting with them separately and not divulging to one what the other has said. I constitute a Chinese Wall between them and their

communications with me. If X eventually makes a deal, he won't know what Y has told me, and vice versa. But these guys are up to their necks in trouble, and I don't expect that the dual representation will end. I want you to understand I'm ready to end the dual representation should it appear that one of their interests is being compromised. . . .

Still another situation in which multiple representation takes place is the case of a targeted employer or company who hires an attorney to represent a number of employees who will be questioned in connection with an investigation of the employer or company. The target of the investigation may have a different attorney, but what is significant here is that the target pays for the employees' attorney, discusses the case with the attorney, and then dispatches him to the employees. It is not uncommon that the employees are confronted with an attorney who is, on the one hand, supposed to represent them but who, on the other hand, acts in the role of a company superior. Early in an investigation an employee may not be able to distinguish his best interests from the company's or employer's interest. If the defense attorney does not have these interests separated clearly in his own mind, the source of his fee will determine his actions, rather than the interest of his client. A prosecutor told me of a witness who came to him without his "assigned attorney" (company-supplied) in order to give his version of the matter in question in an "atmosphere free of the intimidation" exercised by his attorney.

PROBLEM 7B

A local "Fraternal Order of Police" retains you to represent several officers in connection with a grand jury investigation. The officers have been subpoenaed to testify concerning bribes that local bar owners allegedly pay for police "protection." The Fraternal Order has a long-standing policy against cooperation by individual members in cases involving corruption or misconduct. Each officer is aware of the policy and has consented to joint representation. The local district attorney has now moved for your disqualification on the ground that you cannot adequately protect the interests of each client and that your attempt to do so will frustrate the grand jury investigation.

If you believe that some of the officers have taken bribes while others simply know of the practice, what is your response? How should a court rule?[9]

As noted earlier, game theorists use the term "prisoners' dilemma" to describe situations in which people find it individually rational to act against their collective best interest because they cannot be sure how another party will act.[10] Joint representation of codefendants in criminal cases often poses such dilemmas. If granted immunity from prosecution, each defendant could give enough incriminating evidence to convict the other; if both refuse to provide the information, it is unlikely that the government could convict either. The possible options appear in simplified form in the "payoff matrix" below. If both defendants refuse to "deal," that is, to cooperate with the government, they have a 75 percent chance of avoiding conviction. This strategy is the best collective outcome for both defendants. If both defendants offer to deal, the government can choose one to receive immunity from prosecution and thereby convict the other; each therefore has a 50 percent chance of avoiding punishment by making the offer. If, however, one defendant offers to deal and the other does not, he has a 100 percent chance of escaping conviction.

		B's Strategies	
		Deal	*No Deal*
	Deal	50/50	0/100
A's Strategies	*No Deal*	100/0	75/75

The paradoxical quality of the prisoners' dilemma lies in its perverse incentives. Even though the "No Deal" strategy is best for both defendants, rational defendants will reject it under conditions of uncertainty. Each party reasons as follows. If the other side deals, I should offer to deal as well since I then have a 50 percent chance of avoiding conviction. If the other party doesn't deal, I will have a 100 percent chance of avoiding conviction rather than 75 percent. No matter what the other side does, I would do best by dealing. Since each defendant reasons the same way, they both lose.

If the facts in Problem 7B present such a dilemma, how should an attorney respond? Would it be enough to follow the "Chinese Wall" procedure described above by one attorney in Kenneth Mann's study of white-collar criminal defense? Suppose some of the defendants could not afford counsel for a lengthy proceeding but would not meet the statutory definition of indigence? Would you have a different view if the case involved a drug conspiracy, and at least one of the defendants consented to a joint defense because he feared for his own or his family's safety?

The advantages of joint representation in criminal cases are obvious. Defendants can minimize costs by avoiding friction and duplication of efforts; obtain fuller information about their codefendants' strategies; and more effectively present a "stonewall" defense by preventing inconsistent statements or cooperation with the government by any single individual. The disadvantages of joint representation are equally apparent. A "lawyer for the situation" may find it difficult to prevent guilt by association, advise cooperation, or present evidence that would benefit one defendant but compromise the interests of another.

Should clients always have the right to make their own evaluation of these competing concerns? How can we ensure that defendants have received a relatively unbiased assessment of their options? How should we handle cases in which the lawyer presenting those options is receiving fees or other business from a third party, such as a corporate employer, a professional association, or an organized crime syndicate? Consider this issue in light of the discussion of attorney-client conflicts in Part F and Disciplinary Rules 5-101 to 5-107, Model Rules 1.7 and 1.8, and the following two Supreme Court decisions that bear on the general problem of multiple representation in criminal cases.

CUYLER v. SULLIVAN, 446 U.S. 335 (1980). In this case, Sullivan and two codefendants faced indictments for the first-degree murder of a labor official and his companion. Two lawyers, DiBona and Peruto, represented all three defendants. Although Sullivan had initially retained separate counsel, he subsequently accepted joint representation because he could not afford his own lawyer. Sullivan went to trial first, and neither he nor his attorneys raised any concerns about possible conflicts. The evidence against him was circumstantial, consisting of an eyewitness who saw the three defendants at the scene of the crime. The witness testified that shortly afterward he heard firecracker-like sounds, and that one of the other defendants told him to leave and say nothing. Sullivan's lawyers rested without presenting any affirmative defense. Sullivan was convicted while his codefendants were later acquitted at separate trials.

On appeal, DiBona and Peruto offered conflicting accounts of who had been Sullivan's lead counsel and why they had presented no affirmative case. DiBona claimed that he had encouraged Sullivan to testify, while Peruto recalled that he had not "want[ed] the defense to go on because I thought we would only be exposing the [defense] witnesses for the other two trials that were coming up." 446 U.S. at 338-339. After his direct appeals were unsuccessful, Sullivan filed a petition for habeas corpus, arguing that his attorneys' conflict of interest violated his sixth amendment right to effective assistance to counsel. The Court of Appeals for the Third Circuit agreed. On appeal by the state, the Supreme Court vacated that decision and remanded the case for further proceedings.

Writing for the majority, Justice Powell noted that the Court's prior decision in Holloway v. Arkansas, 435 U.S. 475 (1978), requires trial judges to investigate timely objections to multiple representation. However, "[u]nless the trial judge knows or reasonably should know that a particular conflict exists, the court need not initiate an inquiry." 446 U.S. at 347. In the majority's view, the facts of *Cuyler* made no inquiry necessary. Separate trials had reduced the possibility of conflicts, and the decision to present no affirmative defense was a reasonable tactical response to the weakness of the prosecution's circumstantial evidence. In order to establish a violation of the sixth amendment, a defendant who raised no objection at trial must demonstrate that an "actual" conflict of interest "adversely affected" his lawyer's performance. Id. at 348. If the defendant could make such a showing, no demonstration of prejudice or the likelihood of a different outcome would be necessary. The case was remanded to determine whether Sullivan could establish an adverse effect.

Two Justices concurred in only part of the *Cuyler* opinion. Justice Brennan maintained that since almost every case of joint representation presents possible conflicts, a trial court should always advise defendants about the potential hazards. Justice Marshall disagreed with the adverse effect standard on grounds that it was inconsistent with prior precedents, "unduly harsh," and "incurably speculative." In his view, a showing of an actual conflict should be sufficient to establish a sixth amendment violation.

WHEAT v. UNITED STATES, 486 U.S. 153 (1988).   In this litigation, the Court revisited some of the same issues involved in *Cuyler* in a different factual posture. Here, Wheat, Bravo, and Gomez-Barajas faced prosecution for participating in a drug conspiracy. Attorney Iredale represented Bravo, who pleaded guilty to reduced charges, and Gomez-Barajas, who was acquitted of some charges in one trial and then entered a guilty plea to lesser charges in order to avoid a second prosecution for other crimes. At the time of Wheat's trial, the court had not yet accepted Gomez-Barajas' guilty plea. Two days before his own trial, Wheat moved to substitute Iredale as his counsel or to add him as co-counsel. The government opposed the motion on grounds that Iredale would face a conflict of interest. If Gomez-Barajas had to go to trial, Wheat would be a witness against him. Bravo was also expected to testify against Wheat. In both instances, the government argued, Iredale would be unable to cross-examine the witnesses vigorously, since they were his own clients.

In response, Wheat emphasized his right to counsel of his choice and argued that the potential conflicts of interest were highly speculative. From his perspective, the government was attempting to manufacture conflicts in order to avoid crossing swords with Iredale, who had just proven his effectiveness. After losing his motion to substitute counsel, Wheat went to trial represented by his original lawyer and was convicted of conspiracy.

He appealed, and both the Ninth Circuit and Supreme Court affirmed. Justice Rehnquist, speaking for the majority, held that a

district court must be allowed substantial latitude in refusing waivers of conflicts of interest not only in those rare cases where an actual conflict may be demonstrated before trial, but in the more common cases where a potential for conflict exists which may or may not burgeon into an actual conflict as the trial progresses.

Id. at 163.

To hold otherwise would, in the majority's view, allow trial courts to be "'whipsawed' by assertions of error no matter which way they rule" on conflicts issues. Id. at 161. If the judge agrees to joint representation, defendants can later claim that they received ineffective assistance of counsel. On the other hand, if the court requires separate representation, defendants can argue that their choice of counsel was unconstitutionally infringed. Although acknowledging the possibility that the government might seek to "manufacture" a conflict to avoid facing a particularly able adversary, the majority concluded that trial judges would "undoubtedly [be] aware of this possibility" and could take it into consideration when ruling on joint representation. Id. at 168. On the facts in *Wheat*, the Court found that the district court had not abused its discretion in refusing to permit a substitution of counsel. Although defendants should have a presumption in favor of their choice of counsel, that presumption could be overcome by a showing of serious potential for conflict.

Justice Marshall, joined by Justice Brennan, dissented. In their view, a trial court's finding of potential conflict should not enjoy "special deference." Moreover, even under a deferential standard, the dissent concluded that reversal was in order. There was no reason to believe that Gomez-Barajas' plea agreement would be rejected or that Wheat would have been asked to testify against him if the case had gone to trial, since the defendants' only connection involved a conspiracy charge on which Gomez-Barajas had already been acquitted. Bravo's testimony presented no serious potential for conflict since he could not identify Wheat. Indeed, Wheat's counsel did not cross-examine Bravo and neither side referred to his testimony in closing arguments. Since all these developments were predictable at the time of the trial court's ruling on substitution of counsel, the dissent saw no "substantial risk of a serious conflict of interest."

Taken together, *Cuyler* and *Wheat* establish a less rigorous "potential conflict" standard at the beginning of trial in order to overcome a defendant's choice of counsel, and a higher standard requiring actual conflict and adverse effect after trial in order to sustain a defendant's claim of ineffective representation. Do you find the majority's rationale for these different approaches convincing? Should trial judges' concerns about being "whipsawed" have controlling importance? If, as the majority acknowledges in both cases, almost any circumstance of joint representation presents potential for conflict, should trial courts have to consider the issue regardless of whether a defendant raises it? In cases like *Wheat*, if a defendant has waived any conflict, how skeptical should courts be about a prosecutor's motive in seeking disqualification? How protective should they be of defense interests in stonewalling? In West Germany during the mid-1970s, lawyers for an anarchist group used stonewalling tactics to defend members charged with bombings and armed robberies. Such tactics were widely denounced as "procedural sabotage," and the West German parliament passed a statute prohibiting multiple representation of criminal defendants.[11] Would such a per se rule be constitutional in this country? Would it be desirable?

Conflicts of interest also occasionally arise for prosecutors in criminal cases. A well-publicized example involves Kenneth Starr, who retained his position as a lawyer and member of the management committee at Kirkland and Ellis while serving as independent counsel in the Clinton/Whitewater investigation. During his term as counsel, Starr and his firm represented clients in several cases involving potential conflicts of interest. For example, Starr represented a group of tobacco companies under investigation by the Justice Department while he exercised power over Department officials for his Whitewater work. His law firm also was sued by the Resolution Trust Corporation for aiding and abetting financial misconduct by a savings and loan client at the same time that Starr was investigating RTC officials concerning Whitewater. Although Starr claimed ignorance of the RTC suit until after his appointment, critics raised issues about the appearance of impropriety and questioned why he had not made a more thorough investigation of potential conflicts.

After such criticism surfaced, Starr hired Georgetown law professor Sam Dash as an ethics advisor. Dash counseled Starr that he did not need to recuse himself from the RTC investigation because he had played no role in representing the savings and loan client or settling the law firm litigation. Would you have given the same advice?[12]

See Chapter XIV, Criminal Law and Procedure
  • Conflicts of Interest: Effective Representation
      (pages 610–621)

3.   Civil Contexts

PROBLEM 7C

1. John and Mary are a middle-aged couple with adult children. Before beginning a trip abroad, they decide to draft parallel wills based on John's instructions. At a preliminary meeting with a trusts and estate lawyer, they explore various options. The lawyer then prepares two wills. Each leaves all property to the surviving spouse. If there is no surviving spouse, the property goes to the children in equal shares. At a second interview, the lawyer presents the wills to the husband and wife separately. John executes his. When the lawyer meets with Mary and asks if the document reflects her wishes, she responds that it does not. She

would change several provisions if she could do so without telling her husband. However, she is not willing to spark the confrontation that would occur if John were to learn that she wanted a different estate plan than what they had discussed.

What should the lawyer do? Is there any way he could (and should) have prevented this dilemma?[13]

2. The facts are the same as in part 1 except that John is substantially older than Mary, and both spouses have agreed to leave their separate estates to the children from each of their first marriages. John's separate property is quite substantial and Mary's is extremely modest. Both parties are willing to sign waivers of their rights as a surviving spouse. The lawyer has done some prior legal work for John and has reason to believe that the couple's relationship has been somewhat rocky. Should the lawyer respond any differently than in part 1? Would it matter if Mary had the more substantial assets?

3. The lawyer has represented John for many years on various business matters. In 1995, after meeting jointly with John and his wife Mary, the lawyer drafted wills with the mirror image provisions described in part 1. Three years later, John comes to the lawyer without his wife and indicates that he has reevaluated his priorities. He would now like to make a substantial bequest to a television evangelist. He also wants to leave his remaining assets in a trust for the benefit of his wife during her lifetime and then to the evangelist after her death. John does not wish to disclose these arrangements to Mary. How should the lawyer proceed?[14]

A threshold issue under part 3 of Problem 7C is whether the case involves simultaneous representation. As Teresa Collet notes,

> the passage of three years may not be sufficient to assume that the attorney-client relationship that existed in [1995] has terminated, particularly if the form of the representation suggested a continuing relationship with the "family" as a separate entity. Comment 3 to Rule 1.3 recognizes the difficulty in determining when representation has ceased, absent a formal letter of termination of representation. In the hypothetical case, [the lawyer] continues to actively represent [the] . . . husband, and it may be reasonable for [the wife] to believe that [the lawyer] continues to be "her" lawyer as well.[15]

If the wife is an ongoing client, then her interests appear sufficiently adverse enough to her husband's that the lawyer should decline to modify the will. Alternatively, if the lawyer makes the changes, he should disclose them to the wife so that she has an opportunity to modify her own estate plan. By contrast, if the wife is regarded as a former client, then under Model Rule 1.9 the lawyer should not make the proposed modifications absent the wife's consent, because the current and prior estate matters are "substantially related." See Part C, infra. Which characterization of the wife's status do you find most persuasive?

In general, a context such as estate planning presents four possible models of representation:

> separate simultaneous representation of each client by separate lawyers;
>
> joint representation of the clients by the same lawyer in which confidences are shared;
>
> separate simultaneous representation by the same lawyer in which confidences are not shared;
>
> representation of the family as a unit, in which the lawyer owes obligations to a relationship that are greater than those owed to any of the individual clients.[16]

Which model seems preferable in Problem 7C? Which is most consistent with bar ethical rules?

In analyzing part 1 of Problem 7C, Thomas Shaffer writes:

> [N]ow that the lawyer has talked to Mary alone, he is in an impossible situation: he cannot allow John to board the plane with the mistaken belief that Mary has agreed with what "they" decided. Nor, for the same reason, can he help Mary to make a different will. And, of course, he cannot allow Mary to execute a will that does not do what she wants it to do.[17]

Do you agree? What guidance do you find in the Code (DR 5-105) and Model Rules (Rules 1.7 and 2.2)? If Mary requests that their conversation remain confidential, must the lawyer withdraw? Suppose that withdrawal would trigger the confrontation Mary wishes to avoid? Could the lawyer have prevented this dilemma by raising the issue of potential conflicts at the outset and having each spouse sign a waiver letter? A typical letter would provide:

> During the course of our estate planning work, some conflicts may arise between you with respect to the ownership of property and its desired disposition upon your deaths. . . . In case such a [serious] conflict arises, each of you should be represented by independent counsel, whose actions would not be influenced by his or her representation of the other. Although such a conflict may arise, each of you has asked us to represent you in connection with the estate planning work described above. . . .
>
> You have each agreed that there will be complete and full disclosure and exchange of all information that we receive from either or both of you in the course of our representation of you. That agreement applies regardless of whether we obtain such information in conferences with both of you or in private conferences with only one of you. . . .
>
> If this letter accurately reflects your understanding and agreement, each of you should sign the enclosed copy in the space provided. . . .[18]

Suppose that Mary signed such a letter but that when the lawyer interviews her in private she indicates that the will is contrary to her wishes. However, she would rather sign it than have the lawyer withdraw and signal problems to John. Can the lawyer adequately represent both parties under those circumstances? Can he inform Mary of the possibility of later adding a codicil to her will without telling John?

In an ABA Journal forum from which part 1 of Problem 7C is adapted, a specialist in estate work maintained that the lawyer could appropriately counsel Mary how to make subsequent changes. As that commentator pointed out, "[i]f John wanted his will to be conditioned on certain dispositions by Mary, legal mechanisms existed (conditional bequests, or mutual wills, or a joint will) to serve those purposes." However, if, as the Problem suggests, the lawyer had not outlined these alternatives, can he ethically assist Mary in drafting a document inconsistent with her husband's expectations?[19]

Another commentator in that forum argued that the lawyer should not have met with Mary separately in order to execute the will. Rather, the lawyer should have probed for conflicts at the initial interview and if he had sensed any undue influence or lack of consensus, he then should have advised separate representation.[20] Do you agree that such an approach would have been sufficient?

According to commentators such as Shaffer, the conventional "separate representation" response to the conflict in Problem 7C builds on a morally impoverished vision of "radical individualism." From his perspective, a preferable role for a lawyer in estate planning would view the client as the family. Then,

> [i]f the family is well represented, it (that is, each person in it) will learn how to take Mary's purposes into account because Mary is in the family. . . . The estate planning issue, therefore, is whether this family is equal to the truth of what it is.[21]

Other commentators, including Thersea Collet and Russell Pearce, have similarly argued for treatment of the family as an entity.[22] Under this conception, the lawyer's responsibility might include facilitating a dialogue between the husband and the wife concerning the parties' true preferences. What is your view? Should the role of a "lawyer for the situation" be to help a family face up to the "truth" about its differences, whatever their source?

How helpful is the entity concept in cases like Problem 7C? According to Geoffrey Hazard, lawyers can represent an entity in commercial contexts because legal and ethical rules governing such representation supply a way of dealing with internal conflicts. For example, Model Rule 1.13 instructs a lawyer to defer to the highest governing authority, usually the board of directors. By contrast, husbands and wives are "legally autonomous persons" and families lack any overarching structure for resolving conflicts of interest between members.[23] Is there an answer to that criticism?

Should the lawyer's response to Problem 7C be affected by the client's preferred disposition? Would it matter on the facts of Part 1 whether Mary wanted to

a. leave a substantial bequest to their son's former wife, whom John dislikes;

b. leave her separate property to a woman with whom she once had an affair, a fact unknown to John;

c. disinherit her daughter, who had married someone of a different race and religion despite her mother's objection?

Would it matter in Part 2 whether the husband's reason for not providing for the surviving spouse was that he assumed (with good reason) that she planned to remarry soon after his death? Or would it be relevant in Part 3 whether John wanted to leave his bequest to a homeless shelter or to a younger woman? See Chapter IV (Advocacy) at pages 139–157.

Some therapists who work with couples and encounter such confidential information have proposed an approach of "accountability with discretion." Under this framework, maintaining confidentiality is justifiable if it does not interfere with the therapist's ability to serve the family. If it does interfere, the therapist should strongly urge the client to make disclosures. If the client refuses, the therapist should terminate the relationship but not force disclosure because under such circumstances the "resources for minimizing destructive consequences" are unlikely to be adequate. The therapist "can encourage (literally, give courage to) family members to face secrets; (s)he cannot do it for them."[24]

Would such an approach be helpful to lawyers? Consider the dilemma facing Edward Bennett Williams when representing Washington Post owner Philip Graham. While suffering from a terminal illness, Graham instructed Williams that he wanted to redraft his will to disinherit his wife of many years. He gave no reason apart from general bitterness concerning their current relationship. Bennett delayed in the hope that Graham would reconsider. Graham died before the will was changed. His wife inherited the Post and gave its legal business to Williams. Is this a case where virtue is not its only reward, or did Williams behave inappropriately? [25]

PROBLEM 7D

1. An associate in your Los Angeles firm represents an employee pro bono in a wrongful discharge case against a large manufacturer. After she files a complaint, it becomes obvious that the employee's claim is not strong on the merits, but that it may produce a modest settlement. While discovery in the case is proceeding, a group of manufacturers, including the defendant employer, approaches your firm's New York office about the possibility of representation in a challenge to Occupational Health and Safety regulations. Can your New York office take the case? If the employee refuses to settle her claim, can the firm withdraw from the pro bono matter? Can both sides consent to the representation?

2. Suppose the sequence of events had been reversed and the manufacturers' group had approached the firm first. If it had discussed any labor problems in context of the OSHA litigation and later decided not to hire the firm, would acceptance of the pro bono matter be permissible?

The American Law Institute's proposed Restatement of the Law Governing Lawyers, §213, provides that "[i]f a lawyer is approached by a prospective client seeking representation in a litigated matter adverse to an existing client, the lawyer may not prematurely withdraw from representing the current client." Should this proposed rule govern Problem 7D? Would the Code or Model Rules governing withdrawal (DR 2-110 and Rule 1.16) justify abandoning the nonprofitable case? Should it matter that the conflict arose in branch offices? Consider one of the most influential precedents on point, Westinghouse v. Kerr McGee.

WESTINGHOUSE ELECTRIC CO. v. KERR MCGEE, 580 F.2d 1311 (7th Cir. 1978).   In this litigation, the Chicago branch of Kirkland and Ellis represented Westinghouse in an antitrust action against its uranium suppliers. At the same time, Kirkland's Washington office represented the American Petroleum Institute (API) in lobbying efforts against proposed antitrust legislation. In the course of its efforts for API, Kirkland's Washington office confidentially surveyed executives of 59 oil companies about aspects of their operations, including the uranium business; three of these companies were defendants in Westinghouse's antitrust suit.

Kirkland's Washington office released its report for API on the same day that Kirkland's Chicago office filed the antitrust action. The API report contended that the energy industry, including the uranium industry, was highly competitive, while the antitrust complaint charged that uranium suppliers had engaged in a massive price-fixing conspiracy. After the trial court denied a motion by the suppliers to disqualify Kirkland, the court of appeals reversed. In the appellate court's view, Kirkland's Washington office had a fiduciary relationship with API members because of the nature of its work and the confidential information it had acquired. Since that information was related to the antitrust litigation, disqualification was appropriate. Although Kirkland had attempted to construct a "Chinese Wall" to screen attorneys in the two offices, it acknowledged that a memo prepared in the antitrust case had been mailed to API members. While the trial court had been sympathetic to large firms' difficulties in avoiding representation of overlapping interests, the appellate court was skeptical about the effectiveness of screening and unwilling to create separate disqualification rules based on the size of firms. Do you find that reasoning persuasive?

Screening arose in large accounting firms in order to prevent damaging leaks of confidential information. The practice gradually spread to law firms, first in contexts involving former government attorneys and then in certain other settings. Screening generally involves (1) physically isolating the screened lawyers from relevant records; (2) forbidding all contact between groups of lawyers subject to screening; (3) preventing screened lawyers from receiving any financial benefit from the cases from which they are screened, including bonuses or augmented partnership shares; (4) requiring affidavits concerning compliance with screening provisions; and (5) providing notice to all affected clients. In some instances, courts have also required posting of a bond to ensure compliance.

Part C explores the risks and benefits of screening as a general response to conflicts of interest. In evaluating those factors, consider how you would have handled *Westinghouse* and Problem 7D. Is there a legitimate concern about divided allegiance and the "appearance of impropriety" if a law firm has "one foot in [two adversarial] camp[s]"?[26] Alternatively, should the focus be on potential misuse of confidential information and the adequacy of screening? How effectively can screening procedures be enforced?

Similar conflicts arise in contexts involving prospective clients. Individuals seeking representation often need to provide some confidential information in order to assess the potential lawyer's capacity to provide cost-effective services. Lawyers need enough information to address prospective clients' concerns as well as to determine whether representation would pose conflicts with existing clients. The difficulty comes in striking a balance that will protect prospective clients' legitimate expectations of confidentiality while preventing unnecessary disqualification of lawyers if they are not hired. That difficulty has assumed increased importance as greater numbers of clients comparison shop for representation, hold "beauty contests" among prospective counsel, and in some instances engage in "taint shopping" — the practice of pretending to seek legal assistance in order to disqualify the lawyer from future adverse representation.

To accommodate all parties' concerns, Geoffrey Hazard recommends that lawyers explicitly discuss with prospective clients the ground rules covering their preliminary conversations. In the absence of an alternative arrangement, it may be reasonable to assume that if representation does not follow, the lawyer will keep confidential information from colleagues, will personally refrain from subsequent adverse representation, and will be screened from any such representation by his firm.[27] Would such considerations adequately address the facts in Problem 7D?

See Chapter XVII, Property
    • Multiple Representation
      (pages 745–752)

See also Chapter XVI, Family Law

See also Chapter XIX, Torts

C. SUCCESSIVE REPRESENTATION OF CONFLICTING INTERESTS

PROBLEM 7E

Under what standards would you analyze the following issues? What further information would you need to decide if representation is appropriate?

1. Luis Gomez is a partner in Kaplan and Kaplan. Several years ago, one of his partners, Barbara Lee, represented First Corporation in a suit against Second, Inc. Third Corporation now approaches Gomez seeking his help in suing First. May he take the case?

2. Gomez leaves Kaplan and joins Brown and Brown. May Brown and Brown represent Third? May Gomez participate in that representation?

3. After Gomez leaves Kaplan and Kaplan, the firm is asked to sue Fourth, Inc. While Gomez had been at the firm, he had represented Fourth in a dispute with the government on a related issue. May Kaplan and Kaplan take the case?

As Part B indicated, both the Code and Model Rules prohibit representation that would impair obligations to other, existing clients, even if the substance of the matters is unrelated. This prohibition rests on concerns of loyalty and confidentiality. For the most part, obligations of loyalty end when representation ends. Any alternative rule would quickly prove unworkable. If lawyers could not accept matters adverse to any former client, their ability to accept new cases in certain geographic areas or substantive specialties would dramatically decline as their careers progressed. Lawyers would become permanently identified with particular positions and the independence of the profession would be seriously compromised.

However, obligations of confidentiality stand on different footing. These persist after representation ends. In order to prevent misuse of confidential information, courts have generally banned representation that is adverse to a former client if the two matters are "substantially related." Although the Code does not directly refer to the problem of former client conflicts, EC 4-5 notes that confidentiality requirements continue after the client relationship terminates. Courts have also interpreted general conflicts provisions to reach the same result as Model Rule 1.9. That rule prohibits lawyers from subsequently representing a client on a matter that is the same or substantially related to a former client's representation if the second client does not consent and its interests are materially adverse to the former client. Rule 1.9 further prohibits such representation where a lawyer's former firm represented a client on a substantially related matter, and the lawyer acquired confidential information relevant to the matter. A final section of the rule bars use of former client confidences to the disadvantage of that client in any matter, unless the information has become generally known.

The rationale for the "substantial relation" test is that former clients should be entitled to a presumption that their lawyer acquired confidential information that is subject to misuse in matters related to the initial representation. If clients were required to prove misuse in order to obtain disqualification, they would lose confidentiality in the process of seeking its protection.[28] Although that rationale for the substantial relationship test is widely accepted, courts and commentators have divided over what exactly needs to be "related," what constitutes confidential information, and whether the presumption of shared confidences should ever be rebuttable.

In determining if matters are related, courts in some jurisdictions focus on whether the issues are legally related, that is, whether they involve a similar cause of action. In other jurisdictions, the test is whether the matters involve similar factual issues: would the lawyer have acquired information about the former client that would be useful in later cases?[29] In determining what qualifies as confidential information, some judges protect only material falling within the attorney-client privilege; other judges look to whether the information might give the attorney greater insight into the matters at issue. Such information might include competitive strategies, long-term objectives, and financial priorities. Consider which tests make most sense on the facts of Problems 7E and 7F.

Where matters are substantially related, courts have differed about whether the presumption of shared confidences is rebuttable. Some courts have refused to allow attempts to rebut the presumption while other judges have distinguished between cases where lawyers change employment and cases where law firms change sides.[30] If an attorney joins a new firm that wants to take a case substantially related to one handled by the lawyer's former firm, some judges will follow the vicarious disqualification provision in Model Rule 1.10(b): they will allow the firm to rebut the presumption of shared confidences. Relevant factors will include the size of the firm, the lawyer's position and specialty within it, and the nature of screening mechanisms. However, where a firm itself seeks to switch sides and to provide representation on a matter substantially related to that of a former client, these courts view the presumption as irrebuttable and will order disqualification. Their reasoning generally tracks the analysis of Judge Posner in Analytica v. N.P.D. Research, 708 F.2d 1263 (7th Cir. 1983):

> The "substantial relationship" test has its problems, but conducting a factual inquiry in every case into whether confidences had actually been revealed would not be a satisfactory alternative, particularly in a case such as this where the issue is not just whether they have been revealed but also whether they will be revealed during a pending litigation. Apart from the difficulty of taking evidence on the question without compromising the confidences themselves, the only witnesses would be the very lawyers whose firm was sought to be disqualified (unlike a case where the issue is what confidences a lawyer received while at a former law firm), and their interest not only in retaining a client but in denying a serious breach of professional ethics might outweigh any felt obligation to "come clean." While "appearance of impropriety" as a principle of professional ethics invites and maybe has undergone uncritical expansion because of its vague and open-ended character, in this case it has meaning and weight. For a law firm to represent one client today, and the client's adversary tomorrow in a closely related matter, creates an unsavory appearance of conflict of interest that is difficult to dispel in the eyes of the lay public, or for that matter the bench and bar.

Id. at 1269.

By contrast, other courts and commentators have criticized the appearance of impropriety standard as speculative and conclusory, and the distinction between side-switching by lawyers and law firms as unpersuasive. As critics note, such approaches can lead to ambiguities and anomalies in certain settings, such as when a firm splits in two and each half merges with a new firm. Should such cases be viewed as lawyers joining new partnerships, or as one part of the original partnership assuming new matters? Partly for these reasons, the Model Rules do not distinguish between firms that switch sides (Model Rule 1.10(b)) and lawyers who switch firms (Model Rule 1.9(b)); both permit the presumption of shared confidences to be rebutted.

Which approach to presumptions do you favor? Consider that issue on the facts of Problem 7E.

D.   VICARIOUS DISQUALIFICATION

PROBLEM 7F

1. You are the partner in charge of conflicts issues at a small Illinois law firm. One of your long-standing bank clients asks you for assistance in a dispute with the county involving sewer access to developments on

bank property. At issue in the litigation is a sewage disposal agreement between the county and a local village.

One of the three associates in your firm formerly served as an assistant state's attorney for the county. Although the sewage agreement had been signed before he joined the government, he had access to documents and discussions about the validity of similar agreements. At one point, he instructed a summer law clerk to begin work on an opinion letter construing the scope of such agreements. The letter was never completed and the lawyer left soon after. The clerk's wife has just joined the firm as one of its four partners

Under what, if any, circumstances may the associate or the firm represent the bank in this dispute?[31]

2. You are a former SEC regional administrator who headed one of the Commission's California offices. Under your leadership, the office brought actions against a number of individuals alleging fraudulent manipulation of the stock of ABC Financial Corporation. Although you signed the complaint, you did not participate in the litigation.

You subsequently joined a Wall Street firm that is suing several of the same defendants as well as other corporations and individuals for violating various securities and racketeering laws. The suit alleges an elaborate scheme for manipulating the securities of several companies, including one that recently merged with ABC. Under what, if any, circumstances can you participate in this litigation? Must the SEC consent to your involvement? Should it?

3. An associate in your firm served for several years in the Justice Department's antitrust division. One of her responsibilities was to draft a general position paper concerning concentrated ownership in photo processing services. In the course of her work, she reviewed a broad range of literature, interviewed several industry executives, and consulted with a number of government experts. The office has now filed suit against several companies, one of which seeks to retain your firm. Can your firm accept the case? Can the associate participate? What, if any, discussions with friends in the agency would be appropriate?[32]

Both the Code and Model Rules generally provide that when lawyers are prohibited by conflict of interest rules from representing a client, no other member of their firm may undertake such representation absent client consent (Rule 1.10 and DR 5-105(D)). However, the Model Rules do not bar a firm from taking a case adverse to the interests of a client represented by a lawyer formerly associated with the firm unless (1) the matter is substantially related to one in which the formerly associated lawyer represented the client, and (2) a member of the firm has relevant confidential information.

Both the Code and Model Rules also include special provisions for successive government and private employment. These rules derive in part from ABA Ethics Committee Formal Opinion 342 (1975). That opinion holds that a government agency can waive the disqualification of former employees who are screened from further participation in a matter in which they participated personally and substantially while in public service. This holding is now codified in Model Rule 1.11 and reflects the prevailing interpretation of DR 9-101(B). See Armstrong v. McAlpin, 625 F.2d 433 (2d Cir. 1980) (en banc), vacated on other grounds, 449 U.S. 1106 (1981). Model Rule 1.11 also prohibits former government attorneys who acquired information about a person while in public office from representing a private client in a manner adverse to that individual; the former employee's firm, however, may undertake the representation if it provides adequate screening.

Federal officials, including lawyers, are governed by a detailed set of regulations in the Ethics in Government Act, 18 U.S.C. §207, and virtually every state has conflicts rules for its own employees. For senior federal employees, these screening regulations include a one-year ban on all efforts to influence their former agencies on pending matters and a two-year ban on appearing before the government on a matter in which they personally and substantially participated during government employment. For other employees, the Act includes a two-year prohibition on private sector work concerning matters under their official responsibility during government service, and a permanent prohibition on private sector activity on matters in which they participated personally and substantially during government service.

These legislative and ethical requirements have generated considerable dispute. Courts and commentators have advanced several justifications for relaxing conflicts rules that apply to government attorneys. Most important, the public sector would find it extremely difficult to recruit talented lawyers if they became unmarketable upon leaving government service. Overly broad conflicts rules would also prevent a valuable exchange of perspectives and expertise between public and private sectors. Private sector attorneys with prior government service can help promote compliance with regulatory norms. And government attorneys who have had, or expect to have, private employment can more easily retain independence than a career civil servant: they can be more open to fresh ideas, more willing to challenge official policy, and less hostage to a supervisor's recommendations.[33]

Yet these advantages have corresponding costs. Critics of the "revolving door" between public and private sectors argue that it promotes high turnover and low morale in government service. Civil service employees often leave before the taxpayer reaps the benefit of expertise acquired at public expense. Attorneys who see government as a temporary way-station also face constant temptations to handle assignments so as to maximize future career options. Even when lawyers resist such pressure, the appearance of government employees switching sides can erode public confidence. If agency lawyers look uncommitted and opportunistic, justice seems for sale to the highest bidder.

Moreover, from critics' perspective, the practical problems in screening are insurmountable. Violations are extremely difficult to detect and it is generally impossible to prevent screened attorneys from indirectly sharing in some financial rewards (if only the contribution to overhead expenses that all paid cases make). Government consent provisions carry obvious potential for bias; current employees may be predisposed toward policies that will benefit them after their government service. Thus, as Geoffrey Hazard once claimed, screening bears some resemblance to the colonial practice of bundling. During the seventeenth and eighteenth centuries, when heat and beds were limited and individuals in a courting relationship lived a considerable distance from each other, they were often allowed to sleep together with a bundling board between them. In Hazard's view, screening, like bundling, has neither the credibility of real protection nor the dignity of real self-control.[34] No one who doubts the integrity of former government employees will be reassured by the practice; no one who has confidence in their honesty will think it necessary. In these critics' view, the answer to the government's recruiting problems is not to validate the revolving door but to upgrade the pay, status, and advancement opportunities of long-term public servants.

These disputes about the revolving door reflect broader public ambivalence about the roles both of government attorneys and government institutions. On the one hand, Americans want a professional civil service with attorneys who are committed to government objectives and who will stay long enough to make use of their expertise. On the other hand, Americans distrust bureaucracies that may become too stable and too resistant to self-criticism, challenge, and change. In effect, we demand a public sector that is accessible, but not hostage to private sector concerns. If these objectives are not always reconcilable, which should have priority? Do current rules on screening reflect a workable accommodation of the competing interests at issue? How would you interpret those rules on the facts of Problem 7F?

If screening can work in contexts of former government attorneys, should it extend equally to all lawyers? According to one trial court, any alternative rule "would logically require a belief that privately employed attorneys are . . . less trustworthy or more voluble than their ex-Government counterparts." Nemours Foundation v. Gilbane, 632 F. Supp. 418 (Del. 1986). Do you agree? Alternatively, does a "double standard" for public and private sector employees suggest that we are willing to tolerate greater risks of inadequate screening in contexts where other crucial values are at issue?

The current draft of The American Law Institute's Restatement of the Law Governing Law (§204) would permit screening among any affiliated lawyers (not just former government employees) if all affected clients have notice and if any confidential information communicated by the former client is "unlikely to be significant" in the current case. Is this an appropriate accommodation of competing interests? Does it place the former client in the difficult position of having to reveal confidences in order to protect them through a disqualification motion?

Is disqualification always the best remedy? Consider Bruce Green's claim that courts should make two inquiries in disqualification hearings. The first should be whether the possibility of misuse of confidences or other tangible harms to the party seeking disqualification outweighs the cost to the opponent. The second inquiry should focus on whether the lawyer violated conflicts rules in accepting representation and, if so, what economic sanctions would be appropriate. Green argues that in some cases, personal sanctions against attorneys would be a fairer and more cost-effective way of enforcing conflicts rules than disqualification. Do you agree?[35]

How should conflicts rules address lawyers in personal relationships? The difficulties for married lawyers reflected in Problem 7F(1) have increased substantially over the last two decades. Women currently account for approximately 40 percent of new entrants to the profession and half of female practitioners are married to other attorneys. Substantial numbers of lawyers also have other intimate relationships with lawyers, clients, or potential clients.[36]

Until the 1980s, ethical codes did not explicitly address the issue of such conflicts. However, early opinions from courts and bar committees generally held that husbands and wives should not represent opposing interests and that any disqualification should be imputed to an entire firm. A more permissive approach emerged in the ABA Ethics Committee Formal Opinion 340 (1975) and in the Model Rules of Professional Conduct. Opinion 340 interpreted the Code's general conflicts provisions to require that lawyers decline employment where their personal or financial interests might reasonably affect judgment and loyalty; disqualification on this basis should then apply vicariously to colleagues. Model Rule 1.8 provides that a "lawyer related to another lawyer as parent, child, sibling or spouse shall not represent a client in a representation directly adverse to a person who the lawyer knows is represented by the other lawyer except upon consent." However, the Comment to Rule 1.8 indicates that the disqualification is "personal and is not imputed to members of firms with whom the lawyers are associated."

These provisions, like the rules concerning former government attorneys, reflect competing concerns. An unduly restrictive approach risks turning one lawyer, frequently a younger, lower-earning woman, into a "Typhoid Mary."[37] Not only would such a rule be unfair to attorneys and potential clients, it would compromise the profession's commitments to equal opportunity. Yet to ignore both the possibility and the appearance of bias where lawyers are intimately related would also disserve public and professional interests.[38]

Does Model Rule 1.8 strike a reasonable balance? How would it apply on the facts of Problem 7F? Should it be extended to cover other intimate relationships? Why do you suppose the rule does not require screening? Under what, if any, circumstances would Chinese Walls be appropriate?

E. POSITIONAL CONFLICTS

PROBLEM 7G

1. Your firm is a prominent specialist in mergers and acquisitions. Last year, you began drafting "poison pill" by-law provisions for several of your corporate clients that would make them unattractive targets in hostile takeover efforts. You are currently defending one of those arrangements in a Delaware trial court. Another company has now asked your assistance in challenging the legality of a similar poison pill. Under what, if any, circumstances, should you accept the matter?[39]

2. You are a partner in a Washington, D.C., firm that has represented a mid-sized corporation in lobbying on various regulatory matters over the past decade. Another member of your firm now wishes to represent a large coalition that is on the opposite side of some of those matters. When you raise the issue with the corporation's general counsel, she is outraged. In her view, if you accept the coalition as a client, you will be exploiting expertise acquired at her company's expense, and will be undermining your future credibility with various government officials and legislators.

How do you respond? Does it matter whether the coalition is seeking assistance on issues unrelated to your lobbying efforts?

3. You are a public defender in the District of Columbia representing a client charged with rape. Your defense is one of mistaken identification and the district attorney is planning to introduce evidence of DNA-typing that would link the defendant's blood with blood and fluid found on the scene. Under existing rules, the evidence is admissible if it is accepted as reliable within the scientific community. You and several colleagues are preparing to launch a major challenge to the reliability of such evidence. If successful, your effort would prevent use of such evidence in any criminal trial in the District. While you expect that the vast majority of your office's clients would be helped by this ruling, some innocent defendants would lose the benefits of exculpating evidence. How should your office handle the potential conflict? If another of your colleagues has a client who might be exonerated by DNA sampling, could the defendant claim ineffective assistance of counsel if the lawyer did not seek a blood test?[40]

4. Consider the pro bono positional conflicts raised in Problem 4B(4) at pages 154–156. Would your decision on firm policy depend on why other clients or lawyers objected to a particular case, whether important principles were involved, or whether the client could readily find other counsel?

Problem 7G presents examples of "positional conflicts" (also sometimes labeled "ideological conflicts" or "issues conflicts"). They arise whenever lawyers take a position on behalf of one client that might adversely affect another client who has no direct involvement in the matter.

Although neither the Code nor the Model Rules prohibit most positional conflicts, both include provisions that could encompass some of these matters. If any representation would involve misuse of client confidences, it falls under the prohibitions of Canon 4 of the Code and Rule 1.6 of the Model Rules. In addition, if accepting representation would compromise a lawyer's "independent professional judgment," it is impermissible under DR 5-105, while if it would "adversely affect" the lawyer-client relationship, it is impermissible under Model Rule 1.7. The Comment to that Rule explains:

> A lawyer may represent parties having antagonistic positions on a legal question that has arisen in different cases, unless representation of either client would be adversely affected. Thus, it is ordinarily not improper to assert such positions in cases pending in different trial courts, but it may be improper to do so in cases pending at the same time in an appellate court.

Do these distinctions make sense? Can a lawyer arguing contradictory legal positions before the same trial judge or administrative agency necessarily assume that both arguments will be credible? What if victory for one client will establish a precedent that could adversely affect another client's case in a different jurisdiction?

One story, perhaps apocryphal, about Abraham Lincoln's litigation practice reports that he was in trial court one morning arguing for a particular interpretation of a statute. The judge ruled against him. That afternoon, Lincoln invoked the recent ruling in support of a different client whose position was directly contrary to that of the first client. "But," the trial court protested, "didn't you argue just the opposite this morning?" "Yes," replied Lincoln, "and Your Honor was quite correct to reject my claim."

If you were one of Lincoln's clients, how would you have felt about the adequacy of your legal assistance? How should an "adverse effect" on representation be measured and from whose perspective? Under conventional definitions, loyalty involves the "thoroughgoing devotion of a person to a cause."[41] Does this suggest that it is the quality of the lawyer's performance, rather than the client's evaluation of that performance, that is crucial? Or are other dimensions of the lawyer-client relationship, such as trust and empathy, worth protecting? What about public perceptions of disloyalty?

The ABA Ethics Committee has taken a different position than the Model Rules Comment on positional conflicts. ABA Formal Opinion 93-377 (1993) suggests that a lawyer should not argue both sides of a legal issue in the same jurisdiction where "there is a substantial risk that the lawyer's advocacy on behalf of one client will create a legal precedent which is likely to materially undercut the legal position being urged on behalf of the other client." In other contexts, when determining whether representation of either client will be materially limited by the dual representation, the lawyer should consider the following three factors: (1) whether the issue on which the lawyer is taking conflicting positions is likely to affect the outcome of at least one case; (2) whether the decision in one case will have precedential force in the determination of the other case; (3) whether the lawyer's choice of litigation strategy might be affected by the dual representation to the detriment of either client through de-emphasizing or reconciling certain arguments. If there is a significant potential for the lawyer's representation to be materially limited, the lawyer should proceed with both cases only after in-formed consent by each client. Do you agree with this approach? How would it affect your decision on the facts of Problem 7G?

What would be the implications of broader prohibitions on positional conflicts? One concern is the effect of such restrictions on pro bono or law reform activity. Thus, EC 8-1 of the Code maintains that lawyers "should participate in proposing and supporting legisla-tion and programs to improve the system, without regard to the general interests or desires of clients or former clients." EC 7-17 in-sists that a lawyer "may take positions on public issues and espouse legal reforms he favors without regard to the individual views of any client." Model Rule 6.4 similarly encourages attorneys' involvement with law reform activities despite their effect on client interests, and Rule 6.3 authorizes lawyers' participation as directors or officers of legal services organizations despite those organizations' assistance to persons with interests adverse to lawyers' own clients.

As a practical matter, however, many attorneys refuse to risk positional conflicts that carry significant financial costs. The most direct effect of such refusals is to restrict pro bono activities if they conflict with paying matters. Many lawyers take pro bono work for economic reasons as a means to attract new business or accommo-date existing clients.[42] Most practitioners also appear "careful not to step on the toes of their client's important interests"; the longer the relationship, the more likely attorneys become to "develop a sense of loyalty and identification with their clients."[43] Such concerns about positional conflicts help explain why many lawyers work only "one side of the street" in their areas of specialty. Moreover, as attorneys often note, "there is an infinite pro bono need," so practitioners can satisfy their public service obligations without compromising client interests.[44]

From a societal perspective, this is not an entirely bad result, considering the likely alternative. Available research suggests that where attorneys accept clients with modest claims that run counter to the interests of larger continuing clients, the smaller matter often may receive less than zealous representation.[45] However, particu-larly in small towns or rural areas, pro bono coordinators report that positional conflicts "dramatically impact" their ability to place certain cases. And these coordinators object to attorney's "dressing up commercial heartburn as an ethical conflict."[46]

Given the full range of economic and ethical interests at issue, how should the bar respond to positional conflicts? Should lawyers be "proud to acknowledge that as detached professionals they are capable of asserting either side" of an issue without adversely affecting their clients?[47] Alternatively, should the bar's professional rules and practices take more explicit account of the costs of such detachment? Could lawyers do more, individually or collectively, to address the restrictions on access that result from positional conflicts? For example, should attorneys be required, or more strongly encouraged, to provide financial contributions to pro bono projects that do not link contributors to any single matter?

F.   LAWYER-CLIENT CONFLICTS OF INTEREST

1.   The Range of Potential Conflicts

Conflicts of interests arise to some extent in almost any attorney-client relationship. Lawyers generally have some financial, ideological, collegial, or other concerns that are not fully coextensive with those of their clients. Obvious examples include:

The Economic Structure of Practice. Depending on the alternative uses for their time, lawyers charging on an hourly basis may have incentives to spend more billable effort on a given matter than the client would prefer or than an objective observer would think necessary. See, for example, the discussion of "meter running" and discovery abuse in Chapter V (The Adversary System) at pages 185–195. Lawyers who are receiving fixed fees or salaries may have the opposite incentives. See, for example, the discussion in Chapter XIV (Criminal Law and Procedure) of the economic structure of criminal defense practice, which encourages quick plea bargains (pages 610–617). Depending on how much time they have already invested or will need to invest in a particular case, attorneys charging contingent fees also may have different incentives to settle than their clients. See the materials on shareholder derivative litigation in Chapter XIII (Corporate Law) at pages 550–560 and personal injury claims in Chapter XIX (Torts). Lawyers and clients who enter into business relationships (such as joint ventures or book contracts) can often develop conflicting interests.

Collegial Relationships. Lawyers have long-term interests in maintaining good relationships with supervising attorneys, with other potential clients, and with other participants in the legal system such as prosecutors, insurance adjusters, agency officials, and court personnel.[48] These interests may conflict with any single client's short-term goals. See Chapter XIV (Criminal Law and Procedure) at pages 610–621.

Ideological Concerns. Especially in law-reform-oriented class actions, lawyers' objectives may run counter to the economic or political goals of certain members of the class. See the materials on public interest representation in Chapter IX (The Lawyer-Client Relationship) at pages 398–419.

The bar's traditional response to such conflicts is codified in Rules 1.7 and 1.8 of the Model Rules and DR 5-101 and 5-104 of the Code. Under Rule 1.7, a lawyer shall not represent a client if the representation would be materially limited by the lawyer's own interests or responsibilities to third parties unless the client consents and the lawyer reasonably believes that the representation will not be adversely affected. The Code prohibits a lawyer from taking a case where his professional judgment on behalf of a client reasonably may be affected by his own interests, except with the client's consent. Both the Code and the Model Rules include more specific regulations on fee agreements and on lawyer-client business transactions.

2. The Attorney Witness Rule as a Case Study

See Chapter XV, Evidence and Trial Advocacy
  • Lawyers as Witnesses
      (pages 674–676)

3. Fees

See Chapter X, Civil Procedure
  • Class Actions and Lawyer-Client Conflicts
      (page 450)

Endnotes

1. Geoffrey C. Hazard, Jr., Ethics and the Practice of Law 58-62 (1978).

2. John P. Frowe, The Legal Ethics of Louis Brandeis, 17 Stan. L. Rev. 683, 702 (1965); John S. Dzienkowski, Lawyers as Intermediaries: The Representation of Multiple Clients, 1992 U. Ill. L. Rev. 741, 784.

3. Hazard, supra note 1, at 69.

4. Id. at 65, 70-73.

5. Klemm v. Superior Court, 142 Cal. Rptr. 509, 512 (Cal. 1977).

6. Dzienkowski, supra note 2, at 774.

7. Id. at 777.

8. Id. As the Comment to Rule 2.2 notes, the prevailing rule is that the privilege does not attach between commonly represented parties and the same rule generally holds for parties relying on lawyer intermediaries.

9. The facts of this problem are modeled on Pirillo v. Takiff, 341 A.2d 896 (Pa.), reaffirmed, 352 A.2d 11 (Pa. 1975), cert. denied, 423 U.S. 1083 (1976).

10. See Robert D. Luce & Howard Raiffa, Games and Decisions 94-102 (1957); R. Axelrod, The Evolution of Cooperation (1983).

11. See Deborah L. Rhode & David Luban, Legal Ethics 495-496 (2d ed. 1995).

12. Jane Mayer, How Independent Is the Counsel?, The New Yorker, Apr. 22, 1996, at 63; Ralph Nader & Wesley J. Smith, No Contest 326 (1996).

13. Part 1 of this problem is based on The Case of the Unwanted Will, 65 A.B.A.J. 484 (1979).

14. Part 3 of this problem is modeled on a hypothetical described by Teresa Stanton Collet, And the Two Shall Become as One . . . Until the Lawyers Are Done, 7 Notre Dame J.L., Ethics & Pub. Poly. 101, 105-106 (1993).

15. Id. at 108.

16. Id.

17. Thomas L. Shaffer, The Legal Ethics of Radical Individualism, 65 Tex. L. Rev. 963, 969 (1987).

18. John R. Price, Professional Responsibility in Estate Planning: Progress or Paralysis? ch. 18 (University of Miami Institute on Estate Planning (1987)).

19. The Case of the Unwanted Will, supra note 13, at 486 (comments from George Overton).

20. Id. (comments from John C. Williams).

21. Shaffer, supra note 17, at 976-979.

22. Collet, supra note 14; Russell G. Pearce, Family Values and Legal Ethics: Competing Approaches to Conflicts in Representing Spouses, 62 Fordham L. Rev. 1253 (1994).

23. Geoffrey C. Hazard, Jr., Conflicts of Interest in Estate Planning for Husband and Wife, 20 Probate Law. 1 (1994).

24. Mark A. Karpel & Eric S. Strauss, Family Evaluation 255-256 (1983).

25. Evan Thomas, The Man to See: Edward Williams, Ultimate Insider, Legendary Trial Lawyer 178-180 (1991). See also Katharine Graham, Personal History 334-335 (1997); Peter Margulies, Access, Connection and Voice: A Contextual Approach to Representing Senior Citizens of Questionable Capacity, 62 Fordham L. Rev., 1085-1086 (1994).

26. Cinema 5 Ltd. v. Cinerama Ltd., 528 F.2d 1384, 1387 (2d Cir. 1976) (affirming disqualification because firm failed to show absence of apparent or actual conflict where one lawyer was a partner in a Buffalo firm defending Cinerama on antitrust charges as well as a partner in a New York firm suing Cinerama in an unrelated corporate takeover).

27. Geoffrey Hazard, The Would Be Client, Natl. L.J., Jan. 29, 1996, at A19, A20.

28. TC Theatre Corp. v. Warner Brothers Pictures, 113 F. Supp. 265, 268 (S.D.N.Y. 1953).

29. See cases cited in Charles Wolfram, Modern Legal Ethics 370-371 (1986), and Current Developments, Conflicts in Representation: Subsequent Representations in a World of Mega Law Firms, 6 Geo. J. Legal Ethics 1023, 1030 (1993). For example, the Second and Seventh Circuit Courts of Appeals focus on legal issues while the Ninth Circuit focuses on factual contexts. Compare La Salle Natl. Bank v. County of Lake, 703 F.2d 252 (7th Cir. 1983) with Trone v. Smith, 621 F.2d 994, 998 (9th Cir. 1980).

30. See cases cited in Current Developments, supra note 29, and Silver Chrysler Plymouth, Inc. v. Chrysler Motor Corp., 518 F.2d 751 (2d Cir. 1975) (lawyer moving to different firm may rebut presumption).

31. This problem draws in part on LaSalle Natl. Bank v. County of Lake, 703 F.2d 252 (7th Cir. 1983).

32. This problem is modeled on facts similar to those in Securities Investor Protection Corp. v. Vigman, 587 F. Supp. 1358 (C.D. Cal. 1984).

33. Lloyd Cutler, New Rule Goes Too Far, 63 A.B.A.J. 725 (1977); Thomas D. Morgan, Appropriate Limits on Participation by a Former Agency Official in Matters Before an Agency, 1980 Duke L.J. 1.

34. Hazard, supra note 1, at 113. See also Mark Green, The Other Government (1975); Monroe H. Freedman, For a New Rule, 63 A.B.A.J. 724 (1977).

35. Bruce A. Green, Conflicts of Interest in Litigation: The Judicial Role, 65 Fordham L. Rev. 71, 104-129 (1996).

36. Stacy De Broff, Lawyers as Lovers: How Far Should Ethical Restrictions on Dating or Married Attorneys Extend?, 1 Geo. J. of Legal Ethics 433, 434 n.12 (1987).

37. Blumenfeld v. Borenstein, 276 S.E.2d 607, 609 (Ga. 1981) (allowing husband's law firm to oppose client formerly represented by wife).

38. See People v. Jackson, 167 Cal. App. 3d 829, 832 (1985) (finding undisclosed dating relationship between prosecutor and court-appointed defense counsel constituted reversible error); Haley v. Boles, 824 S.W.2d 796 (Tex. 1992) (disqualifying attorney appointed to represent an indigent defendant where prosecutor was married to attorney's law partner).

39. Skadden Arps Poison Pill Stance Raises Conflict of Interest Concern, Wall St. J., July 23, 1986, at 23.

40. This example draws on the experience of Professor Kim Taylor Thompson, New York University Law School, during her prior employment at the Washington, D.C., Public Defender Service. For a related case, see Federal Defenders v. United States Sentencing Commission, 680 F. Supp. 26 (D.D.C. 1988).

41. Josiah Royce, The Philosophy of Loyalty, in Josiah Royce, Basic Writings 855, 861 (1909); Robert Lawry, The Meaning of Loyalty, 19 Cap. U.L. Rev. 1089, 1102 (1990).

42. See sources cited in Deborah L. Rhode, Ethical Perspectives on Legal Practice, 37 Stan. L. Rev. 589, 610 (1985); Sharon Tischer, Bringing the Bar to Justice: A Comparative Study of Six Bar Associations 134-135 (Public Citizen Report (1977)) (quoting chair of the Boston bar's Legal Services to the Indigent Committee, who notes that there were many issues on which he "backed off" to avoid embarrassing paying clients; in the last analysis, he asserted, "We're not here to be doing pro bono. We're here to be lawyers.").

43. Abe Krash, Professional Responsibility to Clients and the Public Interest: Is There a Conflict?, 55 Chi. Bar Rec. 31, 45 (Centennial Issue (1974)).

44. Norman W. Spaulding, The Prophet and the Bureaucrat Stan. L. Rev. (forthcoming) (quoting San Francisco attorney).

45. See, e.g., Stewart Macaulay, Lawyers and Consumer Protection Laws, 14 Law & Socy. Rev. 115, 136-139 (1979).

46. Spaulding, supra note 44 (quoting a director of a legal services organization and a public environmental litigator).

47. Geoffrey C. Hazard & W. William Hodes, I The Law of Lawyering 227 (2d. ed. 1990) (for illustrations of permissible positional conflicts, see §1.7:106; for disabling positional conflicts, see §1.7:105).

48. For an overview of these potential conflicts, see Deborah L. Rhode, Institutionalizing Ethics, 44 Case Western L. Rev. 665 (1994); Jonathan R. Macey & Geoffrey P. Miller, Reflections on Professional Responsibility in a Regulatory State, 63 Geo. Wash. L. Rev. 1105, 1106-1111 (1995).

Chapter VIII

Negotiation and Mediation

A. INTRODUCTION

Negotiation is a central feature of legal practice, both in settling disputes and structuring transactions. Almost 90 percent of all civil and criminal litigation is resolved through negotiated agreements, and much of lawyers' daily work involves some form of bargaining or mediation. Ethical issues are an equally central feature of this landscape. Problems 8A to 8D present a representative range of problems involving deception, distortion, nondisclosure, and coercive tactics.

These ethical dilemmas raise more general questions about effective negotiating strategies and regulatory policies. Many lawyers view hard bargaining as an essential part of good lawyering and assume that codified standards must tolerate certain behavior that would be unacceptable in other contexts. Experts on negotiation often disagree, and argue that current ethical standards are unduly permissive toward conduct that ill serves client, professional, and societal interests.

Underlying this dispute are deeper debates about the effectiveness of different bargaining strategies. Theorists have classified negotiation into three rough categories. The first type, pro-forma negotiation, occurs where the parties are not really bargaining at all. When the stakes are relatively low and the transaction costs of tailor-made agreements are relatively high, the terms of the transaction may follow standardized guidelines. A second form of bargaining is competitive, or concession-oriented; parties adopting this style focus on maximizing their own interests. In a third approach, cooperative or consensus-oriented negotiation, participants aim for mutually advantageous solutions, fair results, and the preservation of good working relationships.[1]

Recent research suggests that cooperative strategies would often prove more effective than the hard-nosed adversarial strategies that many lawyers employ. As this research indicates, the paradigm case for competitive frameworks involves a "zero-sum" situation in which parties lack a continuing relationship and are unlikely to detect deception. These circumstances are less typical than is commonly assumed. Most bargaining contexts present "value-creating" as well as "value-claiming" opportunities. Adversarial approaches may preempt the discovery of mutually advantageous solutions to joint problems. Recent work on game theory also verifies what common sense suggests. Negotiators who encounter each other repeatedly will penalize aggressive bargainers; cooperation works better over the long run.[2] By selecting lawyers with a reputation for cooperativeness, clients sometimes avoid entrapment in prisoners' dilemmas.[3] Effective cooperative strategies include settling differences by appealing to principled, objective criteria; staying focused on the clients' real needs, not simply money; avoiding deadlocks by identifying other issues to trade; and refusing to initiate sharp practices or to hold grudges.[4]

Commentators argue for cooperation, candor, and fairness on normative grounds. Drawing on a wide range of frameworks, including communitarian, religious, feminist, and critical legal studies approaches, these theorists argue that adversarial bargaining can undermine core values. From this perspective, values of honesty, empathy, and fairness need to inform lawyers' bargaining strategies.

In proposing limits on deceptive or exploitive negotiating practices, ethics experts have identified several critical factors: the harms and benefits of such practices both in the short and long term; the motives of the parties; their conduct before and during the negotiation process; and the alternatives available.[5] Under this framework, common excuses for deceptive or manipulative tactics often are unpersuasive. Rationalizations such as "everyone does it" or "the other side is worse" are not justifications that most lawyers would be prepared to generalize and to view as adequate in other contexts. If we know that our adversary is lying, then a retaliatory lie is not simply corrective justice; rather, it is an attempt to impose the kind of injury that we have avoided by discovering the deception. As Chapter II suggested (Traditions of Moral Reasoning, pages 12–36, a morally defensible analysis would focus not on whether others rely on sharp practices but on whether we would want such practices to be a universal norm.

Another common problem in the way that negotiators rationalize cutting ethical corners lies in the selective evaluation of the consequences. Consciously or unconsciously, individuals tend to overvalue the personal short-term benefits from questionable tactics and to disregard the long-term systemic costs. As is clear from the materials in Part D of Chapter II (Traditions of Moral Reasoning) and Part B below, honesty and fairness are to some extent collective goods. The more that lawyers seek to become "free riders," the greater the profession's difficulty in maintaining a climate of trust, credibility, and fair dealing.

So too, an unqualified willingness to exploit an opponent's ignorance or mistake carries broader costs. Disparities in talent, resources, and information inevitably skew negotiation results. While it may be unrealistic to expect parties to forgo all the advantages that arise from such inequalities, it may be reasonable to expect negotiators to forgo some. Particularly where parties lack equal access to relevant facts, it will often be both equitable and efficient to impose minimal disclosure obligations. Thus, Gerald Wetlaufer argues that we need to accept

> the proposition that ethics and integrity are things for which a price may have to be paid. . . . [To that end] we might clearly define winning in a way that leaves room for ethics. It might, for instance, be understood not as "getting as much as we can" but as "winning as much as possible without engaging in unacceptable behavior," and "unacceptable behavior" might then be understood to exclude not just those things that are stupid or illegal but also those other things that are unethical. And finally . . . [we must] do our best to understand and confront the choices between the harsh individualist reality of instrumental effectiveness and . . . the elusive possibilities of ethics, integrity, reciprocity and community.[6]

Consider that argument in evaluating the professional conduct in Problems 8A to 8C. What actions are permitted or required under existing rules? What actions should be? What factors would be relevant to your decision to prohibit, tolerate, or engage in similar behavior? Consider the ethical frameworks in Chapter II (Traditions of Moral Reasoning) at pages 18–26.

ROGER FISHER, A CODE OF NEGOTIATION PRACTICES FOR LAWYERS

1 Negotiation Journal 105, 105-108 (1985)

Most ethical problems facing lawyers in a negotiation stem from a conflict of interest between the lawyer's obligation to the client (presumably to get the best deal) and two of the lawyer's other interests: behaving honorably toward others involved in the negotiation and self-interest in preserving reputation and self-esteem. . . .

It may be possible to limit these ethical problems by conducting a preliminary negotiation between lawyer and client, clarifying the basis on which the lawyer is conducting the negotiation. The following two drafts are intended to stimulate discussion of this possibility.

The first is in the form of a memorandum that a lawyer might give to a new client, and the second an attached draft code of negotiating behavior. . . .

MEMORANDUM TO A NEW CLIENT:
HOW I PROPOSE TO NEGOTIATE

Attached to this memorandum is a Code of Negotiation Practices for Lawyers. It has been prepared for lawyers and other professional experts in the negotiation process and is based on a draft first produced by the Harvard Negotiation Project at Harvard Law School.

I would like to obtain your approval for my accepting this Code as providing the general guidelines for any negotiations I may conduct on your behalf. . . .

I believe that it is not a sound practice to negotiate in a way that rewards deception, stubbornness, dirty tricks, and taking risks. I think it wiser for our clients, ourselves, and our society to deal with differences in a way that optimizes the chance of reaching a fair outcome efficiently and amicably; that rewards those who are better prepared, more skillful and efficient, and who have the better case as measured by objective standards of fairness; and that makes each successive negotiation likely to be even better. (This does not mean that a negotiator should disclose everything or make unjustified concessions.)

A Code of Negotiation Practices for Lawyers

I.   Roles

1. Professional.   You and those with whom you negotiate are members of an international profession of problem-solvers. Do not look upon those on the other side as enemies but rather as partners with whom cooperation is essential and greatly in the interest of your client. You are colleagues in the difficult task of reconciling, as well as possible, interests that are sometimes shared but often conflict.

2. Advocate.   You are also an advocate for your client's interests. You have a fiduciary obligation to look after the needs and concerns of your client, to make sure that they are taken into account, and to act in ways that will tend to ensure that they are well satisfied. It is not enough to seek a fair result. Among results that fall within the range of fairness, you should press with diligence and skill toward that result that best satisfies your client's interests consistent with being fair and socially acceptable.

3. Counsellor.   Clients, motivated by anger or short-term considerations, sometimes act, and may ask you to act, in ways that are contrary to their own best interests. Another of your roles is to help your clients take long-term considerations properly into account, come to understand their enlightened self-interest, and to pursue it.

4. Mediator. Further, a negotiator often has to serve as a mediator between a client and those on the other side. Two lawyers, negotiating with each other, sometimes best function as co-mediators, trying to bring their clients together.

5. Model of Just Behavior. Finally, as a lawyer and negotiator, you should behave toward those with whom you negotiate in ways that incorporate the highest moral standards of civilization. Your conduct should be such that you regard it as a praiseworthy model for others to emulate and such that, if it became known, it would reflect credit on you and the bar. You should feel no obligation to be less candid for a client than you would be for yourself, and should not behave in ways that would justifiably damage your reputation for integrity.

II. Goals

As a negotiator, your goal is a good outcome. Such an outcome appears to depend on at least seven elements:

1. Alternatives. The outcome should be better for your client than the best available alternative that could be reached without negotiating.

2. Interests. Your client's interests should be well-satisfied. The interests of other parties and the community should be sufficiently satisfied to make the outcome acceptable to them and durable.

3. Options. Among the many possible outcomes, an agreement should be the best possible,or as near to it as can reasonably be developed without incurring undue transaction costs. Possible joint gains and mutually advantageous tradeoffs should be diligently sought, explored, and put to use. The result should be an elegant solution with no waste. This means that it could not be significantly better for your client without being significantly worse for others.

4. Legitimacy. The outcome should be reasonably fair to all as measured by objective criteria such as law, precedent, community practice, and expert opinion. No one should feel "taken."

5. Communication. If negotiations are to reach a wise outcome without waste of time or other resources, there must be effective communication among the parties. Communication should not halt when one or more of the parties wants to express disagreement. Even when a given negotiation fails to produce satisfactory results, communication lines should remain open.

6. Commitments. Pledges as to what you will or won't do should be made not at the outset of a negotiation but after differences of perception, interest, and values are fully appreciated.

Commitments should be mutually understood and carefully crafted to be realistic and easy to implement.

7. Relationship. Both the way each negotiation is conducted and its outcome should be such that in future negotiations it will be easier rather than harder for the parties to reach equally good or better outcomes.

PROBLEM 8A

For this problem, you should be assigned to represent either the plaintiff or the defendant and you should be given additional instructions for your side, available from the Teacher's Manual.

Ralph Grimes, 62, was terminated after 31 years of employment with Emco, a mid-sized corporation headquartered in Los Angeles; Grimes worked at Emco's small plant in San Francisco. Grimes' lawyer is a specialist in employment litigation. Emco is represented by the largest firm in California.

Grimes claims that the corporation fired him because of age and replaced him with the president's son, age 25. Grimes seeks three years of future lost wages in the amount of $180,000, an additional $60,000 in lost benefits, and $300,000 in punitive damages. Emco management responds that plaintiff's position became obsolete due to technology, and that although it did hire the president's son, it did so not as a replacement. Only about a third of plaintiff's duties were absorbed by the son. The rest of Grimes' prior responsibilities are now being performed by a new computer. Both sides are willing to pursue arbitration.

Under the applicable Age Discrimination in Employment Act, the plaintiff has the burden of proof to establish by a preponderance of evidence that he was terminated, that he was over the age of 40, and that his termination was based on age. The burden then shifts to the defendant to prove that it had a legitimate reason for terminating plaintiff. The plaintiff then must establish that the defendant's reason was based on pretext.[7]

B. CANDOR IN NEGOTIATION

1. Representations of Fact and Value

a. Introduction

In his nineteenth-century Essay on Professional Ethics, George Sharswood cautioned that it is not only morally wrong but also damaging to mislead opponents. By contrast, some contemporary commentators believe that success in negotiation, as in poker, becomes more likely when an adversary misjudges the bottom line. As law professor James White puts it, good bargaining requires the "capacity both to mislead and not to be misled."[8]

Other contemporary negotiation experts disagree. In their view, deception adversely affects both parties and the process. When misrepresentation is suspected or revealed, it compromises the lawyer's credibility and may provoke retaliatory or defensive responses. Bluffing about what is truly important may also prevent individuals from discovering opportunities for mutual advantage.[9] Even lies that remain undiscovered can have corrosive consequences. As commentators often note, there is much truth to the cliche that it is easy to tell one lie but difficult to tell only one. Deception that remains undetected encourages more deception and ultimately may diminish parties' level of trust, their capacity to reach fair agreements, their ability to exchange credible commitments, and their sense of personal integrity.[10]

In framing general principles, lawyers thus need to measure their gains in particular cases against the broader social costs: the damage to third party interests and to community norms of honesty and fair dealing. If, following Kant, we test the justification for a lie by generalizing "what if everyone did that," then most deception in negotiation would be difficult to justify.

Difficult does not, of course, mean impossible; not all deceptions are created equal. Under conventional definitions, a lie is any effort to create a belief at variance with one's own understanding of the truth, and may occur through concealment or omissions as well as direct statements. Yet moral and legal frameworks distinguish among false statements; misrepresentations such as "it's good to see you again," "this is a great deal," and "this house has never had flooding in the basement" stand on different footing. As noted in Chapter II (Traditions of Moral Reasoning), most ethical approaches justify or excuse a lie under certain circumstances. Deception may be justified by a greater moral obligation (saving a life), or excused by factors such as the low probability of injury (the tactful white lie) or the countervailing benefits (encouraging client confidences).

Such distinctions are to some extent reflected in the Code, the Model Rules, and the legal doctrine on which these ethical standards rely. Disciplinary Rule 2-102(A)(4) prohibits conduct involving "dishonesty, fraud, deceit, or misrepresentation," and DR 7-102(A) provides that a lawyer "shall not ... knowingly make a false statement of law or fact" or "conceal or knowingly fail to disclose that which he is required by law to reveal." Model Rule 4.1 has a slightly more restrictive scope. It provides that a lawyer shall not knowingly

(a) make a false statement of <u>material fact</u> or law to a third person; or

(b) fail to disclose a material fact to a third person when disclosure is necessary to avoid assisting a criminal or fraudulent act by a client, unless disclosure is prohibited by Rule 1.6.

The Comment to Rule 4.1 offers further qualifications. It notes that "[a] lawyer is required to be truthful . . . but generally has no affirmative duty to inform an opposing party of relevant facts." Although the Comment points out that misrepresentation can occur through omission or through incorporation of another person's false statement, it expressly limits the scope of the rule to statements of fact. Moreover,

> [w]hether a particular statement should be regarded as one of fact can depend on the circumstances. Under generally accepted conventions in negotiation, certain types of statements ordinarily are not taken as statements of material fact. Estimates of price or value placed on the subject of a transaction and a party's intentions as to an acceptable settlement of a claim are in this category.

These rules also incorporate common law prohibitions on fraud, which forbid knowing misrepresentations of fact on which another party relies to his or her detriment. What conduct in Problems 8A and 8B falls within these prohibitions? What conduct would you find acceptable negotiating behavior for yourself or an adversary?

PROBLEM 8B

1. In negotiations over a hotel's breach of contract to host a conference, the defendant's attorney makes an initial settlement offer of $15,000. Counsel for the plaintiff organization maintains that his client's officers would never accept such an offer, that damages from the breach are likely to be much higher, and that any jury award would be more substantial. Counsel actually believes that if the case went to trial, his client would receive a substantially smaller sum. Based on that advice, the plaintiff's president has authorized counsel to settle for any amount over $10,000.

2. In negotiations over criminal charges, counsel represents that the evidence will not sustain, and his client will not plead guilty to, certain statutory violations. In fact, the evidence is overwhelming, and the client has agreed to accept a plea on those charges if no better disposition is possible.

3. In negotiating the sale of a ranch, the seller's lawyer states that the property is an outstanding business opportunity and that its acreage and crop yield should produce an income of at least $160,000 per year. The out-of-state buyer, who is unfamiliar with the layout of the ranch, relies on that representation, which significantly overstates the ranch's profitability.

4. In negotiations over a claim that a bank erroneously canceled a small company's loan and ruined its business, the lawyer for the owners states that his clients have suffered severe emotional distress. However, in initial conversations with the lawyer, the clients describe themselves as quite "upbeat," and indicate that they have several important contracts "in the offing."

5. In the negotiations described in Part 1, the plaintiff's attorney represented in settlement negotiations that it would be impossible for his client's organization to find another suitable hotel under such short notice. When the attorney contacted his client to report the settlement offer, he learned that another hotel had orally agreed to host the conference. When he then called the defendant's lawyer to accept the settlement, the lawyer opened the conversation by asking, "How are your efforts to mitigate the damages coming along?" Plaintiff's counsel responded, "Nothing definite yet." The settlement was then finalized at $15,000.

b. Settlement Authority

Are the types of statements in Problem 8B(1) and (2) misrepresentations within the meaning of the Code? Are they "ordinarily" not statements of fact within the meaning of Rule 4.1? If so, have the Model Rule drafters taken undue liberty with the definition of "fact"? What do they mean by "ordinarily?" Are there circumstances in which misrepresentations about settlement would constitute a violation? Are those circumstances present in Problem 8B(1) or (2)?

Lewis Van Deusen, former chair of the ABA Ethics Committee, was once asked point-blank if it was ever proper for a lawyer to lie. Van Deusen answered unequivocally. Lying was ungentlemanly, unlawyerlike, and wrongful. He was then presented with circumstances similar to those in Problem 8B(1) and asked to comment on the lawyer's lie. "Oh," explained Van Deusen, "That's different.... [That's] tactics."[11] Do you agree?

In a more recent survey of experts on legal ethics, six participants believed that it was impermissible for a lawyer directly to misrepresent whether a client had authorized settlement for a specific amount; six participants indicated that it was permissible but that they would not do it. One other expert felt that lying was perfectly acceptable since an opponent didn't have a "right to the information."[12] Which position do you find most persuasive? To many negotiators, the rationale for lying about settlement limits is especially unconvincing, given the availability of other alternatives. Experienced practitioners often sidestep a direct inquiry about their authority to settle for a given amount with responses such as "I would advise my client that the case justifies $20,000" or "I'm authorized to get the best result I can."[13] Would it be preferable to require that lawyers avoid direct misrepresentations about their clients' willingness to accept certain settlements?

c. Statements of Value and Opinion

Do the statements in Problem 8B(3) come within an acceptable definition of puffing? Do they suggest a clear distinction between statements of fact and estimates of value? The traditional rule on

puffing, reflected in Model Rule 4.1 and its Comment, is that statements of value are opinions on which opposing parties cannot
reasonably rely.[14] However, a growing body of common law restricts
rights of exaggeration or misrepresentation. The more a negotiator's
opinion invokes or implies actual knowledge, the more likely courts
will be to find the buyer's reliance justifiable. Liability is also increasingly common for negotiators who deliberately attempt to
deceive, who deal with an unusually gullible party, who have information not available to the other side, or who are reasonably believed to have special skill and judgment related to the matter in
question.[15]

Problem 8B(3) is modeled on Bails v. Wheeler, 559 P.2d 1180
(Mont. 1977). There, the Montana Supreme Court held that the
buyer of a ranch could justifiably rely on an opinion by the seller's
real estate agents about the profitability of ranch property if the
agents possessed superior knowledge that reasonably implied
knowledge of facts supporting the opinion, or if the opinion was so
"blended with facts" that it amounted to a factual statement. Id. at
1181. The court remanded for a determination of these issues. If the
case involved a lawyer, should similar standards apply?

Do the representations in Problem 8B(4) fall within legitimate
boundaries of puffing? In a survey of ethics experts, eight responded
no and five responded yes. Of those who found the representations
acceptable, one reasoned that "obviously some [emotional] distress
had occurred." If the clients "didn't care at all there wouldn't be a
legal matter. . . . [The lawyer is just] embellishing the concern."[16]
James White agreed that the exaggeration was acceptable and drew
analogies to bargaining over the sale of a car. To White, the fundamental question was "what are your and my legitimate expectations"
as opposing negotiators?[17] Ronald Rotunda invoked the same analogy
to arrive at a different conclusion. In his view, the misrepresentation
in Problem 8B(4) was unethical: "If lawyers want to be like used car
salesmen, this is a good place to start."[18] Is it? Would your answer
differ if, in response to their lawyer's prompting, the clients indicated that they were distressed about the possibility of litigating the
claim?[19]

The case on which Problem 8(B)(1) is based arose during the
1960s, when the Washington, D.C., Mattachine Society planned
what it billed as the first national conference to focus on gay and
lesbian rights. The Manger Hotel agreed to host the conference with
knowledge of its subject. Then, two weeks before the event, after
publicity and invitations had been mailed, management in the hotel
chain's home office ordered cancellation of the agreement. Monroe
Freedman, the Society's lawyer, later defended his conduct:

> Was anything definite about mitigation at that point? Is anything
> ever definite in this life? After all, the Mattachine Society had
> thought that the deal with the Manger was definite, and it turned out
> that it wasn't. . . . The statement about mitigation wasn't a flat-out
> denial: it was equivocal — an evasion that a careful listener could have

picked up on. "What do you mean 'nothing definite'?" he might have said. . . .[20]

According to Freedman, the new offer of a hotel site was confidential information and as long as he did not make a false statement of material fact, he did not need to disclose it under Model Rule 4.1. Do you find his reasoning persuasive? What would you have done in his circumstances?

Those who argue that exaggeration or equivocation is harmless generally assume that the opposing party will recognize puffing for what it is. But if that were always true, the practice would also be ineffective. Puffing continues because sometimes it works and some opponents are deceived. To commentators such as Judge Alvin Rubin, parties dealing with a lawyer should not need to exercise the same degree of caution as they would if trading at a Far Eastern bazaar.[21] What is your view? How much prudence is it reasonable to expect concerning statements of value? What interpretation of existing rules would best serve societal interests?

2.   Disclosure Obligations

PROBLEM 8C

1. In settlement negotiations, counsel for the plaintiff makes certain statements revealing that he is unaware of controlling legal precedents favorable to his client. Counsel for the defendant does not affirmatively misstate the law but frames his responses to suggest that opposing counsel's assumptions are correct. The case is settled for an amount that substantially underrepresents what a neutral decision-maker would fix as the fair value of the claim.

2. In negotiations over an eviction action, the tenant is unaware that conditions she has complained about would establish housing code violations entitling her to a setoff against the rent. The tenant has no lawyer. Counsel for the landlord advises her to accept a stipulated settlement without such a setoff and to avoid looking doubtful in front of the judge who will approve the agreement. Otherwise, "If [the judge] thinks I'm taking advantage of you, it'll take hours," and the landlord might reconsider.[22]

3. In negotiating a claim on behalf of a federal agency, counsel for the government does not disclose that the claim would be barred by the statute of limitations. Opposing counsel is unaware of the statutory defense.

4. In negotiations over the lender liability case described in Problem 8B(4), the bank's counsel makes it clear that he believes the owners have gone out of business. The opposing attorney does not misstate the company's status but does nothing to correct his adversary's misimpression before settling the case.

5. In negotiations for the sale of a business, counsel for the seller has supplied profit-loss statements for a period ending two months prior

to the closing. In the last two months, profits have fallen off dramatically due to obscure new export restrictions. The lawyer for the potential buyer makes no inquiry about current sales. Counsel for the seller fails to disclose the change in volume.

6. In settlement negotiations, counsel for the plaintiff fails to disclose that a key witness has recalled certain material facts that are inconsistent with prior deposition testimony.

7. In negotiations over the property settlement in an uncontested divorce, the husband and wife disagree about the value of certain assets, including real estate and stock in a family corporation. When reviewing the wife's proposed settlement, the husband's lawyer notices a $50,000 calculation error by opposing counsel that understates her alleged interest in jointly owned real estate. The lawyer brings the matter to the attention of his client, who believes that the understated figure is a more accurate reflection of the property's true worth. Accordingly, the lawyer prepares a counteroffer replicating the error in a way that minimizes the likelihood of its discovery. On the mistaken belief that the husband has surrendered his challenge to the value of the real estate, the wife abandons her challenge to the value and ownership of the stock. Both parties ultimately accept a version of the husband's counteroffer and sign a final agreement that recites the disposition of assets without specifying their value.

a.   *Mistakes of Law*

How would you evaluate the conduct in Problem 8C(1)? Under the traditional view, misrepresentations of law do not constitute fraud because reasonable individuals should not rely on their adversaries' legal analysis or trade on their opponents' legal preparation. More recent cases suggest that in certain circumstances, such as when a lawyer deals with an unrepresented opponent, a purposely distorted legal opinion can become a basis for liability.[23] Similarly, some commentators support disclosure requirements for mistakes in law when necessary to ensure a reasonably just result. In commenting on the factual situation in Problem 8C(1), William Simon argues that the critical concern

> should be whether the settlement likely to occur in the absence of disclosure [of relevant law] would be fair (in the sense that it reasonably vindicates the merits of the relevant claims). . . . [The] duty [of disclosure] is triggered by the fact that, without some assistance from defense counsel, the procedure cannot be relied on to produce a just resolution. The [opponent's] mistake is a major breakdown in the procedure, and . . . there will be no other opportunities for counsel, judge, or jury to remedy the breakdown.[24]

Do you agree? If counsel is obligated under DR 7-106(B) and Model Rule 3.3(a)(3) to make disclosure of controlling adverse precedent to a tribunal, should similar duties arise in pretrial settlement negotiations?[25] Do the government attorneys in 8C(3) "owe a higher duty to the public that transcend those found in the Model Rules"?[26]

What about lawyers dealing with unrepresented, unsophisticated adversaries? Is it enough for lawyers in cases like 8C(2) to refrain from giving legal advice (DR 7-104(a)(2)); to avoid implying that they are disinterested (Model Rule 4.3); and to correct misunderstandings regarding their role (Model Rule 4.3)? An earlier draft of the Model Rules would have required lawyers to avoid "exploiting unrepresented parties' ignorance of the law or the practices of the tribunal." Discussion Draft Rule 8.6 (1980). Would you support such a rule? Did the lawyer in 8C(2) behave ethically?[27]

b. Mistakes of Fact

Contemporary contract law generally requires negotiators to disclose facts necessary to rectify another person's "misunderstanding of a fundamental fact so central to the transaction that failure to disclose the information would not comport with 'reasonable standards of fair dealing.'"[28] What constitutes fair dealing on the facts of Problem 8C(4)? In commenting on a related set of facts, 57 percent of some 1,600 surveyed lawyers felt that nondisclosure was appropriate; only a third of some 360 surveyed non-lawyers agreed.[29] Surveyed ethics experts agreed that a lawyer must not say anything to ratify or further the opponent's misimpression, but they divided about whether disclosure of the true facts was necessary. Some took the position that it is not the lawyer's job to "educate" opponents; others felt that disclosure obligations should depend on whether the misimpression related to facts that opponents could not discover on their own. A third group, including Geoffrey Hazard, reporter for the Model Rules, maintained that nondisclosure would be fraudulent since the opponent's belief was "a manifest misapprehension that goes to the bargain itself."[30] Which position do you find most convincing?

Does Problem 8C(5) present the same issues? Judge Rubin, in exploring that case and related circumstances, argues that a lawyer should not participate in an unconscionable transaction. Rather, the lawyer should seek the client's permission to disclose current sales information and, if the client refuses, should withdraw from representation. Rubin writes:

> [A lawyer] must not perpetrate the kind of fraud or deception that would vitiate a bargain if practiced by his [client]. Beyond that, the profession should embrace an affirmative ethical standard for attorneys' professional relationships with courts, other lawyers and the public: *The lawyer must act honestly and in good faith.* Another lawyer, or a layman, who deals with a lawyer should not need to exercise the same degree of caution that he would if trading for reputedly antique copper jugs in an oriental bazaar. It is inherent in the concept of an ethic, as a principle of good conduct, that it is morally binding on

the conscience of the professional, and not merely a rule of the game adopted because other players observe . . . the same rule. Good conduct exacts more than mere convenience. It is not sufficient to call on personal self-interest; this is the standard created by the thesis that the same adversary met today may be faced again tomorrow, and one had best not prejudice that future engagement. . . . Substantial rules of law in some areas already exact of principals the duty to perform legal obligations honestly and in good faith. Equivalent standards should pervade the lawyer's professional environment.

While it might strain present concepts of the role of the lawyer in an adversary system, surely the professional standards must ultimately impose upon him a duty not to accept an unconscionable deal. . . . The unconscionable result in these circumstances is in part created by the relative power, knowledge and skill of the principals and their negotiators. While it is the unconscionable result that is to be avoided, the question of whether the result is indeed intolerable depends in part on examination of the relative status of the parties. The imposition of a duty to tell the truth and to bargain in good faith would reduce their relative inequality, and tend to produce negotiation results that are within relatively tolerable bounds. . . .

It is inherent in the concept of professionalism that the profession will regulate itself, adhering to an ethos that imposes standards higher than mere law observance. Client avarice and hostility neither control the lawyer's conscience nor measure his ethics. Surely if its practitioners are principled, a profession that dominates the legal process in our law-oriented society would not expect too much if it required its members to adhere to two simple principles when they negotiate as professionals: Negotiate honestly and in good faith; and do not take unfair advantage of another, regardless of his relative expertise or sophistication. This is inherent in the oath the ABA recommends be taken by all who are admitted to the bar: "I will employ for the purpose of maintaining the causes confided to me such means only as are consistent with truth and honor."[31]

Do you agree?

How would you handle Problem 8C(6)? Must the lawyer disclose the new facts or withdraw from representation under DR 7-102, Rule 4.1, and Rule 1.16? Similar situations occur whenever changes in circumstances make a prior representation misleading. In general, courts have held that failure to correct an error will result in a voidable contract or tort damages where the injured party justifiably relies on the earlier assertion.[32] Similarly, Rule 26 of the Federal Rules of Civil Procedure and its state analogues impose a duty to update materials provided in discovery that have become inaccurate.

Should existing ethical codes be interpreted to require comparable duties? On the facts of Problem 8C(6), a survey of over 1,500 large-firm litigators from around the nation and 1,000 Michigan litigators found that about half of the Michigan lawyers and a third of the national lawyers saw no need to correct the deposition before entering into settlement if the client would not agree to the corrections. Slightly over half of the national litigators and slightly over a third of the Michigan litigators felt that the lawyer must seek to withdraw if the client refused to authorize a correction. Yet approximately half the attorneys in both samples felt that unfair and inadequate pretrial disclosure of material information is a regular or frequent problem; three-quarters felt that incomplete information presents such a problem.[33] Do existing ethical rules respond adequately to those perceived problems?

A prior Model Rules provision would have required a lawyer to disclose material facts in negotiation when necessary to correct a manifest misapprehension of fact or law resulting from the lawyer's previous representations.[34] That proposal would have made attorneys' ethical duties consistent with current tort and contract law governing their clients. Would you support such a provision? Can you identify convincing ethical reasons for its withdrawal?

c. Scrivener's Errors

STARE v. TATE, 21 CAL. APP. 3D 432, 98 CAL. RPTR. 264 (1971). Problem 8C(7) is based on this case. There, as the court noted:

> The mistake might never have come to light had not the husband desired to have the exquisite last word. A few days after [the wife] had obtained the divorce he mailed her a copy of the offer which contained the errant computation. On top of the page he wrote with evident satisfaction: "PLEASE NOTE ... MISTAKE IN YOUR FIGURES." A month later the wife filed suit action to reform the agreement.

98 Cal. Rptr. at 266.

The court reformed the agreement under §3399 of the California Civil Code to conform to the wife's understanding. The Code provides: "When through fraud or mutual mistake of the parties, or a mistake of one party, which the other at the time knew or suspected, a written contract does not truly express the intention of the parties, it may be revised on the application of a party aggrieved, so as to express that intention, so far as it can be done without prejudice to rights acquired by third persons, in good faith and for value." In justifying its decision, the court noted:

> Settlement negotiations of the kind that were had between the parties are usually nothing but a high stake game of poker. . . . By permitting [his wife] to enter into the contract in the belief that he had accepted her value, [the husband] simply took the risk that if she discovered the mistake and sought judicial redress, the contract would be enforced on the terms which she mistakenly thought she had already received.

98 Cal. Rptr. at 269.

The court made no comment about the conduct of the husband's attorney. Should it have? How would you characterize his actions?

What would you have done as counsel for the husband in Stare v. Tate? If you had consulted your client and he had refused to authorize disclosures of the mistake, how would you have responded? What factors would have been most relevant in guiding your conduct? Consider, for example, ethical rules and contract law; your personal feelings about the husband; his value as a source of future business; your personal feelings about the wife and opposing counsel; the likely effect of nondisclosure on your reputation; and your sense of the fairness of the underlying divorce settlement.

Should lawyers have an obligation to seek their clients' approval before correcting a scrivener's error? In Informal Opinion 86-1518 (Feb. 9, 1986), the ABA's standing Committee on Ethics reviewed a situation in which a lawyer discovered that the final draft of a contract prepared by opposing counsel's office did not contain a material, previously disputed, provision. In the Committee's view, the lawyer had no obligation under either the Model Rules or the Code to obtain the client's permission before correcting the error. Rule 1.2(a) provides that lawyers "shall abide by a client's decisions concerning the objectives of representation and shall consult with the client as to the means by which they are to be served." However, the Comment to the Rule acknowledges the lawyer's responsibility for technical and strategic issues. Rule 1.4 requires lawyers to explain matters "reasonably necessary to permit the client to make informed decisions regarding the representation." Under the Committee's analysis, once the client had accepted the disputed provision, no informed decision remained to be made. On similar reasoning, the Committee concluded that the scrivener's error was not a "relevant consideration or material development" that must be communicated to the client under EC 7-8 or 9-2 of the Code.

In addition, the Committee relied on general prohibitions on conduct involving dishonesty, fraud, deceit, or misrepresentation in Rule 8.4(c) and DR 1-102(A)(4), and the provision in Rule 4.1(b) that lawyers shall not fail to disclose a material fact to a third person when disclosure is necessary to avoid assisting a fraudulent act by a client unless the information is privileged. Therefore, the Committee concluded, "the lawyer . . . should contact the [opposing] lawyer to correct the error and need not consult [his client] about the error." Do you agree? Would failure to disclose an error constitute fraud?

Suppose in Problem 8C(7) the attorney had not noticed the scrivener's error until the husband showed him the letter about to be sent to the wife. How should the attorney have responded? Is the reasoning in Opinion 86-1518 helpful? See the readings at pages 27–32 of Chapter II (Traditions of Moral Reasoning), pages 522–523 of Chapter XII (Contracts), pages 699–704 of Chapter XVI (Family Law), and pages 777–778 of Chapter XVIII (Tax).

C.   FAIRNESS IN NEGOTIATION

A recurring entry in lawyer humor collections involves the client who receives a triumphant message from his attorney announcing "reached settlement fair to everyone." The client's exasperated response: "a fair result I could have managed myself."

PROBLEM 8D

1. In negotiating a personal injury case, defense counsel states that facts about the injured plaintiff's undocumented immigration status and about the opposing attorney's solicitation of the claim may come out at trial if the plaintiff refuses to accept the insurance company's extremely modest settlement offer.

2. While negotiating an acrimonious divorce settlement, the husband's lawyer tells the wife's lawyer that his client will have no problem with the wife's claims for legal fees if everything else "works out reasonably."

3. During a divorce action, the husband files a claim for joint custody. Prevailing legal standards base custody decisions on the best interest of the child and give preference to the "friendly parent"—that is, the parent who has demonstrated most willingness to share custody or to grant extensive visitation rights. The wife tells her lawyer that she won't agree to joint custody but that she might make other concessions to spare herself and the children an acrimonious battle. The lawyer for the husband, anticipating such a response, offers to withdraw the custody claim if the wife will relinquish claims to spousal support and to certain jointly owned property. The lawyer knows that the husband does not in fact want joint custody and believes that such an arrangement would not be in the best interests of the children.

The lawyer also suspects that the husband might gain more concessions if he negotiates directly with his wife rather than working through her attorney.

4. In the divorce negotiations described in Part 3, counsel for the wife indicates that if a custody battle develops, certain facts about the husband's gay relationship prior to the marriage might emerge at trial.

RICHARD NEELY, THE PRIMARY CARETAKER PARENT RULE: CHILD CUSTODY AND THE DYNAMICS OF GREED

3 Yale L. & Poly. Rev. 168, 177-179 (1984)

Divorce decrees are typically drafted for the parties after compromises reached through private negotiation. These compromises are then approved by a judge, who generally gives them only the most

perfunctory sort of review. The result is that parties (usually husbands) are free to use whatever leverage is available to obtain a
favorable settlement. In practice this tends to mean that husbands
will threaten custody fights, with all of the accompanying traumas
and uncertainties discussed above, as a means of intimidating wives
into accepting less child support and alimony than is sufficient to
allow the mother to live and raise the children appropriately as a
single parent. Because women are usually unwilling to accept even a
minor risk of losing custody, such techniques are generally successful.

To make these abstract statements more concrete, I would like
to use an example from my own experience. My first encounter with
the manner in which the unpredictability of divorce proceedings can
be used to terrorize women came early in my career as a small-town
lawyer. My client was a railroad brakeman who had fallen out of
love with his wife and in love with motorcycles. Along the way, he
had met a woman who was as taken with motorcycles as he. After
about a year, my client's wife filed for divorce. My client had two
children at home, one about nine and the other about twelve. Unfortunately for him, the judge in the county where his wife had filed her
suit was notorious for giving high alimony and child support awards.
The last thing that I wanted to do was go to trial. The wife had a
strong case of adultery against my client, and the best my client
could come up with was a lame countersuit for "cruel and inhuman
treatment"—not exactly a showstopper in a rural domestic court.

During the initial interview, I asked my client about his children, and he told me that he got along well with them. He also
indicated, however, that two children were the last thing he wanted
from his divorce. Nonetheless, it occurred to me in my role as zealous
advocate that if my client developed a passionate attachment to his
children and told his wife that he would fight for custody all the way
to the state supreme court, we might settle the whole divorce fairly
cheaply. My client was a quick study: That night he went home and
began a campaign for his children. His chance of actually getting
custody from the judge was virtually nonexistent, but that did not
discourage our blustering threats.

My client's wife was unwilling to take any chance, no matter
how slight, on losing her children. Consequently, the divorce was
settled exactly as we wanted. The wife got the children by agreement, along with rather modest alimony and child support. All we
had needed to defeat her legitimate claims in the settlement process
was the halfway credible threat of a protracted custody battle. As
Solomon showed us, the better a mother is as a parent, the less likely
she is to allow a destructive fight over her children.

The above story is more than just a homey example, for it is
repeated across the nation every day. Under our purportedly
sex-neutral system, women on statistical average come out of divorce
settlements with the worst of all possible results: They get the
children, but insufficient money with which to support them. They

are forced to scrape along to support their families at inadequate standards of living, and the children are forced to grow up poor, or at least poorer than they should be. Yet the dynamic demonstrated above is seldom discussed, despite its importance in promoting the growth of a rapidly-expanding class of poor people, the female-headed household. . . .

The everyday occurrence of children being traded for money should be sufficient in and of itself to prompt a reevaluation of a system that turns custody awards into bargaining chips. The fact that such trading also has contributed to the impoverishment of women makes the need for change still more urgent.

See Chapter XVI, Family Law
• Divorce Negotiations
(pages 699–702)

Problem 8D raises questions about the legitimacy of certain bargaining tactics. Which are permissible under relevant standards? Which would you feel justified in using? Would your answer depend on the fairness of your client's proposed settlement? What other factors might influence your judgment on those questions?

Bar ethical standards impose relatively few restrictions on bargaining tactics. Both the Code and Model Rules provide that lawyers must refrain from fraud and may decline to take actions that are "offensive" or personally "repugnant." DR 7-101(A), DR 7-102(A), Model Rule 1.2. In addition, DR 7-105 enjoins lawyers from "presenting or threatening to present criminal charges solely to obtain an advantage in a civil matter," and California Rule 5-100 also prohibits threats of administrative or disciplinary charges. Drafters of the Model Rules intentionally excluded such prohibitions, although the Rules do forbid criminal conduct adversely reflecting on fitness, a ban that presumably includes extortion. Some, but not all, statutory definitions of extortion include attempts to secure financial advantage by threatening to expose criminal conduct or secrets that could impair reputation or livelihood. The laws governing duress also bar wrongful threats that induce a party to enter into a transaction without exercising free will.[35] Do any of these prohibitions govern the conduct described in Problem 8D?

On the facts of Problem 8D(1), roughly half of 2,500 surveyed litigators felt that it would be permissible to report plaintiffs to the INS and to stress the risk of deportation in settlement negotiations. However, most respondents did not perceive any professional obligation to use such a tactic, and only 15 percent felt that they could explicitly threaten to make an INS report in order to obtain a lower settlement.[36] Is the line most litigators draw a convincing one? Would mentioning the possibility of a deportation report constitute an implicit threat? Are there circumstances that might prompt you to make such threats? Would the fairness of your client's proposed settlement be significant?

How would you evaluate the conduct in Problem 8D(2)? The example is drawn from Roy Cohn's Tips to Men on the Divorce Game. Cohn noted that raising the issue of fees might make the other lawyer "much more reasonable," and adds:

> [T]he first job of any good matrimonial lawyer is to try to get a recon-
> ciliation. If that fails, my first question is, "What have you got on
> her?" Then, "What are our vulnerable points, how much does she
> know about them, and are they provable?" Immediately hire a private
> detective and have him dig for adverse information on your wife's per-
> sonal life and spending habits. . . . All this might sound a little cold,
> but when it gets to that point you're at war. Only one side wins.[37]

What constitutes "winning" in a divorce case?

Cohn added that he never discussed fees until after reaching a settlement on the merits. Should the bar require such a practice? How else could it respond to fee-related conflicts of interest? Compare Evans v. Jeff D., 475 U.S. 717 (1986) (excerpted at page 450), in which the Supreme Court refused to ban simultaneous negotiation of a substantive claim and of fees available under the Civil Rights Attorneys Fees Awards Act on the ground that parties had a right to know their total liability.

Both the Code (DR 5-101(A)) and the Model Rules (Rule 1.7(b)) prohibit lawyers from allowing representation of a client to be materially limited by their own interests unless the client gives informed consent. Would lawyers' concerns about maintaining their own reputation ever create a conflict of interest that requires disclosure to a client? Are reputational interests different in kind or degree from financial interests? Should attorneys who do not wish to play the role of "bomber" ever have an obligation to discuss that fact and its implications with the client? Consider Roger Fisher's negotiating code, excerpted at pages 339–342. Of course, lawyers' interests in maintaining their own reputation and moral standards are potentially implicated in all cases. See Chapter II (Traditions of Moral Reasoning) at pages 27–36. Under what circumstances should these interests become a subject for discussion with clients?

May lawyers advise their clients to deal directly with an oppos-
ing party who is represented by counsel where bar rules prohibit lawyers from making such contacts themselves? See Model Rule 4.2 and DR 7-104(A)(1). Bar ethics opinions suggest that attorneys need not dissuade clients from such direct communications but may not propose or assist them. City of New York Opinion 1991-2; California Formal Opinion 1993-131. How should the lawyer proceed in Problem 8D(3)?

What dialogue should take place on the facts of Problem 8D(3)? Maurice Franks offers the following advice to men in divorce cases:

[Perhaps your wife at first seems reasonable.] If you can get through to her at this stage, get her to a lawyer of your choosing *immediately*, for a mutually agreed-upon divorce on your terms. Get it typed and signed today. With the passage of every day, her anger and greed will only increase. So will the unreasonableness of her demands.

The general pattern is that the lady sees a lawyer of her choosing. He quickly straightens her out on divorce protocol. After all, if he can't get her to go straight for your jugular, how is he going to get his fee?

[Once your wife has retained such a lawyer, your best strategy is to be thoroughly prepared for trial, and to make your wife painfully] aware of this. Has it occurred to you that in a divorce action, children can be a valuable commodity? That a child in the home is like money drawing interest in the bank, or rather like money invested in solid municipal bonds, paying tax-free dividends?

Well, think about it. There's a good chance that your children's mother has thought about it.[38]

How would you evaluate this advice? How does it compare to the conduct described in Problem 8D(3)? Compare the following Standards of Conduct of the American Academy of Matrimonial Lawyers:

Comment to Standard 2.2

Children. One of the most troubling issues in family law is determining a lawyer's obligations to children. The lawyer must represent the client zealously, but not at the expense of children. The parents' fiduciary obligations for the well being of a child provide a basis for the attorney's consideration of the child's best interests consistent with traditional adversary and client loyalty principles.

STANDARD 2.25

An attorney should not contest child custody or visitation for either financial leverage or vindictiveness.

Comment:

Clients in contested dissolutions sometimes ask attorneys to contest custody even though they concede that the other spouse is the better parent. It is improper for the matrimonial lawyer to assist the client in such conduct. Proper consideration of the welfare of the children requires that they not be used as pawns in the adversary process. If despite the attorney's advice the client persists, the attorney should seek to withdraw.

Should bar ethical codes and court decisions incorporate such standards? Would they be enforceable?

Although the frequency of "custody blackmail" is subject to dispute, one large-scale California survey found no evidence that custody threats to gain financial advantage were common, while researchers in other states have found such behavior routine. Part of the variation may be due to differences in research methodologies and in state standards governing property, custody, and support obligations.[39] However, in one recent survey, divorce lawyers estimated that in about a fifth of their cases, a parent (almost always the mother) makes financial concessions to avoid custody battles.[40]

To what extent can, or should, we rely on changes in the substantive law to curb bargaining behavior of the type described in Problem 8D(3)? Some jurisdictions, including West Virginia where former Justice Neely served, have adopted presumptions favoring primary caretakers in custody disputes. While some commentators applaud such presumptions as a way to curtail strategic bargaining, others object that the price is to reinforce stereotypes that caretaking is only one parent's (usually the mother's) primary responsibility. (See Chapter XVI (Family Law) at pages 702-704.) Moreover, even in jurisdictions that have adopted such presumptions, some aspects of custody agreements can still be open to negotiation (i.e., how much time will each parent have with the child, may the custodial parent move out of state, etc.).

If parents and their lawyers will inevitably have opportunities for coercive bargaining, what considerations should be relevant to their decisions? How significant would you find the following factors: the reasonableness of the parties' respective settlement proposals; the parties' relative financial circumstances; your assessment of the children's interests; your relationships with the client and opposing counsel.

Does the threat to reveal the husband's prior gay relationship in Problem 8D(4) present significantly different considerations? Suppose that you are aware of a substantial body of research indicating that a parent's homosexuality does not generally have any adverse effect on the children and does not affect the children's sexual orientation. You are also aware that such research is unlikely to prevent many judges from drawing unfavorable inferences from a prior gay relationship.[41] If a client insists on using such a relationship as a bargaining chip, how should the lawyer respond? Would it matter whether the husband had made unreasonable property demands or had threatened to reveal potentially compromising financial dealings by the wife?

Consider the costs of hardball strategies noted earlier, together with Geoffrey Hazard's claim that a lawyer's bargaining tactics should not depend on the equities between the parties. In Hazard's view, it should not matter if one side is vengefully trying to "strip" the other's assets, or alternatively is "out in the cold and rain" because the client "has squirreled [all the marital property] away in the Caribbean." If the equities of a case become a justification for otherwise unjustifiable hardball tactics, Hazard asks: "Where the hell are we? You can't make these cases turn on the underlying merits."[42] Do you agree?

Would you prefer the dialogue that Carrie Menkel-Meadow proposes:

In considering the acceptability of a particular solution, both lawyer and client might engage in a dialogue about the fairness or justness of their proposals. Putting aside for the moment philosophical debates about the appropriate measures of justness or fairness, lawyer and client might simply ask each other what, if any, detrimental effect their solution has on themselves, the other party, third parties, or the larger society. No current rule requires the lawyer or her client to act on such a dialogue. However, . . . the withdrawal rules will govern those lawyers and clients who may have a differing sense of justice or fairness and who choose to part company over their differences.

In one sense this moral dialogue is simply part of ascertaining the client's needs and thus falls squarely within the problem-solving model. By not discussing these issues with her client, the lawyer may be assuming the standardized, self-interested profit maximizer that dominates the adversarial model. Thus, to the extent that the client does have a need to act fairly, morally, or justly, the lawyer must determine such needs as carefully as she determines how much money the client needs. . . .

In a sense, consideration of the justness of the solution may [also] be a "need" of the lawyer who seeks to participate in a process that accomplishes just results, or at least is conducted in a manner which gives full expression to the autonomy and dignity of the participants. Some commentators would go further and suggest that consideration of the justness or fairness of a solution is not a need, but an obligation derived either from the special duties and obligations of our profession, or from the ordinary duties and obligations of our humanity. . . .[43]

D. THE ROLE OF RULES

An earlier draft of the Model Rules of Professional Conduct required a lawyer to "be fair in dealing with other participants."[44] Would you support such a provision? Would it help in dealing with any of the conduct in Problems 8A to 8D? James White, in a much-quoted article on "Machiavelli and the Bar," criticized proposed rules requiring fairness and candor on the ground that they were "set at too high a level of generality" and failed to appreciate the wide variation in bargaining approaches across lawyers' geographic locations, substantive fields, and practice settings.[45] In White's view, it would be "better to have no rule than to have one so widely violated as to be a continuing hypocrisy that may (compromise) the application of the remaining rules."[46]

Do you agree? Legal standards governing highway speed or driving under the influence of alcohol are frequently violated. Does it follow that such violations erode respect for law generally or that such standards should be abolished? Even where noncompliance is common, legal and ethical requirements serve important societal functions. They clarify standards, remove excuses, and provide some support for lawyers who wish to resist client or collegial pressure to cut ethical corners.[47] In the ABA study of 2,500 litigators noted earlier, most attorneys found that ethical codes provided some guidance on negotiating behavior, and over 40 percent believed that revising codified rules would be an effective way of improving standards.[48] The risk of undemanding ethical provisions may be "socialization to the lowest common denominator of conduct that a highly self-interested constituency will publicly brand as deviant."[49] The Model Rules' approach, which invokes generally "accepted conventions" to permit puffing, has aroused particular concern. In critics' view, this approach offers no criteria for identifying which conventions count, and tolerates practices that should be subject to critical reexamination.[50]

What is your view? Would you support greater obligations of candor and fairness in bar ethical codes? Should disciplinary committees play a more active role in policing negotiations? Would sanctions be appropriate for any of the conduct in Problems 8A to 8D?

E.   MEDIATION

1.   Introduction

AMERICAN BAR ASSOCIATION, STANDING COMMITTEE ON DISPUTE RESOLUTION, PROPOSED MODEL RULE ON LAWYERS ACTING AS MEDIATORS FOR NON-CLIENTS

Dispute Resolution News 2 (Fall 1991)

LAWYERS ACTING AS MEDIATORS FOR NON-CLIENTS

(a) A lawyer may act as a mediator but must inform the parties of the difference between the lawyer's role as mediator and the lawyer's role as advocate. The lawyer shall act as mediator only with the parties' consent, unless the parties are attending the session pursuant to a legal mandate.

(b) The lawyer who acts as mediator shall advise and encourage the parties to seek independent legal counsel before a settlement agreement is executed.

(c) If either of the parties do not have independent legal counsel, the lawyer-mediator shall give legal information to a party only in the presence of all parties in the matter. The lawyer-mediator shall advise unrepresented parties or those parties whose independent counsel does not accompany them about the importance of reviewing the lawyer-mediator's legal information with an independent counsel.

(d) A lawyer may act as mediator only if the lawyer has not previously nor is currently representing one of the parties in connection with the subject matter of the mediation.

(e) A lawyer may act as mediator in a dispute involving a past or present client, who was or is represented in a matter unrelated to the mediation, provided (i) there is full disclosure of the representation, (ii) in light of the disclosure, obtain the parties' informed consent, (iii) there is no breach of confidentiality, and (iv) the mediator is impartial. This does not prohibit intermediation between clients, which is interpreted by Rule 2.2 [or EC 5-20].

(f) A lawyer may not act on behalf of any party to a mediation, nor represent one such party against the other, in any legal proceeding related to the subject of the mediation.

(g) A lawyer shall withdraw as mediator if any of the conditions stated in this rule are no longer satisfied or if any of the parties to the mediation so request except when the parties are attending pursuant to a legal mandate. Upon withdrawal, the lawyer shall not represent any of the parties in any present or future matters that were the subject of the mediation.

(h) A lawyer mediator shall not charge a fee contingent on the outcome of the mediation.

PROBLEM 8E

With some reservations, you agreed to serve as a mediator in a divorce action involving the son of an old friend. The couple insisted that they had no substantial disagreements and wished to avoid the costs of separate representation. Each spouse willingly signed an informed consent form acknowledging that you were serving as a mediator rather than an advocate, and that you had advised them to obtain independent counsel.

The couple had been married 12 years. The wife worked to put the husband through law school and then deferred paid employment for several years in order to care for their two children. She recently returned to her job teaching high school English. The couple plans to share legal custody of the children; the wife will have physical custody.

After several sessions, the parties have reached an agreement. Although the terms clearly favor the husband, the disposition is still within the range of what you believe a court would approve. The agreement does, however, have three unsettling aspects. First, you have reason to believe that the husband, a personal injury attorney, may not have been entirely candid in disclosing financial assets. You suspect that he receives consulting income that does not appear on the couple's tax returns and that he has understated the potential value of certain contingent-fee cases that are nearing settlement. A second difficulty is that the wife has waived spousal maintenance and all interest in community property purchased by the husband with his salary income during the marriage. You are uncertain whether the waiver is attributable to feminist principles, guilt, or unwillingness to take a strong bargaining stance that would provoke conflict. A final problem is that, in exchange for the wife's financial concessions, the husband has agreed to restrict his time with the children to vacations and holidays, and to cease bringing them for visits to their paternal grandparents.

What is your role if you believe that the financial agreement is unreasonably lopsided? How should you handle the disclosure issue? Suppose that you discuss the matter with the husband separately and that he affirms his original financial statements without responding fully to your concerns? Are you obligated or permitted to raise the issue with the wife or to conduct any independent investigation? How should you handle the husband's concessions concerning custody if you believe that they are not in the children's best interest?

Assume that the parties obtain their divorce and that their mediated settlement is incorporated in the final decree. Subsequently, the wife decides to return to graduate school and seeks to reopen the decree. Among other things, she claims that her husband fraudulently concealed certain assets and that you were negligent in failing to disclose that risk or to provide adequate financial counseling. She also threatens to sue you for malpractice and seeks damages based on the cost of relitigating the original agreement. What is your likely liability?

Like other forms of alternative dispute resolution discussed in Chapter V (The Adversary System), mediation often has advantages over traditional adversarial processes. In some circumstances, mediation can be cheaper, quicker, more capable of focusing on the underlying sources of conflict, and more likely to promote party satisfaction and compliance with any agreement.

At an abstract level, the goals and structure of mediation command broad consensus: an impartial facilitator assists parties in identifying their interests, understanding their legal options, and reaching an acceptable agreement. At a more concrete level, disagreement centers on what constitutes impartiality and acceptability; how to deal with confidential disclosures; what cases are inappropriate for mediation; what training is essential for mediators; and how to respond to inequalities in the bargaining process. Because formal recognition of lawyers' mediation role is relatively recent, many of these questions remain unsettled under bar ethical codes and committee interpretations.

In an effort to fill this gap, groups such as the American Arbitration Association, American Bar Association, and Society of Professionals in Dispute Resolution have cooperated in developing model Standards of Conduct for Mediators. However, the influence of such standards is not yet clear, and many are formulated at such an abstract level that controversies over mediation ethics are likely to persist.

2.   The Regulatory Framework

The Code of Professional Responsibility mentions mediation only in the Ethical Considerations, not the Disciplinary Rules, and provides little guidance to attorneys who function in that role. EC 5-20 notes:

> A lawyer is often asked to serve as an impartial arbitrator or mediator in matters which involve present or former clients. He may serve in either capacity if he first discloses such present or former relationships. After a lawyer has undertaken to act as an impartial arbitrator or mediator, he should not thereafter represent in the dispute any of the parties involved.

The only Disciplinary Rules governing mediators are the general provisions on conflicts of interest discussed in Chapter VII.

Model Rule 2.2 provides more explicit guidance:

> (a) A lawyer may act as intermediary between clients if:
>
> (1) The lawyer consults with each client concerning the implications of the common representation, including the advantages and risks involved, and the effect on the attorney-client privileges, and obtains each client's consent to the common representation;
>
> (2) the lawyer reasonably believes that the matter can be resolved on terms compatible with the clients' best interests, that each client will be able to make adequately informed decisions in the matter and that there is little risk of material prejudice to the interest of any of the clients if the contemplated resolution is unsuccessful; and
>
> (3) the lawyer reasonably believes that the common representation can be undertaken impartially and without improper effect on other responsibilities the lawyer has to any of the clients. . . .
>
> (c) A lawyer shall withdraw as intermediary if any of the clients so request, or if any of the conditions stated in paragraph (a) is no longer satisfied. Upon withdrawal, the lawyer shall not continue to represent any of the clients in the matter that was the subject of the intermediation.

As Chapter VII indicated, the application of this rule to some common mediation contexts, including divorce, is not entirely clear. Unlike earlier drafts, the final version of Rule 2.2 and its Comment does not mention divorce mediation as an example of the intermediary role. The Comment also advises that a "lawyer cannot undertake common representation of clients between whom contentious litigation is imminent or who contemplate contentious negotiations." For the many divorce mediations that are potentially acrimonious, this admonition raises doubts about the applicability of Rule 2.2 and the appropriateness of the intermediary role more generally. Moreover, the Comment to Rule 2.2 indicates that the provision does not apply to a "lawyer acting as arbitrator or mediator between or among parties who are not clients of the lawyer, even where the lawyer has been appointed with the concurrence of the parties." Since some state bar ethics opinions have held that an attorney-mediator in divorce cases represents neither of the parties, Rule 2.2 would be inapplicable to mediation in those jurisdictions.[51] To fill this regulatory gap, the ABA Standing Committee on Dispute Resolution proposed a Model Rule of Professional Conduct to cover lawyers mediating between nonclients. That rule is set forth above at pages 360–361. Such a rule, like the proposed standards for family law mediators excerpted in Chapter XVI at pages 704–709, would help clear up the current confusion and inconsistencies in ethical standards.

For example, some state bar committee opinions prohibit conventional forms of divorce mediation by lawyers; underlying these decisions are concerns about the inherent potential for conflicting interests and inadequate protection for confidentiality.[52] Other bar committees have authorized divorce mediation on the theory that the lawyer represents neither party.[53] By contrast, many experts take the view that the lawyer-intermediary represents both parties, which would trigger application of Rule 2.2. States also have varying approaches to lawyers' participation in court-annexed mandatory mediation programs.[54]

Of these approaches, the flat ban seems unduly restrictive, while the practical differences between the other permissive approaches remain unduly ambiguous. Recent surveys suggest that in most uncontested divorces, one party goes without a lawyer. Where parties' resources are limited, joint access to an attorney-mediator may be preferable to leaving one spouse unrepresented.[55] Whether mediators are nominally "representing" both or neither party seems less critical than the concrete obligations that the relationship entails, such as requirements of informed consent and rejection of cases involving excessive power disparities.

3. Independent Legal Advice

Some bar ethics committees, in an effort to minimize conflicts of interest, have prohibited mediators from drafting a final agreement or have required that they advise parties to obtain an independent attorney's assessment of any proposed settlement.[56] Although such review may often be helpful, it can also create its own set of problems. If independent counsel intervenes after parties have become psychologically committed to an agreement, the advice may be futile or it may require reopening the entire mediation process. For that reason, Standard VI of the American Bar Association's Standards of Practice for Family Mediators (1984) advises consultation with an independent advisor during the mediation process, prior to agreement. Yet such consultation can also risk duplicating or subverting mediators' own work. The result could be the financial costs and contentiousness that the parties chose mediation to avoid. Thus, lawyers who provide such outside review services need a clear understanding of what functions would be useful. Common examples include assistance in evaluating assets and provision of tax advice.[57]

4.   Professional Skills and Unauthorized Practice

Another area of controversy involves the appropriate training and scope of practice for mediators. In some areas such as divorce mediation, the majority of practitioners are mental health professionals.[58] Their ability to offer services on problems with legal consequences or to affiliate with attorneys has been constrained by prohibitions on unauthorized practice of law. Every state has some form of prohibition on non-lawyer practice that is reinforced by bar ethical codes. Disciplinary Rule 3-101 and Model Rule 5.5 prohibit lawyers from aiding non-lawyers in the practice of law; DR 3-102 and Model Rule 5.4(a) prohibit lawyers from sharing fees with non-lawyers; and DR 3-103 and Model Rule 5.4(b) prohibit forming partnerships with non-lawyers if any of the activities of the partnership involve the practice of law.

The application of these rules to divorce mediators is unclear, in part because prevailing definitions of unauthorized practice are unclear. Decisions regarding the permissible scope of lay services are "consistent only in their inconsistency."[59] In theory, non-lawyer-mediators do not purport to give legal assistance; in practice, they often cannot provide competent services without considering legal issues. As bar leaders have themselves recognized, "all kinds of professional people are practicing the law almost out of necessity."[60]

In response to that reality, some courts have carved out exceptions to broad unauthorized practice prohibitions. Common exemptions include lay legal practice that is widespread in the community, that is incidental to another profession or business, or that serves the public interest.[61] Many commentators believe that mediation in areas such as divorce should fall under at least one of these exceptions. From this perspective, the primary justifications for prohibiting non-lawyer practice, protecting the public from unqualified or unscrupulous practitioners, do not support unqualified bans on lay mediation. Lawyers have not "cornered the market on morality" or expertise in this area, and often have less mediation training than competitors.[62] Many lay mediators are psychologists or social workers who must already satisfy standards of competence and good moral character. Other practitioners could be subject to comparable certification requirements.

So too, while not all lay mediators have legal expertise, not all lawyer-mediators have therapeutic skills. The best answer for both groups may be to expand the training available, both in professional schools and post-licensing programs. An increasing array of educational options are available, ranging from a two-year post-graduate degree program to a five-day training course followed by 250 hours of practice with an experienced family mediator.[63] Yet while cross-professional collaboration has obvious advantages for clients, it is discouraged by bar ethical requirements. Although lawyers and therapists can work together under existing rules by avoiding formal partnerships and joint billing arrangements, these current code limitations may require rethinking.

If mediation services continue to attract increasing public support, they should also have a more carefully tailored regulatory and education structure. For example, the Society of Professionals in Dispute Resolution (SPIDR) has recommended the following principles regarding qualifications:

A. that no single entity (rather, a variety of organizations) should establish qualifications for neutrals;
B. that the greater the degree of choice the parties have over the dispute resolution process, . . . the less mandatory should be the qualification requirements; and
C. that qualification criteria should be based on performance, rather than paper credentials.[64]

How would you apply those principles to attorneys? Should any qualifications apart from a license to practice law be applicable to lawyer-mediators?

5.   Confidentiality

In contexts of joint representation, the attorney-client privilege generally protects the confidentiality of statements only from disclosure to third parties; the privilege does not apply between the joint clients in any subsequent dispute. The privilege also may not protect disclosures to lay practitioners or to lawyers who do not "represent" either party unless the jurisdiction has specifically extended protection to mediation.[65] However, in the absence of such specific provisions, some confidentiality safeguards may be available from other sources. Rule 408 of the Federal Rules of Evidence and its state analogues hold that statements made in settlement negotiations are not admissible in subsequent proceedings. The Standards of Conduct for Mediators require mediators to "maintain the reasonable expectations of the parties with regard to confidentiality." Many mediators also have parties sign confidentiality agreements, although these may not always be enforceable in subsequent disputes.[66]

During the mediation process itself, practitioners differ in the arrangements they make with parties concerning the use of separate caucuses and the sharing of confidential information. In some litigation and labor contexts, shuttle diplomacy between opposing camps is the norm; disclosures from these sessions will not be revealed without a party's authorization. By contrast, in domestic relations, separate meetings with one party are far less common and all information is generally shared.

On the facts of Problem 8E, is it obvious whether the lawyer can provide "adequate representation" (DR 5-105(C)) and ensure that the wife is able to reach an informed agreement compatible with her best interests (Model Rule 2.2)? If the attorney withdraws from representation, can or should she indicate the basis for doing so? If the attorney does not withdraw because she lacks firm evidence of the husband's fraud, could the wife recover in subsequent malpractice litigation?

On facts similar to Problem 8E, a Missouri appellate court rejected the plaintiff's claim. Her complaint alleged that the attorney was negligent in failing (1) to inquire into the husband's financial affairs; (2) to advise her of her full legal rights; and (3) to obtain a more advantageous settlement or to inform her that she would do better if she litigated the matter. Although the court assumed arguendo that the attorney breached his duties and acknowledged that the wife had received a better settlement through litigation, it dismissed her complaint because she failed to establish that the alleged negligence proximately caused any damages. In essence, she failed to demonstrate that if the defendant had properly discharged his duties, she would have obtained a higher mediated settlement without the expense of litigation.[67] Was that the right result? Compare the appellate court's holding in Ishmael v. Millington, 241 Cal. App. 2d 520, 50 Cal. Rptr. 599 (1966), holding that an attorney of ordinary professional skill advising the wife in a divorce action would demand some verification of the husband's financial statement or would at least inform the wife that the statement was unconfirmed and that investigation would be prudent. What advice would you give the attorney on the facts of Problem 8E?

6.   Fairness and Impartiality

The most difficult ethical issue for mediators generally involves their dual responsibility to remain impartial and to ensure a defensible process and result. That issue arises on two levels: how to structure a process that will in general promote just results and how to promote such results in particular cases. Those objectives raise a threshold definitional issue: how do we assess fairness? Does it turn solely on parties' satisfaction or should it have a transformative dimension that develops parties' sense of empowerment and empathy? That issue in turn raises more specific ethical questions: for example, how to present options and their legal implications; how actively to intervene in the face of coercion or disparities in bargaining skills; and how to handle inequities in a proposed settlement. On all of these questions, mediators vary widely, and current standards provide inadequate guidance.[68]

One perspective, dominant in commercial and labor contexts, assumes that impartiality requires neutrality; the mediator's role is to help parties reach a resolution that they find acceptable, whether or not it conforms to the mediator's own views of fairness. This role has the advantage of protecting parties' autonomy, preserving mediators' credibility, and maximizing the chances that participants with superior bargaining leverage will agree to mediated solutions.[69]

At the opposite end of the spectrum are those who define impartiality as fairness; in their view, the mediator's responsibility is to ensure a process and result that meet some minimum standards of justice. This role may require active intervention to maintain a "balanced dialogue" and a settlement that reasonably accommodates the concerns of the parties as well as unrepresented groups or broader societal interests. So, for example, some commentators believe that mediators in environmental disputes should take account of long-term societal effects, and that mediators in divorce cases should consider children's interests as well as those of more vulnerable spouses.[70] From this perspective, mediators' obligation of impartiality requires them to avoid accepting cases where prior loyalties distort their ability to be even-handed and to disclose any substantive commitments that might affect their role.[71]

Between these two positions lie several intermediate options. One approach, reportedly the most common in divorce mediation, seeks to balance concerns for fairness and autonomy.[72] The ABA's Task Force on Mediation for the Section on Family Law attempts such a balance in its Divorce and Mediation Standards of Practice (1985), excerpted in Chapter XVI (Family Law) at pages 704–709. They provide:

> III. D. Impartiality is not the same as neutrality. While the mediator must be impartial as between the mediation participants, the mediator should be concerned with fairness. The mediator has an obligation to avoid an unreasonable result.
>
> E. The mediator has a duty to promote the best interest of the children.
>
> V. The mediator has a duty to suspend or terminate mediation whenever continuation of the process would harm or prejudice one or more of the participants. . . .
>
> E. The mediator has a duty to assure balanced dialogue and must attempt to diffuse any manipulative or intimidating negotiation techniques utilized by either of the participants.

The Standards also emphasize the need for full disclosure and equal understanding of relevant financial and legal information, as well as communication of "biases or strong views" that would affect the mediator's conduct.

Other commentators and professional groups have proposed alternative approaches. Judith Maute suggests that the Model Rules include a requirement that lawyers may not knowingly finalize an agreement that they reasonably believe to be illegal, grossly inequitable, or based on false information.[73] By contrast, Robert Baruch Bush argues that mediators' preeminent responsibilities are to empower the parties to exercise autonomy and to promote the parties' mutual respect for each other's needs and concerns. If mediators sense unfairness in a potential agreement, they should test the "exploited" party's comprehension of the terms and consequences of that agreement. If that party is fully aware of the implications, then a mediator's termination of the process would be an inappropriate "act of disempowerment."[74] Which of these approaches do you find preferable?

For cases falling short of grossly inequitable or misinformed agreements, many mediators simply recommend that each party seek review by separate outside counsel. How often such recommendations prevent unfairness is open to question. It is often difficult or impossible for a reviewing attorney to know whether a proposed settlement is in the client's best interest without engaging in precisely the process that the parties entered mediation to avoid.

In recognition of this fact, some commentators, including many feminists and critical race theorists, argue that mediation is inappropriate for cases involving substantial power disparities. These commentators also object to mandatory mediation programs, such as those established by some jurisdictions for domestic violence or child custody cases. Because mediation places the parties on equal footing and invites compromise, it may lead to inappropriate concessions from more vulnerable participants and may fail adequately to deter abusive conduct or coercive bargaining.[75] Some evidence suggests that women as a group are less willing than men to assert their own needs or to tolerate conflict, and that a conciliatory process may not provide adequate checks for racial, ethnic, and gender bias.[76]

By contrast, defenders of mediation note that women and subordinate groups do not necessarily fare better in more adversarial processes and that they report greater satisfaction.[77] The material in Chapter V on "Why the Haves Come Out Ahead" (pages 176–177) and Judge Neely's discussion of coercion in nonmediated divorce cases suggest as much. As Jay Folberg and Alison Taylor explain:

> The voiced concern about the fairness aspect of mediated agreements tends to compare mediation with a romanticized notion of formal justice. In considering whether mediated settlements will be fair and just, we must ask "compared to what?"... Many disputes resolved outside of mediation are the result of unequal bargaining power due to different levels of experience, patterns of dominance, different propensities for risk avoidance, the greater emotional needs of one disputant, or psychological obstacles in the path to settlement. Should the matter proceed to litigation, the same items may skew the fairness of the outcome in court as in the bargaining phase, and in addition there may be unequal resources to bear the costs of litigation, different levels of sophistication in choosing the best attorneys, and just plain luck as to which judge is assigned to make a decision. These comments are not intended as unique criticisms of our adversarial or judicial systems; no dispute resolution mechanism is devoid of problems concern-

ing fair outcomes, and none of the alternatives is the best for every dispute.[78]

From this perspective, the most productive strategy is not to require or to remove the mediation option for a given set of cases, but rather to provide a choice of processes seeking to minimize unjust tactics and results. Some commentators argue that these processes should meet certain minimum standards. So, for example, Carrie Menkel-Meadow argues that parties should give genuine uncoerced consent to the process and its outcome; parties should have a fair opportunity to choose and participate in the process; and the process should be conducted by a neutral, nonpartisan third party.[79]

Which of these preceding positions would you find most appropriate on the facts of Problem 8E? Is mediation the right strategy for this case? Would either the confidentiality or fairness problems be easier if the mediator had made clear at the outset how she would respond to incomplete disclosures or biased results? If you had been the mediator, what clarification would you have provided?

Endnotes

1. Herbert M. Krietzer, Let's Make a Deal: Understanding the Negotiation Process in Ordinary Litigation, (1991); Paul M. Lisnek, A Lawyer's Guide to Effective Negotiation and Mediation (1993) (arguing for cooperative model).

2. See Robert Axelrod, The Evolution of Cooperation (1984). For general arguments favoring cooperative styles, see Carrie Menkel-Meadow, Toward Another View of Negotiation: The Structure of Legal Problem Solving, 31 UCLA L. Rev. 754 (1984).

3. As Chapter V and Chapter VII indicate, these dilemmas arise when it would serve both parties' interests to deal fairly and cooperatively but if one negotiator is doubtful about an opponent's willingness to engage in such behavior, then noncooperation is preferable. Under circumstances of uncertainty, rational bargainers will not cooperate and will thus undermine their own interests. For discussion of how lawyers can help clients avoid prisoners' dilemmas, see Ronald Gilson & Robert Mnookin, Disputing Through Agents: Cooperation and Competition in Litigation: Can Lawyers Dampen Conflict?, 94 Colum. L. Rev. 509 (1994).

4. Axelrod, supra note 2, at 20, 54.

5. Reed Elizabeth Loder, Moral Truthseeking and the Virtuous Negotiator, 8 Geo. J. Legal Ethics 45, 58 (1994).

6. Gerald B. Wetlaufer, The Ethics of Lying in Negotiations, 75 Iowa L. Rev. 1219, 1272-1273 (1990).

7. This exercise is based on a simulation developed by Richard Burke of the Center for Dispute Resolution at Willamette Law School.

8. James J. White, Machiavelli and the Bar: Ethical Limitations on Lying in Negotiations, 1980 Am. B. Found. Res. J. 926, 927.

9. Sissela Bok, Lying: Moral Choice in Public and Private Life 17-32 (1978); Wetlaufer, supra note 6, at 1228-1229; Loder, supra note 5, at 57-58.

10. Leonard Greenhalgh, The Case Against Winning in Negotiations, 3 Negotiation J. 167, 170 (1987). See also Roger Fisher & William Ury, Getting to Yes 137-140 (1981).

11. Jethro K. Lieberman, Crisis at the Bar 32 (1978).

12. Larry Lempert, In Settlement Talks Does Telling the Truth Have Its Limits?, 2 Inside Litig. 1, 16 (1988). See also David Genenemus, Lies,

Damn Lies and Unethical Lies, Bus. Law Today, May/June 1992, at 11, 12 (suggesting that a lawyer's misrepresentation of settlement authority might not be considered a lie because a client who was present at the negotiation would not authorize an unnecessarily generous result).

13. White, supra note 8, at 942 (suggesting evasive responses); Wetlaufer, supra note 6, at 1237 (suggesting that lawyers can challenge the question as inappropriate or justify their preferred figure); Loder, supra note 5, at 76.

14. Wetlaufer, supra note 6, at 1242 n.73; Gary Tobias Lowenthal, The Bar's Failure to Require Truthful Bargaining by Lawyers, 2 Geo. J. Legal Ethics 383, 421 (1988).

15. Lowenthal, supra note 14, at 421; Restatement (Second) of Contracts §§159, 168 (1993).

16. Lempert, supra note 12, at 18 (quoting Charles Craver).

17. Id. (quoting James White).

18. Id. (quoting Ronald Rotunda).

19. See the materials on witness preparation in Part E of Chapter V (The Adversary System).

20. Monroe Freedman, Lying: Is It Ethical? Legal Times, Dec. 12, 1994, at 20; Monroe Freedman, Acceptable Lies, Legal Times, Feb. 20, 1995, at 24.

21. Alvin B. Rubin, A Causerie on Lawyers' Ethics in Negotiations, 35 La. L. Rev. 577 (1975).

22. Russell Engler, Out of Sight and Out of Line, The Need for Regulation of Lawyers Negotiating with Unrepresented Poor Persons, 85 Cal. L. Rev. 79 (1997).

23. Samuel Williston, A Treatise on the Law of Contracts §1515B (3d ed. 1970); Wetlaufer, supra note 6, at 1242 n.74; Lowenthal, supra note 14, at 439 n.129.

24. William H. Simon, Ethical Discretion in Lawyering, 101 Harv. L. Rev. 1083, 1099 (1988).

25. See the discussion of discovery strategies in Chapter X (Civil Procedure), infra.

26. ABA Standing Committee on Ethics and Professional Responsibility, Formal Op. 94-387 (1994).

27. Engler, supra note 22, describing Housing Courts where 90 percent of the tenants lack lawyers and often experience over-reaching by landlords' lawyers.

28. Lowenthal, supra note 14, at 427. See also Restatement Second of Contracts §161B (1979).

29. Wes Hanson, Lawyers, Lawyers, Lawyers, Ethics: Easier Said Than Done (Joseph and Edna Josephson Institute, 1993).

30. Lempert, supra note 12, at 18 (quoting Hazard).

31. Rubin, supra note 21, at 589-592.

32. Lowenthal, supra note 14, at 429.

33. Stephen D. Pepe, Standards of Legal Negotiations: Interim Report for ABA Commission on Evaluation of Professional Standards and ABA House of Delegates (1983).

34. Model Rules of Professional Conduct, Rule 4.2(b) and (c) (Discussion Draft 1980), discussed in Lowenthal, supra note 14, at 429.

35. See Joseph M. Livermore, Lawyer Extortion, 20 Ariz. L. Rev. 403 (1978); DR 7-101(A)(1); Model Rule 1.16; Restatement of Contracts §492 (1980); Alan Wertheimer, Coercion 29-46 (1987). Other jurisdictions' extortion statutes follow the Model Penal Code, which explicitly exempts

threats to bring criminal charges made during negotiation of a civil claim. Model Penal Code §233.4 (1980).

36. Pepe, supra note 33.

37. Roy Cohn, Roy Cohn's Tips to Men on the Divorce Game, People Magazine, Jan. 24, 1983, at 17.

38. Maurice Franks, Winning Custody 32, 34 (1983).

39. Compare Eleanor Maccoby & Robert H. Mnookin, Dividing the Child (1993) with Jana B. Singer & William L. Reynolds, A Dissent on Joint Custody, 47 Md. L. Rev. 497, 515-516 (1988).

40. Scott Altman, Lurking in the Shadow, 68 U.S. Cal. L. Rev. 493, 497-504 (1995).

41. See sources cited in Deborah L. Rhode, Speaking of Sex 189 (1997), and Problem 11A in Chapter XI (Constitutional Law) at page 459.

42. Panel Discussion, A Gathering of Legal Scholars to Discuss Professional Responsibility and the Model Rules of Professional Conduct, 35 U. Miami L. Rev. 639, 654 (1981).

43. Menkel-Meadow, supra note 2, at 815-817.

44. Model Rule 4.2(a), discussed in White, supra note 8, at 928.

45. Id. at 929-931.

46. Id. at 937-938.

47. Deborah L. Rhode, Ethical Perspectives on Legal Practice, 37 Stan. L. Rev. 589, 647-649 (1985); Lowenthal, supra note 14, at 442-443.

48. Pepe, supra note 33.

49. Rhode, supra note 47, at 647.

50. Eleanor Holmes Norton, Bargaining and the Ethic of Process, 64 N.Y.U. L. Rev. 493, 538 (1989).

51. Boston Bar Ethics Committee, No. 78-1 (1978); Association of the Bar of the City of New York, Op. 80-23 (1981).

52. See Rita Henley Jensen, Divorce, Mediation Style, A.B.A.J., Feb. 1997, at 56; Andrew S. Morrison, Is Divorce Mediation the Practice of Law? A Matter of Perspective, 75 Cal. L. Rev. 1093, 1119 (1987); Linda Silberman, Professional Responsibility Problems of Divorce Mediation, 16 Fam. L.Q. 109, 111-123, 128-134 (1982).

53. See opinions cited in note 51, supra.

54. See Morrison, supra note 52, at 1140. For discussion of Rule 2.2, see Silberman, supra note 52. For court programs, see Jensen, supra note 52, at 56.

55. Patricia Winks, Divorce Mediation: A Nonadversary Procedure for the No-Fault Divorce, 19 J. Fam. L. 615, 625-626 (1981).

56. See Morrison, supra note 52, at 1117. For example, the Boston Bar Ethics opinion contemplates that the lawyer-mediator will both advise independent review and refrain from representing either party in subsequent divorce proceedings. Boston Bar Ethics Committee, supra note 51.

57. M. Dee Samuels & Joel A. Shawn, The Role of the Lawyer Outside the Mediation Process, 2 Mediation 13, 15 (1983).

58. Emily Brown, Divorce Mediation in a Mental Health Setting, in Divorce Mediation 127 (J. Folberg & Ann Milne eds., 1988).

59. Morrison, supra note 52, at 1095 (quoting Comment).

60. James Podgers, Statements of Principles: Are They on the Way Out?, 66 A.B.A.J. 129 (1980) (quoting J.P. Strauss).

61. Deborah L. Rhode, The Delivery of Legal Services by Nonlawyers, 4 Geo. J. Legal Ethics 209 (1990).

62. Jensen, supra note 52, at 57. See Morrison, supra note 52, at 1115; Rhode, supra note 61; and Deborah L. Rhode, Professionalism in Perspec-

tive: Alternative Approaches to Nonlawyer Practice, 22 N.Y.U. Rev. L. & Soc. Change 701 (1996). For discussion of lawyers' training, see Scott H. Hughes, Elizabeth's Story: Exploring Power Imbalances in Divorce Mediation, 8 Geo. J. Legal Ethics 553, 571 (1995).

63. Alan J. Cornblatt, Matrimonial Mediation, 23 J. Fam. L. 99, 104-105 (1984-1985).

64. See generally Society of Professionals in Dispute Resolution (SPIDR), Report of the SPIDR Commission on Qualifications (1989); Carrie Menkel-Meadow, Measuring Both the Art and Science of Mediation, 9 Negotiation J. 321 (1993); Jensen, supra note 52, at 57; Jay Folberg & Alison Taylor, Mediation: A Comprehensive Guide to Resolving Conflicts Without Litigation 255-260 (1984); Lois Gold, Interdisciplinary Team Mediation, 36 Mediation Q. 27 (1984).

65. Cletus Hess, To Disclose or Not to Disclose: The Relationship Between Confidentiality in Mediation and the Model Rules of Professional Conduct, 95 Dick. L. Rev. 601, 605 (1991).

66. See id.; Carrie Menkel-Meadow, Ethics in Alternative Dispute Resolution: New Issues, No Answers from the Adversary Conception of Lawyers' Responsibilities, 38 S. Tex. L. Rev. 407, 441-443 (1997). Lawrence Freedman & Michael L. Prigoff, Confidentiality in Mediation: The Need for Protection, 2 Ohio St. J. on Disp. Resol. 37 (1986).

67. Lange v. Marshall, 622 S.W.2d 237, 238-239 (Mo. 1981).

68. Hughes, supra note 62, at 585-591. See also Robert A. Baruch Bush & Joseph P. Folger, The Promise of Mediation: Responding to Conflict through Empowerment and Recognition (1994) (describing varying conceptions of fairness).

69. Joseph B. Stulberg, The Theory and Practice of Mediation: A Reply to Professor Susskind, 6 Vt. L. Rev. 85, 89 (1981); Leonard L. Riskin & James E. Westbrook, Dispute Resolution and Lawyers 209-212 (1987).

70. Phyllis Gangel-Jacob, Some Words of Caution About Divorce Mediation, 23 Hofstra L. Rev. 825 (1995); Lawrence Susskind, Environmental Mediation and the Accountability Problem, 6 Vt. L. Rev. 1, 46-47 (1981); Sara Cobb & Janet Rifkin, Practice and Paradox: Deconstructing Neutrality in Mediation, 16 Law & Socy. Inquiry 35 (1991).

71. Christopher Honeyman, Bias and Mediators' Ethics, 1986 Negotiation J. 175, 176-177; Jonathan G. Shailor, Empowerment in Dispute Mediation: A Critical Analysis of Communication (1994); Leo F. Smyth, Intractable Conflicts and the Role of Identity, 10 Negotiation J. 311, 314 (1994); Joseph P. Folger & Sydney E. Bernard, Divorce Mediation: When Mediators Challenge the Divorcing Parties, Mediation Q., Dec. 1985, at 5, 19.

72. Folger & Bernard, supra note 71, at 5, 19. See generally Mark D. Bennett & Michele S.G. Hermann, The Art of Mediation 118 (1996).

73. See Judith Maute, Public Values and Private Judging: A Case for Mediator Acceptability, 4 Geo. J. Legal Ethics 503, 515 (1991).

74. Robert A. Baruch Bush, Efficiency and Protection of Empowerment and Recognition? The Mediator's Role and Ethical Standards in Mediation, 41 Fla. L. Rev. 253, 272, 284 (1989).

75. Demie Kurz, For Richer, for Poorer: Mothers Confront Divorce 137 (1996) (one-third of surveyed women feared violence or retaliation for pressing legal claims in divorce negotiations). See also Trina Grillo, The Mediation Alternative: Process Dangers for Women, 100 Yale L.J. 1545, 1599 (1991).

76. Hughes, supra note 62; Jessica Pearson & Nancy Thoennes, Divorce Mediation Research Results, in Divorce Mediation 429, 440-441 (Jay Folberg & Ann Milne eds., 1988); Richard Delgado et al., Fairness and Formality: Minimizing the Risk of Prejudice in Alternative Dispute Resolution, 1985 Wis. L. Rev. 1359; Penelope E. Bryan, Killing Us Softly: Divorce Mediation and the Politics of Power, 40 Buff. L. Rev. 441 (1991).

77. Marc Galanter & Mia Cahill, "Most Cases Settle": Judicial Promotion and Regulation of Settlements, 46 Stan. L. Rev. 1339, 1354-1355 (1994) (summarizing research finding higher satisfaction with mediation than adjudication, and greatest satisfaction among disempowered groups); Carol Bohmer & Marilyn L. Ray, Effects of Different Dispute Resolution Methods on Women and Children After Divorce, 28 Fam. L.Q. 223 (1994) (summarizing mixed results); Jessica Pearson, The Equity of Mediated Arguments, 9 Mediation Q. 179 (1991) (finding mediation no worse than adversarial processes in generating agreements perceived to be equitable); J. Kelly, Empirical Research in Divorce and Family Mediation, 24 Mediation Q. 86 (1989) (finding women who participated in divorce mediation more satisfied). See generally Menkel-Meadow, supra note 2; Joshua D. Rosenberg, In Defense of Mediation, 33 Ariz. L. Rev. 467 (1991).

78. Folberg & Taylor, supra note 64, at 246-247. See Menkel-Meadow, supra note 2.

79. Menkel-Meadow, supra note 66, at 451.

Chapter IX

The Lawyer-Client Relationship

A. LAWYER-CLIENT DECISION-MAKING: PROBLEMS OF PATERNALISM

1. Introduction

Paternalism in lawyer-client relationships is seldom preached but often practiced. As conventionally defined, paternalism involves imposing restrictions on individuals' freedom of choice in order to promote their own interests. Such restrictions implicate two competing principles: autonomy and benevolence. Our respect for personal liberty and dignity counsels deference to clients' own choices; our desire to do good sometimes argues for overriding clients' choices for their own benefit.[1]

According to philosopher Richard Wasserstrom, some measure of paternalism is inherent in professional practice:

> For the professional is, in some respects at least, always in a position of dominance vis-à-vis the client, and the client in a position of dependence vis-à-vis the professional. To be sure, the client can often decide whether or not to enter into a relationship with a professional. And often, too, the client has the power to decide whether to terminate the relationship. But the significant thing I want to focus upon is

that while the relationship exists, there are important respects in which the relationship cannot be a relationship between equals and must be one in which it is the professional who is in control. . . .

To begin with, there is the fact that one characteristic of professions is that the professional is the possessor of expert knowledge of a sort not readily or easily attainable by members of the community at large. . . . Moreover, virtually every profession has its own technical language, a private terminology which can only be fully understood by the members of the profession. . . . These circumstances, together with others, produce the added consequence that the client is in a poor position effectively to evaluate how well or badly the professional performs. In the professions, the professional does not look primarily to the client to evaluate the professional's work. . . .

In addition, because the matters for which professional assistance is sought usually involve things of great personal concern to the client, it is the received wisdom within the professions that the client lacks the perspective necessary to pursue in a satisfactory way his or her own best interests, and that the client requires a detached, disinterested representative to look after his or her interests. . . .

Finally, as I have indicated, to be a professional is to have been acculturated in a certain way. It is to have satisfactorily passed through a lengthy and allegedly difficult period of study and training. . . . Almost all professions encourage this way of viewing oneself: as having joined an elect group by virtue of hard work and mastery of the mysteries of the profession. In addition, the society at large treats members of a profession as members of an elite. . . . If one is a member of a collection of individuals who are accorded high prestige by the society at large, it is equally easy to believe that one is better and knows better than most people.[2]

In some contexts, such as those involving poverty or criminal law, inequalities of class, education, and race further increase the likelihood of professional dominance and paternalistic intervention.

Of course, the leverage in most lawyer-client relationships runs in both directions. Private practitioners depend on clients for their livelihood and, as David Luban emphasizes, "this economic dependence is fundamental in the distribution of power."[3] Sophisticated business clients also may have less difficulty evaluating their own interests or their lawyers' performance than Wasserstrom assumes. Yet even granting these qualifications, experts generally agree that legal practice presents considerable opportunity for paternalism. Simply by diagnosing client needs and presenting potential responses, lawyers inevitably shape the choices available. Research across a broad range of contexts suggests that the boundary between counseling and manipulation is easily overstepped, particularly when the clients are one-shot, unsophisticated consumers of legal services. For example, attorneys in criminal, family, and personal injury cases often attempt to revise client expectations and decisions in accordance with the attorneys' own (not always disinterested) evaluations of the client's best interest.[4] Even in corporate settings, lawyers' technical expertise and experience may enable them to exercise substantial influence over client decision-making.[5]

These opportunities for professional authority provoke three common responses. Some observers, including many attorneys, find nothing wrong with paternalism because they believe either that the client consents implicitly or explicitly to such influence, or that the exercise of professional expertise generally results in less harm than good. As Elihu Root once put it, "about half the practice of a decent lawyer consists in telling would-be clients that they are damn fools and should stop."

By contrast, a second view finds nothing right in attorneys' paternalism, except when the client is under some disability, such as youth or mental impairment. This is, in general, the bar's official position. Unless the client is under a disability as defined below, Model Rule 1.2 requires that a lawyer shall "abide by a client's decisions concerning the objectives of representation . . . and shall consult with the client as to the means by which they are to be pursued." Ethical Consideration 7-7 similarly provides:

> In certain areas of legal representation not affecting the merits of the cause or substantially prejudicing the rights of a client, a lawyer is entitled to make decisions on his own. But otherwise the authority to make decisions is exclusively that of the client and, if made within the framework of the law, such decisions are binding on his lawyer.

This view builds on principles that John Stuart Mill elaborated in his book, On Liberty. For the most part, Mill maintained that the only justification for infringement of a sane adult's freedom was prevention of harm to others. Mill defended this position on utilitarian grounds. Under his analysis, each person ordinarily is the best judge of his own interests as well as the person most intensely concerned with his own welfare; allowing each individual to maximize his own preferences would therefore result in the greatest good for the greatest number.

Mill did, however, recognize certain exceptions to this general principle. They form the starting point for a third approach to paternalism, which calls for a contextual assessment of its justification in particular practice settings. One circumstance in which paternalism generally appears acceptable is when individuals lack sufficient information on which to base some irrevocable action or to make a judgment about what will serve their future interests. Mill's paradigm case for paternalism involves a man about to cross a bridge that he does not realize is unsafe, and a bystander who does not have time to explain the danger but could prevent the man's crossing. Intervention would be legitimate under those circumstances because, as Mill noted, true freedom consists in doing what one desires, and the man presumably does not desire to drown. Mill also recognized a role for paternalistic actions in order to "raise the character" of "uncultivated" individuals. As he put it, "those who most need to be made wiser and better usually desire it least and if they desired it would be incapable of finding the way by their own lights."[6]

Contemporary theorists have made similar efforts to accommodate principles of autonomy and benevolence. Although commentators generally acknowledge the need for some paternalism in legal doctrine, they tend to be more wary of it in lawyer-client relationships given the absence of formal measures of accountability and the dangers of professional elitism or self-interest. Thus, writers on legal ethics have sought to identify certain objective conditions or limiting principles that can constrain the scope of paternalistic interventions.

a. *Objective Conditions*

Philosopher Dennis Thompson argues that paternalism is justifiable only if it meets three conditions:

> First, the decision of the person who is to be constrained must be *impaired.* . . . Second, the restriction is as *limited* as possible. . . . Finally, the restriction prevents a serious and irreversible *harm.*[7]

Bar ethical codes make similar provision for lawyer paternalism. Model Rule 1.14 provides:

> (a) When a client's ability to make adequately considered decisions in connection with the representation is impaired, whether because of minority, mental disability or for some other reason, the lawyer shall, as far as reasonably possible, maintain a normal client-lawyer relationship with the client.
> (b) A lawyer may seek the appointment of a guardian or take other protective action with respect to a client, only when the lawyer reasonably believes that the client cannot adequately act in the client's own interest.

As the Comment to Rule 1.14 notes, the law recognizes intermediate stages of competence. Even if clients lack legal competence, they often have the ability to "understand, deliberate upon, and reach conclusions about matters affecting . . . [their] own well-being." Ethical Consideration 7-11 similarly recognizes that "[t]he responsibilities of a lawyer may vary according to the intelligence, experience, mental condition or age of a client, the obligation of a public officer, or the nature of a particular proceeding." Ethical Consideration 7-12 adds that if the client "is capable of understanding the matter in question or of contributing to the advancement of his interests, regardless of whether he is legally disqualified from performing certain acts, the lawyer should obtain from him all possible aid."

Most commentators, however, recognize that what constitutes impaired decision-making is less readily, and less objectively, determined than codified standards imply. As Thompson notes:

> Many decisions that we may wish to restrict are not impaired in so temporary and easily correctable a way as that of the person who does not know that the bridge is unsafe. The variety of possible impair-

ments is great, including not only ignorance, but also psychological compulsion. . . . [An individual] may be incapable of appreciating what facts are relevant to his decision because he weighs evidence incorrectly, [or] does not recognize what counts as evidence at all. . . . Psychological compulsions range from physiological necessity (such as drug addiction), which may be irresistible in most circumstances, to mere temptation.[8]

As psychological research makes painfully clear, we are all victims of "bounded rationality"; our methods of assessing, recalling, and applying information suffer from systematic biases and limitations.[9] According to some commentators, including Duncan Kennedy, "there is no such 'thing' as capacity" in the abstract. Except in cases of extreme impairment (such as infant or comatose patients), our assessments of a client's capacity will be affected by our assessments of what the client wants to do in the particular case.[10] For example, Mill's man at the bridge was legally competent but situationally incompetent. He would meet any objective test of sanity, but was incapable of acting in his own best interest under a particular set of circumstances.

b. *Hypothetical Consent*

The need for a more contextual understanding of capacity has led some commentators to focus on "hypothetical consent"—that is, what forms of paternalism would a reasonable person accept in advance. Like Odysseus, who ordered himself bound to the mast to protect himself from the lure of the Sirens, we often are willing to protect ourselves from ourselves. As philosopher Gerald Dworkin explains:

> [S]ince we are all aware of our irrational propensities, deficiencies in cognitive and emotive capacities, and avoidable and unavoidable ignorance, it is rational and prudent for us to in effect take out "social insurance policies." We may argue for and against proposed paternalistic measures in terms of what fully rational individuals would accept as forms of protection.[11]

The difficulty, of course, lies in determining what "fully rational" individuals would want since, as Dworkin notes, none of us are fully rational. If we accept our own frailties, we may also wish to preserve some space for our occasionally imprudent or self-indulgent acts. For lawyers, the ethical problems of paternalism arise precisely when it is not self-evident what a rational person with the client's values would do in the client's circumstances. Nor is it clear that most individuals, even those who might agree with a particular paternalistic action, want lawyers to have the power to decide when paternalism is justified. Many potential clients would be reluctant to cede such authority without further limiting principles.

c. *Values, Wants, and Interests*

In their search for such principles, some theorists attempt to ground justifications for paternalism in the distinction between individuals' values, wants, and interests. As David Luban explains:

> Briefly, values are *reasons for acting*, while wants are not. . . . Values are in principle intersubjective, and susceptible to argument and disputation. A want, on the other hand, such as lust in one's heart, is a subjective event and is not to be refuted. . . .
>
> Different from both a person's values and wants are his *interests* . . . [such as] to freedom, money, health and control over other people's actions: what I have earlier called "generalized means to any ultimate ends." . . . The concept of interests that I am employing is meant to be an objective concept. A person's interests can be understood as those goods that enable the person to undertake the normal range of socially available actions. . . .
>
> This objective sense of "interests" is meant to capture the meaning of the concept in sentences such as "Like it or not, I'm going to look out for your best interests." Whether or not a person wants money or values freedom, in our society it is the person's *interest* to have money and freedom. And just as the concept of liberty is ambiguous, in that it can mean either liberty to act on your values or liberty to do what you want, so the concept of *a person's own good* is ambiguous: it can refer either to what is good according to a person's own values, or to what is in the person's best interest. Sometimes these coincide, but often they do not.[12]

Luban argues that paternalism is justified when it involves constraining, on behalf of someone's values, his liberty to do what he wants. Intervention is also appropriate if his values conflict and some of those values have been distorted or overly weighted because of momentary wants. When we know the other person's true values, Luban maintains that we may presume his consent to our paternalism. However, we must be sure of our judgments, for if we are wrong, we have overridden values that form the core of human identity. Luban further argues that paternalism is illegitimate when it involves constraining, on behalf of a person's interests, his liberty to act according to his values. Many people are willing to sacrifice interests of money, freedom, or health in the service of ideological, family, or other personal commitments. As long as individuals have coherent reasons for acting in non-self-interested ways, their choices deserve respect.[13]

To some theorists, the problem with this approach is not that it is wrong but rather that it is unhelpful. How can we be confident that we know someone else's values? When can we be sure that some of those values have been unduly distorted? What counts as a coherent reason for disabling self-sacrifice? Should values based on fear or prejudice ever be overridden?

d. Ad Hoc Paternalism

Some commentators maintain that it is impossible to resolve such questions through any theoretical principle. Thus, for example, Duncan Kennedy argues that the only real basis for paternalism is empathy:

> The actor feels he has intuitive access to the other's feelings and perceptions about the world, and that he participates directly in the suffering and the happiness of the other. . . .
>   In this condition of unity, [paternalism is justifiable if] the actor comes to believe that the other is suffering from some form of false consciousness that will cause him to do something that will hurt him, physically or financially or morally or in some other way. . . . The basis of this kind of intuition is one's own experience of being mistaken, and of having other people sense one's mistake.[14]

Of course, as Kennedy acknowledges, these intuitions may be erroneous. We may misjudge others' true objectives or deny individuals an important opportunity to learn from their own mistakes. Thus, we should approach each case with "fear and trembling, . . . recognizing that influencing another's choice, another's life, in the wrong direction, or so as to reinforce their condition of dependence, is a crime against them."[15]

How would you evaluate these approaches in contexts such as Problems 9A to 9C? Do any of the general considerations regarding paternalism require modification for lawyer-client relationships?

2. Representing Criminal Defendants

PROBLEM 9A

In The Executioner's Song, Norman Mailer chronicles the dialogue between convicted murderer Gary Gilmore and his attorneys:

> Gilmore said, "Now, don't I have the right to die?" . . .
> Gary told [his lawyers] of his belief that he had been executed once before, in eighteenth-century England. He said, "I feel like I've been here before. There is some crime from my past." He got quiet, and said, "I feel I have to atone for the thing I did then." Esplin couldn't help thinking that this stuff about eighteenth-century England would sure have made a difference with the psychiatrists if they had heard it.
> Gilmore now began to say that his life wouldn't end with this life. He would still be in existence after he was dead. It all seemed part of a logical discussion. Esplin finally said, "Gary, we can see your point of view, but we still feel duty bound to go ahead on that appeal."
> When Gary said again, "What can I do about it?" Snyder answered, "Well, I don't know."

Gary then said, "Can I fire you?"

Esplin said, "Gary, we'll make the judge aware that you want to can us, but we're going to file anyway." . . .

On the 3rd of November, Esplin got a letter from Gary. It read: *"Mike, butt out. Quit fucking around with my life. You're fired."*

Despite being dismissed, the two defense attorneys later Wednesday filed a notice of appeal—in their names. . . .

They said it was "in the best interest" of the defendant.[16]

Was it?

Under what circumstances would it constitute ineffective assistance of counsel for a lawyer to follow a client's wishes and waive possible defenses or fail to object to a death sentence?[17]

JONES v. BARNES, 463 U.S. 745 (1983). In this case, the Supreme Court cast some light on the division of authority between criminal defendants and their appointed counsel. Following his conviction for robbery and assault, Barnes requested his court-appointed attorney to raise certain issues on appeal. Although the issues were not frivolous, the lawyer declined to present them on the grounds that they would not succeed and would detract from the persuasiveness of his argument. Barnes submitted a pro se brief raising these additional issues. When his appeal failed, he filed for federal habeas corpus relief. The Second Circuit Court of Appeals granted his petition and the United States Supreme Court reversed.

Speaking for the majority, Chief Justice Burger began by limiting the scope of the Court's prior decisions in Anders v. California, 386 U.S. 738 (1966), and Faretta v. California, 422 U.S. 806 (1975). *Anders* held that even when appointed counsel believe an appeal has no merit, they must provide a brief covering all arguable grounds for appeal so that the client may "raise any points that he chooses." 386 U.S. at 744. *Faretta* recognized that criminal defendants had a right to proceed pro se and to have their appointed counsel provide assistance. According to the majority in *Jones*, neither precedent entitled a defendant who was not proceeding pro se to decide what issues to raise on appeal. Recognition of such a right would "seriously undermine the ability of counsel to present the client's case in accord with counsel's professional evaluation," and would "disserve the very goal of vigorous and effective advocacy that underlies *Anders*." 463 U.S. at 754. Any competent professional evaluation would necessarily involve selecting the best arguments because raising "every colorable issue runs the risk of burying good arguments." Id.

Justice Brennan, joined by Justice Marshall, dissented. Under their analysis, defendants should not be forced to make an "all-or-nothing" choice between "forgoing the assistance of counsel altogether or relinquishing control over every aspect of [their] case." Id. at 759 (Brennan, J., dissenting). In reaching that conclusion, the dissenters relied on the Comment to Standard 21-3.2 of the ABA's Standards for Criminal Justice (1980), which recognizes that the ultimate decision "to press a particular contention on appeal" is a decision to be made by the client. Id. at 759-760. As Justice Brennan also noted, "indigent clients often mistrust the lawyer appointed to represent them. . . . A constitutional rule that encourages lawyers to disregard their clients' wishes without compelling need can only exacerbate the clients' suspicions of their lawyers . . . and denigrat[e] the values of individual autonomy and dignity central to . . . Fifth and Sixth Amendment rights." 463 U.S. at 761-763.

Which of these positions do you find most persuasive? Did it matter that Barnes had submitted a pro se brief? If so, which way did his submission cut? Did he have the worst of both worlds: too many arguments with too little expert assistance? Or did his own presentation of the omitted arguments neutralize any possible prejudice from his counsel's refusal to include them?

Is this a case where utilitarian and rights-based frameworks point to different outcomes? The *Jones* majority focuses on consequences and finds no prejudice because the defendant got what experts would consider the most competent brief. By contrast, the dissent focuses on the defendant's rights to self-determination and assumes that major decisions should be made by the person who will have to live with their implications. Which framework do you find most helpful?

Was the majority's decision in *Jones* an example of justifiable paternalism under any of the frameworks described above? Does the answer depend on how you define the defendant's "interest"? Should that interest be gauged primarily in substantive terms — that is, in having what reasonably competent counsel would consider the most effective argument? Or should the controlling issue be the defendant's assessment of the process: whether it gave him a fair hearing? Recent research generally suggests that "procedural issues are more important than outcome issues" in shaping accused persons' perceptions of fairness in their criminal trials.[18] Other studies indicate that individuals who exercise control over decisions are more likely to be satisfied with the results, and that clients who participate actively in decisions tend to achieve better outcomes.[19]

How should courts and counsel respond to that research? If you had been the defense lawyer in *Jones*, how would you have proceeded? Could you have raised the issues Barnes wanted raised without discussing them at any length? Or would that strategy have compromised both the lawyer's and the client's goals?

PROBLEM 9B

William Simon recounts an incident from his early years in practice when he represented, pro bono, a 65-year-old black woman who worked as a housekeeper. His client, Ms. Jones, faced criminal charges of leaving the scene of an accident. Simon had strong evidence that the charges were unfounded and racially motivated. He was convinced that the defendant would prevail at trial, but concerns about his own inexperience prompted him to enlist the aid of an established criminal defense practitioner as co-counsel. Just before the case was called, the prosecutor offered to allow Jones to plead nolo contendere with six months' probation. Simon was bothered by the prospect that his client would lose the chance for full vindication and exposure of police misconduct. However, he presented the plea in neutral form to Ms. Jones and her minister (who had accompanied her to the courthouse as a character witness).

> I insisted that, because the decision was hers, I couldn't tell her what to do. I then spelled out the pros and cons. . . . However, I mentioned the cons last, and the last thing I said was, "If you took their offer, there probably wouldn't be any bad practical consequences, but it wouldn't be total justice." Up to that point, Mrs. Jones and her minister seemed anxiously ambivalent, but that last phrase seemed to have a dramatic effect on them. In unison, they said, "We want justice."
>
> I went back to my friend and said, "No deal. She wants justice." My friend stared in disbelief and then said, "What? Let me talk to her." He then proceeded to give her his advice. He didn't tell her what he thought she should do, and he went over the same considerations I did. The main differences in his presentation were that he discussed the disadvantages of trial last, while I had gone over them first; he described the remote possibility of jail in slightly more detail than I had, and he didn't conclude by saying, "It wouldn't be total justice." At the end of his presentation, Mrs. Jones and her minister decided to accept the plea bargain, and as I said nothing further, that's what they did.[20]

How would you evaluate the two lawyers' conduct in this case? Should the experienced criminal defense attorney have done anything differently? Should Simon?

Thomas Shaffer and James Elkins observe:

[L]awyers are criticized for providing too much and too little information, but almost certainly for allowing the client too little freedom. The one fault is to leave the client in a state of ignorance; the other is to lecture to the client and leave him no room to make a choice that is his own.

One helpful distinction here is the distinction between tough personal choices and collaborative decisions. A client sometimes needs to decide what he wants. Sometimes he knows what he wants but needs to decide what to do. The difference is that a choice about *what one wants* calls for freedom (acceptance, concern, support), and a decision about *what to do* calls more for information, and for an active and collaborative style in the counselor. The counselor has more openings for providing information, and even for giving his own opinions, when the issue is what to do. He has more openings for providing understanding, acceptance, and care, when the issue is what the client wants. . . .

"Freedom" means leaving the client room to move. Many counselors smother their clients with advice, information, legal knowledge, and personal theories about how the world works. All counseling requires freedom; counseling when the client cannot decide what he wants requires a great deal of freedom.[21]

What kind of choice was Mrs. Jones making? Did the lawyers here respect her freedom in the sense Shaffer and Elkins advocate? How would you have handled the situation?

3. Representing Juveniles

PROBLEM 9C

1. You represent a 15-year-old charged with vandalism and burglary. She comes from a troubled home and has a history of drug abuse. If she is willing to identify the other participant in the crime, the prosecutor will allow her to plead to vandalism and will support her placement in a local halfway house with an excellent reputation. If she refuses, you believe that it might still be possible, on the eve of trial, to talk the prosecutor into a diversion program. Under that program, all charges will be dropped if your client successfully completes two years of probation, including participation in a youth-center counseling program. If your client fails to complete the program, the prosecutor can reinstate both charges and proceed against her as an adult-felony offender. If you take the case to a bench trial in juvenile court, you estimate that the chances of acquittal are about 40 percent. A conviction would probably result in a sentence of anywhere from 6 to 18 months at the state's correctional facility, an outcome that is likely to worsen your client's problems.

You believe that the halfway house is by far the best option. Given your client's current attitudes and closest friends, you doubt that she could manage to stay out of trouble for a two-year probation term. Since failure to complete that term might well result in a felony record, you believe that diversion is not a particularly desirable strategy.

Your client's parents agree. They would like their daughter to live in the halfway house, since it would provide the supervision that they are finding burdensome and unpleasant to impose. After preliminary conversations, your client appears adamantly opposed to the idea. She is unwilling to "squeal" on her accomplice, who appears responsible for supplying her occasional drug habit. She also appears more concerned about losing the ability to stay out late and watch her favorite television programs if she moves to the halfway house than about the possibility of acquiring a felony record. She is frightened by the prospect of the state correctional facility, but has an unrealistic faith that she could talk her way out of a conviction if the case goes to trial. You do not raise the possibility of a diversion program, since the prosecutor has not made such an offer and probably will not unless you insist. How do you proceed?

2. The facts are the same as in part I, except that your client, after obtaining assurances of confidentiality, tells you that her stepfather is sexually abusing her and that her mother refuses to believe it. The daughter doesn't want to "destroy the family" by reporting the abuse, and believes that she has the situation under control by locking her door and managing not to be in the house alone with her stepfather. Your state has laws requiring health professionals, but not lawyers, to report any suspicion of child abuse. How do you proceed?

Experts disagree about the role of lawyers representing minors, and the relevant statutory and common law provides little clarification. Typically, provisions governing appointment of counsel for juveniles in family, civil commitment, or delinquency proceedings refer to representation of their rights, interests, welfare, or well-being. What that means when lawyers and their clients disagree is a matter largely unresolved in law and highly controversial in practice.

In earlier eras, appointment of a guardian ad litem generally signified that the client was not competent to identify his or her own interests. Under current usage, the term is often used interchangeably with court-appointed counsel. However, some courts and commentators, in recognition of this historical legacy, use the guardian description to identify lawyers who represent what they consider to be the client's best interest. By contrast, other attorneys adopt the conventional advocacy role, endorsed by the ABA Juvenile Justice Standards and other children's rights groups. This approach defers to the client's own preferences unless the client is impaired (i.e., lacks "capacity to direct the representation").[22] A third approach is an amicus curiae role, in which the lawyer places before the judge any information that would further the decision-making process and acts as an intermediary between the client and the legal system.[23]

Each of these approaches has been subject to considerable criticism. The conventional advocacy model gives priority to individual dignity and autonomy by allowing persons to make their own choices. However, as Sarah Ramsey argues, that value has little meaning

> without some consideration of the individual's capacity to understand the significance of the choice he is making. . . . The ideal of autonomy depends upon the individual's being capable of shaping his life through his own choices . . . [but] the ability to express a preference is not a sufficient test of capacity.[24]

According to many commentators, the distinctive features of childhood and adolescence make paternalism especially appropriate. Minors may overvalue short-term concerns and lack sufficient experience to understand the full implications of certain choices. Younger clients are particularly vulnerable; the opportunities for positive intervention are correspondingly greater than with most adults. Accordingly, these commentators reason that autonomy should not be the preeminent value in legal representation. As one leading expert put it, "my role is to help a juvenile with the problem as he or she defines it, but to provide help as I define it. That's why I'm involved with these kinds of cases and clients."[25]

Other experts criticize this degree of paternalism as too insensitive to values of autonomy and too inattentive to the distinctive features of the lawyer's role. Why should attorneys be involved in a case if they function just like a judge or a social worker? The point of zealous advocacy is to provide one person to articulate the concerns of the client as the client perceives them; after all, it is the client who will have to live with the consequences. As these commentators also note, most empirical literature does not find strong differences in the decision-making capacity of adults and of older minors, particularly those over age 14.[26] Nor does the history of juvenile and family courts suggest that experts are generally able to determine the "best interest" of children in any objective sense.[27]

From this perspective, once minors reach a certain age, or demonstrate what the ABA Standards refer to as "considered judgment," their decisions should be controlling for the attorney. When representing adults, lawyers do not equate competence with an ability to weigh accurately all the costs and benefits of available options. It is, as the ABA Standards note, "ordinarily sufficient that clients understand the nature and purposes of the proceedings and its general consequences and be able to formulate their desires . . . with some degree of clarity. Most adolescents can meet this standard, and more ought not to be required of them."[28]

The third, amicus curiae, approach attempts to accommodate concerns of both autonomy and protection by presenting all information to the decision-maker, including the client's preferences and the lawyer's assessments. This strategy, however, risks compromising both concerns. An attorney who reports the juvenile's desires but then proceeds to undermine them by disclosing further, often confidential, information has hardly respected individual dignity and autonomy. Yet an attorney who fails to make such disclosures or who attempts to present all facts neutrally may be unable to provide the guidance that an overburdened and understaffed court requires.

In recognition of these difficulties, some commentators have advocated a more contextual approach. This framework recognizes that age is not an adequate proxy for competence, and that a minor who is able to make considered decisions in some circumstances may be unable to do so in others.[29] Under this approach, an attorney should focus on factors such as the risks of a "wrong" decision and the minor's age, mental capacity, psychological stability, strength of preferences, and ability to make rational, consistent judgments without undue influence by others.[30]

Which of these frameworks do you find most helpful? Given the facts of Problem 9C, would it be justifiable for you not to raise the possibility of the diversion program? For the issues in Part 2, consider the materials on confidentiality in Chapter VI. What information would you need about incest and abuse victims in general, or about this family situation in particular, before you decide how to proceed?

Consider the Proposed Standards of Practice for Lawyers who Represent Children in Abuse and Neglect Cases (1995) by the Council of the ABA Family Law Section. Standard B-4(3) provides:

> If the child's attorney determines that the child's expressed preference would be seriously injurious to the child (as opposed to merely being contrary to the lawyer's opinion of what would be in the child's interest), the lawyer may request appointment of a separate guardian ad litem and continue to represent the child's expressed preference. . . . The child's attorney shall not reveal the basis of the request for appointment of a guardian ad litem which would compromise the client's position.

The Comment adds that one of the "most difficult ethical issues for lawyers representing children occurs when the child is able to express a position . . . that could result in serious injury." This is particularly likely when the child desires to "live in a dangerous situation because it is all he or she knows, because of a feeling of blame or of responsibility to take care of the parents, or because of threats. The child may choose to deal with a known situation rather than risk the unknown world of a foster home or other out-of-home placement." In most cases, the Comment suggests that this dilemma can be resolved by effective counseling. However, if the child "cannot be persuaded [to abandon a dangerous position], the attorney has a duty to safeguard the child's interests by requesting appointment of a guardian ad litem, who will be charged with advocating the child's best interest." Yet as the Comment also acknowledges, "as a practical matter, this may not adequately protect the child if the danger to the child was revealed only in a confidential disclosure to the lawyer because the guardian ad litem may never learn of the disclosed danger."

Does this Standard provide appropriate guidance on the facts of Problem 9C(2)? If not, what would you propose?

B.   THE COUNSELING ROLE

See Chapter VI, Confidentiality and Client Counseling
   • Whistle-Blowing in Organizational Contexts
     (pages 278-292)

See Chapter XV, Evidence and Trial Advocacy
  • Witness Preparation
    (pages 662–669)

See also Chapter XVI, Family Law
  • Competing Perspectives on Divorce Practice
    (pages 681–699)

GEOFFREY HAZARD, JR., ETHICS IN THE PRACTICE OF LAW

143-148 (1978)

In recent years, some critics of the legal profession have suggested that a lawyer for a corporation is responsible for its conduct in at least two related respects: his advice to such a client should consist not merely of what the client legally might do but also of what the client morally ought to do; and he should not serve a client who is not disposed to follow advice of that character. . . .

The attack is a difficult one to meet. The response conventionally made by the bar is to suggest that the same criticism would apply to a lawyer for a criminal accused. If it did, the argument runs, the consequence would be that an accused could not obtain representation by a lawyer of standing; since the latter is inadmissible, it must be that the criticism is invalid. Hence, a lawyer is not responsible for what his client does. . . . [Yet it] is perfectly possible to think that the lawyer for the criminal accused is not "responsible" for him, while at the same time thinking that the general counsel for a corporation or agency is, in some sense of the word, "responsible" for it. The point is made by suggesting that it is one thing to represent a sometime murderer, quite another to be on retainer to the Mafia. . . .

The obvious answer for the adviser whose advice is ignored is that he can resign. In some circumstances that is the only honorable course to be followed, but it is impractical as a response to all except fundamental disagreements. More important, though not often recognized by the critics of legal and other advisers to corporations, the sanction of resignation involves some ethical problems of its own. If taken seriously, it should be applicable only when any right-thinking adviser would resign. But this is to say that such a client ought to have no right-thinking adviser at all, at least until the client redirects his conduct so that it would no longer be objectionable to a right-thinking adviser. There are situations in which it seems proper that the client should suffer that kind of penalty, for example if he insists on fabricating evidence or carrying out a swindle. But if the case is less extreme than this, the sanction of resignation is too severe. It implies that the client should have to function without proper guidance, or perhaps cease functioning at all, because its managers do not see fit to follow the advice of its advisers.

If this were the consequence that should ensue from a client's refusal to follow advice, it would mean that the advice was in effect peremptory, not an informed suggestion but a command. When an adviser's advice is in effect peremptory, however, the result is a reversal of the underlying structure of responsibility for the organization's conduct. The adviser becomes the ultimate arbiter and the client a subordinate. . . . Furthermore, in the meantime the nominal principal has the excuse that he was merely following directions and so is not responsible for action taken in his name. Putting the point differently, when responsibility is transferred to an adviser, it is also transferred from his principal.

It seems unlikely that such a transfer of responsibility is contemplated by those who say that an adviser has some kind of responsibility for what his principal does. Probably it is assumed that the organization will not be left helpless for want of essential assistance, but rather that some other adviser will come along to take the place of the right-thinking adviser who resigns. This assumption, however, has some curious implications. It may mean that an equally high-minded adviser can step in as successor because he was not involved before. As a result, that which is reprehensible when done by one adviser in continuous service becomes acceptable when done by multiple advisers acting in a relay. A lot of moral knots are cut this way but it surely is an Alexandrine technique. On the other hand, the assumption may be that a less high-minded successor can be expected to take over. If so, it reduces the significance of resignation to a merely personal matter and perhaps a case of narcissism. (It may also have the result of simply insulating the client from conscientious advisers in the future.) Still another possibility is that the client will figure out how to retain high-minded advisers without creating situations in which they will feel impelled to resign; the client will learn not to ask for advice in the cases that might put his counsel under that kind of pressure. . . .

Advice is made peremptory when it is cast in purely technical terms compelling a single conclusion about what to do. If the advice acknowledges that more than one course of action might be countenanced, it obviously leaves the responsibility for choice with the client. If the advice is not cast in purely technical terms — if it refers to questions of right and wrong or to "policy" — it is also not peremptory. This is because the lawyer as such has no monopoly on moral virtue or the capacity to decide questions of policy; indeed, the definition of his role at most permits him to comment on these dimensions of the matter under deliberation. A legal adviser should be reticent about incorporating morals or policy into his advice: "You can't play God"; "Who the hell are you to tell him what he ought to do?" This can be taken as indifference to questions of morals and policy. It can also be taken as an assertion that expatiation on morals and policy is not within the narrower definition of a legal adviser's domain.

ROBERT W. GORDON, THE INDEPENDENCE OF LAWYERS

68 B.U. L. Rev. 1, 26-28, 71-74 (1988)

Take one of the most routine contexts of business law practice, compliance counseling. The client hopes to seize a profitable opportunity. The plan is routed through the lawyer's office and is seen to pose a potential problem: some legal doctrine or regulation arguably prohibits the plan. What can the lawyer do? . . .

[Options include arguing that a plan:

- may comply with the technical language of the law but not conform to its spirit or to general norms of responsible social conduct, and it should be altered for the sake of appearance or morality;
- may conform to the general purpose of the law but does not comply with its technical requirements and the company may not wish to take the risk of sanctions;
- may be legal but could be altered to accomplish the same business purpose while also promoting other legal and social objectives.

If the lawyer opposes the plan but is overruled, available courses of action include:

- carrying objections to a higher level of management or the board of directors;
- seeking discreetly to modify the most objectionable parts of the plan, or insist on recording objections and reservations in board minutes, opinions, or memos to the file;
- refusing to participate further in the plan;
- withdrawing from representation;
- warning the client that if the proposed course of action proceeds, the lawyer will make public disclosures.] . . .

These are naturally just a tiny handful of the choices to be made regarding the form and content of advice given in the course of compliance counseling. . . . All these choices, except disclosure and withdrawal, which may be regulated, are well within the conventional boundaries of the counselor's role. Which choices are actually made will be a function of the lawyer's situation and convictions, the lawyer's personal courage and confidence, the relations of authority and trust the lawyer has with the managers involved, the lawyer's own position in the hierarchy of the company or outside firm, the importance of the client to the firm, the firm's place in the legal services market, the lawyer's degree of practical knowledge of the business (which will crucially affect the lawyer's ability to suggest alternatives), the form of advice managers prefer to hear from their lawyers, and the general compliance culture of the company (does it walk the line and play hardball with regulators or try to anticipate regulatory problems and initiate its own solutions?).

Obviously most lawyers, or at least lawyers for big, powerful companies, will avoid abrasive and unnecessary confrontations with their clients. They will phrase negative advice as prudential rather than moralistic, supporting their recommendations with reasons that sound much more like statements of technical rules or empirical predictions of risks and results than political or moral judgments. . . .

[Some argue that the lawyer should not act as a morally independent advisor because] it either conflicts with the ideal of client loyalty or arrogates to lawyers an improper role in political decisionmaking, or both. . . .

Underlying the illegitimacy critique is the central belief that lawyers' roles begin and end with vigorously pursuing their clients' interests within the limits of the law. Rather than injecting any of their own political views into the lawyering process, they should simply function as an extension of their clients' interests, accepting those interests according to the terms the clients use to characterize them. . . .

Although this position is *very* commonplace, I think it rests on incoherent premises and leads to indefensible conclusions. . . . [The] position appears to license an untempered adversarial advocacy which when aggregated could easily nullify the purposes of any and every legal regime. Take any simple case of compliance counseling: suppose the legal rule is clear, yet the chance of detecting violations low, the penalties small in relation to the gains from noncompliance, or the terrorizing of regulators into settlement by a deluge of paper predictably easy. The mass of lawyers who advise and then assist with noncompliance in such a situation could, in the vigorous pursuit of their clients' interests, effectively nullify the laws. The only justification for their doing so would have to be their confidence that the system was self-equilibrating, so that some countervailing force would operate to offset their efforts. But such confidence is unfounded. Examples of aggressive advocates virtually precluding the fulfillment of any conceivable purposes of a legal regime — except of course the purpose of enacting symbolic laws never intended to have any effect — are plentiful. Even when legislators prodded by mass opinion have moved to stiffen penalties and strengthen enforcement, lawyers have moved to nullify that too. It is at least questionable whether a social system maintained primarily through the internalization of legal norms rather than state terror can survive much of such behavior. Yes, lawyers must pursue clients' interests within the framework of the rules of the game. But the issue of lawyers' public responsibility is precisely that of what their position should be vis-à-vis those rules.

The principal fallacy implicit in the view of lawyering underlying the illegitimacy critique, is that lawyers must reconcile two sets of social purposes — clients' interests and the law's plain meaning — that arrive at their offices already fully formed and filled in with some definite determinate content. But in fact part of the lawyer's job is to interpret both sets of purposes. . . . [B]oth the client's "interests" and the "law" governing the situation will gradually take the shapes sculpted by the social agents who interpret and transmit them.

But the critic then says: all right, lawyers play legitimate roles in helping both to define the clients' interests and to predict the legal consequences likely to flow from various definitions. But in this capacity lawyers have no right to intrude their opinions, their influence, their political values. They are neither elected officials nor their agents; lawyers have no special authority to go around telling people how they should behave.

The traditional response to this is simple: lawyers do indeed have an official status as licensed fiduciaries for the public interest, charged with encouraging compliance with legal norms. In contexts like counseling, where there is no official third party like a judge to oversee the interaction between the client and the state, the lawyer is not only supposed to predict the empirical consequences of certain behavior, but also to represent the viewpoint of the legal system to the client. Lawyers can't coerce anyone; they can only advise and persuade, sometimes only under the threat of resignation rather than disclosure. Surely the right of the lawyer to encourage compliance with the law's purposes through persuasion is at least as clear as the client's right to demand the lawyer's help in exploiting the law's ambiguities and procedural opportunities and in engaging in strategic behavior designed to evade the law. The other and even better response to the critic is that even conceding that lawyers have no special authority to guide their clients, neither do they have any special immunity from responsibility for the things they help their clients do. . . .

More fundamentally, it seems rather extreme to refrain from trying to develop and act on a commitment to a particular view of legal purposes simply because others may arrive at a different view. That may be a reason for caution, for avoiding dogmatism, for empathizing with and taking account of the view of opponents, but not for paralysis. After all, as William Simon points out, the legal system routinely grants judges and administrators discretionary authority to interpret legal purposes. Judges and administrators, in turn, routinely engage in such interpretive exercises, believing that they can do so reliably despite their knowledge that other judges and officials are constantly disputing them and reaching contrary views. . . .

The Competence Critique. The position that lawyers have no special competence to bring to counseling, nor any special contribution to make to political life, makes sense as a critique of the most pompously inflated view of political independence. According to that view, expressed in the nineteenth century, lawyers belong to a distinct elevated estate uniquely endowed with political wisdom and insight into everybody's long-term best interests. That was always ridiculous, and has become more so with the specialization of the profession. We are bright technicians, for the most part, not philosopher-kings (or queens).

Most of the arguments in favor of lawyers playing an independent role in counseling and politics, however, are much more modest. One such argument concerns the nature of legal training and experience. Legal education is to some extent an education in applied political theory. Lawyers are articulate in one of the major media of public discourse, legal language. They often have diverse experience — government work, different kinds of clients, different kinds of corruption and evil, all the myriad ways in which plans can misfire and go askew. They are professionally capable of detachment, able to see different sides of a problem and analyze motivations. They know powerful people and something about what makes them tick and what will move them. Thus legal training and experience provide a firm foundation for the exercise of independent judgment.

Arguments from good motivations also have some modest force. The legal profession attracts, along with a lot of fairly venal and opportunistic types, a large number of the most public-regarding, socially-conscious people in our society. It's a total waste to define a lawyer's role in a way that will deny such people the chance to act on altruistic intentions. The lawyers too diffident to advise are probably the ones whose advice would be most valuable.

Finally, there are arguments from opportunity. The main idea is just that the chances to act independently are *there*. Lawyers are scattered all over civil society in intermediary and advisory positions from which they have opportunities to exercise influence.

It's easy to say lawyering is not a club for superhumans, and that especially in this century lawyers have been joined, and in many areas of political life displaced, by rival interpreters and articulators and mediators of social purposes. What's absurd is to argue that because of this lawyers are uniquely *disqualified* as citizens or moral and political actors — the one group of individuals in the world who should conscientiously attempt to reduce themselves to ciphers, pure media of transmission. Why should everybody else around the corporation — the engineers, the financial people, the safety and health division — be permitted to deliberate upon and engage in the internal politics of the corporation to promote their views of its best interests, but not the lawyers?

JAMES FREUND, LAWYERING: A REALISTIC APPROACH TO LEGAL PRACTICE

155 (1979)

Particularly for lawyers who practice in the business area, it's impossible to ignore the businessman's popular conception of a lawyer as a breaker, not maker, of deals, and thus to be avoided if at all possible. This unfortunate reputation as obstructionist — prone to talking but not doing, given to raising more problems than we solve — plagues us in all our endeavors.

So, always make an effort to stand back a little and ponder how you *appear* to the client. Not how you *are* — because no one goes out of his way to be non-constructive — but how you're being perceived by the party in interest who doesn't appreciate the obstacles to be overcome. Is it possible that most of your remarks during the course of a lengthy meeting could be construed as throwing up roadblocks in the way of the client's desired goals? Have you served solely as the bearer of bad tax tidings, the Paul Revere of regulatory problems, the harbinger of protracted litigation? Look at yourself through the client's eyes; and if you don't like what you see, then change the image.

Be constructive. When you raise a problem, don't dwell on its magnitude but move quickly to a discussion of possible solutions. Be practical. Get off the theoretical plane and down to your client's level of reality. . . .

PROBLEM 9D

1. Assume that an Environmental Protection Agency water pollution regulation prohibits discharge of ammonia at amounts greater than .050 grams per liter of effluent. One of your clients owns a rural plant that discharges ammonia. Removal of that ammonia from plant effluents is very expensive. You know from informal sources that violations of .075 grams per liter or less are ignored because of a limited enforcement budget and that EPA inspection in rural areas is rare. Enforcement officials usually issue a warning prior to applying sanctions unless the violation is extreme (more than 1.5 grams per liter).

Should you provide full information to your client's management concerning enforcement-related facts even though it may encourage violations of the .050-gram limit? What factors would be relevant to your analysis? If management decides to exceed the EPA limit, under what circumstances might you request the board of directors to reconsider that decision?

2. You represent the owner of a small chain of low-budget motels. He has just discovered that some of his motels' aging water heaters are starting to malfunction and to release scalding hot water with no warning. He does not have adequate funds to replace all the units and already carries so much debt that financing to remedy the problem is unavailable. He seeks your advice. You believe that the severity and foreseeability of potential injuries to guests make further use of the heaters negligent. However, the probability of significant liability is unclear because an injured party is unlikely to know of the pattern of malfunction absent litigation and full discovery. The client's liability insurance is sufficient to cover compensatory but not punitive damages.

What is your advice? Could you propose installing new water heaters on credit, with the motels as security, knowing that the owner would have to default on the obligations? This might allow him to work out a repayment schedule with creditors, who are likely to prefer that option to repossession of the heaters or a forced sale of the motels.[31]

As courts, commentators, and bar ethics codes note, one of lawyers' most valuable roles involves providing advice on the full range of "moral, economic, social, and political factors that may be relevant to the client's situation." Model Rule 2.1. See EC 7-8. In part, this role arises from the collective interests of lawyers, clients, and society generally in maintaining a rule of law, an effective system of justice, and a functional regulatory structure. In addition, as many commentators note, individuals seeking legal advice often benefit from counselors who help them live up to their best, not their worst, self-image.

How to realize this role in practice will, of course, depend on a wide variety of circumstances. But, as Robert Gordon notes, lawyers often have opportunities for "influence at the margins," and a chance to help the client decide whether to engage in regulatory resistance, cosmetic compliance, or genuine efforts to live within the law.[32]

How should lawyers exercise that influence in Problem 9D? If you were the attorney, what factors would be most relevant to your decisions?

C. REPRESENTING THE PUBLIC INTEREST

1. Introduction

Although the term "public interest law" is relatively recent, the concept has its roots in earlier social movements, including legal services for the poor, civil liberties, and civil rights. The legal services tradition began in the late nineteenth century as part of an effort to assist immigrants. With modest support from local governments and private charities, poverty law programs gradually expanded to include other low-income communities. The social activism of the 1960s and 1970s brought a substantial influx of federal and foundation funding as well as a greater commitment to law reform in legal services practice.[33]

An organized civil liberties movement began in 1916, when a small group of pacifists formed an organization to defend conscientious objectors and to pursue other anti-militarist objectives. Several years later, one of its branches split off to become the American Civil Liberties Union. Its activities expanded during the Cold War and again in subsequent decades as similar organizations and specialized ACLU projects began focusing on new areas such as reproductive rights and gay/lesbian issues.[34]

The legal arm of the civil rights movement evolved in parallel fashion. The National Association for the Advancement of Colored People was founded in the early twentieth century in the aftermath of a bloody race riot. Its initial focus was on lobbying and public education, but in 1939 its Legal Defense Fund became a separate organization and began orchestrating a systematic litigation campaign against racial discrimination. During the 1960s, the Legal Defense Fund broadened its agenda to include death penalty cases and became a model for other public interest organizations.[35]

The last quarter century has witnessed a substantial increase in such organizations. As defined by the Council on Public Interest Law, they include tax-exempt, nonprofit groups that employ at least one attorney and devote at least 30 percent of their total resources to the legal representation of previously unrepresented interests on matters of public policy. By that definition, the number of public interest law centers grew from under 30 in 1969 to over 200 by 1990.[36] A significant number of private practitioners also handle public interest legal work on a pro bono or reduced fee basis. The result has been major victories on a wide variety of issues involving discrimination, poverty, civil liberties, and consumer and environmental concerns.

Such activities have drawn criticism from all points on the political spectrum. Critics from the right complain that public interest law vests too much power in non-majoritarian institutions, while critics from the left complain that such power is too limited to produce lasting social change. Conservative objections build on a long tradition of challenges to judicial review, but they also direct particular opposition at public interest lawyers. Cases that avowedly aim at reconstructing social institutions or redistributing substantial resources have drawn fire on the ground that neither courts nor counsel have the competence and accountability for such a role. Liberal critics have also pointed up various limitations of litigation as a means of achieving major social change. Consider the following objections.

Expense. Public interest litigation can be protracted and expensive. The money spent on legal battles may deflect resources from other priorities, and delays or interim defeats can sap organizational strength.

Conflicts of Interest. As the readings below suggest, current procedural and ethical rules do not effectively respond to conflicts within a plaintiff class or between lawyers and clients.

Dependence and Elitism. Traditional forms of advocacy can reinforce the client dependence and passivity that reform efforts seek to counteract. As Joel Handler notes, lawyers "often assume a dominant position with regard to tactics and strategy once the group goes the legal route. The membership is confronted with mysterious procedures and trade language; the specialists take over."[37] Such an approach runs counter to a central insight of organizational theory that "self esteem is increased by doing something for one's self instead of having it done by others."[38]

Limitations of Doctrinal Change.

Limitations of Doctrinal Change. Public interest lawyers may place undue reliance on test-case litigation because their funding, credibility, and professional reputations depend on such visible achievements, and because neither their professional nor personal background equips them for other strategies. This reliance on doctrinal victories is often misconceived. As Gary Bellow explains:

> The problem of unjust laws is almost invariably a problem of distribution of political and economic power; the rules merely reflect a series of choices made in response to these distributions. If a major goal of the unorganized poor is to redistribute power, it is debatable whether judicial process is a very effective means toward that end. This is particularly true of problems arising out of disparities of wealth and income. There is generally not much doctrinal judicial basis for adequately dealing with such problems, and lawyers find themselves developing cases whose outcomes are peripheral to the basic issues that these problems raise.
>
> Secondly, "rule" change, without a political base to support it, just doesn't produce any substantial result because rules are not self-executing; they require an enforcement mechanism. California has the best laws governing working conditions of farm laborers in the United States. . . . But when you drive into the San Joaquin Valley, you find there are no toilets in field after field, and the drinking water is neither cool, nor clean, nor covered. . . . It doesn't matter that there's a law on the books. . . . Enforcement decisions are dominated by a political structure which has no interest in prosecuting, disciplining or regulating the state's agricultural interests. It's nonsense to devote all available lawyer resources to changing rules.[39]

In responding to these challenges, supporters of public interest law generally acknowledge its limitations but also emphasize its potential capacity to redistribute social power. The relative value of law reform strategies, like the value of legal rights more generally, cannot be resolved in the abstract. There is always a risk that the struggle for formal entitlements will deflect attention from more significant political action, and that lawyers' own interests will skew reform priorities. Yet it is also possible for advocates to use law as an effective vehicle to organize groups and reshape social policy. Consider the following contributions of public interest practice.

Group Mobilization and Social Movements.

Group Mobilization and Social Movements. One central contribution of public interest law has been to empower disempowered groups. Cases like Brown v. Board of Education may not have achieved desegregation with "deliberate speed," but they certainly were a major catalyst of the civil rights movement. Much law reform serves multiple purposes; it serves to mobilize groups, increase their legitimacy, enhance their bargaining credibility, attract financial support, and delay harmful actions long enough to build opposition. Threats of a protracted court challenge also may cause readjustments of priorities in socially desirable directions. For each suit brought, there may be several that need not be filed.

Public Attention and Political Responses. So too, lawsuits can help organize communities and focus public attention in ways that will be useful whatever the narrow doctrinal outcome. John Denvir cites several examples. In one suit against the Atomic Energy Commission concerning the scope of environmental impact statements, the resulting disclosure of information reopened a crucial debate on safety issues. Another suit, which challenged the use of culturally biased, English-only intelligence tests to determine school placement, was weak on doctrinal grounds but never required trial. Once the facts of the case received media coverage, the state agreed to change its testing procedures.[40]

Even unsuccessful litigation can focus public attention in ways that generate political reform. The United States Supreme Court's conclusion that discrimination on the basis of pregnancy did not constitute discrimination on the basis of sex led to federal legislation effectively reversing that decision.[41] Similarly, in San Antonio School District v. Rodriguez, 411 U.S. 1 (1973), the Court's rejection of theories requiring equalization of school financing spurred legislative responses. The publicity surrounding the litigation and the possibility of similar suits encouraged many legislators to reevaluate school finance schemes.[42]

Moreover, litigation is not the only tool of public interest lawyers. When the prospects of major legal victories decline, attorneys' reliance on other strategies increases. Lobbying, education, counseling, research, and coalition-building are integral parts of contemporary public interest practice.

Defenders of public interest law not only emphasize these contributions but also challenge conservative objections about the lack of accountability. Part of their challenge focuses on the value of non-majoritarian institutions like courts to protect the needs of "discrete and insular" minorities. Similar protection is also crucial for diffuse majorities that lack resources to organize in a political system increasingly captive to well-financed interests. Moreover, as public interest lawyers emphasize, their efforts are not necessarily inconsistent with democratic authority. For example, environmental litigators' objective is often to make administrative decisions more consistent with legislative intent and more accessible to citizens' oversight.

So too, many public interest lawyers make substantial efforts to maintain accountability to clients and other affected groups. The strategies that lawyers choose vary widely depending on the context. Different approaches are appropriate for representing diffuse interests such as the environment than for acting on behalf of particular client groups. However, in the final analysis, the effectiveness of any public interest work depends on lawyers' capacity to justify their actions to the constituency they claim to represent as well as to others whose interests are at issue.[43]

Consider what strategies for group representation would be most effective in Problems 9E and 9F. When should lawyers withdraw from representing divergent interests? Under what circumstances would such withdrawal simply relocate the problem and result in actions having class-wide significance without class-wide accountability? To what extent can attorneys prevent disabling conflicts by having groups specify a procedure for resolving later disagreements? How active should courts and counsel be in structuring opportunities for broad-based client participation in shaping legal strategies?[44]

2.   Class Action Litigation

PROBLEM 9E

You are the NAACP attorney representing the plaintiff class in Morgan v. Kerrigan, the lawsuit discussed in Derrick Bell's article, Serving Two Masters. As certified, the class consists of all black children who are attending, or will attend, Boston public schools, speaking through their parents. During the course of litigation, it becomes clear that a great number of black parents would prefer to improve Roxbury schools rather than to bus their children to schools of below-average quality in hostile white neighborhoods.

However, studies of other metropolitan areas indicate that most black parents support court-ordered busing plans after they have been implemented and that black graduates of integrated high schools have higher incomes and higher status jobs than black graduates of comparable segregated schools. The NAACP's consistent position has been that full desegregation promises a more stable funding base for inner-city schools than settlements offering remedial expenditures subject to erosion over time. With the eyes of the nation fastened on Boston, a shift in NAACP strategy away from integration would look like surrender in the face of opposition. Accordingly, you believe it would be a great disservice to local students and to the nation generally if the litigation focused on upgrading rather than desegregating ghetto schools.

What are your obligations to the class and to the court?[45]

DERRICK A. BELL, JR., SERVING TWO MASTERS: INTEGRATION IDEALS AND CLIENT INTERESTS IN SCHOOL DESEGREGATION LITIGATION

85 Yale L.J. 470-472, 482-486, 504-505 (1976)

> In the name of equity we . . . seek dramatic im-
> provement in the quality of the education
> available to our children. Any steps to achieve
> desegregation must be reviewed in light of the
> black community's interest in improved pupil
> performance as the primary characteristic of
> educational equity. We define educational equity
> as the absence of discriminatory pupil placement
> and improved performance for all children who
> have been the objects of discrimination. We
> think it neither necessary, nor proper to endure
> the dislocations of desegregation without
> reasonable assurances that our children will in-
> structionally profit.
>
> *Coalition of black community*
> *groups in Boston*[1]

The espousal of educational improvement as the appropriate goal of school desegregation efforts is out of phase with the current state of the law. Largely through the efforts of civil rights lawyers, most courts have come to construe Brown v. Board of Education as mandating "equal educational opportunities" through school deseg-regation plans aimed at achieving racial balance, whether or not those plans will improve the education received by the children affected. To the extent that "instructional profit" accurately defines the school priorities of black parents in Boston and elsewhere, questions of professional responsibility are raised that can no longer be ignored:

How should the term "client" be defined in school desegregation cases that are litigated for decades, determine critically important

---

1. Freedom House Institute on Schools and Education, Critique of the Boston School Committee Plan, 1975, at 2. . . . The statement was a critique of a desegregation plan filed by the Boston School Committee in the Boston school case [Morgan v. Kerrigan]. It was written during two all-day sessions sponsored by the Freedom House Institute, a community house in Boston's black Roxbury area. Judge Garrity had solicited comments on the School Committee's plan from community groups. [The two dozen black community leaders who submitted] this statement did so on behalf of the Coordinated Social Services Council, a confederation of 46 public and private agencies serving minority groups in the Boston area. . . .

Plaintiff's counsel in the Boston school case expressed sympathy with the black community leaders' emphasis on educational improvement, but contended that the law required giving priority to the desegregation process. Few of the group's concerns were reflected in the plaintiffs' proposed desegregation plan rejected by the court.

constitutional rights for thousands of minority children, and usually involve major restructuring of a public school system? How should civil rights attorneys represent the often diverse interests of clients and class in school suits? Do they owe any special obligation to class members who emphasize educational quality and who probably cannot obtain counsel to advocate their divergent views? Do the political, organizational, and even philosophical complexities of school desegregation litigation justify a higher standard of professional responsibility on the part of civil rights lawyers to their clients, or more diligent oversight of the lawyer-client relationship by the bench and bar?

As is so often the case, a crisis of events motivated this long overdue inquiry. The great crusade to desegregate the public schools has faltered. There is increasing opposition to desegregation at both local and national levels (not all of which can now be simply condemned as "racist"), while the once vigorous support of federal courts is on the decline. New barriers have arisen — inflation makes the attainment of racial balance more expensive, the growth of black populations in urban areas renders it more difficult, an increasing number of social science studies question the validity of its educational assumptions.

Civil rights lawyers dismiss these new obstacles as legally irrelevant. Having achieved so much by courageous persistence, they have not waivered in their determination to implement *Brown* using racial balance measures developed in the hard-fought legal battles of the last two decades. This stance involves great risk for clients whose educational interests may no longer accord with the integration ideals of their attorneys. Indeed, muffled but increasing criticism of "unconditional integration" policies by vocal minorities in black communities is not limited to Boston. Now that traditional racial balance remedies are becoming increasingly difficult to achieve or maintain, there is tardy concern that racial balance may not be the relief actually desired by the victims of segregated schools.

This article will review the development of school desegregation litigation and the unique lawyer-client relationship that has evolved out of it. It will not be the first such inquiry. During the era of "massive resistance," Southern states charged that this relationship violated professional canons of conduct. A majority of the Supreme Court rejected those challenges [in NAACP v. Button, 371 U.S. 415 (1963)], creating in the process constitutional protection for conduct that, under other circumstances, would contravene basic precepts of professional behavior. The potential for ethical problems in these constitutionally protected lawyer-client relationships was recognized by the American Bar Association Code of Professional Responsibility, but it is difficult to provide standards for the attorney and protection for the client where the source of the conflict is the attorney's ideals. The magnitude of the difficulty is more accurately gauged in a much older code that warns: "No servant can serve two masters: for either he will hate the one, and love the other; or else he will hold to one, and despise the other."[4]

II. LAWYER-CLIENT CONFLICTS: SOURCES AND RATIONALE

A. Civil Rights Rigidity Surveyed

Having convinced themselves that *Brown* stands for desegregation and not education, the established civil rights organizations steadfastly refuse to recognize reverses in the school desegregation campaign, reverses which, to some extent, have been precipitated by their rigidity. They seem to be reluctant to evaluate objectively the high risks inherent in a continuation of current policies.

1. *The Boston Case*

The Boston school litigation provides an instructive example of what, I fear, is a widespread situation. Early in 1975, I was invited by representatives of Boston's black community groups to meet with them and NAACP lawyers over plans for Phase II of Boston's desegregation effort. Implementation of the 1974 plan had met with violent resistance that received nationwide attention. Even in the lulls between the violent incidents, it is unlikely that much in the way of effective instruction was occurring at many of the schools. NAACP lawyers had retained experts whose proposals for the 1975-1976 school year would have required even more busing between black and lower class white communities. The black representatives were ambivalent about the busing plans. They did not wish to back away after years of effort to desegregate Boston's schools, but they wished to place greater emphasis on upgrading the schools' educational quality, to maintain existing assignments at schools which were already integrated, and to minimize busing to the poorest and most violent white districts. In response to a proposal filed by the Boston School Committee, they sent a lengthy statement of their position directly to District Judge W. Arthur Garrity. . . .

3. *The Atlanta Case*

Prior to Detroit, the most open confrontation between NAACP views of school integration and those of local blacks who favored plans oriented toward improving educational quality occurred in

4. Luke 16:13 (King James). At the outset, it should be made clear that the problems growing out of the lawyer-client relationship in civil rights cases are not limited to the public interest field. . . .

Atlanta. There, a group of plaintiffs became discouraged by the difficulty of achieving meaningful desegregation in a district which had gone from 32 percent black in 1952 to 82 percent black in 1974. Lawyers for the local NAACP branch, who had gained control of the litigation, worked out a compromise plan with the Atlanta School Board that called for full faculty and employee desegregation but for only limited pupil desegregation. In exchange, the school board promised to hire a number of blacks in top administrative positions, including a black superintendent of schools.

The federal court approved the plan. The court's approval was apparently influenced by petitions favoring the plan's adoption signed by several thousand members of the plaintiffs' class. Nevertheless the national NAACP office and LDF lawyers were horrified by the compromise. The NAACP ousted the Atlanta branch president who had supported the compromise. Then, acting on behalf of some local blacks who shared their views, LDF lawyers filed an appeal in the Atlanta case. The appeal also raised a number of procedural issues concerning the lack of notice and the refusal of the district court to grant hearings on the Compromise Plan. These issues gave the Fifth Circuit an opportunity to remand the case to the district court without reaching the merits of the settlement agreement. Undaunted, LDF lawyers again attacked the plan for failing to require busing of whites into the predominantly black schools in which a majority of the students in the system were enrolled. But the district court's finding that the system had achieved unitary status was upheld by the same Fifth Circuit panel.

As in Detroit, NAACP opposition to the Atlanta Compromise Plan was not deterred by the fact that local leaders, including black school board members, supported the settlement. Defending the Compromise Plan, Dr. Benjamin E. Mays, one of the most respected black educators in the country, stated:

> We have never argued that the Atlanta Compromise Plan is the best plan, nor have we encouraged any other school system to adopt it. This plan is the most viable plan for Atlanta — a city school system, that is 82 percent Black and 18 percent white and is continuing to lose whites each year to five counties that are more than 90 percent white. . . .
>
> More importantly, Black people must not resign themselves to the pessimistic view that a non-integrated school cannot provide Black children with an excellent educational setting. Instead, Black people, while working to implement *Brown*, should recognize that integration alone does not provide a quality education, and that much of the substance of quality education can be provided to Black children in the interim. . . .

Idealism, though perhaps rarer than greed, is harder to control. [In NAACP v. Button] Justice Harlan accurately prophesied the excesses of derailed benevolence, but a retreat from the group representational concepts set out in *Button* would be a disaster, not an improvement. State legislatures are less likely than the ABA to draft standards that effectively guide practitioners and protect clients. Even well intentioned and carefully drawn standards might hinder rather than facilitate the always difficult task of achieving social change through legal action. And too stringent rules could encourage officials in some states to institute groundless disciplinary proceedings against lawyers in school cases, which in many areas are hardly more popular today than they were during the massive resistance era.

Client involvement in school litigation is more likely to increase if civil rights lawyers themselves come to realize that the special status accorded them by the courts and the bar demands in return an extraordinary display of ethical sensitivity and self-restraint. The "divided allegiance" between client and employer which Justice Harlan feared would interfere with the civil rights lawyer's "full compliance with his basic professional obligation"[114] has developed in a far more idealistic and thus a far more dangerous form. For it is more the civil rights lawyers' commitment to an integrated society than any policy directives or pressures from their employers which leads to their assumptions of client acceptance and their condemnations of all dissent.

DEBORAH L. RHODE, CLASS CONFLICTS IN CLASS ACTIONS

34 Stan. L. Rev. 1183-1191, 1204-1207, 1209-1212, 1258, 1261-1262 (1982)

A fundamental promise of American adjudicative structures is that clients, not their counsel, define litigation objectives. Thus, the American Bar Association's current and proposed ethical codes both emphasize that an attorney must defer to the client's wishes on matters affecting the merits of legal action. However, by presupposing an individual client with clearly identifiable views, these codes elide a frequent and fundamental difficulty in class action proceedings. In many such cases, the lawyer represents an aggregation of litigants with unstable, inchoate, or conflicting preferences. The more diffuse and divided the class, the greater the problems in defining its objectives.

This article examines those problems in one selected context: plaintiff class actions seeking structural reforms in public and private institutions. Such cases merit special attention on two grounds. First, the often indeterminate quality of relief available makes conflicts within plaintiff classes particularly likely. Most school desegregation, employment discrimination, prison reform, and related cases present no obvious single solution flowing ineluctably from the nature of the violation. Nor will all class members

114. NAACP v. Button, 371 U.S. 415, 460-62 (1963) (Harlan, J., dissenting).

alleging unlawful conduct agree on what should be done about it. Moreover, the prominence of institutional reform litigation vests these intra-class cleavages with particular significance. Such cases account for a high percentage of all class suits and an even greater proportion of legal claims attracting widespread societal concern. Thus, institutional reform litigation provides a useful paradigm for analyzing some of the most vexing issues in class representation.

In exploring these issues, this article takes one central proposition for granted. On the whole, institutional reform class actions have made and continue to make an enormous contribution to the realization of fundamental constitutional values — a contribution that no other governmental construct has proven able to duplicate. That contention has been defended at length elsewhere, and the arguments need not be recounted here. Thus, the following discussion should not be taken to suggest that institutional reform class actions are misused or misconceived, or that there are preferable alternatives. The point, rather, is that the framework in which such actions proceed could benefit from both conceptual and mechanical refurbishing.

Much of the renovation required concerns our concept of class representation. In particular, we need a more coherent theory of class interests and of the role plaintiff preferences should play in defining class objectives. As a first cut at reconceptualization, this article posits a theory of representation mandating full disclosure of, although not necessarily deference to, class sentiment. A central premise is that the class as an entity has interests that may not be coextensive with the preferences of its current membership. Often those able to register views will be insufficiently disinterested or informed to speak for the entire constituency of present and future class members who will be affected by the court's decree. Nonetheless, preferences matter, not because they are conclusive of class interests, but because their disclosure is critical to the efficacy and legitimacy of judicial intervention. . . .

INTRA-CLASS CONFLICTS AND DISCLOSURE OBLIGATIONS

. . . The importance, complexity, and protracted character of structural reform lawsuits create opportunities for conflict at every stage of litigation. Class members who prefer the certainty of the status quo to the risks of judicial rearrangement may oppose litigation from the outset. For example, some parents who anticipate busing or closure of institutional facilities as a consequence of legal intervention will prefer to never initiate proceedings. So too, minority employees have feared retaliation by coworkers and management, or loss of job-related advantages in the aftermath of Title VII actions. . . .

Far more common, however, are schisms that surface during settlement or remedial deliberations. Often when a suit is filed, plaintiffs will not have focused on issues of relief. The impetus for the action will be a general sense that rights have been infringed or needs ignored, rather than a shared conviction about the appropriate remedy. Thus, there may be consensus only on relatively abstract questions—that ghetto schools are bad, institutional conditions unbearable, or special education programs inadequate. During the liability phase of litigation, class members may not be sufficiently informed or interested to participate in decisionmaking. However, once it becomes clear that some relief will be forthcoming, factions emerge. Also, where proceedings are protracted, changes in legal doctrine, contested practices, or plaintiff preferences can create new sources of dissension.

School desegregation cases provide the most well-documented instances of conflict. Both commentators and litigators have described in some detail the balkanization within minority communities over fundamental questions of educational policy. Dispute has centered on the relative importance of integration, financial resources, minority control, and ethnic identification in enriching school environments. Constituencies that support integration in principle have disputed its value in particular settings where extended bus rides, racial tension, or white flight seem likely concomitants of judicial redistricting. . . .

Comparable cleavages arise in various other institutional reform contexts. Parents challenging the adequacy of existing bilingual or special education programs have differed over whether mainstreaming or upgrading separate classes represents the better solution. Suits involving rights of the disabled have divided their families over whether to demand institutional improvement or creation of community care alternatives. . . . In employment cases, controversy has centered on tradeoffs between back-pay awards and prospective relief, the formula used to compute damages, and the means chosen to restructure hiring, promotion, and transfer systems.

Moreover, as with any form of collective litigation, parties often differ in their amenability to compromise and their assessment of particular proposals. Given the uncertainty of outcome and indeterminacy of relief in many institutional reform class actions, risk-averse plaintiffs will often be prepared to make substantial concessions. Other class members will prefer to fight, if not to the death, at least until the Supreme Court denies certiorari. Particularly where the proffered settlement provides generously for a few named plaintiffs, or where some individuals have special reasons for wanting expeditious relief, dissension may arise within the ranks. And, as the following discussion will suggest, all of these problems are compounded by class counsels' own interests and by a doctrinal framework that fails to raise, let alone resolve, the most difficult issues. . . .

THE PARTICIPANTS' ROLES IN DISCLOSING CONFLICT: RULES AND REALITIES

Class Counsel

A familiar refrain among courts and commentators is that lawyers assume special responsibilities in class litigation. According to one circuit court of appeals, the duty to ensure adequate representation rests "primarily upon counsel for the class. . . . [I]n addition to the normal obligations of an officer of the court, and . . . counsel to parties of the litigation, class action counsel possess, in a very real sense, fiduciary obligations to those not before the court." Principal among those duties is the responsibility to apprise the trial judge of conflicting interests that may warrant separate representation or other corrective measures.

Although unobjectionable in concept, that role definition has frequently proved unworkable in practice. To be sure, many attorneys make considerable efforts to appreciate and accommodate the broadest possible spectrum of class sentiment. . . . [But] where the range and intensity of divergent preferences within the class are unlikely to surface without counsel's assistance, he often has strong prudential and ideological reasons not to provide it. One need not be a raving realist to suppose that such motivations play a more dominant role in shaping attorneys' conduct than Rule 23's directives and the accompanying judicial gloss.

1.   Prudential Interests

An attorney active in institutional reform class actions is subject to a variety of financial, tactical, and professional pressures that constrain his response to class conflicts. Of course, none of these constraints is unique to this form of litigation. And [while] the intensity of such pressures varies considerably . . . [more attention should focus on] the inadequacy of conventional correctives.

The most patent of these interests arises from the financial underpinnings of institutional reform litigation. Support for such cases derives largely from limited public interest funding and from court-awarded counsel fees to prevailing parties. Among the factors affecting the attorney's fee award are the relief obtained, the costs of attaining it, and the number of other counsel who have contributed to the result. Given the expense of institutional reform class actions, few litigators can remain impervious to fee-related considerations or organizational budget constraints. And flushing out dissension among class members can prove costly in several respects.

For example, opposing parties often seek to capitalize on class dissension by filing motions for decertification. If such efforts prove successful, class counsel may lose a substantial investment that he cannot, as a practical matter, recoup from former class members. At a minimum, such motions result in expense, delay, and loss of bargaining leverage, and deflect resources from trial preparation. Certification disputes may also trigger involvement of additional lawyers, who would share the limelight, the control over litigation decisions and, under some circumstances, the resources available for attorneys' fees.

Exposing conflict can also impede settlement arrangements that are attractive to class counsel on a number of grounds. As in many other litigation contexts, attorneys often have a bias to settle not shared by their clients. Since institutional reform plaintiffs generally do not underwrite the costs of litigation, their primary interest is in the result attained; the time and effort necessary to attain it are of less concern. Yet from the attorney's perspective, a modest settlement may generate a result "bearing a higher ratio to the cost of the work than a much larger recovery obtained only after extensive discovery, a long trial and an appeal." For example, if the prospects for prevailing on the merits are uncertain, some plaintiffs will see little to lose and everything to gain from persistence. That viewpoint may be inadequately aired by class counsel, who has concerns for his reputation as well as competing claims on his time and his organization's resources to consider.

The potential for attorney-client conflicts is compounded when a proposed settlement makes extremely generous, or totally inadequate, provision for class counsel. Of course a lawyer may attempt to avoid compromising influences by refusing to discuss fees until agreement on all other issues is final. However, that strategy is not necessarily in anyone's interest if it inhibits favorable settlement offers, and many defendants are reluctant to compromise without some understanding of their total liability. Moreover, in an escalating number of civil rights cases, defendants have sought to make settlement on the merits conditional on counsel's waiver or curtailment of claims to statutory compensation. . . .

A final set of problems emerges in test-case litigation. In some instances, counsel may be reluctant to espouse positions that are at odds with those he has taken or intends to take in other proceedings or that could establish an unwelcome precedent. Moreover, test-case litigation often generates settlement biases directly converse to those discussed above. Once a lawyer has prepared a claim with potentially significant impact, he may be disinclined to settle. He almost certainly would not share some plaintiffs' enthusiasm for pre- or post-trial agreements promising generous terms for the litigants but little recognition and no precedential value for similarly situated victims. Few professionals, class attorneys included, can make decisions wholly independent of concerns about their careers and reputations among peers, potential clients, and funding sources. Litigating well-publicized institutional reform cases can provide desirable trial experience, generate attractive new cases, legitimate organizational objectives in the eyes of private donors, and enhance attorneys' personal standing in the legal community. Where such rewards are likely, counsel may tend to discount preferences for a low-visibility settlement, particularly if it falls short of achieving ideological objectives to which he is strongly committed. . . .

2. Ideological Interests

. . . Relying on case histories from Boston, Atlanta, and Detroit, Derrick Bell submits that NAACP attorneys' "single-minded commitment" to maximum integration has led them to ignore a shift in priorities among many black parents from racial balance to quality education.

Similar indictments have been leveled against attorneys in other civil rights contexts. For example, in 1974, a number of parents and guardians brought suit in behalf of all present and future residents of Pennsylvania's Pennhurst facility for the retarded. Class counsel took the position that his obligations ran solely to the residents, and that their interests dictated Pennhurst's closure and replacement with community facilities. Accordingly, counsel made little effort to expose or espouse the views of parents and guardians preferring institutionalization. Indeed, according to one of the lawyers subsequently involved, class counsel sought to avoid "stir[ring] people up" by deemphasizing the possibility of Pennhurst's closure in his out-of-court statements. After the district judge ordered removal of Pennhurst residents to community facilities, a systematic survey of their parents and guardians revealed that only 19% of respondents favored deinstitutionalization. Accounts of other civil rights litigation suggest that *Pennhurst* is not an isolated example.

It does not follow, of course, that attorneys in these and comparable cases failed to represent class interests. Much depends on who one views as appropriate spokesmen for the class and how broadly one defines "interest." . . . [P]arents are often poorly situated to speak for all children who will be affected by judicial decree. But neither is an attorney with strong prudential or ideological preferences well positioned to decide which class members or guardians deserve a hearing and which do not. And one critical problem with existing class action procedures is that they fail to assure adequate disclosure of counsel's own interests or of countervailing client concerns. . . .

[Discussion is omitted concerning limitations in the two most common procedural approaches to class conflicts. The current pluralist approach, which is to rely on separate counsel for separate interests, may, in some instances, exacerbate problems of delay, expense, manageability, and accountability. In other contexts, that strategy can bias results toward those with the organizational ability and financial resources to make themselves heard. The majoritarian alternative is to provide for direct class participation through surveys and public hearings. Yet that approach cannot adequately respond to circumstances where those registering preferences are uninformed, unrepresentative, or unresponsive to the needs of most current or future class members. For example, the complexity of remedial trade-offs may be difficult to convey to large constituencies. And parents whose children will bear the short-term costs of certain desegregation and deinstitutionalization remedies may be poorly situated to evaluate their long-range benefits.

However, granting these difficulties, the article considers various strategies to encourage more reflective resort to pluralist or majoritarian strategies in appropriate circumstances. Among other things, courts could be required to make a record concerning their responsiveness to class conflicts. To assist judicial determinations, class counsel could submit statements detailing contacts with class members, and attorneys' fee awards might be structured to create greater incentives for lawyer-client communication.]

ALTERNATIVES AND APOLOGIA

The Bounded Potential of Procedural Solutions

The ultimate effect of procedural reforms is difficult to predict. There remains the possibility that greater reliance on separate counsel or court-appointed experts will simply increase the numbers of platonic guardians involved in institutional reform litigation. And requiring fact-finders to make more detailed records in support of their conclusions has had mixed success in other contexts. According to Joseph Sax, "emphasis on the redemptive quality of [such] procedural reform" in administrative decisionmaking is "about nine parts myth and one part coconut oil." Yet while systematic data are lacking, most commentators would probably agree with Richard Stewart's less dire assessment. In his view, forcing the decision-maker to "direct attention to factors that may have been disregarded" has in some instances proved of real prophylactic value.

Moreover, clearer mandates to class counsel than those provided by existing procedural and ethical rules could serve important socialization functions. [The lawyer's role could] encompass more explicit fiduciary obligations to dissenting constituencies. Requiring attorneys to record contacts with the class and perceptions of conflict would, if nothing else, narrow their capacity for self-delusion about whose views they were or were not representing. Explicit professional obligations, even those unlikely to trigger any formal sanction, often affect behavioral norms simply by sensitizing individuals to the full implications of their conduct. . . .

To be sure, none of the proposals outlined here can guarantee better results in [institutional reform cases]. But that conclusion, if disconcerting, is not necessarily damning. Given the values at issue in institutional reform cases, conflicts are an ineradicable feature of the legal landscape. Virtually all of the pluralist and majoritarian deficiencies that impede judicial management of such conflicts would arise with equal force if the underlying issues were addressed in legislative or bureaucratic settings. Indeed, one of the strongest justifications for those governance structures is equally available to class actions: While we cannot depend on disinterested and informed judgment by any single group of decisionmakers, we can at least create sufficient procedural checks and balances to prevent the worst abuses.

Moreover, to acknowledge that the formal mandates governing class actions promise far more than they deliver is not to condemn the pretense. No hypothesized procedures can insure that all class interests will be "adequately represented" or that counsel will single-mindedly pursue his "client's" objectives. But the risks of abandoning either fiction may be too great.

No matter how faulty the enforcement mechanism, such mandates serve important legitimating functions. Broad injunctions concerning client autonomy and adequate representation allow us to affirm the individual's right to be heard without in fact paying the entire price. Giving overly fixed content to those terms could propel us toward some generic prescription that raises more difficulties than it resolves. An unqualified embrace of pluralism would entail problems of increased expense and diminished effectiveness. To totter towards majoritarianism would require confrontation with the awkward fact that paternalism is often offensive in principle but desirable in practice. Like other "white lies" of the law, those governing class adjudication have spared us such discomfiting choices by masking certain "weak spots in our intellectual structure."

[And, given the extraordinary achievements of this form of litigation, that is a useful, if sometimes unbecoming, role.]

See Chapter XI, Constitutional Law
• Identifying the Client's Interest in Social Reform
  Litigation: Equal Protection Contexts
  (pages 468–475)

Class action attorneys often take the position that the responsibility for airing conflicts of interest lies elsewhere: with named class representatives, with dissatisfied class members, with opposing parties, or with trial courts. In some contexts, however, none of these participants have the necessary information or incentive to monitor the adequacy of representation. Named representatives or dissenting members may be uninformed, unaccountable, or unrepresentative of the class as a whole; they may also be unwilling to assume the costs of complaining about counsel's performance, or feel that they lack power to affect it. Opposing parties may not always be able to discover the extent of conflict within a class. Nor will they necessarily be interested in drawing the problem to a court's attention if the likely result is to multiply counsel. That is particularly true where opponents could be liable for prevailing parties' attorneys' fees under state or federal statutes. The absence of such oversight also helps account for the absence of malpractice and disciplinary sanctions for class counsel's performance.[46]

Although procedural rules and due process standards require judges to ensure adequate class representation, practical constraints often discourage active oversight. In many cases, finding class representatives or their counsel inadequate will not terminate proceedings; it will prolong them. From a trial court's perspective, "more is seldom merrier. . . . Multiple representation generally multiplies problems. . . . More parties means more papers, more scheduling difficulties, and more potential for objection to any given ruling or settlement proposal."[47]

How should courts and counsel respond to these incentive structures? Would you support the measures that are proposed above, such as requiring a record concerning conflicts and the measures taken to address them, expanding resources for separate counsel, and making greater use of opportunities to be heard as well as notice and survey procedures to determine class views?[48] Or, as William Rubenstein argues, where the civil rights of some defined community are at issue, such as in the gay/lesbian challenges to marriage laws in the mid-1990s, should counsel have an obligation to consult with organizations representing that community?[49]

Would any of these measures help on the facts of Problems 9E, 9F, and 9G? Which interests should be heard? How loudly? Who should decide? And who should pay? For example, in desegregation suits, if communities are divided along economic, racial, and ethnic lines, should each have its own counsel? In such cases, the result may be a trial with 25 to 30 attorneys. Every time one of them sneezes, "the gesundheits [will take] ten pages of transcript."[50] Critics of this approach question how much it helps to have "lawyers representing ten different interest groups objecting to ten different aspects of a proposed decree if the court has no sense of how substantial a constituency each represents."[51] William Simon, responding to Derrick Bell's article, also points out that

> division among plaintiffs might contribute to a result less satisfactory to both plaintiff groups than the one favored by either group would be to the other. This might happen if each group succeeded in discrediting the other's position without establishing the credibility of its own, and the court decided to defer to the school board. In a conflict between the school board and the larger class of blacks, a unified plaintiff class may be better able than competing subclasses to achieve a remedy that is satisfactory to all blacks.
>
> Nor does Bell consider that disaffiliation may sacrifice long term benefits that might accrue from an alternative response to class conflict: intraclass resolution. One option for black parents dissatisfied with the position of class counsel would be to seek to further their views within the Legal Defense Fund or other organizations represen-

tative of the undivided class. A potential byproduct of such efforts is to contribute to the democratization of the organization or class, to strengthen it by making its leadership more sensitive to its members or by broadening patterns of member participation. When this occurs, the litigation provides the occasion for the development of organizational capacity that provides more general benefits to its members. These types of benefits have to be sacrificed when, instead of promoting intraclass resolution, lawyers promote disaffiliation, in effect submitting the conflict to the state. Of course, there are many situations in which state resolution of disputes within a disadvantaged class might be in the interests of some members, and the situation Bell describes may be one of these. But the doctrines to which he appeals do not help determine if it is. The problem with the presumption of disaffiliation is that, to the extent it provides any guidance at all, it does so only by obscuring considerations favoring collective practice.[52]

How would Bell respond to that claim? How would you?

The conflicting objectives that Bell discusses remain common in civil rights litigation. Desegregation is a divisive remedy in many communities for multiple reasons: segregated tracks prevent significant mixing during the school day; the burden of busing has fallen disproportionately on black communities; black administrators and teachers have lost opportunities; and the quality of education has not always improved with integration. Although national surveys find that a majority of blacks support integration, resistance has surfaced in some cities where NAACP suits are pending. For example, three-quarters of Minneapolis residents supported neighborhood schools even if they were predominantly white or minority. Only 16 percent favored efforts such as voluntary busing to achieve racial balance.[53]

Should such preferences play a more central role in class action litigation? If so, how should information be gathered? Neither town meetings nor written questionnaires will necessarily ensure a cross-section of views, and efforts are rarely undertaken to assess the representativeness of responses.[54] Telephone surveys or mass mailings will have difficulty presenting enough factual material to permit informed choices. The problems are well illustrated by a class action antitrust case seeking damages from several major drug companies on behalf of antibiotics purchasers. Class members received a notice stating that unless they indicated a desire to opt out of the litigation, they would be bound by its result. The following responses suggest the limitations of such procedures:

> Dear Sir:
>   I received your pamphlet on drugs which I think will be of great value to me in the future.
>   Due to circumstances beyond my control I will not be able to attend this class at the time prescribed on your letter due to the fact that my working hours are from 7:00 until 4:30.

Dear Sir:
   Our son is in the Navy, stationed in the Caribbean some place.
Please let us know exactly what kind of drugs he is accused of taking.
   From a mother who will help if properly informed.[55]

Deferring to a majority of class members also may provide inadequate protection for the minority and may be impractical where choices are too complicated for simple explanation.[56] Yet if neither the separate representation model nor the majoritarian survey procedure will always be adequate, what follows from that fact? Under what circumstances would such strategies be of some assistance? Are other approaches to conflicts in class actions desirable? Where the remedies are largely financial, should courts or attorneys try to ensure that every class member do at least as well in a settlement as the expected court outcome?[57] Would it make more sense in some cases to dispense with the fiction of the class and allow lawyers or ombudsmen to sue directly?

PROBLEM 9F

1. You are a lawyer for a public interest civil rights organization that is suing a city fire department for race and sex discrimination. The original plaintiff in the suit was a firefighter's union, which claimed that the department's written hiring exam was racially biased and not job-related, and that the department discriminated against African Americans and Hispanics in promotion. After filing suit, the union instituted a coaching program for minority applicants. Some female participants who performed better than their male counterparts on the written test, but worse on the physical strength and agility examination, claimed that many of the required physical skills were also unrelated to job performance and that they discriminated against women. These participants joined the suit along with white women who had passed the written but not the physical exam.

The city has now offered a settlement that you consider grossly inadequate. It eliminates objectionable provisions of the written and physical exams and sets hiring and promotion "goals" for women and minorities, but it establishes no minimum requirements to ensure that its goals are met and provides no back pay or retroactive seniority remedies. When you indicate your dissatisfaction with the proposal, opposing counsel indicates that if the city's offer is not acceptable, he will move for your disqualification on grounds of conflict of interest.

How do you proceed? You believe that it is in the interests of the entire plaintiff class to avoid any settlement that does not provide adequate relief to all subgroups. Otherwise, the financially strapped city will attempt a divide-and-conquer strategy. You also recognize that various subgroups of the plaintiff class have different remedial interests and that some members question whether you have their concerns at heart. You worry that if each subclass has its own attorney, there will be unnecessary expense, friction, and duplication of effort, as well as difficulties in presenting a united front. Court-awarded counsel fees would also need to be divided. On the other hand, if the city comes up with a better compromise settlement, you may have difficulty selling it to some members. How do you proceed?

2. You are a solo practitioner who used to work for the civil rights organization described above. At the request of your former colleague, the lawyer for the plaintiffs in the firefighters' case, you have agreed to represent the women as a subclass in that suit. The city has now made a slightly better settlement offer, which is quite favorable to your clients. It does not, however, meet a number of the union's basic demands. At an open meeting, the women of color in your subclass strongly object to accepting the settlement. They feel an obligation to support the union, which assisted them in the past and would be an important ally in any future struggles with the department. By contrast, most of the white women are satisfied with the terms of the offer, which promises immediate jobs and back pay to applicants who scored above a certain level on prior written exams. How do you proceed?[58]

3.   Environmental Litigation

PROBLEM 9G

1. You are staff counsel for the National Conservation League (NCL), a membership organization that litigates environmental issues primarily relating to wilderness and wildlife preservation. NCL lawyers have become increasingly involved with energy issues, and recently brought class action suits against several coal-fired power plants in the Pacific Northwest. These proceedings, approved by the NCL board of trustees and filed on behalf of NCL members residing in the Northwest, seek to force installation of additional air pollution controls. Defendants estimate that these improvements would raise the average customer's electricity bill by about $150 annually.

You have briefly discussed the litigation with the two NCL members in whose name it was filed. No other members have received formal notice of the actions or the progress of settlement negotiations, although a summary announcement of the cases appeared in the League's monthly journal.

Recent electricity rate increases in the areas served by these plants have provoked some consumer opposition. You have no direct information as to the NCL members' views on the matter but hope that most of them would support your position if fully informed.

2. Two of the trustees of your environmental organization have asked you to challenge their city's plans to construct a baseball stadium on the only site that planners believe is economically feasible. The proposed stadium is necessary to attract a major league team, but its construction on that site would threaten crucial wetlands that are used by endangered wildlife. If you file suit, you may be able to cause sufficient expense and delay to convince the team's owners to relocate in another city. Although you share the trustees' objections to the proposed devel-

opment, you worry about the effects of opposition on the city's racial minorities and on your group's reputation as elitist and insensitive to such concerns. Various civil rights coalitions support the stadium as a way to increase inner-city jobs, expand tax revenues, build morale, and assist minority-owned businesses. Under the proposed plans, minority contractors, vending services, and professional firms (including lawyers, engineers, and architects) would receive a substantial share of the work connected with the stadium.

When you raise your concerns with the trustees, they respond that your organization's mission is to protect environmental interests; it is up to the civil rights coalitions to address minority needs. As one individual puts it, "[w]ildlife has fewer and fewer places to go and paving over wetlands is an unacceptable way of providing cheap development sites."[59] How do you proceed?

3. You represent the Maine Citizens for Environmental Quality in a suit against a small coastal town. Your client is challenging the proposed construction of a causeway linking the town to a nearby island, which will destroy clam beds in the surrounding mud flats. The coalition's leadership and funding come primarily from owners of expensive summer homes on the island, who fear that the causeway will attract increased development. Support for the causeway comes from residents whose economic circumstances have worsened in the aftermath of a major plant closing. They welcome development. No one except you appears much concerned about the clams or the long-term effects on the ecosystem. Does this case pose different considerations than the one described in Part 2?

4. Your environmental organization has been asked to represent a coalition whose members are opposed to construction of a desalinization plant in their low-income Latino community. The water district views the plant as a long-term solution to the risk of periodic drought. The community coalition sees the plant as a major source of pollution, given the additional electric power that its operation would require.

The only logical other location is in Baja, just over the Mexican border. Your organization is generally uncomfortable with any strategy that advocates exporting pollution; however, you believe that the community coalition may be equally uncomfortable with a no-growth stance that would restrict consumption through zoning and immigration policies. How should you proceed?

4. Representing Subordinate Groups

LUCIE E. WHITE, TO LEARN AND TEACH: LESSONS FROM DRIEFONTEIN ON LAWYERING AND POWER

1988 Wis. L. Rev. 699

In this article, White draws on theories about power to "identify methods of lawyering that can alter the processes of subordination rather than merely minister to the injuries that those processes generate." Id. at 754. She begins by analyzing the framework of political scientist Steven Lukes in Power: A Radical View (1974). There, Lukes sets out three dimensions of power that White then employs as a basis for three models of lawyering for social change.

The first dimension of power is that of interest-group politics. Groups gain this form of power by pursuing their interests through established political channels. This process assumes that individuals can make rational, informed decisions about when and how to act on their interests. As both White and Lukes note, this analysis of power is quite limited. It fails to account for systematic inequalities of information and resources that affect the outcome of political contests and the capacity of groups to participate in the process.

The second dimension of power focuses on the suppression of interests and the cultural values and institutional practices that exclude certain concerns from the political sphere. Fear of economic, social, or physical retaliation is most common. For example, tenants who fear eviction will be reluctant to complain about housing conditions, and workers who fear employer reprisals or co-worker ostracism may not support union activity. Other barriers include the failure to recognize certain grievances as legitimate legal or political claims, or the inadequacy of enforcement structures for existing rights. This second dimension of power is also limited. Although it focuses on the suppression of grievances, it fails to account for the structures that keep individuals from recognizing or acting on their interests.

A third dimension of power focuses on the social processes through which individuals understand their experience. Central to this analysis is the way that subordinate groups are socialized into the norms and practices of dominant groups, and the way that dominant groups learn to denigrate, fear, and stigmatize their subordinates. Yet from White's perspective, this dimension of power is also inadequate. It fails to account for the practices of survival and resistance among subordinate groups that can lay the foundations for social change.

White then identifies models of public interest practice that correspond to these dimensions of power.

> The first image of lawyering corresponds to the first dimension of power. In this image, the role of the public interest lawyer is straight-forward and familiar. He is charged with designing and winning lawsuits that will further the substantive interests of client groups. The lawyer "translates" client grievances into legal claims. He crafts the lawsuit so that the judicial remedy, if granted, will directly remove, or at least ameliorate, those grievances. . . .
>
> [Public interest practice along these lines] has brought about substantial change, and continues to do so. However, in some circumstances where institutional practices are challenged, courts have difficulty fashioning effective remedies. . . . When the structure of a bureaucracy or its discretionary, routine functioning is challenged, . . . courts find it difficult to craft and implement effective relief.

Furthermore, when an inadequate appropriation of public funds is the root of the problem, the courts have limited legitimacy to redress it.

In addition to these practical limits on the court-ordered remedy as a device for shifting social power, there is a deeper limitation in the litigation-centered approach to public interest lawyering. . . .

In order to get into court, litigants must present their claims as similar to precedent claims that courts have already accepted. In order to get relief, litigants must propose remedies that are coextensive with these confined claims and that can be feasibly administered by the courts. The result of these pressures is the oft-observed risk that litigation will co-opt social mobilization. Through the process of voicing grievances in terms to which courts can respond, social groups risk stunting their own aspirations.

Id. at 755-757.

A second image of lawyering acknowledges litigation as a means of reallocating social resources but views that function as secondary to its broader role in structuring discourse about social justice. On this view:

[T]he measure of the case's success is not who wins. Rather, success is measured by such factors as whether the case widens the public imagination about right and wrong, mobilizes political action behind new social arrangements, or pressures those in power to make concessions. . . . [I]n order to make the case into an effective vehicle for changing public consciousness . . . [t]he lawyer must learn to read public sentiment, framing cases in which the public will readily see injustice and can be led to see that conventional legal remedies do not really right the wrong. Furthermore, the lawyer must be able to coordinate the lawsuit with any direct political action that the litigation might spark. She must support such mobilization when it arises without either diverting its energy into litigation support or confining its own demands to be the legally feasible remedies. . . .

However, for all of the power of second-dimension lawyering, it also has limits. In the second-dimension, the lawyer assumes that her clients perceive their grievances clearly and stand ready to challenge the responsible parties directly, regardless of the risks. Second-dimensional lawyering cannot respond to subordinated clients who come to them with a more guarded interpretation of their own suffering or a more realistic assessment of their options.

If third order mechanisms of power do indeed operate, the clients that are most fully subordinated never get the second-dimensional lawyer's attention. These are the people who feel cheated but have no clear sense of who is responsible, people who describe their suffering to outsiders as their lot in life, or people who distrust the "system" and the remedial processes that it offers. Such people will not give the right answers when the well-meaning lawyer innocently asks, "What's wrong?"

The lawyer then has three choices. She can work for more assimilated groups, those who ask for help in terms that lawyers more readily understand. She can set her own priorities for social change, recruiting token clients to stand for the issues that her own political analysis has led her to pursue. Or, finally, she can take on the dangerous project of listening carefully to the answers that at first might seem "non-responsive." She can work with those groups in a joint project of translating felt experience into understandings and actions that can increase their power. This is the project of lawyering on the third dimension.

Id. at 758-760.

The third vision of lawyering views law as an opportunity to increase critical consciousness. Drawing on consciousness-raising techniques developed by feminists and writers such as Paulo Freire in the Pedagogy of the Oppressed (1970), the lawyer seeks ways to enable subordinate groups to reflect about concrete injustices and strategies for change. Unlike more traditional practice, the lawyer does not claim to possess "privileged knowledge" about politics or reality. Instead,

> [s]he takes the lead in questioning her own expertise and the values on which it is based and invites other group members to deepen the critique. Rather than manipulating the group to preserve her own authority, she tries to engage the group to displace her as authority, and to relocate the very concept, transformed, in their own process of conversation. This does not mean that she withholds her own judgments. Rather, she tries to speak honestly, as a person with a different experience, and to demand that her views be taken seriously in the group's practice of understanding. . . .
>
> The lawyer cannot simply dictate to the group what actions they must take. Neither the lawyer nor any single individual is positioned to know what actions the group should take at a particular moment. Sound decisions will come only as those who know the landscape and will suffer the risks deliberate together. The role of the lawyer is to help the group learn a *method* of deliberation that will lead to effective and responsible strategic action. . . .
>
> This third-dimensional image of lawyering may seem very remote from our conceptions of lawyering, even lawyering specifically directed toward social change. Yet some writers, in exploring alternative visions of lawyering, have pointed toward it. Its outlines were suggested in 1970 in an article by Steven Wexler. He observed that the problems of poor people are fundamentally social rather than individual in nature and concluded that in order to effect lasting change, the poor must organize and act for themselves. . . . Gerald Lopez has [similarly] explored a concept of "lay lawyering," in which lawyer and client, recognizing each other's skills, learn together how to persuade an adversary of their position. Through this practice, they challenge the client's subordination in the work and in the relationship. . . .

Id at 763-766.

How would the model White describes help lawyers in responding to Problems 9F and 9G?

Endnotes

1. See Dennis F. Thompson, Paternalism in Medicine, Law and Public Policy, in Ethics Teaching in Higher Education 245 (Daniel Callahan & Sissela Bok eds., 1980); Samuel Gorovitz, Doctors' Dilemmas: Moral Conflict and Medical Care 36-37 (1982).

2. Richard Wasserstrom, Lawyers as Professionals: Some Moral Issues, 5 Human Rights 1, 16-21 (1975).

3. David Luban, Partisanship, Betrayal and Autonomy in the Lawyer-Client Relationship: A Reply to Stephen Ellmann, 90 Colum. L. Rev. 1004, 1037 (1990).

4. For examples, see Douglas E. Rosenthal, Lawyer and Client: Who's in Charge? (1974) (personal injury claims); Austin Sarat & William L.E. Felstiner, Law and Strategy in the Divorce Lawyer's Office, 20 Law & Soc. Rev. 93 (1986) (divorce cases). For criminal law, see the discussion of the structure of representation in Chapter XIV (Criminal Law and Procedure) at pages 610–617.

5. This is not necessarily undesirable. See, e.g., Robert W. Gordon, The Independence of Lawyers, 68 B.U. L. Rev. 1 (1988); William Simon, Visions of Practice in Legal Thought, 36 Stan. L. Rev. 469 (1984).

6. Gerald Dworkin, Paternalism, in Morality and the Law 107 (Richard Wasserstrom ed., 1971) (discussing John Stuart Mill's On Liberty); Thompson, supra note 1, at 231, 245.

7. Thompson, supra note 1, at 250-251 (emphasis in original).

8. Id. at 251.

9. See Amos Tversky, Decision Making (1988), and Judgment Under Uncertainty (1982); Leon Festinger, A Theory of Cognitive Dissonance (1957).

10. Duncan Kennedy, Distributive and Paternalist Motives in Contract and Tort Law, with Special References to Compulsory Terms and Unequal Bargaining Power, 41 Md. L. Rev. 563, 644 (1982).

11. Dworkin, supra note 6, at 120.

12. David Luban, Paternalism and the Legal Profession, 1981 Wis. L. Rev. 454, 468, 471-472 (1981).

13. Id. at 472-474.

14. Kennedy, supra note 10, at 638-639.

15. Id. at 644.

16. Norman Mailer, The Executioner's Song 490, 513-514 (1979).

17. For competing precedents, see Deborah L. Rhode & David Luban, Legal Ethics 580 & n.3 (2d ed. 1995); Rodney J. Uphoff, The Role of the Criminal Defense Lawyer in Representing the Mentally Impaired Defendant: Zealous Advocate or Officer of the Court?, 1988 Wis. L. Rev. 65 (1988). For a recent case, see "Volunteer" Gets His Last Day in Court, Dayton Daily News, Sept. 22, 1997, at 38.

18. Jean M. Landis & Lynne Goodstein, When Is Justice Fair? An Integrated Approach to the Outcome Versus Procedure Debate, 1986 ABF Res. J. 675, 701 (1986); John W. Thibaut & Laurens Walker, Procedural Justice: A Psychological Analysis (1975).

19. See Stephen Ellman, Lawyers and Clients, 34 UCLA L. Rev. 717 (1987); Mary Strauss, Toward a Revised Model of Attorney-Client Relationship: The Argument for Autonomy, 65 N.C.L. Rev. 315, 338-339 & n.107 (1987); Rosenthal, supra note 4, at 29-61.

20. William H. Simon, Lawyer Advice and Client Autonomy: Mrs. Jones's Case, 50 Md. L. Rev. 213, 215-216 (1991).

21. Thomas L. Shaffer & James R. Elkins, Legal Interviewing and Counseling 270-271 (1987).

22. Institute of Judicial Administration, American Bar Association, Juvenile Justice Standards (1979). These provide that where a juvenile client is capable of considered judgment, the determination of that client's interest is his or her responsibility. See also Recommendations of the Conference on Ethical Issues in the Legal Representation of Children, 64 Fordham L. Rev. 1301, 1302 (1996).

23. Juvenile Justice Standards, supra note 22; see also Jan C. Costello, Ethical Issues in Representing Juvenile Clients: A Review of the IJA-ABA Standards on Representing Private Parties, 10 N.M.L. Rev. 255 (1980).

24. Sarah H. Ramsey, Representation of the Child in Protection Proceedings: The Determination of Decision-Making Capacity, 17 Fam. L.Q. 287, 306 (1983).

25. Interview with Michael Wald, Professor, Stanford Law School, in Stanford, Cal. (August 1993).

26. Lois A. Weithorn, Involving Children in Decisions Affecting Their Own Welfare, in Children's Competence to Consent 235, 245 (Gary B. Melton et al. eds., 1983). See also David G. Scherer, The Capacities of Minors to Exercise Voluntariness in Medical Treatment Decisions, 15 Law & Hum. Behav. 431 (1991).

27. Ramsey, supra note 24; Jean Koh Peters, The Roles and Content of Best Interests in Client-Directed Lawyering for Children in Child Protective Proceedings, 64 Fordham L. Rev. 1505 (1996).

28. ABA Standards, supra note 22. See also Martin Guggenheim, A Paradigm for Determining the Role of Counsel for Children, 64 Fordham L. Rev. 1399, 1424 (1996).

29. Lois A. Weithorn, Children's Capacities in Legal Contexts, in Children, Mental Health and the Law 25 (N. Dickon Reppucci et al. eds., 1984).

30. Peter Margulies, The Lawyer as Caregiver: Child Clients' Competence in Context, 64 Fordham L. Rev. 1473, 1487-1493 (1996); Randall A. Butz, Comment, Lawyering for the Abused Child: "You Can't Go Home Again," 29 UCLA L. Rev. 1216, 1238-1244 (1982); Willard Gaylin, The "Competence" of Children: No Longer All or None, 21 J. Am. Acad. Child Psychiatry 153 (1982).

31. These problems are drawn from Steven Pepper, Jurisprudence and the Ethics of Lawyering, 104 Yale L.J. 1545, 1551, 1563, 1580 (1995).

32. Robert W. Gordon, Corporate Law Practice as a Public Calling, 49 Md. L. Rev. 255, 288-289 (1990).

33. Earl Johnson, Jr., Justice and Reform: The Formative Years of the American Legal Services Program (1978); Jack Katz, Poor People's Lawyers in Transition (1982).

34. Donald Johnson, The Challenge to American Freedoms (1963); Robert Rabin, Lawyers for Social Change: Perspectives on Public Interest Law, 28 Stan. L. Rev. 207, 210-214 (1976).

35. Id. at 216-218; Charles F. Kellogg, NAACP: A History of the National Association for the Advancement of Colored People, vol. 1 (1967).

36. Nan Aron, Liberty and Justice for All: Public Interest Law in the 1980s and Beyond 4-5 (1989); Nan Aron & Samuel S. Jackson, Jr., Non-Traditional Models for Legal Services Delivery, in Civil Justice: An Agenda for the 1990s, at 145, 146 (American Bar Assn. ed., 1991).

37. Susan M. Olson, Clients and Lawyers: Securing the Rights of Disabled Persons 26 (1984) (quoting Joel Handler). See also Gerald P. Lopez, Rebellious Lawyering: One Chicano's Vision of Progressive Law Practice (1992); Steve Bachmann, Lawyers, Law, and Social Change, 13 N.Y. Rev. L. & Soc. Change 1, 31 (1984).

38. Olson, supra note 37, at 32 (quoting Saul Alinsky).

39. Gary Bellow, quoted in Comment, The New Public Interest Lawyers, 79 Yale L.J. 1069, 1077-1078 (1970). See Gerald N. Rosenberg: The Hollow Hope: Can Courts Bring About Social Change 11-18 (1991). For related problems, see Susan Poser, The Ethics of Implementation: Institutional Remedies and the Lawyer's Role, 10 Geo. J. Legal Ethics 15 (1996).

40. John Denvir, Towards a Political Theory of Public Interest Litigation, 54 N.C.L. Rev. 1133, 1137-1138 (1976) (citing SIPI v. AECI, 481 F.2d 1079 (D.C. Cir. 1973), and complaint filed in Diana v. California State Bd. of Educ.).

41. In the aftermath of Geduldig v. Aiello, 417 U.S. 484 (1974), and General Elec. Co. v. Gilbert, 429 U.S. 125 (1976), Congress passed the Pregnancy Discrimination Act, 42 U.S.C. §2000e.

42. Denvir, supra note 40, at 1140.

43. Martha Minow, From Class Actions to *Miss Saigon*: The Concept of Representation in the Law, 39 Clev. St. L. Rev. 269, 284 (1991).

44. Stephen Ellman, Client Centeredness Multiplied: Individual Autonomy and Collective Mobilization in Public Interest Lawyers' Representation of Groups, 78 Va. L. Rev. 1103 (1992).

45. Rhode & Luban, supra note 17, at 544. For studies on black performance and preference, see Steven A. Holmes, Look Who's Saying Separate Is Equal, N.Y. Times, Oct. 1, 1995, at E5.

46. Susan Koniak, Through the Looking Glass of Ethics and the Wrong Rights We Find There, 9 Geo. J. Legal Ethics 1, 14-19 (1995).

47. For examples, see Deborah L. Rhode, Class Conflicts in Class Actions, 34 Stan. L. Rev. 1183, 1219 (1982). See also Koniak, supra note 46, at 16-19.

48. Patrick Woolley, Rethinking the Adequacy of Adequate Representation, 75 Tex. L. Rev. 572 (1997).

49. William B. Rubenstein, Divided We Litigate: Addressing Disputes Among Clients and Lawyers in Civil Rights Campaigns, 106 Yale L. Rev. 1623 (1997).

50. Rhode, supra note 47, at 1228.

51. Id. at 1229.

52. Simon, supra note 5, at 481-482.

53. Peter Applebome, Wave of Suits Seeks Reversal of School Busing, N.Y. Times, Sept. 26, 1995, at B6; James S. Kunen, Integration Forever?, Time, July 21, 1997, at 39; Drew Days, *Brown* Blues: Rethinking the Integrative Ideal, 38 Wm. & Mary L. Rev. 53 (1992).

54. Rhode, supra note 47, at 1233.

55. Id. at 1235.

56. Nancy Morawetz, Bargaining Class Representation and Fairness, 54 Ohio St. L.J. 1, 37-38 (1993).

57. Id. at 42.

58. Shauna Marshall, Class Actions as Instruments of Social Change: Reflections on *Davis v. City of San Francisco,* 29 U.S.F. L. Rev. 911 (1995).

59. Part 2 of this problem draws on a controversy over San Jose's proposed site for a Giants Stadium in the spring of 1992. The local chapters of the Sierra Club and the Audubon Society opposed the location. The quoted phrase is from Wetlands Committee chairperson Tom Esperson in a Sierra Club Press Release, Sierra Club Calls Zanker Site for Stadium a Strikeout for Wildlife and People (May 27, 1992).

PART II

Legal Ethics in Legal Context

Chapter X

Civil
Procedure

A course in civil procedure makes clear the ethical dimensions of everyday lawyering. To explore those dimensions, the following analysis focuses on the relationships between formal rules, practice norms, and moral values. Attention centers on the way that procedural frameworks accommodate personal, professional, and societal interests. The balance we strike in dispute resolution structures does much to define the ethical possibilities of the lawyer's role.

A.   THE ADVERSARY SYSTEM

See Chapter V, The Adversary System

B. PROCEDURAL VALUES AND LITIGATION STRATEGIES

1. Discovery

See Chapter V, The Adversary System
  • Part C. The Tactical Use of Procedure
      (pages 185–194)

PROBLEM 10A[1]

1. A friend who teaches at a local law school seeks your assistance. He has had long-standing feuds with his next-door neighbor because she rents out her garage apartment to students who hold late and noisy parties. The professor has recently returned from a leave of absence to discover that the neighbor is well into the process of building an extension that slightly encroaches onto his property. Although he is completely unconcerned with the building itself, he sees this as an opportunity to exact promises regarding future renters and retribution for prior insensitivity. May you file suit to enjoin the building or to recover damages?

2. You work for the Missouri Attorney General's office. Several years ago the legislature enacted a statute with various restrictions on access to abortion that the Supreme Court subsequently upheld. The preamble to the legislation defined life as beginning at the moment of conception. Pro-choice organizations have now filed several "guerilla lawsuits" to enforce the preamble in other contexts in which age is significant. One suit seeks to permit voting at age 17 and 3 months because, if life begins at conception, such individuals would in fact be 18. In other cases, the organizations seek to accelerate entitlements concerning drinking, driving, and payments of social security retirement benefits.

It seems clear that plaintiffs are bringing these suits not because they care about winning, but because they wish to dramatize a problem with the legislative preamble. Attorneys in your office are divided about whether to seek sanctions for frivolous litigation. How do you respond?

3. If you were the judge ruling on sanctions motions in the two preceding cases, what would you decide? Assume that the evidence suggests that the professor has a valid claim but is pursuing it to punish and gain bargaining leverage over his neighbor. By contrast, the pro-choice plaintiffs have a far weaker case but are not seeking to harass. How much does motive matter? Are these claims different from those in Problems 5B and 5C (pages 190–191)? Is your decision on sanctions likely to be affected by your personal feelings about late-night parties and restrictions on abortion?

Courts have long asserted inherent authority to impose sanctions for lawyers' misconduct in litigation. In addition, a number of procedural and ethical rules govern the filing of nonmeritorious pleadings. The most important is Rule 11 of the Federal Rules of Civil Procedure and its analogues in state codes. Rule 11 provides in part:

> (b) *Representations to Court.* By presenting to the court . . . a pleading, written motion, or other paper, an attorney or unrepresented party is certifying that to the best of the person's knowledge, information, and belief, formed after an inquiry reasonable under the circumstances
>
> (1) it is not being presented for any improper purpose, such as to harass or to cause unnecessary delay or needless increase in the cost of litigation;
>
> (2) the claims, defenses, and other legal contentions therein are warranted by existing law or by a nonfrivolous argument for the extension, modification, or reversal of existing law or the establishment of new law;
>
> (3) the allegations and other factual contentions have evidentiary support or, if specifically so identified, are likely to have evidentiary support after a reasonable opportunity for further investigation or discovery; and
>
> (4) the denials of factual contentions are warranted on the evidence or, if specifically so identified, are reasonably based on a lack of information or belief.
>
> (c) *Sanctions.* If, after notice and a reasonable opportunity to respond, the court determines that subdivision (b) has been violated, the court may . . . impose an appropriate sanction upon the attorneys, law firms, or parties that have violated subdivision (b) or are responsible for the violation.

Rule 11 parallels and to some extent replicates the prohibitions in bar disciplinary codes. Disciplinary Rule 7-102(A)(1) provides that "a lawyer shall not file a suit, assert a position, conduct a defense, delay a trial, or take other action on behalf of his client when he knows or when it is obvious that such action would serve merely to harass or maliciously injure another." Disciplinary Rule 7-102(A)(2) adds that "a lawyer shall not knowingly advance a claim or defense that is unwarranted under existing law, except that he may advance such claim or defense if it can be supported by good faith argument for an extension, modification, or reversal of existing law." Model Rule 3.1 explicitly enjoins a lawyer from "frivolous" actions, and defines frivolity in language identical to Rule 11 and DR 7-102(A)(2): "A lawyer shall not bring or defend a proceeding, or assert or controvert an issue therein, unless there is a basis for doing so that is not frivolous, which includes a good faith argument for an extension, modification or reversal of existing law."

In addition to Rule 11, courts have other statutory and procedural provisions to deter abuse. For example, under 28 U.S.C. §1927, an attorney who multiplies proceedings unreasonably and vexatiously may be required to pay the costs and attorneys' fees that result from such conduct. Federal Rule of Civil Procedure 37 authorizes sanctions for failures to make disclosures or cooperate in discovery, and Rules 16 and 26 seek to deter abuse through judicial management of pretrial proceedings. Under its inherent power, a court may also award reasonable attorneys' fees for bad faith litigation conduct.

These procedural rules track the bar's traditional ethical prohibition against procedural abuse. In practice, they have been more powerful regulatory mechanisms. Efforts to discipline lawyers for frivolous litigation are extremely rare; motions for procedural sanctions are increasingly common. The reasons for the difference stem largely from amendments strengthening the procedural rules during the 1980s. Most important, the amendments to Rule 11 made impositions of sanctions mandatory, not discretionary, and required a reasonable inquiry into the factual and legal basis of a pleading. Drafters of the amendment believed that subjective bad faith was too difficult to prove and that lawyers should not be rewarded for ignorance, for having a "pure heart and empty head." Rule 11's fee-shifting provisions also provided a monetary incentive generally lacking in disciplinary processes, and their availability during the course of litigation offered strategic advantages absent in bar reporting systems.

To critics, the amended Rule 11 increased problems it was intended to resolve. Motions for sanctions have now become a standard part of the litigator's arsenal and can generate harassing satellite litigation. In the five years following the 1983 amendments, there were almost a thousand reported cases involving Rule 11, compared with only about sixty in the preceding three decades.[2]

The greater frequency of procedural oversight offers greater potential for abuse. Part of the problem involves the ambiguity of standards governing "reasonable inquiry," "good faith arguments," or "well-grounded" in fact. One influential study asked 300 judges to consider ten hypothetical cases based on reported Rule 11 decisions. In six of those cases, judges divided almost evenly on whether to impose sanctions. The indeterminacy of standards makes it possible for judges to impose their own biases in penalizing creative claims.[3] According to some, although not all, studies, Rule 11 sanctions have been imposed disproportionately on civil rights plaintiffs.[4] Because public interest lawyers generally have fewer resources than private practitioners, they are more vulnerable to financial penalties. The result, critics claim, is that Rule 11 has chilled public interest actions.[5]

Both the extent and implications of this deterrent impact are disputed. In some surveys of Rule 11, public interest or legal services lawyers do not receive an exceptional number of sanctions.[6] Other commentators question whether curtailing the rule would make a significant difference. As David Wilkins notes,

[e]ven in the absence of rule 11, judges have a great variety of embedded weapons at their disposal to punish lawyers and clients who bring claims to which the judge is substantively opposed. . . . For example, judges can impose unreasonable but difficult to overturn discovery restrictions, subtly signal their distaste for the plaintiff's claims to jurors and witnesses, enforce formally justifiable but otherwise unnecessary evidentiary requirements, and most importantly, rule in favor of the opposing party on the merits.[7]

To the defenders of Rule 11, the appropriate response to the harassing use of sanctions motions is more sanctions, and the appropriate check on biased trial court rulings is clearer and more consistent appellate guidelines. According to these commentators, empirical studies show that courts are overly reluctant to impose sanctions rather than the converse. All too often, judges lack knowledge to be sure that sanctions are appropriate, or are unwilling to exacerbate acrimony and invite retaliation in election campaigns or judicial performance evaluations.[8]

In an effort to accommodate these varying perspectives, a Judicial Conference Advisory Committee recommended additional amendments to Rule 11. In 1993, the United States Supreme Court approved these modifications. One of the most significant changes in the 1993 amendment was a "safe harbor" provision. After an opponent moves for sanctions, a party has 21 days to withdraw or modify the claims at issue. Absent "exceptional circumstances," law firms are now jointly responsible for violations committed by partners, associates, and employees. The 1993 amendments also made sanctions discretionary rather than mandatory. They can be monetary or nonmonetary, and can include issuing reprimands, requiring participation in educational programs, or referring matters to a disciplinary committee. Financial penalties are now normally paid to the court and attorney's fees for the party seeking sanctions are appropriate only in "unusual circumstances" where necessary for effective deterrence. See Advisory Committee Note.

Justice Scalia, joined by Justice Thomas, dissented from the Court's approval of these modifications. In their view, the return to discretionary sanctions, coupled with a safe harbor provision, would render Rule 11 "toothless" and would inappropriately allow parties filing frivolous claims to escape unpunished. Do you agree? If you had been on the Advisory Committee, what modifications in Rule 11 would you have supported?

Another central question dividing the courts is whether sanctions should be available for a claim that is motivated by an improper purpose but warranted by existing law and facts, as in Problem 10A. How would you resolve that issue? Does the improper purpose need to be the only purpose or the predominant purpose to make conduct sanctionable? Will problems of proof make any subjective standard difficult to apply in principled fashion?[9]

PROBLEM 10B

1. You are the junior partner working on the defense of a sex harassment case. At issue is the conduct of several male supervisors in one of your client's automobile factories. These supervisors allegedly made sexually explicit comments to female subordinates, questioned these women about their sex lives, referred to them in lewd graffiti, and left magazines with nude centerfolds in work areas. The disputed issues in the case are whether the conduct was so pervasive and offensive as to adversely affect working conditions, whether female employees made sufficiently clear that all sexual comments were unwelcome, and whether they suffered substantial damages.

The senior partner has developed a line of deposition questions that he believes might encourage the plaintiffs to accept a modest settlement rather than risk a public trial. For example, he proposes to ask them whether they have ever read sexually explicit magazines or watched sexually explicit movies; whether they have had extramarital affairs or told a sexually explicit joke at work; and whether they are having difficulties in intimate relationships that might contribute to the psychological damages that they are claiming. One of the plaintiffs is from a quite traditional Asian-American family, and you believe she may find such questions particularly intrusive. Another has a history of therapy for problems that are likely to be painful to discuss at a deposition or trial. Are you willing to pursue such inquiries if they might yield evidence relevant at trial?[10]

2. You learn that your opponent's key expert witness is about to leave for a long-planned vacation that will extend until the trial begins. The expert's deposition, already rescheduled once because of opposing counsel's illness, is currently set for just before the expert's departure. If you suddenly become unable to make that date and insist on rescheduling during the expert's vacation, you suspect that she will drop out of the case. May you arrange your calendar to require rescheduling?

3. You are on the federal court of appeals that is reviewing a district court's imposition of Rule 11 sanctions in the Golden Eagle case below. What would you decide?

GOLDEN EAGLE DISTRIBUTING CORP. v. BURROUGHS, 801 F.2D 1531 (9TH CIR. 1986). The case arose when Golden Eagle Distributing Corporation filed an action in Minnesota state court for fraud, negligence, and breach of contract against Burroughs Corporation because of an allegedly defective computer system that Burroughs sold to Golden Eagle. Burroughs successfully moved to transfer the action to the Northern District of California where almost all of the relevant evidence was located.

Kirkland and Ellis lawyers, representing the defendant Burroughs, moved for summary judgment on the ground that Golden

Eagle's claims were barred by California's three-year statute of limitations. Golden Eagle's lawyers responded that under the generally accepted rule, the law of the transferor state, here Minnesota, continued to apply and its statute of limitations did not bar the claim. Resolution of this disputed issue depended on interpretation of the Supreme Court's decision in Van Dusen v. Barrack, 376 U.S. 612 (1964). Kirkland lawyers described the holding there as follows:

> In *Van Dusen*, the Supreme Court declined to state a per se rule requiring a transfer court to apply the original forum's choice-of-law rules under all circumstances. Although the Court held that in that case the transferee court should apply the state law that would have applied had there been no change of venue, the Court stated specifically that the original state's law should not necessarily apply "if it was contended that the transferor State would simply have dismissed the action on the ground of forum non conveniens." This case falls squarely within the forum non conveniens exception noted by the Court in *Van Dusen*.

801 F.2d at 1535.

What the *Van Dusen* Court actually said was:

> [W]e do not and need not consider whether in all cases [the operative statute] would require the application of the law of the transferor, as opposed to the transferee, State. We do not attempt to determine whether, for example, the same considerations would govern . . . if it was contended that the transferor State would simply have dismissed the action on the ground of forum non conveniens.

376 U.S. at 639.

The district court sanctioned Kirkland lawyers for making a misleading suggestion that there already exists a forum non conveniens exception to the general rule that the transferor's law applies when, in fact, the Court raised, but did not resolve, that issue. From the district judge's perspective, Kirkland's claims could have qualified as a "good faith argument" for the extension of existing law if they had been presented as such. However, the failure to be clear about federal law, together with a misrepresentation of Minnesota law governing forum non conveniens and a failure to cite contrary California authority, constituted sanctionable conduct.

An appellate panel reversed. In its view, the rule does not authorize sanctions for a nonfrivolous motion simply because a particular argument on behalf of that motion is unjustified. Counsel would not always be able to tell "whether an argument is based on established law or is an argument for the extension of existing law." 801 F.2d at 1540. Imposing sanctions on an attorney who guesses wrong, or who fails to discuss all the cases that a court finds relevant, would chill zealous advocacy. From the appellate court's perspective, it is "not in the nature of our adversary system to require lawyers to demonstrate to the court that they have exhausted every theory, both for and against their client. Nor does that requirement further the interests of the court. It blurs the role of judge and advocate." 801 F.2d at 1542.

Several members of the circuit disagree with the appellate panel, and would like to have the court hear the case en banc. They question "how . . . a brief [could] be warranted to be 'a good faith argument for the extension, modification, or reversal of existing law' when there is not the slightest indication that the brief is arguing for extension, modification, or reversal?" 801 F.2d at 1542. In the dissenters' view, Kirkland lawyers had not simply exaggerated the state of the law; they had misrepresented it.

How would you vote?

PROBLEM 10C

The plaintiff, a discharged deputy county sheriff, filed a civil rights complaint against his former employer alleging that the defendant had deprived him of a property interest in public employment without due process. The defendant responded with an authenticated 50-page factual stipulation that the plaintiff had filed in a criminal case, admitting to facts establishing his mail fraud and extortion during the course of his employment. In light of this stipulation, the defendant moved for summary judgment dismissing the plaintiff's case for failure to state a claim upon which relief can be granted. The defendant also sought sanctions in the form of attorneys' fees under Rule 11 on the ground that the action was vexatious, unreasonable, and in bad faith. Both parties were represented by counsel from reputable law firms.

Uncontested evidence established that the plaintiff had been a deputy county sheriff for 12 years when he was fired without written notice or a statement of reasons for his termination. The defendant's failure to afford the plaintiff procedural safeguards before termination was inconsistent with a commitment, under a general order of the County Court Services Department, to provide the plaintiff with notice and a hearing on the reasons for termination. The defendant's position is that the order's language establishes as a matter of law its inapplicability to the plaintiff's termination: "The procedure does not purport to govern all terminations, is not stated to be a right of all terminated deputies, and creates no property interest in employment."

The plaintiff, after indictment on numerous counts of mail fraud and extortion, stipulated to the facts underlying the indictment. He was then dismissed from his job. He and his codefendants were subsequently tried via a "stipulated bench trial" (i.e., based solely on the facts agreed on in the stipulation without the presentation of other evidence). The plaintiff's defense was that the facts as stipulated did not constitute federal offenses. He was convicted on 28 of 39 counts. In this suit, he claimed that defendant deprived him of due process by failing to follow prescribed procedures in terminating his employment.

The defendant seeks sanctions against the plaintiff for bringing a claim that obviously lacks merit. According to the defendant, the "plaintiff has absolutely no right to a hearing, and no basis for the belief that one would serve any useful purpose, even if he had such a right."

The plaintiff responds by asserting the court should not prejudge the issues in his discharge solely on the basis of the stipulation. If he had been given notice and a hearing, he would have attempted to show that the stipulated facts were not job-related and did not constitute good cause for discharge. Finally, the plaintiff argues that sanctions should not be imposed because they would have a chilling effect on future civil rights claims. If you were the trial court, how would you rule on the request for sanctions?[11]

2. Fee-Shifting Proposals

Given the difficulties of deterring meritless litigation through Rule 11 and bar disciplinary rules, some commentators have proposed greater reliance on fee-shifting provisions. The theory is that requiring losers to pay their opponents' costs as well as their own would discourage vexatious but not patently frivolous claims. Such strike suits now sometimes yield lucrative settlements because they are too expensive to contest. Consider whether you would support fee-shifting proposals to address this problem in light of the excerpt below.

DEBORAH L. RHODE, INSTITUTIONALIZING ETHICS
44 Case W.L. Rev. 665, 720-722 (1994)

The American rule that parties generally pay their own expenses is a relatively recent and highly exceptional practice. In almost every other country, courts routinely award legal fees as well as costs to a prevailing party. Most evidence suggests that similar practices failed to survive in America largely out of animosity toward lawyers. Ironically enough, some opponents of the current American rule want to replace it for the same reason.

The alternatives involve award of fees to any prevailing party (the English "two-way" fee-shifting rule) or only to a successful plaintiff or defendant (one-way fee-shifting approaches). Either rule can apply across the board (as with the English rule); only for certain types of actions (such as civil rights); only in response to certain conduct (such as sanctions for frivolous, unreasonable, or bad faith claims); or only in a court's discretion under specified circumstances. In this country, judges traditionally have been reluctant to exercise discretion to award fees, and legislatures generally have mandated such awards only for plaintiffs in certain actions that are thought to deserve special encouragement. Proponents of fee-shifting maintain that its wider use would help deter nonmeritorious claims and encourage small but valid ones, particularly among parties of limited means.

Opponents of routine fee-shifting dispute the latter argument. They argue that the risk of paying two sets of fees would unduly chill meritorious but not clear-cut claims, and disproportionately deter suits by public interest and other underrepresented groups. In the early 1990s, Vice President Quayle's Council on Competitiveness revived this debate with a call for experimental adoption of a two-way fee-shifting system in certain federal diversity cases.

It is by no means clear that any such system would address the ethical problems of greatest concern here. Experts generally conclude that the overall effects of adopting the rule are impossible to predict. Too many complex factors enter the calculus. Results depend on cost-cutting incentives, diverse risk preferences, and varied amounts at stake among both parties and their lawyers. Generalizations from other nations' experience are equally risky. In the United Kingdom, for example, application of the "loser pay" system is far more complicated than the label implies. Only about 40 percent of individual plaintiffs are in fact potentially liable for their opponents' fees because litigants receiving legal aid qualify for exemptions and other parties have legal-expense insurance or receive third-party payments from organizations such as labor unions. If American courts adopted a similar two-way fee-shifting rule, comparable exemptions or insurance systems might develop. Indeed, contingent-fee lawyers might themselves underwrite such schemes and thus remove some of the deterrent effect that proponents of reform are seeking to achieve.

As Charles Wolfram maintains, the only reasonable general conclusion about altering fee structures is that any such conclusion should be "viewed with great caution." [As other commentators note,] we also have "no empirical evidence that either the integrity or the efficiency of the judicial process is improved, or indeed affected, by exceptions to the American rule." Before we further expand those exceptions, we should have more systematic evaluations of the state and federal fee-shifting rules already in place.

Although currently available evidence suggests little reason to adopt loser pay rules for all cases, it does point up the need for greater redistribution in selected cases. The rationale for one-way prevailing plaintiff fee awards is much stronger than for categorical loser pay systems, at least where plaintiffs are likely to have fewer resources for litigation. Even more compelling is the rationale for more effective sanctions against bad faith conduct.

Ralph Nader claims that "loser pays is a loser for consumers."[12] Is he right? Consider Florida's experience. There, after intensive lobbying by doctors, the state legislature established a loser-pay system for medical malpractice cases. After five years, legislators repealed the system, also at doctors' urging. Although the threat of additional legal fees did somewhat reduce the number of malpractice cases, it also increased the number that went to trial. Plaintiffs fought harder because the stakes were higher. And since a significant number of losing plaintiffs had insufficient assets to pay opponents' costs, defendants' overall expenses were higher.[13]

3.   Disclosure of Facts and Law

a.   *Disclosure of Facts*

PROBLEM 10D

You are a lawyer with a large law firm in the Pacific Northwest. You are representing Fisons Corporation, a pharmaceutical manufacturer and one of your firm's largest clients, in a products liability suit. One of Fisons' products, Somophyllin Oral Liquid (Somophyllin), is a brand name for the generic drug theophylline. The product, available by prescription, was one of a number that Fisons marketed to alleviate the effects of asthma.

In January 1994, a two-year-old suffered severe and permanent brain damage after being treated with Somophyllin while she was experiencing a viral infection. Shortly thereafter, her parents sued your client and Dr. Klipcera, the pediatrician who prescribed the drug. The federal district court with jurisdiction over the claim has opted out of the automatic disclosure provisions in Rule 26 of the Federal Rules of Civil Procedure. The doctor (along with his insurer) settled with the family and cross-claimed against Fisons, seeking compensation for his settlement and for injury to his reputation. The doctor alleged that Fisons failed to warn him about the dangers of the drug, particularly the toxic effects of its use by a child with a viral infection. Your client's primary defense is that it was not aware of the potential toxicity of the drug, and therefore could not have warned the doctor.

In November 1994, Klipcera's lawyers served your client with requests for production of documents. Those requests and your responses included:

Request for Production No. 2: All documents pertaining to any warning letters, including "Dear Doctor letters" or warning correspondence to the medical professions regarding the use of the drug Somophyllin Oral Liquid.
Answer: Documents responsive to this request, if any, will be produced at a reasonable time and place convenient to Fisons and its counsel of record.

Request for Production No. 3: Produce genuine copies of any letters sent by your company to physicians concerning theophylline
toxicity in children.
Answer: Such letters, if any, regarding Somophyllin Oral Liquid will
be produced at reasonable time and place convenient to Fisons
and its counsel of record. . . .
Request for Production No. 6: All documents contained in all files
from the regulating department, marketing department, drug surveillance department, pharmaceutical development department,
product manager department and the medical departments regarding all cromolyn products of Fisons. [Although Somophyllin is not a
cromolyn product, other cromolyn products developed by Fisons
were also used to treat asthma.]
Answer: Defendant objects to this discovery request as over broad,
not reasonably calculated to lead to the discovery of admissible
evidence, and as incredibly burdensome and harassing. This discovery request encompasses millions of pages of completely irrelevant documents. Neither cromolyn, nor any cromolyn product, nor
the properties or efficacy of cromolyn is at issue in this litigation.

Your response to discovery requests also contained the following
general objection:

*Requests Regarding Fisons' Products Other Than Somophyl-
lin Oral Liquid.* Fisons objects to all discovery requests regarding
Fisons Corp.'s products other than Somophyllin Oral Liquid as
overly broad, unduly burdensome, harassing, and not reasonably
calculated to lead to the discovery of admissible evidence.

You and Fisons' in-house counsel each made a cursory review of
the files sought in request number 6. You both concluded that they did
not contain relevant documents. To avoid production, you made a
motion for a protective order and drafted a supporting affidavit signed by
in-house counsel. That affidavit stated:

I have personally examined the scope and extent of documents responsive to the plaintiff's request number 6. Producing all
documents responsive to the plaintiff's request would be extremely
burdensome and oppressive to the defendant. Between one and
two million pages of documents, most of which have no colorable
relevance to the issues in this action, would have to be located, as-
sembled, and made available for review or copying. The time, expense, and intrusion upon the day-to-day business of defendant
would be immense.
I have identified those documents reasonably related to the
claims asserted by plaintiffs in this litigation and arranged to have
them copied and forwarded to the plaintiffs.

The court granted the motion for a protective order. Further discovery followed, including depositions and your client's production of

thousands of documents to the doctor. None of this material suggested that anyone at Fisons was aware, before the child's illness, of the potentially toxic effects of an interaction between Somophyllin and a viral infection. In preparation for the summary judgment motion, you conducted a final file search and discovered the following documents regarding a drug called Intal. The drug is a cromolyn product that is also used to treat asthma.

> *Document 1.* In June 1989, Fisons' manager of medical communications sent a letter to a select group of 2,000 physicians (not including Dr. Klipcera). Addressed "Dear Doctor," and entitled "Re: Theophylline and Viral Infections," the letter warned that theophylline "can be a capricious drug." The manager cited a published study showing "life-threatening theophylline toxicity when pediatric asthmatics on previously well-tolerated doses of theophylline contract viral infections." The letter promoted another Fisons' product for treatment of asthma, Intal, as safer than competing drugs based on theophylline.
>
> *Document 2.* A July 1993 internal memorandum from the manager to a vice president of Fisons reported the dangers of theophylline and suggested that the company end its promotion of theophylline products. The memo began: "An alarming trend seems to be surfacing in the medical literature. . . . [There has been] a dramatic increase in reports of serious toxicity to theophylline in 1993 medical journals." The memo concluded by asserting that an "epidemic of theophylline toxicity provides strong justification for our corporate decision to cease promotion activities with our theophylline line of products and encourage the use of cromolyn-based drugs."

Both documents contradict your client's primary defense to the failure-to-warn claim by showing that the company knew of the risk of theophylline at least four years before the child was severely disabled by the drug, and that it had seriously considered removing the drug from the market several months before her injury. Production of the documents will eliminate the possibility of obtaining summary judgment against the doctor, will result in reopening of discovery, and will likely lead to a substantial judgment in favor of the doctor at trial. The documents might also adversely affect the litigation with the parents, which was nearing a favorable settlement.

Your client's in-house counsel believes that these documents need not be produced because they were kept in files dealing with Intal, a product distinct from Somophyllin that does not contain theophylline. How do you respond?[14]

PROBLEM 10E

You represent the manufacturer of a profitable pesticide that a state environmental protection agency is seeking to ban. Under prevailing statutory standards, the issue is whether the product is unreasonably dangerous to human health. Although you are convinced that the pesticide should be banned, you have been unable to convince management of that fact. As proceedings progress, it becomes clear that the inexperienced, overworked, and underprepared EPA lawyers will be equally unsuccessful in persuading the state trial judge that the pesticide is dangerous.

1. Agency attorneys have overlooked some highly damaging data buried in one of your expert's reports and have failed to point out severe methodological problems in the principal study on which you rely. At several points during the trial, the judge makes statements that reflect serious misunderstandings or assumptions contrary to the facts in the record. He also makes two procedural rulings in your favor that appear inconsistent with other precedents. On neither occasion does the judge ask for written submissions on those issues, and opposing counsel fail to mention the precedents when arguing against the rulings. Should you draw the judge's attention to information adverse to your client's interests on any of these matters?

2. As expected, the trial court rules in your favor and the case is now on appeal. The associate working with you on the brief has cited frequently to portions of the record that are not directly, but only inferentially or arguably, supportive of the proposition advanced. Based on prior experience, you think it extremely unlikely that EPA counsel will file a reply brief to quibble about the cites or that any state appellate judges will have the time or interest to check the record. Do you alter the references?

3. Just before filing your brief, you learn that an appellate court in another district of your state has ruled on a significant procedural question at issue in your case. Although the ruling is in their favor, EPA counsel have not cited the case.

How do you handle the new authority? Would it be sufficient to add it as a *but see* or *cf.* cite to arguments favoring your position on the procedural issue? Alternatively, suppose you had discovered the case after filing your brief. Under what, if any, circumstances would you file a supplemental statement of authorities?

In a well-known passage from his autobiography, Samuel Williston described an incident from practice involving a financial dispute. As counsel for the defendant, Williston had carefully reviewed his client's correspondence with the plaintiff. Opposing counsel had made no inquiries concerning certain letters relevant to the controversy, and no one mentioned them at trial. The court ruled in favor of the defendant and gave an oral explanation of its reasoning that Williston describes as follows:

> In the course of his remarks the Chief Justice stated as one reason for his decision a supposed fact which I knew to be unfounded. I had in front of me a letter that showed his error. Though I have no doubt of the propriety of my behavior in keeping silent, I was somewhat uncom-

fortable at the time. . . . The lawyer must decide when he takes a case whether it is a suitable one for him to undertake and after this decision is made, he is not justified in turning against his client by exposing injurious evidence entrusted to him. If that evidence was unknown to him when he took the case, he may sometimes withdraw from it, but while he is engaged as counsel he is not only not obligated to disclose unfavorable evidence, but it is a violation of his duty to his client if he does so.[15]

In another often-discussed case from around the same period, the New York County Bar Ethics Committee was asked for an opinion about disclosures in tort litigation. The plaintiff was a three-year-old child who suffered injuries from falling off a porch, allegedly because of the defendant owner's negligence. The defendant's attorney successfully moved to dismiss the case for lack of evidence without disclosing that he had an eyewitness to the accident present in court. Neither the judge nor the plaintiff's attorney was aware that any witness existed. The Committee's entire assessment of the case was as follows: "In the opinion of the Committee the conduct of the defendant's attorney is not professionally improper. The fact of infancy does not call for a different reply."[16]

Such dead ends in the search for truth are not uncommon, as is clear from Wayne Brazil's study of discovery problems, reviewed in Chapter V (The Adversary System), at pages 187–188.[17] Nor are the costs insubstantial: consider the nondisclosure of an opponent's life-threatening disease, discussed in Chapter VI (Confidentiality and Client Counseling), at pages 229–232. The rationale for withholding information in such cases rests on two considerations. One involves the need to protect confidential information in order to ensure trust and candor in lawyer-client relationships. The other consideration involves the need to provide incentives in a competitive adversarial structure. If parties begin to assume that they can rely on an opponent's disclosure of material information, they may cease to do adequate preparation themselves. The result would be inequity and inefficiency. One party could end up subsidizing both sides of a lawsuit. And the more that individuals attempted to freeload on their adversaries, the greater the risk that neither side would prepare adequately.

Are these considerations sufficient to justify the bar's current ethical rules concerning disclosure of facts? Disciplinary Rule 7-102(A) provides that a lawyer "shall not conceal or knowingly fail to disclose that which he is required by law to reveal" and "shall not knowingly make a false statement of law or fact." Model Rule 3.3(a) similarly prohibits lawyers from making a "false statement of material fact or law to a tribunal," and from failing "to disclose a material fact to a tribunal when disclosure is necessary to avoid assisting a criminal or fraudulent act by the client." In ex parte proceedings, a lawyer must "inform the tribunal of all material facts known to the lawyer which will enable the tribunal to make an informed decision, whether or not the facts are adverse."

Should the rule governing ex parte proceedings apply to all litigation? This is, in essence, the obligation Marvin Frankel proposed in the article excerpted in Chapter V at pages 180–181. A similar obligation applies to prosecutors, who must reveal exculpatory facts under Brady v. Maryland, (373 U.S. 83 (1963)), Model Rule 3.8, and DR 7-103(B). Defenders of a broader duty of disclosure in civil cases point out that these analogous provisions have worked reasonably well without undermining incentive structures or trusting relationships in contexts such as criminal prosecutions or securities regulation. Advocates also argue that additional disclosure requirements would not chill client confidences for reasons explored more fully in Chapter VI (Confidentiality and Client Counseling), at pages 225–232. From this perspective:

- clients often have no realistic alternative to confiding in counsel;
- lawyers acquire much adverse information through means other than direct client communication;
- clients already are unaware of the scope of confidentiality protections; and
- the bar in many countries and in this nation historically has managed to provide adequate representation without sweeping confidentiality protections.

What is your view? Would you support an initial proposal by the Model Rules Commission that (1) would have required disclosure of adverse facts if they would "probably have a substantial affect on the determination of a material issue"; and (2) would have permitted disclosure of favorable evidence to opposing parties? Would such rules lead to better or worse results on the facts of Problem 10D and 10E?

In 1993, the Supreme Court approved proposed changes in Rule 26a of the Federal Rules of Civil Procedure requiring litigators to disclose certain information automatically to the opposing party without specific request. That information includes copies or descriptions of relevant documents and the names and location of witnesses likely to have "discoverable information relevant to disputed facts alleged with particularity in the pleadings." Initial disclosures must be supplemented at "timely intervals." Justice Scalia, joined by Justices Souter and Thomas, objected to these amendments:

> By placing upon lawyers the obligation to disclose information damaging to their clients—on their own initiative, and in a context where the lines between what must be disclosed and what need not be disclosed are not clear but require the exercise of considerable judgment—the new rule would place intolerable strain upon lawyers' ethical duty to represent their clients and not to assist the opposing side.

Requiring a lawyer to make a judgment as to what information is "relevant to disputed facts" plainly requires him to use his professional skills in the service of his adversary.

Fed. R. Civ. P. 26, dissent.

Such objections have prompted some district courts to opt out of the new disclosure provisions. Consider what you would recommend on the facts of Problem 10F. How effective do you believe that this mandatory discovery provision would be in addressing problems of undisclosed facts, such as those in Problems 10D and 10E? What other remedies might you propose?

PROBLEM 10F

You are the president of your city's bar association. The local federal district court is considering whether to opt in or out of the initial disclosure requirements of Rule 26a. The presiding judge has asked your association for a recommendation. You have received written comments from members and have held one open meeting on the subject. The results suggest that lawyers in the district are more or less evenly divided. Some believe that mandatory disclosure will undercut the adversary system, create constant disputes about coverage, and invite arbitrary judicial enforcement. Other lawyers view initial disclosure mandates as a reasonably effective way to curtail delay, expense, and withholding of clearly relevant material.

You have agreed to evaluate both sides of the debate and to present your position at the bar association's next meeting. Prepare a summary of your presentation, including the reasons for your recommendation.

b. Disclosure of Law

What justifies attorneys' greater obligation to disclose law than facts? Disciplinary Rule 7-106(B) and Model Rule 3.3(a)(3) require a lawyer to reveal to a tribunal "legal authority in the controlling jurisdiction known to the lawyer to be directly adverse to the position of the client and not disclosed by the opposing counsel." Arguments supporting this higher obligation fall into several categories:

Confidentiality.   Disclosure of facts implicates the values of confidentiality to a much greater extent than disclosure of law.

Systemic.   The costs of nondisclosure of facts may be less than those resulting from nondisclosure of law since a factual mistake generally affects only the instant litigation, while ignorance of relevant legal authority may point judicial decision-making in the wrong direction for a series of cases. Errors of law are also more likely to result in inefficient use of judicial resources, since such errors are more likely to be discovered and to be reversed on appeal.

Prudential.　Nondisclosure of law is likely to be more risky for attorneys than nondisclosure of facts since there is always the likelihood that a court or an adversary will subsequently discover the authority. A lawyer who fails to make disclosures under such circumstances may have alienated the judge and missed opportunities to distinguish relevant materials.

While not disputing these arguments, critics of the fact/law distinction argue that a court is in a much better position to supplement counsel's presentation of legal than factual issues. If, as EC 7-23 suggests, the goal of an adversary system is to "enable a court to make a fair and accurate determination of the matter before it," should lawyers' disclosure obligations be the same on both factual and legal questions?

If accuracy and fairness are the goal, is the "controlling authority" requirement too limited? The ABA's Committee on Professional Ethics Formal Opinion 280 (1949) argued that "[t]he test in every case should be, is the decision which opposing counsel has overlooked one which the court should clearly consider in deciding the case?" If you were determining whether to discipline a lawyer for nondisclosure, is that the standard you would use? How would it apply on the facts of Problem 10E?

C.　THE SUBORDINATE LAWYER

See Chapter III, Regulation of the Profession
  • Part E. Supervisory and Subordinate Lawyers
      (pages 82–89)

D.　FORMAL RIGHTS AND JUST RESULTS

1.　Venue

There is little drama in the routine collection cases that make up most of the civil litigation in most state courts of general jurisdiction. Each of these examples, however, occurs tens of thousands of times a year. Although the amounts of money at issue are small and the defendant's freedom is not at hazard, these are the only experiences with lawyers and the legal system that most people have in their lifetimes. For example, they find that, although they may have borrowed money in Austin, Texas where they reside and made their payments in Austin, the lawsuit is brought in Amarillo, nearly five hundred miles distant. This practice was and, to a fair extent, is still lawful in many states.

What of the lawyers who, by glancing at the files, know that this is what they are doing? They zealously represent their clients by taking advantage of the venue laws to create defaults. In this setting, that single-mindedness of purpose seems less attractive. I believe it is wicked for the lawyers representing Montgomery Ward to zealously represent their client by suing consumer debtors a thousand miles or more from their residences. It is not an adequate excuse to reply that the legislatures or the courts should change these laws. Those lawyers who start collection actions in courts at great distances from the defendant's residence are not acting unethically within the meaning of the [Code of Professional Responsibility]. If the lawyer failed to take advantage of the venue laws and the contractual provisions of the loan contract, he would be considered derelict in his duties to his client.[18]

Do you agree? Consider the materials on the advocate's role in Chapter IV at pages 125–162. Does the "lawyer as friend" of the finance company have an ethical obligation to maximize his client's chances of obtaining a default judgment?[19] Or is this a case where the lawyer might echo Abraham Lincoln's reported advice to a client who was technically entitled to evade his debt to a widow with young children: surely a "sprightly, energetic [manager like you could] . . . try your hand at making . . . [a few hundred] dollars in some other way."[20]

See Chapter IV, Advocacy
  • Part B. The Traditional Rationale and Contemporary
    Challenges
      (pages 133–146)

2. Service of Process

ROVINSKI v. ROWE, 131 F.2D 687 (6TH CIR. 1942). This case arose from an automobile accident in Michigan. Rowe sued Rovinski in Michigan state court under the Michigan nonresident motorist statute. Rovinski objected on the ground that he was a resident of Michigan and therefore not subject to suit under the statute. The court agreed and dismissed the action. Rowe then brought a diversity action against Rovinski in federal court. Under Rule 4(d)(1),[21] Rowe served Rovinski by leaving a copy of the complaint with Rovinski's mother at the address he had claimed as his residence in the prior suit. Again Rovinski challenged service of process, this time on the ground that it was improper because it was not made at his "dwelling house or usual place of abode," which he asserted was in Minnesota. The trial court upheld the service, and the court of appeals affirmed. Its stated rationale was that Rule

4(d)(1) deserved a "liberal construction." 131 F.2d at 689. Its unstated rationale may have been that Rovinski did not deserve to have
it both ways by avoiding a complaint and summons that he had in
fact received twice.

In effect, Rovinski's lawyer initially claimed Michigan as his
client's residence and then denied that residence to be his client's
usual dwelling. Was this strategy unethical? Consider, for example,
law students who have their "dwelling house or usual place of abode"
near where they are attending a state law school, but are not considered residents of that state for purposes of tuition. If residence
and domicile are distinguishable for such purposes, should Rovinski
be able to rely on the distinction for other purposes?

How should the court have handled his action? Did the judges
effectively rewrite Rule 4(d) by upholding service on Rovinski's
residence when the drafters specified a dwelling house or usual place
of abode? What will best serve justice in most cases—a focus on the
literal meaning or the underlying purpose of the rule?

How would you evaluate the quality of lawyering for Rovinski?
Note that in the end, the client paid both for the procedural maneuvering and for defending the case on the merits. Does this suggest an
error in judgment by Rovinski's counsel or were the challenges to
service of process worth making? Does your answer depend on
whether Rovinski had a persuasive defense on the merits? If he did
not, would that affect your assessment of the lawyer's conduct?
Consider the materials on procedural tactics in Chapter V (The
Adversary System) and the advocate's role in Chapter IV (Advocacy),
particularly the discussion of alternative visions of practice and
technical defenses in Chapter IV, Part C. How would defenders and
critics of the traditional advocate's role have evaluated the ethics of
Rovinski's counsel? What is your view?[22]

TICKLE v. BARTON, 95 S.E.2D 427 (W. VA. 1956). Richard
Tickle, a resident of West Virginia, sued Raymond Barton of Virginia
for injuries arising out of an automobile accident in West Virginia.
Tickle made service of process while Barton was attending a football
team banquet at a West Virginia high school. Barton moved to quash
the service of process on the ground that he was fraudulently in-
duced to come within the West Virginia court's jurisdiction by
Tickle's lawyer. More specifically, Barton alleged that the lawyer
telephoned him anonymously and falsely stated that he was calling
on behalf of the sponsors of the banquet to issue a special invitation
to Barton. In fact, the sole purpose of that call allegedly was to
"inveigle" Barton into the state for the purpose of serving process.
The trial court overruled Tickle's demurrer to the motion to quash,
and the West Virginia Court of Appeals affirmed, with two judges
dissenting.

What should happen if the motion in such a case then goes to a hearing? Should it matter whether the lawyer in fact made the alleged telephone call or whether he misrepresented his status? Suppose that he had convinced the sponsors of the banquet to allow him to issue the special invitation. Consider the view of the dissenting judges in *Tickle*, who believed that the facts "properly alleged" did not constitute fraud:

> At most they would simply show that the attorney took advantage of an opportunity, the holding of the social function [in West Virginia] and the interest of the defendant's son in the holding of the function, to try to obtain proper service of process, which was no more than a duty owed his client. . . . [I]t should be kept in mind that defendant had full knowledge of the institution of the action against him . . . [and] of the fact that he had questioned the validity of the service of other process issued in that action.

95 S.E.2d at 434 (Given, J., dissenting). Do you agree? When Barton chose to attend the banquet, did he assume the risk of receiving formal notice of the litigation?

If the conduct of Tickle's lawyer becomes material, what should happen if he is called to testify by either Barton or his client? Compare DR 5-102(A) and (B), Model Rule 3.7, and the discussion of lawyer witnesses in Chapter XV (Evidence and Trial Advocacy) at pages 674–676. If Barton wants to call Tickle's lawyer to testify, should the trial court require his disqualification? What if Tickle wants to call the attorney to rebut Barton's claims? Is disqualification appropriate then? If so, could another lawyer in Tickle's firm handle the case? If not, is withdrawal too high a price to pay to satisfy formal notice requirements? Do the responses to these questions suggest problems either in the rules governing lawyer witnesses or in the procedures for service of process on out-of-state residents?[23]

See Chapter IV, Advocacy
   • Part C. Alternative Visions
      (pages 146–162)

E. FAIR NOTICE, ADEQUATE REPRESENTATION, AND LAWYER-CLIENT CONFLICTS

1. Due Process and Notice Requirements

MULLANE v. CENTRAL HANOVER BANK AND TRUST CO., 339 U.S. 306 (1950). *Mullane* is famous for what the Supreme Court decided about due process and fair notice; under its reasoning, personal service, not service by publication, was necessary for individual beneficiaries of trusts that participated in a common fund. The decision is also noteworthy for what the Court did not decide about the responsibilities of lawyers like Mullane, the court-appointed lawyer for the trust beneficiaries. As Richard Matasar argues, Mullane's conduct can lend itself to either a skeptical or a romantic interpretation. The skeptic sees Mullane's fight for personal notice for each beneficiary as "pure self interest." The struggle increased his hours, his fees, and his reputation as a litigator. The costs of that struggle, as well as the resulting personal service, will be borne by the beneficiaries, who are extremely unlikely to act on the notice that they receive. By contrast, the romantic sees Mullane as a forerunner to the modern public interest attorney, who forgoes normal billing rates for the reduced fees available to court-appointed fiduciaries and who then battles to preserve the rights of beneficiaries he does not know and probably will never represent again. Establishing their entitlement to notice has value irrespective of how many will act on it in that case.[24]

Which view strikes you as most plausible? How should lawyers representing classes of uninformed members determine how much process they should pay for? Did Mullane have any obligation to consult beneficiaries about their preferences? Is it hypocritical for him to demand rights of participation for individuals whose participation he never enlisted? Or would it have been unfair to expect Mullane to consult members before the court justified the expense of their notification?

2. Class Actions and Lawyer-Client Conflicts

See Chapter IX, The Lawyer-Client Relationship
    Part C. Representing the Public Interest
        (pages 398–419)

(Public Interest case)

EVANS v. JEFF D.
475 U.S. 717 (1986)

[At issue was whether the district court abused its discretion in refusing to award attorney's fees where the parties' settlement agreement waived such fees. The defendant petitioners were Idaho public officials responsible for the education and treatment of children with emotional and mental disabilities. The plaintiff respondents were a class of children under petitioners' care, represented by the Idaho Legal Aid Society.]

Justice STEVENS delivered the opinion of the Court.

I

In March 1983, one week before trial, petitioners presented respondents with a new settlement proposal. As respondents themselves characterize it, the proposal "offered virtually all of the injunctive relief [they] had sought in their complaint." . . . The Court of Appeals agreed with this characterization, and further noted that the proposed relief was "more than the district court in earlier hearings had indicated it was willing to grant." 743 F.2d 648, 650. As was true of the earlier partial settlement, however, petitioners' offer included a provision for a waiver by respondents of any claim to fees or costs. Originally, this waiver was unacceptable to the Idaho Legal Aid Society, which had instructed Johnson to reject any settlement offer conditioned upon a waiver of fees, but Johnson ultimately determined that his ethical obligation to his clients mandated acceptance of the proposal. The parties conditioned the waiver on approval by the District Court.

After the stipulation was signed, Johnson filed a written motion requesting the District Court to approve the settlement "except for the provision on costs and attorney's fees," and to allow respondents to present a bill of costs and fees for consideration by the court. App. 87. At the oral argument on that motion, Johnson contended that petitioners' offer had exploited his ethical duty to his clients—that he was "forced," by an offer giving his clients "the best result [they] could have gotten in this court or any other court," to waive his attorney's fees. The District Court, however, evaluated the waiver in the context of the entire settlement and rejected the ethical underpinnings of Johnson's argument. . . . The Court of Appeals . . . after ordering preliminary relief . . . invalidated the fee waiver and left standing the remainder of the settlement; it then instructed the District Court to "make its own determination of the fees that are reasonable" and remanded for that limited purpose. 743 F.2d, at 652.

In explaining its holding, the Court of Appeals emphasized that Rule 23(e) of the Federal Rules of Civil Procedure gives the court the power to approve the terms of all settlements of class actions. . . . The court added that "[w]hen attorney's fees are negotiated as part of a class action settlement, a conflict frequently exists between the class lawyers' interest in compensation and the class members' interest in relief." 743 F.2d, at 651-652. "To avoid this conflict," the Court of Appeals relied on Circuit precedent which had "disapproved simultaneous negotiation of settlements and attorney's fees" absent a showing of "unusual circumstances." Id., at 652. In

this case, the Court of Appeals found no such "unusual circumstances" and therefore held that an agreement on fees "should not
have been a part of the settlement of the claims of the class." . . . We
now reverse.

II

[The question we must decide] is whether the District Court had a
duty to reject the proposed settlement because it included a waiver of
statutorily authorized attorney's fees.
    That duty, whether it takes the form of a general prophylactic
rule or arises out of the special circumstances of this case, derives
ultimately from the Fees Act rather than from the strictures of
professional ethics. Although respondents contend that Johnson, as
counsel for the class, was faced with an "ethical dilemma" when
petitioners offered him relief greater than that which he could
reasonably have expected to obtain for his clients at trial (if only he
would stipulate to a waiver of the statutory fee award), and although
we recognize Johnson's conflicting interests between pursuing relief
for the class and a fee for the Idaho Legal Aid Society, we do not
believe that the "dilemma" was an "ethical" one in the sense that
Johnson had to choose between conflicting duties under the prevailing norms of professional conduct. Plainly, Johnson had no *ethical*
obligation to seek a statutory fee award. His ethical duty was to
serve his clients loyally and competently. Since the proposal to settle
the merits was more favorable than the probable outcome of the
trial, Johnson's decision to recommend acceptance was consistent
with the highest standards of our profession. The District Court,
therefore, correctly concluded that approval of the settlement involved no breach of ethics in this case. . . .

III

The text of the Fees Act provides no support for the proposition that
Congress intended to ban all fee waivers offered in connection with
substantial relief on the merits.
    In fact, we believe that a general proscription against negotiated
waiver of attorney's fees in exchange for a settlement on the merits
would itself impede vindication of civil rights, at least in some cases,
by reducing the attractiveness of settlement. . . .
    Most defendants are unlikely to settle unless the cost of the
predicted judgment, discounted by its probability, plus the transaction costs of further litigation, are greater than the cost of the
settlement package. If fee waivers cannot be negotiated, the settlement package must either contain an attorney's fee component of
potentially large and typically uncertain magnitude, or else the

parties must agree to have the fee fixed by the court. Although either of these alternatives may well be acceptable in many cases, there surely is a significant number in which neither alternative will be as satisfactory as a decision to try the entire case. . . ."[30] Petitioners and the amici who support them never suggest that the district court is obligated to place its stamp of approval on every settlement in which the plaintiffs' attorneys have agreed to a fee waiver. The Solicitor General, for example, has suggested that a fee waiver need not be approved when the defendant has "no realistic defense on the merits," or if the waiver was part of a "vindictive effort . . . to teach counsel that they had better not bring such cases."

We find it unnecessary to evaluate this argument, however, because the record in this case does not indicate that Idaho has adopted such a statute, policy, or practice. Nor does the record support the narrower proposition that petitioners' request to waive fees was a vindictive effort to deter attorneys from representing plaintiffs in civil rights suits against Idaho.[34] . . . In this case, the District Court did not abuse its discretion in upholding the settlement.

The judgment of the Court of Appeals is reversed.

It is so ordered.

Justice BRENNAN, with whom Justice MARSHALL and Justice BLACKMUN join, dissenting.

Ultimately, enforcement of the laws is what really counts. It was with this in mind that Congress enacted the Civil Rights Attorney's Fees Awards Act of 1976. Congress authorized fee shifting to improve enforcement of civil rights legislation by making it easier for victims of civil rights violations to find lawyers willing to take their

30. . . . Although the dissent would allow simultaneous negotiations, it would require that "whatever fee the parties agree to" be "found by the court to be a 'reasonable' one under the Fees Act." The dissent's proposal is imaginative, but not very practical. . . . [T]he dissent's proposal would require district courts to evaluate the reasonableness of fee agreements in several thousand civil rights cases annually while they make that determination in slightly over 100 civil rights class actions now. Moreover, if this novel procedure really is necessary to carry out the purposes of the Fees Act, presumably it should be applied to all cases arising under federal statutes that provide for fee shifting.

34. We are cognizant of the possibility that decisions by individual clients to bargain away fee awards may, in the aggregate and in the long run, diminish lawyers' expectations of statutory fees in civil rights cases. If this occurred, the pool of lawyers willing to represent plaintiffs in such cases might shrink, constricting the "effective access to the judicial process" for persons with civil rights grievances which the Fees Act was intended to provide. H.R. Rep. No. 94-1558, p.1 (1976). That the "tyranny of small decisions" may operate in this fashion is not to say that there is any reason or documentation to support such a concern at the present time. Comment on this issue is therefore premature at this juncture. We believe, however, that as a practical matter the likelihood of this circumstance arising is remote.

cases. Because today's decision will make it more difficult for civil rights plaintiffs to obtain legal assistance, a result plainly contrary to Congress' purpose, I dissent.

I

The Court begins its analysis by emphasizing that neither the language nor the legislative history of the Fees Act supports "the proposition that Congress intended to ban all fee waivers offered in connection with substantial relief on the merits." I agree. There is no evidence that Congress gave the question of fee waivers any thought at all. However, the Court mistakenly assumes that this omission somehow supports the conclusion that fee waivers are permissible. . . . However, the legislative history of the Fees Act discloses that this is not the case. Rather, Congress provided fee awards to ensure that there would be lawyers available to plaintiffs who could not otherwise afford counsel, so that these plaintiffs could fulfill their role in the federal enforcement scheme as "private attorneys general," vindicating the public interest.

It seems obvious that allowing defendants in civil rights cases to condition settlement of the merits on a waiver of statutory attorney's fees will diminish lawyers' expectations of receiving fees and decrease the willingness of lawyers to accept civil rights cases. Even the Court acknowledges "the possibility that decisions by individual clients to bargain away fee awards may, in the aggregate and in the long run, diminish lawyers' expectations of statutory fees in civil rights cases." Ante, at n.34. The Court tells us, however, that "[c]omment on this issue" is "premature at this juncture" because there is not yet supporting "documentation." Ibid. The Court then goes on anyway to observe that "as a practical matter the likelihood of this circumstance arising is remote." Ibid.

I must say that I find the Court's assertions somewhat difficult to understand. . . . [E]xperience surely provides an indication of the immediate hardship suffered by civil rights claimants whenever there is a reduction in the availability of attorney's fee awards. . . .

And, of course, once fee waivers are permitted, defendants will seek them as a matter of course, since this is a logical way to minimize liability. . . .

This all seems so obvious that it is puzzling that the Court reaches a different result. The Court's rationale is that, unless fee waivers are permitted, "parties to a significant number of civil rights cases will refuse to settle. . . ." This is a wholly inadequate justification for the Court's result.

First, the effect of prohibiting fee waivers on settlement offers is just not an important concern in the context of the Fees Act. I agree with the Court that encouraging settlements is desirable policy. But it is *judicially* created policy, applicable to litigation of any kind and having no special force in the context of civil rights cases. The *congressional* policy underlying the Fees Act is, as I have argued throughout, to create incentives for lawyers to devote time to civil rights cases by making it economically feasible for them to do so. . . .

Second, even assuming that settlement practices are relevant, the Court greatly exaggerates the effect that prohibiting fee waivers will have on defendants' willingness to make settlement offers. This is largely due to the Court's failure to distinguish the fee waiver issue from the issue of simultaneous negotiation of fees and merits claims. The Court's discussion mixes concerns over a defendant's reluctance to settle because total liability remains uncertain with reluctance to settle because the cost of settling is too high. However, it is a prohibition on simultaneous negotiation, not a prohibition on fee waivers, that makes it difficult for the defendant to ascertain his total liability at the time he agrees to settle the merits. . . .

The Court asserts, without factual support, that requiring defendants to pay statutory fee awards will prevent a "significant number" of settlements. It is, of course, ironic that the same absence of "documentation" which makes comment on the effects of *permitting* fee waivers "premature at this juncture," does not similarly affect the Court's willingness to speculate about what to expect if fee waivers are *prohibited*. Be that as it may, I believe that the Court overstates the extent to which prohibiting fee waivers will deter defendants from making settlement offers. Because the parties can negotiate a fee (or a range of fees) that is not unduly high and condition their settlement on the court's approval of this fee, the magnitude of a defendant's liability for fees in the settlement context need be neither uncertain nor particularly great. . . .

I would, on the other hand, permit simultaneous negotiation of fees and merits claims, since this would not contravene the purpose of the Fees Act. . . .

How should public interest attorneys handle fee negotiations? According to the majority in Evans v. Jeff D., a settlement offer requiring a waiver of attorney's fees presents no ethical conflict since lawyers are under no ethical obligation to seek statutory fees. Is this view convincing, or should the Court have considered lawyers' obligations to other pro bono clients, whose representation is subsidized in part by statutory fee awards? For example, Charles Silvers argues that the fee-waiver issue reflects a trade-off. Some victims who sue do better if waivers are allowed because defendants will be more willing to settle. Other plaintiffs do worse because less funding will be available for their attorneys. In Silvers' view, the majority opinion in *Jeff D.* is problematic in that it "cites no evidence tending to show that the former [victims] gain more than the latter lose, and

offers no guidance on how to compare the effects on the two groups."[25]
If Silvers is right, how could the effects be compared?

At the close of his separate dissent in *Jeff D.*, Justice Marshall
urges more bar associations to prohibit defendants from demanding
fee waivers as a condition of settlement. He also suggests that public
interest organizations might obtain agreements from their clients
not to waive fees. If you were a member of a state bar ethics committee or a public interest lawyer, would you follow such advice?

Prof: S. ct. went against the conventional
wisdom.

— certain cases where parties who win eat
their fees paid for.

→ This case: settlement terms created an
ethical dilemma?

For public interest the fees aren't that
important.

→ Should there be a rule that
prohibit this, even if S. ct.
disagrees?
Should there be an ethical rule?

Endnotes

1. I am indebted for these examples to Professor Fred Lawrence, Boston University Law School.

2. See sources cited in Deborah L. Rhode & David Luban, Legal Ethics 201 (2d ed. 1995).

3. Saul M. Kassin, An Empirical Study of Rule 11 Sanctions (Federal Judicial Center 1985). See also George P. Joseph, Redrafting Rule 11, Natl. L.J., Oct. 1, 1990, at 13 (noting that trial courts have also imposed sanctions for "meritless" positions that appellate courts have upheld).

4. Kassin, supra note 3, and studies discussed in David B. Wilkins, Who Should Regulate Lawyers?, 105 Harv. L. Rev. 799, 869 n.308 (1989), and note 9 infra.

5. Arthur B. LaFrance, Federal Rule 11 and Public Interest Litigation, 22 Val. U.L. Rev. 331, 352-354 (1988); Carl Tobias, Rule 11 and Civil Rights Litigation, 37 Buff. L. Rev. 485, 503-506 (1989); NAACP Resolutions, The Crisis, Dec. 1988, at 27, 29-30; sources cited in note 4, supra.

6. Thomas E. Willging, The Rule 11 Sanctioning Process (Federal Judicial Center 1988).

7. Wilkins, supra note 4, at 885 n.377.

8. Charles W. Sorenson, Jr., Disclosure Under Federal Rule of Civil Procedure 26a—"Much Ado About Nothing?," 46 Hastings L.J. 679, 712 (1995).

9. The courts are divided on whether improperly motivated but legally warranted suits are sanctionable. See Rob Atkinson, A Dissenter's Commentary on the Professional Crusade, 74 Tex. L. Rev. 259, 287 n.120 (1995); Sussman v. Bank of Israel, 56 F.3d 450 (2d Cir. 1995). Disciplinary actions under bar ethical rules for wrongfully motivated but technically warranted claims are extremely rare. See id. at n.119. For one of the exceptional cases, see In re Levine, 847 P.2d 1093 (Ariz. Sup. 1993) (lawyer's improper purpose in suing former colleagues may subject him to discipline even if his claim is not frivolous).

10. For examples of such questioning, see Kerry Segrove, The Sexual Harassment of Women in the Workforce 221 (1994); Ellen E. Schulz & Junda Woo, Plaintiffs' Sex Lives Are Being Laid Bare in Harassment Cases,

Wall St. J., Sept. 19, 1994, at A1; Andrea Bernstein, Sex Harassment Suits: The Fight for Damages Gets Uglier, Ms., July-Aug., 1996, at 18-19.

11. This problem is drawn from a survey of 292 federal court judges. Kassin, supra note 3, at pages 53-54.

12. Ralph Nader & Wesley J. Smith, No Contest 313 (1996).

13. Herbert J. Kritzer, Prepared Statement, Hearings Before the Subcomm. on Courts and Intellectual Property of the House Comm. on the Judiciary, 104th Cong., 1st Sess., Feb. 6, 1995; Thomas D. Rowe, Prepared Comment, in id., 70, 57.

14. This problem is based on one developed by Roger Cramton, Cornell Law School.

15. Samuel Williston, Life and Law 271-272 (1940).

16. New York City Lawyers Assn. Comm. on Professional Ethics, Op. 309 (1933).

17. Surveyed litigators reported that in about half the cases that were settled and about 30 percent of those that went to trial, opponents failed to discover significant information. Wayne D. Brazil, Civil Discovery: How Bad Are the Problems, 67 A.B.A.J. 450 (1981); Wayne D. Brazil, Views from the Front Lines: Observations by Chicago Lawyers About the System of Civil Discovery, 1980 Am. B. Found. Res. J. 219. See Chapter V (The Adversary System) at page 187.

18. Philip Schuchman, Relations Between Lawyers, in Ethics and Advocacy 73, 78 (American Trial Lawyer's Foundation ed., 1978).

19. Charles Fried, The Lawyer as Friend: The Moral Foundations of the Lawyer-Client Relation, 85 Yale L.J. 1060 (1976).

20. William H. Herndon & Jesse W. Weik, 2 Herndon's Lincoln 346 (1890).

21. Federal Rule of Civil Procedure 4(d)(1) permits service upon an individual "by leaving copies [of the summons and of the complaint] at the individual's dwelling house or unusual place of abode with some person of suitable age and discretion then residing therein. . . ."

22. For fuller discussion, see Richard A. Matasar, Teaching Ethics in Civil Procedure Courses, 39 J. Legal Educ. 587, 593 (1989).

23. For an extended discussion of these issues, see Matasar, id., at 598-599.

24. Id. at 602.

25. Charles Silvers, A Restitutionary Theory of Attorneys' Fees in Class Actions, 76 Cornell L. Rev. 656, 700 (1991).

Chapter XI

Constitutional Law

A. THE ADVOCATE'S ROLE

1. The Pursuit of Principles: Unpopular Positions and Constitutional Values

See Chapter IV, Advocacy
- Moral Principles and Unpopular Positions
  (Problem 4B, pages 154–157)

PROBLEM 11A

You are a member of the New York University moot court board. A hypothetical case that your board has authorized for the student competition provoked the controversy described below. The case involves a constitutional challenge to a lower court decision holding that "award of child custody to a homosexual parent is presumptively contrary to the child's best interest." How do you vote on whether to withdraw the problem?

BOB VAN VORIS, MARDEN
PROBLEM PULLED, REINSTATED

The Commentator (Oct. 18, 1990)

Within the space of several days, the Moot Court Board has withdrawn and then partially reinstated a controversial problem concerning the child custody rights of a lesbian parent, which was to have formed the basis for the Fall Elimination Round of the 1990-1991 Marden Moot Court Competition. The substitution was made after several students complained to the board that the original issue was offensive and one-sided. A subsequent decision to allow students to argue the original issue was an attempt by the Moot Court Board to back away from what the editors came to view as an ill-considered compromise.

The original problem, Mike Brody v. Carol Brody, was conceived as an appeal to the Supreme Court of Hawaii in which a divorced father contests an order awarding primary custody of the couple's child to the mother, a lesbian. The parents are separated and both have live-in lovers. The child has been living with her mother during the week and with her father on the weekends. The record is structured so that, absent the issue of the mother's sexual preference, both parents appear equally capable of caring for the child.

After picking up her copy of the Marden record on Friday, October 5, Nina Ruskin, a third-year student who was assigned to argue the side of the petitioner-father, did some preliminary research on the issue and felt that the authority for the petitioner's position was offensive. "I found that I had a real problem, that I couldn't write the arguments [for the petitioner's side] into a brief." In a letter to the 34 other students assigned to argue the petitioner's case, Ruskin quoted excerpts from some of the relevant cases: "maintaining and exposing the child to an active male homosexual . . . is not conducive to raising this boy in a wholesome environment," and ". . . it is unacceptable to subject children to any course of conduct that might influence them to develop homosexual traits." Ruskin's letter argued that the petitioner's side was "offensive and fueled by hatred" and that Marden participants arguing the petitioner's case were disadvantaged in the competition because of the paucity of legal arguments in support.

The Board initially determined to offer a noncontroversial replacement of the problem and to allow students to choose which to brief. All oral arguments would be made on the replacement problem. In explaining its decision, the Board stated: . . .

> This child custody problem struck the Board as being an interesting and challenging exercise. However, further consideration of the implications of the problem, partly brought to our attention by Marden participants, has led a majority of the Board to conclude that adherence to the problem was not appropriate. The choice of problem, its content, and the decision to withdraw it are solely the responsibility of the Board.

For some members of the Moot Court Board, the issue of whether awarding custody to a homosexual parent is presumptively contrary to a child's best interests was not an open question in a law school community that has a policy of condemning anti-gay biases, both in the law and in society. For these members, the problem was an affront to our law school's values and thus there was no need for further debate. They argued that debate concerning the suitability of custody by an African-American parent would be inappropriate and that the Marden problem was similarly inappropriate.

Other members of the Moot Court Board felt that the nature of the petitioner's argument would hinder those assigned to argue that side in presenting a strong case. Still others believed the Moot Court Board should adhere to the problem because it raised an unsettled question of law and fostered productive debate. Ultimately, the Board concluded that continuing with the problem was not advisable and decided to discontinue its use. The Marden program is designed to improve advocacy skills and the Board believes that changing the problem will enable all participants to realize this goal. We ask for your understanding. . . .

That letter prompted a series of faculty letters excerpted below.

CORRESPONDENCE: ANTHONY AMSTERDAM, BURT NEUBORNE, NORMAN DORSEN, STEPHEN GILLERS, CLAUDIA ANGELOS, PEGGY DAVIS, SYLVIA LAW, NANCY MORAWETZ, SARAH BURNS

I hope that the Moot Court Board will reconsider its decision to discontinue use of the child custody case in the Marden Competition. The decision is seriously damaging to the moot court program, the law school, and your fellow students. Consider just four points:

1. Your October 11 memo attributes to some members of the Board the position that "the issue . . . whether awarding custody to a homosexual parent is presumptively contrary to a child's best interests [is] . . . not an open question in a law school that has a policy of condemning anti-gay biases, both in the law and in society." With all respect, the declaration that *any* legal issue is "not an open question in a law school" is a declaration of war upon everything that a law school is. Most fundamentally, a law school is a place of intellectual inquiry, where the acceptability of ideas can only be determined by examining them.

Members of your Board apparently believe that the idea that "awarding custody to a homosexual parent is presumptively contrary to a child's best interests" is a wrong idea. I agree that it is a wrong idea. But the only acceptable or enduring way to demonstrate that it is a wrong idea is by putting it to the test of debate, not by putting it beyond the pale of debate.

2. Your October 11 memo says that the "Marden program is designed to improve advocacy skills." A critical advocacy skill is to be

able to formulate an argument that you do not believe in, particularly one which leads to conclusions you abhor, and which you identify with people you detest, so that you can contest against it most effectively.

This is not an abstract platitude. A number of years ago I was involved in a Kentucky case in which a divorced mother was denied custody of her children because she was white, she married a black man after the divorce, and the judge believed that the children's best interests would not be served by putting them under the pressures of life in an interracial household. One of the finest and most dedicated civil rights lawyers in the United States led the mother's defense team. This lawyer didn't do it by declaring that the judge's reasoning and the opposition's arguments were unthinkable. The lawyer did it by thinking through every conceivable argument that could be advanced in support of the judge or the opposition and formulating those arguments as strongly as they could be formulated, so as to be able to rebut them before any court in the land.

That is what advocacy is all about. The Marden program cannot responsibly or credibly profess to be designed to improve advocacy skills when you run it in a way that advertises that you don't know the first thing about advocacy.

3. Your October 11 memo attributes to some members of the Board the view that "the nature of the petitioner's argument would hinder those assigned to argue that side in presenting a strong case." This is a wholly unjustified public slur on your fellow students. It accuses them of inability to exercise a level of self-control indispensable to any lawyer. I do not believe that NYU students are the intellectual and moral weaklings you assert they are, but if I took your word for it I would regard that as a serious condemnation of the student body.

4. Your action in discontinuing use of the child custody case disserves the very interests that you seem to think you are promoting:

a. How can we ever rid our society of anti-gay biases unless we formulate the strongest arguments we can possibly make against those biases? And how can we do that if we don't also formulate the strongest arguments that could be made to support the biases?

b. Courageous spokespersons, at high personal cost, have finally begun to bring homosexuality and the issues surrounding it out of the closet. Now you want to put it back in. Can't you see the message you are sending?

c. More basically, once you begin to exclude ideas from the discourse of a community on the ground that they are wrong or offensive, you start in motion a process that inevitably ends up justifying suppression of the unpopular ideas of unpopular minorities. It is fanciful to think that bigots cannot beat you at the game you have begun. They always have and they always will. . . .

Anthony G. Amsterdam

I have just read Tony Amsterdam's letter to you in connection with the Moot Court problem. I could not agree with his position more strongly. Your important pedagogical role in the law school would be seriously undermined if you ruled certain legal controversies beyond the pale of open debate.

Moreover, as Tony points out, you do no service to the gay community by appearing to be afraid of opening certain issues for public debate. Worse, you hobble the effort to expose the fallacies in anti-gay laws by removing them from public discussion. Most troubling, you impede the ability of NYU trained students to combat anti-gay laws in the real world by depriving them of the training needed to be effective advocates. Effective advocacy in the real world does not consist of pronouncing moral anathemas upon your opponents' positions. It requires painstaking analysis and persuasive refutation, and that requires a sophisticated understanding of the arguments on the other side.

Finally, I am sympathetic to your obvious concern that the competition be viewed as "inclusionary" rather than "exclusionary." There are, however, alternative methods of assuring that certain students do not feel excluded from the competition. In my opinion, the one unacceptable method is the censoring of the competition's subject matter on moral grounds.

Burt Neuborne

We write to urge you to reconsider your decision with regard to the child custody case and to reinstate that case in the Marden Competition. . . .

We underscore a point that we urge you to consider carefully: In our judgment, the predictable effect of removing the child custody case from the Marden Competition will be to damage the very cause that those who would take this action seek to promote. The academic community and the wider public will conclude, not unreasonably, that advocates of gay rights lack confidence in their position because they are not willing to subject it to open debate and will also conclude that such persons would sacrifice a long tradition of free discourse, particularly in universities, because of their particular substantive goals. This would be a tragedy for all who favor, as we do, equal rights for the homosexual community.

We recognize that some students assigned to argue against the rights of the homosexual couple may have a deep and abiding personal opposition to making that argument. As in practice, when that happens it is appropriate — perhaps even obligatory — for the student (or lawyer) to refuse to represent the client or to ask that a supervisor not assign the particular case to him or her. On the other hand, we do not think this or any other problem ought to be subject to refusal because a student would prefer to argue the opposing side, because the student would rule against the particular position if he or she were the judge, or because the student believes the position to be wrong and unwise.

Norman Dorsen and Stephen Gillers

We are writing concerning your efforts to grapple with concerns raised about the Moot Court Board's initial issue for its competition: "the issue . . . whether awarding custody to a homosexual parent is presumptively contrary to a child's best interest. . . ." We believe it was appropriate for the Moot Court Board to respond to student concerns about the problem and to consider alternatives. Rather than being "censorship," such reevaluation and consideration of alternatives is an integral part of the Moot Court Board's responsibility to ensure that it is providing a pedagogically valuable experience for Moot Court participants. . . .

As you are well aware, there are many aspects to formulating a good problem for Moot Court. We expect that you look for problems that raise difficult legal issues; that are evenly divided; and that will engage the interest of students. We believe that it is also appropriate for you to consider whether a problem will require students to espouse views that they find deeply morally abhorrent, and to seek out alternatives that allow students to benefit from Moot Court without paying that price of conscience.

Our belief that it is appropriate to consider the possibility of conscientious objection to advocacy of a position in Moot Court is based on the structure of the program. In Moot Court, students must prepare and argue both sides of a case. They not only think through and plan for opposing arguments; they actually stand on their feet, in public, and present those arguments. Obviously, this structure means that students will often be presenting views that they disagree with. This is in the nature of Moot Court and can be a fruitful way for students to explore issues and refine their thinking. But the obligation to argue either side of a problem also raises the possibility that students may be able to participate in Moot Court only if they are willing publicly and forcefully to espouse positions that they find not just disagreeable, but fundamentally morally abhorrent. It is appropriate for you to respond to student concerns when they are put to such a choice.

Your responsiveness to such concerns was particularly reasonable in light of the precise issue presented this year by the first Moot Court problem. . . . As the problem is framed, the argument for the appellant is little more than a recapitulation of old prejudices, and compels the advocate to argue that homosexuals should not share and participate in the most fundamental human experience, having a family. It is unsurprising that a number of students found the prospect of presenting that position morally repugnant.

We do not agree that you "censor" debate when you consider whether a Moot Court problem will present dilemmas of conscience for participants, and we believe that reevaluation of an initial failure to consider such a dilemma is equally appropriate. We hope and

trust that sensitive exploration and debate on controversial issues
will flourish at the Law School in a wide variety of contexts. But we
do not believe that the Moot Court Board is compelled by any first
principles to impose dilemmas of conscience on unwilling advocates
in the circumscribed, if important, context of the Marden Competition.

Professors Claudia Angelos, Peggy Davis,
Sylvia Law and Nancy Morawetz

. . . As lawyers and law students, we learn rather easily to argue
for and against legal presumptions and to defend the rules protecting freedom of speech. I would suggest that it is more challenging to
protect the disenfranchised and disempowered so that freedom of
political action, of speech and of conscience, are not only rights of the
privileged.

That the Marden problem presents a current issue in the law
forcefully demonstrates how readily society dehumanizes lesbians
and gay men. Although cloaked in the language of "best interests of
the child," the presumption operates to equate homosexual orientation with parental unfitness. In other words, lesbians and gay men
are unqualified to have a family. Even the more liberal version of the
presumption's rationale, that in the "best interests of the child" we
should protect the child from the prejudice directed at the par-
ent-child bond, . . . legitimizes society's prejudice by force of law.

However phrased, the presumption is law in a number of states
and enforces the view that lesbians and gay men are unfit to parent.
The result is that many lesbian and gay parents lose their children
through the legal process. Even in jurisdictions where no legal
presumption exists, many more lesbian and gay people relinquish
custody of their children so as not to fight bitter legal battles
through which their children suffer and which homosexual parents
are likely to lose. This is the consequence of biases that disapprove of
homosexuals in general and homosexual parents in particular.
Prejudice destroys not only the familial and social bonds but also the
work opportunities, the economic well being, the health and the very
lives of lesbians and gay men.

Evidence is strong that hatred and discrimination are deeply
embedded in our culture, our social structure, our thinking and
indeed our daily speech. As a result, speech alone cannot overcome
discrimination. More is needed, a thorough and thoughtful examination of the deep assumptions which govern our devaluation of people
based on class memberships. This examination is more elusive and
exacting than legal analysis.

Apparently those who expressed alarm about the change in the
Moot Court problem are concerned that outcry about one side of the
issue is censorious "moralizing" of the kind that generates oppression of lesbians and gay men. Those who hold this view tell us that
the solution obviously cannot be more moralizing. Where group bias
is concerned, it is unchecked prejudice, fear and hatred, not princi-

pled moral claims, that silence and oppress. Forceful normative criticism of words and acts reflecting prejudice, fear or hatred is necessary to end oppression of minorities so that minority group members, in this case lesbians and gay men, might speak and act with the same freedom that the non-minority can now take as a given.

Because some Moot Court participants and some lesbian and gay law students expressed to the Moot Court Board that the Marden problem is not a particularly good problem on lesbian and gay issues, the inference has been drawn that the participants and the lesbian and gay law student advocates are somehow lacking in courage, or "lack confidence in their position." This is a particularly tragic and ironic aspect of the debate. Neither the conscientious objectors nor the lesbian and gay law student community sought to stop the debate. They did suggest alternative moot court problems that are fairer and richer competitively, pedagogically and ideologically.

Those who imply that the lesbian and gay law students (or their supporters) lack courage or confidence in this matter are discounting the nature of the oppression. That the overwhelming majority of lesbians and gay men are still "in the closet" is testament to the power of that oppression. Today even in the streets of Greenwich Village, lesbian and gay people, and those perceived to be, are brutalized. Blame and punishment for openness and honesty about one's identity are part of the terrible oppression of homophobia, for the lesbian or gay man a socially compelled denial of one's self, one's commitments and one's conscience. Indeed, this social compulsion to hide is a pressure for gay and non-gay alike to disavow "gayness" and can be a further excuse to punish those who do not do so. Given such pressures, the courage of those who are openly gay cannot and should not be questioned, disparaged or abused under any guise.

Professor Sarah E. Burns

---

2. Collective Action: The Role of Bar Associations

PROBLEM 11B

You have just begun your term as president of the American Bar Association (ABA), which represents about 40 percent of the nation's lawyers. The Association's purposes include supporting the United States Constitution, promoting the administration of justice and the uniformity of legislation, and "applying professional knowledge for the public good." In pursuing those objectives, the Association's House of Delegates often considers recommendations concerning proposed legislation. In February 1990, the House passed Resolution 160, which provided:

BE IT RESOLVED, That the American Bar Association recognizes the fundamental rights of privacy and equality guaranteed by the United States Constitution, and opposes legislation or other governmental action that interferes with the confidential relationship between a pregnant woman and her physician, or with the decision to terminate the pregnancy at any time before the fetus is capable of independent life, as determined by her physician, or thereafter when termination of the pregnancy is necessary to protect the woman's life or health.

After passage of this resolution, the Association received some 3,000 angry letters and 1,500 members resigned. At the next annual meeting, by a narrowly divided vote, the Association rescinded its earlier resolution and replaced it with the following provision:

BE IT RESOLVED, that the ABA, without adopting a policy supportive of a particular viewpoint, recognizes and respects the right of individual ABA members to hold and express personal convictions, beliefs and views on the profound issues presented by a decision to terminate pregnancy; and BE IT FURTHER RESOLVED, that the ABA recognizes that the questions presented by a decision to terminate pregnancy are extremely divisive, and that the ABA, for the good of the association, will not adopt a policy supportive of a particular viewpoint with respect to constitutional, moral, medical or other questions involved in a decision to terminate pregnancy; and BE IT FURTHER RESOLVED, that the foregoing statement of policy relating to the decision to terminate pregnancy is substituted in place of the policy adopted by the ABA House of Delegates on Feb. 13, 1990, and this resolution shall not be construed as either pro-life or pro-choice.[1]

Pro-choice supporters then succeeded in convincing the House to reverse itself again and reaffirm the original resolution. Another, larger wave of resignations followed and abortion opponents insist that the issue be reconsidered. What is your position?

The dispute over the ABA abortion resolution arose in the context of women's long-standing concerns about their status within the Association. Although about a fifth of ABA members are women, their representation in the House of Delegates and in bar leadership positions has been far lower.[2]

Proponents of the pro-choice resolution pointed out that the ABA previously made recommendations on controversial issues and supported the right to reproductive liberty in the Uniform Abortion Act. According to then-president Talbot D'Alemberte,

[i]n the 1950s, I'm ashamed to say we were neutral when issues of racial justice were before the courts. The ABA may not, without grave risk to our credibility, withdraw from the debate over this vital issue today.

D'Alemberte further argued that the ABA had grown in size and stature after it finally decided to become involved with civil rights, and that the Association should now address the "one issue that women most care about."[3]

By contrast, opponents claimed that the broader mission of the ABA would be compromised by taking a position on an extremely divisive question that would run counter to the moral and religious convictions of many members. According to a letter from former Attorney General William Barr,

> [t]he ABA endangers the perception that it is an impartial and objective professional association. The perception of impartiality and political neutrality is essential if the ABA is to fulfill its various roles and functions.[4]

Echoing that sentiment, one House delegate later noted that the ABA has nearly 1,000 official policies on everything from health care benefits to a "fundamental right to food." These positions are adopted by less than one tenth of the ABA members — those who belong to the House of Delegates — and "do not necessarily reflect the views of the group's 385,000 members, much less the views of the nation's 900,000 lawyers."[5] Are you persuaded by this critique?

In Keller v. State Bar of California, 496 U.S. 1 (1990), the Supreme Court held that lawyers belonging to a mandatory state bar association cannot be compelled to pay dues that the association would use to lobby for controversial political causes. As a matter of organizational policy, should voluntary associations exercise any similar restraints? What consideration should be most central in making that decision? Consider the materials on bar regulatory frameworks in Chapter III (Regulation of the Profession) at pages 40–59. What role should voluntary professional organizations play in reform efforts?

B. REPRESENTING GROUPS: IDENTIFYING THE CLIENT'S INTEREST IN SOCIAL REFORM LITIGATION

1. Equal Protection Contexts: School Desegregation

See Chapter IX, The Lawyer-Client Relationship
- Representing the Public Interest: Class Action Litigation
    (pages 402–418)

PROBLEM 11C

You are chair of the litigation committee of a civil rights public interest law organization. After the Supreme Court's decision in United States v. Fordice, discussed below, a citizen's group from another southern state approaches your organization. The group would like your representation in litigation against its system of higher education. That system has a history and pattern of segregation similar to the one at issue in *Fordice*. Black citizens and educators are divided on the question. How should your organization decide whether to accept the case and what remedy to seek?

UNITED STATES v. FORDICE, 505 U.S. 717 (1992).   This case involved a suit by the federal government claiming that Mississippi had failed to dismantle a system of prior de jure segregation in higher education.   In essence, the Court held that race-neutral policies are insufficient when the state "perpetuates policies and practices traceable to its prior system that continue to have segregative effects, whether by influencing student enrollment decisions or by fostering segregation in other facets of the university system." If these policies lack "sound educational justification and can be practicably eliminated," the state is under an affirmative obligation to do so. Constitutionally suspect policies in the Mississippi system included the use of minimum test scores in admissions, program duplication at predominantly black and white schools, university "mission designations" that affected curricular offerings and funding levels, and the perpetuation of eight institutions rather than some lesser number. The Court remanded the case for determination of whether the state had met its affirmative obligation to dismantle its prior dual system.

Reactions to the *Fordice* decision within the black community were mixed. Although a number of predominantly black organizations had filed amicus briefs in support of the government's case against the university, some commentators questioned that position as well as the Court's subsequent ruling.[6] For example, student editors of the Harvard Law Review maintained:

> *Fordice* fails to make any distinction between racial stratification that results from the free choices of black students and that is thrust upon them by discriminatory policies. For the Court, the preferences of students are irrelevant; merely giving the students the choice of a predominantly black university is suspect. . . . [As a result of the Court's ruling,] black students may be deprived of the option of attending a predominantly black university without receiving a corresponding benefit. The option of attending an integrated university already exists. Thirty percent of Mississippi's black four-year college students currently attend one of the State's historically white com-

prehensive universities. . . . *Fordice* displays the Court's hostility to the survival of the state-supported predominantly black university and its indifference to those black students who prefer to receive their education in the cultural and social environment of the historically black institution.[7]

Other commentators worried about the loss of jobs for black faculty and administrators and perpetuation of the assumption that black schools were inferior.[8]

In 1995, the Southern Education Foundation released a report finding that none of the 12 states that formerly administered segregated universities or colleges could demonstrate an "acceptable level of success in desegregating its higher education system." The report found that most "flagship" universities in the South remain more than 80 percent white, that 60 percent of black freshman attend historically black colleges or junior colleges, and that blacks' graduation rates and enrollment in graduate or professional schools are stagnant or falling in all 12 states.[9]

How should civil rights lawyers respond to these challenges? Compare Drew Days' view in the article below with Derek Bell's position, excerpted in Chapter IX (The Lawyer-Client Relationship) at pages 403–407. Should lawyers in civil rights litigation seek to ensure the preservation of traditionally all-black schools? Alternatively, should they focus on making all public institutions respond adequately to the needs of black students?[10] Who should decide these questions? If you were the lawyer in Problem 11C or Problem 9D, how would you proceed?

DREW S. DAYS, III, *BROWN* BLUES: RETHINKING THE INTEGRATIVE IDEAL

34 Wm. & Mary L. Rev. 53 (1992)

I. INTRODUCTION

Thirty-eight years have passed since the Supreme Court's Brown v. Board of Education decision declaring unconstitutional state-imposed segregation of public schools. One would have thought that by now American society would have arrived at a consensus with respect to the substance and scope of *Brown*. The truth is otherwise. Even in the education sector of our national life that *Brown* specifically addressed, deep differences remain over what changes that decision was designed to effect. . . .

Several developments in recent years suggest . . . that growing numbers of blacks may be turning away from [an] integrative ideal. Four examples of this shift are worth noting: first, black parents now express support for school board efforts to end desegregation plans that involve busing, favoring instead a return to neighborhood schools, even though this would result in increases in the number of virtually all-black schools in the inner city; second, at the urging of black parents, school boards in a number of major cities have attempted to create all-black male academies; third, black administrators, faculty, students, and alumni of historically black colleges in the South have joined state officials in opposition to court-ordered higher education desegregation plans; and fourth, black students on predominantly white college campuses have urged administrators to provide special facilities for the black students' social and cultural events. Some critics have dismissed these developments as perverse efforts by blacks to return to a "separate but equal" regime. In fact, these developments raise serious and complex questions about the future of race relations in America that deserve careful analysis, not simplistic characterization.

II. BLACKS AND NEIGHBORHOOD SCHOOLS

The school desegregation process has not been unproblematic, to say the least. Almost forty years after *Brown*, there is still active litigation alleging constitutional violations. There is no gainsaying, however, that as a result of *Brown* and its progeny, thousands of black, white, and Hispanic children have been able to receive integrated educations and develop both educational and social skills that will stand them in good stead in later life. At the very least, the mandatory presence of white children has saved some black and other minority children from the physically inferior facilities — and inferior resources — to which they had been assigned under segregation.

Acknowledging the important gains of desegregation, however, should not blind us to the continuing legacy of segregation within desegregated systems. In many schools, racially segregated classes make it unlikely that children of different races will have meaningful interaction during the school day. Moreover, the black community has paid, in some instances, a high price for desegregation. For example, schools that served not only as educational institutions but as community centers in predominantly black neighborhoods have been closed; the burden of busing has fallen disproportionately upon black children; black teachers and administrators have been dismissed and demoted disproportionately; and black students have encountered increased disciplinary action in recently desegregated schools.

Most important, perhaps, given the initial hope that desegregation would increase the quality of educational opportunity for black students, is the fact that the desegregation process has not necessarily brought about improvements. Indeed, in some cases, desegregation has limited opportunity. For example, where magnet schools offering innovative educational programs have replaced formerly all-black facilities, black student enrollment in the special programs has been limited by the need to maintain racial balance. This record establishes, contrary to common assumptions, that desegregation has not been an unmitigated benefit to previously segregated black students, teachers, and administrators.

One need not conclude that these negative consequences are the inevitable result of desegregation, however, and that the black community might have been better off seeking to improve educational opportunities within a segregated system. The more plausible explanation is that the same racist tendencies in America that created and maintained segregated schools did not disappear overnight once desegregation was mandated. Rather, they merely found new opportunities in this new arrangement to disadvantage the black community.

Whatever the pros and cons of desegregation, however, the reality is that demographic changes in the United States since 1954 have produced a pattern of residential segregation. This makes further progress in school desegregation in certain areas difficult to envision. . . .

There is also a sense among some blacks that although some desegregation plans no longer produce meaningful numbers of whites and blacks studying together, the plans are maintained because of the mistaken belief that blacks cannot learn unless whites are sitting next to them in class. The blacks who challenge the continuation of such plans argue that a return to neighborhood school assignment makes more sense because parental and community involvement in the schools would be more likely to increase. Moreover, government resources expended on busing could be redirected to increasing the quality of materials and instruction available at those schools.

Blacks and whites who oppose efforts to roll back desegregation plans do so for a variety of reasons. First, they fear that such proposals are yet another attempt by school boards guilty of past intentional segregation to escape any further role in avoiding resegregation. Second, they suspect blacks who support such roll-backs of acting more in their own political and economic interests than in the interests of black children. What roll-back proponents seek, in fact, are more and better jobs for black administrators and teachers in exchange for reduced pressure for increasing or maintaining desegregation levels. Third, roll-back opponents fear that a return to all-black schools will result in "benign neglect" of those schools in terms of resources allocated for facilities, materials, and personnel.

The debate has taken on a new dimension, however, because black mayors, city council members, and school superintendents have begun to express similar concerns about the wisdom of what they see as "desegregation at any cost." Courts are justifiably perplexed over how to evaluate the views of this group, because their authority, as elected and appointed blacks, to speak for the black community certainly is equal to, if not greater than, that of plaintiffs and their lawyers in school desegregation cases. . . .

Black higher education groups [have been] at odds with federal agencies and the NAACP Legal Defense Fund . . . regarding the wisdom of pressing desegregation of public colleges and universities. Black college presidents, faculty, and alumni were undoubtedly mindful of the burdens the black community had been forced to bear during desegregation of public primary and secondary systems. They feared that desegregation of higher education would result, at best, in whites displacing black teachers and administrators, as well as black students. At worst, given the relative inferiority of their institutions, desegregation might result in the closing of schools, or the absorption of traditionally black institutions into historically white schools. In either event, institutions important to the black community would lose their identity, and opportunities in higher education for black administrators, faculty, and students would be significantly diminished.

Despite similar concerns, however, proponents of desegregation in higher education believed that both litigation and administrative enforcement could increase resources available to historically black institutions. Reducing program duplication and forcing the states to locate especially attractive academic programs at traditionally black schools would also enhance the schools' long-term viability.

It is fair to say that this desegregation effort has not been very successful. Significant segregation between historically black and white institutions is still apparent. Since 1973, state officials have effectively utilized the administrative process to delay meaningful change. . . .

It is [the] fear that black institutions will be the inevitable casualties of higher education desegregation that has complicated the dismantling of dual systems. Take for example, the ostensibly odd alignment of parties in the Louisiana case. After concluding that Louisiana's desegregation plans were inadequate, the federal court commissioned its own strategy. That plan envisioned, among other things, merging the traditionally black Southern University Law Center into the law school of Louisiana State University (LSU), the state's traditionally white flagship institution. The two law schools are located in Baton Rouge, only a few miles apart.

That the state opposed the merger plan was not surprising. However, it was joined by the Southern University Board of Supervisors, which viewed the court's order as a step backward, rather than forward, for black education in Louisiana. The board claimed that blacks, the victims of the state's history of segregation and discrimination in higher education, were being required to bear a disproportionate burden in rectifying that situation. Specifically, they contended that the merger of Southern University's law school into LSU's would undoubtedly displace black faculty and staff and curtail opportunities for blacks seeking legal education. The court's plan did not envision LSU's absorbing Southern's faculty and staff, nor did it require LSU to expand to ensure against a net loss of law school seats for black students after the merger.

In defense of its plan, the court took the position that the merger was required by the Constitution and was in the long-term interests of the citizens of Louisiana, black and white. But for the state's creation and maintenance of segregated higher education, the court pointed out, there would not still be two public law schools in the same city, one white and the other black. The court concluded that desegregation could occur only if one of the institutions closed. Moreover, the court observed that in a fiscally strapped state, maintaining two law schools in Baton Rouge made no economic sense.

Because Southern University's law school had been denied adequate state support due to its status as a black institution, the condition of its physical plant and the quality of its educational program were inferior to those of LSU. Consequently, the court concluded that Southern's law school should be the one to close. In response to the Southern University Board of Supervisors' concerns about the desegregation process, the court suggested that the board was interested in protecting the jobs of Southern faculty and administrators, rather than in improving educational opportunities for blacks.

This controversy delineates starkly the dilemma confronting proponents of higher education desegregation. The court clearly was correct that the maintenance of dual, segregated law schools in one city makes no legal or fiscal sense and that merging the institutions would require blacks and whites to study law together rather than apart. But the black opponents of the merger also have compelling arguments. Absent the state's history of discriminatory treatment of Southern University Law Center, the school's facilities and program probably would not be so inferior to those of LSU. Had there been "tangible" equality over the years between the two institutions, white students might have opted to attend Southern rather than LSU based upon "intangible" considerations, such as the presence of particular faculty members or curricular emphases. Moreover, there is no reason why Southern's board should apologize for seeking to protect the jobs of faculty and administrators. They too are victims of the state's segregative practices.

Finally, Southern University Law Center and LSU Law School have different admissions criteria. As a consequence, Southern has been able to admit some black students who, based upon objective indicators such as GPA and LSAT scores, would not be competitive candidates at LSU. Southern nevertheless has been able to train and graduate generations of black lawyers who provide competent legal services to poor and minority communities in the state. Unless LSU ensured that black students whom Southern would have admitted would find seats at LSU, the merger would represent a net loss of educational opportunities for black students in Louisiana.

The Louisiana case eventually was dismissed in light of the Fifth Circuit's ruling in the Mississippi case. Solving the dilemma in Louisiana and in other states where higher education desegregation is underway will not be easy now that the Supreme Court has vacated that decision. The solution cannot be achieved overnight, however. It must operate within the twin constraints of constitutional requirements and economic reality. At the same time, it must address responsibly the displacement effects of the desegregation process and the ironic price that the black community must pay for desegregation.

---

2. First Amendment Contexts: Pornography

PROBLEM 11D

1. You are one of two staff lawyers for a women's rights organization in a midwestern city. Your group is not a membership organization; it receives financial support from individual women, foundations, and occasional attorney fee awards. A board of directors makes fundamental decisions concerning the organization's goals and structure and must approve any litigation filed in the organization's name. The board meets twice annually and generally does not intervene in day-to-day activities. Its members are chosen largely for their capacities in fund-raising.

The head of a conservative religious coalition has asked for your organization's co-sponsorship of a local ordinance to curb the spread of pornography. The group would also like your advice about what legal restrictions would be constitutional. In particular, they would like you to consider a provision banning violent pornographic materials or a provision modeled on federal legislative proposals that would enable victims of sexual crimes to recover from publishers and sellers of obscene material if the victims can prove that material was a "proximate cause" of their injury.[11]

The local chapter of the American Civil Liberties Union has asked for your assistance in fighting any such ordinance. How do you respond? How would you make the decision? What advice would you give to the conservative coalition?

2. A faculty member from the University of Michigan Law School seeks your help. The school's Journal of Gender and Law recently sponsored a conference on prostitution. A number of key anti-prostitution advocates were unwilling to speak if activists supporting repeal of prostitution laws were also invited. Student organizers agreed not to include such activists but arranged for an art exhibit that would present their views. A Detroit artist critical of pornography and prostitution prohibitions prepared the exhibit, which included video interviews with prostitutes and footage from sexually explicit films in which sex workers appeared. When two speakers at the conference objected to the film, students removed it. After the artist objected to censorship of part of the exhibit, they asked her to remove the entire display. She did.

The incident has attracted widespread publicity. Catherine MacKinnon, who teaches at Michigan Law School but was not involved in the decision, told the New York Times that she supported the students' action:

> It is one thing to talk about trafficking women, and it is another thing to traffic women. . . . There is nothing in [the] First Amendment to require that this school, or students in it, be forced to traffic women. If these materials are pornography, and I haven't seen them so I can't say, it is not a question of their offensiveness, but of safety and equality for women. Showing pornography sets women up for harassment and rape. . . . I don't see it as a fight within feminism but a fight between those who wish to end male supremacy and those who wish to do better under it.[12]

The director of the ACLU National Arts Censorship project responded:

> Censorship of sexually explicit material is not in women's interest. It's also unconstitutional. Michigan is a state school, and when any government institution removes an art exhibit or book because it expresses ideas some people find offensive, there's a First Amendment problem.[13]
> I think it's particularly alarming that at a public university, this group of students . . . seem to take the view that they have no obligation to present the views of others and they feel it is OK to use the university's resources to show the views of only one side of an important issue.[14]

The Dean has formed a committee to consider how the law school administration should respond. Its chair asks your advice. How should the students have handled the complaint about the exhibit in the first instance? How should the law school respond?

The problems for lawyers representing groups have both theoretical and practical dimensions. At the theoretical level, the issue is how to make claims for, by, or about particular constituencies without homogenizing their concerns. At the practical level, the issue is how to represent those group interests in legal actions that have class-wide significance without adequate mechanisms for class-wide accountability.

A representative example involves divisions within the women's movement over antipornography ordinances. In the early 1970s, feminists began organizing protests against the growing industry of pornography, which they defined as material eroticizing female subordination. In their view, such material contributed to women's inequality and victimization in several respects: it encouraged individuals to model abusive or degrading behavior in their own sexual relationships; it posed risks of severe physical and psychological injury to individuals featured in pornography; and, when coupled with violence, heightened viewers' acceptance of rape myths and aggression toward women.[15]

Activists in the antipornography campaign generally claim to speak from women's experience and to represent women's interests. Yet much contemporary feminist and critical race theory has challenged assertions of any universal experience cutting across other boundaries such as race, class, ethnicity, and sexual orientation. Leading feminists have also challenged the claims that suppressing pornography reflects women's interests. These anticensorship activists often maintain that pornographic material expresses "a radical [liberating] impulse" and can be a source of pleasure as well as degradation for women.[16] As any review of mass-market romances or lesbian erotica makes clear, some women find portrayals of sexual subordination arousing. Even if this view is the product of sexist social conditioning, anticensorship groups believe that the last thing women need is "more sexual shame, guilt and hypocrisy, this time served up as feminism."[17]

This division among feminists came to a head in struggles over local antipornography ordinances. The most well-known involved an Indianapolis initiative struck down in American Booksellers Assn., Inc. v. Hudnut, 771 F.2d 323 (7th Cir. 1985), aff'd mem., 475 U.S. 1001, reh'g denied, 475 U.S. 1132 (1986). The ordinance defined pornography as the "graphic sexually explicit subordination of women, whether in pictures or words," which also included one or more of certain specified portrayals, such as the presentation of women as "sexual objects" who enjoy pain, humiliation, or rape; the presentation of women in scenarios of "degradation, injury, abasement, or torture"; or the presentation of women as sexual objects for "domination, conquest, violation, exploitation, . . . possession or use, or through postures or positions of servility or submission or display." Supporting the ordinance were Catherine MacKinnon and various antipornography groups, as well as organizations such as Citizens for Decency Through Law, which claimed that pornography "cause[d] crime, venereal disease, and dangerous societal change."[18] Opposing the ordinance were an association of booksellers, a lesbian and gay rights organization, the ACLU, and the National Feminist Anticensorship Task Force (FACT).

The FACT brief challenged the Indianapolis ordinance as ambiguous, overinclusive, and repressive. It noted that most evidence linking pornography with increased aggressive tendencies toward women was based on laboratory studies of violent visual imagery; researchers had not discovered similar effects with nonviolent or exclusively written materials. The brief also raised concerns that sexually explicit lesbian materials would be targeted for censorship, and expressed doubt that misogynist images were central enough factors in the oppression of women to justify censorship. In conclusion, the brief argued:

> The suppression authorized by the Indianapolis ordinance of a potentially enormous range of sexual imagery and texts reinforces the notion that women are too fragile and men too uncontrollable, absent

the aid of the censor, to be trusted to reject or enjoy sexually explicit speech themselves. By identifying "subordination of women" as the concept that distinguishes sexually explicit material which is tolerable from that to be condemned, the ordinance incorporates a vague and asymmetric standard for censorship that can as readily be used to curtail feminist speech about sexuality, or to target the speech of sexual minorities, as to halt hateful speech about women. Worse, perpetuation of the concept of gender determined roles in regard to sexuality strengthens one of the main obstacles to achieving real change and ending sexual violence.[19]

The court in *American Booksellers* refused to consider most arguments advanced by feminists on both sides because it declined to balance the harms of pornography against the harms of censorship; rather, the court found that the ordinance was per se unconstitutional given its content-based restriction on speech. 771 F.2d at 332. However, the divisions within the feminist movement continued, and surfaced in other cities that were considering ordinances, boycotts, or zoning restrictions. Such disputes also arose in Congress during debates over statutes regulating the Internet and authorizing civil damages for victims of pornography-related violence.

Antipornography activists, in response to their feminist opponents, challenged whether any substantial part of the materials at issue constituted a "liberating radical impulse" for most women — materials that depicted women as "bound, battered, tortured, humiliated and sometimes killed . . . hung from a meat hook, forced to eat excrement, penetrated by eels and rats and knives and pistols."[20] In a celebrated passage, MacKinnon denounced feminists who challenged the antipornography ordinance as "collaborators" with pornographers:

> I really want you to stop your lies and misrepresentations of our position. I want you to do something about your thundering ignorance about the way women are treated. I want you to remember your own lives. I also really want you on our side. But failing that, I want you to stop claiming that your liberalism, with its elitism, and your Freudianism, with its sexualized misogyny, has anything in common with feminism.[21]

If you were the lawyer in Problem 11D, is there any way you could minimize the risks of alienating some important allies? Does it make sense to assist conservative groups that have historically opposed your organization on gender-related issues at the expense of antagonizing civil liberties groups that have generally supported your efforts? Would coalitions with conservatives be a way of building bridges to women with traditional values? Consider Phyllis Schlafly's claim that liberal feminists

> prove their hypocrisy by their nonattitude toward pornography. [Women's liberationists] profess outrage at the role concept fostered by school textbooks that include pictures of women in the home as

wives and mothers, but they raise no protest about the role concept fostered by obscene pictures of women as playthings for male lust and sadism.[22]

Is Schlafly's position any different from MacKinnon's on this issue? If not, what does that suggest about lawyers' representation of women's interests in the antipornography campaign? Are there other educational or protest issues on which most women could find common ground? Should these assume priority over more divisive claims? Or is taking a controversial position an essential strategy for raising public awareness and preserving organizational principles?

C.   CAUSES AND CLIENTS: GROUP INTERESTS AND INDIVIDUAL CLAIMS IN THE REPRODUCTIVE RIGHTS CAMPAIGN

PROBLEM 11E

You are a Texas lawyer during the early 1970s who is involved with women's rights and reproductive health issues. You are anxious to challenge a Texas law prohibiting abortion unless necessary to save the life of the mother. You have had difficulty locating a pregnant plaintiff who is willing to forgo obtaining an abortion (through either an illegal or out-of-state provider) long enough for a court to act. Finally, you receive a referral of a woman, Norma McCorvey, who wants to terminate her pregnancy but lacks money to go out of state and is afraid to risk an illegal abortion. In discussions about a challenge to the Texas statute, she asks if it "would help" if she had been raped. You explain that Texas law includes no exception for rape. Although McCorvey claims that her pregnancy resulted from rape, she has no corroberating witnesses or police reports.

McCorvey then asks what being a plaintiff would involve. You respond that she would only need to sign a brief affidavit describing her situation. She could remain anonymous, and would not need to attend any hearings or pay any part of the legal costs. Based on that information, McCorvey agrees to challenge the statute. She does not request, and you do not volunteer, information about how long it will likely take to get a trial court ruling. Nor do you discuss how far advanced her pregnancy is.

You subsequently draft an affidavit stating that "Jane Roe" desires to terminate her pregnancy because of the economic hardship it entails and the social stigma attached to illegitimate births. You do not include the allegations of rape because you lack proof and because you don't want the court to invalidate the statute only for involuntary pregnancies. McCorvey signs the affidavit and you file a class action with her as the name plaintiff. You also file a companion suit on behalf of a married couple, "John and Mary Doe," who have been warned that neither pregnancy nor birth control pills are medically advisable given the wife's neurochemical disorder.

Your claim in *Roe* is successful in the trial court; *Doe* is dismissed for lack of standing. By the time you receive the ruling, McCorvey's pregnancy is too far advanced to obtain an abortion. She gives birth and places the baby for adoption.[23]

McCorvey's claim results in the Supreme Court's landmark decision Roe v. Wade. Two decades after that ruling, a number of publications, including McCorvey's own autobiography, raise questions about your conduct in the case. Critics fault you for not consulting McCorvey about the decision to file the case as a class action and to make no reference to the rape. You are also criticized for failing to counsel McCorvey about the likely timing of the lower court's ruling and its affect on her ability to obtain an abortion. According to McCorvey, she was nothing to you other than "a name on a piece of paper."[24]

How do you respond? With the benefit of hindsight, would you have done anything differently?

In commenting on the conduct of Sarah Weddington, the lawyer in *Roe*, Kevin McMunigal identifies a central irony:

> Weddington's dominant point . . . is that women should have choice — the power to decide questions that seriously affect their lives. Restrictive abortion laws fail to accept women as individuals capable of choice and render them powerless over such questions. Weddington, though . . . allows McCorvey virtually no choice or power concerning the *Roe* case, a matter that seriously and immediately affects McCorvey's life and reproductive choices. Weddington also criticizes restrictive abortion laws as treating women as merely a means to an end, a reproductive vehicle or carrying case for a fetus. Yet Weddington treated McCorvey almost exclusively as a means to serve the end of changing the law of abortion.[25]

Do you agree with that criticism? Who was entitled to make the choice about proceeding as a class action or including a rape allegation? Would it affect your view to learn that McCorvey later admitted that her claim of rape was false? See DR 7-101A and Model Rule 1.2, discussed in Chapter IV (Advocacy) at pages 135 and 159. The Model Rule grants clients the right to decide the "objectives of representation" and "the means by which they are to be pursued." The Comment adds that lawyers should assume responsibility for "technical and legal tactical issues." Was Weddington's conduct consistent with this Rule? If Weddington had believed that discussion of the timing of the litigation would have convinced McCorvey to obtain an illegal abortion rather than to challenge the statute, was it ethical for her not to raise the issue?[26]

D.   REPRESENTING THE GOVERNMENT: IDENTIFYING THE CLIENT'S INTEREST IN CONSTITUTIONAL LITIGATION

1.   First Amendment Contexts: The Separation of Church and State

PROBLEM 11F

1. You are the attorney general of New Jersey. The state legislature has passed legislation requiring a minute of silence each day in state public schools. The governor vetoed the legislation on the ground that its intent was to sanction prayer, and that it therefore violated constitutional requirements of separation between church and state. You agree with that decision. The state senate overrode the veto.

Just before the override vote, you advised the legislature that your office would not defend the law if a suit was brought to challenge it. The majority leader of the state senate has publicly requested that you reconsider your decision. Several prominent members have threatened to take further legislative action if you do not. In their view,

[t]he Attorney General is sworn to uphold the laws of New Jersey and this is a law of New Jersey whatever the Attorney General thinks of it.

[If the Attorney General has the right to refuse to defend a law,] we should do something about it. The State of New Jersey is entitled to representation. It's not for the Attorney General to act as judge and jury.[27]

How do you respond? If you decline to defend the law, should the court appoint counsel for the state, to be paid out of state funds?[28]

2. The United States Secretary of Education decides to provide federal funds to parochial schools for the removal of hazardous asbestos insulation. You are a young lawyer in the Education Department honors program who is assigned to legal work involving the program. You discover a recent six-three opinion of the Supreme Court striking down, on establishment clause grounds, a program of federal aid for new fire escapes in parochial schools. In addition, you find an Attorney General's opinion, issued during the prior administration, holding that an earlier asbestos removal proposal was both outside the Secretary's statutory powers and unconstitutional. You know that the current Education Secretary's decision is based on a pragmatic desire for political support from parents of parochial school children and on a principled personal commitment to school choice. How should you proceed?[29]

Problems 11F and 11G raise a fundamental and frequently disputed issue: who is the client of the government lawyer? If, as many commentators insist, it is the public generally, and not any particular government agency or decision-maker, how is the public's interest to be determined?[30] These questions assume constitutional dimensions when government lawyers doubt the legality of government action or the propriety of strategies that might support it.

Problem 11F(2) involves a variation on these themes. In commenting on the church-state issue, Geoffrey Miller notes:

> One common intuition is that the government attorney should do what she considers to be right under the circumstances, and that in appropriate cases doing what is right can and should trump the attorney's duties of loyalty to her agency, the President, or even the government as a whole. Assume, for example, that [the lawyer] feels strongly that the separation of church and state is crucial to the maintenance of American values and freedoms. In this circumstance he may have an easy out by requesting reassignment to something less problematic. Yet, [the lawyer] may want to participate in order to prevent a result he perceives as dangerous and unjust. Would it be unethical for him to accept the assignment but leak the details to the press or the ACLU in hopes that the program will be politically stymied? What about working on the project but attempting to blunt its force with fine-print restrictions, thus knowingly frustrating the Secretary's policy objectives? Government attorneys have been known to engage in these tactics and more when they strongly opposed the policies of their superiors.
>
> The intuition that might justify sabotage of this type is, I think, based on the premise that government attorneys owe special ethical duties not applicable to the ordinary lawyer. They represent the "public interest." The unique nature of that representation carries with it special responsibilities. . . . Despite its surface plausibility, the notion that government attorneys represent some transcendental "public interest" is, I believe, incoherent. It is commonplace that there are as many ideas of the "public interest" as there are people who think about the subject. The lawyer may believe in the separation of church and state; his superior may believe that church-state separation is inconsistent with the nation's historical experience and present needs. If attorneys could freely sabotage the actions of their agencies out of a subjective sense of the public interest, the result would be a disorganized, inefficient bureaucracy, and a public distrustful of its own government. More fundamentally, the idea that government attorneys serve some higher purpose fails to place the attorney within a structure of democratic government.[31]

Accordingly, Miller concludes that government attorneys should not substitute their judgment for the outcome of a political process that is generally accepted as legitimate. To be sure, lawyers should refuse to assist an action that lacks any constitutional authority. However, they may defend or participate in projects that appear inconsistent with Supreme Court precedents if such projects are not contrary to any binding legal judgment and if the executive branch makes a "bona fide claim" that the Court's prior decision is incorrect.[32] Under Miller's analysis, the government lawyers in contexts like Problem 11F should defer to their superiors' judgments about the appropriate course of conduct.

Many practitioners take a similar view. As one study concluded, "most Justice Department lawyers continue to believe that most agencies, most of the time, are entitled to their day in court and to have the best said in their behalf that the legal imagination can devise, the more so because the agencies are captive clients who cannot seek representation elsewhere."[33] On this analysis, a government lawyer who attempts to further the public interest as she perceives it is "not a lawyer representing a client but a lawyer representing herself."[34]

By contrast, other lawyers argue that government counsel have obligations as public servants to "pursue justice" and to avoid assisting an action that they believe is unconstitutional. From this perspective, "where the client is the Government itself, he who represents this vague entity often becomes its conscience, bearing a heavier responsibility than usually encountered by . . . lawyers."[35]

What is your view? Neither the Code nor the Model Rules provide specific guidance, although EC 7-14 speaks generally to the issue:

> A government lawyer in a civil action . . . has the responsibility to seek justice and to develop a full and fair record, and he should not use his position or the economic power of the government to harass parties or to bring about unjust settlements or results.

Does this provision help resolve the issue facing the attorney general in Part 1 of Problem 11F? What would you have done in his position? What would EC 7-14 require on the facts in Problem 11G below?

2. Equal Protection Contexts: The Japanese-American Evacuation

PROBLEM 11G

Assume that you were in the position of Edward Ennis under the circumstances that Peter Irons describes below. What would you do?

PETER IRONS, JUSTICE AT WAR (1993). Irons' book chronicles the ethical dilemmas for attorneys defending the detention and relocation of Japanese Americans during World War II. One such dilemma involved Edward Ennis, the director of the Alien Enemy Control Unit in the Justice Department. Ennis had primary responsibility for presenting the Department's position in Hirabayashi v. United States, 320 U.S. 81 (1943), and Korematsu v. United States, 323 U.S. 214, 220 (1944).[36] Although Ennis had opposed the evacuation, he was prepared to defend the government's policy. However, during the course of his work on *Hirabayashi*, he discovered a crucial internal memorandum by staffers in the Office of Naval Intelligence. That memo, by the military unit most knowledgeable on the issue, reached conclusions that directly undercut the rationale for the military's wholesale evacuation. In particular, it concluded that the "Japanese Problem" had been magnified out of proportion, that the small number of Japanese Americans who posed potential threats were in custody or were already known and subject to apprehension, and that case-by-case determinations of dangerousness were preferable to a categorical evacuation.

Ennis believed that this report should be called to the Supreme Court's attention, and he so advised the Solicitor General, Charles Fahy.

Appealing to Fahy's sense of rectitude and his responsibility as Solicitor-General, Ennis argued that "in view of the fact that the Department of Justice is now representing the Army in the Supreme Court of the United States and is arguing that a partial, selective evacuation was impracticable, we must consider most carefully what our obligation to the Court is in view of the fact that the responsible Intelligence agency regarded a selective evacuation as not only sufficient but preferable." Ennis further noted that "one of the most difficult questions" in the Hirabayashi case "is raised by the fact that the Army did not evacuate people after any hearing or any individual determination of dangerousness, but evacuated the entire racial group." . . . On "one of the crucial points" raised in the Hirabayashi case, he noted, "the Government is forced to argue that individual selective evacuation would have been impractical and insufficient when we have positive knowledge that the only Intelligence agency responsible for advising General DeWitt gave him advice directly to the contrary." Ennis phrased his final plea to Fahy in terms that waved a warning flag before the Solicitor General: "I think we should consider very carefully whether we do not have a duty to advise the Court of the existence of the [internal] memorandum and of the fact that this represents the view of the Office of Naval Intelligence. It occurs to me that any other course of conduct might approximate the suppression of evidence." [p.204]

Ennis' position did not prevail. Rather, Arnold Raum, the author of the brief for the government in *Hirabayashi*, contended that issues of loyalty were irrelevant. In his view,

[t]he rationale behind [military] orders was "not the loyalty or disloyalty of individuals but the danger from the residence of the class as such within a vital military area." Such a judgment about the "danger" posed by Japanese Americans as a group, however, necessarily required as the "rational basis" demanded by the due process clause some reasonable estimation of loyalty within the group. In searching for such rationality, Raum retreated to speculation and supposition. Japanese Americans had been "treated as a group," he wrote, because some of them were "thought" to be dangerous. Raum did not identify those who harbored these thoughts, nor did he explain why it would be a "virtually impossible task" to determine loyalty on the basis of

hearings. . . . Rebuffed in his attempt to alert the Supreme Court . . . , Ennis gave up for the time his objection to Fahy's "suppression of evidence." As a loyal government lawyer, Ennis swallowed his doubts and added his name to the Hirabayashi brief along with those of Fahy [and] Raum. [pp.205-206]

A similar problem arose a year later in preparing the government's brief in *Korematsu*. Ennis had cause to be skeptical of certain assertions in the military's final report justifying the evacuation. At his request, the Attorney General authorized an FBI and FCC investigation of allegations regarding Japanese espionage efforts (including radio signaling) on the West Coast. Both agencies concluded that certain assertions in the report justifying evacuation were false. General DeWitt, who had authorized the report and supported the evacuation, knew of these errors.

Ennis and one of his staff members, John Burling, who was working on the *Korematsu* brief, were determined to avoid reliance on the final report in presenting the government's case.

The sole concession in Burling's [brief] to the "military necessity" claim advanced by the War Department was an admission that Army officials, in the period that preceded evacuation, had "ample ground to believe that imminent danger then existed of an attack by Japan upon the West Coast." Burling appended to this statement . . . a footnote designed to alert the Court to the Justice Department's disavowal of the DeWitt report:

> The Final Report of General DeWitt is relied on in this brief for statistics and other details concerning the actual evacuation and the events that took place subsequent thereto. The recital of the circumstances justifying the evacuation as a matter of military necessity, however, is in several respects, particularly with reference to the use of illegal radio transmitters and to shore-to-ship signaling by persons of Japanese ancestry, in conflict with information in the possession of the Department of Justice. In view of the contrariety of the reports on this matter we do not ask the Court to take judicial notice of the recital of those facts contained in the Report.

Burling's attempt to wave this red flag before the Supreme Court first encountered opposition from Solicitor General Fahy. Unwilling to disclose to the Court the existence of the FBI and FCC reports, Fahy amended the footnote to read simply that "the views of this Department" differed from those of the War Department on the contested issues. Although the change in wording seemed minor, it concealed the existence of the FBI and FCC reports that refuted DeWitt's espionage charges. Burling promptly appealed to Assistant Attorney General Herbert Wechsler in an effort to retain the footnote in its original form. A former Columbia Law School professor, Wechsler had replaced Fahy as director of the War Division over the summer and now shared supervision of the Korematsu brief with the Solicitor General. [pp.286-287]

Burling was temporarily successful, but protests from Assistant Secretary John J. McCloy in the War Department caused the Solicitor General to halt printing of the government's brief that contained the contested footnote. This, in turn, caused Ennis and Burling to urge that Wechsler take the issue directly to the Attorney General.

> "We have proved unable to cope with the military authorities on their own ground in these matters," they told Wechsler. "If we fail to act forthrightly on our own ground in the courts, the whole historical record of this matter will be as the military choose to state it. The Attorney General should not be deprived of the present, and perhaps only, chance to set the record straight." [p.288]

When Wechsler and Fahy proposed an alternative "toned down" footnote, Ennis and Burling threatened to refuse signing the brief.

> This tactic confronted Wechsler with a serious dilemma. It was likely, he recognized, that a sharp-eyed member of the Supreme Court (or one of the law clerks) would notice the omission of Ennis's and Burling's names from the brief, since both lawyers had signed the government's brief on the Hirabayashi case, and surmise that there was dissension within the Justice Department over the Korematsu case. Confronted with rebellion on the part of his subordinates, Wechsler placed a call to Ralph F. Fuchs, the lawyer on Fahy's staff who had been delegated responsibility for the final drafting and printing of the Korematsu brief, and ordered a second halt of the printing presses.
>   Ennis and Burling soon learned that their last-second tactic had failed. Wechsler promptly drafted an alternative to the footnote that Fahy had handed him earlier that morning. Designed to break the impasse with the War Department, this substitute eliminated any reference to the espionage allegations in the DeWitt report: "We have specifically recited in this brief the facts relating to the justification for the evacuation, of which we ask the Court to take judicial notice; and we rely upon the Final Report only to the extent that it relates to such facts." . . . Semantic ambiguity had replaced forthright repudiation. The final page of the brief, urging that the Supreme Court affirm Korematsu's conviction, included the names of Edward Ennis and John Burling. Institutional loyalty had prevailed over personal conscience. [pp.290-291]

In subsequent interviews reflecting on these incidents,

Ennis offered an explanation of why he and John Burling (who died in 1959) had swallowed their doubts and continued to work on the internment cases. He raised, in discussing this question, the option of resignation as an alternative to internal opposition. "I'm still wondering why Burling and I didn't just throw up our hands and quit. Why didn't we throw the whole thing up? I really believe we didn't throw it up because we didn't want to put it in the hands of Justice Department lawyers who were gung-ho for the Army's position. I think we felt that we'd just stay with it and do the best that we could, which wasn't a hell of a lot." Ennis also confessed . . . that "when I look back on it now I don't know why I didn't resign."
  Ennis had in fact talked of resigning after the showdown with McCloy in Attorney General Biddle's living room on February 17, 1942, after Biddle abandoned his opposition to evacuation. There

seems little doubt that his resignation at that point would not have affected Roosevelt's decision to sign the executive order approved at this meeting. It seems more likely, however, that had Ennis and Burling resigned in October 1944, in protest at Solicitor General Fahy's capitulation to McCloy over the disputed footnote in the Korematsu brief, such a dramatic step might well have changed the outcome of that crucial case. [pp.350-351]

How would you have handled the problems confronting Ennis and Burling in the wartime evacuation cases? Did they violate their obligations to develop a "full and fair record" (EC 7-14)? Does preparing a brief from the Solicitor General's office carry special responsibilities? Consider the view of former Solicitor General Archibald Cox, who maintained that if the office were willing to take a "somewhat disinterested and wholly candid position even when it means surrendering a victory," then its position in other cases would retain greater credibility.[37]

Does it follow that Ennis or Burling should have refused to sign the government's briefs or threatened to resign their positions? How would you analyze their dilemma under the ethical frameworks described in Chapter II (Traditions of Moral Reasoning)? Under a rights-based analysis, could you find a universal, generalizable principle that would justify Ennis' and Burling's conduct? Consider one obvious candidate: less than full candor to the Court is permissible in a case of national security. Are there problems with such a principle?

On a utilitarian analysis, is the case for disclosure any different? On one hand, it is clear that the record was inadequate to support the military's justification for the evacuation. A fuller factual record might have led to a better Supreme Court decision. Concealment ultimately damaged the credibility of all concerned: the Court, the army, the government's lawyers. Given the enormous human costs for Japanese Americans, should government lawyers have taken special care to ensure the integrity of military and judicial decision-making? Consider Sissela Bok's approach, which assesses the moral justifications for and against disclosure from the perspective of those affected by the deception. Is Ennis' and Burling's conduct defensible from that perspective?

On the other hand, how would you assess the costs of provoking a confrontation with high-level army officials during wartime and eroding their trust in government attorneys? Are you persuaded by Ennis' argument that he wanted to prevent the case from falling into the hands of more "gung-ho" pro-military lawyers? Consider Bernard Williams' observation that the rationale of "working from within" has kept many "queazy people tied to many appalling ventures for remarkably long periods."[38] Was Ennis an example?

The preceding materials pose ethical issues on two levels. One involves what moral theorists label dilemmas of "dirty hands."[39] To accomplish ethically defensible ends, it may be necessary to use ethically disagreeable means. Whether to withhold information or concede principles for the sake of larger political goals are the kinds of questions that may face any public servant. A second set of ethical issues is specific to lawyers in government service; these involve problems of identifying the client and the client's interest.

George Bernard Shaw captured the dirty hands dilemma in commenting on a Labour Party colleague who lost his seat in Parliament after refusing to compromise on an issue:

> When I think of my own unfortunate character, smirched with compromise, rotted with opportunism, mildewed by expediency . . . I do think Joe might have put up with just a speck or two on those white robes of his for the sake of the millions of poor devils who cannot afford any character at all because they have no friend in Parliament. Oh, these moral dandies, these spiritual toffs, these superior persons. Who is Joe anyhow, that he should not risk his soul occasionally like the rest of us?[40]

Some trade-offs between moral means and moral ends appear particularly necessary in government, because success is often "measured by a historian's yardstick" and undue insistence on principle can prevent publicly desirable outcomes.[41]

Although dilemmas of dirty hands do not yield simple or categorical solutions, most commentators agree on one general principle. Bernard Williams suggests that conflating Plato's question "how can the good rule" and Machiavelli's question "how to rule the world as it is" leads to cynicism unless one adjusts the question: "the good need not be pure, so long as they retain some active sense of moral costs and moral limits and [the culture] has some genuinely settled expectations of civic respectability."[42] So, for example, under circumstances like Problem 11G, decision-makers need to engage in ethical analysis along the lines described in Chapter II. Could they justify nondisclosure in such contexts under some generalizable principle? What would be the costs of a nondeceptive alternative — that is, of revealing weaknesses in the government's position? What would be the costs of not revealing such weaknesses if the truth came to light?

For lawyers, the difficulties of making such moral judgments are further complicated by questions of role. Where trade-offs between ethical principles and political expediency appear necessary, who should decide what balance to strike? When should an attorney defer to elected officials who are more directly accountable to the public? The Code of Ethics for Government Service (1958) provides that "[a]ny person in Government service should: Put loyalty to the highest moral principles and to country above loyalty to persons, party or Government department." Did Ennis and Burling adhere to this provision? Would you find it helpful in their position? Under what circumstances does a government lawyer owe direct obligations to the public that cannot be countermanded by legislative or executive directive?

3. Due Process and Double Jeopardy in First Amendment Contexts: Prosecutorial Vindictiveness in Obscenity Prosecutions

PROBLEM 11H

You are the new head of the Justice Department's General Litigation and Legal Advocacy Section. Until the late 1980s, the Department's Manual for District Attorneys provided that simultaneous prosecutions of the same defendant in multiple jurisdictions were "not favored," and required special Department approval from your section. Department officials subsequently revised the Manual to "encourage" multidistrict prosecutions in obscenity cases, and launched Project PostPorn, a series of multidistrict enforcement efforts.

Following a change in administration, you have been asked to review the Department policy on multiple prosecutions and make a recommendation to the Attorney General. What do you propose?

According to proponents, the antipornography initiative has been "one of the most successful prosecution strategies in the history of the Department of Justice."[43] By the early 1990s, the costs of defending multiple suits had caused some major distributors to cease dealing in sexually explicit materials. Their response spared the government the expense of proving the obscenity of each targeted item in the community of each recipient.[44] Since every mailing of obscene material is a separate offense, government attorneys have maintained that the strategy presents no double jeopardy problems.

Some, although not all, courts have disagreed. According to the district court for the District of Columbia, while a distributor who mails allegedly obscene material could appropriately be prosecuted by each state,

> the same may not hold true for the federal judicial system. . . . [If distributors] may be successively prosecuted by the United States in each of the 95 federal judicial districts for mailing the identical material, the rule would render the Double Jeopardy clause meaningless in obscenity cases involving mass mailings. The United States would have nearly a hundred opportunities to convince a local jury that the same sexually oriented materials are obscene, according to their contemporary community rights, and any one conviction might suffice to put the distributor out of business, if the ordeal had not already done so.

Freedberg v. United States Dept. of Justice, 703 F. Supp. 107, 110 (D.D.C. 1988) (granting a preliminary injunction enjoining multiple prosecutions).

The multiple prosecution strategy again came under scrutiny in United States v. P.H.E., 965 F.2d 848 (10th Cir. 1992). There, a distributor of adult materials moved to dismiss the indictment on grounds of vindictive prosecution. The Tenth Circuit Court of Appeals remanded the case for trial. Under its analysis, P.H.E. had met its burden of showing actual vindictiveness or a reasonable likelihood of vindictiveness. The burden therefore shifted to the government on remand to justify its decision with "legitimate, articulable, objective reasons." 965 F.2d at 860. In considering whether the government could meet that burden, the trial court was to consider whether the prosecution would have occurred but for the hostility or punitive response to P.H.E.'s exercise of legal rights.

What evidence would be relevant to that determination? If you were drafting the Justice Department guidelines on multidistrict prosecutions, how would you respond to these cases? When, if ever, should such enforcement efforts be permissible? Could they ever be a legitimate response to the enormous costs of prosecuting pornography on an item-by-item, jurisdiction-by-jurisdiction basis?

E. FREEDOM OF EXPRESSION AND ASSOCIATION

1. Group Legal Services

Group legal services plans began during the latter part of the nineteenth century.[45] Most were sponsored by organizations such as policemen's benevolent associations and railway brotherhoods. These programs sought to ensure the availability of legal assistance primarily for employment-related claims. However, until the 1960s, bar ethical restrictions on solicitation by attorneys and unauthorized practice of law by non-attorneys inhibited the growth of such plans. Until recently, the legal profession's preferred alternatives were bar programs that would refer clients to attorneys who agreed to abide by certain specified conditions.

Such referral plans have not, however, provided the same advantages to the consumer as group or prepaid legal services. Referral plans are open to all attorneys and are most popular among lawyers least busy with other work. Because such plans make no effort to screen for competence or expense, the participating lawyers are not necessarily those most likely to be attractive to consumers. By contrast, group plans can provide some control over the cost and quality of services and, in the case of some nonprofit organizations, can identify members interested in raising certain claims. So too, any prepaid system offers cost-spreading features; individuals can protect themselves from incurring substantial financial obligations in any given year through modest premiums.

Such advantages have prompted various challenges to bar ethical restrictions. In a series of cases in the 1960s, the Supreme Court extended first amendment protection for group legal services.

The first of these cases, NAACP v. Button, 371 U.S. 415 (1963), recognized the NAACP's rights of association through seeking plaintiffs and providing them with counsel for civil rights suits. Subsequent decisions in Brotherhood of R.R. Trainmen v. Virginia State Bar, 377 U.S. 1 (1964), and United Mine Workers v. Illinois State Bar Assn., 389 U.S. 217 (1967), extended *Button* to protect union practices of referring members to selected lawyers or of employing attorneys to handle members' workers' compensation claims. As the Court subsequently summarized its holdings, the "common thread" running through these decisions was that "collective activity undertaken to obtain meaningful access to the courts is a fundamental right within the protection of the First Amendment." United Transp. Union v. State Bar, 401 U.S. 576, 585 (1971).

Although these rulings established basic constitutional safeguards for group legal services, restrictions in the ABA's Code of Professional Responsibility, DR 2-103, inhibit plans that are operated by attorneys for their economic benefit and "for profit plans" that require selection of an attorney from a "closed panel" of approved participants. Those restrictions, however, have been largely abandoned or liberalized in the Model Rules (Rules 5.4, 7.3(d)), and group programs have become an increasingly important means of broadening access to legal services among middle-income consumers.[46]

The Model Rules do, however, include certain restrictions that have inhibited the growth of for-profit legal service plans. Rule 5.4 prohibits lawyers from forming partnerships with non-lawyers to engage in practicing law, and from working for any organization in which a non-lawyer has the right to direct or control the professional judgment of a lawyer. During debates over an earlier, more liberal version of this Rule, a member of the ABA House of Delegates asked if this proposed provision would allow Sears, Roebuck to open a law office. Under the terms of the proposed Rule, such an office would have been permissible if it complied with specified requirements. For example, the office would have been required to permit participating lawyers to exercise independent professional judgment on behalf of clients; to maintain client confidences; to provide competent services; to avoid conflicts of interest; and to refrain from improper solicitation, advertising, or fee-sharing arrangements. When lawyers in the House of Delegates considered competition with non-lawyer-owned organizations under these requirements, then, according to Geoffrey Hazard, "that was the end of the debate."[47]

Should it have been?

2. Lawyer Advertising

See Chapter III, Regulation of the Profession
  • Part G. Competition
     (pages 92–95)

3. Solicitation

See Chapter III, Regulation of the Profession
  • Part G. Competition
      (pages 95–100)

4. The Fair Trial/Free Press Balance

PROBLEM 11I

In 1991, William Kennedy Smith faced prosecution for raping a
Florida woman whom he had picked up in a nightclub. The alleged rape
occurred after she drove him back to the Kennedy beachfront estate
from the club where he, Senator Edward Kennedy, and another family
member had been drinking. Although the media traditionally has not
disclosed the names of rape victims, a number of newspapers and
broadcast networks identified the complainant and revealed a wide array
of unfavorable details about her life, including her mediocre high school
grades, her traffic violations, her single motherhood, her prior abortions,
her cocaine use, her mother's divorce, her alleged "wild streak," her
possible psychological disorders, and her family's reputation for social
climbing. According to widespread rumors, reporters obtained much of
this information from investigators for the defense. Most stories did not
include sources for the claims about the victim's past. Nor did early
coverage report unfavorable information concerning the defendant's
prior sexual activities.[48]

Such information did, however, subsequently emerge when the
prosecutor filed, and released to the press, a pretrial motion indicating
her intent to call three witnesses who claimed that Smith had raped or
attempted to rape them while on dates. Their testimony would be
admissible at trial only if the court found that these prior acts were so
similar to the Palm Beach charges as to indicate a common pattern and
that their probative value outweighed their prejudicial impact. Critics of
the prosecutor's action claimed that publicly releasing the document
(rather than filing it under seal) was unethical and prejudicial, particularly
since the defense counsel was under a no-comment order to refrain from
further public discussion of the case. Supporters of the prosecutor's
conduct argued that it was appropriate to counteract earlier negative
images of acquaintance rape victims in general and the Palm Beach
complainant in particular.

What is your view? How would you have handled press disclosures
if you had been the lead prosecutor or defense counsel? If you had been
the lawyer for a leading national newspaper, what would your advice
have been concerning publication of the complainant's name and
personal background?

Lawyers' first "no comment" rule, Canon 20 of the 1908 Canons of Professional Conduct, was precisely that. Statements to the press about pending or anticipated litigation were "generally to be condemned" and were not to extend beyond quotations from the record or papers on file with the court. Subsequent rules have been more permissive, a trend encouraged by litigation challenging the constitutionality of restrictive standards. The Code of Professional Responsibility, DR 7-107, provides in part:

> (B) A lawyer or law firm associated with the prosecution or defense of a criminal matter shall not, from the time of the filing of a complaint, information, or indictment, the issuance of an arrest warrant, or arrest until the commencement of the trial of disposition without trial, make or participate in making an extrajudicial statement that a reasonable person would expect to be disseminated by means of public communication and that relates to:
>> (1) The character, reputation, or prior criminal record (including arrests, indictments, or other charges of crime) of the accused.
>
> (C) DR 7-107(B) does not preclude a lawyer during such period from announcing:
>> (9) Quotations from or references to public records of the court in the case.

Rule 3.6 of the Model Rules of Professional Conduct provides in part:

> (a) A lawyer shall not make an extrajudicial statement that a reasonable person would expect to be disseminated by means of public communication if the lawyer knows or reasonably should know that it will have a substantial likelihood of materially prejudicing an adjudicative proceeding.
>
> (b) A statement referred to in paragraph (a) ordinarily is likely to have such an effect when it refers to a civil matter triable to a jury, a criminal matter, or any other proceeding that could result in incarceration, and the statement relates to:
>> (1) the character, credibility, reputation or criminal record of a party, suspect in a criminal investigation or witness, or the identity of a witness, or the expected testimony of a party or witness. . . .
>
> (c) Notwithstanding paragraphs (a) and (b)(1), a lawyer involved in the investigation or litigation of a matter may state without elaboration:
>> (1) the general nature of the claim or defense;
>> (2) the information contained in a public record. . . .

Some lower courts, following the 1978 ABA Fair Trial-Free Press Standards, hold that a lawyer cannot be punished for statements unless they present a "serious and imminent threat" of interference with the "fair administration of justice."

These codified rules and standards seek to accommodate competing values. On one hand, litigants have rights to a fair trial untainted by prejudicial publicity. Participants in certain categories of cases such as rape and sexual abuse also have interests in keeping their identities or prior intimate relationships confidential. On the other hand, individuals subject to possibly false accusations have interests in clearing their names, and the public in general has a right to "guard against the miscarriage of justice by subjecting the legal process to extensive public scrutiny and criticism."[49] How would you balance these competing values in light of the Supreme Court's decision in Gentile v. State Bar of Nevada?

GENTILE v. STATE BAR OF NEVADA, 501 U.S. 1030 (1991). This case gave rise to the Supreme Court's first decision on the constitutionality of bar ethical restrictions on trial comment. A divided Court struck down part of Nevada's rules governing public statements. Rule 177(1) prohibited a lawyer from making extrajudicial statements to the press that he knew or reasonably should have known would have a "substantial likelihood of materially prejudicing" an adjudicative proceeding. Rule 177(2) listed statements that would "ordinarily" be prejudicial. Rule 177(3) provided that "[n]otwithstanding subsection 1 and [2], a lawyer involved in the investigation or litigation of a matter may state without elaboration . . . the general nature of the claim or defense."

The case arose from a brief press statement petitioner Gentile made six months before the trial of his client, Grady Sanders. Sanders faced prosecution for stealing drugs and travelers' checks. In the statement at issue, Gentile claimed:

> When this case goes to trial, and as it develops, you're going to see that the evidence will prove not only that Grady Sanders is an innocent person and had nothing to do with any of the charges that are being leveled against him, but that the person that was in the most direct position to have stolen the drugs and money, the American Express Travelers' checks, is Detective Steve Scholl. . . . And I have to say that I feel that Grady Sanders is being used as a scapegoat to try to cover up for what has to be obvious to people at Las Vegas Metropolitan Police Department and at the District Attorney's office.

Although Gentile declined to provide further details, the Nevada state bar reprimanded him and the state supreme court affirmed.

The United States Supreme Court reversed. Chief Justice Rehnquist and Justice Kennedy each wrote opinions in which four Justices joined; Justice O'Connor as the swing vote joined part of both opinions. In the portion of the Chief Justice's opinion commanding a majority (White, Scalia, Souter, and O'Connor), the Court held that states could permissibly restrict attorney speech that posed a "substantial likelihood of material prejudice"; a more rigorous "clear and present danger test" was not constitutionally required. In the majority's view:

> Because lawyers have special access to information through discovery and client communications, their extrajudicial statements pose a threat to the fairness of a pending proceeding since lawyers' statements are likely to be received as especially authoritative. . . . We

agree with the majority of the States that the "substantial likelihood of material prejudice" standard constitutes a constitutionally permissible balance between the First Amendment rights of attorneys in pending cases and the state's interest in fair trials. . . .

The "substantial likelihood" test embodied in Rule 177 is constitutional under this analysis, for it is designed to protect the integrity and fairness of a state's judicial system, and it imposes only narrow and necessary limitations on lawyers' speech. . . . Few, if any, interests under the Constitution are more fundamental than the right to a fair trial by "impartial" jurors, and an outcome affected by extrajudicial statements would violate that fundamental right. . . . Even if a fair trial can ultimately be ensured through voir dire, change of venue, or some other device, these measures entail serious costs to the system. Extensive voir dire may not be able to filter out all of the effects of pretrial publicity, and with increasingly widespread media coverage of criminal trials, a change of venue may not suffice to undo the effects of statements such as those made by petitioner. The State has a substantial interest in preventing officers of the court, such as lawyers, from imposing such costs on the judicial system and on the litigants.

The restraint on speech is narrowly tailored to achieve those objectives. The regulation of attorneys' speech is limited — it applies only to speech that is substantially likely to have a materially prejudicial effect; it is neutral as to points of view, applying equally to all attorneys participating in a pending case; and it merely postpones the attorney's comments until after the trial. . . .

However, a majority of the Court (Justice Kennedy, joined by Blackmun, Marshall, Stevens, and O'Connor) found that subsection 3 of the Rule rendered it void for vagueness. By permitting a lawyer to state "without elaboration" the "general nature of the claim or defense," Nevada had created a "safe harbor" provision and had therefore provided insufficient notice of prohibited conduct.

In the dissenting portion of his opinion not joined by Justice O'Connor, Justice Rehnquist disagreed. He found Rule 177 constitutional as applied because, in his view, petitioner had ample notice that the statement was improper. Not only were Gentile's claims inflammatory; he had also "called the press conference for the express purpose of influencing the venue. It is difficult to believe that he went to such trouble, and took such a risk, if there was no substantial likelihood that he would succeed."

Which of these opinions do you find most persuasive? Consider the majority's assertion that the Rule "merely postpones the attorney's comment until after the trial." Does that statement adequately acknowledge the interests of the accused before and during trial? Critics of the Court's approach argue that this is the period when the public's interest is most intense and when defendants and their families are suffering considerable injury from the stigma of criminal charges. The delay before vindication can be years; even then, an acquittal or reversal on appeal may be insufficient to counter specific prejudicial comments.[50]

In noting that "lawyers' statements are likely to be received as especially authoritative," the *Gentile* majority does not distinguish between prosecutors' and defense attorneys' statements. Should it? Are prosecutors' comments likely to have greater credibility with the public, given prevailing attitudes toward accused criminals?

If you were a member of the Nevada state bar's governing body, how would you respond to the Court's ruling in *Gentile*? Would you support rules modeled on the District of Columbia approach that Monroe Freedman endorses below?

MONROE FREEDMAN, MUZZLING TRIAL PUBLICITY: NEW RULE NEEDED

Legal Times, Apr. 5, 1993, p.24*

Even in the wake of *Gentile*, though, there's hardly a need for bar groups to rush to write a new rule governing trial publicity. For one thing, the old one was almost never enforced. . . .

Hal Lieberman, chief counsel to the disciplinary committee for New York's First Judicial Department, gives three reasons why the rule hasn't been enforced. First, Lieberman says, are the thorny First Amendment problems of enforcing restrictions on speech. Second, given the priorities of an underfunded office, he has more serious matters (like theft of client funds) that take precedence. And third, it is virtually impossible to prosecute a case of trial publicity successfully [given the difficulties of proving substantial likelihood of material prejudice]. . . .

Another problem with MR 3.6 and DR 7-107 is that they expressly permit trial publicity based upon information in a public record. Prosecutors have been far ahead of defense lawyers in using this exception effectively to nullify the rule. . . . Prosecutors who want to hold dramatic press conferences damning the accused have developed the "speaking indictment," in which every conceivably prejudicial detail is laid out. One defendant said he had never known that his nickname was "The Snake" until he saw it stated as an alias in an indictment,and then heard the prosecutor repeatedly calling him that on television.

Defense lawyers have missed the opportunity to create their own "public record" to avoid the trial-publicity rule. For example, just about everything that Dominic Gentile said in his press conference — and things he carefully avoided saying — could have been made a public record in a bail application or in a motion in limine.

*Monroe Freedman is the Lichtenstein Distinguished Professor of Legal Ethics at Hofstra University. This issue is discussed at greater length in his book, Understanding Lawyers' Ethics (Matthew Bender 1990).

Then, as prosecutors have been doing for years, Gentile could have prejudiced the trial with impunity.

But the problem, alas, has never been prejudice to the trial. Unfortunately, the Supreme Court has been unable to find prejudice, even in cases of "pervasive, adverse" publicity against an accused that has been "instigated" and "actively promoted" by the prosecution. . . . Recently, the Court found no prejudice in a capital-murder case where the publicity included numerous references to inflammatory and inadmissible evidence. Mu'Min v. Virginia, 111 S. Ct. 1899 (1991).

SILENCE DURING TRIAL

Should there, then, be no rule at all restricting trial publicity? I think there should, in fact, be two of them, based on Rules 3.6 and 3.8(f) of the D.C. Rules of Professional Conduct.

The District's Rule 3.6 says: "A lawyer engaged in a case being tried to a judge or jury shall not make an extrajudicial statement that a reasonable person would expect to be disseminated by means of mass public communication if the lawyer knows or reasonably should know that the statement will create a serious and imminent threat to the impartiality of the judge or jury." . . . [It] is reprehensible for a lawyer during trial to dodge a judge's ruling by broadcasting inadmissible evidence to jurors through the news media. Freedom of speech is adequately protected by the "serious and imminent threat" standard and by limiting the rule to the period when the case is "being tried." Before trial, however, the defendant should be free to respond publicly to the public charges made in the indictment or information — charges that, in any other context, would be actionable defamation.

Even better as a model is the version of Rule 3.6 that was unanimously approved by the Jordan Committee (which drafted the D.C. rules) and by the board of governors of the D.C. Bar. In that version, only jury trials (and not bench trials) were covered. The bar's comment, quoting Craig v. Harney, 331 U.S. 367 (1947), explained that judges need not be protected from trial publicity because they are people of "fortitude, able to thrive in a hardy climate." But the D.C. Court of Appeals (which lays claim to knowing more than the bar about the mettle of judges) rewrote the rule to include bench trials as well.

PROSECUTORIAL RESTRAINT

In addition, the District has a special rule governing publicity by prosecutors. Rule 3.8(f) recognizes that the real prejudice of extrajudicial comment, an often irreparable one, is to the defendant's reputation. That means that the prosecutor abuses her governmental powers when she gratuitously imposes the punishment of public condemnation upon the defendant without the due process of a trial.

Thus, Rule 3.8(f) provides: "Except for statements which are necessary to inform the public of the nature and extent of the prosecutor's action and which serve a legitimate law enforcement purpose, [the prosecutor shall not] make extrajudicial comments which serve to heighten condemnation of the accused."

The comment makes it clear, however, that the prosecutor is free to respond to any extrajudicial allegations by the defense of unprofessional or unlawful conduct on the part of the prosecutor's office.

How would you evaluate the issue facing the prosecutor in Problem 11I? Did release of the motions describing prior rape allegations pose a substantial likelihood of material prejudice? Or was the disclosure consistent with government counsel's general obligation to inform the public and to "do justice"? Alan Dershowitz, in commenting on the prosecutor's conduct, argued that even if the judge excluded testimony about the prior allegations, public release of the motion would irrevocably prejudice the defendant's interests:

> [I]f jurors in the Smith case learn of the three previous alleged crimes, they will no longer think he is a nice boy. They will think that maybe one woman or even two could be overreacting, mistaken or on a vendetta. But all four? No way! This guy is a rapist, the jurors will think, even if the evidence is less than entirely convincing. They will see the Florida woman as someone who finally had the courage to blow the whistle on Mr. Smith.
>
> Even if Judge Lupo eventually rules the evidence inadmissible . . . it is likely to have a pervasive influence on the jury as well as on Mr. Smith's ongoing trial in the court of public opinion. This kind of evidence is called "skunk evidence" by criminal lawyers because even if you get rid of the skunk, the smell remains.[51]

By contrast, defenders of the prosecutor's conduct claimed that her actions ensured a more accurate public understanding the rationale for prosecuting Smith.

How would you have resolved the issue? Is your opinion affected by the ultimate outcome in the case? The judge excluded evidence of Smith's prior sexual conduct, and the jury acquitted despite the prosecutor's media disclosures. Would your decision be influenced by social science evidence? Research findings are mixed. Some studies suggest that exposure to adverse pretrial publicity may predispose jurors to convict. However, even in those cases, jurors often appear able to base their verdict on evidence presented in court.[52]

Do statements concerning judicial performance stand on any different constitutional footing? Disciplinary Rule 8-102(B) prohibits lawyers from knowingly making false accusations against judges and judicial candidates. Model Rule 8.2 provides that a lawyer "shall not make a statement that the lawyer knows to be false or with reckless disregard as to its truth or falsity concerning the qualifications or integrity of a judge [or candidate for judicial office]." Both DR 2-102 and Model Rule 8.4 prohibit lawyers from engaging in conduct "prejudicial to the administration of justice." Consider whether any of the following examples violate those rules.

PROBLEM 11J

Which of the following comments should be subject to sanctions? Should courts attempt to determine the factual basis for the claims?

1. "The judge's decision is overt racism. He clearly regards it as his special mission and perhaps his last mission to keep the defendants incarcerated."[53]

2. "The judge has a penchant for sanctioning Jewish lawyers: me, David Kenner and Hugh Manes. I find this to be evidence of anti-Semitism."[54]

3. "The judge sitting on this bench is a danger to the people of the city."[55]

4. "What the judge did today was outrageous. It was vindictive, it was petty, it was uncalled for. . . . I am sick and tired of this judge not treating the prosecution fairly. The defense gets away with murder; we get hit. What the judge did today was outrageous." The judge's ruling was "outrageous, specious, and unspeakable."[56]

5. "The judge's decision to vacate the death penalty was the most shocking and outrageous decision in the history of the Supreme Court of this State. Faced with the almost insurmountable task of reacquiring witnesses after some six or seven years and retrying the case . . . I feel that it's an example of judicial legislation at its very worst."[57]

6. The state's appellate judges are "whores who become madames. I would like to [be a judge]. . . . But the only way you can get it is to be in politics or buy it—and I don't even know the going price."[58]

7. The jury selection process is a "legalized lynching." Given the judge's racial insensitivity, unless he recuses himself, this will be a "kangaroo court."[59]

F.   ACCESS TO THE LEGAL PROFESSION: ADMISSION TO THE BAR

See Chapter III, Regulation of the Profession
- Admission to the Bar
    - Competence
        (pages 60–61)

- Character
        (pages 61–65)

As Chapter III indicated, the Supreme Court has established constitutional safeguards concerning admission to the bar; any criteria for exclusion must bear a "rational connection with the applicant's fitness or capacity to practice law." Schware v. Board of Bar Examiners, 353 U.S. 232, 239 (1957). In applying that standard, the Court has upheld denial of applicants who failed to supply information regarding their membership in the Communist Party, In re Anastaplo, 366 U.S. 82 (1961); failed to take an oath promising to join the state militia in times of war, In re Summers, 325 U.S. 561 (1945); or refused to take an oath to uphold the Constitution, Law Students Civil Rights Research Council v. Wadmond, 401 U.S. 154 (1971). By contrast, the Court also has overturned state decisions to exclude applicants who knowingly joined organizations advocating violent overthrow of the government, finding that "a state may not inquire about a man's views or associations solely for the purpose of withholding a right or benefit because of what he believes." Baird v. State Bar, 401 U.S. 1, 7 (1971) (plurality opinion). See also In re Stolar, 401 U.S. 23 (1971).

Consider the materials on character requirements in Part C of Chapter III (Regulation of the Profession), at page 61. Should any recent activity reflecting disrespect for law be grounds for scrutiny? How would you vote in Problem 3C? How would you assess the constitutionality of decisions delaying or excluding applicants on the following grounds:

1. Committing private noncommercial sexual acts with a consenting adult in a jurisdiction that criminalizes such acts.[60]
2. Misrepresenting personal views and intentions regarding military service to ROTC officials in order to avoid being drafted during the Vietnam war.
3. Refusing to authorize the release of psychological treatment records for problems that a therapist certifies are unrelated to professional performance.[61]
4. Failing to disclose expunged convictions.[62]
5. Failing to pay full child support.[63]

G.   ACCESS TO LEGAL SERVICES AND THE LEGAL SYSTEM

As the Supreme Court has long recognized, "the right to sue and defend . . . in an organized society . . . is the right conservative of all other rights, and lies at the foundation of orderly government."

Chambers v. Baltimore & Ohio R.R., 277 U.S. 142, 148 (1907). That right, the Court has also noted, "would in many cases be of little avail if it did not also comprehend the right to be heard by counsel." Powell v. Alabama, 287 U.S. 45, 68-69 (1932). Thus, access to legal assistance and to the legal system are often related and rest on several constitutional provisions: the sixth amendment guarantee of effective assistance of counsel for criminal defendants; the fifth and fourteenth amendments' due process clause; the fourteenth amendment's equal protection clause; and the first amendment's protection for freedom of speech.

1. Rights to Counsel in Criminal Cases

At the time of the American Revolution, England prohibited defendants in ordinary felony prosecutions from having counsel at their trials. The framers of the sixth amendment sought to prevent any such prohibition in federal cases; 12 of the original 13 states also eliminated it in their courts.

The expansion of constitutional guarantees from permitting to requiring counsel in criminal cases has occurred gradually over the last half-century. In 1938, the Court interpreted the sixth amendment to mandate counsel for indigent defendants in federal criminal cases. Johnson v. Zerbst, 304 U.S. 458 (1938). Around the same time, the Supreme Court held that a state's failure to provide adequate legal assistance could violate the due process clause under certain circumstances. Powell v. Alabama, 287 U.S. 45, 68-69 (1932) (reversing conviction of indigent black Scottsboro youths charged with raping white women). Subsequent decisions applied a standard of "fundamental fairness" to determine if counsel was necessary. Betts v. Brady, 316 U.S. 455 (1942). Relevant considerations were whether the proceedings were complicated, the penalties were severe, or the defendants were particularly ill-equipped to represent themselves due to youth, illiteracy, or unfamiliarity with the English language. Id. at 462.

Finally in 1963, in response to a handwritten in forma pauperis petition from a jailed defendant, the Supreme Court held that an indigent defendant in a state felony proceeding was entitled to an attorney. As Gideon v. Wainwright, 372 U.S. 335, 344 (1963), acknowledged, the ideal of ensuring that "every defendant stands equal before the law . . . cannot be realized if the poor man charged with a crime has to face his accusers without a lawyer to assist him." Id.

The Court subsequently extended the guarantee of court-appointed counsel to juveniles, In re Gault, 387 U.S. 1 (1967), and to misdemeanor defendants threatened with incarceration, Argersinger v. Hamlin, 407 U.S. 25 (1972). In other proceedings involving the possibility of imprisonment, such as probation revocation hearings, the Court left decisions about appointment of counsel to be made on a case-by-case basis. Gagnon v. Scarpelli, 411 U.S. 778 (1973).

A related series of equal protection decisions evolved in similar fashion. In Griffin v. Illinois, 351 U.S. 12 (1956), the Court required states to provide a free trial transcript to indigents appealing their criminal convictions; there was, as Justice Black noted, no "rational relationship" between a defendant's guilt and ability to pay. Similarly, in Douglas v. California, 372 U.S. 353 (1963), the Court also required appointment of counsel for indigents appealing by right from a criminal conviction. However, in Ross v. Moffitt, 417 U.S. 600 (1974), the Court found no constitutionally protected right to counsel's assistance in optional criminal appeals in federal court, and in Pennsylvania v. Finley, 481 U.S. 551 (1987), it extended that reasoning to post-conviction proceedings in state court. Under the *Ross* majority's analysis, the government's duty was not to "duplicate the legal arsenal that may be privately retained by a criminal defendant [but] only to assure the indigent defendant an adequate opportunity to press his claims fairly." 417 U.S. at 616. Consider how well states are discharging that duty in light of the materials on effective assistance of counsel in Chapter XIV (Criminal Law and Procedure) at pages 610–621.

2. Access to the Courts in Civil Cases

The Court has recognized no corresponding rights to legal assistance in civil matters except under highly limited circumstances. However, certain other restrictions on access have not survived scrutiny. In Boddie v. Connecticut, 401 U.S. 371 (1971), the Court struck down filing fees for indigents in divorce cases on the ground that such fees unduly restricted access to the legal system. However, subsequent decisions upholding filing fees for bankruptcy proceedings and welfare appeals distinguished *Boddie* as applicable only to circumstances where fundamental interests were at issue and where judicial procedures offered the only means of resolving disputes over those interests. United States v. Kras, 409 U.S. 434 (1973); Ortwein v. Schwab, 410 U.S. 656 (1973).

The Court again qualified *Boddie*'s logic in Lassiter v. Department of Social Services, 452 U.S. 18 (1981). There, a woman imprisoned for second-degree murder lost parental rights to her 3-year-old son after a hearing at which she lacked assistance of counsel. Although the case implicated a fundamental interest and the state held a monopoly over procedures for resolving the issue, a majority of Justices concluded that a court-appointed lawyer was not necessarily required. Applying the due process standards of Mathews v. Eldridge, 424 U.S. 319, 335 (1976), and Gagnon v. Scarpelli, 411 U.S. 778 (1973), the Court held that decisions about whether to provide counsel in the absence of a "potential deprivation of physical liberty" should depend on evaluation of three factors: the private interest at stake, the government's interest, and the risk that lack of counsel at the civil hearing would result in an erroneous decision. 452 U.S. at 26-27, 31. Under those standards, a majority of Justices found no reversible error in *Lassiter* because the assistance of counsel would not have made a "determinable difference." Given the state's strong factual case and the absence of "troublesome" issues of law, the failure to provide a lawyer did not make the procedure "fundamentally unfair." 452 U.S. at 32, 33. By contrast, in Little v. Streater, 452 U.S. 1 (1981), the Court held that due process required the state to subsidize a blood test for an indigent defendant in a paternity action. Because the proceeding was quasi-criminal, no alternative forum was available, and the interests at issue were of constitutional significance, governmental assistance was necessary.

Are you persuaded by the Court's analysis in these cases? If not, what alternative framework would you propose?

3. Access Decisions Reconsidered

Critics have challenged decisions concerning legal access on several grounds. One line of criticism charges courts with failing to enforce their own principles. As Chapter XIV (Criminal Law and Procedure) suggests, the inadequate resources for criminal defense counsel undercut the ideals that constitutional decision-making has embraced. Under current plea-bargaining pressures, the vast majority of criminal defendants have "access" to courts or counsel only in the most formalistic sense.

A related argument is that the results of the Court's decisions in civil cases square poorly with its underlying theories. Some civil proceedings, such as those in *Lassiter*, implicate interests at least as significant as those at issue in many misdemeanor criminal proceedings where counsel is required. Accordingly, commentators often have argued that minimal legal assistance for indigents in civil cases is itself a fundamental right. On this reasoning, access to counsel is necessary for access to the legal system, access to the legal system is necessary to realize equality before the law, and equality before the law is necessary to the legitimacy of our form of government.[64] Frank Michelman, in a celebrated article, has drawn parallels between voting and litigating: both are "preservative of all rights"; both provide an "orderly method of resolving disputes" that prevent resort to force; and both give legitimacy to the state's coercive power.[65]

These arguments for rights to counsel in civil cases have met resistance on both practical and theoretical grounds. As a threshold matter, how could such rights be limited? If money were no object, what would deter parties from pursuing trivial claims and inflicting unwarranted costs, not only on the state but also on innocent opponents? In response to such concerns, commentators have noted that a number of European countries have recognized rights to legal assistance that are limited through screening mechanisms and restrictions on the fees recoverable by subsidized counsel.[66] The experience of civil legal aid programs in the United States also suggests strategies for screening cases and allocating resources.

A more fundamental concern involves the magnitude of assistance necessary to assure truly effective representation in civil matters. Recent studies estimate that well over three-quarters of the needs of low-income households remain unmet.[67] Moreover, these studies have obvious limitations. They measure only reported individual needs and omit claims that parties don't recognize or that reflect common problems such as environmental risks or inequitable educational financing.

Can you imagine any constitutional or legislative entitlement to assistance that could address needs of this dimension? Do any limiting principles suggest themselves? Of all the unmet needs of poor people, is it clear that access to lawyers should have priority?

Some critics also challenge arguments for a right to counsel because such arguments often assume that what people need is more of the same: more access to law, lawyers, and formal legal proceedings. An alternative approach would be to reduce the need for legal intervention and assistance. Plain English statutes, no-fault insurance schemes, simplified divorce and probate proceedings, increased alternative dispute resolution opportunities, and improved employee and consumer grievance procedures are representative illustrations. So too, greater reliance could be placed on less costly service providers than lawyers, including paralegals, hotlines, routine form-processing services, citizens' advice bureaus, courthouse ombudsmen for pro se litigants, and so forth.[68] Which of these approaches strike you as most promising? What would make them politically realistic?

4. Mandatory Pro Bono Representation

Courts' authority to require that lawyers provide uncompensated representation for indigents has been a matter of considerable historical as well as contemporary dispute. According to Thomas Cooley, a nineteenth-century constitutional authority, "[n]o one is at liberty to decline such [a pro bono] appointment and it is to be hoped that few would be disposed to do so."[69] Other authorities disagreed, and comparable disputes in recent years often have resulted in constitutional challenges.[70]

The Supreme Court has never ruled directly on the scope of judicial authority to compel uncompensated assistance. However, in dicta and in one summary dismissal, the Court approved the exercise of such authority in criminal cases. According to Powell v. Alabama, 287 U.S. 45, 73 (1932), "[a]ttorneys are officers of the court, and are bound to render service when required by such an appointment." In Sparks v. Parker, 368 So. 2d 528 (Ala. 1979), the Alabama Supreme Court upheld an uncompensated assignment system for indigent criminal defense, and the Supreme Court summarily dismissed an appeal. 444 U.S. 803 (1979). See also Barnard v. Thorstenn, 489 U.S. 546 (1989) (implicitly acknowledging courts' appointment power in the context of distinctions between resident and nonresident attorneys). In civil cases, since the courts have found no right of counsel except under narrow circumstances, the scope of judicial appointment powers is less clear. The Supreme Court reserved decision on the issue in one case involving interpretation of federal statutory authority. Mallard v. United States District Court for Southern District of Iowa, 490 U.S. 296 (1989).

In the absence of explicit Supreme Court holdings, lawyers have challenged mandatory pro bono appointments on two primary grounds. Such appointments are alleged to impose involuntary servitude in violation of the thirteenth amendment and to be unjustified takings in violation of the fifth amendment. Neither claim has commanded substantial support.

A well-established line of precedent holds that thirteenth amendment prohibitions extend only to physical restraint or threat of legal confinement; they do not apply if the individual may choose freedom at the cost of economic losses. Since refusal to accept appointments can result in disciplinary sanctions other than incarceration, courts generally have rejected involuntary servitude challenges. Family Division of Trial Lawyers v. Moultrie, 725 F.2d 695 (D.C. Cir. 1984); Stephan v. Smith, 747 P.2d 816 (Kan. 1987); Amendments to Rules Regulating the Florida Bar, Rules 1-3(a) (Dec. 13, 1990).

Most courts also have dismissed objections based on the takings clause. Their reasoning is that "[t]he Fifth Amendment does not require that the Government pay for the performance of a public duty if it is already owed." Hurtado v. United States, 410 U.S. 578, 588 (1973). According to United States v. Dillon, 346 F.2d 633 (9th Cir. 1965), cert. denied, 382 U.S. 978 (1966), a frequently cited federal appellate decision:

> An applicant for admission to practice law may justly be deemed to be aware of the traditions of the profession which he is joining, and to know that one of these traditions is that a lawyer is an officer of the court obligated to represent indigents for little or no compensation upon court order. Thus, the lawyer has consented to, and assumed, this obligation.

Id. at 635. Some lower courts agree, at least as long as the required amount of service is not unreasonable. *Moultrie*, 725 F.2d at 704-710. Other decisions have questioned the historical basis for such claims about the bar's pro bono traditions.[71]

Commentators' response to this line of cases has been mixed. Critics have objected to the analysis of cases like *Dillon*, which seems to permit the state to enlarge its authority over attorneys simply by providing notice of the conditions attaching to legal practice. Other commentators have objected to the inequalities and inefficiencies of mandatory appointment systems. As Charles Wolfram has noted, such systems tend disproportionately to draft lawyers who practice in areas where services are most needed, such as criminal and family law. Some of these lawyers are already providing assistance to the poor, and they are likely to be among the least well-compensated members of the bar.[72] Yet if the appointment system sweeps more broadly and compels service from all lawyers, then obvious problems of cost-effectiveness arise. To have corporate lawyers dabble in criminal representation may result in unduly expensive, incompetent assistance and relieve the government from making more adequate provision for indigent defense.

Other commentators, while agreeing with the need for greater legal aid subsidies, believe that lawyers also have a special professional obligation to offer some pro bono service, given their exclusive entitlement to legal practice. To these commentators, thirteenth amendment challenges are particularly problematic:

> It is surprising — surprising is a polite word — to hear some of the most wealthy, unregulated, and successful entrepreneurs in the modern economic world invoke the amendment that abolished slavery to justify their refusal to provide a little legal help to those, who in today's society, are most like the freed slaves.[73]

From this perspective, lawyers appear hypocritical when they claim special status as professionals but disavow any special responsibilities accompanying that status. According to Stephen Gillers, "we'd rather wave the flag of professionalism, and insist that everyone else salute it, than dig into our pockets and help realize the promise of equal access to justice as our institutional responsibility."[74]

What is your view? Consider the arguments for pro bono service set forth in Chapter II (Traditions of Moral Reasoning) at pages 25–27. How do these arguments affect your assessment of the constitutional claims at issue?

Endnotes

1. ABA Section of Individual Rights and Responsibilities, Recommendation to the House of Delegates (Feb. 1990); Monica Bay, ABA: Neutral on Abortion, The Recorder, Aug. 9, 1990, at 1.

2. It was not until 1981 that a woman sat on the ABA Board of Governors and not until 1991 that women reached 10 percent of the House of Delegates. Marilyn Loftus, Making a Difference: Women on the Bench, 12 Women's Rts. L. Rep. 255, 267 (1991).

3. Mark Curriden, ABA Leadership Votes to Back Abortion Rights: Bush May Stop Seeking Group's Advice on Judges, The Atlanta Constitution, Aug. 12, 1992, at A2; Jenifer Warren, Bar Association Renews Fight on Abortion, L.A. Times, Aug. 11, 1992, at A3.

4. Curriden, supra note 3, at A2.

5. Theodore Olson, It's Politics as Usual at the ABA, Wall St. J., July 30, 1997, at A15.

6. Organizations included the National Bar Association, the National Association for Equal Opportunity in Higher Education, the Congressional Black Caucus, the National Alumni Association, the National Conference of Black Lawyers, and Alcorn State University.

7. The Supreme Court, 1991 Term, Desegregation of Public Systems of Higher Education, 106 Harv. L. Rev. 236 (1992).

8. See Kevin Brown, Has the Supreme Court Allowed the Cure for De Jure Segregation to Replicate the Disease?, 78 Cornell L. Rev. 1 (1992).

9. Southern Education Foundation, Redeeming the American Promise (1995).

10. Id.; Peter Applegome, Epilogue to Integration Fight: Blacks Favor Own Colleges, N.Y. Times, May 19, 1991, at A1. See generally Steven A. Holmes, Look Who's Saying Separate Is Equal, N.Y. Times, Oct. 1, 1995, at E5.

11. The analogous proposed federal legislation is the Women's Equal Opportunity Act, H.R. 1149, 102d Cong., 1st Sess., tit. II, subtit. C (1991).

12. Tamer Lewin, Furor on Exhibit at Law School Splits Feminists, N.Y. Times, Nov. 13, 1992, at B16 (quoting Catherine MacKinnon).

13. Id. (quoting Marjorie Heins, director of the Art Censorship Program at the ACLU in New York).

14. Ken Myers, Porn Fight, Natl. L.J., Dec. 14, 1992, at 4 (quoting Marjorie Heins).

15. For an overview, see Deborah L. Rhode, Speaking of Sex 129–139 (1997).

16. Ellen Willis, Feminism, Moralism, and Pornography, in Powers of Desire: The Politics of Sexuality 460, 462 (Ann Snitow, Christine Stansell & Sharon Thompson eds., 1983); Pleasure and Danger: Exploring Female Sexuality (Carole S. Vance ed., 1984); Robin West, The Feminist Conservative Antipornography Alliance and the 1986 Attorney General's Commission on Pornography Report, 1987 Am. B. Fed. Res. J. 681.

17. Willis, supra note 16, at 462.

18. Lisa Duggan, Censorship in the Name of Feminism, The Village Voice, Oct. 16, 1984, at 11.

19. Nan D. Hunter & Sylvia Law, Brief Amici Curiae of Feminist Censorship Taskforce et al.: *American Booksellers Association v. Hudnut*, reprinted in 21 U. Mich. J.L. Ref. 69 (1987).

20. Catherine MacKinnon, quoted in Paul Brest & Amy Vandenberg, Politics, Feminism, and the Constitution: The AntiPornography Movement in Minneapolis, 39 Stan. L. Rev. 611, 623 (1987).

21. Catherine MacKinnon, Feminism Unmodified 146 (1989).

22. Phyllis Schlafly, The Power of the Positive Woman 153, 158 (1977).

23. These facts are adapted from the account of the lawyer in the case. Sarah Wellington, A Question of Choice 50-69 (1992).

24. Norma McCorvey, I Am Roe 127 (1994). For a critical review of Weddington's conduct, see Kevin C. McMunigal, Of Causes and Clients: Two Tales of *Roe v. Wade*, 47 Hast. L.J. 779 (1996).

25. McMunigal, supra note 24, at 806.

26. Id.

27. Clifford D. May, A Dispute Arises on Silent Period Voted in Trenton, N.Y. Times, Dec. 20, 1982, at B1 (quoting legislators).

28. See Clerk of Superior Court v. Treasurer, 437 N.E.2d 158, 163-164 (Mass. 1982).

29. This fact situation is from Geoffrey P. Miller, Government Lawyers' Ethics in a System of Checks and Balances, 54 U. Chi. L. Rev. 1293 (1987).

30. Jack B. Weinstein & Gay A. Crosthweit, Some Reflections on Conflicts Between Government Attorneys and Clients, 1 Touro L. Rev. 1 (1985); William Josephson & Russell Pearce, To Whom Does the Government Lawyer Owe the Duty of Loyalty When Clients Are in Conflict?, 29 How. L.J. 539 (1986); Catharine J. Lanctot, The Duty of Zealous Advocacy and the Ethics of the Federal Government Lawyer: The Three Hardest Questions, 64 S. Cal. L. Rev. 951 (1991).

31. Miller, supra note 29, at 1294-1295.

32. Id. at 1295.

33. Donald Horowitz, The Jurocracy: Government, Agency Programs and Judicial Decisions 21 (1977). See also Roger Cramton, The Lawyer as Whistleblower: Confidentiality and Government Lawyer, 5 Geo. J. Legal Ethics 291, 301 (1991).

34. Josephson & Pearce, supra note 30, at 565.

35. Judge Charles Fahy, Special Ethical Problems of Counsel for the Government, 33 Fed. B.J. 331, 333-334 (1974); accord Weinstein & Crosthweit, supra note 30. See also Lanctot, supra note 30.

36. *Hirabayashi* upheld the validity of curfews on Japanese Americans in selected areas, and *Korematsu* upheld the validity of the evacuations.

37. Lincoln Caplan, The Tenth Justice: The Solicitor General and the Rule of Law 10 (1987).

38. Bernard Williams, Politics and Moral Character, in Public and Private Morality 58 (Stuart Hampshire et al. eds., 1978).

39. The phrase comes from Jean-Paul Sartre's play, Dirty Hands, in No Exit and Three Other Plays 224 (Lionel Abel trans., 1956), where the protagonist, a Communist leader, notes, "I have dirty hands right up to the elbow. . . . Do you think you can govern innocently?" Michael Walzer, Political Action: The Problem of Dirty Hands, 2 Phil. & Public Aff. 160, 168 (1973).

40. Bernard Shaw, quoted in John Rohr, Ethics for Bureaucrats 8-9 (1978), and Stephen K. Bailey, Ethics and the Politician 6 (1960).

41. Stuart Hampshire, Public and Private Morality, in Public and Private Morality, supra note 38, at 50.

42. Williams, supra note 38, at 69.

43. Jim McGee, U.S. Crusade Against Pornography Tests the Limits of Fairness, Wash. Post, Jan. 11, 1993 (quoting Brent Ward, former U.S. attorney).

44. Id.

45. Group legal services include any type of plan by which a group makes legal assistance available to its members. Some plans involve prepayment (i.e., insurance) programs under which premiums are paid by individuals or third parties, such as employers, in order to cover future services. Other group plans do not involve prepayment but instead provide referrals to cooperating attorneys or employ lawyers to handle members' claims.

46. By the close of the 1980s, over 15 million Americans had some form of group legal services coverage. See Deborah L. Rhode & David Luban, Legal Ethics 669 (2d. ed. 1995).

47. David Kaplan, Want to Invest in a Law Firm?, National L.J. Jan. 19, 1987, at 28 (quoting Geoffrey Hazard, Jr.). See ABA Formal Op. 355 (1987) (setting forth guidelines for lawyers' participation in for-profit plans under the Model Rules).

48. Katha Pollitt, Media Goes Wilding in Palm Beach, Nation, June 24, 1991, at 833; Laura Parker, Palm Beach Accuser's Ordeal of Proof: Alleged Rape Victim Forfeits Privacy as Prosecutors Build Case, Wash. Post, June 2, 1991, at A1. For general discussion of policies concerning disclosure of rape victims' identity, see Deborah W. Denno, Perspectives on Disclosing Rape Victims' Names, 61 Fordham L. Rev. 1113 (1993).

49. Monroe H. Freedman & Janet Starwood, Prior Restraints on Freedom of Expression by Defendants and Defense Attorneys: Ratio Decidendi v. Obiter Dictum, 29 Stan. L. Rev. 607 (1977) (quoting Nebraska Press Assn. v. Stuart, 423 U.S. 1319 (1975) (citations omitted)).

50. Freedman & Starwood, supra note 49, at 613; Joel H. Swift, Restraints on Defense Publicity in Criminal Jury Cases, 1984 Utah L. Rev. 45, 76-84.

51. Alan Dershowitz, Two Rape Cases — Justice on Trial: Florida Scores Against Smith, N.Y. Times, July 26, 1991, at A27.

52. For evidence regarding predispositions, see Norbert L. Kerr et al., On the Effectiveness of Voir Dire in Criminal Cases with Prejudicial Pretrial Publicity: An Empirical Study, 40 Am. U.L. Rev. 665, 666-667 (1991). For evidence concerning fair verdicts, see Newton N. Minow & Fred H. Cate, Who Is an Impartial Juror in an Age of Mass Media?, 40 Am. U.L. Rev. 631, 635 (1991); Rita J. Simon, Does the Court's Decision in *Nebraska*

Press Association Fit the Research Evidence on the Impact on Jurors of News Coverage?, 29 Stan. L. Rev. 515 (1977); Robert E. Drechsel, An Alternative View of Media-Judiciary Relations: What the Non-Legal Evidence Suggests About the Fair Trial-Free Press Issue, 18 Hofstra L. Rev. 1 (1989).

53. In re Kuby (D. Conn. 1993), discussed in Monroe Freedman, Blasting the Bench, Legal Times, Mar. 6, 1996, at 8.

54. Standing Committee on Discipline v. Yagman, 55 F.3d 1430 (9th Cir. 1995).

55. Freedman, supra note 53, quoting New York Mayor Rudolph Guiliani's characterization of a New York City criminal court judge.

56. Andrea Fored & Jim Newton, Prosecutors Opt Not to Include Simpson Chase, L.A. Times, Sept. 14, 1995, at A1, A17 (quoting Los Angeles County District Attorney Gil Garcetti); Nancy McCartny, Bar Reproves 2 Simpson Lawyers, Cal. Bar. J., July 1997, at 1.

57. In re Raggio, 487 P.2d 499 (Nev. 1971).

58. Matter of Justices v. Erdmann, 301 N.E.2d 426, 427 (1973).

59. In re Hinds, 499 A.2d 483, 486 (N.J. Sup. Ct. 1982). See generally Monroe H. Freedman, The Threat to Judicial Independence by Criticism of Judges — A Proposed Solution to the Real Problem, 25 Hofstra L. Rev. 729 (1997).

60. In re N.R.S., 403 So. 2d 1315 (Fla. 1981) (granting admission); Deborah L. Rhode, Moral Character as a Professional Credential, 94 Yale L.J. 491, 576-579 (1985) (discussing attitudes of 40 percent of surveyed character examiners, who find such sexual conduct troubling).

61. Cf. In re Applicant, 443 So. 2d 71 (Fla. 1983) (no constitutional right to withhold psychological and medical or health records).

62. Rhode, supra note 60, at 576 (noting that 24 percent of jurisdictions request such information).

63. Id. at 541.

64. David Luban, Lawyers and Justice: An Ethical Study 263-264 (1988).

65. Frank Michelman, The Supreme Court and Litigation Access Fees: The Right to Protect One's Rights, Part 1, 1973 Duke L.J. 1153.

66. Honorable Earl Johnson, Jr., The Right to Counsel in Civil Cases: An International Perspective, 19 Loy. L.A.L. Rev. 341 (1985).

67. See sources cited in Deborah L. Rhode, Lawyers, Wm. & Mary L. Rev. (forthcoming 1997).

68. Nan Aron & Samuel S. Jackson, Jr., Nontraditional Models for Legal Services Delivery, in Civil Justice: An Agenda for the 1990s, at 143 (Papers of the American Bar Association National Conference on Access to Justice in the 1990s, Esther F. Lardent ed., 1991).

69. Thomas Cooley, A Treatise on the Constitutional Limitations Which Rest upon the Legislative Power of the States of the American Union (1871).

70. See David Shapiro, The Enigma of the Lawyer's Duty to Serve, 55 N.Y.U.L. Rev. 735 (1980); Michael Millemann, Mandatory Pro Bono in Civil Cases: A Partial Answer to the Right Question, 49 Md. L. Rev. 18, 33-35 (1990).

71. See Shapiro, supra note 70; State ex rel. Scott v. Roper, 688 S.W.2d 757 (Mo. 1985).

72. Charles Wolfram, Modern Legal Ethics 952 (1986).

73. Millemann, supra note 70, at 70.

74. Stephen Gillers, Words into Deeds: Counselor, Can You Spare a Buck?, 76 A.B.A.J., Nov. 1990, at 81.

Chapter XII

Contracts

A. THE MORALITY OF ROLES

1. The Advocate's Role

See Chapter IV, Advocacy
- Part B. The Traditional Rationale and Contemporary
  Challenges
    (pages 133–146)

2. Legal Ethics, Judicial Ethics, and Fraudulent Representations

VOKES v. ARTHUR MURRAY

212 So. 2d 906 (Fla. Ct. App. 1968)

Judge PIERCE delivered the opinion of the court.

Plaintiff Mrs. Audrey E. Vokes, a widow of 51 years and without family, had a yen to be "an accomplished dancer" with the hopes of finding "new interest in life." So, . . . [she attended] a "dance party" at Davenport's "School of Dancing" where she whiled away the pleasant hours, sometimes in a private room, absorbing . . . accomplished sales technique, during which her grace and poise were elaborated upon and her rosy future as "an excellent dancer" was painted for her in vivid and glowing colors. As an incident to this interlude, . . . [the defendants] sold her eight 1/2-hour dance lessons to be utilized within one calendar month therefrom, for the sum of $14.50 cash in hand paid, obviously a baited "come-on."

Thus she embarked upon an almost endless pursuit of the terpsichorean art during which, over a period of less than sixteen months, she was sold fourteen "dance courses" totalling in the aggregate 2302 hours of dancing lessons for a total cash outlay of $31,090.45, all at Davenport's dance emporium. . . .

These dance lesson contracts and the monetary consideration therefor of over $31,000 were procured from her by means and methods of Davenport and his associates which went beyond the unsavory, yet legally, permissible, perimeter of "sales puffing" and intruded well into the forbidden area of undue influence, the suggestion of falsehood, the suppression of truth, and the free exercise of rational judgment, if what plaintiff alleged in her complaint was true. From the time of her first contact with the dancing school in February, 1961, she was influenced unwittingly by a constant and continuous barrage of flattery, false praise, excessive compliments, and panegyric encomiums, to such extent that it would be not only inequitable, but unconscionable, for a Court exercising inherent chancery power to allow such contracts to stand.

She was incessantly subjected to overreaching blandishment and cajolery. She was assured she had "grace and poise"; that she was "rapidly improving and developing in her dancing skill"; that the additional lessons would "make her a beautiful dancer, capable of dancing with the most accomplished dancers"; that she was "rapidly progressing in the development of her dancing skill and gracefulness," etc., etc. . . . [In] truth and in fact she did not develop in her dancing ability, she had no "dance aptitude," and in fact had difficulty in "hearing the musical beat." The complaint alleged that such representations to her "were in fact false and known by the defendants to be false and contrary to the plaintiff's true ability, the truth of plaintiff's ability being fully known to the defendants, but withheld from the plaintiff for the sole and specific intent to deceive and defraud the plaintiff and to induce her in the purchasing of additional hours of dance lessons." It was averred that the lessons were sold to her "in total disregard to the true physical, rhythm, and mental ability of the plaintiff." In other words, while she first exulted that she was entering the "spring of her life," she finally was awakened to the fact there was "spring" neither in her life nor in her feet.

The complaint prayed that the Court decree the dance contracts to be null and void and to be cancelled, that an accounting be had, and judgment entered against the defendants "for that portion of the $31,090.45 not charged against specific hours of instruction given to the plaintiff." The Court held the complaint not to state a cause of action and dismissed it with prejudice. We disagree and reverse.

The material allegations of the complaint must, of course, be accepted as true for the purpose of testing its legal sufficiency. Defendants contend that contracts can only be rescinded for fraud or misrepresentation when the alleged misrepresentation is as to a material fact, rather than an opinion, prediction or expectation, and that the statements and representations set forth at length in the complaint were in the category of "trade puffing," within its legal orbit.

It is true that "generally a misrepresentation, to be actionable, must be one of fact rather than of opinion." . . . But this rule has significant qualifications, applicable here. It does not apply where there is a fiduciary relationship between the parties, or where there has been some artifice or trick employed by the representor, or where the parties do not in general deal at "arm's length" as we understand the phrase, or where the representee does not have equal opportunity to become apprised of the truth or falsity of the fact represented. . . .

It could be reasonably supposed here that defendants had "superior knowledge" as to whether plaintiff had "dance potential" and as to whether she was noticeably improving in the art of terpsichore. . . .

Even in contractual situations where a party to a transaction owes no duty to disclose facts within his knowledge or to answer inquiries respecting such facts, the law is if he undertakes to do so he must disclose the *whole truth*. . . .

It accordingly follows that the order dismissing plaintiff's last amended complaint with prejudice should be and is reversed.

PROBLEM 12A

1. If you had been Judge Pierce's law clerk, would you have raised any questions about the tone of his decision? Why do you think the judge drafted the opinion in the way that he did? Who was his intended audience? Should he have considered the impact of his colorful phrasing on the plaintiff or on other potential plaintiffs?

2. If you had been the lawyer for the plaintiff in *Vokes*, what conversations would you have had with your client about trial strategy? Consider Model Rule 1.2, which recognizes the client's prerogative to decide the "objectives" of representation, but acknowledges the lawyer's responsibility to decide questions of legal tactics. Was the portrait of the plaintiff that emerged in the *Vokes* complaint an issue of objectives or tactics?

3. If you had been representing the defendant in *Vokes*, what would you have advised the dance studio to do when the plaintiff first attempted to cancel the contract? What would you have advised after the appellate court reinstated the complaint? Consider the materials on counseling in Part B of Chapter IX (The Lawyer-Client Relationship). What was your client selling to women like Ms. Vokes? Was it only, or primarily, instruction in the "terpsichorean art"? If not, what implications does that have for your client's employees?

Consider Robert Gordon's observations in the excerpt that follows.

ROBERT W. GORDON, UNFREEZING LEGAL REALITY: CRITICAL APPROACHES TO LAW

15 Fla. St. U.L. Rev. 195, 205-210 (1987)

Through the briefly sketched images of the court, our rational consumer has been transformed into a lonely, vulnerable woman in search of excitement and companionship — the dance studio, from a seller of dancing skills, into a sort of surrogate lover. A 51-year-old widow who would not dream of going, for example, to a singles bar wants safe and respectable ways to find male companionship. Learning how to dance is such a way. The dance studio becomes not just a way of getting there, but the destination itself: a place where attractive and charming instructors discover in her unsuspected graces and talents, and encourage her to feel desirable and at home among friends. They put her in a hierarchy of achievement and reward her efforts with medals and promotions. Was she really misled by being told how graceful and talented she was? Would things have been better, and she happier, if she had been given a coldly critical appraisal of her dancing ability? Perhaps the flattery and attention, even the lies if one must label a seducer's compliments as such, were not a distortion of the service the studio should have been rendering her, but an essential part of the service itself. The commodity the studio men are supplying is much more than dancing skills; it is the sensation of being alive and exciting. . . . One might also paint just such a tragic picture of the managers of the dance studio, small business people just barely scraping a profit from their franchise, depending on income streams from long-term contracts to pay the rent, feed the kids, and keep instructors employed. Should they run a business dependent upon good customer relations by first insulting the customers — coldly appraising their dancing abilities and telling them, if they have none, to get lost?

Besides, the lawyer might say, all this circumstantial detail you have added just makes the studio's case stronger. If Audrey Vokes *wanted* to hear half-truths about her ability, if flattery and cajolement is all part of the service, then there has been no "distortion" of rational choice. She has contracted for what she wants — what we all want — the illusion of endless youth and erotic vitality, powers expanding rather than contracting with age. If the courts deny dance studios the right to sell this commodity by insisting on flatly factual dealings with their customers, then people like Audrey Vokes will have many more restricted choices, maybe nowhere to go, or at least will have to pay higher prices to compensate the studios for the risk of ad hoc judicial invalidation of some of the other customers' contracts. . . .

[Judge Pierce's decision, with all its details, is invoking] what might be called an underground jurisprudence of equity. The jurisprudence is not actually all underground. Some of it has been formalized in the categories of "undue influence" or (more vaguely) of "fiduciary relationships." The idea is that in relationships in which people have achieved a certain level of intimacy and an expectation of mutual trust there should be a big change in the legal ground rules affecting their interaction. Once a party has come to expect that the other will not take every advantage of her that he can, and her guard is down, the other's room for self-interested strategic maneuvering should be limited. . . . The outrage of the court, reflected in the law of undue influence or of advantage taking of fiduciary relations, comes in part from the sense of betrayal that we all experience when "we realize that a lover, or an intimate, someone whom we trusted to take care of us, has all along had nothing in mind but his own profit. The plaintiff says: 'You've seduced me and abandoned me, and now, to add insult to injury, you expect me to pay for the experience.'" . . .

The argument just made is one that asks us to see nonenforcement in this case not as an interference with, but a promotion of, the goals of free contracting in the market. Obviously, it is not the only such argument that can be made. To list briefly a few more:

1. [T]he studio knows a key fact about these deals that customers do not know: the appetite for commercial dancing services rather rapidly reaches a saturation point. Few people end up actually wanting anything like the vast total of hours they sign up for. . . . The studio knows this from long experience and the customers do not and will not usually be able to find out until it is too late. . . .

2. The previous set of arguments suggests a second: the customer's capacity for "free contracting" in the present has to be limited to preserve her capacity for free choice in the future. The studio should not be able to bind her to this agreement because it ties up too many of her assets and too much of her time for too long. . . .

3. The addictive drugs analogy suggests yet another line of argument, going to contractual *capacity*. The particular seduction techniques used to sell the contract have suspended Ms. Vokes' capacity for rational choice. The studio hooks her on glamorizing flattery, then threatens to withhold the drug unless she keeps signing contracts. The main evidence for this is simply the outlandish quantity of lessons: if she danced for two hours a day, every day, for the next ten years she still would not have consumed all the hours purchased.

What follows from Gordon's observations? Was the remedy available in *Vokes* an effective way to handle the situation, or would more fundamental changes be preferable? Consider, for example, legislative limits on the hours of dance studio instruction a consumer can purchase at given intervals or more community services for individuals like Audrey Vokes.[1] In the absence of such initiatives, how should attorneys for buyers and sellers respond?

3.   Formal Justice and Substantive Justice

PROBLEM 12B

1. A wealthy businessman whom you have represented in the past asks for your assistance in a contractual dispute. Your former client orally agreed to pay an elderly couple several thousand dollars if they would manage certain property while he was out of the country. The couple basically fulfilled the contract but a disagreement over a minor matter has led him to withhold payment. If he is unaware that the Statute of Frauds might enable him to avoid ever paying for the services, must you alert him to the possibility? Suppose that no quasi-contractual remedies are available for the couple and they now need the money for medical expenses. How do you proceed?[2]

Consider the materials on technical defenses in Chapter IV (Advocacy) at pages 157–161. Is this a case where Abraham Lincoln's advice to employ professional skills elsewhere would be appropriate? Would your answer be different if the couple were not in need of money or you were not in need of clients?

2. Consider the contractual counseling issues in Problem 9D in Chapter IX (The Lawyer-Client Relationship) at page 397. Could you ethically advise a client to assume debt obligations that he has no intentions of fulfilling?

See Chapter IV, Advocacy

4.   Adversarial Structures and Professional Constraints: Implied Contracts, Witness Preparation, and Counseling Responsibilities

PROBLEM 12C

From 1990 to 1996, Cliff and Nancy lived together in one half of a Los Angeles duplex. Cliff had purchased the duplex in his own name, using his separate funds for a down payment. The other half of the duplex was rented out, and Nancy helped to maintain it by cleaning and painting between tenants, showing it to prospective tenants, and so forth. Nancy and Cliff deposited both their separate earnings and rental payments in joint savings and checking accounts. The couple used these accounts for mortgage payments as well as household purchases.

Neither individual kept careful records of their respective earnings during this period of cohabitation, but Cliff's salary was significantly higher than Nancy's. In 1991, Nancy gave birth to a child, whom Cliff acknowledges is his, and left the paid labor force.

Some property ownership issues are complicated. The couple had several automobiles during the period, all of which were registered solely in Cliff's name. Some of their household items were gifts from their parents. Nancy had purchased a car before they had begun living together, but when she left her job after giving birth, she transferred title to Cliff. Cliff took over the payments and when he later sold that car, he used the proceeds to purchase a truck registered in his own name.

At various times during their relationship, Nancy asked Cliff to put her name on the title to the duplex or the cars, but he always refused. She also asked him to marry her on several occasions, but he was unwilling. When she gave birth, she was hospitalized under his name and his health insurer paid her bills. Nancy claims that Cliff assured her that if he died, all his property would go to her and the child.

1. Suppose that Nancy seeks your advice when she realizes that she is pregnant. She wants to know whether it is important that she and Cliff marry. She knows that Cliff wants the child, and probably would marry her if she insisted upon it as a condition of her carrying the pregnancy to term. She wonders whether you think she should insist and exactly how it would matter if she doesn't. What do you tell her?

2. Suppose that Nancy decides to press for marriage. Cliff is willing only if she signs a premarital agreement providing that neither party will have any obligation to the other in the event of divorce. What advice would you give her?

3. Suppose that Cliff comes to you for advice. He would like you to draft an agreement that will protect him from any claims by Nancy if their relationship ends. He discloses that a few years ago he came into a significant inheritance, which he invested in his brother's software company. The company has done very well, but he has been unwilling to tell Nancy. He predicts that she will want to spend the additional income on purchases like a nicer home or better car. He prefers to reinvest the profits, which he considers to be his own separate property. What do you advise?

4. Suppose that neither party consulted you while they were living together and that they made no written agreements. After the relationship ends, Nancy seeks your legal advice. When and how would you explain the relevant law on cohabitation? What action would you propose that she take?[3]

MARVIN v. MARVIN

557 P.2d 106, 110-111, 116, 121-123 (Cal. 1976)

[P]laintiff and defendant lived together for seven years without marrying; all property acquired during this period was taken in defendant's name. When plaintiff sued to enforce a contract under which she was entitled to half the property and to support payments, the trial court granted judgment on the pleadings for defendant.... [T]he trial court denied plaintiff a trial on the merits ... and must be reversed.

1. THE FACTUAL SETTING OF THIS APPEAL

... Plaintiff avers that in October of 1964 she and defendant "entered into an oral agreement" that while "the parties lived together they would combine their efforts and earnings and would share equally any and all property accumulated as a result of their efforts whether individual or combined." Furthermore, they agreed to "hold themselves out to the general public as husband and wife" and that "plaintiff would further render her services as a companion, homemaker, housekeeper and cook to ... defendant."

Shortly thereafter plaintiff agreed to "give up her lucrative career as an entertainer [and] singer" in order to "devote her full time to defendant ... as a companion, homemaker, housekeeper and cook"; in return defendant agreed to "provide for all of plaintiff's financial support and needs for the rest of her life."

Plaintiff alleges that she lived with defendant from October of 1964 through May of 1970 and fulfilled her obligations under the agreement. During this period the parties as a result of their efforts and earnings acquired in defendant's name substantial real and personal property, including motion picture rights worth over $1 million. In May of 1970, however, defendant compelled plaintiff to leave his household. He continued to support plaintiff until November of 1971, but thereafter refused to provide further support.

On the basis of these allegations plaintiff asserts two causes of action. The first, for declaratory relief, asks the court to determine her contract and property rights; the second seeks to impose a constructive trust upon one half of the property acquired during the course of the relationship. ...

2. PLAINTIFF'S COMPLAINT STATES A CAUSE OF ACTION FOR BREACH OF AN EXPRESS CONTRACT

... [We] base our opinion on the principle that adults who voluntarily live together and engage in sexual relations are nonetheless as competent as any other persons to contract respecting their earnings and property rights. Of course, they cannot lawfully contract to pay for the performance of sexual services, for such a contract is, in essence, an agreement for prostitution and unlawful for that reason. But they may agree to pool their earnings and to hold all property acquired during the relationship in accord with the law governing community property; conversely they may agree that each partner's earnings and the property acquired from those earnings remains the separate property of the earning partner. So long as the agreement does not rest upon illicit meretricious consideration, the parties may order their economic affairs as they choose, and no policy precludes the courts from enforcing such agreements.

In the present instance, plaintiff alleges that the parties agreed to pool their earnings, that they contracted to share equally in all property acquired, and that defendant agreed to support plaintiff. The terms of the contract as alleged do not rest upon any unlawful consideration. . . .

3. PLAINTIFF'S COMPLAINT CAN BE AMENDED TO STATE A CAUSE OF ACTION FOUNDED UPON THEORIES OF IMPLIED CONTRACT OR EQUITABLE RELIEF

. . . First, we note that the cases denying relief [to cohabiting couples] do not rest their refusal upon any theory of "punishing" a "guilty" partner. Indeed, to the extent that denial of relief "punishes" one partner, it necessarily rewards the other by permitting him to retain a disproportionate amount of the property. Concepts of "guilt" thus cannot justify an unequal division of property between two equally "guilty" persons.

Other reasons advanced in the decisions [denying relief] fare no better. The principal argument seems to be that "[e]quitable considerations arising from the reasonable expectation of . . . benefits attending the status of marriage . . . are not present [in a nonmarital relationship]." (Vallera v. Vallera, 21 Cal. 2d at 685, 134 P.2d 761, 763.) But, although parties to a nonmarital relationship obviously cannot have based any expectations upon the belief that they were married, other expectations and equitable considerations remain. The parties may well expect that property will be divided in accord with the parties' own tacit understanding and that in the absence of such understanding the courts will fairly apportion property accumulated through mutual effort. We need not treat nonmarital partners as putatively married persons in order to apply principles of implied contract, or extend equitable remedies; we need to treat them only as we do any other unmarried persons.

The remaining arguments advanced from time to time to deny remedies to the nonmarital partners are of less moment. There is no more reason to presume that services are contributed as a gift than to presume that funds are contributed as a gift; in any event the better approach is to presume, as Justice Peters suggested, "that the parties intend to deal fairly with each other."

. . . The argument that granting remedies to the nonmarital partners would discourage marriage must fail; as *Cary* pointed out, "with equal or greater force the point might be made that the pre-1970 rule was calculated to cause the income-producing partner to avoid marriage and thus retain the benefit of all of his or her accumulated earnings." [In re Marriage v. Cary, 34 Cal. App. 3d 345,

353, 109 Cal. Rptr. 862, 866 (1973).] Although we recognize the well-established public policy to foster and promote the institution of marriage, perpetuation of judicial rules which result in an inequitable distribution of property accumulated during a nonmarital relationship is neither a just nor an effective way of carrying out that policy.

In summary, we believe that the prevalence of nonmarital relationships in modern society and the social acceptance of them marks this as a time when our courts should by no means apply the doctrine of the unlawfulness of the so-called meretricious relationship to the instant case. As we have explained, the nonenforceability of agreements expressly providing for meretricious conduct rested upon the fact that such conduct, as the word suggests, pertained to and encompassed prostitution. To equate the nonmarital relationship of today to such a subject matter is to do violence to an accepted and wholly different practice.

We are aware that many young couples live together without the solemnization of marriage, in order to make sure that they can successfully later undertake marriage. This trial period, preliminary to marriage, serves as some assurance that the marriage will not subsequently end in dissolution to the harm of both parties. We are aware, as we have stated, of the pervasiveness of nonmarital relationships in other situations.

The mores of the society have indeed changed so radically in regard to cohabitation that we cannot impose a standard based on alleged moral considerations that have apparently been so widely abandoned by so many. Lest we be misunderstood, however, we take this occasion to point out that the structure of society itself largely depends upon the institution of marriage, and nothing we have said in this opinion should be taken to derogate from that institution. The joining of the man and woman in marriage is at once the most socially productive and individually fulfilling relationship that one can enjoy in the course of a lifetime.

We conclude that the judicial barriers that may stand in the way of a policy based upon the fulfillment of the reasonable expectations of the parties to a nonmarital relationship should be removed. As we have explained, the courts now hold that express agreements will be enforced unless they rest on an unlawful meretricious consideration. We add that in the absence of an express agreement, the courts may look to a variety of other remedies in order to protect the parties' lawful expectations.

The courts may inquire into the conduct of the parties to determine whether that conduct demonstrates an implied contract or implied agreement of partnership or joint venture or some other tacit understanding between the parties. The courts may, when appropriate, employ principles of constructive trust or resulting trust. Finally, a nonmarital partner may recover in quantum meruit for the reasonable value of household services rendered less the reasonable value of support received if he can show that he rendered services with the expectation of monetary reward.

———————————

In *Marvin*, the plaintiff, Michelle Marvin, alleged that she and the defendant, Lee Marvin, entered into an oral agreement providing that while they lived together they would combine their efforts and earnings, "share equally" in any accumulated property, and hold themselves out to the public as husband and wife. In addition, Michelle allegedly would give up her lucrative career to provide services as a companion, homemaker, and cook, and Lee in return would "provide for all of [her] financial support and needs for the rest of her life." Do you think that is what Michelle initially told her lawyer during their first interview? Is that alleged agreement difficult to reconcile with the parties' decision not to marry after Lee's divorce became final? What other problems of proof might such claims present? In contexts involving private, unwritten agreements, where do you draw the line between helping clients recollect, and helping them reconstruct, their relationships?

Consider the materials on witness preparation in Chapter V (The Adversary System) at pages 195–200. How would you counsel Michelle regarding her trial testimony? How would you counsel her regarding settlement?

Of the parties most directly involved in *Marvin*, not everyone lived happily ever after. On remand, the trial involved 11 weeks of testimony by 60 witnesses concerning the most intimate and indelicate aspects of the Marvins' relationship, including Lee's alcoholism and Michelle's infidelities. Legal fees for Michelle alone totaled half a million dollars, and the cumulative efforts of counsel pointed to no clear resolution of the questions at issue: whether Lee's "idle male promises" were binding and whether he had been unjustly enriched by Michelle's services.[4]

In an attempted Solomonic gesture, the trial court found no agreement between the parties but granted Michelle $104,000 in rehabilitative support to enable her to acquire new job skills.[5] Lee, who by that point in the process appeared more willing to pay such sums to his current lawyer than to his former partner, contested the award. He prevailed in an intermediate court of appeals and the California Supreme Court declined to reenter the dispute. Under the appellate court's analysis:

> [T]he trial court expressly found that plaintiff benefitted economically and socially from her relationship with defendant and suffered no damage therefrom, even with respect to its termination. Furthermore, the trial court also expressly found that defendant never had any obligation to pay plaintiff a reasonable sum . . . for her maintenance and that defendant had not been unjustly enriched by reason of the relationship or its termination and that defendant had never acquired anything of value from plaintiff by any wrongful act.

Furthermore, the special findings in support of the challenged re-
habilitative award merely established plaintiff's need therefor and defendant's ability to respond to that need. This is not enough. The
award, being nonconsensual in nature, must be supported by some
recognized underlying obligation in law or in equity. A court of equity
admittedly has broad powers, but it may not create totally new substantive rights under the guise of doing equity.

Marvin v. Marvin, 122 Cal. App. 3d 871, 876, 176 Cal. Rptr. 555,
558-559 (1981).

If the facts were as the trial court found, how would you analyze
the effectiveness of the parties' legal representation in *Marvin*?

B.   CLIENT CONFIDENCES AND
DISCLOSURE OBLIGATIONS

1.   Bargaining in the Shadow of the Law

PROBLEM 12D

How should the attorney proceed in the following cases?

1. "A is negotiating with B to sell the All-American Hamburger
Stand. A makes full disclosure of all sales records and answers all of B's
questions. B agrees to buy the stand. At the closing, B says, 'I'm glad
there's no competition for a hamburger stand in this area. You don't
know of any plans for any, do you?' A looks at her lawyer, C, who says
nothing. A says, 'There's always a lot of rumors, but nothing definite.'
They sign the papers. A few days later, B learns that a McDonald's
restaurant is going to open across the street. Did A have an obligation to
tell what she knew in response to B's question? If attorney C knew of
McDonald's plans, did C act ethically?"[6] See Chapter XVII (Property),
Part C, at pages 743–745. See also Problem 13E in Chapter XIII
(Corporate Law) at page 571.

2. Consider the settlement negotiations for the breach of contract in
Problem 8B(1), (4), and (5) in Chapter VIII (Negotiation and Mediation)
at pages 344–345. Did the lawyers there breach any ethical obligation?

Restatement (Second) of Contracts, §161, comment d (1979), at
433-434, provides:

In many situations, if one party knows that the other is mistaken as
to a basic assumption, he is expected to disclose the fact that would
correct the mistake. A seller of real or personal property is, for example, ordinarily expected to disclose a known latent defect of quality or
title that is of such character as would probably prevent the buyer
from buying at the contract price. An owner is ordinarily expected to
disclose a known error in a bid that he has received from a contrac-

tor. . . . Nevertheless, a party need not correct all mistakes of the other and is expected only to act in good faith and in accordance with reasonable standards of fair dealing, as reflected in prevailing business ethics. A party may, therefore, reasonably expect the other to take normal steps to inform himself and to draw his own conclusions. If the other is indolent, inexperienced or ignorant, or if his judgment is bad or he lacks access to adequate information, his adversary is not generally expected to compensate for these deficiencies. A buyer of property, for example, is not ordinarily expected to disclose circumstances that make the property more valuable than the seller supposes.

2. Misstatements of Law and Fact

See Chapter VIII, Negotiation and Mediation
- Representations of Fact and Value
    (Problem 8A, parts 1 and 4, page 342)
- Disclosure Obligations
    (pages 347–353)

C. CONFLICTS OF INTEREST AND LAWYER-CLIENT RELATIONSHIPS

1. Identifying the Client's Interests

PROBLEM 12E

You are a legal services attorney. Your client is a single mother who works as a laundress. She comes to you for representation in a dispute with a local modeling agency. The controversy arose after her 15-year-old daughter saw an advertisement for a course on fashion modeling and sent away for information. A week later, the agency sold the family a course for $3,300 with tuition due in three installments: $300 on signing the contract, $900 at the beginning of the course, and $2,100 by the final week. In your view, the daughter has few of the physical features, apart from thinness, necessary for success in the world of fashion modeling.

She nonetheless completed the course, and the agency is now suing for the unpaid balance of $2,100. Your client is close to judgment-proof, and she now bitterly regrets her investment. The daughter still has aspirations for a career in modeling. How do you proceed?[7]

In the dispute on which this problem is based, the lawyer decided that because the mother had little to lose financially, the case would offer a good trial opportunity for law student interns. As they structured the litigation, the defense was based on fraud and misrepresentation, and involved evidence suggesting that the daughter had no realistic chance of a career in modeling. As the trial proceeded, friction intensified between the mother and daughter. The daughter was not a good witness, and the lawyer negotiated a settlement prior to judgment for $1,200. The students reported that they "enjoyed the whole experience, even if we did lose."[8]

In commenting on the result, one prominent litigator faulted the attorney for not counseling the client about the "psychic hurts" that the process might impose. As he noted, clients' "pride, self-image, ability to bear stress are essential considerations in deciding available alternatives." And, he added, "can anyone doubt that only the most callous person could permit a young girl to be adjudicated ugly for the sum of [$2,100]"?[9]

Do you agree? Was such an adjudication the only way to win? Suppose the mother and the daughter had different views about the price of such psychic hurts. If the lawyer represents the mother, what, if any, obligations does he owe to her daughter?

2.   Fiduciary Obligations: Excessive Fees, Referral Fees, and Modification of Fee Agreements

PROBLEM 12F

1. A close friend has consulted you in connection with a suit by her former attorney for breach of their fee agreement. Your friend initially sought the attorney's help in connection with a dispute over an estate matter. He is a prominent practitioner who has handled some high-profile cases but who lacks experience in estate law. He agreed to represent her on a contingent fee basis under a graduated formula, giving him approximately 33 percent of any recovery reached prior to trial and 40 percent of any recovery thereafter. Midway through the course of representation, the defendant proposed a settlement that the lawyer considered inadequate. He advised your friend to proceed to trial and presented her with another fee contract altering the terms of the formula. According to his explanation, the original arrangement provided inadequate compensation for unforeseen work in connection with discovery. She signed the new agreement, which promised the lawyer 40 percent of any pretrial recovery and 48 percent of any recovery received after trial.

Later, on your advice, she consulted another attorney. He advised her that the new fee would be in excess of the customary fees of similarly qualified litigators. She subsequently discharged her first attorney, hired the second, and settled the case. The first attorney is now suing her for his fee based on the modified agreement. What is your advice?

2. Suppose that the new fee formula had granted the lawyer 55 percent of any post-trial recovery, but that the client did not discharge him. The case proceeds to trial and the client ends up with a judgment slightly in excess of the settlement offer. She then learns that the fee is

grossly in excess of conventional charges. She refuses to pay and submits the dispute to arbitration. The lawyer claims that the client was purchasing his reputation as well as his time and that she got what she bargained for. You are the arbiter. What do you advise?

3. Assume that the first attorney, instead of proposing a new fee agreement midway through representation, suggested shortly after accepting the case that a more experienced lawyer handle the matter. The first attorney referred the matter to a litigator who agreed to take the case for a fee approximately 12 percent higher than the original agreement. When the client asked about her liability to the first attorney, she was told not to worry, that the second lawyer's fee would cover both. She subsequently learned that the first attorney received a 12 percent fee for forwarding the case. After settlement of the action, she consults you about her obligations to each attorney. What do you advise?

a. Excessive Fees

IN RE KUTNER, 399 N.E.2D 963 (1979). Luis Kutner was an Illinois lawyer with a national reputation who was especially well known for his pro bono work in civil cases. Warren Fisher consulted him in connection with battery charges arising from a dispute with his sister-in-law. Although Kutner had no experience in defending such criminal charges, he agreed to represent Fisher for a $5,000 retainer. On the day of trial, Kutner sent another attorney to seek a continuance. When the attorney did so, the complainant requested the judge to drop the charges. The case was then dismissed.

After consultation with two other attorneys, Fisher requested a refund of $4,000. Kutner initially refused to return any portion of the fees. After an adverse decision by the bar committee's Review Board, he offered to settle the matter by refunding $1,OOO. The case reached the Illinois Supreme Court on the issue of whether Kutner had violated DR 2-106. It prohibits a lawyer from charging a "clearly excessive fee," and provides: "A fee is clearly excessive when, after a review of the facts, a lawyer of ordinary prudence would be left with a definite and firm conviction that the fee is in excess of a reasonable fee." Relevant factors in determining the reasonableness of the fee include the time and labor required; the novelty and difficulty of the questions involved; the skill needed to perform the legal service properly; the fees customarily charged in the locality; and the experience, reputation, and ability of the lawyer.

Expert testimony suggested that the fee charged for defending a client in Fisher's position at trial would be between $750 and $1,250. When charges were dismissed before trial, the customary practice was to return a portion of the retainer to the client. The bar's Hearing Board concluded that Kutner had spent between five and six hours on the case. Kutner claimed that his total time was closer to ten hours and that one of the reasons that Fisher had hired him was that his reputation might discourage the sister-in-law from proceeding with the complaint.

A majority of the Illinois Supreme Court concluded that the $5,000 fee for a routine battery case that never went to trial was not only excessive but unconscionable. The court imposed censure.

Justice Clark, dissenting, maintained that

> Fisher thought he was getting fair value for his money since respondent had a favorable reputation and 49 years of experience. While it is our duty to scrutinize lawyer client dealings where an injustice has been done, I do not think we should pierce the veil of lawyer-client relations where no fraud or wrongdoing has been shown. . . . My opinion might be different had coercion, overreaching or deception been shown here. But those elements simply are not present. . . .
>
> In this connection the question may be asked whether the fee in this case would be excessive if the attorney involved were a nationally famous criminal lawyer? . . . The result should not differ here, simply because the respondent does not possess a reputation as "high powered" [in criminal cases] and the case involved a simple battery. I do not think it is appropriate for the court to rate an attorney's worth over another, which is precisely what this case sets a precedent for doing. . . .

399 N.E.2d at 967-968.

Do you agree? The traditional rationale for policing fee agreements is that lawyers and clients stand in a fiduciary relationship and that deterring exploitation in such relationships is necessary to preserve trust in the profession. Many courts and bar committees reason that unsophisticated clients cannot readily gain access to information about the appropriate value of services prior to representation. Do you find those justifications persuasive on the facts in *Kutner*?

Should attorneys who violate DR 2-106 or the corresponding Model Rule 1.5 be denied a quantum meruit recovery or be subject to significant disciplinary sanctions? Consider the reasoning of the Tennessee Supreme Court. In its view, lawyers should not be penalized for "innocent snafus" that render their fees unexpectedly large, but lawyers who attempt to collect fees that are "clearly excessive" should forfeit any recovery. To hold otherwise would "encourage attorneys to enter exorbitant fee contracts, secure that the safety net of quantum meruit is there in case of a subsequent fall." White v. McBride, 937 S.W.2d 796 (Tenn. 1996). Would you come to a similar conclusion as an arbiter in Problem 12F(2)? What sanctions should be appropriate by bar disciplinary committees? See In re Thonert, (Ind. Supreme Ct.), ABA/BNA Law. Man. Prof. Conduct 215 (1997) (imposing 30-day suspension of lawyer who refused to return unearned portion of $4,500 nonrefundable retainer).

b. Terminating Representation

FRACASSE v. BRENT, 494 P.2d 9 (Cal. 1972). In this case, the California Supreme Court held that if a client exercises his or her absolute right to discharge an attorney who is working under a contingent fee agreement, the attorney will be "limited to a quantum meruit recovery for the reasonable value of his [or her] services upon the occurrence of any contingency contemplated by his [or her] contract." 494 P.2d at 10. The case arose after the defendant Ray Raka Brent retained George Fracasse to represent her in a personal injury claim. Under the retainer agreement, Fracasse's compensation would be 33 percent of any settlement obtained 30 days prior to trial and 40 percent of any recovery obtained after that date. Before she obtained any recovery, Brent discharged Fracasse and hired another attorney. Fracasse then filed an action for declaratory judgment alleging that his dismissal was without cause and that he was entitled to one-third of any recovery in the personal injury case.

In rejecting that claim, the majority noted that

> [t]he client's power to discharge an attorney, with or without cause, is absolute. . . . This court [has] stated that "The interest of the client in the successful prosecution or defense of the action is superior to that of the attorney, and he has the right to employ such attorney as will in his opinion best subserve his interest. The relation between them is such that the client is justified in seeking to dissolve that relation whenever he ceases to have absolute confidence in either the integrity or the judgment or the capacity of the attorney. . . .
>
> Such a discharge does not constitute a breach of contract for the reason that it is a basic term of the contract, implied by law into it by reason of the special relationship between the contracting parties, that the client may terminate that contract at will. It would be anomalous and unjust to hold the client liable in damages for exercising that basic implied right. . . . [W]e believe it would be improper to burden the client with an absolute obligation to pay his former attorney regardless of the outcome of the litigation. The client may and often is very likely to be a person of limited means for whom the contingent fee arrangement offers the only realistic hope of establishing a legal claim. Having determined that he no longer has the trust and confidence in his attorney necessary to sustain that unique relationship, he should not be held to have incurred an absolute obligation to compensate his former attorney. Rather, since the attorney agreed initially to take his chances on recovering any fee whatever, we believe that the fact that the success of the litigation is no longer under his control is insufficient to justify imposing a new and more onerous burden on the client. Hence, we believe that the attorney's action for reasonable compensation accrues only when the contingency stated in the original agreement has occurred — i.e., the client has had a recovery by settlement or judgment. It follows that the attorney will be denied compensation in the event such recovery is not obtained.

494 P.2d at 9, 13.

Two judges, dissenting, argued:

> For well over a century it has been the settled rule in California that when an attorney is wrongfully discharged by his client before he has completely performed his contract, he may recover from the client damages for breach, the measure of the damages being the fee specified in the contract, or he may recover on a quantum meruit for the reasonable value of his services.
>
> By their decision today, the majority repudiate a rule supported by an impressive array of authority and replace it with one which will reduce an attorney-client contract to a hollow and meaningless act. . . . [W]here the fee arrangement between attorney and client is on a contingency basis, quantum meruit is an inherently imprecise and inadequate basis for determining compensation. In many instances, the most valuable and difficult services are rendered by the attorney in the early stages of his employment in advising the client of his legal rights; in investigating the case, interviewing witnesses and initiating other preparatory procedures; and in making basic decisions as to strategy and tactics. Where the attorney is then discharged without cause, these services are frequently imponderable elements in any equation for determining his loss . . . and their value can only be guessed at by a court. An attorney who is discharged for "cause" cannot reasonably complain about having his fees determined in this manner, but an attorney who is blameless should not in all fairness be relegated to such an uncertain recovery. . . . Contrary to the majority's position, an attorney bargains for a *limited* risk, the risk that the personal injury action may be unsuccessful under his management. He does not expect to hazard compensation for his services on the client's choice of a substitute attorney when the client may have made an arbitrary and ill-considered decision to change counsel.

494 P.2d at 17-18.

Which position do you find most convincing? If the dissenters' view had prevailed, would plaintiffs in a contingent fee case have been able to discharge their attorneys without the frequent risk of expensive disputes over cause? Would the risk of quantum meruit liability generally be sufficient to deter the bad faith that the dissenting justices fear? Suppose in *Fracasse* that if the lawyer's services were compensated at his standard hourly rate, his recovery would exceed one-third of the plaintiff's recovery. How would the contingency of a low verdict affect the plaintiff's liability for fees? See Rosenberg v. Levin, 409 So. 2d 1016 (Fla. 1982) (relevant factors in assessing a discharged attorney's fees include time expended, skill demanded, results obtained, and contract provisions). If a retainer agreement includes a maximum-fee restriction, should it limit any quantum meruit recovery? See id. Suppose that the client fires the lawyer for misconduct or for arguably unreasonable conduct such as failure to be available for trial? See Polen v. Melonakos (Mich. App.), 13 ABA/BNA Law Man. Prof. Conduct 172 (1997) (permitting quantum meruit recovery for unreasonable but not wrongful conduct).

c. Referral Fees

In theory, the American bar has imposed stringent restrictions on the use of referral fee contracts. In practice, these restrictions have been frequently ignored and seldom enforced. Disciplinary Rule 2-107(A) provides that lawyers should not divide fees outside their law firm unless

> (1) The client consents to employment of the other lawyer after a full disclosure that a division of fees will be made.
> (2) The division is made in proportion to the services performed and responsibility assumed by each.
> (3) The total fee of the lawyers does not clearly exceed reasonable compensation for all legal services they rendered the client.

Model Rule 1.5(e) similarly provides:

> a division of fee between lawyers who are not in the same firm may be made only if:
> (1) the division is in proportion to the services performed by each lawyer or, by written agreement with the client, each lawyer assumes joint responsibility for the representation;
> (2) the client is advised of and does not object to the participation of all the lawyers involved; and
> (3) the total fee is reasonable.

Despite these requirements, lawyers who forward a case and agree to assume nominal responsibility for its resolution routinely receive substantial fees, often one-third of the total amount.

The reasons for both the theory and the practice are straightforward. As an ethical matter, fees for referring a client are difficult to justify: why should a lawyer "get paid for no work"?[10] As a prudential matter, however, enforcing rules against referral fees could encourage attorneys to retain matters that they cannot effectively or efficiently pursue rather than directing the client toward a more qualified practitioner. Some commentators also argue that as long as lawyers within the same firm can share fees irrespective of how their work is divided, it is hypocritical to ban fee-splitting outside of firms.

Note that neither the Code nor the Model Rules require that clients receive information concerning the percentage of a fee division or the allocation of work. Should they? What, if any, remedy should be available to clients who are not so informed?

D.   POLICING THE BARGAIN: INEQUALITY, UNCONSCIONABILITY, AND PROFESSIONAL RESPONSIBILITY

1.   Partnership Agreements and Covenants Not to Compete

PROBLEM 12G

1. Your law firm has a clause in its partnership agreement providing that a member who withdraws and joins a competing practice is entitled to "no proportion of the net profits of the partnership collected thereafter whether for services rendered before or after the member's withdrawal." The agreement further restricts the amount that defecting partners can retain from their pension plan and their initial investment in the partnership.

One of your partners has recently left the firm, taking two associates and several clients with him. He challenges the departure provision as a violation of the bar's prohibitions on covenants not to compete. He seeks several hundred thousand dollars of revenue attributable to work he did before departure, as well as several hundred thousand dollars in partnership equity. Should your firm settle or contest the claim?

2. Suppose that the partner had not left voluntarily. Rather, he was forced out in a cost-cutting decision to close the branch office where he practiced. If the partnership agreement had no provision for termination without cause, could he sue for compensatory and punitive damages?

In Cohen v. Lord, Day & Lord, 144 A.2d 277, 534 N.Y.S.2d 161 (N.Y. App. Div. 1st Dept. 1988), a New York appellate panel reversed a lower court ruling that had found the same clause on profit shares a violation of DR 2-108. That rule provides:

(A) A lawyer shall not be a party to or participate in a partnership or employment agreement with another lawyer that restricts the right of a lawyer to practice law after the termination of a relationship created by the agreement, except as a condition to payment of retirement benefits.

(B) In connection with the settlement of a controversy or suit, a lawyer shall not enter into an agreement that restricts his right to practice law.

Model Rule 5.6(a) includes a similar provision:

A lawyer shall not participate in offering or making:

(a) a partnership or employment agreement that restricts the rights of a lawyer to practice after termination of the relationship, except an agreement concerning benefits upon retirement. . . .

In the appellate court's view, the objective of these rules is to protect clients' right to "select and repose confidence in lawyers of their choice without restriction by providing full availability of legal counsel." 144 A.2d at 280, 534 N.Y.S.2d at 163. See EC 2-26 and 2-31. However, a contractual restriction that does not directly seek to prevent a departing lawyer from establishing a competing practice is permissible under the court's analysis; such a restraint simply "protects departing partners who are likely to cause potential economic injury to the firm from either reaping . . . windfalls or from eating into what could be shrinking profits due to loss of business." Id.

Do you agree? Should there be any limits on the economic punishment that partnership agreements can impose on defecting lawyers? Other courts and bar committees have found that forfeiture clauses violate Model Rule 5.6.[11] In Katchen v. Wolff & Samson, 610 A.2d 415 (N.J. 1992), a New Jersey appellate court struck down a contractual provision stating that if a lawyer "shall voluntarily withdraw from the [professional] Corporation, he shall be deemed to have forfeited his equitable interest in the Corporation." Id. at 417. Under that provision, the lawyer would have lost close to a million dollars' worth of business that he had originated. According to the appellate court, such a clause inappropriately forced the lawyer "to make the Hobson's choice of staying with a firm that was not affording him sufficient support to effectively represent his clients, or withdrawing from it and joining a new firm that would give him more support, in which case he would forfeit his equitable interest in the defendant firm. . . . In such circumstances, the forfeiture provision of the agreement constitutes a restriction on the practice of law in so far as it impacts on client representation and is unenforceable." Id. at 420.

Which approach to foreclosure provisions do you find most persuasive? How would you respond to discharges for economic reasons? In a case on which Problem 12G(2) is modeled, a Florida court awarded the former Caldwalder, Wickersham & Taft partner $2.5 million, including $500,000 in punitive damages.[12] How would you respond to partnership agreements that impose financial disincentives on departing lawyers who take clients with them? What balance would you strike between the lawyer's right to leave unproductive workplace settings and the firm's desire to prevent lawyers from gaining experience and contacts and then eroding the client base that makes such benefits possible?[13]

Some research suggests that about half of the nation's firms do not have formal partnership agreements. Many firms that do have agreements skirt certain awkward issues about colleagues who are unproductive or who "grab and run."[14] If you were the managing partner of a small firm, how explicit and punitive would you want to be toward departing members?

2.   Bargaining Inequalities and Lack of Consideration

PROBLEM 12H

1. You represent the agent and manager for a rock group. He has proposed to have its members sign a standard form contract that is complicated, jargon-laden, and one-sided. Among other things, the contract gives the agent an exclusive copyright over any song composed by group members for five years with an option to renew for five years. One member of the group is required to complete at least one new song each month. The agent-manager agrees only to use his "best efforts to launch the composer's works to the fullest possible extent." The agent has the right to assign any composition or to do nothing with whatever music he considers unmarketable. None of the group members has independent legal counsel. How do you advise the agent-manager?

2. Suppose that you were the group's manager as well as lawyer on the facts above. Would any different considerations arise? Consult DR 5-101(A), DR 5-104(A), Model Rule 1.7(b), and the discussion in Part F of Chapter VII (Conflicts of Interest) at pages 331–332.

In Clifford Davis Management v. WEA Records, 1 All E.R. 237 (1975), the English Court of Appeal refused to uphold the clause in Problem 12H. The case involved a claim against Fleetwood Mac by the group's former manager, Clifford Davis. According to Lord Denning, the contract terms were "manifestly unfair," the composers were "talented in music . . . but not in business," and they had no legal counsel. 1 All E.R. at 240. Thus, "if the [manager] wished to . . . drive so unconscionable a bargain, he ought to have seen that the composer had independent advice." 1 All E.R. at 241. Would an American court agree? Would it have been enough if the manager had given group members advice to obtain independent legal counsel and they had declined? Alternatively, what if they had done so, and the manager had indicated that the contract terms were non-negotiable?

PROBLEM 12I

You practice commercial law in a jurisdiction that has declared cross-collateral clauses void as a matter of public policy. One of your clients has such a clause in its standard purchase agreement and is reluctant to delete it. In your client's view, such a clause could prove to be useful bargaining leverage in a dispute with a client who doesn't have a lawyer or whose counsel is unaware of the prohibition. What do you do?

An early discussion draft of the Model Rules of Professional Conduct provided:

> A lawyer shall not conclude an agreement, or assist a client in concluding an agreement, that the lawyer knows or reasonably should know is illegal, contains legally prohibited terms, would work a fraud, or would be held to be unconscionable as a matter of law.

Comments to that draft added:

> Although a lawyer is generally not responsible for the substantive fairness of the result of a negotiation, the lawyer has a duty to see that the product is not offensive to the law. . . . Modern commercial law provides that grossly unfair contracts are unconscionable and may therefore be invalid. Such proscriptions are intended to secure definite legal rights. As an officer of the legal system, a lawyer is required to observe them.

In its final form, Model Rule 1.2 provides:

> A lawyer shall not counsel a client to engage, or assist a client, in conduct that the lawyer knows is criminal or fraudulent, but a lawyer may discuss the legal consequences of any proposed course of conduct with a client and may counsel or assist a client to make a good faith effort to determine the validity, scope, meaning or application of the law.

If you had been a member of the ABA House of Delegates, which version of the Rule would you have supported? Why do you suppose that the current Rule includes no reference to prohibited terms? If a group more representative than the organized bar were formulating ethical requirements, would the earlier version have been likely to prevail?

Most other Western democracies closely regulate the terms of adhesion contracts. In a concept paper on consumer protection for the Bulgarian government, the ABA'S Central and East European Law Initiative proposed two strategies:

> First, enact a law that generally prohibits unfair contract terms and provides a relatively short, nonexclusive list of clauses that are prohibited. . . . Second, when laws concerning specific types of consumer transactions are under consideration, such as laws governing insurance, banking, consumer credit, product liability, or warranty, provide that consumer rights and remedies granted by the law cannot be diluted by contract.[15]

Would you support such strategies for this country? In their absence, would you agree with the approach that some legal ethics experts have recommended: hold attorneys accountable under disciplinary rules and civil liability standards if they knowingly draft unenforceable clauses?[16] As these commentators note, current oversight of standard form contracts through administrative regulation and judicial decisions has been ineffective because those who include unenforceable terms risk little or no cost. Legal challenges have been rare because parties subject to such clauses generally lack the knowledge, resources, or incentives to sue.[17]

What strategies would you recommend to address that problem? What difficulties do you predict in implementing them?

WILLIAMS v. WALKER-THOMAS FURNITURE CO., 350 F.2d 445 (D.C. Cir. 1965). This landmark decision on unconscionability involved contracts that predated adoption of U.C.C. §2-302. The plaintiff-appellee, Walker-Thomas Furniture Company, operated a retail furniture store that sold goods on credit. The contracts at issue included cross-collateral clauses in extremely small type providing that "all payments . . . shall be credited pro rata on all outstanding leases, bills, and accounts due . . . at the time each payment is made." 350 F.2d at 447. The effect of those clauses was to keep a lien on all prior purchases until a buyer paid for everything.

In 1962, Ms. Ora Williams, one of the defendant-appellees in the *Walker-Thomas* case, bought a stereo for $514.95. After she defaulted, the store sought to repossess all prior purchases she had made since 1957. At the time of repossession, Ms. Williams owed a total of $444 on some $1,500 worth of goods. Her debts included 25 cents on an item purchased on December 23, 1957, 3 cents on an item purchased a week later, and so forth. The salesman for the store was aware of Ms. Williams' financial position, since the reverse side of the contract indicated that she received $218 a month in welfare payments and had seven children to support. Ms. Williams did not receive copies of the contracts and apparently signed some of them blank, without the terms filled in.

The court, speaking through Judge Wright, remanded the case for findings on whether the contractual terms were unreasonable in light of the general commercial background and needs, and on whether the buyer had an absence of "meaningful choice." 350 F.2d at 449. If the case were to arise today, the focus would also be on the commercial setting, purpose, and effect of such cross-collateral clauses. According to the comment to §2-302, the principle is "prevention of oppression and unfair surprise, and not the disturbance of allocation of risks because of superior bargaining power."

Shortly after the appellate court's decision, the legal aid lawyer for Ms. Williams commented to researchers that the case

> should never have been permitted by [Walker-Thomas] to reach the appeals court. Poor cases make poor law. The law of these cases is not what I would call poor law; the problem of limitation of the effect of the decision is, however, difficult and subject to variation, thus creating a degree of uncertainty. The best effect of [Judge Wright's] decision lies in the fact that it is a dormant threat to unconscionable conduct. . . . When the case enters the defense at trial level, plaintiffs seem to be much more disposed towards settlement. . . . I decided to

take . . . [the case] as far as necessary to achieve a precedent which would afford some protection to the lesser members of the community. . . . Trial, appeal to the D.C. Court of Appeals, and then to the U.S. Circuit Court of Appeals took 210 man-hours of legal time, for which the appellants were not obligated to pay.[18]

PROBLEM 12J

1. Suppose that before the *Williams* case reached Judge Wright, but after the vast majority of work had been completed, the store had offered to settle on very favorable terms for Ms. Williams. What would the lawyer's obligations be? Consult EC 7-7 and Model Rule I.2, and the materials on public interest representation in Part C of Chapter IX (The Lawyer-Client Relationship).

2. Suppose that after the *Williams* case, Walker-Thomas stops using cross-collateral clauses. However, because the resale value of repossessed goods is low and the costs of repossession are high, the effect of outlawing such terms is to increase the price and restrict the availability of credit to the poor.[19] If you had been the lawyer for Ms. Williams, would you consider the case a victory? Would your client? Who should make decisions about the trade-offs between easy credit and hard terms for individuals like Ms. Williams? Consider the materials on paternalism in Part A of Chapter IX.

How the law in general, and lawyers in particular, should respond to apparently inequitable bargains has sparked some of the most fundamental debates in contemporary contract law. A central contested issue involves identifying defects in the bargaining process. Critics of unconscionability doctrine have claimed that assumptions about low-income consumers' bargaining incompetence are often conclusory, unsupported, and patronizing. Too often, courts' analysis has been circular; one party is assumed to be incompetent because the deal is bad, while the deal is assumed to be bad because the party appears incompetent. Despite frequent assertions about poor consumers' impulsiveness, escapism, and insensibility to contractual terms, available research does not, on the whole, find that economic status correlates with uninformed or unwise purchase decisions.[20]

Critics also worry that encouraging lawyers to contest, and courts to invalidate, contracts based on ill-defined criteria of commercial fairness is a costly way to redistribute resources. Many of those costs will be borne by the nonlitigious poor in the form of higher prices, larger down-payment requirements, and reduced access to credit. Letting a few consumers off the hook for their bad bargains may also create the wrong incentives for future conduct.

Defenders of broad unconscionability prohibitions make several responses. From their perspective, easy credit erodes opportunities

for true economic self-determination and perpetuates the market for
shoddy goods. Low-income consumers who are lured into purchases
that they cannot afford will end up with less income to spend on
essential items. Ad hoc paternalism can at least deter the most
egregious exploitation and affirm values of fundamental fairness for
parties most vulnerable to over-reaching.[21] As Karl Llewellyn once
noted, many individuals will lay their heads "into the mouth of a
lion, either . . . without reading the fine print, or occasionally in hope
and expectation . . . that it will be a sweet and gentle lion."[22] Particularly where those individuals and their families are at the
economic margin, lawyers may want to set limits on how large a bite
the lion will be able to take.

What is your view?

3. Contractual Provisions and Public Policy Considerations

PROBLEM 12K

You are the lawyer for the founder of a computer franchise company. Your client sold the company to a larger corporation, Spectrum
Information Technologies. As part of the purchase price, the founder
accepted 12.3 million shares of Spectrum stock. Spectrum subsequently
discovered faulty accounting practices at the acquired company that
substantially diminished its earnings. In settlement of any potential
liability claims, your client has agreed to return 3.5 million shares of the
stock. He has also tentatively accepted a provision in the settlement
agreement stating that neither he nor Spectrum will "instigate an investigation by, or voluntarily forward information to, any persons, including
any local, state and [f]ederal authorities regarding the [accounting]
adjustments, or voluntarily assist in any investigation thereof except [as]
required by applicable law or court order."[23]

Your client now seeks advice as to the appropriateness and enforceability of this provision. What is your response?

E. EMPLOYMENT AT WILL AND WHISTLE-BLOWING RESPONSIBILITIES

PROBLEM 12L

1. You are an associate at a New York firm. At your request, the
firm is handling the financing and closing on a condominium that you
have decided to purchase. For several months, the associate assigned
to the case has assured you that he has gotten favorable mortgage
terms and has maintained frequent contact with a bank loan officer.
Several days before the closing, you learn that he has neither secured
the mortgage nor even spoken with the loan officer. After considerable

difficulty, you manage to find financing in time to complete the closing but you incur about $27,000 in additional financing costs.

You describe this incident to the firm's name partners, and subsequently learn that the associate has engaged in similar conduct on prior occasions. When you propose that the firm report the matter to the state bar, you are informed that it will be handled internally instead. How should you proceed?

2. Assume that you are a member of the state bar disciplinary staff, and that neither the associate nor the firm partners reported the misconduct described in Part 1. A year later, a client who has a similar experience with the real estate associate files a complaint with your office and sues the firm for malpractice. Your investigators learn of the prior incident. Should you initiate proceedings against the associate or the partners?

One strategy for increasing lawyers' willingness to report professional misconduct is to provide greater safeguards against retaliation. The New York Court of Appeals set an important example along those lines in Wieder v. Skala, 80 N.Y.2d 628 (1992), the case on which Problem 12L is based.

WIEDER v. SKALA

609 N.E.2d 105 (N.Y. 1992)

HANCOCK, Judge.

[The court began by summarizing the allegations of the complaint, which it accepted as true for purposes of the appeal. Howard Wieder, an associate of Feder, Kasovitz, Weber & Skala, demanded that the firm file a disciplinary report concerning the real estate associate, Larry Lubin, whose conduct is described in Problem 12L. The complaint set forth the following events.]

[Two senior partners] conceded that the firm was aware "that L.L. [Larry Lubin] was a pathological liar and that [he] had previously lied to [members of the firm] regarding the status of other pending legal matters." When plaintiff confronted L.L., he acknowledged that he had lied about the real estate transaction and later admitted in writing that he had committed "several acts of legal malpractice and fraud and deceit upon plaintiff and several other clients of the firm."

The complaint further alleges that, after plaintiff asked the firm partners to report L.L.'s misconduct to the Appellate Division Disciplinary Committee as required under DR 1-103(A) of the Code of Professional Responsibility,[1] they declined to act. Later, in an effort to dissuade plaintiff from making the report himself, the partners told him that they would reimburse his losses. Plaintiff nonetheless met with the Committee "to discuss the entire matter." He withdrew his complaint, however, "because the [f]irm had indicated that it would fire plaintiff if he reported [L.L.'s] misconduct." Ultimately, in December 1987—as a result of plaintiff's insistence— the firm made a report concerning L.L.'s "numerous misrepresentations and [acts of] malpractice against clients of the [f]irm and acts of forgery of checks drawn on the [f]irm's account." Thereafter, two partners "continuously berated plaintiff for having caused them to report [the] misconduct." The firm nevertheless continued to employ plaintiff "because he was in charge of handling the most important litigation in the [f]irm." Plaintiff was fired in March 1988, a few days after he filed motion papers in that important case. . . .

[Wieder responded with a $500,000 suit in state court against Lubin and the firm's name partners. Among other things, his complaint alleged wrongful discharge and breach of contract. The lower courts dismissed his claim as legally insufficient under New York employment at will doctrine. Thirteen ethics and labor law specialists, as well as the Bar Association of the City of New York, supported Wieder's appeal as amicus curiae.]

The employment-at-will doctrine is a judicially created common-law rule "that where an employment is for an indefinite term it is presumed to be a hiring at will which may be freely terminated by either party at any time for any reason or even for no reason" (Murphy v. American Home Prods. Corp., 58 N.Y.2d 293, 300 . . .). In *Murphy*, this Court dismissed the claim of an employee who alleged he had been discharged in bad faith in retaliation for his disclosure of accounting improprieties. In so doing, we expressly declined to follow other jurisdictions in adopting the tort-based abusive discharge cause of action for imposing "liability on employers where employees have been discharged for disclosing illegal activities on the part of their employers," being of the view "that such a significant change in our law is best left to the Legislature" (id.).

[The Court reached a similar result in Sabetay v. Sterling Drug, where the employee alleged he was fired for blowing the whistle and refusing to assist unlawful activities.] . . .

As plaintiff points out, his employment as a lawyer to render professional services as an associate with a law firm differs in several respects from the employments in *Murphy*. . . . The plaintiffs in those cases were in the financial departments of their employers, both large companies. Although they performed accounting services,

---

1. DR 1-103(A) provides: "A lawyer possessing knowledge, not protected as a confidence or secret, of a violation of DR 1-103 that raises a substantial question as to another lawyer's honesty, trustworthiness or fitness in other respects as a lawyer shall report such knowledge to a tribunal or other authority empowered to investigate or act upon such violation."

they did so in furtherance of their primary line responsibilities as part of corporate management. In contrast, plaintiff's performance of professional services for the firm's clients as a duly admitted member of the Bar was at the very core and, indeed, the only purpose of his association with defendants. Associates are, to be sure, employees of the firm but they remain independent officers of the court responsible in a broader public sense for their professional obligations. . . .

We agree with plaintiff that in any hiring of an attorney as an associate to practice law with a firm there is implied an understanding so fundamental to the relationship and essential to its purpose as to require no expression: that both the associate and the firm in conducting the practice will do so in accordance with the ethical standards of the profession. Erecting or countenancing disincentives to compliance with the applicable rules of professional conduct, plaintiff contends, would subvert the central professional purpose of his relationship with the firm — the lawful and ethical practice of law.

The particular rule of professional conduct implicated here (DR 1-103[A]), it must be noted, is critical to the unique function of self-regulation belonging to the legal profession. . . .

Moreover, as plaintiff points out, failure to comply with the reporting requirement may result in suspension or disbarment (see, e.g., Matter of Dowd, 160 A.D.2d 78, 559 N.Y.S.2d 365). Thus, by insisting that plaintiff disregard DR 1-103(A) defendants were not only making it impossible for plaintiff to fulfill his professional obligations but placing him in the position of having to choose between continued employment and his own potential suspension and disbarment. We agree with plaintiff that these unique characteristics of the legal profession in respect to this core Disciplinary Rule make the relationship of an associate to a law firm employer intrinsically different from that of the financial managers to the corporate employers in *Murphy* and *Sabetay*. The critical question is whether this distinction calls for a different rule regarding the implied obligation of good faith and fair dealing from that applied in *Murphy* and *Sabetay*. We believe that it does in this case, but we, by no means, suggest that each provision of the Code of Professional Responsibility should be deemed incorporated as an implied-in-law term in every contractual relationship between or among lawyers.

It is the law that in "every contract there is an implied undertaking on the part of each party that he will not intentionally and purposely do anything to prevent the other party from carrying out the agreement on his part." . . .

"What courts are doing [when an omitted term is implied]," Professor Corbin explains, "whether calling the process 'implication' of promises, or interpreting the requirements of 'good faith,' as the current fashion may be, is but a recognition that the parties occasionally have understandings of expectations that were so funda-

mental that they did not need to negotiate about those expectations"
(3 Corbin, Contracts §570, 1992 Supp. at 411).

Just such fundamental understanding, though unexpressed, was
inherent in the relationship between plaintiff and defendant law
firm. . . . Intrinsic to this relationship, of course, was the unstated
but essential compact that in conducting the firm's legal practice
both plaintiff and the firm would do so in compliance with the
prevailing rules of conduct and ethical standards of the profession.
Insisting that as an associate in their employ plaintiff must act
unethically and in violation of one of the primary professional rules
amounted to nothing less than a frustration of the only legitimate
purpose of the employment relationship. . . . We conclude . . . that
plaintiff has stated a valid claim for breach of contract based on an
implied-in-law obligation in his relationship with defendants.

[In an omitted section of the opinion, the court refused to
recognize the tort of abusive discharge and concluded that "any
additional protection must come from the legislature."]

Although ethics experts generally applauded the New York
court's ruling, the decision also highlighted the inadequacies of
prevailing law concerning whistle-blowing. As Chapter VI (Confidentiality and Client Counseling) reflects, most jurisdictions have
not provided adequate safeguards against retaliatory discharge.[24]
Moreover, even where formal safeguards are in place, the cost of
invoking them is often prohibitive. As Wieder noted after the court
of appeals decision, "I've been portrayed as crazed, eccentric, and
litigation prone. I was unemployed for nine months. I've gone into
massive debt."[25] And he had not yet even begun to try the case.

What strategies would be most effective in reducing the barriers
to reporting misconduct in cases such as Wieder's? Consider the
following materials on whistle-blowing:

See Chapter III, Regulation of the Profession
  • The Disciplinary Process
      (pages 68–82)

See Chapter VI, Confidentiality and Client Counseling
  • Whistle-Blowing in Organizational Contexts
      (pages 278–292)

Endnotes

1. Cal. Civ. Code §§1812.50-1812.54 (West 1985). Gordon reports that these statutes were drafted by Stanford students who had read cases like *Vokes* in their contracts class. Robert W. Gordon, Unfreezing Legal Reality: Critical Approaches to Law, 15 Fla. St. U.L. Rev. 195, 219 n.30 (1987).

2. This problem is adapted from Michael D. Bayles, A Problem of Clean Hands: Refusal to Provide Professional Services, 5 Soc. Theory & Prac., Spring 1979, at 165, reprinted in Michael Davis & Frederick A. Elliston, Ethics and the Legal Profession 428 (1986).

3. This problem is based on one appearing in Ira M. Ellman, Paul M. Kurtz & Katharine T. Bartlett, Family Law: Cases, Texts, Problems 843-845 (1991).

4. Marlene A. Marks, The Suing of America 22 (1981); Larry Bodine, Marvin v. Marvin, Natl. L.J., Apr. 16, 1979, at 1 (noting Lee Marvin's characterization of his love letters as "idle male promises" and his description of the relationship as "light and airy" and "free of responsibility").

5. Marks, supra note 4, at 21. In reaching that decision, the trial court noted that Lee had not urged Michelle to give up her career and, in fact, had helped further it.

6. Scott J. Burnham, Teaching Ethics in Contracts, 41 J. Legal Educ. 113 (1991). This problem is suggested by Kardon v. Natl. Gypsum Co., 69 F. Supp. 512 (E.D. Pa. 1946), 73 F. Supp. 798, 801 (E.D. Pa. 1947).

7. This problem is based on Lawyers, Clients, and Ethics 88-91 (Murray Tiegh Bloom ed., 1974).

8. Id. at 91.

9. Id. at 92-93 (comments of Bruce S. Rogow).

10. Larry Bodine, Forwarding Fees: Ethical?, Natl. L.J., Feb. 5, 1979, at 1 (quoting Geoffrey Hazard). According to Hazard, paying lawyers for referrals "amounts to saying that a lawyer should be bribed to act ethically. For it happens to be the unambiguous rule . . . that lawyers not competent to handle cases should not handle them. . . . [I]f a lawyer can afford to forego some percentage of his fee in favor of a lawyer who does no work on the case, then that [first] lawyer . . . is charging too much." Id.

11. For other cases, see 9 ABA/BNA Manual on Professional Conduct 359 (Dec. 15, 1993); 10 ABA/BNA Manual on Professional Conduct 392 (Dec. 28, 1994); and Jacob v. Norris, McLaughlin & Marcus, 607 A.2d 142 (N.J. 1992) (invalidating provision that financially penalized lawyers who took clients with them when they left a law firm).

12. Mark Hansen, Cost Cutting Proves Costly, A.B.A.J., Nov. 1996, at 28.

13. See Mark W. Bennett, Now You *Can* Take It with You: The Ethics of Lawyer Departure and Solicitation of Firm Clients, 10 Geo. J. Legal Ethics 395 (1997).

14. See Gail Diane Cox, Smile When You Say That, Partner, Natl. L.J., Apr. 3, 1989, at 1, 49.

15. Ralph Nader & Wesley J. Smith, No Contest 367 (1996).

16. William T. Vukowich, Lawyers and the Standard Form Contract System: A Model Rule That Should Have Been, 6 Geo. J. Legal Ethics 799 (1993).

17. Id. at 847-848.

18. Robert H. Skilton & Orrin L. Helstad, Protection of the Installment Buyer of Goods Under the Uniform Commercial Code, 65 Mich. L. Rev. 1465, 1479-1480 & n.38 (1967).

19. For such arguments, see Richard A. Epstein, Unconscionability: A Critical Appraisal, 18 J.L. & Econ. 293, 307 (1975). See also Federal Trade Commission, Economic Report on Installment Credit and Retail Sales Practices of District of Columbia Retailers (1968) (finding that retailers of household furnishings and appliances to low-income D.C. consumers did not make substantially higher profits than general market retailers; their higher prices reflected higher costs of doing business, including higher losses on credit sales).

20. See evidence reviewed in Alan Schwartz, A Reexamination of Nonsubstantive Unconscionability, 63 Va. L. Rev. 1053, 1079-1081 (1977); Jan M. Newton, Economic Rationality of the Poor, 36 Human Organization 50, 58 (1977).

21. See, e.g., Duncan Kennedy, Distributive and Paternalist Motives in Contract and Tort Law, with Special Reference to Compulsory Terms and Unequal Bargaining Power, 41 Md. L. Rev. 563 (1982).

22. Karl N. Llewellyn, The Common Law Tradition: Deciding Appeals 362 (1960).

23. Susan Antilla, Former Apple Chairman Causes a Stir in New Job, N.Y. Times, Oct. 19, 1993, at D22.

24. Anthony J. Blackwell, Wieder's Paradox: Reporting Legal Misconduct in Law Firms, 1992-1993 Annual Survey of American Law 9, 36-37, 42 (noting that less than half of all jurisdictions have recognized wrongful discharge actions when employees reported illegal or unethical action, and only three states have explicitly indicated that professional codes may be a source of public policy that justifies an exception to employment at will).

25. David Margolick, N.Y. Court Shields Lawyers Who Report Dishonest Colleagues, N.Y. Times, Dec. 23, 1992, at B4 (quoting Wieder).

Chapter XIII

Corporate Law

A. REPRESENTING THE CORPORATE ENTITY

1. Introduction

A well-established principle of legal ethics is that lawyers representing corporations "owe [their] allegiance to the entity and not to a stockholder, director, officer, employee, representative, or other person connected with the entity." EC 5-18. The Model Rules add a note of realism in providing that "[a] lawyer employed or retained by an organization represents the organization acting through its duly authorized constituents." Rule 1.13. The Comment to Rule 1.13 further acknowledges that "[t]here are times when the organization's interest may be or become adverse to those of one or more of its constituents. In such circumstances the lawyer should advise any constituent, whose interest the lawyer finds adverse to that of the organization of the conflict or potential conflict of interest, that the lawyer cannot represent such constituent, and that such person may wish to obtain independent representation."

This Comment assumes that lawyers can readily identify the "organization's interest." Yet the "entity" theory of representation has what one commentator characterizes as an "Alice in Wonderland" quality where interests among corporate constituencies diverge:

> The client to which [the lawyer] owes undivided loyalty, fealty, and al-
> legiance cannot speak to him except through voices that may have in-
> terests adverse to his client. He is hired and may be fired by people
> who may or may not have interests diametrically opposed to those of
> his client. And finally, his client is itself an illusion, a fictional "per-
> son" that exists or expires at the whim of its shareholders, whom the
> lawyer does not represent.[1]

Most economists accept the view propounded by Ronald Coase, Oliver Hart, and Oliver Williamson that a corporation is simply a "nexus of contracts." At any given point, the organization represents an equilibrium of agreements between capital, labor, management, creditors, and so forth. Under this view, there is no entity apart from its various constituencies. Treating the corporation as an entity is a harmless abstraction as long as the equilibrium holds. However, when major conflicts arise, the practical implications of this simpli-fied construct become highly problematic. Difficulties in identifying the organization's interest routinely arise in two contexts explored more fully below: corporate takeovers and shareholder derivative litigation. In assessing these problems, consider whether the concept of representing an entity makes sense. Should lawyers have abstractions as clients? What are the plausible alternatives?

2.   Mergers and Acquisitions

PROBLEM 13A

You are in-house counsel for Driscoll Lab, a small drug company listed on the New York Stock Exchange, incorporated in Delaware, and located in a small midwestern city. You have been worried for some time about a potential takeover, in part because of the company's low debt, recent earnings slump, and top-heavy management structure. In anticipation of a hostile raid, you have retained a New York firm, Chase & Chen (C&C), well known for its merger and acquisition defense.

Two days ago, Global Industries announced a cash tender for Driscoll stock at $75 per share, $25 above the current share price. Global is controlled by a flamboyant Chicago investor, Edward Rey-nolds, and many of his recent targets have not survived intact. Driscoll officers are concerned not only about their own job security after a takeover, but also about the effect that liquidation might have on the local economy. Driscoll is its city's largest employer and the region has recently lost several manufacturing plants to overseas locations.

At a recent meeting with C&C's major takeover specialist, you reviewed several strategies. You could buy about a week's time by filing for a temporary restraining order under your state's takeover statute. Although such an injunction would not last because Delaware law governs, it would take some time for Global attorneys to dissolve the order. In the interim, you could ensure a longer delay by arranging for a "poison pill" that would make Driscoll less attractive.[2]

C&C believes that the best long-term strategy for staving off the acquisition would be a management-sponsored leveraged buyout. In essence, management would form a new corporation that would acquire Driscoll. Financing this purchase would require borrowing the maximum cash that banks will provide, offering a generous package of debt securities and cash for Driscoll's outstanding shares, and granting substantial stock options to management. In order to meet the debt service on that package, Driscoll would have to sell its two most profitable divisions. Although such sales would have an extremely adverse effect on Driscoll's ability to finance the drug research and development that is critical to its long-term survival, the short-term result would keep the current management structure intact and would provide a handsome payout to current shareholders. After the sale of the divisions, the company also would be less attractive as a target.

In connection with a disclosure statement to security holders, the SEC requires a filing with the Commission concerning the company's financial status. Among other things, that filing (Schedule 14D-9) must disclose whether any "negotiation is being undertaken or is underway by the subject company in response to the tender offer which relates to . . . [a] purchase, sale, or transfer of a material amount of assets." SEC rules also require prompt amendment in the event of "any material change" in the information provided. For obvious reasons, it would be disadvantageous to disclose any negotiations about the sale of the profitable Driscoll divisions before the loans and refinancing packages are complete. C&C lawyers accordingly advise that discussions with potential purchasers of the Driscoll divisions be phrased as preliminary inquiries rather than as negotiations.

C&C lawyers also propose to use certain rumors concerning Reynolds' personal life and professional ventures that might discourage his pursuit of Driscoll. In depositions, C&C lawyers are prepared to question him about questionable campaign contributions to Chicago politicians, dubious savings and loan transactions by one Global subsidiary, and drug use at the Reynolds penthouse. Although these allegations may be of limited interest to investors, they could attract considerable notice in the press. Given Reynolds' reported efforts to gain acceptance among Chicago's social elite and to obtain membership on highly selective charitable boards, these hardball tactics might give him second thoughts about pursuing the acquisition.

Driscoll's board of directors has nine members. Four are officers of the corporation. Of the five "independent" directors, two own substantial shares, two are "professional" directors owning no shares, and one is an attorney with the firm that serves as the corporation's outside counsel. All of the independent directors receive substantial compensation for their services.[3]

1. How should you advise the corporation concerning C&C's proposed strategies? Would your obligations be any different if you were outside counsel serving on the board?

2. At what point are negotiations "underway" and "material" regarding the sale of Driscoll divisions? If a potential buyer indicates that the divisions would be attractive at a specified price, can that statement be construed as a preliminary expression of interest rather than as a

negotiation? Who should make that decision? If the relevant corporate officer maintains that such a statement is not yet part of negotiations, what should be the responsibilities of a lawyer who disagrees?

3. What are corporate counsel's obligations concerning possible requests for a temporary restraining order or deposition inquiries about Reynolds' other activities? Would these be frivolous tactics within the prohibition of DR 7-102(A)(1) and (2), Model Rule 3.1, and Rule 11 of the Federal Rules of Civil Procedure? See Chapter V (The Adversary System) at pages 186–195 and Chapter X (Civil Procedure) at pages 430–445. Suppose that Driscoll management is willing to run the risk of sanctions in order to gain the time and in terrorem value that such tactics could provide.

Conflicts of interest in corporate takeovers are probably less the exception than the rule. Often, as in Problem 13A, managers and directors will lose their position if the acquisition effort succeeds. In other instances, the corporate raider may offer "sweetheart deals" to officers and board members who cooperate with the takeover. For shareholders, the incentive structure can be quite different. They may either collect a windfall premium for their shares or confront a squeeze-out for less than fair value. Changes in organizational ownership and structure can also affect other corporate stake-holders. A number of state legislatures have recognized as much by explicitly authorizing directors faced with takeover offers to consider the interests of employees, suppliers, customers, consumers, and other affected parties.[4] By the same token, these different corporate constituencies may be affected differently by various takeover de-fenses. Obvious examples include provision of expensive "golden parachutes" for corporate officers and directors, or financial re-structuring that creates onerous long-term debt burdens to provide unprecedented short-term dividends for existing shareholders.

None of the conventional responses to these conflicting interests are entirely satisfactory. The prevailing view in this, as in other corporate contexts, is that the attorney normally defers to the board of directors' judgment, even if its "utility or prudence is doubtful." Model Rule 1.13, Comment. The rationale for this approach is that although the "potential for divergent interests exists, the board is still bound by its fiduciary duty to the shareholders and therefore, absent a determination of a specific conflict, the board remains in the best position to represent the entity's interest."[5] Yet even such a deferential approach still presents problems in determining when a conflict is so direct as to require an alternative decision-making structure.

Where such conflicts are present, one response is to create a committee of the board composed of independent directors. This committee typically retains counsel that has no prior affiliation with the entity.[6] Management and inside directors may also obtain advice from their own separate counsel concerning measures such as golden parachutes or financial restructuring in leveraged buyouts.

One difficulty with this approach is that the independent directors are seldom wholly independent. They owe their selection and retention to insiders; they have ongoing friendships with insiders; and they have interests in defending their past judgments or in maintaining their existing positions.[7] Such biases may prompt these directors to select independent counsel whose advice also is not wholly independent. By picking a firm with a reputation of advising for, or more commonly against, takeovers, a board committee can often confirm its own predispositions.

Moreover, as one commentator notes, it seems bizarre for corporate counsel to represent the "interests of [the corporation] to the exclusion of the interests of its officers, directors and shareholders, all of whom are safely represented by other lawyers."[8] Under such an allocation of responsibility, what is left for corporate lawyers to do, particularly if they must defer to the business judgment of the board or of an independent committee?[9]

Would any alternative approach to conflicts of interest in takeover litigation be preferable? How much could be accomplished through stricter enforcement of ethical rules governing litigation tactics? Herbert Wachtell's classic article on strategies in takeover litigation advises lawyers for target corporations as follows:

> You are operating in a pressure atmosphere where you have constant surprise. You have very little turnaround time. The company goes running for counsel: help us. You have to commence litigation immediately. . . .
>
> This . . . means that if you want to have any prayer whatsoever of getting an injunction, you have to have *evidence*, and the way you're going to get evidence means you have to fire out immediate notices of deposition and immediate document demands. And by immediately, I mean within hours (24 hours at the outside), you have to file the complaint.[10]

The objective of this lawsuit is not simply to attempt to enjoin the offer but also to build morale, rally the troops, "chill the arbitrage," and delay the consummation so that bankers might look for some other partner.[11]

Can this advice be reconciled with DR 7-102(A) and Model Rule 3.1 and Rule 11 of the Federal Rules of Civil Procedure? Should attorneys or their firms be subject to disciplinary action and heavy fines for strategies such as those contemplated in Problem 13A? See Part D of Chapter III (Regulation of the Profession) and Part E of Chapter V (The Adversary System). Should we abandon the premise that lawyers represent entities and instead define their client as the board? Alternatively, would a better approach be changes in the substantive law, such as limitations on the use of certain takeover defenses or on inquiries concerning fitness for corporate office? If you were convinced that some substantive reforms were desirable, how would you regulate professional conduct in the interim, before their adoption?

See Chapter V, The Adversary System
  • Tactical Use of Procedure
        (pages 186–195)

See Chapter X, Civil Procedure
  • Discovery
        (pages 430–437)

3.   Lawyers as Directors

One further ethical issue that can arise in contexts such as Problem 13A involves the role of attorneys who serve as members of a client's board of directors. Although many commentators have condemned such membership because of its inherent potential for conflicts of interest, the practice remains common. According to recent estimates, more than one in six American public corporations have outside counsel sitting on their boards.[12]

The reasons are obvious. Corporations receive legal advice at no additional charge beyond the normal director fee that they would pay to any other board member. Moreover, lawyers generally make good directors. They may recognize problems that others miss, and the knowledge of the business that they obtain from board discussion can inform their legal advice. Lawyer-directors' sense of loyalty and accountability also may be heightened by their dual role.[13] For attorneys, board service is a way of gaining credibility and solidifying relationships with corporate decision-makers. Some board memberships can also confer significant prestige and generous directors' fees.

There are, however, corresponding disadvantages in this dual lawyer-director role. It decreases the possibility of disinterested advice and increases the possibility of malpractice liability, a risk that some insurance policies will not cover. Plaintiffs who sue lawyer-directors or plan to call them as witnesses can generally force their disqualification as outside counsel. And disclosures made by or to lawyers in their director capacity do not fall within the lawyer-client privilege.[14]

Given these competing concerns, bar ethical codes do not categorically prohibit a lawyer from serving as a director, but they do require that any lawyer considering such service comply with general rules on conflicts of interest. The Code allows attorneys faced with competing obligations either to recuse themselves or, if it is "obvious" that they can provide "adequate" representation, to continue in both roles after the client's informed consent. DR 5-105(C). Model Rule 1.7's comment provides more explicit guidance:

> A lawyer for a corporation or other organization who is also a member of its board of directors should determine whether the responsibilities of the two roles may conflict. The lawyer may be called on to advise the corporation in matters involving actions of the directors. Consideration should be given to the frequency with which such situations may arise, the potential intensity of the conflict, the effect of the lawyer's resignation from the board and the possibility of the corporation's obtaining legal advice from another lawyer in such situations. If there is material risk that the dual role will compromise the lawyer's independence of professional judgment, the lawyer should not serve as a director.

Some commentators have argued that such material risks are always present, and that ethics rules should follow the example of accountants' codes, which prohibit such a dual role.[15] Other experts argue that a categorical prohibition is unwise and unnecessary, and that courts can curb abuses by imposing higher standards of liability on lawyers who serve as directors as well as counsel for their clients.[16] These commentators emphasize the fundamental difference between lawyers' and accountants' roles. A central feature of attorneys' professional responsibility is zealous representation of the client's objectives; a core obligation of accountants is independence from an audit client.

Some of the potential problems under circumstances like Problem 13A are suggested by In re Kern.[17] There, the SEC brought injunctive proceedings against a lawyer who served on a board of directors while defending the corporation against a hostile takeover. The Commission alleged that Kern was partly responsible for his client's inadequate disclosure of certain defense maneuvers as required under §14(d) of the 1934 Securities Exchange Act. The administrative law judge acknowledged that Kern would not normally face liability as a legal advisor, but found that he should be accountable for his acceptance of discretionary authority as a director to determine whether disclosure was necessary.[18] The implications of *Kern* remain open to dispute. Among the unresolved questions are:

> What should someone in Kern's position do when the client says, "Look, you know more about this stuff than I do. I'm leaving this in your hands." Should it make a great deal of difference if Kern had gotten someone at the company to "take him off the hook" by seemingly making the decision, when in fact Kern's expertise and judgment were the key elements in the process?[19]

How would you resolve those questions? As a general matter, how would you regulate the practice of lawyers serving on clients' boards?

4. Shareholders' Derivative Litigation

PROBLEM 13B

You are one of Ford Motor Company's in-house lawyers. Assume that the following facts described in the American Lawyer are true. Would you recommend accepting the settlement? If the settlement is approved, what if any action would you recommend concerning Cohn's conduct?

Event #1: A lawyer, using his partner's children as the aggrieved "shareholders," decides to bring a shareholders' derivative suit against a company, charging the chairman with stealing. The charges are so scandalous, and the company and its chairman so well known, that the suit makes big headlines.

Event #2: After he files the suit he tells a reporter, as he waves various papers in the air, that he has "an open and shut" case on all the charges.

Event #3: The suit has not been filed in the right jurisdiction. It is thrown out.

Event #4: The lawyer vows to file the suit in the right jurisdiction.

Event #5: Telling the other side that he plans to file again, and that this will mean a rehash of the charges in the press, the lawyer inquires if a "settlement" might be possible.

Event #6: The company, which has denied all the charges but is beset by bad publicity on other fronts, including a criminal trial for allegedly having made dangerous products, gives the lawyer $100,000 in "legal fees" on the condition that he not bring the suit in the right jurisdiction.

Event #7: The lawyer declares that "it now appears" that the company chairman was not guilty of any wrongdoing.

The lawyer's supposed clients, the shareholders, get nothing. Nor do they give up anything: the shareholders can sue again on the same charges. It's just that the headline-making lawyer can't represent them. Contrary to what would be required in any other shareholders' suit, a judge does not have to approve this settlement. With the first suit thrown out and the second one only threatened, there is no suit pending and, therefore, no judge with jurisdiction.

In short, the lawyer, having filed a claim in the wrong jurisdiction, having produced no proof, and having now admitted that the charges were unsupportable, gets $100,000 in return for dropping his client and not generating any more bad headlines.

In many circles this would be called extortion. At Hughes Hubbard & Reed, it is called a "settlement." And Cohn's $100,000 is called "legal fees," although Hughes Hubbard lawyers say that his time and work were not documented in any way.

How can it be a "settlement" if no suit was pending and if the shareholders can sue again on the same charges?

"Because we weren't buying off the lawsuit," says Hughes Hubbard senior partner Jerome Shapiro, who negotiated the deal with Cohn. "We were buying off Roy Cohn. It's Cohn we were interested in, and what he said he could do to us in the press if he started the suit again in Michigan [the correct jurisdiction]. Cohn has a special relationship with the press," Shapiro continues. "He can get a headline in The Wall Street Journal or

The New York Times by picking up a phone. . . . These papers printed uncritical, big-headline accounts of Cohn's charges." . . .

"No, he doesn't deserve this as a fee, and it doesn't make me happy that he's received anything," Shapiro concludes. Then won't this just encourage him to go after other big-business targets? "Of course it will," Shapiro says, "but I represent the Ford Motor Company, not the next guy." . . . [20]

PROBLEM 13C

Daufuskie Investors, Ltd. ("Daufuskie") is a closely held corporation, with fewer than 20 shareholders. Daufuskie's assets are a portfolio of investment securities, which is valued at some $27 million. Henry Driessen, who is a partner in the law firm of Driessen, Morgan & Rose (DM&R), is a shareholder in Daufuskie, Inc., which holds a wide range of investments. Daufuskie's portfolio of securities includes 100 shares of common stock in Savannah Savings & Loan (the S&L). The S&L stock is worth about $30 per share.

The S&L's board has just entered into an agreement to acquire a large number of highly questionable mortgages from Metropolitan Bank of Atlanta. In exchange for those mortgages, Metropolitan will receive a 51 percent stake in the S&L and will provide golden parachutes for all of the S&L's directors. After reading about the proposed acquisition in the newspaper, Driessen calls a meeting of Daufuskie shareholders. At first, the shareholders wonder why Driessen cares about the S&L acquisition, because collectively they stand to lose at most $3,000 if the S&L collapses. But Driessen explains how important it is to keep the S&L independent and strong, and he notes that many people have their life savings tied up in S&L stock. The shareholders unenthusiastically agree to file a derivative action against the S&L board and to retain DM&R as counsel.

After the first round of extensive discovery and establishment of an independent review committee by the S&L board, settlement negotiations begin. The S&L management offers to renegotiate with Metropolitan and to offer only 45 percent of the S&L's voting power instead of 51 percent. Although this arrangement ostensibly would leave Metropolitan with less than majority control, at least 15 percent of the shares are not voted each year. Metropolitan would also add two independent directors to its board. DM&R would receive $750,000 as "reasonable attorney's fees."

Driessen presents this offer to a poorly attended meeting of the Daufuskie stockholders. In his view, the company has no alternative but to accept. If it does not, the S&L board committee would almost certainly decide to dismiss the shareholder action and its decision would be upheld by the business judgment rule. Daufuskie's shareholders agree, and the appropriate court approves the settlement. Driessen's share in DM&R's profits from the fee settlement is around $100,000, which leaves him enough to buy generous Christmas gifts for the Daufuskie shareholders. The retirees who depended on their S&L stock may need to anticipate some less festive holiday seasons.

How would you assess Driessen's conduct? Does it violate any Code or Model Rule provisions? How would you assess the adequacy of those provisions in regulating shareholder derivative litigation?

JONATHAN R. MACEY & GEOFFREY MILLER, THE PLAINTIFF'S ATTORNEY'S ROLE IN CLASS ACTION AND DERIVATIVE LITIGATION: ECONOMIC ANALYSIS AND RECOMMENDATIONS FOR REFORM

58 U. Chi. L. Rev. 1, 22-26 (1991)

[C]onsider incentive effects in class and derivative litigation. The lack of monitoring [by nominal plaintiffs] . . . in these settings would not be especially problematic if the interests of plaintiffs' counsel were closely aligned with those of their clients. Unfortunately, there is a substantial deviation of interests between attorney and client. The nature of the conflict varies depending on the type of litigation involved and the procedure used in the jurisdiction for determining the attorney's fee. But at least under the existing regulatory system, the conflict remains significant in all cases.

In "common fund" cases, where the plaintiffs' attorney generates a fund for the benefit of the class, the majority of American courts award fees out of the fund based on the lodestar calculation. Under this approach, the hours reasonably expended by the lawyer are multiplied by the lawyer's reasonable hourly fee to calculate a lodestar. The lodestar is then adjusted by a multiplier to account for a variety of factors including [any unusual degree of skill, superior or inferior, and,] most significantly, the risk of the litigation. Attorneys in these cases thus have an incentive to run up excessive hours, delay the litigation unnecessarily, or even to exaggerate the number of hours expended in order to obtain a larger fee. Plaintiffs' attorneys may also wish to settle for a relatively low sum on the eve of trial, knowing that in so doing they obtain most of the benefits they can expect from the litigation while eliminating their downside risk. These abuses are checked, to a degree, by the required judicial scrutiny of fee awards and settlements in class and derivative litigation. Nevertheless, agency costs in cases where fees are calculated using the lodestar method are no doubt substantial.

Further, plaintiffs' attorneys may sometimes substantially reduce their risk by reaching an understanding with defense counsel early on about the contours of the eventual settlement. Then they can expend a mutually acceptable number of additional hours on the case, charging them against the settlement fund under the lodestar calculation. The social disutility of this procedure is obvious; it represents an essentially meaningless exercise that ties up the resources of plaintiffs' counsel, defense counsel, and others such as witnesses who must submit to depositions that all parties understand will never be used in court. The principal losers are members of the plaintiff class who must pay over part of their recovery to counsel for work that serves no purpose other than to justify an enhanced attorney's fee.

The other method of calculating attorneys' fees in common fund cases, which has become more popular recently, is the "percentage" method, in which fees are awarded based on some fixed percentage of the fund. There are obvious incentive problems with this arrangement as well. First, plaintiffs' attorneys will earn windfall profits, at the expense of the class members, in cases presenting large damages and low proof costs. . . .

The second incentive problem in percentage-of-the-recovery cases is settlement. Attorneys compensated on a percentage method have an incentive to settle early for an amount lower than what might be obtained by further efforts. The attorney who puts in relatively few hours to obtain an early settlement is likely to earn a much greater compensation per hour of effort than an attorney who expends greater efforts and litigates a case to the point where the plaintiffs' recovery is maximized. Again the plaintiff class loses.

Consider now common benefit . . . cases. Common benefit cases are typically shareholder's derivative suits in which the plaintiffs' attorney does not generate a fund, but rather causes the defendant to do something that confers a nonpecuniary benefit on the corporation. . . . In common benefit . . . cases the attorneys' fee comes from the defendant rather than from the class recovery. Unlike common fund cases, therefore, there is a counter-party in common benefit and fee-shifting cases with an incentive to bargain over the fee in order to keep it within reasonable limits.

This feature, however, does not effectively obviate the attorney-client conflict. Defendants in common benefit and fee-shifting cases typically wish to minimize the sum of three costs: the costs of the relief on the merits, the costs of their own attorney's fees, and the costs of the plaintiff's attorney's fees. Defendants are typically indifferent about how the total cost of litigation is distributed among these elements. Plaintiffs' attorneys, on the other hand, have an interest in increasing their own fees, even at the expense of a reduction in the relief afforded to the putative client. Thus the conditions are present for a bargain under which the plaintiffs' attorneys agree to a lower overall settlement on the merits of the litigation in exchange for a higher fee.

A related problem occurs when the defendant offers a relatively generous settlement on the merits on condition that the plaintiffs' attorney agrees to waive any fee request (or to accept a low fee). This conflict has led some courts and commentators to call for a mandatory rule separating the fee negotiation from the settlement on the merits in fee-shifting cases. Whether such a rule could be effectively enforced is open to question, however. Moreover, separating the fee negotiation from the merits determination raises the possibility that plaintiffs' attorneys who believe that a favorable settlement will eventually be reached will string out litigation well past the point where settlement first becomes possible in order to justify a higher fee request. Splitting the fee and merits negotiations is no panacea for the agency problems in the common benefit and fee-shifting contexts.

Shareholder derivative suits, a form of class action brought by one or more stockholders on behalf of a corporation, play a central role in policing managerial abuses and self-dealing. Because such oversight is often expensive and exceeds the potential value to any single shareholder, the primary incentive for derivative actions is court-awarded attorneys' fees. Yet although such claims can provide a cost-effective form of deterring misconduct, they create their own set of regulatory problems, as the preceding excerpt reflects.[21] Just as shareholders have difficulty monitoring the performance of management, they also have difficulty monitoring the performance of class counsel. The free rider and collective action problems that prevent stockholders from policing opportunistic behavior by corporate decision-makers prevent comparable policing of attorneys. These problems are not unique to derivative litigation. However, such contexts well illustrate the ethical tensions that often arise in class actions.

a.   *Ethical Problems in Monitoring Plaintiff's Counsel*

Ethical problems in shareholder litigation have an extended history. A report prepared for Governor Thomas Dewey in 1945 analyzed 1,400 New York shareholder suits filed in the preceding decade and sharply criticized the lack of meaningful shareholder involvement in many actions filed in their name.

> [Nominal plaintiffs] rarely figure in the case, and on their infrequent appearances as witnesses commonly display astonishing lapses of memory, both about the reasons they brought the action and many other pertinent circumstances. It is by no means unknown for these crusaders to be so heedless of their crusade that they sell their stock during its course . . . or overlook the fact that they have voted for the transactions they assail, but a Providence kindly to lawyers whose fee position is thus menaced seems always to supply a qualified substitute client in the nick of time.[22]

More recent commentary on the derivative suit has also noted the sham nature of the nominal client's role and related ethical violations by counsel. One concern involves disregard of rules prohibiting personal solicitation of plaintiffs (DR 2-104 and Model Rule 7.3, discussed in Chapter III (Regulation of the Profession) at pages 102–103. A related ethical violation involves "maintenance," in which attorneys advance litigation costs without requiring that clients remain ultimately liable for their repayment.[23] Bar prohibitions of these practices seek to prevent lawyers from stirring up unnecessary litigation, from pressuring clients to accept representation, and from acquiring financial interests that might run counter to those of clients.

In much shareholder litigation, however, the prohibitions on solicitation and maintenance are widely ignored and frequently criticized. Without in-person solicitation, shareholders are often unaware of abuses, unlikely to respond to written notices, and unwilling to subsidize litigation costs.[24] As the Macey and Miller excerpt notes, the justification for prohibiting maintenance is also questionable because current fee structures already give lawyers incentives that diverge from those of shareholders.

Accordingly, some commentators have suggested either eliminating the fiction of "the client" entirely or relaxing restrictions on attorneys' solicitation and financing of derivative suits. The first approach would allow lawyers to sue directly or even establish an auction procedure for lawyers seeking to pursue a given claim.[25] Alternatively, in place of categorical bans on in-person solicitation, bar ethical codes could rely on more carefully tailored measures to prevent abuse, such as time, place, and manner restrictions and stricter judicial regulation of baseless claims. See Chapter III (Regulation of the Profession) at pages 100–109. Limitations on attorney financing of litigation costs could be eliminated entirely, since in the derivative context these restrictions cannot accomplish their intended objective. Any conflict of interest arising from payment of litigation costs is likely to be insignificant in the context of broader fee-related influences on lawyer judgment. According to most commentators, the central ethical challenge in derivative suits is to reduce these influences and to discourage suits or settlements that privilege attorneys' interests over those of their clients.

The reasons for lawyer-client conflicts are explored in the preceding article by Macey and Miller as well as in much of John Coffee's work.[26] As these experts point out, nominal plaintiffs generally lack incentives or capacities for monitoring shareholder suits while defendants often agree both to settlements that are insufficiently related to the merits of the litigation and to fee awards that are insufficiently related to opposing counsel's performance. In general, Coffee notes, defendants lose leverage in settlement negotiations because they face greater expenses than plaintiffs. This disadvantage reflects several factors:

> the extreme difficulty of obtaining dismissal on the pleadings; the costly nature of the discovery process for defendants, who must respond to voluminous discovery requests that plaintiffs can make cheaply; the need for multiple attorneys to represent the different defendants in a derivative action; and the plaintiff's attorney's typically lower overhead costs. In combination, these factors create a signifi-

cant cost differential that favors plaintiffs and may give a case settlement value largely unrelated to its litigation odds.[27]

As Janet Alexander's research suggests, corporate directors and
managers are particularly likely to favor overly generous dispositions where an adverse judgment might threaten their own jobs or
stock holdings.[28] And since most corporate defendants in derivative
suits are not repeat players, they may be unwilling to mount an
expensive defense in order to deter other baseless claims.[29]

Nor are trial courts necessarily able to fill the gap when approving settlements. For overburdened judges, accepting agreements
that parties have negotiated is generally the "course of least resistance."[30] Rejecting settlements increases the trial docket that most
courts are trying desperately to clear and creates a possibility of
reversal on appeal. If fee awards are part of a package settlement,
judges who second-guess the parties' agreement risk upsetting the
entire bargain. As a consequence, settlement hearings are "typically
pep rallies jointly orchestrated by plaintiff's counsel and defense
counsel" and concluded with little searching scrutiny from the
court.[31]

b.   Ethical Issues for Corporate Counsel

Corporate counsel face a different set of ethical issues than
shareholders' attorneys. For the corporation's lawyers, the central
issue in derivative litigation is generally whether to represent both
the organization and its individual officers and directors. The
Comment to Model Rule 1.13 speaks to this issue:

> The proposition that the organization is the lawyer's client does not
> alone resolve the issue. Most derivative actions are a normal incident
> of an organization's affairs, to be defended by the organization's law-
> yer like any other suit. However, if the claim involves serious charges
> of wrongdoing by those in control of the organization, a conflict may
> arise between the lawyer's duty to the organization and the lawyer's
> relationship with the board. In those circumstances, Rule 1.7 governs
> who should represent the directors and the organization.

Rule 1.7 provides, in language that largely tracks a similar provision
in the Code (DR 5-101):

> (a) A lawyer shall not represent a client if the representation of
> that client will be directly adverse to another client, unless:
>> (1) the lawyer reasonably believes the representation will not
>> adversely affect the relationship with the other client; and
>> (2) each client consents after consultation.
> (b) A lawyer shall not represent a client if the representation of
> that client may be materially limited by the lawyer's responsibilities
> to another client or to a third person or by the lawyer's own interests,
> unless

(1) the lawyer reasonably believes the representation will not be adversely affected; and

(2) the client consents after consultation. . . .

In derivative litigation, the application of rules governing conflicts poses several difficulties. One is whether directors of a corporation whose performance is at issue are capable of giving valid consent to a conflict. A second question is whether it makes sense to allow dual representation prior to the point of an actual conflict.

In addressing these issues, courts and commentators have generally focused on whether the complaint is patently frivolous, seeks only minor relief, or does not charge officers and directors with significant wrongdoing. For those cases, as the Model Rule commentary suggests, separate representation appears unnecessary. In more serious cases, dual representation is likely to be inappropriate even before actual conflicts have materialized because loyalty to individual defendants may prevent an unbiased inquiry concerning the corporation's interest. An attorney with competing responsibilities might proceed in a way that avoids actual conflict but does not well serve each client.[32]

Accordingly, recent decisions have been increasingly sensitive to the likelihood of conflict when substantial shareholder claims are at issue and have prohibited dual representation from the outset, or from the time that the corporation seeks to take an active litigation role.[33] One standard practice is for the corporation to create an independent committee of outside directors not named as defendants to review the merits of the derivative claim and to have this committee choose separate legal representation for the corporation. Another less common practice is for trial courts to select an independent corporate counsel. Whatever the selection mechanism, separate representation has obvious advantages. As one leading Seventh Circuit decision summarized them:

> [Decisions about the corporation's role in litigation] will be made without the possibility of any influence emanating from the representation of the individual defendants, and will also eliminate the problem of confidences and secrets reposed by the individual defendants being used adverse to their interests.

Cannon v. U.S. Acoustics Corp., 398 F. Supp. 209, 220 (E.D. Ill. 1975), aff'd in part, 532 F.2d 1178 (7th Cir. 1976).

Although most experts agree that separate counsel in nonfrivolous derivative suits is generally advisable, this approach is not without difficulties. Outside counsel can often add considerably to the expense without assisting the decision-making process. As in the takeover context, independent committees are not necessarily independent; they almost always recommend dismissal of the derivative suit and courts almost always defer to a committee's business judgment.[34] Although some experts have advocated a more active role for trial judges in scrutinizing corporate decisions, other commentators question how effective this strategy would be in practice. Courts frequently lack the time, expertise, or information to assess a company's best interest.[35] Moreover, recent research suggests that the central problem in derivative suits is not inappropriate dismissals but inappropriate settlements. As noted earlier, the expense of responding to derivative suits (even if an independent committee might eventually recommend dismissal) generally leads to settlement, and on terms that bear too little relationship to the merits. According to most experts, addressing that problem should be the primary focus of reform efforts.

c. *Strategies for Reform*

One cluster of reform proposals involves increasing judicial oversight of settlements. For example, courts have been urged to give closer scrutiny to agreements that provide a significant fee award for plaintiffs' counsel but little tangible benefits for shareholders.[36] Such claims often should not have been filed at all or should not have been settled without a more substantial remedy. To facilitate judicial review, some commentators have proposed appointing lawyers as guardians ad litem for the shareholder class in cases involving large stakes but small individual claims. These lawyers could have access to discovery materials and offer an independent assessment of the merits of proposed agreements.[37] However, as commentators generally acknowledge, separate representation is no panacea. One difficulty is that "independent" guardians ad litem are often repeat players who have an incentive to cultivate reputations for cooperativeness in settlement negotiations.

To control attorneys' fees, courts and bar ethical rules could require separate negotiation of the substantive terms of settlement and the compensation for plaintiffs' counsel. This practice could minimize collusion and encourage judicial adjustments of excessive attorney compensation without jeopardizing the entire agreement.[38] The American Law Institute considered such proposals during debate on its Corporate Governance Project. Proponents (including Coffee) argued that banning fee discussions prior to judicial approval of a settlement would help deter frivolous litigation because plaintiffs' lawyers would run the risk that defendants would oppose any fee award once the substantive claims were resolved. The defense bar objected to the proposal on the ground that it would make settling derivative suits more difficult and that its deterrent value was speculative at best.

This argument parallels the debate over simultaneous negotiations of substantive claims and attorneys' fees in civil rights actions, discussed in Chapter X (Civil Procedure) at pages 450–456. In Evans v. Jeff D., 475 U.S. 717 (1986), the Supreme Court declined to ban such simultaneous bargaining, in part out of deference to defendants' justifiable interests in determining their total liability. The dissenting Justices, joined by civil rights attorneys, argued that finalizing both substantive and fee-related issues at the same time exposed counsel and their clients to an inherent conflict of interest. Some leading ethics experts have agreed with the dissenters and have argued that the majority's reasoning in *Jeff D.* has little force in derivative suits, where the corporation is effectively subsidizing both sides of a successful lawsuit. Which side of this debate do you find most persuasive? Would you have supported the ALI proposal?

What formula for settling the amount of attorneys' fees do you favor? Although all approaches have their drawbacks, many commentators endorse a percentage fee, adjusted for special factors. Thus, courts might grant counsel between 15 and 33 percent of the recovery, based on the amount of risk assumed and effort expended.[39] Such a formula discourages counsel from padding hours and encourages them to maximize shareholder relief. Where complex fee calculations are required, appointment of special masters should be more common. By contrast, other commentators worry that guaranteeing lawyers a percentage fee will simply add to their incentives to ignore the merits; the temptation will be to accept early offers without doing adequate investigation.[40] Whether a graduated formula can minimize such effects is not entirely clear. In the absence of definite evidence, what approach would you advocate?

Finally, and most fundamentally, many experts emphasize the need to rethink the structure of derivative actions. Particularly in cases involving large stakes and small individual claims, the named plaintiff functions largely as a "figurehead [who does] little, indeed, usually does nothing, to monitor the attorney."[41] By requiring the pretense of a lawyer-client relationship, procedural rules invite ethical violations involving solicitation and maintenance, while providing inadequate protection of class interests. One alternative worth considering would be to allow attorneys to bring Jane Doe or Richard Roe actions directly on behalf of a class or a corporation.[42]

Jonathan Macey and Geoffrey Miller advocate a more fundamental change, an auction procedure, which has attracted some support and experimentation among trial courts. As they describe it,

[a] pure form of auction would simply sell the plaintiffs' claims outright to the winning bidder, with the proceeds to be distributed immediately to the class or corporation. Under such an approach, the winner of the auction would have litigation incentives that are very similar to those which a claimholder would have in traditional, two-party litigation. There would be no need for any rules on typicality or adequacy of representation or for judicial scrutiny of settlements and fee awards. Class members would receive a certain and quick recovery rather than an uncertain and delayed one. The result would be more effective private enforcement of the law. Other possibilities . . . involve partial bids or bids for lead counsel rights based on the percentage of the recovery that the attorney would be willing to take as a fee; these may be more feasible to implement, although they retain some of the problems of misalignment between the interests of the attorney and client.[43]

What is your view of such a procedure? In In re Oracle Securities Litigation, 132 F.R.D. 538 (N.D. Cal. 1990), Judge Walker auctioned off the right to serve as class counsel among four attorney bidders.[44] Is that approach desirable, or preferable to dispensing with plaintiffs entirely? Would eliminating plaintiffs prove unacceptable on symbolic grounds by implying that "justice is for sale"? Do auction procedures create incentives for bids too low to ensure adequate representation? Could courts deal with that risk by allowing additional fees if costs prove unexpectedly high? Or would such exceptions undercut the point of an auction? Consider the difficulties raised in Problems 13B and 13C. To what extent will recent reforms in federal law address such problems by imposing higher pleading standards, delaying discovery, and insulating management from suits for mistaken predictions?[45]

B. CONFIDENTIALITY AND DISCLOSURE OBLIGATIONS

1. The Attorney-Client Privilege in Organizational Settings

a. Introduction

As noted earlier, lawyers representing organizations owe their fundamental allegiance to the entity, not to any of its officers, directors, or employees. EC 5-18; Model Rule 1.13. This allocation of responsibility raises obvious questions concerning the attorney-client privilege. Whose confidences must be kept? From whom?

Those questions have generated considerable dispute among courts and commentators. While some early opinions suggested that any officer's or employee's statement to counsel should be privileged, other decisions held that none of these statements should be protected because the privilege was "fundamentally personal in nature."[46] By the 1980s, two intermediate approaches had become dominant. Under one approach, the "control group" test, the privilege applies only to persons in a position to control or take substantial part in a decision based on legal advice. Under an alternative "subject matter" test:

> The attorney-client privilege is applicable to an employee's communication if (1) the communication was made for the purpose of securing legal advice; (2) the employee making the communication did so at the direction of his corporate superior; (3) the superior made the request so that the corporation could secure legal advice; (4) the subject matter of the communication is within the scope of the employee's corporate duties; and (5) the communication is not disseminated beyond those persons who, because of the corporate structure, need to know its contents.

Diversified Industries, Inc. v. Meredith, 572 F.2d 596, 609 (8th Cir. 1977) (expanding on Harper & Row Publishers, Inc. v. Decker, 423 F.2d 487 (7th Cir.), aff'd, 400 U.S. 348 (1970)).

In 1981, the Supreme Court attempted to resolve the dispute within the federal courts in Upjohn Co. v. United States.

UPJOHN CO. v. UNITED STATES
449 U.S. 383 (1981)

Justice REHNQUIST delivered the opinion of the Court.

We granted certiorari in this case to address important questions concerning the scope of the attorney-client privilege in the corporate context. . . . 445 U.S. 925. With respect to the privilege question the parties and various amici have described our task as one of choosing between two "tests" which have gained adherents in the courts of appeals. We are acutely aware, however, that we sit to decide concrete cases and not abstract propositions of law. We decline to lay down a broad rule or series of rules to govern all conceivable future questions in this area, even were we able to do so. We can and do, however, conclude that the attorney-client privilege protects the communications involved in this case from compelled disclosure. . . .

I

Petitioner Upjohn Co. manufactures and sells pharmaceuticals here and abroad. In January 1976 independent accountants conducting an audit of one of Upjohn's foreign subsidiaries discovered that the subsidiary made payments to or for the benefit of foreign government officials in order to secure government business. The accountants so informed petitioner Mr. Gerard Thomas, Upjohn's Vice President, Secretary, and General Counsel. . . .

He consulted with outside counsel and R.T. Parfet, Jr., Upjohn's Chairman of the Board. It was decided that the company would conduct an internal investigation of what were termed "questionable payments." As part of this investigation the attorneys prepared a letter containing a questionnaire which was sent to "All Foreign General and Area Managers" over the Chairman's signature. The letter began by noting recent disclosures that several American companies made "possible illegal" payments to foreign government officials and emphasized that the management needed full information concerning any such payments made by Upjohn. The letter indicated that the Chairman had asked Thomas, identified as "the company's General Counsel," "to conduct an investigation for the purpose of determining the nature and magnitude of any payments made by the Upjohn Company or any of its subsidiaries to any employee or official of a foreign government." The questionnaire sought detailed information concerning such payments. Managers were instructed to treat the investigation as "highly confidential" and not to discuss it with anyone other than Upjohn employees who might be helpful in providing the requested information. . . . Thomas and outside counsel also interviewed the recipients of the question- naire and some 33 other Upjohn officers or employees as part of the investigation.

[The company voluntarily submitted a preliminary report disclosing certain questionable payments to the SEC and the IRS. Government authorities subsequently demanded production of Upjohn's investigative files, including written questionnaires. The company declined to produce the questionnaires, claiming they were protected by the attorney-client privilege. On appeal of an order directing production, the Sixth Circuit Court of Appeals held that the privilege did not apply to communications made by "agents not responsible for directing Upjohn's actions in response to legal advice." The court reasoned that a broader application of the privi- lege would encourage too broad a "zone of silence," and remanded the case for a determination of who was within the control group. The Supreme Court reversed.]

. . . The attorney-client privilege is the oldest of the privileges for confidential communications known to the common law. 8 J. Wigmore, Evidence §2290 (McNaughton rev. 1961). Its purpose is to encourage full and frank communication between attorneys and their clients and thereby promote broader public interests in the observance of law and administration of justice. The privilege recognizes that sound legal advice or advocacy serves public ends and that such advice or advocacy depends upon the lawyer's being fully informed by the client. . . .

The Court of Appeals, however, considered the application of the privilege in the corporate context to present a "different problem," since the client was an inanimate entity and "only the senior man- agement, guiding and integrating the several operations, . . . can be said to possess an identity analogous to the corporation as a whole." . . . Such a view, we think, overlooks the fact that the privilege exists to protect not only the giving of professional advice to those who can act on it but also the giving of information to the lawyer to enable him to give sound and informed advice. The first step in the resolution of any legal problem is ascertaining the factual background with an eye to the legally relevant. . . . In the corporate context, however, it will frequently be employees beyond the control group as defined by the court below, "officers and agents . . . respon- sible for directing [the company's] actions in response to legal advice," who will possess the information needed by the corporation's lawyers. Middle-level, and indeed lower-level, employees can, by actions within the scope of their employment, embroil the corpora- tion in serious legal difficulties, and it is only natural that these employees would have the relevant information needed by corporate counsel if he is adequately to advise the client with respect to such actual or potential difficulties. . . .

The control group test adopted by the court below thus frustrates the very purpose of the privilege by discouraging the communication of relevant information by employees of the client to attorneys seeking to render legal advice to the client corporation. The attorney's advice will also frequently be more significant to noncontrol group members than to those who officially sanction the advice, and the control group test makes it more difficult to convey full and frank legal advice to the employees who will put into effect the client corporation's policy. . . .

An uncertain privilege, or one which purports to be certain but results in widely varying applications by the courts, is little better than no privilege at all. The very terms of the test adopted by the court below suggest the unpredictability of its application. The test restricts the availability of the privilege to those officers who play a "substantial role" in deciding and directing a corporation's legal response. Disparate decisions in cases applying this test illustrate its unpredictability. . . .

[The Court then discounted the appellate panel's concern that extension of the privilege beyond the control group would unduly burden discovery and create a zone of silence over corporate affairs. In addressing this issue, Justice Rehnquist noted:] Here the Government was free to question the employees who communicated with Thomas and outside counsel. Upjohn has provided the IRS with a list of such employees, and the IRS has already interviewed some 25 of them. While it would probably be more convenient for the Government to secure the results of petitioner's internal investigation by simply subpoenaing the questionnaires and notes taken by petitioner's attorneys, such considerations of convenience do not overcome the policies served by the attorney-client privilege. As Justice Jackson noted in his concurring opinion in Hickman v. Taylor, 329 U.S., at 516: "Discovery was hardly intended to enable a learned profession to perform its functions . . . on wits borrowed from the adversary."

---

b. The Rationale for the Privilege

As discussion in Chapter VI (Confidentiality and Client Counseling) at page 223 indicates, the attorney-client privilege has two fundamental justifications: preserving individual rights, such as privacy, autonomy, and the freedom from self-incrimination; and promoting compliance with law through candid attorney-client relationships. Rights-based concerns, however, have much less relevance in organizational settings because the privilege belongs to the corporate entity rather than its individual agents. Unless those agents who communicate with counsel reasonably believe that the lawyer represents them personally, they may not claim protection for any of their statements: the corporation decides whether to assert or waive confidentiality.[47] Accordingly, the rationale for the corporate privilege rests largely on its second justification: effectiveness in promoting effective legal counseling.

This rationale is one of the justifications that *Upjohn* offers to support a broad privilege. Does Justice Rehnquist's opinion provide evidence for the claim that such a privilege is necessary or sufficient for adequate legal representation? Is that claim self-evident? Would lower-level employees usually have sufficient reasons to cooperate apart from promises of confidentiality? How significant are those promises if the corporation rather than the individual employee determines whether to keep or waive the privilege? One of the only empirical studies on point found that although corporate counsel raise the confidentiality issue almost 70 percent of the time, only about one-quarter of corporate employees express concern about whether their communication will be protected.[48]

Some commentators have argued that the most significant advantage of a broad privilege is that it will encourage organizations to make their own investigations of potentially illegal conduct and to involve counsel in that process. Without a privilege, lawyers will be "cut out of the loop" of sensitive legal information.[49] Critics of broad confidentiality protections respond that corporations often have sufficient independent reasons to undertake internal investigations and to require cooperation with lawyers; such cooperation may be essential to preparing a defense or minimizing damages. A broad privilege, critics argue, creates "black holes" of information. Attorneys who investigate misconduct may be the only individuals with a clear sense of what happened. Their communications are protected; thus, information goes in the hole but never comes out.[50]

Which argument do you find most convincing? Justice Rehnquist in *Upjohn* responds to concerns about "zones of silence" by noting that only legal communications are privileged, not underlying facts. Opponents can still question employees about illegal conduct. And, he concludes, a learned profession should not rely on "wits borrowed from its adversary." Is this an adequate response? Depositions are a quite costly means of acquiring information, especially in corporate settings where outsiders may not know who has the relevant facts or which account to credit if sources conflict. Consider Bentham's critique of those who look on the legal system through "fox-hunting eyes," and regard the trial as a "sort of game . . . in which the proper end to be aimed at is, not that the truth may be discovered, but that both parties may have fair play."[51] How might Justice Rehnquist respond to this criticism? How would you?

c. *The Implications of* Upjohn

Although the court in *Upjohn* stressed the need for certainty in the scope of the privilege, Justice Rehnquist's opinion declined to endorse any broad rule. However, its ad hoc approach was certainly consistent with the subject matter test of *Diversified Industries*. Many states, which are free to fashion their own rules of privilege, have adopted an approach similar to *Upjohn*. Other courts have offered less sweeping protections, and some commentators have endorsed a case-by-case balancing approach similar to the framework governing attorneys' work product.[52] Under a balancing approach, adversaries could have access to materials not otherwise reasonably available. What would be the costs and benefits of such an alternative framework?

Arguments for replacing the per se corporate privilege standard with a balancing test have won favor primarily in the context of shareholder derivative suits. The leading case carving out a corporate fiduciary exception to the privilege is Garner v. Wolfinbarger, 430 F.2d 1093 (5th Cir. 1970), cert. denied, 401 U.S. 974 (1971). There, the court permitted plaintiff stockholders to "show cause" why they should have access to otherwise privileged material and indicated that the result would depend on factors such as the number of shareholders and the percentage of stock they represent; the necessity or desirability of granting plaintiffs access to the information; the nature or wrongfulness of the corporate action at issue; and any interests of the corporation in protecting the information, such as concerns about trade secrets. Subsequent decisions have extended that analysis to litigation involving other fiduciary relationships, including those between limited partners and partnerships, insurers and insured parties, and labor unions and union members.[53]

d. *The Lawyer's Counseling Role*

Model Rule 1.13(d) provides that

> [i]n dealing with an organization's directors, officers, employees, members, shareholders or other constituents, a lawyer shall explain the identity of the client when it is apparent that the organization's interests are adverse to those of the constituents with whom the lawyer is dealing.

The Comment to that Rule further notes that when the organization's interest may be adverse to that of its constituents, the lawyer should "advise such persons that they may wish to obtain independent representation." In addition:

> (1)... Care must be taken to assure that the individual understands that, when there is such adversity of interest, the lawyer for the organization cannot provide legal representation for that con-

stituent individual, and that discussion between the lawyer for the organization and the individual may not be privileged.

(2) Whether such a warning should be given by the lawyer for the organization to any constituent individual may turn on the facts of each case.

Model Rule 4.3 further requires that

[w]hen the lawyer knows or reasonably should know that the unrepresented person misunderstands the lawyer's role in the matter, the lawyer shall make reasonable efforts to correct the misunderstanding.

The Code of Professional Responsibility does not speak explicitly to conflicts of interest and confidentiality obligations for attorneys in organizational contexts. However, DR 7-104(A)(2) provides that a lawyer should not "[g]ive advice to a person who is not represented by a lawyer, other than the advice to secure counsel, if the interests of such person are or have a reasonable possibility of being in conflict with the interest of his client."

These rules attempt to accommodate competing concerns. It is usually in the organization's interest to gain full information from employees and to encourage their cooperation in team defense efforts. It is not necessarily in the interest of individual employees to comply. The more explicit the discussion of potential conflicts and limits of confidentiality protections, the less the likelihood of confusion about the lawyer's role but the greater the risks of noncooperation. A difficult question for corporate counsel involves deciding when conflicts have materialized to such an extent that such an explicit discussion is necessary.

The Code does not speak to that issue, and some commentators have criticized the Model Rules for giving priority to organizational over employee concerns.[54] What is your view? Should corporate counsel routinely inform employees about the scope of the attorney-client privilege and the organization's right to waive it? Should the lawyer in Problem 13D provide the functional equivalent of *Miranda* warnings? See Problem 15C at pages 663.

e.   *Confidentiality and Conflicts of Interest*

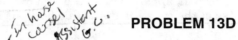

PROBLEM 13D

Lisa Rosaldo is a fifth-year associate in a firm that serves as outside counsel for a drug company. A senior manager has asked the firm for a review of health risks and potential legal liability of the company's breast implants. As a preliminary matter, the supervising partner asks Rosaldo to talk with the company's assistant research director, John Barrett, with whom she has worked before on unrelated matters. The manager has reason to question Barrett's competence in handling implant research and complaints, but does not want Rosaldo to say anything that would cause alarm and discourage his candid cooperation. The senior partner conveys this to Rosaldo with advice to be particularly careful in any statements about confidentiality.

At the outset of her interview with Barrett, Rosaldo tells him that the firm has asked her to "conduct this interview as the company's lawyer." She also indicates that everything they discuss will be "covered under the attorney-client privilege" and that he should "keep these matters confidential."

During the course of the interview, Rosaldo learns that in seeking FDA approval, the company ran large numbers of animal tests but never put silicone implants in or under human breast tissue. Most company tests involved only two-year follow-ups rather than the seven-year animal "lifetime" design that the FDA increasingly has been demanding. Sixteen months after the product was released, the chair of an internal corporate task force expressed concerns that the company still lacked any "truly quantitative data" about the risks of implant leakage. Over the next decade, a series of complaints, including leaks, painful scarring, and adverse reactions by the body's immune system, prompted the director to promise the FDA that the company would undertake additional tests. These have not yet begun. Rather, the company has reviewed a sample of doctors' records involving about 1,000 patients. These showed a serious complaint rate of only 1 percent. However, few of those complaints involved women who had implants for more than five years, and other research indicates that the most serious complications have taken between five to ten years to materialize.

When Rosaldo presses Barrett for an explanation of why more adequate research had not been undertaken, he becomes defensive. From the beginning, he points out, his division was under heavy pressure to come up with a product to counter a rival softer gel that had seized half of the company's implant market. The company's initial research had disclosed no substantial safety problems, and the FDA had not demanded further study. The vast majority of women who have the implants appear satisfied, and a significant number (about 20 percent) are in a high-need category: they seek breast reconstruction following cancer.

Finally, the director adds that certain personal problems may have contributed to his delays in launching additional implant research. He has recently been through an acrimonious divorce and has developed stress-related back problems. To combat the tension and pain, he began drinking heavily. However, he is now in a treatment program and is preparing a full-scale investigation of reported complications as well as additional tests.

When Rosaldo indicates that she will need to summarize the status of implant research for senior management, the interview becomes highly strained. Barrett tells her that he believed that everything he said would be confidential. Rosaldo explains that she meant that he should keep matters confidential. At that point, Barrett becomes furious:

> Remember that you're my lawyer too. I've worked for this company for over a quarter century, and I can tell a good product from a bad one. These complaints have almost all involved cosmetic surgery

patients, the world's most dissatisfied women. They expect perfection without problems, and then if the doctor misleads them or messes up the operation, everyone blames the product. There's nothing to be concerned about here, and if you suggest otherwise, then you'll have something to worry about.

Rosaldo prepares a report detailing this interview and her criticisms of the product trials. She concludes her report by quoting the director's comments about cosmetic surgery patients and suggesting that his attitude might be contributing to an undervaluation of serious complaints. The supervising partner directs her to delete this discussion in the final version of the report; it strikes him as "strident feminism."

Six months later, Rosaldo learns that her report was never circulated and that no further testing has begun. When she expresses concern, the supervising partner responds that her responsibility has ended, and that it is up to senior management to handle the situation.

Consider Model Rules 1.13 and 4.3 discussed above. Did the associate provide adequate disclosures to the research director? Did the supervising attorney provide appropriate guidance to the associate? How would you have handled those issues? Given the confusion about roles, should Rosaldo have disclosed the research director's personal problems?[55]

---

f. Decision-Making Authority

Consider the material on external and internal whistle-blowing in Chapter VI (Confidentiality) at pages 278–292 and Model Rule 1.13(b). The Rule provides in part that when an officer intends to act in a manner that is a

> violation of a legal obligation to the organization, or a violation of law which reasonably might be imputed to the organization, and is likely to result in substantial injury to the organization, the lawyer should proceed as is reasonably necessary in the best interests of the organization.

Any response should be "designed to minimize disruption of the organization" and may include advising that a separate legal opinion be sought and referring the matter to higher authority in the organization. The Comment to that Rule adds that "[c]lear justification should exist for seeking review over the head of the constituent normally responsible for it. . . . Review by the chief executive officer or by the board of directors may be required when the matter is of importance commensurate with their authority."

Could inadequacies in testing, review of complaints, or warnings to implant users constitute a "legal violation" within the meaning of this rule? If not, should that foreclose outside counsel from seeking review of the matter from a higher authority within the corporation? Evaluate that issue in light of the excerpts from Coffee and Williams below.

How should the associate respond to the supervisor's directives? Consider the materials on supervisory and subordinate attorneys in Chapter III (Regulation of the Profession), pages 82–89, and Model Rule 5.2. Is this a case where the associate may or should "act in accordance with a supervisory lawyer's reasonable resolution of an arguable question of professional duty"? Model Rule 5.2.

JOHN C. COFFEE, JR., BEYOND THE SHUT-EYED SENTRY: TOWARD A THEORETICAL VIEW OF CORPORATE MISCONDUCT AND AN EFFECTIVE LEGAL RESPONSE

63 Va. L. Rev. 1099, 1131-1139 (1977)

[Adverse information about possibly illegal corporate conduct often fails to reach the board of directors until a crisis has become unavoidable.] A variety of reasons appear to share responsibility for these information blockages: (a) a shared feeling on the part of subordinate officials that they owe their loyalty chiefly to senior management and not to the board; (b) a belief that the board is interested only in "hard" quantitative information, such as capital costs, financial ratios, and expected rates of return; (c) a sense that "everybody knows anyway," coupled with the perception that the board would rather not be put on formal notice as to the ugly "facts of life" of doing business . . . and (d) a "lack of congruence" between the interests of the corporation and the career aspirations of individual corporate officials. More simply, this last point means that what is good for General Motors is not necessarily good for its Assistant Vice President. If he fails to use [ethically questionable methods such as payoffs to corrupt foreign officers] or if he discloses to his superiors any questionable practices he does use, he may appear less successful than his compatriots who hide such information from their superiors. To be sure, the tendency to report information selectively, emphasizing the positive while filtering out the negative, is characteristic of all bureaucratic organizations (whether the information relates to . . . environmental hazards of a major governmental project, or the illegal means by which a profitable contract has been secured). But distinguishing the corporate context is the comparative absence of any institutionalized mechanisms by which to penetrate and break down these information blockages. While armies have inspectors general, and governmental projects face the necessity of environmental impact studies, no currently enforced legal norm requires the corporation to internalize a means of forcing potentially adverse information to the attention of the board.

HAROLD WILLIAMS, PROFESSIONALISM AND THE CORPORATE BAR

36 Bus. Law. 159, 166-167 (1980)

COMMUNICATING WITH THE CLIENT

One of the cardinal attributes of the attorney-client relationship is free and frank communication. In the corporate context, that should entail an obligation to communicate to the corporation, meaning its officers or, if necessary, its board, if he or she is aware that the corporation is embarked on a course of conduct which, while arguably lawful, may be questionable and is of such significance that the corporation's interests, not limited to legal liability, may be materially affected.

I doubt that explicit recognition of this duty would mean, as some have suggested, that the attorney would be isolated from candid discussion or full information because of management's concern that the lawyer would be a conduit of the board. But, to the extent that it does, it is a responsibility the client must assume. This is not a basis for compromising the lawyer's appropriate ethical standards. Further, we must recognize that management itself may well have obligations to report to the board in similar circumstances. And, if management is not inclined to be open with its board or would choose not to consult counsel rather than risk counsel's going to the board, counsel may well be on notice of larger potential problems with his client's candor and integrity. And, finally, all who deal with an attorney must understand that a lawyer should not be used as a value-neutral technician and that a necessary adjunct to his technical skills is sensitivity to ethical considerations. In my opinion, the prestige that such integrity engenders will enhance, rather than diminish, the role of the lawyer as a counsellor.

My concerns in this area go far beyond the possibility that a corporation may risk legal penalties or serious damage to its reputation. More significant in the long-run to the American economic system is the fact that, in some situations, the corporate conduct is incompatible with the continuation of the corporate system as we know it. And, by acquiescence, the lawyer becomes a party to its further erosion. It would not be consistent with the bar's professional obligation if it insulates attorneys from their responsibility to prevent situations which could contribute to the erosion of the corporate system which they serve.

But I do not take comfort from the fact that the [Model Rules] would *permit* the attorney to refer particular matters to higher client authority, including, if necessary, the board of directors or a similar governing body. [Rule 1.13,] taken together with the related commentary, erects a number of additional hurdles which would frustrate, rather than facilitate, the attorney's communication with the client. Worse still, these hurdles may be used by timorous corporate lawyers to justify standing mute. For example, the commentary suggests that counsel must have a "clear justification" before going over the head of a corporate officer; in my judgment, the dictates of the attorney's own sense of professional responsibility ought to be justification enough for bringing a matter to higher levels of corporate authority. Further, the comments caution that lawyers must be confident that the question is one of law and not merely policy. To the extent that considerations of matters which are not strictly legal, such as damage to reputation or considerations with ethical overtones, would be considered as a policy, rather than legal, concern, it would seem that the [Rule] restricts the lawyer to the role of legal technician, rather than encourages the corporate attorney to exercise the broader sensitivity and judgment which are the hallmark of a profession.

---

2. Client Loyalty, Public Safety, and Conflicts of Interest

See Chapter XV, Evidence and Trial Advocacy
  • Witness Preparation
      (Problem 15C, page 663)

See Chapter VI, Confidentiality and Client Counseling
  • Part A. The Attorney-Client Privilege and Bar Ethical Obligations
      (pages 223–225)
  • Part B. Justification and Critiques
      (pages 225–229)

3. Client Fraud

PROBLEM 13E

For the past eight years, you have occasionally represented a small family-owned corporation. You are currently participating in the final stages of negotiation on the sale of the corporation, and the buyer has asked for a standard net worth statement. After briefly glancing at the document, you have difficulty reconciling its bottom line with what you know of corporate assets and performance over the past several years.

1. You have not been asked to review the document. May you include it in materials provided to the buyer without comment or further inquiry?

2. Suppose that you raise the issue with the company's president and primary stockholder. She reminds you that no one has requested your opinion and that an accountant has certified the statement as accurate. How do you respond?

3. Alternatively, assume that you are asked to draft an update letter in connection with the final closing of the sale. That letter will discuss whether any material changes have occurred between the completion of the net worth statement and the final closing date. May you compose a letter that truthfully denies any awareness of material changes, but fails to disclose information raising doubts about the accuracy of the original statement?

4. If you decline to draft the letter, should you withdraw from representation? If you withdraw, what, if any, information about your withdrawal should you provide to the buyer or to your replacement counsel?

SCHATZ v. WEINBERG & GREEN, 943 F.2D 485 (4TH CIR. 1991), CERT. DENIED, 503 U.S. 936 (1992). In 1986, the plaintiffs, Ivan and Joanne Schatz, arranged to sell an 80 percent interest in two companies to Mark Rosenberg. The purchase price was $1.2 million in promissory notes that a holding company issued and that Rosenberg personally guaranteed. Prior to the closing, the plaintiffs relied on a financial statement and update letter describing Rosenberg's net worth. The documents, prepared by his law firm, Weinberg & Green, contained material misstatements. Over the next several years, the Schatzes loaned an additional $150,000 to the companies while Rosenberg siphoned off all available corporate assets. When he declared bankruptcy, the Schatzes were left with worthless notes. They then sued the law firm and argued that the attorneys should be accountable for providing information that they knew was false and that was incorporated into a document on which third parties will reasonably rely.

In affirming the dismissal of plaintiffs' complaint, the Fourth Circuit reasoned that attorneys owed common law duties only to clients and to direct beneficiaries of the lawyer-client relationship, not to other third parties such as the Schatzes.

> Any other result may prevent a client from reposing complete trust in his lawyer for fear that he might reveal a fact which would trigger the lawyer's duty to the third party. Similarly, if attorneys had a duty to disclose information to third parties, attorneys would have an incentive not to press clients for information. The net result would not be less securities fraud. Instead, attorneys would more often be unwitting accomplices to the fraud as a result of being kept in the dark by their clients or by their own reluctance to obtain information. The better rule, that attorneys have no duty to "blow the whistle" on their clients, allows clients to repose complete trust in their lawyers. Under those circumstances, the client is more likely to disclose damaging or problematic information, and the lawyer will more likely be able to counsel his client against misconduct.

Under the court's analysis, the lawyers could be liable only if they had the specific intent to aid the client's fraud.

In criticizing the *Schatz* holding, commentators often note that recent decisions generally hold professionals other than lawyers to a higher standard than the Fourth Circuit's. For example, "conscious avoidance" of facts indicating fraud will establish federal criminal liability for professionals such as underwriters. These commentators argue on public policy grounds that attorneys in civil cases should have no greater protection from liability.[56]

Moreover, from critics' perspective, the *Schatz* holding ill serves the bar as well as the public. In economic terms, the decision undermines the value of having attorneys prepare financial documents. Paying a law firm to complete a net worth statement is valuable largely because the firm's reputation serves to corroborate the client's assertions. On this reasoning, the outcome in *Schatz* is inefficient because it permits negligent or willfully ignorant attorneys to devalue other lawyers' reputational signals.[57] If this is true, would malpractice liability be an appropriate response?

A number of courts have imposed more rigorous fiduciary standards than *Schatz*. For example, in litigation involving failures of savings and loan institutions, lawyers have been held accountable for failure to make reasonable investigation.[58] Consider the frequently cited statement by the Committee on Counsel Responsibility and Liability of the ABA Section of Corporation, Banking and Business Law. Would it establish an appropriate standard in malpractice cases?

REPORT OF THE COMMITTEE ON COUNSEL RESPONSIBILITY AND LIABILITY OF THE SECTION OF CORPORATION, BANKING AND BUSINESS LAW, THE CODE OF PROFESSIONAL RESPONSIBILITY AND THE RESPONSIBILITY OF LAWYERS ENGAGED IN SECURITIES LAW PRACTICE, 30 BUS. LAW. 1289 (1975). The focus of this report involves

the circumstances under which, and the extent to which, a lawyer should verify or supplement the facts presented to him as the basis for [a legal] opinion. . . . [T]he lawyer should, in the first instance, make inquiry of his client as to the relevant facts and receive answers. If any of the alleged facts, or the alleged facts taken as a whole, are incomplete in a material respect; or are suspect; or are inconsistent; or either on their face or on the basis of other known facts are open to question, the lawyer should make further inquiry. The extent of this inquiry will depend in each case upon the circumstances; for example, it would be less where the lawyer's past relationship with the client is sufficient to give him a basis for trusting the client's probity than where the client has recently engaged the lawyer, and less where the lawyer's inquiries are answered fully than when there appears a reluctance to disclose information. . . .

The essence of this opinion . . . is that, while a lawyer should make adequate preparation including inquiry into the relevant facts that is consistent with the above guidelines, and while he should not accept as true that which he should not reasonably believe to be true, he does not have the responsibility to "audit" the affairs of his client or to assume, without reasonable cause, that a client's statement of the facts cannot be relied upon.

See Chapter VIII, Negotiation and Mediation
  • Disclosure Obligations
      (pages 347–353)

C.   LAWYER'S OBLIGATIONS IN SELECTED REGULATORY CONTEXTS

1.   Securities Regulation

PROBLEM 13F

Your firm is outside counsel for International Construction, Inc. (ICON), whose stock is traded on the New York Stock Exchange and is subject to the reporting and disclosure requirements of the Securities and Exchange Act of 1934. ICON's business consists of major construction projects, including airports, oil refining installations, and port facilities.

In recent years the rate of growth in ICON revenues has declined, although total revenue continues to increase. To compensate for a projected slowdown in the economies of developed nations, ICON's chairman and chief executive has launched a diversification program. Through expanded marketing activities, ICON has increased its revenues from Middle Eastern projects from 0.5 percent to 8 percent of total revenue in only three years. The company's annual shareholder reports glowingly describe this achievement as "heralding an era of substantial growth." These increased revenues also have served as the basis for income projections reflecting an impressive climb in corporate profits.

Your firm is preparing a registration statement for an issue of debentures. Its proceeds would provide the working capital necessary to service ICON's continued growth. During the course of preparing that statement, you discover correspondence disclosing substantial payments made to Middle Eastern nationals that were recorded in ICON's books as "sales commissions." ICON's management is aware that the Foreign Corrupt Practices Act bars only payments made to foreign "officials." In an effort to preempt future difficulties, ICON's in-house counsel has obtained opinion letters from local law firms in the countries in which the payments were made, stating that none of the recipients were government employees. When pressed, the chief executive officer does concede that these individuals apparently have remarkable influence with the government officials responsible for selecting contractors. He also informs you that ICON's marketing efforts would be unsuccessful in the absence of such payments.

You believe that the nature of ICON's marketing efforts must be disclosed both in the pending registration statement and in the annual report to shareholders. Even if the payments do not clearly violate the Corrupt Practices Act, the Securities Act of 1933 (which governs the registration statement) and the Securities Exchange Act of 1934 (which covers all public statements, including registration documents) nonetheless require disclosure of all "material information." In your view, ICON's conduct might be considered a commercial bribe that the Securities and Exchange Commission considers "material," since it reflects on the integrity of management. Moreover, 8 percent of the company's revenues and the validity of the publicized growth projections depend on a form of doing business that is at least questionable.

1. ICON's chairman is understandably concerned that disclosure of this marketing practice would interfere with the contemplated financing and, more important, make it difficult to obtain contracts for substantial Mideast projects. Accordingly, he asks you to estimate the probability that nondisclosure would be considered to be a violation of the securities laws, thereby exposing the company to civil and criminal sanctions and to damage claims by those who have traded in the company's stock. After some reflection, you project that if the nondisclosure became public, there would be an 85 percent probability that ICON would be found guilty of securities act violations. The chairman then considers the likelihood that nondisclosure would come to light, the 15 percent chance that no securities violations would be found, and the potential damage to the company if the payments were publicized. After a lengthy discussion, he directs you not to make disclosure. What is your response?

2. Suppose that you raise concerns with ICON's board of directors. The board backs the chair and the independent directors resign. What should your firm do? If it withdraws from representation, what, if any, disclosures could you make to ICON's new outside counsel?

3. If you were the managing partner of ICON's new firm, what information would you seek to obtain from your predecessors? Suppose that ICON's inside counsel insisted that all disclosures to their former lawyers were privileged?[59]

As courts and commentators often have recognized, "the legal profession plays a unique and pivotal role in the effective implementation of the securities laws."[60] That role arises because of the extent of lawyers' involvement with securities issues, the importance of preventing financial disasters like the crash of 1929, and the limitations on regulators' ability to prevent or remedy misconduct. Attorneys participate in various aspects of securities transactions such as rendering legal opinions in connection with public offerings of securities and helping to prepare registration statements and prospectuses. In general, courts and bar ethics committees have required that lawyers providing such assistance proceed with "due diligence" and check material facts that are easily verifiable or matters that raise reasonable doubts.[61]

Attorneys' more specific responsibilities in securities-related work are defined by various statutory provisions and SEC rules as well as bar ethical codes.[62] Rule 10b-5 of the 1934 Securities Exchange Act, 17 C.F.R. §240.10b-5 (1992), prohibits the use of manipulative or deceptive devices or material misrepresentations to defraud in connection with the purchase or sale of securities. Section 17(a) of the 1933 Securities Act, 15 U.S.C §77a, prohibits schemes to defraud in connection with the offer or sale of securities. The SEC has authority to enjoin violations of these provisions, including aiding and abetting by attorneys, and private citizens may also initiate 10b-5 actions. In addition, Rule 2(e)(1), 17 C.F.R. §201.2(e)(1) (1992), authorizes the SEC to deny the "privilege of appearing or practicing before it" to any person who "lacks the requisite qualifications, lacks character or integrity, [or] engages in unethical or unprofessional conduct, or willfully violates or aids and abets a violation of securities laws." Finally, the Remedies Act of 1990, 15 U.S.C. §77h-1, allows the SEC to enter cease-and-desist orders in administrative proceedings against any person that "is, was, or would be a cause of [a securities] violation." Such orders may include steps to ensure future compliance and to recover illicit profits.

This regulatory framework creates a central tension for securities lawyers; they are "paid by one side but potentially disciplined by the other."[63] Over the last two decades, this tension has resulted in several major confrontations between the SEC and the corporate bar concerning attorneys' ethical obligations.

The first of these battlegrounds was SEC v. National Student Marketing Corp., 457 F. Supp. 682 (D.D.C. 1978). The case arose after shareholders of National Student Marketing (NSM) and Interstate National Corporation (INC) approved a merger agreement between the companies. At a meeting to close the transaction, one of the essential documents was a "comfort letter" from NSM accountants. Under normal circumstances, such a letter states that there has been no material change from the financial statements on which the merger had been negotiated. In this case, the comfort letter was not comforting; it disclosed that a prior unaudited statement for NSM showing net earnings of $700,000 was in error and that an accurate accounting would have revealed a loss for the nine-month period in question. Interstate's officers and lawyers nevertheless determined to proceed with the merger without disclosing the accountant's corrections to other directors or shareholders. From management's perspective, a $700,000 discrepancy might be "material" within technical SEC definitions, but it did not call for reassessment of the merger. The risk of a delay and resolicitation of shareholders was that NSM might look elsewhere for a partner, and INC would lose what appeared to be a quite attractive multimillion-dollar deal.

As it turned out, the deal was not so attractive, and the SEC filed charges under Rule 10b-5, §10(b), and §17(a) against all the major participants. Included in the suit as aiders and abetters were two law firms, White & Case and Lord, Bissell & Brooks. What gained the case particular notoriety was the SEC's claim that the lawyers had an obligation not only to interfere with the closing, but also to disclose the error to the SEC or to INC shareholders if the companies declined to do so. The federal district court found it unnecessary to reach the latter claim or to determine the "precise scope" of the attorneys' obligations

> since it is undisputed that they took no steps whatsoever to delay the closing pending disclosure to and resolicitation of the Interstate shareholders. But, at the very least, they were required to speak out at the closing concerning the obvious materiality of the information and the concomitant requirement that the merger not be closed until the adjustments were disclosed and approval of the merger was again obtained from the Interstate shareholders. Their silence was not only a breach of this duty to speak, but in addition lent the appearance of legitimacy to the closing.[64]

A similar issue arose several years later in Rule 2(e) administrative proceedings, In re Carter, SEC Reg. & Law Rep. No. 593 (March 4, 1981). There, an administrative law judge suspended two partners in Brown, Wood, Ivey, Mitchell & Perry from appearing before the SEC because their client, National Telephone Company, ignored advice concerning misleading financial disclosures. During the period in question, the company had issued press releases, stockholder reports, and earnings and revenue figures that overstated the corporation's profitability. The Commission subsequently reversed the ALJ's holding on the ground that the lawyers lacked the requisite degree of recklessness, but used the case to define the general obligations of securities lawyers:

> When a lawyer with significant responsibilities in the effectuation of a company's compliance with the disclosure requirements of the federal securities laws becomes aware that his client is engaged in a substantial and continuing failure to satisfy those disclosure requirements, his continued participation violates professional standards unless he takes prompt steps to end the client's noncompliance.[65]

Those steps might include enlisting the aid of other managers, officers, or members of the board of directors. Although "the lawyer's continued interaction with his client will ordinarily hold the greatest promise of corrective action," there could be situations where the misconduct is "so extreme and irretrievable, or the involvement of his client's management and board in the misconduct is so thoroughgoing and pervasive, that any action short of resignation would be futile." In a footnote, the Commission noted:

> This case does not involve, nor do we here deal with, the additional question of when a lawyer aware of his client's intention to commit fraud or an illegal act, has a professional duty to disclose that fact publicly or to an affected third party. Our interpretation today does

not require such action at any point although other existing standards of professional conduct may be so interpreted. See, e.g., ABA DR 7-102(B).[66]

Following the *Carter* decision, the SEC also sought comment on a proposed "Standard of Conduct Constituting Unethical or Improper Professional Practice before the Commission." That standard would have codified *Carter*'s requirement that lawyers take "prompt steps" to end the client's noncompliance with disclosure requirements.[67]

This series of Commission pronouncements evoked mixed reactions. Most securities lawyers were relieved that the SEC was no longer claiming, as it had in *National Student Marketing*, that lawyers should publicly disclose a client's misconduct. However, the organized bar was also disturbed that the Commission was proposing a specific regulatory standard for lawyers and was using Rule 2(e) proceedings to duplicate the function of bar disciplinary committees. To express these concerns, the Board of Governors of the American Bar Association adopted a comment on the proposed standard. That comment concluded that the SEC had no power to issue such a regulation and added:

> The willingness or ability of the lawyer involved to do what is ethical . . . is not likely to be aided by a proliferation of essentially redundant, or even worse, possibly inconsistent standards. . . . [The SEC's proposal and the possibility that other agencies will take similar action] might cause clients to be concerned whether their lawyers will regard themselves as owing a primary duty to them or to the agencies.[68]

Although the proposed SEC standard was never promulgated, the use of agency disciplinary proceedings continues to be a source of dispute. Partly to allay such concerns, the Commission issued a Final Rule on Rule 2(e) proceedings indicating that

> [w]ith respect to attorneys, the Commission generally has not sought to develop or apply independent standards of professional conduct. The great majority of Rule 2(e) proceedings against attorneys involve allegations of violations of the law (not of professional standards). . . . Indeed, the Commission has *generally* utilized Rule 2(e) proceedings against attorneys only where the attorneys' conduct has already provided the basis for a judicial or administrative order finding a securities law violation in a non-Rule 2(e) proceeding. (Emphasis added.)[69]

Surveys of Rule 2(e) proceedings in the decade following *Carter* confirm that the SEC has "generally" adhered to that pattern.[70] However, as some commentators note, "[g]enerally is not a policy. It reflects a practice that the SEC has, for the time being, found convenient . . . and reflects more the views of the General Counsel than of the five SEC Commissioners."[71] Experts' assessment of that practice is mixed. Some commentators believe that the limited use of Rule 2(e) proceedings is appropriate, given the unwillingness of state bar disciplinary agencies to proceed against lawyers for securities violations.[72] By contrast, many practitioners believe that the Commission is an improper forum for enforcing attorneys' responsibilities. The risk, as Jonathan Macey and Geoffrey Miller describe it, is that agencies can intimidate lawyers who are repeat players from effectively representing clients, especially when such representation involves challenging regulatory policies.[73]

Many practitioners also have expressed concern about the SEC's use of other authority apart from Rule 2(e) to accomplish similar results.[74] That concern intensified in the early 1990s after the SEC initiated proceedings against top executives at Salomon Brothers and a Report of Investigation concerning the firm's general counsel, Donald Feuerstein.[75]

IN RE GUTFREUND, SECURITIES EXCHANGE RELEASE NO. 34-31554 (DEC 3, 1992). The case arose after Salomon officers and the general counsel Feuerstein learned that the head of the firm's government trading desk had submitted a false bid in the auction of United States treasury securities. According to the Commission's findings, Feuerstein advised the officers

> that the submission of the bid was a criminal act and should be reported to the government, and he urged them on several occasions to proceed with disclosure when he learned that the report had not been made. However, Feuerstein did not direct that an inquiry be undertaken, and he did not recommend that appropriate procedures, reasonably designed to prevent and detect future misconduct, be instituted, or that other limitations be placed on [the trader's] activities. Feuerstein also did not inform the Compliance Department, for which he was responsible as Salomon's chief legal officer, of the false bid.

No investigation or report of the trader's conduct occurred until six months after its discovery, and only after other events prompted an internal inquiry by an outside firm. Prior to that inquiry, the trader engaged in further misconduct.

Because the attorney was not a direct supervisor of the trader, the SEC found it inappropriate to name him in its complaint against the other officers for violations of §15(b)(4)(E) of the 1934 Securities Exchange Act. That section authorizes the Commission to impose sanctions against a broker dealer who "failed reasonably to supervise, with a view to preventing violations [of federal securities laws], another person who commits such a violation, if such person is subject to his supervision." However, the Commission also viewed the proceeding as an

> appropriate opportunity to amplify our views on the supervisory responsibilities of legal and compliance officers in Feuerstein's position. . . .

Once a person in Feuerstein's position becomes involved in formulating management's response to the problem, he or she is obligated to take affirmative steps to insure that appropriate action is taken to address the misconduct. For example, such a person could direct or monitor an investigation of the conduct at issue, make appropriate recommendations for limiting the activities of the employee, or for the institution of appropriate procedures, reasonably designed to prevent and detect future misconduct, and verify that his or her recommendations, or acceptable alternatives, are implemented. If such a person takes appropriate steps but management fails to act and that person knows or has reason to know of that failure, he or she should consider what additional steps are appropriate to address the matter. These steps may include disclosure of the matter to the entity's board of directors, resignation from the firm, or disclosure to regulatory authorities.

In a footnote, the Commission added, "[o]f course, in the case of an attorney, the applicable Code of Professional Responsibility and the Canons of Ethics may bear upon what course of conduct that individual may properly pursue."

One other interesting aspect of the Salomon Brothers case involves the diffusion of responsibility that so frequently contributes to ethical problems in organizational settings. As the SEC's report notes:

[E]ach of the four executives who attended meetings . . . placed the responsibility for investigating Mozer's [the trader's] conduct and placing limits on his activities on someone else. Meriwether [the vice chairman and Mozer's direct supervisor] stated that he believed that once he had taken the matter of Mozer's conduct to Strauss [the president] and Strauss had brought Feuerstein and Gutfreund [the CEO] into the process, he had no further responsibility to take action with respect to the false bid unless instructed to do so by one of those individuals. Meriwether stated that he also believed that, though he had the authority to recommend that action be taken to discipline Mozer or limit his activities, he had no authority to take such action unilaterally. Strauss stated that he believed that Meriwether, who was Mozer's direct supervisor, and Feuerstein, who was responsible for the legal and compliance activities of the firm, would take whatever steps were necessary or required as a result of Mozer's disclosure. Feuerstein stated that he believed that, once a report to the government was made, the government would instruct Salomon about how to investigate the matter. Gutfreund stated that he believed that the other executives would take whatever steps were necessary to properly handle the matter. According to the executives, there was no discussion among them about any action that would be taken to investigate Mozer's conduct or to place limitations on his activities.

Do you think this was actually what happened, or how the officers later rationalized their inaction? Note that the SEC's statements of fact are negotiated with the principals involved. Would you

find this account convincing if you were a neutral third party
decision-maker? If not, why do you suppose the SEC accepted such a
narrative? Alternatively, if this description is accurate, does it
reflect the pathology that Hannah Arendt described as "rule by
Nobody"? To Arendt, this form of bureaucracy was the most dangerous of all, "since there is no one left who could even be asked to
answer for what is being done."[76]

According to prominent Wall Street practitioners such as
Dennis Block and Jonathan Hoff, the Salomon Brothers report
raised several concerns. In their view, the Commission offered
inadequate guidelines for misconduct less clear than that facing
Feuerstein:

> [The report provides] little guidance as to the kinds of steps which
> should be taken: what level of investigation, restrictions or discipli-
> nary action is required and what new obligations do the firm, line
> management and legal/compliance officers undertake if the wrongdo-
> ing is not terminated? . . . [H]olding [lawyers] accountable may create
> a reluctance on the part of capable professionals to assume or retain
> significant compliance authority; dampen the legal/compliance staff's
> motivation [to intervene; and] . . . "dilute the emphasis on responsibil-
> ity of the line manager, who in most firms is the only person who can,
> in fact, have significant impact on practices."
>
> Moreover, the Commission's suggestion that legal/compliance
> personnel should consider resigning if management is uncooperative
> appears at odds with the desire to see these individuals gain influence
> within their organizations. In the words of one industry spokesman,
> to target lawyers and compliance personnel who are on the same side
> as the SEC "seems to me from a regulatory policy point of view to be
> shooting at your own troops."[77]

Do you agree? Professor David Wilkins, in an extended article
on bar regulatory structures, argues that

> [d]espite protestations to the contrary, there is very little evidence
> that corporate lawyers have been unduly "chilled" by [Commission]
> regulatory measures. . . . Because of the financial and other rewards
> of a "cutting edge" corporate legal practice, the fear of liability in this
> context is not sufficient to deter even clearly questionable conduct, let
> alone legitimate advice that might be made to appear questionable af-
> ter the fact.[78]

Given lawyers' self-interest in the formulation and enforcement of
bar disciplinary rules, some commentators have argued that government agencies can add a useful supplemental framework. See
generally Chapter III (Regulation of the Profession). Enlisting lawyers as "gatekeepers" of regulatory policy may be more cost-effective
than the plausible alternatives.[79]

What is your view? Although debates over cases like *Gutfreund,
National Student Marketing,* and *Carter* typically proceed as if
lawyers' and clients' interests are in conflict, not all experts agree.
Jonathan Macey points out that

[b]oth the lawyers and clients lose if the bad news being covered up gets disclosed. The lawyers are urged to cover it up, not because the cover-up benefits the clients at the expense of the lawyers, but because clients often will have different assumptions than lawyers about (1) the severity of the sanctions for such a cover-up and (2) the probability of detection. As such the lawyers' job is to educate the clients about these issues. After all, in a public corporation, why should management want to risk a jail sentence to benefit the shareholders? This point also seems relevant in the S&L context where lawyers often got their clients into a lot of trouble by not advising them to disclose damaging information to regulators.[80]

If Macey is right, what are the implications for regulatory policy? Does the current balance of authority between the SEC and the private bar make sense? Who should decide that question?

2. Banking

PROBLEM 13G

Following the Kaye, Scholer settlement described below, the Office of Thrift Supervision counsel Harris Weinstein proposed that, in the future, the bank examination process should include a letter to lawyers for thrifts asking them to confirm that they had "informed the thrift's management of transactions in which there is a possible question of compliance with law, rule, or regulation." The proposed letter also would request confirmation that the lawyers had sought review "up to the corporate board of directors [when] necessary" if they "recognized that management intended to proceed with a transaction that did not comply with applicable law, rule, or regulation, or with the requirements of fiduciary responsibility." Initial drafts of the proposed letter would also have asked counsel to confirm that they "declined and/or will decline to assist any such transaction."[81] This provision was subsequently deleted.[82]

Would you support either version of such a letter? Is it broader than Model Rule 1.13? If so, is such an expanded concept of attorney responsibility appropriate?

Lawyers who represent banking institutions work within a complicated regulatory framework. Its basic structure was established during the Depression of the 1930s and was strengthened following the savings and loan crisis of the 1980s. In order to insure the safety of customer accounts, stabilize mortgage funding, and avoid future panics, Congress created a national system of deposit insurance. That system included a Federal Home Loan Bank Board with various investigatory, injunctive, and remedial powers. Until the 1980s, most federal agencies' enforcement authority did not explicitly extend to attorneys; government powers were largely limited to enforcing common law remedies, such as aiding and abetting of fraud, breach of contract, and unjust enrichment.[83] The Financial Institution Reform, Recovery and Enforcement Act of 1989 (FIRREA), Pub. L. No. 101-73, 103 Stat. 183 (1989), expanded those powers by expressly including lawyers as "institution-affiliated parties" subject to the enforcement authority of the Office of Thrift Supervision (OTS). That Office replaced the Board as chief overseer of savings and loan institutions (S&Ls).

During the early 1990s, controversies over the role of lawyers for these institutions raised broader questions of professional ethics. The failure of over 700 S&Ls exposed massive misconduct, resulting in over 1,000 criminal and 2,000 civil cases. Taxpayers ended up with a bill likely to total half a trillion dollars.[84] According to Harris Weinstein, the general counsel of OTS, "few of the frauds and none of the high-risk schemes could have been undertaken without the active assistance of professionals, including lawyers and accountants." It was striking "how many cases there are in which professionals provided little or no resistance to abusive activity to which they contributed some form of paper, counsel, or cover."[85] Loans and investments required opinion letters as to their legality, and lawyers proved happy to oblige. According to one lawyer/banker, by the 1980s "[f]or a half a million dollars you could buy any legal opinion you wanted from any law firm in New York."[86]

Similarly, federal judge Stanley Sporkin, hearing a challenge to the Lincoln Savings and Loan seizure, noted:

> Keating testified that he was so bent on doing the "right thing" that he surrounded himself with literally scores of accountants and lawyers to make sure all the transactions were legal. The questions that must be asked are:
> Where were these professionals, a number of whom are now asserting their rights under the Fifth Amendment, when these clearly improper transactions were being consummated?
> Why didn't any of them speak up or disassociate themselves from the transactions?
> Where also were the outside accountants and attorneys when these transactions were effectuated?[87]

A substantial number of lawyers involved in S&L work have faced similar questions that are not rhetorical. Several leading decisions have held attorneys accountable for failure to make reasonable investigations or reports of client fraud.[88] The most celebrated case involves Kaye, Scholer, Fierman, Hays & Handler, the Wall Street firm that served as counsel for Lincoln.

DIRECTOR OF THE OFFICE OF THRIFT SUPERVISION v. KAYE, SCHOLER, FIERMAN, HAYS AND HANDLER, 1992 WL 57983 (D.D.C. 1992). OTS filed suit against the firm, alleging reckless or knowing breaches of ethical rules and regulations, and concealment and omissions of material information. Among other things, OTS claimed that firm lawyers became "institution-affiliated parties" when they took on the role of intermediaries for all communications between Lincoln and federal investigators.[89] In that role, counsel allegedly had the same obligations as their clients not to make knowingly incomplete statements. In particular, OTS claimed that Kaye, Scholer lawyers should have disclosed compromising facts surrounding Arthur Anderson's resignation as accountant for Lincoln, as well as material facts concerning Lincoln's net worth and questionable transactions.

Kaye, Scholer lawyers responded that the government had access to such information through other sources. They also claimed that OTS's complaint was that the firm failed to volunteer negative information and instead put the client's position as "persuasively as possible where they had a reasonable basis" in doing so.[90] Geoffrey Hazard, Jr., whom Kaye, Scholer had hired as an ethics consultant, agreed, and issued an opinion letter concluding that the firm was acting as litigation counsel and, in that capacity, did not assume the client's disclosure obligations.[91]

What gained the case particular notoriety was OTS's decision to place a freeze order on Kaye, Scholer assets. The freeze order followed the firm's refusal to comply with OTS subpoenas and to supply certain information, including facts about its insurance coverage. Under 12 U.S.C. §1818(c), a federal banking agency may issue a temporary order against institutions or institution-affiliated parties to prevent the dissipation of assets that is likely to prejudice the interests of the institution's depositors. Such orders are based on an evidentiary review by the agency's director without a judicial hearing and they can be challenged in federal court. To justify a freeze, the government must establish a prima facie case of likely dissipation, not a reasonable probability of success.

From OTS's perspective, the order was appropriate in the Kaye, Scholer proceeding, partly because of the size of the remedy requested: $275 million in restitution for losses from the firm's alleged misconduct. The government claimed that the firm had threatened to amend its insurance policy and that such a possibility, coupled with the risk that some partners might resign, could impair the firm's ability to provide restitution. By contrast, many observers viewed the order as a "hardball tactic" designed to force Kaye, Scholer to settle and to ensure other firms' cooperation with OTS investigations.[92]

Most commentary was highly critical of that tactic. According to some critics, the government's action constituted a "Draconian" procedure, a "sledgehammer" designed to extort an unreasonable judgment, to scapegoat wealthy lawyers, and to consolidate prosecutorial power verging on "gestapo dimensions."[93] Kaye, Scholer lawyers echoed these complaints and maintained that the freeze prompted New York banks to threaten to pull the firm's line of credit if the case wasn't settled. Since the firm couldn't meet its payroll without credit, it had to accept a settlement demanding $41 million and restrictions preventing two partners from subsequently representing federally insured depository institutions, terms it had rejected a week before.

Some commentators rejected such characterizations of government abuse. As they noted, Kaye, Scholer could have promptly challenged the freeze order. The firm's determination not to do so reportedly gave it an excuse to settle that diverted attention from its own misconduct.[94] As one commentator noted, "OTS zealously represented the government; Kaye, Scholer would have done nothing different if the shoe was on the other foot."[95]

Is that an adequate justification? Should the government exercise more restraint in playing "hardball" than private litigants? Are the advantages of such tactics worth the backlash that they risk? According to Peter Fishbein, one of the sanctioned Kaye, Scholer lawyers, "we have gotten a tremendous amount of support from lawyers, judges, the bar, and the financial community. . . . The general feeling in the world we deal with is that there are a bunch of Nazis at the OTS who took advantage of a public crisis situation and abused the power of the agency to coerce an unjustified settlement."[96] By contrast, OTS defenders argue that government lawyers are more justified than other practitioners in using hardball tactics since the results serve public rather than private interests. Who has the stronger argument? Would a fair compromise position be the proposal of the New York Bar Association to require judicial authorization of freeze orders?

Following the Kaye, Scholer agreement, government regulators settled a similar case against Jones, Day, Reavis & Polk on similar terms, without a freeze order. According to the government's complaint, Jones, Day lawyers, as counsel for Lincoln Savings & Loan, had information that they failed to disclose to appropriate Lincoln officials (particularly the board of directors) concerning misconduct by Charles Keating and other managers. This failure allegedly helped delay the government's seizure of Lincoln, whose collapse ultimately cost taxpayers over $2 billion. Jones, Day settled the case for $51 million; its insurer was to pay approximately $31.5 million of the judgment. According to industry sources, such settlements contributed to steep hikes in malpractice insurance rates for many firms.[97]

As part of the settlement, Jones, Day agreed to take certain measures if one of its attorneys acquired knowledge of illegal actions by an employee, officer, or director of a federally insured depository institution. Under such circumstances, the attorney must notify the firm's designated financial institution supervising partner, who must then go up the thrift's chain of command. If the breach of duty so warrants, the partner must inform the thrift's board of directors.[98]

These cases raise broader questions about lawyers' disclosure responsibilities in civil cases generally and in banking contexts in particular. Following the Kaye, Scholer controversy, then-OTS counsel Weinstein made several speeches concerning the bar's ethical obligations. According to Weinstein, in circumstances other than litigation, attorneys should recognize distinctions between acting as advocates and acting as clients' agents in presenting factual information. As an advocate, a lawyer "may have an obligation of due diligence, and the lawyer may not argue facts he knows [or should know] to be false." But a lawyer who takes responsibility for presenting the facts should also be subject to "whatever requirements govern factual submissions to the agency"; in effect, that lawyer should assume the client's full disclosure obligations.[99]

To Weinstein, the "[k]nowledge relevant to a lawyer's conduct is not a narrow, cramped beast, that a lawyer can avoid simply by closing his eyes."[100] A lawyer must "determine the accuracy of the facts stated by the client if the lawyer has reason to suspect that they are inaccurate or incomplete."[101] More broadly, lawyers should avoid "loophole lawyering," which Weinstein defines as "reliance on an implied exception to a statute or regulation that mistakenly disregards the significance of principles of general applicability."[102] For example, banking regulations provide no exceptions to the general fiduciary duties of bank officers and directors to operate their institutions safely and soundly. Even if lawyers believe that they have found a legal loophole, or that they are counseling in a grey area, they must advise banking clients to discharge these overarching fiduciary duties.[103]

Unsurprisingly, such arguments have commanded greater enthusiasm among ethics experts than corporate practitioners.[104] One lawyer captured widespread views in commenting on Weinstein's disapproval of loophole lawyering: "[f]or those attorneys who have thought of this as their job, this will indeed be news."[105] According to prominent bar leaders like Lawrence Fox, the policy that Weinstein was advocating and OTS was attempting to impose would turn the private practitioner "into an enforcer for the government. In effect then, the client pays for the lawyer to represent the regulatory agency. And who then 'fulfills the role of the lawyer for the client?'"[106] Other practitioners similarly warned that Weinstein's views would prove not "prophylactic" but "corrosive"; they would "cause lawyers to look at their representation of troubled thrifts . . . very carefully and cause them to be less zealous."[107]

Given recent history, many ethics experts do not find that troubling. As David Luban argues, the problem with zealous lawyering in this context is that individual attorneys could each readily rationalize their own actions. Their willingness to overlook client over-reaching often was not especially egregious and was not of itself responsible for any S&L collapses. But, collectively, the "thrifts died the Death by a Thousand Cuts. As in many other financial crashes, each of the transactions was systemically inconsequential until a threshold or tipping point was reached." Together, however, they caused a collapse of financial responsibility and a societal cost of unprecedented proportions.[108]

In the final analysis, increasing lawyers' third party obligations inevitably forces trade-offs. The benefit is that attorneys often have access to information that is extremely difficult and expensive for regulators to acquire.[109] The cost is that sophisticated clients may be able to shield attorneys as well as regulators from such information and to frustrate counsels' internal efforts in promoting compliance.[110] Holding lawyers accountable for failure to prevent or remedy client misconduct will also increase third party claims and malpractice rates, and a large part of those expenses will be passed on to other consumers in the form of higher fees.

How these costs and benefits will play out in any given context is impossible to determine in the abstract. Thus, David Wilkins argues that cases like Kaye, Scholer point up the need for "making context count," and for developing regulatory structures that vary in light of particular substantive obligations, legal tasks, and market forces. In banking contexts, Wilkins argues that lawyers should have three primary obligations: to provide independent counseling (including the duty to inform boards of directors of potential misconduct); to cooperate with regulators' efforts in collecting relevant information; and to disclose the existence and reasons for legal positions that might cause withholding of relevant information.[111] In Wilkins' view, such an approach could strike a balance between preserving lawyer-client trust and recognizing that most banking regulatory procedures are not adversarial in the traditional sense; they lack an impartial judge and parties are required to cooperate.[112]

What is your view? How would you accommodate the competing interests? Do you agree with Wilkins that the appropriate accommodation might differ in particular regulatory contexts? Is it troubling that OTS's counsel, although referring repeatedly to Kaye, Scholer's and Jones, Day's ethical violations, declined to seek bar disciplinary action and proceeded instead in the agency's own forum? That decision is not surprising, given the inadequacies of disciplinary processes discussed in Part D of Chapter III (Regulation of the Profession). Susan Koniak has argued that the increasing judicial and administrative activism in defining ethical responsibilities stems largely from deficiencies in the profession's own regulatory structures. In her view, the organized bar's objections to OTS's assertions of power "ring hollow" in light of its own success in making lawyer liability standards responsive to lawyers' rather than society's interests.[113]

If that is a fair criticism, what are its implications for bar regulatory structures? Would a disciplinary system more independent both from state bar and federal administrative agencies be desirable?

Endnotes

1. Ralph Jonas, Who Is the Client? The Corporate Lawyer's Dilemma, 39 Hastings L.J. 617, 619 (1988).

2. In its most common form, a poison pill offers stockholders a dividend convertible into shares of common stock with rights of redemption into preferred shares. The effect is to dilute a raider's ownership and possibly to depress the price of its common shares. See Herbert M. Wachtell, Special Tender Offer Litigation Tactics, 32 Bus. Law. 1433 (1977).

3. This problem is modeled on a hypothetical presented by John C. Coffee, Jr. at an AALS workshop on Securities Law and Ethical Considerations (January 1991).

4. Roberta S. Karmel, Duty to the Target: Is an Attorney's Duty to the Corporation a Paradigm for Directors?, 39 Hastings L.J. 677, 695 (1988).

5. See id.; Frederick W. Kanner, Overview of Professional Responsibility Issues for the Corporate Lawyer, in Conflicts of Interest in Legal Representation 211, 221-225 (1989).

6. Marc I. Steinberg, Attorney Conflicts of Interest in Corporate Acquisitions, 39 Hastings L.J. 579, 592 (1988).

7. Panter v. Marshall Field & Co., 646 F.2d 272, 300-301 (7th Cir.) (Cudahy, J., concurring in part and dissenting in part), cert. denied, 454 U.S. 1092 (1981); see Steinberg, supra note 6, at 589.

8. Jonas, supra note 1, at 622.

9. Id. at 621.

10. Wachtell, supra note 2.

11. Id.

12. Craig C. Albert, The Lawyer-Director: An Oxymoron?, 9 Geo. J. Legal Ethics 413, 415 (1955).

13. Id. at 416-419.

14. Dean Starkman, Lawyers Debate Ethics of Role in Boardrooms, Wall St. J., Aug. 5, 1996, at B1, B3; Albert, supra note 12, at 436-444.

15. See Charles W. Wolfram, Modern Legal Ethics at 739 & n.12 (1986); Lawyers as Directors: Panel Discussion, 30 Bus. Law. 41, 51 (1975) (remarks of David S. Ruder); American Assn. of Certified Public Account-

ants, Code of Professional Ethics, Rule 101 (1980). In addition to potential conflicts, problems may arise as to the confidentiality of statements made to lawyer/directors. Albert, supra note 12.

16. For a general overview of the debate, see SEC Staff Report on Corporate Accountability F26-F31 (1980).

17. [1988-1989 Transfer Binder] Fed. Sec. L. Rep. (CCH) ⁋84,342 (Nov. 14, 1988), aff'd, [1991 Transfer Binder] Fed. Sec. L. Rep. (CCH) ⁋997 (June 21, 1991).

18. However, the administrative law judge discontinued the proceedings on grounds that Kern had subsequently left the corporation and that the Commission lacked authority to compel the lawyer to correct the company's filings or to comply with the law in future filings by other clients. *Kern*, [1988-1989 Transfer Binder] Fed. Sec. L. Rep. (CCH) at 89,580. In 1990, Congress granted the Commission authority to issue the kind of order involved in *Kern*. David Wilkins, Who Should Regulate Lawyers?, 105 Harv. L. Rev. 799, 857 n.256 (1992) (citations omitted).

19. Kanner, supra note 5, at 270-271.

20. Steven Brill, Roy Cohn Rides Again, Am. Law., Mar. 1980, at 5.

21. See Jonathan R. Macey & Geoffrey P. Miller, The Plaintiffs' Attorney's Role in Class Action and Derivative Litigation: Economic Analysis and Recommendations for Reform, 58 U. Chi. L. Rev. 1, 20-23 (1991); Kenneth E. Scott, Corporation Law and the American Law Institute Corporate Governance Project, 35 Stan. L. Rev. 927, 940 (1980).

22. Deiter F. Vagts, Materials on Basic Corporation Law 459 (3d ed. 1989) (quoting report prepared by Franklin Wood, Esq., for Gov. Thomas Dewey, 1945).

23. Maintenance, under common law prohibitions, referred to lawyers' assistance to clients in pursuing legal actions. See V W. Blackstone, Commentaries ch. X, §12, at 135 (Tucker ed., 1803). Both the Code and Model Rules allow lawyers to advance litigation costs, but the Code requires clients to remain liable in all cases. The Model Rules permit repayment contingent on the outcome and, for indigent clients, allow lawyers to subsidize costs. Cf. DR 5-103(B) and Model Rule 1.8.

24. See Macey & Miller, supra note 21, at 99-102.

25. Id. at 6, 105-116.

26. See, e.g., John C. Coffee, Jr., Understanding the Plaintiff's Attorney: The Implications of Economic Theory for Private Enforcement of Law Through Class and Derivative Actions, 86 Colum. L. Rev. 669 (1986) [hereinafter Plaintiff's Attorney]; John C. Coffee, Jr., The Unfaithful Champion: The Plaintiff as Monitor in Shareholder Litigation, 48 Law & Contemp. Probs. 5 (1985) [hereinafter Unfaithful Champion].

27. Coffee, Plaintiff's Attorney, supra note 26, at 702.

28. Janet Cooper Alexander, Do the Merits Matter? A Study of Settlements in Securities Class Actions, 43 Stan. L. Rev. 497, 532 (1991).

29. Id. at 533-534.

30. Coffee, Unfaithful Champion, supra note 26, at 27.

31. Macey & Miller, supra note 21, at 46-47.

32. See Developments in the Law, Conflicts of Interest in Private Practice, 94 Harv. L. Rev. 1284, 1307 (1981); S. Kendall Patton, Disqualification of Corporate Counsel in Derivative Actions: Jacuzzi and the Inadequacy of Dual Representation, 31 Hastings L.J. 347, 357 (1979).

33. H. Henn & J. Lawson, Laws of Corporations §370, at 1082 (3d ed. 1983); Patton, supra note 32; Rice v. Baron, 456 F. Supp. 676 (S.D.N.Y. 1978).

34. Macey & Miller, supra note 21, at 39.

35. Compare Macey & Miller, supra note 21, at 38-41 (noting the limitations of courts) with Coffee, Unfaithful Champion, supra note 26, at 70 & n.205 (acknowledging these limitations but nonetheless advocating adoption of a proposal by the American Law Institute that would allow judges to inquire into the reasons behind dismissal of a derivative suit).

36. See Coffee, Unfaithful Champion, supra note 26, at 26-32.

37. Macey & Miller, supra note 21, at 47-48.

38. Id. at 59-61; Coffee, Unfaithful Champion, supra note 26, at 40-48. But cf. Evans v. Jeff D., 475 U.S. 717 (1986) (holding that simultaneous negotiation of fees and merits is not impermissible for cases falling under the Civil Rights Attorney's Fees Awards Act of 1976 and that defendants could insist on plaintiff's waiver of counsel fees as a condition of settlement).

39. Macey & Miller, supra note 21, at 59-61; Coffee, Unfaithful Champion, supra note 26, at 40-48.

40. Alexander, supra note 28, at 579.

41. Macey & Miller, supra note 21, at 5.

42. Id. at 6.

43. Id.

44. For discussion of Oracle Securities and recommendations of competitive bidding as long as proposed fees allow adjustments for extraordinary circumstances, see Steven A. Burns, Note: Setting Class Action Attorney Fees: Reform Efforts Raise Ethical Concerns, 6 Geo. J. Legal Ethics 1161 (1993).

45. Securities Litigation Reform Acts, 104 Pub. L. No. 67, 109 Stat. 737 (1995).

46. Radiant Burners v. American Gas Assn., 207 F. Supp. 771, 773 (N.D. Ill. 1962), rev'd, 320 F.2d 314 (7th Cir.), cert. denied, 375 U.S. 929 (1963).

47. Wolfram, supra note 15, at 283-287 (discussing cases and noting that rights-based justifications do not support the corporate privilege).

48. Corporate Legal Ethics: An Empirical Study, 1983 J. Corp. L. 601, 622-625 (1983). About one-fifth of managers indicated that they had withheld information during the investigation. See also John C. Coffee, Jr., Beyond the Shut-Eyed Sentry: Toward a Theoretical View of Corporate Misconduct and an Effective Legal Response, 63 Va. L. Rev. 1099 (1977).

49. Steven Shavell, Legal Advice About Contemplated Acts: The Decision to Obtain Advice, Its Social Desirability, and Protection of Confidentiality, 17 J. Legal Stud. 123 (1988).

50. Deborah L. Rhode & David Luban, Legal Ethics 275 (2d. ed. 1995).

51. Jeremy Bentham, 5 Rationale of Judicial Evidence, Specially Applied to English Practice 318 (1827).

52. Wolfram, supra note 15, at 286-287.

53. Developments in the Law, Privileged Communications, 98 Harv. L. Rev. 1450, 1524-1529 (1985). See also Wendy Kilbride, Identifying the Client in the Corporate Setting and the Attorney-Client Privilege, 6 Geo. J. Legal Ethics 1140-1142 (1993).

54. Kathryn W. Tate, Lawyer Ethics and the Corporate Employee: Is the Employee Owed More Protection Than the Model Rules Provide?, 23 Ind. L. Rev. 1 (1990).

55. This problem's discussion of testing issues is loosely based on reports of Dow Corning Corporation's procedures for its breast implant. See Philip J. Hilts, Maker Is Depicted as Fighting Tests on Implant Safety,

N.Y. Times, Jan. 13, 1992, at A1, C6; Maker of Silicone Breast Implants Says Data Show Them to Be Safe, N.Y. Times, Jan. 14, 1992, at A1, C3; Andrew D. Dyer, Todd E. Himstead & N. Craig Smith, Dow Corning Corporation: Product Stewardship, in Cases on Leadership, Ethics, and Organizational Integrity: A Strategic Perspective 298 (Lynn Sharp Paine ed., 1996). Although the safety of implants remains controversial, manufacturer failure to do more adequate testing has had devastating impact in legal costs. Estimates in the mid-1990s indicated that over 12,000 lawsuits had been filed. Zoe Panarites, Breast Implants: Choices Women Thought They Made, 11 N.Y.L. Sch. J. Hum. Rts. 163 (1993). The discussion of the lawyer's interview with the research director draws on a similar pattern in a video, "Representing the Corporate Client: The Saga of Albinox," in the Professional Responsibility for Lawyers series published by Commerce Clearinghouse in cooperation with the Center on Professionalism at University of Pennsylvania Law School. For a thorough analysis of the ethics issues raised in this problem, see E. Michelle Rabouin, Walking the Talk: Transforming Law Students into Ethical Transactional Lawyers, 9 DePaul Bus. L.J. 1 (1996).

56. John M. Freeman & Nathan M. Crystal, Scienter in Professional Liability Cases, 42 S.C.L. Rev. 783 (1991).

57. I am indebted to Jonathan Macey for this point.

58. See Stephen Gillers, Cleaning Up the S&L Mess, A.B.A.J., Feb. 1993, at 93; and Part C, section 2, infra.

59. For a case involving similar issues, see Stuart Taylor, Ethics and the Law: A Case History, New York Times Magazine, June 9, 1983, and OPM Leasing Services, Inc., in The Social Responsibility of Lawyers 184 (Philip Heymann & Lance Liebman eds., 1988).

60. Securities and Exchange Commn. v. Spectrum, 489 F.2d 535, 541-542 (2d Cir. 1973).

61. See Escott v. BarChris Constr. Corp., 183 F. Supp. 643, 690 (S.D.N.Y. 1968); ABA Comm. on Ethics & Professional Responsibility, Formal Op. 335 (Feb. 2, 1974).

62. For an overview, see Robert J. Haft, Liability of Attorneys and Accountants for Securities Transactions §8.01 (1991).

63. Robert W. Emerson, Rule 2e Revisited: SEC Disciplining of Attorneys Since *In re Carter*, 29 Am. Bus. L.J. 156, 242 (1991).

64. SEC v. National Student Marketing Corp., 457 F. Supp. 682, 713 (D.D.C. 1978).

65. In re Carter, [1981 Transfer Binder] Fed. Sec. L. Rep. (CCH) ⁋82,847 (Feb. 28, 1981), at 84,172.

66. Id. at note 78.

67. See Securities Act Release No. 6344, Securities Exchange Act Release No. 18106, Public Utility Holding Company Act Release No. 22200, Trust Investment Act Release No. 656, Investment Company Act Release No. 11942, Investment Act Release No. 775 (Sept. 21, 1981).

68. David Ranii, SEC Standard of Conduct for Lawyers, 37 Bus. Law. 915, 921-922 (1981). See ABA Opposes Securities Lawyers' Code, Natl. L.J., Dec. 7, 1981, at 5.

69. SEC Final Rule on Rule 2(e) Proceedings, Securities Act Release No. 6783, Exchange Act Release No. 25893 (July 7, 1988), 20 Sec. Rel. & L. Rep. (BNA) 1116 (July 15, 1988) (quoted in Emerson, supra note 63, at 241).

70. Emerson, supra note 63, at 161.

71. Id. at 214.

72. See id. at 208.

73. Jonathan R. Macey & Geoffrey P. Miller, Reflections on Professional Responsibility in a Regulatory State, 63 Geo. Wash. L. Rev. 1105, 1111 (1995).

74. See Daniel L. Goelzer & Susan Ferris Wyderko, Rule 2(e): Securities and Exchange Commission Discipline of Professionals, 85 Nw. U.L. Rev. 652, 670-675 (1991); Robert G. Day, Note, Administrative Watchdogs or Zealous Advocates? Implications for Legal Ethics in the Face of Expanded Attorney Liability, 45 Stan. L. Rev. 645, 678-680 (1993).

75. In re Gutfreund, Sec. Exch. Release No. 34-31554 (Dec. 3, 1992). John Gutfreund, the chair and CEO, was ordered to pay a $100,000 fine and to refrain from associating in the future in the capacity of chair or CEO with any broker, dealer, or investment advisor regulated by the Commission. The president and vice chair were suspended from similar association for six and three months respectively and ordered to pay fines of $75,000 and $50,000. Salomon stock declined substantially. See Lynn Sharp Paine & Michael A. Santero, Forging the New Solomon, in Cases on Leadership, Ethics, and Organizational Integrity, supra note 55, at 111.

76. Hannah Arendt, On Violence 38-39 (1970).

77. Dennis J. Block & Jonathan M. Hoff, Mergers and Acquisitions: Liability Extended to Legal and Compliance Officers, New York L.J., Mar. 18, 1993, at 10, 11 (citations omitted).

78. Wilkins, supra note 18, at 870-871.

79. Renier H. Kraakman, Gatekeepers: The Anatomy of a Third-Party Enforcement Strategy, 1 J.L. Econ. & Org. 53 (l986).

80. Jonathan Macey, Correspondence, May 26, 1993 (on file with the author).

81. Rita Henley Jensen, Agency Tries to Rein in S&L Lawyers, Natl. L.J., July 27, 1992, at 38.

82. Revised Attorney Letter, Office of Thrift Supervision, Apr. 15, 1993.

83. Day, supra note 74.

84. Harris Weinstein, Attorney Liability in the Savings and Loan Crisis, 1993 U. Ill. L. Rev. 53 (reporting that 90 of the civil cases were brought against lawyers); David Luban, The Social Responsibilities of Lawyers: A Green Perspective, 63 Geo. Wash. L. Rev. 955, 958 (1995).

85. Susan Schmidt, Panel: Where Were the Lawyers During S&L Crisis?, Wash. Post, Mar. 23, 1991, at B1 (quoting Harris Weinstein); Marianne Lavelle, How OTS Set the Stage for Order Against Firm, Natl. L.J., Mar. 16, 1992, at 32 (quoting Harris Weinstein).

86. Martin Mayer, The Greatest Ever Bank Robbery 20 (1990).

87. Lincoln Sav. & Loan Assn. v. Wall, 743 F. Supp. 190, 191-220 (D.D.C. 1990). Judge Sporkin is a former head of the enforcement division of the SEC.

88. See FDIC v. O'Melveny and Myers, 969 F.2d 744 (9th Cir. 1992); FDIC v. Clark, 958 F.2d 1079 (10th Cir. 1992); see also In re American Continental/Lincoln S&L Secs. Litig., 794 F. Supp. 1424 (D. Ariz. 1992); Stephen Gillers, Cleaning Up the S&L Mess, supra note 58.

89. Steve France, Just Deserts: Don't Cry for Kaye, Scholer, Legal Times, Apr. 6, 1992, at 28-29.

90. Verbatim: OTS Faces Off Against Kaye, Scholer, Legal Times, Mar. 9, 1992, at 11-12 (excerpting OTS complaint and Kaye, Scholer answer).

91. France, supra note 89, at 28.

92. Stephen Labaton, S&L's Lawyers Pressured by Suit, N.Y. Times, Mar. 8, 1992, at 22 (quoting John C. Coffee, Jr.).

93. Marvin E. Frankel, Lawyers Can't Be Stool Pigeons, N.Y. Times, Mar. 14, 1992, at 15; Steve France, supra note 89, at 28; Paul Craig Roberts, Big Brother Makes Lawyers Turn Snitch, L.A. Times, Mar. 16, 1992, at B5.

94. France, supra note 89, at 29.

95. Edward A. Adams, Repercussions of Kaye, Scholer Suit Discussed by Ethics Experts, New York L.J., Mar. 23, 1992, at 1 (quoting Mary C. Daly).

96. Ralph Nader & Wesley J. Smith, No Contest 46 (1996) (quoting Peter Fishbein).

97. Jones, Day's carrier, Attorneys Liability Assurance Society, which insures about 370 firms, increased 1993 rates about 20 percent for large firms. Saundra Torry, Paying the Price and Bearing the Burden, Wash. Post, Apr. 26, 1993, at F7.

98. Rita Henley Jensen, Jones, Day Pact Sets Conditions, Natl. L.J., May 3, 1993, at 42.

99. ABA, OTS Square-off on Lawyer Liability, ABA/BNA Lawyers Manual on Professional Conduct: Current Reports, Aug. 26, 1992, at 264, 266.

100. Remarks of Harris Weinstein, University of Michigan Law School, Mar. 24, 1992, at 16 [hereinafter Weinstein].

101. Id. (quoting Wolfram, supra note 15, at 709-710).

102. Weinstein, supra note 100, at 11.

103. Id. at 11-12.

104. Daniel Drapiewski, Lawyers Must Fight Back: Political Potshots Are Part of a Broader Assault on the Legal Profession, Los Angeles Daily J., Sept. 24, 1992, at 4.

105. Id. For views similar to Weinstein's on loophole lawyering, see William H. Simon, Ethical Discretion in Lawyering, 101 Harv. L. Rev. 1083 (1988), excerpted in Chapter IV (Advocacy); and Kenney Hegland, Quibbles, 67 Tex. L. Rev. 1491 (1989), discussed in Chapter IV at pages 159–160.

106. Lawrence J. Fox, OTS v. Kaye, Scholer: An Assault on the Citadel, 48 Bus. Law. 1521, 1524 (1993).

107. Jensen, supra note 81, at 1, 38 (quoting Michael Bloom). See generally Day, supra note 74.

108. Luban, supra note 84, at 959.

109. David B. Wilkins, Making Context Count: Regulating Lawyers After Kaye, Scholer, 66 U.S.C.L. Rev. 1145 (1993); see also Kraakman, supra note 79.

110. Day, supra note 74, at 666-669.

111. Wilkins, supra note 109.

112. Id.

113. Susan Koniak, When Courts Refuse to Frame the Law and Others Frame It to Their Will, 66 U.S.C.L. Rev. 1075 (1993).

Chapter XIV

Criminal Law and Procedure

A. THE LAWYER'S ROLE: CRIMINAL DEFENSE

1. Introduction

PROBLEM 14A

1. You are the lawyer representing David Keith in the case that Randy Bellows describes below. How would you proceed?

2. Richard Haynes, a highly successful defense lawyer, was known for his technique of presenting multiple defenses. According to one account,

> [h]e develops several scenarios simultaneously, and when it gets to final arguments, he picks the one he thinks will work. In defending . . . two Houston policemen, for example, Mr. Haynes contended that the beaten prisoner had in fact suffered the severe internal injuries while trying to escape. Or that he had died of an overdose of morphine. Or that the deep laceration in the victim's liver had actually been made during the autopsy.
>
> Mr. Haynes summed up this defense strategy before a recent American Bar Association seminar in New York. "Say you sue me because you say my dog bit you," he told them, holstering his thumbs in his vest pockets. "Well, now this is my defense: My dog doesn't bite. And, second, in the alternative, my dog was tied up that night. And third, I don't believe you really got bit. And fourth"—he grins slyly—"I don't have a dog."[1]

If this strategy does not involve knowing use of perjured or false information, is it ethically permissible? Should it be?

3. You are defending a client on charges of robbery. He has acknowledged committing the crime, which he knows took place around 4 P.M. The victim gives a statement to the police that mistakenly fixes the time at 2 P.M. Your client has a truthful and unshakable alibi for that period. May you present the alibi?[2]

RANDY BELLOWS, NOTES
OF A PUBLIC DEFENDER

The Social Responsibility of Lawyers: Case Studies
69-72, 78-79, 82, 88, 97, 99 (Philip B. Heymann &
Lance Liebman eds., 1988)

My name is Randy Bellows. I am a public defender [in Washington, D.C.] and this is my story or, more precisely, a collection of my stories. It is all true, with the following caveats: I have changed the names of all my clients and the names of certain other individuals. Where necessary to protect attorney-client confidences, I have changed material and immaterial facts. . . .

This is the story of David Keith and a marriage that was almost broken.

David Keith was charged with four brutal murders of elderly men and women in a once-peaceful Southeast Washington neighborhood. Murder by strangulation and asphyxiation. Murder by stomping. Murder by concussion/shock/fear. Several of the elderly women had also been raped. One morning, my co-counsel and I trekked over to the medical examiner's office and reviewed color glossy photographs of the carnage. Long after the case was over, long after the Keith case was replaced in the newspaper by other rapes and other robberies and other murders, I would remember the photograph of a sneaker print on the head of an 87-year-old man.

David Keith was just 18 years old, a veteran of the juvenile justice system. He had escaped several years earlier from a juvenile detention facility and had not been apprehended. He seldom lived at home. Much of the time, he would stay in condemned apartments, smoking reefer, getting high.

The police were led to David after he was caught in possession of a car stolen in one of the robberies. At the time of arrest, 4:00 A.M., he was tired, high, and scared. Sometime during the next seven hours he signed a nine page, single-spaced confession, admitting to dozens of different crimes, including the murders. . . .

I try hard, when I visit my clients, to ignore the crimes with which they are charged, to give them my own presumption of innocence. But when I would go to see David, particularly when I was the emissary of bad news, I would think of John Daniels, whose head had been stomped in two dozen times. I would think of 65-year-old

Rita Davis, who had been raped and strangled and left to rot under a mound of her own clothing. Visiting David was not really a lot of fun.

I remember the cross-examination of the homicide detective. David had decided that he stood nothing to gain from pleading guilty to multiple life offenses. It was not an inappropriate decision. As we prepared for trial, it became readily apparent that the only conceivable defense, in light of the nine page confession, was that the confession itself was a fraud.

I did not personally know the detective responsible for the confession. And that was a good thing. Because those colleagues of mine who did know him considered him to be one of the most honorable, decent, honest, and compassionate men on the police force. As one of my colleagues said, "If I murdered someone, he's the guy I'd want to confess to." It was my job to convince the jury that this man was not worthy of their trust, that it was really the detective, not David, who had composed the confession, that it was really the detective who had included all the voluminous details that gave it authenticity. It was my job to convince the jury that David had signed this document, not out of guilt and remorse, but as the last desperate act of a tired and strung-out youngster who had been questioned from 5:00 A.M. to noon and who just wanted to be left alone.

I cross-examined the detective for hours. The questioning was harsh, unfriendly. I intentionally sought to come across as hostile and disbelieving. I could not expect a jury to find this detective guilty of the malevolence with which I was charging him if it did not appear that I was angry, incensed by his conduct. When it was over, I did not really feel very good about the whole thing. I did what I had to do. I did not regret it then and I do not regret it today. But I had tried to make an honorable man appear dishonorable. And that is a sad thing to have to do, even if you are a public defender and even if that is your job. I remember my closing argument. . . . I did everything in my power to make David the victim and the detective his assailant. I argued until I was hoarse. I savaged the so-called confession, arguing that it was authored by the police to justify David's arrest and thereby, at least momentarily, squelch the public clamor for an end to the crime spree. I poked holes in all the other evidence: an inconclusive fingerprint, an ambiguous shoeprint, a weak identification.

Finally, it was over. The jury retired to deliberate. The next day they returned with a verdict. David was acquitted of every offense in which the sole evidence of guilt was the confession. He was convicted of every offense in which there was other evidence, like the fingerprint, to corroborate the confession. He was acquitted of a lifetime of offenses. Unfortunately for David, he was also convicted of a lifetime of offenses. And, so, he was ultimately sentenced to life in prison.

David Keith was a watershed case in my life as a public defender. It also turned out to be a watershed in my marriage.

Barbara had encouraged me to be a public defender. It sounded idealistic. It certainly sounded more idealistic than being a prosecutor. I would be a latter-day Atticus Finch. Instead, I was representing rapists and robbers, many of whom were obviously guilty, and many of whom would certainly pillage again upon release. Worse still, I was working feverishly to free these guys, even acting sometimes like this was not a job but a holy mission. And did I really have to help these people on Sundays, too? Did I have to work all night and get sick from lack of sleep? This was incomprehensible to her. These men were evil. What in hell was I doing working desperately to free them? Intellectually, Barb understood all the rationales and was tired of them. This was not law school, where we had stayed up late into the night talking abstractly about justice. This was for real. I was for real helping child molesters go free. I was for real getting stick-up men out on technicalities. Barb began to wonder if the man she was married to was not unwittingly serving evil. He certainly was not serving justice. . . . [T]his was not Atticus Finch at all. This was just bad. Maybe even immoral, certainly amoral.

And then came David Keith, sort of a distilled nightmare, all the gruesome crimes that had come down the pike rolled into one neat indictment. And Barb could not get away from it. Not only was she hearing about it from me. . . . Her teacher colleagues were asking whether that was her husband they had read about and, if so, how could he possibly be representing an animal like that? Barb had no answer to give them.

For a while, and long after the Keith case was over, things were touch-and-go at home. Ultimately, we worked out a fragile compromise. I stopped telling her about my bad clients and she stopped thinking about them. When I did talk about PDS, it was about our friends who worked there. When I did talk about my clients, I tip-toed, limiting myself to those innocent or innocuous clients about whom one could easily feel good.

It has worked. We no longer fight about PDS. We were eyeball to eyeball. To preserve our love, and out of our love, we both blinked. . . .

I try not to think about victims too much. The more I think about them, the more difficult it is to represent my clients. And, of course, sometimes victims are not victims at all. Sometimes victims are liars, fabricating incidents that never occurred; sometimes victims are really assailants who have managed to cloak themselves in innocence; sometimes victims pick the wrong man and your client becomes a victim too. But often it is none of those things. A victim is a victim is a victim and your client is a victimizer. Those are the cases where I try hardest not to think of the victim.

To represent a client properly, you have to be able to develop an enormous amount of empathy. You have to be able not only to advocate, but to advocate passionately. Thus, again and again, I found myself becoming almost overwrought at sentencings, pleading for one more chance, pleading to keep families together, pleading for a judge to reach out to my client, pleading for freedom. At a few sentencings I nearly cried and, as I stood there awaiting pronouncement of sentence, I felt transfixed, as if it were my life and liberty hanging in the balance.

This kind of intense involvement is a necessity. If you care about your client, maybe, just maybe, the judge will care about your client. But if you do not care, if you feel no bond to your client, that fact will be so obvious to the court that all your carefully architectured blandishments will go unheeded. The same is true, only more so, with a jury. If the jury senses that you do not like your client, that you just do not care if he goes down the drain, sure as anything they will flush him. . . .

An incarcerated client is filled with anxiety. And why not? Here he is completely dependent on his public defender lawyer, someone he does not know and did not hire. The jail abounds with stories about clients being screwed by their lawyers. About incompetent lawyers. About lazy lawyers. About lawyers who just do not care. Am I the one who is going to sell him down the river? Is it really true that PDS stands for Plea Delivery Service? . . .

[Why should clients trust me?] They do not know me from beans; they do not trust anyone who works in the court system; I am white and they are usually black; they are not paying me a dime and since when does that get you anything; even worse, they know that the people who are paying me are the same people, more or less, who pay the cops and the D.A.'s. . . .

I became a public defender because I believe passionately in our system of justice, in the adversary system. Without a lawyer fighting with all of his strength to advocate for his client, without a lawyer as competent and able as the prosecutor, the system simply is not legitimate. I help make it legitimate and that is why I do what I do. Lawyers who do not care about their clients, who do not represent them competently, who do not provide even a shadow of effective assistance of counsel render the system null and void. . . .

I am leaving PDS. I need more money to raise a growing family. (Have you not heard that refrain before?) I find myself burned out, a syndrome which I thought afflicted only other lawyers. I am tired of being a public defender. I am sick of representing so many bad people, though I will certainly miss the many good people I have helped. I am sick, in particular, of representing rapists. I am sick of being afraid to walk in my own parking lot yet helping people who mug citizens in other parking lots. I have lost much of the empathy I once had for my clients. It is time to go.

I also leave because I want to be a prosecutor. There are people in my office who could no more conceive of themselves as prosecutors than they can conceive of themselves as police officers. They consider prosecutors persecutors and could not possibly picture themselves trying to get someone locked up. I can. It is an imperfect world with imperfect solutions. Lorton [Jail] is one of them.

I want to be a prosecutor because I want to be in a position where I can do good more of the time. As a public defender, I do good when I represent innocent persons. I do good when I represent guilty men who deserve a break. But I do not do good when I help bad men go free, except, that is, in the broad, philosophical sense that I have vindicated the judicial system and upheld our constitutional principles.

I am at a point right now where I need more than a philosophical construct, even one as noble as the Sixth Amendment. I want direct, not circumstantial, evidence that I am doing good, that I am doing justice.

I am through now, and I can say it: I saved some lives. Of course, that is only part of the story. Many lives I did not save; many lives I could not save. But I did save some lives.

I kept a number of innocent men and women from going to prison. Will I ever do anything more significant than that? I helped people who needed help, people who *had* committed the crimes they were charged with but who did not deserve to go to prison or who did not deserve to spend the rest of their lives in prison. I earned the trust of men for whom trust comes hard.

JOHN B. MITCHELL, THE ETHICS OF THE CRIMINAL DEFENSE ATTORNEY— NEW ANSWERS TO OLD QUESTIONS

32 Stan. L. Rev. 293, 320, 334 (1980)

II. WHY I DEFEND THE GUILTY

[T]he defense attorney plays a critical role in "making the screens work." By defending the guilty at trial, the defense attorney assures that those who are supposed to operate the screens do so properly. By defending the guilty at trial, the defense attorney dispels at least some of the coercive effects of the plea-bargaining system. In short, by defending the guilty, the defense attorney protects the freedom of the innocent. But I defend the guilty not simply to protect all of us but also to protect the guilty from the corrupting influences of the criminal justice system. . . .

Many judges in large urban court systems, interested only in clearing their dockets, and often given to a martinet's temperament, shuttle the 20 or so new faces represented by the same public defender each day from arraignment through guilty plea. Police often lie, while prosecutors suppress evidence favorable to the defense. This governmental lawbreaking passes without the slightest notice. Under the umbrella of almost limitless discretion, judges are often guided only by their inclinations. . . .

Our criminal courts must teach better lessons. It is to this end that I defend the guilty, for they, above all, must be taught the right lesson. It is not that I naively believe that most convicted defendants would thank a judge for being "fair" while sending them to prison. From my experience, however, the prevalent injustice in the current process does do harm by further lessening respect for the law, not just in the criminal defendants, but also in friends, family, witnesses, and spectators. The lessons are communicated to all of those who are touched by the process. . . .

B.   The Ravages of Conviction

1.   The Prisons

A lengthy exposition on the nightmarish conditions in our jails and prisons would cover little new ground. Literature and reports documenting the horror are extensive. . . .

I will not dwell on this. Those guilty of serious crimes merit the wrath of our society. But almost no one deserves the hell holes that we call jails and prisons. There is almost no case I would not defend if that meant keeping a human being, as condemnable as he or she may be, from suffering the total, brutal inhumanity of our jails and prisons. . . .

When people ask how I can defend someone who is "dangerous," they are referring to a person who is more than just factually guilty of a crime; they mean someone who poses immediate physical danger to them in a very special sense. Statistically, drunk or negligent drivers are responsible for more deaths annually than murderers. But this kind of immediate physical danger does not frighten us. We do not like it, but we understand it. It does not involve some stranger totally disregarding our personal integrity by violently entering our world and using us as an object of his wishes. When people say "dangerous," they mean the violent offender.

I do not consider every person who commits a violent offense to be dangerous. When I speak of "dangerous" I refer to a quality of the person, not of the crime. While the nature of the crime may reflect this quality, it will not necessarily do so. Murderers rarely endanger lives a second time, and even those who assault their victim in the course of a robbery generally do so only when surprised by the victim's resistance. . . .

In my view a dangerous person is one for whom violence is a customary response, who is willing to attack a stranger without reason, and who is likely to do so in the future. The type of person I consider dangerous in a way that poses ethical problems greater than the basic problem of defending the factually guilty is a person likely to commit another act of violence the very same day. The question that arises, then, is how certain must I be that a person is "dangerous" before I will consider that factor in my ethical calculus?

Scientific studies attempting to predict future dangerous behavior have been unable to do so to a standard of "more likely than not," let alone "beyond a reasonable doubt." Nevertheless, there are defendants who, after interviews and review of their present charge and past criminal history, I have reasonably believed to be dangerous. The fact that I cannot validate this belief by some scientifically devised scale of deviance does not mean that this belief has no importance in my own calculation of the morality of my actions. A reasonable belief is a sufficient level of certainty to define a defendant as dangerous for my purposes.

Even if the defendant is guilty and dangerous, I can yet posit several reasons to justify his or her defense. First, it is through the defense of just such cases that an attorney can most influence the functioning of the screens. Government can best be educated in a serious case, especially one in which the police and prosecutor perceive the defendant as dangerous. The agents of the government really want to win convictions in such cases and it is in just such cases that all of the abuses the system generates are most likely to appear. Acquittals or even difficulties at trial due to inadequate investigation or the use of poor evidence will be remembered. In addition, making the screens operate effectively when serious charges are involved is especially important because the consequences of convicting an innocent person of a serious offense are so severe.

Second, it is important to ensure that the dangerous are treated fairly in the process. Such persons are the last ones in whom to reinforce values that disregard the worth of other human beings. Finally, aside from the general aversion I have to seeing anyone go to prison, incarceration presents some special problems for me when dealing with the dangerous offender. Almost all of the defendants I have met who I believed were dangerous had committed assaults, not murders. Their prison sentences would therefore be short — especially since over half of all violent crimes are committed by persons under 18 years of age. Even if we lock them up for quite a while, when they get out they will still be young and strong and probably more dangerous to the society than they were before they entered prison.

---

2.   The Rationale for Zealous Representation

> When employed to defend those charged with
> crimes of the deepest dye, and the evidence
> against them, whether legal, or moral, be such
> as to leave no just doubt of their guilt, I shall not
> hold myself privileged, much less obliged, to use
> my endeavors to arrest, or to impede the course
> of justice, by special resorts to ingenuity, the

artifices of eloquence, to appeals to the morbid and fleeting sympathies of weak juries. . . . Persons of atrocious character, who have violated the laws of God and man, are entitled to no such special exertions from any member of our pure and honourable profession.

David Hoffman[3]

In 25 years, Martin Erdmann has defended more than 100,000 criminals. He has saved them tens of thousands of years in prison and in those years they have robbed, raped, burglarized and murdered tens upon tens of thousands of people. The idea of having had a very personal and direct hand in all that mayhem strikes him as boring and irrelevant. "I have nothing to do with justice," he says. "Justice is not even part of the equation. If you say I have no moral reaction to what I do, you are right."

And *he* is right. As right as our adversary judicial system, as right as jury trials, as right as the presumption of innocence and the Fifth Amendment. If there is a fault in Erdmann's eagerness to free defendants, it is not with Erdmann himself, but with the system. Criminal law to the defense lawyer does not mean equity or fairness or proper punishment or vengeance. It means getting everything he can for his client. And in perhaps 98% of his cases, the clients *are* guilty. Justice is a luxury enjoyed by the district attorney. He alone is sworn "to see that justice is done." The defense lawyer does not bask in the grandeur of any such noble oath. He finds himself most often working for the guilty and for a judicial system based upon the sound but paradoxical principle that the guilty must be freed to protect the innocent.

James Mills[4]

No issue is more central to the American legal system and more controversial among the American public than the criminal defense lawyer's obligations in defending the guilty. As an abstract proposition, most individuals agree that persons accused of a crime should be presumed innocent and should be entitled to force the government to make its case. But when that presumption becomes concrete and the lawyer's role in freeing guilty, often dangerous, offenders becomes explicit, popular sentiment shifts.

The moral boundaries of defense lawyers' obligations are troubling to many individuals within the profession as well as outside it. Long-standing debates have centered on whether counsel in criminal cases should have "something to do with justice" in particular cases as well as in the system as a whole. While virtually all commentators agree that a defendant has, and should have, a constitutional right to put the government to its proof, they disagree about what that right implies for defense counsel. At the most general level, the controversy involves defense lawyers' duties to truth when defending the guilty. More specific questions concern attorneys' obligations in misleading a jury, impeaching honest witnesses, or presenting evidence that is probably, but not certainly, false. These questions are explored in subsequent sections below and in Chapter VI (Confidentiality and Client Counseling), pages 236–262, and Chapter V (The Adversary System), pages 203–208. Discussion here centers on the general issue of whether defendants believed to be guilty have a right to all techniques of partisanship that are not specifically prohibited.

The two most common justifications for zealous representation on behalf of guilty defendants parallel the arguments on behalf of the adversary system and the advocate's role more generally discussed in Chapters IV and V. One rationale involves the pursuit of truth and the other involves the defense of rights.[5] Many commentators who reject these arguments for unqualified neutral partisanship in the civil context accept them in criminal cases because of certain distinctive procedural features and practical consequences of the penal system.

a. Truth

The first justification for zealous representation of clients whom an attorney believes to be factually guilty is that it is necessary to protect those who are factually or legally innocent. Attorneys may be wrong in their assessments, particularly since defendants seldom have reason to confess their culpability to an attorney. As former public defender Barbara Babcock notes: "[F]acts are indeterminate, contingent, and in criminal cases, often evanescent. . . . [And] there is a difference between legal and moral guilt."[6] Accordingly, our system proceeds on the assumption that defendants are entitled to have their guilt determined "not in the privacy of one lawyer's office but in open court under due process."[7] As Lord Erskine observed in the trial of Thomas Paine for publishing The Rights of Man (1792), "If the advocate refuses to defend from what he may think of the charge or the defense, [the lawyer] assumes the character of the judge . . . before the hour of judgment."[8]

The risks of allowing lawyers to curtail their efforts in accordance with their own perceptions of guilt are particularly great under a system in which over 90 percent of all defendants never go to trial, acquittal is rare, and resources for pretrial preparation are generally minimal.[9] In one study, almost half of defense counsel entered pleas without interviewing any prosecution witnesses and almost a third without interviewing any defense witnesses.[10] In another survey of New York assigned attorneys, 90 percent of lawyers in felony cases submitted no reimbursement requests for interviewing witnesses and 80 percent made no defense motions.[11] The costs of licensing attorneys to judge, not defend, their clients were well illustrated by a Texas habeas corpus case in which a defendant won release after seven years of imprisonment on the basis of incompetent assistance of counsel. In his lawyer's view, the appointment to provide representation did not include "going out to sleazy bars to look for witnesses," particularly since he believed the defendant was guilty.[12]

The disincentives for adequate representation are especially great where the crime is heinous or the accused is a member of a particularly unpopular group. To take only the most obvious example, for most of this nation's history, southern blacks accused of an offense against a white victim stood little chance of anything approximating a fair trial.[13] Despite substantial progress, discrimination against racial and ethnic minorities remains common.[14] So too, in many dictatorships and totalitarian countries, where defense counsel's role is to "serve justice," what passes for "justice" does not commend itself for export. Often the roles of counsel for the defendant and the state are functionally identical and the price is paid in innocent lives.[15]

Moreover, in this country, the legal system's heavy dependence on plea-bargaining makes it essential that the government's case receive vigorous challenge in the small percentage of proceedings that do reach a jury. As John Mitchell argues, without the prospect of a zealous defense in those cases, prosecutors and police have far fewer incentives to investigate the facts thoroughly, to corroborate a complainant's story, and to ensure, in short, that they are not trying the wrong person.

Critics of this rationale for unqualified partisanship make several responses. In William Simon's view, arguments that the fact-finding role rests properly with judges or jurors, not lawyers, are convincing only to the extent that those triers of fact have all relevant information. The difficult ethical issue, however, arises where that is not the case, where, for example, only the attorney knows that the defendant offered other patently implausible alibis before settling on the current version. We need not attribute "cosmic certainty" to the lawyer to believe that she is sometimes better able to make a judgment about guilt than a judge or juror.[16]

On similar reasoning, Harry Subin argues that lawyers can provide appropriate law enforcement incentives without resorting to the kind of "special . . . ingenuity" that David Hoffman deplored and Randy Bellows describes. In his view,

> it is one thing to attack a weak government case by pointing out its weakness. It is another . . . to attack a strong government case by confusing the jury with falsehoods. . . . [Accordingly] I would limit my representation at that stage to putting forth the strongest argument I could that the facts presented by the state did not sustain its burden.

In these ways, the defendant would receive the services of an attorney in subjecting the state's case to the final stage of the screening process provided by the system to insure against unjust convictions. That, however, would be all that the defense attorney could do.[17]

Where defense counsel lack the resources or inclination to provide effective representation, many commentators argue that the appropriate response is to address those problems directly, not to inculcate an ideology oblivious to truth. Thus, greater resources could be available for appointed counsel to make adequate investigations, and more effective oversight of lawyers' performance could be institutionalized through civil and disciplinary liability as well as through reversals on appeal. While none of these strategies may be wholly successful in ensuring adequate representation of poor and unpopular defendants, neither is the current system.[18]

Finally, some commentators have questioned whether "unqualified partisanship in the small percentage of cases that go to trial, and almost no formal scrutiny of the 90% resolved through plea bargains, is the most just way of resolving criminal charges."[19] For example, some European systems rely far less on plea-bargaining and impose more procedural protections to reduce the likelihood that innocent defendants will be pressured into guilty pleas.[20] Consider the merits of such a structure in light of the concerns about rights and the constraints on resources discussed below.

b. Rights

The second principal justification for zealous representation of the guilty involves the protection of rights. Where individual's lives, liberty, and reputation are so directly at risk, they deserve one advocate without competing loyalties to the state. That is particularly the case when, as Babcock notes, those who commit crimes often are "themselves the victims of horrible injustice."[21] Political abuses of the law enforcement system have figured too prominently in American history to discount the risks of government repression. David Luban recounts some of the more well-known examples in the last half-century: "McCarthyism, FBI and CIA infiltration of domestic protest movements during the civil rights and Viet Nam War eras, Nixon's Enemies List."[22]

Rights-based concerns also arise from the conditions of confinement in most of this nation's prisons, the inadequacy of alternatives to incarceration, the extended length of sentences for relatively minor offenses, and the disabling consequences of a criminal record, especially for poor, low-skilled, and minority defendants. These distinctive features of penal sanctions, coupled with the potential for governmental repression, justify many of the special protections of the criminal process, including the sixth amendment right to effective assistance of counsel and the fifth amendment privilege against

self-incrimination. For many commentators, these protections also
entail a commitment of unqualified partisanship beyond that justifiable in civil proceedings.[23] To penalize clients for making disclosures
to their lawyers that suggest guilt would effectively force an impermissible choice between fifth and sixth amendment guarantees.

These justifications for partisanship have been subject to several
lines of challenge. One obvious response to concerns about self-
incrimination is that voluntary disclosures to a lawyer do not involve
the same risk of abuses and inaccuracies associated with confessions
to law enforcement officials. While acknowledging the unique
features of criminal punishment, some commentators argue that it
would be preferable to address these concerns directly. In William
Simon's view, lawyers should press for changes in the sanctioning
process and dispositional alternatives rather than legitimate an
ideology of zealous advocacy that is both under- and over-inclusive.
Misleading the judge and jury in the few cases that go to trial does
nothing to address the problems in the vast number of cases that do
not: more attention should focus directly on disproportionate
sentences, inhuman prison conditions, and inadequate opportunities
for ex-offenders.

Moreover, a categorical distinction between civil and criminal
proceedings fails to take account of relevant factors. In some civil
cases, the potential for abuse of private power and the consequences
for the parties are far more substantial than in some routine criminal cases involving petty offenses and offenders for whom one
additional conviction will have little practical significance. To the
extent that our concern is with protecting individual rights, many
commentators argue that the rights of victims deserve some consideration in defense counsel's moral universe. As Charles Ogletree
notes, while many defendants are victims of injustice, often the
targets of their crimes have had similar or worse experiences.[24]
"Private" conduct by criminal offenders can constitute no less a
threat to personal liberty than misuse of "public" authority by the
state.

Accordingly, some commentators maintain that lawyers should
make contextual, not categorical, judgments about whether to
engage in aggressive defense tactics, that is, tactics that are legal
but that are likely to distort the fact-finding process. For example,
William Simon argues that attorneys should consider the extent to
which values justifying zealous partisanship are in fact implicated in
particular prosecutions. Does the case involve abuses of state power,
racial bias, or disproportionate sentences? Fred Zacharias adds
factors such as the disparity of resources between the parities and
the quality of the lawyer-client relationship. Are the clients so
legally unsophisticated or distrustful that only zealous partisanship
will ensure their candor and confidence?[25]

David Luban offers the following characterization of the debate
between those who, like himself, support a categorical presumption

favoring zealous advocacy in criminal cases, and critics like Simon who favor a more contextual approach:

> Simon writes as though aggressive defense is a norm among criminal defense lawyers; as though aggressive defense ties prosecutors in knots and has a significant impact on law enforcement and conviction rates; as though aggressive defense tangibly diminishes public safety and inflicts moral harms on substantial numbers of crime victims; as though defense lawyers would typically be reluctant to forego aggressive defense and the advantages it confers on them and their clients.
>
> I, on the other hand, have portrayed a world of lawyers for whom no defense at all, rather than aggressive defense or even desultory defense, is the norm; a world of minuscule acquittal rates; a world where advocacy is rare and defense investigation virtually nonexistent; a world . . . in which individualized scrutiny is replaced by the indifferent mass processing of interchangeable defendants.
>
> We are both right, for there are in reality two criminal justice systems, two criminal populations, and two criminal defense bars [divided by wealth]. . . . The typical client is poor, and the typical defender is not paid enough to engage in individualized advocacy, let alone zealous advocacy. . . .
>
> My own view is that [defense counsel] should utilize her scarce resources on behalf of those clients who are in greater jeopardy and who are less dangerous, rather than the other way around; probably Simon would agree. However . . . I think that a blanket permission (or even encouragement) for indigent defenders to engage in aggressive advocacy is better than an injunction to assess each candidate for aggressive defense on its merits, because the latter rule would lead to too many wrong decisions to curtail zeal.[26]

In a sense, this argument parallels the debate between rule utilitarians and act utilitarians described in Chapter II. How would you evaluate each position? Where would you draw the line on representing defendants whom you believe to be both guilty and dangerous?

B. DESTRUCTION OF EVIDENCE

PROBLEM 14B

In The Superlawyers, Joseph Goulden relates the following exchange:

> "You are looking," the Washington Lawyer told me, "at one of the dumbest sons of bitches in Western civilization." He nodded across the [room]. . . .
>
> "This fellow," the Washington Lawyer was saying to me, with three-martini candor, ". . . came to me, on recommendation of a friend of mine in Baltimore, and said he needed some help in a bad way. He had been doing some odd-ball discounting to some customers and not to others, and the way he admitted it to me, it was a clear-cut violation of the Robinson-Patman act, because it was as discriminatory as hell. Apparently

one of the unfavored customers had complained to his lawyer, who in turn had complained to the Federal Trade Commission. Trouble was coming; it was just a matter of time.

"Now, in a situation like this, the documents should tell the whole story, and I don't see any reason why a man should help the Federal government build a gallows for himself. At the same time, the bar rules are pretty simple: If I advise him to go burn everything, I can be disbarred for interfering with the processes of justice.

"So I take another route. I tell him just what I told you—without all his sales records, the FTC will have a hell of a time making a case. Oh, they could, but only by backtracking to customers. But I know the FTC is so short-handed they won't do that except in a major case. 'Do you *still* have any documents around that could hurt you?' I asked him. 'Some of this stuff must be getting pretty old, and most people turn over their records fairly *fast*.'

"'Oh, no,' he said, 'I've got everything. My bookkeeper is meticulous.'

"I tried again. 'You know,' I said, 'there's no law that says how long you've got to keep stuff, so long as you have enough to substantiate your records. That must be quite a storage problem, maintaining all those old outdated files.'

"God, he didn't even blink. 'Oh, we have plenty of space,' he said. 'We just put it in crates and put it in the back of the warehouse. It's all right there.'

"I gave up. He was so damned dense he wasn't about to tumble to what I was saying and I didn't dare take it a step further and tell him to go home and have himself one hell of a big bonfire. I kind of like being a lawyer, you know. Just as I feared, the FTC subpoenaed enough to make a case, and it cost the poor bastard one hell of a lot of time and trouble. 'But why didn't you just tell me I should have cleaned out the files?' he kept asking me. I finally unloaded on him and gave him an informative little talk.

"He's still mad at me. He haggled over the bill, and he cussed me all over Washington and Baltimore. I don't give a damn, though; I still have my law license."

Id. at 287-289.

Should he? Consider the materials on destruction of evidence in Chapter VI (Confidentiality and Client Counseling), at pages 239–248.

C. CLIENT PERJURY

See Chapter VI, Confidentiality and Client Counseling
   • Part F. Client Perjury
      (pages 251–262)

D. TRIAL TACTICS

See Chapter V, The Adversary System
   • Witness Preparation
      (pages 195–200)
   • Impeachment
      (pages 200–203)

See Chapter XV, Evidence and Trial Advocacy
          Trial Tactics
          (pages 655–662)

E.   EFFECTIVE REPRESENTATION, PLEA-BARGAINING, AND CONFLICTS OF INTEREST

1.   The Structure of Representation

> [A prominent British justice] expressed surprise
> when the defendant requested an attorney. "You
> were caught with your hand inside a man's
> pocket. What can a lawyer say in your defense?"
> There was a pause and then the response,
> "That's what I am anxious to know."
>
> *Patrick Mahony*[27]

PROBLEM 14C

1. You are the prosecutor in a routine drug case. Defense counsel is not providing what you consider adequate representation. Under what, if any circumstances, do you have any ethical obligation to intervene? What form of intervention would be appropriate? Consider, for example, the following possibilities:

   a. The court-appointed defense counsel makes no effort to mount an affirmative defense despite obvious weaknesses in your case. He also seems wholly without trial skills.
   b. The public defender assigned to the case appears to be under the influence of alcohol. Her cross-examinations are totally ineffectual and she has failed to make relevant evidentiary objections. The trial judge, known for his bias against defendants, claims not to notice any performance problems.
   c. The court-appointed attorney's direct and cross-examinations are satisfactory and make it appear as if he has mounted an adequate defense. However, he has not investigated the facts or filed what would probably be a successful motion to suppress evidence. Prior dealings with this attorney suggest that he accepts far too many appointed cases to prepare adequately for trial.
   d. Same facts as in (c), except that the attorney has been privately retained. Since the defendant has no apparent resources, you suspect that counsel fees are being paid by someone whose interests are not entirely consistent with the defendant's.[28]

2. You are the trial judge in a capital murder case. The privately retained defense lawyer, a 72-year-old veteran of the local criminal court, has fallen asleep several times during witnesses' testimony. On your own motion, you appoint co-counsel. When a reporter covering the trial questions the first attorney about his midafternoon naps, the attorney responds that the trial is "boring." Co-counsel expresses hope that these sleeping habits will "make the jury feel sorry for us." By his own account, co-counsel has spent between five and seven hours preparing the case. The lead attorney has read the state's case file. Neither has done any factual investigation.

You believe that the defendant is guilty. However, the prosecution's case has several weaknesses. Prior to a lineup, one key eyewitness expressed some uncertainty about her ability to identify the perpetrator. The other primary witness is a paid informant with three prior convictions who received a favorable plea in exchange for his testimony. You believe that defense counsel is doing a reasonable job of exposing these weaknesses but that the failure to mount a convincing affirmative defense makes conviction quite likely.

How should you proceed? What would you do if you were a member of the bar disciplinary committee reviewing the conduct of these attorneys after the defendant is convicted? What would you do as an appellate judge if the defendant is convicted and claims ineffective assistance of counsel?[29]

Under the sixth amendment, criminal defendants have a constitutional right to effective assistance of counsel. However, that right has lost much of its meaning in practice.

In most jurisdictions, defendants in about two-thirds of felony cases qualify as "indigents" for purposes of obtaining court-appointed lawyers. Between one-third and one-half of misdemeanor defendants also meet indigency requirements and have a right to state-subsidized representation before being sentenced to incarceration.

A majority of judicial districts use court-appointed private practitioners for these cases. A growing number of jurisdictions are instituting competitive contract systems in which lawyers bid to provide representation for a specified percentage of cases for an annual fee, irrespective of the volume or complexity of that caseload. Such systems often present serious quality control problems since little or no effort is made to monitor the adequacy of training, support staff, or representation.[30] Similar oversight problems occur in jurisdictions that rely on private practitioners who seek assignment on a case-by-case basis.[31] Payment takes the form of a flat fee or an hourly rate, coupled with a ceiling on total compensation. Under all of these systems, fee awards are usually quite low. Limits of $500 to $1,000 are common for felony cases and some states enforce such ceilings even in capital cases. Caps for hourly rates can be as low as $40. In jurisdictions with low ceilings on total compensation, hourly rates can dip to below $2.[32] A small number of court systems also require pro bono assistance from the bar in general or the criminal defense bar in particular.[33]

About a third of all counties, representing some 60 percent of the nation's population, have a public defender office. In most of these districts, the office provides representation for all defendants except in cases of conflict of interest. Other jurisdictions rely on a mix of public defenders and private practitioners. In some jurisdictions, indigent caseloads are extremely heavy and can sometimes total over 500 cases per year per attorney.[34] However, in jurisdictions where caseloads are manageable, the quality of representation tends to be quite high, and the training and mentoring of defense attorneys are impressive. Even in areas where caseloads are demanding, the level of representation compares favorably with that of private practitioners, who often depend on large volumes to compensate for low fees.

Criminal defendants who can afford counsel fall into several categories. Most of those individuals are just over the line of indigency and rely on a small number of attorneys who specialize in handling a high volume of criminal cases, and who almost always charge a flat fee, payable in advance.[35] Defendants who can afford to pay substantial fees, usually in white-collar or organized crime cases, have access to an elite group of highly skilled trial lawyers. Often these lawyers will also take on pro bono cases with special appeal.

For the vast majority of criminal cases, the pressures on attorneys to settle before trial are quite intense. Both privately retained lawyers, who rely on flat fees, and court-appointed attorneys, who work for unrealistic hourly rates with statutory caps, depend on a high turnover of cases. Seldom do these practitioners have any interest in going to trial, and a complex case that does not settle can be financially disastrous.

Although salaried public defenders do not operate under the same financial constraints, caseload pressures often push in similar directions. Out of all state and local expenditures for criminal justice, less than 2 percent goes to legal defense.[36] Inadequate salaries, facilities, and support staff compound the problem.[37]

The inadequacy of resources for criminal representation creates obvious conflicts of interest between lawyer and client. Attorneys have every incentive to plead clients guilty except in the rare cases where statutory fee levels and caseloads are set at realistic levels or where the client is able to pay. These financial incentives are reinforced by the psychological dynamics and professional reward structures that Albert Alschuler describes below. A quick plea spares lawyers the pressures and risks of trial, and preserves good working relationships with other participants in an overburdened system.

Thus, almost by necessity, much criminal defense work falls into the classic pattern that Abraham Blumberg described in "The Practice of Law as Confidence Game." Clients who expect vindication through their "day in court" are "cooled out" by the risks of trial that their attorney projects.[38] Yet this risk assessment is inevitably influenced, whether consciously or unconsciously, by attorneys' own concerns. And the lack of time or resources for pretrial investigation noted earlier makes it easier for counsel to assume that defendants generally are not giving up valid defenses by a quick plea. Yet all too often that plea may be based on inadequate preparation and therefore inadequate bargaining leverage. The dedication that Bellows describes is extremely difficult to sustain under current resource constraints.

Conflicts of interest between lawyers and clients are especially problematic in criminal defense, given the inadequacy of market or regulatory oversight mechanisms. Defendants typically lack sufficient information to second-guess lawyers' plea recommendations; rarely do they have access to knowledge about prosecutorial, juror, and judicial behavior in comparable cases.[39] Even if clients doubt the reliability or disinterest of their appointed lawyer, they cannot do much about it. Indigent defendants have no right to select their attorneys, and court-appointed lawyers do not depend for their livelihood on the satisfaction of clients.[40] Indeed, a reputation for singled-minded zeal on behalf of the accused is unlikely to work to counsel's advantage among the court officials who control appointments or negotiate bargains.[41] Some trial judges who are themselves under intense caseload pressures will refuse to appoint "obstructionist" lawyers who frequently raise "technical defenses" or insist on trials.[42]

Other non-market forms of oversight are equally inadequate to counteract these structural pressures. Indigent criminal defendants rarely are sympathetic malpractice clients and generally must establish their innocence to prevail.[43] Bar disciplinary authorities rarely consider complaints of "mere" negligence against criminal defense attorneys. Only the most egregious lawyering will lead to a finding of ineffective assistance of counsel and a reversal of conviction.[44] In one nine-state survey, less than 1 percent of ineffective assistance claims were successful.[45] The extent of judicial tolerance is well illustrated by the Texas case on which Problem 14C(2) is based. In rejecting the defendant's claim of ineffective representation, the district judge noted, "[t]he Constitution says that everyone is entitled to an attorney of their choice. But the Constitution does not say that the lawyer has to be awake."[46]

For the vast majority of clients who plea-bargain, no relief will be available for a bad bargain based on inadequate preparation or investigation. Courts have granted remedies only to the very few clients who can demonstrate that but for the ineffective assistance of counsel, they would never have pled guilty. Hill v. Lockhart, 474 U.S. 52, 59 (1985).

These structural problems have prompted a variety of reform proposals. The most obvious response is also the most unpopular: a substantial increase in resources for criminal defense. What makes this approach politically unpalatable is equally obvious. Public officials are likely to win far more support promising to be tough on criminals than subsidizing their defense. Yet as federal judge Frank Easterbrook has argued, a society that professes the "inestimable value of liberty" and that is willing to pay more than $20,000 a year for each individual it incarcerates should be prepared to pay more than $250 to determine whether imprisonment is in fact justifiable.[47] According to many commentators, if this position is unpopular with the electorate, that is all the more reason for non-elected judges to require adequate appropriations. For the same reasons that it has fallen on courts to set threshold standards for prisons, it may be necessary for them to set realistic benchmarks for criminal defense fees and caseloads.[48]

Other commentators propose making counsel more accountable in fact and appearance through a system of vouchers. Clients with court-appointed counsel report significantly less satisfaction with their lawyers' performance than clients who have retained their own counsel, even where there is no measurable difference in case outcomes.[49] In general, defendants see assigned attorneys as "part of the system" and assume that they have "nothing to gain" by fighting hard; they "get [their] money either way."[50] These attitudes are well-captured by the title of Jonathan Casper's landmark article, "Did You Have a Lawyer When You Went to Court? No, I Had a Public Defender."[51] A system that gives defendants some choice in their counsel is likely to improve lawyer-client relationships and may slightly enhance market controls over lawyer performance. Voucher structures with clearly visible ceilings on expenditures might also increase pressure for change. Giving criminal defendants a voucher for under $100 is more likely to arouse judicial (if not popular) concern than retaining a system that in fact provides such limited funding per case.[52]

Yet neither increased resources nor greater client control will address all of the conflicts of interest noted above. Even with more adequate compensation and realistic caseloads, appointed counsel will often have personal and professional reasons to avoid trial. Retained counsel who charge flat fees will still have incentives to plea-bargain cases that defendants might prefer to litigate. Moreover, any criminal defense lawyer may be pressured to trade off a particular client's interest to preserve judicial and prosecutorial relationships that will benefit other clients. As Martin Guggenheim notes, even lawyers who "never give an inch [may be making trade-offs. They] may think that they are obeying the injunction to represent each client zealously . . . but they are sure to fail. . . . [N]obody makes reasonable deals with them. [Some of their] clients always seem to be the losers." Moreover, as Guggenheim adds, "[t]he danger is that [those of us who represent indigent defendants] may fool ourselves into believing that a particular result is best for the client, without realizing that we came to that conclusion only, or mainly, because it is best for us."[53]

Thus, conflicts of interest are not readily avoided under the American criminal justice system; however, it may be possible to mitigate their worst consequences by providing more responsive civil liability and bar disciplinary systems and more rigorous standards for assessing effective assistance of counsel. Given the difficulties of ensuring adequate resources and regulatory oversight, changes in the plea-bargaining structure also may be appropriate. Consider the merits of these reform strategies in light of the materials that follow.

ALBERT W. ALSCHULER, PERSONAL FAILURE, INSTITUTIONAL FAILURE, AND THE SIXTH AMENDMENT

14 N.Y.U. Rev. L. & Soc. Change 149, 149-153 (1986)

. . . A system of plea negotiation is a catalyst for inadequate representation. It subjects defense attorneys to serious temptations to disregard their clients' interests, engenders suspicion of betrayal on the part of defendants, and aggravates the harmful impact of inadequate representation when it occurs. . . . [Also], a plea negotiation system insulates attorneys from review and often makes it impossible to determine whether inadequate representation has occurred. . . . A regime of plea negotiation lends itself to ineffective assistance and aggravates its harmful consequences in at least six ways that an adjudicative system does not.

First, like other people, defense attorneys like money. A plea bargaining system subjects these attorneys to powerful financial temptations to disregard their clients' interests. For obvious practical reasons, privately retained defense attorneys usually collect their fees in advance; and once an attorney has pocketed his fee, his economic interests lie in disposing of the case as rapidly as possible. The most rapid way to dispose of a case is usually to enter a bargained plea. A similar conflict of interest besets some appointed attorneys, those who receive small statutory payments for every case in which they appear. . . .[7]

Second, apart from the desire to make money, attorneys like to minimize work. Plea negotiation offers defense attorneys a more comfortable way of life than does adjudication. As salaried lawyers whose compensation does not depend on the ways in which their

---

7. Although a defense attorney's financial interests usually favor the entry of a plea of guilty, these interests occasionally push in the opposite direction. Consider, for example, an assigned counsel system that compensates attorneys on an hourly basis. Attorneys who regard the prescribed hourly rate as inadequate may be tempted to put the burdens of their assignments behind them by entering bargained pleas of guilty. Attorneys who lack more remunerative uses of their time, by contrast, may be tempted to "milk" their assignments. These attorneys may take cases to trial when that course would not be in their clients' interests. The point is simply that a defense attorney often has personal interests in his client's choice of plea that differ from those of the client himself.

cases are resolved, public defenders are not subject to the same economic temptations as private defense attorneys. Nevertheless, all lawyers are subject to the temptation to promote their own convenience at the expense of their clients. As with the economic temptations noted above, the danger is not so much deliberate betrayal as warped judgment and excessive use of shortcuts. . . .

Somewhat similar conflicts of interest would influence the performance of defense attorneys in an adjudicative system. There are a variety of ways to bluff, cut corners, and "wing it" when a case is tried. Nevertheless, the trial process constrains the ability of lawyers to shrug off most forms of hard work as unnecessary. . . . Even if the attorney has conducted no pretrial investigation, his client may have suggested some defense witnesses (including the client himself). The attorney must either call these witnesses to testify or explain to his client why he has not. In addition, the attorney must participate in the formulation of the court's instructions, argue to the jury, and more. An attorney who wished to appear competent in performing these visible tasks would be likely to investigate the facts before trial, speak to his witnesses, research the relevant law and prepare in other ways. He would not have an easy way to conclude his representation in minutes and rationalize his lack of vigorous advocacy as the best possible representation of his client. . . .

Third, like other people, attorneys like to be liked and to enjoy good relationships with co-workers. This personal interest, like the others, can lead defense attorneys to represent their clients less vigorously. In a plea bargaining system, prosecutors and trial judges, the group with whom a defense attorney works every day, are likely to become a more important constituency than the attorney's more transient clients. . . . An important virtue of the administration of justice by juries and other impartial tribunals is that it maximizes the extent to which outcomes depend on the facts of each case and minimizes the influence of personal favoritism and favor-seeking. . . .

Plea bargaining promotes inadequate representation for a fourth reason. Defense attorneys, like other people, do not want to be proven wrong. A decision to plead guilty, unlike a decision to stand trial, cannot be proven wrong. A guilty plea not only masks prior errors and professional deficiencies but also ensures the impregnability of a lawyer's professional judgment. Once a guilty plea has been entered, no one can know what result a trial would have reached. From the defendant's perspective, one can always suppose that the outcome would have been worse. When an attorney takes a case to trial, by contrast, he knows (and his client usually knows) what offer or bargaining opportunity has been declined. At the conclusion of a trial, it may be evident that the rejection of an offer has cost a defendant several years of his life. This moment of recognition is unlikely to enhance a lawyer's self-esteem or make future contact with the client more pleasant. . . .

A fifth reason why a regime of plea bargaining promotes inadequate representation is its secrecy and unwritten rules. These characteristics maximize the dangers of inexperience. . . . Moreover, the danger is not simply that an inexperienced lawyer may be unable to distinguish a good offer from a bad offer. In addition, the lawyer may not know how to get a good offer. When does a lawyer push too hard and harm his clients because courthouse insiders conclude that he is a "shotgun who goes off half-cocked"? When does he fail to push hard enough and harm his clients because insiders realize that they can take advantage of him? How "reasonable" is too reasonable, and how "reasonable" is not reasonable enough? These questions are difficult, and defendants may suffer while attorneys try to figure them out.

By contrast, trial is an open system — a system with reasonably well-defined roles and a system than can be studied, learned, and eventually mastered. Moreover, even when an inexperienced attorney founders at trial, the witnesses usually tell their stories in a coherent fashion; the judge usually gives reasonably accurate instructions on the law; the jurors usually follow both the evidence and their consciences; and if the defendant is convicted, the judge imposes the sentence that he thinks fair. An inexperienced defense lawyer can harm his clients greatly at trial, but to a far greater extent than plea negotiation, trial is a system of checks and balances.

There is a sixth way in which the performance of defense attorneys in a plea bargaining system differs from their performance in an adjudicative system. A conscientious lawyer in a plea bargaining system cannot be only an advocate for his client. The lawyer must also be the point man or woman for a coercive system of justice. It is the defense attorney who must deliver the message that the client does not have an unfettered right to trial. It is the defense attorney who must explain how the plea bargaining leverage works. . . .

---

2. Plea-Bargaining

A recent Yale Law Journal symposium captured the flavor of long-standing debates in a sequence of articles titled Plea Bargaining as Contract, Plea Bargaining as Compromise, and Plea Bargaining as Disaster.[54] These competing characterizations, and the public policies they imply, have obvious relevance in assessing lawyers' individual and collective responsibilities. Since less than about 15 percent of all criminal cases go to trial, how we evaluate plea-bargaining inevitably will shape how we evaluate the criminal justice system in general and lawyers' roles in particular.[55]

To some commentators, plea-bargaining violates individuals' most fundamental rights and society's most fundamental values. From this perspective, our elaborate constitutional protections serve largely as window dressing for a system that in fact dispenses justice with no greater safeguards than a street bazaar. In an influential as well as evocative analysis, John Langbein suggests that contemporary plea-bargaining functions in much the same fashion as medieval torture. Extorting confessions became an apparent necessity in order to bypass the European criminal justice system's idealistic but unworkable prohibition against the use of circumstantial evidence. In Langbein's view, the level of complexity and safeguards in our current criminal procedures has produced similar reliance on coercive methods. "Like the medieval Europeans," he argues, "we have preserved an unworkable trial procedure in form, we have devised a substitute nontrial procedure to subvert the formal procedure, and we have arranged to place defendants under fierce pressure to 'choose' the substitute."[56]

What is particularly objectionable about this system is that it leads to "innocent defendants being offered (and taking) the same deals as guilty ones."[57] For an increasing number of crimes, the severity of possible sentences creates intense pressures to plead even for individuals with strong defenses. This bargaining structure also encourages ineffective assistance of counsel because any inadequacy in the defense lawyer's preparation remains largely invisible when cases quickly settle.[58] Since prosecutors are particularly disposed to plead their weakest cases, the incentives to forgo trial are strongest for those at greatest risk of an unjust conviction.

The problem is compounded by the horrendous conditions in many jails, which sometimes encourage defendants to take any bargain that ensures their immediate transfer or release. The paradox was captured in an interchange between a New York public defender and an incarcerated client:

> "I'm innocent. I didn't do nothing. But I got to get out of here. I got to . . ."
> "Well, if you *did* do anything and you are a little guilty, they'll give you time served and you'll walk."
> "I'll take a plea. But I didn't do nothing." . . .
> "No one's going to let you take the plea if you aren't guilty."
> "But I didn't *do* nothing."
> "Then you'll have to stay in and go to trial."
> "When will that be?"
> "In a couple of months. Maybe longer."
> [The client] has a grip on the bars. "You mean if I'm guilty I get out today?"
> "Yes." . . .
> "But if I'm innocent, I got to stay in?"
> "That's right."[59]

As critics also note, plea-bargaining fosters a corrosive value structure that aggravates rather than corrects the typical mentality of most pleading defendants. Most criminals view the world at large as a con game. . . . This is, of course, the attitude which brings them into court in the first place. Plea bargaining appears as just another con game where deceit, bravado, and putting on a good front can get a good deal. The goal of criminal rehabilitation is thus seriously compromised from the start because the system reinforces the very mentality it seeks to eradicate.[60]

As an alternative to bargaining, some critics have proposed a system of non-negotiable sentencing concessions for avoiding trial, fixed either by statute or rules of court. Jurisdictions could also provide the option of a brief mini-trial before a judge, without the time-consuming processes of jury selection, instruction, deliberation, and opening and closing arguments. Under a system of fixed, predictable concessions, those who elected trial would be those most likely to have a chance of acquittal (rather than those most worried about an arbitrarily high sentence).[61] Such an alternative bargaining structure also might reduce the significance of resource disparities and accompanying class biases that plague the current process.[62]

By contrast, other commentators see plea-bargaining as an acceptable compromise of competing values.[63] Given the highly limited resources that American society is willing to invest in criminal justice, plea-bargaining offers something for everyone. Both sides can make offers that will avoid the delays, expense, and uncertainty of trial.[64] Although the plea-bargaining process may not always separate the innocent from the guilty, the same is true of trials. Defense lawyers are free to present exculpating evidence during negotiations and if they lack the resources or incentive to do so, the problem is not attributable to plea-bargaining per se. Nor would these problems of inadequate representation be eliminated by eliminating plea negotiation; they are also likely to emerge at trial if resource constraints remain unchanged. Under this reasoning, reform efforts should focus on reducing caseloads and increasing investigatory support, compensation, and regulatory oversight for defense counsel rather than on tinkering with the bargaining process.

A final group of commentators believe that some tinkering would be helpful, particularly if other reform efforts prove unsuccessful. As these critics note, enhancing the accuracy and consistency of the criminal justice system serves societal interests apart from those of individual defendants or prosecutors. From this perspective, modest changes are appropriate to reduce the arbitrariness and coercion of the current bargaining process. Recent proposals include enforcing prosecutors' sentencing promises, encouraging judicial review of unusually stiff punishments, eliminating mandatory minimum sentences that induce risk-averse but innocent defendants to plead guilty, and using financial incentives to discourage overcharging as a coercive tactic.[65]

Which of these positions do you find most persuasive? How effective do you believe that any of these reform proposals would be in avoiding unjust convictions? Can you identify other measures to address the structural problems that critics have noted?

3.   Ineffective Assistance of Counsel

In Strickland v. Washington, 466 U.S. 668 (1984), the Supreme Court held that a criminal defendant had a right to reasonably effective representation under prevailing professional norms, but that counsel should be "strongly presumed to have rendered adequate assistance." Convictions should be overturned only if the attorney's performance falls below "prevailing professional norms," and there is a "reasonable probability that, absent [counsel's] errors, the factfinder would have a reasonable doubt respecting guilt." 466 U.S. at 695.

This burden has proven extremely difficult to meet. Courts' reluctance to find ineffective assistance rests on several considerations: a desire to encourage finality and discourage frivolous appeals; a disinclination to second-guess trial tactics with the benefit of hindsight; an unwillingness to humiliate defense counsel and discourage their acceptance of court assignments; and a reluctance to reward lawyers who commit deliberate errors to save an otherwise hopeless case. Appellate judges' refusal to overturn convictions, together with the economic pressures noted above, makes inadequate representation a chronic problem.

Reforms could take various shapes. Some courts and commentators have proposed a preventive approach: the establishment of specific performance requirements based on ABA Standards Relating to the Defense Function.[66] For example, courts could establish processes for certifying criminal defense lawyers or require minimum qualifications of training and experience for assigned counsel in criminal cases.[67] Trial judges also could meet with defense lawyers at a pretrial conference and monitor their performance through worksheets disclosing how frequently they have met with a client, what discovery requests they have made, what witnesses they have interviewed, and so forth.[68] The failure to satisfy minimum requirements could constitute a violation of sixth amendment guarantees regardless of whether defendants can prove an adverse effect on their trial or plea-bargain.

Would you support such performance standards? What enforcement difficulties would you anticipate? Could prosecutors play a greater role in assisting such oversight? Fred Zacharias argues that prosecutors' duty to "do justice" includes monitoring defense counsel.[69] In his view, a prosecutor who becomes aware of inadequate representation should alert the judge while there is still time to remedy the matter. Is this a realistic proposal? How would you enforce it?

Several other strategies have met with mixed success. One has been to challenge either statutory caps on fee compensation or the constitutionality of state systems for providing indigent criminal representation.[70] Other efforts have included requiring pro bono service from local attorneys; paying for indigent defense with funds from lawyer registration fees or the interest on lawyer trust accounts; and strikes by public defenders for higher compensation, lower caseloads, and structural reforms in indigent defense systems.[71] What problems might these approaches present? What other alternatives are promising?

4. Multiple Representation

See Chapter VII, Conflicts of Interest
  • Simultaneous Representation of Multiple Interests in
    Criminal Defense
      (pages 307–314)

F.   PROBLEMS OF PATERNALISM

See Chapter IX, The Lawyer-Client Relationship
  • Paternalism in Representing Criminal Defendants
      (pages 383–387)

G.   THE LAWYER'S ROLE: PROSECUTION

1. The Pursuit of Justice[72]

Codes and commentary on prosecutorial ethics generally build on a shared premise. Prosecutors have a dual role as advocates and ministers of justice; their obligation is to "seek justice, not merely to convict."[73] Yet what that obligation entails is subject to considerable dispute. To some commentators, "seek justice" is an unhelpful and unenforceable truism; what prosecutor would admit to any other objective? As Justice Jackson once put it, "the qualities of a good prosecutor are as elusive and as impossible to define as those which [mark] a gentleman. And those who need to be told would not understand it anyway."[74]

To other commentators, the prosecutor's unique role imposes unique ethical responsibilities that can and should be specified. Those responsibilities arise from the value that American society attaches to individual freedom and to the particular constraints it imposes on the state. As the Report of the ABA Joint Conference on Professional Responsibility emphasized, prosecutors have exceptional power: they have full access to the coercive and investigatory resources of the government, but none of the accountability demanded by an identifiable client. Misconduct that occurs under color of law erodes public confidence in the legal system, and prosecutors must exercise special self-restraint.

Such restraint is particularly important in light of the ineffectiveness of other review mechanisms discussed in section 2 below. Judicial oversight has been minimal. Concerns about separation of powers, together with the absence of workable legal standards, have made courts reluctant to second-guess prosecutors' charging decisions and enforcement priorities. Except in extreme cases, most judges have been equally unwilling to overturn convictions of guilty defendants in response to violations of ethical rules, typically on the theory that the violations are harmless errors.

In theory, violations that do not rise to constitutional dimension should be addressed through professional disciplinary proceedings. In practice, such proceedings are rare because few individuals have incentives to file complaints and bar enforcement agents seldom proceed on their own initiative. Judges and defense counsel have little to gain from arousing a district attorney's ire, and prosecutorial immunity from civil liability discourages citizens' grievances. Rory Little's review of some 600,000 reported state disciplinary decisions found only 18 instances of sanctions for prosecutorial misconduct.[75] So too, the Department of Justice's Internal Office of Professional Responsibility (OPR) lacks adequate resources, independence, and incentive for effective oversight of federal prosecutors. Despite recent improvements, the ratio of OPR personnel to reviewable attorneys is about 1 to 1,000.[76]

Although state DAs are generally elected and U.S. attorneys are high-level political appointees, their subordinates are not, and the electoral process provides an inadequate referendum on prosecutorial discretion. The vast majority of enforcement decisions are not publicized and not memorable. Nor are most voters and politicians who control appointments adequately informed about the complex considerations underlying enforcement practices. That is not to deny the influence of public opinion on many prosecutorial decisions. But where public sentiment plays a role, it often reinforces pressures to "get tough on crime" at the expense of other values.

These pressures arise from multiple sources. For most prosecutors, conviction records are the most tangible measure of status and success; acquittals may look like evidence of incompetence or overzealousness.[77] Law enforcement agents and victims of crime often function as surrogate clients, and their concerns are communicated more directly than those of defendants and their families. These factors, together with the dynamics of adversarial processes, can make winning — or at least not losing — the preeminent value. When prosecutors think, "I know I've got the right man but can I prove it?," the temptations to cut corners escalate.[78]

Then-Attorney General Richard Thornburgh captured prevailing views in his description of federal prosecutors' role:

> Law enforcement is basically a conservative business. You're putting bad guys in jail. You're trying to get every edge you can on those people who are devising increasingly more intricate schemes to rip off the public, hiring the best lawyers, providing the best defenses.
>
> So you're constantly pushing the edge of the envelope out to see if you can get an edge for the prosecution . . . not to abolish constitutional rights, but to give the law enforcement officer an even break.[79]

Consider where that envelope edge should end in the problems that follow.

2. Prosecutorial Discretion

a. Introduction

PROBLEM 14D

Consider the following exercises of professional discretion. Which are justifiable under existing standards? Which should be?

1. Where unable to obtain sufficient evidence to prosecute certain labor leaders for suspected corruption, the Department of Justice has sought proof of income tax violations. Some of those leaders had previously been critical of administration policy in general and the Attorney General in particular.[80]

2. A state district attorney refuses to offer certain standard plea concessions to a defendant whose lawyer previously has engaged in hardball tactics on behalf of organized crime leaders.[81]

3. Washington, D.C. prosecutors have information indicating that Mayor Marion Barry has violated various drug laws and has lied about his offenses following a federal "sting" operation. The government offers to allow Barry to plead to misdemeanors if he resigns his office.[82]

4. Under New York City's "federal day" program, local district attorneys referred for federal prosecution all drug offenders charged on a certain day of the week. Prosecutors' hope was that the random risk of harsh penalties under federal law would provide more deterrence than the less stringent sanctions authorized by state law.[83]

5. State law enforcement authorities who completed investigation of a drug trafficker referred the case for federal prosecution to take advantage of less demanding federal safeguards governing wiretaps, search warrants, and informants.[84]

6. A prosecutor offers to request probation for a mother charged with abusing two of her children if she agrees to obtain counseling, attend parenting classes, refrain from physically disciplining her children, and have the contraceptive Norplant implanted in her arm.[85]

7. A prosecutor offers to dismiss criminal charges on the condition that the defendant release law enforcement officers from claims of civil liability.[86]

AMERICAN BAR ASSOCIATION STANDARDS RELATING TO THE ADMINISTRATION OF CRIMINAL JUSTICE, THE PROSECUTION FUNCTION

(1978)

STANDARD 3-1.1   THE FUNCTION OF THE PROSECUTOR

. . . (b) The prosecutor is both an administrator of justice and an advocate. The prosecutor must exercise sound discretion in the performance of his or her functions.

(c) The duty of the prosecutor is to seek justice, not merely to convict.

STANDARD 3-2.5   PROSECUTOR'S HANDBOOK: POLICY GUIDELINES AND PROCEDURES

(a) Each prosecutor's office should develop a statement of
    (i) general policies to guide the exercise of prosecutorial discretion, and
    (ii) procedures of the office.
The objectives of these policies as to discretion and procedures should be to achieve a fair, efficient, and effective enforcement of the criminal law.

(b) In the interest of continuity and clarity, such statement of policies and procedures should be maintained in an office handbook. This handbook should be available to the public, except for subject matters declared "confidential," when it is reasonably believed that public access to their contents would adversely affect the prosecution function.

STANDARD 3-3.9   DISCRETION IN THE CHARGING DECISION

(a) It is unprofessional conduct for a prosecutor to institute, or cause to be instituted, or to permit the continued pendency of criminal charges when it is known that the charges are not supported by probable cause. A prosecutor should not institute, cause to be instituted, or permit the continued pendency of criminal charges in the absence of sufficient admissible evidence to support a conviction.

(b) The prosecutor is not obliged to present all charges which the evidence might support. The prosecutor may in some circumstances and for good cause consistent with the public interest decline to prosecute, notwithstanding that sufficient evidence may exist which would support a conviction. Illustrative of the factors which the prosecutor may properly consider in exercising his or her discretion are:

(i) the prosecutor's reasonable doubt that the accused is in fact guilty;

(ii) the extent of the harm caused by the offense;

(iii) the disproportion of the authorized punishment in relation to the particular offense or the offender;

(iv) possible improper motives of a complainant;

(v) reluctance of the victim to testify;

(vi) cooperation of the accused in the apprehension or conviction of others; and

(vii) availability and likelihood of prosecution by another jurisdiction.

(c) In making the decision to prosecute, the prosecutor should give no weight to the personal or political advantages or disadvantages which might be involved or to a desire to enhance his or her record of convictions.

(d) In cases which involve a serious threat to the community, the prosecutor should not be deterred from prosecution by the fact that in the jurisdiction juries have tended to acquit persons accused of the particular kind of criminal act in question.

(e) The prosecutor should not bring or seek charges greater in number or degree than can reasonably be supported with evidence at trial.

UNITED STATES DEPARTMENT OF JUSTICE, PRINCIPLES OF FEDERAL PROSECUTION

27 Crim. L. Rep. (BNA) 3277-3279 (1980)

In determining whether prosecution should be declined because no substantial federal interest would be served by prosecution, the attorney for the government should weigh all relevant considerations, including:

(a) federal law enforcement priorities;
(b) the nature and seriousness of the offense;
(c) the deterrent effect of prosecution;
(d) the person's culpability in connection with the offense;
(e) the person's history with respect to criminal activity;
(f) the person's willingness to cooperate in the investigation or prosecution of others; and
(g) the probable sentence or other consequences if the person is convicted.

H. RICHARD UVILLER, THE VIRTUOUS PROSECUTOR IN QUEST OF AN ETHICAL STANDARD: GUIDANCE FROM THE ABA

71 Mich. L. Rev. 1145, 1145-1156 (1978)

At first encounter, the widely supported brief for uniformity in the enforcement of the criminal laws appears to need little argumentation. To most, the proposition "Equal justice under law," chiseled on the courthouse pediment, is both elegant and self-evident. Indeed, this slogan expresses for many the quintessence of the American system of justice. Yet, the phrase is fundamentally deceptive. While wide or irrational disparities in treatment are deplorable, equality in the sense of uniformity in result is neither the fact nor the ideal in the system of justice. A given piece of human behavior, described grossly by statute as a crime, does not and should not generate an automatic and standardized response from police, juries, or judges. Nor should we expect an undiscriminated prosecutorial reflex. . . . Professor Monroe H. Freedman . . . uses a blunter instrument to probe prosecutorial ethics. He attacks . . . the prosecutor who singles out a target for determined prosecution. Citing Al Capone and James Hoffa as the victims of overzealous prosecution, he decries "prosecutions that are directed at individuals rather than at crimes."

The ethical standard so casually suggested by Professor Freedman is somewhat baffling. What does he mean by a prosecution directed against an individual? Does he mean that in deciding where to investigate or how vigorously to prosecute, the district attorney should have no regard for the personal characteristics of the actual or potential defendant? Surely, he does not argue that in deciding on the acceptability of a lesser plea, the prosecutor should pay no heed to whether the offender is a novice or a seasoned professional, treating all cases alike according to the deed that was done. But if the prosecutor may ethically take the background or reputation of the defendant into consideration in electing an appropriate disposition, why not in fixing his investigative sights? Would the ban on individuals as targets preclude the decision to devote prosecutorial energy to discovering evidence of a crime committed by a known underworld loanshark? Or would Professor Freedman only countenance a prosecution of such a target for usury, regardless of the evidence of other reprehensible conduct unearthed by the investigation? . . . Apparently, a prosecutor who cracked down relentlessly on gambling, pot-smoking, or prostitution (directing his attention to crimes, not individuals) need fear no censure from Professor Freedman, even though he did nothing about street muggings or corruption and was motivated solely by his own personal antipathy to vice. . . .

I recognize the significance of my disparagement of objective consequences. Unequal results are unequal regardless of the motivation of the official who achieved them. But if Robert Kennedy, as Attorney General, was convinced that the Teamsters Union, and Hoffa in particular, was destructive to trade unionism and a powerful, dangerous, and gangster-ridden force in the economy of the nation, would not his pursuit of Hoffa seem more ethical than if (as Freedman hypothesizes) Kennedy resolved to imprison Hoffa in revenge for a trivial personal insult and brought the armies of the Justice Department against him on that account? The prosecutor who senses the outrage of his constituency against the aggressive and unsightly hordes of prostitutes infesting the streets may ethically respond by stricter application of valid laws against prostitution. More questionable, it seems to me, is the same campaign waged by the prosecutor as self-appointed custodian of community morality, impelled by personal distaste generated by his own values. I do not suggest that the honorable prosecutor be the slave of his electorate. Indeed, in many matters his duty clearly lies in the defiance of community pressures. But, within the confines of law, I would rather see his discretion guided by an honest effort to discern public needs and community concerns than by personal pique or moralistic impertinence.

It may be argued, with some merit, that my distinction is as artificial as Freedman's, and far less workable than the measured advice of the ABA standards. What prosecutor in his senses would admit to being motivated by personal pique? What action could not be rationalized as a good faith effort to discern community needs? And what possible scheme of enforcement of professional canons could hinge on the purity of official motivation? . . .

While [the current] ABA standard 3.9(a) condemns in its strongest terms the prosecutor who institutes or causes to be instituted criminal charges when he knows them to be unsupported by "probable cause," paragraph (b)(i) of the same standard suggests that the prosecutor may decline to prosecute a case when he himself entertains a "reasonable doubt that the accused is in fact guilty." . . .

Read together, then, the trio of provisions sounds like this: The prosecutor *must* abjure prosecution without probable cause, *should* refuse to charge without a durable prima facie case, and *may* decline to proceed if the evidence fails to satisfy him beyond a reasonable doubt.

The interesting part of the standard is the suggestion that if the prosecutor, imagining himself in the seat of a juror, would not vote for a verdict of guilty, he may decline to present the matter to the system's designated fact finder. I have heard prosecutors, as a matter of personal conscience, take this notion as an ethical imperative. "I never try a defendant," so runs the credo, "unless I am personally convinced of his guilt beyond a reasonable doubt." Or, for some: "beyond any doubt." Realistically, the prosecutor figures that, inflamed by the brutal facts of the crime or for some other reason, the jury may overlook the basis for the doubt which nags his own judgment. And he could not sleep at night having contributed to the conviction of a man who might just possibly be innocent. Of course, in reaching this extra-judicial judgment, the prosecutor will allow himself to consider relevant items which might be excluded from trial evidence. Nor would his refusal to prosecute the case necessarily mean he would decline to recommend the acceptance of a guilty plea, for the confession which normally accompanies the plea may remove the prosecutor's doubt.

Yet withal, the prosecutor's conscientious stand represents a notable modification of our system of determining truth and adjudicating guilt. At the least it creates a new subtrial, informal and often ex parte, interposed between the determinations of the accusing and judging authorities.

Can there be any objection to the prosecutor's transformation of the standard's "may" into a personal "must"? A defendant, of course, can only benefit from this additional safety procedure, and its adoption may move the prosecutor to more diligent and painstaking pretrial investigation, including an open-minded search for persuasive defense evidence. This latter effort comports nicely with the familiar injunction duly intoned by standard 1.1(c): "The duty of the prosecutor is to seek justice, not merely to convict." From these features it may appear that the standards should have placed this burden of internal persuasion on the prosecutor in every case. I think not.

A concrete, commonplace example may illustrate the operation of the precept and flesh out our appraisal of its wisdom. Practitioners know too well a sticky item: the one-eye-witness-identification case. For instance, an elderly white person is suddenly grabbed from behind in a dimly lit vestibule by a black youth who shows a knife and takes the victim's wallet. The entire incident occupies thirty seconds. Some days later, the victim spots the defendant in the neighborhood and has him arrested by the nearest policeman. Although the prosecutor presses him hard, the victim swears he has picked the right man. There is nothing unusual about the defendant's appearance, the victim never saw him before the crime, and he admits he does not know many [blacks] personally, but his certainty cannot be shaken. He insists that in those few moments of terror his attacker's face was "indelibly engraved on his memory." The defendant may have an alibi: his mother will testify that at the time of the crime he was at home watching television with her (not evidence readily credited). And that is the entire case.

Many prosecutors, I think, would concede that as jurors they would hesitate to vote "guilty" on this evidence. His sincerity unmistakable, the victim might well be correct in his identification of the defendant; perhaps it is more likely than not that the defendant is the perpetrator. And juries regularly convict in such cases. But since he knows the fallibility of identification under such circumstances, the basis for reasonable doubt is clear to the prosecutor.

Should the ethical prosecutor refuse to put this sort of evidence before the jury, withhold from the regular fact-finding process the opportunity to decide the issue? Indeed, should the conscientious prosecutor set himself the arduous task of deciding whether in this instance the complainant is right? If it is his duty to do so, how does he rationally reach a conclusion? For this purpose, are his mental processes superior to the jurors' or the judge's? Or may he — should he — abstain from prejudging the case and simply pass the responsibility to those who cannot escape it?

Let us take the problem in a somewhat different, equally common form. The defendant, let us assume, is charged with the illegal possession of a quantity of narcotics. There is little doubt of his guilt; indeed, he is ready to plead guilty. However, he claims that the drug was obtained by an illegal search of his automobile and should therefore be suppressed. The police officer insists that he retrieved the bag of drugs after the defendant abandoned it by throwing it from the window of the vehicle at the officer's approach. Now, the prosecutor knows that some drug carriers do try to divest themselves of the contraband when approached by police, but he also knows that many police seek to escape the strictures of the exclusionary rule by reciting an abandonment to cover an illegal search and seizure. Despite his general suspicion, however, the prosecutor has no reason to believe that the case in question is based on false testimony. Moreover, he has every reason to believe that on the ultimate issue of the defendant's guilt, justice will be done. What is his ethical course?

I confess I have no clear release from the prosecutor's predicament. I recognize as laudable the taking of one more precaution to avert the horror of convicting an innocent person. Yet, on balance, I do not believe the prosecutor must, or should, decide to proceed only in those cases where he, as a fact finder, would resolve the issue for the prosecution.

Where the prosecutor, from all he knows of the case, believes that there is a substantial likelihood that the defendant is innocent of the charge, he should, of course, not prosecute. Similarly, if he has good reason to believe that a witness is lying about a material fact, he should not put the witness on the stand, and if his case fails without the witness' testimony he should dismiss it regardless of whether inadmissible evidence persuades him of the culpability of the defendant. Short of these grounds for declining prosecution on the merits, I deem the ethical obligations of the prosecutor satisfied if he makes known to the court, or the defense, discovered adverse evidence and defects of credibility in witnesses.

Thus, when the issue stands in equipoise in his own mind, when he is honestly unable to judge where the truth of the matter lies, I see no flaw in the conduct of the prosecutor who fairly lays the matter before the judge or jury. [The prosecutor] is, let us remember, an advocate as well as a minister of public justice. . . .

It is widely agreed that prosecutors should seek justice but how to realize that aspiration evokes no such consensus. Disputes have focused on how much discretion prosecutors should exercise, what considerations should be foremost in their decision-making, and what forms of external review are appropriate.

Unlike some countries, in which the state is expected to file indictments for every felony supported by sufficient evidence, American prosecutors have substantial discretion in selecting cases to pursue.[87] State district attorneys decline to file charges in an estimated 45 to 55 percent of potential felony proceedings, and federal district attorneys decline to pursue over three-quarters of potential cases.[88] Principal reasons for nonprosecution include the insufficiency of admissible evidence, the unavailability of parties, the appropriateness of alternative remedies, the characteristics of defendants, the relative significance of the offense, and the limitations on enforcement resources.[89]

Which of these considerations should be most crucial and how they should be interpreted in particular cases remain matters of considerable dispute. Consider the ABA's Standards for the Charging Decision and the federal guidelines set forth above. What practical problems might their implementation present?

b.   Prosecutorial Intent

Kenneth Culp Davis notes that it is theoretically possible to construct a system in which enforcement occurs in only a fraction of possible cases and in which "all the cases prosecuted are more deserving of prosecution than any of the cases not prosecuted." However, in his view,

> [t]he degree of probability of such an achievement is . . . the same as the degree of probability that all public administrators will act with 100 percent integrity, will never be influenced by political considerations, will never tend to favor their friends, will never take into account their own advantage or disadvantage in exercising discretionary power, . . . will always subordinate their own social values to those adopted by the legislative body, and will make every decision on a strictly rational basis.[90]

Should bar ethical standards seek to reinforce this ideal, however difficult it is to realize in practice? Or is some more pragmatic approach appropriate? What standard should govern Problems 14D(1) and (2)?

c.   The Allocation of Power and Referral Policies

UNITED STATES v. RICHMOND, 550 F. SUPP. 605 (E.D.N.Y. 1982). In this proceeding, Judge Jack Weinstein held unconstitutional a plea-bargain requiring resignation from public office. The case involved a congressman who agreed to plead guilty to income tax evasion, possession of marijuana, and unlawfully supplementing the salary of a federal employee. He also agreed to resign from Congress and to terminate his reelection campaign. In return, the prosecutor agreed to forgo prosecution for various other crimes. Judge Weinstein concluded:

> This portion of the agreement [concerning resignation and reelection] was invalid for three reasons. First, it conflicted with the fundamental right of the people to elect their representatives. Second, it interfered with the principle of separation of powers. Third, it contravened public policy by utilizing a technique latent with the possibility of Executive domination of members of Congress through the threat of forced resignations. . . .
>
> Power to strip a member of Congress of elective office was committed to neither the executive nor the judiciary. It was explicitly reserved to Congress itself. . . . The possibility of the executive utilizing the threat of prosecution to force the resignation of a congressional representative involves potentially dangerous political consequences. It represents an opportunity for an assault on the composition and integrity of a coordinate branch of government. Taken together, . . . the enormous spectrum of criminal laws that can be violated, the powerful investigative and prosecutorial machine available to the executive, and forced resignations through plea bargaining would provide an intolerable threat to a free and independent Congress. . . .

Would you come to a similar conclusion? In response to the *Richmond* decision, the Justice Department promulgated guidelines that encourage U.S. attorneys to consider voluntary offers of resignation from office as a desirable objective in plea negotiations. *Richmond*'s reasoning has not been followed elsewhere in the nation, and attorneys divide about the propriety of including resignation as part of a formal plea agreement.[91] Under the circumstances described in Problem 14D(3), what factors should be relevant to the prosecutor's negotiations concerning resignation?

Other issues concerning the distribution of power arise under referral practices between state and federal authorities. Some commentators have criticized strategies such as the "federal day" policy in Problem 14D(4) on the ground that they subject similarly situated defendants to different treatment for reasons unrelated to their personal characteristics or offense.[92]

Criticism has also centered on the use of referral policies to evade procedural protections. In United States v. Ucciferri, 960 F.2d 953, 954 (11th Cir. 1992), the case on which Problem 14D(5) is based, the court of appeals acknowledged that "the systematic transfer of what may properly be called 'state' cases to federal court is a legitimate source of concern." However, the court rejected the defendant's claim that dismissal of the indictment was appropriate because the case lacked federal ties and was transferred in order to evade state constitutional protections.

What is your view? Should courts require that referral decisions be justified by some legitimate reason apart from a desire simply to increase penalties or to avoid procedural safeguards?

d.   Legislative Overbreadth, Public Notice, and Political Accountability

One of the most common justifications for prosecutorial discretion rests on concerns about legislative overbreadth. Criminal codes tend to prohibit "everything that people are against, with little regard to enforceability, changing social concepts, etc."[93] For administrative convenience, such codes will often retain overinclusive provisions, such as prohibitions on gambling that encompass casual poker games; or aspirational provisions, such as bans on adultery, which express ideals that society wishes to affirm in principle but not necessarily in practice.

Does it follow that any statute that is rarely enforced should never be enforced, or does the reason for its disuse and resurrection matter? Consider, for example, contemporary officials' reliance on post-Civil War civil rights statutes that had not been invoked in the South for almost a century. Compare that strategy with the decision to prosecute Michael Hardwick for violating Georgia's sodomy statute in the privacy of his own home, although enforcement almost never occurred under such circumstances. Bowers v. Hardwick, 478 U.S. 186 (1986). Presumably, the prosecutors in both contexts considered their options to be morally justified. Are the cases nonetheless distinguishable?

According to Alexander Bickel's well-known analysis, the resurrection of a long unenforced statute has "all the vices of an ad hoc official decision," unrelated to anything that may realistically be taken as present legislative policy.[94] Although the Supreme Court has permitted prosecutions despite a statute's long disuse, the Justices have acknowledged that the resulting lack of notice should be an "ameliorating factor in enforcement." District of Columbia v. John R. Thompson Co., 346 U.S. 100, 117 (1953) (permitting prosecution under statute not used for 78 years that prohibited refusal to serve African Americans). In cases of desuetude, should prosecutors' primary concern be fair notice to a defendant, accountability to the popular will, or an independent assessment of the morality of the technically prohibited conduct?

Similar questions arise concerning resource priorities, as Problem 14E indicates.

PROBLEM 14E

Assume that a large majority of the local electorate:

1. opposes prosecution of rape cases where the victim behaved "irresponsibly" by drinking heavily, wearing seductive clothing, or accompanying the assailant to his residence alone;
2. opposes prosecution of police officers for lying about justifications for searches and seizures or for using excessive force during drug raids in low-income minority communities;
3. opposes prosecution of illegal but private homosexual activity between consenting adults;
4. supports prosecution of street walkers but not their clients;
5. supports prosecution of pregnant drug users even if they have been unable to find placement at treatment facilities;
6. opposes prosecution of crimes involving small amounts of powder cocaine (an offense committed disproportionately by whites) but supports prosecution of crimes involving small amounts of crack cocaine (an offense committed disproportionately by African Americans).

What effect should such community attitudes have on prosecutors' enforcement decisions?

e.   Standards of Proof

A related issue concerns the level of proof that prosecutors should demand before filing charges. Some commentators agree with Richard Uviller that prosecutors who insist on proof beyond a reasonable doubt usurp the functions of the judge and jury. Critics, including Monroe Freedman in the article Uviller cites, point out that such functions are already supplanted by plea-bargaining in about 85 to 90 percent of all cases. From critics' perspective, anything short of a "reasonable doubt" standard creates the risk that an innocent person will suffer criminal penalties.

Similarly, Kenneth J. Melilli argues that the probable cause approach, reflected in the ABA Prosecution Standards, is "essentially meaningless" as an ethical mandate. It requires "little more than heightened suspicion, and it is not even remotely sufficient to screen out individuals who are factually not guilty."[95] Melilli contends that if the case does go to trial, "it is entirely possible that both the prosecutor and the jury will have deferred, at least in part, to the presumed independent determination of guilt made by the other."[96] The prosecutor will assume that questionable cases should be decided by a jury, and the jury will assume that the prosecutor wouldn't have brought the case if there was any question of innocence.

What standard would you apply as a prosecutor? How do the materials on plea-bargaining in Part E affect your decision?

f.   Selective Enforcement

Uviller and Freedman also disagree about the practice of focusing enforcement resources on particular individuals. In the article that Uviller discusses, Freedman takes issue with the contention that "if the individual is in fact guilty of the crime with which he is charged, the motive of the prosecutor is immaterial." In Freedman's view, "[t]his contention overlooks the fact that there are few of us who have led such unblemished lives as to prevent a determined prosecutor from finding some basis for an indictment."[97] Do you agree? Is there anything unjust about a prosecutor drawing up an "enemies list" if its membership is based on suspected criminal activity other than the offense charged and not on the prosecutor's personal or political considerations?

Does selective treatment favoring certain categories of offenders, such as law enforcement officers, stand on different footing? When prosecutors depend on cooperation from police, how should they respond to implausible testimony in search and seizure cases? Compare Uviller's account of "dropsy" testimony at page 629 with Alan Dershowitz's criticisms of police testimony supporting a warrantless search of O.J. Simpson's residence. If prosecutors doubted officers' assertions that they were trying to protect Simpson and did not suspect him of murder, what was the appropriate response?[98] See the discussion of perjured testimony in Chapter VI (Confidentiality and Client Counseling) at pages 251–262.

g.   Review of Prosecutorial Discretion

Do any of the examples discussed in these materials suggest a need for greater review of prosecutorial discretion? In general, the judiciary has been extremely reluctant to second-guess charging decisions. Courts have held that such decisions may not discriminate on the basis of race, religion, or the exercise of constitutionally protected interests such as freedom of speech.[99] However, prevailing doctrine imposes a heavy burden of proof on individuals who claim such improper exercise of discretion: evidence of discriminatory purpose and discriminatory impact is necessary.[100]

Some commentators have urged greater review of prosecutorial decision-making. Kenneth Culp Davis summarizes the argument:

> Even if we assume that a prosecutor has to have a power of selective enforcement, why do we not require him to state publicly his general policies and require him to follow those policies in individual cases in order to protect evenhanded justice? Why not subject prosecutor's decisions to a simple and general requirement of open findings, open reasons, and open precedents, except when special reason for confidentiality exists? Why not strive to protect prosecutors' decisions from political or other ulterior influence in the same way we strive to protect judges' decisions? . . .

I think we Americans should learn from other nations that the huge discretionary power of prosecutors need not be unconfined, unstructured, and unchecked. We should reexamine the assumptions to which our drifting has led us — that a prosecutor should have uncontrolled discretion to choose one out of six cases to prosecute, without any requirement that the one most deserving of prosecution be chosen, or to trade a lesser charge for a plea of guilty in one case but not in another, with no guiding rules or standards, without disclosing findings or reasons, without any requirement of consistency, without supervision or check, and without judicial review.[101]

To address these concerns, some commentators have urged prosecutors to establish internal guidelines or presumptive policies to ensure consistent responses to similar offenses.[102] The National Advisory Commission on Criminal Justice Standards recommended that victims and complaining witnesses be granted standing to challenge decisions not to prosecute and that courts be permitted to order prosecution in cases involving an abuse of discretion.[103]

Would you favor such a policy? Opponents have expressed reservations along several lines. If internal policies and priorities become public and enforceable, some of the deterrent power of criminal sanctions might be lost, incentives for defendants to cooperate would be reduced, and courts could become enmeshed in difficult evidentiary issues. Commentators have also worried that supervisors would respond by withdrawing guidelines or framing them at a level of generality that would eliminate their usefulness.[104] Greater judicial oversight presents related problems, as the following case suggests.

INMATES OF ATTICA CORRECTIONAL FACILITY v. ROCKEFELLER

477 F.2d 375 (2d Cir. 1973)

[The plaintiff brought a class action seeking to require federal and state officials to investigate and prosecute persons who allegedly had violated federal and state criminal statutes by mistreating inmates during and following the Attica prison uprising. The district court dismissed the complaint, and the court of appeals affirmed.]

MANSFIELD, J. . . . Federal mandamus is, of course, available only "to compel an officer or employee of the United States . . . to perform a duty owed to the plaintiff." 28 U.S.C. §1361. And the legislative history of §1361 makes it clear that ordinarily the courts are "'not to direct or influence the exercise of discretion of the officer or agency in the making of the decision.'" More particularly, federal courts have traditionally and, to our knowledge, uniformly refrained from overturning, at the instance of a private person, discretionary decisions of federal prosecuting authorities not to prosecute persons regarding whom a complaint of criminal conduct is made.

This judicial reluctance to direct federal prosecutions at the instance of a private party asserting the failure of United States officials to prosecute alleged criminal violations has been applied even in cases such as the present one where, according to the allegations of the complaint, which we must accept as true for purposes of this appeal, serious questions are raised as to the protection of the civil rights and physical security of a definable class of victims of crime and as to the fair administration of the criminal justice system.

The primary ground upon which this traditional judicial aversion to compelling prosecutions has been based is the separation of powers doctrine. . . . In the absence of statutorily defined standards governing reviewability, or regulatory or statutory policies of prosecution, the problems inherent in the task of supervising prosecutorial decisions do not lend themselves to resolution by the judiciary. The reviewing courts would be placed in the undesirable and injudicious posture of becoming "superprosecutors." In the normal case of review of executive acts of discretion, the administrative record is open, public and reviewable on the basis of what it contains. The decision not to prosecute, on the other hand, may be based upon the insufficiency of the available evidence, in which event the secrecy of the grand jury and the prosecutor's file may serve to protect the accused's reputation from public damage based upon insufficient, improper, or even malicious charges. In camera review would not be meaningful without access by the complaining party to the evidence before the grand jury or the U.S. Attorney. Such interference with the normal operations of criminal investigations, in turn, based solely upon allegations of criminal conduct, raises serious questions of potential abuse by persons seeking to have other persons prosecuted. . . .

Nor is it clear what the judiciary's role of supervision should be were it to undertake such a review. At what point would the prosecutor be entitled to call a halt to further investigation as unlikely to be productive? What evidentiary standard would be used to decide whether prosecution should be compelled? How much judgment would the United States Attorney be allowed? Would he be permitted to limit himself to a strong "test" case rather than pursue weaker cases? What collateral factors would be permissible bases for a decision not to prosecute, e.g., the pendency of another criminal proceeding elsewhere against the same parties? . . . With limited personnel and facilities at his disposal, what priority would the prosecutor be required to give to cases in which investigation or prosecution was directed by the court?

These difficult questions engender serious doubts as to the judiciary's capacity to review and as to the problem of arbitrariness inherent in any judicial decision to order prosecution. On balance, we believe that substitution of a court's decision to compel prosecution for the U.S. Attorney's decision not to prosecute, even upon an abuse of discretion standard of review and even if limited to directing that a prosecution be undertaken in good faith, would be unwise.

Would you reach a similar decision? Should courts be more willing to review prosecutorial conduct under principles analogous to those developed for monitoring abuse of discretion by administrative agencies?[105] What would be the costs and advantages of such review? Would it make a difference in circumstances such as those in Problems 14D and 14E?

3. Trial Conduct

PROBLEM 14F

You are a member of the Illinois Attorney Registration Disciplinary Commission. The following cases have been referred to your office. What, if any, sanctions would you vote to impose?

1. Attorney Marvin Glass learned that he was a target of a major federal "Greylord" investigation of corruption in Cook County, Illinois. In an effort to reduce any criminal charges, Glass offered to cooperate with the government in identifying possible drug traffickers. He subsequently met with Assistant United States Attorney Scott Turow and mentioned one of his clients, who was facing Florida cocaine charges, as a possible target for investigation. Turow warned Glass not to reveal any privileged attorney-client conversations, but encouraged him to act as an informant concerning other criminal activity. Turow also arranged for Glass to carry a hidden electronic surveillance transmitter in his subsequent meetings with the defendant. For ten months, the government allowed Glass to continue to act as counsel for the defendant, and recorded conversations about future drug crimes.

The defendant subsequently moved to dismiss the Florida indictment, alleging, among other things, that the surreptitious surveillance violated his fifth and sixth amendment rights. The trial court denied the motion and the court of appeals affirmed. United States v. Ofshe, 817 F.2d 1508 (11th Cir. 1987). Since the tape recordings had not revealed anything pertinent to the cocaine charges, the appellate court found no violation of the attorney-client privilege, no ineffective assistance of counsel, and no law enforcement activity sufficiently "shocking to the universal sense of justice [as to violate] . . . the Due Process clause of the Fifth Amendment." 817 F.2d at 1516, quoting United States v. Russell, 411 U.S. 423, 432 (1973). In a footnote, however, the court added that while it did not find the government conduct outrageous enough to warrant the dismissal of the indictment, it viewed the behavior of both Glass and Turow as "reprehensible," and assumed that the trial judge would refer the matter to the Illinois Attorney Registration and Disciplinary Commission. 817 F.2d at 1516, n.6.

In a New York Times Magazine article, former prosecutor and well-known author Scott Turow described Ofshe as the most "dismal" case in his professional career. He was, however, subsequently vindicated by a Justice Department investigation and he continued to defend his actions on the ground that "neither clients nor lawyers have the right to plan crimes secure from government enforcement efforts."[106] Do you agree? How would you vote concerning sanctions?

2. In order to obtain proof of bribery by two defense lawyers, Illinois prosecutor Morton Friedman arranged with police officers to have them perform the services that the attorneys had solicited. In one instance, an officer arranged for the absence of a key witness and falsely advised the court that the witness was unavailable. In a second case, a police officer falsely informed the trial judge that the complaining witness had decided to drop certain charges. In both instances, after the officers collected their bribes, an assistant state's attorney informed the court of the deception and the charges were reinstated.

A complaint against Friedman was then filed with the Illinois Disciplinary Commission. If you were a member of the Commission, how would you rule?

IN RE FRIEDMAN, 392 N.E.2D 1333 (ILL. 1979).   After the Illinois Disciplinary Commission voted five to three to censure the prosecutor, a sharply divided supreme court reversed. Chief Justice Goldenhersh's opinion for the court, joined by one other justice, concluded that the prosecutor had acted improperly but that since he was motivated by "a sincere, if misguided, desire to bring corrupt attorneys to justice," no discipline should be imposed. Id. at 1336. In holding the action improper, the court quoted from Justice Brandeis' celebrated dissent in Olmstead v. United States, 277 U.S. 438, 485 (1928):

> In a government of laws, existence of the government will be imperiled if it fails to observe the law scrupulously. Our Government is the potent, the omnipresent teacher. For good or for ill, it teaches the whole people by its example. Crime is contagious. If the Government becomes a lawbreaker, it breeds contempt for law; it invites every man to become a law unto himself; it invites anarchy. To declare that in the administration of the criminal law the end justifies the means — to declare that the Government may commit crimes in order to secure the conviction of a private criminal — would bring terrible retribution. Against that pernicious doctrine this Court should resolutely set its face.

Id. at 1335-1336.

By contrast, Justice Underwood, joined by one colleague, concurred in the judgment but concluded that the prosecutor's temporary deception, "motivated and circumscribed as it was, did not breach the disciplinary rules." Id. at 1339. According to these concurring justices, the prosecutor had no adequate alternative because bribery convictions of an attorney "rarely succeed" based on testimony of a single uncorroborated witness. As these justices emphasized:

The fact is that no one, other than the dishonest lawyers, was injured by respondent's conduct. The courts were promptly informed. One case was reinstated, and the other could have been. And respondent created a substantial and obviously needed deterrent to similar misconduct by other attorneys. I should make clear that I abhor the thought of intentionally deceiving a judge, even temporarily, by the presentation of false testimony. But I abhor even more those members of my profession who seek to prostitute our courts. Since corrupt lawyers will not make payment of the bribe until that which they seek has been done, and payment is, in my judgment, a practical necessity to conviction of the lawyer, some form of misrepresentation to the judge is required if the evidence of payment is to be secured. What was done here, much as I dislike it, seems to me preferable to informing the judge in advance, thereby making him a participant, or immunizing the corrupt lawyer from investigation and prosecution.

Id. at 1338.

Several ethics experts, including Monroe Freedman and the former assistant chief counsel of the Senate Watergate Committee, reached a similar conclusion. Both filed affidavits supporting the prosecutor's conduct; indeed, the former counsel characterized it as "in the highest traditions of law enforcement." Id. at 1337.

Two justices, in separate dissenting opinions, disagreed sharply with that assessment. Assuming for the sake of argument that deception was necessary to ensure prompt payment of the bribe and to secure conviction, Justice Clark concluded that the prosecutor should have sought approval from the trial court or chief judge and that the failure to do so justified censure. Justice Moran also concluded that censure was appropriate, but wrote separately to emphasize his disagreement with Justice Underwood's concurring opinion:

Under the more palatable term "necessary," [that opinion] avoids stating its assention to the cliche that the end justifies the means. . . . In my view, the concurrence sets an intolerably dangerous precedent. . . . Respondent's conduct is of the genre that has undermined the public's confidence in the profession, in the courts and, ultimately, in the law.

Id. at 1342-1343.

Which opinion do you find most persuasive?

PROBLEM 14G

Consider the following prosecutorial statements. Which violate ABA Standards and ethical rules? What should be the appropriate sanctions? Should it matter whether defense counsel failed to object or also made improper comments?

1. A prediction that "if this man goes free, you have chalked up one point for the criminal."[107]

2. References to defense expert witnesses as "mercenary soldiers" and as "the two happiness boys . . . ignorant, stupid, and incompetent."[108]

3. An assertion that a police witness' testimony was credible because "[she] is black and the defendant is black. . . . If [the officer] is lying, she's lying against . . . a person who is black . . . a member of her own race."[109]

4. Repeated references to the defendant's failure to challenge the prosecution's case.[110]

5. A claim that the "defense's role in this case is to try to confuse you."[111]

6. An assertion that defense counsel "has said things to you that are frankly outrageous [and] . . . absolutely preposterous."[112]

Consider the race-based appeals and peremptory challenges described in Problem 15A, Chapter XV (Evidence and Trial Advocacy). Which violate professional rules and/or constitutional standards?

Ethical rules governing argument to the jury illustrate the tensions in the prosecutor's dual role as zealous advocate and officer of justice. In principle, courts often embrace Justice Sutherland's classic statement in Berger v. United States, 295 U.S. 78, 88 (1935):

> The United States Attorney is the representative not of an ordinary party to a controversy, but of a sovereignty . . . whose interest . . . in a criminal prosecution is not that it shall win a case but that justice shall be done. . . . [W]hile he may strike hard blows, he is not at liberty to strike foul ones.

In practice, however, courts are equally willing to acknowledge that if every improper comment were grounds for reversal, "comparatively few verdicts would stand, since in the ardor of advocacy and in the excitement of trial, even the most experienced counsel are occasionally carried away by this temptation." Dunlop v. United States, 165 U.S. 486, 498 (1897).

This ambivalence is apparent in the bench and bar's responses to prosecutorial "temptations." Prevailing rules set forth mandates that are clear in form but often murky in application. The Code and Model Rules both prohibit lawyers from alluding to matters not supported by admissible evidence, asserting their personal knowledge of the facts, or offering their personal opinion as to facts, credibility, or culpability. DR 7-103(c)(4); Model Rule 3.4e. The ABA Standards on Prosecutorial Conduct further provide:

STANDARD 3-5.8   ARGUMENT TO THE JURY

(a) The prosecutor may argue all reasonable inferences from evidence in the record. It is unprofessional conduct for the prosecutor intentionally to misstate the evidence or mislead the jury as to the inferences it may draw.

(b) It is unprofessional conduct for the prosecutor to express his or her personal belief or opinion as to the truth or falsity of any testimony or evidence or the guilt of the defendant.

(c) The prosecutor should not use arguments calculated to inflame the passions or prejudices of the jury.

(d) The prosecutor should refrain from argument which would divert the jury from its duty to decide the case on the evidence, by injecting issues broader than the guilt or innocence of the accused under the controlling law, or by making predictions of the consequences of the jury's verdict.

(e) It is the responsibility of the court to ensure that final argument to the jury is kept within proper, accepted bounds.

Current case law enforces these general rules and also bars comments that undermine the privilege against self-incrimination, such as references to defendants' failure to testify.

Compliance with these prohibitions has been uneven, in part because of inherent ambiguities in their scope and in part because the rewards for courtroom excess typically overshadow the penalties. Prosecutors push the limits of the permissible not only because they want to win, but also because they are generally convinced that winning serves justice.[113] As a consequence, a substantial body of case law has developed in response to comments such as those reflected in Problem 14G.

Appeals to passion or prejudice take various forms. Some trial courts disallow abusive references to the defendant on the ground that they offend the dignity of the court, unduly influence jurors, and often suggest prior criminal behavior that is inadmissible as evidence. Other courts allow comments that are a "reasonable deduction from the evidence," and vary widely in their definitions of "reasonable". References that courts have held impermissible include "hoodlum," "deviant homosexual," "boss," "hippie," and "dope peddler." References that courts have allowed include "creature of the jungle," "monster," "trash," "mad dog," and "trafficker in human misery."[114] What does this pattern suggest about the difficulties of regulating prosecutorial misconduct? Where would you draw the line between fair and unfair comment in such cases?

Other areas of recurrent abuse involve appeals to law and order and family ties. In general, court will disallow "safe streets" and "civic duty" references once they become focused on the accused or on the jurors themselves. Even the most tolerant judges draw the line at comments such as "[I]f you want to, you can believe all of it and turn him loose, and *we'll send him down in the elevator with you and his gun*,"[115] or "[I]f you find this man not guilty . . . [y]ou will approve and say, 'Okay, Tulsa citizens, it is open season on spouses. Take your shot.'"[116] Yet slightly less inflammatory appeals, such as assertions that the family of a rape victim was entitled to the same protection as jurors' own mothers and daughters, have been upheld.[117]

A similar subjectivity in standards is apparent in other contexts. For example, the Supreme Court has held that explicit comment on the defendant's silence violates the fifth amendment privilege against self-incrimination. Griffin v. California, 380 U.S. 609 (1965).

However, more oblique references to the government's "undisputed" case or to defense counsel's failure to counter certain evidence will be permissible unless the prosecutor manifestly intended, or jurors "naturally and necessarily" interpreted, the references as comments on the defendant's silence.[118] So too, in most but not all states, a prosecutor must refrain from vouching for a witness' credibility or lack of credibility. However, courts have divided over characterizations such as "lies" and "unworthy of belief," or references to plea bargains that include a witness' promise of truthful testimony.[119]

Related controversies center on the appropriate response for inappropriate conduct. Whether reversal is necessary hinges on whether the defendant suffered prejudice. That determination will, in turn, depend on several factors, such as whether the conduct was egregious; whether it was an isolated or brief episode in an otherwise proper argument; whether the defense counsel invited, provoked, or promptly objected to the impropriety; whether the trial judge took corrective action such as instructing the jury to disregard the remarks; and whether there was overwhelming evidence of guilt.

The relative significance of these factors has, however, provoked frequent dispute. In a representative case, United States v. Young, 470 U.S. 1 (1985), the defendant's attorney made several references to the prosecution's "unfair" and "reprehensible" conduct, and submitted that there was not a person in the courtroom who thought that the defendant had the required intent to defraud. Id. at 4-5. The prosecutor did not object to opposing counsel's comments but offered his own rejoinder. He pointed out that he was sitting in the courtroom, and he believed that the defendant intended to defraud, "[i]f we are allowed to give our personal impressions since it was asked of me." Id. at 5. Defense counsel did not object at the time but raised the point on appeal. A majority of the Supreme Court paid lip service to the cliche that "two apparent wrongs do not make for a right result," but held that neither did they amount to plain error. Id. at 11. Viewing the comments in context of the government's overwhelming case, the majority felt they did not deprive the defendant of a fair trial.

However, the Court also emphasized that such vouching was improper because it could "convey the impression that evidence not presented to the jury, but known to the prosecutor, supports the charges," and because the prosecutor's opinion carries with it the "imprimatur of the Government" and could bias jurors' assessment of the evidence. Id. at 18. In the majority's view, the prosecutor should have objected to defense counsel's comment and asked for a curative instruction.

Justice Brennan, joined by Justices Marshall and Blackmun, agreed with the majority that the prosecutor had no automatic right of reply in response to improper argument by opposing counsel, but disagreed that the conviction should nonetheless be affirmed. As the dissenters read the record, the evidence of guilt was not unequivocal. At the very least, they wanted a remand to determine whether this and other prosecutorial improprieties cumulatively had compromised the integrity of the trial. Id. at 22 (Brennan, J., dissenting).

The *Young* case highlights the bar's difficulties in developing appropriate sanctions for prosecutorial misconduct. As in other contexts, courts are reluctant to reverse convictions where guilt seems clear, but neither do they have adequate regulatory alternatives. One appellate court, expressing frustration with the limited options available, noted that "[t]en years ago we were commenting on a 'sense of futility from persistent disregard of prior admonitions.' These rebukes seem to have little effect, no doubt because of the harmless error rule." United States v. Pallais, 921 F.2d 684, 691-692 (7th Cir. 1990).

The assumption that curative instructions are sufficient is, as courts have noted elsewhere, "an unmitigated fiction." Jackson v. Denno, 378 U.S. 368, 388 n.15 (1964). Often the effect is like asking jurors to "unring a bell." United States v. Murray, 784 F.2d 188, 189 (6th Cir. 1986). Given the frequent inadequacy of such instructions, defense counsel often see little to gain from requesting them. That is particularly true when frequent objections may irritate the jury, draw additional attention to the improper reference, or invite further prejudicial disclosures if prosecutors are allowed to defend their comment in open court.

Reliance on disciplinary sanctions is similarly misplaced. As a general matter, neither defendants nor their lawyers have incentives to bring a complaint that might invite retaliation, and courts rarely make referrals to bar regulatory agencies. Empirical surveys indicate that disciplinary actions for improper argument are extremely rare.[120] In response to these inadequacies, an ABA report has recommended an automatic referral to bar disciplinary authorities whenever a conviction is overturned because of prosecutorial misconduct. Some courts and commentators also recommend referrals, reversals, or dismissals in any case suggesting bad faith conduct on the part of prosecutors.[121] Tracy Meares proposes withholding financial rewards from prosecutors whose improper trial argument provokes a judicial rebuke or bar disciplinary sanctions.[122]

Which of these proposals seems most likely to be effective? How would you handle problems of prosecutorial misconduct described in Problem 15A in Chapter XV (Evidence and Trial Advocacy) at page 655.

H.   DISCLOSURE OBLIGATIONS

PROBLEM 14H

1. You are the prosecutor in a robbery case with extremely strong evidence of guilt. The victim had an excellent opportunity to observe the robber and readily identified him at a lineup shortly after the incident. Defense counsel is a private practitioner whose high volume of cases

generally prevents pretrial investigation. Several days before your scheduled plea negotiation on the eve of trial, you learn that the complaining witness has fled the jurisdiction and cannot be located. Must you disclose that fact in plea negotiations? Should you?[123]

2. In another case involving the same defense attorney, you have charged the defendant with aggravated assault. The victim is his former girlfriend, and shortly before trial you learn that she is unwilling to testify. In part her reluctance stems from fear that the defendant or his friends will retaliate; in part she is afraid that facts about her history of psychiatric treatment will become public.

How do you proceed? What factors would be most relevant to your judgment? Should a victim's reluctance to press charges be conclusive in your decision whether to drop the case or accept a plea? Do you have any obligations to disclose the witness' prior psychiatric history?

Model Rule 3.8, DR 7-103, and Standard 3-3.11(a) of the ABA Prosecution Standards require prosecutors to make timely disclosure of evidence that tends to negate guilt or mitigate the offense. These rules have constitutional foundations. Under standards first set forth in Brady v. Maryland, 373 U.S. 83 (1963), and more recently clarified in United States v. Bagley, 473 U.S. 667 (1985), a government must reveal "evidence favorable to the accused and 'material either to guilt or to punishment.'" 373 U.S. at 87. Noncompliance will result in reversal of the conviction if there is a "reasonable probability" that the result of the proceeding would have been different had disclosure been made. 473 U.S. at 681.

The application of these requirements in plea-bargaining remains unsettled. It is equally unclear whether all information involving the availability or credibility of witnesses is "material" or "exculpatory" under existing doctrine. In People v. Jones, 375 N.E.2d 41 (N.Y. Ct. App.), cert. denied, 439 U.S. 846 (1978), the New York Court of Appeals found no denial of due process where the prosecutor failed to disclose that the complaining witness in a robbery prosecution had died four days before the entry of the plea. In the court's view, although such information would have been a significant factor influencing the defendant's determination to plead guilty, it was not relevant to the legal issue of guilt. The prosecutor was not "obliged to share his appraisal of the weaknesses of his own case (as opposed to specific exculpatory evidence)," and the witness' unavailability was not "evidence." However, somewhat inconsistently, the court left open the possibility that a prosecutor might have disclosure obligations if a defendant "staunchly and plausibly maintains his innocence" but explicitly states he will accept a plea to avoid the risk of a stiffer sentence. 375 N.E.2d at 44.

Is the court's reasoning persuasive? Compare Arizona Ethics Opinion 94-07 (1994), which concluded that if a prosecutor lists a witness who later dies, the defendant must receive notice of the death. Consider the materials on candor in negotiation in Chapter

VIII at pages 342–353. What constitutes "fair dealing" in criminal cases? Is any evidence that discredits a witness subject to disclosure? Alternatively, are prosecutors entitled to make their own assessment that some material's prejudicial value outweighs its relevance? In Problem 14H(2), what kind of psychiatric treatment would be material and exculpatory?

Under Kyles v. Whiteley, 115 S. Ct. 1555 (1995), courts must consider the cumulative effect of all undisclosed evidence in determining whether a prosecutor has withheld material information in violation of *Brady*. What guidance does that standard provide on the facts of Problem 14H(2)? If evidence is subject to disclosure requirements, should the defendant have a right to receive it before entering a plea? Neither Supreme Court decisions nor bar ethical rules discuss disclosure in plea contexts. ABA Prosecution Standard 3-3.11a requires disclosure at the "earliest feasible opportunity," and some, but not all, lower courts have ruled that defendants should receive information before they enter a plea.[124]

May a prosecutor decide not to pursue certain leads for fear of discovering exculpatory material? Do the government's obligations increase where defense counsel's trial preparation is inadequate?[125] Most prosecutors think not, and many claim that opposing attorneys rely too heavily on *Brady* instead of doing their own work.[126] By contrast, defense lawyers argue that public pressure and an "adversarial mindset" encourage prosecutors to withhold *Brady* materials and that neither judges nor disciplinary committees have provided adequate enforcement. This latter perception is consistent with a study of the first quarter century following *Brady*, which found only nine cases in which discipline was even considered for suppressing discoverable material.[127] The problems of monitoring disclosure obligations have led about a half dozen states to mandate "open file" policies for prosecutors by statute or court order. Would you support such a policy? Why or why not?

I. THE ALLOCATION OF RULE-MAKING AUTHORITY

PROBLEM 14I

You are a federal prosecutor in the Southern District of New York who is licensed to practice law in New York State. You are supervising a mail fraud investigation of an individual, Jones, who was recently indicted by your office on unrelated tax evasion charges. When Jones learns of the new investigation, the lawyer representing him on the tax charges meets with you in an attempt to persuade you that Jones is innocent of mail fraud. Not entirely convinced, you plan to direct federal investigators to go unannounced to Jones' home in New Jersey and to question him about the alleged fraud.[128]

Would your conduct violate bar ethical rules? Should it?

Circumstances like those in Problem 14I have provoked considerable controversy between federal officials and state bar leaders. As recently amended, Model Rule 4.2 provides:

> In representing a client, a lawyer shall not communicate about the subject of representation with a person the lawyer knows to be represented by another lawyer in the matter, unless the lawyer has the consent of the other lawyer or is authorized by law to do so.

DR 7-104(A)(1) has a similar prohibition.[129]

During the early 1990s, then-Attorney General Richard Thornburgh issued a memorandum authorizing ex parte contacts under certain circumstances without notifying a party's lawyer. Attorney General Janet Reno subsequently issued regulations providing similar authorization. Prosecutors have maintained that conversations outside a defense attorney's presence at times are essential, especially in organized crime cases. Some defendants wish to cooperate with the government but are afraid to inform lawyers who are being paid by higher-level organized crime figures. Federal prosecutors conducting multistate investigations also need uniform rules. According to the Justice Department, the supremacy clause permits federal regulations to satisfy the "authorized by law" exception in ex parte contact rules.

Several courts have held otherwise, and ABA leaders have sharply criticized the claim that "ethics standards for [federal] prosecutors should be only written by prosecutors."[130] By contrast, several prominent ethics experts have questioned whether either the ABA or the Justice Department should have exclusive regulatory authority. Some commentators support proposed congressional legislation authorizing ex parte contacts; others believe that federal courts offer the greatest likelihood of balanced and disinterested decision-making.[131]

Which position do you find most convincing? Similar controversies have arisen over conflicting state and federal rules governing subpoenas of defense attorneys.[132] Who should regulate federal prosecutors and who should regulate the regulators?

Endnotes

1. Beth Nissen, For the Defense: Texas Attorney Gains Fame Winning Cases That Seem Impossible, Wall St. J., Oct. 31, 1978, at 1, 35.

2. When presented with these facts, the Michigan State Bar Committee on Professional and Judicial Ethics held that the lawyer could introduce the truthful testimony despite its potential to mislead the finder of fact. Op. CI-1164, 3 Law. Man. Prof. Conduct 41 (Jan. 23, 1987), discussed in Murray L. Schwartz, On Making the True Look False and the False Look True, 41 Sw. L.J. 1135 (1988).

3. David Hoffman, 2 A Course of Legal Study 755-756 (2d ed. 1836).

4. James Mills, I Have Nothing to Do with Justice, Life, Mar. 12, 1971, at 56, 57.

5. The commentary on criminal defense lawyers' ethical obligations to guilty clients is extensive. For representative selections, see Alan H. Goldman, The Moral Foundations of Professional Ethics 90-155 (1980); Barbara A. Babcock, Defending the Guilty, 32 Clev. St. L. Rev. 175 (1983): Stephen Gillers, Can a Good Lawyer Be a Bad Person?, 84 Mich. L. Rev. 1011 (1986); Stephen L. Pepper, The Lawyer's Amoral Ethical Role: A Defense, a Problem, and Some Possibilities, 1986 A.B.F. Res. J. 613; A. Kenneth Pye, The Role of Counsel in the Suppression of Truth, 4 Duke L.J. 921 (1978); and sources cited in notes 9, 15, 16 infra.

6. See Babcock, supra note 5, at 177. For discussion of defendants' unwillingness to fully trust court-appointed counsel, see Part E, section 1, infra.

7. Deborah L. Rhode, An Adversarial Exchange on Adversarial Ethics: Text, Subtext, and Context, 41 J. of Legal Educ. 29, 32 (1991).

8. Lloyd P. Stryker, For the Defense 217 (1947) (quoting Erskine).

9. Felony acquittal rates in the state courts are about 1 percent and in the federal district courts about 2.8 percent. See sources cited in David Luban, Are Criminal Defenders Different?, 91 Mich. L. Rev. 1729 (1993).

10. Margaret L. Steiner, Adequacy of Fact Investigation in Criminal Lawyer's Trial Preparation, 1981 Ariz. St. L.J. 523, 538.

11. Mike McConville & Chester Mirsky, Guilty Plea Courts: A Social Disciplinary Model of Criminal Justice, 42 Soc. Probs. 216 (1995).

12. William A. Mintz, Lawyer Wouldn't Go to "Sleazy Bar," Client Wins Freedom from Life Term, Natl. L.J., Nov. 24, 1980, at 7. At the district attorney's insistence, the defendant agreed, as part of the bargain for his release, to waive any malpractice claims against his former lawyer. Id. (discussing Rummel v. Estelle, 445 U.S. 263 (1980)).

13. For representative examples, see Dan T. Carter, Scottsboro: A Tragedy of the American South (1969); Richard Kluger, Simple Justice (1976); Daniel H. Pollitt, Counsel for the Unpopular Cause: The Hazard of Being Undone, 43 N.C.L. Rev. 9 (1964).

14. See Clem Turner, What's the Story? An Analysis of Juror Discrimination and a Plea for Affirmative Jury Selection, 34 Am. Crim. L. Rev. 289 (1996) (summarizing evidence finding black defendants are significantly more likely to be found guilty and to receive capital sentences). For an illustration, see Peter Aplebome, Alabama Releases Man Held on Death Row for Six Years, N.Y. Times, Mar. 3, 1993, at A1.

15. See John Kaplan, Jerome H. Skolnick & Malcolm M. Feeley, Criminal Justice: Introductory Cases and Materials 323-324 (5th ed. 1991); Rhode, supra note 7, at 33; Jesse Berman, The Cuban Popular Tribunals, 69 Colum. L. Rev. 1317, 1341 (1969) (quoting law professors at the University of Havana: "the first job of a revolutionary lawyer is not to argue that his client is innocent, but rather to determine if his client is guilty, and if so, to seek the sanction which will best rehabilitate him").

16. William Simon, The Ethics of Criminal Defense, 91 Mich. L. Rev. 1703 (1993).

17. Harry I. Subin, The Criminal Defense Lawyer's "Different Mission": Reflections on the "Right" to Present a False Case, 1 Geo. J. Legal Ethics 125, 148, 151 (1987).

18. See Part E, section 1, and Gary Goodpaster, The Adversary System, Advocacy, and Effective Assistance of Counsel in Criminal Cases, 14 N.Y.U. Rev. L. & Soc. Change 59 (1986).

19. Deborah L. Rhode & David Luban, Legal Ethics 305 (1992).

20. See Markus Dirk Drubber, American Plea Bargains, German Lay Judges, and the Crisis of Criminal Procedure, 49 Stan. L. Rev. 547 (1997); John H. Langbein, Land Without Plea Bargaining: How the Germans Do It, 78 Mich. L. Rev. 204 (1979).

21. Babcock, supra note 5, at 178.

22. Luban, supra note 9, at 1749.

23. See David Luban, Lawyers and Justice (1988); Richard Wasserstrom, Lawyers as Professionals: Some Moral Issues, 5 Human Rights 1 (1975).

24. Charles J. Ogletree, Jr., Beyond Justifications: Seeking Motivations to Sustain Public Defenders, 106 Harv. L. Rev. 1239, 1270 (1993).

25. Simon, supra note 16; Fred C. Zacharias, The Civil-Criminal Distinction in Professional Responsibility, 7 J. of Law & Contemp. Issues 165, 182-194 (1996).

26. Luban, supra note 9, at 1762-1763, 1765.

27. Patrick Mahony, Barbed Wit and Malicious Humor 126 (1956).

28. For variations on these possibilities, see Fred Zacharias, Structuring the Ethics of Prosecutorial Trial Practice: Can Prosecutors Do Justice?, 44 Vand. L. Rev. 45, 68-69 (1991).

29. Bruce Shapiro, Sleeping Lawyer Syndrome, The Nation, Apr. 7, 1997, at 27-29.

30. Chester Mersky, Quality Legal Aid: Going, Going, Gone, Natl. L.J., Dec. 4, 1995, at A19.

31. Robert L. Spangenberg et al., U.S. Dept. of Justice, National Criminal Defense Systems Study: Final Report (1986); Jerold H. Israel, Yale Kamisar & Wayne R. La Fave, Criminal Procedure and the Constitution 25 (1991).

32. See Luban, supra note 9; Albert L. Vreeland, II, The Breath of the Unfee'd Lawyer: Statutory Fee Limitations and Ineffective Assistance of Counsel in Capital Litigation, 90 Mich. L. Rev. 626 (1991); Ronald Smothers, Court-Appointed Defense Offers the Poor a Lawyer, but the Cost May Be High, N.Y. Times, Feb. 14, 1994, at A12; Richard Klein & Robert Spanenberg, The Indigent Defense Crisis, for the American Bar Association Section of Criminal Justice, Ad Hoc Committee on the Indigent Defense Crisis (1993). See, e.g., Huskey v. State, 688 S.W.2d 417 (Tenn. 1985) (upholding fee of $500 for 181 hours in murder trial).

33. See David Margolick, Volunteers or Not, Tennessee Lawyers Help Poor, N.Y. Times, Jan. 17, 1992, at B16. See also Chapter XI (Constitutional Law), at pages 504–506.

34. Stephen B. Bright, Course for the Poor: The Death Sentence Not for the Worst Crime but for the Worst Lawyer, 103 Yale L.J. 1835, 1850-1854 (1994); Public Defenders Are Overloaded, The Hartford Courant, Jan. 10, 1995, at A10; Christopher Johns, "Slaughterhouse Justice": Crushing Workloads, Underfunded Public Defenders Shortchange Indigent Clients, The Arizona Republic, May 23, 1993, at C1; J. Michael McWilliams, The Erosion of Indigent Rights: Excessive Caseloads Resulting in Ineffective Counsel for Poor, 79 A.B.A.J. 8 (1993).

35. Stephen J. Schulhofer, Plea Bargaining as Disaster, 101 Yale L.J. 1979, 1988 (1992).

36. U.S. Dept. of Justice, Sourcebook of Criminal Justice Statistics, 1990, at 2, tbl. 1.1 (Kathleen Maguire & Timothy J. Flanagan eds., 1991) (45 percent of the funding goes to police, 33.5 percent to corrections, 12.1 percent to courts, and 6.1 percent to prosecution).

37. Kenneth B. Mann, The Trial as Text: Allegory, Myth, and Symbol in the Adversarial Criminal Process—A Critique of the Role of Public Defender and a Proposal for Reform, 32 Am. Crim. L. Rev. 743, 803-812 (1995).

38. Abraham S. Blumberg, The Practice of Law as Confidence Game, 1 Law & Soc. Rev., June 1967, at 15, 27.

39. Schulhofer, supra note 35, at 1990; Robert E. Scott & William J. Stuntz, Plea Bargaining as Contract, 101 Yale L.J. 1909, 1959 (1992).

40. See Morris v. Slappy, 461 U.S. 1 (1983) (rejecting right to appointed counsel of choice). For a cynical explanation of this rule, see James S. Kunen, How Can You Defend Those People? 50 (1985) ("The court won't let an indigent client dump his lawyer just because he happens to think the lawyer's doing a lousy job. Half of the defendants have lawyers who *are* doing a lousy job").

41. Schulhofer, supra note 35, at 1990.

42. McConville & Mirsky, supra note 11, at 219, 224.

43. See, e.g., Shaw v. State of Alaska, 861 P.2d 566, 572 (Alaska 1993); Glenn v. Aiken, 409 Mass. 699, 707 (1991).

44. Stephen J. Schulhofer, Effective Assistance on the Assembly Line, 14 N.Y.U. Rev. L. & Soc. Change 137 (1986); Scott & Stuntz, supra note 39, at 1957-1958; Goodpaster, supra note 18, at 80; Bruce A. Green, Lethal Fiction: The Meaning of "Counsel" in the Sixth Amendment, 78 Iowa L. Rev. 433, 499-501 (1993).

45. Victor E. Flango & Patricia McKenna, Federal Habeas Corpus Review of State Court Convictions, 31 Cal. W.L. Rev. 237, 259-260 (1995).

46. Shapiro, supra note 29, at 27 (quoting Judge Doug Shaver).

47. Frank H. Easterbrook, Plea Bargaining as Compromise, 101 Yale L.J. 1969, 1974 (1992). See Schulhofer, supra note 35.

48. United States v. Peart, 621 So. 2d 780, 791 (La. 1993) (finding constitutional violation in New Orleans indigent defense system); Makemson v. Martin Cty., 491 So. 2d 1109 (Fla. 1986), cert. denied, 479 U.S. 1043 (1987) (holding that statutory maximum fees violated rights to effective assistance of counsel in cases involving extraordinary circumstances). Other courts that doubt their authority to appropriate public funds have refused to hear cases in which counsel is inadequately compensated or have refused to require counsel to accept appointments. Cf. State ex rel. Wolff v. Ruddy, 617 S.W.2d 64 (Mo. 1981) (en banc) (rejecting claim); Bradshaw v. Ball, 487 S.W.2d 294 (Ky. 1972); State ex rel. Partain v. Oakley, 227 S.E.2d 314 (W. Va. 1976).

49. See research summarized in Roy B. Fleming, Client Games: Defense Attorney Perspectives on Their Relations with Criminal Clients, 1986 A.B.F. Res. J. 253, 254 n.3, 276.

50. Jonathan D. Casper, Did You Have a Lawyer When You Went to Court? No, I Had a Public Defender, 1 Yale Rev. L. & Soc. Action 4 (1971). See Rodney Thaxton, Professionalism and Life in the Trenches: The Case of the Public Defender, 8 St. Thom. L. Rev. 185 (1995).

51. Casper, supra note 50.

52. Schulhofer, supra note 35, at 1999 (noting that our present methods "hide the real value of defense services afforded the indigent . . . [and] tend to approximate [a system] in which there is no meaningful representation").

53. Martin Guggenheim, Divided Loyalties: Musings on Some Ethical Dilemmas for the Institutional Criminal Defense Attorney, 14 N.Y.U. Rev. L. & Soc. Change 13, 19 (1986).

54. Scott & Stuntz, supra note 39, at 1909; Easterbrook, supra note 47; Schulhofer, supra note 35.

55. See U.S. Dept. of Justice, Sourcebook of Criminal Justice Statistics, supra note 36, at 502, tbls. 5.25, 5.26, 5.51.

56. John H. Langbein, Torture and Plea Bargaining, 46 U. Chi. L. Rev. 3, 20 (1978).

57. Scott & Stuntz, supra note 39, at 1911. See Malcolm M. Feeley, The Process Is the Punishment (1979); Stephen J. Schulhofer, Is Plea Bargaining Inevitable?, 97 Harv. L. Rev. 1037 (1984); Albert W. Alschuler, The Changing Plea Bargaining Debate, 69 Cal. L. Rev. 652 (1981).

58. Stephen J. Schulhofer, A Wake-Up Call from the Plea-Bargaining Trenches, 19 Law & Soc. Inq. 135, 140-143 (1994).

59. Mills, supra note 4, at 56.

60. Rudolph Gerber, A System in Collapse: Appearance vs. Reality in Criminal Justice, 12 St. Louis U. Pub. L. Rev. 225, 227 (1993).

61. Schulhofer, supra note 35, at 1994; Schulhofer, supra note 58, at 142.

62. See Christopher H. Schmitt, Plea Bargaining Favors Whites as Blacks, Hispanics Pay Price, San Jose Mercury News, Dec. 8, 1991, at A1 (reporting study of almost 700,000 California criminal cases that showed that "whites as a group get significantly better deals than Hispanics or blacks who are accused of similar crimes and have similar criminal backgrounds"; whites fared better in categories such as charges dropped,

charges reduced, cases dismissed, prison time, special charges, and alternative punishment).

63. Scott & Stuntz, supra note 39, at 1910; Milton Heumann, Plea Bargaining (1978).

64. Easterbrook, supra note 47, at 1975.

65. Scott & Stuntz, supra note 39; Tracy L. Meares, Rewards for Good Behavior: Influencing Prosecutorial Discretion and Conduct with Financial Incentives, 64 Fordham L. Rev. 851 (1995) (advocating rewards for prosecutors who obtain a conviction on the same charge they pursued at the outset of a case).

66. United States v. DeCoster, 624 F.2d 196, 276 (en banc) (D.C. Cir. 1979) (Bazelon, J. dissenting); William J. Genego, The Future of Effective Assistance of Counsel: Performance Standards and Competent Representation, 22 Am. Crim. L. Rev. 181 (1984).

67. Green, supra note 44, at 435, 437, 492-493.

68. Richard Klein, The Relationship of the Court and Defense Counsel: The Impact on Competent Representation and Proposals for Reform, 29 B.C.L. Rev. 531, 582-584 (1988); Green, supra note 44, at 492-493.

69. Zacharias, supra note 28, at 66-74.

70. See sources cited in notes 34 and 48; see cases discussed in Rodger Citron, Note: (un)Luckey v. Miller: The Case for a Structural Injunction to Improve Indigent Defense Services, 101 Yale L.J. 481 (1991); Klein, supra note 68.

71. William Glaberson, Change Proposed in Legal Aid Representation, N.Y. Times, Mar. 3, 1991, at 44; FTC v. Superior Court Trial Lawyers Assn., 493 U.S. 411 (1990) (finding strike by a District of Columbia association of court-appointed private attorneys amounted to conspiracy to fix prices).

72. Similar introductory material also appears in Deborah L. Rhode & David Luban, Legal Ethics 322-323 (2d ed. 1995).

73. See Berger v. United States, 295 U.S. 78 (1935); ABA Standards Relating to the Administration of Criminal Justice 3-1.1(b)(c) (2d ed. 1980). See also Model Rules, Rule 3.8 cmt. (1983) ("A prosecutor has the responsibility of a minister of justice and not simply that of an advocate"); EC 7-13 (1981).

74. Robert Jackson, The Federal Prosecutor, 24 J. Judicature Soc. 18 (1940), quoted in Stanley Z. Fisher, In Search of the Virtuous Prosecutor: A Conceptual Framework, 15 Am. J. Crim. L. 197, 219 (1988).

75. 13 ABA/BNA Manual on Prof. Conduct 165 (June 11, 1997).

76. Meares, supra note 65, at 901; Bruce A. Green, Policing Federal Prosecutors: Do Too Many Regulators Produce Too Little Enforcement?, 8 St. Thom. L. Rev. 69 (1995) (noting temptations for OPR staff to sympathize with colleagues and to avoid public acknowledgement of wrongdoing).

77. Fisher, supra note 74, at 205. See Kenneth Bresler, "I Never Lost a Trial": When Prosecutors Keep Score of Criminal Convictions, 9 Geo. J. Legal Ethics 537 (1996).

78. Scott Pendleton, When Innocence Gets Short Shrift, Christian Science Monitor, June 26, 1995, at 9 (quoting James Liebman).

79. Jim McGee, War on Crime Expands U.S. Prosecutors' Powers: Aggressive Tactics Put Fairness at Issue, Wash. Post, Jan. 10, 1993, at A1, 36.

80. This problem draws on Monroe H. Freedman, Lawyers' Ethics in an Adversary System 82-83 (1975) (describing Kennedy Administration's prosecution of James Hoffa). See also David Burnham, Misuse of the IRS: The Abuse of Power, N.Y. Times Magazine, Sept. 3, 1989, at 25.

81. See In re Complaint of Rook, 556 P.2d 1351 (Or. 1976) (per curiam).

82. See United States v. Richmond, 550 F. Supp. 605 (E.D.N.Y. 1982) (invalidating that portion of a plea agreement requiring resignation of a congressman charged with income tax violation).

83. Greg Hollon, After the Federalization Binge: A Civil Liberties Hangover, 31 Harv. C.R.-C.L. L. Rev. 499, 614 (1995).

84. United States v. Ucciferri, 960 F.2d 953 (11th Cir. 1992).

85. People v. Johnson, No. 29390 (Cal. Super. Ct., Tulare Cty., Jan. 2, 1991).

86. Monroe Freedman, Treading On, or Trading Off, Rights, The Recorder, May 17, 1995, at 6. In Town of Newton v. Rumery, 480 U.S. 386 (1987), the Court held that release-dismissal agreements are valid if the government can prove that the defendant's consent was "voluntary, deliberate and informed," and that the prosecutor was motivated by an "independent, legitimate reason."

87. Donald G. Gifford, Equal Protection and the Prosecutor's Charging Decision: Enforcing an Ideal, 49 Geo. Wash. L. Rev. 659, 660 (1981).

88. Id. at 666; Richard S. Frase, The Decision to File Federal Criminal Charges: A Quantitative Study of Prosecutorial Discretion, 47 U. Chi. L. Rev. 246, 251 (1980).

89. Frase, supra note 88, at 265.

90. Kenneth C. Davis, Discretionary Justice: A Preliminary Inquiry 167 (1969).

91. Elsa Walsh, U.S. Plea Guidelines Encourage Resignations, Wash. Post, June 2, 1990, at A8.

92. Hollon, supra note 83, at 514-515.

93. Statement by an FBI representative, quoted in Wayne R. La Fave, The Prosecutor's Discretion in the United States, 18 Am. J. Comp. L. 532, 533 (1970).

94. Alexander M. Bickel, The Supreme Court, 1960 Term, Foreword: The Passive Virtue, 75 Harv. L. Rev. 40, 63 (1962).

95. Kenneth J. Melilli, Prosecutorial Discretion in an Adversary System, 1992 B.Y.U.L. Rev. 669, 680-681.

96. Id. at 700, n.257 (noting that jurors may defer to prosecutors on the presumption that prosecutors have other evidence of guilt not available at trial).

97. Monroe H. Freedman, The Professional Responsibility of the Prosecuting Attorney, 55 Geo. L.J. 1030, 1034-1035 (1967).

98. Alan M. Dershowitz, Reasonable Doubts: The OJ Simpson Case and the Criminal Justice System (1996).

99. Oyler v. Boles, 368 U.S. 448 (1962). Nor may a prosecutor punish defendants for exercise of a right related to the criminal process, though they may file additional charges against defendants who refuse to plead guilty. See Gifford, supra note 87, at 686-687; Bennet L. Gershman, Prosecutorial Misconduct §4.3 (1985).

100. United States v. Armstrong, 116 S. Ct. 1480 (1996); Oyler v. Boles, 368 U.S. 448 (1962).

101. Davis, supra note 90, at 189-190, 224-225.

102. Gifford, supra note 87, at 717-718; Abrams, Internal Policy: Guiding the Exercise of Prosecutorial Discretion, 19 U.C.L.A.L. Rev. 1 (1971).

103. National Advisory Commission on Criminal Justice Standards and Goals, Standard 1.2, at 24 (1973), discussed in Frase, supra note 88, at 299.

104. Frase, supra note 88, at 296-297.

105. The Administrative Procedure Act, 5 U.S.C. §§701-706 (1982), authorizes courts to set aside executive branch agency actions that are "arbitrary, capricious, an abuse of discretion, or otherwise not in accordance with law," §706(2)(A), contrary to constitutional protections, §706(2)(C), without observance of procedural requirements, §706(2)(D), or "unwarranted by the facts," §706(2)(F).

106. Scott Turow, Law School v. Reality, N.Y. Times Magazine, Sept. 18, 1988, at 52.

107. United States v. Wiley et al., 534 F.2d 659, 665 (6th Cir. 1976).

108. Commonwealth v. Shelley, 373 N.E.2d 951, 954-955 (Mass. 1978); People v. Wood, 187 N.E.2d 116, 122 (N.Y. Ct. App. 1962).

109. McFarland v. Smith, 611 F.2d 414, 416 (2d Cir. 1979).

110. United States v. Hasting et al., 461 U.S. 499, 502 (1983).

111. State v. Pindale, 249 N.J. Super. 266, 286 (App. Div. 1991).

112. State v. Acker, 265 N.J. Super. 351 (App. Div. 1993).

113. Gershman, supra note 99, at §10.1, at 10-4; Whitney N. Seymour, Jr., Why Prosecutors Act Like Prosecutors, 11 Rec. Assn. Bar City N.Y. 302 (1956).

114. Gershman, supra note 99, at §102(b), at 10-11; Dennis N. Balske, Prosecutorial Misconduct During Closing Argument: The Art of Knowing When and How to Object and of Avoiding the "Invited Response" Doctrine, 37 Mercer L. Rev. 1033, 1038 (1986).

115. United States v. McRae, 593 F.2d 700, 706 (5th Cir.) (emphasis in original), cert. denied, 444 U.S. 862 (1979).

116. Meggett v. State, 599 P.2d 1110, 1114 n.3 (Okla. Crim. App. 1979).

117. People v. Wilson, 264 N.E.2d 492, 498 (Ill. App. 1970).

118. Gershman, supra note 99, at §10.3, at 10-23; Balske, supra note 114, at 1043; Ellen S. Podgor & Jeffrey S. Weiner, Prosecutorial Misconduct: Alive and Well, and Living in Indiana?, 33 Geo. J. Legal Ethics 657, 675-676 (1990).

119. See Balske, supra note 114, at 1052-1053; Gershman, supra note 99, at §10.5(c), at 10-37. California does not prohibit vouching, which left prosecutors an unusual degree of leeway in the O.J. Simpson case.

120. ABA/BNA Manual, supra note 75; Meares, supra note 65, at 897-898; Albert W. Alschuler, Courtroom Misconduct by Prosecutors and Trial Judges, 50 Tex. L. Rev. 629, 671 (1972) (finding only one reported instance of disciplinary sanctions for improper argument).

121. ABA Standing Commission on Professional Discipline, The Judicial Response to Lawyer Misconduct 1.14 (1984); Richard A. Rosen, Disciplinary Sanctions Against Prosecutors for *Brady* Violations: A Paper Tiger, 65 N.C.L. Rev. 693, at 735-736 (1987) (finding only nine reported cases of discipline for perjured testimony or failure to disclose exculpatory testimony); Podgor & Weiner, supra note 118, at 686-688.

122. Meares, supra note 65, at 903-907.

123. People v. Jones, 375 N.E.2d 41 (N.Y. Ct. App.), cert. denied, 439 U.S. 846 (1978).

124. See Sanchez v. United States, 50 F.3d 1448 (9th Cir. 1995); Kevin C. McMunigal, Disclosure and Accuracy in the Guilty Plea Process, 40 Hastings L.J. 957 (1989).

125. See Fisher, supra note 74, at 222-226; Zacharias, supra note 28.

126. Cris Carmody, The *Brady* Rule: Is It Working?, Natl. L.J., May 17, 1993, at 30.

127. Id.; Rosen, supra note 121, at 720; Meares, supra note 65.

128. Bruce A. Green, Federal Prosecutors' Ethics: Who Should Draw the Lines, 7 Prof. Law. 1 (Nov. 1995).

129. The principal difference is that the Code applies to communications with represented "parties" while the Model Rule applies to "persons." The original version of Model Rule 4.2 also referred to parties but was amended in 1995 to reflect what drafters viewed as a clarification of the Rule rather than a substantive change. Green, supra note 128, at 8 n.1.

130. William Glaberson, Thornburgh Policy Leads to a Sharp Ethics Battle, N.Y. Times, Mar. 1, 1991, at B14.

131. Fred C. Zacharias, Who Can Best Regulate the Ethics of Federal Prosecutors, Or, Who Should Regulate the Regulators?: Response to Little, 65 Fordham L. Rev. 429 (1996).

132. Charles F. Williams, Who Wears the Badge?, A.B.A.J., May 1997, at 34.

Chapter XV

Evidence and Trial Advocacy

A. THE ADVERSARY SYSTEM AND THE ADVOCATE'S ROLE

B. TRIAL TACTICS

PROBLEM 15A

Consider the following trial tactics. Which are violations of bar disciplinary rules? Which should be violations?

1. Civil Litigation

(a) In an employee's suit for injuries resulting from a railroad's allegedly unsafe working conditions, the plaintiff's lawyer referred to the defendant's agents as "inhuman cheapskates," who were willing to send the plaintiff "down the tubes" onto a "human trashpile" and to use a "smoke-screen" of deceit to deny recovery. Defense counsel did not object or request an admonition to the jury to disregard such remarks.[1]

(b) The defense attorney in a wrongful death action attempted to "humanize" his client insurance company through several strategies. The case involved a failure by the insured elevator company to take certain safety precautions common in the industry. The attorney had the company's superintendent from the accident site dress in work clothes and sit at defense counsel's table at trial. After the superintendent gave an emotional account of his safety and rescue efforts, the attorney asserted in closing argument that to hold the defendant liable would be to blame the superintendent for the worker's death.

Defense counsel also arranged for an attractive male employee of the insured to be present during the entire trial and to make seemingly intimate conversation with the plaintiff's widow whenever her lawyer was absent. This strategy conveyed to the jury the impression that she already had a new relationship. The lawyer also attempted to distract the jury by "snickering" and "smirking" during opposing counsel's cross-examination.[2]

(c) In litigation over contractual and property rights in a real estate development project, a male lawyer repeatedly directed demeaning remarks at opposing counsel, such as "Be quiet, little girl," "What do you know, young girl," and "I don't have to talk to you, little lady."[3]

2. Criminal Defense

(a) The defense attorney represents a prominent white labor leader on criminal charges before a predominantly black jury. Midway through the trial, the attorney arranges for a prominent black boxing champion to appear in court and, in full view of the jury, to pose for a photograph with the defendant. The attorney also has two young black associates sit at defense counsel's table, although neither takes any active role in the trial. During the course of cross-examining a key government witness, defense counsel asks if the witness had ever been involved in breaking up an Alabama bus boycott, a question bearing no relevance to any issue in the case and one ruled out of order by the trial judge.[4]

(b) In a case involving hate crimes against gays and lesbians by American Nazi Party members, the defense attorney uses peremptory challenges to exclude Jews.

(c) The attorney for Bernard Goetz characterizes the African Americans whom his client allegedly shot in self-defense as "savages" and "vicious predators."[5]

(d) The lawyer representing a defendant convicted of kidnapping, raping, and murdering a 23-year-old artist states during the penalty phase of the trial, "Now I didn't know [the victim] personally, but I would expect, and from what I know about her, that she would not be interested in retribution or vengeance."[6]

(e) In the prosecution of a famous African-American athlete for the murder of his white ex-spouse, defense counsel accuses the police of racism and asks the jury to "send a message" through acquittal.[7]

3. Criminal Prosecution

(a) The prosecutor characterizes the defendant police officer as a "punk behind a badge" who used "Gestapo tactics," and refers to defense counsel as "tricky."[8]

(b) The prosecutor states that defense counsel's function is to "get his client off" by bringing out "insignificant facts" and "legal technicalities."[9]

(c) The prosecutor states that he "would quit" rather than send an innocent person to prison.[10]

(d) The prosecutor characterizes the testimony of a black defense witness as "shucking and jiving on the stand."[11]

(e) The prosecutor states:

> I know what the ethical obligations are of a prosecutor. I took a cut in pay to join this office because I believe in this job. . . . I have the luxury on any case . . . of [saying] "Don't convict, it's not here." . . . This job gives me that luxury. Doesn't give me a lot of money, but it gives me that luxury. I can get up in the morning and look at myself in the mirror and say, "I tell you the truth." I will never ask for a conviction unless I should.[12]

1. Introduction

Trial tactics like those at issue in Problem 15A are subject to both formal and informal norms. Formal prohibitions include a ban on

- engaging in conduct intended to disrupt a tribunal or to influence a juror by means prohibited by law (Model Rule 3.5);
- engaging in undignified or discourteous conduct which is degrading to a tribunal (DR 7-106(C)(6));
- communicating with a juror concerning a case at trial except in official proceedings (DR 7-108(A));
- alluding to any matter that the lawyer does not reasonably believe is relevant or that will not be supported by admissible evidence, asserting personal knowledge of facts in issue except when testifying as a witness, or stating a personal opinion as to the justness of a case, the credibility of a witness, the culpability of a civil litigant, or the guilt or innocence of an accused (Model Rule 3.4(e) and DR 7-106(C));

- engaging in conduct involving dishonesty, fraud, deceit, misrepresentation, or conduct prejudicial to the administration of justice (DR 1-102).

In addition, other standards not codified as disciplinary rules provide that a lawyer

- should not ask a witness a question "solely for the purpose of harassing or embarrassing him . . . and should not by subterfuge put before a jury matters which it cannot properly consider" (EC 7-25);
- should refrain from argument "calculated to inflame the passions or prejudices of the jury" or "divert the jury from its duty to decide the case on the evidence, by injecting issues broader than the guilt or innocence of the accused under the controlling law, or by making predictions of the consequences of the jury's verdict" (Standard 3-5.8, ABA Standards Relating to the Administration of Criminal Justice, The Prosecution Function);
- should refrain from knowingly offering inadmissible evidence or asking legally objectionable questions "for the purpose of bringing inadmissible matter to the attention of the judge or jury" (Standard 4-7.5, ABA Standards, The Defense Function; Standard 3-5.6, ABA Standards, The Prosecution Function).

As economists suggest, such rules can serve both the profession's and the public's interest by fostering honesty, trust, and equitable decision-making. Their ability to serve such functions, in turn, depends on the effectiveness of their enforcement.[13] Problems are most likely to arise when the application of norms is unclear or controversial, when the sanctions for noncompliance are weak in comparison with the advantages, and when individual practitioners can persuade themselves that deviance is justifiable. Common excuses are that justice is served, that the cause is meritorious, or that everyone does it.

Does the material on deception in Chapter II (Traditions of Moral Reasoning) at pages 27–32 and moral psychology in Chapter I (Introduction) at pages 6–7 suggest ways to counter such arguments? Could the legal system operate effectively if in fact "everyone did it"? Does applying Kant's categorical imperative suggest useful insights about the tactics in Problem 15A? Would the lawyers in any of those circumstances have been prepared to see their conduct become a universal norm for everyone?

2. Civil Litigation

How should courts and bar ethics committees respond to inflammatory language or to questions introducing inadmissible evidence? Many lawyers believe that such conduct reflects a serious and growing problem of incivility that has damaged the profession's image in the eyes of the public. Other practitioners believe that "searing, goading, caustic" tactics may be legitimate parts of the litigator's role.[14] What is your view? How would you respond as a judge or bar disciplinary official to the conduct in Problem 15A? Would instructions to the jury be a sufficient remedy for a tactic like the bus boycott question? Should it matter whether opposing counsel asks for such instructions? Experimental data suggest that courts' reliance on jury admonitions is often misplaced. Directing individuals to disregard evidence often draws special attention to that evidence and provokes what psychologists label "reactance." Many people respond to efforts to curtail their freedom by resisting those efforts. Thus, attempts by the court to have jurors disregard what they consider probative evidence can readily backfire. In one representative study of a mock personal injury trial, when evidence of the defendant's insurance coverage was kept from the jury, verdicts averaged $34,000. When existence of insurance was mentioned, average verdicts rose to $37,000. When insurance was mentioned but the jury was instructed to disregard it, average verdicts climbed to $46,000.[15]

Mock jury studies also make clear that legally irrelevant material can substantially influence verdicts. In one representative case involving a woman charged with murdering her husband, jurors responded differently when given information about whether she was a good mother, although the facts were unrelated to her possible defenses of temporary insanity, duress, or self-defense.[16]

At what point do attempts to personify a corporate defendant become so misleading as to be unethical? Insurance defense counsel frequently claim that such efforts are necessary to counteract the jury biases that arise when a needy individual sues a company with a deep pocket. As counsel note, increased insurance rates also carry a cost for real people. Does it follow that the attorney's reliance on the superintendent in Problem 15A(1)(b) was permissible? What about the courtroom romance orchestrated by the defense? Would it matter whether the woman was in fact involved in another relationship? Should more stringent sanctions such as fines, mistrials, or suspension be available for prejudicial courtroom conduct? Would such sanctions be appropriate for any of the conduct described in Problem 15A?

3.   Criminal Trials

> I try to get a jury with little education but with
> much human emotion. The Irish are always the
> best jurymen for the defense. I don't want a
> Scotchman, for he has too little human feelings; I
> don't want a Scandinavian, for he has too strong
> a respect for law as law. In general, I don't want
> a religious person, for he believes in sin and

> punishment. The defense should avoid rich men
> who have a high regard for the law, as they make
> and use it. The smug and ultra-respectable think
> they are the guardians of society, and they be-
> lieve the law is for them.
>
> *Clarence S. Darrow, Attorney for*
> *the Defense, in Verdicts out of*
> *Court 313 (Arthur Weinberg*
> *& Lila Weinberg eds., 1963).*

Under what circumstances is it ethical for lawyers to play on racial, ethnic, gender, religious, or related biases? Consider the anti-bias rules discussed in Chapter III (Regulation of the Profession) at pages 50–59. Would any of the current or proposed rules be effective in dealing with the conduct at issue in Problem 15A? Do "send a message" appeals like Cochran's in the O.J. Simpson case invite racially-based jury nullification that discredits the justice system? Or do such appeals, by providing a check on law enforcement abuses, help the system function more fairly over the long run?

Anecdotal evidence suggests that appeals to factors like race, ethnicity, and gender are increasing in cases where their connection to disputed issues is doubtful. However, the limited data available fail to find corresponding increases in the rate of jury nullification.[17] Would comprehensive evidence on these trends affect your views? How should attorneys respond in cases where they believe that race or gender is socially but not legally relevant?

Does discrimination in the exercise of peremptory challenges stand on different footing? The Supreme Court has prohibited use of peremptory challenges based on race or sex, but has not yet determined whether such prohibitions extend to other forms of discrimination in jury selection. See Batson v. Kentucky, 476 U.S. 79 (1986); J.E.B. v. Alabama ex rel. T.B., 511 U.S. 127 (1994). The Court has also established a standard of proof that makes proof of discrimination extremely difficult. Under Purckett v. Elem, 514 U.S. 765, 839 (1995) (per curiam), a facially neutral reason, even one that is "implausible or fantastic," can justify a peremptory challenge.

These decisions attempt to accommodate competing concerns. As a matter of principle, we believe that jurors should be chosen on the basis of individual capabilities not group identities, and that exclusions based on race, gender, ethnicity, or related factors compromise the legitimacy of the justice system. In criticizing gender-based peremptory challenges, Barbara Babcock notes:

> The unexplained strike of a woman says that she does not belong on the jury, that she could not be impartial or that she is incompetent. The crude stereotypical message is summed in the trial manuals and jury selection tracts that typically advise that "women are more suspicious of other women, especially as plaintiffs in civil cases or defendants in criminal cases" and that "women are more likely than men to

be influenced by the physical attractiveness and personality traits of witnesses." . . .

Again it will be said, all peremptory challenges are based on stereotypes, expressing various intuitive biases. When a postman or Presbyterian is struck, unpleasant stereotypes are also at work, so goes the refrain. But in the case of the postman or the Presbyterian, the same ancient stereotypes about their competence and predispositions have not been used to prevent them from voting, being summoned for juries, pursuing their chosen professions and vocations or otherwise participating in public life and discourse.[18]

Yet many attorneys who deplore the influence of stereotypes also recognize their inevitability. Factors such as ethnicity, race, and gender profoundly shape our life experiences. It is implausible to expect that either jurors, or the lawyers who select them, can entirely remove these influences from their decision-making. Intuitions about whether to strike a particular juror generally reflect multiple characteristics, and courts have had enormous difficulty in distinguishing between pretextual and permissible reasons for exclusion. As one jury consultant noted, lawyers can "always find something" to explain a particular challenge other than race or sex.[19] Reasons that courts have accepted for peremptory strikes include:

- exclusion of three black males wearing blue jeans on the ground that their choice of clothing showed disrespect for the court;[20]
- exclusion of a black female because she was "overweight and poorly groomed," which suggested that she "might not have been in the mainstream of people's thinking";[21]
- exclusion of a black male because he had "long, curly, . . . unkempt hair," and a "mustache and a goatee";[22]
- exclusion of two Hispanics who had family members with criminal records, and two other Hispanics who were proficient in Spanish and allegedly might be reluctant to "accept the interpreter as the final arbiter of what was said by . . . [Spanish-speaking] witness" in a prosecution of a Hispanic defendant.[23]

If such reasons satisfy constitutional standards, has the Supreme Court in fact established a burden that critics characterize as "impossible to meet"?[24] Are there alternative ways to enforce antidiscrimination principles in jury selection? For example, some commentators have proposed more extensive use of written questionnaires, as well as voir dires out of the presence of other potential jurors. Such questionnaires could provide a basis for inquiry that "neither humiliates the potential juror nor rouses the ire of the others in the venire."[25] Other commentators propose restricting the number of preemptory challenges. In their view, three or four challenges are sufficient to exclude individuals with actual bias, but twenty invite wholesale reliance on group stereotypes.[26]

Would you support any of these proposals? If you were a defense lawyer, what would you do if you believed that excluding jurors on the basis of race, gender, or religion would work to your client's advantage and you could construct facially neutral explanations for your challenges? Should more stringent standards govern prosecutors than defense counsel since they have the obligation to "seek justice, not merely to convict"?[27]

C.   RELATIONS WITH WITNESSES

1.   Witness Preparation

See Chapter V, The Adversary System
   • Witness Preparation
        (pages 195–200)

PROBLEM 15B

"[Y]our client's building has burned down. Whether insurance covers the loss depends on reconstruction of a telephone conversation between the insurance company's agent and the employee in charge of insurance for your client. The agent said he was issuing a property insurance binder on the building, but that the policy would contain a sprinkler clause (i.e., no coverage if sprinklers are not operational). After the binder was issued, but before the policy itself was delivered, fire destroyed the building. The sprinklers did not operate. The insurance agent claims he told your [client's employee] that if there were a fire and sprinklers were not in operating order, there would be no coverage.

"In the first fact-gathering session, your client's employee is candid. His recollection of the telephone conversation is hazy. He thinks he remembers the agent's saying that the sprinkler clause affected only rate, not coverage. But he is hesitant to deny the agent's story."[28]

How do you proceed?

_____

Consider the rules on witness preparation reviewed in Part E of Chapter V (The Adversary System) at pages 195–200. Where is the line between refreshing and reconstructing recollection in this case?

In the article on which Problem 15B is based, the authors offer the following general advice:

> [B]efore you have the witness say anything, be sure you know where the trouble spots are in the case and in his view of events. With that knowledge firmly in mind, be sure you ask questions the first time around that do not invite, or stampede, the witness into an unhelpful narrative.[29]

On the facts in Problem 15B, the authors suggest that the lawyer not "focus on the deponent's doubt. That will reinforce it."[30] Instead, they propose recounting the scene described by the agent and exploring what the employee would have done if the agent was right. For example, would the employee have said to himself, "I should call Charlie Johnson to check if the sprinklers are operational"?[31] Would he have just decided "to take a chance and hope for the best" even though this was a $1.5 million policy?[32]

After exploring these possibilities, the authors propose trying "various alternative formulations to find the most positive one the deponent agrees with":

> He might prefer "To the best of my recollection, Mr. X mentioned only rate, not coverage, in telling me about the clause." Or he might like, "Although I do not recall the conversation verbatim, Mr. Z said something to the effect that the clause concerned rate. I feel certain that if Mr. X had mentioned that we would not have coverage if the sprinklers were not operational, I would remember that." And so on.[33]

Do you see any ethical problems in proceeding in this fashion? In reaching your conclusion, consider the studies finding that individuals' recollections of an event can be distorted by misleading questions. For example, in one such study, participants viewed slides in which an accident occurs after a car comes to a halt at a stop sign. Participants who were asked "what happened at the yield sign" later tended to remember having seen a yield rather than stop sign.[34]

If it would be imprudent to "stampede" an employee into an "unhelpful narrative," would it be unethical to stampede him into a helpful one through the use of suggestive questions? Consider the comparative materials on inquisitorial systems in Chapter V at pages 182–184. Such systems generally prohibit pretrial contact with witnesses. What advantages and disadvantages do you see in such a prohibition?

Trial attorneys generally argue that a flat ban on pretrial contact would prove too costly; witness preparation serves legitimate functions, such as helping individuals provide responsive and admissible testimony. Given the difficulties of policing such preparation, some commentators have proposed that courts instruct the jury about the practice.[35] Under current procedures, jurors are encouraged to assess credibility based in part on the demeanor of the witness. Where extensive coaching has occurred, demeanor may be misleading. Advising jurors about pretrial preparation may prevent them from attaching undue weight to carefully scripted performances.

PROBLEM 15C

From 1987 to 1996, the International Chemical Organization (ICO) manufactured chlorine at its facility on the edge of a riverside industrial park. The manufacturing process produced waste in the form of wet, mercury-contaminated sludge. Before the introduction of its state-of-the-art disposal process in 1990, ICO placed the sludge into concrete-lined basins and allowed it to settle. Following the settling process, ICO separated reusable brine at the top of the basins from the heavy sludge, which sank to the bottom of the basins. In 1996, ICO sold the chlorine facility to Horizon General Chemical (HGC) under a sales agreement including a broad but ambiguous indemnification clause.

In 1997, following an unusual number of neurological disorders and other health problems in the neighborhood, 200 area residents sued HGC, other manufacturing facilities located in the industrial park, and scores of individual employees. Included in the suit is Joseph Bliss, ICO's director of quality control from 1987 to 1996 and HGC's current director. The residents have demanded $100 million in compensatory damages for personal injuries and diminution of property values, and $200 million in punitive damages for knowing concealment of the contamination. Although mercury was among the contaminants alleged in the class action complaint, plaintiffs' preliminary studies have not detected the presence of any mercury in area wells.

HGC has retained, at its expense, separate counsel to defend Bliss. One of HGC's in-house lawyers has negotiated a joint defense agreement with Bliss' attorney. Under that agreement, HGC promises to keep confidential anything Bliss discloses during the course of representation and will not make any use of such confidences for purposes other than the defense of the current civil proceedings.

Plaintiffs' initial round of discovery names Bliss as the first deposition witness. In the course of preparing for his deposition, Bliss informs his lawyer and HGC's counsel that on three different occasions between 1987 and 1991, he observed Sidney Sterling, ICO's cost containment manager, oversee company employees as they emptied sludge basins into a drainage facility. That facility channeled materials through an industrial sewer directly into the nearby river. Under the company's official operating procedures, such materials were supposed to be recycled through the treatment system at the plant. On each of these occasions, Bliss also saw liquid contents at the bottom of the basins that appeared to be seeping into the ground. He does not know whether the seepage he observed reached the groundwater table near residential wells, but he assumes that mercury-contaminated liquid probably did, or probably will, leak into the groundwater.

At the time of these incidents, Bliss was responsible for the quality of the manufactured product. He had no authority over the waste disposal process. Sterling, who did have authority, subsequently advanced through the ranks. He now holds the positions of corporate treasurer, chief financial officer, and chair of the newly established quality management committee of the HGC board of directors.

ICO never had permits to dispose of hazardous wastes and never reported such disposal to any regulatory authority. At all times since 1987, federal and state laws have prohibited the disposal of hazardous waste (including mercury-contaminated sludge) into the environment (including the groundwater) without a permit. Any individual, corporation, or other entity who "knows or should know" of an unlicensed disposal of hazardous waste may be subject to felony prosecution and civil penalties of $25,000 per day.

Two years ago, HGC initiated applications for federal and state hazardous waste disposal permits. Such permits are necessary for disposing of by-products of certain new product lines that the corporation wishes to launch. Both state and federal agency rules provide

> [n]o person shall file a permit application to this agency containing any false or misleading information concerning the applicant or the application. Every permit application filed with the agency shall be signed and sworn to by the applicant and, in any case of a corporate applicant, by the applicant's responsible corporate officer.

A joint meeting is now scheduled with federal and state regulators. Such meetings generally serve to finalize permit conditions and update information in the original permit applications. HGC's vice president for environmental affairs, Maria Cabrillo, is handling the licensing proceedings with legal representation by the company's in-house counsel and outside general counsel. Cabrillo's prior monitoring efforts failed to develop any facts concerning either the 1987-1991 events that Bliss observed or any resulting groundwater contamination. In her initial permit applications, Cabrillo made sworn declarations denying knowledge of any impermissible waste disposal at the manufacturing facility.

Bliss must be prepared for his deposition testimony. Cabrillo must be prepared for her joint meeting with federal and state regulators on HGC's pending waste disposal applications.

1. You are a white-collar criminal defense lawyer who is representing Bliss. HGC's general counsel, a casual acquaintance and the source of some referrals in the past, contacted you about taking the case. Because of scheduling conflicts, the two of you do not meet with Bliss until the day before his deposition. During that meeting, he reveals a number of crucial facts in addition to the disclosures noted above. After he saw Sterling empty the basins, which struck him as highly irregular and potentially dangerous, he may have discussed the incidents with other plant employees, although not with Cabrillo. He also "probably" described the conduct in notes for the file that he was keeping at the time to protect himself "just in case." No one asked him to make notes, no one knows of their existence, and he wrote them at home, not "on company time." He has not reread them recently, but he believes that they may also disclose knowledge of the disposal among ICO managers during this period.

Bliss never discussed waste disposal with Sterling, who appeared "willing to do anything to get ahead" and would "never have held up production to check for leakage." Bliss seems to envy as well as dislike Sterling, who "advanced everywhere" while Bliss "advanced nowhere." According to Bliss, the hazardous drainage was just the "tip of the iceberg" as far as Sterling's environmental record was concerned.

On close questioning by HGC's general counsel, Bliss acknowledges that he did not actually see sludge seeping into the ground. He assumed that seepage occurred because of the amount of sludge he saw left in the tank, but he never took any precise measurements. Nor does he know for sure that mercury was left in the liquid that may have leaked into the groundwater table. In response to questions about whether he had ever tested the liquid or heard of such tests, Bliss indicated that the unit under Sterling's control was not interested in such procedures. When pressed on this point, the following exchange between Bliss and the general counsel occurred:

Counsel: You will be asked on deposition whether you know of any hazardous discharges.

Bliss: I believe that some occurred.

Counsel: But the question is what did you *know*. Was your belief based on actual knowledge and expertise or simply what you inferred as a matter of common sense?

Bliss: Common sense had a lot to do with it.

Counsel: This was not an area of the plant under your supervision, and you were not trained as an expert in waste disposal, were you?

Bliss: You don't have to be a chemist to have an opinion. This was not an area of technological sophistication. But if what you're driving at is that I could say "I don't know," I guess I could say that. Is that what I'm supposed to do?

Following this exchange, the general counsel has to leave for another meeting, but she indicates that the conversation needs to continue and that she will be back in touch with you later.

After her departure, Bliss states that he is relieved that she has gone because he did not feel comfortable with her present. He wants to know whether he personally risks any significant liability and what he should do about his notes. Since he is eligible for early retirement, he wonders if he would be best off cooperating with government regulators and opposing parties.

In your judgment, the liability issue is unclear. Knowing involvement in the discharge of hazardous waste is a crime, and under some circumstances "willful blindness" may be sufficient to establish liability. In this case, much may depend on what Bliss' notes reveal. Since these notes were not corporate documents prepared in the course of business, they are not subject to any current discovery request. Nor has Bliss been served with a personal subpoena or pretrial order requiring him to preserve or produce documents. Plaintiffs' counsel, however, will almost certainly ask whether he reviewed any written material prior to the deposition, and may ask whether he kept any notes or records at the time. If he destroys the notes now, it will create extremely adverse inferences and may trigger a criminal investigation. If he denies having such materials, he will be committing perjury, although only you, HGC's general counsel, and Bliss will be aware of that fact. The best strategy would be for Bliss to give you the notes unread. However, he may be reluctant to trust you with potentially explosive material, particularly since you have no prior relationship with him and your fees are being paid by the company.

How do you respond to Bliss' questions? If he asks whether it is unlawful for him to destroy the notes, what do you say? See Part E of

Chapter VI (Confidentiality and Client Counseling) at pages 239–251. Suppose you counsel him against destruction, and he questions whether you are looking out for his interest or that of the company?

Should you be concerned that HGC's counsel may not observe the joint defense agreement? Are you satisfied with your representation up to this point?

2. You are HGC's general counsel. After Bliss' disclosures, you have some doubts about how to proceed. You have promised not to disclose Bliss' confidential statements or to use them for any purpose other than joint defense. But you are also concerned that if you do not propose an investigation of possible continuing contamination, both you and the company may face criminal as well as civil liability. You are also unsure about whether you should contact Cabrillo, who will be making sworn statements about waste disposal compliance in the course of permit renewal proceedings.

The CEO is a good friend of Sterling's, and you suspect that raising the issue with him will trigger a tirade against Bliss, who is known as a "whiner." You also worry that management will want you to put pressure on Bliss' counsel concerning his deposition strategies or his recommendations about potential cooperation with regulatory authorities. In the past, the company has taken the position that it will pay the legal expenses of employees who maintain that they are innocent of wrongdoing. However, management has been unwilling to subsidize the defense of someone who admits culpability and takes the fifth amendment or negotiates an individual settlement. As Sterling once put it, if "someone wants to shoot us in the back, why should we subsidize the gun and the ammunition?"

How do you proceed?

3. You are a partner at the law firm that handles HGC's environmental matters. You are working with the company's assistant general counsel to prepare Cabrillo for her final meeting with governmental regulators. Cabrillo has just learned of Bliss' allegations and is unsure whether she has any duty to investigate their accuracy and to disclose her findings to government regulators. Neither the federal nor state agency's administrative rules have explicit requirements to supplement or correct permit statements that were accurate when made. However, Cabrillo anticipates some questions at the meeting about whether she has additional information concerning the company's waste disposal practices.

HGC's assistant general counsel maintains that Cabrillo has no disclosure obligations based on one disgruntled employee's uncorroborated allegations of events occurring over a decade earlier. He notes that for every week the permits are delayed, HGC loses about a quarter of a million dollars in projected sales revenues. Given the heightened sensitivity that the civil suit has generated, any disclosure to the agency is likely to trigger substantial adverse publicity, delays, and legal costs. If an investigation corroborates any aspect of Bliss' story, the chances of civil and criminal liability also escalate. Accordingly, the assistant general counsel recommends that Cabrillo confine herself to "facts" and indicate that her office has no data on waste discharges beyond what she has provided. By restricting her statements to records available for certain periods, she can avoid disclosing Bliss' allegations and prevent a "feeding frenzy" among plaintiffs. Since an adequate disposal treatment process has been in place since HGC acquired the property, Cabrillo can make truthful statements about the company's own safety perform-ance.

Cabrillo expresses concerns both about the possibility of continuing safety risks and about her reputation and liability if she remains silent. Even if she is under no legal duty to disclose Bliss' allegations, her credibility with the agency and her career in environmental compliance would be destroyed if those assertions ever became public and she had done nothing to assess their accuracy. She also recalls the criticism targeted at management in prior environmental cases such as those involving asbestos and Love Canal. She does not want to share a similar fate. If someone writes a sequel to Jonathan Harr's A Civil Action (1996), Cabrillo does not want to discover herself in a prominent role. But she is equally concerned that any full-fledged investigation would violate the corporation's joint defense agreement, cause Bliss to go public, and expose the limitations of her own prior monitoring efforts. As the assistant general counsel notes, such an investigation would also delay the permits and increase the risk of a crippling liability judgment against the company. What do you advise her to do?

Cabrillo would like you to attend the meeting with regulators in order to ensure that she can invoke an "advice of counsel" defense to any subsequent claims against her personally. You and the assistant general counsel are reluctant to agree. He points out that a lawyer's presence at this usually pro forma stage of the process is quite unusual and is likely to wave a red flag. Cabrillo responds that the civil suit has already had that effect. You, however, have further concerns that the greater your involvement in the regulatory process, the greater your own potential liability. In two recent cases, one involving a savings and loan proceeding and the other involving an environmental clean-up, prose-cutors sought to hold attorneys liable for not disclosing their clients' misconduct. No court has ruled on the scope of lawyers' accountability under circumstances analogous to those facing HGC, but you are reluctant to become part of a test case. Yet you are also reluctant to let personal liability concerns color your representation, and if you were in Cabrillo's position, you would want an outside lawyer present as well. How do you proceed?[36]

See Chapter VI, Confidentiality and Client Counseling
- Destruction and Disclosure of Evidence
    (pages 239–251)
- Whistle-Blowing in Organizational Contexts
    (pages 278–292)

See Chapter IX, The Lawyer-Client Relationship
- Part B. The Counseling Role
    (pages 390–398)

2.   Impeachment

PROBLEM 15D

You are one of the lawyers defending A.H. Robins in some of the 14,000 cases filed by Dalkon Shield users. "Wicking" action by the Shield caused dangerous bacteria to accumulate in the uterus of some wearers, causing pelvic inflammatory disease. The result was stillbirths, hysterectomies, sterilization, infants with congenital defects, and, occasionally, death. Certain sexual activities can enhance the environment for the disease, even if they do not cause it. Some judges have accordingly permitted pretrial inquiries on virtually all aspects of women's sexual histories; other courts have required a connection between the questions and the injuries alleged.

Your colleagues have found that extensive inquiries concerning plaintiffs' sexual partners and practices tend to discourage claims and to encourage early settlement. Effective questions have included the age at which women became sexually active, their use of devices such as vibrators, and any sexual problems prior to use of the Shield. When you object to such questions, your colleagues accuse you of imposing your own personal morality on a company verging on bankruptcy. They insist that any limitations on effective cross-examination should come from judges, not from counsel hired to provide a vigorous defense.[37]

How do you respond?

2. Consider the strategies of lawyers defending sex harassment cases described in Problem 10B in Chapter X (Civil Procedure) at page 434. When questioned by a reporter concerning his intrusive questioning of a plaintiff, one lawyer responded, "I may feel uncomfortable doing it. It's certainly something I'd prefer not to do—but I don't allow myself the luxury of regret."[38] Should he?

3.   Misleading the Witness

PROBLEM 15E

1. You are a member of the Hawaii Supreme Court hearing an appeal of disciplinary sanctions. The charges involve a defense attorney's impeachment of the prosecution's expert witness through deception. By substituting a fake document for an exhibit with the defendant's handwriting, counsel succeeded in having the expert inaccurately identify the fake as the defendant's writing. In a divided opinion, the lower court suspended the attorney for ten days. Even though the defendants were "on trial for their lives," the majority found the use of falsehood unjustifiable. One judge dissented on the ground that the attorney had experience in handwriting analysis and believed that his client had not written the incriminating material in the exhibit. Thus, his purpose

was not the evil one of misleading the jury as to a fact which he knew existed, but the laudable one of exposing what he believed to be an erroneous opinion. This was in the interest of justice and not against it. [The attorney] also testified that he had been unable after a long cross examination of [the expert] to discredit his opinion and there was no other handwriting expert available whom he could consult or to whose opinion he could submit writings. His only alternative therefore was in some way to lead [the expert] to disclose his own fallibility.[39]

How would you vote? Suppose that the reason no other expert was available was that the defendant could not afford to bring a witness over from the mainland?

2. What if the defense attorney, rather than switching the exhibits, had asked the witness about his familiarity with leading treatises, and had included both well-known and fictitious authorities? After the witness claimed to have studied a non-existent book, the attorney revealed that fact to the jury.[40] Would sanctions be appropriate?

––––––––––––––

In a case similar to Problem 15E, United States v. Thoreen, 653 F.2d 1332 (9th Cir. 1981), the lawyer had a man resembling the defendant sit at counsel's table while the defendant sat with the general audience. Counsel consulted with the look-alike and did not correct the trial judge when he referred to the look-alike as the defendant. Various witnesses identified the look-alike as the person involved in the crime. Although the defendant was ultimately convicted, counsel's conduct caused considerable delays and confusion. In upholding a criminal contempt finding against the lawyer, the appellate court reasoned that his conduct "crossed over the line from zealous advocacy to actual obstruction." Not only had counsel violated a court custom, he had delayed and impeded the search for truth. 653 F.2d at 1339. Other courts have reached similar conclusions on similar facts and have suggested that counsel should request the judge's permission for such tactics.[41] Under what circumstance do you believe courts would, and should, grant such permission?

Consider the following practice described in Mark Lazerson's study of the Bronx Housing Court. Before bringing a summary eviction proceeding, landlords had to make an oral or written demand for rent. As Lazerson explains:

Landlords usually do not mail such a notice because of the problems involved in proving delivery. Nor do they make the demand by telephone because many tenants either have no telephone or unlisted numbers and lawyers have difficulty developing the necessary foundation for telephone testimony. Thus most landlords or their agents testified that they had personally visited the tenant at the apartment to demand the rent. In a substantial number of cases this was a lie. Such casual perjury may have been encouraged by the fact that both court officials and landlords viewed summary proceedings as a collection machinery, not as a fact-finding inquiry, and that hearing officers consistently discredited the assertions by poor black or Hispanic tenants that they had never received a rent demand.

Legal Services [lawyers] responded by having someone other than the tenant sit at the defense table. When examined, the landlord invariably pointed to the individual at the defense table as the one upon whom the demand had been made. Once the real tenant was identified in the spectator's section, pandemonium would erupt in the hearing room. This tactic never resulted in a perjury indictment against landlords; landlord criminality was not a major concern of the Bronx district attorney's office. But it did have an effect on the hearing officers. If their tacit assumption that tenants lie and landlords tell the truth was only slightly shaken, it did make them realize that the litigation skills of [South Bronx Legal Services] could prove an embarrassment to the Housing Court.[42]

If you had been a hearing officer, how would you have responded? Would you have recommended either perjury charges against the landlords or disciplinary proceedings against the attorneys?

4.   The Role of Experts

PROBLEM 15F

You represent plaintiffs on a contingent fee basis in a product liability claim. They have a strong case but are unable to afford the costs of litigation. You explain that the bar's ethics code requires them to remain liable for all costs but that, as a practical matter, you would not seek to recover any expenses unless the suit is successful. Is such a practice permissible? Can you describe the plaintiffs' circumstances to your expert witness and indicate your hope that she would not seek to collect her fee if the claim is unsuccessful?

Anglo-American courts have long recognized a need for expert testimony; physicians, for example, have offered such evidence since at least the fourteenth century.[43] However, in recent years, reliance on experts has increased, partly in response to the growing technical complexity of many cases. For example, specialists from various fields provide testimony concerning the nature and cause of injuries, the appropriate standard of care, the reliability of evidence, and the sanity or dangerousness of defendants. To qualify as an expert, individuals generally must have relevant specialized knowledge that is based on information reasonably relied on by others in the field. The standard, as applied in Daubert v. Merrell Dow Pharmaceuticals, 509 U.S. 579 (1993), does not require that the expert's testimony meet with "general acceptance." Rather, it is enough that such evidence rest on a "reliable foundation." Id. at 597 (interpreting Rule 702 of the Federal Rules of Evidence).

In theory, experts are obligated to maintain an unbiased allegiance to truth, to respect the limits of their own competence, and to separate research findings from personal opinions.[44] In practice, such ethical obligations have been difficult to enforce, and the role of experts has been widely criticized.

Problems arise on several levels and are symptomatic of more general difficulties with adversarial processes. First, parties do not have equal capacity to hire experts, and poorer litigants suffer disproportionally from prohibitions on contingent fees for such testimony. Such prohibitions appear in DR 7-109 and in the common law of most states. Model Rule 3.4(b) bans any "inducement to a witness that is prohibited by law," which includes state common law mandates.

Although the purpose of these rules is to prevent experts from having incentives to shade their testimony, such provisions are hardly adequate to that end. Many witnesses have ongoing relations with the attorney who has retained them and do not request payment in cases that are unsuccessful.[45] As long as parties are free to shop for experts, some bias in experts' testimony is inevitable. According to some commentators, the current system does a poor job of exposing that bias because it encourages de facto rather than explicit contingency arrangements, and such tacit understandings are harder to explore in cross-examination.

A related problem is that lawyers select experts on the basis of how helpful they will be to a client's case, not on the basis of their qualifications or the merits of their positions. Thus, one consulting organization promises lawyers that if the "first doctor we refer doesn't agree with your legal theory, we will provide you with the name of a second."[46] This selection process inevitably skews the evidence that reaches the tribunal.

Experts who function as hired guns also may have greater credibility than they deserve. That was, for example, the objection to evidence by a Texas "Doctor of Doom," who by 1980 had testified for prosecutors in over 70 death penalty cases. All but one resulted in death sentences. In each trial he concluded, whether he had personally examined the accused or not, that the defendant was a remorseless "sociopath" who would kill again.[47]

Critics of the current system have proposed various reforms. Some commentators support the approach of civil law countries like Germany, in which courts decide whether an expert is necessary and, if so, whom to select. Typically, judges will make selections from a list approved by an official licensing body or another public agency. Parties may object to a particular choice on grounds of bias, and request appointment of a second expert or hire their own. Although such a system reduces risks of partisanship, it introduces other difficulties. Judges may be less motivated than parties to identify the most appropriate experts, and litigants may be unable effectively to challenge court-appointed witnesses even where opposing opinions exist.[48] Some evidence also suggests that fact-finders are best able to assess evidence when it is presented through adversarial exchanges rather than from a single source.[49]

In response to such criticism, some commentators have proposed a system in which courts could appoint a panel of experts from a list chosen by the parties. Alternatively, when parties cannot resolve a material issue, courts could establish a panel with one expert that they select, one that the plaintiff chooses, and one that the defendant selects.[50] Other less sweeping reform proposals include allowing explicit contingency agreements for experts' fees; encouraging more judicial appointments of experts under existing rules; and permitting only expert testimony that reflects accepted views among similar experts.[51]

Which of these possible reforms strikes you as most desirable? In rejecting a "general acceptance" standard as a prerequisite for admitting expert testimony, the Court in *Daubert* reasoned that "[v]igorous cross examination, presentation of contrary evidence and careful [jury] instruction . . . are the traditional and appropriate means of attacking shaky but admissible evidence." 509 U.S. at 596. Are those "traditional" measures an adequate response to the problems noted above? Should Congress consider overturning that decision by amendment of the Federal Rules of Evidence?

If you agree with the Court's holding in *Daubert*, would you permit the "vigorous cross examination" that occurred in Problem 15D? See also Chapter XIX (Torts) at pages 794–795.

D.   TRIAL PUBLICITY

See Chapter XI, Constitutional Law
- Fair Trial/Free Press Balance
    (pages 492–499)

E.   THE ATTORNEY-CLIENT PRIVILEGE AND CONFIDENTIALITY

See Chapter VI, Confidentiality and Client Counseling
- Part A. The Attorney-Client Privilege and Bar Ethical
    Obligations
        (pages 223–225)
- Part B. Justifications and Critiques
        (pages 225–229)
- Part C. The Moral Limits of Confidentiality
        (pages 229–232)

F.   THE LAWYER-CLIENT WITNESS RULE

1.   Introduction

Both the Code and the Model Rules prohibit lawyers from acting simultaneously as both advocates and witnesses under certain circumstances. Disciplinary Rule 5-101(B) provides that lawyers should not accept or continue representation if they know or it is obvious that they or other lawyers in their firm should be called as a witness, unless the testimony will relate to uncontested matters (including matters of formality) or to the nature and value of legal services, or unless refusal of the case would work a substantial hardship to the client because of the distinctive value of counsel's services. Disciplinary Rule 5-102(A) requires that if lawyers learn after undertaking representation that they or other lawyers in their firm ought to be called as witnesses for their clients, then they must withdraw from representation except under the circumstances noted above. However, if the lawyers will be called as witnesses by parties other than the client, DR 5-102(B) requires withdrawal only if it becomes apparent that the testimony may be prejudicial to the client.

Model Rule 3.7 makes no distinction based on who will call the lawyer as a witness and prohibits the witness from acting as an advocate unless the testimony relates to an uncontested matter or to the nature and value of legal services, or unless disqualification would work substantial hardship. Lawyers may, however, act as advocates when other lawyers in their firm will be called as witnesses, unless precluded from doing so by general conflict of interest provisions in Rules 1.7 or 1.9. For example, the Comment to Rule 1.7 explains that if there is a conflict between the testimony of the client and that of the lawyer or member of the lawyer's firm, then representation is improper. However, in all but rare cases, client consent can eliminate the need for vicarious disqualification.

These rules against lawyer-witnesses originated from the common law prohibition against clients testifying on their own behalf. It followed as a matter of evidence law that counsel who were acting as agents for the client should be subject to similar disqualification. Once the ban on client testimony eroded, other rationales for the advocate-witness prohibition developed, some based on interests of the client and others based on interests of opposing parties.

2.   Client Interests

The dual role of advocate and witness may create obvious conflicts of interest if the lawyer's testimony and the client's testimony are inconsistent. A related concern is that advocates will be ineffective witnesses because they will be impeached for bias and will have difficulty arguing for their own credibility. See EC 5-9. Some commentators find this rationale unpersuasive because the ban has never extended to former lawyers of the client, who could just as readily be subject to impeachment on the same ground. Moreover, if client injury were the only consideration, then many commentators believe that a client's informed consent should be sufficient to prevent disqualification.[52]

3.   Opposing Parties

A second rationale for the prohibition on advocate-witnesses rests on the interests of opposing parties. One concern is that opponents' lawyers will have difficulty conducting an adequate cross-examination of a witness who is also their opposing counsel. In part, the difficulties may arise from professional courtesy and in part from the lawyer-witness' presumed familiarity with what would be effective testimony. This justification has also met with some skepticism. It is not clear how often opponents in fact are disabled by professional politeness in conducting cross-examination. A genuine sense of courtesy might argue just as strongly against disqualification, which generally creates far more material hardships on opposing counsel than zealous cross-examination. Many commentators believe that the best response to impaired advocacy is to place incentives on opponents to obtain skilled and zealous counsel rather than to allow disqualification of a lawyer-witness.[53]

4.   Confusion of Roles

The Comment to Model Rule 3.7 suggests an additional rationale for discouraging the dual role of advocate-witness:

> A witness is required to testify on the basis of personal knowledge, while an advocate is expected to explain and comment on evidence given by others. It may not be clear whether a statement by an advocate-witness should be taken as proof or as an analysis of the proof.

Whether consciously or unconsciously, lawyer-witnesses may find it difficult to avoid slanting testimony. The prohibition on their dual role reflects considerations similar to those supporting prohibitions on advocates voicing personal opinions about the merits of a cause. See Model Rule 3.4(e) and DR 7-106(c)(3).[54]

Which of these rationales do you find most convincing? Under what circumstances is it "obvious" that lawyers must testify? When would the hardship to a client from disqualification be significant enough to outweigh other concerns? Courts vary in the importance that they attach to the relevant considerations. At one extreme are cases imposing a high threshold of necessity before a lawyer is subject to disqualification. These holdings require a lawyer to be "indispensible" or to have "crucial" information that is not otherwise available. Other courts have permitted disqualification if the lawyer's testimony "could be significantly useful" or if the testimony might "conceivably be used at trial."[55] Some courts are also more tolerant of attorneys serving as witnesses when the trial is before a judge rather than a jury. In your view, which of these approaches best accommodates the values at stake?

5. Vicarious Disqualification

The Code of Professional Responsibility subjects every lawyer in the firm of an advocate-witness to imputed disqualification. The Model Rules are more permissive and, in effect, limit vicarious disqualification to the rare situations involving non-waivable conflicts. See Model Rules 3.7(b), 1.7(b), and 1.10(a) and (c). In interpreting the Code, some courts have declined to apply the imputed disqualification rules literally in certain circumstances, such as where an entire prosecutor's office would otherwise be barred from representation or where the lawyer is a party to litigation.[56]

Which approach to vicarious disqualification makes most sense, given the justifications for prohibiting advocate-witnesses and the costs of overbroad application of those justifications? In response to the bar's protest of highly restrictive lawyer-witness case law, California adopted an ethical rule that permits such testimony with client consent. Is that a preferable strategy?[57] What would be its costs?

Endnotes

1. Sabella v. Southern Pac. Co., 449 P.2d 750, 753 (Cal. 1969).

2. Jeffrey O'Connell, Ending Insult to Injury 6 (1975); Lawyer Fined for Natural Charisma, Natl. L.J., July 8, 1997, at A8.

3. Principe v. Assay Partners, 586 N.Y.S.2d 182, 184 (N.Y. Sup. Ct. 1992); Daniel Wise, Attorney Sanctioned for Sexist Insults, N.Y.L.J., May 8, 1992, at 1.

4. Robert S. Anson, Why Fast Eddie Williams Keeps on Running, 1 Am. Law., May 1979, at 1, 25 (describing Edward Bennett William's defense of Teamster boss Jimmy Hoffa).

5. Ellen Yaroshefsky, Balancing Victim's Rights and Vigorous Advocacy for the Defendant, Ann. Surv. Am. L. 135, 149 (1989).

6. Stephen Wermiel, Lawyers' Public Image Is Dreadful, Spurring Concern by Attorneys, Wall St. J., Oct. 11, 1983, at A1 (quoting Allen Sheperd).

7. Roger C. Park, Proving the Case: Character and Prior Acts: Character Evidence Issues in the O.J. Simpson Case — or, Rationales of the Character of Evidence Ban, with Illustrations from the O.J. Simpson Case, 67 U. Colo. L. Rev. 747, 775 (1996).

8. Commonwealth v. Baranyai, 442 A.2d 800, 801 (Pa. Super. Ct. 1982).

9. Johnson v. State, 453 N.E.2d 365, 368 (Ind. App. 1983).

10. United States v. Garza, 608 F.2d 659, 662 (5th Cir. 1979).

11. Smith v. State, 516 N.E.2d 1055, 1064 (2d Cir. 1987), cert. denied, 488 U.S. 934 (1988). For other examples, see Sherri Lynn Johnson, Racial Imagery in Criminal Cases, 67 Tul. L. Rev. 1739, 1751-1755 (1993).

12. Marcia Clark, Without A Doubt 458 (1997).

13. Roland N. McKean, Some Economic Aspects of Ethical Behavior Codes, 27 Pol. Stud. 251 (June 1979); Phillip L. Schuchman, Relations Between Lawyers in Ethics and Advocacy 73, 93 (American Trial Lawyers' Foundation ed., 1978).

14. Raoul Lionel Felder, I'm Paid to Be Rude, N.Y. Times, July 15, 1997, at A15.

15. Harry Kalven Jr., A Report on the Jury Project of the University of Chicago Law School, 24 Ins. Counsel J. 368, 377-378 (1957). For similar findings, see Sharon Wolf & David A. Montgomery, Effects of Inadmissible

Evidence and Level of Judicial Admonishment to Disregard on the Judgments of Mock Jurors, 7 J. App. Soc. Psychol. 205 (July-Sept. 1977). For general discussion of reactance and the inadequacy of juror instructions, see D.M. Wegner et al., Paradoxical Effects of Thought Suppression, 53 J. Personality & Soc. Psychol. 5 (1987).

16. James Q. Wilson, Keep Social-Science "Experts" Out of the Courtroom, Chron. Higher Educ., June 6, 1997, at A52.

17. Compare Mark Curriden, Blowing Smoke, A.B.A.J., Oct. 1995, at 56 (describing increase in such tactics) with Roger Parloff, Race and Juries: If It Ain't Broke . . . , Am. Law., June 1997, at 5 (discussing lack of evidence)

18. Barbara Babcock, A Place in the Palladium: Women's Rights and Jury Service, 61 U. Cin. L. Rev. 1139, 1173 (1993).

19. Carey Goldberg, Simpson Again, Race Again, N.Y. Times, Sept. 29, 1996, at E4 (quoting Wendy Alderson).

20. Id.

21. People v. Johnson, 767 P.2d 1047, 1055 (Cal. 1989), cert. denied, 494 U.S. 1038 (1990).

22. Purkett v. Elem, 115 S. Ct. 1769 (1996).

23. Hernandez v. New York, 600 U.S. 352, 356 (1991) (affirming exclusion where victim and witnesses, as well as defendant, were Hispanic and prosecutor offered race-neutral reason).

24. Richard C. Reuben, Excuses, Excuses, A.B.A.J., Feb. 1996, at 20.

25. Babcock, supra note 18, at 1161 n.77.

26. Stuart Taylor, Jr., Bouncing the Jury-Picking Process, Am. Law., June 1997, at 40.

27. Standards Relating to the Administration of Criminal Justice, The Prosecution Function, Standard 3-1.1(c).

28. Dennis R. Suplee & Diana S. Donaldson, Reconstructing Reality: Preparing the Deponent to Testify, 15 Litig. 19, 22 (Fall 1988).

29. Id. at 21.

30. Id. at 22.

31. Id.

32. Id.

33. Id. at 23.

34. Daniel L. Schacter, Searching for Memory 115 (1996) (discussing research by Elizabeth Loftus).

35. Bruce A. Green, The Whole Truth?: How Rules of Evidence Make Lawyers Deceitful, 25 Loy. L.A.L. Rev. 699, 705 (1992).

36. This problem draws on a similar hypothetical fact pattern prepared by John J. O'Leary for the ABA Litigation Section meeting (Phoenix, Nov. 1992). For another hypothetical case raising comparable issues, see Stephen Gillers, A Fine Kettle of Fish (and Arsenic?), Am. Law, Mar. 1993, at 9.

37. This problem is based on the treatment of plaintiffs described in Morton Mintz, At Any Cost: Corporate Greed, Women, and the Dalkon Shield 194-195 (1985); Susan Perry & Jim Dawson, Nightmare 192 (1985).

38. Ellen E. Schultz & Junda Woo, The Bedroom Ploy: Plaintiff's Sex Lives Are Being Laid Bare in Harassment Cases, Wall St. J., Sept. 19, 1994, at A1 (quoting Ronald M. Green).

39. In re Metzger, 31 Haw. 929 (1931).

40. See generally R. Keeton, Trial Tactics and Methods 159-163 (1973).

41. People v. Simac, 641 N.E.2d 416 (Ill. 1994).

42. Mark Lazerson, In the Halls of Justice, the Only Justice Is in the Halls, in 1 The Politics of Informal Justice 152-153 (Richard Abel ed., 1982).

43. Jack B. Weinstein, Improving Expert Witness Testimony, 20 U. Rich. L. Rev. 473, 474 (1986); Robert Kargon, Expert Testimony in Historical Perspective, 10 Law & Hum. Behav. 15 (1986).

44. Committee on Ethical Guidelines for Forensic Psychologists, Specialty Guidelines for Forensic Psychologists, 15 Law & Hum. Behav. 655 (1991); Christopher Slobogin, Dangerousness and Expertise, 133 U. Pa. L. Rev. 97, 128-129 (1984).

45. Person v. Association of the Bar of the City of New York, 554 F.2d 534 (2d Cir.), cert. denied, 434 U.S. 924 (1977) (rejecting constitutional challenges to ban on contingent agreements with experts but noting that some experts do not expect to collect their fee unless the party retaining them is successful); Jeffrey Parker, Note, Contingent Expert Witness Fees: Access and Regulation, 64 U.S.C.L. Rev. 1363, 1387 (1991) (describing experts' practice of forgoing collection of fees from unsuccessful litigants).

46. Peter Huber, Galileo's Revenge: Junk Science in the Courtroom 207 (1992) (describing Medical Legal Consulting Service). See Patrick R. Anderson & L. Thomas Winfree, Jr., Pragmatism and Advocacy in Criminal Justice Expert Witnessing, in Expert Witnesses: Criminologists in the Courtroom 36 (Patrick R. Anderson & L. Thomas Winfree, Jr., eds., 1987) (finding that specialists who had been hired as experts were more advocacy-oriented than other specialists).

47. Charles P. Ewing, Dr. Death and the Case for an Ethical Bar on Psychiatric and Psychological Predictions of Dangerousness in Capital Sentencing Proceedings, 8 Am. J.L. & Med. 407, 410 (1983). See also Ralph A. Cohen, Dallas' Unreliable Expert Witness Testimony, For the Defense, Apr. 1990, at 8.

48. John H. Langbein, The German Advantage in Civil Procedure, 52 U. Chi. L. Rev. 823, 835-841 (1985); John H. Langbein, Comparative Criminal Procedure: Germany 76 (1977).

49. Steven D. Penrod & Brian L. Cutler, Eyewitness Expert Testimony and Jury Decisionmaking, 52 Law & Contemp. Probs. 43, 79-82 (Fall 1989).

50. Barton L. Ingraham, The Ethics of Testimony: Conflicting Views on The Role of the Criminologist as Expert Witness, in Expert Witnesses, supra note 46, at 178.

51. See, e.g., The President's Council on Competitiveness, Agenda for Civil Justice Reform in America 21 (1991) (proposing that expert's view must reflect widespread views); Parker, supra note 45, at 1378-1379 & n.83 (evaluating jurors' ability to identify bias and reviewing proposals for nonpercentage (i.e., hourly) expert witness fees contingent on the outcome).

52. Geoffrey Hazard, Jr. & William Hodes, The Law of Lawyering §3.7, at 406 (1988 Supp.).

53. Id.; Charles Wolfram, Modern Legal Ethics 378 (1986).

54. Hazard & Hodes, supra note 52, at 679; Wolfram, supra note 53, at 378-379.

55. See cases cited in ABA/BNA Lawyers Man. on Prof. Conduct, at 61:501 (1995).

56. Wolfram, supra note 53, at 387.

57. Rule 2-111(A)(4). Under Rule 2-111(A)(5), however, clients' consent may be insufficient if the testimony would be prejudicial to their interests. Comden v. Superior Court, 145 Cal. Rptr. 9, 576 P.2d 791, cert. denied, 439 U.S. 981 (1978). For subsequent discussion of the California approach, see Maxwell v. Superior Court, 180 Cal. Rptr. 177, 639 P.2d 248 (1982).

Chapter XVI

Family Law

Ethical dilemmas arise with greater frequency and higher stakes in family law than in most other areas of practice. The reasons are readily apparent. Legal issues involving divorce, custody, adoption, prenuptial agreements, domestic partnerships, and related issues carry considerable emotional freight. Parties often care more and experience greater difficulties making rational decisions than in other contexts. Moreover, many family law settings involve the interests of vulnerable parties. Children often are directly implicated but not formally represented. Lawyers' multiple, and sometimes competing, responsibilities to clients, to other family members, and to the system of justice more generally are the subject of this chapter.

A. THE LAWYER'S ROLE

1. Competing Perspectives on Divorce Practice

a. Introduction

Lawyers who specialize in divorce cases take quite different views of their professional role, as the following comments suggest:

In matrimonial cases clients are primarily interested in money. If you represent the wife, then your job is to get as much as possible for her. If you represent the husband, pay out as little as possible.[1]

Suppose I get a huge alimony for a wife and I know that it is more than the man can afford in terms of spendable income. Well the wife thinks it's wonderful and I'm a great lawyer in her eyes. But in a few years he won't pay it any more; he can't afford it. He was anxious to get divorced and wasn't too cautious, but now it is impossible. Maybe he wants to remarry. He's angry. He can't pay. The situation deteriorates. Why? Because the contract was not feasible to begin with. . . . I try for fairness in such situations, a settlement which can serve as a guide for my client for a long time.[2]

The first job of any good matrimonial lawyer is to try to get a reconciliation. If that fails, my first question is "What have you got on her?" Then, "What are our vulnerable points, how much does she know about them, and are they provable?" Immediately hire a private detective and have him dig for adverse information on your wife's personal life and spending habits. Meanwhile, let your wife know as little as possible about your income and assets.[3]

I am tough because I assume the lawyer who opposes me will also be tough. It is not my intention to stand in judgment. I am not a moralist. . . . As a lawyer I am a technician, a how-to man. . . .
    When I take a case I am not concerned with whether my client is right or wrong. As far as I am concerned, my client is always right.[4]

As an officer of the court, counsel will have (and indeed has) a clear and affirmative duty to reach toward this goal [of fostering the best interest of the child]. . . . Public policy certainly dictates that the attorney vigorously press for the appropriate resolution for the child.[5]

We have three techniques in a contested case, one is nasty and two are just abusive. . . . We enjoin him from touching all his assets before he knows about the divorce, first. Then we harass him like hell by delving into his business dealings and talking with his business associates. Finally, we haul him into court on every pretext. He gets tired of it happening every day.
[Question to lawyer:] "Do you ever wish you were in some other line of work?"
[Response:] "Oh no. I just feel I help people in trouble."[6]

[Question to client:] "[W]hat did he [the lawyer] do for you?"
[Response:] "He just drew up the papers."
[Question to client in different case:] "What if anything did this attorney tell you about the law of child support and the law of custody?"
[Response:] "He handed me some kind of pamphlet or brochure, which I don't even think I read."[7]

AUSTIN SARAT, LAWYERS AND CLIENTS: PUTTING PROFESSIONAL SERVICE ON THE AGENDA OF LEGAL EDUCATION

41 J. Legal Educ. 43, 46-53 (1991)

I. THE EMPIRICAL RESEARCH

For thirty-three months William Felstiner and I observed law-yer/client interaction in forty divorce cases in two sites, one in Massachusetts, the other in California. We followed one side of each case, ideally from the first lawyer/client interview until the divorce was final. We taped 115 lawyer/client sessions and interviewed the lawyers and clients about the meetings. We chose to examine divorce because it is an important social problem in which the role of law-yers has been and remains particularly salient and controversial. For the remainder of this article, I plan to examine briefly two causes of strain in the lawyer/client relation in divorce: conflicting understandings of the nature of the dispute and differing under-standings of the nature of the legal process. In fact, I will tell two stories, one about the emotional unresponsiveness of divorce law-yers, the other about their cynicism, and I will speculate about how both shape lawyer/client interaction in divorce.

Before telling the stories, two observations about the context of lawyer/client interaction in divorce are necessary. First, unlike the conventional image of the divorce lawyer as shark, the lawyers I observed were eager, indeed, sometimes too eager, to reach negoti-ated settlements. In divorce as in other areas of personal service practice, lawyers often try to cool out their clients and discourage the full assertion of formal legal rights. This is not to say that lawyers in divorce are cooperative or acquiescent. In the cases we observed, negotiations were quite adversarial. Nevertheless, lawyers work hard to sell settlement to their clients and to avoid contested hearings and trials. The negotiation between lawyer and client over how to understand the nature of the divorce dispute and the nature of the legal process is, in most cases, intertwined with the efforts of lawyers to sell settlement.

Second, lawyer/client interaction in divorce occurs against a background of mutual suspicion, if not antagonism, between lawyers and clients. Clients worry that their lawyers will be inattentive or disloyal. They are often quite frustrated by the length of time it takes to negotiate a settlement or obtain a divorce. They insist that lawyers attend to issues beyond those that are technically relevant, and they often regard lawyers' resistance to those issues as insensi-tive or inappropriate. For lawyers, divorce clients are an uncertain, if not difficult and dangerous, commodity. They are emotional, irrational, have unrealistic goals and expectations, and demand constant attention. Clients are volatile and unreliable; given their sometimes precarious emotional states, they must be treated quite gingerly lest they "explode." For divorce lawyers the client is the enemy, or, if not an enemy, then an uncertain and unreliable partner and ally. It is in a context of mutual suspicion that divorce lawyers and their clients negotiate a shared understanding of the nature of the divorce dispute and the nature of the legal process.

II.   WHAT IS THIS DISPUTE ABOUT?

Although no-fault divorce is the prevailing legal regime in California and an important component of the legal regime in Massachusetts, many divorce clients insist that the divorce dispute is really about who did what to whom and why. They focus their energies on, and attempt to enlist their lawyers in, constructing an explanation for the past and for the failure of their marriage that assigns blame and fault to their spouse. They are angry or hurt, they feel victimized or guilty, and they seek to bring that emotional material to bear in the legal process.

For lawyers in a no-fault regime, the question of who did what to whom and why is largely irrelevant. Because they regard the client's emotional agenda as volatile and dangerous, lawyers often avoid responding to clients' characterizations of their spouse or of some event during the marriage; they try to discourage the expression of emotion in or through the divorce and make a professional practice of being emotionally unresponsive to what are for many of their clients the central issues in the divorce. In this sense, "clients largely talk past their lawyers." Lawyers seek to define or redefine the divorce dispute by focusing on the financial rather than emotional aspects of the dispute and by trying to get their clients to think about the future rather than the past.

Client stories about the breakup of the marriage sometimes emerge when lawyers ask them to explain some aspect of their own or their spouse's behavior; more often, such stories are embedded in discussions of other subjects. They seem to emerge ad hoc, to be introduced out of context, or to take the form of editorial commentary. These stories are told with unusual intensity and interest, but lawyers typically respond with flat affect or by trying to move the discussion along. . . .

Consider, for instance, the following excerpt from a conference in Massachusetts between a woman and her male lawyer. The lawyer and client were talking about her future educational needs. The client responded by focusing not on the future but on the past, on her sense that her husband had discouraged her from pursuing her education and had emphasized her duties as a wife.

Client: There was harassment and verbal degradation. No interest at all in furthering my education. None whatsoever . . . If there was ever any time when I did need or want sex, I was subject to, you know, there I was . . .

Lawyer: Mmm uh.

Client: . . . When he undertook to lecturing me and I'd say, "I don't want to hear this. I don't have time right now." I could lock myself in the bathroom and he would break in. And I was just to listen, whether I wanted to or not. And he would lecture me for hours . . . There was no escaping him, short of getting in the car and driving away. But then he would stand outside in the driveway and yell, anyhow. The man was not well.

Lawyer: Okay. Now how about any courses you took.

The lawyer simply ignores the client's characterization of her husband. Although his "okay" may seem out of place in response to what he has just been told, it is part of his determined effort to get the conversation back on track. His response is typical of the way lawyers respond to clients' efforts to talk about the reasons for the divorce or at least to enlist a sympathetic response from their lawyers.

When discussion turns to the client's conduct in the marriage, clients emphasize their own innocence, vulnerability, and injury. They suggest that any undesirable conduct on their part was the product of provocation and duress. They attempt to blame their spouse and to present their own behavior as reasonable and justifiable. Lawyers generally do not challenge such characterizations nor do they generally validate them. Throughout their meetings with lawyers, clients insist that the dispute should be seen in the context of the marriage failure. Even though law reform makes such questions legally irrelevant, clients continue to think in terms of fault. Most lawyers resist by avoidance. Client and lawyers are like performer and bored audience: although the lawyer will not interrupt the aria, she will not applaud too much either for fear of inviting an encore. If lawyers were to join clients in the project of reconstructing the marriage failure and the moral standing of the spouse, they would enter a domain that is, in principle, irrelevant to no-fault divorce and that seems beyond their expertise. If they were directly to challenge client characterizations or to dismiss them as legally irrelevant, they would risk alienating their clients. Yet when lawyers refuse to engage with clients' efforts to give meaning to the past, clients often end up dissatisfied because they believe their lawyers do not understand or empathize with them.

Although divorce lawyers were reluctant to engage in the moral or psychological reconstruction of the marriage or the marriage failure, they were ready to engage in moral or psychological talk when they tried to negotiate an appropriate "legal self" for the client. This negotiation is necessary because the legal process will not or cannot deal with many aspects of the dispute. Thus, divorce lawyers typically stress the need to separate the emotional from the financial aspects of the divorce and stress that the legal process can only work well if emotional material is kept under control.

Lawyers present supposedly authoritative insights into the psychological dynamics of the divorce process and urge clients not to trust their own feelings. Clients are told directly and indirectly that they are unreliable judges of their own interests. Lawyers openly criticize their clients' emotionalism and urge them not to be short-sighted, not to act on short-term emotions. Sometimes the warnings are used to caution clients against making what the lawyers perceive to be unreasonable demands; sometimes they occur when lawyers warn against despairing or desiring just to get the divorce over. Consider the following discussion of a client's expressed willingness to waive spousal support:

Lawyer: . . . As I have told you, whatever you take out of this marriage has got to last you the rest of your life. Prince Charming just has not been known, you know, to come along and sweep up my clients.

Client: There's a lot of frogs out there . . .

Lawyer: A lot of toads, even more than frogs. Not only that, but if they sweep you up and take you to the castle, it's because they want you to sweep it. So you can't count on him coming along and saying, "Oh, you need money you sweet little darling. Let me help you. . . ." Hold out a little bit longer and don't just agree to, you know, giving him Grandma's undershorts and everything else, simply to get rid of him and be done with it.

As this lawyer sees it, the client will only be able to make an adequate arrangement with her husband when she can contemplate their relationship unemotionally. For the client, thinking about her husband unemotionally seems impossible. The program divorce lawyers present to their clients places marriage in the realm of property; clients, however, typically see property issues as insepara-ble from a broader context of emotion and blame. Although the market does not exhaust the client's realm of values, putting aside the context of emotion and morality is exactly what the law requires.

From one perspective, the effort to keep emotion out of the divorce may be just the sort of wise counseling that one would expect of divorce lawyers. Although it does exact an emotional toll, concen-trating on the instrumental, tangible aspects of the divorce may produce a more satisfactory disposition of divorce cases. Thus, divorce lawyers can be seen as helping clients who will in the long run be more interested in the economics of settlement than in the vindication of immediate emotions. Putting aside emotional matters may also serve the interest of lawyers untrained in dealing with emotional problems and unwilling to find ways to cope with them. It allows lawyers to sidestep what is clearly one of the most difficult and least rewarding aspects of divorce practice. . . . Clients, however, come to the divorce process expecting that their emotions will matter and that lawyers will care; they come away disappointed.

III. WHOSE LAW IS IT ANYWAY?

Clients bring to their encounters with lawyers an expectation that the justice system will impartially sort the facts, that the "truth" counts. They expect the legal process to follow its own rules, to proceed in an orderly fashion and to be fair and error free. Most clients begin with a fairly strong belief in formal justice; they want vindication, protection of their rights, a zealous advocate, and a conscientious third party. It is the job of lawyers to bring these expectations and images of law and legal justice closer to reality and, at the same time, to maintain respect for the law. . . .

Although lawyers might offer their clients a subtle interpretation of, or education in, the nuances of the legal process, they tend to offer cynicism instead. They "trash" the legal process, critiquing its key premises and criticizing the motivations and competence of judges and other lawyers. . . .

When lawyers bring rules into the foreground, it is generally to disparage them as useless or irrelevant. Judges and others, lawyers say, ignore relevant rules or find ways around them. One Massachusetts lawyer described the way judges deal with property: "[I]n this state the statute requires judges to consider fifteen separate things. . . . They just hear a few and then divide things up. Things generally come out roughly even, but not because the rules require it." . . .

Lawyers are equally critical of opposing counsel and of the tendency of the divorce process to be drawn out and to turn those who go through the legal process into victims. One lawyer counseled a client as follows: "It is wearing and tearing. Just how much wear and tear can you take?" . . .

As clients hear that rules are not central to the divorce process, sooner or later it must dawn on them that the purported technical expertise of lawyers is of limited value. Yet the cynicism of lawyers, even as it relegates rules to the background and stresses the peculiar dispositions of legal actors, prepares the way for an alternative defense of professional power, one based not on rules but on local knowledge, insider access, connections, and reputation. Lawyers suggest that what clients buy is knowledge of the ropes rather than knowledge of the rules; when they describe the legal system as idiosyncratic and personalistic, they endow themselves with the mystique of insider knowledge. They suggest that the service lawyers provide is experience with the personalities of judges and the back corridors of legal institutions. They imply a "private knowledge," the full details of which cannot be shared with clients. They try to impress their clients with their contacts and their reputation. One Massachusetts lawyer offered the following assurances to a client:

> Now, I think I have a good reputation with the registrar of pro-
> bate here. Judge Murdoch is married to, no, what am I saying. Judge
> Murdoch's sister is married to Bob's wife. My God, try again. His sis-
> ter is Bob's wife. Okay. They talk all the time. Bob likes me very, very
> much. We get along very, very well. And I have a good reputation in
> this court and I think it's going to get through to the judge.

Although this kind of talk may be intended to give clients a reason to
trust or at least depend on their lawyers, it may also create doubts
about the legal process.

IV. CONCLUSION

The emotional unresponsiveness and the cynicism of divorce lawyers
serve to enhance their power and control over divorce clients.
Because clients come to the divorce system with unrealistic expectations, part of the lawyer's job, as in any lawyer/client interaction, is
to teach the client about the legal process. Much of their interaction
in divorce involves the lawyer's talking the client into a frame of
mind "appropriate" to do business effectively. Clients come to the law
expecting concern for the things they care about and a rational and
responsive legal system. They want to believe that lawyers can
navigate them safely through the troubled waters of a divorce.
Clients want predictions and certainty; lawyers, however, emphasize
the undisciplined and unpredictable nature of the legal process.
Divorce lawyers are almost constantly on their guard against clients
who seek what cannot be delivered. Because they define the goal in
terms of property, divorce lawyers present the law as indifferent to
those parts of the self that are most salient to the client. As a result,
the legal process becomes at best a distraction and at worst an
additional trauma.

Is dealing with the emotionally insensitive and cynical divorce
lawyer beneath the dignity or beyond the competence of legal education? Some may dismiss the problems as unique to divorce practice
or to people who were educated at someone else's law school. The
problems may, however, be more common than we suspect. Indeed,
the more familiar and experienced lay people are with the legal
process, the less they like or respect it. Legal education needs to
confront the issue of client service. The client and client service
should become part of every course. Learning how to identify and
respond to the distinct problems and perspectives of clients is as
important for the future securities lawyer as it is for the future
divorce lawyer. Attention to clients and client service should become
a high priority for law schools and a pervasive part of the law school
curriculum. By investing in the education of lawyers in their cli-
ent-serving roles, law schools can do something concrete and positive
in response to the public's diminishing respect for the law and the
increasing malaise in the legal profession.

PROBLEM 16A

1. You are a member of the American Academy of Divorce Lawyers and generally subscribe to its Standards of Conduct, set forth at pages 691–693 below. When dealing with another member of the Academy, you typically exchange all discoverable material without formal requests, a practice that saves considerable time and money. One of your current clients is unwilling to disclose financial information that you believe is clearly relevant. However, despite your best efforts at persuasion, the client insists on remaining silent in the hope that the other side's lawyer will not specifically request the information.

How should you respond? Could you alert opposing counsel to the need to make formal discovery requests, or would this improperly betray a confidence of your client? See DR 4-101 and Model Rule 1.6. Alternatively, should you remain silent and allow opposing counsel to rely on a customary practice of automatic disclosure that you are not following in this case?[8] Are such customary practices desirable? If so, can they survive if lawyers disregard them at a client's insistence? Who should decide whether to disclose discoverable information without an explicit request? How much importance should you attach to your own interest in maintaining a reputation for fair dealing?

Would a reasonable compromise position be to inform your client that you intend to advise opposing counsel of the need for formal discovery and, if the client objects, to withdraw from representation? Should you have described your practice regarding full disclosure at the initial interview before the client retained your services?[9]

2. You represent a middle-aged woman who is deeply depressed about her husband's decision to terminate their marriage. For almost a year she has delayed making any decisions about a financial agreement in the unrealistic hope that her husband will reconsider. When opposing counsel intensifies pressure for a settlement, you press your client for some decisions. She becomes emotionally distraught and tells you that she can't bear a fight. She wants to accept her husband's proposal for an equal division of marital property and no spousal support.

You believe that if the case went to trial a court would order a property arrangement more favorable to the wife, given her career sacrifices and low earning potential. You also predict that the husband might make a better offer if you delay.

Can you drag your feet without violating any ethical rules? For how long? What reasons could you give to your client and opposing counsel?[10]

3. You are a partner in a law firm that accepts women but not men clients in divorce cases. Your firm has been sanctioned under the circumstances described in Problem 4B (Chapter IV) at pages 154–157. How do you proceed?

PROBLEM 16B

One of your current matrimonial clients is an especially anxious and lonely older man. He calls frequently for advice about matters somewhat related to his divorce, but you suspect that he primarily wants to talk with someone. You have made clear to him that all time spent in telephone conversations will be billed at your standard hourly rates. He says he understands and pays your fees regularly without complaint. The frequency of his calls is increasing, and the press of other work leaves you unwilling to return some of those calls.

How does your conduct square with the following ABA rules and Matrimonial Lawyers' Standards of Conduct? Should you be subject to any sanctions for failing to make prompt responses? Consider Austin Sarat's call for greater sensitivity to client needs. What strategies might an empathetic lawyer adopt in this case?[11]

MODEL RULE 1.1.   COMPETENCE

A lawyer shall provide competent representation to a client. Competent representation requires the legal knowledge, skill, thoroughness and preparation reasonably necessary for the representation.

DR 6-101.   FAILING TO ACT COMPETENTLY

(A) A lawyer shall not: . . .

> (2) Handle a legal matter without preparation. . . .
>
> (3) Neglect a legal matter entrusted to him.

STANDARDS OF CONDUCT OF THE AMERICAN ACADEMY OF MATRIMONIAL LAWYERS (1992): COMMUNICATION AND DECISION-MAKING RESPONSIBILITY

In no area of law is the relationship of trust between attorney and client more important than in matrimonial law. Clients come to matrimonial lawyers when there is a significant problem in the family relationship. Emotions often render rational decision-making difficult. Clients seek the advice and judgment of their attorneys, even about non-legal matters. Therefore, issues of communication and decision-making in the attorney-client relationship arise frequently.

STANDARD 2.6

An attorney should keep the client informed of developments in the representation and promptly respond to letters and telephone calls.

Comment

The duty of keeping the client reasonably informed and complying promptly with reasonable requests for information, includes the attorney or a staff member responding to telephone calls, normally by the end of the next business day. The client should be informed at the outset, however, that communications with the attorney are chargeable.

As the preceding excerpts suggest, lawyers in divorce cases play a variety of roles. Which roles a practitioner assumes depend in part on clients' objectives, but also on the attorney's own sense of professional responsibilities. Most matrimonial lawyers fall somewhere on a continuum defined by two extreme types: lawyers as bombers and lawyers as scriveners.

b. *Zealous Advocacy and Ethical Constraints*

At one end of the spectrum are "bombers," lawyers who identify strongly with the partisan role discussed in Chapter IV (Advocacy) at pages 131–147. From their perspective, the attorney's job is to get clients "the result they want . . . provided it's not illegal and can be done."[12] Since divorce rarely brings out the best in the human spirit, clients' anger and anxieties drive many of the tactics described above. Although no-fault procedural reforms and increasing judicial sanctions have helped to curb the most egregious conduct, a minority of cases present substantial opportunities for abuse. In these cases, lawyers for "warring husbands and wives have dropped the equivalent of tactical nuclear weapons on families, destroying all within range — children included."[13]

Consider the ethical prohibitions concerning such abuses discussed more fully in Chapter V (The Adversary System) at pages 186–195. Rule 3.1 of the Model Rules prohibits lawyers from asserting claims unless there is a basis for doing so that is not frivolous. Model Rule 3.2 requires lawyers to make "reasonable efforts to expedite litigation consistent with the interest of the client." Disciplinary Rule 7-102(A) similarly provides that "a lawyer shall not assert a position or delay a trial . . . when he knows or when it is obvious that such action would serve merely to harass or maliciously injure another." How would these apply to the conduct at issue in Problem 16A and the views of divorce lawyers' roles described earlier?

Consider also the barriers to enforcement of ethical rules discussed in Chapter III (Regulation of the Profession) at pages 69–73. As that discussion makes clear, neither courts nor bar disciplinary committees often have sufficient resources, information, or inclination to respond to abusive pretrial maneuvers. Richard Crouch, a former chair of the ABA Family Section's Ethics Committee, sums up the problem: "nearly all divorce practitioners criticize the bomber . . . but in the current moral climate nothing succeeds like success."[14]

Yet lawyers who accept this combative role often disserve their clients' long-term interests. Abusive tactics increase delay, divisiveness, and expense, which can undermine opportunities for durable agreements and cooperative co-parenting relations after divorce.[15] In recognition of this fact, the Standards of Conduct of the American Academy of Matrimonial Lawyers discourage highly partisan practices.

STANDARD 2.11 [COMMUNICATION AND DECISION-MAKING RESPONSIBILITY]

When the client's decision-making ability is affected by emotional problems . . . an attorney should recommend counseling or treatment.

Comment

. . . [A]n angry client may demand a course of action that will escalate costs, prolong litigation, irritate the judge and raise the animosity level, but a course entirely within his or her legal rights. Even though the ultimate decision must be that of the client, before accepting a clearly detrimental decision, the attorney should attempt to dissuade the client and, if that fails, urge the client to counsel with others who might have a stabilizing influence: family, friends, therapists, doctor or clergymen. When rejection of the attorney's advice is likely to adversely affect the client's interests, the attorney should document both the advice and the client's refusal to follow it. Such documentation makes the risk even more clear to the client and protects the attorney from subsequent allegations of complicity in the conduct. In appropriate cases, the attorney may withdraw from representation.

STANDARD 2.27   [CHILDREN]

An attorney should refuse to assist in vindictive conduct toward a spouse or third person and should not do anything to increase the emotional level of the dispute.

Comment

Although the client has the right to determine the "objectives of representation," after consulting with the client the attorney may limit the objectives and the means by which the objectives are to be pursued. The matrimonial lawyer should make every effort to lower the emotional level of the interaction between the parties and their counsel. Some dissension and bad feelings can be avoided by a frank discussion with the client at the outset of how the attorney handles cases, including what the attorney will and will not do regarding vindictive conduct or actions likely to adversely affect the children's interests. Although not essential, a letter to the client confirming the understanding, before specific issues or requests arise, is advisable. To the extent that the client is unwilling to accept any limitations or objectives or means, the attorney should decline the representation.

If such a discussion did not occur, or the client despite a prior understanding asks the attorney to engage in conduct the attorney believes to be imprudent or repugnant, the attorney should attempt to convince the client to work toward family harmony or the interests of the children. Conduct in the interests of the children or family will almost always be in the client's long term best interests.

STANDARD 3.6   [PROFESSIONAL COOPERATION AND THE ADMINISTRATION OF JUSTICE]

An attorney should cooperate in the exchange of information and documents whenever possible. An attorney should not use the discovery process for delay or harassment, or engage in obstructionist tactics.

Comment

. . . The discovery rules are designed to eliminate or reduce unfair surprise, excessive delay and expense, unnecessary and futile litigation, and the emotional and financial cost of extended and overly-adversarial litigation. In addition, pretrial discovery often results in settlements more beneficial than protracted litigation. In no area of the law are these benefits more important than in matrimonial law, where the necessity of future dealings between the parties and the interest in protecting the emotional and psychological stability of children necessitate avoiding unnecessary litigation and acrimony. It is in the interest of all parties (including the client) to assist, rather than resist, legitimate discovery.

In an effort to effectuate the interests of their clients, attorneys may be tempted to wear down the opposing party or counsel by means of "hardball" tactics. These tactics do not support the *legitimate* interests of clients, and are clearly improper.

Do these standards provide practical and appropriate guidance? How do they compare with bar ethical rules? Can either set of requirements work if opposing counsel believes in "bombing"? Should the American Academy standards be adopted by courts or bar associations? Are other informal sanctioning strategies appropriate? For example, should voluntary organizations such as the American Academy attempt to exclude lawyers who engage in hardball tactics?

c.   *Lawyers as Scriveners*

If lawyers as bombers occupy one end of the advocacy spectrum, lawyers as scriveners occupy the other. In many divorce cases, attorneys' primary or exclusive function is to provide basic legal information, prepare the necessary forms, and translate agreements that parties have reached independently into proper terminology. For some clients, lawyers assist a process frequently characterized as "bargaining in the shadow of the law."[16] Attorneys explain the statutory guidelines and legal norms that courts apply in reviewing agreements or deciding contested cases; the parties then work out their own settlements. In other cases, the absence of any disagreement or of any significant property and custodial issues makes extensive legal advice unnecessary.

According to the limited empirical data available, a large percentage of divorce cases involve only the most routine legal assistance. One study of uncontested Connecticut divorces found that 60 percent of divorcing couples reached agreement without assistance from an attorney and that only 3 percent modified their agreements based on counsels' advice.[17] Similarly, in an Illinois survey, the lawyers' functions that clients viewed as most important were providing legal information (74 percent) and preparing forms (70 percent). A substantially smaller proportion of clients relied on their lawyer for more extensive assistance, such as negotiation (38 percent), counseling (17 percent), and litigation (8 percent).[18]

The dominance of routine clerical and informational functions raises larger questions about the structure of divorce procedures and the nature of the lawyer's role. A wide array of evidence suggests that the current system is an unnecessarily expensive and unreliable way of assisting many parties in terminating their marriage. Some empirical research, such as the study by Austin Sarat and William Felstiner described above, finds that lawyers often provide skewed information about the legal process. Attorneys' overstatements of their own "insider" role and of judges' arbitrary rulings reinforce clients' dependence as well as cynicism. Other studies indicate that many lawyers do not provide adequate advice about financial and custodial issues.[19] In the only comparative study on point, individuals who received help from nonlawyer form-preparation specialists were more satisfied than those who received assistance from lawyers.[20]

Such data raise questions on several levels. First, do current restrictions on lay services serve the public interest? See Part B at pages 699–709. Second, do we need more effective structures of lawyer regulation? See Part B at pages 699–709. Third, does the current adjudicative structure make sense for uncontested divorces? In many countries, such cases are handled administratively, and, in most nations, parties can receive legal advice from government clerks or advice bureaus staffed by non-lawyer experts.[21] Would such a streamlined structure be desirable in this country?

d.   *The Counseling and Negotiation Role*

For some clients, lawyers provide crucial emotional support, psychological assistance, and referrals for appropriate counseling services. Many divorces trigger depression, anxiety, stress, anger, guilt, low self-esteem, and a profound sense of personal failure.[22] Yet individuals who experience such difficulties often do not obtain assistance from mental health experts.[23] Clients who are deterred by the cost or perceived stigma of therapy may seek similar assistance from their attorneys. Many divorce practitioners have the necessary expertise, experience, or simply distance from the divorcing party's situation to provide significant help. Their advice may encourage clients to take the long view, to place higher priority on children's welfare, or to obtain support from other sources. So too, individuals whose anger or guilt prevents fruitful communication with their spouse can benefit from having their attorneys conduct the negotiations.

Yet how effectively some lawyers perform these functions is open to question. Many law schools do not adequately prepare students for the counseling and negotiating strategies necessary in family practice.[24] Nor do many practitioners want to become enmeshed in the explosive dynamics that often accompany divorce proceedings. As the Sarat and Felstiner study reflects, attorneys who focus only on legal issues often end up talking past the concerns that are most central to the client. Participants are often occupied with "two different divorces: lawyers with the financial and legal consequences of separation and clients with the social ones."[25] This mismatch leads to the unresponsive counseling that Sarat describes, the patterns of unreturned phone calls that Problem 16B exemplifies, and the exceptionally high rates of client dissatisfaction with divorce lawyer performance that various studies document. In one such study, over 70 percent of women and 90 percent of men were disappointed or angered by their representation. Many felt "helpless and unimportant, victimized by their ex-spouses and their own attorneys."[26]

Of course, the emotional freight of divorce cases often places lawyers as well as clients in "no-win" situations. Attorneys readily become scapegoats for much of the resentment that parties feel toward their spouses and the legal process generally. Yet given the inevitable traumas involved in divorce, many experts believe that lawyers should not accept such cases without some special training for, and commitment to, the personal counseling role.

Conversely, other experts worry that if lawyers act as amateur psychologists, they may second-guess or substitute for more expert assistance. Feminists also have been critical of some divorce attorneys' patronizing and paternalistic attitudes toward their female clients, as well as some practitioners' failure to explore domestic violence issues.[27] By contrast, lawyers have sometimes been equally critical of feminist colleagues who, in their effort to empower women clients, reportedly lose sight of when "enough is enough."[28]

What is your view? Is a "little knowledge" of therapeutic techniques a dangerous thing, or exactly what family practitioners should, at a minimum, acquire? How would you counsel the lawyer with the needy client in Problem 16B and the lawyers in the Sarat and Felstiner study?

2. The Delivery of Legal Services in Divorce Cases

a. Non-Lawyer Competition

The simplification of divorce procedures and the rise in consumer activism has created an increasing market for self-help kits and form-preparation services. Surveys during the 1980s and early 1990s found that pro se filings in sampled counties accounted for between 40 and 60 percent of family cases. In some states such as California, summary divorce procedures are available for couples without custodial or complicated financial issues to resolve. In one of the only studies on usage of non-lawyer services, 70 to 80 percent of California pro se divorce applicants relied on lay form-preparation assistance.[29]

The organized bar's response to such competition has been generally unenthusiastic. Both economic and status issues are at stake, and acceptance of non-lawyer practitioners in matters such as uncontested divorces has implications for other substantive areas. The more the profession openly acknowledges that non-lawyers can effectively perform legal tasks, the greater the bar's difficulty in claiming special prestige, high levels of compensation, and regulatory autonomy. Particularly among attorneys serving primarily individuals rather than business, the desire to differentiate themselves from low-cost lay providers is likely to persist.[30]

Since the Depression, bar opposition to lay competitors has been expressed largely through prohibitions against the unauthorized practice of law.[31] Application of these prohibitions to divorce services has generated frequent controversy. Until the mid-1970s, many courts banned written divorce kits on the theory that they provided legal instructions "in lieu" of attorneys. More recent cases have permitted the sale of kits and typing services but not personalized legal advice from non-lawyers, including correction of errors.[32] This compromise has prompted continuing challenges because many customers require some oral assistance. It is not self-evident that their interests are served by doctrines requiring knowledgeable practitioners to refrain from answering simple questions or to complete forms with obvious mistakes.

This issue attracted increased attention during the Florida bar's campaign against one well-known service provider, Rosemary Furman. Furman, a former legal secretary, was found guilty of criminal contempt for violating a prohibition on providing basic advice as well as typing services.[33] In her view, the bar's action reflected self-interest rather than public interest: "Every time I make $50, some lawyer loses between $500 and $5,000." According to Furman, uncontested divorces "shouldn't need to go to a judge at all"; the current system is an "extortion racket of the first order."[34] In the aftermath of adverse publicity, the Florida Supreme Court promulgated a rule permitting non-lawyers to give oral advice regarding routine procedures and completion of court-approved legal forms.

In other jurisdictions, the increasing volume of pro se litigants and declining availability of legal aid have encouraged similar innovations, such as bar association and legal aid clinics or interactive courthouse computer services for unrepresented parties.[35] Recent surveys of family courts find that around two-thirds of litigants have no lawyer.[36] A significant number of these individuals experience difficulties due to the lack of affordable assistance.[37]

In the United States, divorce-related services are less readily available for low- and middle-income individuals than in many nations. Most countries do not prohibit oral advice by non-lawyers and some handle uncontested divorces through simple administrative procedures.[38] Whether the United States should follow suit is an issue worth closer consideration.

In advocating such reforms, commentators stress several points. First, current legal aid programs meet only a small part of the need for divorce-related services and the wait for assistance is often quite long, even for cases involving domestic violence.[39] Second, existing research suggests no persuasive justification for restricting uncontested divorce services to lawyers. Three years of law school or passage of a bar exam appears neither a necessary nor sufficient guarantee of competence in counseling or form-processing skills. Studies of uncontested divorce practice do not reflect greater evidence of incompetence among non-lawyers than lawyers.[40] Not only are consumer complaints regarding lay specialists infrequent, but the only survey to date of customer satisfaction found higher rates of satisfaction with assistance from lay specialists than from lawyers.[41]

Third, concerns about incompetent or unethical assistance could be addressed by measures short of prohibiting all lay practice. Such measures could include effective consumer complaint mechanisms, client security funds, mandatory malpractice insurance, and, if necessary, limited licensing or registration systems for non-lawyer providers.[42] Finally, although increased competition may adversely affect some lawyers, consumers will benefit from the pressures toward increased efficiency. And the legal profession's public image is also likely to improve if the organized bar abandons self-serving efforts to police its own monopoly.

Are you persuaded by these arguments? If you were a state policy-maker, how would you regulate non-lawyer services?

b.   Fees

Lawyers' fees in divorce and custody contexts give rise to a number of ethical concerns. Some are common to all areas of practice, and some have particular force in family cases. Bar committees report that the number of fee disputes arising in family law practice are several times greater than those in any other field.[43] Several factors account for that disparity. Many divorce clients are legally unsophisticated and psychologically vulnerable; they lack ongoing relationships with their lawyers, experience with billing practices, and emotional detachment in assessing the costs and benefits of various strategies. If, as is often the case, the divorce has an unhappy ending, lawyers are a convenient, though often unjustified, target for blame.

Further problems arise from limitations and inequalities in parties' resources. The financially weaker party, usually the wife, may find it difficult to find adequate representation given the traditional bans on contingent fees or inadequate and long-delayed judicial fee awards.[44] All of these factors contribute both to special problems for lawyers in collecting fees and to special vulnerabilities for clients to over-reaching by their own attorneys.

Recent studies document both sorts of problems. Common complaints about lawyers' practices include:

- failure to itemize charges or to provide adequate information about probable costs;

- excessive charges for actions of minimal or no benefit (i.e., "motion churning");
- insistence on large nonrefundable retainers;
- coercive collection practices (e.g., pressuring clients into signing promissory notes or confessions of judgment, placing liens on homes, and retaining files or other personal documents without legal justification).[45]

Other examples involve the bargaining strategies described in Chapter VIII (Negotiation and Mediation) at pages 353–359, and an Illinois attorney's bills for time spent having sex with a client.[46] Such practices have contributed to the situation that one prominent practitioner describes: "Divorce may be a financial disaster for all but the wealthy, but it is a financial blessing for the matrimonial bar."[47]

Bar ethical rules offer general prohibitions on fee-related abuses. Disciplinary Rule 2-106 bans "clearly excessive fees" and EC 2-20 notes that contingent fees in domestic relations cases are "rarely justified" because of the "human relations involved and the unique character of the proceedings." Model Rule 1.5 requires that lawyers' fees be "reasonable," and that "where the lawyer has not regularly represented the client, the basis or rate of the fee shall be communicated to the client, preferably in writing, before or within a reasonable time after commencing the representation." Are these requirements adequate to deal with the problems noted above or would more specific prohibitions be desirable? What provisions would you suggest? Consider, for example, Standard 2.1 of the American Academy of Matrimonial Lawyers Standards of Conduct, which recommends that fees be written and be presented to the client in a manner that allows opportunity for reflection, consultation with another attorney, and answers to any questions.

Recent studies suggest that bar ethical mandates are inadequate because many clients do not know how or where to complain; disputes over fees can be unpleasant and expensive; and fee arbitration systems are not mandatory. In response to such inadequacies, groups such as the New York Department of Consumer Affairs have recommended a range of initiatives, and some courts have adopted many of those recommendations. For example, under New York's rules, lawyers must submit to arbitration at a client's request and prepare written retainer agreements specifying fee-related terms in plain language. Nonrefundable retainers are impermissible. Clients also must receive a standardized bill of rights that includes information on available complaint channels and clarifies their entitlements regarding fee arrangements.[48] Should any of these proposals be part of bar ethical codes or common law requirements? What other fee-related regulations would you propose? See Chapter XII (Contracts) at pages 524–529.

Is the traditional ban on contingent fees in matrimonial cases appropriate? Justifications for this prohibition include the desire to protect vulnerable clients from over-reaching and to avoid giving lawyers a stake either in discouraging reconciliation or in maximizing financial awards at the expense of clients' long term interests. However, some courts and commentators have questioned whether contingent fees in fact pose greater risks than hourly arrangements. Accordingly, some jurisdictions permit contingency arrangements in certain matrimonial cases, such as proceedings to enforce a divorce decree. If you were an appellate judge or bar ethics committee member, would you permit greater use of contingency agreements? Alternatively, would it be preferable to encourage more judicial awards of legal fees to financially vulnerable parties in divorce proceedings?[49]

3.   Antenuptial Agreements and Counseling Responsibilities

See Chapter XII, Contracts
- Adversarial Structures and Professional Constraints Involving Cohabitation Agreements
(pages 516–522)

4.   Representing Juveniles

See Chapter IX, The Lawyer-Client Relationship
- Paternalism in Juvenile Cases
(pages 387–390)

5.   Common Law and Community Property Issues in Estate Planning

See Chapter XVII, Property
(pages 740–741)

B.   NEGOTIATION AND MEDIATION

1.   Divorce Negotiations

PROBLEM 16C

The Smith Case

General Instructions for Negotiation

1. Class members should divide into teams of two or three persons, depending on the professor's instructions. Half the teams should repre-

sent the wife, Mary Smith, and the other half should represent the husband, Fred Smith. If the teams include three students, one should play the role of the client.

2. The wife, the husband, and their attorneys all have separate instructions, (available from the professor) as well as the joint factual statement below. Do not read the separate instructions for the other side until after your negotiation is finished.

3. After reading your instructions, meet with your partner to discuss the goals that you hope to achieve in the negotiation and the strategies that you intend to use. Your team should then meet with the opposing team, negotiate, and attempt to reach a settlement. Allow at least one hour for the negotiation session as well as additional time to discuss the outcome with your opposing team. Do not discuss the problem with other persons in the class until both you and they have completed negotiations. You should not know the terms of other settlements before your team attempts to reach a settlement.

5. If you reach a settlement with opposing counsel (subject, of course, to your client's final approval), you should sign and record the terms on the form provided. If you cannot reach a settlement, that also should be recorded, together with the last offer on either side, signed again by the four team members.

If students are playing the role of Fred and Mary Smith, each team should meet with its client following the negotiation. Allow at least one hour to discuss the proposed settlement and the negotiation exercise. Record the terms that the client will accept on the form provided.

6. Assume that your jurisdiction has adopted the Uniform Marriage and Divorce Act. Relevant provisions are included in your instructions.

7. After completing the negotiation, each pair of teams should meet together to compare strategies and address ethical concerns. Consider whether the relevant bar ethical standards of your jurisdiction and of the American Academy of Matrimonial Lawyers have been followed. If not, what factors made compliance difficult?

8. Write a short memo, no more than one typewritten page, describing the basic terms of your accepted or rejected agreement and the major ethical issues that you faced.[50]

Facts Agreed To by Both Parties

Mary and Fred Smith were married in 1977. At the time of the marriage, Mary had graduated from a two-year college program and was working as an executive secretary. Fred had just graduated from college. Fred then entered an MBA program and received his degree three years later. During this period, the couple lived entirely on Mary's income. They paid tuition through a combination of her income, student loans, and Fred's part-time student employment. Each of these sources covered about one-third of the school expenses.

After Fred completed the MBA, he took an executive position with a major international corporation. Mary left the paid labor force shortly afterwards. She cared for their two sons, did volunteer work for various church, school, and charitable causes, and helped her husband with business-related travel and entertaining.

Fred and Mary are now getting a divorce. Both are in their mid-forties and in good physical health. Fred is a corporate vice-president and is earning an annual salary of $350,000. One son, John, is 18 and about to begin college; the other, Mark, is a freshman in high school.

The major assets that the parties have accumulated are as follows:

Household furniture	$ 26,000
Auto, hers	7,000
Auto, his	19,000
Jointly owned home	450,000
Husband's pension and life insurance (present value)	400,000
Vacation condominium (husband's)	300,000
Cash, savings	20,000
Husband's stock in husband's corporate employer	20,000
Wife's stock (inherited from her mother)	20,000

The parties agree that the values stated reflect the fair market value of those assets. The couple also has a $150,000 mortgage on their home and an $80,000 mortgage on their vacation condo. Fred currently carries medical insurance for the entire family.

Under the law of your jurisdiction, courts may not grant a divorce until all questions concerning custody, maintenance, and property division have been decided, either by written agreement or by judicial order. Your state's supreme court has not ruled on whether a professional degree is marital property, and lower courts have reached conflicting results. Some decisions recognize no spousal interest in a degree, others reimburse the spouse's contribution or foregone alternatives, and a third group awards a percentage of future earnings attributable to the degree.

State law imposes no obligations to support a child over 18. Child support guidelines applicable to the minor son would probably require a monthly support payment between $1,000 to $1,200. Child support payments are not taxable to the recipient and are not deductible for the payor. Spousal maintenance payments are taxable to the recipient and are deductible to the payor. You may ignore the other tax implications of the settlement.

If the couple is unable to reach a settlement, the case will not proceed to trial for at least a year. Litigation costs are likely to range between $15,000 and $55,000 for each party, depending on which issues are contested. One of your jurisdiction's three family court judges tends to favor wage-earners over homemakers in property disputes. The other two judges are hard to classify, and it is impossible for parties to know or affect who hears their case.

Confidential Instructions for Husband's and Wife's Attorneys and the Clients and Uniform Marriage and Divorce Act Provisions

These materials will be available from your professor and are included in the Teachers Manual for this text.

2. Custody

See Chapter VIII, Negotiation and Mediation
- Candor in Negotiation: Representations of Fact and Value
  (pages 342–347)
- Fairness in Negotiation: Custody Agreements
  (pages 353–359)

Most divorce proceedings involve minor children. Except in a
small percentage of cases involving contested custody litigation,
their interests are not formally represented. How lawyers should respond to these unrepresented interests is a matter of long-standing
debate. Recurring problems involve clients who, consciously or unconsciously, want to use child custody and visitation as a bargaining
chip in financial negotiations, or who seek objectives that the attorney believes will compromise children's interests.

Reported cases rarely address these problems directly, and those
that do so reach varying results. In In re Marriage of Lauren A, 642
P.2d 1043 (Mont. 1982), the wife moved to set aside a settlement
agreement that she had previously accepted on grounds that its
terms were unconscionable, that her husband had threatened to
contest custody if she did not agree, and that he had implied that his
claim would include evidence of her adultery. In rejecting the wife's
petition, the court noted that "custody is frequently a bargaining
chip whether we like it or not." Id. at 1049. In the court's view, it
would be imprudent to encourage challenges of prior agreements,
particularly where the wife had advice of separate counsel. By
contrast, in Brockman v. Brockman, 194 Cal. App. 3d 1035 (1987), a
California appellate court ruled that a wife must have the chance to
prove that she was coerced into giving up substantial community
property in exchange for the husband's agreement to forfeit a
$100,000 bond if he ever contested a custody or support order.

How would you evaluate these decisions? Do existing ethical
rules adequately acknowledge the interests of unrepresented third
parties? Consider as an alternative the Standards of Conduct of the
American Academy of Matrimonial Lawyers. Standard 2.23 provides
that "[i]n representing a parent, an attorney should consider the
welfare of children," and the Comment explains that obligation as
follows:

> One of the most troubling issues in family law is determining a
> lawyer's obligations to children. The lawyer must represent the client
> zealously, but not at the expense of children. The parents' fiduciary
> obligations for the well-being of a child provide a basis for the attor-
> ney's consideration of the child's best interests consistent with tradi-
> tional adversary and client loyalty principles. It is accepted doctrine
> that the attorney for a trustee or other fiduciary has an ethical obliga-
> tion to the beneficiaries to whom the fiduciary's obligations run.

In particular, Standard 2.25 provides:

> An attorney should not contest child custody or visitation for either financial leverage or vindictiveness.

Its Comment states:

> Clients in contested dissolutions sometimes ask attorneys to contest custody even though they concede that the other spouse is the better parent. It is improper for the matrimonial lawyer to assist the client in such conduct. Proper consideration of the welfare of the children requires that they not be used as pawns in the adversary process. If despite the attorney's advice the client persists, the attorney should seek to withdraw.

Would (or did) you follow that standard on the facts of Problem 8A at page 342 in Chapter VIII (Negotiation and Mediation)? If not, why? If you believe that such a standard is appropriate, how would you determine what is "best" for the children?

The difficulties of policing "custody blackmail" through bar ethical codes, as well as the indeterminacy of best interest standards, have led many commentators to endorse the primary caretaker presumption that former West Virginia Justice Richard Neely advocated. Other commentators, including feminists such as Katharine Bartlett and Carol Stack, have argued that such a presumption carries too great a cost. It reinforces stereotypes that child-rearing is the responsibility of one parent, typically the mother, and fails adequately to acknowledge the children's interests in maintaining attachments to both parents.[51]

Some empirical research also casts doubt on the necessity or effectiveness of such presumptions in curtailing strategic custody demands. One study in Minnesota found that the primary caretaker standard was not as determinate as proponents had hoped. Where parents perceived the quality of their prior caretaking to be at issue, the rule proved highly divisive.[52] In response to such problems, the legislature subsequently eliminated the presumption. Another major study on point, Eleanor Maccoby and Robert Mnookin's analysis of 1,100 California families, found no statistically persuasive evidence of custody blackmail. The authors speculate that specific child support guidelines had dramatically reduced the possibilities for strategic bargaining. However, they also note that those guidelines do not made adequate provision for children's financial needs. On balance, they support a rule presuming that primary caretakers should receive physical custody on the ground that such parents have demonstrated and developed caretaking abilities.[53] Other commentators come to similar conclusions for younger children, in part because of the additional psychological cost to primary caretakers of losing custody.[54]

What is your view? What are the responsibilities of the parents' lawyers to protect children's interests? Should legal representation for children be more common in divorce proceedings? If so, what reform strategies would you propose?[55]

3.   Fairness and Disclosure Obligations in Mediation

See Chapter VIII, Negotiation and Mediation
   • Part E. Mediation
      (pages 360–367)

TASK FORCE ON MEDIATION, SECTION OF FAMILY LAW, AMERICAN BAR ASSOCIATION, DIVORCE AND FAMILY MEDIATION: STANDARDS OF PRACTICE

(1986)

PREAMBLE

For the purposes of these standards, family mediation is defined as a process in which a lawyer helps family members resolve their disputes in an informative and consensual manner. This process requires that the mediator be qualified by training, experience and temperament; that the mediator be impartial; that the participants reach decisions voluntarily; that their decisions be based on sufficient factual data; and, that each participant understands the information upon which decisions are reached. While family mediation may be viewed as an alternative means of conflict resolution, it is not a substitute for the benefit of independent legal advice.

STANDARD I.   THE MEDIATOR HAS A DUTY TO DEFINE AND DESCRIBE THE PROCESS OF MEDIATION AND ITS COSTS BEFORE THE PARTIES REACH AN AGREEMENT TO MEDIATE

Before the actual mediation sessions begin, the mediator shall conduct an orientation session to give an overview of the process and to assess the appropriateness of mediation for the participants. Among the topics covered, the mediator shall discuss the following:

A. The mediator shall define the process in context so that the participants understand the differences between mediation and other means of conflict resolution available to them. In defining the process, the mediator shall also distinguish it from therapy or marriage counseling.

B. The mediator shall obtain sufficient information from the participants so they can mutually define the issues to be resolved in mediation.

C. It should be emphasized that the mediator may make suggestions for the participants to consider, such as alternative ways of resolving problems and may draft proposals for the participants' consideration, but that all decisions are to be made voluntarily by the participants themselves, and the mediator's views are to be given no independent weight or credence.

D. The duties and responsibilities that the mediator and the participants accept in the mediation process shall be agreed upon. The mediator shall instruct the participants that either of them or the mediator has the right to suspend or terminate the process at any time.

E. The mediator shall assess the ability and willingness of the participants to mediate. The mediator has a continuing duty to assess his or her own ability and willingness to undertake mediation with the particular participants and the issues to be mediated. The mediator shall not continue and shall terminate the process, if in his or her judgment, one of the parties is not able or willing to participate in good faith.

F. The mediator shall explain the fees for mediation. It is inappropriate for a mediator to charge a contingency fee or to base the fee on the outcome of the mediation process.

G. The mediator shall inform the participants of the need to employ independent legal counsel for advice throughout the mediation process. The mediator shall inform the participants that the mediator cannot represent either or both of them in a marital dissolution or in any legal action. The mediator cannot act as lawyer for either party or for them jointly and should make that clear to both parties.

H. The mediator shall discuss the issues of separate sessions. The mediator shall reach an understanding with the participants as to whether and under what circumstances the mediator may meet alone with either of them or with any third party.

I. It should be brought to the participants' attention that emotions play a part in the decision-making process. The mediator shall attempt to elicit from each of the participants a confirmation that each understands the connection between one's own emotions and the bargaining process.

STANDARD II.   THE MEDIATOR SHALL NOT VOLUNTARILY DISCLOSE INFORMATION OBTAINED THROUGH THE MEDIATION PROCESS WITHOUT THE PRIOR CONSENT OF BOTH PARTICIPANTS

A. At the outset of mediation, the participants should agree in writing not to require the mediator to disclose to any third party any statements made in the course of mediation. The mediator shall inform the participants that the mediator will not voluntarily disclose to any third party any of the information obtained through the mediation process, unless such disclosure is required by law, without the prior consent of the participants. The mediator also shall inform the participants of the limitations of confidentiality such as statutory or judicially mandated reporting.

B. If subpoenaed or otherwise noticed to testify, the mediator shall inform the participants immediately so as to afford them an opportunity to quash the process.

C. The mediator shall inform the participants of the mediator's inability to bind third parties to an agreement not to disclose information furnished during the mediation in the absence of any absolute privilege.

STANDARD III.   THE MEDIATOR HAS A DUTY TO BE IMPARTIAL

A. The mediator shall not represent either party during or after the mediation process in any legal matters. In the event the mediator has represented one of the participants beforehand, the mediator shall not undertake the mediation.

B. The mediator shall disclose to the participants any biases or strong views relating to the issues to be mediated, both in the orientation session, and also before these issues are discussed in mediation.

C. The mediator must be impartial as between the mediation participants. The mediator's task is to facilitate the ability of the participants to negotiate their own agreement, while raising questions as to the fairness, equity and feasibility of proposed options for settlement.

D. The mediator has a duty to ensure that the participants consider fully the best interests of the children, that they understand the consequences of any decision they reach concerning the children. The mediator also has a duty to assist parents to examine the separate and individual needs of their children and to consider those needs apart from their own desires for any particular parenting formula. If the mediator believes that any proposed agreement of the parents does not protect the best interests of the children, the mediator has a duty to inform them of this belief and its basis.

E. The mediator shall not communicate with either party alone or with any third party to discuss mediation issues without the prior written consent of the mediation participants. The mediator shall obtain an agreement from the participants during the orientation session as to whether and under what circumstances the mediator may speak directly and separately with each of their lawyers during the mediation process.

STANDARD IV.   THE MEDIATOR HAS A DUTY TO ASSURE THAT THE MEDIATION PARTICIPANTS MAKE DECISIONS BASED UPON SUFFICIENT INFORMATION AND KNOWLEDGE

A. The mediator shall assure that there is full financial disclosure, evaluation and development of relevant factual information in the mediation process, such as each would reasonably receive in the discovery process, or that the parties have sufficient information to intelligently waive the right to such disclosure.

B. In addition to requiring this disclosure, evaluation and development of information, the mediator shall promote the equal understanding of such information before any agreement is reached. This consideration may require the mediator to recommend that either or both obtain expert consultation in the event that it appears that additional knowledge or understanding is necessary for balanced negotiations.

C. The mediator may define the legal issues, but shall not direct the decision of the mediation participants based upon the mediator's interpretation of the law as applied to the facts of the situation. The mediator shall endeavor to assure that the participants have a sufficient understanding of appropriate statutory and case law as well as local judicial tradition, before reaching an agreement by recommending to the participants that they obtain independent legal representation during the process.

STANDARD V.   THE MEDIATOR HAS A DUTY TO SUSPEND OR TERMINATE MEDIATION WHENEVER CONTINUATION OF THE PROCESS WOULD HARM ONE OR MORE OF THE PARTICIPANTS

A. If the mediator believes that the participants are unable or unwilling to meaningfully participate in the process or that reasonable agreement is unlikely, the mediator may suspend or terminate mediation and should encourage the parties to seek appropriate professional help. The mediator shall recognize that the decisions are to be made by the parties on the basis of adequate information. The mediator shall not, however, participate in a process that the mediator believes will result in harm to a participant.

B. The mediator shall assure that each person has had the opportunity to understand fully the implications and ramifications of all options available.

C. The mediator has a duty to assure a balanced dialogue and must attempt to diffuse any manipulative or intimidating negotiation techniques utilized by either of the participants.

D. If the mediator has suspended or terminated the process, the mediator should suggest that the participants obtain additional professional services as may be appropriate.

STANDARD VI.   THE MEDIATOR HAS A CONTINUING DUTY TO ADVISE EACH OF THE MEDIATION PARTICIPANTS TO OBTAIN LEGAL REVIEW PRIOR TO REACHING ANY AGREEMENT

A. Each of the mediation participants should have independent legal counsel before reaching final agreement. At the beginning of the mediation process, the mediator should inform the participants that each should employ independent legal counsel for advice at the beginning of the process and that the independent legal counsel should be utilized throughout the process and before the participants have reached any accord to which they have made an emotional commitment. In order to promote the integrity of the process, the mediator shall not refer either of the participants to any particular lawyers. When an attorney referral is requested, the parties should be referred to a Bar Association list if available. In the absence of such a list, the mediator may only provide a list of qualified family law attorneys in the community.

B. The mediator shall inform the participants that the mediator cannot represent either or both of them in a marital dissolution.

C. The mediator shall obtain an agreement from the husband and wife that each lawyer, upon request, shall be entitled to review all the factual documentation provided by the participants in the mediation process.

D. Any memo of understanding or proposed agreement which is prepared in the mediation process should be separately reviewed by independent counsel for each participant before it is signed. While a mediator cannot insist that each participant have separate counsel, they should be discouraged from signing any agreement which has not been so reviewed. If the participants, or either of them, choose to proceed without independent counsel, the mediator shall warn them of any risk involved in not being represented, including where appropriate, the possibility that the agreement they submit to a court may be rejected as unreasonable in light of both parties' legal rights or may not be binding on them.

Compare these standards for mediators with the norms for advocates set forth in Part A of this chapter at pages 681–699. What are the advantages and disadvantages of these different roles? If you were advising individuals involved in family law disputes whether to pursue mediation, what factors would you emphasize?

Is it plausible to expect any mediator to be entirely free of personal biases concerning the matters typically at issue in family cases? If not, what "biases or strong views" are subject to disclosure under Standard III? If the mediator believes that a proposed parental agreement "does not protect the best interest of the children," should the mediator have obligations beyond the disclosure responsibilities specified in Standard IIID?

C. CONFIDENTIALITY

1. Introduction

Chapter VI (Confidentiality and Client Counseling) sets forth rules governing confidentiality and the attorney-client privilege and explores their underlying justifications. In general, the attorney-client privilege prevents lawyers from testifying in court regarding confidential communications from clients. The Code and Model Rules prohibit disclosure of confidential information obtained in the course of representation, whether from clients or other sources.

These mandates also include exceptions. The privilege does not protect communications that are intended to further crimes or frauds, and bar ethical rules have similar limitations. Disciplinary Rule 4-101(C)(3) allows a lawyer to reveal "the intention of his client to commit a crime and the information necessary to prevent the crime." One version of DR 7-102(B), applicable in some states, calls on lawyers to rectify frauds perpetrated during the course of representation. Model Rule 1.6(b)(1) permits (but does not require) a lawyer to disclose confidential information "to the extent the lawyer reasonably believes necessary to prevent the client from committing a criminal act that the lawyer believes is likely to result in imminent death or substantial bodily harm."

Both the Code and Model Rules prohibit lawyers from assisting fraud (DR 7-102, 1-102(a)(4); Model Rule 1.6, Comment), and both allow withdrawal to avoid such assistance (Model Rule 1.16, Comment; DR 2-110(C)). Model Rule 1.2(d) provides that "[a] lawyer may not counsel a client to engage, or assist a client, in conduct that the lawyer knows is criminal or fraudulent, but a lawyer may discuss the legal consequences of any proposed course of conduct with a client and may counsel or assist a client to make a good faith effort to determine the validity, scope, meaning or application of the law." The Comment to that provision adds:

> There is a critical distinction between presenting an analysis of legal aspects of questionable conduct and recommending the means by which a crime or fraud might be committed with impunity.

When the client's course of action has already begun and is continuing, the lawyer's responsibility is especially delicate. The lawyer is not permitted to reveal the client's wrongdoing, except where permitted by Rule 1.6. However, the lawyer is required to avoid furthering the purpose, for example, by suggesting how it might be concealed. A lawyer may not continue assisting a client in conduct that the lawyer originally supposes is legally proper but then discovers is criminal or fraudulent. Withdrawal from the representation, therefore, may be required.

Model Rule 3.3(a) provides that

(a) A lawyer shall not knowingly:
(1) make a false statement of material fact or law to a tribunal;
(2) fail to disclose a material fact to a tribunal when disclosure is necessary to avoid assisting a criminal or fraudulent act by the client; . . .
(4) offer evidence that the lawyer knows to be false. If a lawyer has offered material evidence and comes to know of its falsity, the lawyer shall take reasonable remedial measures.
(b) The duties stated in paragraph (a) continue to the conclusion of the proceeding, and apply even if compliance requires disclosure of information otherwise protected by rule 1.6.
(c) A lawyer may refuse to offer evidence that the lawyer reasonably believes is false.

Disciplinary Rule 7-102 similarly provides:

(A) In his representation of a client, a lawyer shall not . . . :
(3) Conceal or knowingly fail to disclose that which he is required by law to reveal.
(4) Knowingly use perjured testimony or false evidence.
(5) Knowingly make a false statement of law or fact.
(6) Participate in the creation or preservation of evidence when he knows or it is obvious that the evidence is false.
(7) Counsel or assist his client in conduct that the lawyer knows to be illegal or fraudulent. . . .
(B) A lawyer who receives information clearly establishing that:
(1) His client has, in the course of the representation, perpetrated a fraud upon a person or tribunal shall promptly call upon his client to rectify the same, and if his client refuses or is unable to do so, he shall reveal the fraud to the affected person or tribunal, except when the information is protected as a privileged communication.
(2) A person other than his client has perpetrated a fraud upon a tribunal shall promptly reveal the fraud to the tribunal.

Finally, DR 4-101 permits lawyers to reveal confidences if required by law or court order, while Model Rule 1.6(a) similarly exempts from confidentiality "disclosures that are impliedly authorized in order to carry out the representation." Most authorities agree that this category includes disclosures required by law.

2. Disclosure of Assets

A common ethical issue in divorce representation arises when lawyers believe that their client has concealed assets or misstated their value, as in Problems 16C and 8B, page 344. Bar ethical rules clearly prohibit knowing assistance in fraud, perjury, or presentation of false evidence. However, they are less clear about what constitutes knowledge and what lawyers must do if they suspect but are not certain that their client has committed or is planning to commit fraud. Some ambiguity and room for discretion also arise concerning lawyers' obligations if they withdraw from representation after learning of clients' fraud.

In speaking to the first issue, the Comment to Standard 2.13 of the American Academy of Matrimonial Lawyers Standards of Conduct indicates that in situations of uncertainty a lawyer should initially give the client the "benefit of any doubt." However, a lawyer who later acquires knowledge of fraudulent conduct must avoid assisting such conduct and may need to withdraw from representation. More specifically, Standard 2.13 provides that lawyers "should never assist a client to hide or dissipate assets" and points out that such actions involve fraud on the spouse and are likely to result in fraud on the court. This standard is consistent with a well-established line of cases invalidating settlements based on misrepresentation of assets.[56]

Lawyers' obligations following withdrawal remain a matter of some dispute. One frequently cited divorce case involving fraud before a tribunal is In re A, 554 P.2d 479 (Or. 1976). There, the client testified at a deposition that his mother was in Salem. He neglected to mention that she was buried there and conveyed the misleading impression that she was still alive and might need his financial support. The lawyer could not persuade the client to correct the misimpression, largely because it might reveal welfare fraud. While his mother was still alive, the client had obtained public assistance for her support by not disclosing trust assets. According to the court in In re A, attorneys who cannot convince clients to correct a misstatement have an obligation to withdraw, but they may not knowingly disclose confidences.[57]

ABA ethics opinions interpreting the Code in its initial form held that when lawyers learn of false testimony after the fact, they may not disclose it. Opinion 341 (1975). However, amendments to the Code, judicial decisions in some states, and Model Rule 3.3 reflect a different view.[58] Under the ABA Committee's interpretation of Rule 3.3, "if, before the conclusion of a proceeding, a lawyer learns that the client has testified falsely, the lawyer must disclose that information to the tribunal." ABA Ethics Committee Formal Opinion 357 (1987). The Comment to Model Rule 1.6 also provides that the lawyer may give "notice of the fact of withdrawal" and may "withdraw or disaffirm any opinion, document, affirmation or the like."

How would you interpret these requirements on the facts of Problems 16C, 16D, and 8B? Under what, if any, circumstances should lawyers have obligations to investigate potentially fraudulent conduct and to "wave the red flag" when withdrawing after the discovery of fraud?

3. Custody and Child Abuse

PROBLEM 16D

Michelle Ramirez is representing a woman, Joanne Reynolds, in a divorce and custody dispute with her husband John Reynolds. The client wants custody of her two sons, ages five and eight. After a year of unsuccessful negotiations, the case will soon go to trial.

The client has recently begun living with a man, Sam Andrews, who has difficulties controlling his temper. After the lawyer learns of the problem through interviews with the boys and potential witnesses, she raises it with her client. The following dialogue then takes place.

Joanne: Well, Sam likes things neat and peaceful. If the house isn't clean or the boys act out, he can get pretty angry. It doesn't happen very often, but sometimes, particularly after he has had a couple of drinks, he has thrown things around.

Michelle: Has he ever hit you or the boys?

Joanne: Would that be important in my custody case?

Michelle: It could be quite important if Sam is abusing the boys.

Joanne: I didn't say he was abusing them. It's just that he gets upset sometimes. It's my fault for not keeping things neater and not making sure that they clean up and behave when Sam's around.

Michelle: Joanne, no children that age are going to be perfect. If Sam likes things neat, couldn't he clean up? In any case, I need to know more about these violent episodes. Has he ever hit the boys?

Joanne: I don't want to talk about this any more. I can deal with Sam, so just forget I said anything about this. John doesn't know anything about Sam's temper, and the boys aren't going to discuss it.

Michelle: Joanne, this is too important to ignore. I can't represent you properly if you don't trust me enough to give me the information I need.

Joanne: Well, Sam is a really wonderful man. But occasionally when he gets into one of his moods, he can be a little frightening. He's only hit me once, but he has lost his temper two or three times with the boys. He didn't hit them hard, but I'm worried about what might have happened if I hadn't been there. He's promised never to do it again, and I'm going to really pressure him to see a therapist if we can't work things out. But believe me, the boys are better off with us than with John who is always too wrapped up in his work to give them the attention that they need.

John Reynolds has challenged his wife's fitness as a parent on the grounds that her extramarital relationship, which began while they were still living together, reflects lack of moral character. He also claims that Sam is a bad influence on the boys, and that they lack adequate supervision. If his wife wins custody, John tells his lawyer, he plans to stop seeing his sons. "She'll ruin them both" is his view. The older boy never does his homework and isn't involved in sports or school activities. Both of his sons spend their free time mainly watching television and playing video games. John believes Joanne is too preoccupied with her relationship with Sam to provide appropriate discipline. John is about to marry a woman who is prepared to adjust her part-time hours to be home with the boys, which is "more than their mother will do."

1. If Joanne provides no further details about Sam's conduct, what are Michelle's responsibilities? Does she have any obligation to investigate his current behavior or his previous relationships for evidence of abuse?

2. Under what circumstances should Michelle disclose what she knows or suspects about child abuse? Assume that the law in her jurisdiction requires physicians and other specified professionals to report suspected child abuse to the state, but exempts attorneys whose knowledge comes from privileged communications.

3. Suppose that Joanne gives deposition testimony concerning Sam that the lawyer later learns is false. What are her obligations? Does it depend on how material the statements are likely to be? Suppose that Joanne describes Sam's caring relationship with the children and denies that he has ever physically abused them. Should it matter whether Michelle believes that John also has made false statements?

4. If Joanne or Michelle terminates the representation, what are the lawyer's obligations? If Michelle does not disclose Sam's abuse and he later seriously injures one of the boys, should the lawyer have any liability?[59]

How lawyers should respond to suspicions of child abuse has been a matter of substantial confusion and concern. The concern arises from the magnitude of the problem and the interests at stake. An estimated one million children suffer from parental abuse or neglect each year, and a substantial percentage are at risk for life-threatening injuries, mental retardation, learning disabilities, severe emotional disorders, and later addictive or violent behaviors.[60] Despite passage of mandatory reporting laws, recent estimates suggest that less than half of the cases of abuse and neglect known to professionals make their way to child protection agencies.[61] The confusion regarding lawyers' responsibilities when they suspect abuse arises partly from the conflicting and ambiguous scope of statutory requirements. By the mid-1990s, about half of American jurisdictions had misdemeanor statutes imposing liability on certain professionals, but not lawyers, for failure to report abuse. Most of the other states had mandatory reporting systems that either included any person or specifically included lawyers.

Statutes applicable to lawyers vary in their treatment of otherwise privileged communications. Some eliminate all privileges, some specifically preserve the attorney-client privilege, some provide that privileged communications should be exempt both from disclosure in court and from reporting requirements, and some leave the reach or applicability of the privilege ambiguous.[62] In the absence of concrete legislative guidance, commentators and state attorney generals have reached different conclusions concerning the effect of the privilege on reporting requirements.[63]

These ambiguities are further compounded by bar ethical requirements, which give attorneys discretion but not obligations to reveal future crimes (DR 4-101(C)(3)(1)) or future crimes that present risk of substantial bodily harm (Model Rule 1.6). Unlike exceptions to the privilege, which only allow disclosure of communications intended to further crimes, bar ethical rules authorize disclosure regardless of whether the client seeks to enlist an attorney's aid in illegal conduct. What complicates decision-making under these discretionary provisions is the difficulty of predicting future criminal acts from past abuse. Rarely (if ever) will individuals acknowledge an intent to engage in future abusive conduct. And although experts believe that a history of repeated abuse should raise a presumption of continuing risk, predictions based on isolated or borderline incidents are far more difficult.[64]

Several bar ethics opinions have confronted this difficulty. For example, New Jersey's Ethics Committee has ruled that "where an attorney for a parent has facts that demonstrate a propensity of that parent to engage in child abuse . . . the attorney-client privilege does not apply and the information must be provided to the Children's Bureau."[65] The Indianapolis Ethics Committee has held that attorneys have discretion to report a client's child abuse, although they may not be required to give testimony based on confidential communications. For attorneys who are unsure about the client's propensity, the Indianapolis Committee suggested consultation with an expert on child abuse.[66]

If you were a member of your state's ethics committee, how would you advise the lawyers in Problems 16D and 16E? Consider the standard justifications for confidentiality protections set forth in Chapter VI (Confidentiality and Client Counseling) at pages 225–229. One rationale is that individuals require lawyers' assistance to protect basic rights, and lawyers cannot provide effective assistance if clients fear to make candid disclosures. A related claim is that confidential communications enable attorneys to promote compliance with legal mandates; only if lawyers are knowledgeable about a client's affairs can they identify potential problems and appropriate responses. In the context of child abuse, other common arguments are that eliminating the attorney-client privilege will infringe clients' constitutional guarantees to effective assistance of counsel and protection from self-incrimination while providing only limited evidentiary assistance. As some commentators note, by the time the case goes to court, the state will normally have obtained sufficient evidence of child abuse without attorneys' testimony.[67]

Of course, the latter argument applies only to testimonial disclosures, not to disclosures in other contexts. Do any of the preceding rationales provide a sufficient reason for absolving lawyers from responsibilities to prevent future abuse? How should the rights of clients be balanced against the rights of children whose health and safety are at issue? Consider the empirical literature reviewed in Chapter VI at pages 226–229, which suggests that limited disclosure obligations may not have broad chilling effects on attorney-client relationships.[68] Note also that, in the context of child abuse, the rationale for encouraging candid communications may be stronger for mental health practitioners who are providing treatment than for lawyers who are providing less crucial forms of assistance. Since virtually all jurisdictions require health professionals to report possible abuse and neglect, should lawyers have similar obligations?[69]

Consider the following Standard of the American Academy of Matrimonial Lawyers:

STANDARD 2.26

An attorney should disclose evidence of a substantial risk of physical or sexual abuse of a child by the attorney's client.

Comment

While engaged in efforts on the client's behalf, the matrimonial lawyer may become convinced that the client has abused one of the children. Or the client, who seems a good parent, has a live-in lover who has abused one of the children. Under traditional analysis in most jurisdictions, the attorney should refuse to assist the client. The attorney may withdraw if the client will not be adversely affected and the courts grant any required permission.

It may also be appropriate to seek the appointment of a guardian ad litem or attorney for the children. . . . However, even the appointment of a guardian or lawyer for the child is insufficient if the matrimonial lawyer is aware of physical abuse or similarly extreme parental deficiency. Nor would withdrawal (even if permitted) solve the problem if the attorney is convinced that the child will suffer adverse treatment by the client.

In the most extreme cases, the attorney may reveal information believed necessary "to prevent the client from committing a criminal act. . . ." The rules do not appear to address, however, revelation of conduct that may be severely detrimental to the well-being of the child, but not criminal.

Notwithstanding the importance of the attorney-client privilege, the obligation of the matrimonial lawyer to consider the welfare of children, coupled with the client's lack of any legitimate interest in preventing his attorney from revealing information to protect the children from likely physical abuse, requires disclosure of a substantial risk of abuse and the information necessary to prevent it. If the client insists on seeking custody or unsupervised visitation, even without the attorney's assistance, the attorney should report specific knowledge of child abuse to the authorities for the protection of the child.

Is this a rule you would support? If not, what changes would you propose? Are other strategies for assisting children more likely to be productive? No adequate research traces the impact that reporting abuse has on children's long-term welfare. Nor have governmental authorities made significant efforts to sanction professionals for nondisclosure. Enforcement of reporting requirements confronts multiple obstacles: the difficulties of proof; the need to secure the professional's cooperation in the case against the parents; the belief that criminal culpability is lacking; and the unwillingness to encourage overreporting that would dwarf the resources of underfunded child welfare authorities.[70] Moreover, as some experts note:

> It is paradoxical to pay such close attention to professionals who fail to report suspected abuse while at the same time ... the child protective system cannot manage those cases which are reported. ... Mandated reporting of child abuse is [an inadequate] ... solution, focusing on damage control. Proactive steps, ... such as identifying and intervening with parents who are at high risk for abuse, will prove to be more effective and cost efficient in the long run.[71]

In the short run, if such proactive measures are unavailable or ineffective, how should lawyers respond to suspicions of abuse? If you believe that reporting is appropriate, how would you respond in other contexts where a past history of abusive behavior suggests some significant risk of recurrence?

4.　Client Perjury and Relocation of the Child

PROBLEM 16E

1. You represent a young mother in an acrimonious custody case. Your client claims that her eight-year-old daughter has made statements suggesting that she has been sexually abused by her father. Two experts, one appointed by the state mediation service and one retained by your firm, have failed to corroborate these charges. You have no independent basis on which to assess your client's claims. But since she has ample reasons to want to punish her husband, you suspect that the charges may be unfounded. If she insists on pursuing them in court, how should you respond? Is it enough to warn her that judges often penalize parents who allege abuse that cannot be substantiated?

2. Assume that your client is unsuccessful in obtaining sole custody and is extremely unhappy with the joint custody provisions approved by the court. A year and a half after the decree, she comes to you for advice. She insists that her ex-husband has physically abused the child

and has left her unsupervised for extended periods. Your client is also convinced that the father is turning her daughter against her. Even though the child's school teacher can verify evidence of physical injury, the mother does not believe that her charges would be believed if the custody proceedings were reopened. She wants information on the risks that she would face if she defied the court order and resettled with her child in another jurisdiction under a new name. In addition, she asks some specific questions about extradition treaties between the United States and Mexico. How do you respond? If at the close of your meeting, you believe that the client may well leave the country with the child, what, if any, action must or should you take?

3. If the mother does in fact vanish with the child and you are called to give testimony about her possible location, what are your obligations?

According to some commentators, perjury is common in custody proceedings because "[p]arents will do anything to keep their children."[72] And, given the stakes involved, some lawyers adopt a "don't ask, don't tell" policy.[73] They lay out the prohibitions and risks concerning perjury and avoid "knowing" assistance of misrepresentations, but they also try to avoid knowledge. In some cases, however, knowledge is inescapable, or fairness to the child and opposing party argues for greater obligations. Under what circumstances in Problems 16D and 16E should lawyers disclose misstatements or withdraw from representation? How certain should attorneys be before they present, or refuse to present, allegations of child abuse? If, as most evidence suggests, fabricated allegations of abuse are highly infrequent in custody cases, should that affect how lawyers and judges respond?[74]

Do similar considerations affect attorneys' involvement in abducting a child? Recent estimates suggest that between 25,000 and 100,000 children are kidnapped by a parent each year.[75] At issue in Problem 16E is how lawyers should respond if a client relocates a child contrary to a court order, or appears likely to do so.

Courts have divided over attorneys' obligations or discretion to disclose information about the client's location and intent.[76] For example, in In the Matter of the Appointment of a Guardian for Jacqueline F., 391 N.E.2d 967 (N.Y. 1979), a child's aunt attempted to evade a court order revoking her guardianship of the child and directing the child's return to the natural parents. To prevent such contempt of court, the lawyer for the guardian was directed to reveal the location of his client. In the court's view, the attorney-client privilege, "which exists to foster lawful and honest purposes, must yield to the best interests of the child." Id. at 972. Similarly, in Bersani v. Bersani, 565 A.2d 1368 (Conn. Super. Ct. 1989), the court held that the attorney-client privilege would not protect a mother who had fled the country with her children in defiance of the court's custody order. Under the court's analysis, two Model Rules permitted disclosure of the client's location: Model Rule 1.6(C)(2), which permits attorneys to "rectify the consequence of a client's criminal or fraudulent act in the commission of which the lawyer's services had been used"; and Model Rule 3.3(A)(2), which provides that "a lawyer shall not knowingly . . . fail to disclose a material fact to a tribunal when disclosure is necessary to avoid assisting a criminal or fraudulent act by the client."

By contrast, in Brennan v. Brennan, 422 A.2d 510 (Pa. 1980), the court reversed an order directing an attorney to disclose his client's location because there had been no adequate showing of the client's crime or fraud. The wife, who was seeking disclosure, had not established that her ex-husband had received notice of a custody conciliation hearing or of an award granting her temporary custody.

How should the attorney in Problem 16E respond to the client's request for information concerning her risks if she removes the child? Would providing such information constitute assistance in a criminal act? Should the attorney warn the client that the privilege would not shield disclosure of her location? Under what, if any, circumstances should the lawyer warn the husband about the risk of the child's removal? Does it matter whether the lawyer shares the client's conclusions both about child abuse and about the likely result of further custody litigation?

See Chapter VI, Confidentiality and Client Counseling
  • Part A. The Attorney-Client Privilege and Bar Ethical
    Obligations
    (pages 223–225)
  • Part B. Justifications and Critiques
    (pages 225–229)

D.   CONFLICTS OF INTEREST

1.   Joint Representation in Antenuptial Counseling

PROBLEM 16F

You are an attorney in the tax department of a large law firm. One of the department's major clients is getting married and wants you to draw up a prenuptial agreement. The proposed agreement provides that the parties will keep separate all of the property that each brought into the marriage. They will share any money that either party earns except income from property accumulated before the marriage.

The client and her fiancee come to your office to discuss the terms of the agreement. During the discussion, it becomes clear that the agreement greatly advantages your client. She is a wealthy artist. Her income comes primarily from investments on a trust fund from her parents, although she earns several thousand dollars each year from her

[handwritten: Lawyer can't effectively represent the fiancee]

art sales, and she is hopeful that such sales will increase. Under the agreement that she is proposing, the bulk of her income will continue to be classified as separate property since it will come from gains on property accumulated before the marriage. Her fiance, a freelance journalist, has few assets and generally earns a steady but quite modest living. Under the proposed contract, almost all of his income will be joint property.

What should you say to your client about the proposal? What should you say to her fiance? Can you represent both parties in the transaction? Either party? Would it matter to you if the reason your client wants to keep her assets separate is to leave them to a child from her first marriage? Alternatively, would it matter to you if the gender roles were reversed and the client were a wealthy man with no children?

[handwritten left margin: If joint rep, Lawyer would have to take a position against the client who hes representing in another matter]

[handwritten right margin: Fiancee must get full disclosure (informed consent) ↓]

DELOREAN v. DELOREAN

511 A.2d 1257 (N.J. 1986)

*[handwritten right margin: * does he know what she has? Under disclosure, he'd have to be told how much she's worth. What he'd be entitled to, absent the prenup]*

[At issue was an antenuptial agreement that the couple signed in 1973, a few hours before their marriage. Under its terms, all property, income, and earnings acquired by each before and after the marriage would remain the separate property of each party. The agreement also recited: "Husband is the owner of substantial real and personal property and he has reasonable prospects of earning large sums of monies; these facts have been fully disclosed to Wife."

After a thirteen-year marriage and the birth of two minor children, the couple sought divorce. Their potential assets could exceed $20 million, and in the absence of the agreement, the wife could have reasonably anticipated receiving approximately half of the property. She argued that the agreement should not be enforced because "(1) she was not provided with a full and complete disclosure of her husband's financial affairs before she signed it and (2) undue influence was exerted upon her by her husband who possessed far greater financial knowledge and experience than she." The court rejected those claims.]

IMBRIANI, J. [For the antenuptial contract to be enforceable, it must be clear first] that there was no fraud or duress in the execution of the agreement, or, to put it another way, that both parties signed voluntarily. The wife alleges she did not sign voluntarily because her husband presented the agreement to her only a few hours before the marriage ceremony was performed and threatened to cancel the marriage if she did not sign. In essence she asserts that she had no choice but to sign. While she did not have independent counsel of her own choosing, she did acknowledge that before she signed she did privately consult with an attorney selected by her husband who advised her not to sign the agreement. Yet, for whatever reason, she rejected the attorney's advice and signed.

While her decision may not have been wise, it appears that she had sufficient time to consider the consequences of signing the agreement and, indeed, although she initially refused to sign it, after conferring with her intended spouse and an attorney, she reconsidered and decided to sign it. Concededly, the husband was 25 years older and a high powered senior executive with General Motors Corporation, but she was not a "babe in the woods." She was 23 years old with some business experience in the modeling and entertainment industry; she had experienced an earlier marriage and the problems wrought by a divorce; and she had advice from an attorney who, although not of her own choosing, did apparently give her competent advice and recommended that she not sign. While it may have been embarrassing to cancel the wedding only a few hours before it was to take place, she certainly was not compelled to go through with the ceremony. There was no fraud or misrepresentation committed by the husband. He made it perfectly clear that he did not want her to receive any portion of the marital assets that were in his name. At no time did she ever make an effort to void the agreement and, of course, it was never voided. Under these circumstances the court is satisfied that the wife entered into the agreement voluntarily and without any fraud or duress being exerted upon her.

Second, the agreement must not be "unconscionable." This is not to say that the agreement should be what a court would determine to be "fair and equitable." The fact that what a spouse receives under an antenuptial agreement is small, inadequate or disproportionate does not in itself render the agreement voidable if the spouse was not overreached and entered into the agreement voluntarily with full knowledge of the financial worth of the other person. . . . So long as a spouse is not left destitute or as a public charge the parties can agree to divide marital assets in any manner they wish. Marschall v. Marschall, 477 A.2d 833 (Ch. Div. 1984). Mrs. DeLorean presently enjoys substantial income from her employment as a talk-show television hostess and was given a life interest in a trust of unknown amount created by Mr. DeLorean, which he testified had assets of between $2 and $5 million dollars. She will not be left destitute. The court is unaware of any public policy which requires that the division of marital assets be made in what the court believes to be fair and equitable if the parties freely and voluntarily agree otherwise. In the final analysis it is for the parties to decide for themselves what is fair and equitable, not the court. So long as a spouse had sufficient opportunity to reflect on her actions, was competent, informed, and had access to legal advice and that of any relevant experts, a court should not, except in the most unusual case, interject its own opinion of what is fair and equitable and reject the wishes of the parties. Since the wife voluntarily agreed to this division of the marital assets and she will not become destitute or a public charge, the agreement is not unconscionable. . . .

The only way that Mrs. DeLorean could knowingly and intelligently waive her legal rights in Mr. DeLorean's assets was if she was fully and completely informed what they were. And for Mr.

DeLorean to merely state that he had an interest in a farm in California, a large tract of land in Montana and a share in a major league baseball club fell far short of a full and complete disclosure. If this issue were decided under New Jersey law the court would conclude that Mr. DeLorean did not make a full and complete disclosure of his financial wealth before his spouse signed the antenuptial agreement and, therefore, it would not be valid and enforceable.

However, . . . the law of California must be applied in this case. . . . [U]nlike New Jersey, California does not treat a party to an antenuptial agreement as a fiduciary on the theory that "parties who are not yet married are not presumed to share a confidential relationship." Marriage of Dawley, 551 P.2d 323 (Cal. Sup. Ct. 1976). So long as the spouse seeking to set aside such an agreement has a general idea of the character and extent of the financial assets and income of the other, that apparently is sufficient in California. Indeed, absent fraud or misrepresentation, there appears to be a duty to make some inquiry to ascertain the full nature and extent of the financial resources of the other. As this court reads California law, the disclosures made by John DeLorean appear to be sufficient for purposes of enforcing this agreement.

In *DeLorean*, the court did not discuss the role of counsel for the husband. How would you evaluate the performance of that attorney concerning the terms and timing of the antenuptial agreement? How would you evaluate the court's reasoning that the wife's acceptance of the agreement was adequately informed, "voluntary," and "without duress"?

If you were the lawyer in Problem 16F, how would you proceed? Consider the observation of leading divorce practitioner Raol Felder: "Prenuptuals are pretty much exploitation devices for men against women."[77] Not all lawyers agree, but many acknowledge that such contracts can cause "a lot of rancor." People don't like prenuptuals because "love and law don't mix."[78] Other commentators point out that "neither sometimes do love and marriage."[79] If they are right, how should lawyers respond?

2. Joint Representation in Uncontested Divorces

Chapter VII (Conflicts of Interest) sets forth bar ethical rules governing joint representation. Under the Code, multiple representation is permissible only if it is "obvious" that the lawyer can "adequately represent" the interests of each party and each consents after full disclosure. DR 5-105(c). The Model Rules allow joint representation only if the lawyer "reasonably believes that the representation will not be adversely affected" and all parties give informed consent. Rule 1.7(2).

Application of these rules to divorce contexts has generated conflicting results. The traditional rule, reflected in the Standards of Conduct of the American Academy of Matrimonial Lawyers, has been that attorneys should not represent both husband and wife in a divorce even with the consent of both. Standard 2.20. However, the recent trend among courts and bar committees has been to permit such joint representation under certain circumstances, such as where no substantial property, custody, or support issues are involved, or where the parties have relatively equal employment and educational status and have resolved all financial issues.[80]

Other jurisdictions have allowed lawyers who represent one party to draft a separation agreement for the couple, provided that they make clear that they are not representing the other party and that the other party has full opportunity to obtain separate counsel.[81] In cases involving unrepresented parties, Model Rule 4.1 cautions that the lawyer "shall not state or imply that the lawyer is disinterested." When the lawyer "knows or reasonably should know that the unrepresented person misunderstands the lawyer's role in the matter, the lawyer shall make reasonable efforts to correct the misunderstanding." Standard 2.21 of the American Academy of Matrimonial Lawyers' Standards of Conduct provides that lawyers should not advise an unrepresented party. The Comment to Standard 2.21 further suggests that in dealing with such a party, the attorney should indicate in writing that the attorney does not represent him or her but will at all times look out for the other spouse's interests, and that he or she should obtain separate counsel.

Problems resulting from joint representation or from agreements involving unrepresented parties generally surface in three contexts: in challenges to the validity of the agreement, in malpractice claims, and in bar disciplinary proceedings. As a general matter, courts will not invalidate a settlement absent evidence of fraud or over-reaching.

Two cases at opposite ends of the spectrum are illustrative. In Levine v. Levine, 436 N.E.2d 476 (N.Y. 1982), the court declined to set aside a separation agreement prepared by an attorney who was related to the husband, who had previously represented him in business matters, and who had known the couple for several years. Under the court's analysis, the wife had failed to demonstrate over-reaching and unfairness. In so ruling, the court noted that the terms of the agreement were not manifestly unjust, and the attorney both had maintained a "position of neutrality" and had advised the wife that she could obtain separate counsel. By contrast, in Adkins v. Adkins, 137 Cal. App. 3d 68, 186 Cal. Rptr. 818 (Cal. App. Div. 1982), the California appellate court disapproved a settlement agreement that the wife's attorney had drafted. There, although the husband had minimal education and legal knowledge, the attorney gave him no opportunity to read the agreement, provided no explanation of its terms or his rights, and advised him not to hire separate counsel. If the husband had known of his community property entitlements, he assertedly would not have agreed to the settlement; accordingly, the court found fraud in its inducement. Difficulties arise in areas between these extremes, particularly if the lawyer makes factual or legal assertions that the unrepresented party later challenges.

Malpractice cases can present similar issues and the results turn on similar considerations concerning the parties' capacities and their lawyers' conduct. In one frequently cited case, Ismael v. Millington, 241 Cal. App. 2d 520, 50 Cal. Rptr. 592 (Cal. App. Div. 1966), the plaintiff signed a property settlement drafted by an attorney who had previously represented her husband and his business. The husband presented her with the agreement and she did not discuss it with the attorney, who was also representing her as the complaining party in the divorce proceedings. Although she knew that she was entitled to half the marital property, the agreement gave her a small fraction of its worth. In defending against her subsequent malpractice claim, the attorney claimed that he assumed that the wife "knew what she was doing" and that her loss was attributable to her negligent failure to make inquiries regarding the true worth of the community property. Id. at 524. In rejecting that claim, the California appellate court found that an attorney of "ordinary professional skill would demand some verification of the husband's financial statement; or, at a minimum, inform the wife that the husband's statement was unconfirmed, that wives may be cheated, [and] that prudence called for investigation and verification." Id. at 527. Without such disclosure, the wife could not make a "free and intelligent choice." Id.

Egregious cases of conflicting interests occasionally result in bar disciplinary proceedings. A representative example is Board of Overseers v. Dineen, 500 A.2d 262 (Me. 1985). There, the court upheld an attorney's suspension for six months based on his representation of a couple in a divorce action and his simultaneous representation of the wife on a drunk driving charge. In affirming disciplinary sanctions, the court emphasized that the lawyer had used confidential information concerning the wife's alcohol problems to the husband's advantage in the divorce proceedings; failed to make "full disclosure of the effect on his judgment of multiple representation"; failed to obtain written consent from the wife; and favored the husband's interests in legal advice and in drafting the agreement. Id. at 266.

Taken together, court holdings and expert commentary suggest several rules of thumb for lawyers in multiple representation contexts. Fully informed consent is necessary but not sufficient. Attorneys may be unable to provide adequate assistance to both parties where they have substantially unequal bargaining power, where one spouse dominates the decision-making of the other, or where the attorney's special relationship to one party makes the fact or appearance of neutrality difficult to sustain.[82]

How would those considerations affect your judgment on the facts of Problem 16F? If the attorney decides to provide joint representation, what precautionary measures would be appropriate?

3. Multiple Representation in Uncontested Adoption Proceedings

MATTER OF SWIHART, 517 N.E.2D 792 (IND. 1988). The lawyer in *Swihart* agreed to help place the baby of an 18-year-old unwed mother. She did not want to know the identity of the adoptive parents and did not want a couple from the local area, but she otherwise gave the attorney discretion to choose a suitable home. The attorney took temporary custody of the baby, and several months later he and his wife decided to adopt the infant themselves. They did not inform the mother of their intent. Rather, the attorney brought a friend, who was a lawyer and notary public, to the mother's house and waited in the car while the friend attempted to obtain signatures on forms consenting to the adoption. On questioning by the natural mother, the friend admitted that the attorney was one of the adoptive parents. The mother was confused but signed the forms, which erroneously stated that she did not know the identity of the adoptive parents. She subsequently sued to set the adoption aside, and obtained custody of the child.

In disciplinary proceedings against the attorney, the court found that he had failed to pursue the client's legitimate objectives, in violation of DR 7-101(A); had abandoned his professional obligations for the sake of a personal interest, in violation of DR 5-101(A); and had engaged in conduct prejudicial to the administration of justice, in violation of DR 1-102(A). In mitigation, the attorney claimed that his wife had formed a close attachment to the child, and that he had paid $4,000 in unreimbursed birth expenses and care of the infant.

The court imposed a 30-day suspension. Its opinion did not discuss the hardship to the natural mother or to the child.

PROBLEM 16G

If you had been the attorney in *Swihart*, how would you have handled the matter? If you had been the friend, what would you have done? If you had been on the court, what sanctions would you have found appropriate? If you had been the mother, how would you have wanted the court to respond?

Recent estimates indicate that close to one-third of all domestic adoptions concerning unrelated parties are handled independently rather than through state agencies. These procedures usually involve private attorneys, although the lawyer's role varies considerably, depending on party preferences and the law of the particular jurisdiction. In many states, attorneys may serve as intermediaries who put birth mothers in contact with possible adoptive parents or who select such parents based on specified criteria. Some of these jurisdictions allow attorneys to represent both the adoptive parents and birth mothers.[83] Such dual representation has both obvious advantages and obvious potential for conflicts of interest.

Recurrent problems involve last-minute changes in intent or differences between the parties concerning disclosure of potentially relevant information. Other difficulties arise if the attorney represents multiple couples who might wish to adopt the same child.

Matter of Petrie, 742 P.2d 796 (Ariz. 1987) (en banc), illustrates some of those problems. There, Gregory and Barbara Pietze contacted an attorney, Petrie, and indicated their desire to adopt. The attorney had no knowledge of infants available at the time but agreed that if the Pietzes located an infant, he would represent them. A year and a half later, the couple had a friend contact the attorney and provide information about a birth mother who was interested in placing a child. The attorney subsequently met with the mother and wrote to the Pietzes, who had moved out of the area. The Pietzes responded that they were interested in adopting the infant and were "very hopeful" that it would work out. The attorney, however, interpreted their response as "equivocal" because they had raised questions about the fees, time of birth, and natural father. Based on the attorney's recommendation, the natural mother agreed to place the baby with another couple that had sought Petrie's assistance. When he informed the Pietzes of that decision, they objected and subsequently filed a complaint with the state bar.

The bar commission found that the attorney had chosen the other couple because they were more cooperative than the Pietzes and were "locally situated." The attorney also was "not excited" about the prospect of making two appearances in the county where the Pietzes had relocated. In defending his actions, Petrie claimed that he represented only the natural mother, who had no obligation to the Pietzes. The Arizona Supreme Court rejected that claim. In its view, the Pietzes had every reason to rely on Petrie's statement that he would represent them if they found a child. Accordingly, Petrie was representing the natural mother and two sets of adoptive parents without informed consent in violation of DR 5-105. At the very least, the court concluded, once the conflict had materialized, the lawyer should have secured counsel for the Pietzes and withdrawn from representing any party.

Would that have been a satisfactory way of handling the matter? Suppose that the attorney believed that the other couple would make better parents and had so indicated when the birth mother had asked for advice. Would that have violated his obligations to the Pietzes? Would the attorney's conduct have been permissible if he had obtained written consent based on disclosures that he represented multiple adoptive parents and birth mothers?

In Informal Opinion 87-1523 (1987), the American Bar Association Committee on Ethics and Professional Responsibility concluded that a lawyer may not ethically represent both the adoptive and biological parents in a private adoption proceeding. In the Committee's view, the biological parents' rights to revoke consent are potentially inconsistent with the objectives of the adoptive parents and the "inherent conflicts [of interest] cannot be reconciled." Do you agree? Would you recommend a flat prohibition on joint representation or a case-by-case approach?

4.   Lawyer-Client Sexual Relations

PROBLEM 16H

You are a partner in a small firm that specializes in family, trusts, and estate work. One of your partners has been spending a considerable amount of time on a divorce settlement for the wife of a wealthy real estate developer. Last week you happened to see your colleague and his client at a local restaurant under circumstances that did not suggest a purely business conversation. When you asked your partner for an explanation, he acknowledged that he was having a "relationship" with the woman, but insisted that it had begun at her initiative and that he had offered to withdraw from representation. She had asked him to finish negotiating her settlement because finding new counsel would add expense and delay, and she trusted him completely. Your partner is serious about the relationship and sensitive to the potential for conflicting interests, but is convinced that he has the situation under control. When you indicate reservations, he responds that his personal affairs are none of your business, and that the firm will be better off if he doesn't antagonize the client by terminating either the personal or professional relationship.

How should you respond? What facts might be relevant to your decision? Would it matter if the gender roles were reversed, and your partner was female? Consider the materials on lawyer-client sexual relationships in Chapter III (Regulation of the Profession) at pages 80–81. If you were chair of your state bar's family law section, what, if any, rules governing lawyer-client sexual relationships would you propose? How helpful would they be in addressing your partner's conduct?

Ethics experts have divided over whether special rules on lawyer-client sexual relationships should apply in divorce cases. According to David Isbell, chair of the ABA's committee on ethics and professional responsibility, "[t]he antitrust lawyer doesn't have to deal with the psychological state of his client. A successful matrimonial lawyer will make the client feel better about things and have a relationship with the client that is almost like being a therapist."[84] However, Isbell opposes any flat ban on lawyer-client sexual involvement: "There are too many circumstances where two consenting adults are involved and it does not impair the ability of the lawyer to render professional services."[85]

Professor Stephen Gillers agrees that a categorical prohibition would be inappropriate. For example, he believes there "would and should be nothing wrong with an associate at a large law firm getting sexually involved with a corporate vice president whose company is a client."[86] However, he concludes that

> [f]rom a policy perspective, it makes sense to protect matrimonial clients as a distinct group because it is among the most vulnerable. . . . [A flat ban makes sense] only where the client is especially dependent on the lawyer, where the risk of abuse is greatest and where we can't be confident that the client's relationship with the lawyer is truly voluntary.[87]

Do you agree?

Women's rights advocates are divided on this issue. Some agree with Gillers about the potential for abuse, but argue that a categorical prohibition compromises rights of privacy and reinforces demeaning stereotypes of women. Restrictions that apply only to sexual relations begun after representation but not before (as in California, Oregon, and New York) suggest that a woman is capable of choosing "her lover as a lawyer but not her lawyer as her lover."[88] From these commentators' perspective, the bar should focus not on sex but on power — on the abuse of a fiduciary relationship.

Other women's rights advocates worry that too many of those abuses will never come to light if the burden is on clients to complain and to establish that the relationship was exploitative. What is your view? Would you prefer a categorical rule prohibiting lawyer-client sexual involvement, no such prohibition, or a special rule governing family and related cases?

Endnotes

1. Hubert J. O'Gorman, Lawyers and Matrimonial Cases 134-136 (1963).

2. Id.

3. Roy Cohn's Tips to Men on the Divorce Game, People, Jan. 24, 1983, at 17.

4. Raol Lionel Felder, Divorce 2-7 (1971).

5. Andrew S. Watson, The Children of Armageddon: Problems of Custody Following Divorce, 21 Syracuse L. Rev. 55, 64 (1969).

6. Petacque & Koval, Chicago Sun Times, Apr. 18, 1971, p.1, col. 3; Apr. 19, p.4, cols. 1, 2, quoted in Harry Krause, Family Law: Cases and Materials 713 (1976).

7. Herbert Jacob, The Elusive Shadow of the Law, 26 Law & Socy. Rev. 565, 579, 580 (1992).

8. See the confidentiality rules discussed at pages 224–225. Model Rule 4.1(b) provides that lawyers shall not "fail to disclose a material fact to a third person when disclosure is necessary to avoid assisting a criminal or fraudulent act by a client, unless disclosure is prohibited by rule 1.6." Model Rule 1.6 requires lawyers to maintain confidences unless disclosure is authorized by the client, and the Comment indicates that lawyers should withdraw rather than assist fraudulent conduct. Rule 1.16 authorizes withdrawal if it can be accomplished without "material adverse effect on the interests of the client," and the client insists on pursuing an objective that the lawyer considers "repugnant or imprudent." Disciplinary Rule 2-102(A)(4) prohibits a lawyer from engaging in conduct involving dishonesty, fraud, deceit, or misrepresentation. Disciplinary Rule 7-102 prohibits a lawyer from assisting fraudulent conduct or knowingly failing "to disclose that which he is required by law to reveal." And DR 2-110(C) permits withdrawal if the client insists that the lawyer engage in conduct "contrary to the judgment and advice of the lawyer."

9. This problem is drawn from interviews for Ronald Gilson & Robert Mnookin, Disputing Through Agents: Cooperation and Conflict Behavior: Lawyers in Litigation, 94 Colum. L. Rev. 509 (1994).

10. See Austin Sarat & William L.F. Felstiner, Divorce Lawyers and Their Clients 67-68 (1995).

11. This problem is drawn from materials presented by David Chambers at a workshop on Teaching Ethics in Family Law at the Association of American Law Schools' annual meeting, 1990.

12. O'Gorman, supra note 1, at 134-136.

13. Floyd Abrams, Why Lawyers Lie, N.Y. Times Mag., Oct. 9, 1994, at 54.

14. Richard E. Crouch, The Matter of Bombers: Unfair Tactics and the Problem of Defining Unethical Behavior in Divorce Litigation, 20 Fam. Law Q. 413, 415 (1986).

15. Gilson & Mnookin, supra note 9, at 563-564; Eleanor E. Maccoby & Robert H. Mnookin, Dividing the Child: Social and Legal Dilemmas of Custody 239 (1992).

16. Robert H. Mnookin & Lewis Kornhauser, Bargaining in the Shadow of the Law: The Case of Divorce, 88 Yale L.J. 950 (1979).

17. Ralph C. Cavanagh & Deborah L. Rhode, Project, The Unauthorized Practice of Law and Pro Se Divorce: An Empirical Analysis, 86 Yale L.J. 104, 138-139 (1976).

18. Jacob, supra note 7, at 579-581. The roles that surveyed lawyers have acknowledged as most important are mediation/negotiation and personal counseling. Cavanagh & Rhode, supra note 17, at 141.

19. Cavanagh & Rhode, supra note 17, at 139; Jacob, supra note 7. In the Connecticut study, approximately four-fifths of surveyed individuals received no information about the tax implications of divorce settlements. In the Illinois survey, many clients received minimal guidance, such as an unread pamphlet on custody.

20. Report of the State Bar of California Commn. on Legal Technicians 14 (July 1990).

21. See Deborah L. Rhode, Policing the Professional Monopoly: A Constitutional and Empirical Analysis of Unauthorized Practice Prohibitions, 34 Stan. L. Rev. 1 (1981).

22. Gay C. Kitson, Portrait of Divorce: Adjustment to Marital Breakdown (1992); Stan L. Albrecht, Hayward M. Bahr & Kirston L. Goodman, Divorce and Remarriage: Problems, Adaptations and Adjustments 122 (1983). See generally Lynn Carol Halem, Separated and Divorced Women (1982).

23. Albrecht, Bahr & Goodman, supra note 22, at 122.

24. For a general critique of law schools' marginalization of such training, see Ann Shalleck, Construction of the Client Within Legal Education: Consequences for Civic Discourse, 45 Stan. L. Rev. 1731 (1993); Deborah L. Rhode, Missing Questions: Feminist Perspectives on Legal Education, 45 Stan. L. Rev. 1547 (1993).

25. Austin Sarat & William Felstiner, Law and Social Relations: Vocabularies of Motive in Lawyer-Client Interaction, 22 Law & Socy. Rev. 737, 746 (1988) (quoting John Griffiths). See also Sarat excerpt at page 683 supra.

26. Halem, supra note 22, at 30-31.

27. Karen Winner, Divorced from Justice (1996); Kathleen Waits, Battered Women and Family Lawyers: The Need for an Identification Protocol, 58 Alb. L. Rev. 1027 (1995).

28. Sarat & Felstiner, supra note 10, at 103.

29. Steven Cox & Mark Dwyer, Self-Help Law: Its Many Perspectives 1-2, 34 (1985) (unpublished survey sponsored by the ABA Special Comm. on Delivery of Legal Services); Report of the State Bar of California Commn. on Legal Technicians, supra note 20, at Appendices 11, 12; Bruce D. Sales,

Connie J. Beck & Richard K. Haan, Self-Representation in Divorce Cases (ABA 1993).

30. Recent estimates suggest that Americans pay lawyers close to $2 billion annually for divorces, bankruptcies, incorporations, and wills, and that lay experts could cut this bill by a substantial amount. See sources cited in Deborah L. Rhode, The Delivery of Legal Services by Nonlawyers, 4 Geo. J. Legal Ethics 209, 220 (1990).

31. State supreme courts have asserted control over all provision of legal services under their inherent power to regulate the practice of law. However, the judiciary generally has permitted legislative initiatives that are consistent with its own authority. See Charles Wolfram, Modern Legal Ethics 58 (1986).

32. For discussion of these holdings, see Deborah L. Rhode, Policing the Professional Monopoly: An Empirical and Constitutional Analysis of Unauthorized Practice Prohibitions, 34 Stan. L. Rev. 1 (1980); Cavanagh & Rhode, supra note 17.

33. Florida Bar v. Furman, 451 So. 2d 808 (Fla. 1984).

34. Vincent Cuppola, Up Against the Bar in Florida, Newsweek, Aug. 22, 1983, at 69; Martha Siegel, Interview with Rosemary Furman, Dec. 12, 1984 (Harvard Program on the Legal Profession).

35. See Deborah L. Rhode, Professionalism in Perspective: Alternative Approaches to Nonlawyer Practice, 22 N.Y.U. Rev. L. & Soc. Change 701 (1996); Douglas Martin, For the Poor, Do-It-Yourself Divorce, N.Y. Times, Nov. 20, 1996, at B1.

36. See Russell Engler, Out of Sight and Out of Line: The Need for Regulation of Lawyers' Negotiations with Unrepresented Poor Persons, 85 Cal. L. Rev. 79 (1997); At a Loss in Family Court, Cal. Law., July 1996, at 17.

37. Engler, supra note 36; At a Loss, supra note 36, at 17.

38. For discussion of procedures in Japan, Denmark, Norway, Iceland, and Sweden, see Max Rheinstein, Marriage Stability, Divorce and the Law 109-131 (1972); Cavanagh & Rhode, supra note 17, at 106.

39. Martin, supra note 35, at B1; City of New York Dept. of Consumer Affairs, Women in Divorce: Lawyers, Ethics, Fees and Fairness 9-10 (Mar. 1992); Pamela A. MacLean, Legal Disservices, Cal. Law., Mar. 1997, at 23.

40. See Rhode, supra note 32, at 77-79, 85-88; Cavanagh & Rhode, supra note 17, at 127-139 (finding that lawyers made frequent readily correctable errors, and did not provide substantial help in resolving financial or custody issues in most uncontested cases); California State Bar Assn. Public Protection Comm. Public Hearing (Oct. 8, 1987) (statement of Fresno clerk indicating no difference in rejection rate of legal documents because of errors between papers drafted by lawyers and non-lawyers).

41. State Bar Commn. report, supra note 20, at 14 (76 percent satisfied with non-lawyers; 64 percent with lawyers).

42. Martin, supra note 35, at 131; Rhode, supra note 35.

43. American Academy of Matrimonial Lawyers, Standards of Conduct, Standard 2.1; Comment.

44. For the ban on contingent fees, see EC 2-20 and Model Rule 1.5(d). Some lawyers have attempted to evade such prohibitions by agreements that give them additional "bonuses" based on results obtained or the complexity of the case.

45. City of New York Dept. of Consumer Affairs, Women in Divorce, supra note 39, at 3, 20, 30, 49; Report of the Comm. to Examine Lawyer Conduct in Matrimonial Actions (May 4, 1993).

46. In re Marriage of Sherry Kantar, 581 N.E.2d 6 (Ill. App. 1 Dist. 1991).

47. Wendy Kaminer, True Love Waits 190 (1996) (quoting Peter Bronstein).

48. See In re Cooperman, 591 N.Y.S.2d 895, aff'd, 633 N.E.2d 1069 (1993); Sarah Ramsey, Survey of New York Law: Family Law, 45 Syracuse L. Rev. 417 (1994).

49. See Louis Parley, The Ethical Family Lawyer 48-52 (1995).

50. This problem is adapted from materials presented by Sarah Ramsey at a workshop on Teaching Ethics in Family Law at the Association of American Law Schools' annual meeting, 1990. For general discussion see Lewis Becker, Ethical Concerns in Negotiating Family Law Agreements, 3 Fam. L.Q. 587 (1996).

51. Katharine T. Bartlett & Carol Stack, Joint Custody, Feminism, and the Dependency Dilemma, 2 Berkeley Women's L.J. 9 (1986).

52. Gary Crippin, Stumbling Beyond Best Interests of the Child: Reexamining Child Custody Standard-Setting in the Wake of Minnesota's Four-Year Experiment with the Primary Caretaker Preference, 75 Minn. L. Rev. 427 (1990).

53. Maccoby & Mnookin, supra note 15.

54. David Chambers, Rethinking the Substantive Rules for Custody Disputes in Divorce, 83 Mich. L. Rev. 477 (1984).

55. Katherine Hunt Federle, Looking for Rights in All the Wrong Places: Resolving Custody Disputes in Divorce Proceedings, 15 Cardozo L. Rev. 1523 (1994).

56. Greger v. Greger, 578 A.2d 162 (Conn. App. 1990). But see Hresko v. Hresko, 574 A.2d 24 (Md. Ct. Spec. App. 1990) (reviewing cases); Sally Burnett Sharp, Fairness Standards and Separation Agreements, 132 U. Pa. L. Rev. 1399, 1424-1428 (1984).

57. The court held, however, that A was not subject to disciplinary action because there was substantial disagreement over the applicable duty at the time of occurrence, and A made several good faith attempts to ascertain the proper course of action.

58. For an overview, see Wolfram, supra note 31, at 641-658.

59. This problem is adopted from hypotheticals in Robert H. Aronson, What About the Children? Are Family Lawyers the Same (Ethically) as Criminal Lawyers? A Morality Play, 1 J. Instit. for Study of Legal Ethics 141 (1996), and in materials presented by Sarah Ramsey at a workshop on Teaching Ethics in Family Law at the Association of American Law Schools' annual meeting, 1990.

60. Robert P. Mosteller, Child Abuse Reporting Laws and Attorney-Client Confidences: The Reality and the Specter of Lawyer as Informant, 42 Duke L.J. 203 (1992); Robin A. Rosencrantz, Note: Rejecting "Hear No Evil Speak No Evil": Expanding the Attorney's Role in Child Abuse Reporting, 8 Geo. J. Legal Ethics 327, 331-335 (1995).

61. National Center on Child Abuse and Neglect, U.S. Dept. of Health and Human Services, Study of National Incidence and Prevalence of Child Abuse and Neglect: 1988, at 6-8 to 6-11 (1988).

62. Mosteller, supra note 60, at 217-222.

63. Compare Mosteller, supra note 60 (arguing that the privilege should override reporting requirements) with Op. Wis. Atty. Gen. 10-87 (1987) and Op. Utah Atty. Gen. 82-87 (Feb. 17, 1983) (privilege should have no impact). See Parley, supra note 49, at 88; Maura Strassberg, Taking

Ethics Seriously: Beyond Positivist Jurisprudence in Legal Ethics, 80 Iowa L. Rev. 901, 944 & n.232 (1995).

64. Ruth E. Thurman, Client Incest and the Lawyers' Duty of Confidentiality 17 (1985).

65. N.J. Sup. Ct. Advisory Comm. on Professional Ethics, Op. 280 (1974), reprinted in 97 N.J.L.J. 753 (1974).

66. Indianapolis Bar Assn. Legal Ethics Comm. Op. 1-1986 (Apr. 29, 1986).

67. Mosteller, supra note 60, at 254.

68. See also Robert Weisberg & Michael Wald, Confidentiality Laws and State Efforts to Protect Abused or Neglected Children, 18 Fam. L.Q. 143, 185-195, 203 (1984) (reviewing studies and concluding that children's physical interest is more critical than less measurable impact on adults' privacy rights).

69. Mosteller, supra note 60, at 265.

70. Douglas Besharov, Recognizing Child Abuse: A Guide for the Concerned 37 (1990).

71. Seth E. Kalichman & Cheryl L. Brosig, Mandatory Child Abuse Reporting Laws: Issues and Implications for Policy, 14 Law & Poly. 153, 164 (1992).

72. William Louis Tabac, Give Them a Sword: Representing a Parent in a Child Custody Case, 28 Loy. L.J. 267, 277 (1996).

73. Id. at 279.

74. A study of some 9,000 cases in a cross-section of American courts found that fewer than 2 percent of the contested custody and visitation cases involved allegations of child sexual abuse. Nancy Thoennes, Child Sex Abuse: Whom Should a Child Believe? What Should a Judge Believe?, 27 Judges J. 14, 14 (Summer 1988). Of the allegations that were found to be false, most appeared to have been made in good faith. Id. See also Catherine Paquette, Handling Sexual Abuse Allegations in Child Custody Cases, 25 New Eng. L. Rev. 1415, 1417 (1991) (concluding that the best research finds only 5 to 8 percent of allegations of child sex abuse in surveyed cases including divorce are fictitious); Meredith Fayn, Allegations of Child Sexual Abuse in Custody Disputes: Getting to the Truth of the Matter, 14 Women's Rights L. Rev. 123 (1992).

75. Steven M. Schuetze, Note, Thompson v. Thompson: The Jurisdictional Dilemma of Child Custody Cases Under the Parental Kidnapping Prevention Act, 16 Pepp. L. Rev. 409 (1989).

76. See generally Parley, supra note 49, at 88-89.

77. Kaminer, supra note 47, at 202 (quoting Felder).

78. Id. (quoting Katherine Thompson and Betty Levinson).

79. Id.

80. Klemm v. Superior Court, 75 Cal. App. 3d 893, 142 Cal. Rptr. 509 (Cal. Super. Ct. 1977); Committee on Legal Ethics of the District of Columbia Bar, Op. 143 (Nov. 13, 1984).

81. Ohio Bar Ethics Comm. Formal Op., No. 30 (May 1975). For a review of case law, see Parley, supra note 49, at 19 and 20.

82. See generally Wolfram, supra note 31, at 546-547.

83. Cal. Civ. Code 2324.10 (West Supp. 1992) (requiring written consent). See generally D. Marianne Brower Blair, Getting the Whole Truth and Nothing but the Truth: The Limits of Liability for Wrongful Adoption, 67 Notre Dame L. Rev. 851, 956-959 (1992).

84. Stephen Labaton, Are Divorce Lawyers Really the Sleaziest?, N.Y. Times, Sept. 5, 1993, at E5.

85. Id.

86. Id.

87. Id.

88. Linda Fitts Mishler, Reconciling Rapture, Representation, and Responsibility: An Argument Against Per Se Bans on Attorney-Client Sex, 10 Geo. J. Legal Ethics 209, 237 (1996).

Chapter XVII

Property

The practice of property law involves a broad variety of legal roles and raises an equally broad range of ethical issues. Lawyers' functions include negotiation, counseling, planning, document preparation, and representation before, or on behalf of, courts, administrative agencies, boards, commissions, and government agencies. Much of this practice is preventive and most does not match the adversarial paradigm, in which all affected parties receive zealous representation before a neutral decision-maker. In analyzing the problems that follow, consider how well existing professional rules, adversarial norms, and regulatory structures respond to the ethical concerns at issue.

A. THE ADVOCATE'S ROLE

PROBLEM 17A

1. You represent the landlord in an eviction suit against a tenant who is two months behind in her rent. The landlord acknowledges to you that, during the period in question, the tenant's heating system worked only sporadically and that plumbing problems and a leak in the roof took several weeks to fix. You believe that the tenant probably has a valid claim for violation of both the local housing code and the implied warranty of habitability. When you point this out to the landlord, he authorizes you to meet with the tenant to try and negotiate a settlement. However, if she cannot make any substantial payments on the back rent,

he wants the eviction to proceed as quickly as possible. The landlord predicts that the tenant has a convincing "tale of woes" but he doesn't want to hear it. His company will never survive if it manages property like a "quasi-charitable institution."

Your client would also like you to redraft his standard lease form to include a clause providing that the tenant must pay all the landlord's attorney fees in any action under the lease. Although such clauses are unenforceable in your jurisdiction, the landlord believes that they might deter tenants from contesting evictions. In addition, he would like you to include a clause like the one he saw in another form, which provided:

> **THERE IS NO IMPLIED WARRANTY THAT THE PREMISES ARE FIT FOR HABITABLE OCCUPATION** except as far as government regulations, legislation, or judicial enactment otherwise requires.

The tenant is a single mother with a small child and an elderly dependent parent. She is behind in her rent because she was temporarily out of work and because her former husband failed to meet his child-support obligations. Although her situation is improving, she cannot pay the accumulated charges in the immediate future. Since she was patient about the repairs, she believes the landlord should be patient about the back rent. The woman appears to have no idea that the heat, plumbing, and leakage problems could entitle her to substantial damages in a counterclaim to an eviction action. Nor does she plan to see a lawyer; she cannot afford the fees, and her local civil legal assistance office does not handle evictions. She would like you to persuade the landlord to grant her an extension. When you indicate that he is unlikely to do so, she asks your advice.

How do you respond to the tenant? Assume that if a reasonable judge knew all the facts, he would find a violation of the housing code as well as a breach of the warranty of habitability. Is it still ethical for you to file for eviction? What guidance do the Code and Model Rules provide? What guidance should they offer?[1]

How do you respond to the landlord? Does what you know about the tenant's circumstances affect your answer?

2. Is it permissible for you to draft a lease form with a clause that you know to be unenforceable? Should it be? Alternatively, suppose that a statute in your jurisdiction makes attorney fee-shifting clauses enforceable but reciprocal; that is, a tenant who successfully sues under a lease has the same right to fees as a landlord. Can you draft the clause to refer only to the landlord's recovery of fees?

3. You represent the landlord under the same circumstances as in Part 1, except that the tenant is more knowledgeable. When the landlord failed promptly to repair the leak, she filed a complaint with the local housing authority. Your client was outraged. He told the tenant that her conduct was totally unreasonable, given his good faith efforts to complete the repairs. Fixing the leak required replacing part of the roof, and it took time to get estimates. Then the contractor with the lowest bid

delayed scheduling the work. The heating and plumbing problems were difficult to trace, and a company partly responsible was tardy in servicing its product. The landlord views the tenant as a "pain in the ass" and now wants her out of the building whether or not she is willing to pay the back rent.

You are preparing your client for testimony at an administrative hearing before the housing authority. As you review the events, the landlord expresses anger about the tenant's charges. You remind him that it is illegal to evict renters for filing complaints, and that any statements at the administrative hearing could later become admissible in eviction proceedings. You also point out that although he is under oath and must testify truthfully, he should not volunteer anything. You then ask if there were other reasons why he found the tenant "unreasonable." He recounts several incidents in which she was rude or noisy, and emphasizes her unrealistic expectations about how quickly the repairs could be completed.

As you prepare the landlord for some possible questions, including ones about his feelings toward the tenant, he relates these concerns but does not volunteer any reference to the housing authority charges. When you press the point, he responds that the tenant has a "perfect right to file a complaint," but that under the circumstances, he felt that he was doing the best he could to make appropriate repairs.

Are you satisfied with that response and with your role in prompting it? Consider the materials on witness preparation in Chapter V (The Adversary System) at pages 195–200. Has the lawyer in this case crossed the boundary between legitimate preparation and facilitating perjury?

4. You represent the tenant in Problem 5B in Chapter V (The Adversary System) at pages 190–191. Should lawyers representing clients in difficult circumstances have greater latitude to engage in zealous advocacy? If so, what circumstances count?

5. You represent the developer in Problem 19B in Chapter XIX (Torts) at page 789. Can you file suit in his behalf without violating ethical rules? What strategies would you be willing to pursue against the neighborhood association?

See Chapter IV, Advocacy
  • The Morality of Means and the Morality of Ends
      (pages 157–161)

See Chapter V, The Adversary System
  • Traditional Rationale and Contemporary Challenges
      (pages 169–179)
  • Tactical Use of Procedure
      (pages 185–195)

See Chapter XIX, Torts
   • The Adversarial Process
      (pages 789–795)

When dealing with an unrepresented adversary, attorneys' sole responsibilities under Model Rule 4.3 are to avoid stating or implying that they are disinterested, and to make reasonable efforts to correct any misunderstanding about their role. An earlier proposed rule would have prevented lawyers from unfairly exploiting the ignorance of pro se opponents or from procuring an unreasonable result. Consider the materials in Chapter VIII (Negotiation and Mediation) at pages 367–370, and in Chapter XII (Contracts) at pages 523–530. Which rule would you support?

What other reforms might be appropriate to deal with the adversarial imbalances reflected in Problem 17A? As indicated in the materials on pro bono service in Part C of Chapter II (Traditions of Moral Reasoning), legal assistance is not available for about 80 percent of the problems that low-income individuals experience. In one representative survey, attorneys represented 72 percent of all landlords but only 27 percent of all tenants appearing before an urban court; in other studies the ratio is worse.[2] To what extent could, and should, these imbalances be addressed by expanding legal aid, simplifying court procedures, or relaxing bans on legal assistance by non-lawyer providers? Would any politically plausible reforms be extensive enough to prevent the kind of dilemma facing the landlord's counsel in Problem 17A?[3]

In analyzing the problems facing unrepresented tenants in housing disputes, Russell Engler notes that the situation has worsened substantially over the last decade. Judicial and bar commissions' calls for increased legal assistance have been largely ineffective. In the absence of such resources, Engler identifies a number of potential reform strategies:

> Procedural changes could . . . require lawyers to disclose to the court facts or potential claims of an unrepresented adversary, through submission of a certification or oral statement to the court. Courts could require the use of standardized settlement agreements, tailored to the proceedings heard in that court. Courts could attempt to restrict the discussions between lawyers and their adversaries, limiting negotiation to the exchange of settlement terms on paper, where the court is able to monitor the face-to-face negotiations.[4]

Consider also William Simon's proposal that lawyers exercise ethical discretion to facilitate the law's overarching purposes. See Chapter IV (Advocacy), pages 147–153. What would be the strengths and limitations of such a framework here?

How should the lawyer respond to the request to include an unenforceable clause? Consider the materials in Chapter XII, Part D. Should such decisions be regulated by ethical rules or by substantive laws that prohibit drafters from knowingly including an unenforceable clause? Should the American Bar Association have adopted a proposed Model Rule that would have prohibited lawyers from assisting a client to conclude an agreement that includes legally prohibited terms or that would be held unconscionable as a matter of law?

Charles Wolfram's treatise, Modern Legal Ethics, speaks to such issues. There, Wolfram considers whether a lawyer may draw up a lease limiting occupancy to "adults only" if the applicable law has recently changed to invalidate such provisions. As he points out, "[t]he lawyer may know that many tenants are unaware of the new law and would comply with the unenforceable term." Id. at 703. In Wolfram's view, "the moral dimensions of such chicanery seem clear" even though the relevant legal precedents are divided. Id.

Do you agree with Wolfram's ethical assessment? If he is right, why do you suppose that the legal rules are not as "clear" as the moral norms? If the landlord insists on including an unenforceable term against the lawyer's advice, how should the lawyer respond?

B. THE COUNSELING ROLE

1. Adverse Possession

PROBLEM 17B

1. You are a solo practitioner in a small New England town. Adverse possession in your jurisdiction takes ten years. An old college friend comes to you for advice about fencing a certain area adjacent to his property. He recently heard that it is possible to acquire land through that method if the true owner fails to object. The area in question belongs to a nonresident who rarely visits and is "unlikely to know or care" about the fence. The friend asks your advice about how to establish legal rights to the area. How do you respond?

2. Assume instead that a local entrepreneur with a reputation for sharp practices seeks such advice. He has had a fence around the area for about nine years on the assumption that he owned it. However, in the course of planning some improvements, he learned that the property in fact belongs to his neighbor. He is quite upset because he has already spent a substantial amount of money on construction in the area. He wants to work things out with the owner, who is rarely there, and asks your advice.

Do you volunteer information that if he retains the fence and says nothing for another year, he may be able to claim the property through adverse possession? If he had heard about that possibility from your college friend, how do you respond?

3. Assume now that you are approached by a local environmental activist. She fenced the area at least a decade ago, although she cannot remember the precise date when the fence was constructed. While she

has suspected all along that the property might not belong to her, she was sure that the real owner would not care. However, that owner now plans to sell to a developer, whose construction is likely to cause major ecological damage to the area. She would like to preserve the fenced area, especially because it has valuable wildlife and fish preserves that would be destroyed by development. She asks your advice.

Adverse possession is sometimes labeled "legal theft."[5] In a sense, it is a contradiction in terms (a characterization that is also sometimes applied to legal ethics). The anomaly in property law arises because an intentional effort to acquire another's land normally constitutes trespass and may be a crime as well as a tort. Yet the common law concept of adverse possession does not require possessors to have a good faith belief that they have any legal right to the property in question.

Consider DR 7-102(A)(7), Model Rule 1.2(d), and the material on witness preparation in Chapter V (The Adversary System) at pages 195–200. Would explaining the legal requirements of adverse possession on the facts of parts 1, 2, or 3 of Problem 17B constitute "counseling or assisting a client in conduct that the lawyer knows to be illegal"? Alternatively, would such an explanation constitute a permissible "discussion of legal consequences" that assists the client to "make a good faith effort to determine the validity, scope, meaning, or application of the law"? Model Rule 1.2.

Do these rules provide adequate ethical guidance for a lawyer in Problem 17B? Would other factors be material, such as your views about the purpose and justifiability of adverse possession doctrine or of the client's conduct?

2. Community and Common Law Property

PROBLEM 17C

1. You have represented an elderly couple on a variety of property matters since they moved to your state after retirement. For most of their 30-year marriage, the couple lived in Ohio, a common law property state. From the husband's earnings during marriage, he accumulated personal property worth about $750,000. Under Ohio law, the wife would have, at the husband's death, an elective share of one-half the property. Under the community property law of your jurisdiction, all the husband's personal property came into the state as his separate property. During probate, your state applies its own law, which does not recognize a wife's elective share because it assumes that she normally has a community property interest in the couple's assets. Thus, the wife would have no rights to any of the husband's separate property, even though

she would have had a half share as community property if they had been living in your state when it had been acquired.

The husband seeks your assistance in drafting a will. He would like to leave the personal property that will make up his probate estate, except his interest in the couple's modest condominium, to a television evangelist. When you explain that this would effectively disinherit the wife, contrary to the intent of the laws in both jurisdictions, the husband persists in his plan. His wife, he believes, can get by on social security if he leaves her the condominium. How should you respond?[6]

2. Would your response differ if:

a. The husband wanted to give the property to a homeless shelter or to a younger woman with whom he is having an affair?
b. The wife knew about the husband's plans and is likely to inherit substantial separate property?
c. The lawyer had no prior contact with the wife?
d. The lawyer knew the wife reasonably well and believed that her alcoholism and unpleasantness were largely responsible for the couple's unhappy marriage?
e. The lawyer knew the husband reasonably well and believed that his alcoholism had caused enormous hardship to the wife and had contributed to her poor health and economic conditions?

Does this problem suggest the need for legal reforms in jurisdictions that would not recognize a "quasi" community property interest in the husband's prior earnings?[7] If so, how should lawyers respond before such reforms are implemented? Would a lawyer under the facts of Problem 17C have any ethical obligation to counsel the client about how to defeat his wife's rights by making a complete transfer during his lifetime? To what extent should an attorney's own view of the equities matter? Consider the materials on alternatives to the conventional advocate's role in Part C of Chapter IV (Advocacy) at pages 146–162, and on conflicts of interest in estate planning in Chapter VII at pages 314–318. Under circumstances such as Problem 17C, does the lawyer have any special ethical obligations to the family unit or to unrepresented third parties? Or does furthering the client's individual autonomy always take precedence?[8]

3. Environmental Proceedings

PROBLEM 17D

You are the lawyer in Problem 9F in Chapter IX (The Lawyer-Client Relationship) at page 417. Whose interests do you represent? How zealously?

See Chapter IX, (The Lawyer-Client Relationship)
    (pages 418–419)

See Chapter XV, Evidence and Trial Advocacy
    • Relations with Witnesses
        (pages 662–673)

4.   Fraudulent Transactions

PROBLEM 17E

1. You represent the buyer in a sale of real estate. During the course of representation you learn of facts suggesting that your client agreed to pay a sum of cash to the seller "under the table" that will not be reflected in the purchase contract. You advise your client about the risks and penalties of filing false returns for the city and state transfer tax. You also indicate that you cannot assist a closing or sign returns based on fraudulent representations. If your client insists on going forward with the transaction, what are your obligations?

2. Suppose that your client acknowledges making the side payment. You withdraw from representation and your former client hires another firm to complete the transaction. What are your obligations? Would your responsibilities be different if you learned of the payment from someone other than your client?

3. If a friend at the new firm asks about the circumstances surrounding your withdrawal, what is your response?[9]

Consider DR 7-102(A)(7), which prohibits assistance in conduct that the lawyer "knows to be illegal or fraudulent"; DR 7-102(B)(2), which requires a lawyer to reveal information clearly establishing that the client has committed a fraud upon a person or a tribunal unless it is protected as a confidence or secret; DR 7-101(c)(3), which gives the lawyer discretion to disclose confidential or secret information if necessary to prevent a future crime; and DR 2-110(B), which requires lawyers to withdraw from representation if it is obvious that their continued employment would result in violation of a Disciplinary Rule. Model Rule 1.2 prohibits lawyers from assisting a client in conduct that the lawyer "knows is criminal or fraudulent"; Model Rule 1.6 prohibits disclosure of confidential information except where necessary to prevent the client from committing a criminal act likely to result in death or substantial bodily harm; and Model Rule 1.16 requires lawyers to withdraw from representation that will result in violation of ethical rules or other laws.

When does a lawyer "know" that an act is fraudulent? See the discussion in Chapter VI (Confidentiality and Client Counseling) at page 261. What factors would you find most relevant in answering that question?

C. THE NEGOTIATOR'S ROLE

PROBLEM 17F

1. You represent a buyer of a small office building who is financing part of the purchase by borrowing money from the seller. At the closing, your client is prepared to sign a deed of trust that lists the building as security for the buyer's debt. The seller's attorney prepared the deed, and as you scan its contents one final time, you notice a typographical error in the lot number describing the property's location. This error means that the deed of trust refers to someone else's property. Such a mistake may or may not invalidate the document, depending on when it is discovered and what actions the seller then takes. After noticing the error, what do you do?

Suppose that you manage to consult your client without arousing the seller's suspicion. The client directs you not to disclose the error. How do you respond? Does it matter whether (a) the seller's attorney is someone you know and respect; (b) the seller's attorney is someone you dislike, distrust, and believe has provided generally incompetent representation to his client; (c) the sellers are an elderly couple living on a fixed income; or (d) the seller is the buyer's former spouse, who has given what you consider to be a grossly inadequate divorce settlement?

2. Assume that the seller was never represented by counsel and that you prepared for the buyer the deed of trust form including the typographical error. Does that change your obligations? Should it?

3. You represent the seller of a local shopping center. The buyer has separate counsel. While you are formalizing the sale agreement, your client receives a geologist's report on several of her company's properties. That report notes that one corner of the center has an unusual subsoil problem. Extremely heavy and prolonged rainfall could cause dangerous settling in that area. This condition was not identified on a previous inspection when your client purchased the property. Your state does not have legislation mandating general disclosure of property defects. Although the sale agreement will include various representations about the property, the seller would like to avoid disclosure of this condition. Normally buyers do their own structural report, and the seller sees no reason to identify a condition that escaped her notice as a purchaser and that is unlikely to cause problems. How do you respond? Does your answer depend on the chances of extremely heavy, protracted rainfall in the area?

4. You represent the seller in the shopping center transaction. There is no adverse geologist's report. However, on the morning of closing, you

learn that the city council just passed a zoning ordinance that the buyer does not realize will defeat his plans for the center.

Do you have any obligation to disclose this information to the other side? Does it matter how you learned about the ordinance? Suppose that your client provided the information and insists that you remain silent. Alternatively, suppose that the ordinance has not yet passed but that you learn about it through a friend before knowledge becomes public.

5. You represent the sellers in a residential home sale. Several years ago, after a small earthquake, your clients had a structural engineer check the house for damage. She discovered some asbestos-insulated piping in the basement. Even a small earthquake could dislodge some of the material and might necessitate expensive removal of the entire system to prevent contamination. The problem is not unique, but neither is it common in the area. During preliminary conversations, the buyer asked about potential earthquake risks, and your clients responded truthfully that the house was "structurally sound." They now wonder if they have any further disclosure obligations. How do you respond?

Consider the materials on disclosure obligations in Chapter VIII (Negotiation and Mediation) at pages 347–353. Should a lawyer be subject to any ethical obligations beyond the Model Rules' prohibitions on fraud and material misstatements (Rule 4.1) and the Code's prohibitions on dishonesty, fraud, deceit, misrepresentation, and knowing failure "to disclose that which he is required by law to reveal" (DR 2-102(A)(4), DR 7-102(A))? Would nondisclosure under any of the facts in Problem 17F void the transaction? Consider the Restatement of Contracts standard mandating disclosure if necessary to "correct a mistake of the other party as to a basic assumption on which that party is making the contract and if nondisclosure of the fact amounts to a failure to act in good faith and in accordance with reasonable standards of fair dealing."[10] If clients want to run the risk that a court would later void their transactions, how should lawyers respond? Should attorneys' responsibilities depend on the accessibility of the information to the other side or on their own sense of the fairness of the transaction?

Would more state regulation of disclosure obligations be desirable? By the late 1990s, at least six states had laws or regulations mandating general disclosure of property defects by sellers. About the same number required disclosure of certain matters (such as underground storage tanks or hazardous materials), and over 20 legislatures had considered enacting compulsory disclosure provisions.[11] Some of this regulation is applicable to real estate brokers as well as sellers. Should it also cover lawyers? Alternatively, could the same result be achieved through extension of malpractice liability or enforcement of existing rules barring assistance in fraudulent activities?

For example, in Petrillo v. Bachenberg, 623 A.2d 272 (N.J. Super. Ct. App. Div. 1993), a New Jersey appellate court held that lawyers' fiduciary duties extended to a third party purchaser of real estate who reasonably relied on information that the lawyer supplied. There, the attorney for the seller gave a realtor a report of percolation tests that sought to demonstrate whether soil conditions could support a septic system. It appeared from the report that two successful tests had been obtained out of seven attempts, rather than out of the thirty efforts that had actually been made. The realtor subsequently decided to purchase the property and put a deposit down while conducting its own percolation tests. These tests revealed that the earlier successful studies were anomalies, based on unrepresentative soil profiles. The buyer then sued for return of the deposit and the court upheld its action against the lawyer as well as the seller. In the court's view, the attorney knew or should have known that the report was misleading and would be relied on by buyers.

If you were a lawyer in New Jersey, or another state with similar precedents, would it affect your conduct on the facts of Problem 17F?

E. MULTIPLE REPRESENTATION

PROBLEM 17G

Assume that in your jurisdiction both the buyer and the seller in real estate transactions generally have legal counsel.

1. You represent a small accounting partnership. One of the partners is selling his house to another partner, and the seller asks you to represent him. This would involve preparing the necessary documents and conducting the closing. What is your response? What factors would be most relevant to your decision?

2. Assume that you decide to represent the seller after talking with the buyer. The buyer then asks if you will represent her as well. As far as you can tell, this is a very straightforward home sale with no complications. The parties propose to retain you for 20 percent more than you would charge the seller alone, and to split your fees. This arrangement seems reasonable because you will have to do little, if any, additional work as the buyer's lawyer, but you will bear additional risks of blame if either side becomes dissatisfied. Assume further that if you decline to represent both parties, the buyer will not retain separate counsel. Instead, she will rely on the good faith of you and her partner. What do you do? Does it matter whether you might be able to frighten the buyer into hiring another attorney?

3. Assume that you agree to represent both parties. In the course of reviewing certain financing documents, you notice what appear to be misstatements in the buyer's statement of assets and liabilities. When you raise the point with her, she becomes evasive and defensive. She

says that she needs to reconcile her disclosures in the financing documents with other information in her tax forms and divorce settlement.
She assures you that none of the "slight irregularities" in the real estate
forms affect her overall credit standing or cast doubt on her ability to
discharge all of her financial obligations. She is "relying on your confidentiality" because if you tell her partner or the deal falls through, the
whole partnership might find out. That would jeopardize her career as
well as expose her to risks of further public disclosures and possible
legal liability.

    How do you respond? Assume that the seller does not have any
direct interest in the buyer's financial status regarding the real estate
transaction if the sale goes through; the arrangement does not include
take-back financing. However, the buyer's potential liability for fraud and
tax evasion and her attitude toward financial "irregularities" have obvious
implications for the accounting partnership. Could (and should) you have
done anything to prevent this dilemma? What do you do at this point?

See Chapter VII, Conflicts of Interest
    • Simultaneous Representation of Multiple Interests:
      Civil Contexts
        (pages 314–321)

AMERICAN BAR ASSOCIATION, RESIDENTIAL REAL ESTATE TRANSACTIONS: THE LAWYER'S PROPOSED ROLE

2-5, 8-9 (1978)

A.   THE BROKERAGE CONTRACT

Any seller signing such a contract [with a real estate broker] should
have it approved by the seller's lawyer before signing. The seller
should have the lawyer explain its meaning and be on hand to see
that it is properly executed. (It is presumed that if the seller consults
a lawyer, the lawyer will advise against entering into any oral
agreement.) In other words, the seller needs the traditional legal
services embraced in the expression "advice, representation and
drafting." The broker needs similar services at one time or another
and receives them from the broker's own lawyer as needed. In
routine transactions the broker is sufficiently familiar with the
details to be able to handle the matter without resort to professional
assistance.

B.   THE PRELIMINARY NEGOTIATIONS

. . . It is generally thought that neither the buyer nor the seller needs a lawyer in the course of negotiations. In theory this assumption is correct because neither party is bound until a written sales contract is signed. In fact, a great deal of trouble can be avoided if both the buyer and the seller consult their own lawyers during the course of the negotiations. If they are to make a proper bargain, they must know what to bargain about.

Aside from the question of price, which seems paramount in the minds of both parties, they should consider such problems as the mode of paying the purchase price and the tax consequences resulting therefrom, the status of various articles as fixtures or personal property, the time set for occupancy and the effect of loss by casualty pending the closing.

They can make whatever agreement they want, but they should anticipate all important questions and be certain a complete understanding has been reached. Failure to do so in the preliminary negotiations may mean, at the time for signing a contract, that they will have to start negotiations all over again. Worse, they may enter into a contract highly disadvantageous to one or the other, so uncertain as to require litigation to determine its meaning, or so ambiguous as to be void for indefiniteness.

C.   THE COMMITMENT FOR FINANCING

. . . The commitment contract between the lender and buyer will normally be prepared by the lender's lawyer. . . . Normally the lender has much greater financial expertise than the buyer. For this reason, when dealing with the lender the buyer is in need of legal assistance.

D.   THE CONTRACT OF SALE . . .

. . . Here again the parties need legal services in the form of drafting, advice, and representation.

This need is not avoided by the use of forms. Even if the form is properly drawn, the printed portion may not adequately express the particular agreement made between the parties, or the words used in filling in blanks may distort its effectiveness. As a matter of practice standardized forms are widely used, and it is recognized that this practice likely will continue. It is recommended that local bar associations draft standard forms of sales agreements, and that joint seminars with real estate brokers and others regarding residential real estate transactions be held regularly. Whenever forms are used, any insertion should be carefully checked by the buyer's and seller's lawyers, and the appropriateness of the form for the particular transaction should be determined by the buyer's and seller's lawyers. The buyer and the seller are often unaware of what the contract means, what they should anticipate, and what steps are needed to make the instrument binding. They should be advised by their own legal counsel.

Prior to the time the contract is signed, the buyer and the seller should have detailed advice about many legal aspects of the transaction. For example, they may not be aware of the need to anticipate the question of who bears the loss of damage to, or destruction of, buildings on the premises between the time the contract is signed and the time of closing. They also may be unaware of the existence of such problems as whether the contract so changes the interest of the seller as to affect insurance policies; whether either the buyer or seller, or both, should execute new wills; whether federal and state gift and death tax matters are involved; whether joint tenancies or tenancies by the entireties will be affected; and the like. . . .

The Conflicts of Interest

At every step set out above it has been said that buyers and sellers should have representation, advice and draftsmanship. This is to say, each needs separate legal representation and should not rely on services rendered by a lawyer for some other party. Why, it will be asked, is so much legal service needed to consummate a routine, uncontested transaction? No two transactions are identical, and none is simple. Because of the complexity of property law a "minor" slip may cause great expense and inconvenience. To the buyer, at least, the purchase of a house may be the most important legal and financial transaction of a lifetime.

All of the parties have conflicting interests. Some of them have wide experience with land transfers. To others the transaction may be a once-in-a-lifetime event. Houses are bought and sold by the inexperienced as well as by the sophisticated. The buyer and seller, without representation, will usually not have as much knowledge of conveyancing as the other parties. Only their own attorneys will be motivated to explain fully the transaction.

It is sometimes said the parties require disinterested advice. This misstates the case. Instead of disinterested advice, each requires the assistance of someone dedicated to that person's interests and equipped with sufficient skill to protect that person. The escrow company used in some sections of the country is theoretically disinterested. Actually its primary loyalty is to the institutions which are the sources of its business.

Most real estate transactions do not match the world envisioned by the American Bar Association excerpt. Many parties wish to minimize expense and acrimony through joint representation and are willing to assume some of the risks.[12] At what point those risks become too great, and who should decide when that point is reached, have been matters of ongoing debate. Three often-cited cases, decided at approximately ten-year intervals, illustrate the concerns.

In In re Kamp, 194 A.2d 236 (N.J. 1963), the buyer contracted to purchase a house that would be built by a home development corporation. The contract specified that the closing of title would be handled by Daniel Kamp, a lawyer who had represented the corporation for several years. Under his arrangement with the corporation, Kamp would perform a tract title search for no fee. In return, when the corporation sold property from the tract, it would "encourage" buyers to use Kamp as the closing lawyer, and the buyers would be billed for his services. In the case at issue, the buyer made progress payments toward a home purchase. However, she hired her own lawyer for the closing and he was unable to locate her property through a normal title search. Kamp refused to assist the buyer's lawyer under the apparent belief that the contract created a binding obligation on the buyer to accept Kamp's legal representation. The buyer never received any title insurance or assurance of marketable title.

The New Jersey Supreme Court held that Kamp had violated the Canons of Professional Ethics. Given the inherent possibility of conflicting interests between buyers and sellers, the court required that any lawyer undertaking multiple representation must obtain the client's informed consent. To ensure that the client has full information, the lawyer should disclose the lawyer's relation to the other party, the possible pitfalls that might arise, and the potential advantages of separate counsel. Disciplinary Rule 5-105 codifies these standards and also requires that it must be "obvious" that the lawyer representing multiple clients can adequately represent the interests of each. Model Rule 1.7 similarly provides that lawyers should not represent multiple clients if the representation of one client will adversely affect the representation of another or if the representation of one client will be materially limited by the lawyer's responsibilities to another. See Chapter VII (Conflicts of Interest) at pages 304–306.

In In re Lanza, 322 A.2d 445 (N.J. 1974), the New Jersey Supreme Court applied these requirements to reprimand a lawyer for representing conflicting interests. There, the attorney agreed to assist the seller in the sale of her home. He then arranged to act for the buyers as well without first obtaining the seller's consent. After a change in the proposed closing date, the buyers asked the seller to accept a postdated check for $1,000 as part of the purchase price. The seller agreed after consulting Lanza, who saw no reason to object. The buyers subsequently refused to honor the check. They claimed that the seller had represented that her cellar was always dry but that after taking possession, they found a serious water condition that would cost $1,000 to repair. The seller denied making any such representation and sought assistance from the lawyer. When he declined to take effective measures, she retained other counsel and sued the buyers.

A majority of justices found the lawyer's conduct deficient in several respects. At the outset, he should have obtained both parties' informed consent to joint representation. Then, when the issue arose over altering the date, he should have insisted that the buyers pay the full purchase price or provide other security. If the buyers had refused, he should have withdrawn from representation. In so holding, the court emphasized that a

> client cannot foresee and cannot be expected to foresee the great variety of potential areas of disagreement that may arise in a real estate transaction of this sort. The attorney is or should be familiar with at least the more common of these and they should be stated and laid before the client at some length and with considerable specificity.

Id. at 448.

One justice concurred in the result but argued that dual representation in buyer-seller transactions should always be forbidden. In his view, because no client could

> ever possibly fully appreciate all the complexities involved . . . full disclosure and informed consent are illusory. What most people typically do is rely upon the representation of their attorney when he reassures them that everything will be properly handled. However, the attorney is, unfortunately, not a clairvoyant who can foresee problem areas, although he realizes that there is certainly the potential for genuine conflict. . . .
>
> Numerous situations like the present instance require affirmative legal action and demand an attorney's undivided loyalty. If two separate attorneys were individually retained, both parties would be sure that they were receiving the best possible legal attention. If and when a conflict developed, they would be duly represented, instead of deserted. The inconvenience in retaining separate attorneys is minimal when weighed against the dangers involved, and the cost differential in the final analysis would be inconsequential.

Id. at 451 (Pashman, J., concurring). If you were resolving this issue as a judge or member of a bar disciplinary committee, what would you decide? Who should determine whether costs are inconsequential?

In a subsequent case, Baldasarre v. Butler, 625 A.2d 458 (N.J. 1993), a majority of New Jersey Supreme Court Justices disapproved of joint representation in complex commercial real estate transactions. The court held that a bright-line rule prohibiting dual representation was necessary in such transactions where "large sums of money are at stake, where contracts contain complex contingencies, or where options are numerous." Id. at 466. Under the court's analysis, "[t]he potential for conflict in that type of complex real estate transaction is too great to permit even consensual dual representation of buyer and seller." Id.

Do you agree? Most courts and bar ethics committees have taken a more permissive view. In re Johnson, 707 P.2d 573 (Or. 1985), is illustrative. There the Oregon Supreme Court absolved an attorney from any ethical misconduct in his multiple representation of two close corporations and their owners. In that capacity, Johnson prepared a lease option for certain corporate property on which one owner had a residence. That owner later instructed the lawyer to prepare a contract of sale for the property. At the time, the owner claimed to be president of both corporations and signed the contract in that dual role. Johnson took him at his word and recorded the contract. It later turned out that the owner had not been president of the seller corporation when he signed the contract, and the lawyer's multiple representation had assisted the fraud.

In absolving Johnson of any impropriety, the Oregon Supreme Court distinguished between (1) actual conflict, where multiple representation is impermissible; (2) likely conflict, where multiple representation is permissible after disclosure and informed consent; and (3) unlikely conflict, where multiple representation is permissible without disclosure and consent. Id. at 576-578. For lawyers to be liable for misconduct, they must have known, or "by the exercise of reasonable care, should have known," of facts suggesting a conflict. Id. at 579. Johnson lacked such knowledge.

Taken together, these and other recent judicial and bar committee opinions establish certain general principles for joint representation in real estate transactions. To minimize difficulties, lawyers should disclose:

1. their relationship to all parties, particularly any financial arrangements that might suggest bias;
2. the nature, seriousness, likelihood, and potential consequences of conflicts;
3. the scope of confidentiality protection (i.e., that the attorney-client privilege does not protect communication among multiple clients).

Even with full disclosure and consent, lawyers should not undertake joint representation in the face of "obvious" conflicts, such as the payment terms in *Lanza*.

Such general principles, however, leave considerable grey areas. How specific must disclosure about potential conflicts be in a case like *Lanza* or those presented in Problem 17G? If, for example, the joint representation involves an institutional lender, must lawyers explain every important provision in a loan agreement and the lender's likely willingness to delete them? If significant bargaining could occur over the terms of the agreement, is joint representation appropriate? See N.Y. City Bar Ethics Opinion 81-4 (1982). Would more bright-line prohibitions on multiple representation be desirable? Would they be likely to increase parties' access to disinterested advice, or would they encourage more parties not to obtain counsel at all? Would an alternative be for lawyers to act as intermediaries? See Chapter VII (Conflicts of Interest) at page 307. Are other structural reforms in the delivery of legal services appropriate, such as those suggested in Part F below?

F. THE DELIVERY OF LEGAL SERVICES

Since the Depression, bar associations have frequently brought suit against lay competitors for the unauthorized practice of law in real estate transactions. Results have varied by jurisdiction. Some courts have prohibited realtors or title companies from preparing real estate documents on the ground that such activities require legal knowledge or are commonly understood to involve legal skills. Other courts have permitted lay competitors to fill in standard forms or to give legal advice only if it is "incidental" or "ancillary" to their primary function. Restrictive judicial holdings have sometimes prompted legislative responses, including state constitutional amendments granting real estate brokers the power to fill in forms.[13] Other state courts have found insufficient evidence of consumer injury to justify banning non-lawyer assistance in routine real estate work. Thus, the New Mexico Supreme Court relied on "uncontroverted evidence" that the use of lawyers increased costs and delays without providing increased protection to clients.[14] Controversies between attorneys and real estate agents are pending in other jurisdictions.[15]

Related controversies have involved competition from lay title insurance companies. In an effort to meet such competition, lawyers in some states have formed their own title insurance organizations, sometimes under state bar auspices. Such organizations have raised concerns about conflicts of interest and antitrust violations. Bar efforts to standardize title examination fees have also been struck down as unlawful price-fixing.[16]

Compare the ABA's arguments favoring separate lawyers for all parties in real estate transactions with arguments favoring increased lay competition and simplified procedures. Which claims do you find most persuasive? According to American Bar Foundation surveys, about 60 percent of all residential real estate purchasers do not consult lawyers.[17] For many of these transactions, admission to the bar is neither a necessary nor sufficient guarantee of the required expertise; in routine sales, hiring a lawyer may be equivalent to "hiring a surgeon to pierce an ear."[18] If lay specialists are likely to be better equipped than lawyer generalists for many real estate matters, what, if any, reforms in current legal practices are appropriate?[19]

Endnotes

1. Part 1 of the problem draws on a related fact pattern in Joseph William Singer, Property Law: Rules, Policies, and Practices 795-796 (1993). The warranty of habitability clause is modeled on a provision at issue in Leardi v. Brown, 474 N.E.2d 1094 (Mass. 1985).

2. See Singer, supra note 1, at 795; Russell Engler, Out of Sight and Out of Line: The Need for Regulation of Lawyers' Negotiations with Unrepresented Poor Persons, 85 Cal. L. Rev. 79 (1997).

3. Kurt E. Olafsen, Note, Preventing the Use of Unenforceable Provisions in Residential Leases, 64 Cornell L. Rev. 522, 533-537 (1979) (proposing legislative requirement that all residential leases include a clause informing tenants that they cannot be required to pay landlords' attorneys' fees or to relinquish specified rights).

4. Engler, supra note 2, at 148.

5. This point and problems analogous to Problem 17B appear in materials developed by Peter A. Joy for Case Western Reserve University School of Law.

6. Part 1 of this problem draws on a similar fact pattern in Jesse Dukeminier & James E. Krier, Property 360 (2d ed. 1988).

7. For example, California and Idaho label as quasi-community property any property (except real property) owned by one spouse that would have been characterized as community property if the couple had been residing in California or Idaho when the property was acquired. During the marriage, such property is treated for most purposes as the separate property of the acquiring spouse. However, upon the death of that spouse, one-half of the quasi-community property belongs to the surviving spouse. Cal. Prob. Code §§66, 101 (1989); Idaho Code §15-2-201 (1979). To prevent a spouse from attempting to defeat a survivor's rights by inter vivos transfer, California gives the surviving spouse the right to reach one-half of any gratuitous transfer where the decedent retained certain ownership rights. Cal. Prob. Code §102 (1989).

8. See Chapter VII (Conflicts of Interest) and Thomas L. Shaffer, The Legal Ethics of Radical Individualism, 65 Tex. L. Rev. 963 (1987).

9. Association of the Bar of the City of New York, Committee on Professional and Judicial Ethics, Formal Op. No. 1994-8 (1994).

10. Restatement of Contracts §161B (1993).

11. Robert M. Washburn, Residential Real Estate Condition Disclosure Legislation, 44 DePaul L. Rev. 381 (1995); James D. Lawlor, Seller Beware, 78 A.B.A.J., Aug. 1992, at 90.

12. See Part F infra, and Jean A. Mortland, Attorneys as Real Estate Brokers: Ethical Considerations, 25 Real Prop., Prob., & Tr. J. 755, 767 (1991).

13. See Merton E. Marks, The Lawyers and the Realtors: Arizona's Experience, 49 A.B.A.L. Rev. 139 (1963); Cultrom v. Heritage House Realtors, Inc., 694 P.2d 630, 633 (Wash. 1985); Deborah L. Rhode, The Delivery of Legal Services by Non-Lawyers, 4 Geo. J. Legal Ethics 209 (1990).

14. State Bar v. Guardian Abstract & Title Co., 575 P.2d 943, 949 (N.M. 1978). For a critical overview of unauthorized practice doctrine, see Rhode, supra note 13, and Deborah L. Rhode, Professionalism in Perspective: Alternative Approaches to Nonlawyer Practice, 22 N.Y.U. Rev. L. & Soc. Change 701 (1991); Deborah L. Rhode, Policing the Professional Monopoly: A Constitutional and Empirical Analysis of Unauthorized Practice Prohibitions, 34 Stan. L. Rev. 1 (1981).

15. In Virginia, the state legislature rejected efforts by the state bar to prevent non-lawyers from concluding closings. See Caroline E. Mayor, Virginia Amends Realty Closing Rules, Wash. Post, Feb. 22, 1997, at F1; Ann Davis, Virginia Bar Wants to Be There at Closings, Natl. L.J., Sept. 16, 1996, at 6 (describing South Carolina decision prohibiting non-lawyers' closing services and New Jersey opinion permitting them).

16. Goldfarb v. Virginia State Bar, 421 U.S. 773 (1975). For a discussion of conflicts of interest created by lawyer referrals of purchasers to real estate transaction insurance companies, see H. Ley Roussel & Moses K. Rosenberg, Lawyer-Controlled Title Insurance Companies: Legal Ethics and the Need for Insurance Department Regulations, 48 Fordham L. Rev. 25 (1979).

17. Barbara A. Curran, The Legal Needs of the Public 135-136 (1977); Barbara A. Curran, The Legal Profession in the 1980s: Selected Statistics from the 1984 Statistical Report (1988).

18. Hal Lancaster, Rating Lawyers, Wall St. J., July 31, 1980, at 1, 8 (quoting Robert Ellickson and describing inadequate performance by half of sampled firms regarding real estate sale).

19. See Rhode, supra note 13; Rhode, Policing the Professional Monopoly, supra note 14.

┌─────────────────────────────────┐

Chapter XVIII

Tax

└─────────────────────────────────┘

A. INTRODUCTION

Ethical issues in tax practice reflect both the particular nature of its regulatory framework and the more general tensions arising from lawyers' competing responsibilities. These issues have become increasingly important as the nation's budget has become increasingly dependent on self-reporting income tax systems. Since both federal and state tax systems depend on voluntary compliance, the ethical norms of taxpayers and their lawyers have considerable societal significance.

Those norms have themselves become a matter of growing concern. The Internal Revenue Service has insufficient resources to audit more than 1 percent of returns for substantive validity, and those audits reveal increasingly high levels of underpayment.[1] Conservative estimates suggest that unreported taxable income averages 10 to 15 percent of taxable income and this "compliance gap" now exceeds $100 billion.[2] According to recent surveys, noncompliance is becoming more difficult to control, partly as a result of taxpayer dissatisfaction with the complexity and seeming inequity of the tax code, as well as skepticism toward government in general and the Internal Revenue Service in particular.[3]

What to do about the compliance gap is the subject of the material that follows. It focuses on lawyers' counseling role concerning personal income taxation under federal laws, because that system attracts widest student and public interest. However, the ethical problems at issue are representative of those arising in all areas of tax practice. To understand these problems, a brief, much simplified, overview of penalty structures and bar interpretations is helpful.

Taxpayers face penalties for both fraud and accuracy-related violations not rising to the level of fraud. For fraudulent underpayments, taxpayers are subject to penalties of 75 percent of the amount due (§6663). For accuracy-related violations, taxpayers are liable for penalties of 20 percent of the resulting underpayment (§6662).

Accuracy-related violations take several forms that are relevant to the ethical discussion that follows. The first involves negligence or disregard of applicable rules (§6662(c)). "Negligence" encompasses failure to make reasonable attempts at compliance, and "disregard" encompasses careless, reckless, or intentional transgressions. A second accuracy-related penalty applies to "substantial understatement" of income tax. An understatement is substantial if it exceeds 10 percent of the correct tax liability or $5,000, whichever is greater (§6662(d)(1)(A)(i) and (ii)). The third accuracy-related penalty concerns "substantial valuation misstatement." This type involves an overstatement of property value or basis of at least 200 percent (§6662(e)(1)(A)) or an understatement of estate or gift tax valuation of at least 50 percent (§6662(g)(1)). A valuation misstatement is considered substantial only if it results in a tax underpayment exceeding $5,000 for individuals. The final accuracy-related penalty applies to substantial overstatement of pension liabilities. This penalty involves a pension liabilities overstatement of at least 200 percent resulting in a tax underpayment exceeding $1,000 (§6662(f)).

Most accuracy-related penalties are inapplicable if taxpayers disclose the basis for a position and the position has a reasonable basis.[4] For certain other violations, penalties are avoidable if the taxpayer establishes good faith and reasonable cause (§6664(c)(1)).

Preparers of tax returns may also be subject to penalties. A $250 penalty is applicable if a return takes an undisclosed or frivolous position for which "there was not a realistic possibility of being sustained on the merits," and the preparer knew or reasonably should have known of the position (§6694(a)). As with the taxpayer penalties under §6662, however, the preparer penalty for an unrealistic position under §6694(a) is inapplicable if there was a reasonable cause for the understatement and the preparer acted in good faith. This exception does not apply to more egregious preparer behavior. For example, preparers are subject to a penalty of $1,000 for willfully attempting to understate the client's liability or for acting with "any reckless or intentional disregard of rules or regulations" (§6694(b)). Similarly, under §6701, a $1,000 penalty ($10,000 for preparers of corporate taxes) applies to practitioners who helped prepare any document that they knew or had reason to believe would be used materially to understate federal tax liability. Preparers who promote abusive tax shelters are subject to a $1,000 penalty or 100 percent of the gross income of the tax shelter, whichever is less (§6700).

Under Circular 230, the IRS may also impose sanctions, including suspension or disbarment from practice before the Service, against any preparers who engage in disreputable conduct. Such conduct includes knowing provision of false or misleading information or commission of violations that are willful, reckless, or a result of gross incompetency.[5] As amended in 1994, Circular 230 provides that a practitioner may not sign a return as a preparer if the return has an undisclosed position that lacks

> a realistic possibility of being sustained on the merits. . . . A position is considered to have a realistic possibility . . . if a reasonable and well-informed analysis by a person knowledgeable in the tax law would lead such a person to conclude that the position has approximately a one-in-three, or greater, likelihood of being sustained on its merits.

31 C.F.R. §10.34. No violation occurs if the position is disclosed and is not frivolous.

Specific statutory efforts to regulate lawyers' tax practice are, for the most part, relatively recent. Although for many years IRS Circular 230 required "due diligence" in preparing or assisting the preparation of tax returns, the Treasury Department offered no interpretive regulations. In 1965, the ABA issued Ethics Opinion 314, which held that a lawyer assisting preparation of a client's tax returns could freely urge the statement of positions most favorable to the client as long as there was a "reasonable basis" for those opinions. In so ruling, the Ethics Committee reasoned that lawyers were acting in a potentially adversarial capacity against the IRS and were not obligated to disclose weaknesses in their clients' position unless the facts indicated beyond a doubt that a crime was being committed. And, the Committee noted, a "wrong or indeed sometimes unjust tax result in the settlement of a controversy is not a crime."

That reasoning provoked considerable criticism. Many commentators challenged the analogy between ex parte administrative filings and adversarial litigation, particularly given the resource constraints and self-reporting aspects of the tax system. Moreover, as a practical matter, the "reasonable basis" standard evolved to what one commentator labeled the "laugh aloud" standard; it would permit any argument you could make with a reasonably straight face.[6]

In response to widespread criticism, the ABA Ethics Committee in 1985 released formal Opinion 85-352, reprinted below. This opinion replaced the "reasonable basis" test with a more stringent standard requiring a realistic possibility of success.

As subsequent discussion indicates, many commentators believe that this regulatory structure remains inadequate. Some experts are dissatisfied with the lack of state ethics opinions dealing with tax issues, the almost total absence of bar disciplinary proceedings involving improper tax advice, and the leniency of "realistic possibility" standards in practice.[7] By contrast, other commentators doubt that "taxpayer conduct can be controlled through practitioner standards of conduct because, in the last analysis, taxpayers act in what they perceive to be their economic self interest."[8] From this perspective, progress is unlikely to occur without fundamental changes in audit and penalty rates.

Under current audit rates, how high would penalties need to be in order to ensure compliance by Holmes' proverbial "bad man," who is concerned only with sanctions? Are penalties at that level even remotely plausible as a political matter? If not, what follows from that fact?

Consider your own position in light of the materials that follow.

B.   TAX RETURN PREPARATION AND ADVICE

1.   Questionable Positions

PROBLEM 18A

1. Your client wishes to take a position on her return that is consistent with a ruling by a U.S. district court in your jurisdiction. However, two U.S. courts of appeals in other circuits have rejected the position. You believe that these appellate decisions offer the more persuasive analysis of the language and legislative history of the legal requirements at issue. However, you could offer some policy arguments to support the district court's conclusion. How do you advise the client?

2. Assume that you conclude that the client's position does not have a realistic possibility of success. If the client disagrees and insists on taking that position without disclosure on her return, how should you proceed?[9]

RANDOLPH PAUL, THE RESPONSIBILITY OF THE TAX ADVISER

63 Harv. L. Rev. 377 (1950)

Tax attorneys know very well that tax avoidance is "in the nature of mortals." Certainly the courts have resigned themselves to the thought that it is almost universal. There is nothing reprehensible or illicit in attempts to avoid by legal means some portion of the burden of taxation or in honest efforts "to reduce taxes to the minimum required by law." Tax avoidance has been said to be "above reproach." At the very least, it is a natural product, in terms of human attitude. . . .

I do not mean to give blanket sanction to the many tax avoidance schemes that are constantly being presented to tax advisers.

Above all things, a tax attorney must be an indefatigable skeptic; he must discount everything he hears and reads. The market place abounds with unsound avoidance schemes which will not stand the test of objective analysis and litigation. The escaped tax, a favorite topic of conversation at the best clubs and the most sumptuous pleasure resorts, expands with repetition into fantastic legends. But clients want opinions with happy endings, and he smiles best who smiles last. It is wiser to state misgivings at the beginning than to have to acknowledge them ungracefully at the end. The tax adviser has, therefore, to spend a large part of his time advising against schemes of this character. I sometimes think that the most important word in his vocabulary is "No"; certainly he must frequently use this word most emphatically when it will be an unwelcome answer to a valuable client, and even when he knows that the client may shop for a more welcome answer in other offices which are more interested in pleasing clients than they are in rendering sound opinions.

I am far from advising undue receptivity on the part of tax advisers to tax avoidance devices though I am dealing with the problem of the tax adviser's attitude toward tax avoidance. Taxes have a statutory base; there is no taxation without legislation. Every tax asserted by the Commissioner must be "authorized by Congress." The question for the tax adviser is not what the law ought to be, but what it is or will become. My point is that in deciding that question the tax adviser must put aside his personal notions of tax policy and make his most intelligent guess as to the meaning of a statute passed by Congress. . . . The tax adviser need not worry about his moral position. It is not his function to improve men's hearts. As Judge Frank has observed, the task of a lawyer is to win specific cases and guide clients to pleasant destinations. . . . Indeed, it is his positive duty to show the client how to avail himself to the full of what the law permits. He is not the keeper of the Congressional conscience.

AMERICAN BAR ASSOCIATION ETHICS COMMITTEE'S FORMAL OPINION 85-352: TAX RETURN ADVICE

(1985)

The Committee has been requested by the Section of Taxation of the American Bar Association to reconsider the "reasonable basis" standard in the Committee's Formal Opinion 314 governing the position a lawyer may advise a client to take on a tax return. . . .

The Committee is informed that the standard of "reasonable basis" has been construed by many lawyers to support the use of any colorable claim on a tax return to justify exploitation of the lottery of the tax return audit selection process. . . . The Committee does not believe that the reasonable basis standard, properly interpreted and applied, permits this construction.

However, the Committee is persuaded that as a result of serious controversy over this standard and its persistent criticism by distinguished members of the tax bar, IRS officials and members of Congress, sufficient doubt has been created regarding the validity of the standard so as to erode its effectiveness as an ethical guideline. For this reason, the Committee has concluded that it should be restated [particularly given changes in bar ethical codes]. . . .

The ethical standards governing the conduct of a lawyer in advising a client on positions that can be taken in a tax return are no different from those governing a lawyer's conduct in advising or taking positions for a client in other civil matters. Although the Model Rules distinguish between the roles of advisor and advocate, both roles are involved here, and the ethical standards applicable to them provide relevant guidance. In many cases a lawyer must realistically anticipate that the filing of the tax return may be the first step in a process that may result in an adversary relationship between the client and the IRS. This normally occurs in situations when a lawyer advises an aggressive position on a tax return, not when the position taken is a safe or conservative one that is unlikely to be challenged by the IRS.

Rule 3.1 of the Model Rules, which is in essence a restatement of DR 7-102(A)(2) of the Model Code, states in pertinent part:

> A lawyer shall not bring or defend a proceeding, or assert or controvert an issue therein, unless there is a basis for doing so that is not frivolous, which includes a good faith argument for an extension, modification or reversal of existing law.

Rule 1.2(d), which applies to representation generally, states:

> A lawyer shall not counsel a client to engage, or assist a client, in conduct that the lawyer knows is criminal or fraudulent, but a lawyer may discuss the legal consequences of any proposed course of conduct with a client and may counsel or assist a client to make a good faith effort to determine the validity, scope, meaning or application of the law.

On the basis of these rules and analogous provisions of the Model Code, a lawyer, in representing a client in the course of the preparation of the client's tax return, may advise the statement of positions most favorable to the client if the lawyer has a good faith belief that those positions are warranted in existing law or can be supported by a good faith argument for an extension, modification or reversal of existing law. A lawyer can have a good faith belief in this context even if the lawyer believes the client's position probably will not prevail. However, good faith requires that there be some realistic possibility of success if the matter is litigated. This formulation of the lawyer's duty in the situation addressed by this opinion is consistent with the basic duty of the lawyer to a client, recognized in ethical standards since the ABA Canons of Professional Ethics, and in the opinions of this Committee: zealously and loyally to represent the interests of the client within the bounds of the law.

Thus, where a lawyer has a good faith belief in the validity of a position in accordance with the standard stated above that a particular transaction does not result in taxable income or that certain expenditures are properly deductible as expenses, the lawyer has no duty to require as a condition of his or her continued representation that riders be attached to the client's tax return explaining the circumstances surrounding the transaction of the expenditures.... Competent representation of the client would require the lawyer to advise the client fully as to whether there is or was substantial authority for the position taken in the tax return. If the lawyer is unable to conclude that the position is supported by substantial authority, the lawyer should advise the client of the penalty the client may suffer and of the opportunity to avoid such penalty by adequately disclosing the facts in the return or in a statement attached to the return. If after receiving such advice the client decides to risk the penalty by making no disclosure and to take the position initially advised by the lawyer in accordance with the standard stated above, the lawyer has met his or her ethical responsibility with respect to the advice.

In all cases, however, with regard both to the preparation of returns and negotiating administrative settlements, the lawyer is under a duty not to mislead the Internal Revenue Service deliberately, either by misstatements or by silence or by permitting the client to mislead. Rules 4.1 and 8.4(c); DRs 1-102(A)(4), 7-102(A)(3) and (5).

In summary, a lawyer may advise reporting a position on a return even where the lawyer believes the position probably will not prevail, there is no "substantial authority" in support of the position, and there will be no disclosure of the position in the return. However, the position to be asserted must be one which the lawyer in good faith believes is warranted in existing law or can be supported by a good faith argument for an extension, modification or reversal of existing law. This requires that there is some realistic possibility of success if the matter is litigated. In addition, in his role as advisor, the lawyer should refer to potential penalties and other legal consequences should the client take the position advised.... His own notions of policy, and his personal view of what the law should be, are irrelevant. The job entrusted to him by his client is to use all his learning and ability to protect his client's rights, not to help in the process of promoting a better tax system. The tax lawyer need not accept his client's economic and social opinions, but the client is paying for technical attention and undivided concentration upon his affairs. He is equally entitled to performance unfettered by his attorney's economic and social predilections.

REPORT OF THE SPECIAL TASK FORCE
ON FORMAL OPINION 85-352

(1985)

[Opinion 352's new standard] requires not only that there be some possibility of success, if litigated, rather than merely a construction that can be argued or that seems reasonable, but also that there be more than just any possibility of success. The possibility of success, if litigated, must be "realistic." A possibility of success cannot be "realistic" if it is only theoretical or impracticable. This clearly implies that there must be a substantial possibility of success, which when taken together with the assumption that the matter will be litigated, measurably elevates what had come to be widely accepted as the minimum ethical standard.

A position having only a 5% or 10% likelihood of success, if litigated, should not meet the new standard. A position having a likelihood of success closely approaching one-third should meet the standard. Ordinarily, there would be some realistic possibility of success where the position is supported by "substantial authority," as that term is used in section 6661 of the Code and applicable regulations. A position to be asserted in the return in the expectation that something could be obtained by way of concession in the bargaining process of settlement negotiations would not meet the new standard, unless accompanied by a realistic possibility of success, if litigated. If there is not a realistic possibility of success, if litigated, the new standard could not be met by disclosure or "flagging" of the position in the return.

IF THE POSITION FALLS BELOW
THE STANDARD

If the standard is not met, the position may be advanced by payment of the tax and claim for refund, which necessarily sets forth in detail each ground upon which a refund is claimed. A position may be advanced in litigation if it is not frivolous. The lawyer may bring a proceeding, and assert an issue therein, if there is a basis for doing so that is not frivolous, which includes a good faith argument for an extension, modification, or reversal of existing law. In such a context good faith does not require that there be a possibility of success that is "realistic." Model Rule 3.1; DR 7-102(A)(2).

If the client determines to proceed to assert a position in a tax return that is not supported by a realistic possibility of success if litigated, the lawyer must withdraw from the engagement, at least to the extent it involves advice as to the position to be taken on the return, subject to usual rules governing withdrawal.

FREDERIC G. CORNEEL, GUIDELINES
TO TAX PRACTICE SECOND

43 Tax Law. 297, 303-306 (1990)

As a result of the "self-assessment" tax system, clients must apply tax law to their own conduct. Uncertainties created by the complexities of the law, doubts as to its fairness, widespread publicity about the exploitation of loopholes, and low audit coverage which, unlike any other lottery, skew the odds of the tax lottery in favor of the client, all tend to make the average person think of a tax lawyer not so much as an expert in the law, but as an expert in what the client might get away with on the client's return.

This attitude on the part of many clients increases the need for us to adhere to the highest ethical standards in our tax practice and to make it clear to our clients that this firm insists on such adherence. . . .

Questions of professional responsibility should not be resolved merely on the basis of individual conscience, but on the basis of rules applicable to the entire office. With this in mind, we are publishing and circulating to every attorney in the firm guidelines to our tax practice, with the exception of criminal tax practice and tax litigation in the courts. . . .

II. OUR RELATIONSHIP TO OUR CLIENTS

a. When a client decides to take an aggressive position, we should usually explain the risks to make sure that the client is aware of what is involved. We should make a record of our warning and of the technical support for the client's position to protect this firm against possible claims from the client or the Service. We should, however, make such record in a manner that preserves the confidentiality of our communications.

b. The general view of tax return professionals is that the applicable rules of professional ethics that bar assistance to a client engaged in "violation of law" are intended solely to prohibit participation in criminal conduct. With respect to client conduct that may lead to certain lesser civil penalties . . . the professional's obligation is merely to warn the client. Nevertheless, it would be highly unusual for this firm to participate in conduct certain to lead to civil tax penalties; indeed we will generally not participate when a civil penalty to the taxpayer would more likely than not result if the return were audited and all of the facts were presented to a court. Further, we will not serve as return preparers if it appears more likely than not that we would be subject to any preparers' penalty if all the facts were known to the Service.

c. Both as a matter of statutory law and as a matter of the common law of taxation, the risk of penalties resulting from aggressive positions may generally be reduced by riders or explanatory statements attached to the return. No matter how complete the disclosure, however, we must in good faith believe that the taxpayer's position is not frivolous.

Most tax practice involves three primary roles: structuring transactions to ensure both compliance and maximum benefits under applicable regulations; reporting transactions to the IRS on tax returns; and representing clients in tax disputes. Many commentators believe that reporting and litigating functions tend to be more adversarial than planning functions, in part because the risks of an aggressive reporting posture are lower than the risks of an unwisely structured transaction. Despite recent reforms, the penalties for underreporting tend to be modest. Moreover, the vast majority of returns are prepared by accountants, and pressures on tax practitioners to compete for business may favor an adversarial stance.

Some clients also tend to be more aggressive at the reporting than at the planning stage. Some of the motives underlying taxpayers' "questionable positions" are captured in columnist Dave Barry's account:

> [W]hen we get to the question about how much, exactly, we spent on "child care," we are going to have some questions of our own, including: What about Captain Skyhawk? Captain Skyhawk is a Nintendo game that we purchased for our son for Christmas because we are bad parents who wish to rot his mind. It cost $41.99, and we definitely view this as a child-care expense on rainy Saturday afternoons when our son has what sounds like 73 friends over, and if they weren't totally engrossed in an effort to get to the last stage of Captain Skyhawk, where you have to kill a giant eyeball that has tentacles, then they would probably be putting spiders into the toaster.
>
> So we say to ourselves, OK, that's $41.99 worth of child care right there, plus mileage to and from the mall, plus psychiatric damage caused by looking for a parking space amidst hundreds of holiday-crazed drivers who are so desperate that not only would they park in a handicapped person's parking space, but some of them would park on an actual handicapped *person*. Pretty soon we realize that just this one item amounts to *thousands of dollars* in tax-deductible child-care expenses, and if the IRS agents don't agree with our calculations, then let *them* clean the charred spiders out of our toaster.[10]

Although commentators generally view ABA Opinion 85-352 as an improvement over its predecessor, many feel that it still does not set high enough ethical standards for practitioners. From critics' perspective, Opinion 314 failed adequately to distinguish the "highly structured, rights-oriented judicial process" and the more "duty-oriented administrative process" that relies on ex parte presentations.[11] ABA Opinion 85-352 has been subject to the same criticism. According to Michael Graetz, replacing the "reasonable basis" approach with the "good faith/realistic possibility of success" framework amounts to replacing the "laugh aloud" standard with a "giggle test."[12]

Similarly, Matthew Ames maintains that

> Opinion 85-352 is based on the belief that filing a tax return creates an adversarial relationship. However, the opinion contains no attempt to justify this belief. . . . [The opinion] states, "[i]n many cases a lawyer must realistically anticipate that the filing of the tax return may be the first step in a process that may result in an adversary relationship between the client and the I.R.S." "May" is the key word in this sentence. In fact, "may" means about one percent of the time, since only that many return filings lead to actual proceedings. . . . [Yet] mere potential for litigation is not enough to create an adversary relationship, since almost any legal transaction could lead to litigation, and lawyers must always be aware of that eventuality. If the opinion's language was the rule, a lawyer in any type of practice would have to behave as an adversary in every role he ever played. That simply is not the case. . . .
>
> The [opinion's] overarching assumption of an adversarial role tends to blur the distinction between advice and advocacy, forcing the client's interest to the fore whether the lawyer is preparing a return or simply advising. In either case, concern solely for loyalty to the client results in a relatively low standard of behavior and effectively creates a single standard under which the client's interests and desires control. For instance, according to the Opinion, the lawyer preparing the return must have a good faith belief in the validity of a position before taking it, but has no duty to require that a rider be attached. The lawyer advising a client on a position only has a duty to determine whether substantial authority exists for the position . . .; if it does not exist, the lawyer must warn the client of the penalty for nondisclosure. The lawyer's own good faith belief in the validity of the position is irrelevant. Consequently, even if the attorney is not willing to sign the return, and the client is willing to assume the risk of a questionable position, the client is free to play the lottery and the attorney is free to continue representing the client. . . . Even if the warning [of penalties] is stated fully and clearly, if the lawyer delivers it with a wink and a nod, or some indication of the low likelihood of an audit, it may not have much of an impact.[13]

Do you find such criticisms persuasive? What would be the costs and benefits of more stringent standards? Some commentators, including members of an early ABA tax section committee, have proposed that lawyers should not advise clients to take undisclosed positions on a return that are not meritorious.[14] Other experts would require preparers to withdraw from representing a client who refuses to disclose a position lacking substantial authority. In advocating higher standards, these commentators are careful not to overstate the likely benefits of the doctrinal change. However, available data also suggest that actions reinforcing taxpayers' sense of social responsibility as well as reminding them of applicable penalties may result in modest improvements in compliance.[15]

Opponents of such proposals make several responses. Where the law is unclear, as is often the case in tax practice, these commentators maintain that individuals should have "broad latitude" in resolving doubts in their own favor.[16] A further argument is that more stringent disclosure requirements will be impracticable. As Boris Bittker notes,

> [W]hen they demand too much, legal and ethical systems fall of their own weight in practice. . . . I fear that the full-disclosure theory of the federal tax return, asking in effect that the taxpayer identify every item that the government might reasonably seek to treat differently, goes beyond what can be reasonably expected of the taxpayer.[17]

Such disclosure requirements may also go beyond what can be reasonably expected of many tax attorneys. In one survey, over two-thirds disagreed that lawyers should withdraw from representation if the client takes an undisclosed position lacking a realistic possibility of success.[18] If standards for preparers extend too far beyond what is acceptable to the general public, they may remain unenforced or taxpayers may simply dispense with professional assistance. In the long run, these commentators argue, it would not promote compliance with tax law to impose disclosure burdens that penalize individuals who hire lawyers. Nor would it be fair, some experts also argue, to hold tax practitioners to higher standards than other attorneys. Theodore Falk maintains

> [i]f a position on a tax return should be "meritorious," then the same is true of a position on an application to an administrative agency for a field-burning permit, a chauffeur's license, a resident visa, or Medicare certification. . . .
>
> If fair dealing with the government requires elevating standards of legal ethics, this should be done by a uniform approach to the ethics of administrative law, rather than by carving out a distinctive set of rules for tax ethics.[19]

Do you agree? In the absence of sufficient political leverage to raise standards for the entire bar, does it follow that reforms are inappropriate for particular groups of lawyers? Jerome Kurtz, former Commissioner of Internal Revenue, points out that securities practitioners must meet special disclosure standards, and these requirements have not led either to erosion in enforcement or unwillingness to hire lawyers.[20] Given current levels of noncompliance with tax mandates and the IRS' highly limited auditing resources, should tax attorneys have special responsibilities to the legal system? Alternatively, would other reforms better address the problem, such as expanding enforcement resources or increasing no-fault penalties for underpayment? Are these options politically plausible? If not, are tighter ethical standards for attorneys an acceptable alternative?

2. Subjective Intent and Objective Circumstances

a. Introduction

Ethical problems involving taxpayer intent arise in a wide variety of settings where favorable tax treatment turns on subjective purposes. Common examples include characterizing an action as a gift, a loan, or a payment for services rendered or anticipated. Intent issues also emerge where the Internal Revenue Code denies certain advantageous tax treatment to transactions whose dominant purpose is tax avoidance. Such circumstances present ethical questions analogous to those involving witness preparation (Chapter V (The Adversary System)) and client perjury (Chapter VI (Confidentiality and Client Counseling)).

A number of bar ethical provisions are relevant to lawyers' responsibilities concerning taxpayer intent. Model Rule 3.3 and DR 7-102 prohibit an attorney from knowingly using false evidence. Model Rule 1.2 further provides that "a lawyer shall not counsel a client to engage or assist a client in conduct that the lawyer knows is criminal or fraudulent . . . but may counsel or assist a client to make a good faith effort to determine the validity, scope, meaning, or application of the law." Knowingly false representations to the IRS can constitute both fraudulent and criminal conduct (§§6663, 7206). Ethical Consideration 7-6 speaks most specifically to intent issues in a tax context:

> Whether the proposed action of a lawyer is within the bounds of the law may be a perplexing question when his client is contemplating a course of conduct having legal consequences that vary according to the client's intent, motive, or desires at the time of the action. Often a lawyer is asked to assist his client in developing evidence to the state of mind of the client at a particular time. He may properly assist his client in the development and preservation of evidence of existing motive, intent, or desire; obviously he may not do anything furthering the creation or preservation of false evidence. In many cases, a lawyer may not be certain as to the state of mind of his client and in those situations he should resolve reasonable doubts in favor of his client.

What constitutes a "reasonable doubt" and "good faith effort" on the facts of Problems 18B to 18D below? If clients alter their story after learning its tax implications, when does the attorney "know" that they are lying? How certain does a lawyer need to be? How would you characterize the practice summarized by Marvin Frankel of "telling the client 'the law' before eliciting the facts — i.e., telling the client what facts would constitute a successful claim or defense, and only then asking the client what the facts happen perchance to be."[21] See the discussion of client perjury in Chapter V at pages 203–204 and Chapter VI at pages 251–262.

In tax contexts, a recurring question is whether clients should be bound by the way they characterize their motives before becoming aware of the tax consequences. For example, a frequently quoted exchange among tax experts involves a hypothetical in which a client indicates that he would like to "save some tax money" by splitting a corporation into two entities after a friend reportedly "divided his business and saved quite a bit."[22] Under regulations then applicable, such savings were not available if the "principal purpose" of the split was to achieve a tax advantage. According to one practitioner, the client's opening statement should not deprive him of the "right to an examination of his factual situation and legal advice as to what his rights are. . . . [An attorney could appropriately] explore the situation to see whether or not . . . there was justifiable basis for proceeding on a basis other than the tax advantage alone."[23] By contrast, David Herwitz, a Harvard Law School business planning specialist, observed:

> [W]hen a fellow has come in and stated his objective in the way described here, . . . [although] there may well be some other quite adequate business reasons [for the split], there is a real question as to whether one could ever overcome the likelihood of the stated purpose being at least a major purpose, since it is the only one the client starts with on his own.[24]

Ethics professors divide along similar lines, as Chapter V's discussion of witness preparation reflects. Monroe Freedman defends the practice of disclosing the law before discussing the facts on the ground that the lawyer should not "presume that the client will make unlawful use of his advice. . . . Before he begins to remember essential facts, the client is entitled to know what his own interests are." Withholding information would, in Freedman's view, "penalize the less well-educated defendant."[25] Other commentators deny that the lawyer's role includes encouraging clients to lie or ensuring that they all have equal advantages in deception.

Where do you fall in this debate? What considerations would be relevant to your decisions to assist the taxpayers in Problems 18B, 18C, and 18D?

b.   *Gifts and Charitable Contributions*

PROBLEM 18B

1. You are the chair of your local philharmonic orchestra, which is in difficult financial circumstances. Your development committee is looking for ways to reward membership without violating tax laws. One committee member proposes establishing free group lessons for talented children. Although the program would not be limited to family members of contributors, neither would it be widely advertised. In selecting among applicants, administrators could give special consideration to candidates

whose family background demonstrated commitment to fostering musical talent. As chair of the committee and its only expert on tax law, what is your assessment of that proposal?

2. One of your clients has heard from a friend that there are tax-deductible ways to send children to compete in European music festivals. She asks whether it would be permissible to make a charitable contribution to a local philharmonic orchestra or to her son's tax-exempt school on the condition that the funds subsidize travel by aspiring violists. How do you respond?

On its face, prevailing law is clear that a "quid pro quo" will defeat charitable intent. In application, however, what constitutes a quid pro quo is not always clear. Two often-cited decisions denying charitable tax deductions for taxpayers who expected something in return are Singer Co. v. United States, 449 F.2d 413 (Ct. Cl. 1971), and Ottawa Silica Co. v. United States, 669 F.2d 1124 (Fed. Cir. 1983) (per curiam). In *Singer*, the taxpayer sold discounted sewing machines to schools with the expectation that students trained on Singer machines would later purchase their own Singer product. In *Ottawa Silica*, the taxpayer mining company donated land to a school district for the construction of a high school and access road. This construction would clearly increase the value of surrounding land that the taxpayer planned to sell for residential development. Both *Singer* and *Ottawa Silica* held that the expectation of a return benefit barred any charitable deduction. In the *Singer* court's view, quoted with approval in *Ottawa*, "if the benefits received . . . or expected to be received, are substantial, and [are] greater than those that inure to the general public . . . then . . . the transferor has received, or expects to receive, a quid pro quo sufficient to remove the transfer from the realm of deductibility." 449 F.2d at 423.

For similar reasons, individuals who purchase tickets for charitable fund-raising events may deduct only that portion of the ticket price that exceeds the fair market value of the event. See, e.g., Rev. Rul. 67-246, 1967-2 C.B. 104. Charities must provide a good faith estimate of that market value.

By contrast, individuals are allowed to make charitable donations to tax-exempt educational institutions even if they receive certain benefits, such as having a building, lecture, or professorship named after them, or ensuring special attention to applications by their children. Similarly, in DeJong v. Commissioner, 309 F.2d 373 (9th Cir. 1962), the court upheld a charitable deduction to a tuition-free parochial school where 70 percent of its income came from parents. Although the school suggested a contribution of the cost per student, no child had ever been refused admission for a parent's failure to contribute. The court allowed parents to deduct that portion of their contributions that exceeded the market value of the education that their children received. In so holding, the court was not concerned with any indirect benefit resulting from the parents' contribution.

Is the logic of these holdings consistent or persuasive? How would you resolve the issues in Problem 18B? Are your ethical responsibilities different in advising charitable organizations about how to structure a fund-raising event than in counseling taxpayers about their tax liability or preparing donors' tax returns?

c. Gifts, Loans, and Payments

PROBLEM 18C

1. Consider the facts in the landmark cohabitation case, Marvin v. Marvin, 557 P.2d 106 (Cal. 1976), excerpted in Chapter XII (Contracts) at page 517. If Michelle Marvin had recovered a judgment from Lee Marvin, what would have been the appropriate tax treatment of the payments? Given the appellate court's ultimate determination, what should be the tax status of property transfers that Lee made to Michelle during the relationship? Should trips, clothing, jewelry, cars, and so forth be considered gifts or payments for services? If you were a lawyer for parties in the Marvins' situation, how might tax considerations color your advice? What other concerns would be relevant, and what ethical issues do you expect your advice to raise?

2. You are a second-year associate in the tax department of a large law firm. Your firm holds a day-long white water rafting outing that is attended by every lawyer in the firm. Although you hate the water and boats make you seasick, you feel an obligation to participate. Aside from a discussion of boat safety on shore, no meetings are held during the event. After the outing you learn that the firm plans to deduct the trip as a business expense.

As a tax specialist, you are concerned about this planned deduction. Roughly speaking, §274 of the Internal Revenue Code and the regulations under that section disallow deductions for entertainment that does not include meetings.[26] If the firm deducts the trip, you believe that the lawyers who attended should pay taxes on its value. However, you are not quite sure what action you should take. Consider the following options. (1) You could suggest to the tax section that the firm should not take the deduction and hope that you will be, if not commended, at least not penalized for spotting the questionable tax issue. (2) You could tell the accounting department that the firm might be able to get away with the deduction if the lawyers are advised to report the value of the outing on their personal taxes. (3) You could say nothing but personally report what little benefit the outing had to you on your income tax return. (4) You could say and report nothing. Which of these or other options make most sense? Would you respond differently if you were the senior partner in the firm's tax section?

Taxpayers generally establish their subjective intent through objective factors. What, then, is the point of having a subjective test? Is the concern simply that bright-line rules would be over- or under-inclusive? Are other considerations relevant? Under what circumstances would it be possible or desirable to reduce ethical tensions by eliminating intent-based standards? For example, a frequent dilemma in tax practice used to involve gifts made "in contemplation of death." IRS rules treated such gifts as part of the donor's estate to prevent avoidance of inheritance taxes. Clients nearing death often wished to avoid taxation by claiming some other motive for their generosity. The difficulties that lawyers, clients, and auditors faced in applying the "contemplation of death" requirement finally resulted in its replacement with a rule that automatically includes gifts made within three years of death as part of the decedent's estate. Should the tax bar lobby more actively for comparable changes in other IRS provisions that employ subjective tests? What would be the costs of such modifications in circumstances like those in Problems 18B and 18C?

d. Hobbies and Employment

PROBLEM 18D

Your client, a full-time physician, raises poodles, which she enters from time to time in local competitions. An acquaintance recently told her that it is possible to deduct the expenses connected with her dogs if she is showing them professionally. She seeks your advice. Although she considers herself "something of a professional," she would never consider selling any of her four dogs, and the prizes at local competitions are far too small to defray her costs.

Under Treasury Regulations §1.183-2, the costs of an activity are nondeductible if the taxpayer engages in it primarily as a hobby, but are deductible if the taxpayer enters into the activity with the objective of making a profit. Factors relevant in determining if the activity is for profit include whether it is carried on in a businesslike fashion with appropriate books and records; whether the taxpayer has expertise in the field; and whether the taxpayer spends significant time and effort on the activity.

How do you advise your client? If she never kept books and records in the past, may you advise her to begin now and prepare a return claiming the expenses as a deduction?

e. Active Versus Passive Investment

PROBLEM 18E

Your client, the poodle owner described in Problem 18D, owns an apartment building. It showed a tax loss of $30,000 in the past year. The loss will be fully deductible only if the client actively managed the apartment building. Under §469(h), the test is whether the taxpayer had "material participation" in management activities. Material participation involves "regular, continuous and substantial" activity. Proposed regulations establish seven standards for meeting this test. For example, the taxpayer must spend more than 600 hours per year on the activity or, alternatively, at least 100 hours and at least as many hours as other individuals. Another standard is qualitative: the taxpayer may introduce other facts and circumstances to establish material participation. Treas. Regs. §1.469-5T(a).

How do you counsel the client concerning the deductibility of her losses? Would your personal knowledge concerning the taxpayer's other activities limit your ability to accept certain claims about her time on real estate management at face value?

C.   CANDOR AND CONFIDENTIALITY

1.   Introduction

As Chapter VI (Confidentiality and Client Counseling) indicates, both the Model Rules and the Code of Professional Responsibility prohibit lawyers from disclosing client confidences, except under quite limited circumstances. Several exceptions are particularly relevant to tax practice. Disciplinary Rule 4-101(C)(3) allows a lawyer to reveal the intention of his client to commit a crime and the information necessary to prevent the crime. An amended version of DR 7-102(B), applicable in some states, calls on lawyers to rectify frauds perpetrated during the course of representation. Model Rule 3.3 provides that a lawyer shall not fail to disclose a material fact to a tribunal when disclosure is necessary to avoid assisting criminal or fraudulent client conduct. That rule also requires lawyers to take reasonable remedial measures if they have offered evidence that they later learn is false. Both the Model Rules and the Code permit lawyers to reveal confidences to protect themselves from accusations of wrongful conduct or to collect a fee. DR 4-101(C)(4); Model Rule 1.6.

Under circumstances raising conflicts between duties of candor and confidentiality, the lawyer's prescribed course of action is generally withdrawal from representation. A lawyer must withdraw if the representation will result in violations of rules of professional conduct or other law (Model Rule 1.16; DR 2-110(B)). A lawyer may withdraw if the client persists in a course of action involving the lawyer's services that the lawyer reasonably believes is criminal or fraudulent. Id. Proposed Guidelines on Tax Practice reflect these rules in prescribing a general standard: "[W]e will not voluntarily disclose confidential information unless so authorized by the client and we will not lie to the Service. We will do our best to resolve any conflict between these two principles, and if we cannot do so, we will resign."[27]

Consider the justifications and critiques of broad confidentiality protection for lawyer-client relationships discussed in Chapter VI. The primary rationale for such protection is to encourage candid disclosures between attorneys and clients. Underlying that rationale are several key assumptions: that exceptions to confidentiality rules would preempt the trust and candor that is necessary for effective representation; that such representation is essential to protect fundamental legal rights, safeguard privacy interests, and promote compliance with the law; and that these functions should have priority over other societal needs.

Critics of unqualified confidentiality protections challenge such assumptions. In their view, limited disclosure obligations would not necessarily preempt candid or effective representation. As they note, clients often make disclosures without an accurate understanding of the scope of confidentiality, many individuals have no realistic alternative but to confide in lawyers, and counsel often learn damaging information from sources other than clients' direct disclosures. Critics also question why attorneys should be allowed to reveal confidential information to protect their own interests in collecting fees but not to serve other societal values. See pages 226–227.

Consider these claims in light of the Problems that follow. Under what circumstances would you insist on disclosure or withdrawal from representation?

2. Material Errors and Prior Returns

PROBLEM 18F

1. In the case that Geoffrey Hazard describes at page 776 below, your client acknowledges that he "left out a lot of income in last year's tax return."[28] He asks for your advice. What considerations would be relevant to your response? How do they compare with the Guidelines set forth below?

2. You represent a client who claimed a deduction for expenses involving a two-week trip to Europe. The applicable law requires an allocation of expenses between deductible business expenses and nondeductible personal expenses. The IRS is now auditing the return and challenging your client's deduction as improper because of the small amount of time spent on business each day. You know, but the IRS agent does not, that the taxpayer has relatives in Europe and spent several days with his family during a period at which he was nominally participating in a conference. How do you proceed?[29]

FREDERIC G. CORNEEL, GUIDELINES TO TAX PRACTICE SECOND

43 Tax Law. 303, 307-311 (1990)

a. We may advise a client even though his return may run the risk of incurring a penalty. As return preparers, however, we will seek to avoid participation in a return likely to subject us to penalties.

b. If, subsequent to our preparation of a return, it comes to our attention that there was a clear and material error on the return, we may wish to withdraw from the representation unless the error is corrected, although the client may not be under a legal obligation to make a correction. We are obliged not to mislead the Service, and by continuing under the circumstances we may do so. Indeed, we may from time to time be asked to assist in the defense of a client who has filed a fraudulent return. If we should ever learn, however, that a client asked us to be return preparers of a fraudulent return, we would immediately terminate all further representation.

A. Prior Years' Returns

If we discover an error in a prior year's return that is not barred by the statute of limitations, whether or not of our own creation, we must advise the client of the error. We should explain that present law does not mandate the filing of an amended return, but that a tax that is owed is a debt that should be paid and, therefore, in general an amended return should be filed to correct any clear and material errors.

1. Although there is no legal obligation to file an amended return, the implications of an uncorrected error on future years' returns must be considered. An uncorrected error having an effect on future returns cannot knowingly be carried forward.

2. If correction gives rise to risk of penalty, we must describe the risk and explore ways of paying the tax due that will minimize exposure to the penalty. In any situation involving potential fraud charges, however, we should carefully explain to the taxpayer the benefits and hazards of the various options available, including any constitutional right not to cooperate with the Service. A lawyer who does not have criminal tax practice experience should consult with one who has such experience.

a. When a clear and material error was made on a return prepared by this firm or in an audit in which we acted as the client's representative, we should explain to the client our own interest in an appropriate correction, and suggest that if the client wants advice not colored by such interest, the client should consult another adviser. Indeed, we may be required to insist that the client consult another adviser, where our own interest is sufficiently disparate from that of the client.

B.   Truthfulness in Dealings with the Service

1. We must at all times be truthful with the Service and use our best efforts to ensure that the client is also truthful.

a. To preserve our reputation for integrity and reliability we must, in communications to the Service, be clear as to the source of any facts we assert. "The Corporation made all relevant elections on a timely basis" is a legitimate statement if we know it to be a fact. If we do not know it, we should say, "We are informed by John Jones, Treasurer of the corporation, that it made all relevant elections on a timely basis."[43]

b. When we become aware of a clear and material error on the client's return, we should generally urge the client to permit disclosure, particularly when the proceeding involves the general correctness of the return rather than focusing on a specific issue. (For instance, we should do so if we find during the course of an audit that a deduction was taken for a particular expenditure that was clearly non-deductible.) Also, any mathematical mistakes whether made by ourselves, the client, or the Service, should be disclosed to the Service.[44]

c. If, in an appropriate case, the client refuses to make the necessary correction or disclosure, in general, we should withdraw from further representation; the need to withdraw is particularly strong when we were the preparers of what is now known to be an erroneous return or when we may otherwise be understood by the Service to have participated in a misrepresentation by the client.

(i) Withdrawal from the engagement must be carefully undertaken so as to balance the desire or obligation to withdraw against the requirements that confidences not be disclosed and the client's interest not be otherwise prejudiced.

(ii) It may be helpful to remind the client that, during the course of an audit, it is customary for the auditing agent to ask whether the taxpayer or taxpayer's representative is aware of any matters requiring adjustment. If there is an undisclosed problem, and we have decided to continue representation in spite of the client's refusal to authorize disclosure, we must provide a truthful answer.

2. Difficult questions occasionally arise whether, in order to avoid misleading the Service, the lawyer should disclose information

---

43. Model Rules of Professional Conduct, Rule 3.3 Comment ("an assertion purporting to be on the lawyer's own knowledge, . . . may properly be made only when the lawyer knows the assertion is true or believes it to be true on the basis of reasonably diligent inquiry.").

44. ABA Comm. on Ethics and Professional Responsibility, Informal Op. 1518 (1986), counsels disclosure of a "scrivener's error" to the opponent without consultation with the client, since raising the issue of disclosure with the client might involve the lawyer in fraud if the client refuses to authorize disclosure. But see Chicago Bar Assn. Prof. Resp. Com., Op. 864, in ABA/BNA, Lawyer's Manual on Professional Conduct, Vol. 4, No. 20, 345 (1988). In a particular case, it may be preferable first to consult with the client and urge disclosure.

not known to the Service. Generally, in an audit, as in other adversarial proceedings, our obligation to tell the truth does not require disclosure of all relevant facts and law.

a. Excepting only the situations referred to in part V.B.1.b above, we are under no legal or ethical obligation to volunteer to the Service information adverse to the client or to urge the client to do so. Nevertheless, in our dealings with the Service, we can often serve our client most effectively by frank recognition of the problems with our client's case and then explaining why, in spite of these problems, our client should prevail.

In a panel discussion on the Model Rules of Professional Conduct, Geoffrey Hazard put the case noted in Problem 18F:

> There is a critical distinction between giving advice and any further step of facilitation. There is, however, no absolutely clean factual boundary there. The problem of perjury, in my opinion, begins with the fact that the lawyer is presenting the case. It would be one thing if the client asked you, "Look, I left out a lot of income in last year's tax return. What should I do?" In that situation a lawyer can say, "There are severe penalties if they catch up with you; they will be heavy. I have to tell you that the auditing is selective. For someone in your income tax bracket with the kind of income you have, as I understand what they do (and they don't generally tell us), the chances are statistically remote that they will question it. It's for you to decide what you want to do. I consider it my obligation to tell you what the enforcement situation is, as well as what the law is." There is no question what the law is and I can't further the client's purpose, and I haven't done so. There's also no doubt that you don't tell anybody. That's it. If the client wants to do it, that's his problem. The same holds true when you're talking about other kinds of violations.
>
> The problem in practice is often trickier than that, however. Frequently, particularly these days, clients not only have the responsibility of compliance, they also have the responsibility to file reports. They may ask you some questions about the reports. Take the case in which an SEC report requires the lawyer's signature. I just don't see how the lawyer is in any different situation than an income tax preparer signing a tax return. On the other hand, the lawyer can say, "I will look at your report and tell you what the law is." Again what you have done is give advice. You can give advice that tells the client what the law is and what enforcement practices are, as long as you are not involved in executing the purpose. In doing so you do not violate the law and you do not violate legal ethics.[30]

Compare Hazard's approach to the ABA Guidelines. Which do you prefer? Would any alternative approach offer a better accommodation of lawyer, client, and societal interests?

3.   Scriveners' Errors

PROBLEM 18G

1. While helping your client respond to an IRS audit, you become aware of a substantial mathematical error by the Service in favor of your client. If you draw the matter to your client's attention, you are confident that she will refuse to authorize disclosure. If you simply make the disclosure yourself, you are not certain that the client will become aware of that fact, but if she does, it is unlikely that your relationship will extend beyond this audit. On the other hand, if anyone at the IRS later discovers the error, your credibility with the Service could suffer.

How do you respond? What factors would influence your decision? Would it be advisable for your firm to have a general policy concerning such issues, or is it preferable to encourage contextual judgments?

2. Suppose that you make no disclosure and the audit agent asks whether you know of any other matters requiring adjustment. How should you respond?

The ABA Taxation Section's first proposed Guidelines to Tax Practice suggested that if the Service makes a mathematical mistake favoring the client, the lawyer should ask the client's permission to inform the Service and should abide by the client's decision.[31] When Committee members were considering a revised version of the Guidelines, Harvard professor Bernard Wolfman called attention to an informal opinion of the ABA Committee on Ethics. It held that a lawyer had an ethical obligation to disclose scriveners' errors to an opposing party without consulting the client, since an informed client might pressure the lawyer into improper conduct.[32] Accordingly, an early draft of the Guidelines' second edition proposed that the norm for practitioners should be correction without consultation. Its author, Frederic Corneel, reports:

> I was moved to accept that position not so much by the ABA Opinion as by reflection on a frequently repeated personal experience: When, by mistake, I give the cashier two bills that are stuck together, [she returns] . . . my extra bill without asking the store owner. She is right to assume that she was hired to act as a decent register clerk; we, as lawyers, have a right to assume that we have been hired to act as decent lawyers.[33]

However, disagreement by other practitioners prompted him to draft a position in the Guidelines that "waffles" on this point.[34] Under the Guidelines excerpted above, lawyers should "generally urge the client to permit disclosures," and should "generally" withdraw from representation if "in an appropriate case, the client

778   Part II. Legal Ethics in Legal Context

refuses to make the necessary correction or disclosure." In clarifying what would be an "appropriate case," the Guidelines refer to circumstances in which the lawyers' firm prepared the return on which the Service might understand the lawyer "to have participated in a misrepresentation." However, the Guidelines also acknowledge the need to "balance" the client's interests in confidentiality.[35]

Is this approach an improvement over the ABA Ethics Committee's opinion and Corneel's first draft? Consider the materials in Chapter VIII (Negotiation and Mediation) at pages 351–353 on scriveners' errors. In what kind of world would you prefer to practice, one where lawyers routinely disclosed such errors or one where they did not? If your preference is disclosure, do you see reasons to treat the IRS differently, either as a general matter or in particular cases?

4. Valuation

PROBLEM 18H

Your client has agreed in principle to pay $1.5 million for an apartment building and the acre of land on which it sits. The building is a wasting asset that can be depreciated. The land is nondepreciable. It is, therefore, in your client's interest to attribute as much of the sale price as possible to the building rather than the land. The seller is indifferent to how the purchase price is allocated. Your client would like you to recommend some real estate appraisers who have been "helpful" in the past in preparing evaluations.

Two of the individuals that you recommend value the building at $700,000 and $800,000 respectively. These figures strike you as somewhat higher than those that an entirely neutral expert would select, but they do not appear grossly inflated. Your client then finds a third appraiser, who values the building at $1 million. Unsurprisingly, your client would like you to prepare sales documents and tax returns using the $1 million figure. How do you respond? Is your advice affected by past experience indicating that if the IRS audits the return, it is likely to assume some overvaluation and may discount the value allocated to the building by about 10 percent?

The "race to the bottom" among appraisers, coupled with the low probability of audits for taxpayers, creates recurrent ethical dilemmas for lawyers. Problem 18H is a variation on a hypothetical put to a sample of Boston tax practitioners before the promulgation of Opinion 85-352. Under that hypothetical, the lawyer needed to price some stock of a closely held family corporation in preparing an estate return. Two neutral experts put the value of the stock at about $50 per share. However, its book value was $30, and because it was a minority interest and would be hard to sell, it could be discounted to

$22.50. Surveyed practitioners were aware of the IRS' practice of assuming some underreporting and attaching a "mendacity premium" to whatever value the taxpayer selected. Under those hypothesized circumstances, none of the surveyed practitioners would report the value of the shares at $50. About a third would report at $40, and the majority at $30 or less.[36]

The ethical temptations inherent in such contexts have prompted several initiatives, including increased penalties for overvaluation and undervaluation of property, bright-line rules concerning issues like amortization, requirements of a qualified appraiser in certain circumstances, and the "good faith/realistic possibility of success" standard of Opinion 85-352. Proposed Guidelines to Tax Practice Second have also attempted to raise practice norms. They provide:

> [W]hile there is nothing wrong in either the appraiser or the preparer giving the client the benefit of the doubt where the value [of property] is uncertain, any valuation involved in a return that we prepare must be responsibly done, make sense, be well-reasoned, and be internally consistent.[37]

If your firm had such a standard, how would you proceed on the facts in Problem 18H?

5. Cash Reporting and Client Identity

Section 6050I of the IRC requires anyone in a trade or business who receives payment of over $10,000 in cash to report it on a special Form 8300. This cash reporting provision is designed both to increase revenue and to assist monitoring of criminal activity. The provision does not exempt attorneys, and their obligation to report the identities of clients making substantial cash payments has become a focus of increasing controversy. In a series of cases during the early 1990s, federal appellate panels rejected claims that Section 6050I violated fourth, fifth, or sixth amendment rights. Although recognizing that client identity may be privileged information, these courts reasoned that clients could preserve secrecy by not paying for legal services in cash.[38] However, a number of state bar ethics committees have taken a more protective view and have authorized lawyers to withhold information that may prejudice client interests.[39]

Resistance to this reporting provision stems in part from the conviction that it functions less to identify tax cheaters than to diminish resources for legal defense, to discourage confidential communications, and to drive a wedge between lawyers and clients. As one practitioner put it, "I do not believe my role as a criminal defense attorney is to be the first witness for the prosecution."[40] According to some commentators, the provision is indefensible as a revenue-enhancing measure since voluntary compliance is minimal and enforcement efforts have been limited.[41]

By contrast, defenders of the cash reporting provision argue that it is a potentially useful strategy in identifying increasingly sophisticated criminal activity. As they also note, it is far less damaging to attorney-client relationships than other law enforcement measures such as racketeering statutes requiring forfeiture of attorneys' fees that are paid with tainted funds.

If you were a member of your state bar ethics committee, how would you advise attorneys who receive cash payments? If you were a criminal defense attorney, could you avoid problems by requesting payment in property such as highly liquid securities?

See Chapter VI, Confidentiality and Client Counseling
  • Scope of the Attorney-Client Privilege: Client Identity
     (pages 234–236)

6. Backdating

PROBLEM 18I

Several months ago, the IRS passed a regulation providing that prepayment of interest will be tax deductible for certain transactions completed before a specified date. Your firm represents several clients in a transaction that almost closed by the prescribed date, and would have done so but for the managing partner's negligence. In order to spare those clients substantial tax losses as well as to absolve themselves of any malpractice claims, the lawyers working on the case have backdated relevant forms.

1. You are an associate in the firm's tax department. You are not asked to do any backdating personally, although you are working on the transaction in which backdated documents will be submitted. What do you do? Consider the materials on supervisory and subordinate attorneys in Part E of Chapter III (Regulation of the Profession). Would it matter why the managing partner failed to complete the transaction or what your expectations were about advancement within the firm?

2. Suppose that the clients had backdated the forms. No one in your firm signs the return or actively assists the backdating, but you are asked to provide further tax-related representation to those clients. What do you do? Would it matter why the clients believed that backdating was necessary or justifiable?

Frederic Corneel's proposed Guidelines to Tax Practice Second provide:

  1. It is unethical to assist the client in the preparation of evidence designed to mislead the Service. . . .

> 2. At times the client in ignorance of the tax law has taken steps resulting in adverse tax consequences or has failed to take steps to prevent such consequences. It is not unethical to make every effort to correct this result, provided that this can be done without destruction of existing documents, backdating of new documents or other steps intended to mislead the Service as to what in fact happened.[42]

Although the IRS and courts will generally allow correction of clerical, mathematical, or drafting errors that do not reflect the true intent of the parties, they will not permit backdating to obtain favorable tax treatment.[43]

It is clear that a lawyer cannot ethically assist backdating; it is less clear what an associate under the facts of Problem 18I is obligated to do about it. In responding to that Problem, surveyed practitioners take different views. Some suggest that the associate could "crank up the rumor mill" and hope that eventually a "version of the events will reach the right people."[44] Other lawyers feel that the associate should refuse to work on any transaction involving backdated forms and should report the conduct to a supervising partner or another senior partner. While acknowledging that advancement within the firm would certainly be a concern, these attorneys feel that lawyers should not want to stay in an environment where "matters were not resolved with integrity."[45] How would you respond?

Consider the materials on supervisory and subordinate attorneys in Chapter III at pages 82–89. Model Rule 5.2 provides that a "lawyer is bound by the rules of professional conduct notwithstanding that the lawyer acted at the direction of another person." However, a subordinate lawyer does not violate the rules by acting "in accordance with a supervisory lawyer's reasonable resolution of an arguable question of professional duty." Both the Code and the Model Rules require attorneys to report violations of disciplinary rules involving dishonesty or fitness to practice unless their knowledge of such violations is protected as a client confidence.

As the materials in Part D of Chapter III indicate, attorneys' reports of collegial misconduct to disciplinary agencies are relatively rare. Disciplinary sanctions against attorneys for failure to report other lawyers are rarer still. Although the reluctance to "inform" on fellow practitioners, particularly one's own superiors, is understandable on pragmatic grounds, it is inconsistent with the bar's commitment to self-regulation. At the very least, many experts believe that associates who confront clearly unethical conduct should disclose it to other members of the firm.[46] As the Berkey-Kodak case history at pages 82–86 in Chapter III indicates, such disclosures can often prove less professionally damaging than silence. For contexts where that is not the case, many commentators would prefer not to absolve associates from responsibility, but rather to alter existing incentive structures.[47] What is your view?

Are the same considerations applicable where the issue is client rather than collegial fraud, as on the facts of part 2 of Problem 18I?

Geoffrey Hazard observes that one of the hardest responsibilities of lawyers

> is to report wrongdoing. . . . [However, if] everyone lets [the wrong-doer] get away with it, [professional regulation is] not going to get done. . . .
>
> So far as what clients think, you have to use good judgment at the margin. You don't go blowing the whistle as your first recourse. One of the things you must have is the courage to tell the client what to do. That brings to mind a good story from the firm I went with. When I was being interviewed, one of the lawyers was writing a resignation letter, firing a client. That impressed the hell out of me. The lawyer was obviously quite distressed by doing it because he had represented the client for quite a while. But this client had been involved in two fraud cases and now had gotten into a third. The lawyer knew these were not accidents. This is just the way the client did business. I'm sure people asked why that firm no longer represented that company, but I believe the firm was far better off without that client. That firm was terribly interested in maintaining its reputation for trustworthiness in its representations. The State Tax Commission and the Internal Revenue Service would believe us if our people made a statement as to what the situation was. That was of great value to the firm; it was of great value to the firm's clients. Most businesses want to be represented by lawyers who have a first class reputation for integrity because their legal counsel's reputation reflects on them. It's just about that simple.[48]

Is it?

D.   COMPETENT REPRESENTATION

PROBLEM 18J

The executive vice president of a long-standing client is about to leave for Japan for a business conference with his wife. He has been assuming that her expenses would be deductible as long as she helps with business entertaining at the conference. However, one of his colleagues has suggested that the issue is not clear-cut, so he wanted to run it by you quickly. He does not want you to invest any significant amount of time researching this issue; he simply wants your best judgment.

1. You vaguely recall a case where the wife hosted a hospitality suite and the expenses were deductible, but you also think that there may be some later holdings on the subject. May you advise the client what you remember and make clear the limits of your knowledge, or should you decline to give the "seat of the pants" response that the vice president has requested?

2. Suppose that the couple attends the conference and the husband wants to deduct her expenses. You have found the dated case support-

ing the deduction but have not done further research. May you help prepare the return without doing additional work on this issue?[49]

Both the Model Rules and Code of Professional Responsibility require lawyers to provide competent representation, which includes preparation "reasonably necessary" (Model Rule 1.1) or "adequate in the circumstances" (DR 6-101(A)(2)). Model Rule 1.2 allows lawyers and clients to agree to limit the scope of representation, provided that it is not so limited as to violate obligations of competence. Comment, Rule 1.2.

In applying these rules to circumstances similar to Problem 18J, Paul Sax, former Chair of the Committee on Standards of Tax Practice, makes the following argument: lawyers may properly restrict their assistance, provided that they "determine that the minimum standard is met for asserting a position in a tax return."[50] If a client declines to pay for adequate assistance, the lawyer must provide it without payment or must refuse to provide representation. In addition, Sax argues that any limits on assistance must be in the client's best interest and must be consistent with any obligations owed to third parties.[51]

Frederic Corneel's Proposed Guidelines to Tax Practice Second come to similar conclusions. Of the three main options facing a lawyer under circumstances in Problem 18J — declining work, performing it without adequate compensation, or limiting it in accordance with client preferences — the Guidelines maintain:

> [T]he last alternative is generally the least desirable. Inadequate work on small jobs is likely to breed a general careless-ness. . . . Except for emergencies, we should refuse to represent a client in matters before a court or in dealings with the Service or other third parties unless we are satisfied that we can provide quality representation. . . . [When limiting efforts,] we should make sure that the client understands the risks resulting from our limited work. For our own protection as well as that of the client, such warning should usually be in writing.[52]

Would a written warning be sufficient on the facts of Problem 18J? In addressing that issue, Allan Samansky argues that an attorney's reliance on a dated opinion with no additional research is highly questionable even if the position simply needs to be nonfrivolous and even if the client receives a written warning.[53] To give advice whether a deduction is worth taking and whether it should be accompanied by disclosures, the attorney needs to know the taxpayer's likelihood of prevailing if audited. And, as Samansky notes, recent case law leaves doubt that spouses' expenses would generally be deductible, absent some specific and clearly justifiable business function for them on the trip.[54] Samansky concludes his observation with the comment that an "attorney will often resolve doubt by doing some extra research even though she knows she will not be paid for it. That result should not be distressing."[55] To whom? What are the alternatives?

A converse issue is what degree of ingenuity should be available to clients willing and able to pay. That issue is the subtext of a cartoon featuring an American in Hindu religious robes explaining to another man similarly attired: "Last week I was running an electric plant in Ohio and today I'm a holy man in Kashmir. What will my tax lawyer think of next?"[56]

Richard Posner touches on similar themes:

> Quality is an elusive concept when one is speaking of legal services. Highly intelligent lawyers may create intricate doctrinal structures that, while ingenious . . . have no social utility. For example, brilliant lawyers create, discover, and enlarge tax loopholes. This activity is purely redistributive; there is no social gain. In fact there is a net social loss, not only because lawyers' time has an opportunity cost but also because their beaver-like activities require more carefully drafted and complex tax codes. Social welfare might increase if the IQs of all tax lawyers could be reduced by 10 percent.[57]

Endnotes

1. Robert Tobias, National Treasury Employees Union Press Release (Jan. 5, 1990), reported in Daily Tax Rep. (BNA, Jan. 8, 1990).

2. Michael J. Graetz, Can the Income Tax Continue to Be the Major Revenue Source?, in Options for Tax Reform (Joseph A. Pechman ed., 1984); Walter T. Henderson, Jr., Criminal Liability Under the Internal Revenue Code: A Proposal to Make the "Voluntary" Compliance System a Little Less "Voluntary," 140 U. Pa. L. Rev. 1429 nn.6-8 (1992). For a summary of public complaints that surfaced in 1997 Senate hearings, see John M. Broder, Demonizing the I.R.S.: Is an Overview Needed or Just Less Posturing?, N.Y. Times, Sept. 20, 1997, at 1.

3. IRS Taxpayer Attitudes Study, Final Report 55-59 (1984); Mark H. Moore, On the Office of Taxpayer and the Social Process of Taxpaying, in Income Tax Compliance: A Report of the ABA Section of Taxation Conference on Income Tax Compliance 275 (Phillip Sawicki ed., 1983).

4. Adequate disclosure will not, however, protect certain violations such as tax shelters; to avoid penalties, taxpayers must have a reasonable belief that their positions were more likely than not to be held proper.

5. 31 C.F.R. §10.50(b) (1993); see also 18 U.S.C. §1001 (making a false statement to government agency constitutes a felony).

6. Michael J. Graetz, Too Little, Too Late, Tax Times, Feb. 1987, at 17.

7. Deborah T. Schenk, Conflicts Between the Tax Lawyer and the Client: Vignettes in the Law Office, 20 Cap. U.L. Rev. 387, 393 n.26 (1991) ("I know of no case where an attorney has been disciplined by a state for improperly advising a client about a tax return position"); Bernard Wolfman, James P. Holden & Deborah H. Schenk, Ethical Problems in Federal Tax Practice 67 (3d ed. 1995) (noting that "there is no known case where a practitioner was disciplined by an admitting authority for violating a rule relating to the quality of income tax advice").

8. James P. Holden, Practitioners' Standard of Practice and the Taxpayer's Reporting Position, 20 Cap. U.L. Rev. 327, 341 (1991).

9. For a similar hypothetical, see Wolfman, Holden & Schenk, supra note 7, at 71.

10. Dave Barry, Tax Advice That Could Get You 1,040 Years, Chi. Trib., Feb. 24, 1991 (Sunday Magazine), at 25.

11. L. Ray Patterson, Tax Shelters for the Client, Ethics Shelters for the Lawyer, 61 Tex. L. Rev. 1163, 1169 (1983).

12. Graetz, supra note 6, at 17.

13. Matthew C. Ames, Formal Opinion 352: Professional Integrity and the Tax Audit Lottery, 1 Geo. J. Legal Ethics 411, 422-424 (1987).

14. Id. at 424 ("[I]f the attorney is not willing to sign the return, . . . this position may, in the short run, dissuade some clients from playing the lottery, since the sight of the lawyer balking may shake their confidence").

15. In one study, approximately 400 taxpayers were divided into four groups matched for reportable income and interviewed a month before they were to file tax returns. The first group was asked questions referring to the penalties for tax evasion. The second group was asked questions designed to evoke a sense of civic obligation. The third group was asked neutral questions, and the fourth group was not interviewed. A comparison of tax returns found that the first two groups reported an increase in income from the previous year and the other two reported a slight decrease. See Nigel Walker, Sentencing in a Rational Society 59 (1969).

16. See Michael C. Durst, The Tax Lawyer's Professional Responsibility, 39 U. Fla. L. Rev. 1027, 1063 (1987). For discussion of complexity, see David Burnham, The Abuse of Power: Misuse of the IRS, N.Y. Times Mag., Sept. 3, 1989, at 24, 27 (noting a survey of tax preparers that revealed wide variations in their treatment of a hypothetical case and a survey of 1,000 IRS employees assigned to answer taxpayer questions that identified one-third of all sampled answers as incorrect or incomplete).

17. Boris I. Bittker, Professional Responsibility in Federal Tax Practice 254-255 (1970).

18. J. Timothy Philipps, Michael W. Mumbach & Morgan W. Alley, What Part of RPOs Don't You Understand? An Update and Survey of Standards for Tax Return Positions, 51 Wash. & Lee L. Rev. 1163, 1191 (1994).

19. Theodore C. Falk, Tax Ethics, Legal Ethics, and Real Ethics: A Critique of ABA Formal Opinion 85-352, 39 Tax Law. 643, 663 (1986).

20. Jerome Kurtz, Remarks to the American Institute of Certified Public Accountants, 103 Daily Tax Rep. J., May 26, 1977, at 3; Jerome Kurtz and Panel, Discussion on "Questionable Positions," Meeting of A.B.A. Section of Taxation, 32 Tax Law. 13 (1987). See also Ames, supra note 13, at 413-414; and Robert G. Mason, A Longitudinal Study of Changes in Income Tax Evasion, in Income Tax Compliance, supra note 3, at 449.

21. Marvin E. Frankel, Partisan Justice 15 (1980).

22. Business Planning and Professional Responsibility, 8 Prac. Law. 17, 29-30 (1962) (comments of Ross L. Malone).

23. Id. at 30.

24. Id. at 32 (comments of David R. Herwitz).

25. Monroe H. Freedman, Professional Responsibility of the Criminal Defense Lawyer: The Three Hardest Questions, 64 Mich. L. Rev. 1469, 1479, 1481 (1966).

26. See Danville Plywood Corp. v. United States, 899 F.2d 3 (Fed. Cir. 1990) (finding that a Superbowl outing is not an ordinary business expense under §162 and that §274 might also disallow the deduction if it was not directly related to, or associated with, the taxpayer's business).

27. Frederic G. Corneel, Guidelines to Tax Practice Second, 43 Tax Law. 297, 301 (1990).

28. Panel Discussion on Professional Responsibility and the Model Rules of Professional Conduct, 35 U. Miami L. Rev. 639, 659-663 (1981) (comments of Geoffrey Hazard, Jr.).

29. This problem is modeled on a hypothetical situation in Wolfman, Holden & Schenk, supra note 7, at 124-125.

30. Panel Discussion, supra note 28, at 659-660.

31. Guidelines to Tax Practice, 31 Tax Law. 551, 554 (1977).

32. ABA Comm. on Ethics and Professional Responsibility, Informal Op. 1518 (1986).

33. Corneel, supra note 27, at 298.

34. Id.

35. Id. at 310.

36. Frederic G. Corneel, Ethical Guidelines for Tax Practice, 28 Tax L. Rev. 1, 11 (1972).

37. Corneel, supra note 27, at 304.

38. United States v. Goldberger & Dubin, 935 F.2d 501 (2d Cir. 1991), and United States v. Leventhal, 961 F.2d 936 (11th Cir. 1992).

39. See Wisconsin Bar Op. E-90-3 (Apr. 1990), reprinted in Man. on Prof. Conduct (ABA/BNA) 901:9111 (1990); Ohio Supreme Court Bar Opinions, Op. 90-4 (Apr. 4, 1990), reprinted in Man. on Prof. Conduct (ABA/BNA) 901:6865 (1990); Washington State Bar Opinions, Op. 189 (1991). See also Updated Advice on Cash Reporting, 18 Natl. Crim. Def. Law. Wash. Dig. (Aug. 15, 1991).

40. Ellen S. Podger, Form 8300: The Demise of Law as a Profession, 5 Geo. J. Legal Ethics 485, 508 (1992) (quoting attorney Donald Samuel). See also Eugene R. Gaetke & Sarah N. Welling, Money Laundering and Lawyers, 43 Syracuse L. Rev. 1165, 1166 (1993).

41. Podger, supra note 40, at 493.

42. Corneel, supra note 27, at 312.

43. See generally Sheldon I. Banoff, Unwinding or Rescinding a Transaction: Good Tax Planning or Tax Fraud?, 62 Taxes 942 (1984). Such backdating can lead to criminal violations under §§7201 and 7206.

44. Dennis J. Herman, Letter to the Editor, Stan. Law Alum., Summer 1995, at 5.

45. Philip S. Wilcox, Letter to the Editor, Stan. Law Alum. Summer 1995, at 5.

46. See Association of the Bar of the City of New York, Commission on Professional and Judicial Ethics, Inq. Rev. 82-79 (1982).

47. See the materials in Chapter III, Parts D and E.

48. Panel Discussion, supra note 28, at 661-662 (comments of Geoffrey Hazard, Jr.).

49. This problem draws on a hypothetical case in Paul J. Sax, When Worlds Collide: Ethics vs. Economics, 20 Cap. U.L. Rev. 365 (1991).

50. Id. at 382.

51. Id.

52. Corneel, supra note 27, at 300.

53. Allan J. Samansky, Comment to When Worlds Collide: Ethics vs. Economics, 20 Cap. U.L. Rev. 383, 385 (1991).

54. See id.; Anchor Natl. Life Ins. Co. v. Commissioner, 93 Tax Court 382 (1989). See also Federal Tax Regs. §1.162-2(c) (1993), U.S. Code Cong. Admin. News.

55. Samansky, supra note 53, at 386.

56. S. Gross, Lawyers, Lawyers, Lawyers 47 (1994).

57. Richard A. Posner, Overcoming Law 54 (1995).

A. THE ADVERSARIAL PROCESS

1. Frivolous Cases and Malicious Prosecution: Libel, Personal Injury, and Malpractice Litigation

PROBLEM 19A

Assume that you are the lawyer for the plaintiff in a case against two defendants alleging their joint and several liability.[1] After filing suit, you discover facts suggesting which of the two opposing parties almost certainly caused the injury. However, for financial or personal reasons the client still wishes to sue both defendants. How do you proceed?

PROBLEM 19B

You represent a prominent developer who is seeking to build a processing plant adjacent to a predominantly Asian-American residential community. A neighborhood association has formed in an effort to block the development. Association members have distributed flyers, published editorials, and staged protests that denounce the project as an "ecological death warrant" and an "environmental Hiroshima." They also describe the developer as a racist, a "shady" operator, and an "environmental Jack the Ripper."

Your client believes that these characterizations are entirely without merit and that the group members are more concerned with their own

property values than with the community's need for economic development. He insists on filing suit for defamation and tortious interference
with a prospective business advantage. How should you proceed?[2]

PROBLEM 19C

The director of a multicultural studies institute at a local university
asks you to represent her in a suit against a right-wing campus
newspaper. The article that sparked this suit described the director as a
"femi-nazi" and a representative of a campus "lesbian lunatic fringe." The
piece also misquoted her book on migrant workers (which it denounced
as "sloppy, strident, pseudo-scholarship") and denounced her participation in picketing activities that allegedly stifled free debate. In fact, she
was not involved in the picketing (although she might have been if she
had been in town).

You believe that there is almost no chance that the case could
succeed. However, the director tells you that she doesn't care. She is
willing to "pay a lot" to make sure that the editors and their financial
backers bear "some fraction of the costs" that they have imposed. Her
reputation among colleagues and students has been damaged and the
credibility of the multicultural studies program has suffered. Although she
supports gay and lesbian issues in principle, she is in fact heterosexual
and fears that the article's characterization has undermined her efforts to
build support among potential donors and "mainstream" students.

May you file the suit? If your state has a provision analogous to
Rule 11 of the Federal Rules of Civil Procedures, would you run any risk
of sanctions? Could (or should) you be liable for malicious prosecution?

Individuals who are targets of meritless litigation have often
sought damages in tort. Friedman v. Dozorc, 312 N.W.2d 585 (Mich.
1981), sets forth the traditional requirements for such claims.

FRIEDMAN v. DOZORC, 312 N.W.2D 585 (MICH. 1981).
Friedman was a physician who had obtained a directed verdict in his
favor in a medical malpractice action after the plaintiff had failed to
present any expert testimony showing a breach of professional standards. The doctor subsequently sued the attorneys who had represented the plaintiff in that action. The Michigan Supreme Court
held first that Friedman had failed to state an actionable claim in
negligence because the "public policy of maintaining a vigorous adversary system outweighs the asserted advantages of finding a duty
of due care to an attorney's legal opponent." Id. at 592. The court also
rejected the doctor's claim of abuse of process because he had failed
to meet the requirements of an "ulterior purpose" and an "irregular"
and "improper" procedural action. Id. at 594-595. Finally, no remedy
for malicious prosecution was available because Friedman had not
established a "special injury" (i.e., an "interference with person or

property") in addition to showing success in prior proceedings, an absence of probable cause for those proceedings, and malice (i.e., a purpose other than securing proper adjudication). Id. at 588.

Under this traditional English "special injury" rule, which the *Friedman* court reaffirmed, parties have no remedy for a frivolous claim in the absence of special damages beyond the normal "expense and travail" of defending a lawsuit. Id. at 595. According to the majority, abandoning the English rule would

> arm all prevailing defendants with an instrument of retaliation. . . .
> This is strong medicine—too strong for the affliction it is intended to cure. To be sure, successful defense of the former action is no assurance of recovery in a subsequent tort action, but the unrestricted availability of such an action introduces a new strategic weapon into the arsenal of defense litigators, particularly those whose clients can afford to devote extensive resources to prophylactic intimidation. . . . Some product manufacturers and insurance companies may routinely file countersuits with a view to inhibiting plaintiffs or their attorneys from commencing actions against them or their insureds. The indiscriminate filing of countersuits may lead to actions for wrongfully proceeding with a wrongful civil proceedings action. Embittered litigants whose differences are more emotional than legal will have added opportunities to continue their strife.
> The cure for an excess of litigation is not more litigation. Meritorious as well as frivolous claims are likely to be deterred. There are sure to be those who would use the courts and such an expanded tort remedy as a retaliatory or punitive device without regard to the likelihood of recovery or who would seek a means of recovering the actual costs of defending the first action without regard to whether it was truly vexatious.

Id. at 601-602.

Three justices dissented in part. As one noted, the special injury requirement prevented "meritorious as well as vexatious actions" and was not "logically related to the actual damages incurred by the defendant as the result of a frivolous suit." Id. at 613 (Moody, J., dissenting in part).

A majority of jurisdictions have repudiated the English rule and abolished the requirement of special damages. However, these jurisdictions generally absolve the attorney from a duty to investigate the basis for the action and from any duty to "prejudge" the claim; as long as the client does not proceed for improper purposes, the attorney may safely provide representation even if the chances for prevailing are slight.[3]

How restrictive should the standards be for malicious prosecution and abuse of process actions? Do any of the claims in Problems 19A, 19B, or 19C meet these standards? If the attorneys in those problems filed suit, would sanctions be appropriate under bar ethical

rules or Federal Rule of Civil Procedure 11 and its state law analogues? See the discussion in Chapter V (The Adversary System) at
pages 190–192, and Chapter X (Civil Procedure) at pages 431–433.
Are other remedies for frivolous lawsuits adequate? If not, what
would be the most desirable response?

Is the proposed lawsuit in Problem 19B an example of the
"strategic weapon" that the majority in *Friedman* feared? Such legal
actions, commonly known as SLAPPs (Strategic Lawsuits Against
Public Participation), have provoked legislative as well as judicial
remedies. For example, a California statute authorizes SLAPP
defendants to file a "special motion to strike" that stays proceedings
and prevents harassing discovery until the court decides the motion.
Other remedies include statutory fee awards to successful SLAPP
defendants and punitive damage in SLAPP-back countersuits.[4]
Would such remedies be appropriate if the developer brought suit in
Problem 19B?

2.   Discovery Abuse

PROBLEM 19D

You are the lawyer for Fisons Corporation in Problem 10E in
Chapter X (Civil Procedure) at page 441. How would you proceed? What
might you have done as in-house counsel at an earlier point to prevent
this case from arising?

See Chapter V, The Adversary System
 • Tactical Use of Procedure: The Scope of the Problem
     (pages 190–195)

See Chapter X, Civil Procedure
 • Discovery
     (pages 430–437)

3.   Witness Preparation and Client Perjury in Personal Injury and Wrongful Birth Litigation

PROBLEM 19E

1. You represent the defendant construction company in the personal injury claim described in Problem 5E of Chapter V (The Adversary
System) at page 195. You are highly skeptical that the plaintiff fell at the
construction site and could prove that your client's negligence caused
the fall. You are also convinced that it would be cheaper to buy her off

with a small settlement than to contest the claim. However, if the company acquires a reputation as a pushover, it will attract other equally dubious lawsuits. To discourage overzealous plaintiffs' attorneys, you could teach this one a lesson by playing hardball discovery and refusing to settle. Since the plaintiff's claims are modest and the lawyer is on a contingent fee, this would probably be an expensive lesson for all concerned. If you are wrong about the merits, it would be, of course, unjust as well.

How do you proceed? Do current procedural and ethical rules provide an adequate response to this dilemma?

2. In Gordon v. American Museum of Natural History, 492 N.E.2d 774 (N.Y. 1986), the plaintiff testified that as he "descended the upper level of steps he slipped on the third step and that while he was in midair he observed a piece of white, waxy paper next to his left foot." He further alleged that this paper came from a concession stand and caused his fall. The court held that the case should not have gone to the jury because there was no evidence in the record that the defendant had actual or constructive notice of the paper. In the court's view:

> [T]o constitute constructive notice, a defect must be visible and apparent and it must exist for a sufficient length of time prior to the accident to permit defendant's employees to discover and remedy it. The record contains no evidence that anyone, including plaintiff, observed the piece of white paper prior to the accident. Nor did he describe the paper as being dirty or worn, which would have provided some indication that it had been present for some period of time. . . . Thus, on the evidence presented, the piece of paper that caused plaintiff's fall could have been deposited there only minutes or seconds before the accident and any other conclusion would be pure speculation.

492 N.E.2d at 775.

If you had been the lawyer for the plaintiff, would you have informed him of the elements of constructive notice before asking about what happened? If the plaintiff did not initially recall the condition of the paper, how would you have proceeded?

PROBLEM 19F

You are a Massachusetts attorney specializing in medical malpractice. A potential client seeks your advice about whether she has a claim against a doctor who performed an unsuccessful sterilization procedure. Under the Massachusetts Supreme Court's decision in Burke v. Rivo, 551 N.E.2d 1 (1990), parents may recover costs associated with the birth and rearing of an initially unwanted child if "their reason for seeking sterilization was founded on economic or financial considerations." Those damages will then be offset against the benefits of having the child. However, child-rearing costs will not be available if the parents' "desire to avoid the birth of a child was founded on eugenic reasons (avoidance of a feared genetic defect) or was founded on therapeutic reasons (concern for the mother's health) and if a healthy normal baby is born." Id. at 5.

Do you explain this holding to the mother before she discusses her motivation for filing suit? If not, are you penalizing ignorance of the law? Are clients entitled to knowledge that may assist them in revising intent?

See Chapter V, The Adversary System
   • Witness Preparation
      (pages 195–200)

4.   The Role of Experts

Over 80 years ago, an article on expert testimony concluded:

> There can be no question but that the attorneys are no less blameworthy than the experts they use. An attorney who would refuse to present fake testimony to the court in ordinary matter does not hesitate to employ biased or fake expert witnesses. It is the practice and demands of lawyers which have created the "plaintiff's expert" and "defendant's expert." If they did not buy, the doctors would not sell. The average accident lawyer wants the doctors properly labeled.[5]

More recent commentary echoes similar views. According to Judge Posner, "[t]here is hardly anything not palpably absurd on its face, that cannot now be proved by some so-called experts."[6] Although jurors may discount the weight they give to the testimony of a paid witness, that approach will not necessarily be helpful if they hear from no impartial experts appointed by the court. Even if such appointed experts testify, some potential for abuse remains as long as parties are free to offer additional conflicting evidence.

The problem is compounded when one side lacks the resources to hire the necessary expertise. Under DR 7-109(C) and prevailing common law rules that Model Rule 3.4(b) incorporates by reference, parties may not pay expert witnesses a fee contingent on the content of their testimony or the outcome of the case. In Person v. Association of the Bar of New York, 554 F.2d 534 (2d Cir. 1977), the Second Circuit Court of Appeals upheld this traditional prohibition against constitutional challenge. In so ruling, the court rejected the plaintiff lawyer's claim that the rule prevented him from adequately financing a lawsuit and therefore foreclosed his access to the courts.

What is your view? Should distinctions be drawn between payments of flat fees (for time and costs) that are contingent on a favorable judgment, and payments of sliding scale fees, whose size depends on the amount of a judgment?[7] Consider the discussion in Chapter XV (Evidence and Trial Advocacy) at pages 671–673. How would you describe the problem, and the most promising solutions, concerning expert witnesses?

See Chapter XV, Evidence and Trial Advocacy
- Expert Witnesses
   (pages 671–673)

5. Trial Strategies

See Chapter XV, Evidence and Trial Advocacy
- Trial Tactics in Tort Proceedings
   (pages 658–659)

B. DILEMMAS OF ADVOCACY

1. Confidentiality and Personal Injury Litigation

See Chapter VI, Confidentiality and Client Counseling
- Part C. The Moral Limits of Confidentiality
   (pages 229–232)

See also Chapter XIII, Corporations
- Attorney-Client Privilege in Organizational Settings
   (Problem 13D, pages 560–571)

2. The Counseling Role: Product Design and Consumer Safety

See Chapter VI, Confidentiality and Client Counseling
- Dilemmas in Counseling
   (pages 262–293)

C. CONFLICTS OF INTEREST

1. Joint Representation

PROBLEM 19G

1. An insurance company retains your firm to defend its insured under the terms of a standard negligence policy. The insured is a sole proprietor of a small self-service gas station. The claim is based on injuries sustained when the plaintiff slipped on oil surrounding a leaky pump. Plaintiff's complaint alleges both negligence and a "conscious and malicious disregard for safety," and seeks $1.5 million in compensatory

damages and $1 million in punitive damages. Defendant's policy excludes intentional torts and limits coverage to $1 million per claim.

Based on your conversations with the insured and two of his employees, you think that the plaintiff has a very strong case on negligence and a weak claim on intentional torts. The defendant failed for several months to repair the defective pump nozzle that caused the leak. He also failed to post warning signs or to instruct and supervise the staff in cleaning the area properly. However, the absence of prior accidents will make it extremely difficult for the plaintiff to establish the kind of malicious, intentional conduct necessary for a punitive damages award.

Two weeks before trial, the plaintiff offers to settle for $1 million. From the insurance company's perspective, this offer appears unacceptable because the plaintiff's compensatory damages request is grossly inflated. However, the insured would prefer to settle to eliminate his risk of liability in excess of the policy. How should you proceed? If the insurance company refuses to settle and the trial judgment exceeds the policy limits, what would your obligations be in a subsequent suit by the insured claiming breach of fiduciary duties? Suppose that the company maintains that the high verdict is attributable to your negligent trial preparation. Could you be liable for malpractice? To whom?

2. Just before trial, you learn from one of the gas station's former employees that a similar accident occurred several months prior to the plaintiff's injury. You now suspect that the defendant may not have been entirely truthful at his deposition when he denied knowing of earlier incidents. How do you proceed?

Lawyers representing insurance companies and their policyholders encounter such chronic conflicts of interest that the relationship is known as the "eternal triangle."[8] Problem 19G illustrates two of the most common ethical dilemmas, for which there is no easy solution.

The first dilemma involves settlement of claims where coverage is undisputed. Where a judgment in excess of policy limits is extremely unlikely, insured parties may prefer to reject a settlement within policy limits, however reasonable the offer. If the verdict at trial proves better than the offer, insured litigants may save their reputation and save money depending on the size of the policy deductible and the terms of the final judgment. If the verdict proves worse than the offer, it still costs the insured nothing if it remains within policy limits. By contrast, where the risks of judgment above policy limits are substantial, the insured might prefer a settlement within its limits, even if the amount seems much larger than the plaintiff could prove at trial.

So too, insurance companies have interests that conflict with those of a particular policyholder. Often the settlement of one claim may affect the resolution of others, and a company's failure to engage in strategic bargaining may lead to overpayment and financial difficulties. If the claim is very large and substantially above policy limits, the insurer sometimes has incentives to gamble with the insured's money by proceeding to trial. Other common conflicts in insurance contexts involve disputes over coverage and litigation expenses. Insured parties who are not bearing the costs of defense will typically prefer greater expenditures than the companies paying the bills.

Under the typical liability policy, the insurer has the right and duty to defend claims against its insured. If the insurer cannot settle the claim through its own internal process, it usually hires an attorney to defend the case. Under these circumstances, a threshold question arises in identifying the client. The majority view is that a lawyer provided by the insurance carrier can jointly represent the insured and insurer. Under this arrangement, if lawyers acquire compromising information from an insured, they generally must withdraw from representation unless they obtain an informed waiver of the conflict and can adequately represent both parties. The general rule that a lawyer may share confidences with joint clients is unavailable because the insured expects confidentiality and does not have free choice in consenting to a different arrangement.[9]

Alternatively, some courts and commentators take the position that lawyers represent only the insured party. On this view, attorneys must maintain confidences and withdraw if they believe that payment by the carrier would compromise their ability to provide adequate representation.[10] Critics of this view believe that is unrealistic because it ignores the extent to which insurance contracts qualify the insured party's rights of representation (particularly concerning settlement), and the extent to which insurance defense lawyers inevitably feel loyalty toward the source of past and future business.[11]

Although the legal and insurance professions have frequently addressed this issue, their proposed resolutions have not met with full acceptance by the courts. In 1972, the ABA House of Delegates approved a set of "Guiding Principles" of the National Conference of Lawyers and Liability Insurers. These principles retain influence although in 1980 the bar repealed all such interprofessional agreements under threat of antitrust liability. Both these principles as well as the ABA Committee on Ethics' Formal Opinion 1476 (1981) provide that if attorneys discover a conflict involving coverage, they should notify both the insurer and the insured, and the insured should be invited to retain separate counsel at the insured's expense. If, however, the insured makes disclosures "under circumstances indicating the insured's belief that such disclosure would not be revealed to the insurance company but would be treated as confidential communication to the attorney," the attorney should not reveal the information to the company. Nor should the lawyer "discuss with the insured the legal significance of the disclosure or the nature of the coverage question."[12]

Most courts and bar ethics committees have provided greater protection for the insured. Under the predominant view, if a question of coverage arises, the preferred course is for an attorney promptly to disclose that fact to an insured without creating the illusion of confidentiality. If the coverage question cannot be resolved, the company must notify the insured and obtain his permission to proceed with the defense under a reservation of rights. That reservation entitles the company to contest coverage if a judgment is entered against the insured. If the company decides to contest coverage or another conflict arises, the insured is entitled to hire an independent lawyer at the insurer's expense.[13]

The proposed American Law Institute's Restatement of the Law Governing Lawyers takes a somewhat different position than most courts. It permits a lawyer to defer to a third party payor such as an insurance company only when the payor bears substantially all of the consequences of the result in litigation. Under that proposed rule, lawyers could not properly follow an insured company's directions in any case where the policyholder faces meaningful excess exposure, a result so far rejected by most judicial decisions.[14]

These differing perspectives concerning attorneys' obligations have resulted in continuing efforts by insurance industry lawyers to draft acceptable guidelines and to encourage consistent judicial rulings.[15] Until those efforts are successful and more authoritative guidance is available, how would you handle Problem 19G(1)? Both the insured and insurer obviously hope for a judgment against the plaintiff, but the carrier may be able to avoid liability by supporting the claim for intentional harm, while the insured would be better off with a finding of negligence or recklessness. Does that suggest a need for separate counsel? If so, who should pay?

When such conflicts arise, insurance carriers sometimes write insured parties an "excess claim" letter, inviting them to obtain separate counsel. Occasionally, these parties will do so. Usually they do not, and the lawyer hired by the insurer remains under a duty to represent their interests or to withdraw. Under such circumstances, prevailing case law provides that the insurance company or its lawyer may be liable for a bad faith refusal to settle.[16] What would constitute bad faith on the facts of Problem 19G? How should the lawyer handle confidential information concerning coverage?

PROBLEM 19H

1. Two sisters retain you to pursue a personal injury claim arising out of an automobile accident. According to their accounts, the older sister was the driver and the younger sister was a passenger in a car that collided with the defendant's taxi. They both claim that the defendant caused the collision by running a stop sign. After you file suit, you discover a eyewitness to the accident who recalls that the sister who was driving also did not observe the stop sign. Your state has a comparative negligence statute. Can you continue to represent both sisters?

2. During a recent deposition, the eyewitness consistently refers to the younger sister as the driver. That sister is uninsured and her license was suspended during the period at issue. The policy only covers accidents occurring while the car owner is driving. How should you proceed?

Suppose that you had been retained not by the sisters but by their insurance company. Would your ethical responsibilities be different?[17]

See Chapter VII, Conflicts of Interest
- Simultaneous Representation of Multiple Interests in Civil Contexts
  (pages 314–321)

2. Lawyer-Client Conflicts: Contingent Fees

PROBLEM 19I

You are a member of the ABA Standing Committee on Ethics and Professional Responsibility. You have been asked for guidance concerning certain contingent fee arrangements described below. How do you respond?

Contingent fees are a way of providing payment for lawyers that is conditional on the outcome of representation. Such arrangements are almost universal in personal injury litigation and common in other areas such as tax referrals, debt collection, eminent domain, employment discrimination and harassment, shareholders' derivative claims, and private antitrust actions. The size of the fee varies, but the most common range is between 33 and 40 percent of the client's recovery.

Contingent fees have prompted long-standing criticisms and restrictions. Early common law banned such fees as a form of three prohibited practices: "barratry" (stirring up litigation by urging others to bring suits); "maintenance" (providing financial assistance for litigation); and "champerty" (providing assistance that would be repaid out of any recovery from the litigation).[18]

Some American jurisdictions initially retained such prohibitions. According to George Sharswood's nineteenth-century Essay on Professional Ethics, contingent fees provided an "undue encouragement to litigation"; turned "lawyers into higglers with their clients"; and invited exploitation of parties "not on an equal footing in making such a bargain."[19]

By the turn of the century, however, pressure for greater access to the courts had prompted liberalization of traditional rules. Contingent fee arrangements under court supervision gradually gained acceptance for most litigation although other forms of financial assistance to clients did not. Disciplinary Rule 5-103(A), Model Rule 1.5, and related case law generally permit "reasonable" contingent fees except in criminal or domestic relations cases; the Model Rules require such agreements to be in writing and to specify the basis for calculation. Yet what constitutes "reasonable" in this context remains a matter of debate, as the following overview suggests.

Defenders of contingent fees generally emphasize three main advantages of such arrangements:

1. they give lawyers an incentive to pursue a case vigorously in contexts where clients would have difficulty evaluating the quality of professional services;
2. they enable clients who could not otherwise afford competent legal representation to borrow against the value of their claims; and
3. they allow such clients to shift most of the risk of an unsuccessful suit to attorneys, who can spread the costs among other claimants.

Critics of prevailing contingency agreements generally challenge the first of these claims. As these commentators note, such fee arrangements do not create a full identity of interest between lawyers and clients. Attorneys' economic interest lies in maximizing the return on their work; clients' interest lies in gaining the highest possible settlement. Depending on the amount of effort and expense lawyers have invested in preparation, and the alternative uses of their time, they may be more or less disposed to settle than their clients. Most commentators have concluded that for claims of low or modest value, contingent fee lawyers have inadequate incentives to prepare a case thoroughly and hold out for the highest possible settlement. Conversely, in high-stakes cases, once lawyers have spent substantial time in preparation, they may be more inclined to gamble for a large recovery than clients with marginal resources and substantial needs.

Critics of contingency arrangements also object that the lawyer's return often bears no necessary relationship to the amount of work performed or to the risk actually assumed. In many cases where liability is clear and damages are substantial, a standard one-third percentage recovery will provide windfalls for the attorney. If defendants make an early settlement offer, the lawyer can end up with huge fees for minimal work, much of it delegable to paralegals. In some widely publicized cases, attorneys' hourly return rate has ranged between $20,000 and $35,000.[20]

Although lawyers frequently defend such recoveries as essential to subsidize other cases with higher risks of nonpayment, it is questionable how often counsel assume such risks. Systematic data are lacking and some of the evidence that defenders invoke can be misleading. For example, a study of California trial courts found that personal injury plaintiffs were successful in only about a third of their cases, as compared with an average plaintiff success rate of about half.[21] However, since over 90 percent of all claims are settled without trial, the crucial issue is the degree of success across attorneys' entire portfolio of claims. At least some evidence suggests that contingent fee lawyers' overall rate of recovery is high because they seldom accept cases that are unlikely to yield a reasonable hourly return.[22]

In any event, even if contingent fee lawyers are undercompensated in some significant number of cases, it by no means follows that they are entitled to make up the difference by overcharging clients in other matters. According to most courts and commentators, fixing a rate that bears no relation to the risk actually assumed for a particular claim violates lawyers' fiduciary obligations. As Professor Charles Wolfram notes: "Courts in general have insisted that a contingent fee be truly contingent. The typically elevated fee reflecting the risk to the lawyer of receiving no fee will be permitted only if the representation indeed involves a significant degree of risk."[23] By that standard, many current contingent fee arrangements would not pass muster. Windfall profits are a chronic problem, particularly in mass tort cases after liability is established, in class actions offering little benefit to individual members, and in other cases where settlement offers are accepted without substantial work.[24]

How best to respond to such problems is subject to considerable controversy. As a threshold matter, it bears emphasis that the potential for attorney-client conflicts and overcharging is not limited to contingent fee agreements; it also arises with standard hourly fee arrangements. Although sytematic evidence is again lacking, the limited data available suggest that lawyers in contingent fee cases do not on average earn more than those charging by the hour.[25] Incentives for under- or overpreparation arise with hourly billing as well as with contingency contracts. Where attorneys' net gain does not depend on the result, their level of preparation may be affected not just by the client's interest but also by the rates they can charge and the alternative uses for their time. For example, compare the meter running in corporate litigation described in Chapter V (the Adversary System) at pages 187–189, with the ineffective representation in indigent criminal defense described in Chapter XIV (Criminal Law and Procedure) at pages 610–614.

Of course, even if the problems surrounding contingent fee arrangements are not unique, the injustices that do occur still demand attention. To that end, scholars and policy-makers have proposed a number of approaches. One strategy is to require advancing percentage formulas. Under this approach, lawyers receive a larger portion of the total recovery as the case progresses and presumably becomes more time-consuming. So, for example, in a matter settled without filing suit, the lawyer receives 25 percent of

the recovery; in a case settled after filing, 33 percent; in a case that
goes to trial, 40 percent; and in a case won on appeal, 50 percent. An
obvious problem with such a formula is that it may encourage
lawyers to prolong proceedings where the stakes are sufficiently
high, and may still permit overcompensation where little work
occurs before settlement.

An alternative approach is to require a graduated scale that
gives lawyers a smaller percentage of recovery as clients' claims
grow larger. Under one such statute designed to prevent windfall
fees, an attorney receives 50 percent of the first $1,000 of recovery,
40 percent of the next $2,000, 33 1/3 percent of the next $47,000, 20
percent of the next $50,000, and 10 percent of amounts over
$100,000. This approach, however, still permits overcompensation of
counsel in small, simple cases and may discourage lawyers from
accepting large, complex claims.

A third, more sophisticated, formula that some commentators
advocate combines an hourly fee for the time spent on a case and a
percentage of the amount by which the client's recovery exceeds the
lawyer's normal hourly charges. Such an approach does not entirely
eliminate lawyer-client conflicts; an attorney who lacks enough
other well-paying work might still overprepare a case. Nor would
this kind of formula be easy to administer.

The most influential recent reform proposal, developed at the
Manhattan Institute and endorsed by some two dozen leaders of the
American bar, offers an alternative approach to windfall fees. Under
this proposal, defendants in civil suits would have an opportunity to
make an early settlement offer, for example, within 60 days of the
filing of the legal action. If they chose not to make an offer, the
plaintiff's lawyers would be free to negotiate contingent fees, subject
to current ethical rules. However, if an offer was made and accepted,
the compensation to those attorneys would be limited to a reasonable
hourly rate or a very modest share of the gross recovery, for
instance, 10 percent. If a settlement offer was made and refused, it
would set a baseline for assessing the reasonableness of the
contingency fee.[26]

In the mid-1990s, supporters of this approach sent a letter to the
American Bar Association Ethics Committee requesting guidance
concerning the use of contingency fees in the absence of any realistic
risk of nonrecovery. In particular, supporters asked the Committee
to consider whether

I.   Is it ethical for an attorney to charge a standard contingency
     fee on the entire recovery if the attorney knows or has reason
     to know that a significant settlement offer is likely to be
     made without the need for significant effort on her part?; and
II. Is there an ethical obligation for an attorney retained under a
     contingency fee contract to assist her client in analyzing the
     risks of a claim by soliciting and conveying early defendant
     settlement offers; and is it ethical to charge the standard, or
     any contingency fee against such early offers?[27]

The Committee, however, answered a somewhat different question: is it "an ethical violation for a lawyer to charge a contingent fee a) to a client who can otherwise afford to pay on a noncontingent basis or b) in a matter where liability is clear and some recovery is likely?"[28] The Committee found both practices permissible. In its view, "all contingent fee agreements carry certain risks" that could justify a premium. For example,

> the risk that the case will require substantially more work than the lawyer anticipated; the risk that there will be no judgement, or only an unenforceable one; the risk of changes in the law; the risk that the client will dismiss the lawyer; and the risk that the client will require the lawyer to reject what the lawyer considers to be a good settlement.[29]

Do you find that reasoning persuasive? What if the risk premium grossly exceeds the actual risks?

Debate over contingent fee regulation continues. In the mid-1990s, Congress held hearings and considered legislative reforms. They included variations on the Manhattan Institute proposal and disclosure requirements obligating lawyers to advise clients about different fee options, to estimate the time their case would likely require, and, at the conclusion of representation, to provide a bill indicating the actual time spent and the fee per hour that resulted.[30] California voters also came close to endorsing a ballot initiative (Proposition 202) that would have capped contingent fees at 15 percent if the client accepted an early settlement offer.

Opponents of such measures claim that they would prove overinclusive. The effect would be to deny lawyers a reasonable recovery in many settled cases and, as a consequence, to limit clients' access to legal services and reduce the deterrent value of liability claims.[31] These commentators prefer voluntary self-restraint by lawyers, and when that fails, sanctions or adjustment of egregious fees through arbitration or bar and judicial oversight.

Critics respond that such efforts have proven demonstrably inadequate, and that the prospects for fundamental improvement seem limited. The American Trial Lawyers' call for members to "exercise sound judgment" in setting percentage fees has gone unheeded in circles where regulation is most needed.[32] Bar sanctions for contingent fee abuses are rare and lenient.[33] Neither courts nor disciplinary agencies have resources to oversee charges in even a small fraction of the approximately one million new contingent fee cases filed each year.[34]

What is your position concerning contingent fee regulation? How would you have answered the two questions put to the ABA Committee? Consider the requirements for contingent fees that Lester Brickman proposes:

> (1) Contingent fees are permissible only if there is a realistic possibility that there will be no recovery; (2) if risk is present, the contin-

gent fee percentage must be proportionate to the risk and the anticipated effort; (3) the lawyer, in fulfillment of his fiduciary obligation must inform the client of the risk involved, the projected amount of time required, the risk premium being charged and whatever other information the client requires to determine whether the contingent fee percentage quoted is fair under the circumstances; (4) the lawyer must also inform the client of the client's right to pay an hourly or fixed fee instead; (5) even if the client consents to paying a contingent fee, if that fee arrangement is not beneficial to the client, the lawyer bears a heavy burden to demonstrate that the consent was truly "informed," and (6) even if the client has given informed consent, if the contingent fee is so disproportionate to risk and anticipated effort as to be excessive and unreasonable, it must be struck down.[35]

Would you agree with these requirements? If so, what enforcement strategies would you propose?

3. Financing Litigation

Bar ethical rules traditionally have prohibited lawyers from advancing financial assistance to clients, other than litigation costs for which the client agrees to remain responsible whatever the outcome of representation. DR 5-103(B). In practice, the requirement of client reimbursement is widely ignored, and commentators have often argued that its strict enforcement would preempt many deserving claims. Class actions and shareholder derivative suits would particularly suffer because an individual client rarely has sufficient economic incentive to underwrite the full costs of litigation.[36] In response to such concerns, the Model Rules permit the lawyer to advance litigation expenses contingent on the result and to pay such expenses for indigent clients irrespective of the outcome. Rule 1.8.

This more liberal approach still falls short of addressing two issues: provision of "humanitarian assistance," that is, payment of clients' living and medical expenses during litigation, or payment of expenses for individuals who are not impoverished but who are not able to bear substantial legal costs. Supporters of such assistance point out that, without a lawyer's help, a client may for "reasons of economic necessity and physical need, be forced to settle his claim for an inadequate amount." Louisiana Bar Assn. v. Edwins, 329 So. 2d 437, 446 (La. 1976). Proponents of the traditional prohibition respond that allowing humanitarian aid would encourage lawyers to compete for business through the size of the loans they are willing to make rather than the quality of representation they are able to offer.[37] Moreover, lawyer financiers could be tempted to settle a case for a lower amount than it is worth in order to guarantee prompt recovery of their loan.

How would you handle this issue? Consider Rule 4-210(A)(2) of the California Rules of Professional Conduct. It permits lawyers "after employment [to] len[d] money to the client upon the client's promise in writing to repay such loan." Are either of these rules preferable to the Code or Model provisions? How significant is the likelihood of abuse?

A related issue arises with recent innovative efforts to finance mass torts and patent claims. In litigation on behalf of victims of Agent Orange (a toxic chemical used in Vietnam), a Plaintiffs Management Committee for consolidated lawsuits worked out a complicated fee-splitting arrangement. That arrangement advantaged lawyers who were subsidizing the case at the expense of lawyers who were trying it. In challenging a fee agreement that he had initially accepted, the plaintiff's chief counsel pointed out that it gave him an effective hourly rate of $55 while a passive investor would recover over $1,700.[38] The Second Circuit Court of Appeals sustained his challenge. In re Agent Orange Product Liability Litigation, 818 F.2d 216 (2d Cir.), cert. denied, 484 U.S. 926 (1987). In the appellate court's view, agreements allocating fees based on the amount of funds advanced rather than on work performed would give investors an undue incentive to accept an early settlement that was not in the best interests of the class. Id. at 224. Peter Schuck's account of the litigation offers a different view. Given the difficulty that the Managing Committee had in attracting financial support, Schuck concludes:

> The legal system cannot have it both ways. If it desires the end, then it must desire (or at least accept) the only practical means to that end. If it wishes to encourage so-called public interest tort litigation on behalf of diffuse, poorly financed interests over extremely complex issues of scientific or technical uncertainty, then it must either transform the government into a tort litigator on behalf of these interests (a solution with enormous problems of its own), or it must countenance, indeed welcome, private arrangements for securing the resources necessary for effectively prosecuting such cases. The truth is that in the fall of 1983, if the Agent Orange litigation was to go forward, the resources of the financiers were desperately needed; it is no exaggeration to say that at that critical moment and thereafter, they were needed far more than the services of the chief trial counsel, valuable as his services were. The otherwise grotesque imbalance revealed by [his] comparisons reflected the relative value that their money and his services had for the survival of the case at that point, a value [counsel] obviously appreciated when he signed the agreement. Although the opportunism of investors is not a pretty or edifying sight, the prospect of meritorious cases failing for want of resources is even less appealing.[39]

Do you agree? How would you have resolved this issue?[40] Would you support ventures like the California-based Judgment Purchase Corporation, which advances cash in exchange for a share in litigation judgments that are pending appeal?[41]

D.   ALTERNATIVE DISPUTE RESOLUTION AND NO-FAULT REFORMS

Criticisms of the lawyer's role in the American tort system parallel criticisms of the system itself. The most commonly cited problems include undercompensation of victims, overcompensation of intermediaries (including lawyers), inadequate checks on fraudulent claims, and inconsistency and unpredictability in outcomes. Almost all major studies indicate that a large proportion of victims fail to recover adequate compensation. For example, Rand researchers have found that only 2 to 3 percent of accident victims sue.[42] In another study of some 30,000 New York hospital records, only about 12 percent of patients who sustained injuries from negligent medical care brought malpractice actions and only half of those received compensation.[43] Among those who do file claims, the most seriously injured victims are grossly undercompensated, while those with less severe injuries and modest economic losses are sometimes overcompensated. For example, one study of Florida medical malpractice cases found that, overall, plaintiffs recovered just over half their costs. Those with the least serious injuries received three times their estimated losses while some of the most seriously injured parties received only a third.[44] Similar patterns hold for automobile and airline accident victims.[45]

Yet while victims with legitimate claims are undercompensated, parties with inflated or fraudulent claims are overcompensated. In some areas of practice such as workers' compensation and vehicle accidents, estimates suggest that at least 10 to 20 percent of claims involve cheating.[46] Indeterminacies in liability standards also expand opportunities for unethical behavior such as strike suits and inflammatory trial tactics. These strategies in turn lead to inconsistent and unjustifiable outcomes.

The current system not only results in high levels of over- and undercompensation, it does so at substantial cost. Of the amounts paid by insurance companies in asbestos cases, victims received only about 37 percent; in effect it cost about $1.71 to place $1.00 in the hands of a plaintiff.[47] Other studies similarly find that about 60 percent of medical malpractice insurance dollars are spent on litigation rather than compensation.[48]

Such problems have sparked a wide variety of reform proposals. The most significant have been no-fault systems, which also have produced the most sustained opposition from the organized bar. Under current procedures, a large proportion of lawyers' income derives from personal injury cases, and it may not be wholly coincidental that the American Bar Association and American Trial Lawyers Association have consistently lobbied against any structural changes.[49] According to the ABA's Special Committee Report on tort reform, the existing system has proven "vital and responsive as a working process . . . for dealing with injuries alleged to be wrongs."

The Report therefore concludes that further experimentation with no-fault systems is unnecessary and unwise.[50]

How would you assess that assessment? Is it plausible to expect the bar to represent the public's rather than the profession's interests on no-fault issues? If not, what strategies are most likely to promote significant reform?[51]

See Chapter V, The Adversary System
   • Part H. Alternative Dispute Resolution
       (pages 208–217)

E.   REGULATION OF THE PROFESSION

1.   Competence and Malpractice

PROBLEM 19J

Consider the conduct of the lawyers in Problem 3D and in In re Himmel in Chapter III (Regulation of the Profession) at pages 66–69. Under what circumstances should lawyers be subject to discipline for failing to report misconduct? How would you have responded in the facts presented in Problem 3D and in *Himmel*?[52]

PROBLEM 19K

You are the insurance company's defense lawyer whom Douglas Rosenthal describes in Chapter V (The Adversary System) at page 176. How do you proceed? Do current malpractice and bar disciplinary processes provide an adequate response to incompetent adversaries?

See Chapter III, Regulation of the Profession
   • Malpractice
       (pages 89–93)

2.   Solicitation

See Chapter III, Regulation of the Profession
   • Solicitation
       (pages 100–113)

As the materials in Chapter III indicate, lawyers' in-person solicitation of tort claims is associated with a variety of abuses:

fraud, over-reaching, and invasion of privacy. These abuses have
their parallel in conduct by insurance agents, who often attempt to
negotiate settlements before victims have an opportunity to consult
lawyers. One controversial approach involves sending accident
victims or their families a version of an "Alpert letter." In its original
form, the letter reads in part:

> Money can never compensate for the loss of a loved one but this is the
> medium recognized by the law for compensating victims and the fami-
> lies of victims in air disasters. . . . It is our intention to see that you
> receive fair compensation for the loss which you have sustained. It is
> also our hope that you will retain as much of the compensation as is
> properly due you without unnecessary diversion of large amounts to
> legal expenses. You may find yourselves under pressure to sign a con-
> tingent fee retainer with an attorney whereby his fee is a percentage
> of the final award. The rationale for such a percentage fee is that the
> lawyer risks getting no fee if there is no recovery. There is no such
> contingency in this case. There is also nothing to be gained by a pre-
> cipitous lawsuit. We do suggest that it would be in your best interest
> to evaluate the offers which will be made to you and obtain the help of
> your attorney based upon a fee for the work involved rather than a
> percentage of the settlement award.[53]

The problems arising from in-person solicitation have generated
various proposals. One approach is to impose time, place, and
manner restrictions on both attorneys and insurance agents along
the lines described in Chapter III. Further variations on this strategy involve a cooling-off period after accidents in which agents
would not negotiate releases and attorneys would not contact victims
or media representatives and would not file lawsuits.[54] Another
possibility raising fewer first amendment concerns is to improve
volunteer outreach efforts by the organized bar, particularly after
mass disasters. Such efforts can include providing published and
personalized information from disinterested sources concerning
claimants' rights and bar disciplinary complaint channels.[55]

Which of these proposals seems most likely to reduce the abuses
associated with solicitation? What other initiatives would you
support?

Endnotes

1. See, e.g., Summers v. Tice, 199 P.2d 1 (Cal. 1948); Ybarra v. Spangard, 154 P.2d 687 (Cal. 1944).

2. See Jennifer E. Sills, SLAPPs (Strategic Lawsuits Against Public Participation): How Can the Legal System Eliminate Their Appeal?, 25 Conn. L. Rev. 547, 553-554 (1993); John C. Barker, Common-Law and Statutory Solutions to the Problem of SLAPPs, 26 Loy. L.A.L. Rev. 395, 422 (1993).

3. Restatement Second of Torts §674 (1977). But see Bull v. McCuskey, 615 P.2d 957 (Nev. 1980) (upholding a jury's finding of abuse of process against an attorney who brought suit against a physician without adequate investigation or expert evidence and who offered to settle for minimal sum of $750); Yost v. Torok, 344 S.E.2d 414 (Ga. 1986) (allowing tort action for frivolous proceeding if brought as a compulsory counterclaim).

4. Barker, supra note 2, at 408, 448-454.

5. Lee M. Friedman, Expert Testimony, Its Abuse and Reformation, 19 Yale L.J. 247 (1910).

6. Chaulk v. Volkswagen of Am., Inc., 808 F.2d 639, 644 (7th Cir. 1986) (Posner, J., dissenting).

7. See Note, Contingent Expert Witness Fees: Access and Legitimacy, 64 S. Cal. L. Rev. 136 (1991).

8. Geoffrey Hazard & William Hodes, The Law of Lawyering §1.7: 303, at 256 (1996 Supp.); Douglas R. Richmond, Lost in the Eternal Triangle of Insurance Defense Ethics, 9 Geo. J. Legal Ethics 475 (1996).

9. Hazard & Hodes, supra note 8. But see Charles Wolfram, Modern Legal Ethics 432 (1986) (information may be shared unless one client understood that it would be confidential or a conflict had arisen).

10. The Comment to Model Rule 1.7 makes passing reference to the problem by requiring that when an insured and insurer have conflicting interests and the insurer is required to provide counsel, the arrangement should assure the special counsel's "professional independence."

11. Charles Silver & Kent Syverud, The Professional Responsibilities of Insurance Defense Lawyers, 45 Duke L.J. 255, 336-339 (1995).

12. 7 Martindale Hubbell Law Directory 76M-77M (1978) (repealed 1980).

13. Wolfram, supra note 9, at 431.

14. Restatement (Third) of the Law Governing Lawyers §215 cmt. d (Tentative Draft No. 4, 1996); Charles Silver, Does Insurance Defense Counsel Represent the Company or the Insured?, 72 Tex. L. Rev. 1583, 1587 (1994).

15. Silver, supra note 14, at 1586 n.13.

16. Wolfram, supra note 9, at 433; Richmond, supra note 8, at 504-509.

17. For analogous problems, see George C. Christie & James E. Meeks, The Law of Torts 1249, 1251 (2d ed. 1990). See also In re Thornton, 421 A.2d 1 (D.C. Ct. App. 1980) (disallowing joint representation of driver and passenger where liability is in dispute).

18. Wolfram, supra note 9, at 490.

19. George Sharswood, An Essay on Professional Ethics 98, 103-106 (2d ed. 1860).

20. For example, see the cases involving a bus accident, chemical plant explosion, and an environmental hazard discussed in Lester A. Brickman, Contingency Fee Abuses, Ethical Mandates and the Disciplinary System: The Case Against Case-by-Case Enforcement, 53 Wash. & Lee L. Rev. 1339, 1345 n.22 (1996).

21. Samuel R. Gross & Kent D. Syverud, Getting to No: A Study of Settlement Negotiations and the Selection of Cases for Trial, 90 Mich. L. Rev. 319, 337 (1992).

22. Lester Brickman, ABA Regulation of Contingency Fees: Money Talks, Ethics Walks, 65 Fordham L. Rev. 247, 279 (1996).

23. Wolfram, supra note 9, at 532.

24. Barry Meier, Math of a Class Action Suit: "Winning" $2.19 Costs $91.33, N.Y. Times, Nov. 21, 1995, at A1; Barry Meier, Fistful of Coupons, N.Y. Times, May 26, 1995, at C1; Brickman, supra note 22.

25. Ralph Nader & Wesley J. Smith, No Contest 311 (1996); Manuel R. Ramos, 57 Ohio L.J. 863, 896 (1996) (noting that hourly billing defense lawyers in California receive substantially more money in legal malpractice cases than contingent fee plaintiffs' lawyers).

26. Peter Passell, Contingency Fees in Injury Cases Under Attack by Legal Scholars, N.Y. Times, Feb. 11, 1994, at B1, B16.

27. Letter to the Standing Comm. on Ethics and Professional Responsibilty, Feb. 10, 1994, reprinted in 65 Fordham L. Rev. 299, 305, 307 (1996).

28. American Bar Assn. Comm. on Ethics and Professional Responsibility, Formal Op. 94-389.

29. Id.

30. Lawyers' Fees Are Subject of Proposed Federal Laws, 11 ABA/BNA Lawyer's Man. Prof. Conduct 12 (1995).

31. See, e.g., Lawrence Fox, Contingent Fees, A.B.A.J., July 1995, at 44.

32. American Trial Lawyers Assn., Keys to the Courthouse: Quick Facts on the Contingent Fee System 4 (1994).

33. Brickman, supra note 22, at 305-308. For an example, see Michael Hytha, "People's Lawyer" Gets Mild Penalty from State Bar, San Francisco Chron., Aug. 8, 1997, at A19 (describing private reproval for lawyer charging up to 46 percent on simple insurance claims).

34. Brickman, supra note 20, at 1349.

35. Lester Brickman, Contingent Fees Without Contingencies: Hamlet Without the Prince of Denmark?, 37 UCLA L. Rev. 29, 99 (1989).

36. Jonathan R. Macey & Geoffrey P. Miller, The Plaintiff's Attorney's Role in Class Action and Derivative Litigation: Economic Analysis and Recommendations for Reform, 58 U. Chi. L. Rev. 1 (1991).

37. For example, in one particularly heated competition for clients whose children died in a bus crash, a lawyer reportedly offered to help a parent buy a new home. Lisa Belken, Where 21 Youths Died, Lawyers Wage a War, N.Y. Times, Jan. 18, 1990, at A1.

38. Peter Schuck, Agent Orange on Trial 120-121 (1986).

39. Id. at 204.

40. See Jack B. Weinstein, Ethical Dilemmas in Mass Tort Litigation, 88 Nw. U.L. Rev. 470, 526-527 (1994). For discussion of alternative compensation structures, see Robert L. Rabin, Some Thoughts on the Efficacy of a Mass Toxics Administrative Compensation Scheme, 52 Md. L. Rev. 951 (1993).

41. Kim Horner, Judgment-Buying Venture Broadens Its Territory, San Francisco Recorder, Aug. 13, 1996, at 1.

42. Deborah R. Hensler et al., Compensation for Accidental Injuries in the United States 110 (1991).

43. Harvard Medical Practice Study, Patients, Doctors and Lawyers— Medical Injury, Malpractice Litigation and Patient Compensation in New York: The Report of the Harvard Medical Practice Study to the State of New York 6-9, 7-1 (1990); Michael Saks, Do We Really Know Anything About the Behavior of the Tort Litigation System—and Why Not?, 140 U. Penn. L. Rev. 1147, 1183-1184 (1992); Kenneth Jost, Still Warring over Medical Malpractice: Time for Something Better, A.B.A.J., May 1993, at 68.

44. Frank A. Sloan & Stephen S. van Wert, Cost and Compensation of Injuries in Medical Malpractice, 52 L. & Contemp. Probs. 131, 155 (1991).

45. Marc Galanter, Real World Torts: An Antidote to Anecdote, 55 Md. L. Rev. 1093, 1117-1118 (1996).

46. Gary T. Schwartz, Waste, Fraud and Abuse in Worker's Compensation: The Recent California Experience, 52 Md. L. Rev. 983, 987-993 (1993); Peter Kerr, The Price of Health: Employee Fraud, N.Y. Times, Dec. 29, 1991, at 1. See also Peter Kerr, "Ghost Riders" Are Target of an Insurance Sting, N.Y. Times, Aug. 18, 1993, at 1 (National Industry Crime Bureau estimates that 10 to 30 percent of payouts for medical bills in vehicle accidents are fraudulent); Stephen Carroll et al., The Costs of Excess Medical Claims for Automobile Personal Injuries 3, 23 (Rand 1995) (estimating that over a third of claimed medical costs in automobile accident claims were excessive).

47. James S. Kakalik, Patricia A. Ebener, William L.F. Felstiner & Michael G. Shanley, Costs of Asbestos Litigation vi, viii (1983); James S. Kakalik & Nicholas M. Pace, Costs and Compensation Paid in Tort Litigation xiii (Rand Institute for Civil Justice 1986) (finding that for non-automobile torts, including medical malpractice, the net compensation remaining in the hands of victims was 43 percent of the total private and social expenditures on the processing and reimbursement of these claims). See also Saks, supra note 43.

48. Paul C. Weiler, The Case for No-Fault Medical Liability, 52 Md. L. Rev. 908, 915 (1993).

49. Brickman, supra note 22, at 261-262; Jeffrey O'Connell, Offers That Can't Be Refused, 77 Nw. L. Rev. 589, 595 (1982).

50. American Bar Assn., Towards a Jurisprudence of Injury (1984), quoted in Stephen D. Sugarman, Taking Advantage of the Torts Crisis, 48 Ohio St. L.J. 329, 343 (1987). A subsequent ABA Commission to Improve

the Tort Liability System proposed certain limited reforms but rejected consideration of no-fault proposals. Id. at 346. See also Brickman, supra note 22, at 261-263.

51. For an overview of structural changes, see Report to the American Law Institute, Enterprise Liability for Personal Injury (1991); Paul Weiler, Medical Malpractice on Trial (1991); Robert Rabin, Some Reflections on the Process of Tort Reform, 25 San Diego L. Rev. 13 (1988); Weiler, supra note 48; Rabin, supra note 40.

52. For a related case finding liability, see Togstad v. Vesley, Otto, Miller & Keeh, 291 N.W.2d 686 (Minn. 1980).

53. Cindy J. Jackson, A Controversial Settlement Approach: The Alpert Letter, 49 J. Air. L. & Comm. 213, 217 (1983).

54. Eric S. Roth, Confronting Solicitation of Mass Disaster Victims, 2 Geo. J. Legal Ethics 967 (1983).

55. Id. at 983-985; Deborah Rhode, Solicitation, 36 J. Legal Educ. 317, 330 (1986).

Index